LOCAL COMMUNITY FACT BOOK CHICAGO METROPOLITAN AREA

BASED ON THE 1970 AND 1980 CENSUSES

Edited by
THE CHICAGO FACT BOOK CONSORTIUM

Executive Committee

William Erbe, The University of Illinois at Chicago, *Project Director*
Richard Glasser, United Way of Metropolitan Chicago, *Chair, Committee on Data Users and Producers*
Albert Hunter, Northwestern University, *Chair, Data Design Committee*
John Johnstone, The University of Illinois at Chicago, *Chairman, Chicago Fact Book Consortium*
Gerald Suttles, University of Chicago, *Chair, Government Relations Committee*

Participants

James Bennett, The University of Illinois at Chicago
Robert Bursik, University of Oklahoma
David Carpenter, The University of Illinois at Chicago
Max Dieber, Northeastern Illinois Planning Commission
Donna Drinan, Private Consultant
Kenneth Fidel, DePaul University
Elizabeth Hershey, Chicago Department of Human Services
Ray Hutchison, DePaul University
Evelyn Kitagawa, University of Chicago
Kathleen McCourt, Loyola University
Barbara Monsor, Youth Guidance
Joseph Puntil, Illinois Institute of Juvenile Research
David Reed, Chicago Area Projects
Dennis Roncek, Kansas State University
Lauren Snowden, United Way of Metropolitan Chicago
Edwin Thomas, The University of Illinois at Chicago
Susan Waldheir, Chicago Department of Planning

Project Staff

John Beggs, The University of Illinois at Chicago
Richard Lee, The University of Illinois at Chicago
Antoinette LoBosco, The University of Illinois at Chicago
Stephanie Rusnak, The University of Ilinois at Chicago

The Chicago Fact Book Consortium
c/o Department of Sociology
The University of Illinois at Chicago
Chicago, Illinois 60680

This publication is made possible by grants from:

The Chicago Community Trust
The John D. and Catherine T. MacArthur Foundation
The Joyce Foundation
Woods Charitable Fund, Inc.

and

The Research Board, The Center for Research in Law and Justice
and the Department of Sociology of
The University of Illinois at Chicago

ISBN 0–914091–60–3 (Casebound)
ISBN 0–914091–61–1 (Paperbound)

Published by
The Chicago Review Press
213 W. Institute Place
Chicago, IL 60610

Phototype conversion and graphics by
The Office of Publications Services,
The University of Illinois at Chicago

Dedicated To

DAVID P. STREET
(1935-1980)

Acknowledgments

The idea of reviving the *Community Fact Book* series for Chicago developed out of discussions in the late 1970s among participants in an inter-university seminar organized by David Street of the University of Illinois at Chicago, Gerald Suttles of the University of Chicago, and Albert Hunter of Northwestern University. All lamented the absence of a 1970 Fact Book, and when Dennis Roncek proposed to David Street that the Sociology Department at the University of Illinois take responsibility for a *1980 Fact Book*, the blueprint was drawn that was to result in this volume. David Street did not live long enough to see this venture launched, and it is in his memory that we dedicate this *Local Community Fact Book: Chicago Metropolitan Area, 1980.*

The Chicago Fact Book Consortium was formed in the early Fall of 1980 to plan and carry out the project. Several early meetings were hosted by Richard Glasser at the United Way of Metropolitan Chicago. This group grew to about 25 persons and eventually became the Chicago Fact Book Consortium.

As the project began to take shape, proposals for funding had to be outlined and written, and a Data Design Committee was established to decide on the overall specifications for the project. Albert Hunter chaired this committee, and the others who worked on it included Robert Bursik, David Carpenter, William Erbe, Richard Glasser, David Reed and Dennis Roncek. Evelyn Kitagawa, who had co-edited the *1960 Community Fact Book* with Karl Taeuber, was also very helpful in providing guidance on data design, as was Edwin Thomas. An early decision of this committee was to include 1970 as well as 1980 data in the new edition of the *Fact Book.*

About this time, James Bennett, of the Office of Sponsored Research at the University of Illinois at Chicago, became involved in the project, and took on a major role in developing the proposal and in contacting and visiting potential funding sources. Gerald Suttles also made important contributions to the development of the project by generating support for it from a broad base of governmental, business and non-profit organizations and associations in the metropolitan area. After some initial setbacks, the first break came in October, 1981, with a grant from the Joyce Foundation to support the first major phase of the work. This was followed by grants from the Chicago Community Trust, the John D. and Catherine T. MacArthur Foundation and the Woods Charitable Fund, as well as from the Research Board of the University of Illinois at Chicago and the UIC Center for Research in Law and Justice. Complete funding for the project had been secured by January of 1983. Additional financial support to help with publication costs was provided by the MacArthur Foundation. Fran Gamwell, of the Community Renewal Society, helped with plans for the distribution of the book, as did Gerald Danzer, of the UIC History Department, the Woods Charitable Fund, and the United Way of Metropolitan Chicago.

William Erbe became Project Director, and his first major task was to organize a staff for the updating and writing of 125 community histories. Eventually, 35 different persons were to author these histories, and each is identified by name at the end of his or her narrative. Many persons authored more than one: Gail Danks Welter and Annie Ruth Leslie each wrote 16; Antoinette LoBosco authored 14; Will Hogan, 13; Marjorie DeVault, 9; Rodney Nelson, 7; and Winston McDowell, 5. Thirty of the histories were prepared by personnel recruited by the Center for Urban Affairs and Policy Studies at Northwestern University, under a subcontract directed by Albert Hunter. Ninety-five of the narratives were prepared by persons recruited by or affiliated with the University of Illinois at Chicago. As many as 17 Sociology graduate students at UIC contributed narratives. William Erbe edited all 125 manuscripts. In 100 of these 125, authors started out with the text that had appeared in the *1960 Fact Book,* and thus owe substantial credits to Beatrice Treiman and Ethel Shanas, who wrote the 1960 community histories — and who in turn acknowledge authorship debts to Vivian Palmer, who wrote the narratives for the first *Community Fact Book* in 1938, published under the direction of Professor Ernest W. Burgess.

Preparation of the 1980 Community Area statistical tables was carried out in the Department of Sociology at UIC. John Beggs, who functioned as a general consultant and troubleshooter on computational problems, was responsible for the preparation of those tables, and Dennis Roncek worked on the early stages of their design. Cathy Fladung assisted in this work. The historical tables reported for each of the 125 communities, as well as the population table for the Consolidated Area as a whole (Table A), were prepared by Richard Lee, under the supervision of William Erbe. Maps for the Chicago Community Areas were provided by the City of Chicago Department of Planning.

The 1970 Community Area tables, the suburban maps, and all tables reported in Sections III and IV were prepared by the Chicago Area Geographical Information Service of the Department of Geography, University of Illinois at Chicago. James Bash was in charge of this work at CAGIS, and William Erbe designed the specifications for the tables.

The first five tables reported in Part II were prepared at the Center for Urban Affairs and Policy Research at Northwestern University, by Marjorie DeVault, Richard Fritz, Rod Nelson, Larry Ouellet and Sandra Schroeder. The table of statistics on police and juvenile court referrals was compiled from data published by the Illinois Institute for Juvenile Research. The Geographical Cross-Reference Table in Part II was prepared by Antoinette LoBosco of the University of Illinois.

Emeritus Professor David Carpenter, former Head of the Department of Sociology at UIC, wrote the Introduction to the *1980 Fact Book,* and also served as editor for many of the statistical tables in the book.

Stephanie Rusnak, of the University of Illinois Sociology Department, was responsible for putting together a coherent final product from the bewildering array of texts, tables and maps. Ms. Rusnak designed the layout for the book, contributed to the copy editing and proofreading, and authored one of the narratives. She and several others gave generously of their time during the Spring of 1984 when the manuscript was being entered into the computer. Assisting in the latter task were members of the UIC Department of Sociology office staff, Rita Bell, Vanessa Miller, Cynthia Smith and, especially, Barbara Nesbary, who entered many of the complex statistical tables which appear in Part II. Other members of the Sociology Department helped out with the final proofreading, including William Erbe, Mildred Schwartz and Wayne Villemez from the faculty, and Helen J. Miller, Administrative Assistant for the department. Mrs. Miller was also responsible for monitoring expenditures on what turned out to be a very complex project budget, with six different accounts.

Acknowledgment should be made here of the services provided by the University of Illinois Computer Center, whose facilities were used to develop most of the statistical tables and all of the text appearing in the book. The textual data were telecommunicated to the University's Office of Publications Services where they were converted electronically to phototypeset copy, a process programmed and supervised by Elizabeth Vandercook, Managing Editor. From the beginning this project has received continuous support from the UIC Administration, and in particular from Richard M. Johnson, Vice Chancellor for Academic Affairs, Irving F. Miller, Dean of the Graduate College, Richard M. Michaels, Associate Dean for Research Development in the Graduate College, and Joseph Peterson, Director of the Center for Research in Law and Justice.

Many persons, groups and organizations thus participated in the production of the *1980 Fact Book*. Any errors contained in the text or tables are the responsibility of the editors, of course, and if any are found we trust that users of the book will communicate them to us.

John W.C. Johnstone
Chicago, Illinois
May, 1984

Table of Contents

Map 1. Chicago-Northwestern Indiana Urbanized Area

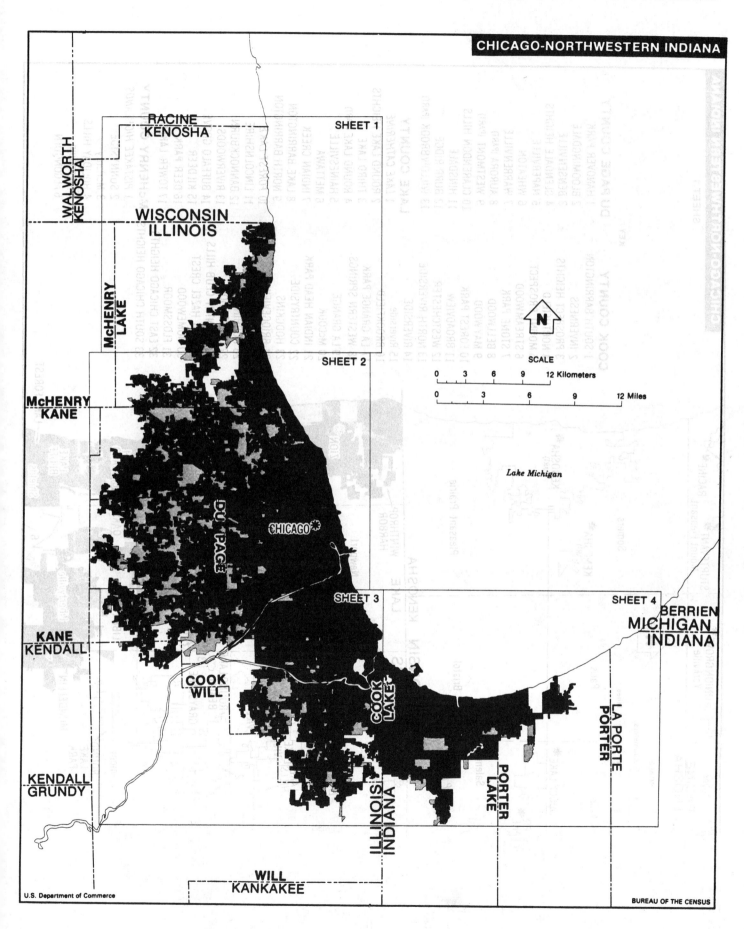

CHICAGO-NORTHWESTERN INDIANA

SHEET 1

RACINE
KENOSHA

WALWORTH
KENOSHA

WISCONSIN
ILLINOIS

McHENRY
LAKE

McHENRY
KANE

SHEET 2

N

SCALE

0   3   6   9   12 Kilometers

0   3   6   9   12 Miles

Lake Michigan

DU PAGE

CHICAGO

SHEET 3

SHEET 4

BERRIEN
MICHIGAN
INDIANA

KANE
KENDALL

COOK
WILL

COOK
LAKE

LA PORTE
PORTER

KENDALL
GRUNDY

PORTER
LAKE

ILLINOIS
INDIANA

WILL
KANKAKEE

U.S. Department of Commerce

BUREAU OF THE CENSUS

Map 1. Chicago-Northwestern Indiana Urbanized Area

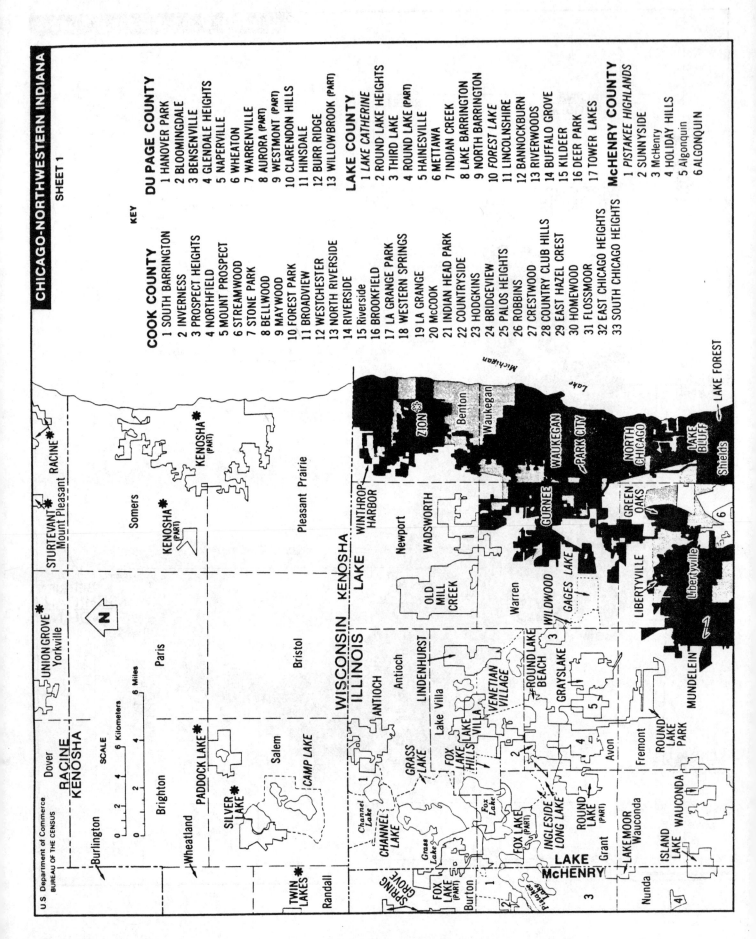

CHICAGO-NORTHWESTERN INDIANA

SHEET 1

KEY

COOK COUNTY
1 SOUTH BARRINGTON
2 INVERNESS
3 PROSPECT HEIGHTS
4 NORTHFIELD
5 MOUNT PROSPECT
6 STREAMWOOD
7 STONE PARK
8 BELLWOOD
9 MAYWOOD
10 FOREST PARK
11 BROADVIEW
12 WESTCHESTER
13 NORTH RIVERSIDE
14 RIVERSIDE
15 Riverside
16 BROOKFIELD
17 LA GRANGE PARK
18 WESTERN SPRINGS
19 LA GRANGE
20 McCOOK
21 INDIAN HEAD PARK
22 COUNTRYSIDE
23 HODGKINS
24 BRIDGEVIEW
25 PALOS HEIGHTS
26 ROBBINS
27 CRESTWOOD
28 COUNTRY CLUB HILLS
29 EAST HAZEL CREST
30 HOMEWOOD
31 FLOSSMOOR
32 EAST CHICAGO HEIGHTS
33 SOUTH CHICAGO HEIGHTS

DU PAGE COUNTY
1 HANOVER PARK
2 BLOOMINGDALE
3 BENSENVILLE
4 GLENDALE HEIGHTS
5 NAPERVILLE
6 WHEATON
7 WARRENVILLE
8 AURORA (PART)
9 WESTMONT (PART)
10 CLARENDON HILLS
11 HINSDALE
12 BURR RIDGE
13 WILLOWBROOK (PART)

LAKE COUNTY
1 *LAKE CATHERINE*
2 ROUND LAKE HEIGHTS
3 THIRD LAKE
4 ROUND LAKE (PART)
5 HAINESVILLE
6 METTAWA
7 INDIAN CREEK
8 LAKE BARRINGTON
9 NORTH BARRINGTON
10 *FOREST LAKE*
11 LINCOLNSHIRE
12 BANNOCKBURN
13 RIVERWOODS
14 BUFFALO GROVE
15 KILDEER
16 DEER PARK
17 TOWER LAKES

McHENRY COUNTY
1 *PISTAKEE HIGHLANDS*
2 SUNNYSIDE
3 McHenry
4 HOLIDAY HILLS
5 Algonquin
6 ALGONQUIN

U S Department of Commerce
BUREAU OF THE CENSUS

SCALE

0   2   4   6 Kilometers

0   2   4   6 Miles

N

RACINE
KENOSHA

Burlington
Dover
Sturtevant
Mount Pleasant
RACINE
Yorkville
UNION GROVE

Brighton
Paris
Somers
KENOSHA (PART)

Wheatland
Salem
Bristol
Pleasant Prairie

PADDOCK LAKE

SILVER LAKE

CAMP LAKE

Randall
TWIN LAKES

WISCONSIN
ILLINOIS

Burton
SPRING GROVE

FOX LAKE (PART)

Nunda
LAKE McHENRY

Grant
LAKEMOOR
Wauconda

ISLAND LAKE
WAUCONDA

FOX LAKE (PART)
INGLESIDE
LONG LAKE
ROUND LAKE (PART)

CHANNEL LAKE

Channel Lake
Grass Lake
Fox Lake

FOX LAKE HILLS

GRASS LAKE

Lake Villa
LAKE VILLA

Antioch
ANTIOCH
LINDENHURST

VENETIAN VILLAGE

Avon
Fremont
ROUND LAKE PARK
ROUND LAKE BEACH
GRAYSLAKE
WILDWOOD
GAGES LAKE

MUNDELEIN
LIBERTYVILLE

KENOSHA
LAKE
WINTHROP HARBOR

Newport
WADSWORTH
OLD MILL CREEK
Warren

GURNEE
GREEN OAKS

Benton
Waukegan
ZION
WAUKEGAN
PARK CITY
NORTH CHICAGO
LAKE BLUFF
Shields

Lake Michigan

LAKE FOREST

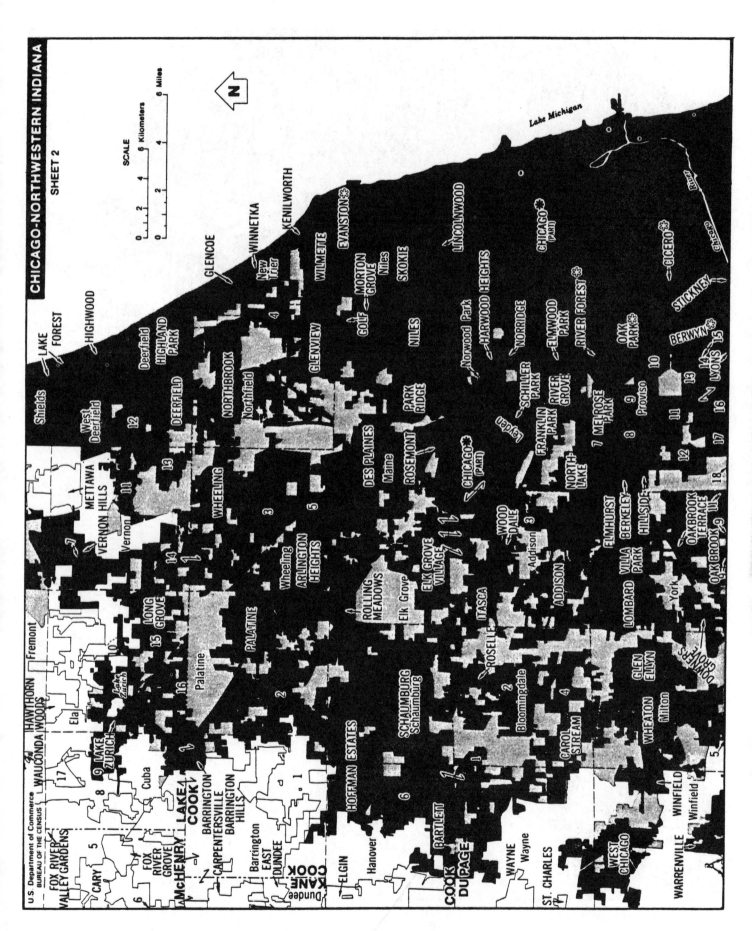

Map 1. Chicago-Northwestern Indiana Urbanized Area

xi

Map 1. Chicago-Northwestern Indiana Urbanized Area

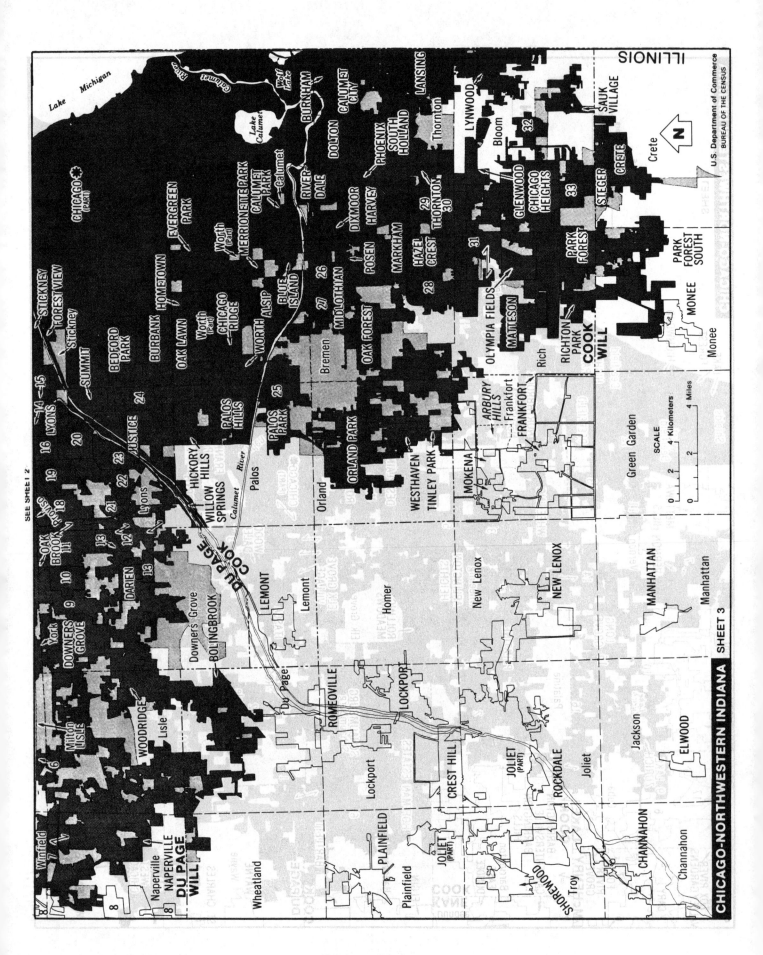

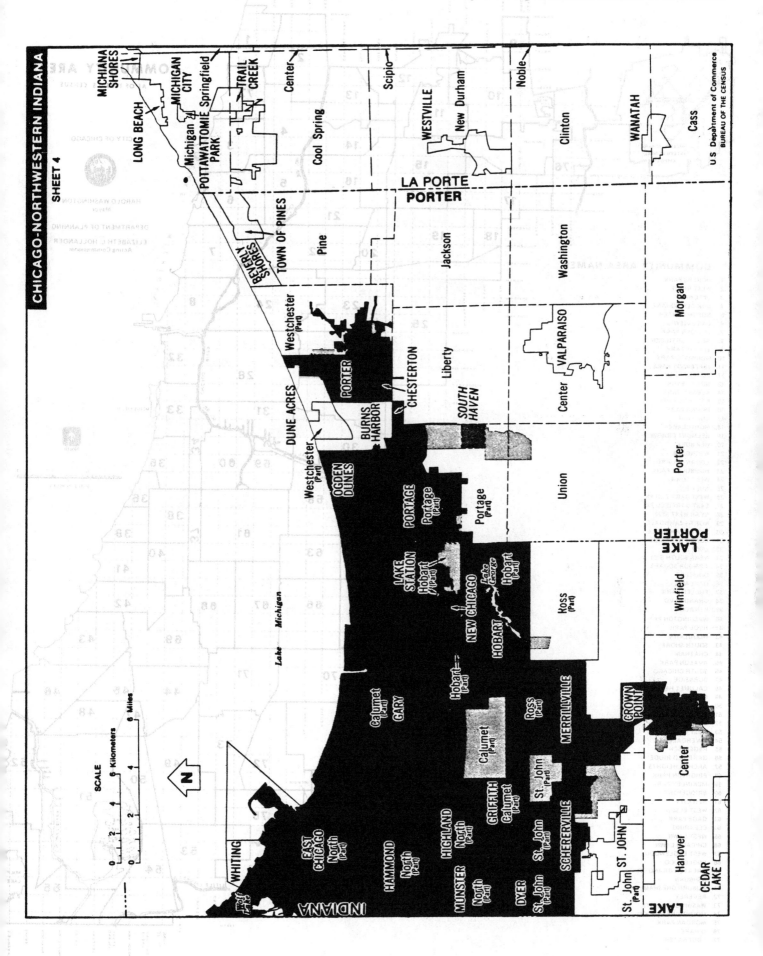

Map 1. Chicago-Northwestern Indiana Urbanized Area

Map 2

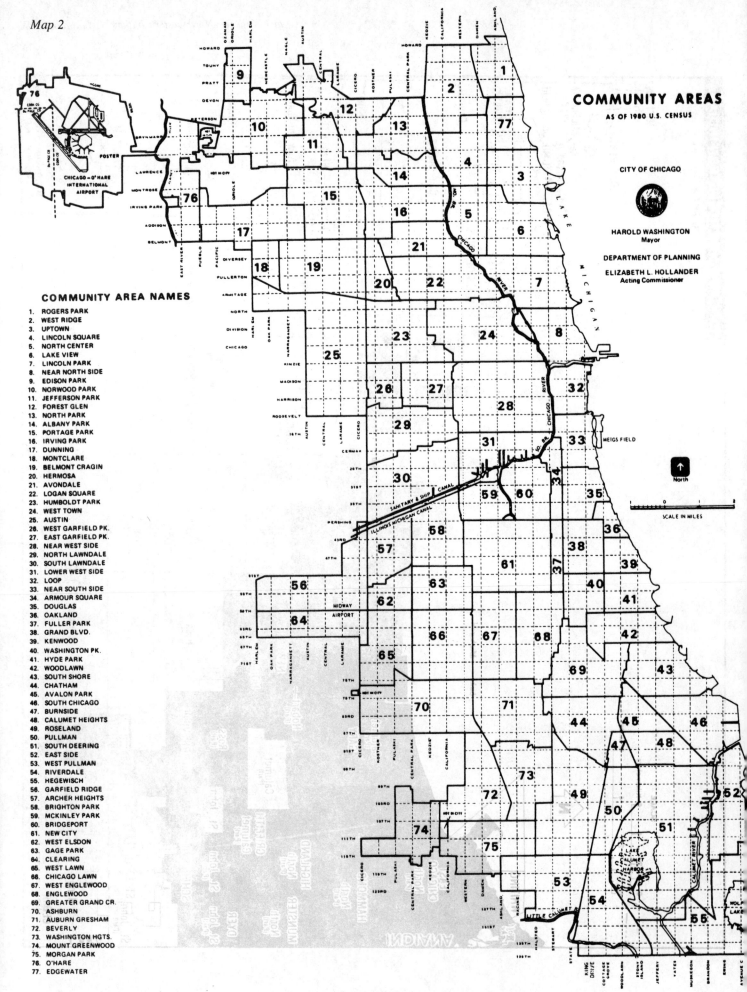

COMMUNITY AREAS

AS OF 1980 U.S. CENSUS

CITY OF CHICAGO

HAROLD WASHINGTON
Mayor

DEPARTMENT OF PLANNING

ELIZABETH L. HOLLANDER
Acting Commissioner

↑
North

SCALE IN MILES

COMMUNITY AREA NAMES

1. ROGERS PARK
2. WEST RIDGE
3. UPTOWN
4. LINCOLN SQUARE
5. NORTH CENTER
6. LAKE VIEW
7. LINCOLN PARK
8. NEAR NORTH SIDE
9. EDISON PARK
10. NORWOOD PARK
11. JEFFERSON PARK
12. FOREST GLEN
13. NORTH PARK
14. ALBANY PARK
15. PORTAGE PARK
16. IRVING PARK
17. DUNNING
18. MONTCLARE
19. BELMONT CRAGIN
20. HERMOSA
21. AVONDALE
22. LOGAN SQUARE
23. HUMBOLDT PARK
24. WEST TOWN
25. AUSTIN
26. WEST GARFIELD PK.
27. EAST GARFIELD PK.
28. NEAR WEST SIDE
29. NORTH LAWNDALE
30. SOUTH LAWNDALE
31. LOWER WEST SIDE
32. LOOP
33. NEAR SOUTH SIDE
34. ARMOUR SQUARE
35. DOUGLAS
36. OAKLAND
37. FULLER PARK
38. GRAND BLVD.
39. KENWOOD
40. WASHINGTON PK.
41. HYDE PARK
42. WOODLAWN
43. SOUTH SHORE
44. CHATHAM
45. AVALON PARK
46. SOUTH CHICAGO
47. BURNSIDE
48. CALUMET HEIGHTS
49. ROSELAND
50. PULLMAN
51. SOUTH DEERING
52. EAST SIDE
53. WEST PULLMAN
54. RIVERDALE
55. HEGEWISCH
56. GARFIELD RIDGE
57. ARCHER HEIGHTS
58. BRIGHTON PARK
59. MCKINLEY PARK
60. BRIDGEPORT
61. NEW CITY
62. WEST ELSDON
63. GAGE PARK
64. CLEARING
65. WEST LAWN
66. CHICAGO LAWN
67. WEST ENGLEWOOD
68. ENGLEWOOD
69. GREATER GRAND CR.
70. ASHBURN
71. AUBURN GRESHAM
72. BEVERLY
73. WASHINGTON HGTS.
74. MOUNT GREENWOOD
75. MORGAN PARK
76. O'HARE
77. EDGEWATER

CHICAGO NEIGHBORHOODS

Map 3

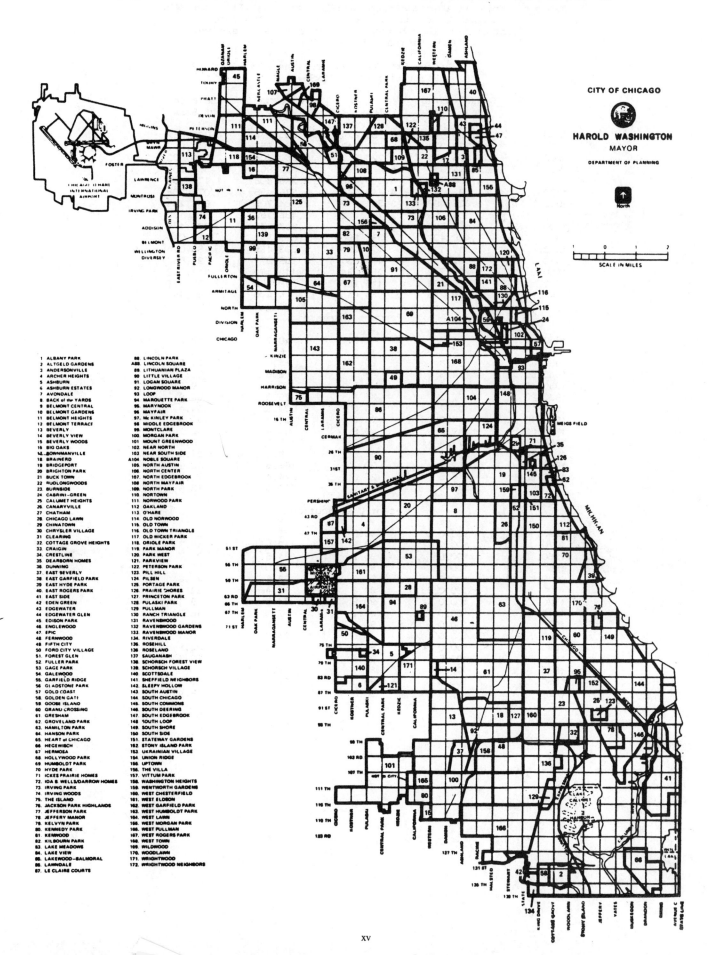

CITY OF CHICAGO

HAROLD WASHINGTON
MAYOR

DEPARTMENT OF PLANNING

North

SCALE IN MILES

1. ALBANY PARK
2. ALTGELD GARDENS
3. ANDERSONVILLE
4. ARCHER HEIGHTS
5. ASHBURN
6. ASHBURN ESTATES
7. AVONDALE
8. BACK of the YARDS
9. BELMONT CENTRAL
10. BELMONT GARDENS
11. BELMONT HEIGHTS
12. BELMONT TERRACE
13. BEVERLY
14. BEVERLY VIEW
15. BEVERLY WOODS
16. BIG OAKS
17. BOWMANVILLE
18. BRAINERD
19. BRIDGEPORT
20. BRIGHTON PARK
21. BUCK TOWN
22. BUDLONGWOODS
23. BURNSIDE
24. CABRINI-GREEN
25. CALUMET HEIGHTS
26. CANARYVILLE
27. CHATHAM
28. CHICAGO LAWN
29. CHINATOWN
30. CHRYSLER VILLAGE
31. CLEARING
32. COTTAGE GROVE HEIGHTS
33. CRAIGIN
34. CRESTLINE
35. DEARBORN HOMES
36. DUNNING
37. EAST BEVERLY
38. EAST GARFIELD PARK
39. EAST HYDE PARK
40. EAST ROGERS PARK
41. EAST SIDE
42. EDEN GREEN
43. EDGEWATER
44. EDGEWATER GLEN
45. EDISON PARK
46. ENGLEWOOD
47. EPIC
48. FERNWOOD
49. FIFTH CITY
50. FORD CITY VILLAGE
51. FOREST GLEN
52. FULLER PARK
53. GAGE PARK
54. GALEWOOD
55. GARFIELD RIDGE
56. GLADSTONE PARK
57. GOLD COAST
58. GOLDEN GATE
59. GOOSE ISLAND
60. GRAND CROSSING
61. GRESHAM
62. GROVELAND PARK
63. HAMILTON PARK
64. HANSON PARK
65. HEART of CHICAGO
66. HEGEWISCH
67. HERMOSA
68. HOLLYWOOD PARK
69. HUMBOLDT PARK
70. HYDE PARK
71. ICKES PRAIRIE HOMES
72. IDA B. WELLS/DARROW HOMES
73. IRVING PARK
74. IRVING WOODS
75. THE ISLAND
76. JACKSON PARK HIGHLANDS
77. JEFFERSON PARK
78. JEFFERY MANOR
79. KELVYN PARK
80. KENNEDY PARK
81. KENWOOD
82. KILBOURN PARK
83. LAKE MEADOWS
84. LAKE VIEW
85. LAKEWOOD
86. LAKEWOOD—BALMORAL
87. LAWNDALE
88. LE CLAIRE COURTS

88. LINCOLN PARK
A88. LINCOLN SQUARE
89. LITHUANIAN PLAZA
90. LITTLE VILLAGE
91. LOGAN SQUARE
92. LONGWOOD MANOR
93. LOOP
94. MARQUETTE PARK
95. MARYNOOK
96. MAYFAIR
97. McKINLEY PARK
98. MIDDLE EDGEBROOK
99. MONTCLARE
100. MORGAN PARK
101. MOUNT GREENWOOD
102. NEAR NORTH
103. NEAR SOUTH SIDE
A104. NOBLE SQUARE
105. NORTH AUSTIN
106. NORTH CENTER
107. NORTH EDGEBROOK
108. NORTH MAYFAIR
109. NORTH PARK
110. NORTOWN
111. NORWOOD PARK
112. OAKLAND
113. O'HARE
114. OLD NORWOOD
115. OLD TOWN
116. OLD TOWN TRIANGLE
117. OLD WICKER PARK
118. ORIOLE PARK
119. PARK MANOR
120. PARK WEST
121. PARKVIEW
122. PETERSON PARK
123. PILL HILL
124. PILSEN
125. PORTAGE PARK
126. PRAIRIE SHORES
127. PRINCETON PARK
128. PULASKI PARK
129. PULLMAN
130. RANCH TRIANGLE
131. RAVENSWOOD
132. RAVENSWOOD GARDENS
133. RAVENSWOOD MANOR
134. RIVERDALE
135. ROSEHILL
136. ROSELAND
137. SAUGANASH
138. SCHORSCH FOREST VIEW
139. SCHORSCH VILLAGE
140. SCOTTSDALE
141. SHEFFIELD NEIGHBORS
142. SLEEPY HOLLOW
143. SOUTH AUSTIN
144. SOUTH CHICAGO
145. SOUTH COMMONS
146. SOUTH DEERING
147. SOUTH EDGEBROOK
148. SOUTH LOOP
149. SOUTH SHORE
150. SOUTH SIDE
151. STATEWAY GARDENS
152. STONY ISLAND PARK
153. UKRAINIAN VILLAGE
154. UNION RIDGE
155. UPTOWN
156. THE VILLA
157. VITTUM PARK
158. WASHINGTON HEIGHTS
159. WENTWORTH GARDENS
160. WEST CHESTERFIELD
161. WEST ELSDON
162. WEST GARFIELD PARK
163. WEST HUMBOLDT PARK
164. WEST LAWN
165. WEST MORGAN PARK
166. WEST PULLMAN
167. WEST ROGERS PARK
168. WEST TOWN
169. WILDWOOD
170. WOODLAWN
171. WRIGHTWOOD
172. WRIGHTWOOD NEIGHBORS

Table A. Total Population of Chicago-Gary-Kenosha, Ill.-Ind.-Wis.
Standard Consolidated Statistical Area, Its Three
Component Standard Metropolitan Statistical Areas and
Their Central Cities: 1840-1980

Chicago Standard Metropolitan
Statistical Area (SMSA)

	Consolidated Area Total	Total	Chicago City	Balance of SMSA
1980.....	7,869,542	7,103,624	3,005,072	4,098,552
1970.....	7,730,231	6,978,947	3,366,957	3,611,990
1960.....	6,895,076	6,220,913	3,550,404	2,670,509
1950.....	5,661,334	5,177,868	3,620,962	1,556,906
1940.....	4,954,179	4,569,643	3,396,808	1,172,835
1930.....	4,797,054	4,449,646	3,376,438	1,073,208
1920.....	3,626,493	3,394,996	2,701,705	693,291
1910.....	2,838,798	2,702,465	2,185,283	517,182
1900.....	2,163,524	2,084,750	1,698,575	386,175
1890.....	1,449,409	1,391,890	1,099,850	292,040
1880.....	817,118	771,250	503,185	268,065
1870.....	532,959	493,531	298,977	194,554
1860.....	292,742	259,384	112,172	147,212
1850.....	135,244	115,285	29,963	85,322
1840.....	39,246	35,616	4,470	31,146

Percent Increase

	Consolidated Area Total	Total	Chicago City	Balance of SMSA
1970-80..	1.8	1.8	-10.7	13.5
1960-70..	12.1	12.2	-5.2	35.3
1950-60..	21.8	20.1	-1.9	71.5
1940-50..	14.3	13.3	6.6	32.7
1930-40..	3.3	2.7	0.6	9.3
1920-30..	32.3	31.1	25.0	54.8
1910-20..	27.7	25.6	23.6	34.1
1900-10..	31.2	29.6	28.7	33.9
1890-00..	49.3	49.8	54.4	32.2
1880-90..	77.4	80.5	118.6	8.9
1870-80..	53.3	56.3	68.3	37.8
1860-70..	82.1	90.3	166.5	32.2
1850-60..	116.5	125.0	274.4	72.5
1840-50..	244.6	223.7	570.3	173.9

Percent Distribution

	Consolidated Area Total	Total	Chicago City	Balance of SMSA
1980.....	100.0	90.3	38.2	52.1
1970.....	100.0	90.3	43.6	46.7
1960.....	100.0	90.2	51.5	38.7
1950.....	100.0	91.5	64.0	27.5
1940.....	100.0	92.2	68.6	23.6
1930.....	100.0	92.8	70.4	22.4
1920.....	100.0	93.6	74.5	19.1
1910.....	100.0	95.2	77.0	18.2
1900.....	100.0	96.4	78.5	17.9
1890.....	100.0	96.0	75.9	20.1
1880.....	100.0	94.4	61.6	32.8
1870.....	100.0	92.6	56.1	36.5
1860.....	100.0	88.6	38.3	50.3
1850.....	100.0	85.2	22.1	63.1
1840.....	100.0	90.8	11.4	79.4

Table A. Total Population of Chicago-Gary-Kenosha, Ill.-Ind.-Wis.
Standard Consolidated Statistical Area, Its Three
Component Standard Metropolitan Statistical Areas and
Their Central Cities: 1840-1980

	Gary -- Hammond -- East Chicago Statistical Area (SMSA)			Kenosha SMSA		
	Total	Gary, Hammond & E. Chicago Cities	Balance of SMSA	Total	Kenosha City	Balance of SMSA
1980.....	642,781	285,453	357,328	123,137	77,685	45,452
1970.....	633,367	330,380	302,987	117,917	78,805	39,112
1960.....	573,548	347,687	225,861	100,615	67,899	32,716
1950.....	408,228	275,768	132,460	75,238	54,368	20,870
1940.....	321,031	236,540	84,491	63,505	48,765	14,740
1930.....	284,131	219,770	64,361	63,277	50,262	13,015
1920.....	180,213	127,349	52,864	51,284	40,472	10,812
1910.....	103,404	56,825	46,579	32,929	21,371	11,558
1900.....	57,067	15,787	41,280	21,707	11,606	10,101
1890.....	41,938	6,683	35,255	15,581	6,532	9,049
1880.....	32,318	...	32,318	13,550	5,039	8,511
1870.....	26,281	...	26,281	13,147	4,309	8,838
1860.....	19.458	...	19,458	13,900	3,990	9,910
1850.....	9,225	...	9,225	10,734	3,455	7,279
1840.....	3,630	.·..	3,630	----	----	----

Percent Increase

	Total	Gary, Hammond & E. Chicago Cities	Balance of SMSA	Total	Kenosha City	Balance of SMSA
1970-80..	1.5	-13.6	17.9	4.4	-1.4	16.2
1960-70..	10.4	-5.0	34.1	17.2	16.1	19.6
1950-60..	40.5	26.1	70.5	33.7	24.9	56.8
1940-50..	27.2	16.6	56.8	18.5	11.5	41.6
1930-40..	13.0	7.6	31.3	0.4	-3.0	13.3
1920-30..	57.7	72.6	21.7	23.4	24.2	20.4
1910-20..	74.3	124.1	13.5	55.7	89.4	-6.5
1900-10..	81.2	260.0	12.8	51.7	84.1	14.4
1890-00..	36.1	136.2	17.1	39.3	77.7	11.6
1880-90..	29.8	...	9.1	15.0	29.6	6.3
1870-80..	23.0	...	23.0	3.1	16.9	-3.7
1860-70..	35.1	...	35.1	-5.4	8.0	-10.8
1850-60..	110.9	...	110.9	29.5	15.5	36.1
1840-50..	154.1	...	154.1	----	----	----

Percent Distribution

	Total	Gary, Hammond & E. Chicago Cities	Balance of SMSA	Total	Kenosha City	Balance of SMSA
1980.....	8.1	3.6	4.5	1.6	1.0	0.6
1970.....	8.2	4.3	3.9	1.5	1.0	0.5
1960.....	8.3	5.0	3.3	1.5	1.0	0.5
1950.....	7.2	4.9	2.3	1.3	1.0	0.3
1940.....	6.5	4.8	1.7	1.3	1.0	0.3
1930.....	5.9	4.6	1.3	1.3	1.0	0.3
1920.....	5.0	3.5	1.5	1.4	1.1	0.3
1910.....	3.6	2.0	1.6	1.2	0.8	0.4
1900.....	2.6	0.7	1.9	1.0	0.5	0.5
1890.....	2.9	0.5	2.4	1.1	0.5	0.6
1880.....	4.0	...	4.0	1.6	0.6	1.0
1870.....	4.9	...	4.9	2.5	0.8	1.7
1860.....	6.7	...	6.7	4.7	1.4	3.3
1850.....	6.8	...	6.8	8.0	2.6	5.4
1840.....	9.2	...	9.2	---	---	---

Introduction

In his introduction to the first *Local Community Fact Book,* published in 1938, Professor Louis Wirth observed that: "The modern metropolis is a city of cities. It is a mosaic of little worlds, an aggregate of local comunities, each one differentiated from the others by its characteristic function in the total economy and cultural complex of city life."

To action agencies — government, business, industry, labor, welfare, health, education, and the like — no less than to the individual, the metropolitan area is also a congeries of political, economic, and social worlds. Problems of day-to-day functioning—whether they be seeking markets, employing labor, distributing newspapers, administering the schools, providing public housing, conducting welfare programs, conserving deteriorating areas, redeveloping slum areas, or selecting industrial sites — necessarily involve consideration of local communities within the vast metropolitan agglomeration. The metropolitan area as a whole or even the City of Chicago is much too large and heterogeneous an area for analysis of these and many other problems.

The *Fact Book* is designed to fulfill the need for a convenient compilation of a variety of information on local communities within the metropolitan area. Early editions of the *Fact Book* were limited to 75 community areas within the City of Chicago. The inadequacies of considering only the central city portion of the metropolitan area, however, were recognized in Professor Wirth's introduction to the first *Fact Book:* "The residential and industrial suburbs of Chicago, such as Evanston, Oak Park, Lake Forest, Glen Ellyn, Cicero, East Chicago, and Hammond are outside of the municipal limits by historical accident; but, by virtue of their role in the economic and social life, they are quite as much a part of the metropolis of Chicago as are the communities within the city limits, such as Beverly Hills, Austin, Norwood Park, South Chicago, Clearing, and New City." The scope of this edition of the *Fact Book* has been enlarged to embrace the entire nine-county Chicago-Gary-Kenosha Standard Consolidated Statistical Area (Cook, DuPage, Kane, Lake, McHenry, and Will Counties in Illinois, Lake and Porter Counties in Indiana, and Kenosha County in Wisconsin). Data are presented for 131 incorporated communities of 10,000 or more population in the Consolidated Areas as well as for 77 community areas within the City of Chicago.

The Concept of Community Areas

The 77 community areas within the City of Chicago were first delineated as 75 areas more than 50 years ago, through the work of the Social Science Research Committee of the University of Chicago, building upon the years of research activity of its predecessor, the Local Community Research Committee, with the cooperation and concerted effort of many local agencies and the United States Bureau of the Census. The boundaries of the 75 community areas were originally drawn on the basis of several considerations, chief among which were: (1) the settlement, growth, and history of the area; (2) local identification with the area; (3) the local trade area; (4) distribution of membership of local institutions; and (5) natural and artificial barriers such as the Chicago River and its branches, railroad lines, local transportation systems, and parks and boulevards. The actual boundaries drawn were necessarily a compromise, involving in addition to these factors the tabulation requirements of the U.S. Bureau of the Census. Community areas comprise complete census tracts, so that the regularly published census data for hundreds of tracts can be compiled into more convenient form for studying the characteristics and changes in the characteristics of local communities.

Community areas at the present time are best regarded as statistical units for the analysis of varying conditions within the City of Chicago at a given time, and for studying changes over time in conditions within local communities. When community area boundaries were delineated more than 50 years ago, the objective was to define a set of subareas of the city each of which could be regarded as having a history of its own as a community, a name, an awareness on the part of its inhabitants of common interests, and a set of local businesses and organizations oriented to the local community. As initially designated, community areas measured up to these criteria in varying degree. Over time, there have been major changes in the distribution of people and in specific patterns of land use. Rather than revising the boundaries of community areas at each census, there has been a deliberate effort to maintain a constant set of subareas within the city in order to analyze changes in the social, economic and residential structure of the city. Redefining boundaries every ten years would destroy the usefulness of the grid for studying change, and would not greatly increase the utility of community areas for the study of characteristics at one point in time. The initial set of community area boundaries represented a compromise, and no single set of boundaries then or now could satisfy everyone interested in studying local communities. For particular analyses, researchers may find other groupings of census tracts more useful, for example, to pinpoint areas of dilapidated housing or areas of high income at a given point in time, but a fixed set of communities with some historical basis — such as that provided by the community areas — is generally most useful for the analysis of changing composition and structure over time. The community areas, for which Chicago statistics have been compiled since 1930, not only serve this purpose admirably, but they remain, in many cases, meaningful local communities. Two additional community areas since 1960 are Area 76 (O'Hare Airport and adjacent area) and Area 77 (Edgewater-formerly part of Area 3-Uptown).

Previous Statistics for Community Areas

Statistics for the 75 community areas were first published in *Census Data of the City of Chicago, 1930,* edited by Ernest W. Burgess and Charles Newcomb, and published by the University of Chicago Press in 1933. Professor Burgess, it should be noted, was chiefly responsible for the research activities which produced the census tract grid of the City of Chicago for the 1920 Census, and for planning the special tabulation of census tract statistics based on the 1920 Census and published in *Census Data of the City of Chicago, 1920,* edited by Ernest W. Burgess and Charles Newcomb (University of Chicago Press, 1931).

Additional statistics for the 75 community areas appeared in the *District Fact Book,* edited by Edward L. Burchard and Martin J. Arvin, and published in 1935 by the Chicago Board of Education, the Chicago Recreation Commission and the Illinois Emergency Relief Commission. This publication, compiled as a manual for civic and social agencies interested in facts about subareas within the City of Chicago, contained 1934 and 1930 census data. The first *Local Community Fact Book,* edited by Louis Wirth and Margaret Furez, was in fact a revised edition of the *District Fact Book* containing, in addition to revisions in form, more detailed statistical data and expanded histories of the community areas. It was published in 1938 by the Chicago Recreation Commission.

Between the publication of the first and second *Fact Books,* the Chicago Plan Commission and Work Projects Administration published a series of pamphlets, *Housing in Chicago Communities* (one for each of the 75 community areas), containing some of the data collected in the Land Use Survey of 1939 and also selected census statistics from the 1934 and preceding censuses. Mention should also be made of the volume, *Census Data of the City of Chicago, 1934,* edited by Charles Newcomb and Richard O. Lang, and published by the University of Chicago Press in 1934. This volume was based on the special 1934 Census of Chicago, which was compiled as a project of the Civil Works Administration, and presented statistics for the 935 census tracts but did not summarize the data by community areas.

The second *Local Community Fact Book of Chicago,* edited by Louis Wirth and Eleanor H. Bernert, published in 1949 under the auspices of the Chicago Community Inventory, contained comparative statistical data for each community area based on the 1940 and 1930 Censuses, together with other selected statistics.

The *Local Community Fact Book for Chicago, 1950,* edited by Philip M. Hauser and Evelyn M. Kitagawa, was published in 1953, under the auspices of the Chicago Community Inventory with the cooperation of a large number of city organizations. A variety of data from the 1950 Census was presented for each community area, together with a history of the area, summary measures for each census tract in the area, comparative statistical data from the 1940 and 1930 Censuses, and selected social statistics from other sources.

The Local Community Fact Book, Chicago Metropolitan Area, 1960, edited by Evelyn M. Kitagawa and Karl E. Taeuber, was published in 1963, under the Chicago Community Inventory, University of Chicago, Philip M. Hauser, Director. Cooperating in the Inventory were a large number of city and metropolitan organizations. A variety of data from the 1960 Census was presented for each community area and for each suburban city of 25,000 or more population, together with a history of each community area and major suburb, summary measures for each census tract in the area, comparative statistical data from earlier Censuses, and selected social statistics from other sources. Additional statistical data were provided for the Chicago-Northwestern Indiana Standard Consolidated Area, for the six counties in Illinois and two counties in Indiana making up the Consolidated Area, and for the 75 cities of 10,000 or more population in the Standard Consolidated Area.

While no 1970 edition of the *Local Community Fact Book, Chicago Metropolitan Area,* was issued, a volume entitled *Community Area Data Book for the City of Chicago: 1970 Census Data by 75 Community Areas* was published by the Chicago Association of Commerce and Industry, Research and Statistical Division, and Osla Financial Services Corporation.

Organization of the 1980 Fact Book

Under the chairmanship of the late Professor David W. Street of the University of Illinois at Chicago, the Chicago Fact Book Consortium was formed to revive the decennial *Fact Book* publication. Following Professor Street's untimely death in 1980, Professor John W. C. Johnstone became chairman of the Consortium, composed of representatives from major universities and from business, social and governmental agencies in the Chicago Metropolitan area. Participants in this Consortium are listed on the cover page.

The content of the *1980 Community Fact Book* is similar to the 1960 version, though the book is organized somewhat differently, and both 1980 and 1970 statistical summaries are presented for the community areas and cities described in Part I. In addition, data are also included for Kenosha County, Wisconsin, as the ninth county in the newly-defined and named Chicago-Gary-Kenosha, Ill.-Ind.-Wis. Standard Consolidated Statistical Area, as designated by the U.S. Office of Management and Budget.

The 1980 edition of the *Fact Book* is organized into four major parts, plus an introductory section. This Introduction includes descriptions of the various geographic areas for which data are presented, definitions and explanations of census statistics, and sources of data for local communities. Three maps appear on the pages immediately preceding the Introduction, including a 5-page Bureau of the Census map of the Chicago-Northwestern Indiana Urbanized Area, which also shows Kenosha County, Wisconsin; an outline map of the Community Areas in the City of Chicago; and a map of Chicago Neighborhoods to indicate the overlap between the original community areas and currently recognized Chicago neighborhoods. The latter two maps were obtained from the City of Chicago Department of Planning. A table of historical statistics for the Consolidated Area is also shown here.

Part I, the main body of the volume, contains statistics and historical narratives for each of the 77 Chicago Community Areas and the 48 other cities in the Standard Consolidated Area which had achieved populations of 25,000 or more by 1980. This section is much expanded over the 1960 edition of the *Fact Book;* it includes data on 24 additional cities in the Metropolitan Area, plus Community Area 77, Edgewater, and also includes community and census tract data from both the 1980 and 1970 U.S. censuses. For each of 125 communities or cities, then, Part I present an updated (or newly written) historical narrative, a map identifying component census tracts, a table summarizing population and housing characteristics from 1930 to 1980, and two tables of selected community and tract characteristics, one for 1980 and one for 1970. Each of the 48 cities outside Chicago is identified in Part I by its census-defined Place number, as well as by name.

Part II presents several tables of non-census statistics for the Chicago Community Areas. Definitions, explanations and sources of these data appear in the Introduction to Part II. This section also includes a chart (Table II-7) which relates City of Chicago census tract boundaries to political, police and educational districts, and to Zip Code areas. For some of the tables in this series separate compilations of data were not available for Uptown and Edgewater, and are reported, combined, under Community Area 3 — Uptown.

Detailed census statistics for Chicago Community Areas are presented in Part III. Comparable data for individual cities of 25,000 or more in the Consolidated Area are not reproduced in Part III, but they are readily available in the regular census tract reports published by the Bureau of the Census.

Finally, Part IV presents tables summarizing selected 1980 and 1970 population and housing characteristics for each of the 77 Community Areas in the City of Chicago, and each of the 131 cities of 10,000 or more population in the Standard Consolidated Area.

Area Classifications

Each person enumerated in the 1980 Census was counted as an inhabitant of his or her usual place of abode, which is generally construed to mean the place where one lives and sleeps most of the time. This place is not necessarily the same as one's legal residence, voting residence, or domicile.

Persons in the Armed Forces quartered on military installations were enumerated as residents of the States, counties, and county subdivisions in which their installations were located. Members of their families were enumerated where they actually resided. College students were considered residents of the communities in which they were residing while attending college. The crews of vessels of the U.S. Navy and the U.S. Merchant Marine in harbors of the United States were counted as part of the population of the ports in which their vessels were berthed on April 1, 1980. Inmates of institutions, who ordinarily live there for long periods of time, were counted as inhabitants of the place in which the institution was located, whereas patients in general hospitals, who ordinarily remain for short periods of time, were counted at, or allocated to, their homes.

Metropolitan Areas. It is clear that the City of Chicago does not include within its legal boundaries the entire population aggregation and the economic and social entity identified with Chicago. There is no single political or governmental unit which defines the total economic and social reality of which the City of Chicago is the central core. For census and general governmental statistical purposes, the U.S. Office of Management and Budget had delineated "Standard Metropolitan Statistical Areas" (SMSA's) around each large city. Each SMSA includes at least one city of 50,000 inhabitants or more, the county in which that city is located and contiguous counties which are essentially metropolitan in character and are socially and economically integrated with the central city.

The Chicago SMSA comprises six counties in Illinois: Cook, Du-Page, Kane, Lake, McHenry, and Will. The Gary-Hammond-East Chicago SMSA comprises two counties in Indiana: Lake and Porter. The Kenosha SMSA comprises one county in Wisconsin: Kenosha. Together, the nine counties of the three SMSA's comprise the Chicago-Gary-Kenosha, Ill.-Ind.-Wis. Standard Consolidated Statistical Area.

The metropolitan areas defined in previous censuses differed from those in the 1980 Census. Throughout this edition of the *Fact Book* the 1980 definitions are used. For the historical statistics on metropolitan growth in Table A, this required assembling county data from previous censuses, and combining them into metropolitan areas as defined in 1980.

Urbanized Area. In order to provide a better separation of urban and rural population in the vicinity of large cities, the U.S. Bureau of the Census has delineated Urbanized Areas. An Urbanized Area comprises an incorporated place and adjacent densely settled surroundings that together have a minimum population of 50,000. The densely settled surrounding area consists of the surrounding closely settled incorporated places and unincorporated areas, contiguous territory with a population density of 1,000 inhabitants or more per square mile, and small blocks of less densely settled territory to eliminate enclaves and gross irregularities in boundaries. Enumeration districts (ED's) were the basic geographic units used in eliminating enclaves and determining population density in contiguous unincorporated territory. The Chicago-Northwestern Indiana Urbanized Area extends north to the Wisconsin border, southeast into Porter County, Indiana and has arms extending west of Palatine, Winfield, and Lisle, and south to Crete. A complete boundary description and detailed map of the Urbanized Area may be found in U.S. Bureau of the Census, *U.S. Census of Housing, 1980: General Housing Characteristics, Illinois,* HC 80-1-A15, pp. 468-472.

All of the population in an Urbanized Area is counted as urban, as is population living in urban places outside of Urbanized Areas. By contrast, a Standard Metropolitan Statistical Area includes both urban and rural population, and is generally larger and more extensive than the corresponding Urbanized Area, especially since the SMSA is comprised of entire counties. The Urbanized Area represents the agglomeration of contiguous dense settlement; the metropolitan area includes in addition the surrounding rural and urban population that is socially and economically integrated with the central city.

Cities within the Consolidated Area. Within the Chicago Standard Consolidated Area, there are 48 incorporated places with a 1980 population of 25,000 or more, and 83 incorporated places with a 1980 population of 10,000-24,999. In general, the range of census data summarized in Part I of the *Fact Book* for places with 25,000 or more inhabitants is the same as that presented for the 77 community areas within Chicago. Selected census characteristics of places with 10,000-24,999 inhabitants are summarized in Part IV. For convenience in tables all 131 incorporated places are referred to as cities,

and the designation of city, village or town is dropped from the place names.

Census Tracts. The entire Consolidated Area has been divided for statistical purposes into small areas known as census tracts, for which a wide range of census data are tabulated and published. Census tract boundaries were established cooperatively by a local Census Tract Committee and the U.S. Bureau of the Census. The average tract in the Consolidated Area has about 5,000 residents. Tract boundaries are established with the intention of being maintained over a long period of time so that comparisons may be made from census to census. Census tracts were first delineated for the City of Chicago for the 1910 Census. The grid of 935 tracts delineated for the 1930 Census remained essentially unaltered through later Censuses. Some revisions in the Chicago tract grid were necessary for the 1980 Census, but the changes took the form mainly of combining two or more tracts with small populations, or of splitting tracts with very large populations into two or more smaller tracts.

Portions of the metropolitan area surrounding the City of Chicago were tracted in 1950, but the 1960 Census was the first for which the entire Consolidated Area was tracted. The rapid rate of growth of much of the area outside Chicago, and the frequency of annexations to the many individual incorporated places, posed a serious problem in designing the census tract grid. Stability of tract boundaries over time is crucial if tracts are to serve their basic function in the study of changes over time in the characteristics of small areas. If tract boundaries were drawn to correspond with the boundaries of incorporated places, however, many of the tracts would have to be altered at each census to take account of annexations. A compromise solution was reached for tracts in the Chicago Consolidated Area. Census tracts were delineated such that their boundaries never cross township boundaries. Within the older close-in suburbs, which have no room for expansion, tract boundaries do not cross the boundaries of incorporated places. Elsewhere, tracts were drawn in a fairly regular fashion, ignoring the current boundaries of specific places. Census tracts spanning the boundaries of any place of 25,000 or more are designated as "split tracts," and census data are published separately for the part of the tract within the place and the part of the tract lying outside the place.

The census tract data presented in Part I for cities of 25,000 or more inhabitants refer, in the case of "split tracts," to the portions that lie wholly within the city boundaries. Split tracts are designated on the city maps by the designation "part" or "pt.," and are footnoted in the tract summary tables.

Census tract comparability between 1970 and 1980 is shown in detail in Tables A and B at the front of the first volume of each 1980 census tract report. For the Chicago-Gary-Kenosha Standard Consolidated Statistical Area, one needs to refer to all three SMSA census tract reports: *Census Tracts, Chicago, Ill. Standard Metropolitan Statistical Area; Census Tracts, Gary-Hammond-East Chicago, Ind. Standard Metropolitan Statistical Area; Census Tracts, Kenosha, Wis. Standard Metropolitan Statistical Area.*

For census tract changes in earlier decades, comparable tables appear in 1970 census tract reports and in earlier reports. For a discussion of the impact of census tract changes on community areas in the City of Chicago between 1950 and 1960, see pages xvii and xviii of the *1960 Community Fact Book.*

Community Areas. The general purpose and history of the system of community areas in the City of Chicago are described in the first part of the Introduction. The system of 75 community areas, delineated for the 1930 Census out of combinations of the 935 census tracts, remained essentially unaltered for later Censuses with two major exceptions.

The largest territorial annexations to the City of Chicago during the last 50 years occurred in the 1950's in connection with the development of O'Hare International Airport. Much of the annexed territory including and surrounding the airport was delineated as a separate community area, number 76, O'Hare, for the 1960 Census.

Community area number 77 was delineated for the 1980 Census in response to local community support in Edgewater for separation of 1970 community area number 3 (Uptown) into a northern area (number 77 — Edgewater) and a southern area (number 3 — Uptown).

Definitions of Census Items

All of the statistics presented in Parts I, III and IV of the *Fact Book* are from the U.S. Censuses of Population and Housing, and the definitions and concepts follow census usage. Brief definitions and explanations of individual items are given below. For the most part, these explanations are excerpted from the published census volumes. For more thorough discussions, consult the introductory sections and appendices of the 1980 Census publications of the U.S. Bureau of the Census, particularly: *U.S. Census of Population and Housing: 1980 Census Tracts. Final Report PHC80-2*, any number. Definitions and explanations of the non-census data in Part II of the *Fact Book* are given in the Introduction to Part II.

The interpretation of census data requires some understanding of the way the data were collected and tabulated. The 1980 census was conducted primarily through self-enumeration. A census questionnaire was delivered by postal carriers to every housing unit several days before Census Day, April 1, 1980. This questionnaire included explanatory information and was accompanied by an instruction guide. Spanish-language versions of the questionnaire and instruction guide were available on request. The questionnaire was also available in narrative translation in 32 languages.

In most areas of the United States, altogether containing about 95 percent of the population, the householder was requested to fill out and mail back the questionnaire on Census Day. Approximately 83 percent of these households returned their forms by mail. Households that did not mail back a form and vacant housing units were visited by an enumerator. Households that returned a form with incomplete or inconsistent information that exceeded a specified tolerance were contacted by telephone or, if necessary, by a personal visit, to obtain the missing information.

In the remaining (mostly sparsely settled) areas of the country, which contained about 5 percent of the population, the householder was requested to fill out the questionnaire and hold until visited by an enumerator. Incomplete and unfilled forms were completed by interview during the enumerator's visit. Vacant units were enumerated by a personal visit and observation.

Each housing unit in the country received one of two versions of the census questionnaire: a short-form questionnaire containing a limited number of basic population and housing questions or a long-form questionnaire containing these basic questions as well as a number of additional questions. A sampling procedure was used to determine those units which were to receive the long-form questionnaire. Two sampling rates were employed. For most of the country, one in every six housing units (about 17 percent) received the long form or sample questionnaire; in counties, incorporated places and minor civil divisions estimated to have fewer than 2,500 inhabitants, every other housing unit (50 percent) received the sample questionnaire to enhance the reliability of sample data in small areas.

Special questionnaires were used for the enumeration of persons in group quarters such as colleges and universities, hospitals, prisons, military installations, and ships. These forms contained the population questions but did not include any housing questions. In addition to the regular census questionnaires, the Supplementary Questionnaire for American Indians was used in conjunction with the short form on Federal and State reservations and in the historic areas of Oklahoma (excluding urbanized areas) for households that had at least one American Indian, Eskimo, or Aleut household member.

The 1980 census questionnaires were processed in a manner similar to that for the 1970 and 1960 censuses. They were designed to be processed electronically by the Film Optical Sensing Device for Input to Computer (FOSDIC). For most items on the questionnaire, the information supplied by the respondent or obtained by the enumerator was indicated by marking the answer in predesignated positions that would be "read" by FOSDIC from a microfilm copy of the questionnaire and transferred onto computer tape with no intervening manual processing. The computer tape did not include information on individual names and addresses.

The data processing was performed in two stages. All 100-percent data, all short forms, and pages 2 and 3 of the long forms (which have the same questions as the short form), were microfilmed, "read" by FOSDIC, and transferred onto computer tape for tabulation. For the sample data, the long form (or sample) questionnaires were processed through manual coding operations since some questions required the respondent to provide write-in entries which could not be read by FOSDIC. Census Bureau coders assigned alphabetical or numerical codes to the write-in answers in FOSDIC readable code boxes on each questionnaire. After all coding was completed, the long forms were microfilmed, and the film was "read" by FOSDIC and transferred onto computer tape.

The tape containing the information from the questionnaires was processed on the Census Bureau's computers through a number of editing and tabulation steps.

A more detailed description of the data collection and processing procedures can be obtained from the 1980 Census of Population and Housing, Users' Guide, PHC80-R1.

Much of the material presented here concerning Census definitions and procedures is taken from Appendices A through F appearing in each of the census tract reports of the 1980 Census of Population and housing. Interested readers are referred to these appendices: *Appendix A. — Area Classifications; Appendix B. — Definitions and Explanations of Subject Characteristics; Appendix C. — General Enumeration and Processing Procedures; Appendix D. — Accuracy of the Data; Appendix E. — Facsimiles of Respondent Instructions and Questionnaires Pages; Appendix F. — Publication and Computer Tape Program.*

Race. The data on race were derived from answers to question 4, which was asked of all persons. The concept of race as used by the Census Bureau reflects self-identification by respondents; it does not denote any clear-cut scientific definition of biological stock. Since the 1980 census obtained information on race through self-identification, the data represent self-classification by people according to the race with which they identify.

For persons who could not provide a single response to the race question, the race of the person's mother was used; however, if a single response could not be provided for the person's mother, the first race reported by the person was used. This is a modification of the 1970 census procedure in which the race of the person's father was used.

The category "White" includes persons who indicated their race as White, as well as persons who did not classify themselves in one of the specific race categories listed on the questionnaire but entered a response such as Canadian, German, Italian, Lebanese, or Polish. In the 1980 census, persons who did not classify themselves in one of the specific race categories but marked "Other" and wrote in entries such as Cuban, Puerto Rican, Mexican, or Dominican were included in the

"Other" race category. In the 1970 census, most of these persons were included in the "White" category.

The category "Black" includes persons who indicated their race as Black or Negro, as well as persons who did not classify themselves in one of the specific race categories listed on the questionnaire but reported entries such as Jamaican, Black Puerto Rican, West Indian, Haitian, or Nigerian.

The category "American Indian, Eskimo, and Aleut" includes persons who classified themselves as such in one of the specific race categories. In addition, persons who did not report themselves in one of the specific race categories but entered the name of an Indian tribe or reported such entries as Canadian Indian, French American Indian, or Spanish American Indian were classified as American Indian.

The category "Asian and Pacific Islander" includes persons who indicated their race as Chinese, Filipino, Japanese, Asian Indian, Korean, Vietnamese, Hawaiian, Samoan, or Guamanian. The category "Other Asian and Pacific Islander" includes persons who provided write-in entries of such Asian and Pacific Islander groups as Cambodian, Laotian, Pakistani, and Fiji Islander under the "Other" race category. Persons who did not classify themselves in one of the specific race categories but wrote in an entry indicating one of the nine categories listed above (e.g., Chinese and Filipino) were classified accordingly. For example, entries of Nipponese and Japanese American were classified as Japanese; entries of Taiwanese and Cantonese as Chinese, etc.

Differences between 1980 census and 1970 census population totals by race seriously affect the comparability for certain race groups. First, a large number of Spanish origin persons reported their race differently in the 1980 census than in the 1970 census; this difference in reporting has a substantial impact on the counts and comparability for the "White" population and the "Race, n.e.c." or "Other" race population (shown as "All other" races in 1970). A much larger proportion of the Spanish origin population in 1980 than in 1970 reported their race in the questionnaire category "Other." Second, in 1970, most persons who marked the "Other" race category and wrote in a Spanish designation such as Mexican, Venezuelan, Latino, etc., were reclassified as "White." In 1980, such persons were not reclassified but remained in the "Other" race category. As a result of this procedural change and the differences in reporting by this population the proportion of the Spanish origin population classified as "Other" race in the 1980 census was substantially higher than that in the 1970 census.

Spanish/Hispanic Origin. The data on Spanish/Hispanic origin or descent were derived from answers to question 7, which was asked of all persons. Information on the Spanish origin population shown in this report is derived from both the 1980 census 100-percent and sample tabulations.

Persons of Spanish/Hispanic origin or descent are those who reported Mexican, Puerto Rican, Cuban or other Spanish/Hispanic origin in question 7. Persons who reported "other Spanish/Hispanic" origin were those whose origins are from Spain or the Spanish-speaking countries of Central or South America, or they are persons identifying their origin or descent as being Spanish, Spanish-American, Hispano, Latino, etc.

Origin or descent can be viewed as the ancestry, nationality group, lineage, or country in which the person or person's parents or ancestors were born before their arrival in the United States. It is important to note that persons of Spanish origin may be of any race.

Persons of more than one type of Spanish origin and persons of both a Spanish and some other origin(s) who were in doubt as to how to report origin were classified according to the origin of the person's mother. If a single origin was not provided for the person's mother the first reported origin of the person was recorded.

The 1980 data on Spanish origin are not directly comparable with those of 1970 because of several factors; namely, overall improvements in the 1980 census, better question design, and an effective public relations campaign by the Census Bureau with the assistance of national and community ethnic groups. These efforts at census improvement explain, in part, the large increase in the number of Hispanics over 1970. Also, these efforts undoubtedly resulted in the inclusion of a sizeable but unknown number of persons of Hispanic origin who are in the country in other than legal status.

Age. The age classification is based on the age of the person in completed years as of April 1, 1980.

Household. A household consists of all the persons who occupy a housing unit (see definition below). Population per household is obtained by dividing the population in households by the number of households.

Group quarters. All persons who are not members of households are classified as living in group quarters. Group quarters are living arrangements for institutional inmates or for other groups containing five or more persons unrelated to the person in charge. Group quarters are located most frequently in lodging and boarding houses, military barracks, college dormitories, homes for nurses, convents, monasteries, and ships, and in formal institutions providing care and custody for the inmates, such as homes for children, the aged, and dependent persons, and places providing specialized medical care for persons with mental disorders or other chronic diseases.

Relationship to householder. The data on relationship to householder were derived from answers to question 2, which was asked of all persons in housing units. Only basic categories of relationship are recognized in this report. More detailed categories of relationship appear in the PC80-1-B, PC80-1-C, and PC80-1-D reports (and summary tape files 2, 4, and 5).

One person in each household is designated as the "householder." In most cases, this is the person or one of the persons in whose name the home is owned or rented, and who is listed in column 1, of the census questionnaire. If there is no such person in the household, any adult household member could be designated as the "householder." Two types of householders are distinguished: a family householder and a nonfamily householder. A family householder is a householder living with one or more persons related to him or her by birth, marriage, or adoption. The householder and all persons in the household related to him or her are family members. A nonfamily householder is a householder living alone or with nonrelatives only.

A spouse is a person married to and living with a householder. This category includes persons in formal marriages as well as persons in common-law marriages.

A child is son, daughter, stepchild, or adopted child of the householder regardless of the child's age or marital status. The category excludes sons-in-law and daughters-in-law. "Own" children are sons and daughters, including stepchildren and adopted children, of the householder who are single (never married) and under 18 years of age. "Related" children in a family include own children and all other persons (except the spouse of the householder) under 18 years of age in the household, regardless of marital status, who are related to the householder by birth, marriage, or adoption.

Other relative is any person related to the householder by birth, marriage, or adoption who is not shown separately in the particular table (e.g., "spouse," "child," "brother or sister," or "parent").

Nonrelative is any person in the household not related to the householder by birth, marriage or adoption. Roomers, boarders, partners, roommates, paid employees, wards, and foster children are included in this category.

Unrelated Individual. An unrelated individual is (1) a householder living alone or with nonrelatives only, (2) a household member who is not related to the householder, or (3) a person living in group quarters who is not an inmate of an institution.

Family. A family consists of a householder and one or more other persons living in the same household who are related to the householder by birth, marriage, or adoption. All persons in a household who are related to the householder are regarded as members of his or her family. A "married-couple family" is a family in which the householder and spouse are enumerated as members of the same household. Not all households contain families, because a household may be composed of a group of unrelated persons or one person living alone. The measure "persons per family" is obtained by dividing the number of persons in families by the total number of families (or family householders).

Marital Status. The data on marital status were derived from answers to question 6, which was asked of all persons. The marital status classification refers to the status at the time of enumeration. Persons classified as "now married" include those who have been married only once and have never been widowed or divorced as well as those currently married persons who remarried after having been widowed or divorced. Persons reported as separated are those living apart because of marital discord, with or without a legal separation. Persons in common-law marriages are classified as now married, persons whose only marriage had been annulled are classified as never married and all persons under 15 years old are classified as never married. All persons classified as never married are shown as "single" in this report.

School enrollment. Persons are classified as enrolled in school if they reported attending a regular school or college at any time between February 1, 1980, and the time of enumeration. Regular schooling is defined as nursery school, kindergarten, elementary school, and schooling which leads to a high school diploma or college degree. Schooling in trade or business schools, company training, or through a tutor was to be reported only if the course credits obtained were regarded as transferable to a regular elementary school, high school, or college. Children were to be reported as enrolled in nursery school if the school included instruction as an integral phase of its program but not if only custodial care was given. Children in Head Start programs were to be reported in nursery school or kindergarten as appropriate.

Elementary school, as defined here, includes grades 1 through 8, and high school includes grades 9 through 12. In general, a public school is defined as any school which is controlled and supported primarily by a local, State or Federal government agency.

Persons whose education was received in a foreign school or an ungraded school were instructed to report the approximate equivalent grade in the regular American school system. If a person was currently attending or did not finish (item 10) the highest grade attended (item 9), he or she was tabulated as having completed the previous grade or year.

If the person did not attend college but finished high school by an equivalency test (GED), the person was instructed to mark grade 12 (high school, 4 years).

"Percent high school graduates" includes persons who completed four years of high school as well as those who completed one or more years of college.

Nativity and place of birth. The data on nativity and place of birth were derived from answers to questions 11 and 12. The category "Native" comprises persons born in the United States, in Puerto Rico, or in an outlying area of the United States. Also included in this category is the small number of persons who were born abroad with at least one American parent. Persons not classified as native are classified as "foreign born."

Native persons are classified according to their State or area of birth. Respondents were instructed to report place of birth as the mother's usual State of residence at the time of the birth rather than as the location of the hospital, if the birth occurred in a hospital.

Language spoken at home and ability to speak English. The data on language spoken at home and ability to speak English were derived from answers to questions 13a,b, and c. Persons who responded in question 13a that they spoke a language other than English at home were asked to report what language they spoke (question 13b) and how well they could speak English (question 13c). Languages were coded using a detailed classification of languages. Ability to speak English was reported as one of the four categories: "Very well," "Well," "Not well," or "Not at all."

The questions were intended to measure the extent to which non-English languages were currently being spoken in the United States and the number of persons who felt that their English ability was limited. The questions were not intended to determine which language was a person's main language, or whether a person was fluent in the non-English language that he or she reported. Therefore, persons who reported speaking a language other than English may have also spoken English at home and they may have been more fluent in English than in non-English language.

Ancestry. The data on ancestry were derived from the answers to question 14. The 1980 census marked the first time that a general question on ancestry (ethnicity) was asked in a decennial census. The question was based on self-identification and was open-ended (respondents were required to write their answers). Ancestry refers to a person's nationality group, lineage, or the country in which the person or the person's parents or ancestors were born before their arrival in the United States. Thus, persons reported their ancestry group regardless of the number of generations removed from their country of origin. Furthermore, responses to the ancestry question reflected the ethnic groups with which persons identified and not necessarily the degree of attachment or association the person had with the particular ethnic group(s).

Ancestry and race are separate characteristics; therefore, persons reporting a particular ancestry may be of any race. Ancestry is also different from other population characteristics that are sometimes regarded as indicators of ethnicity; namely, country of birth and language spoken at home.

A large number of persons reported their ancestry by specifying a single ancestry but some reported two, three, or more ancestry categories. All responses were coded manually by a procedure that allowed for identification of all single- and double-ancestry groups reported. In addition, 17 triple-ancestry categories were identified by unique codes (these categories were selected since they were reported frequently in Census Bureau surveys taken prior to the 1980 census). All other multiple responses were coded according only to the first and second ancestry categories reported.

Residence in 1975. Persons 5 years old and over were asked their usual place of residence as of April 1, 1975. Persons reporting "same house as in 1980" are counted as non-movers. Everyone reporting a different house is counted as a mover, and further classified according to location of residence in 1975.

Income in 1979. Information on total income for the calendar year 1979 was requested from persons 15 years old and over. Family income represents the combined incomes of all members of the family.

Labor force and employment status. The "labor force" includes all persons in the civilian labor force plus members of the Armed Forces (persons 16 years old and over the active duty with the U.S. Army, Navy, Air Force, Marine Corps, or Coast Guard). The "civilian labor force" consists of persons classified as employed or unemployed in accordance with the criteria described below.

All persons 16 years old and over who are not classified as members of the labor force are defined as "not in labor force." This category consists mainly of students, housewives, retired workers, seasonal workers enumerated in an "off" season who were not looking for work, inmates of institutions, disabled persons, and persons doing only incidental unpaid family work (less than 15 hours during the reference week).

"Employed persons" include all civilians 16 years old and over who were either (a) "at work" - those who did any work at all during the reference week as paid employees or in their own business or profession, or on their own farm, or who worked 15 hours or more as unpaid workers on a family farm or in a family business; or (b) were "with a job but not at work" - those who did not work during the reference week but had jobs or businesses from which they were temporarily absent due to illness, bad weather, industrial dispute, vacation, or other personal reasons. Excluded from the employed are persons whose only activity consisted of work around the house or volunteer work for religious, charitable, and similar organizations.

Persons are classified as "unemployed" if they were civilians 16 years old and over and (a) were neither "at work" nor "with a job but not at work" during the reference week, (b) were looking for work during the last 4 weeks, and (c) were available to accept a job. Also included as unemployed are persons who did not work at all during the reference week and were waiting to be called back to a job from which they had been laid off.

Industry and occupation. The data on industry and occupation were derived from answers to questions 28 and 29, respectively, and are shown here for employed persons 16 years old and over. For persons who worked at two or more jobs, the data refer to the job at which the person worked the greatest number of hours. The industry and occupation statistics are based on the detailed classification systems developed for the 1980 census. The 1980 industry classification is based on the U.S. Standard Industrial Classification (SIC) and is similar to the 1970 system; the 1980 occupation classification is based on the new U.S. Standard Occupational Classification (SOC).

Means of transportation to work. Persons 16 years old and over who worked during the reference week were asked how they got to work that week. Answers refer to "principal means," i.e., the one covering the greatest distance if more than one means was used in daily travel or the one used most frequently if different means were used on different days. The percent riding to work by auto includes those reporting "private auto or car pool" as their principal means, but excludes "taxicab." The base of the percentage is all workers reporting means of transportation.

Place of work. Persons 16 years old and over who worked during the reference week were asked the geographic location of their workplace. Persons working at more than one job were asked to report the job at which they worked the greatest number of hours during the reference week. Salesmen, deliverymen, and others who work in several places each week were requested to name the place in which they began work each day, if they reported to a central headquarters, and otherwise to name the place in which they worked the greatest number of hours during the reference week.

Housing unit. A housing unit is a house, an apartment, a group of rooms, or a single room, occupied as a separate living quarters or, if vacant, intended for occupancy as a separate living quarters. Separate living quarters are those in which the occupants live and eat separately from any other persons in the building and which have direct access from the outside of the building or through a common hall. The occupants may be a single family, one person living alone, two or more families living together, or any other group of related or unrelated persons who share living arrangements (except those in Group Quarters). For vacant units, the criteria of separateness and direct access are applied to the intended occupants whenever possible. If that information cannot be obtained, the criteria are applied to the previous occupants. Both occupied and vacant housing units are included in housing unit inventory except that boats, tents, vans, caves, and the like are included only if they are occupied as someone's usual place of residence. Vacant mobile homes are included, provided they are intended for occupancy on the site where they stand. Vacant mobile homes on dealers' sales lots, at the factory, or in storage are excluded from the housing inventory.

Occupancy status. A housing unit is "occupied" if it was (a) the usual place of residence for the person or group of persons living in it at the time of enumeration; (b) usually occupied by persons who were only temporarily absent; or (c) occupied by persons with no usual place of residence elsewhere.

A housing unit is "vacant" if no persons were living in it at the time of enumeration and it was not the usual residence of persons temporarily absent. Units temporarily occupied by persons having a usual place of residence elsewhere were also considered vacant. Available vacant units are those which are on the market for year-round occupancy, are in either sound or deteriorating condition, and are offered for rent or for sale. Units "for rent" include those "for rent or sale." "Other vacant units" include dilapidated units, seasonal units, units awaiting occupancy, and so forth.

Tenure. Occupied housing units are classified as "owner occupied" if the owner or co-owner lives in the unit, even if it is mortgaged or not fully paid for. All other occupied units are classified as "renter occupied," whether or not cash rent is paid. The percent owner-occupied is based on all housing units.

Persons. All persons enumerated as members of the household, including lodgers, were counted in determining the number of persons who occupied the housing unit.

Rooms. The number of rooms is the count of whole rooms used for living purposes, such as living rooms, dining rooms, bedrooms, kitchens, and finished attic or basement rooms. Not counted as rooms are bathrooms, halls and foyers, closets, strip or pullman kitchens, or space used for storage.

Persons per room. The number of persons per room was computed for each occupied housing unit by dividing the number of persons by the number of rooms in the unit. Percent with 1 (1.01) or more persons per room is based on occupied housing units. In interpreting persons per room, note that one-person households must have 1.0 or fewer persons per room.

Year moved into unit. Data on year moved into unit are based on the information reported for the head of the household. The question relates to the year of latest move.

Year structure built. "Year built" refers to the date the original construction of the structure was completed, not to any later remodeling, addition, or conversion. Percent built in 1960 or later, or 1970 or later is based on all housing units.

Units in structure. A structure is a separate building that either has open space on all sides or is separated from other structures by dividing walls that extend from ground to roof. In the determination of the number of units in a structure, all housing units, both occupied and vacant, were counted. The statistics are presented for the number of housing units in structures of specified type and size, not for the number of residential buildings. Included in the count of mobile homes or trailers are units classified as boats, tents, vans, etc.

Plumbing facilities. The category "Complete plumbing for exclusive use" consists of units which have hot and cold piped water, a flush toilet, and a bathtub or shower inside the housing unit for the exclusive use of the occupants of the unit. "Lacking complete plumbing for exclusive use" includes those conditions when (1) all three specified plumbing facilities are present inside the unit, but are also used by another household; (2) some but not all the facilities are present; or (3) none of the three specified plumbing facilities is present.

In 1970, there were separate questions on the presence of hot and cold piped water, a bathtub or shower, and a flush toilet. For 1980, these three items were combined into a single question on plumbing facilities. In addition, the facilities must be inside the housing unit rather than inside the structure as in 1970.

Bathroom. A complete bathroom is a room with a flush toilet, bathtub or shower, and a wash basin with piped hot and cold water for the exclusive use of the occupants of the housing unit. (Although the instructions on the questionnaire do not specify that a complete bathroom must have hot water, this requirement was applied during the processing of the data in an edit combining the items on complete bathrooms and complete plumbing facilities for the exclusive use of the household). A half-bathroom has at least a flush toilet or a bathtub or shower for exclusive use, but does not have all the facilities for a complete bathroom. The equipment must be inside the unit being enumerated.

Heating equipment. Housing units use specific types of heating equipment as their primary source of heat. The categories for types used are: (1) a steam or hot water system; (2) a central warm-air furnace with ducts to the individual rooms; (3) an electric heat pump; (4) other built-in electric units which are permanently installed in the floors, walls, ceilings, or baseboards, and are a part of the electrical installation of the building; and (5) other means which include a floor, wall, or pipeless furnace; room heaters with flue or vent that burn gas, oil, or kerosene; nonportable room heaters without flue or vent that burn gas, oil, or kerosene; and fireplaces, stoves, or portable room heaters of any kind that can be picked up and moved. For vacant units which have had the heating equipment removed, the kind of equipment used by the previous occupants is considered to be the heating equipment for the unit.

Air-conditioning. Air-conditioning is defined as the cooling of air by a refrigeration unit. It does not include evaporative coolers, fans, or blowers which are not connected to a refrigeration unit; however, it does include heat pumps. A central system is an installation which air-conditions a number of rooms. In an apartment building, such a system may cool all apartments in the building, each apartment may have its own central system, or there may be several systems, each providing central air-conditioning for a group of apartments. A system with individual room controls is a central system.

Vehicles available. Data for this item refer to the number of households with vehicles available at home for the use of the members of the household. Included in this item are passenger cars, pickup trucks, small panel trucks of 1-ton capacity or less, as well as station wagons, company cars, and taxicabs kept at home for the use of household members. Cars rented or leased for 1 month or more; police and government cars kept at home; and company vans and trucks of 1-ton capacity or less are also included if kept at home and used for nonbusiness purposes. Dismantled cars; immobile cars used as a source of power for some piece of machinery; and vans and trucks kept at home but used only for business purposes are excluded. The statistics do not reflect the number of vehicles privately owned or the number of households owning vehicles.

Telephone in housing unit. A unit is classified as having a telephone if there is a telephone in the living quarters. Units where the respondent uses a telephone located inside the building but not in the respondent's living quarters are classified as having no telephone.

Value. Value data are restricted to owner-occupied units having only one housing unit in the property and no business. Units in multi-unit structures and trailers were excluded from the tabulations. Value is the respondent's estimate of how much the property would sell for on today's market (April, 1970 or April, 1980).

Rent. Contract rent is the monthly rent agreed upon, regardless of any furnishings, utilities, or services that may be included. Gross rent is the contract rent plus the estimated average monthly cost of utilities and fuels if these items are paid for by the renter in addition to contract rent. Thus gross rent eliminates rent differentials which result from varying practices with respect to the inclusion of heat and utilities as part of the rental payment.

Renter-occupied units for which no cash rent was paid are excluded from the base in computing median rent.

Notes on Fact Book Contents

Medians, averages and percentages are not shown where the base is smaller than a required minimum. If fewer than 100 persons live in a census tract, then nothing is reported for the tract except the total count. If there are more than 100 persons in a tract, but they live in fewer than 50 housing units, then housing data are not reported. Similarly, median values of owner-occupied units are not reported when the base is fewer than 50. In census tracts consisting principally of persons living in group quarters, income data and other family characteristics are not reported. A dash (-) in a table indicates that data have been omitted for one of these reasons. In percentage distributions the symbol 0.0 is used if there is at least one case in that category but the percent is 0.05 or less. Percentages for specific items shown separately in one table and as part of a percent distribution in another table may differ slightly due to rounding.

The median is used as a type of average. It is that value which divides the distribution into two equal parts — one-half of the cases falling below this value and one-half above. Medians used are those provided by the Census Bureau except for those reported for Chicago Community Areas, a small number of split census tracts, and for years of schooling.

Community area, census tract, and city data. The detailed 1980 statistics for community areas in the City of Chicago were derived from census tract tabulations contained on Bureau of Census computer tapes for Illinois: Summary Tape Files 1A (STF 1) and STF 3. Community area data for 1970 were derived from census tract tabulations contained on Bureau of Census computer tapes for Illinois: Census First Count, Third Count, and Fifth Count Summary Tapes. Census tract data and data for cities in 1980 and 1970 were obtained from the same computer tape sources for Illinois, Indiana, and Wisconsin.

Community area statistics for 1930 to 1960 were taken from the *Local Community Fact Book, Chicago Metropolitan Area, 1960.*

Data for the Metropolitan Area. The historical statistics presented in Table A for the Chicago, Gary, Kenosha, Ill.-Ind.-Wis. Standard Consolidated Statistical Area and its three component Standard Metropolitan Statistical Areas (SMSA's) were complied from statistics for counties in the regular U.S. Census publications for 1900 and subsequent years. The *Twelfth Census of the United States, 1900,* Volume I, *Population,* Part 1, Table 4, reports the population of counties from 1790 to 1900.

Historical statistics for the cities of Chicago, Gary, Hammond, East Chicago and Kenosha were also complied from the regular census publications. Each of these cities experienced boundary changes during the period covered. Consequently, their population growth statistics by decades reflect not only changes in population within a given area but also changes in city boundaries.

Histories. Community histories in the 1980 edition of the *Fact Book* are for the first time identified by author. The debt of these authors to the anonymous historians of earlier editions is extensive and obvious from text comparisons. The histories of community areas were revised and updated on the basis of 1970 and 1980 Census data, as well as professional and amateur scholarship on earlier times. The 1980 historians used information on community area history and problems available from the files of the Municipal Reference Library, City of Chicago, and the Chicago Historical Society; newspaper articles appearing in the metropolitan and community press; books on Chicago and community area history, especially Ron Grossman, *Guide to Chicago Neighborhoods* (Piscataway, N.J.: New Century Publishers, Inc., 1981); Glen E. Holt and Dominic A. Pacyga, *Chicago: A Historical Guide to the Neighborhoods* (Chicago: Chicago Historical Society, 1979) and Harold M. Mayer and Richard C. Wade, *Chicago: Growth of a Metropolis* (Chicago: University of Chicago Press, 1969). Local history collections at branches of the Chicago Public Library were useful, as was material provided by community area historical societies, community organizations and chambers of commerce. Several of the community area texts were written by members of the local historical societies. Professor Richard Taub, of the University of Chicago, made available draft chapters of a book he is preparing about nine Chicago community areas.

The histories of suburban municipalities of 25,000 or more population are, in half the cases, updated revisions of narratives appearing in the 1960 edition of the *Fact Book.* The roster of suburbs was doubled by the addition of 24 cities which have grown to a population of 25,000 in the last twenty years, whose histories appear for the first time in this edition. The help of municipal librarians and the members of suburban historical societies was again of great value, especially in locating city histories of limited or private circulation, and these informants have supplied the narrative text itself in several instances. The Meyer and Wade book noted above is a useful reference, as well as the Federal Writers Project, *Illinois: A Descriptive and Historical Guide* (Chicago: A.C. McClurg & Co., 1939) and Paul M. Angle (ed. for the Illinois Sesquicentennial Commission), *Illinois Guide and Gazetteer* (Chicago: Rand McNally & Company, 1969). Census tract data and community area computations covering Chicago and suburban communities for 1970 were supplied by the Chicago Area Geographical Information Study (CAGIS), Department of Geography, University of Illinois at Chicago. Errors and additions to community area and suburban histories should be brought to the attention of the editors.

Maps. The sources for the maps appearing in the introductory section are noted on the maps themselves. For extensive work with census tract data, it will be helpful to consult the maps in the Census Tracts report (PHC80-2) published by the Bureau of the Census. The maps in Part I of this *Fact Book* show the boundaries of census tracts within community areas and municipalities. The Chicago community area maps were provided by the Department of Planning, City of Chicago, and the suburban maps were prepared by CAGIS. Suburban census tracts often overlap city limits. In these cases, the entire tract is shown, but the portion that is part of the municipality itself is indicated.

Non-census data. Sources for the non-census statistics in Part II are cited in the introduction to Part II.

Other features. The chart in Part II which relates census tracts to other administrative or marketing districts, was prepared with the aid of overlay maps provided by the Citizens Information Service of Illinois. Some problems of placement proved to be insoluble due to differing boundary principles or different map scales. In census tracts which fall into more than one civic district, the agencies which have jurisdiction over the boundaries should be consulted for their exact location.

Other data on local communities. No attempt can be made here to cover all additional sources of statistics for local communities, but a few sources can be noted which are particularly likely to be of interest to users of the *Fact Book.*

For individual census tracts in the nine-county Chicago-Gary-Kenosha SCSA, three SMSA reports are available in printed form for the 1980 Census of Population and Housing: *Census Tracts, Chicago, Ill. Standard Metropolitan Statistical Area, PHC 80-2-119; Census Tracts, Gary-Hammond-East Chicago, Ind. Standard Metropolitan Statistical Area, PHC 80-2-169; Census Tracts, Kenosha, Wis. Standard Metropolitan Statistical Area, PHC 80-2-201.* Similar census tract reports are available for 1970.

Data are also available by blocks *(PHC 80-1, Block Statistics)* for principal cities in the nine-county metropolitan area for 1980, but issued on microfiche rather than in print form. Present population and housing unit totals and statistics on selected characteristics which are based on complete count tabulations are shown for blocks in urbanized areas and selected adjacent areas, for blocks in places of 10,000 or more inhabitants, and for blocks in areas which contracted with the Census Bureau to provide block statistics. The set of reports consists of 374 sets of microfiche and includes a report for each SMSA, showing blocked areas within the SMSA, and a report for each state.

For suburban municipalities in the Chicago Standard Metropolitan Statistical Area, data from the 1980 Census and from a variety of public and private agencies are published in reports issued by the Northeastern Illinois Planning Commission.

The City of Chicago Department of Planning — City and Community Development, issues frequent reports and analyses, including data on subareas of Chicago.

Data from the 1980 Census of Population and Housing are also available for counties, cities, towns, townships, and villages in the nine-county Chicago-Gary-Kenosha Standard Consolidated Statistical Area in separate reports for the states of Illinois, Indiana, and Wisconsin: *Characteristics of the Population, Number of Inhabitants, PC80-1-A; Characteristics of the Population, General Population Characteristics, PC80-1-B; Characteristics of the Population, General Social and Economic Characteristics, PC80-1-C; Characteristics of Housing Units, General Housing Characteristics, HC80-1-A.*

Part I
Histories and Census Tract Statistics

Chicago Community Areas

Community Area 1

Rogers Park

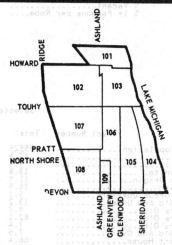

The Rogers Park community is located approximately 10 miles north of Chicago's Loop, at the northeast city limits. It has grown from a small farming community of a few hundred people in the 19th century to one of the most densely populated areas of Chicago.

The Pottawatomie Indians had established villages in the area. The first mark left by white people was a tavern built about 1809 on Ridge Avenue just south of Pratt Avenue, which served as a stop along the stagecoach line. Treaties made with the Indians resulted in their ceding the land south of the "Indian Boundary Line" (now Rogers Avenue) by 1821. The first white settler in the area was Phillip Rogers, an Irishman who had moved west from upstate New York. In 1839, having cleared his land and sold the wood as charcoal, he built a cabin at the present intersection of Ridge and Lunt avenues. With proceeds from his successful truck farm, which he called "Rogers Ridge," he was able to acquire 1,600 acres of land by the time of his death in 1856. Farmers of Irish, Scotch, German and English descent settled along the western boundary of the community, which was always known as "The Ridge" because it was a raised shelf of land, part of the old lake shore. Ridge Road was an important military, trade, mail and stagecoach route and the only north-south passageway through Rogers Park.

The land owned by Rogers passed to his daughter Catherine and her husband, Captain Patrick L. Touhy, who became the chief developer of Rogers Park. The Touhys were involved in establishing the first churches in the area, and their 24-room mansion, located near what is now the intersection of Clark Street and Touhy Avenue, was a symbol of elegance at the time. More important, Touhy helped to organize other early settlers (among them Paul and George Pratt, Stephen P. Lunt, Charles S. Morse, John V. Farwell, Luther L. Greenleaf and George Estes) into a cohesive group to further community development. This association culminated in the organization of the Rogers Park Building and Land Company in 1873. Interest in Rogers Park had increased after the Chicago Fire of 1871, and the Chicago and North Western Railroad had completed a route through the area in 1873. Five commuter trains made daily stops in the area. A period of residential construction and expansion followed, but the area did not develop as expected, because of bad economic times and distance from the downtown area.

Touhy and the others persevered and, in 1878, the village of Rogers Park was incorporated, encompassing the area from Rogers Avenue to Devon, Ridge Avenue to the lake. Not much happened in the following 10 years, the next growth surge coming in 1888 through 1893. Most of the residential development had occurred around the Northwestern Station at Greenleaf and Ravenswood avenues but, during this period,

the community began to spread out in all directions. In 1885, the Chicago, Milwaukee and St. Paul railroad built a Chicago-Evanston line along the current elevated tracks in the eastern part of Rogers Park. The area east of Ashland Avenue had been, for all practical purposes, a swamp due to the constant tidal activity of Lake Michigan but, because of the railroad, homes were now built along Sheridan Road. By 1893, the population reached 3,500 and the area had two schoolhouses, a sewage system, paved streets, a fire department and a two-man police force. It was formally annexed to the city in April of 1893. A fire in 1894 destroyed much of the business center along Clark Street and Ravenswood Avenue, but the area was rebuilt with brick buildings and continued to flourish.

Around the turn of the century, the two-story apartment building began to appear, and while the western part of the community was predominantly single-family dwellings (having been settled earlier), the eastern portion benefited by this trend. By 1904, the population had more than doubled to 7,500. In 1906, the Jesuits, who had operated a college on the Near West Side, moved to the southeastern section of the community and started building Loyola University, chartered in 1909. Many of their older Irish parishoners, from St. Ignatius, moved with them from the West Side and settled in the area. In 1907, the Northwestern elevated line extended service to Howard Street, which helped to develop the northeastern section of the community. In 1915, the old Key farm north of Rogers Avenue and the section of Evanston south of Calvary Cemetery were annexed to the city and completed the Rogers Park area as we know it today. This northern section was known as "Germania" in the early 20th century because of the large number of Germans living there.

Rogers Park grew from a population of 6,761 in 1910 to 57,094 in 1930. Larger residential buildings, such as hotels and apartment buildings were being constructed in the eastern section while the section west of the railroad tracks remained in smaller units. Germans, Irish and English settled and dominated the area until about 1930. By that time, Russian Jews, who began moving into the community in 1910, were second only in number to the Germans. From 1930 to 1950

Community Area 1 — Rogers Park
Population and Housing Characteristics, 1930-1980

	1980	1970	1960	1950	1940	1930
Total Population.......	55,525	60,787	56,888	62,252	60,565	57,094
% Male..................	47.8	45.7	45.3	46.1	45.6	46.4
% Female................	52.2	54.3	54.7	53.9	54.4	53.6
% White.................	76.8	95.5	99.3	99.7	99.7	99.6
% Black.................	9.4	1.3	0.1	0.2	0.2	0.3
% Other Nonwhite Races..	13.8	3.2	0.6	0.1	0.1	0.1
% Under 5 Years Old.....	5.4	6.5	7.8	8.3	5.5	6.9
% 5-19 Years Old........	15.2	16.5	15.3	13.7	15.9	17.3
% 20-44 Years Old.......	49.7	38.9	33.1	40.2	48.7	52.4
% 45-64 Years Old.......	14.7	22.5	29.6	28.6	23.5	19.0
% 65 Years and Older....	15.0	15.6	14.2	9.2	6.4	4.4
Median School Years....	12.9	12.4	12.2	12.4	12.2	*
Total Housing Units....	28,400	28,031	24,523	22,620	21,106	*
% In One-Unit Structures.	4.7	5.4	7.5	*	*	*
% Owner Occupied........	12.7	9.9	11.3	11.6	7.7	*
% Renter Occupied.......	79.9	86.2	83.2	86.3	85.6	*
% Vacant................	7.4	3.9	5.5	2.1	6.7	*
% 1+ Persons per Room...	6.3	3.3	4.2	11.7	*	*

Community Area 1 — Rogers Park
Selected Characteristics of Census Tracts: 1980

Tract Number	Total	101	102	103	104	105	106	107	108	109
Total Population..............	55525	6309	8087	6470	4856	9747	6620	8471	3742	1223
% Male........................	47.8	54.0	45.0	46.4	48.6	45.8	48.6	47.6	48.0	48.4
% Black.......................	9.4	30.7	9.0	6.6	4.9	8.3	5.8	6.7	2.7	2.7
% Other Nonwhite..............	13.8	20.0	12.0	13.9	5.4	10.3	14.5	15.9	17.2	23.8
% Of Spanish Origin...........	11.9	26.9	11.6	13.9	4.4	9.6	10.6	13.5	15.0	12.8
% Foreign Born................	28.9	36.4	25.9	24.8	16.7	28.6	32.1	31.6	34.8	30.0
% Living In Group Quarters....	5.1	1.7	4.5	13.9	26.2	0.0	2.4	0.5	0.2	0.0
% 13 Years Old And Under......	13.2	21.4	13.9	8.5	5.7	9.1	13.9	16.6	16.2	17.8
% 14-20 Years Old.............	9.7	11.5	7.4	5.4	24.0	6.2	8.3	9.0	10.2	12.2
% 21-64 Years Old.............	62.1	61.2	62.3	63.4	55.0	64.1	63.3	63.3	60.7	61.3
% 65-74 Years Old.............	7.4	2.9	8.4	9.2	8.9	9.0	7.5	6.4	7.5	4.7
% 75 Years Old And Over.......	7.5	3.0	8.0	13.4	6.4	10.7	7.0	4.7	5.5	3.9
% In Different House..........	66.4	71.7	63.6	70.8	66.5	70.1	64.1	62.0	63.6	54.8
% Families With Female Head...	25.2	32.4	23.1	22.5	24.3	27.3	21.3	25.6	22.4	20.9
Median School Years Completed...	12.9	12.5	12.9	13.5	14.9	12.9	13.0	12.9	12.6	12.9
Median Family Income, 1979...$$	18784	11828	20415	22016	21058	17141	19583	17439	18600	21674
% Income Below Poverty Level...	11.9	27.0	6.7	8.4	5.8	13.4	10.8	10.1	14.0	4.7
% Income Of $30,000 Or More...	22.3	12.7	25.0	26.5	35.6	20.4	22.8	20.9	19.8	26.5
% White Collar Workers........	66.6	50.2	66.2	74.3	77.0	71.3	67.1	65.3	56.3	55.9
% Civilian Labor Force Unemployed.	6.3	12.9	3.9	4.9	6.3	7.6	4.0	5.9	7.3	4.0
% Riding To Work By Automobile....	42.7	41.6	53.5	40.9	35.5	36.6	41.1	44.0	46.0	51.7
Mean Commuting Time - Minutes...	32.1	32.3	29.8	33.9	32.9	32.9	32.0	33.4	30.0	28.3
Population Per Household..........	2.0	2.4	2.1	1.8	1.6	1.7	2.1	2.2	2.2	2.7
Total Housing Units..........	28400	2975	3970	3359	2363	6181	3269	4003	1794	486
% Condominiums................	6.4	2.5	6.5	17.0	12.0	4.3	5.2	5.0	0.0	0.0
% Built 1970 Or Later.........	4.9	2.1	3.3	6.2	2.6	8.0	6.3	4.9	2.1	0.0
% Owner Occupied..............	12.7	5.6	15.1	16.6	12.6	7.3	15.0	17.6	12.7	23.5
% With 1+ Persons Per Room....	6.3	16.5	4.8	5.6	2.9	4.4	4.9	6.5	7.0	5.0
Median Value: Owner Units....$$	66100	70000	64600	71600	-	67500	69400	64400	58200	-
Median Rent: Rental Units....$$	235	213	250	247	250	223	239	241	219	247
Median Number Of Rooms: All Units.	3.8	3.4	4.2	3.7	3.5	3.2	4.0	4.2	3.9	5.0

Community Area 01 — Rogers Park
Selected Characteristics of Census Tracts: 1970

Tract Number	TOTAL	0101	0102	0103	0104	0105	0106	0107	0108	0109
Total Population.............	60787	6937	8771	6751	5584	11118	7181	8848	4037	1560
% Male........................	45.7	48.3	44.7	45.0	41.3	46.7	45.4	46.1	46.2	47.9
% Black.......................	1.3	5.6	0.5	0.8	1.6	1.0	0.2	0.6	0.2	0.1
% Other Nonwhite..............	3.2	3.7	3.7	3.1	1.4	2.9	3.5	2.7	2.7	6.5
% Of Spanish Language.........	4.6	9.4	3.4	3.1	1.2	3.9	3.8	5.5	4.0	14.5
% Foreign Born................	19.8	19.7	15.5	21.6	19.1	21.0	19.7	21.1	22.5	17.5
% Living In Group Quarters....	3.4	0.5	1.1	6.8	18.4	0.3	0.5	0.0	0.4	0.4
% 13 Years Old And Under......	15.2	15.3	16.7	11.3	9.3	12.7	15.5	18.4	21.0	26.7
% 14-20 Years Old.............	10.1	9.0	7.9	6.1	19.6	11.2	9.9	8.9	9.0	12.1
% 21-64 Years Old.............	59.1	64.0	60.0	62.5	54.7	58.3	59.1	58.4	56.2	51.3
% 65-74 Years Old.............	10.1	7.6	10.1	11.3	10.3	11.5	10.4	9.4	9.0	7.2
% 75 Years Old And Over.......	5.5	4.1	5.3	8.8	6.1	6.3	5.0	4.5	4.7	2.0
% In Different House..........	34.8	31.9	39.8	29.2	33.2	32.2	36.4	37.3	39.8	35.0
% Families With Female Head...	14.3	13.7	13.7	12.5	13.6	15.2	14.9	15.4	14.5	13.4
Median School Years Completed...	12.4	12.5	12.5	12.5	12.5	12.6	12.5	12.3	12.1	12.2
Median Family Income, 1969...$$	11306	9678	11830	12423	12152	10990	11110	11330	9716	12868
% Income Below Poverty Level...	4.7	7.7	3.7	3.2	2.4	5.6	5.7	4.4	7.0	3.2
% Income of $15,000 or More...	27.8	23.6	27.8	34.2	33.2	26.8	29.4	26.3	18.3	35.2
% White Collar Workers........	40.6	38.9	40.8	50.5	43.9	40.1	39.0	37.8	32.2	38.2
% Civilian Labor Force Unemployed.	2.9	3.9	1.9	3.7	2.1	3.3	3.7	2.5	2.1	0.8
% Riding To Work By Automobile....	44.9	43.3	51.1	47.8	33.6	39.8	42.8	51.7	49.8	46.0
Population Per Household..........	2.2	2.2	2.1	2.3	2.0	1.9	2.0	2.3	2.4	3.3
Total Housing Units..........	28042	3523	3908	3324	2416	5516	3265	3861	1744	485
% Condominiums & Cooperatives.....	1.8	0.6	2.3	4.8	3.8	0.2	2.3	1.2	0.0	0.0
% Built 1960 Or Later.........	15.9	6.1	14.8	19.1	21.8	20.8	17.7	17.5	4.8	1.0
% Owner Occupied..............	8.1	4.0	10.2	5.7	5.5	5.6	7.5	13.0	13.6	21.0
% With 1+ Persons Per Room....	3.7	5.6	2.2	2.2	2.9	3.8	3.2	4.5	4.9	9.1
Median Value: Owner Units....$$	24500	29500	24000	29200	30000	-	24800	24000	21000	-
Median Rent: Rental Units....$$	132	114	138	141	146	132	132	132	117	134
Median Number Of Rooms: All Units.	3.8	3.3	4.1	3.6	3.5	3.4	4.0	4.1	3.9	5.0

the total population of Rogers Park decreased 6 percent, while the Jewish population nearly tripled. In 1960, the largest ethnic group in the area was Russian Jews, followed by Poles and Germans.

After 1930, there was a sharp drop in construction, which did not resume again until after World War II. Most of the postwar construction has been in multiple family dwellings. The majority of the structures in the community, however, predate 1939. Of the housing units in 1960, 93 percent were renter-occupied and 68 percent were in structures containing more than 10 units, and these figures remained virtually unchanged over the next decade.

Educational and commercial activities dominate the major thoroughfares of Rogers Park today. These include Sheridan Road, site of Mundelein College, and many shops catering to the college population. There are a number of luxury apartment buildings on the side streets east of Sheridan Road, many converted to condominums.

A major shopping area is located along Howard Street. Clark Street running south from Howard is one of the longest continuous strips of business and commercial activity in Rogers Park. All but one small section is zoned business or commercial. Along this street, one may find anything from a taffy apple manufacturing company to the local American Legion post, as well as the local branch of the Chicago Public Library, warehousing and storage areas, and two financial institutions. Several businesses have been located along Clark Street for many decades. As with the residential housing in Rogers Park, many of the commercial buildings are aging and in need of constant maintenance. After years of community request, a new Rogers Park (24th) Police District was formed, and a new building erected on Clark Street.

Morse Avenue includes a number of retail shops now owned by Koreans, and more shops are found along the "EL" tracks on Glenwood Avenue, both north and south of Morse. Finally, a major area of commercial and business activity is located along Devon Avenue, which is a major east-west artery, the dividing line between the Rogers Park and Edgewater community areas. The far southwestern corner of the community (Ridge and Devon avenues) is the site of an electrical equipment manufacturing firm, today the only major industry remaining in the community area.

Several trends in Rogers Park over the last 20 years have contributed to changes in the area. First, there have been changes in ethnic composition. In 1970, while Russian Jews, Poles and Germans still predominated, blacks and persons of Spanish-speaking origin had begun to move in. Half of the black population and a fourth of the Latinos lived in the area north of Howard Street. Population figures for 1980 indicate another decrease since 1970 of 8.7 percent, to 55,525. Of this number, 9.4 percent are black and 11.9 percent are of Hispanic origin. Much of this may be a result of the greater availability of low-income housing north of Howard Street and the changing ethnic composition of the city as a whole.

Although there still is a large number of Jews in the community, and Russian immigration continued in the 1970's, the Jewish population is aging. Seventy-two percent are more than 45 and 42 percent are more than 65 years old. Several nursing homes had been constructed along Sheridan Road during the 1970's to accommodate the needs of the elderly. Many of these facilities are built on the sites of razed older homes and a continuation of this trend could decrease significantly the number of housing units available in the future.

Along with this, there has been an increase in the number of multiple family units converted into condominiums. This trend will most likely decrease the number of rental units available in the future. Most of this conversion is going on in the area east of Clark Street. It has brought greater numbers of Asians, Middle Easterners, Europeans, students and single professionals into the area, since rents and housing prices are more reasonable than in some other areas of the city.

The area north of Howard Street, which was a bar strip during and after World War II, is undergoing major changes through urban renewal. Many older deteriorated buildings have been demolished and a neighborhood redevelopment corporation has purchased 240 rental units for renovation. There are also plans to build low-income housing in Rogers Park, which have met with opposition. The only subsidized housing in the area currently is for the elderly, at Devon and Sheridan Road. Some of the population decline of the last decade has been caused by the consequently tightened housing market. The construction of new housing units in Rogers Park under urban renewal could ease this shortage in the coming decade, with a resultant increase in the population.

Maria L. Ule
Gail Danks Welter

West Ridge

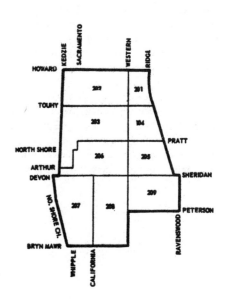

The West Ridge community area is also variously referred to as North Town or West Rogers Park. Settlement dates back to the 1830s with the purchase by Phillip Rogers of 1,600 acres of land south of what is today Rogers Avenue. In the 1830s and 1840s a community of Luxembourg farmers began to form along the elevated ridge of land that ran through the area. The Ridge was the only north-south road into the area and it served as a military trade and mail road and as a stage coach line. The early settlers were joined by additional Luxembourgers and Germans and their settlement at what is today Ridge and Devon avenues became known as Ridgeville. These settlers converted the prairie land into truck farms and the West Ridge area acquired a rural farming character that it maintained until the turn of the century.

Some subdivisions of tracts occurred in the mid-1870s, but this produced little further residential development. In 1885 there were only 44 frame residential structures in the area and of the estimated 300 residents of West Ridge in 1891, two-thirds were farmers.

Relations between the communities of West Ridge and Rogers Park — the ridge formed a natural boundary between the two areas — were frequently acrimonious during the latter part of the century. West Ridge remained a largely rural area while Rogers Park developed a more suburban character as Chicago's population expanded northward during the late 1880s. Disagreements between the neighboring areas over local improvements led to the incorporation of West Ridge as a village in 1890 although only three years later the village was annexed to Chicago. A dispute over the formation of separate Park Districts for the two areas led to a brief skirmish between residents of the two communities in 1897 and other conflicts developed over the paving of Ridge Avenue and prohibition.

By 1895 there were still only 127 residential structures in West Ridge. No prominent business thoroughfares had developed in the community and most of the streets were unpaved sandy trails. Poor transportation into the area was improved somewhat by the extension of cable car service to Devon Avenue in 1890. At the turn of the century the residential community of West Ridge remained clustered along Ridge Avenue. West of what is now Western Avenue was prairie or farmland, except for some brickyards which had been built along the western boundary of Touhy Avenue in order to take advantage of the natural deposits of clay and sand in the area. Some of these yards had moved to West Ridge from sites along the North Branch of the Chicago River. A number of greenhouse businesses also became established in the 1890s, supplying flowers to Chicago families.

The brickyard area became a scene of great activity after 1900. In 1905 a large tract of land south of Touhy Avenue between Kedzie and Western avenues was sold to a brick company. In addition the construction of the canal in 1909 provided the yards with ample clay dumps. This expansion brought new workers — primarily Germans and Scandinavians — into the area, and these workers built small cottages near the brickyards. A real estate drive was launched between 1912 and 1915 and West Ridge was advertised nationally. Although the subdivision of West Ridge was underway at this time, actual residential construction lagged behind. The estimated population of West Ridge in 1910 was 3,000.

West Ridge developed phenomenally after World War I and by 1930 the community had reached residential maturity. The area east of California Avenue was the site of most of the early residential construction in the 1920s. Indian Boundary Park was opened in 1922 — named in commemoration of the treaty signed in 1816 — and several large apartment buildings were constructed next to the park. Most of the construction, however, was of brick bungalows and duplexes which soon supplanted the older one-family frame and stucco homes in the area. Parts of the southeastern side of West Ridge were also built up during the 1920s primarily with single-family dwellings but also with some two-flats and apartment buildings. West of California Avenue there were fewer improvements and less development and most of the northern section of West Ridge remained undeveloped. Transportation for West Ridge residents improved with the extension of the Devon Avenue cable car line from Western Avenue to Kedzie Avenue in 1925.

The population of West Ridge increased from 7,500 in 1920 to almost 40,000 10 years later. The leading ethnic groups in the area were Germans and Swedes who came north from the communities of Uptown, Lincoln, and Lake View as those areas became more crowded during the 1920s. Some Irish also moved into West Ridge at this time.

Commercial ventures were still few and scattered in West Ridge in 1930, although there were the beginnings of a business district on Western Avenue following the construction of a bank building. The greenhouses that flourished at the turn of the century were rapidly disappearing as residential development encroached upon them. Along the North Shore Channel from Touhy to Pratt avenues there were still some brick plants and a few factories. In 1929 a new post office was built at Devon and Talman avenues and the use of the name "North Town" as an alternative to West Ridge dates from that year.

Unlike most Chicago community areas, West Ridge experienced a 10 percent population growth during the 1930s. The Depression curtailed residential construction through most of this time, but building picked up somewhat late in the decade. In 1938 the Granville Garden Apartments, one of the largest building projects in Chicago in those years, was built at Granville and Hoyne avenues. Construction tapered off during World War II, but then spurted ahead during the 1950s, when West Ridge had its second great growth period, and the population increased by a third. The number of inhabitants edged over 65,000 in 1970 but declined in the following decade as the baby-boom generation reached maturity and began to establish residence elsewhere.

During the 1950s many Russian and Polish Jews began moving into West Ridge, and by 1960 they were the most numerous ethnic group in the area, although the German, Irish and English nationalities were still substantially represented. Greeks began to move in during the following decade. A large Jewish population remains in West Ridge along with thousands of German, Irish and Greek extraction. The greatest increase in recent years has come from an influx of Asiatics, principally Koreans, Asian Indians, Filipinos and Chinese. Non-whites now comprise more than 10 percent of the population, and within that group Asiatics outnumber blacks by 10-to-1. Many of the Asian immigrants have established businesses along Devon Avenue.

Since the dispersion of the brick manufacturing industry that was centered along the western edge of the community, there has been little industry in West Ridge. The area is primarily residential, and most residents commute to work in downtown Chicago by bus or elevated trains. The housing units are a mixture of rental apartments (about 60 percent), condominium apartments and single-family homes, the latter comprising about one-fourth of the housing stock. Many of the apartment buildings have resident owners, and almost half the dwelling units in West Ridge are owner-occupied. The median value of an owner-occupied single-family home in West Ridge exceeds $72,000, and this puts West Ridge among the top 10 Chicago communities in this respect. The main shopping areas in West Ridge are along Devon Avenue from Western to California avenues; on Western Avenue near Howard Street; and on Touhy Avenue between Kedzie and Western avenues. Recent changes in West Ridge include the establishment of Warren Park in the area bounded by Damen, Pratt, Western and Ridge avenues, and the widening of Pratt Boulevard from Western to Ridge avenues.

Rodney Nelson

Community Area 2 -- West Ridge
Population and Housing Characteristics, 1930-1980

	1980	1970	1960	1950	1940	1930
Total Population.......	61,129	65,432	63,884	47,930	43,553	39,759
% Male...................	45.8	46.7	47.6	47.9	47.8	48.6
% Female.................	54.2	53.3	52.4	52.1	52.2	51.4
% White..................	89.3	98.9	99.7	99.7	99.6	99.9
% Black..................	0.7	0.1	0.1	0.2	0.3	0.1
% Other Nonwhite Races...	10.0	1.0	0.2	0.1	0.1	0.0
% Under 5 Years Old......	4.8	5.2	7.0	8.7	6.9	9.9
% 5-19 Years Old.........	15.9	19.1	22.4	19.4	22.3	23.2
% 20-44 Years Old........	33.1	26.9	29.1	36.8	42.8	47.2
% 45-64 Years Old........	23.5	32.4	31.2	27.4	22.4	16.0
% 65 Years and Older.....	22.7	16.4	10.3	7.7	5.6	3.7
Median School Years....	12.8	12.4	12.2	12.3	11.3	*
Total Housing Units....	26,064	24,389	21,281	15,092	12,787	*
% In One-Unit Structures.	22.3	23.2	27.0	*	*	*
% Owner Occupied.........	46.0	44.1	45.7	37.5	25.4	*
% Renter Occupied........	49.9	54.4	52.4	60.8	71.0	*
% Vacant.................	4.1	1.5	1.9	1.7	3.6	*
% 1+ Persons per Room....	2.3	1.6	1.9	5.4	*	*

Community Area 2 -- West Ridge
Selected Characteristics of Census Tracts: 1980

Tract Number	Total	201	202	203	204	205	206	207	208	209
Total Population.............	61129	3182	5842	8426	3943	4938	8785	7521	10640	7852
% Male.......................	45.8	43.4	46.8	44.3	45.1	45.4	46.8	45.3	46.1	47.1
% Black......................	0.7	1.9	0.2	0.6	0.6	0.1	0.1	0.4	0.2	1.7
% Other Nonwhite.............	10.0	5.5	11.2	5.0	7.6	14.1	8.2	9.5	10.6	16.2
% Of Spanish Origin..........	3.7	3.4	3.2	1.9	3.7	4.7	2.7	3.1	4.6	6.0
% Foreign Born...............	32.3	20.1	28.1	26.2	18.2	41.9	34.4	32.7	34.3	42.2
% Living In Group Quarters...	1.9	2.5	1.9	5.1	0.1	5.1	0.4	2.1	0.1	1.2
% 13 Years Old And Under.....	13.6	9.2	15.7	10.3	11.4	13.4	14.3	13.8	14.9	15.8
% 14-20 Years Old............	8.4	6.3	9.4	7.0	9.2	6.3	8.8	9.3	10.0	7.3
% 21-64 Years Old............	55.4	57.6	56.8	48.7	58.7	58.7	54.4	54.4	56.5	57.3
% 65-74 Years Old............	14.1	16.8	12.6	21.3	12.8	13.1	14.1	13.7	10.7	12.9
% 75 Years Old And Over......	8.5	10.1	5.5	12.7	7.9	8.5	8.4	8.8	8.0	6.7
% In Different House.........	45.4	43.5	32.4	34.7	46.4	55.9	44.4	43.0	45.7	63.8
% Families With Female Head..	13.6	22.1	10.9	10.7	15.4	16.7	12.6	12.6	12.5	16.5
Median School Years Completed...	12.8	12.8	13.1	12.8	13.2	12.7	12.7	12.8	12.5	12.8
Median Family Income, 1979...$$	25109	24813	32763	28626	25574	20945	23803	25061	23756	21708
% Income Below Poverty Level.	4.4	1.8	3.3	2.8	5.0	7.5	3.7	4.2	3.6	8.2
% Income Of $30,000 Or More..	37.3	35.9	59.4	46.1	36.2	29.9	35.2	35.8	31.1	27.9
% White Collar Workers.......	71.6	73.7	77.4	78.4	78.8	66.2	69.3	72.1	66.4	68.2
% Civilian Labor Force Unemployed.	4.0	3.2	2.7	3.5	2.0	4.3	3.7	4.8	5.4	4.8
% Riding To Work By Automobile...	67.4	62.7	71.9	74.3	63.6	62.6	69.5	65.7	66.1	65.4
Mean Commuting Time - Minutes...	31.1	27.4	31.5	30.1	30.3	34.9	30.1	31.0	30.8	32.4
Population Per Household.........	2.4	2.0	2.8	2.2	2.2	2.3	2.5	2.6	2.5	2.3
Total Housing Units..........	26064	1583	2091	3763	1867	2165	3646	2965	4369	3615
% Condominiums...............	14.0	16.9	3.9	39.2	14.3	15.2	3.3	6.1	0.8	25.0
% Built 1970 Or Later........	4.0	3.9	3.2	10.2	6.4	3.1	3.6	2.2	1.3	2.4
% Owner Occupied.............	46.0	34.0	82.0	68.4	39.5	26.3	43.2	48.9	36.5	34.4
% With 1+ Persons Per Room...	2.3	1.1	1.4	0.9	1.6	2.9	2.2	2.6	3.0	3.5
Median Value: Owner Units......$$	72300	65600	78100	75700	71000	57500	70800	73400	65500	60800
Median Rent: Rental Units......$$	269	285	279	280	284	267	258	278	256	266
Median Number Of Rooms: All Units.	5.0	4.6	5.6	5.1	4.8	4.5	5.1	5.3	5.1	4.6

Community Area 02 -- West Ridge
Selected Characteristics of Census Tracts: 1970

Tract Number	TOTAL	0201	0202	0203	0204	0205	0206	0207	0208	0209
Total Population.............	65432	3575	6309	8924	4316	5948	9346	7509	11466	8039
% Male.......................	46.7	43.9	48.5	46.4	47.1	46.4	47.1	46.8	46.7	46.5
% Black......................	0.1	0.3	0.1	0.1	0.3	0.7	0.1	0.0	0.0	0.0
% Other Nonwhite.............	1.0	0.4	0.5	0.6	1.0	1.4	0.8	1.3	1.4	1.3
% Of Spanish Language........	1.7	1.8	2.7	0.9	0.3	1.7	1.5	1.3	1.5	3.6
% Foreign Born...............	22.4	18.7	20.9	22.3	15.5	20.3	28.8	25.5	22.0	20.6
% Living In Group Quarters...	1.6	2.6	1.8	0.0	0.2	12.5	0.1	0.4	0.1	0.1
% 13 Years Old And Under.....	15.7	12.6	16.2	13.3	17.7	18.9	14.2	14.4	17.1	17.1
% 14-20 Years Old............	10.0	7.6	13.3	10.2	8.5	10.4	10.8	11.4	9.5	7.3
% 21-64 Years Old............	57.9	60.7	59.8	59.4	57.6	54.2	56.7	58.7	55.8	60.1
% 65-74 Years Old............	11.1	13.0	6.7	12.1	10.7	10.0	12.4	10.9	11.7	11.4
% 75 Years Old And Over......	5.3	6.0	4.0	4.9	5.5	6.5	5.8	4.5	5.9	4.2
% In Different House.........	53.6	49.3	73.8	45.1	49.8	47.1	58.0	54.9	56.7	44.9
% Families With Female Head..	9.5	11.5	7.1	8.4	9.9	11.3	8.7	8.7	10.6	10.5
Median School Years Completed..	12.4	12.6	12.6	12.5	12.5	12.3	12.2	12.3	12.1	12.4
Median Family Income, 1969.....$$	13531	14376	16634	14976	13660	12041	13409	13161	12309	12788
% Income Below Poverty Level...	3.2	1.6	2.3	2.5	3.1	5.2	3.2	3.8	2.9	3.8
% Income of $15,000 or More...	41.4	45.6	56.1	49.9	41.6	34.6	40.2	38.1	35.3	36.9
% White Collar Workers.......	48.6	46.0	53.1	55.8	51.1	46.5	48.1	50.3	41.2	47.6
% Civilian Labor Force Unemployed.	2.8	2.1	3.1	3.0	1.0	4.1	3.4	3.1	1.9	2.5
% Riding To Work By Automobile....	63.3	55.4	66.7	70.7	66.7	54.8	62.1	63.0	62.1	63.5
Population Per Household..........	2.7	2.4	3.1	3.1	2.6	2.6	2.7	2.8	2.7	2.5
Total Housing Units..........	24384	1491	1981	3423	1683	2064	3484	2731	4277	3250
% Condominiums & Cooperatives.....	10.4	5.7	2.2	31.8	12.7	13.3	4.6	7.7	1.5	12.2
% Built 1960 Or Later.............	13.6	26.5	10.0	34.9	22.7	10.7	3.6	8.2	4.6	11.7
% Owner Occupied.................	33.7	21.2	80.7	34.2	25.7	11.2	40.2	40.6	36.2	12.8
% With 1+ Persons Per Room........	1.7	1.3	0.9	0.6	2.2	2.6	1.3	1.2	2.7	2.1
Median Value: Owner Units.......$$	30500	25800	32600	32300	27500	-	30300	31400	26000	26400
Median Rent: Rental Units.......$$	154	171	168	161	163	147	144	165	143	159
Median Number Of Rooms: All Units.	5.0	4.5	6.0	5.1	4.7	4.4	5.2	5.3	5.1	4.5

Uptown

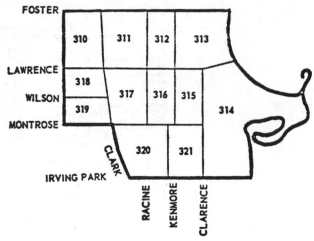

The community of Uptown includes several older neighborhoods which were once the northern part of the township and later the city of Lake View. When the township of Lake View was organized in 1857, this area was almost completely prairie, forest, or swampy wasteland. There was a small settlement just to the southeast of this territory.

There were two railroads in the territory, the Chicago and Milwaukee along the lake shore, and the predecessor of the Chicago and North Western along what is now the western boundary. The earliest settlements were along the latter route which was laid out along a ridge of higher land. The land to the east of this ridge was for the most part swamp and marsh and, therefore, its subdivision came later. An exception was the southeastern corner of the community where, in the late 1860s, some large homes were built in the vicinity of the newly-erected Marine Hospital.

The years from 1870 through 1890 were years of relatively substantial growth for Uptown. The community settlers were predominantly German or of German descent, although they included an increasing number of Swedes. They lived in modest frame cottages or farmhouses, although there were more elaborate residences in the community belonging to wealthy Chicagoans who sought a suburban life reasonably close to the city. In 1889, Uptown became part of Chicago when the city of Lake View elected to be annexed.

The decades between 1890 and 1920 witnessed the most rapid growth of the community, primarily as a result of improvement in transportation facilities. By 1920, the Swedes were the dominant foreign-born group, although there were still many Germans and persons of German descent in the community. Many Germans and Irish, or those of German or Irish descent, moved into Uptown from older residential areas in Chicago which were being occupied by newer groups such as the Italians, Poles, and Russian Jews.

By 1919, Uptown had reached residential maturity. Its growth, however, was not uniform. The older area west of Clark Street, a section chiefly of single family and one- or two-story frame homes, developed gradually but steadily. It was in the area east of Clark Street, however, that the greatest strides were made in residential and commercial development during the period between 1890 and 1920. New transit lines such as the Lawrence Avenue car line, the extension of others, such as the Broadway Avenue and Clark Street lines, and the extension in 1900 of the North Western elevated line to Wilson Avenue, fostered this growth. In the southern part of the community, apartment houses, apartment hotels, and hotels sprang up alongside of the old frame and stone homes. The development of transit facilities, along with the development of the Wilson Avenue and Clarendon Avenue beaches, were the initial factors in determining the residential, commercial, and recreational characteristics of the area. A rapid increase in land values checked the construction of residences in the section east of Clark Street and promoted instead the erection of multiple-apartment buildings, apartment hotels, and hotels. The desirability of location and the excellent transportation facilities attracted many young single people or young married couples to this section. As a result, some of the older residences were converted into rooming houses, a practice which gathered momentum in the ensuing decades.

During the 1920s, the population of Uptown continued to increase, but more slowly. The area west of Clark Street was inhabited chiefly by Germans and Swedes or those of German or Swedish descent. The small black population was concentrated in Census Tract 316. This settlement probably started when the Uptown area was one of single-family homes of wealthy people who had black servants.

The area west of Clark Street remained predominantly residential, except for some industrial use along Ravenswood Avenue. The tendency of the time was to tear down the older homes and small apartment buildings and erect new multiple-apartment buildings, apartment hotels, and hotels. East of Clark Street, apartment buildings were rapidly replacing single-family residences. A city-wide housing shortage during World War II encouraged the conversion of many apartments in Uptown into even smaller units, especially in the central section along Winthrop and Kenmore avenues. Housing continued to be in demand after the War, and Uptown became a section of the city offering many one- and two-room units at relatively low rents.

From 1930 to 1950, the population of Uptown increased slowly. During the 1950s it declined for the first time, and it has continued to decline since. The area currently designated as Uptown had a population of 76,103 in 1960, 74,838 in 1970 and 64,414 in 1980. (Earlier editions of this book have combined the community areas of Uptown and Edgewater, but in 1980 Edgewater, north of Foster Avenue, was designated a separate community area.) Most of Uptown's population loss has occurred in the central section of the community. Population along the lakefront increased between 1960 and 1970, and then decreased slightly between 1970 and 1980.

The nature of its housing supply has helped to make Uptown a port of entry for many groups entering the city with limited resources, and has contributed to a high degree of transience. During the 1950s and 1960s there was an influx of white Southerners (mainly from Kentucky, Tennessee and West Virginia), who were displaced by automation in the mining industry. During the 1960s, when changes in the Bureau of Indian Affairs' policy brought many Native Americans to the cities, most of those who came to Chicago settled in Uptown. Japanese-Americans, Mexican-Americans and Indo-Chinese refugees have also moved into the area as they have arrived in the city. In addition, a large number of former mental patients were resettled in the Uptown area during the 1970s as part of a statewide program of deinstitutionalization. A number of old hotels were converted to half-way houses or sheltered care homes for these individuals. Still, Uptown continues to have wealthy residents who have stayed in the area along with its more transient population. Overall, the area is characterized by great heterogeneity. The black population has increased steadily over the past two decades, both in numbers and as a percentage of the total population, as some Appalachian whites have left the area.

Since World War II, the western section of Uptown has been relatively stable. It is an area of predominantly middle-income families and good housing stock. The lakefront section of Uptown is also inhabited by a population of relatively high socioeconomic status, primarily in high-rise apartment buildings constructed in recent decades. The commerical section of the community is centered around the major retail center at Broadway and Wilson Avenue and along Lawrence Avenue. The central section, bounded by Clark, Montrose, Broadway and Leland, and the Winthrop-Kenmore Corridor, which

Community Area 3 -- Uptown
Population and Housing Characteristics, 1930-1980

	1980	1970	1960	1950	1940	1930
Total Population.......	64,414	74,838	76,103	84,462	77,677	67,699
% Male.................	51.1	49.7	49.4	48.2	47.2	49.4
% Female...............	48.9	50.3	50.6	51.8	52.8	50.6
% White................	57.2	87.7	94.8	98.1	99.2	98.9
% Black................	15.1	4.1	0.5	0.5	0.5	0.7
% Other Nonwhite Races.	27.7	8.2	4.7	1.4	0.3	0.4
% Under 5 Years Old....	7.8	8.5	8.7	6.7	4.9	4.3
% 5-19 Years Old.......	18.5	18.7	14.5	10.7	12.7	12.8
% 20-44 Years Old......	42.7	36.6	35.7	43.7	49.4	57.4
% 45-64 Years Old......	17.1	20.6	27.6	29.1	25.3	20.0
% 65 Years and Older...	13.9	15.6	13.5	9.8	7.7	5.1
Median School Years....	12.3	11.5	11.1	11.7	10.6	*
Total Housing Units....	33,714	36,864	40,487	34,228	28,576	*
% In One Unit Structures.	2.4	2.9	1.7	*	*	*
% Owner Occupied........	11.1	4.9	5.1	5.9	3.8	*
% Renter Occupied.......	72.6	84.9	82.5	91.6	87.7	*
% Vacant................	16.3	10.2	12.4	2.5	8.5	*
% 1+ Person per Room....	12.2	10.7	11.9	19.1	*	*

Community Area 3 -- Uptown
Selected Characteristics of Census Tracts: 1980

Tract Number	Total	310	311	312	313	314	315	316	317	318	319
Total Population..............	64414	4906	5863	5558	7283	5043	9567	3031	8644	2276	3135
% Male.......	51.1	46.6	50.0	53.5	46.2	45.5	50.6	56.4	54.1	51.1	54.7
% Black.......	15.1	1.8	7.2	26.5	17.9	7.9	23.7	27.8	12.7	0.9	3.4
% Other Nonwhite.....	27.7	31.5	37.1	26.1	15.4	7.7	38.2	22.6	25.0	34.0	34.7
% Of Spanish Origin.....	23.3	31.4	29.1	18.5	5.8	4.2	17.4	14.6	24.7	40.6	40.5
% Foreign Born........	31.7	41.0	42.8	31.4	32.0	20.1	37.3	16.9	22.9	39.6	38.9
% Living In Group Quarters........	6.5	4.1	3.6	5.7	16.1	4.7	6.3	18.3	5.0	0.0	5.4
% 13 Years Old And Under.	18.8	20.0	19.9	19.4	8.3	5.7	22.9	21.4	23.7	19.1	20.0
% 14-20 Years Old........	9.1	11.1	10.6	8.6	5.5	3.0	9.2	8.7	11.7	11.0	10.5
% 21-64 Years Old........	58.2	53.5	57.3	50.1	62.8	66.6	55.8	58.7	57.1	59.0	60.4
% 65-74 Years Old........	7.2	6.7	5.7	11.6	10.3	14.1	6.1	5.7	4.2	7.1	5.6
% 75 Years Old And Over..	6.7	8.7	6.5	10.3	13.1	10.5	6.0	5.4	3.3	3.9	3.4
% In Different House.....	66.8	62.4	66.6	70.7	72.6	66.7	67.8	53.6	65.3	71.3	65.7
% Families With Female Head.....	33.5	24.5	26.3	42.2	27.4	23.2	31.0	53.5	40.8	23.1	25.5
Median School Years Completed....	12.3	12.3	12.1	11.2	12.9	14.5	12.4	11.3	11.5	12.5	12.5
Median Family Income, 1979.....$$	14455	19022	14777	8701	16310	29614	15101	8661	11649	16575	16015
% Income Below Poverty Level....	22.6	10.4	18.0	42.1	9.5	2.9	19.7	39.5	33.1	8.5	19.6
% Income Of $30,000 Or More.....	14.7	21.0	11.9	5.0	21.6	49.2	8.2	2.6	7.5	15.8	13.5
% White Collar Workers.....	52.0	36.9	40.7	30.1	71.3	90.3	52.4	40.0	47.5	44.5	41.1
% Civilian Labor Force Unemployed.	10.3	5.7	12.7	16.5	7.6	1.8	12.4	14.6	11.8	6.9	14.3
% Riding To Work By Automobile....	45.8	50.6	48.0	36.9	47.0	52.6	39.0	27.5	44.7	51.5	52.4
Mean Commuting Time - Minutes...	31.2	28.6	26.3	37.2	32.6	32.7	31.5	29.9	32.4	29.1	29.3
Population Per Household...	2.1	2.6	2.6	1.9	1.7	1.6	2.3	2.3	2.4	2.5	2.5
Total Housing Units..........	33714	1913	2557	3352	4244	3628	4775	1484	4183	969	1346
% Condominiums...........	11.3	1.6	0.8	1.1	23.3	65.2	1.0	0.0	0.2	9.5	2.5
% Built 1970 Or Later........	8.1	0.8	1.6	6.1	10.9	22.0	10.4	9.4	3.3	0.8	1.7
% Owner Occupied........	11.1	18.6	13.9	2.9	13.9	41.6	1.9	1.9	4.5	18.7	14.3
% With 1+ Persons Per Room.	12.2	10.3	12.2	12.7	4.9	1.9	17.2	14.9	16.6	15.9	13.6
Median Value: Owner Units.......$$	61400	49600	49700	-	227	317	204	153	66200	58700	62200
Median Rent: Rental Units.....$$	196	210	207	164	227	317	204	153	171	201	205
Median Number Of Rooms: All Units.	3.1	4.2	4.2	2.1	3.0	3.4	2.8	2.9	2.8	3.6	3.9

Tract Number	320	321
Total Population..............	1123	7985
% Male.......	53.2	54.4
% Black.......	4.8	20.3
% Other Nonwhite.....	29.8	30.8
% Of Spanish Origin.....	34.9	40.7
% Foreign Born........	20.6	29.9
% Living In Group Quarters........	0.0	3.4
% 13 Years Old And Under.	28.1	21.9
% 14-20 Years Old........	9.5	10.2
% 21-64 Years Old........	57.7	60.6
% 65-74 Years Old........	3.0	4.8
% 75 Years Old And Over..	1.6	2.6
% In Different House.....	41.8	69.2
% Families With Female Head.....	30.2	39.9
Median School Years Completed....	10.1	12.1
Median Family Income, 1979......$$	5833	10766
% Income Below Poverty Level....	55.6	34.7
% Income Of $30,000 Or More.....	4.8	9.3
% White Collar Workers.....	24.3	39.0
% Civilian Labor Force Unemployed.	14.7	12.6
% Riding To Work By Automobile....	55.3	44.4
Mean Commuting Time - Minutes...	29.1	32.0
Population Per Household...	2.3	2.2
Total Housing Units..........	674	4589
% Condominiums...........	0.0	4.2
% Built 1970 Or Later........	2.9	8.3
% Owner Occupied........	1.8	3.4
% With 1+ Persons Per Room.....$$	25.7	15.2
Median Value: Owner Units.......$$	-	-
Median Rent: Rental Units.....$$	145	185
Median Number Of Rooms: All Units.	2.1	2.9

extends northward into Edgewater, is inhabited primarily by lower-income people and contains the poorest housing; these are the areas that have given Uptown its reputation as a poor community.

During the 1970s a variety of government-funded social programs was established to serve Uptown's troubled residents. Many of these services have been discontinued since then, as funding for such efforts has diminished. However, Uptown still has a number of active community organizations which concern themselves with the course of future development. Several groups became involved in debate over the planning of Truman College, which opened in 1976 in a new building at Wilson and Racine. While various interests supported the opening of the college as a stimulus to revitalization of the area, some were concerned about the displacement of poor residents from approximately 200 housing units which were destroyed. More recently, debate has focused on the desirability of increasing the amount of subsidized housing in the area. Both controversies illustrate the type of debate which continues in Uptown, over how to promote development of the area, while maintaining a balance between the interests of poor people already in the area and new development more directly serving middle-income residents.

Marjorie DeVault

Community Area 03 — Uptown
Selected Characteristics of Census Tracts: 1970

Tract Number	TOTAL	0310	0311	0312	0313	0314	0315	0316	0317	0318	0319
Total Population............	74838	4605	6537	6728	7819	5430	10919	4662	10885	2212	3347
% Male......................	49.7	42.5	46.6	54.5	45.3	45.2	50.0	53.2	52.6	48.6	49.4
% Black.....................	4.1	0.2	0.8	5.1	3.6	0.4	8.4	17.2	1.3	0.4	0.3
% Other Nonwhite............	8.2	4.8	13.3	8.7	6.9	2.3	10.3	10.9	7.5	9.3	6.3
% Of Spanish Language.......	13.3	6.6	18.6	16.8	7.4	1.9	18.4	10.2	8.1	23.2	7.7
% Foreign Born..............	19.8	26.4	30.8	20.5	26.8	20.1	20.3	7.9	9.3	30.3	18.5
% Living In Group Quarters..	3.8	7.0	4.2	1.7	2.7	3.4	4.6	5.9	4.3	2.9	1.6
% 13 Years Old And Under....	20.7	17.3	21.0	20.1	14.3	10.2	21.7	30.7	24.7	19.8	18.3
% 14-20 Years Old...........	8.0	8.5	10.2	7.4	6.4	4.0	8.3	9.5	9.0	8.7	8.3
% 21-64 Years Old...........	55.7	51.9	53.0	55.7	58.0	66.4	53.4	49.7	54.3	57.5	57.1
% 65-74 Years Old...........	9.3	11.0	8.4	10.5	11.9	14.2	9.6	6.7	7.1	9.2	10.1
% 75 Years Old And Over.....	6.2	11.2	7.4	6.4	9.3	5.2	6.9	3.5	4.9	4.7	6.2
% In Different House........	29.2	42.2	40.4	22.4	24.5	42.8	18.6	21.5	27.2	46.4	39.0
% Families With Female Head.	16.3	12.8	14.3	15.0	16.1	12.0	19.6	23.8	15.2	15.1	14.0
Median School Years Completed	11.4	11.7	11.4	10.8	12.4	12.9	10.6	8.9	10.2	12.1	12.1
Median Family Income, 1969....$$	8524	10052	10192	7500	9915	14926	6985	5533	7703	10967	10098
% Income Below Poverty Level....	15.8	5.7	10.5	16.8	9.9	4.9	21.8	35.0	17.9	12.1	7.2
% Income of $15,000 or More.....	18.1	21.0	22.7	10.9	24.5	49.7	8.0	6.2	10.3	27.3	26.4
% White Collar Workers.........	27.8	26.7	24.1	17.8	45.7	60.6	24.4	14.0	12.4	23.7	27.3
% Civilian Labor Force Unemployed.	4.9	3.3	2.6	6.1	4.2	1.9	5.6	6.7	6.5	2.6	4.5
% Riding To Work By Automobile....	44.4	45.8	47.5	40.6	45.0	54.7	35.1	37.5	49.8	56.1	49.3
Population Per Household.........	2.2	2.4	2.6	1.9	1.9	1.9	2.1	2.6	2.3	2.3	2.2
Total Housing Units.........	36859	1864	2525	4051	4326	2831	5780	2127	4913	966	1537
% Condominiums & Cooperatives.....	0.4	0.0	1.0	0.0	1.9	0.2	0.1	0.0	0.0	0.5	1.2
% Built 1960 Or Later.............	12.6	4.6	2.0	6.5	26.1	40.6	20.6	10.5	3.1	8.1	2.3
% Owner Occupied..................	4.5	17.5	13.3	1.8	2.1	2.3	1.5	2.6	4.1	14.0	10.0
% With 1+ Persons Per Room........	10.7	4.6	9.1	11.3	7.0	2.8	12.7	17.6	16.8	6.7	5.7
Median Value: Owner Units.......$$	21800	18700	17600	-	-	-	-	-	-	23100	20600
Median Rent: Rental Units.......$$	111	111	112	94	133	185	111	97	102	111	105
Median Number Of Rooms: All Units.	2.9	4.2	4.2	1.9	2.8	3.3	2.3	2.8	2.5	3.6	3.5

Tract Number	0320	0321
Total Population............	1402	10292
% Male......................	54.1	52.2
% Black.....................	1.8	4.2
% Other Nonwhite............	6.7	8.1
% Of Spanish Language.......	17.8	21.2
% Foreign Born..............	10.0	19.0
% Living In Group Quarters..	0.0	3.4
% 13 Years Old And Under....	28.2	23.3
% 14-20 Years Old...........	10.2	7.9
% 21-64 Years Old...........	54.6	57.2
% 65-74 Years Old...........	4.4	7.5
% 75 Years Old And Over.....	2.6	4.1
% In Different House........	38.0	24.8
% Families With Female Head.	18.6	19.3
Median School Years Completed	9.5	10.6
Median Family Income, 1969....$$	6250	7268
% Income Below Poverty Level....	24.5	19.7
% Income of $15,000 or More.....	3.9	11.0
% White Collar Workers.........	14.5	23.0
% Civilian Labor Force Unemployed.	7.6	6.8
% Riding To Work By Automobile....	38.8	37.1
Population Per Household.........	2.3	2.2
Total Housing Units.........	716	5223
% Condominiums & Cooperatives.....	0.0	0.0
% Built 1960 Or Later.............	0.0	5.5
% Owner Occupied..................	2.1	2.5
% With 1+ Persons Per Room........	18.1	12.8
Median Value: Owner Units.......$$	-	-
Median Rent: Rental Units.......$$	85	103
Median Number Of Rooms: All Units.	2.2	2.6

Community Area 4

Lincoln Square

The community area of Lincoln Square includes part or all of five previous communities. These were formerly Bowmanville, Budlong Woods, Ravenswood, Summerdale, and Winnemac. The neighborhood was first settled by whites in the late 1830s and 1840s. The "Little Fort Road" (Lincoln Avenue) ran through the area connecting Chicago with Waukegan (then known as "Little Fort"). The Lincoln Square vicinity became a stopping point for travellers on the road and in 1845 the Bowmanville Hotel was built at the corner of what is today Lincoln Avenue and Ainslie Street. The community of Bowmanville was established five years later when Jesse Bowman laid out a subdivision bounded by Foster, Western, Lawrence, and California avenues. It was later discovered that Bowman's title to this area was not legal and the buyers of his lots were forced to repurchase their land. Bowman, in the meantime, had left town.

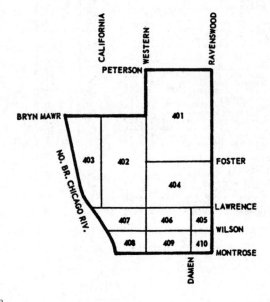

The early settlers in the area were predominantly English, German, Luxembourger, and American farmers. They cultivated the land and established truck farms in the 1850s and 1860s. A major factory was established in the area when, in 1857, Lyman A. Budlong built the Budlong Pickle Factory at the intersection of Lincoln and Berwyn avenues. Labor needed to work on the farms and in the pickle factories of the area was obtained from the foreign settlements west of the Loop. Men, women, and children, mostly Polish, were transported to the community daily by wagons.

Bowmanville was regarded as a bright spot in the sparsely settled township of Jefferson. The community consisted of a few frame houses, the Bowmanville Hotel, some saloons, and a store, all located along Lincoln Avenue. In 1859 a large tract of land in the northeastern section of Lincoln Square was purchased and a cemetery was laid out. A typographic error resulted in its becoming known as the Rosehill Cemetery. A tavern on a small hill in the area was run by Hiram Roe and the reference to the area as Roe's Hill gave way to that of Rose Hill. Expansion of this cemetery in the following years made about one-fourth of the Lincoln Square area unavailable for residential use.

The southern part of the Lincoln Square area remained prairie and farmland during the 1850s and 1860s. Events that were to change this situation were, however, set in motion in 1868 when the Ravenswood Land Company was formed. Led by Martin Van Allen, this company purchased 194 acres on either side of the Chicago and North Western Railroad tracks in 1869 and set about subdividing this area which was then part of the Lake View Township. Chicago streets such as Wilson, Leland, Kedzie, and Greenleaf were named after members of the Ravenswood Land Company.

Moderate growth took place in the community between 1875 and 1895. Although horse cars had started to operate on Lincoln Avenue in 1874, residents in the southern part of the community tended to build close to the railroad which was then the chief means of transportation to the city. Development of the Ravenswood section of Lincoln Square proceeded and in 1876 and 1877 a sewage system and waterworks were installed in this area. The northwestern section of Lincoln Square began to be transformed into a flower-growing area in the 1880s when the Budlong brothers set up a number of greenhouses. By 1897 they had constructed 18 greenhouses in this vicinity. In 1889, Lincoln Square became part of Chicago with the annexation of the townships of Jefferson and Lake View.

Lincoln Square's real growth came after annexation, during the years from 1895 through 1924. In the 1890s electric car lines were running on Lawrence, Montrose, Lincoln, and Western avenues and in subsequent years the lines on Lincoln and Western avenues were extended. The western section of Lincoln Square began to be developed after the Albany Park branch of the elevated line was opened in 1907.

Community Area 4 -- Lincoln Square
Population and Housing Characteristics, 1930-1980

	1980	1970	1960	1950	1940	1930
Total Population.......	43,954	47,751	49,850	47,298	47,179	46,419
% Male...................	46.6	46.0	46.4	47.0	47.7	48.5
% Female.................	53.4	54.0	53.6	53.0	52.3	51.5
% White..................	84.3	97.9	99.3	99.8	99.9	100.0
% Black..................	0.5	0.1	0.1	0.1	0.0	0.0
% Other Nonwhite Races...	15.2	2.0	0.6	0.1	0.1	0.0
% Under 5 Years Old......	6.0	6.4	7.9	8.0	5.5	6.9
% 5-19 Years Old.........	17.6	18.7	17.7	15.6	18.6	19.8
% 20-44 Years Old........	37.0	30.5	30.7	38.1	44.1	48.1
% 45-64 Years Old........	21.4	27.1	30.3	28.6	24.6	20.0
% 65 Years and Older.....	18.0	17.3	13.4	9.7	7.2	5.2
Median School Years......	12.4	11.8	11.2	11.3	9.1	*
Total Housing Units....	19,454	19,428	18,964	15,764	14,921	*
% In One-Unit Structures.	11.3	11.2	12.0	*	*	*
% Owner Occupied.........	26.6	26.8	28.0	24.8	18.8	*
% Renter Occupied........	69.4	71.0	69.0	74.5	78.0	*
% Vacant.................	4.0	2.2	3.0	1.7	3.2	*
% 1+ Persons per Room....	4.7	4.1	3.8	8.5	*	*

Community Area 4 -- Lincoln Square
Selected Characteristics of Census Tracts: 1980

Tract Number	Total	401	402	403	404	405	406	407	408	409	410
Total Population.............	43954	4168	13786	3113	8539	1166	2988	4199	1811	2368	1816
% Male..........................	46.6	45.8	45.6	48.3	45.5	46.9	48.6	49.4	47.5	46.0	46.9
% Black.........................	0.5	0.7	0.5	1.9	0.3	0.3	0.2	0.7	0.2	0.1	0.3
% Other Nonwhite................	15.2	12.4	13.1	12.8	15.0	21.5	14.4	18.5	12.1	14.6	35.0
% Of Spanish Origin.............	11.3	8.8	6.5	3.2	15.3	17.8	12.6	16.0	8.9	14.5	30.4
% Foreign Born..................	35.4	23.8	43.3	38.9	31.4	35.5	34.3	41.6	18.4	28.2	30.0
% Living In Group Quarters......	1.8	5.2	2.3	2.3	5.3	0.0	0.0	0.0	0.4	0.2	4.7
% 13 Years Old And Under........	15.6	13.6	15.3	15.0	15.8	13.4	14.2	21.5	12.9	14.3	17.3
% 14-20 Years Old...............	9.8	10.1	8.8	12.6	9.7	7.8	8.8	11.7	12.5	9.7	8.6
% 21-64 Years Old...............	56.6	55.7	55.4	53.1	57.0	62.4	59.2	55.8	59.0	57.7	62.6
% 65-74 Years Old...............	10.2	10.8	11.3	11.6	11.6	9.5	10.7	6.3	9.3	11.0	6.8
% 75 Years Old And Over.........	7.8	9.9	9.3	7.7	7.1	6.9	7.0	4.7	6.3	7.3	4.8
% In Different House............	50.3	48.7	49.2	37.4	56.4	49.0	48.9	54.6	41.8	49.8	57.6
% Families With Female Head.....	19.0	19.8	14.1	9.3	21.9	21.9	19.7	24.1	29.1	22.1	25.9
Median School Years Completed...	12.4	12.3	12.3	12.8	12.4	12.5	12.4	12.5	12.5	12.4	12.3
Median Family Income, 1979......$$	20170	21368	20418	27995	18654	20597	21158	17299	23621	17357	15444
% Income Below Poverty Level....	7.2	6.1	5.6	5.5	4.3	7.1	4.8	14.4	5.6	10.1	13.7
% Income Of $30,000 Or More.....	23.4	26.2	23.6	45.8	15.6	12.5	25.2	21.8	34.7	12.8	15.1
% White Collar Workers..........	55.5	51.9	56.4	67.9	55.2	54.8	46.6	49.2	66.2	56.9	54.6
% Civilian Labor Force Unemployed.	6.4	7.4	5.4	4.5	5.4	9.2	7.1	8.8	7.3	10.5	4.9
% Riding To Work By Automobile...	56.6	60.3	62.3	69.6	49.0	41.2	52.9	55.0	64.3	49.8	42.0
Mean Commuting Time - Minutes...	27.9	27.3	27.3	26.6	28.9	26.3	26.1	30.5	25.2	29.0	29.3
Population Per Household........	2.3	2.3	2.4	2.7	2.2	2.0	2.2	2.2	2.6	2.1	2.2
Total Housing Units..........	19454	1794	5951	1129	3981	618	1418	1692	827	1201	843
% Condominiums..................	3.2	0.0	7.0	11.3	1.3	0.0	0.0	0.0	3.0	0.0	0.0
% Built 1970 Or Later...........	1.7	3.0	2.6	0.4	0.5	1.5	0.0	1.5	4.9	1.6	0.8
% Owner Occupied................	26.6	32.7	26.9	64.0	22.9	9.9	22.3	24.3	30.4	20.6	7.9
% With 1+ Persons Per Room......	4.7	3.5	4.8	1.7	3.5	7.1	3.4	9.3	2.6	3.7	11.1
Median Value: Owner Units......$$	60100	50200	62900	86700	49600	-	50400	62800	64700	49000	-
Median Rent: Rental Units.....$$	217	222	239	273	211	192	194	207	214	190	192
Median Number Of Rooms: All Units.	4.4	4.5	4.4	5.4	4.4	3.7	4.5	4.6	4.9	3.9	3.7

Community Area 04 -- Lincoln Square
Selected Characteristics of Census Tracts: 1970

Tract Number	TOTAL	0401	0402	0403	0404	0405	0406	0407	0408	0409	0410
Total Population.............	47751	4486	14280	3263	9597	1289	3423	4561	2305	2575	1972
% Male........................	46.0	44.5	45.8	47.6	45.5	48.6	46.9	47.8	46.7	45.0	44.2
% Black.......................	0.1	0.1	0.1	0.9	0.0	0.0	0.0	0.0	0.0	0.0	0.3
% Other Nonwhite..............	2.0	2.0	1.6	1.4	1.8	2.6	2.5	2.7	2.1	1.4	3.7
% Of Spanish Language.........	4.2	3.3	2.5	0.6	4.4	7.0	5.4	8.6	3.4	3.1	11.4
% Foreign Born................	25.3	17.3	31.5	22.4	22.2	11.8	26.2	31.2	25.8	18.8	19.7
% Living In Group Quarters....	1.3	5.0	1.0	4.3	0.1	1.2	0.0	0.0	0.7	0.6	3.4
% 13 Years Old And Under......	17.4	17.3	16.1	15.8	17.8	13.5	17.4	22.2	21.6	16.4	15.9
% 14-20 Years Old.............	9.0	8.9	8.3	11.2	8.7	8.8	9.0	9.8	11.2	7.8	10.5
% 21-64 Years Old.............	56.3	53.9	57.3	55.8	55.9	61.5	56.8	55.1	51.5	57.0	59.5
% 65-74 Years Old.............	11.1	11.3	11.9	11.8	11.6	9.7	11.2	8.0	9.9	12.1	8.8
% 75 Years Old And Over.......	6.2	8.6	6.4	5.5	6.1	6.4	5.6	4.8	5.8	6.8	5.3
% In Different House..........	53.4	48.0	54.1	63.9	56.0	49.2	53.7	48.6	58.1	55.8	35.4
% Families With Female Head...	12.7	14.4	12.5	8.0	13.6	13.2	13.4	11.5	15.2	12.1	13.5
Median School Years Completed.	11.8	11.1	12.0	12.4	11.6	11.9	11.2	11.5	12.2	10.7	11.7
Median Family Income, 1969..$$	11246	11333	11700	14689	10490	10592	10324	11615	10500	11131	9758
% Income Below Poverty Level..	5.0	3.2	4.8	2.9	5.1	5.3	3.7	8.4	6.9	6.3	5.4
% Income of $15,000 or More...	27.6	25.2	30.9	48.5	21.3	19.6	24.6	28.7	29.5	23.7	13.3
% White Collar Workers........	29.0	27.9	35.1	55.5	22.4	19.8	24.8	18.1	32.0	22.3	21.0
% Civilian Labor Force Unemployed.	2.9	2.1	2.7	0.4	3.9	1.6	3.0	3.0	4.9	2.5	4.0
% Riding To Work By Automobile.	51.1	56.3	54.1	72.5	48.1	35.2	52.1	41.8	48.0	41.5	42.9
Population Per Household......	2.5	2.5	2.5	2.8	2.4	2.1	2.5	2.8	2.8	2.2	2.1
Total Housing Units..........	19396	1747	5726	1109	4077	647	1433	1687	844	1194	932
% Condominiums & Cooperatives.	3.5	0.3	7.7	17.8	0.6	0.0	0.5	0.3	0.0	0.0	0.0
% Built 1960 Or Later.........	5.2	4.9	11.6	2.0	1.2	5.8	1.3	2.3	0.0	5.1	4.5
% Owner Occupied..............	23.4	33.0	20.3	47.7	21.4	12.2	23.2	25.4	29.3	20.3	6.4
% With 1+ Persons Per Room....	4.0	3.0	3.5	2.4	3.8	4.5	3.2	7.5	5.7	3.1	5.1
Median Value: Owner Units...$$	22500	19100	25600	37600	19200	-	18600	22600	24400	19200	-
Median Rent: Rental Units...$$	117	117	138	165	112	108	103	113	112	104	110
Median Number Of Rooms: All Units.	4.4	4.5	4.5	5.4	4.4	3.7	4.5	4.7	4.8	3.8	3.6

Lincoln Square's population jumped from 12,169 in 1910 to 27,990 in 1920 in conjunction with an expansion of residential construction in the community. The residents were still predominantly German and Swedish, with some Poles and Luxembourgers in the northwestern part of the community. After 1915, many Germans and persons of German descent moved into Lincoln Square from the older, more crowded communities to the south which were receiving influxes of newer ethnic groups.

Lincoln Square's building boom continued through the 1920s. The northern section had its greatest development during this decade. The early frame houses on Lincoln Avenue began to be replaced by large apartment buildings and new brick bungalows and two- and three-flat buildings were constructed in the area west of Lincoln Avenue. Beautiful brick houses were constructed along the Chicago River at the western edge of Lincoln Square. East of Lincoln Avenue, however, the old wood and stucco one- and two-story frame building prevailed. The building trend in other parts of the community was toward the construction of brick bungalows and two-story flats. By 1925, Lincoln Square had become residentially developed.

A large increase in population accompanied the building boom in Lincoln Square during the twenties with a rise from 27,990 in 1920 to 46,419 in 1930. Germans and Swedes were still the predominant ethnic groups in 1930. The Poles, who originally had settled in the northern sector, increased in number but were more diffused throughout the community. Other ethnic groups attracted to Lincoln Square by the building boom included Italians, Russian Jews, and Greeks.

Paralleling the residential development was the growth of Lincoln Square's industrial and business sections. The business center along Ravenswood Avenue gave way to an array of light manufacturing and assembling plants. The old stores were remodeled for light factory use. As the industries expanded and needed larger quarters, the old structures were razed and modern-type factories were built. Lincoln Avenue remained the main business thoroughfare, although in the mid-1940s some vacant store fronts began to appear in the stretch of Lincoln Avenue north of Lawrence Avenue.

Between 1930 and 1960, the population of Lincoln Square grew slowly, reaching a historic peak, just under 50,000, at the end of that period. Germans, Russians, Swedes, and Poles were the dominant ethnic groups in 1960. The stretch along Lincoln Avenue remained predominantly German through the sixties, but during the 1970s Greeks, Koreans, Latinos, and some East Europeans began moving into this area. The postwar increase in residential construction benefited mainly the northwestern section of the community and included both single-family structures.

The population of Lincoln Square has dropped off about 12 percent since 1960, standing today just under 44,000. The racial composition is predominantly white (84 percent), with a small number of blacks and the rest other non-whites. The Spanish-origin population is 11 percent of the total. The prevailing housing structure is the small apartment building; more than two-thirds of all units are located in buildings containing less than 10 apartments. The median value of single-family owner-occupied homes puts Lincoln Square among the top 20 community areas in the city in this respect.

Lincoln Square contains a major retail center, consisting of the stores along Foster Avenue, between Damen and Western avenues. The community acquired a symbol in 1956, with the erection of the Abraham Lincoln Monument at the intersection of Lincoln, Lawrence and Western avenues. The Lincoln Avenue shopping area was revitalized with the completion of the Lincoln Square Mall in 1978. This is a pedestrian mall which stretches from Leland Avenue to Lawrence Avenue on Lincoln and is closed to the northbound traffic. The establishment of public parking lots in 1980 near the mall has somewhat alleviated parking problems in the area. There is a major retail center in Lincoln Square located on Lawrence Avenue from Ravenswood to Damen avenues, anchored by the Sears store on Lawrence Avenue. Another landmark in Lincoln Square, the new Hild Regional Library building, is to be constructed soon at Montrose and Lincoln avenues.

Rodney Nelson

North Center

The community of North Center is located approximately seven miles northwest of Chicago's Loop. As the name implies, it is situated practically in the center of the North Side. The area was sparsely settled and given over to prairie and farmland largely until after the Chicago fire of 1871. This was due, in part, to the limited accessibility of the area from the city since there were only two main routes — Green Bay Road (now Clark Street) and Little Fort Road (now Lincoln Avenue), an old Indian trail leading to the northwest. The community area, as it is known today, was formed out of parts of the old townships of Lakeview and Jefferson, both annexed to the city of Chicago in 1889.

Much of the North Center area is built on what was once the farmland of John Turner, an Englishman. His 80-acre farm was purchased in the 1850s from William B. Ogden, but Turner did not live there until after the fire. He became a truck farmer and sheep breeder and leased portions of his land to newly arrived German settlers. Truck farming was the dominant occupation of these people and it flourished until nearly 1890. At one time North Center was part of the greatest celery-growing region in America and it was here, historically, that greenhouse technology was developed. The Chicago and North Western Railroad tracks were laid in 1854 and truck farming communities, such as the one at Cuyler Station, developed along the tracks. At the close of the 1880s the population of North Center lived mainly south of Addison Avenue from Leavitt Avenue to the North Western tracks, with the greatest concentration of population east of Damen Avenue. Farther south, between the present Wrightwood and Diversey avenues, east of Damen, was located a livestock market for the buying, selling and trading of horses, cows and goat.

While farming was predominant in the northern half of the community, industry predominated in the southern portion and spread along the North Branch of the Chicago River. There were many clay pits along Belmont Avenue from the North Western tracks to the river and at one time the area was a nationally known center of the brick-making industry. In 1880, William Deering located his harvester works in the southwestern part of the community. It employed 1,500 men and covered 25 acres. In that time, one of the residential subdivisions was called Deering. Other industries located there were Northwestern Terra Cotta, Lassig Iron Works, Clybourn's Slaughterhouse and the Luetgart Sausage Company.

During the 1890s, residential housing construction expanded northward and westward in North Center. While the main group of settlers was German, there were also sizeable numbers of Irish, Swedes and English coming into the area. The center of German social life was located along Belmont Avenue, and the Irish center was located south of the area, around Fullerton. A real estate developer, Sam Brown, Jr., loaned money for lumber to anyone buying a lot from him, thus allowing new settlers to build small houses on their lots. When they were able to save enough money, they built larger houses on the front of the lot. Many of these double-housed lots can still be seen around North Center today.

Also in the 1890s, the North Western tracks, which originally had been built at the street level, were elevated and this caused some subdivisions, such as Cuyler and Gross Park, to be separated from one another. This split created the business district that is located at the intersections of Lincoln, Damen and Irving Park avenues, which became the heart of North Center. Transportation was improved during this period and into the 1900s, with the extension of the Ravenswood branch of the "L" in 1907, the development of a new streetcar line on Western Avenue and the extension of routes along Irving Park Road, Lincoln and Clybourn avenues. The community was largely residential with frame and brick homes and two-flat buildings. The southern part

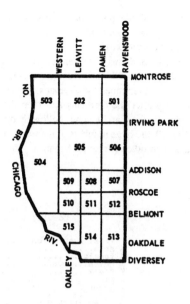

of the community, the area of first settlement, was beginning to show signs of decay.

Even though new nationality groups, among them Hungarians, Poles and Slovaks, began to enter the area around World War I, the largest nationality remained the Germans. The new group settled in the southern part of the community, while Germans and Swedes settled in the northern half. The population in the area increased 40 percent during the years from 1910 to 1920.

During the 1900s the old clay pits in the southern half of the community began to close down, due in part to opposition to their noxious odor. These pits were used for garbage dumps for some time until the land could be used for other purposes. Light manufacturing firms began to predominate on Ravenswood Avenue from Montrose to Diversey and still do so today. The southern fringe of the community along Diversey and the river has heavier industry and fewer residential units.

In 1903, William Schmidt opened the Schuetzen Park rifle and gun range in the vicinity of Belmont and Western. It was located on the North Branch of the river, on a filled-in portion of a clay pit. In 1905, the name was changed to Riverview Sharpshooter's Park and the area expanded into an amusement park. During its era of prominence, it was referred to as the "Coney Island" of Chicago. Due to decreasing interest and changing area composition, the park closed its doors in 1967.

In 1923, in the western part of the community, the Mid-City Golf links were developed on another clay pit landfill. In 1934, the land was taken over for the construction of Lane Technical High School and, to the northwest of Addison and Western avenues, a large industrial park. Light industrial plants have also developed along Western Avenue and Irving Park Road. In the 1930s, on the site of yet another landfill, the Julia C. Lathrop Homes were built, in the vicinity of Diversey, Clybourn and the river. About one-half of this lies in North Center and it is low-income housing, administered by the Chicago Housing Authority. The project has one highrise for the elderly and 63 lowrises. It contains approximately 990 families, of which more than one-half are white and the remainder black or Hispanic. Virtually all (99 percent) of the housing units in North Center were built before 1940, the majority being in one to three flat buildings and single-family homes.

After a slight increase in population between 1930-1940, North Center has been experiencing a decline since a high of 48,759 in 1940. In 1970 the population was 39,443. The 1980 census shows that North Center's population has decreased 10.8 percent to a total of 35,161. This decrease is equal to the city's loss for the same period. The black population increased to 1.2 percent of the total and Hispanics now constitute 19 percent of the population. This is due to residential spillover from the Uptown area to the northeast and expansion of the Lathrop Homes in the southwest.

After World War II, Serbians, Croatians and other Eastern Europeans moved into the area. In 1970 the predominant ethnic group of both native and foreign stock remained the Germans. Italians constitute the second largest group after the Germans and then the Irish. Among foreign born, Yugoslavians are second, followed by Austrians and Hungarians. In the 1970s, large numbers of Koreans and other Asians, South Americans, and other Hispanics began to move in.

More than 60 percent of the housing units in North Center are renter occupied. With the encroachment of heavy industry in the southern and western parts of the community, housing in that area is deteriorating and being demolished. The North Center shopping area is also waning and it would seem that the trend in the community is more to manufacturing and industry.

Marie L. Ule

Community Area 5 — North Center
Population and Housing Characteristics, 1930–1980

	1980	1970	1960	1950	1940	1930
Total Population	35,161	39,410	43,877	47,787	48,759	47,651
% Male	47.4	46.9	47.5	48.1	49.2	50.1
% Female	52.6	53.1	52.5	51.9	50.8	49.9
% White	84.5	98.3	99.4	99.9	100.0	100.0
% Black	1.2	0.3	0.1	0.0	0.0	0.0
% Other Nonwhite Races	14.3	1.4	0.5	0.1	0.0	0.0
% Under 5 Years Old	6.9	7.5	9.6	8.3	6.1	7.0
% 5-19 Years Old	21.1	23.1	20.3	18.2	20.2	22.4
% 20-44 Years Old	37.7	30.7	31.2	37.3	42.2	44.5
% 45-64 Years Old	20.7	24.5	26.4	26.5	24.0	20.4
% 65 Years and Older	13.6	14.2	12.5	9.7	7.5	5.7
Median School Years	12.0	10.6	9.4	9.0	8.4	*
Total Housing Units	14,969	15,183	15,531	15,402	14,815	*
% In One-Unit Structures	15.5	16.0	17.2	*	*	*
% Owner Occupied	35.2	35.1	36.4	35.3	29.9	*
% Renter Occupied	58.5	60.5	61.1	63.6	68.0	*
% Vacant	6.3	4.4	2.5	1.1	2.1	*
% 1+ Persons per Room	4.4	4.6	5.5	8.1	*	*

Community Area 5 — North Center
Selected Characteristics of Census Tracts: 1980

Tract Number	Total	501	502	503	504	505	506	507	508	509	510
Total Population	35161	2765	5272	2542	627	5647	2066	1410	1529	1668	1511
% Male	47.4	47.1	48.4	47.4	50.1	45.5	45.8	45.8	49.0	46.0	49.0
% Black	1.2	0.6	0.1	0.0	1.1	0.2	0.4	0.4	0.1	0.2	0.7
% Other Nonwhite	14.2	17.8	11.9	9.8	14.0	7.7	8.9	16.5	12.4	15.9	17.1
% Of Spanish Origin	19.0	16.5	13.1	10.7	9.3	9.4	14.5	21.4	17.1	22.0	25.7
% Foreign Born	18.8	25.1	23.5	22.9	47.1	17.0	16.0	13.5	17.4	14.1	18.5
% Living In Group Quarters	0.2	0.0	0.2	0.0	3.2	0.2	0.0	0.0	0.0	0.0	0.0
% 13 Years Old And Under	18.8	15.7	17.9	14.4	15.0	15.8	17.3	16.2	20.8	17.7	20.5
% 14-20 Years Old	10.9	11.0	12.0	8.8	11.0	10.3	9.1	11.8	12.0	10.7	11.1
% 21-64 Years Old	56.6	59.8	57.1	59.0	58.5	57.0	57.9	57.7	54.4	56.5	57.6
% 65-74 Years Old	8.3	8.8	8.5	9.7	9.6	10.2	8.8	9.2	6.4	9.4	6.8
% 75 Years Old And Over	5.3	4.6	4.5	8.1	5.9	6.7	6.9	5.1	6.4	5.8	4.0
% In Different House	45.3	49.3	46.8	38.1	25.8	37.5	39.1	47.1	46.8	49.9	51.1
% Families With Female Head	25.2	21.3	21.2	18.6	12.3	21.3	22.4	22.0	22.9	28.6	26.7
Median School Years Completed	12.0	12.1	12.1	12.1	12.2	12.2	12.2	12.1	12.1	11.9	11.0
Median Family Income, 1979 $$	19361	16541	20265	22579	23594	21187	21894	17654	23963	20469	16613
% Income Below Poverty Level	9.9	8.7	7.4	4.7	3.9	7.4	6.8	7.3	10.1	9.6	7.9
% Income Of $30,000 Or More	20.8	20.9	22.4	21.4	32.9	26.2	22.8	19.4	26.3	17.9	18.5
% White Collar Workers	48.8	51.9	49.8	50.1	49.5	56.5	54.5	43.8	53.5	45.8	42.7
% Civilian Labor Force Unemployed	7.3	6.8	5.9	8.2	6.4	5.4	9.8	6.9	4.2	4.2	12.1
% Riding To Work By Automobile	56.7	49.4	55.6	64.0	59.0	57.7	46.0	53.3	61.4	53.2	62.0
Mean Commuting Time - Minutes	27.0	26.6	29.7	26.7	26.1	26.6	26.0	31.2	31.0	26.7	21.9
Population Per Household	2.5	2.4	2.6	2.4	2.7	2.4	2.3	2.5	2.7	2.4	2.5
Total Housing Units	14969	1254	2150	1095	250	2388	920	603	642	739	661
% Condominiums	0.0	0.0	0.0	0.0	0.0	0.0	0.0	0.0	0.0	0.0	0.0
% Built 1970 Or Later	0.4	0.7	0.3	0.0	0.0	0.5	0.0	0.0	0.0	0.0	2.9
% Owner Occupied	35.3	26.3	41.0	46.0	54.4	38.5	30.4	39.6	38.3	33.4	29.7
% With 1+ Persons Per Room	4.4	3.8	4.1	2.5	4.0	1.9	2.3	5.4	5.4	3.7	3.6
Median Value: Owner Units $$	42900	48200	44200	44200	54900	48100	45000	44000	39600	-	41900
Median Rent: Rental Units $$	183	197	195	188	205	197	197	191	172	190	176
Median Number Of Rooms: All Units	4.8	4.8	4.9	4.9	5.2	5.2	4.8	5.0	4.7	4.8	4.7

Community Area 5 — North Center
Selected Characteristics of Census Tracts: 1980

Tract Number	511	512	513	514	515
Total Population	1666	1935	2180	2896	1447
% Male	48.6	48.8	49.0	46.3	47.9
% Black	0.4	0.9	0.6	9.6	1.6
% Other Nonwhite	16.2	12.7	18.1	27.5	18.9
% Of Spanish Origin	25.8	28.0	25.1	38.6	29.2
% Foreign Born	24.5	11.7	11.5	12.6	19.5
% Living In Group Quarters	0.0	2.4	0.0	0.0	0.0
% 13 Years Old And Under	22.4	20.3	20.6	28.4	23.4
% 14-20 Years Old	10.7	11.1	10.7	11.7	12.8
% 21-64 Years Old	56.3	56.9	55.5	50.8	54.6
% 65-74 Years Old	6.1	7.5	8.0	5.3	7.0
% 75 Years Old And Over	4.4	4.2	5.2	3.8	2.2
% In Different House	59.8	44.8	47.7	49.7	49.2
% Families With Female Head	23.9	30.0	16.0	47.5	30.5
Median School Years Completed	11.2	12.0	11.9	11.5	10.1
Median Family Income, 1979 $$	18586	18445	17750	12464	16007
% Income Below Poverty Level	7.6	11.5	7.6	28.7	20.1
% Income Of $30,000 Or More	21.6	15.8	20.2	10.9	10.3
% White Collar Workers	35.9	52.5	41.3	36.0	41.8
% Civilian Labor Force Unemployed	10.7	7.8	5.8	12.5	7.7
% Riding To Work By Automobile	62.7	55.9	59.4	60.8	55.5
Mean Commuting Time - Minutes	22.7	25.5	25.2	23.8	33.3
Population Per Household	2.5	2.5	2.6	2.7	2.7
Total Housing Units	717	831	931	1219	569
% Condominiums	0.0	0.0	0.0	0.0	0.0
% Built 1970 Or Later	0.0	0.6	0.7	0.0	0.9
% Owner Occupied	32.4	25.8	46.2	20.7	30.4
% With 1+ Persons Per Room	4.7	6.5	5.6	10.7	7.0
Median Value: Owner Units $$	39500	–	35600	34400	29200
Median Rent: Rental Units $$	162	168	168	118	159
Median Number Of Rooms: All Units	4.5	4.6	4.9	4.2	4.5

Community Area 05 — North Center
Selected Characteristics of Census Tracts: 1970

Tract Number	TOTAL	0501	0502	0503	0504	0505	0506	0507	0508	0509	0510
Total Population	39410	3216	5877	3049	754	6513	2395	1511	1634	1888	1635
% Male	46.9	46.3	47.8	47.2	50.9	46.4	46.4	46.3	46.4	47.5	48.2
% Black	0.4	0.3	0.1	0.0	0.0	0.1	0.0	0.0	0.2	0.0	0.0
% Other Nonwhite	1.4	2.9	1.1	0.8	1.2	0.8	1.4	2.4	0.4	1.6	1.2
% Of Spanish Language	5.4	3.1	3.1	4.8	1.2	3.7	2.7	3.9	6.8	4.6	1.7
% Foreign Born	17.3	17.9	20.1	22.4	17.0	18.8	21.3	12.7	18.0	16.9	18.7
% Living In Group Quarters	0.4	0.2	0.3	0.0	0.0	0.8	0.8	0.5	0.0	0.0	0.0
% 13 Years Old And Under	21.6	18.6	21.5	20.6	20.6	19.8	19.3	19.5	20.6	21.4	22.5
% 14-20 Years Old	10.4	9.5	9.9	9.6	11.4	10.5	10.1	11.1	11.3	9.9	10.7
% 21-64 Years Old	53.8	57.2	55.3	55.6	58.8	53.8	53.4	52.7	52.1	55.1	54.1
% 65-74 Years Old	9.0	9.2	8.7	9.2	5.3	10.1	11.4	9.7	11.0	9.2	8.0
% 75 Years Old And Over	5.2	5.4	4.6	4.6	4.0	5.8	5.8	7.0	5.1	4.4	4.6
% In Different House	57.8	45.0	60.5	67.9	66.5	62.2	68.3	55.3	55.7	55.8	55.9
% Families With Female Head	14.2	11.8	13.6	10.3	11.3	11.7	14.4	17.6	13.8	11.4	14.6
Median School Years Completed	10.6	11.2	11.3	10.2	10.5	11.3	11.3	10.3	10.1	10.2	9.6
Median Family Income, 1969 $$	10600	10744	11094	12071	10843	11609	11212	10474	9442	11013	8889
% Income Below Poverty Level	6.3	8.2	5.3	2.6	2.2	3.1	4.5	3.1	9.8	3.1	7.3
% Income of $15,000 or More	20.6	18.3	26.1	30.5	12.8	23.8	24.5	11.5	16.6	19.7	23.1
% White Collar Workers	19.8	25.8	20.6	20.7	18.7	22.1	25.0	16.3	18.8	18.3	14.0
% Civilian Labor Force Unemployed	2.6	3.5	1.9	2.9	0.0	2.1	3.1	5.8	0.5	3.5	2.8
% Riding To Work By Automobile	53.0	53.0	55.4	57.1	51.5	53.1	42.3	29.6	53.3	57.4	58.9
Population Per Household	2.7	2.5	2.7	2.7	3.0	2.8	2.6	2.7	2.6	2.7	2.7
Total Housing Units	15182	1308	2209	1130	263	2393	927	594	657	757	664
% Condominiums & Cooperatives	0.3	0.5	0.7	0.6	0.0	0.4	0.0	0.0	0.0	0.7	0.0
% Built 1960 Or Later	2.2	5.6	7.4	3.8	0.0	0.2	0.0	0.0	0.0	0.0	1.4
% Owner Occupied	35.0	25.0	39.2	44.5	54.4	38.0	30.1	37.5	39.0	31.3	31.0
% With 1+ Persons Per Room	4.8	3.0	5.2	4.6	5.6	3.2	4.3	3.9	4.0	4.1	5.4
Median Value: Owner Units $$	17400	18400	17200	18200	21500	20000	20300	16600	16400	–	15100
Median Rent: Rental Units $$	93	103	91	101	109	106	101	95	89	103	83
Median Number Of Rooms: All Units	4.7	4.7	4.8	4.9	5.1	5.2	4.8	4.8	4.5	4.7	4.4

Tract Number	0511	0512	0513	0514	0515
Total Population	1841	2023	2420	2953	1701
% Male	47.3	45.7	47.5	44.5	48.3
% Black	0.0	0.0	0.3	3.6	0.2
% Other Nonwhite	1.6	2.2	0.5	1.3	3.1
% Of Spanish Language	7.1	0.8	6.4	22.7	10.8
% Foreign Born	15.2	15.0	12.6	9.0	12.0
% Living In Group Quarters	0.0	2.6	0.0	0.1	0.0
% 13 Years Old And Under	23.8	22.4	23.9	27.8	25.3
% 14-20 Years Old	10.5	10.4	10.9	10.5	12.3
% 21-64 Years Old	53.8	53.6	52.6	46.5	53.1
% 65-74 Years Old	7.9	7.3	7.5	8.8	6.3
% 75 Years Old And Over	4.0	6.3	5.1	6.4	3.0
% In Different House	47.5	45.1	65.1	54.1	45.3
% Families With Female Head	15.2	14.3	14.7	26.8	16.2
Median School Years Completed	10.0	10.6	10.0	9.6	9.6
Median Family Income, 1969 $$	9663	9594	10833	7284	9475
% Income Below Poverty Level	6.0	10.4	4.7	20.3	7.9
% Income of $15,000 or More	19.1	11.5	20.6	6.5	14.0
% White Collar Workers	18.3	22.9	12.1	14.5	12.1
% Civilian Labor Force Unemployed	3.0	2.8	2.6	2.3	3.3
% Riding To Work By Automobile	55.2	57.5	54.7	48.0	57.2
Population Per Household	2.7	2.7	2.8	2.7	2.9
Total Housing Units	722	782	935	1218	623
% Condominiums & Cooperatives	1.0	0.0	0.0	0.0	0.0
% Built 1960 Or Later	3.2	0.9	0.0	1.3	0.0
% Owner Occupied	32.8	30.1	45.6	22.9	29.2
% With 1+ Persons Per Room	6.2	3.3	5.4	9.1	8.8
Median Value: Owner Units $$	16400	–	15300	15500	12800
Median Rent: Rental Units $$	82	83	84	73	81
Median Number Of Rooms: All Units	4.4	4.6	4.8	4.1	4.4

Lake View

The Lake View community area takes its name from the City of Lake View, of which it was once part. In 1836, Conrad Sulzer and his wife came to Chicago from Switzerland and purchased 100 acres of land in what is now the north section of Lake View. The Sulzers were soon followed by more immigrants from Germany, Luxembourg and Sweden. These early settlers were mostly farmers, but some built fine homes along the lakefront. In 1854 the Lake View House, a three-story wooden hotel, was opened on the lake shore just south of Graceland Avenue (Irving Park Road). This became the nucleus around which wealthy Chicagoans built large residences, primarily summer homes, situated on extensive tracts of land.

In 1857 the Township of Lake View was organized. Eight years later the township was incorporated as the Town of Lake View. The Town Hall was built in 1872, providing a governmental and cultural center. Throughout the 1870s the Lake View area remained predominatly farmland. The land just east of Green Bay Road (Clark Street) was divided into large estates, and to the west it was mostly small farms. Lake View remained predominantly settled by Germans and Swedes. The dominant industry at the time was truck farming. The area was widely noted as a celery-growing region.

In 1887 Lake View was incorporated as a city. The city extended from the lake to Western Avenue, between Fullerton and Devon avenues. Soon after, in 1889, Lake View was annexed to the city of Chicago. During the 1880s and 1890s several large industrial plants were established along the southern edge of the community, leading to the development of nearby residential neighborhoods. Another major commerical development of the 1890s was the emergence of two shopping areas located at Lincoln Avenue and Belmont Avenue, and at Diversey Parkway and Clark Street. Between 1885 and 1894 there was much construction in Lake View. This was the result of improvements in transportation, an increase in the city population, and the movement of people from more crowded areas south of Lake View. The building boom resulted in a substanial change in land use. Single-family, one- or two-story homes and small multiple-family frame and brick structures were built in the section west of Clark Street. The large estates along the lake shore were subdivided to accommodate frame and brick homes and a few apartment buildings.

Lake View reached residential maturity between 1910 and 1920, when the population grew from 60,535 to 96,482. Those of German and Swedish origin were still most numerous. Hungarians, Polish, Slovaks and Italian immigrants moved into the south part of the community area, close to an industrial development to the southwest.

Industry also grew at the turn of the century. Lake View's southwestern industrial area grew considerably between the years 1900 and 1920, extending to residential areas north and east. A light factory area developed on the east side of Ravenswood Avenue, from Montrose Avenue to south of Irving Park Road. Business establishments continued to grow along the leading streets and in the two shopping areas. In 1914 Wrigley Field was built at Clark Street and Addison Avenue, for the Whalers, a Chicago Federal Baseball League franchise. It was taken over by the Chicago Cubs when they merged with the Federals in 1916. The Wrigley family bought the team and the ballpark shortly after World War I and named the field. It was also used by the Chicago Bears to play football until 1971. Despite commercial and industrial growth, Lake View remained essentially a residential community. By 1920, more than 95,000 lived there.

Population and dwelling construction continued to increase, as the number of inhabitants grew to nearly 115,000 in 1930. After 1920, dwellings were built to accommodate the population. Highrises, multiple-family apartment buildings, and apartment hotels were built

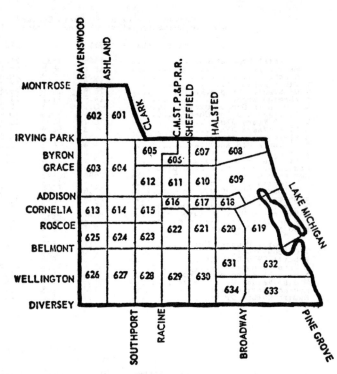

in the district east of Clark Street, especially on the lakefront. These buildings were erected on sites formerly occupied by one- or two-story dwellings or small multiple-family structures. As a result of the increase of commercial and industrial land use after World War I, residential areas were invaded. The main industrial area located in the southern half of Lake View spread into the surrounding residential areas.

Population growth continued during the Depression and after World War II, to a historic high of almost 125,000 in 1950. During the 1950s, persons of Asiatic descent began to move into the community. By 1960 this non-white population made up 3 percent of the total. Among the white population, those of German and Russian descent were predominant. During the 1950s residential construction was concentrated mostly along the lakefront in the form of high-rent multi-family structures because this area had a low turnover of residents. The remainder of the community was experiencing a rapid rate of conversion. In 1960 only 13 percent of the housing units were owner-occupied, and 52 percent of the population lived in structures containing 10 or more units. Because of the lack of construction activity, the quality of the residential units in the community was declining. In 1960, only 9 percent of all residential structures were less than 20 years old.

The population in Lake View has been declining continuously since 1950, dropping by more than 17,000 in the last decade. Since 1970, there has been a net loss of 33,000 whites, many of whom moved to the community areas farther north and west, or to the suburbs surrounding Chicago. Their place has been taken, to some extent, by others. The Asiatic population has been increasing steadily since 1960, making up 5 percent of the community area total in 1980. The principal Asiatic nationalities are Filipino and Japanese. The black population has increased to nearly 7,000, almost all of whom moved in during the 1970s. The population of Hispanic origin, which began to grow in the 1960s, has increased to 19 percent of the total, largely concentrated in a central corridor bounded by Halsted Street, Diversey Parkway, Southport Avenue, and Grace Street. Among the whites, those of German and Irish descent are most numerous.

Owner occupation in residential housing units rose from 13 percent to 22 percent in 1980. The rise in residential ownership is the result of

Community Area 6 — Lakeview
Population and Housing Characteristics, 1930-1980

	1980	1970	1960	1950	1940	1930
Total Population.......	97,519	114,943	118,764	124,824	121,455	114,872
% Male.................	48.2	46.6	47.2	47.4	47.4	48.9
% Female...............	51.8	53.4	52.8	52.6	52.6	51.1
% White................	77.1	94.0	76.9	99.2	99.6	99.6
% Black................	6.9	0.8	0.1	0.2	0.2	0.2
% Other Nonwhite Races...	16.0	5.2	3.0	0.6	0.2	0.2
% Under 5 Years Old......	5.0	6.5	8.4	7.4	5.2	5.7
% 5-19 Years Old.........	13.4	17.7	16.4	14.4	17.0	18.0
% 20-44 Years Old........	50.4	37.9	33.2	40.3	45.7	50.6
% 45-64 Years Old........	16.4	22.5	29.1	28.5	25.0	20.4
% 65 Years and Older.....	14.8	15.4	12.9	9.4	7.1	5.3
Median School Years....	13.2	12.1	10.7	10.8	8.9	*
Total Housing Units....	56,794	56,554	52,931	45,079	40,402	*
% In One-Unit Structures.	3.6	4.4	4.9	*	*	*
% Owner Occupied........	20.4	10.9	13.0	14.0	11.2	*
% Renter Occupied........	71.1	81.8	80.1	84.2	83.3	*
% Vacant................	8.5	7.3	6.9	1.8	5.5	*
% 1+ Persons per Room....	4.5	5.3	6.4	11.7	*	*

Community Area 6 — Lakeview
Selected Characteristics of Census Tracts: 1980

Tract Number	Total	601	602	603	604	605	606	607	608	609	610
Total Population.............	97519	3314	2467	3231	3438	1343	790	2597	5225	6311	2089
% Male......................	48.2	49.9	51.5	46.0	47.0	41.3	55.2	54.0	46.9	42.3	52.1
% Black.....................	6.9	3.5	0.7	0.2	1.4	3.8	10.0	10.7	17.9	17.1	14.8
% Other Nonwhite............	16.0	28.2	19.1	19.9	24.3	19.7	12.5	43.8	10.3	7.2	27.4
% Of Spanish Origin.........	18.8	38.9	27.8	23.0	29.4	26.7	15.9	33.8	7.3	5.9	31.1
% Foreign Born..............	20.3	30.1	28.3	21.6	24.4	17.5	12.8	34.2	19.0	17.9	10.5
% Living In Group Quarters..	1.0	0.0	0.0	0.0	0.0	0.0	9.1	0.0	0.0	0.8	0.0
% 13 Years Old And Under....	12.4	20.5	17.4	19.3	18.1	13.4	9.6	19.4	7.8	7.2	19.0
% 14-20 Years Old...........	7.1	13.5	8.6	11.5	10.6	8.1	4.3	9.2	5.1	3.8	8.0
% 21-64 Years Old...........	65.7	58.5	63.0	57.8	60.2	48.3	76.2	61.0	70.2	60.9	65.9
% 65-74 Years Old...........	7.9	4.3	6.9	6.5	6.5	12.1	5.6	6.5	9.0	14.3	3.7
% 75 Years Old And Over.....	6.8	3.2	4.1	4.9	4.7	18.1	4.3	3.9	7.9	13.8	3.4
% In Different House........	61.2	66.0	57.9	43.1	54.4	39.8	52.7	54.0	73.0	59.6	70.6
% Families With Female Head...	27.5	23.6	24.9	22.0	28.0	23.6	20.8	24.9	29.4	37.0	36.2
Median School Years Completed...	13.2	12.5	12.7	12.0	12.3	11.2	14.7	13.0	15.1	13.4	13.1
Median Family Income, 1979....$$	20716	17417	20284	18167	18723	18650	11700	15183	27214	19621	18269
% Income Below Poverty Level..	10.2	20.6	15.1	12.4	9.7	10.4	11.0	18.3	1.7	5.3	14.6
% Income Of $30,000 Or More....	30.0	16.7	29.3	20.4	17.3	18.6	26.6	10.0	42.5	31.7	29.4
% White Collar Workers......	69.8	56.1	58.1	54.5	53.0	45.7	85.7	56.4	79.7	81.7	53.9
% Civilian Labor Force Unemployed.	5.5	6.4	6.4	7.9	8.8	4.1	6.0	11.6	5.8	4.8	8.3
% Riding To Work By Automobile...	39.7	56.2	57.1	67.7	53.1	37.4	35.2	32.1	40.0	32.3	25.4
Mean Commuting Time - Minutes....	28.7	27.1	33.0	26.0	27.2	27.2	31.1	31.6	29.7	32.2	29.7
Population Per Household..........	1.9	2.7	2.2	2.6	2.6	2.3	1.9	2.1	1.6	1.5	2.3
Total Housing Units..........	56794	1354	1192	1334	1624	811	474	1468	3643	4590	1028
% Condominiums..............	16.5	2.1	3.9	0.0	0.0	0.0	7.8	3.9	42.1	41.1	2.9
% Built 1970 Or Later.......	9.0	0.6	0.9	2.1	0.4	18.9	2.7	5.7	38.0	21.2	1.1
% Owner Occupied............	20.4	25.0	21.0	32.8	21.9	11.6	16.9	4.8	27.0	26.6	12.2
% With 1+ Persons Per Room.......	4.5	8.6	6.6	4.1	5.3	3.6	2.1	17.8	3.6	3.1	7.1
Median Value: Owner Units.......$$	52300	59200	58600	40000	42700	-	-	-	-	-	-
Median Rent: Rental Units....$$	239	222	201	191	205	91	214	190	355	242	223
Median Number Of Rooms: All Units.	3.7	4.8	4.1	5.0	4.7	3.3	4.4	3.0	3.3	3.1	4.4

Community Area 6 — Lakeview
Selected Characteristics of Census Tracts: 1980

Tract Number	611	612	613	614	615	616	617	618	619	620	621
Total Population.............	1336	2174	1464	1553	2042	462	1238	1327	7756	2623	3332
% Male......................	52.0	47.7	48.0	48.2	48.2	51.9	56.4	48.1	43.6	57.6	52.9
% Black.....................	5.1	2.4	2.5	2.1	1.2	7.1	10.7	15.7	6.4	11.3	15.0
% Other Nonwhite............	28.4	25.8	21.7	14.7	21.7	24.5	33.4	11.8	5.2	8.1	28.2
% Of Spanish Origin.........	31.0	31.3	27.4	20.5	26.3	34.8	41.6	8.9	4.7	7.5	31.0
% Foreign Born..............	15.5	29.0	20.4	13.4	20.0	18.0	30.5	14.5	18.5	10.7	16.5
% Living In Group Quarters..	0.0	0.0	4.6	0.0	0.0	2.4	0.0	9.1	0.0	0.0	1.7
% 13 Years Old And Under....	16.7	15.5	18.6	12.9	15.9	12.6	15.0	9.8	5.6	7.6	17.3
% 14-20 Years Old...........	9.7	10.6	12.5	8.8	9.2	8.7	10.4	4.6	3.0	4.7	9.2
% 21-64 Years Old...........	66.5	64.7	56.5	67.2	61.9	69.9	67.5	76.6	66.7	81.6	64.8
% 65-74 Years Old...........	4.6	4.6	7.4	7.0	7.6	5.0	5.0	5.7	13.3	3.4	4.3
% 75 Years Old And Over.....	2.5	4.6	5.1	4.1	5.5	3.9	2.0	3.4	11.3	2.8	4.4
% In Different House........	60.5	62.7	42.2	67.7	52.5	76.4	48.5	74.4	62.5	76.9	68.3
% Families With Female Head...	30.0	23.4	29.0	17.8	22.2	20.0	22.3	31.9	33.2	31.5	41.4
Median School Years Completed...	12.5	12.7	11.8	13.2	12.6	14.1	12.4	15.4	14.8	15.6	12.6
Median Family Income, 1979......$$	18203	19316	17204	19667	20000	19722	20714	20559	26099	22207	13235
% Income Below Poverty Level..	12.6	14.1	16.6	15.9	3.2	0.0	7.1	7.3	8.5	7.0	23.8
% Income Of $30,000 Or More....	23.6	22.0	21.5	26.9	22.3	15.6	14.7	26.9	43.8	39.4	14.0
% White Collar Workers......	64.1	52.2	57.5	67.9	56.2	78.9	52.3	78.5	85.8	73.6	63.1
% Civilian Labor Force Unemployed.	8.1	3.4	3.5	3.2	3.5	3.4	3.9	2.9	2.5	5.8	9.3
% Riding To Work By Automobile...	52.9	48.6	50.1	52.5	46.7	63.7	38.2	28.5	33.1	29.0	37.4
Mean Commuting Time - Minutes...	29.6	30.7	21.1	29.7	24.6	21.5	28.7	35.1	29.4	29.8	27.7
Population Per Household..........	2.3	2.4	2.5	2.2	2.3	2.3	2.1	1.6	1.5	1.6	2.1
Total Housing Units..........	657	992	612	758	966	232	635	772	5455	1770	1785
% Condominiums..............	5.8	3.2	0.0	0.0	1.6	0.0	5.7	14.1	25.6	3.8	0.0
% Built 1970 Or Later.......	0.0	0.6	0.0	1.5	1.2	0.0	0.0	9.7	9.5	3.0	3.1
% Owner Occupied............	17.8	22.3	26.6	21.2	21.0	14.2	16.5	17.7	16.8	9.3	10.0
% With 1+ Persons Per Room.......	5.3	5.2	5.7	2.8	5.4	4.1	10.2	3.5	3.4	3.7	6.0
Median Value: Owner Units.......$$	-	-	34500	-	-	-	-	-	-	-	-
Median Rent: Rental Units....$$	228	236	195	225	230	254	200	241	283	259	207
Median Number Of Rooms: All Units.	4.8	5.1	4.5	4.7	5.0	4.3	4.6	3.5	3.0	3.6	4.1

Community Area 6 -- Lakeview
Selected Characteristics of Census Tracts: 1980

Tract Number	622	623	624	625	626	627	628	629	630	631	632
Total Population	2569	1488	1445	1471	1313	2761	3118	3905	3328	2029	7910
% Male	50.9	49.5	49.5	57.8	47.9	48.3	51.6	50.6	49.9	56.8	43.7
% Black	6.7	0.9	1.3	2.6	0.7	1.8	2.6	3.6	11.1	8.3	4.7
% Other Nonwhite	29.0	16.1	14.8	14.1	15.9	15.3	16.8	18.9	26.1	11.1	5.0
% Of Spanish Origin	30.9	36.4	28.1	23.0	22.3	28.4	32.9	31.7	22.2	12.4	3.1
% Foreign Born	27.4	29.9	26.5	17.7	19.6	24.7	24.5	23.4	19.8	17.4	18.4
% Living In Group Quarters	2.0	0.0	3.9	17.4	0.0	0.0	0.0	0.0	2.6	1.7	1.2
% 13 Years Old And Under	19.5	20.9	18.7	15.0	17.8	18.6	19.7	16.7	13.1	7.5	5.2
% 14-20 Years Old	11.4	9.8	11.1	8.0	10.0	11.0	11.5	10.2	7.9	4.4	2.9
% 21-64 Years Old	61.4	59.2	58.0	61.8	57.8	57.4	60.7	65.1	72.7	80.0	68.8
% 65-74 Years Old	4.9	6.0	6.9	9.2	8.4	8.2	5.0	4.9	3.8	4.3	10.8
% 75 Years Old And Over	2.8	4.1	5.3	6.1	6.0	4.8	3.1	3.1	2.4	3.8	12.3
% In Different House	74.7	39.2	46.7	60.4	44.7	43.8	60.5	69.2	60.7	62.6	62.2
% Families With Female Head	30.0	27.1	32.8	27.5	21.3	21.4	24.8	25.4	27.7	32.8	22.3
Median School Years Completed	12.4	11.3	11.0	11.6	11.9	10.9	12.1	12.8	14.8	14.9	15.7
Median Family Income, 1979 $$	16210	14000	19786	14167	13468	18547	17068	20755	20658	18542	37997
% Income Below Poverty Level	12.7	18.4	11.4	35.9	18.6	14.7	13.7	8.9	7.4	6.0	1.7
% Income Of $30,000 Or More	15.5	11.0	27.0	20.8	15.8	20.4	22.3	21.8	31.9	28.4	60.2
% White Collar Workers	51.6	38.5	52.8	38.8	41.5	45.2	50.7	61.5	70.4	68.6	86.2
% Civilian Labor Force Unemployed	5.4	7.9	7.9	6.6	9.4	7.4	6.9	7.4	4.8	3.7	3.7
% Riding To Work By Automobile	45.1	54.2	44.8	43.3	46.0	47.9	47.3	45.7	31.5	26.5	40.1
Mean Commuting Time - Minutes	26.5	23.8	27.8	25.5	28.6	24.7	23.0	27.4	26.6	29.2	30.4
Population Per Household	2.5	2.4	2.5	2.2	2.3	2.5	2.5	2.5	1.9	1.6	1.5
Total Housing Units	1129	671	590	599	604	1193	1401	1920	1954	1354	5558
% Condominiums	0.0	0.0	0.0	0.0	0.0	0.0	0.0	0.6	15.2	7.1	30.7
% Built 1970 Or Later	2.8	0.7	0.0	1.5	0.8	1.9	1.6	1.9	15.1	9.2	12.3
% Owner Occupied	14.3	24.4	30.3	23.0	28.8	30.8	22.0	18.9	18.2	9.7	25.3
% With 1+ Persons Per Room	8.1	6.5	3.8	5.7	4.7	8.4	7.5	6.0	6.3	2.9	1.7
Median Value: Owner Units $$	-	-	-	-	-	40200	36700	55000	-	-	-
Median Rent: Rental Units $$	202	176	178	181	162	161	175	213	240	241	299
Median Number Of Rooms: All Units	4.7	4.6	4.9	4.7	4.4	4.4	4.5	4.7	3.8	3.6	3.1

Community Area 6 -- Lakeview
Selected Characteristics of Census Tracts: 1980

Tract Number	633	634
Total Population	8001	2069
% Male	42.2	55.4
% Black	4.4	8.4
% Other Nonwhite	6.1	8.7
% Of Spanish Origin	2.6	11.5
% Foreign Born	14.6	15.2
% Living In Group Quarters	0.5	0.0
% 13 Years Old And Under	3.9	8.4
% 14-20 Years Old	2.0	4.3
% 21-64 Years Old	71.3	79.2
% 65-74 Years Old	11.1	4.9
% 75 Years Old And Over	11.6	3.2
% In Different House	62.2	79.5
% Families With Female Head	26.1	31.8
Median School Years Completed	15.5	14.2
Median Family Income, 1979 $$	29932	21645
% Income Below Poverty Level	2.7	11.1
% Income Of $30,000 Or More	49.8	27.5
% White Collar Workers	88.5	74.8
% Civilian Labor Force Unemployed	2.6	5.0
% Riding To Work By Automobile	30.8	28.0
Mean Commuting Time - Minutes	29.3	27.9
Population Per Household	1.4	1.6
Total Housing Units	6270	1399
% Condominiums	29.7	5.4
% Built 1970 Or Later	7.1	4.3
% Owner Occupied	21.9	8.6
% With 1+ Persons Per Room	1.8	4.1
Median Value: Owner Units $$	-	-
Median Rent: Rental Units $$	274	250
Median Number Of Rooms: All Units	2.9	3.3

Community Area 06 -- Lakeview
Selected Characteristics of Census Tracts: 1970

Tract Number	0633	0634
Total Population	8757	2421
% Male	38.9	52.3
% Black	0.6	1.7
% Other Nonwhite	2.3	8.4
% Of Spanish Language	3.2	15.1
% Foreign Born	16.6	18.1
% Living In Group Quarters	2.0	0.5
% 13 Years Old And Under	4.8	9.1
% 14-20 Years Old	3.5	7.9
% 21-64 Years Old	67.3	68.9
% 65-74 Years Old	16.1	8.0
% 75 Years Old And Over	8.3	6.1
% In Different House	36.7	31.6
% Families With Female Head	15.4	17.8
Median School Years Completed	12.8	12.4
Median Family Income, 1969 $$	13714	10966
% Income Below Poverty Level	3.1	13.4
% Income Of $15,000 or More	43.4	29.1
% White Collar Workers	55.5	40.7
% Civilian Labor Force Unemployed	2.2	2.1
% Riding To Work By Automobile	32.5	40.2
Population Per Household	1.5	1.8
Total Housing Units	6190	1422
% Condominiums & Cooperatives	1.4	0.0
% Built 1960 Or Later	25.3	6.3
% Owner Occupied	1.3	5.9
% With 1+ Persons Per Room	1.9	4.4
Median Value: Owner Units $$	-	-
Median Rent: Rental Units $$	159	127
Median Number Of Rooms: All Units	2.8	3.4

Community Area 06 -- Lakeview
Selected Characteristics of Census Tracts: 1970

Tract Number	TOTAL	0601	0602	0603	0604	0605	0606	0607	0608	0609	0610
Total Population	114943	3584	2738	3758	4038	1444	1366	3074	4313	6764	2696
% Male	46.6	48.0	47.8	45.6	47.3	45.5	51.5	53.5	47.1	41.6	49.6
% Black	0.8	0.3	0.0	0.1	0.2	0.1	1.3	2.9	1.3	0.9	0.2
% Other Nonwhite	5.2	4.0	3.1	2.3	3.3	3.2	6.2	11.8	3.5	2.3	14.1
% Of Spanish Language	13.5	12.7	7.7	6.9	10.9	14.0	28.7	28.1	5.0	5.6	39.9
% Foreign Born	17.5	19.2	14.3	14.7	24.6	14.6	12.1	24.1	17.5	18.6	14.5
% Living In Group Quarters	1.1	0.2	0.5	0.5	0.2	0.0	8.3	0.6	0.2	2.4	0.2
% 13 Years Old And Under	17.3	23.2	18.6	23.9	22.1	17.3	20.1	21.1	8.0	7.6	25.4
% 14-20 Years Old	8.5	11.6	10.8	10.0	10.2	9.8	14.9	8.6	4.7	4.7	12.2
% 21-64 Years Old	58.9	54.0	56.2	53.1	54.7	45.5	56.1	58.3	67.4	62.2	52.1
% 65-74 Years Old	10.0	7.2	9.0	8.2	8.4	15.7	5.6	8.0	13.5	17.1	6.5
% 75 Years Old And Over	5.3	4.0	5.4	4.8	4.5	11.6	3.2	4.0	6.3	8.5	3.9
% In Different House	40.4	41.8	51.1	55.5	51.5	38.6	34.1	20.3	36.4	42.7	48.8
% Families With Female Head	15.4	14.1	15.8	15.2	13.7	11.3	12.2	17.9	15.4	17.1	17.1
Median School Years Completed	12.1	12.0	11.9	10.9	10.9	9.9	10.9	10.8	12.7	12.5	10.4
Median Family Income, 1969 $$	10484	10037	11342	10444	9614	9152	7350	8041	13211	12793	8730
% Income Below Poverty Level	8.9	8.6	4.2	6.9	8.9	7.5	22.6	14.3	8.0	7.4	19.0
% Income of $15,000 or More	26.6	14.5	29.4	20.1	17.9	18.7	11.8	10.0	40.8	41.8	15.3
% White Collar Workers	35.2	19.1	23.5	21.1	19.1	15.9	23.1	24.5	53.4	47.4	20.5
% Civilian Labor Force Unemployed	3.7	3.9	2.4	2.5	4.3	5.8	0.0	10.2	3.5	3.0	5.0
% Riding To Work By Automobile	42.5	54.2	58.0	55.1	50.4	39.4	38.5	36.0	47.5	36.3	45.5
Population Per Household	2.2	2.9	2.4	2.5	2.6	2.2	2.3	2.4	2.5	2.5	2.8
Total Housing Units	56572	1291	1202	1401	1582	764	609	1591	2771	4213	1024
% Condominiums & Cooperatives	1.0	0.4	0.0	0.0	0.0	0.0	0.0	0.0	1.1	4.6	0.0
% Built 1960 Or Later	18.8	1.6	3.8	1.0	3.6	50.6	0.0	15.5	31.5	41.8	2.3
% Owner Occupied	9.8	23.9	18.1	33.3	23.4	13.5	12.6	2.1	0.7	0.5	11.5
% With 1+ Persons Per Room	5.3	4.6	4.6	5.2	5.4	4.1	9.9	12.4	2.8	3.1	10.8
Median Value: Owner Units $$	17900	19300	20400	15400	17300	-	-	-	-	-	-
Median Rent: Rental Units $$	121	113	110	94	102	68	86	99	176	157	104
Median Number Of Rooms: All Units	3.6	4.6	4.0	4.9	4.6	3.3	3.1	2.5	3.3	3.0	4.1

Community Area 06 -- Lakeview
Selected Characteristics of Census Tracts: 1970

Tract Number	0611	0612	0613	0614	0615	0616	0617	0618	0619	0620	0621
Total Population	1812	2792	1557	1862	2498	659	1930	1603	9259	3680	4757
% Male	50.8	47.4	45.2	46.5	47.1	53.6	51.0	45.9	41.1	49.8	48.3
% Black	0.3	0.4	0.0	0.1	0.0	1.4	0.9	2.3	1.1	1.2	1.4
% Other Nonwhite	9.2	6.3	2.6	2.0	6.6	8.5	16.4	4.4	1.8	7.1	14.5
% Of Spanish Language	16.0	19.3	13.1	2.9	9.9	16.6	44.3	8.0	2.8	24.5	38.6
% Foreign Born	24.2	27.3	18.2	15.7	20.3	15.2	22.8	17.4	15.3	17.1	13.4
% Living In Group Quarters	3.1	0.0	0.0	0.0	0.0	0.0	2.4	3.4	0.4	2.4	1.4
% 13 Years Old And Under	25.4	22.9	19.6	18.3	21.3	23.8	30.5	13.0	7.4	19.1	28.5
% 14-20 Years Old	12.5	10.2	9.1	10.5	10.0	9.0	13.3	9.4	4.7	9.1	11.4
% 21-64 Years Old	51.3	54.1	56.5	56.2	55.4	56.3	48.6	63.0	68.7	60.4	47.8
% 65-74 Years Old	7.5	8.7	10.3	9.4	8.5	6.2	5.0	9.3	13.8	6.3	7.7
% 75 Years Old And Over	3.4	4.0	4.5	5.6	4.8	4.7	2.7	5.4	5.5	5.1	4.7
% In Different House	48.2	46.8	56.1	54.4	51.2	29.0	33.2	26.2	24.5	32.5	42.7
% Families With Female Head	17.0	15.1	16.9	15.9	15.4	15.6	18.7	12.4	15.2	16.3	18.7
Median School Years Completed	11.4	10.7	9.9	10.9	10.6	9.0	10.1	12.4	12.9	11.9	9.5
Median Family Income, 1969 $$	9402	10313	9600	10586	10238	8600	8517	9310	14268	8931	7590
% Income Below Poverty Level	11.2	9.8	6.8	4.9	8.4	4.6	15.6	18.5	3.5	11.3	21.4
% Income of $15,000 or More	18.7	23.2	14.2	24.0	21.6	2.8	15.1	26.8	47.4	13.0	9.7
% White Collar Workers	24.1	20.7	12.0	18.8	21.7	12.2	14.6	45.4	55.1	33.9	16.8
% Civilian Labor Force Unemployed	4.6	4.0	9.8	3.0	3.6	7.1	5.3	4.9	1.9	4.0	5.3
% Riding To Work By Automobile	49.2	53.8	32.3	48.0	58.5	41.4	47.2	39.8	39.6	36.6	36.3
Population Per Household	2.9	2.8	2.4	2.5	2.7	2.5	3.2	2.0	1.7	2.2	2.8
Total Housing Units	648	1010	695	798	974	277	624	834	5766	1820	1787
% Condominiums & Cooperatives	0.0	0.0	0.0	0.0	0.0	0.0	0.0	6.4	1.5	0.4	0.0
% Built 1960 Or Later	0.0	1.5	0.7	0.0	0.0	0.0	0.0	28.2	49.7	1.8	6.6
% Owner Occupied	19.4	22.1	24.3	20.6	23.0	12.6	15.5	2.5	1.7	6.3	9.1
% With 1+ Persons Per Room	8.8	5.8	4.9	4.5	4.9	8.0	15.5	5.1	2.5	7.6	12.9
Median Value: Owner Units $$	-	-	16800	-	-	-	-	-	-	-	-
Median Rent: Rental Units $$	96	108	97	105	107	102	101	124	172	107	92
Median Number Of Rooms: All Units	4.6	5.0	4.2	4.4	4.9	4.1	4.6	3.5	3.1	3.3	4.0

Community Area 06 -- Lakeview
Selected Characteristics of Census Tracts: 1970

Tract Number	0622	0623	0624	0625	0626	0627	0628	0629	0630	0631	0632
Total Population	3335	1868	1709	1512	1635	3258	3892	5165	4418	2413	8376
% Male	51.2	47.9	47.6	56.5	49.4	46.9	51.0	50.1	50.1	53.3	40.6
% Black	0.4	0.0	0.1	0.2	0.1	0.0	0.1	0.7	1.7	1.7	0.9
% Other Nonwhite	5.7	2.4	3.3	1.5	1.8	2.1	4.0	8.9	12.5	6.1	1.4
% Of Spanish Language	22.8	11.4	9.3	13.7	5.2	11.1	12.4	15.7	25.7	21.4	2.3
% Foreign Born	11.8	15.6	21.6	19.7	10.0	12.7	11.7	19.0	27.9	20.0	14.6
% Living In Group Quarters	0.0	0.0	0.0	0.5	0.0	1.5	0.4	0.3	2.6	0.7	1.3
% 13 Years Old And Under	27.8	25.1	23.6	18.0	21.0	23.6	25.3	26.5	20.6	14.3	7.3
% 14-20 Years Old	12.4	10.7	9.9	9.9	9.2	12.0	11.3	9.9	10.7	7.7	4.3
% 21-64 Years Old	51.7	53.7	52.4	57.1	56.0	52.6	53.1	53.5	59.2	64.8	67.4
% 65-74 Years Old	5.2	6.3	9.2	9.4	8.4	7.2	6.3	6.5	6.4	9.3	14.3
% 75 Years Old And Over	2.9	4.3	4.9	5.6	5.4	4.6	4.0	3.7	3.1	4.0	6.8
% In Different House	49.8	35.5	49.2	48.8	52.4	59.6	51.6	48.2	38.5	29.5	28.7
% Families With Female Head	15.9	15.8	12.4	15.2	16.2	16.5	14.0	13.7	13.2	15.5	14.3
Median School Years Completed	9.4	10.3	10.0	9.8	9.7	9.7	10.1	10.2	11.7	12.0	13.0
Median Family Income, 1969 $$	8222	9636	9702	10278	8952	10564	10126	8365	8412	9466	17887
% Income Below Poverty Level	16.4	7.1	9.2	8.4	12.3	9.7	6.7	9.6	8.3	9.2	2.2
% Income of $15,000 or More	9.7	16.5	19.1	20.3	15.2	18.3	20.1	14.1	14.0	13.4	56.8
% White Collar Workers	11.0	18.4	21.7	12.4	13.0	19.5	10.8	19.7	29.9	34.8	60.7
% Civilian Labor Force Unemployed	3.6	3.7	3.6	5.4	3.1	4.0	4.8	5.6	7.1	5.3	1.0
% Riding To Work By Automobile	50.4	55.2	32.6	38.7	49.3	45.6	46.9	45.3	32.6	36.5	43.3
Population Per Household	3.0	2.8	2.7	2.1	2.4	2.8	2.8	2.8	2.4	1.9	1.7
Total Housing Units	1234	703	692	790	724	1199	1455	1983	1986	1441	5072
% Condominiums & Cooperatives	0.0	0.0	0.0	0.0	0.0	0.0	0.3	0.0	0.0	0.6	1.9
% Built 1960 Or Later	0.5	0.0	0.0	0.0	0.5	0.0	0.3	0.8	2.5	1.3	42.9
% Owner Occupied	14.9	24.3	26.9	15.2	26.5	27.8	21.6	19.1	7.7	6.9	1.7
% With 1+ Persons Per Room	9.4	7.0	6.1	5.2	5.9	7.4	9.4	9.4	7.9	4.7	1.9
Median Value: Owner Units $$	-	-	-	-	16000	14300	14600	16000	-	-	-
Median Rent: Rental Units $$	88	82	78	80	84	78	81	90	99	107	171
Median Number Of Rooms: All Units	4.5	4.4	4.5	3.5	4.1	4.4	4.5	4.5	3.6	3.0	3.0

renovation projects undertaken by individual building owners. Many of the building rehabilitation efforts occurred in structures located along the Ravenswood and Howard Street elevated train tracks, which were deteriorating faster than the rest of the community. Elsewhere, many apartment buildings have been rehabilitated and converted into condominiums. The median value of owner-occupied condominiums is slightly higher, and the median value of single-family dwellings is about $5,000 higher than the city median. On the other hand, the number of subsidized housing units in the community has increased, due to federally-sponsored housing projects that were built during the 1970s, against strong opposition from Lake View residents.

Lake View retains a major retail center in the southwest corner of the community, centered on the Belmont-Lincoln-Ashland Avenue intersection. Another commercial development that has grown noticeably is the Asiatic shopping area, a scattering of restaurants and stores offering Asiatic goods located on Clark Street, between Belmont Avenue and Addison Avenue. The area began to grow in the 1950s due to the growing population of Asiatic persons. The most recent major commercial development in Lake View is New Town, the area (formerly called East Lake View) along Broadway between Diversey Parkway and Belmont Avenue. In the 1960s this neighborhood changed from a predominantly residential district served by small business to a large business area with high-priced housing. In the last 20 years Broadway has become a brightly-lit and crowded street. In the face of extensive commercial development since the 1960s Lake View is still a predominantly residential community.

The latest threat to the equilibrium between business and residential use centers around Wrigley Field, where the Cubs' organization, no longer managed by the Wrigley Family, has indicated an interest in staging night baseball games. A large number of residents in the central area of Lake View believe that this would create many problems — parking, noise, vandalism, crime — that would lower the quality of life. However, some say baseball contributes to many businesses in the vicinity, and the introduction of night games would create more opportunities. Development of Lake View seems likely to be determined by further variants of this continuing conflict between business and residential interests.

Angela M. Fadragas

Lincoln Park

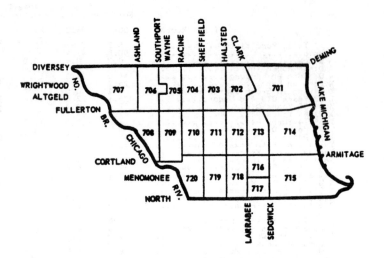

The Lincoln Park community area, the center of which is located two and a half miles north of the Loop, takes its name from the large and popular city park that forms its eastern boundary. In the early 19th century, this region was primarily forest, with stretches of grassland made dangerous by patches of quicksand. In the 1820s, the United States Army built a small post near the center of the area, which was supplied with meat from the Archibald Clybourne slaughterhouse, located nearby on the North Branch of the Chicago River. Most of the land comprising the southern two-thirds of the community area was deeded to the trustees of the Illinois and Michigan Canal in 1830. When the City of Chicago was incorporated in 1837, a small portion of the southeast side of the community was included within the city limits. The land was used for a smallpox hospital and the city cemetery.

After Green Bay Road (Clark Street) was improved in the 1830s, speculators and farmers began to buy land from the trustees. These included Henry and Horatio Cleveland, and Joseph Sheffield, a settler from Connecticut who established a truck farm and nursery. In the 1840s the land began to fill up with German immigrants, driven to migrate by political upheavals in their native states. They settled in the southeast sector, west of Green Bay Road, in the area now called the Old Town Triangle. Like the earlier settlers, they took up produce farming. In 1850 a channel known as the Ten-Mile Ditch was dug east of Green Bay Road, to drain the lowlands near the lake. On the west side of Green Bay Road was an expansive celery garden. Fullerton Avenue, then a dirt road, became the northern boundary of Chicago with the annexation of the area east of Sedgwick Street in 1847. The land west of Sedgwick to the river was added in 1853. The celery patch was subdivided in 1856 and frame houses were constructed. A horse-drawn streetcar line began operating on Central (Armitage) Avenue in the 1860s. More than 400 people lived in the Lincoln Park area at that time.

At the outset of the Civil War, the area east of Clark Street, where the park is now, was a succession of ridges and hollows. The hollows contained 5 to 6 feet of water during the wet seasons. The ridges were covered with large, aromatic pine trees and sturdy oaks. The city council provided for the establishment of a city park in 1864, to be known as Lake Park. To do this, it was necessary to move the old city cemetery, which contained the remains of a thousand Confederate prisoners who had died at the Camp Douglas stockade and in the hospital. The park was renamed for President Lincoln after his death in 1865.

The Great Fire of 1871 destroyed virtually every home in the community. Relief shanties were built to house victims of the Fire. Like many other peripheral Chicago communities, Lincoln Park was not included in the new strict building codes. Many workingmen could afford only frame homes and, within a few years, the area between Fullerton and North avenues, west of Lincoln Avenue, was covered with such "Chicago cottages." The population increased by 10,000. When large industrial plants located along the river in the 1880s, Germans, Irish, and some Polish workingmen settled in the northwestern corner. In 1889, the northern third of the community area was added with the annexation of the City of Lake View. Public transportation was improved with the establishment of cable cars on Clark Street in 1888 and on Lincoln Avenue soon after. The elevated train tracks came up Sheffield Avenue in 1896. By 1895, the area was completely built up. Scarcely a generation earlier it had been covered with truck farms, woody ridges and drainage ditches.

Factory construction along the river continued from the turn of the century to World War I and workers from many nations moved in. The wealthier Germans lived in the north and northeast (parkfront) sec-

tions, while the less fortunate clustered farther west and south. The Irish lived in the vicinity of Ogden, Belden, Webster and Sheffield avenues, in the parish of St. Vincent DePaul, near St. Vincent's College which was founded in 1898, and which became DePaul University in 1907. The Poles located farther west, near St. Josaphat's Church at Belden and Southport, while Romanians lived farther south, around Webster Avenue and Wayne Street, where the Assumption of the Holy Virgin Greek Orthodox parish was established in 1912. West of Old Town, the Italian colony was an extension across North Avenue of the Little Sicily area in the neighboring Near North Side. By 1920, almost 95,000 people lived in the Lincoln Park neighborhood.

German and Irish residents had begun to move out with the influx of the new immigrants. Between 1920 and 1940, the population of Linclon Park drifted upward to more than 100,000. Persons of German stock still constituted nearly one-fourth of the total. Hungarians moved near the Romanians in the west on Clybourn Avenue and adjacent streets. There was a Serbian colony around the intersection of Fullerton and Southport avenues. A small black population settled in the area near Armitage and Racine avenues in the mid-1920s. During these decades new residential construction was minimal. High-rise apartment buildings, apartment hotels, hotels and some luxury townhouses were built east of Clark Street, facing the Park. Elsewhere, some of the larger structures were being converted into rooming houses, especially west of Halsted Street to Racine Avenue, to where light industry had begun to expand. By 1940 10 percent of all residential structures were in need of major repairs or unfit for use. This included some of the relief shanties built after the Great Fire, still used as residences 70 years later.

After World War II, the population of Lincoln Park increased to an all time high of more than 102,000 in 1950. However, the future of Lincoln Park as a residential area was problematic. Only 10 housing units had been built in the entire community area in the 1940s, nevertheless the number of housing units had increased by more than 4,000, due to conversions. Most of the housing consisted of two-family units built before 1895, and more than three-fourths of the housing units predated 1920. Almost one-fourth of all housing units were in sub-standard condition. Home ownership was declining steadily, and the 1950 edition of the *Fact Book* forecast "the end of much of Lincoln Park as a residential community." Ten years later, the number of residents had decreased by almost 14,000, a net out-migration of more than 22,000 having been obscured by the baby-boom fertility rates of the 1950s.

Despite all this, proximity to the Loop, racial turnover and over-crowding in other areas, and the solid structures of many of the old homes attracted homeowners to Lincoln Park. Residents of Old Town and the relatively unsubstructed area to the north founded neighbor-

Community Area 7 — Lincoln Park
Population and Housing Characteristics, 1930-1980

	1980	1970	1960	1950	1940	1930
Total Population	57,146	67,416	88,836	102,396	100,826	97,873
% Male	48.7	49.1	49.2	48.9	49.5	51.4
% Female	51.3	50.9	50.8	51.1	50.5	48.6
% White	83.3	88.6	95.3	98.2	99.8	99.4
% Black	8.6	7.3	1.5	0.2	0.1	0.1
% Other Nonwhite Races	8.1	4.7	3.2	1.6	0.1	0.4
% Under 5 Years Old	4.4	7.7	9.9	8.1	6.4	6.8
% 5-19 Years Old	11.5	19.8	19.6	16.7	19.7	22.0
% 20-44 Years Old	59.5	42.6	35.5	41.8	44.3	47.9
% 45-64 Years Old	14.7	18.8	23.9	24.6	23.2	18.7
% 65 Years and Older	9.9	11.1	11.1	8.8	6.4	4.6
Median School Years	15.7	12.2	9.8	9.7	8.5	*
Total Housing Units	35,315	33,026	37,538	35,929	31,633	*
% In One-Unit Structures	6.8	5.8	6.9	*	*	*
% Owner Occupied	23.0	12.2	14.0	14.5	12.1	*
% Renter Occupied	66.6	75.9	79.1	83.0	83.3	*
% Vacant	10.4	11.9	6.9	2.5	4.6	*
% 1+ Persons per Room	2.9	6.4	10.5	14.9	*	*

Community Area 7 — Lincoln Park
Selected Characteristics of Census Tracts: 1980

Tract Number	Total	701	702	703	704	705	706	707	708	709	710
Total Population	57146	8230	3765	2988	2812	2148	2097	2927	1136	1120	3025
% Male	48.7	45.8	47.8	53.5	48.2	49.8	50.8	47.1	56.0	51.6	50.0
% Black	8.6	5.3	2.3	3.1	2.0	1.5	1.3	10.2	5.6	2.2	5.8
% Other Nonwhite	8.1	6.7	8.6	11.8	8.6	11.6	19.9	17.8	9.9	8.0	7.0
% Of Spanish Origin	10.5	4.0	4.7	16.6	6.8	15.7	38.1	32.2	34.9	19.5	12.7
% Foreign Born	12.3	12.6	11.6	17.7	13.9	17.0	21.1	18.2	24.5	12.0	13.0
% Living In Group Quarters	3.4	1.8	5.8	0.0	0.0	0.0	0.0	0.0	9.2	0.0	16.0
% 13 Years Old And Under	11.1	5.4	7.7	10.4	8.9	13.5	20.6	25.5	19.3	15.6	9.9
% 14-20 Years Old	6.1	3.1	2.9	5.5	6.0	8.1	11.9	11.5	10.0	8.9	12.5
% 21-64 Years Old	72.9	79.2	77.2	76.8	64.8	66.3	58.9	49.4	61.9	67.4	69.2
% 65-74 Years Old	5.3	7.3	6.7	4.1	7.9	7.5	5.3	7.9	6.7	6.3	4.1
% 75 Years Old And Over	4.6	4.9	5.5	3.2	12.4	4.6	3.3	5.7	2.1	1.7	4.3
% In Different House	63.1	69.8	73.0	72.6	52.7	52.9	55.5	37.5	57.9	49.1	70.2
% Families With Female Head	29.3	28.9	31.8	23.9	19.3	20.5	23.9	43.5	22.8	27.4	20.1
Median School Years Completed	15.7	16.1	16.1	15.3	12.9	12.8	10.5	10.1	11.0	12.3	15.4
Median Family Income, 1979....$$	24509	40696	26272	21503	26050	19565	17538	8857	14648	21326	25083
% Income Below Poverty Level	12.0	2.4	15.3	7.5	2.5	12.0	13.0	37.7	15.9	11.8	8.2
% Income Of $30,000 Or More	41.2	64.7	40.3	35.2	42.1	25.3	14.8	7.6	5.6	29.0	42.2
% White Collar Workers	78.5	86.4	86.3	71.9	70.6	59.0	47.3	37.3	31.6	62.7	75.0
% Civilian Labor Force Unemployed	4.1	2.5	4.6	3.3	1.7	3.6	6.9	10.7	6.7	0.0	3.6
% Riding To Work By Automobile	41.3	30.9	37.3	39.3	52.3	54.3	48.2	41.5	55.8	44.2	44.3
Mean Commuting Time - Minutes	24.7	25.9	25.9	24.2	24.3	22.5	30.4	25.8	27.4	18.0	21.7
Population Per Household	1.7	1.4	1.6	1.9	1.7	2.1	2.6	2.5	2.7	2.2	2.0
Total Housing Units	35315	6325	2383	1775	1757	1169	948	1318	437	651	1476
% Condominiums	15.9	31.0	8.6	4.7	3.8	1.9	0.0	0.0	0.0	2.6	8.5
% Built 1970 Or Later	17.9	25.1	9.5	11.0	7.1	4.8	1.3	3.3	5.6	14.0	0.0
% Owner Occupied	23.0	22.9	17.8	18.9	19.9	24.4	21.7	16.3	22.9	25.7	24.1
% With 1+ Persons Per Room	2.9	2.6	1.5	4.5	1.9	4.3	14.5	10.4	10.1	3.7	1.8
Median Value: Owner Units....$$	123700	200100	116700	93100	72500	53900	-	-	-	-	162500
Median Rent: Rental Units....$$	269	273	259	273	188	199	165	100	158	225	315
Median Number Of Rooms: All Units	3.8	2.7	3.5	4.4	4.2	4.6	4.0	3.9	4.4	4.6	4.9

Tract Number	711	712	713	714	715	716	717	718	719	720
Total Population	3030	1907	3667	4532	5530	1595	1370	2332	2325	610
% Male	51.0	48.8	47.4	43.7	49.3	49.0	47.6	51.8	51.5	50.5
% Black	5.0	8.8	4.2	3.5	8.8	9.5	18.3	34.5	40.5	40.5
% Other Nonwhite	7.6	4.4	4.9	4.0	3.9	6.3	7.7	8.8	7.7	10.7
% Of Spanish Origin	8.9	4.8	3.6	2.7	3.5	5.8	7.4	13.7	12.6	17.7
% Foreign Born	7.5	12.8	8.6	12.1	7.6	14.2	10.1	9.2	3.9	12.1
% Living In Group Quarters	10.3	9.8	3.2	5.8	1.4	0.4	2.0	0.0	0.0	0.0
% 13 Years Old And Under	12.3	12.2	9.4	5.5	5.1	10.1	15.0	19.0	18.8	22.1
% 14-20 Years Old	9.8	3.4	3.4	3.8	2.6	3.2	5.3	8.1	7.8	12.0
% 21-64 Years Old	72.8	70.6	80.6	77.2	85.2	78.6	69.9	68.2	68.0	61.8
% 65-74 Years Old	3.0	6.4	3.2	6.6	3.0	3.6	3.4	3.8	3.4	2.1
% 75 Years Old And Over	2.0	7.4	3.0	8.1	3.5	2.3	3.6	1.8	2.0	2.0
% In Different House	68.2	50.4	56.0	66.2	69.8	71.5	47.1	58.1	75.4	50.7
% Families With Female Head	25.9	25.7	23.8	23.6	26.4	25.6	32.9	42.4	46.1	26.2
Median School Years Completed	16.1	15.9	16.1	16.1	16.1	16.1	16.1	14.5	13.2	14.0
Median Family Income, 1979....$$	30279	27545	33417	36665	31688	34464	27679	22000	11299	23170
% Income Below Poverty Level	6.1	3.9	6.3	6.6	7.7	14.2	11.5	20.4	36.8	4.3
% Income Of $30,000 Or More	50.8	41.8	56.9	59.5	55.7	58.3	44.0	36.4	20.1	25.2
% White Collar Workers	86.7	84.4	86.2	89.0	87.1	80.6	80.6	71.7	73.1	61.3
% Civilian Labor Force Unemployed	6.0	2.4	0.8	2.6	3.3	4.6	5.7	7.3	16.1	4.8
% Riding To Work By Automobile	37.8	34.8	33.6	39.0	34.7	66.2	63.0	67.9	44.4	46.4
Mean Commuting Time - Minutes	21.9	24.8	23.2	26.5	25.1	27.5	27.1	24.5	21.5	21.8
Population Per Household	1.9	1.8	1.6	1.5	1.4	1.8	2.1	2.2	2.2	2.5
Total Housing Units	1564	1038	2262	3334	4152	927	685	1356	1430	328
% Condominiums	0.9	12.8	13.3	13.9	47.1	12.9	2.2	8.8	1.5	0.0
% Built 1970 Or Later	2.0	19.8	18.8	30.8	33.1	39.4	17.9	22.6	5.5	4.5
% Owner Occupied	26.0	24.4	24.8	11.6	38.0	31.3	27.0	22.3	15.8	17.4
% With 1+ Persons Per Room	0.9	1.2	0.9	1.2	1.1	1.0	5.0	3.1	3.7	5.8
Median Value: Owner Units....$$	172200	156800	177300	-	186300	148700	156800	118400	111800	-
Median Rent: Rental Units....$$	290	320	295	366	326	314	267	227	222	179
Median Number Of Rooms: All Units	5.0	4.3	4.0	3.3	3.1	5.1	4.4	4.6	4.6	4.4

19

Community Area 07 -- Lincoln Park
Selected Characteristics of Census Tracts: 1970

Tract Number	TOTAL	0701	0702	0703	0704	0705	0706	0707	0708	0709	0710
Total Population.............	67416	6967	4437	4251	3736	2836	2419	3317	1763	2256	4272
% Male........................	49.1	46.7	47.8	49.9	47.9	49.1	50.6	47.1	52.1	50.7	51.4
% Black.......................	7.2	1.2	1.1	0.8	0.5	0.6	10.3	3.4	5.8	1.7	0.8
% Other Nonwhite..............	4.6	6.5	9.6	7.0	6.9	2.9	1.2	1.5	1.5	3.1	4.2
% Of Spanish Language.........	14.6	2.7	6.7	21.7	16.4	12.2	15.9	19.4	13.7	24.8	28.1
% Foreign Born................	14.0	17.5	14.5	21.5	23.0	12.1	12.3	13.7	9.8	18.3	21.3
% Living In Group Quarters....	2.9	1.4	0.7	0.5	0.0	0.0	0.0	0.5	4.2	18.0	5.9
% 13 Years Old And Under......	20.4	6.7	14.4	24.4	22.4	23.1	28.0	26.4	31.2	25.0	25.4
% 14-20 Years Old.............	8.7	4.6	6.7	10.6	9.6	10.4	11.9	12.5	10.5	10.6	10.6
% 21-64 Years Old.............	59.9	73.6	66.1	55.5	54.5	54.7	51.1	49.8	51.4	54.7	53.6
% 65-74 Years Old.............	6.8	9.7	8.3	6.1	7.9	8.0	5.7	6.6	4.4	5.5	5.3
% 75 Years Old And Over.......	4.2	5.3	4.5	3.4	5.6	3.8	3.4	4.8	2.5	4.2	5.1
% In Different House..........	41.0	28.5	36.5	43.3	40.5	50.8	47.8	63.8	41.1	39.0	47.3
% Families With Female Head...	15.7	14.1	15.5	14.2	13.7	13.3	18.5	19.5	19.9	14.8	13.8
Median School Years Completed...	12.2	13.4	12.5	10.7	9.7	9.7	8.9	8.9	9.0	9.1	11.0
Median Family Income, 1969......$$	9652	13168	9904	8615	9091	9350	9529	7852	7770	9370	9375
% Income Below Poverty Level..	12.6	6.8	9.9	12.9	14.2	7.3	13.9	19.5	20.6	11.6	13.3
% Income of $15,000 or More.....	24.0	42.1	21.0	19.6	18.3	14.5	18.8	14.3	10.1	19.2	12.2
% White Collar Workers........	39.8	55.7	39.9	25.2	24.6	20.7	10.2	15.2	12.4	21.5	26.8
% Civilian Labor Force Unemployed.	4.0	3.4	2.0	5.3	4.2	5.1	7.4	3.7	5.7	2.8	5.0
% Riding To Work By Automobile....	39.9	30.4	35.8	40.5	43.9	53.3	41.0	50.9	40.9	51.8	42.8
Population Per Household..........	2.3	1.6	1.9	2.7	2.6	2.7	2.9	2.8	3.1	3.3	2.?
Total Housing Units..........	33042	5532	2535	1714	1764	1149	785	1256	863	609	1588
% Condominiums & Cooperatives.....	0.6	2.1	0.0	0.5	0.0	0.0	0.0	0.0	0.0	0.0	0.0
% Built 1960 Or Later..............	12.1	34.6	7.7	7.1	21.7	2.6	0.4	3.5	0.4	0.0	0.4
% Owner Occupied.................	11.5	2.2	11.1	16.5	15.2	22.5	21.1	18.8	20.2	22.2	13.0
% With 1+ Persons Per Room......$$	7.0	4.7	4.2	10.5	6.6	7.3	11.4	11.9	15.4	13.7	11.0
Median Value: Owner Units.......$$	19500	45000	24500	16100	15300	16200	-	13800	-	-	-
Median Rent: Rental Units.......$$	111	142	116	106	89	80	68	74	71	79	93
Median Number Of Rooms: All Units.	3.8	2.3	3.3	4.4	4.0	4.3	4.2	4.1	4.2	4.8	4.5

Tract Number	0711	0712	0713	0714	0715	0716	0717	0718	0719	0720
Total Population.............	3978	2174	3512	3919	4019	1764	1492	4250	4937	1117
% Male........................	51.9	50.4	49.4	42.2	50.0	51.5	49.5	51.5	48.4	48.8
% Black.......................	2.6	3.5	1.4	2.3	2.9	3.2	8.2	24.2	43.1	35.1
% Other Nonwhite..............	7.3	3.4	4.3	2.9	2.2	4.4	0.9	5.0	4.3	3.0
% Of Spanish Language.........	15.6	7.6	4.3	2.0	1.6	11.1	12.0	26.8	31.9	28.3
% Foreign Born................	10.3	12.6	11.2	14.0	9.7	12.4	11.3	8.5	7.8	6.6
% Living In Group Quarters....	6.1	2.1	4.2	9.3	2.1	1.7	3.8	0.6	0.2	0.0
% 13 Years Old And Under......	20.6	14.8	9.8	5.7	8.4	17.9	20.0	34.4	36.5	33.6
% 14-20 Years Old.............	10.0	4.9	5.0	3.3	4.8	7.9	10.6	11.3	13.1	13.3
% 21-64 Years Old.............	63.7	63.4	74.7	66.9	76.6	65.2	59.5	47.2	45.4	47.8
% 65-74 Years Old.............	3.5	11.1	6.3	15.3	5.9	5.6	5.7	4.4	3.3	3.4
% 75 Years Old And Over.......	2.2	5.7	4.1	8.8	4.3	3.5	4.3	2.7	1.7	1.9
% In Different House..........	43.2	52.5	28.3	37.6	30.3	38.0	51.1	53.9	35.5	46.4
% Families With Female Head...	11.2	11.8	9.4	12.9	15.3	12.3	17.0	16.4	26.0	27.4
Median School Years Completed...	12.6	12.5	14.0	13.3	15.5	12.9	12.1	9.1	9.1	8.8
Median Family Income, 1969......$$	11392	9529	13685	16432	15375	10569	10393	7296	6988	6118
% Income Below Poverty Level..	6.4	9.6	3.5	4.3	2.0	5.9	4.1	17.3	27.7	35.6
% Income of $15,000 or More.....	32.5	29.4	44.7	53.7	51.2	26.1	19.9	4.3	9.3	9.1
% White Collar Workers........	41.7	53.2	60.6	62.6	64.9	48.9	33.6	18.6	20.1	15.7
% Civilian Labor Force Unemployed.	2.9	4.0	2.0	3.5	3.0	2.9	3.8	7.7	6.6	4.5
% Riding To Work By Automobile....	40.9	40.1	38.5	33.7	37.9	44.4	41.2	48.8	40.6	46.3
Population Per Household..........	2.5	1.9	1.7	1.6	1.7	2.4	2.5	3.2	3.3	3.1
Total Housing Units..........	1736	1279	2048	2461	2696	835	617	1483	1705	387
% Condominiums & Cooperatives.....	0.0	0.0	0.2	2.4	0.0	0.0	0.0	0.0	0.0	0.0
% Built 1960 Or Later..............	1.8	15.6	7.3	11.6	18.2	8.1	6.8	0.4	0.7	0.0
% Owner Occupied.................	16.2	10.9	10.0	3.2	8.2	20.4	19.9	13.5	13.0	12.7
% With 1+ Persons Per Room......	6.1	3.1	2.6	2.2	2.4	3.0	8.3	14.5	15.9	14.0
Median Value: Owner Units.......$$	23800	-	49600	-	44000	-	-	-	-	-
Median Rent: Rental Units.......$$	107	107	126	166	164	129	100	84	81	74
Median Number Of Rooms: All Units.	4.6	3.6	3.4	2.8	3.1	4.9	4.7	4.5	4.4	4.3

hood associations, concerned with building code enforcement, neighborhood clean-up and the maintenance of city services. In 1954, representatives of neighborhood organizations and the major educational, religious, medical and banking institutions formed the Lincoln Park Conservation Association. In addition to providing information and support to individual and neighborhood renovation efforts, the Association approached the city Department of Urban Renewal. In 1956, the Community Conservation Board designated a Lincoln Park Urban Renewal Area, 266 acres, which covered the entire community except for the northwest corners. The first phase was funded in 1964.

Construction and rehabilitation have brought the number of dwelling units in Lincoln Park to more than 35,000, within 600 of the inflated number reported in 1950. Today 37 percent of all housing units are located in structures containing 10 or more units, compared to 34 percent 30 years ago. However, the number of single-family dwelling units has increased substantially in the last decade. More than 14 percent of all units are single today, compared with 6 percent during the three previous decades. In 1950, the median value of single-family homes in Lincoln Park was 20 percent below that of the city, but the most recent estimate, $123,700, is more than two and a half times the city median, second among all Chicago community areas.

Although the number of dwelling units has remained relatively stable since 1950, the population has dropped from 102,000 to 57,000 in that time, a decrease of 44 percent. The number of households in Lincoln Park has dropped from 37,500 to 31,700, and this accounts for about a third of the loss. However, the key element in the population decline has been a drop in the size of the average household, which was 2.7 in 1950, but is 1.8 today. This decrease accounts for two-thirds of the population decline. In 1950, 60 percent of all residents of Lincoln Park aged 15 and older were married; today there are fewer than 35 percent. Forty-eight percent of all residents, including more than half the men, never have been married. Almost half (47.8 percent) of the residents are young adults between the ages of 18 and 34 years, triple the concentration in that age group of the city population.

While the renewal and renovation of Lincoln Park has made it a more attractive residential area, the increase in housing values had made it less affordable to those with low and moderate incomes, and this is reflected in most figures showing changes in population composition. Thirty years ago, fewer than 7 percent of all residents 25 years old or more had completed four or more years of college, although 44 percent of the resident labor force were white-collar workers, about half of them in clerical occupations. Today, almost half (48.6 percent) have at least four years of college and many have completed more. More than three-fourths are white-collar workers, and more than half the labor force is in professional, technical or managerial occupations. The population of Lincoln Park is more than 80 percent white, the rest consisting of about equal parts black and an assortment of other non-white races. The 1980 black population is the same as that a decade ago, but turnover between working-class and middle-class residents has undoubtedly taken place. Among the other non-whites, Filipinos and Japanese are the most numerous nationality groups.

Specialty shops, boutiques, restaurants, bars, theaters and nightclubs have turned the grim thoroughfares of the 1950s into an attractive brightly-lit district, to which Chicagoans as well as tourists come evenings and weekends. These and the active young resident population, moving about, shopping and driving automobiles on the narrow streets, have made Lincoln Park an area more lively and congested than it was 30 years ago, although twice as many people lived there then.

M.W.H.
Marcia Chaimowitz

Community Area 8

Near North Side

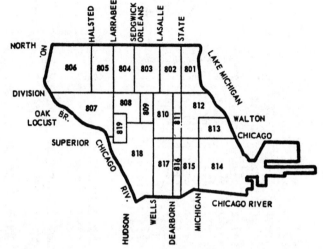

The Near North Side is one of the older areas of Chicago. The first manufacturing establishments appeared along the north bank of the river — a tannery, a meat-packing plant, a soap factory, and a brickyard. All of the community was included in the city of Chicago, incorporated in 1837.

During the 1840s, most of the city's development took place south and west of the river. The delays involved in crossing the river impeded development of the North Side, although there were some fashionable frame residences. The first slum was already in the making in the section situated near the fork in the North Branch of the river, settled chiefly by Irish immigrants. Soon shipyards, iron foundries, and breweries were located along the river. The first railroad, the Galena and Chicago Union (later the Chicago and North Western), ran down the center of Kinzie Street in 1847.

Bridges were constructed over the river at Rush Street in 1856 and at Erie Street and Grand Avenue in 1857, thus connecting the North Side with the rest of the city. As a result, several large industries, including the McCormick reaper works, located on the north bank of the river. Hundreds of small frame cottages, homes of workingmen, were constructed on the Near North Side, especially west of Wells Street. The eastern fringe had the fashionable residences of the leading families of Chicago. By 1860, the population of the North Side was reputed to have been 29,922, of whom many were Irish and German immigrants. Most of the Irish settled along the river and as far east as State Street. For the most part, they worked as laborers in the neighboring factories, mills, railroad yards, and shops. The majority of the Germans, who ran truck gardens, lived north of Chicago Avenue and east of Clark Street in their small frame cottages. During the 1850s, Swedes settled in the southwestern part of the community.

By 1864, new construction had built up the city solidly for three miles in every direction except east. There was a great demand for land adjacent to occupied areas along the recently-established horsecar lines. New plants and factories built during the 1860s expanded the industrial area northward and eastward from the river. The North Side area was becoming increasingly surrounded by factories and slums. The population doubled in the years from 1862 to 1870, from 35,000 to 70,000, mainly due to the influx of workers, mostly Irish and German.

The Great Fire of 1871 almost wiped out the North Side of Chicago. The old neighborhood patterns were repeated in the rebuilding after the fire, and the Near North Side continued to grow during the 1880s and 1890s. In the 1890s, the Chicago and North Western Railway laid its tracks along the North Branch of the river, cable lines were installed, and the Chicago and Evanston Railroad operated parallel to Evanston Avenue, now Broadway. In the late 1890s, electric surface lines began to replace the cable lines and the North Western elevated line was started.

In 1882 Potter Palmer, whose State Street development projects had revolutionized the spatial arrangements of the Loop, bought land covered by frog ponds on what became North Lake Shore Drive and built an imposing mansion there. His wife, Bertha, was the acknowledged leader of Chicago society, which deserted existing upper class areas on Prairie Avenue, Ashland and Jackson Boulevards for Lake Shore Drive and the streets adjacent to it. Land values there increased by 400 percent within a decade and this "Gold Coast" became the home of the leaders of the city's "Four Hundred." Even in the late 1880s and early 1890s North Clark Street was declining as a residential area and becoming a district of rooming houses and cheap cabarets. At the same time, the area west of Wells Street was becoming a slum.

The land east of Michigan Avenue and north of the Chicago River was created during this period. In 1886, Captain George Wellington Streeter, an adventurer who had outfitted a boat for gun-running in the South, ran aground in Lake Michigan on a sandbar near what is now Superior Street. He stayed on the boat where it was grounded, and convinced city contractors to dump hard fill in the section surrounding his boat. Later, he laid claim to the 186-acre tract created in this way and called it the "Free District of Lake Michigan," an independent territory. He sold lots to squatters and survived skirmishes with the the police until 1918, when he finally was evicted. His descendants continued to press claims to the land until 1940. Today the name "Streeterville" is generally associated with the area north of Pearson Street and east of Michigan Avenue to Lake Shore Drive.

The first two decades of the 20th century saw the movement of warehouses and wholesale houses into the area east of Michigan Avenue and south of Ohio Street. The old manufacturing area extended west along the river, then north along the east side of the river and back to Hudson Street. Clark Street had become a street of cheap hotels, second-hand stores, theatres, and dance halls. The encroachment of business, the trend toward rooming houses, and the invasion of the area by new foreign-born groups, primarily Italians, accelerated the exodus of society from the old fashionable residential streets. New mansions were built on Lake Shore Drive and on the side streets from Bellevue Place to Lincoln Park, the section known as the "Gold Coast." West of Wells Street the blighted area spread almost to North Avenue.

Community Area 8 — Near North Side
Population and Housing Characteristics, 1930-1980

	1980	1970	1960	1950	1940	1930
Total Population.......	67,167	70,269	75,509	89,196	76,954	79,554
% Male..................	46.8	46.5	50.4	50.7	51.7	53.2
% Female................	53.2	53.5	49.6	49.3	48.3	46.8
% White.................	64.2	61.3	67.0	76.5	92.3	93.7
% Black.................	32.8	37.1	30.6	20.0	6.7	5.3
% Other Nonwhite Races...	3.0	1.6	2.4	3.5	1.0	1.0
% Under 5 Years Old.....	5.7	6.4	10.6	7.3	4.6	5.3
% 5-19 Years Old........	15.5	21.5	18.2	14.1	14.0	17.4
% 20-44 Years Old.......	45.9	38.5	36.4	44.8	47.7	50.5
% 45-64 Years Old.......	19.9	21.5	24.6	25.4	26.6	22.4
% 65 Years and Older.....	13.0	12.1	10.2	8.4	7.1	4.4
Median School Years....	15.1	12.8	12.0	10.9	9.1	*
Total Housing Units....	41,289	38,958	38,243	27,248	22,934	*
% In One-Unit Structures.	2.2	3.4	8.4	*	*	*
% Owner Occupied........	24.1	5.4	6.0	8.7	6.1	*
% Renter Occupied.......	64.0	79.6	83.5	87.5	82.6	*
% Vacant...............	11.9	15.0	10.5	3.8	11.3	*
% 1+ Persons per Room....	4.9	8.5	12.8	21.4	*	*

Community Area 8 — Near North Side
Selected Characteristics of Census Tracts: 1980

Tract Number	Total	801	802	803	804	805	806	807	808	809	810
Total Population.............	67167	7544	7187	2408	4659	4346	9	124	6663	840	4632
% Male....................	46.8	42.9	44.8	58.1	43.2	42.3	–	47.6	40.4	50.5	49.6
% Black..................	32.8	1.2	3.8	40.1	96.9	98.3	–	93.5	99.4	57.5	13.7
% Other Nonwhite........	3.0	1.4	2.7	5.9	2.3	1.1	–	6.5	0.5	1.3	4.9
% Of Spanish Origin.......	2.9	1.9	1.7	8.6	2.6	1.9	–	0.0	0.7	0.8	3.0
% Foreign Born..........	8.2	10.0	8.4	9.3	1.9	0.6	–	4.7	0.2	9.1	10.3
% Living In Group Quarters.	5.0	0.1	2.3	7.4	0.0	0.0	–	0.0	0.0	15.5	31.5
% 13 Years Old And Under..	15.0	5.7	4.8	10.8	36.6	43.5	–	16.1	50.2	10.6	1.6
% 14-20 Years Old........	7.7	3.1	2.9	8.3	15.0	20.4	–	9.7	14.1	5.5	15.0
% 21-64 Years Old........	64.2	71.7	87.4	70.7	45.1	29.5	–	50.0	34.9	72.5	59.2
% 65-74 Years Old........	7.6	11.5	2.9	6.1	2.5	2.9	–	8.9	0.5	8.0	12.9
% 75 Years Old And Over...	5.4	8.1	1.9	4.1	0.9	3.7	–	15.3	0.3	3.5	11.3
% In Different House......	55.4	57.7	72.2	39.2	55.8	77.7	–	0.0	44.2	66.3	72.1
% Families With Female Head.	61.1	14.8	23.0	51.9	64.3	79.2	–	71.4	87.9	55.4	40.0
Median School Years Completed.	15.1	16.1	16.1	14.7	12.1	9.4	–	7.9	11.0	12.6	12.9
Median Family Income, 1979.....$$	23408	56097	46824	15854	10616	4484	–	4833	4363	11950	11250
% Income Below Poverty Level....	26.2	2.2	3.1	18.8	42.3	89.5	–	53.6	76.5	9.2	25.4
% Income Of $30,000 Or More.....	44.6	79.3	75.3	22.1	11.7	0.0	–	0.0	0.3	9.2	7.7
% White Collar Workers......	80.4	89.9	89.8	72.5	45.9	50.2	–	75.9	29.5	79.3	59.7
% Civilian Labor Force Unemployed.	5.5	1.5	1.9	10.2	13.4	21.2	–	0.0	37.6	17.2	5.1
% Riding To Work By Automobile....	24.9	34.1	29.0	12.5	25.5	28.6	–	0.0	20.0	28.7	18.5
Mean Commuting Time - Minutes...	20.6	22.5	23.5	21.5	27.8	29.8	–	0.0	26.0	19.8	17.6
Population Per Household...	1.8	1.5	1.4	1.8	3.3	4.0	–	2.3	3.7	1.9	1.2
Total Housing Units...........	41289	5240	5420	1422	1637	1200	16	54	1837	451	2937
% Condominiums.............	29.5	41.6	63.2	14.8	0.0	0.0	–	0.0	2.5	0.0	1.8
% Built 1970 Or Later.......	19.4	19.1	20.3	6.3	18.8	2.1	–	0.0	2.1	64.7	29.0
% Owner Occupied...........	22.4	37.3	40.6	17.2	5.1	1.2	–	11.1	3.0	2.4	2.3
% With 1+ Persons Per Room...	4.9	0.6	1.2	3.8	12.9	26.3	–	9.3	23.3	2.7	3.7
Median Value: Owner Units......$$	200100	200100	200100	–	–	–	–	–	–	–	–
Median Rent: Rental Units....$$	322	383	403	187	217	63	–	131	76	285	219
Median Number Of Rooms: All Units.	3.1	3.4	3.0	3.8	4.3	4.3	–	4.2	4.2	3.7	2.0

Tract Number	811	812	813	814	815	816	817	818	819
Total Population.............	2458	7234	6716	5091	2025	1350	1158	834	1889
% Male....................	59.0	47.2	43.1	50.4	60.4	48.1	71.8	51.9	41.3
% Black..................	16.3	3.0	1.7	7.3	7.8	0.6	16.8	81.3	99.3
% Other Nonwhite........	8.0	2.6	3.5	4.6	5.5	1.6	9.8	2.2	0.4
% Of Spanish Origin.......	7.2	2.9	1.9	2.4	7.2	1.7	18.8	5.6	0.7
% Foreign Born..........	11.9	10.8	10.7	11.6	18.0	20.0	11.3	9.5	0.9
% Living In Group Quarters.	2.2	0.0	4.8	12.6	2.8	0.0	23.8	6.2	0.0
% 13 Years Old And Under..	3.5	4.7	3.4	3.4	2.5	1.5	8.5	30.1	35.5
% 14-20 Years Old........	3.7	3.1	3.6	2.9	2.4	1.6	5.4	11.8	18.3
% 21-64 Years Old........	84.5	73.2	69.1	77.4	76.4	80.9	69.9	51.1	42.6
% 65-74 Years Old........	5.3	11.1	13.7	9.8	11.9	10.9	8.6	4.4	2.3
% 75 Years Old And Over...	3.0	8.0	10.2	6.5	6.8	5.1	7.4	2.6	1.3
% In Different House......	81.4	53.6	59.4	65.6	60.0	44.9	53.8	41.7	23.5
% Families With Female Head.	36.6	19.5	14.7	18.4	18.2	6.3	25.0	65.9	80.4
Median School Years Completed.	14.7	16.1	16.1	16.1	16.1	16.1	12.1	11.9	9.9
Median Family Income, 1979.....$$	24000	55751	54852	38387	20833	35196	8958	15347	5887
% Income Below Poverty Level....	9.1	0.8	2.2	5.0	0.0	4.7	12.9	40.9	51.6
% Income Of $30,000 Or More.....	38.1	75.8	78.1	65.7	39.9	67.1	0.0	0.0	1.2
% White Collar Workers......	72.9	88.5	89.0	89.4	71.6	85.2	51.4	35.3	22.5
% Civilian Labor Force Unemployed.	2.4	2.8	1.7	4.4	11.0	1.9	12.9	19.5	39.3
% Riding To Work By Automobile....	15.8	28.2	26.2	23.6	7.3	9.4	29.2	31.0	39.0
Mean Commuting Time - Minutes...	16.8	21.0	20.3	17.0	16.1	14.8	13.1	11.6	24.7
Population Per Household...	1.3	1.5	1.5	1.4	1.3	1.4	1.7	2.8	3.3
Total Housing Units...........	2145	5488	4863	3823	2073	1070	734	291	588
% Condominiums.............	0.7	46.5	61.1	19.0	0.0	0.0	0.0	0.0	0.0
% Built 1970 Or Later.......	25.7	31.6	14.7	13.4	36.2	1.2	0.0	0.0	1.6
% Owner Occupied...........	1.4	35.6	45.8	8.9	0.6	0.0	3.3	4.1	1.0
% With 1+ Persons Per Room...	3.7	1.6	1.7	3.3	5.5	1.8	13.0	16.2	18.4
Median Value: Owner Units......$$	–	–	–	–	–	–	–	–	–
Median Rent: Rental Units....$$	295	406	403	460	307	501	163	112	49
Median Number Of Rooms: All Units.	1.5	3.3	3.2	2.5	1.4	2.8	1.4	4.4	4.0

Many Italians entered the Irish and Swedish community between Sedgwick Avenue and the industrial belt along the river. While blacks and Persians had also started to move into the area around 1900, they did not enter in considerable numbers until after World War I. In 1920, the population of the Near North Side was 83,936.

With the construction of the Boulevard Link Bridge, connecting the parts of Michigan Avenue north and south of the river, in 1920, the Near North Side experienced a decade of vigorous development. The retail shopping that expanded from the downtown area onto North Michigan Avenue, especially that section from Ohio Street to Chicago Avenue where the street was at ground level, was of the sophisticated boutique type. Additionally, several fine new office buildings, hotels and a bank were attracted to Chicago Avenue. Northwestern University's Chicago campus was established south of Chicago Avenue and east of St. Clair Street. New, fashionable, high-rise apartment buildings were constructed in the Streeterville area. The former fashionable

Community Area 08 -- Near North Side
Selected Characteristics of Census Tracts: 1970

Tract Number	TOTAL	0801	0802	0803	0804	0805	0806	0807	0808	0809	0810
Total Population	70269	6656	6855	3763	5892	6752	54	279	6717	1089	3989
% Male	46.5	40.7	42.2	52.7	46.1	45.8	-	41.2	43.2	46.2	50.2
% Black	37.1	0.9	1.7	50.9	93.1	94.3	-	91.0	98.9	97.4	9.9
% Other Nonwhite	1.6	0.4	1.3	2.6	0.6	0.6	-	6.1	0.1	0.7	4.9
% Of Spanish Language	3.2	1.5	1.5	10.6	3.0	3.1	-	11.3	1.6	0.0	5.8
% Foreign Born	6.4	8.0	8.4	5.9	1.2	0.5	-	0.0	0.0	0.0	13.1
% Living In Group Quarters	4.8	1.1	1.5	2.1	0.4	0.3	-	0.0	0.0	1.8	26.4
% 13 Years Old And Under	19.5	5.5	3.6	23.4	42.9	47.8	-	32.6	50.5	30.0	3.4
% 14-20 Years Old	10.2	2.9	3.2	10.5	15.5	18.6	-	12.9	17.8	14.6	16.9
% 21-64 Years Old	58.2	70.8	85.8	56.1	38.8	28.0	-	45.5	29.7	47.7	63.0
% 65-74 Years Old	8.3	14.6	4.9	6.6	2.0	3.9	-	5.0	1.4	5.3	11.1
% 75 Years Old And Over	3.8	6.3	2.5	3.3	0.8	1.6	-	3.9	0.6	2.4	5.6
% In Different House	40.1	39.6	21.4	41.1	46.5	60.1	-	78.9	64.1	47.3	33.8
% Families With Female Head	25.9	10.7	10.9	28.5	39.7	47.4	-	50.0	60.0	37.7	16.9
Median School Years Completed	12.7	14.7	16.1	10.9	9.5	9.5	-	8.7	9.7	8.2	12.6
Median Family Income, 1969 $$	11274	30812	19228	8061	6496	5345	-	3667	4555	5342	9471
% Income Below Poverty Level	22.2	2.0	4.3	24.8	34.6	44.7	-	67.4	50.7	33.8	10.9
% Income of $15,000 or More	39.4	78.0	61.9	12.8	10.6	5.5	-	10.6	1.3	7.1	23.7
% White Collar Workers	49.3	67.5	62.4	30.3	10.6	9.4	-	0.0	11.8	9.4	33.7
% Civilian Labor Force Unemployed	4.1	1.6	1.6	4.8	9.7	13.0	-	7.9	11.5	11.6	4.4
% Riding To Work By Automobile	24.6	36.8	28.8	31.7	26.2	32.5	-	38.0	24.8	26.2	10.2
Population Per Household	2.0	1.7	1.5	2.3	4.0	4.5	-	3.3	4.6	3.3	1.3
Total Housing Units	38946	4627	4682	1819	2023	1689	28	94	1661	385	2691
% Condominiums & Cooperatives	3.9	11.6	1.4	0.4	0.0	0.0	-	0.0	0.0	1.3	0.3
% Built 1960 Or Later	29.6	36.0	55.0	3.3	9.2	57.7	-	17.2	9.3	0.0	10.3
% Owner Occupied	1.7	0.8	1.9	6.2	5.6	2.8	-	9.6	1.0	3.4	1.0
% With 1+ Persons Per Room	9.0	0.8	2.9	9.0	26.0	41.5	-	11.8	42.8	17.1	6.0
Median Value: Owner Units $$	50100	-	50100	-	-	-	-	-	-	-	-
Median Rent: Rental Units $$	160	232	203	87	85	72	-	80	81	74	113
Median Number Of Rooms: All Units	2.9	3.3	2.6	3.6	4.5	4.4	-	4.8	4.3	4.4	1.4

Tract Number	0811	0812	0813	0814	0815	0816	0817	0818	0819
Total Population	1910	5914	6974	4878	1248	1774	2093	1194	2238
% Male	54.6	42.6	38.8	52.3	65.7	54.9	73.1	49.7	42.9
% Black	8.2	1.3	0.4	3.3	2.0	0.5	13.1	72.8	97.1
% Other Nonwhite	2.7	1.3	1.5	2.4	4.3	3.4	4.2	0.0	1.0
% Of Spanish Language	2.3	1.4	2.0	0.5	4.6	2.9	5.7	22.4	2.1
% Foreign Born	14.2	8.1	11.9	21.1	13.9	17.8	5.9	2.8	0.0
% Living In Group Quarters	0.6	0.5	5.0	21.1	2.6	1.6	21.8	1.8	0.0
% 13 Years Old And Under	2.8	3.9	6.1	2.2	1.4	2.4	11.3	33.8	44.8
% 14-20 Years Old	8.0	5.8	8.7	4.5	3.8	2.7	2.7	17.1	18.1
% 21-64 Years Old	74.9	71.2	64.8	76.4	75.4	77.8	65.5	42.8	33.4
% 65-74 Years Old	10.1	12.5	14.1	12.5	13.1	12.0	14.4	4.3	2.5
% 75 Years Old And Over	4.3	6.7	6.3	4.5	6.4	5.1	6.2	2.1	1.3
% In Different House	35.0	34.9	29.8	15.2	43.5	39.0	41.6	75.0	53.3
% Families With Female Head	15.7	12.0	8.8	14.7	7.1	10.6	9.9	36.1	60.6
Median School Years Completed	12.5	14.2	15.0	13.3	12.5	12.7	8.8	8.7	10.2
Median Family Income, 1969 $$	10000	20651	23225	21250	10400	19802	6000	5100	5265
% Income Below Poverty Level	4.1	4.7	2.8	3.6	5.6	2.9	22.9	38.3	32.5
% Income of $15,000 or More	28.0	63.5	72.7	63.1	22.1	64.9	9.6	2.5	5.3
% White Collar Workers	37.3	57.7	71.5	68.1	36.7	51.6	18.4	19.9	8.9
% Civilian Labor Force Unemployed	5.2	1.3	1.0	3.1	3.4	3.5	8.0	13.5	14.2
% Riding To Work By Automobile	9.3	20.4	25.8	23.1	13.9	15.6	16.9	33.0	30.8
Population Per Household	1.3	1.6	1.7	1.5	1.2	1.4	1.3	3.2	3.9
Total Housing Units	1974	4441	4487	3108	1200	1369	1660	399	609
% Condominiums & Cooperatives	0.0	7.3	12.5	0.0	0.0	0.0	0.0	0.0	0.0
% Built 1960 Or Later	0.6	15.2	38.1	73.5	0.0	63.3	0.4	2.8	1.6
% Owner Occupied	0.8	2.0	0.2	0.2	0.7	0.9	0.8	1.8	0.7
% With 1+ Persons Per Room	1.3	3.5	3.0	4.0	9.6	3.3	6.5	22.4	31.9
Median Value: Owner Units $$	-	-	-	-	-	-	-	-	-
Median Rent: Rental Units $$	107	216	249	259	116	178	65	74	68
Median Number Of Rooms: All Units	1.4	2.8	3.2	2.4	1.1	2.3	1.2	4.0	4.0

residences on LaSalle, Dearborn, and Rush streets were increasingly converted into small apartments or rooming houses.

The western part of the community continued as a blighted area. The Italians began to move out of the southwestern part of the slum area as it was increasingly invaded by industry. They moved westward and northward, pushing the Germans across North Avenue. Blacks were moving into the old deteriorating buildings in the southern part of the slum area. In 1930, the leading nationalities among the foreign stock were still the Italians, Germans and Irish.

The first attempt at rehabilitation of the area was a private enterprise, the Marshall Field Garden Apartments (now the Town and Garden Apartments), built in 1928 between Hudson Avenue and Sedgwick Street from Evergreen Avenue to Blackhawk Street. This project, however, did not provide better housing for families in the blighted section, since its rents were too high. In the southwestern part of the community, light manufacturing plants, wholesale and storage houses pushed northward and eastward into the slum area. The Merchandise Mart, finished in 1930, occupied two square blocks in this section.

The population of the Near North Side remained relatively stable during the 1930s, increased by 16 percent during the 1940s as a result of an influx of blacks and Japanese, and then declined 15 percent during the 1950s as a result of extensive demolition for various redevelopment projects. Since 1960, the population has continued to decline, though more slowly. The black population increased to about 31 percent of the total during the 1950s and has stayed near that level since.

The residential pattern of the Near North Side community has not altered substantially since 1930, in spite of new construction. In 1943, the Chicago Housing Authority built the Frances Cabrini Homes in the blighted area to the west. This 586-unit project, located in Census Tract 819, consists of row houses and garden apartments. In 1958, a 1,921-unit extension to the Cabrini Homes was completed in Census Tracts 808 and 818. The Green Homes, with 1,096 units, were built north of Division Street in 1962. In recent years, there has been some additional construction of low-income housing. Private residential construction had moved slowly westward from the eastern section of the community. During the 1950s, expensive high-rise apartments were built in the fashionable eastern Gold Coast section. In 1956, the Chicago Land Clearance Commission designated the "North-LaSalle" or "Carl Sandburg" urban renewal project in Census Tract 802 for residential development. The Carl Sandburg complex was built and expanded during the 1960s and '70s, and eventually converted to condominium housing. In recent years, the construction of apartment complexes in the area has continued, making the Near North one of the few areas in the city which has had significant additions to its housing stock. In 1980, most of the black population and only a small portion of the white population (about 4 percent) lived west of LaSalle Street. This residential segregation is accompanied by economic constrast: the median family income in Cabrini-Green homes was $4,600 in 1980, while the median value of an owner-occupied house in the Near North area was $200,000, the highest in the city.

Since 1930, there has been constant commercial development along Michigan Avenue and the streets running into it. During the 1960s, and '70s the nucleus of commercial activity has moved northward from the central city, and the Magnificent Mile on North Michigan Avenue has become a major retail area attracting shoppers from around the world as well as the metropolitan area. The construction of the John Hancock Center, with mixed office, residential and commercial space, in 1970 and 1971, and the Water Tower Place-Ritz Carlton Hotel complex within the next five years, provided a center for the area. The retail strip complements the Loop shopping district, catering to a higher-income clientele, and has had continuing success, even during difficult economic times.

In the southwestern part of the Near North Side, the recent trend has been for light industry to move out, and for industrial loft space to be converted to mixed residential and commercial use. Some light industry remains in the Goose Island Area. Overall, the number of manufacturing jobs has declined in the area. Non-manufacturing jobs have increased in the Gold Coast section, but decreased somewhat in the western portions of the community.

The rapid and successful development of the Gold Coast area has led to some controversy. Some residents have argued in favor of downzoning or preservation efforts to mitigate problems associated with increasing population density, while others contend that such problems have been over-stated, and that continued development can only help the area.

Marjorie DeVault

Community Area 9

Edison Park

Edison Park, the farthest northwest community in the City of Chicago, shares its earliest beginnings with the adjacent village of Niles. The 1834 arrival of a German family, the Ebingers, and their subsequent settlement southwest of Touhy and Milwaukee avenues, led the area to be dubbed "Dutchman's Point." The farm of the youngest son, the Rev. Christian Ebinger, Sr., stretched west across Harlem Avenue and was the first in what is now Edison Park. Today, a public grade school, located on a portion of that farm, is named after him.

The first organized land development attempt came in 1853 when the Illinois and Wisconsin Railroad laid tracks northwest from Chicago. A stop was established and named "Canfield." The name may be that of a nearby farmer or because the "station" was a wooden platform for milk cans, located in a field. The Illinois and Wisconsin Land Company laid out on paper a town of 300 acres, but made few sales before the Panic of 1857 collapsed the railroad line. The I&W line was reorganized as part of the Chicago and North Western Railroad, but development did not resume.

An awakened interest in suburban property after the 1871 Chicago Fire prompted two developers, A.C. Bandeau and George H. Pierce, to buy parts of the former Canfield subdivision. The more successful Norwood Park development east of Harlem Avenue overshadowed Canfield's "Ridgelawn" re-subdivision. The community was more successful after Chicago annexed the Town of Jefferson in 1889. In December, 1890 Canfield was renamed "Roseneath," a name that lasted only six months. Six electric streetlights, installed at an intersection north of the railroad station, inspired the sobriquet "The Electric Suburb" and the community's new name. The Village of Edison Park was incorporated May 17, 1881, named for inventor Thomas A. Edison.

Developers Butler and McCabe built homes and a hotel north of the railroad tracks. Another firm, McLean and Bierbach, developed several blocks of houses south of the railroad station. The village grew from about 20 families in the mid-1890s to about 300 people in 1910. The balance shifted from farmers to middle- and upper-middle-class families dependent on the train for transportation to the city. In 1910, the perceived advantages of city services over rising costs for private utility contracts prompted Edison Park voters to decide to annex themselves to Chicago. Until this time, all of the community's affili-

ations had been with Maine Township. The early settlers, mostly first- and second-generation Germans and Swedes, had built their one- and two-story frame residences in a scattered fashion around the village area, although there were more houses in the development north of the tracks. By 1920, the business center consisted of a block along the north side of Olmsted Avenue, across from the railroad station. In 1918, efforts had been initiated to pave the streets of the area, and this contributed to the rapid development of Edison Park in the following decade.

Housing growth began before the First World War, but the greatest residential growth came in the 1920s. Between 1920 and 1930, the population grew from 950 to 5,370 people. Subdivisions filled much of the land between Devon and Touhy avenues, although sidewalks, street paving and other amenities had to wait in some of these areas. Annexation of segments of Maine Township in 1922 and 1924 completed the community area as it now stands. The Ebinger School, built in 1927, replaced the former four-room school. The growth of neighborhood churches kept pace with the community expansion. The Edison Park Methodist Church built a sanctuary addition. Three new churches joined it: the Edison Park Evangelical Church (First Edison Park United Church of Christ), Edison Park Lutheran Church, and St. Juliana Roman Catholic Church.

Community Area 9 — Edison Park
Population and Housing Characteristics, 1930-1980

	1980	1970	1960	1950	1940	1930
Total Population.......	12,457	13,241	12,568	7,843	5,999	5,370
% Male.................	45.8	46.6	47.8	48.6	48.9	48.7
% Female...............	54.2	53.4	52.2	51.4	51.1	51.3
% White................	98.9	99.8	100.0	100.0	100.0	99.9
% Black................	0.0	0.0	–	–	–	0.1
% Other Nonwhite Races...	1.1	0.2	0.0	0.0	0.0	0.0
% Under 5 Years Old......	3.7	5.3	9.2	9.3	6.8	9.8
% 5-19 Years Old........	20.4	26.9	26.5	21.5	23.9	26.6
% 20-44 Years Old........	29.2	24.9	28.0	33.8	40.1	43.9
% 45-64 Years Old........	28.1	29.4	26.6	28.0	23.2	15.8
% 65 Years and Older......	18.6	13.5	9.7	7.4	6.0	3.9
Median School Years....	12.5	12.2	12.1	12.2	11.0	*
Total Housing Units....	4,777	4,389	3,777	2,274	1,675	*
% In One-Unit Structures.	67.4	71.9	83.3	*	*	*
% Owner Occupied.........	78.3	77.9	83.1	77.8	61.9	*
% Renter Occupied........	20.0	21.0	15.0	21.1	35.8	*
% Vacant.................	1.7	1.1	1.9	1.1	2.3	*
% 1+ Persons per Room....	1.9	4.2	5.9	6.6	*	*

Community Area 9 — Edison Park
Selected Characteristics of Census Tracts: 1980

Tract Number	Total	901	902	903
Total Population.............	12457	4007	6964	1486
% Male........................	45.8	47.8	44.6	46.3
% Black.......................	0.0	0.0	0.0	0.0
% Other Nonwhite..............	1.1	1.1	1.1	0.7
% Of Spanish Origin...........	1.0	0.5	1.2	1.2
% Foreign Born................	10.7	13.6	9.6	8.5
% Living In Group Quarters....	0.0	0.0	0.0	0.0
% 13 Years Old And Under......	13.3	12.1	13.7	15.0
% 14-20 Years Old.............	12.4	12.3	12.6	11.3
% 21-64 Years Old.............	55.6	59.2	53.7	54.9
% 65-74 Years Old.............	11.4	11.2	11.5	11.5
% 75 Years Old And Over.......	7.2	5.2	8.4	7.3
% In Different House..........	29.0	25.7	30.8	29.3
% Families With Female Head...	9.1	7.3	9.6	11.4
Median School Years Completed...	12.5	12.3	12.6	12.5
Median Family Income, 1979.....$$	27325	27087	27714	26339
% Income Below Poverty Level...	1.5	1.0	1.9	1.0
% Income Of $30,000 Or More.....	43.7	42.5	45.0	40.9
% White Collar Workers.........	61.8	61.8	62.2	59.9
% Civilian Labor Force Unemployed.	3.6	4.1	3.7	2.0
% Riding To Work By Automobile....	73.1	82.5	68.2	70.8
Mean Commuting Time - Minutes...	28.8	25.8	30.3	30.6
Population Per Household..........	2.7	2.8	2.6	2.7
Total Housing Units..........	4777	1429	2790	558
% Condominiums...................	9.9	0.0	16.9	0.2
% Built 1970 Or Later............	7.9	0.9	12.0	4.8
% Owner Occupied.................	78.4	87.7	72.8	82.3
% With 1+ Persons Per Room.......	1.9	2.6	1.5	2.0
Median Value: Owner Units.......$$	72500	73700	72600	68800
Median Rent: Rental Units.......$$	275	278	274	269
Median Number Of Rooms: All Units.	5.2	5.3	5.2	5.2

Community Area 09 — Edison Park
Selected Characteristics of Census Tracts: 1970

Tract Number	TOTAL	0901	0902	0903
Total Population.............	13241	4699	7150	1392
% Male........................	46.6	48.1	45.7	46.2
% Black.......................	0.0	0.0	0.0	0.0
% Other Nonwhite..............	0.2	0.2	0.2	0.7
% Of Spanish Language.........	0.3	0.0	0.5	0.0
% Foreign Born................	7.1	7.7	6.2	9.6
% Living In Group Quarters....	0.2	0.4	0.1	0.0
% 13 Years Old And Under......	21.2	20.5	22.1	19.2
% 14-20 Years Old.............	12.3	15.7	10.5	10.0
% 21-64 Years Old.............	53.0	54.7	51.5	55.5
% 65-74 Years Old.............	8.8	6.0	10.4	9.8
% 75 Years Old And Over.......	4.7	3.0	5.6	5.5
% In Different House..........	72.2	80.2	66.9	71.9
% Families With Female Head...	9.2	6.3	11.4	7.7
Median School Years Completed....	12.2	12.2	12.2	12.3
Median Family Income, 1969.....$$	13536	13784	13333	13500
% Income Below Poverty Level...	2.4	1.5	2.6	4.9
% Income of $15,000 or More.....	38.3	38.7	37.6	40.6
% White Collar Workers..........	31.7	30.7	32.5	30.8
% Civilian Labor Force Unemployed.	1.9	1.3	2.4	1.5
% Riding To Work By Automobile....	67.2	72.1	65.3	54.0
Population Per Household..........	3.0	3.3	2.9	2.8
Total Housing Units..........	4393	1404	2494	495
% Condominiums & Cooperatives.....	4.8	0.0	8.5	0.0
% Built 1960 Or Later.............	17.0	10.0	22.4	9.9
% Owner Occupied.................	73.2	88.5	62.8	82.6
% With 1+ Persons Per Room.......	4.1	5.6	3.7	2.4
Median Value: Owner Units.......$$	29500	30300	29200	27400
Median Rent: Rental Units.......$$	157	170	152	155
Median Number Of Rooms: All Units.	5.2	5.2	5.2	5.2

The whole community, except along the Northwest Highway and along Harlem Avenue, was zoned for single-family dwellings, and that was the predominant type of residential structure. By 1929, Edison Park had achieved residential maturity, even though the section north of Touhy Avenue remained virtually unsettled and there were many open spaces in the community. Some of this land was undeveloped, and some was "marooned." The earlier subdivisions had been into 25-foot lots, but a new zoning ordinance required at least 30-foot fronts for residential construction, leaving some of the vacant 25-foot lots "marooned" between two dwellings. The only industrial property was a small printing plant, the Edison Press, south of the railroad tracks, and strenuous efforts were made by the residents to keep out other industrial establishments. Germans, English and Swedes led all other nationalities among the foreign stock in 1930.

The arrival of the Great Depression caught many building programs mid-stream. The four churches struggled to maintain their mortgages. The Edison Park State Savings Bank failed, although it paid back its depositors. Many families lost their mortgages; others abandoned building their homes and lived in small houses or garages at the back of their lots until conditions improved. Parts of the community streets were paved by the WPA, with no curbs or sewers. During the 1930s, the population grew by fewer than 700 people.

The decade of the 1940s brought some recovery. After a long fight for an area high school, Taft High School was opened in Norwood Park in 1939. The Chicago Transit Authority added bus service on Northwest Highway to supplement suburban United Motor Coach service. The Douglas Aircraft Company opened a plant at Orchard Airport (later O'Hare). After the war, a development of inexpensive housing was erected near Touhy Avenue for returning servicemen. The census of 1950 showed a 30 percent population growth in the decade. North of Touhy, developers built a series of small brick homes, suitable for small families but with limited room for expansion. A survey in the early 1950s showed the need for a public school to supplement Ebinger School. Stock School branch was built to meet the expectations of the post-war baby boom.

The expectation proved to be well-founded, as the population increased 62 percent during the decade, to more than 12,000 in 1960. Germans and Poles were now the most numerous foreign-stock nationalities. Residential construction, almost entirely single-family units, had increased the housing stock by two-thirds during the 1950s. A growing population led community groups, including the Edison Park Community Council and the Edison Park Chamber of Commerce, to petition for stop signs and lights and better community services. Resurrection Hospital was opened in 1953, the first hospital in the immediate area. Taft High School and local churches expanded.

In the early 1960s, the single-family character of the community was threatened when a number of older homes along main street in central Edison Park were razed to make room for apartments and condominiums. The council fought zoning changes and the building of tiny brick houses on the old marooned 25-foot lots. In two landmark cases, some zoning guidelines were established to prevent large houses built on a series of 25-foot lots from being replaced by small houses on each lot.

The last two decades have changed the community. The opening of O'Hare International Airport brought roars from jet planes. The new Northwest (Kennedy) Expressway just south of Edison Park cut travel time to downtown Chicago. Dutch Elm disease devastated the cathedral arches of trees which had lined community streets. The Edison Park Community Council initiated a winter snowplowing program which continued until 1979. The community council devoted its efforts to obtaining full field house facilities for Olympia Park (completed 1971) and Brooks Park (1981).

In 1970, the number of residents surpassed 13,000, the highest recorded to this date. Today, about a hundred fewer live in Edison Park than lived there 20 years ago, but the 6 percent falloff in the 1970s is not large compared to the 11 percent drop for the city. The population of Edison Park is 99 percent white, and includes 120 of Spanish descent, the majority of whom are Mexicans. More than 19 percent of the total population is 65 years of age or older, about twice as many as in 1960. There are almost as many elderly as young people of school age, who constitute just more than 20 percent of the total, compared to more than 34 percent 20 years ago. The community has retained its single-family home atmosphere; 69 percent of all households are in such units, but this is down 14 percent from 1960. The rate of home ownership continues high, 79 percent of all units are occupied by an owner, compared to a high of 83 percent 20 years ago. The median value of owner-occupied homes is more than $72,000, more than 50 percent higher than the city median, putting Edison Park residential values among the top 10 for community areas in the city.

The community's single-family, suburban atmosphere has attracted many city workers, policemen and firemen who must live within the city limits. A successful year-round sports program, Edison Park Youth, Inc., and a strong Chamber of Commerce (sponsor of the annual Edison Park Fest), are additional attractions. Entering the 1980s, the community faces problems with declining public school populations (Stock School was closed in 1981), the large senior citizen population, escalating real estate taxes, and sharp curtailment of its public transit network as the O'Hare rapid transit extension threatens service cuts for most local bus routes.

Anne Lund

Norwood Park

The Norwood Park community traces its roots to pioneer settlers, the Mark Noble family, who arrived from the settlement of Chicago in 1883. Direct access to Chicago along the Indian Trail that would later become Milwaukee Avenue, good drainage along glacial ridges, and proximity to the Des Plaines River and the North Branch of the Chicago River made the area attractive for farmers. The Illinois and Wisconsin Railway (later the Chicago and North Western's northwest line), built in 1853, and the completion of the Milwaukee Plank Road increased access to the area.

In 1868, a group of Chicagoans led by educator John Eberhart formed the Norwood Land and Building Association. They made arrangements to purchase six parcels of farmland, totaling 860 acres, between Nagle and Harlem avenues, north of Bryn Mawr Avenue to the present city limits with Niles. They subdivided them, platting a village with the distinctive Circle Avenue as a hub of arched and

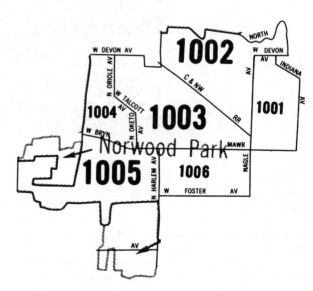

Community Area 10 — Norwood Park
Population and Housing Characteristics, 1930-1980

	1980	1970	1960	1950	1940	1930
Total Population.......	40,459	41,827	40,953	26,798	16,466	14,408
% Male...................	46.8	47.4	48.5	49.3	49.4	49.5
% Female.................	53.2	52.6	51.5	50.7	50.6	50.5
% White..................	98.5	99.7	99.9	99.8	100.0	100.0
% Black..................	0.0	0.0	0.0	0.1	0.0	0.0
% Other Nonwhite Races...	1.5	0.3	0.1	0.1	0.0	0.0
% Under 5 Years Old......	3.8	5.3	8.0	10.4	6.7	10.3
% 5-19 Years Old.........	18.6	24.9	25.7	22.0	26.1	29.1
% 20-44 Years Old........	28.7	25.6	29.6	38.5	40.2	41.5
% 45-64 Years Old........	29.5	31.8	27.7	22.9	21.3	14.7
% 65 Years and Older.....	19.4	12.4	9.0	6.2	5.7	4.4
Median School Years.....	12.4	12.1	11.0	11.0	8.9	*
Total Housing Units.....	15,180	13,659	12,295	7,621	4,355	*
% In One-Unit Structures.	71.7	74.6	81.7	*	*	*
% Owner Occupied.........	78.6	79.5	83.3	78.0	59.8	*
% Renter Occupied........	19.7	19.1	14.8	19.8	38.0	*
% Vacant.................	1.7	1.4	1.9	2.2	2.2	*
% 1+ Persons per Room....	1.8	4.5	4.9	6.7	*	*

Community Area 10 — Norwood Park
Selected Characteristics of Census Tracts: 1980

Tract Number	Total	1001	1002	1003	1004	1005	1006	1007	8104
Total Population.............	40585	5721	7112	6794	3461	6781	5178	5412	126
% Male.......................	46.8	45.1	47.3	45.0	48.1	47.4	46.7	48.5	49.2
% Black......................	0.0	0.0	0.0	0.0	0.0	0.0	0.0	0.0	0.8
% Other Nonwhite.............	1.5	1.0	1.1	1.7	1.4	1.9	2.2	0.9	0.0
% Of Spanish Origin..........	1.0	0.7	0.8	1.2	0.8	1.1	0.9	1.0	0.0
% Foreign Born...............	12.9	16.7	10.4	11.2	9.3	13.1	14.2	15.1	5.5
% Living In Group Quarters...	1.1	0.0	0.1	5.7	0.7	0.2	0.0	0.0	0.0
% 13 Years Old And Under.....	12.9	11.7	13.0	14.1	14.1	14.1	12.2	11.0	8.7
% 14-20 Years Old............	11.2	9.7	11.6	12.1	10.7	11.7	10.4	11.5	11.9
% 21-64 Years Old............	56.5	55.4	56.8	51.8	57.7	57.3	58.0	60.3	54.8
% 65-74 Years Old............	12.4	14.9	11.8	10.5	12.9	11.8	13.2	12.6	18.3
% 75 Years Old And Over......	7.0	8.3	6.7	11.6	4.6	5.0	6.2	4.6	6.3
% In Different House.........	28.2	25.4	29.6	35.5	28.8	25.2	29.8	21.6	54.3
% Families With Female Head..	8.4	8.5	10.1	6.6	6.6	9.3	9.9	7.1	0.0
Median School Years Completed	12.4	12.3	12.5	12.5	12.6	12.4	12.2	12.3	11.6
Median Family Income, 1979...$$	27596	25654	26658	29015	28676	27308	27756	28139	26563
% Income Below Poverty Level..	2.4	1.7	4.1	2.4	2.4	2.7	0.9	2.3	0.0
% Income Of $30,000 Or More...	42.2	38.8	39.8	46.6	44.9	40.5	40.2	46.0	42.5
% White Collar Workers........	56.9	58.6	58.9	59.6	61.6	54.9	51.2	53.9	58.6
% Civilian Labor Force Unemployed.	4.0	3.9	4.6	4.1	3.2	3.4	4.1	4.1	0.0
% Riding To Work By Automobile....	73.0	69.6	69.5	72.0	80.6	77.2	73.7	71.2	84.5
Mean Commuting Time - Minutes.	28.8	27.7	29.5	28.7	26.2	27.7	30.0	31.0	20.9
Population Per Household......	2.7	2.5	2.6	2.7	2.8	2.9	2.6	2.8	2.6
Total Housing Units..........	15180	2343	2807	2403	1244	2377	1989	1968	49
% Condominiums................	3.4	0.0	9.5	4.2	0.0	3.8	0.0	2.7	–
% Built 1970 Or Later.........	7.0	3.2	13.4	16.1	2.0	5.2	2.7	1.1	–
% Owner Occupied..............	78.6	63.2	70.1	71.8	94.6	91.5	80.5	89.1	–
% With 1+ Persons Per Room....	1.8	1.7	1.6	1.9	1.9	1.8	1.8	2.0	–
Median Value: Owner Units....$$	70400	66600	68700	78000	71000	71500	65700	71600	–
Median Rent: Rental Units....$$	269	239	269	287	280	288	271	308	–
Median Number Of Rooms: All Units.	5.3	5.0	5.1	5.4	5.6	5.6	5.1	5.4	–

Community Area 10 — Norwood Park
Selected Characteristics of Census Tracts: 1970

Tract Number	TOTAL	1001	1002	1003	1004	1005	1006	1007
Total Population.............	41827	6145	7245	6672	3934	5817	5714	6300
% Male.......................	47.4	46.4	47.1	46.5	47.9	48.8	48.0	47.4
% Black......................	0.0	0.0	0.0	0.0	0.0	0.0	0.0	0.0
% Other Nonwhite.............	0.3	0.0	0.1	0.2	0.4	0.2	0.3	0.3
% Of Spanish Language........	0.7	0.0	0.0	0.4	1.4	0.0	1.2	1.2
% Foreign Born...............	10.0	11.8	8.8	9.9	7.2	9.4	10.8	10.9
% Living In Group Quarters...	0.8	0.3	0.3	4.3	0.0	0.1	0.0	0.3
% 13 Years Old And Under.....	19.5	16.6	20.4	20.0	19.1	21.5	18.3	20.1
% 14-20 Years Old............	12.1	10.1	11.4	12.8	12.9	11.7	12.1	13.6
% 21-64 Years Old............	56.0	57.0	54.1	52.4	58.1	57.1	58.0	57.2
% 65-74 Years Old............	7.9	10.7	9.4	7.8	6.0	6.8	7.7	5.9
% 75 Years Old And Over......	4.5	5.7	4.7	6.9	3.8	2.9	3.8	3.2
% In Different House.........	72.2	72.1	69.1	64.0	79.1	77.2	70.1	77.6
% Families With Female Head..	8.3	10.0	9.6	8.6	6.3	7.5	7.1	8.1
Median School Years Completed.	12.1	11.6	12.1	12.3	12.3	12.2	11.6	11.9
Median Family Income, 1969.....$$	13699	12930	12816	14686	14068	13890	13485	14207
% Income Below Poverty Level....	2.5	3.0	3.9	1.2	2.5	2.3	1.6	2.4
% Income of $15,000 or More.....	40.8	36.7	35.8	47.7	43.0	41.8	37.8	44.6
% White Collar Workers..........	27.4	25.1	24.5	32.8	34.6	27.4	25.9	24.1
% Civilian Labor Force Unemployed.	2.5	2.2	1.8	3.1	2.4	2.6	2.7	2.8
% Riding To Work By Automobile....	67.5	60.3	63.2	66.2	72.2	78.9	67.9	67.2
Population Per Household........	3.1	2.8	2.9	3.2	3.2	3.2	3.0	3.4
Total Housing Units..........	13641	2237	2496	2037	1246	1831	1914	1880
% Condominiums & Cooperatives.....	1.1	0.7	1.5	0.7	0.7	4.0	0.0	0.0
% Built 1960 Or Later.............	13.6	10.8	14.2	16.4	6.6	11.6	15.8	17.5
% Owner Occupied.................	78.4	65.4	67.5	76.0	93.7	87.5	81.3	89.3
% With 1+ Persons Per Room.......	4.6	3.1	4.2	5.1	4.0	4.6	4.7	6.4
Median Value: Owner Units.......$$	28200	27600	27300	30200	29000	26800	26200	30200
Median Rent: Rental Units.......$$	147	136	139	145	166	152	164	177
Median Number Of Rooms: All Units.	5.2	5.0	5.0	5.4	5.4	5.3	5.0	5.3

curving streets. The name "Norwood" was taken from the popular novel by Henry Ward Beecher. Since there was already an Illinois post office by that name, the word "Park" was added to the community's official designation. Houses, a railroad station and a hotel were built. Real estate sales were brisk, especially after the 1871 Chicago Fire.

The subdivision was located at the northwest corner of Jefferson Township where it intersected with Niles, Maine and Leyden Townships. Township services and roads were nearly non-existent, since

attention was focused on access with Chicago. Area farmers petitioned the Cook County Board for a township of their own. Although the board granted permission in 1873, it wasn't until the state legislature passed a law in March 1874 that the new Norwood Park Township became official: 1½ miles on either side of Harlem Avenue, north from Irving Park Road to Devon Avenue, with small corners from Maine and Niles Township added. The Norwood Park subdivision was incorporated as a village following an election July 25, 1874.

By the mid-1880s, the community had a population of about 400. Most homes were built west of Newark Avenue, the ascending side of the glacial ridge, and south of the railroad tracks. It wasn't until after 1910 that the remainder of the subdivision was thoroughly developed, helped by drainage of the marshy river flood plain between Newark and the Chicago River.

After Chicago annexed all of the land up to the Norwood Park Township boundaries in the late 1880s, Norwood Park Village and several adjacent small subdivisions voted to join Chicago in 1893, primarily to gain city services. During its first 25 years in the city, the Norwood Park population grew steadily, principally native whites of English, German, Scandinavian and Polish descent. Local civic organizations worked tirelessly for improvements. The Norwood Park School, opened in 1916, had the first lighted school program in the city. The Norwegian Old People's Home (1896) and the Danish Old People's Home (1906) chose Norwood Park to establish retirement homes to serve the metropolitan area. The Passionist Fathers established the Immaculate Conception Monastery in 1904 at the corner of Harlem and Talcott avenues, and later helped to found many area Roman Catholic parishes. Chicago's Girl Scout Troop No. 1 was founded at Immaculate Conception parish in 1919. The Sisters of the Resurrection bought a series of adjacent farms west of Harlem along Talcott in 1912, and would later found Resurrection High School and Academy (1913), Resurrection Hospital (1953) and Resurrection Retirement Community (1977).

The 1920s brought a substantial increase in population, from 2,857 in 1920 to 14,408 in 1930. Onahan School was built in 1928 to supplement the needs of Norwood Park School. The advent of the automobile brought a demand for better roads and public transportation. Although streetcar service was available along Milwaukee Avenue, the Chicago and North Western trains were the major link to the rest of the city. By 1930, the largest foreign-stock nationality was German, followed by Polish and Scandinavian.

Part of the population increase resulted from annexation of additional Norwood Park Township land in 1924 and 1927. Since they had been part of the township, they were linked to the Norwood Park Community area. Additional small annexations over the years gradually increased the size of the community, whether or not there were any direct connections to the former village. Two other areas were separately incorporated as Harwood Heights and Norridge in the 1940s, and some sections of Norwood Park Township are still unincorporated, although surrounded by Chicago.

The Oriole Park subdivision (Census Tract 1005) was developed in the late 1930s. It grew during the war years with a housing development for Douglas Aircraft workers employed at the future O'Hare Airport. Oriole Park has maintained its identity since the 1940s, although it is part of the Norwood Park Community Area. Located there are the Oriole Park School, Oriole Park Field House and park, and Oriole Park Library Branch. The section west of Harlem between Devon and the Kennedy Expressway developed after World War II. Thomas Edison School was built there in 1950.

The population of the Norwood Park neighborhood grew by 2,000 through the lean years of the Depression and World War II. Taft High School opened in 1939 after years of pressure for a local high school. A Civil Defense block captain program, developed in Norwood Park,

became the model for the city and country. Bus lines were opened on major arteries. Some light industry developed along the Northwest Highway corridor. Growth came quickly after the end of the war. By 1950, the population had increased by more than 60 percent to almost 27,000. Construction thrived in Norwood Park as more than 3,000 units were added.

Half again as many units were added in the following decade, and by 1960 the number of Norwood Park residents exceeded 40,000, more than 10 percent of whom lived on additional territory, south of the new expressway, annexed to the city in that year. Efforts of several Norwood Park leaders helped to insure that the new superhighway being constructed along the southern end of the community would be a freeway, not a tollway, through the city limits. The Northwest (Kennedy) Expressway opened in 1960, further isolating Oriole Park and other southern sections of the community area from the core. In 1970, the population of Norwood Park reached a historic high, just under 42,000.

The Norwood Park Citizens Association was organized to provide snowplowing and other services to its neighborhood, within the boundaries of the original village. The Citizens Association took a leading role in a number of community projects, including obtaining a new library building (Roden Branch, 1969), and a paramedic ambulance (1976); and preserving area zoning. Multi-unit buildings replaced some houses near major streets during the 1960s and seventies, but the community's single-family residential character was preserved. The association also sponsored the Norwood Park Centennial Committee (1973-74), an omnibus group of more than 100 representatives of area organizations and institutions, which planned 32 events over a 14-month period to celebrate the best things the community had to offer. A historical society was formed and a Memorial Association established to maintain the tradition of the Norwood Park Memorial Day parades. The interest in history, spawned by the centennial and subsequent Bicentennial celebration, led to a community drive to have an 1851 farmhouse at Devon and Milwaukee avenues declared a city landmark in 1980. The Henry W. Rincker House became a landmark in another sense in 1981 when it became the first city-designated landmark to be illegally destroyed.

Today, 40,585 persons live in Norwood Park, down 3 percent from the 1970 peak. The population is 99 percent white, a hundred or so Koreans and Filipinos, constituting the largest non-white groups. Nearly one in five Norwood Park residents is at least 65 years old (compared to one in 10 in the city), and the Bank of Commerce and Industry's Senior Citizens Club is the largest in Chicago. There are more than 15,000 housing units in Norwood Park now, twice as many as 30 years ago, and almost three-fourths of them are single-family homes. Only 7 percent live in large structures containing 10 or more housing units. Eighty percent of all household are located in owner-occupied units, and the median value of such single-family units is almost 50 percent greater than the city median. More than 800 units are valued at $100,000 or more. Norwood Park works hard to continue its single-family character and "suburban" charm, despite nearly 90 years in the city. As it entered the 1980s, its problems were those of an aging but affluent white neighborhood. Residents are concerned about high property assessments, threatened transit sevice cuts, and the need to repair, maintain and enhance services and facilities.

Anne Lund

Jefferson Park

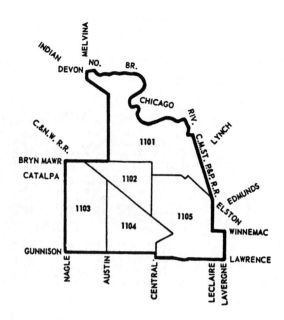

The history of Jefferson Park dates back to the early 1830s when the first white settler, John Kinzie Clark, arrived in the area. He was followed by a few others who began to farm the prairie land. The construction of the Northwestern Plank Road — now Milwaukee Avenue — in 1844 enabled the area farmers to get their produce to Chicago and also helped attract more settlers to the area. In 1845 a post office was built and the residents chose to name it after President James Monroe. However, as "Monroe" was discovered to be already in use by another community, they opted for the name "Jefferson" instead.

In 1850 the Township of Jefferson was organized by local farmers. That township originally extended from Harlem to Western avenues and from North to Devon avenues, its nucleus being the Jefferson village at Milwaukee and Lawrence avenues. In the 1850s more permanent settlers, the English and Luxembourger truck farmers who were establishing themselves throughout the northwestern communities, arrived. They tended to settle along the Northwestern Plank Road. In 1855 the village was platted on the land that now constitutes the southeastern corner of the community. Nearly 50 frame dwellings were constructed, but further construction was halted by the economic panic of 1857. The village was re-subdivided in 1868, and again in 1870, especially that part of the tract lying east of the Chicago and North Western Railroad. In 1872 the Village of Jefferson was incorporated.

The population of the village was approximately 800 in the early 1870s. It was a popular stopping place for travellers on the plank road and served as a market town for the surrounding farmers of Jefferson Township. The attractiveness of the village as a surburb was boosted with the opening of a station on the Chicago and North Western line between what are now Edmunds and Gale streets. In 1889 the community was annexed to Chicago as part of Jefferson Township. In the 1890s Jefferson Park was still mainly a region of mud flats and truck farms where a profit could be made in growing onions. Settlement was still confined for the most part to the original village site in the southeast. The Chicago and North Western Railroad provided the only transportation to the heart of the city. Milwaukee Avenue and Elston Avenue (first called the Lower Road) were the two main tollroads through the community area.

The annexation brought much vacant land within the city limits. At the same time, Jefferson Park benefited from the local improvements that came as the city gradually expanded to the north and northwest. No substantial subdivision occurred in Jefferson Park, however, until after the turn of the century, when the extension of streetcar service on Lawrence, Milwaukee, and Elston avenues brought laborers, artisans, and small tradesmen to settle in the community. During the years from 1900 to 1920, first- and second-generation Poles, Germans, Russians, Italians, and Czechoslovakians arrived in Jefferson Park and settled in the old Jefferson village bounded by Foster, Elston, Lawrence, and Central avenues. World War I and the high cost of construction immediately after the war arrested development of a new subdivision to the north and west of the old village for some time. The next decade, 1920 to 1930, brought renewed construction activity. Old subdivisions boomed and the remaining district, the northern and eastern parts of the community, was subdivided during this period. There was a sharp increase in population from 5,825 in 1920 to 20,532 in 1930. The influx of Poles, Czechoslovakians, Scandinavians, and Italians continued, and the largest foreign-born groups in the 1930 were the Germans, Poles and Italians.

The residential character of Jefferson Park was well-established by 1930. A manufacturing region had developed in the district between Avondale Avenue and Northwest Highway on either side of the

Chicago and North Western tracks, and scattered along Milwaukee Avenue. Another manufacturing area began to develop in the vicinity of Ardmore Avenue between Elston Avenue and the Chicago, Milwaukee and St. Paul tracks and along those tracks at Catalpa Avenue. There was still a considerable amount of vacant land in the western and northern parts of Jefferson Park in 1930.

Jefferson Park continued to grow after the last wave of immigration in the 1920s, but at a greatly reduced pace. The population of the community increased by 34 percent between 1930 and 1960, most of the growth coming after World War II. During the 1960s, modern two- and three-story apartment flats began to be built along major streets like Higgins Avenue. The old business district around Lawrence and Milwaukee maintained its vitality in the 1960s despite growing competition from the surrounding shopping centers. The leading nationality groups in the sixties continued to be Poles, Germans, and Italians.

The lack of adequate transportation to the Loop and other areas was a problem for Jefferson Park residents until the opening of the Northwest (Kennedy) Expressway in 1960. This highway, which forms a physical barrier dividing the area in half, runs diagonally through Jefferson Park. In 1970 the Kennedy Rapid Transit Facility Terminal, on Milwaukee Avenue, was completed. This terminal has become a major transportation hub linking several major bus and train routes. Unfortunately, the advantages of accessible rapid transportation for Jefferson Park have been offset by a chronic lack of parking space.

The community area population grew to an all-time high, greater than 27,500, by 1970 but dropped by 3,000 in the most recent decade. The residential loss was comparable to that experienced by many neighborhoods, probably part of the overall trend. Jefferson Park is almost all white; a handful of blacks and about 500 other non-whites live there. Nearly 400 residents are Hispanic. Among the whites, those claiming Polish, German, Irish and Italian descent are most numerous. Housing units are almost evenly distributed between single and multiple dwelling structures. About two-thirds of the non-vacant units are owner-occupied. The median value of single-family dwellings in Jefferson Park is almost $65,000, which is 13th ranked among the 77 Chicago community areas.

The busiest retail area in Jefferson Park is located at Higgins Road extending southward along Milwaukee Avenue and including the stores on Lawrence Avenue. A second business section includes the businesses on Milwaukee Avenue north of Lawrence Avenue. With the closing of Wolke's Department Store in 1982, Jefferson Park's central shopping area was left with only one major department store. Wolke's building is currently being converted into an outpatient treatment center for Grant Hospital.

Jefferson Park has gained an important cultural attraction with the construction of the Copernicus Civic and Cultural Center at Lawrence and Lipps avenues. The first phase of this Center was completed in December, 1981. The Center sponsors various language classes, exhibits, workshops, and ethnic events for Polish and other nationality groups in Jefferson Park and Chicago.

Rodney Nelson

Community Area 11 -- Jefferson Park
Population and Housing Characteristics, 1930-1980

	1980	1970	1960	1950	1940	1930
Total Population.......	24,583	27,553	27,494	23,556	21,537	20,532
% Male.................	46.0	46.8	48.3	49.4	50.6	50.6
% Female...............	54.0	53.2	51.7	50.6	49.4	49.4
% White................	98.1	99.8	99.9	100.0	100.0	100.0
% Black................	0.0	0.0	-	0.0	0.0	0.0
% Other Nonwhite Races...	1.9	0.2	0.1	0.0	0.0	0.0
% Under 5 Years Old......	3.9	6.1	8.3	9.3	7.0	9.8
% 5-19 Years Old.........	16.9	21.3	21.4	19.3	24.6	30.3
% 20-44 Years Old........	30.4	27.1	30.8	38.9	41.5	43.2
% 45-64 Years Old........	28.4	30.9	28.2	25.9	22.4	13.8
% 65 Years and Older.....	20.4	14.6	11.3	6.6	4.5	2.9
Median School Years....	12.2	11.3	10.2	9.0	8.4	*
Total Housing Units......	10,175	9,951	9,011	6,947	5,880	*
% In One-Unit Structures...	47.9	48.6	53.4	*	*	*
% Owner Occupied.........	65.2	64.9	67.8	64.1	49.6	*
% Renter Occupied........	32.7	33.1	30.2	35.1	48.5	*
% Vacant................	2.1	2.0	2.0	0.8	1.9	*
% 1+ Persons per Room....	1.9	3.3	4.5	8.1	*	*

Community Area 11 -- Jefferson Park
Selected Characteristics of Census Tracts: 1980

Tract Number	Total	1101	1102	1103	1104	1105
Total Population.............	24583	5205	2560	5060	4089	7669
% Male.......................	46.0	46.5	45.5	47.0	45.1	45.6
% Black......................	0.0	0.1	0.0	0.0	0.0	0.0
% Other Nonwhite.............	1.9	1.8	1.2	1.3	1.6	2.6
% Of Spanish Origin..........	1.6	1.1	1.2	1.7	0.9	2.4
% Foreign Born...............	15.3	15.3	11.8	15.5	19.1	14.2
% Living In Group Quarters........	0.0	0.0	0.0	0.0	0.0	0.0
% 13 Years Old And Under.....	12.4	13.2	13.4	11.1	11.4	12.9
% 14-20 Years Old............	9.9	9.4	9.8	10.7	9.2	10.2
% 21-64 Years Old............	57.3	57.1	57.4	56.6	57.4	57.7
% 65-74 Years Old............	13.0	12.2	11.8	15.0	14.6	11.8
% 75 Years Old And Over......	7.4	8.1	7.7	6.6	7.3	7.4
% In Different House.........	31.0	27.7	35.6	19.6	32.9	38.5
% Families With Female Head...	12.4	11.5	9.4	10.0	12.8	15.2
Median School Years Completed...	12.2	12.3	12.2	12.1	12.3	12.3
Median Family Income, 1979......$$	25083	25403	25599	24650	26190	24593
% Income Below Poverty Level....	2.1	2.2	2.2	2.3	2.0	2.0
% Income Of $30,000 Or More.....	34.9	37.4	30.4	32.6	39.0	34.1
% White Collar Workers.......	58.3	56.6	53.3	55.9	60.7	61.2
% Civilian Labor Force Unemployed....	4.0	3.7	3.3	4.5	4.7	3.8
% Riding To Work By Automobile....	67.6	71.7	68.7	72.7	66.0	62.5
Mean Commuting Time - Minutes...	28.2	27.7	28.4	28.1	30.2	27.4
Population Per Household......	2.5	2.5	2.5	2.6	2.4	2.4
Total Housing Units..........	10175	2105	1068	1985	1713	3304
% Condominiums...............	2.7	0.0	0.0	5.4	0.8	4.8
% Built 1970 Or Later........	5.0	3.0	1.7	5.1	3.6	8.1
% Owner Occupied.............	65.2	67.6	59.0	84.7	59.3	57.0
% With 1+ Persons Per Room...	1.9	1.5	1.6	2.4	1.7	2.0
Median Value: Owner Units.......$$	64800	66700	63100	65300	65900	62300
Median Rent: Rental Units.......$$	233	233	216	228	247	233
Median Number Of Rooms: All Units.	5.0	5.1	5.0	5.0	5.0	4.8

Community Area 11 -- Jefferson Park
Selected Characteristics of Census Tracts: 1970

Tract Number	TOTAL	1101	1102	1103	1104	1105
Total Population.............	27553	5958	2964	5838	4569	8224
% Male.......................	46.8	47.4	46.2	48.1	46.1	46.1
% Black......................	0.0	0.0	0.0	0.0	0.0	0.0
% Other Nonwhite.............	0.2	0.2	0.2	0.2	0.1	0.3
% Of Spanish Language........	0.4	0.0	0.2	1.8	0.0	0.1
% Foreign Born...............	12.4	11.5	11.8	12.1	14.3	12.4
% Living In Group Quarters........	0.2	0.0	0.0	0.0	0.3	0.4
% 13 Years Old And Under.....	18.8	18.6	20.4	18.2	16.8	19.7
% 14-20 Years Old............	10.0	10.1	9.9	10.6	9.8	9.6
% 21-64 Years Old............	56.7	55.7	55.5	59.2	58.3	55.2
% 65-74 Years Old............	9.3	10.3	9.3	7.6	9.2	9.8
% 75 Years Old And Over......	5.3	5.3	4.9	4.4	5.8	5.7
% In Different House.........	68.6	67.1	67.6	73.2	67.0	67.8
% Families With Female Head...	10.7	9.6	11.5	8.7	11.0	12.6
Median School Years Completed...	11.3	11.8	10.8	10.7	11.5	11.5
Median Family Income, 1969......$$	12353	12302	12262	12649	12399	12216
% Income Below Poverty Level.....	3.3	4.4	0.5	1.9	3.6	4.2
% Income of $15,000 or More.....	31.3	30.2	25.5	34.7	33.1	30.5
% White Collar Workers.......	24.8	24.3	24.4	24.0	23.9	26.5
% Civilian Labor Force Unemployed.	2.4	2.5	5.2	2.9	1.0	1.8
% Riding To Work By Automobile....	63.2	64.5	58.1	70.0	62.6	59.5
Population Per Household......	2.8	2.9	2.8	3.0	2.8	2.7
Total Housing Units..........	9950	2110	1071	1991	1677	3101
% Condominiums & Cooperatives.....	0.9	0.8	0.5	1.4	0.4	1.0
% Built 1960 Or Later........	12.8	9.6	8.0	13.2	16.6	14.4
% Owner Occupied.............	63.9	68.5	62.3	80.4	58.1	54.0
% With 1+ Persons Per Room...	3.7	3.6	3.9	4.6	3.0	3.6
Median Value: Owner Units.......$$	25200	25800	23600	26000	27700	23300
Median Rent: Rental Units.......$$	128	126	119	127	144	123
Median Number Of Rooms: All Units.	4.9	5.0	5.0	4.9	4.9	4.8

Forest Glen

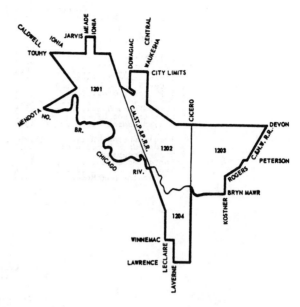

Forest Glen is an insulated enclave on the northern edge of the city of Chicago, surrounded by forest preserves, golf courses, city parks and cemeteries. The community is an odd-shaped area, which roughly resembles a set of triangles pushed together, about 14 miles from the Loop. Peterson Avenue, which runs through the center of the community area from east to west, serves as something of a main street. The land in Forest Glen is slightly more rugged than elsewhere around Chicago and it is heavily wooded. The North Branch of the Chicago River, which runs through the community area from southeast to northwest, adds considerably to its physical attractiveness.

Forest Glen contains two prestigious neighborhoods, Edgebrook and Sauganash. In many ways Forest Glen is as suburban as the sylvan North Shore municipalities. The dense forest preserves surrounding the neighborhoods of Edgebrook and Sauganash were once hunting grounds for Pottawattomi Indians. There are still occasional newspaper reports of today's residents uncovering arrowheads and tomahawks in their gardens. The Indian legacy remains in streets named Hiawatha, Minnetonka, Dowagiac and Minnehaha.

A considerable portion of the area within the present community of Forest Glen was once contained in what was known as Billy Caldwell's Reserve. Billy Caldwell, a half-breed Indian who was a chief of the Pottawattomies, was better known as "The Sauganash," his Indian name meaning "the Englishman." The land Edgebrook and Sauganash now occupy, approximately 1,600 acres along the river, was granted to Caldwell by the federal government in 1828 to be used as an Indian reservation. The land was payment for his services as a mediator in treaties signed by his tribe, and also for saving the lives of the John Kinzie family after the Fort Dearborn Massacre in 1812. In 1836, after the tribe left the area, Caldwell sold most of the land to farmers. Later, a considerable portion of this land was set aside by Cook County as a forest preserve which is known today as the Sauganash or Caldwell Reserve.

In 1872 the Chicago, Milwaukee and St. Paul Railway Company purchased a right-of-way through the area and railroad officials started to buy land to build houses nearby. The first urban settlement in Forest Glen dates from the 1880s when 10 acres from the farm of W.C. Hazelton was subdivided. The Edgebrook railroad station was built in 1883 and was replaced in 1896 by a stone and frame building at Lehigh and Devon avenues. This structure, which was located north of the current station, was also used for community meetings, parties, dances and musicals. It burned to the ground in 1930, and was later rebuilt closer to Edgebrook's business district.

Most of Forest Glen, except for the elongated section north of Devon Avenue, was annexed to Chicago by election in 1889 as part of the Town of Jefferson, but subdivision and development in the modern sense did not begin until the mid-1920s, when two area realtors, Henry G. Zander and George F. Koester, started to promote the Sauganash neighborhood.

In 1920 Forest Glen's population was only 446 and growing slowly. Early settlers were farmers and railroad officials of English stock who built large frame houses on substantial lots. A few Swedes, many of them in the construction industry, moved in subsequently. Businesses in the community were scarce and were concentrated along the railroad tracks just north of the junction of the tracks and Elston Avenue.

The major reason for this slow growth was probably the lack of transportation for most of the community. Only the southernmost section south of Foster Avenue, which was part of the old Village of Jefferson Park, and the settlement clustered around the Forest Glen station had access to the railroad. The influx of residents began in the mid-1920s in response to a spurt in construction activity. The building boom of the early 1920s, which characterized most of the neighboring Chicago communities, did not reach Forest Glen until middle and late 1920s. Once begun, the peak of residential construction covered the years between 1925 and 1934. Although construction took place in all parts of the community, it was especially pronounced in the area west of Cicero Avenue and north of Bryn Mawr Avenue. From 1922 through 1928 small parts of Niles township were also periodically annexed either by elections or ordinance to Chicago and became part of the community of Forest Glen. By 1940, Forest Glen was firmly established as a community of high-grade expensive homes. In addition to golf courses and forest preserves, Forest Glen had large stretches of undeveloped land and vacant lots scattered throughout the community, particularly in the northern parts, until the late sixties.

The population of Forest Glen rose from 400 to 4,000 between 1920 and 1930, a 911 percent increase. Unlike most other Chicago communities, Forest Glen experienced a substantial population increase during the 1930s, which continued in the following decades. The leading nationalities were Germans, Swedes, Czechs and Russians. By 1940, bus service began on some of the major streets, and some minor manufacturing districts developed, mostly along railroad tracks. The population increased to 6,600 in 1940 and then almost doubled to 12,200 in 1950. It reached 19,200 in 1960, thus tripling in two decades between 1940 and 1960. Germans, Swedes and Poles were the leading ethnic groups.

Since 1960, Forest Glen has continued to grow and fill in vacant land with considerable building activity of mostly single-family high-grade residential homes. Peak population growth came in 1970, when it reached 20,531.

Since World War II, Forest Glen, especially the Sauganash section, has gradually become known as a neighborhood of wealth and power. The median family income for the community in 1979 was $31,872, one and a half times the Chicago average of $18,776. The median value of single-family homes, more than $89,000, puts Forest Glen among the top 10 communities in the city. More high-ranking city administrators, judges and top echelon police and fire department officials live in the Sauganash and Edgebrook neighborhoods than in any other Chicago community area. In the mid-1970s Mayor Richard Daley, attempting to stem the white flight from Chicago to the suburbs, let it be known that he wanted all city workers to live within the city. For years Chicago police and fire personnel, like all city workers, had been required to live in the city, but the rule never had been strongly enforced. Following the mayor's announcement, many government

Community Area 12 -- Forest Glen
Population and Housing Characteristics, 1930-1980

	1980	1970	1960	1950	1940	1930
Total Population.......	18,991	20,531	19,228	12,189	6,630	4,065
% Male..................	46.9	47.2	47.7	48.3	48.9	50.7
% Female................	53.1	52.8	52.3	51.7	51.1	49.3
% White.................	96.8	99.5	99.9	99.9	99.8	99.8
% Black.................	0.1	0.0	0.0	0.1	0.2	0.0
% Other Nonwhite Races...	3.1	0.5	0.1	0.0	0.0	0.2
% Under 5 Years Old......	3.9	5.8	6.8	8.2	7.7	9.6
% 5-19 Years Old.........	21.1	24.0	23.9	22.0	24.0	28.0
% 20-44 Years Old........	28.2	24.4	25.3	34.4	42.9	43.4
% 45-64 Years Old........	27.8	31.4	34.4	29.1	21.1	15.9
% 65 Years and Older.....	19.0	14.4	9.6	6.3	4.3	3.1
Median School Years....	12.9	12.6	12.2	12.2	10.1	*
Total Housing Units....	6,907	6,766	5,374	3,106	1,359	*
% In One-Unit Structures.	85.9	86.4	84.7	*	*	*
% Owner Occupied.........	87.1	87.6	87.1	86.6	71.4	*
% Renter Occupied........	11.5	11.0	9.4	10.8	21.8	*
% Vacant.................	1.4	1.4	3.5	2.6	6.8	*
% 1+ Persons per Room....	1.5	2.0	2.5	3.9	*	*

Community Area 12 -- Forest Glen
Selected Characteristics of Census Tracts: 1980

Tract Number	Total	1201	1202	1203	1204
Total Population..............	18991	4524	4871	6274	3322
% Male..............................	46.9	48.1	46.3	46.3	47.5
% Black.............................	0.1	0.0	0.2	0.0	0.0
% Other Nonwhite..............	3.1	1.9	3.1	3.7	3.8
% Of Spanish Origin...........	1.6	1.1	1.4	1.9	2.1
% Foreign Born................	15.4	11.1	15.9	17.4	16.8
% Living In Group Quarters.........	0.0	0.0	0.0	0.0	0.0
% 13 Years Old And Under..........	15.0	15.9	15.3	14.1	14.8
% 14-20 Years Old..............	11.3	12.8	11.8	10.6	9.9
% 21-64 Years Old..............	54.7	53.5	53.8	55.2	56.9
% 65-74 Years Old..............	12.1	11.5	12.3	12.8	11.3
% 75 Years Old And Over.........	6.9	6.3	6.8	7.4	7.1
% In Different House............	25.9	29.9	20.4	22.8	34.6
% Families With Female Head.....	7.9	8.3	7.2	8.0	8.0
Median School Years Completed....	12.9	13.3	12.9	13.0	12.5
Median Family Income, 1979.....$$	31872	33639	35507	31209	27067
% Income Below Poverty Level....	1.8	1.9	1.5	2.6	0.8
% Income Of $30,000 Or More.....	54.2	56.7	63.3	53.4	39.4
% White Collar Workers...........	68.9	70.2	73.4	72.8	53.5
% Civilian Labor Force Unemployed.	3.6	4.6	3.0	2.9	4.3
% Riding To Work By Automobile....	73.5	73.1	74.8	76.7	66.3
Mean Commuting Time - Minutes...	27.3	27.0	26.5	27.5	28.6
Population Per Household..........	2.8	3.0	2.8	2.7	2.6
Total Housing Units..........	6907	1552	1752	2317	1286
% Condominiums.................	0.0	0.0	0.0	0.0	0.0
% Built 1970 Or Later...........	4.9	2.8	9.8	2.4	5.3
% Owner Occupied................	87.2	93.8	86.1	89.1	77.2
% With 1+ Persons Per Room......	1.5	1.5	1.6	1.1	2.2
Median Value: Owner Units.......$$	87100	90600	93800	88800	67100
Median Rent: Rental Units.......$$	265	324	290	272	216
Median Number Of Rooms: All Units.	5.6	5.6	5.6	5.6	5.2

Community Area 12 -- Forest Glen
Selected Characteristics of Census Tracts: 1970

Tract Number	TOTAL	1201	1202	1203	1204
Total Population.............	20531	4947	4757	7116	3711
% Male..............................	47.2	47.6	47.2	46.7	47.4
% Black.............................	0.0	0.0	0.0	0.0	0.0
% Other Nonwhite...............	0.5	0.3	0.8	0.4	0.6
% Of Spanish Language..........	0.4	0.0	0.3	1.0	0.0
% Foreign Born.................	10.9	5.9	13.2	12.5	11.2
% Living In Group Quarters.........	0.1	0.2	0.0	0.3	0.0
% 13 Years Old And Under..........	20.2	23.2	19.7	18.7	19.9
% 14-20 Years Old..............	10.7	11.7	8.9	11.6	9.9
% 21-64 Years Old..............	54.7	52.1	56.6	54.8	55.6
% 65-74 Years Old..............	10.0	9.2	10.3	10.6	9.7
% 75 Years Old And Over.........	4.3	3.8	4.4	4.4	4.9
% In Different House............	68.2	71.2	60.9	70.4	69.3
% Families With Female Head.......	8.4	6.2	8.3	9.0	10.2
Median School Years Completed....	12.6	12.7	12.7	12.6	12.1
Median Family Income, 1969......$$	16868	18791	16738	17588	13829
% Income Below Poverty Level....	2.9	1.3	4.9	2.1	3.8
% Income of $15,000 or More.....	57.0	65.0	56.6	59.3	42.6
% White Collar Workers...........	46.2	48.1	54.2	51.1	25.6
% Civilian Labor Force Unemployed.	2.0	2.8	1.9	1.3	2.5
% Riding To Work By Automobile....	71.7	72.2	70.2	73.7	69.2
Population Per Household..........	3.1	3.3	3.0	3.1	2.9
Total Housing Units...........	6770	1530	1635	2312	1293
% Condominiums & Cooperatives.....	0.1	0.0	0.3	0.0	0.0
% Built 1960 Or Later...........	10.2	2.4	19.3	8.9	10.2
% Owner Occupied................	87.3	95.4	84.6	89.7	76.8
% With 1+ Persons Per Room......	2.2	1.8	1.6	2.0	2.8
Median Value: Owner Units.......$$	34700	36400	39300	35900	27000
Median Rent: Rental Units.......$$	145	184	161	165	113
Median Number Of Rooms: All Units.	5.8	6.0	6.0	5.9	5.1

officials and workers scrambled to get back inside city limits, particularly into the nicer "suburban type" neighborhoods, causing the housing values to rise. These newcomers were welcomed in the Forest Glen neighborhoods because they added a stable and safe younger element, they worked for the city, were white and Catholic, like the people who already lived there. Thus, the most recent groups moving into the community were of Irish or Italian descent.

The population of Forest Glen is predominantly native white. There are only a hundred non-whites, three hundred Hispanics, in a total of almost 19,000. The number of residents dropped by 1,500 in the most recent decade. There is no evidence however, of any physical decline or of any signs of mass migration out of this very secluded, quiet community. The loss is due rather to a change in household composition, created by grown children away at college or starting their own families.

Forest Glen contains some of the best of the newer residential development to be found within the city limits of Chicago. Land use in the area is predominantly residential. In 1980 the majority of housing units, 88 percent, were owner-occupied single-family residences, well above the Chicago average. A variety of designs from turreted Old English-style and gracious two-story Colonial houses to contemporary raised ranches in varied materials such as stone, brick or cedar exteriors, set off individual buildings on wooded streets. Some of the newer developments on the nothern part of the community are clustered around a cul-de-sac, further secluded behind brick and cedar walls.

Commercial land use is minimal. Most of the commercial activity within Forest Glen is scattered along the main north and south axis of the area, Cicero Avenue. Some businesses are located also at the intersection of Devon and Lehigh avenues.

Ariela Royer

Community Area 13

North Park

Settlement of the North Park area began in the 1850s when it was part of the newly-organized Jefferson Township. A village was laid out in 1855 and 50 dwellings were erected. This small settlement developed into a market town and as a result achieved economic independence from the city of Chicago. The original settlers of North Park were German and Swedish farmers who grew vegetables along the south bank of the North Branch of the Chicago River. They were later joined by an emigration of Czechoslovakians into the northwestern corner of the community after the opening of the Bohemian National Cemetery in 1877. The Czechoslovakian presence was short-lived, however, and they began to move out around the turn of the century.

In 1889, North Park was annexed to Chicago as part of the Town of Jefferson. At this time there were only a few frame houses in the area, the rest of the land was covered with brush and woods. The name North Park was given to the community because of its location in northern Chicago and its naturally wooded environment.

In 1893, the Swedish University Association of the Swedish Evangelical Mission Covenant, looking for a site where they could establish a college, purchased more than 97 acres of land north of Albany Park. About eight and one-half acres, between Kedzie and Spaulding avenues along the river in the southeastern corner of North Park, were donated to the Mission Covenant for the college. The first buildings of North Park College were erected in 1894 and the remainder of the tract was subdivided. The next two years saw the laying out of streets, a few board sidewalks, and the construction of sewer lines in North Park.

The establishment of North Park College attracted an increasing number of Swedes and other Scandinavians into the community. More residents were attracted by the extension of the streetcar service on Lawrence and Elston avenues after the turn of the century. Although the subdivision and sale of lots increased at this time, the population of North Park was only 478 in 1910. The ample vacant acreage in the area was a factor in the decision of the city to establish the Chicago Parental School at Foster and Central Park avenues in 1900 and the Chicago Municipal Tuberculosis Sanitarium at Bryn Mawr Avenue and Pulaski Road in 1905.

After 1910 North Park entered a period of extensive residential development. Subdivision and construction of residential dwellings was concentrated in the region bounded by Bryn Mawr and Kedzie

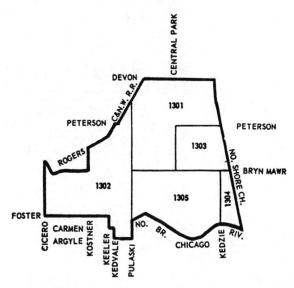

avenues, the river and Pulaski, and to a lesser extent in the section just north of Bryn Mawr Avenue. Until the early 1920s, no apartment buildings were permitted in the community. By the mid-1920s, however, two- and three-flats and a number of small apartment buildings were erected. By 1930, North Park had reached residential maturity despite the fact that there was still some vacant land in the community and some of the recently subdivided sections had yet to be occupied. Except for its few frame structures and the older college buildings, North Park was at this time a young residential community which had developed, within 15 years, from a neighborhood of prairie and woods to one of bungalows and two-flats. During the 1910 to 1930 period, there was virtually no industrial development in North Park.

North Park grew during this period in spite of inadequate transit facilities. The Ravenswood branch of the elevated lines was the only rapid transit line near the community, and its terminal at Kimball and Lawrence avenues was located at least four blocks from North Park's southern boundary. Eventually bus and feeder lines were installed on Foster and Kimball avenues and the Kedzie Avenue car line was extended to Bryn Mawr Avenue, but during the 1930s, North Park was still without direct rapid transportation to downtown Chicago. Lack of adequate transportation was a deterrent to the development of the northern part of the community. The Peterson Industrial District, the

Community Area 13 — North Park
Population and Housing Characteristics, 1930-1980

	1980	1970	1960	1950	1940	1930
Total Population.......	15,273	16,732	17,866	15,291	12,271	11,052
% Male..................	46.4	47.9	48.3	48.3	45.9	48.5
% Female................	53.6	52.1	51.7	51.7	54.1	51.5
% White.................	86.7	95.8	96.7	96.2	98.8	99.1
% Black.................	0.9	2.6	2.9	3.6	0.2	0.6
% Other Nonwhite Races...	12.4	1.6	0.4	0.2	-	0.3
% Under 5 Years Old......	5.0	4.6	5.1	9.4	5.5	8.7
% 5-19 Years Old........	19.8	21.1	25.3	21.0	20.9	23.7
% 20-44 Years Old........	34.6	27.9	27.9	39.9	46.9	49.1
% 45-64 Years Old........	22.6	31.2	31.1	23.6	22.1	15.2
% 65 Years and Older.....	18.0	15.2	10.6	6.1	4.6	3.3
% Median School Years....	12.8	12.4	12.0	12.1	9.3	*
Total Housing Units....	5,582	5,358	5,111	4,039	3,063	*
% In One-Unit Structures.	40.3	43.4	45.3	*	*	*
% Owner Occupied.........	55.2	57.2	60.2	46.5	32.5	*
% Renter Occupied........	41.7	42.0	38.4	51.4	65.5	*
% Vacant.................	3.1	0.8	1.4	2.1	2.0	*
% 1+ Persons per Room....	2.2	1.8	1.8	8.9	*	*

Community Area 13 — North Park
Selected Characteristics of Census Tracts: 1980

Tract Number	Total	1301	1302	1303	1304	1305
Total Population.............	15273	3859	797	4521	81	6015
% Male........................	46.4	46.1	42.4	47.0	-	46.7
% Black.......................	0.9	0.3	3.6	0.2	-	1.5
% Other Nonwhite..............	12.3	13.8	1.9	11.0	-	13.9
% Of Spanish Origin...........	5.5	4.7	2.5	3.5	-	7.9
% Foreign Born................	30.3	29.7	13.7	34.6	-	30.0
% Living In Group Quarters....	7.6	9.3	6.6	0.0	-	12.5
% 13 Years Old And Under......	14.6	15.8	13.3	15.1	-	13.6
% 14-20 Years Old.............	12.5	8.9	14.9	9.6	-	16.8
% 21-64 Years Old.............	55.0	54.3	56.5	55.1	-	55.0
% 65-74 Years Old.............	11.0	12.5	8.8	13.6	-	8.4
% 75 Years Old And Over.......	6.9	8.5	6.5	6.6	-	6.1
% In Different House..........	49.1	43.0	36.8	41.5	-	60.7
% Families With Female Head...	10.1	5.3	12.0	11.7	-	11.7
Median School Years Completed.	12.8	13.3	12.3	12.7	-	12.8
Median Family Income, 1979.....$$	25975	35332	24625	26168	-	22166
% Income Below Poverty Level..	3.1	2.4	3.4	1.8	-	4.1
% Income Of $30,000 Or More...	39.3	62.0	30.1	40.1	-	24.3
% White Collar Workers........	68.1	76.7	54.5	67.9	-	64.7
% Civilian Labor Force Unemployed.	4.5	3.5	5.6	4.7	-	4.9
% Riding To Work By Automobile....	62.1	73.9	76.3	66.6	-	50.2
Mean Commuting Time - Minutes....	27.4	28.3	31.0	29.8	-	24.7
Population Per Household..........	2.6	3.0	2.4	2.5	-	2.5
Total Housing Units..........	5582	1175	316	1865	51	2175
% Condominiums................	2.2	3.1	0.0	1.9	-	2.4
% Built 1970 Or Later.........	3.3	3.6	1.6	1.2	-	5.3
% Owner Occupied..............	55.2	91.7	62.7	47.2	-	42.3
% With 1+ Persons Per Room....	2.2	2.4	0.6	1.9	-	2.6
Median Value: Owner Units.....$$	75000	85200	61300	75700	-	64500
Median Rent: Rental Units......$$	253	299	180	269	-	242
Median Number Of Rooms: All Units.	5.4	5.6	5.1	5.4	-	5.0

Community Area 13 — North Park
Selected Characteristics of Census Tracts: 1970

Tract Number	TOTAL	1301	1302	1303	1304	1305
Total Population.............	16732	4618	895	4748	53	6418
% Male........................	47.9	50.1	43.9	47.7	-	47.1
% Black.......................	2.6	5.7	2.2	0.1	-	2.3
% Other Nonwhite..............	1.6	1.6	1.2	1.0	-	2.0
% Of Spanish Language.........	2.3	0.4	0.0	2.5	-	3.8
% Foreign Born................	23.0	20.4	19.2	26.7	-	22.3
% Living In Group Quarters....	10.4	19.5	8.7	0.1	-	11.8
% 13 Years Old And Under......	14.5	13.0	18.8	14.2	-	15.0
% 14-20 Years Old.............	13.6	12.8	14.3	10.8	-	16.3
% 21-64 Years Old.............	56.6	59.7	52.4	60.2	-	52.6
% 65-74 Years Old.............	9.7	7.8	9.2	10.2	-	10.8
% 75 Years Old And Over.......	5.5	6.7	4.7	4.7	-	5.4
% In Different House..........	57.3	66.1	61.8	59.0	-	49.4
% Families With Female Head...	7.9	4.8	6.8	7.7	-	10.1
Median School Years Completed...	12.4	12.6	11.7	12.3	-	12.3
Median Family Income, 1969.....$$	13695	20207	13542	13163	-	11535
% Income Below Poverty Level....	2.7	2.3	0.0	3.0	-	2.9
% Income of $15,000 or More.....	43.8	69.9	41.8	39.5	-	31.4
% White Collar Workers..........	47.0	63.8	18.4	48.0	-	39.9
% Civilian Labor Force Unemployed.	2.7	1.7	5.9	2.3	-	3.3
% Riding To Work By Automobile....	60.8	73.1	59.3	62.7	-	52.2
Population Per Household..........	2.8	3.3	2.6	2.7	-	2.6
Total Housing Units..........	5389	1129	320	1753	14	2173
% Condominiums & Cooperatives.....	2.5	0.0	0.0	5.2	-	2.0
% Built 1960 Or Later.............	5.3	5.1	2.0	6.7	-	4.8
% Owner Occupied..............	54.2	93.6	62.8	44.4	-	40.3
% With 1+ Persons Per Room....	1.6	1.1	1.9	1.3	-	2.0
Median Value: Owner Units.......$$	31000	34800	22200	31400	-	25500
Median Rent: Rental Units........	137	177	102	145	-	132
Median Number Of Rooms: All Units.	5.4	6.4	5.0	5.4	-	5.0

only industrial section developed in the 1930s, in the northwestern corner of North Park, was isolated from the rest of the community by the Chicago and North Western tracks, the Sanitarium, the cemetery, and the Parental School.

Nevertheless, North Park's population tripled from 3,376 in 1920 to 11,052 in 1930. Swedes remained the dominant ethnic group during this period. During the mid-1920s, Russian Jews began to move into the community. This movement continued through the 1930s as they continued to move northward from Albany Park. A smaller number of Poles were also taking up residence in North Park.

The residential development of North Park slackened during the 1930s. The population increased by less than 10 percent from 11,052 in 1930 to 12,271 in 1940. Most of the increase in population was due to the movement of Russian Jews into the area. By the end of the thirties, the Jewish population was almost as large as the Swedish. The closing of many of the County's junior colleges during the Depression years contributed to the ethnic diversification of North Park College, which became an attractive institution for residents of other Chicago communities.

Residential construction dropped off considerably during World War II, but picked up again in the 1950s. This decade saw the development of a well-to-do residential district in the northern sections of the community in the Hollywood Park and Peterson Park areas. After 1940 new plants and additions to old ones were constructed in the Peterson Industrial District in the northwest corner which, although in decline, still constitutes the manufacturing area of North Park.

During the Second World War and the post-war decades, the population of North Park increased by 46 percent, to a historic high of nearly 18,000 in 1960. Since then, the number of residents has been decreasing, and the current population is about the same as that reported in 1950. Russian Jews were the largest foreign-stock group in 1960, followed by Polish, and these are still the largest descent groups in the community area. As in the past, North Park is for the most part white, but a sizeable number of Asians (especially Koreans and Filipinos) have moved in during the last decade, and they comprise more than 10 percent of the population total. The great majority of residents lives in single or small multiple-dwelling units. More than 43 percent of all units are single-family homes, and 56 percent of all occupied units are lived in by their owners. The median value of owner-occupied homes in North Park is almost $75,000, a figure among the top 10 community area medians in Chicago.

The Municipal Tuberculosis Sanitarium was closed in 1974 and its main building at Pulaski Road and Bryn Mawr Avenue is being converted into a 180-unit senior citizen housing complex called North Park Village. The rest of the 160-acre site will be used for a school for the mentally handicapped and a nature study preserve. Felician College, Northeastern Illinois University, and North Park College are important institutions in North Park. Although they have added parking problems, they have brought young people and cultural activities into the community, and have helped to keep the property values high. North Park College is currently undergoing a major building renovation and expansion.

North Park shares a major retail center with suburban Lincolnwood, to the north, that runs north along Lincoln Avenue from Lincoln Village to Lincolnwood Plaza. Other shopping areas in North Park are on Bryn Mawr, Foster and Peterson avenues. The area is served by the Ravenswood elevated train line.

Rodney Nelson

Community Area 14

Albany Park

Albany Park is located on the Northwest Side of Chicago, about eight miles from the Loop. Irregularly shaped, it is centered at the intersection of Lawrence and Kimball avenues. The community is said to be named after Albany, New York, the home town of De Lancey Lauderbach, one of the earliest real estate developers, who did much to interest settlers in the new community. The name appeared for the first time on the front of the Chicago and North Western elevated trains in 1892. Unlike many northwest communities that grew from initially independent villages, Albany Park was settled in the course of the peripheral expansion of Chicago itself, and particularly through the growth of nearby older and established residential areas such as Irving Park, Ravenswood and Mayfair. The region west of Pulaski Road in northwest Albany Park developed as a part of Mayfair and was settled by many Bohemians during the 1870s and 1880s.

Albany Park was annexed to Chicago in 1889, as part of the Town of Jefferson, and subdivision in the modern sense began in 1905. During the 1880s and early 1890s, many Chicagoans came to the area to attend horse races at the Rusk and Diamond Tracks. After the World's Fair of 1893, a syndicate, which included Lauderbach, purchased 640 acres for subdivision, mostly south of Lawrence Avenue, from the farm of the McAllister family. The installation of an electric streetcar line in 1896 on Lawrence Avenue stimulated development of the area. Later, Lauderbach developed land north of Lawrence Avenue. The completion of the Ravenswood branch of the elevated to Kimball and

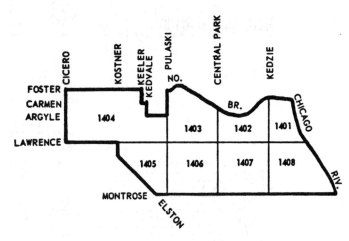

Lawrence avenues in 1907 started a building boom, and lots were widely sought in the area between Montrose, Kedzie, Kimball and Lawrence avenues. In 1909, a tract east of Sacramento and south of Lawrence avenues was subdivided as Ravenswood Manor, and it was settled mainly by Germans, Swedes and some Irish.

The residential community expanded very rapidly after 1910. The population increased from 7,000 in that year to 26,676 in 1920, and to 55,577 in 1930. Albany Park developed into a major commercial and residential district after the completion of the Ravenswood elevated line. A spectacular rise of land values took place at that time, continuing into the 1920s, at which time the community achieved resi-

Community Area 14 -- Albany Park
Population and Housing Characteristics, 1930-1980

	1980	1970	1960	1950	1940	1930
Total Population.......	46,075	47,092	49,450	52,995	56,692	55,577
% Male....................	48.8	47.7	48.2	48.9	48.9	49.1
% Female..................	51.2	52.3	51.8	51.1	51.1	50.9
% White...................	74.0	97.6	99.6	99.8	99.8	99.8
% Black...................	0.6	0.1	0.0	0.1	0.1	0.1
% Other Nonwhite Races...	25.4	2.3	0.4	0.1	0.1	0.1
% Under 5 Years Old......	8.5	8.4	7.6	7.9	5.4	7.3
% 5-19 Years Old.........	22.2	22.9	21.4	18.4	21.6	24.9
% 20-44 Years Old........	40.0	32.9	28.6	37.6	43.3	45.9
% 45-64 Years Old........	18.2	22.7	27.9	27.5	23.9	18.0
% 65 Years and Older.....	11.1	13.1	14.5	8.6	5.8	3.9
Median School Years....	12.2	11.3	10.1	12.4	*	*
Total Housing Units....	17,119	17,081	17,028	16,211	15,740	*
% In One-Unit Structures.	19.1	18.5	18.6	*	8.7	*
% Owner Occupied.........	31.8	32.8	34.3	33.0	24.0	*
% Renter Occupied........	63.3	64.5	63.4	66.1	72.9	*
% Vacant.................	4.9	2.7	2.3	0.9	3.1	*
% 1+ Persons per Room....	9.0	5.4	4.4	9.7	*	*

Community Area 14 -- Albany Park
Selected Characteristics of Census Tracts: 1980

Tract Number	Total	1401	1402	1403	1404	1405	1406	1407	1408
Total Population.............	46075	4096	5499	6352	5467	2946	6904	7640	7171
% Male.......................	48.9	51.7	50.5	48.2	47.4	47.3	48.1	49.3	49.1
% Black......................	0.6	1.7	0.8	0.5	0.0	0.0	0.7	0.8	0.3
% Other Nonwhite.............	25.4	42.3	34.2	27.3	5.3	8.1	22.3	30.9	27.3
% Of Spanish Origin..........	19.7	27.6	20.5	16.2	3.5	7.0	17.9	28.2	27.9
% Foreign Born...............	36.3	54.0	44.2	42.1	17.6	19.6	34.1	38.2	36.1
% Living In Group Quarters...	0.8	0.0	3.3	2.9	0.0	0.0	0.0	0.0	0.3
% 13 Years Old And Under.....	21.4	28.0	22.4	22.2	15.3	15.6	22.2	22.2	21.5
% 14-20 Years Old............	11.3	12.1	11.7	10.8	9.8	9.6	11.8	11.8	11.2
% 21-64 Years Old............	56.2	54.1	54.7	55.6	57.5	56.7	55.6	57.0	57.7
% 65-74 Years Old............	6.5	3.7	5.8	5.8	10.6	11.5	6.2	5.6	5.5
% 75 Years Old And Over......	4.6	2.1	5.3	5.6	6.8	6.6	3.8	3.4	4.1
% In Different House.........	59.6	72.3	80.6	66.3	34.1	42.0	62.7	56.5	57.9
% Families With Female Head..	19.7	20.6	20.3	18.6	11.5	17.2	22.0	21.1	21.6
Median School Years Completed	12.2	12.2	12.3	12.3	12.3	12.1	12.1	12.1	12.4
Median Family Income, 1979...$$	19793	17551	16205	19653	25160	21780	19181	19000	19433
% Income Below Poverty Level.	10.5	15.4	15.0	9.5	1.3	6.2	12.4	10.5	13.6
% Income Of $30,000 Or More..	23.8	17.3	16.2	25.4	33.4	29.0	21.6	23.5	23.4
% White Collar Workers.......	49.9	44.7	50.5	49.2	59.7	48.2	46.3	47.2	51.8
% Civilian Labor Force Unemployed.	6.9	7.2	9.3	6.0	4.2	4.2	7.9	7.0	8.2
% Riding To Work By Automobile....	61.1	58.0	52.6	60.5	68.3	62.8	64.6	57.3	63.5
Mean Commuting Time - Minutes...	30.3	30.4	33.3	31.9	27.7	28.2	29.8	31.4	29.2
Population Per Household..........	2.8	3.2	2.9	2.9	2.6	2.4	2.8	2.8	2.8
Total Housing Units..........	17119	1387	1917	2244	2202	1276	2559	2906	2628
% Condominiums...............	0.1	0.0	1.2	0.0	0.0	0.0	0.0	0.0	0.0
% Built 1970 Or Later........	1.2	2.9	0.5	1.1	1.3	1.5	0.7	1.2	1.0
% Owner Occupied.............	31.8	15.9	17.5	29.4	63.9	45.3	30.6	21.9	31.6
% With 1+ Persons Per Room...	9.0	20.1	14.4	8.1	1.7	3.0	8.0	9.7	9.1
Median Value: Owner Units.......$$	59400	-	49800	60200	62500	54500	54300	47800	63500
Median Rent: Rental Units.......$$	212	214	204	220	223	206	215	208	211
Median Number Of Rooms: All Units.	4.7	4.3	4.2	4.6	5.3	4.8	4.7	4.5	4.8

Community Area 14 -- Albany Park
Selected Characteristics of Census Tracts: 1970

Tract Number	TOTAL	1401	1402	1403	1404	1405	1406	1407	1408
Total Population.............	47092	3762	5270	6217	6123	3398	7326	7724	7272
% Male.......................	47.7	48.2	48.9	47.2	46.8	46.8	48.1	48.4	47.2
% Black......................	0.1	0.2	0.0	0.1	0.0	0.0	0.0	0.1	0.1
% Other Nonwhite.............	2.3	3.8	2.5	2.8	0.6	0.6	2.2	2.3	3.4
% Of Spanish Language........	6.1	14.0	8.6	4.0	1.0	1.2	5.7	6.4	8.5
% Foreign Born...............	22.2	36.1	33.8	24.1	12.3	18.5	20.1	18.8	20.9
% Living In Group Quarters...	0.6	0.1	1.5	2.8	0.0	0.0	0.0	0.0	0.3
% 13 Years Old And Under.....	23.0	26.4	20.9	23.6	20.2	21.4	25.6	23.5	22.2
% 14-20 Years Old............	9.9	9.6	11.1	9.2	10.2	7.7	9.3	10.0	10.7
% 21-64 Years Old............	54.1	52.6	53.7	53.5	54.4	56.4	54.1	55.0	53.3
% 65-74 Years Old............	7.7	6.9	8.3	7.3	9.2	8.5	7.0	6.8	8.3
% 75 Years Old And Over......	5.3	4.5	6.1	6.4	6.0	5.9	4.0	4.7	5.4
% In Different House.........	50.1	32.6	50.2	49.7	67.3	61.4	46.3	43.6	49.7
% Families With Female Head..	12.1	12.6	13.1	11.5	10.6	12.0	12.9	12.7	11.4
Median School Years Completed	11.3	10.2	10.7	10.9	12.0	11.1	11.0	11.3	12.1
Median Family Income, 1969...$$	11021	10032	9581	11288	12497	11258	11140	10748	10944
% Income Below Poverty Level.	6.2	11.5	5.4	6.9	3.7	2.1	6.6	6.4	6.5
% Income of $15,000 or More..	23.7	14.0	21.9	28.0	33.2	20.3	23.5	20.7	23.2
% White Collar Workers.......	23.2	21.9	24.7	25.3	22.0	22.8	21.6	21.3	26.1
% Civilian Labor Force Unemployed.	2.5	7.7	1.0	3.6	2.1	2.4	1.7	2.4	2.1
% Riding To Work By Automobile....	55.6	50.5	49.9	59.7	63.1	60.8	59.1	54.6	47.7
Population Per Household..........	2.8	2.9	2.7	2.9	2.8	2.6	2.9	2.8	2.8
Total Housing Units..........	17079	1349	2035	2162	2199	1323	2541	2852	2618
% Condominiums & Cooperatives.....	0.9	0.6	1.3	1.6	0.6	0.6	0.4	1.1	0.5
% Built 1960 Or Later........	2.3	2.9	0.7	2.6	3.6	3.9	3.4	0.8	1.5
% Owner Occupied.............	32.0	15.6	16.4	29.0	64.5	44.1	30.8	22.4	33.0
% With 1+ Persons Per Room...	5.5	7.3	6.7	4.9	3.1	4.4	6.6	5.6	5.6
Median Value: Owner Units.......$$	22800	-	20700	22800	24200	21100	20900	19400	24000
Median Rent: Rental Units.......$$	113	115	108	118	121	104	115	113	112
Median Number Of Rooms: All Units.	4.7	4.4	4.2	4.6	5.2	4.8	4.7	4.6	4.7

dential maturity. Property in this area was prized highly and changed hands frequently at big profits. Many fine houses were built on Bernard Street north of Ainslee, in the northcentral section. The corner of Lawrence and Pulaski, a street-car intersection, became an important business center and, in the boom of the 1920s, land there sold for $1,000 a front foot. Peak population came in 1940 with a total of 56,692. Since then, the number of inhabitants has declined slowly. In 1960, the population was 49,450; in the 1970 it was 47,092; in 1980, 46,075; a decrease of 2 percent in the last decade. Historically, Albany Park has served as a first stop for many European immigrants, and also as a steppingstone for successive population groups moving away from the older and denser parts of the city, on their way to the outlying areas of the city and the suburbs. The early settlers were Germans and Swedes. Many of them eventually moved farther north, although some emained in the northern and eastern areas of Albany Park, especially in Ravenswood Manor. After 1912, there was a large influx of Russian Jews. Many of them had moved from around Division and Western avenues, in West Town, and from Lawndale. By 1930, they formed the largest group among the foreign-born whites. By the late 1920s, some of the Jews, especially those in the middle- and upper-classes, already had started moving north to Rogers Park, North Park or to the lakefront section of Lakeview. Yet the community maintained a large Jewish population through the 1950s. The majority of these people, more than 70 percent, were native-born, first-generation Americans. In the late 1960s and early 1970s, however, as the Jewish community continued to move north, especially to the northern suburbs, they were replaced by non-English speaking immigrants from Korea, India, Pakistan, Greece, Iran, Yugoslavia and from different Spanish speaking countries. Albany Park is also a first stop for young Israeli immigrants. In addition, a large population of Appalachian whites have moved to the central section south of Lawrence Avenue. In 1950, there were 48 blacks, and in 1980 their number had increased to 279, still less than 1 percent of the total.

Albany Park now has an extremely diversified ethnic mix. Almost two-thirds of the residents are of mixed European origins; 14 percent are Asian, mainly Korean, Asian, Indian and Filipino; 20 percent are Hispanic, mostly Mexican and Puerto Rican but also South American. Von Steuben, one of two high schools serving the community area, reports more than 30 languages are spoken by students' families. A marketing study disclosed that there are 27 identifiable ethnic groups, mostly white and lower middle class in Albany Park now. In the last decade, the groups which have grown most are the east and southeast Asians, from 3 percent of the area's population in 1970 to 11 percent in 1980. The Korean population has jumped from a few individuals to 2,230, by far the largest concentration of Koreans in the city.

With the exception of the rapidly increasing Hispanic and Greek subcommunities, proportions of the other major ethnic groups comprising the area's population, Italians and Scandinavians, have remained fairly constant. The Eastern European group has changed in composition while remaining about the same in numbers. Russian and Polish Jews who died or moved out have been replaced by Yugoslavs, who are also counted in that category.

Very little residential development has taken place since 1930. Nearly all (87 percent) of the housing stock was built before 1939. In the early 1960s, the Albany Park area began to deteriorate. The shopping strip along Lawrence Avenue, large buildings especially, was showing signs of deferred maintenance. Absentee ownership became common. Retail locations closed up, while clusters of blocks along business streets on Kedzie, Lawrence, Montrose, Elston or Pulaski avenues were becoming slums. The city began to consider the possibility of urban renewal, in particular for the central business area around Lawrence and Kedzie avenues. This aroused a great deal of controversy, because many residents had been pushed out of Lincoln Park and the South Side by urban renewal and feared that it meant wholesale demolition again with little rebuilding. The city eventually gave up its plans, presumably because community opposition was too strong to make the project feasible. After that, community leaders attempted to deal with the problems of the area by instituting several programs. Two of these major attempts were the "model block" programs sponsored by the North River Commission and other community groups and a small business loan program administered by the Lawrence Avenue Development Corporation (LADCOR). The North River Commission was founded in 1962 by North Park College, Swedish Covenant Hospital, and the Albany Park Bank, to "provide a framework within the North River community that would clarify common concerns and interests, establish priorities, choose programs of action and mobilize the community's resources." They have been instrumental in the construction of a new CTA terminal at Lawrence and Kimball, the establishment of the North River Mental Health Center in the same central location, the development of the North River Youth Services Program and various other projects.

Today there is a large variety of housing types in Albany Park, but the multi-unit structure predominates. These are made of brick, ranging from the two- and three-flat to the large court apartment buildings of 10 units or more. More than two-thirds of all Albany Park housing units are located at addresses including two-to-nine housing units, while 9 percent are in structures with 10 or more. These large buildings, mostly three- or four-story walk-ups, are especially prevalent in the central sections of the community between Central Park and Kimball avenues. Although larger apartment buildings constitute less than 10 percent of all residential structures, they contain more than 40 percent of the dwelling units, resulting in high density areas in the center of Albany Park.

On the other hand, a large part of the community area, especially in the northwest and southeast corners is covered by single- and two-family dwellings, with well-kept lawns, located on pleasant tree-lined streets. About a third of all housing units are owner-occupied, and 23 percent of all households are located in single-family dwellings, principally bungalows. Approximately three-fourths of the single-family dwellings are one-story, and the rest are two-stories. While the proportions living in single-family and owner-occupied units are lower than those of the city as a whole, single-family housing in Albany Park is expensive. The median value of such homes is $12,000 higher than the city median. There are no large areas of land suitable for residential development. Except for the industrial areas on the west and east fringes of the community, all the land is occupied.

Ariela Royer

Portage Park

In the early 19th century the site of the Portage Park community area was a flat marshy prairie transversed by two parallel ridges — now Cicero and Narragansett avenues — that formed a natural watershed between the drainage systems of the Mississippi River and the Great Lakes. These ridges, and the trail that was to later become Irving Park Road, were popular portage routes for the various Indian tribes and explorers of the time seeking a passage from the Chicago River to the Des Plaines River. Settlement of the area did not start until after the Indian treaty of 1816 and substantial numbers of settlers did not begin arriving until the mid-1830s, at the end of the Blackhawk war.

The major transportation route for settlers in the 1840s was the newly-constructed Northwest Plank Road — now Milwaukee Avenue — and in 1841 E.B. Sutherland build a small combination tavern and inn alongside the road located approximately at the intersection of what is now Milwaukee and Belle Plaine avenues. Sutherland's Inn was sold to Chester Dickinson in 1846 and the Dickinson Tavern, as it was then named, became a well-known gathering place and landmark. In 1850 the town of Jefferson was organized at the Dickinson Tavern with Dickinson becoming the first town supervisor.

Transportation into the Portage Park area was comparatively good in these early years due to the existence of the Northwest Plank Road. The Chicago and North Western Railroad built a track on the eastern boundary which provided access to employment and shopping downtown. The Chicago, Milwaukee and St. Paul Railroad built a spur off its main line to the Cook County poor farm and asylum at Irving Park Road and Narragansett Avenue and this new transportation facility encouraged new settlers to come into the area. In 1862 the Jefferson Town Hall was built at the southeast corner of Irving Park Road and Cicero Avenue, at Milwaukee Avenue, an intersection commonly known today as "Six Corners."

Until the turn of the century the original Portage Park settlement grew slowly but steadily while remaining a quiet suburban community. The 1870s and 1880s witnessed the development of several subdivisions principally in the northern and eastern sections of the Portage Park area. The southern and western sections of the community remained largely prairie land containing truck farms up until the end of the 19th century.

In 1889, when the town of Jefferson was annexed to Chicago by election, most of what is now Portage Park became part of the city. This year also saw the first major real estate deal in Portage Park with the sale of the southwest corner of Cicero Avenue and Irving Park Road to developers Koester and Zander. These developers, along with the Schorsh brothers, are largely credited with the development of the Six Corners shopping area. Most of the settlers in Portage Park at this time were Germans, English, and Swedes.

In 1912 the Portage Park District was organized for the purpose of developing a park in the area. The name "Portage Park" was soon adopted by the residents of the community. In 1915 the city took over a small eight-acre tract bounded by Irving Park Road, Berteau, Central, and Long avenues as the site of the new park. A community house was built and in 1917 an outdoor swimming pool opened. The swimming pool, in reality a large mud hole, proved to be an immediate success, attracting thousands of people, and as a result the Portage Park area became well publicized in the rest of Chicago. The popularity of the park, in combination with the expanded streetcar service, led to the development of more property in Portage Park, particularly in the immediate vicinity of the park. The population of Portage Park had reached 24,439 by 1920.

Although building in Portage Park was interrupted by World War I, residential development quickly resumed during the 1920s as part of

the general northwestern expansion of Chicago.

Residential construction was so widespread in the community during the early twenties that Portage Park may be said to have reached residential maturity by 1924, notwithstanding the fact that small stretches of vacant property remained west of Central Avenue and south of Addison Street. The majority of residential dwellings built in Portage Park during the twenties were one- and two-family homes. In 1930, 80 percent of the dwelling units were single-family homes.

The population of Portage Park nearly tripled during the decade of the twenties. Poles began to move into the community in larger numbers during this decade, chiefly in the southern section of Portage Park. In the northeast corner of the community was a concentration of Czechoslovakians, a continuation of a group to be found north of Lawrence Avenue. The Swedes were beginning to move to communities farther north and northwest of Portage Park. By 1930, Germans, Poles, and Scandinavians were the leading immigrant groups in Portage Park. The population had risen to 64,203 by 1930 and remained roughly stable for 30 years after that.

In 1924, annexation by election of the town of Norwood Park brought the western boundary of the community to its present location by the addition of a small section west of Austin Avenue between Irving Park Road and Gunnison Avenue. In the 1920s an industrial area developed along the railroad tracks on the community's eastern border and in the northeastern corner. This industrial development was especially concentrated at the intersection of two railroad lines, the Chicago and North Western and the Chicago, Milwaukee and St. Paul. Commercial and business activity continued to be concentrated at the Six Corners area, although some commercial activity was scattered along the major streets.

The phenomenal growth of Portage Park in the 1920s and the onset of the Depression combined to inhibit residential growth in the 1930s, although the population reached its historic high, more than 66,000, in 1940. The poor transportation between Portage Park and downtown Chicago helped the Six Corners area to grow during the thirties and a second shopping area developed at Belmont and Central avenues.

Portage Park remained a stable, primarily residential community throughout the 1940s and 1950s. After the Depression industrial construction continued with the building of new plants and additions of old ones in the extreme northeastern corner of the community and the expansion of the industrial area all along the eastern border, from the railraod tracks west to Cicero Avenue. However, the industrial areas of Portage Park are not extensive and are confined for the most part to the

Community Area 15 -- Portage Park
Population and Housing Characteristics, 1930-1980

	1980	1970	1960	1950	1940	1930
Total Population.......	57,349	63,608	65,925	64,736	66,357	64,203
% Male.................	46.2	46.6	47.6	48.6	49.6	50.4
% Female...............	53.8	53.4	52.4	51.4	50.4	49.6
% White................	97.5	99.6	99.9	99.8	100.0	100.0
% Black................	0.1	0.0	0.0	0.1	0.0	0.0
% Other Nonwhite Races...	2.4	0.4	0.1	0.1	0.0	0.0
% Under 5 Years Old......	4.6	6.4	8.1	8.1	5.7	7.7
% 5-19 Years Old.........	18.4	22.2	20.5	18.0	22.0	27.9
% 20-44 Years Old........	32.2	27.7	30.0	37.9	42.7	44.2
% 45-64 Years Old........	25.7	28.3	28.3	28.1	24.5	16.7
% 65 Years and Older.....	19.1	15.4	13.1	7.9	5.1	3.5
Median School Years....	12.2	11.1	10.0	9.5	8.5	*
Total Housing Units....	23,422	23,115	22,342	19,560	18,521	*
% In One-Unit Structures.	37.9	38.8	41.0	*	*	*
% Owner Occupied........	55.9	54.9	56.9	56.1	46.5	*
% Renter Occupied........	41.5	42.9	41.3	43.3	52.0	*
% Vacant................	2.6	2.2	1.8	0.6	1.5	*
% 1+ Persons per Room....	2.0	4.0	4.4	7.1	*	*

Community Area 15 -- Portage Park
Selected Characteristics of Census Tracts: 1980

Tract Number	Total	1501	1502	1503	1504	1505	1506	1507	1508	1509	1510
Total Population.............	57349	302	7055	7067	8120	7218	3815	4135	4375	1549	6267
% Male........................	46.2	52.0	46.6	45.9	44.5	46.8	46.9	47.0	45.9	48.2	47.6
% Black.......................	0.1	0.0	0.1	0.0	0.2	0.3	0.1	0.0	0.0	0.0	0.1
% Other Nonwhite..............	2.4	6.6	3.2	1.4	1.5	1.7	3.1	1.6	2.5	7.6	3.9
% Of Spanish Origin...........	2.6	5.3	3.5	1.8	1.4	2.2	2.3	1.3	3.3	10.3	4.3
% Foreign Born................	18.2	16.8	16.4	17.2	18.1	23.1	16.9	14.4	14.7	16.1	22.0
% Living In Group Quarters....	0.6	0.0	0.0	0.2	1.5	1.9	0.0	0.0	0.0	0.0	0.0
% 13 Years Old And Under......	13.9	18.2	14.2	12.9	12.7	13.9	16.5	14.3	16.6	16.5	14.7
% 14-20 Years Old.............	10.6	8.9	10.6	10.1	10.8	11.9	11.7	11.4	10.7	11.9	9.7
% 21-64 Years Old.............	56.3	60.9	57.8	56.4	55.3	57.1	54.7	54.9	55.7	56.4	58.0
% 65-74 Years Old.............	11.7	8.6	10.7	12.5	12.8	10.8	10.2	11.9	10.3	10.3	11.2
% 75 Years Old And Over.......	7.4	3.3	6.7	8.0	8.3	6.2	6.8	7.5	6.7	5.0	6.5
% In Different House..........	36.9	48.1	42.6	31.5	36.6	37.9	32.5	32.1	38.1	40.2	38.9
% Families With Female Head...	13.6	13.3	16.4	12.0	11.9	14.5	10.3	13.8	14.7	12.5	15.7
Median School Years Completed..	12.2	12.6	12.3	12.0	12.4	12.1	12.1	12.3	12.2	12.2	12.1
Median Family Income, 1979.....$$	23402	28646	22324	25273	24017	25325	21969	24382	20819	18438	21250
% Income Below Poverty Level....	3.4	2.5	4.9	2.5	1.2	1.5	5.5	3.5	5.2	4.0	4.5
% Income Of $30,000 Or More.....	30.0	41.3	28.1	35.1	31.0	35.8	26.6	33.8	25.2	12.8	24.3
% White Collar Workers..........	54.7	56.8	54.3	60.1	53.6	53.6	54.9	58.5	51.5	49.0	51.6
% Civilian Labor Force Unemployed.	4.8	0.0	5.2	3.3	6.1	6.2	3.9	5.9	4.9	6.8	3.5
% Riding To Work By Automobile....	66.4	54.1	58.7	63.1	65.1	72.4	69.7	73.8	64.3	66.2	67.6
Mean Commuting Time - Minutes...	29.2	28.1	27.5	30.2	29.7	30.3	28.4	28.6	30.4	25.9	29.1
Population Per Household.........	2.5	2.4	2.4	2.5	2.5	2.6	2.6	2.7	2.6	2.6	2.4
Total Housing Units..........	23422	129	3050	2955	3237	2774	1469	1629	1783	613	2700
% Condominiums..............	1.4	0.0	0.8	8.1	1.0	0.0	1.6	0.0	1.1	0.0	0.0
% Built 1970 Or Later.......	3.6	5.8	2.9	9.2	3.9	6.2	1.7	0.9	2.3	2.7	2.4
% Owner Occupied............	55.8	44.2	42.3	56.2	63.1	65.9	65.0	63.4	53.6	53.5	43.1
% With 1+ Persons Per Room..	2.0	3.2	2.2	1.1	1.6	2.6	2.0	1.4	1.5	4.6	2.9
Median Value: Owner Units.......$$	61100	-	60700	63700	63800	61800	60800	60300	57500	46500	57700
Median Rent: Rental Units.......$$	216	219	210	231	229	229	221	222	205	206	208
Median Number Of Rooms: All Units.	5.0	4.8	4.9	5.1	5.0	5.0	5.2	5.2	5.0	5.0	4.8

Tract Number	1511	1512
Total Population.............	4134	3312
% Male........................	45.0	45.4
% Black.......................	0.0	0.0
% Other Nonwhite..............	2.2	1.7
% Of Spanish Origin...........	1.4	1.5
% Foreign Born................	21.9	13.9
% Living In Group Quarters....	0.3	0.8
% 13 Years Old And Under......	12.2	11.1
% 14-20 Years Old.............	8.2	10.8
% 21-64 Years Old.............	56.0	55.4
% 65-74 Years Old.............	13.9	13.6
% 75 Years Old And Over.......	9.7	9.0
% In Different House..........	45.6	27.4
% Families With Female Head...	13.7	11.2
Median School Years Completed..	12.0	12.3
Median Family Income, 1979.....$$	22762	25953
% Income Below Poverty Level....	5.7	1.4
% Income Of $30,000 Or More.....	25.0	36.2
% White Collar Workers..........	55.6	55.6
% Civilian Labor Force Unemployed.	5.5	1.8
% Riding To Work By Automobile....	69.7	65.3
Mean Commuting Time - Minutes...	28.3	29.4
Population Per Household.........	2.3	2.6
Total Housing Units..........	1797	1286
% Condominiums..............	0.0	0.0
% Built 1970 Or Later.......	0.7	0.5
% Owner Occupied............	48.6	69.5
% With 1+ Persons Per Room..	1.8	1.5
Median Value: Owner Units.......$$	60200	62500
Median Rent: Rental Units.......$$	210	218
Median Number Of Rooms: All Units.	4.9	5.2

eastern section of the community. In the 1950s the remaining vacant lots in Portage Park were covered with residential dwellings, and a large drainage system improvement to remedy the problem of flooded basements and streets was constructed.

Transportation facilities continued to improve with the extension of bus service through to Harlem Avenue in the fifties. In the late 1950s and early 1960s the Northwest (Kennedy) Expressway was constructed, cutting through the northeast corner of the community area. Other transportation improvements resulted from the construction of the Milwaukee subway line, especially its extension up the Kennedy Expressway to O'Hare Airport, and the development of the Kennedy Rapid Transit terminal in neighboring Jefferson Park. However, in the 1970s local residents, led by Six Corners business owners, became part of a general movement that successfully opposed the construction of the proposed Crosstown Expressway, which would have run parallel to Cicero Avenue.

After hovering around 65,000 for three decades, the population of Portage Park began to decline after 1960, dropping below 60,000 for the first time since 1930 in the most recent 10 years. However, the percentage loss during the 1970s was about the same as that experienced by the city as a whole. Poles, Germans and Italians were the leading ethnic groups in 1960 and have remained so through the last 20 years. About 1,500 Hispanic Americans now live there. Portage Park has always been a white community. Only a few blacks live there now, but about a thousand other non-whites, principally Filipinos and Koreans, have moved in during the last decade.

Community Area 15 -- Portage Park
Selected Characteristics of Census Tracts: 1970

Tract Number	TOTAL	1501	1502	1503	1504	1505	1506	1507	1508	1509	1510
Total Population	63608	297	7957	7724	8682	8282	4171	4587	4942	1719	6878
% Male	46.6	50.2	46.2	46.6	46.3	45.9	46.9	46.6	47.2	48.1	46.8
% Black	0.0	0.0	0.0	0.0	0.0	0.1	0.1	0.0	0.0	0.0	0.0
% Other Nonwhite	0.4	0.3	0.3	0.4	0.1	0.4	0.6	0.3	0.6	0.3	0.6
% Of Spanish Language	1.1	4.4	0.8	0.4	0.8	1.3	1.2	0.1	2.7	1.6	0.5
% Foreign Born	14.5	23.5	14.9	12.9	16.3	12.8	12.0	13.2	9.8	10.7	15.7
% Living In Group Quarters	0.5	0.0	0.1	0.3	0.0	0.0	2.9	0.0	0.0	0.0	0.4
% 13 Years Old And Under	19.4	16.5	19.7	19.3	18.4	21.5	20.1	19.4	21.1	21.2	19.5
% 14-20 Years Old	10.6	7.1	11.0	10.7	9.4	11.8	10.9	10.6	10.2	10.0	9.8
% 21-64 Years Old	54.7	63.3	53.8	53.9	55.4	54.5	53.5	53.5	54.5	58.0	56.1
% 65-74 Years Old	9.5	10.4	10.0	9.2	10.4	7.5	9.6	10.2	9.1	7.6	8.8
% 75 Years Old And Over	5.9	2.7	5.5	6.9	6.3	4.6	5.8	6.3	5.1	3.2	5.8
% In Different House	63.8	50.2	60.5	66.2	61.4	63.3	66.3	67.4	64.0	66.9	60.8
% Families With Female Head	11.8	9.0	11.9	12.3	11.2	10.7	11.2	10.6	12.5	12.7	12.5
Median School Years Completed	11.1	10.0	11.3	11.6	11.1	11.4	11.1	11.6	11.2	10.8	10.4
Median Family Income, 1969 $$	11916	13167	11513	12415	12256	12339	11740	12710	11546	11270	11105
% Income Below Poverty Level	3.9	12.8	4.3	1.7	4.1	3.2	1.6	2.6	7.6	5.3	3.3
% Income of $15,000 or More	29.1	28.0	28.7	35.8	30.4	32.1	25.4	29.1	23.1	20.4	24.3
% White Collar Workers	24.0	24.3	22.9	28.8	24.6	24.6	22.5	22.7	22.5	19.5	22.8
% Civilian Labor Force Unemployed	2.5	3.5	2.5	2.6	1.8	2.7	3.0	2.5	4.4	2.8	2.7
% Riding To Work By Automobile	61.5	61.8	55.6	58.7	62.0	61.9	68.4	69.6	62.8	60.1	62.8
Population Per Household	2.8	2.5	2.7	2.9	2.8	2.9	2.9	2.9	2.8	2.8	2.7
Total Housing Units	23110	126	3014	2757	3204	2778	1475	1603	1814	618	2634
% Condominiums & Cooperatives	0.7	0.0	0.2	2.5	0.2	0.4	0.5	0.5	0.9	0.0	0.8
% Built 1960 Or Later	5.7	8.5	1.4	7.3	8.6	14.8	3.6	5.3	4.1	1.7	2.8
% Owner Occupied	54.2	38.9	41.0	52.1	60.9	64.2	62.8	62.8	50.6	51.8	42.4
% With 1+ Persons Per Room	3.8	4.2	3.8	3.0	3.0	6.2	3.8	3.1	3.9	4.5	4.4
Median Value: Owner Units $$	23600	-	22800	25400	25400	23500	23400	22700	22000	19700	22100
Median Rent: Rental Units $$	116	111	112	126	129	120	114	121	108	104	111
Median Number Of Rooms: All Units	4.9	4.6	4.9	5.1	5.0	4.9	5.0	5.1	4.9	4.9	4.7

Tract Number	1511	1512
Total Population	4634	3735
% Male	46.0	47.5
% Black	0.0	0.0
% Other Nonwhite	0.1	0.5
% Of Spanish Language	0.5	3.1
% Foreign Born	21.4	17.4
% Living In Group Quarters	0.2	0.1
% 13 Years Old And Under	15.3	17.1
% 14-20 Years Old	10.4	11.0
% 21-64 Years Old	55.8	54.1
% 65-74 Years Old	10.8	11.4
% 75 Years Old And Over	7.7	6.4
% In Different House	66.8	65.8
% Families With Female Head	13.7	12.1
Median School Years Completed	10.5	10.8
Median Family Income, 1969 $$	11685	12200
% Income Below Poverty Level	7.2	3.8
% Income of $15,000 or More	29.8	31.3
% White Collar Workers	24.0	23.3
% Civilian Labor Force Unemployed	0.9	1.7
% Riding To Work By Automobile	61.5	56.9
Population Per Household	2.6	2.9
Total Housing Units	1771	1316
% Condominiums & Cooperatives	0.3	0.4
% Built 1960 Or Later	2.3	3.4
% Owner Occupied	49.2	68.6
% With 1+ Persons Per Room	3.1	3.7
Median Value: Owner Units $$	24300	25500
Median Rent: Rental Units $$	118	123
Median Number Of Rooms: All Units	4.9	5.0

Almost 40 percent of all housing units in Portage Park are single-family dwellings, well-kept brick bungalows, many of which were built during the 1920s construction boom. Almost all of the remainder of the housing is in small apartment buildings, of two to nine units, with the owner often in residence, as the 56 percent owner-occupation rate indicates. The median value of a single-family home, more than $60,000, is among the 20 highest in the city.

Few changes have occurred in Portage Park since 1960. In 1959 an Olympic-size swimming pool was built on the site of the old open swimming hole, and the 1972 American Olympic team trials were held there. The park itself was expanded to 36 and a half acres and now includes two recreation houses, tennis courts and baseball diamonds. The main shopping areas, Six Corners, which in 1980 contained approximately 150 stores, and Belmont-Central, which is shared with the neighboring Belmont Cragin community, are major retail centers whose sales volumes were in 1977, respectively, the third and fourth largest in Chicago. However, competiton from the nearby new Brickyard Mall may reduce their sales in the future.

Rodney Nelson

Community Area 16

Irving Park

Located on Chicago's northwest side, the community of Irving Park grew by accretion around the suburban settlements of Montrose, Garyland, and Irving Park. The earliest histories indicate that present-day Milwaukee Avenue and Irving Park Road were old Indian trails. Stagecoaches and truck farmers transporting their goods to the city passed through this area on the muddy and dusty Milwaukee Plank Road.

Montrose, Garyland, and Irving Park each developed around railroad stations. The earliest settlement, located near the present-day crossing of Irving Park Road and the Chicago North Western Railroad, originated on the site of a farm purchased by the Race family in 1869.

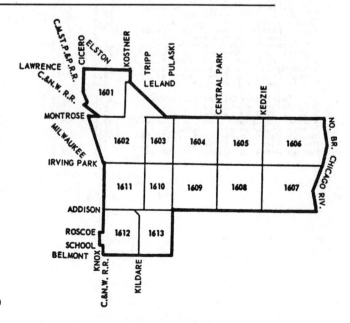

Community Area 16 -- Irving Park
Population and Housing Characteristics, 1930-1980

	1980	1970	1960	1950	1940	1930
Total Population.......	49,489	54,900	58,298	64,881	66,553	66,783
% Male...................	47.2	47.0	47.7	48.4	49.1	49.5
% Female.................	52.8	53.0	52.3	51.6	50.9	50.5
% White..................	90.6	99.1	99.7	99.9	99.9	99.9
% Black..................	0.1	0.1	0.0	0.0	0.0	0.1
% Other Nonwhite Races...	9.3	0.8	0.3	0.1	0.1	0.0
% Under 5 Years Old......	6.1	7.7	9.1	8.6	6.0	7.5
% 5-19 Years Old.........	19.0	21.5	19.6	17.2	20.2	23.9
% 20-44 Years Old........	37.5	31.4	31.8	38.8	44.3	46.0
% 45-64 Years Old........	21.8	25.4	27.3	26.5	22.9	18.1
% 65 Years and Older.....	15.6	8.5	12.2	8.9	6.6	4.5
Median School Years....	12.3	11.1	10.2	9.9	8.7	*
Total Housing Units....	21,350	21,353	20,769	20,614	19,834	*
% In One-Unit Structures.	19.6	19.7	19.7	*	*	*
% Owner Occupied.........	38.1	38.0	38.2	38.2	30.8	*
% Renter Occupied........	58.4	59.1	59.3	60.6	66.8	*
% Vacant.................	3.5	2.9	2.5	1.2	3.4	*
% 1+ Persons per Room....	2.9	4.0	4.7	8.5	*	*

Community Area 16 -- Irving Park
Selected Characteristics of Census Tracts: 1980

Tract Number	Total	1601	1602	1603	1604	1605	1606	1607	1608	1609	1610
Total Population............	49489	2270	3455	3739	4526	6269	6613	5327	4436	2771	2142
% Male......................	47.2	46.9	47.2	43.2	47.2	47.4	47.6	47.5	45.9	47.6	49.1
% Black.....................	0.1	0.0	0.1	0.2	0.1	0.2	0.1	0.4	0.1	0.0	0.0
% Other Nonwhite............	9.3	4.3	5.3	9.2	7.7	13.5	16.6	9.9	9.3	5.6	3.1
% Of Spanish Origin.........	8.6	3.3	4.5	5.9	8.9	13.6	13.8	9.9	9.2	6.1	5.4
% Foreign Born..............	19.4	13.7	12.2	20.7	17.0	22.9	25.5	23.0	17.2	16.9	13.3
% Living In Group Quarters..	1.0	0.0	1.7	3.5	0.0	0.0	0.2	4.6	0.0	1.3	0.0
% 13 Years Old And Under....	16.5	17.4	18.2	9.9	16.2	18.7	18.0	17.3	16.5	17.4	14.1
% 14-20 Years Old...........	10.4	11.2	11.6	7.0	10.4	11.0	10.7	10.2	10.1	11.8	11.7
% 21-64 Years Old...........	57.5	55.4	55.7	60.8	57.7	57.6	58.3	55.1	56.3	56.2	59.0
% 65-74 Years Old...........	9.4	10.4	9.4	12.5	9.5	7.5	7.9	9.1	10.7	9.1	9.5
% 75 Years Old And Over.....	6.2	5.6	5.1	9.7	6.1	5.2	5.1	8.4	6.4	5.5	5.7
% In Different House........	43.5	42.0	36.8	57.4	41.3	45.5	46.6	43.4	41.6	34.9	42.8
% Families With Female Head..	18.8	13.2	11.8	23.8	19.1	21.2	21.0	19.9	18.7	16.8	18.9
Median School Years Completed	12.3	12.4	12.3	12.5	12.3	12.2	12.3	12.2	12.2	12.3	12.5
Median Family Income, 1979....$$	21089	26307	24338	18611	21209	20117	20553	21464	20263	22470	21455
% Income Below Poverty Level....	6.6	2.0	5.3	6.5	7.3	8.8	10.0	5.9	6.7	4.3	2.6
% Income Of $30,000 Or More....	24.8	35.8	32.6	18.5	23.6	17.6	22.7	26.0	23.6	27.6	29.2
% White Collar Workers.........	54.3	56.6	58.0	61.5	50.4	51.3	54.7	55.9	54.3	58.7	60.5
% Civilian Labor Force Unemployed.	6.2	7.5	5.4	5.6	4.7	6.1	8.4	5.0	4.9	7.9	5.6
% Riding To Work By Automobile....	62.3	64.2	62.0	55.4	63.2	62.9	66.5	70.2	61.0	56.1	57.6
Mean Commuting Time - Minutes...	27.8	27.8	24.8	30.4	29.3	27.6	28.2	27.9	25.1	27.6	32.6
Population Per Household........	2.4	2.6	2.6	1.8	2.3	2.5	2.4	2.5	2.5	2.6	2.4
Total Housing Units.........	21350	911	1352	2027	2012	2637	2847	2121	1882	1102	933
% Condominiums..............	2.2	2.5	0.0	21.3	0.0	0.0	0.4	0.0	0.0	0.0	0.0
% Built 1970 Or Later.......	1.9	3.1	1.6	9.1	0.4	0.1	1.2	0.8	1.3	0.0	1.0
% Owner Occupied............	38.1	51.4	50.5	28.5	35.3	34.4	27.7	43.4	42.7	46.8	36.3
% With 1+ Persons Per Room....	2.9	2.3	2.3	2.1	2.6	4.2	4.0	2.8	2.4	2.2	2.1
Median Value: Owner Units......$$	53800	58900	57800	58600	52500	45000	47700	49100	47600	61400	59300
Median Rent: Rental Units....	201	212	189	216	192	202	214	198	196	207	206
Median Number Of Rooms: All Units.	4.7	5.1	5.1	3.9	4.6	4.7	4.5	4.9	5.0	5.2	4.8

Tract Number	1611	1612	1613
Total Population............	2320	2444	4046
% Male......................	52.9	49.0	46.4
% Black.....................	0.1	0.0	0.0
% Other Nonwhite............	0.3	0.6	1.3
% Of Spanish Language.......	1.6	0.0	2.2
% Foreign Born..............	11.1	10.5	14.9
% Living In Group Quarters..	0.3	0.5	0.2
% 13 Years Old And Under....	21.7	22.0	18.4
% 14-20 Years Old...........	12.4	10.0	9.7
% 21-64 Years Old...........	54.4	54.9	56.8
% 65-74 Years Old...........	7.5	8.6	9.6
% 75 Years Old And Over.....	4.0	4.6	5.5
% In Different House........	59.0	62.6	59.5
% Families With Female Head..	10.3	9.7	12.7
Median School Years Completed	12.2	10.0	10.9
Median Family Income, 1969....$$	12677	11769	10674
% Income Below Poverty Level....	1.3	1.3	1.3
% Income Of $15,000 Or More....	29.0	23.3	21.0
% White Collar Workers.........	23.6	17.4	15.7
% Civilian Labor Force Unemployed.	5.2	3.6	1.4
% Riding To Work By Automobile....	56.1	54.3	50.9
Population Per Household........	2.6	2.9	2.4
Total Housing Units.........	931	870	1703
% Condominiums & Cooperatives.....	0.5	1.1	0.3
% Built 1960 Or Later.............	4.0	5.1	1.5
% Owner Occupied..................	37.8	53.2	32.9
% With 1+ Persons Per Room........	3.9	5.6	3.9
Median Value: Owner Units......$$	23400	21500	20500
Median Rent: Rental Units....$$	92	99	101
Median Number Of Rooms: All Units.	4.6	4.8	4.4

Abandoning plans to farm the area and start a business, the family subdivided and sold the land after the Chicago and North Western Railroad agreed to stop its trains at the proposed town. Named after Washington Irving, the village was originally called Irvington, but was renamed Irving Park. The advantages of transportation and good drainage drew settlers to the area, especially after the Chicago Fire of 1871. By 1875, Irving Park and its 60 homes was considered a very fashionable suburb. The village continued to grow by subdividing to the south and west.

At the same time, the suburban town of Montrose (later called Mayfair) was established at the crossing of two railroads, the Chicago, Milwaukee, and St. Paul and the Chicago and North Western. Located in the northwest section of the present community, this 80-acre tract was purchased in 1864 for $800. Montrose was laid out 10 years later following the heavy exodus of settlers toward Jefferson Township after the Chicago Fire. Like Irving Park, its original settlers were English, Germans, and Swedes. Through subdivisions and additions, Montrose grew until its southern boundary lay adjacent to the village of Irving Park.

In the southwestern section of the community, the village of Garyland grew up around the station by that name on the Chicago, Milwaukee, and St. Paul Railroad near Milwaukee Avenue. Originally the farm of John Gray, the area was subdivided in 1873.

These three communities became part of the city of Chicago in 1889 when the township of Jefferson was annexed by election. As the areas around Mayfair and Irving Park were further subdivided, the present community area continued to attract residents because of its excellent water supply, good drainage, and easy access to transportation. The installation of electric surface and car lines on many of the community's major streets tied Irving Park to the heart of the city.

The turn of the century was accompanied by the urbanization and growth of Irving Park. Although subdivision into town lots had begun 30 years earlier, the years between 1900 and 1920 saw the development of Irving Park's present residential form. The intensity of residential construction activity during these two decades is indicated by the fact that 85 percent of the housing units in 1940 had been constructed between 1895 and 1925. The distinctive suburban atmosphere of Irving Park, characterized by new one- and two-story homes as well as fashionable apartment buildings, attracted so many new residents that by 1910 its population had grown to 14,748. Residential construction was accompanied by business development along Irving Park Road and scattered commercial development along several other thoroughfares.

41

Community Area 16 — Irving Park
Selected Characteristics of Census Tracts: 1970

Tract Number	TOTAL	1601	1602	1603	1604	1605	1606	1607	1608	1609	1610
Total Population.............	54900	2636	3795	3905	5075	6985	7112	5985	5111	2986	2500
% Male.......................	47.0	47.9	47.2	43.1	46.6	47.5	46.8	47.5	46.1	47.2	46.8
% Black......................	0.0	0.0	0.0	0.1	0.0	0.0	0.1	0.2	0.0	0.1	0.0
% Other Nonwhite.............	0.8	0.6	0.8	1.1	0.7	0.5	1.1	0.7	1.0	1.0	0.6
% Of Spanish Language........	2.9	3.7	2.9	1.4	3.3	4.2	4.4	4.0	1.6	1.8	2.6
% Foreign Born...............	14.7	12.3	10.1	14.6	14.3	16.2	19.9	16.5	15.0	12.7	9.4
% Living In Group Quarters...	0.8	0.3	1.6	3.2	0.3	0.1	0.0	2.2	0.2	1.3	1.2
% 13 Years Old And Under.....	20.7	23.2	22.7	14.1	21.0	22.5	21.5	21.3	20.3	19.7	20.0
% 14-20 Years Old............	10.0	10.3	12.0	6.3	9.8	9.9	9.5	9.5	9.4	11.9	13.1
% 21-64 Years Old............	55.3	54.8	53.0	59.2	54.3	54.9	55.9	55.6	55.0	54.5	53.5
% 65-74 Years Old............	8.8	7.0	7.7	12.5	9.5	8.0	8.4	8.4	10.0	8.7	7.8
% 75 Years Old And Over......	5.2	4.7	4.6	8.0	5.5	4.6	4.6	5.2	5.3	5.1	5.6
% In Different House.........	54.7	53.3	64.0	39.3	52.9	47.5	49.6	58.0	59.7	58.6	62.0
% Families With Female Head..	12.5	12.1	13.5	12.6	12.9	12.9	12.7	11.1	13.4	10.3	14.5
Median School Years Completed	11.1	11.8	12.0	11.7	11.0	10.9	11.1	10.5	10.3	11.8	12.0
Median Family Income, 1969......$$	11254	12691	11775	12246	10456	10892	10797	11438	10996	11652	11398
% Income Below Poverty Level....	4.6	3.3	4.1	6.2	4.7	6.7	4.4	3.4	4.2	7.3	7.3
% Income of $15,000 or More....	24.5	36.4	28.9	30.6	18.2	23.5	19.5	26.2	23.7	25.9	27.1
% White Collar Workers.......	21.8	24.8	26.2	31.2	22.6	18.8	21.0	19.3	18.8	24.5	27.0
% Civilian Labor Force Unemployed.	2.6	1.1	1.3	2.7	2.9	2.5	2.8	2.7	2.2	1.7	5.2
% Riding To Work By Automobile....	56.2	59.4	62.3	58.6	56.1	55.6	55.5	53.9	52.7	61.6	61.9
Population Per Household......	2.6	2.9	2.8	2.1	2.6	2.7	2.6	2.8	2.7	2.7	2.7
Total Housing Units.........	21357	936	1350	1907	2030	2670	2840	2181	1916	1098	925
% Condominiums & Cooperatives....	1.7	3.0	0.0	12.7	0.3	0.4	0.9	0.7	0.4	0.5	0.0
% Built 1960 Or Later........	4.6	6.9	4.1	25.4	1.2	1.1	3.3	2.8	1.1	0.9	2.7
% Owner Occupied.............	36.4	48.5	49.3	9.4	37.0	34.6	28.1	44.0	43.3	46.1	36.0
% With 1+ Persons Per Room...	3.8	4.7	5.3	2.2	3.1	4.9	3.6	3.8	3.2	2.8	4.0
Median Value: Owner Units.......$$	21100	22600	21400	24000	19600	18500	19000	20400	20400	23500	22500
Median Rent: Rental Units.......$$	107	113	103	113	104	107	112	107	106	107	113
Median Number Of Rooms: All Units.	4.7	5.0	5.0	3.8	4.6	4.7	4.5	4.9	5.0	5.1	4.7

Tract Number	1611	1612	1613
Total Population.............	2100	2167	3674
% Male.......................	52.7	48.1	46.1
% Black......................	0.0	0.1	0.1
% Other Nonwhite.............	5.3	7.0	6.9
% Of Spanish Origin..........	3.3	6.6	5.9
% Foreign Born...............	13.2	16.7	21.9
% Living In Group Quarters...	0.0	0.0	0.1
% 13 Years Old And Under.....	15.8	16.2	14.6
% 14-20 Years Old............	11.0	11.4	9.0
% 21-64 Years Old............	59.6	57.5	59.2
% 65-74 Years Old............	9.0	9.2	11.1
% 75 Years Old And Over......	4.7	5.7	6.0
% In Different House.........	34.9	33.8	49.9
% Families With Female Head..	18.4	16.2	18.0
Median School Years Completed	12.4	11.7	11.5
Median Family Income, 1979......$$	24631	20500	18025
% Income Below Poverty Level....	10.6	2.3	5.2
% Income Of $30,000 Or More....	39.5	28.7	18.9
% White Collar Workers.......	53.8	46.9	47.0
% Civilian Labor Force Unemployed.	8.5	4.4	6.4
% Riding To Work By Automobile....	58.8	65.6	57.2
Mean Commuting Time - Minutes...	25.6	27.8	28.2
Population Per Household......	2.3	2.6	2.2
Total Housing Units.........	944	864	1718
% Condominiums...............	0.0	0.0	0.0
% Built 1970 Or Later........	2.8	3.1	0.0
% Owner Occupied.............	39.1	55.3	33.2
% With 1+ Persons Per Room...	1.6	4.0	3.2
Median Value: Owner Units.......$$	61900	53700	48800
Median Rent: Rental Units.......$$	155	187	187
Median Number Of Rooms: All Units.	4.8	4.9	4.4

Prior to 1920, various industries were also established on Montrose Avenue and Irving Park Road near the North Branch of the Chicago River and along the railroad in the western section of the community.

Beginning in 1900, the intensive settlement of several ethnic groups, particularly the Germans and the Swedes, contributed to the dramatic increase in population from 14,748 in 1910 to 42,467 in 1920. The planning, subdivision, and development of Irving Park Villa — a small residential triangle bounded by Addison, Pulaski, and the Chicago and North Western — occurred during this period. By 1920, then, the present spatial layout of Irving already had been well established.

Irving Park felt the impact of the general expansion of the city to the north and northwest during the 1920s, but to lesser extent than neighboring communities to the north and west. Whereas the previous two decades saw the residential development of the community, the 1920s was a period of intensive business development. A commercial real estate boom provided the impetus for heavy development along Irving Park Road. Other thoroughfares were also lined with stores, offices, and apartment buildings. By this time, the area of thickest residential settlement was around the Irving Park railroad station. Construction of bungalows and apartment buildings continued in Mayfair, while the area east of Kedzie Avenue (known as California Park) remained sparsely settled.

Large numbers of Germans and Scandinavians left the community during the 1920s, but their exodus was compensated for by a heavy influx of Poles. Russians and Czechoslvakians also moved in along the northern boundary. The community reached its peak population of 66,783 in 1930, with Germans, Scandinavians, Poles, and Russians dominating the foreign stock.

The population of Irving Park declined in each decade after 1930, with a total decline of almost 26 percent between 1930 and 1980. In 1940, Germans and Swedes were the leading nationalities, and 20 years later Germans, Poles, and Italians made up much of the foreign stock. However, the number of foreign-born declined, and by 1960 national origins were quite heterogeneous, with no one group making up more than 10 percent of the population. People of German, Irish and Polish descent are most numerous today. The last decade has seen a significant increase of Hispanics and Asiatics, especially Filipinos.

By 1940, land use in Irving Park was 87 percent residential, 10 percent commercial or business, and 2 percent industrial. Manufacturing expanded along the western railroad boundary of the community in the 1940s. At the same time, a new industrial district developed along Addison Avenue from the Chicago and North Western to Kedzie. Otherwise, older manufacturing plants remained confined to the eastern and western sections of the community. Commercial development also stabilized by mid-century. The major thoroughfares continued to be characterized by a dense concentration of business establishments serving the community. New residential contruction virtually stopped; 96 percent of the 1960 housing units were built before 1940. By 1980, 23 percent of the residences were single-family structures, 38 percent were owner-occupied. The median value of owner-occupied single units is among the top third of all community areas in the city.

Since 1960, the rate of population decrease has leveled out and the proportion of residents of foreign stock has continued to decline. Some new residential construction occurred during the 1960s, and the amount of land used for business lining the major streets of the community remains excessive. Although many of Irving Park's major streets do not have the capacity to carry present traffic loads, transportation has been improved by the completion of the Northwest Expressway (renamed the John F. Kennedy Expressway) in 1960, which cuts diagonally across the western portion of the community. The extension of the CTA subway line down the middle of the expressway was completed in 1970.

Peter Vukosavich

Dunning

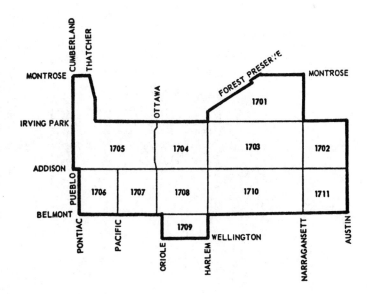

White settlers began arriving in the area shortly after the Indian treaty of 1833 and began farming the prairie land. At the close of the Civil War, an officer named Andrew Dunning arrived in the area and settled on a 120-acre farm. Dunning later became a land developer in Jefferson Township and platted the area around Irving Park Road and Nashville Avenue which became the nucleus of the settlement named after him.

An important factor in the early history of the Dunning area was the decision to locate the Cook County Infirmary and Insane Asylum just north of Irving Park Road outside the city limits. The Asylum, later renamed the Chicago State Hospital, was constructed in 1868 on land donated by Andrew Dunning.

To facilitate transportation to and from the county institutions, the city arranged with the Chicago, Milwaukee and St. Paul Railroad for the construction of a spur connecting with the main line of the railroad. In 1882 a small wooden depot was built adjacent to the Dunning settlement at Irving Park Road and Nashville. The depot was named Dunning after the settlement. Swedes, Germans, and native Americans were the dominant nationalities among settlers in the Dunning area at this time.

In 1889 portions of Dunning were annexed to Chicago as part of the township of Jefferson. At the turn of the century, Dunning was widely known for a number of picnic groves along Irving Park Road. Particularly popular was Kolze's Grove, an 8-acre wooded tract at the corner of Narragansett Avenue and Irving Park Road. Housing at this time was primarily located in the northeastern section in the vicinity of the Dunning railroad station, but other houses were scattered throughout Dunning. Until 1910, Dunning remained a detached suburban community, primarily a region of truck farms, with a few small stores and saloons on Irving Park Road near Neenah Avenue which did business with visitors to the County institutions.

Residential growth increased in Dunning in the decade after 1910 despite the interruption due to World War I. The population of Dunning had grown to 4,019 by 1920. Although hampered by generally poor transportaion facilities, the great building boom during the '20s on the north and northwest side of Chicago encompassed parts of Dunning as well and by 1930 the community's population had swelled to 19,659. By the mid-1920s, with the western boundary then at Harlem Avenue, one-seventh of the land in Dunning was occupied by cemeteries and one-half of the remaining land was vacant. Germans, Poles, and Swedes continued to be the dominant ethnic groups in Dunning in 1930.

Settlement began west of Harlem Avenue in the 1920s when this area was still outside the city limits. Poorly-constructed houses were built at random on what was mostly a vast weed-ridden prairie. Some of these structures were nothing more than shanties. This district, which included parts of the towns of Leyden and Norwood Park and the village of River Grove, was annexed to Chicago by ordinance in 1928 and 1929. The only manufacturing area in Dunning had developed on Dakin Street in the northeastern portion of the community in the vicinity of the railroad tracks.

The population of Dunning continued to grow at a steady rate after 1930 reaching 41,626 in 1960. An increasing number of Italians moved into the community after 1930 and by 1960 they were the third largest ethnic group in the community behind the Poles and Germans.

Residential construction also continued steadily after 1930. As late as 1940, the area west of Harlem Avenue was considered an area of arrested residential development, virtually a rural slum area. There were many vacant lots with poorly constructed cheap frame houses scattered among them. Since this region was not annexed to the city until 1928 and therefore not protected by the city building laws, many poorly constructed frame dwellings were erected on small lots. Even after annexation, while new construction was better and more substantial, there was still no zoning in this area. Without zoning protection, residential construction was hampered by the possible future threat of invasion by commercial and industrial buildings. When this area was zoned, active residential construction began. While residential construction since 1930 has been scattered throughout the community, it has tended to concentrate in this area west of Harlem Avenue.

The number of residents in Dunning continued to increase in the decades after World War II, peaking at almost 44,000 in 1970. In the last 10 years, the population has gone down by 6,000, a loss proportionately greater than that experienced by the city in the same period. The population of Dunning is almost entirely white, with fewer than 400 non-whites living there now. Six hundred residents are of Spanish origin. The neighborhood is stable and quiet with a low crime rate.

Although there are some office and industrial buildings in Dunning, the area is primarily residential. Most of the residential growth occurred between 1940 and 1960. At the end of that period, about half of the housing in the community area had been built during the preceding 20 years. Construction has slowed down since then, but today there are more than 14,000 units, 70 percent of which are single-family dwellings. Home ownership is prevalent, 78 percent of all occupied units are owner occupied. The median value of owner-occupied single-family dwellings in Dunning is among the top fifth of Chicago community area medians.

The main shopping and business area is located in the adjacent suburb of Norridge. The Harlem-Irving Plaza is the centerpoint of this area and the Norridge Commons shopping facilities are located across from the Plaza. The Harlem-Irving Plaza underwent expansion during the 1970s in an attempt to halt the trend of shoppers going to shopping malls in the surrounding communities. There is also a shopping area along Belmont Avenue in the southern section of Dunning.

Wright Junior College, which was established in 1934, is a prominent educational institution located on Austin Avenue on the eastern border of the community. The Chicago-Read Mental Health Center is located in the northeast corner.

Rodney Nelson

43

Community Area 17 — Dunning
Population and Housing Characteristics, 1930-1980

	1980	1970	1960	1950	1940	1930
Total Population.......	37,860	43,856	41,626	32,231	23,328	19,659
% Male..................	47.7	48.0	48.9	49.5	50.9	51.7
% Female................	52.3	52.0	51.1	50.5	49.1	48.3
% White.................	98.2	99.1	99.8	100.0	99.9	99.9
% Black.................	0.5	0.7	0.0	0.0	0.0	0.0
% Other Nonwhite Races...	1.3	0.2	0.2	0.0	0.1	0.0
% Under 5 Years Old......	4.2	5.6	8.4	9.5	7.2	10.8
% 5-19 Years Old.........	19.1	23.5	24.2	22.4	28.3	31.8
% 20-44 Years Old........	30.1	27.5	30.3	38.8	40.8	42.4
% 45-64 Years Old........	28.3	30.3	28.0	24.1	20.3	13.0
% 65 Years and Older.....	18.3	13.1	9.1	5.2	3.4	2.0
Median School Years....	12.1	10.9	9.9	9.4	8.4	*
Total Housing Units....	14,161	14,185	12,897	9,154	6,205	*
% In One-Unit Structures.	70.4	72.3	78.5	*	*	*
% Owner Occupied.........	76.2	76.9	80.5	79.7	65.7	*
% Renter Occupied........	21.9	21.7	17.9	18.3	32.4	*
% Vacant.................	1.9	1.4	1.6	2.0	2.9	*
% 1+ Persons per Room....	2.3	4.9	6.3	9.2	*	*

Community Area 17 — Dunning
Selected Characteristics of Census Tracts: 1980

Tract Number	Total	1701	1702	1703	1704	1705	1706	1707	1708	1709	1710
Total Population.............	37860	509	3500	4691	3853	4893	2605	3075	3467	1517	6352
% Male........................	47.7	63.1	46.9	48.0	47.7	49.0	47.8	47.6	47.3	47.2	47.0
% Black.......................	0.5	35.6	0.0	0.0	0.0	0.0	0.0	0.0	0.0	0.0	0.0
% Other Nonwhite..............	1.3	2.2	1.1	1.6	1.4	2.0	1.7	0.7	1.2	0.8	0.8
% Of Spanish Origin...........	1.6	5.1	1.3	1.6	1.5	1.3	1.5	2.0	1.0	1.5	1.9
% Foreign Born................	17.3	6.6	16.0	13.8	21.4	15.2	16.9	22.8	18.8	18.4	15.1
% Living In Group Quarters....	1.3	100.0	0.0	0.0	0.0	0.0	0.0	0.0	0.0	0.0	0.0
% 13 Years Old And Under......	13.9	11.6	15.2	14.5	14.9	15.4	14.1	14.2	13.9	11.4	11.9
% 14-20 Years Old.............	11.1	21.4	12.7	11.0	10.8	10.9	11.2	11.3	11.1	10.3	10.5
% 21-64 Years Old.............	56.7	62.5	54.8	57.6	56.3	57.3	55.6	56.6	56.8	57.9	56.1
% 65-74 Years Old.............	11.9	3.1	10.9	10.9	12.1	11.1	12.2	11.6	11.6	13.7	14.3
% 75 Years Old And Over.......	6.4	1.4	6.3	6.0	5.8	5.3	6.4	6.2	6.7	6.7	7.1
% In Different House..........	29.1	98.1	22.4	31.0	25.4	26.4	27.6	35.8	22.4	34.8	28.3
% Families With Female Head...	10.6	-	8.7	9.6	12.4	12.4	11.2	9.8	12.3	12.0	9.3
Median School Years Completed..	12.1	12.3	12.2	12.2	12.2	12.2	12.1	12.0	12.0	12.0	12.1
Median Family Income, 1979......$$	24446	-	25271	24708	25531	24893	24175	23482	22816	23281	24748
% Income Below Poverty Level....	2.9	-	0.8	2.6	0.4	3.0	4.7	5.6	5.1	4.5	2.3
% Income Of $30,000 Or More.....	34.8	-	35.1	31.3	39.0	35.7	39.6	31.6	31.3	26.6	35.9
% White Collar Workers..........	50.9	-	52.5	52.2	45.3	49.5	52.5	48.6	46.8	46.0	54.3
% Civilian Labor Force Unemployed.	4.5	-	3.6	2.9	6.0	4.2	4.0	3.7	5.2	8.3	4.5
% Riding To Work By Automobile....	74.8	-	73.6	71.4	74.9	77.0	80.8	76.6	75.0	78.6	74.4
Mean Commuting Time - Minutes....	30.8	-	30.2	28.7	33.3	30.1	28.7	29.3	33.3	33.5	30.9
Population Per Household..........	2.7	-	2.9	2.7	2.7	2.8	2.8	2.6	2.6	2.6	2.6
Total Housing Units...........	14161	0	1240	1770	1429	1789	950	1192	1351	664	2449
% Condominiums................	0.8	-	0.0	1.2	0.0	0.0	1.1	0.0	3.6	0.0	1.6
% Built 1970 Or Later.........	4.8	-	0.0	4.7	5.8	4.5	10.2	6.5	5.4	3.8	3.6
% Owner Occupied..............	76.1	-	77.7	70.3	79.8	82.4	84.2	72.5	74.5	63.4	76.4
% With 1+ Persons Per Room....	2.3	-	1.9	2.5	2.6	2.3	2.8	3.0	2.4	2.4	1.6
Median Value: Owner Units.......$$	63500	-	61800	62900	62100	64700	63700	60800	62200	61600	66700
Median Rent: Rental Units.....$$	240	-	217	250	255	260	239	234	239	249	244
Median Number Of Rooms: All Units.	5.1	-	5.4	5.0	5.0	5.3	5.1	4.9	4.9	4.8	5.2

Tract Number	1711
Total Population.............	3834
% Male........................	46.1
% Black.......................	0.0
% Other Nonwhite..............	0.2
% Of Spanish Language.........	1.6
% Foreign Born................	18.9
% Living In Group Quarters....	0.0
% 13 Years Old And Under......	17.4
% 14-20 Years Old.............	11.2
% 21-64 Years Old.............	54.0
% 65-74 Years Old.............	12.0
% 75 Years Old And Over.......	5.3
% In Different House..........	60.0
% Families With Female Head...	12.0
Median School Years Completed..	11.2
Median Family Income, 1969......$$	12624
% Income Below Poverty Level....	4.7
% Income of $15,000 or More.....	35.4
% White Collar Workers..........	33.1
% Civilian Labor Force Unemployed.	2.1
% Riding To Work By Automobile....	55.6
Population Per Household..........	2.9
Total Housing Units...........	1335
% Condominiums & Cooperatives.....	0.0
% Built 1960 Or Later.........	9.5
% Owner Occupied..............	74.9
% With 1+ Persons Per Room....	4.1
Median Value: Owner Units.......$$	26300
Median Rent: Rental Units.....$$	121
Median Number Of Rooms: All Units.	5.1

Community Area 17 — Dunning
Selected Characteristics of Census Tracts: 1970

Tract Number	TOTAL	1701	1702	1703	1704	1705	1706	1707	1708	1709	1710
Total Population..............	43856	1668	3812	5126	5264	5330	2929	3498	3822	1681	6892
% Male....................	48.0	52.2	46.1	47.8	48.7	48.8	48.2	49.2	47.5	49.1	47.7
% Black...................	0.7	17.9	0.0	0.0	0.1	0.1	0.0	0.0	0.0	0.0	0.0
% Other Nonwhite..........	0.2	0.4	0.2	0.1	0.1	0.6	0.4	0.1	0.1	0.1	0.2
% Of Spanish Language......	0.8	3.9	0.3	1.3	0.0	0.4	0.0	2.0	0.3	0.0	0.6
% Foreign Born............	14.8	11.9	10.1	16.0	16.3	12.5	14.4	19.6	14.1	16.9	13.0
% Living In Group Quarters........	3.8	95.9	0.6	0.0	0.0	0.0	0.5	0.1	0.0	0.0	0.2
% 13 Years Old And Under.........	19.2	6.1	21.7	20.7	21.5	21.4	19.1	20.6	20.1	15.7	16.8
% 14-20 Years Old.........	11.3	9.7	11.9	11.0	11.3	12.4	12.9	10.6	11.2	11.3	10.7
% 21-64 Years Old.........	56.4	57.1	52.0	57.0	55.7	56.5	57.3	57.1	57.2	59.9	58.0
% 65-74 Years Old.........	8.6	14.2	8.8	7.3	7.5	6.7	7.2	8.1	7.9	9.0	9.9
% 75 Years Old And Over...	4.5	12.9	5.6	3.9	4.1	3.0	3.6	3.5	3.7	4.1	4.6
% In Different House......	65.5	45.7	65.7	63.5	66.0	68.9	70.3	60.5	64.3	71.5	71.3
% Families With Female Head.......	9.4	11.1	11.2	10.3	8.1	7.4	7.2	8.8	8.9	8.6	10.6
Median School Years Completed.....	10.9	8.2	11.4	11.5	10.8	11.6	10.8	10.0	10.5	10.2	11.0
Median Family Income, 1969.....$$	12129	18235	12913	12177	11377	12622	12265	12000	11284	11265	12650
% Income Below Poverty Level....	3.6	0.0	2.6	4.8	3.8	4.1	4.2	4.6	2.4	4.2	2.2
% Income of $15,000 or More....	30.8	73.9	31.5	29.5	27.9	33.7	33.7	25.0	24.2	28.9	34.2
% White Collar Workers....	24.8	13.3	27.2	22.5	21.8	26.6	27.4	18.5	20.3	24.5	26.2
% Civilian Labor Force Unemployed.	2.7	0.0	3.8	2.5	3.3	1.4	4.1	3.3	1.6	0.6	3.5
% Riding To Work By Automobile....	66.3	77.8	57.4	66.7	72.6	71.6	73.7	67.0	63.9	75.8	63.5
Population Per Household..........	3.0	3.0	3.1	3.0	3.1	3.2	3.2	3.0	3.0	2.8	2.9
Total Housing Units........	14184	25	1251	1738	1719	1722	921	1201	1285	605	2382
% Condominiums & Cooperatives.....	0.1	—	0.0	0.0	0.0	0.0	0.0	0.0	1.2	0.0	0.0
% Built 1960 Or Later.....	12.7	—	2.8	15.6	11.3	13.8	10.3	17.0	20.1	19.4	10.9
% Owner Occupied..........	76.7	—	77.3	68.7	81.8	82.3	85.0	72.7	76.1	68.1	77.0
% With 1+ Persons Per Room.	4.8	—	5.4	4.8	5.8	4.3	6.2	6.2	4.5	4.3	3.6
Median Value: Owner Units.......$$	25300	—	24600	25600	23800	24800	25800	23300	23500	24800	28800
Median Rent: Rental Units.......$$	131	—	111	142	118	153	141	133	129	136	133
Median Number Of Rooms: All Units.	5.0	—	5.2	4.9	4.9	5.1	5.0	4.8	4.9	4.8	5.1

Tract Number	1711
Total Population..............	3398
% Male....................	45.9
% Black...................	0.0
% Other Nonwhite..........	0.9
% Of Spanish Origin.......	1.9
% Foreign Born............	21.5
% Living In Group Quarters........	0.0
% 13 Years Old And Under.........	13.3
% 14-20 Years Old.........	10.1
% 21-64 Years Old.........	56.9
% 65-74 Years Old.........	11.4
% 75 Years Old And Over...	8.3
% In Different House......	31.5
% Families With Female Head.......	9.0
Median School Years Completed.....	12.1
Median Family Income, 1979.....$$	24564
% Income Below Poverty Level....	2.6
% Income Of $30,000 Or More.....	36.8
% White Collar Workers....	56.9
% Civilian Labor Force Unemployed.	5.0
% Riding To Work By Automobile....	70.3
Mean Commuting Time - Minutes...	30.6
Population Per Household..........	2.6
Total Housing Units........	1327
% Condominiums............	0.0
% Built 1970 Or Later.....	5.0
% Owner Occupied..........	75.0
% With 1+ Persons Per Room......	1.9
Median Value: Owner Units.......$$	63100
Median Rent: Rental Units.......$$	214
Median Number Of Rooms: All Units.	5.2

Community Area 18

Montclare

Located about nine miles northwest of Chicago's Loop on the western border of the city, the Montclare community is predominately residential, with quiet streets lined with single-family bungalow-style housing. Railroad tracks on the east and south mark two of the four boundaries which form the borders of the community area, and the railroad made an important contribution to its early historical development.

The first frame house in what would later be known as Montclare was built in 1840 by William E. Sayre on his 90-acre farm. Sayre had moved from Orange County, New York to what was then Jefferson Township in 1836. His marriage to Harriet Lovett in 1839 was the first recorded there. Sayre and the other farmers who settled in the area hauled produce to Chicago over a road which became Grand Avenue. In 1872 the Chicago and Pacific Railroad Company was granted a

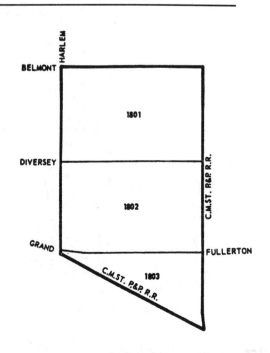

45

Community Area 18 — Montclare
Population and Housing Characteristics, 1930-1980

	1980	1970	1960	1950	1940	1930
Total Population.......	10,793	11,675	11,802	11,166	9,693	8,500
% Male.................	45.8	47.0	48.4	49.6	50.2	50.7
% Female...............	54.2	53.0	51.6	50.4	49.8	49.3
% White................	98.7	99.7	99.9	100.0	99.9	99.9
% Black................	0.0	0.0	0.0	0.0	0.0	0.1
% Other Nonwhite Races...	1.3	0.3	0.1	0.0	0.1	0.0
% Under 5 Years Old.....	4.0	5.6	7.5	9.2	6.7	9.3
% 5-19 Years Old........	18.4	21.7	21.8	20.0	25.9	30.7
% 20-44 Years Old........	29.3	27.5	30.6	40.3	41.5	42.4
% 45-64 Years Old......	27.8	30.2	28.0	23.7	21.5	14.3
% 65 Years and Older....	20.5	15.0	12.1	6.8	4.4	3.3
Median School Years....	12.1	10.7	9.6	9.4	8.4	*
Total Housing Units....	4,328	4,143	3,772	3,189	2,528	*
% In One-Unit Structures.	49.8	49.6	57.8	*	*	*
% Owner Occupied.........	60.7	60.1	65.7	62.8	53.6	*
% Renter Occupied........	34.6	38.1	32.0	36.2	45.6	*
% Vacant................	4.7	1.8	2.3	1.0	1.8	*
% 1+ Persons per Room....	2.8	4.4	5.3	11.6	*	*

Community Area 18 — Montclare
Selected Characteristics of Census Tracts: 1980

Tract Number	Total	1801	1802	1803
Total Population.............	10793	5139	4853	801
% Male.......................	45.8	45.2	46.8	43.4
% Black......................	0.0	0.0	0.0	0.0
% Other Nonwhite.............	1.3	1.3	1.4	0.5
% Of Spanish Origin..........	1.7	1.2	1.8	4.1
% Foreign Born...............	22.4	21.5	23.5	20.9
% Living In Group Quarters....	1.1	1.9	0.3	0.5
% 13 Years Old And Under.....	13.3	11.8	14.9	13.7
% 14-20 Years Old............	10.7	10.4	11.5	7.6
% 21-64 Years Old............	55.5	56.2	54.7	55.6
% 65-74 Years Old............	12.3	12.6	11.8	13.7
% 75 Years Old And Over......	8.2	9.1	7.0	9.4
% In Different House.........	33.1	29.6	32.3	60.1
% Families With Female Head......	12.1	13.3	11.3	11.0
Median School Years Completed....	12.1	11.9	12.1	12.2
Median Family Income, 1979......$$	24006	24930	23629	19145
% Income Below Poverty Level...	3.9	2.1	4.9	10.1
% Income Of $30,000 Or More.....	31.1	35.8	28.6	15.4
% White Collar Workers.........	49.9	46.5	52.4	58.6
% Civilian Labor Force Unemployed.	4.0	2.8	5.4	3.1
% Riding To Work By Automobile....	70.8	73.9	69.6	58.0
Mean Commuting Time - Minutes...	29.1	28.8	29.7	28.3
Population Per Household.........	2.6	2.6	2.6	2.3
Total Housing Units..........	4328	1998	1928	402
% Condominiums...............	0.0	0.0	0.0	0.0
% Built 1970 Or Later.........	2.2	3.1	1.3	2.1
% Owner Occupied.............	60.8	68.8	56.1	43.3
% With 1+ Persons Per Room...	2.8	2.1	3.9	0.9
Median Value: Owner Units......$$	61800	64400	56900	64500
Median Rent: Rental Units......$$	225	254	206	224
Median Number Of Rooms: All Units.	4.9	5.0	4.9	4.7

Community Area 18 — Montclare
Selected Characteristics of Census Tracts: 1970

Tract Number	TOTAL	1801	1802	1803
Total Population.............	11675	5549	5209	917
% Male.......................	47.0	47.0	47.3	45.1
% Black......................	0.0	0.0	0.0	0.1
% Other Nonwhite.............	0.3	0.2	0.3	0.4
% Of Spanish Language.........	0.7	0.0	1.3	1.5
% Foreign Born...............	16.8	17.9	16.0	15.1
% Living In Group Quarters........	1.4	2.6	0.4	0.0
% 13 Years Old And Under........	18.0	16.9	19.5	15.8
% 14-20 Years Old................	10.7	10.2	11.2	10.0
% 21-64 Years Old................	56.4	57.4	55.3	56.2
% 65-74 Years Old............	9.2	9.1	8.8	11.8
% 75 Years Old And Over........	5.9	6.4	5.3	6.2
% In Different House..........	62.9	61.6	64.6	61.6
% Families With Female Head.......	9.9	9.8	10.2	8.8
Median School Years Completed.....	10.7	10.7	10.5	11.6
Median Family Income, 1969......$$	11700	11967	11128	12245
% Income Below Poverty Level...	3.5	2.8	4.2	4.4
% Income of $15,000 or More.....	28.3	30.8	24.8	32.0
% White Collar Workers.........	21.2	20.5	21.7	22.4
% Civilian Labor Force Unemployed.	3.4	2.6	4.1	4.1
% Riding To Work By Automobile....	62.4	62.4	64.5	52.1
Population Per Household.........	2.8	2.9	2.8	2.6
Total Housing Units..........	4137	1902	1879	356
% Condominiums & Cooperatives.....	0.0	0.0	0.0	0.0
% Built 1960 Or Later.........	12.1	12.9	11.2	12.2
% Owner Occupied.............	60.5	69.0	54.8	44.9
% With 1+ Persons Per Room.......	4.4	4.1	4.5	5.7
Median Value: Owner Units......$$	24600	26600	22000	25700
Median Rent: Rental Units......$$	122	135	117	119
Median Number Of Rooms: All Units.	4.8	4.9	4.7	4.6

right-of-way over the Sayre farm. In return, the company established what was originally called "Sayre" station, with a telegraph outlet, on the farm. This original depot was located in the vicinity of Sayre and Medill avenues.

In 1873, an economic panic forced the Chicago and Pacific Railroad into receivership and it was eventually purchased by the Chicago, Milwaukee and St. Paul Railroad. The new company provided only limited service through the location and this change, along with the general economic conditions, slowed development in the area. The first significant subdivision of property took place at this time, but the lots were difficult if not impossible to sell.

That same year Sayre station was renamed Montclare after the community of Montclair, New Jersey. The origin of the name has been attributed by some to a local minister who had invested in the area. Others credit the new name to Mary Sayre Allen, daughter of the early settlers William and Harriet Sayre, who was said to have visited and been impressed with the New Jersey town. The post office at Montclare was established in December, 1873, with Thomas A. Rutherford commissioned as the first postmaster. In 1874 Herbert Merrill was appointed as the first station agent at the Montclare depot.

By 1884, the village of Montclare consisted of 14 houses with a population of about 120. Most residences clustered near the railway station in the southeast part of the community. The earliest settlers were predominantly of native American origin, English and German. Despite the annexation of Montclare, as part of the Town of Jefferson, to Chicago in 1889, growth in the area was slow, primarily due to inadequate transportation and a lack of residential amenities. By 1910 there were only about 50 houses in the community area. The extension of the Grand Avenue streetcar line to Montclare in 1912 stimulated greater residential and commercial development. In 1916, the Sayre family donated a parcel of land to the community which was later combined with land donated by Thomas A. Rutherford, the first postmaster, to form the Rutherford-Sayre Park. The park is traversed by railroad tracks which mark the southern border of Montclare.

By 1920, the population of Montclare had increased to nearly 2,000, about one-third foreign-born, chiefly Norwegians and Germans. Residential growth still was hampered by inadequate suburban railroad service and lack of local facilities. Between 1920 and 1930, improvements were initiated, resulting in the paving of streets, the installation of utilities and the development of community services. This decade proved to be a time of remarkable residential growth for Montclare, and it was at this time that the community began to assume its present pattern of single-family frame, brick and stucco bungalow-type structures. The majority of these homes were brick. Some two-flats and small apartment houses were also built in the section between Fullerton and Diversey avenues. New dwellings were rapidly constructed during this time, primarily in the northern part of the community. The intersection of Harlem and Grand avenues emerged during this decade as an important shopping area. Manufacturing establishments were constructed, primarily in the southeastern corner of the community, bordering on the railroad tracks. In 1926 the Shriners Hospital for Crippled Children was established. It was located in a building on Oak Park Avenue in the southeast section of Montclare across from the Rutherford-Sayre Park.

By 1930 Montclare's population had increased to 8,500. Many of these new residents were of Italian origin, and by 1930, there were more Italians than Germans among the foreign born. The Italian and Polish immigrants tended to be laborers who found employment in the surrounding area's growing industries.

The population of Montclare grew by 30 percent during the years between 1930 and 1950, despite the Depression and the Second World War. Residential development followed the pattern established during the 1920s, with most new dwellings being single-story one-family brick homes. Some two-flats and apartment buildings were also constructed. Most new residences were built in the area north of Diversey Avenue, which was less densely settled until 1930.

Between 1930 and 1960, the intersection of Grand and Harlem avenues became one of the city's busiest commercial intersections, with many local retail businesses thriving as a result of the high rate of residential growth in the area. By 1960, Montclare's population had grown steadily to nearly 12,000.

The period of 1960 to 1970 was a time of relative stability for the Montclare community. The number of housing units increased by about 10 percent due primarily to an increase in rental units. However, total population declined slightly during the decade.

Population decline continued through the 1970s, the community's total population decreasing by 8 percent during the decade. In 1980, those reporting Italian ancestry were the largest ethnic group, constituting 26 percent of the total population. More than 12 percent of Montclare's residents reported Polish ancestry. Twenty-two percent of the total population were foreign-born. The racial composition of Montclare has remained stable throughout its history. In 1980, 99 percent of the residents were white and there were no blacks living there.

Montclare's stability was reflected by the fact that 65 percent of the residents were living in the same house in 1980 as they were in 1975. Since 1960, the proportion of residents older than 65 had increased from 12 to 20 percent. Sixty-one percent of the residential units in Montclare were owner-occupied and half of the units were single-family dwellings. In 1980 there were no condominium units in the community. Median value of single-family units was $62,000, about a third higher than the city median. Median family income in 1979 was more than $24,000, also well above the city average.

The last decade has also brought a gradual but definite decline in the Grand and Harlem avenues commercial section in Montclare, reflected by the departure of some businesses and the deterioration of some buildings. The Brickyard, a modern, large regional shopping center was opened in March, 1977. It is located on Montclare's eastern border in the neighboring Belmont-Cragin community. Its proximity to Montclare has affected local business and traffic flow. In 1981, the old Shriners Hospital building on Oak Park Avenue was replaced at the same location by a new and modern facility.

Three structures in Montclare are considered of "special interest" by the Illinois Department of Conservation because of their architectural characteristics. These include two private residences on Oak Park and on Neva avenues and the Montclare Congregational Church, located at the corner of Newland and Medill avenues. True to its origins, Montclare remains a commuter stop on the Milwaukee Road, with its present depot located not far from the original site on the old Sayre farm.

Kathryn Golden

Belmont Cragin

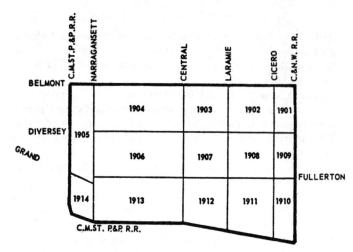

In the 1840s the present-day community of Belmont Cragin was mostly farmland, prairie, and woodland laced with Indian trails. The oldest known settlement centered around Whiskey Point, located at the present intersection of Armitage and Grand avenues. Legend has it that this early trading post and saloon was purchased from the Indians for one bottle of whiskey. In the years to follow, the area was incorporated into the larger township of Jefferson.

The first of two historic periods of great activity in Belmont Cragin began in the 1870s coincident to the extension of the Chicago, Milwaukee, and St. Paul Railroad into the area. During this period, three early communities developed along these tracks, which today serve as the southern boundary of Belmont Cragin. The first originated in 1883 near Whiskey Point, when the Cragin brothers introduced metals manufacturing into the area by building the Cragin Manufacturing Company. A railroad station was established near the plant and the community of Cragin developed as a suburban industrial town. A year later, Cragin had a population of more than 200. At the same time, Hanson Park developed around another railroad station off Central Avenue along the tracks. Like Cragin, Hanson Park was the result of industrial development along the tracks, with the railroad serving to bring in workers who then settled in the community. Finally, the town of Galewood developed around a third station on the Chicago, Milwaukee, and St. Paul near Naragansett Avenue. The station was named after Abram Gale, whose farm was converted into a subdivision.

Apart from these communities, Belmont Cragin remained largely prairie and woodland. In 1889, all these communities and rural sections were annexed by election to Chicago as part of the township of Jefferson. By 1910, Belmont Cragin's population reached 3,826, the result of many first- and second-generation Germans, Scandinavians, and Irish settling in the south and southeastern parts of the community and working in nearby factories and railroad yards. People were drawn to these communities because work was readily available there and houses and lots were reasonably priced. In 1913, the area between Diversey and Belmont avenues and west of the Chicago and North Western tracks to Laramie Street was subdivided into a residential area known as Belmont Park. By 1920, Belmont Cragin's population had increased to 13,492, with Poles, Italians, and Germans dominating the foreign stock.

The second surge of growth in Belmont Cragin occurred during the 1920s and was the result of the general outward expansion of the city to the north and west. Growth was facilitated by an improvement in transportation to the area, which had depended on the few daily trains of the Chicago, Milwaukee, and St. Paul. Surface and bus lines were now installed on many of the community's major thoroughfares. During this decade, Belmont Cragin underwent dramatic growth in three respects. First, the industrial area along the railroad tracks underwent intensive development. The already well-established Cragin industrial district expanded and increased in density through the addition of many new factories. The Galewood industrial district was established during this decade, as was the industrial concentration in the southwest corner of the community. While metals manufacturing dominated, the printing industry also made its appearance. Secondly, residential construction reached its peak during this decade. The building boom of the first 18 months of the 1920s alone exceeded that of the previous 10-year period. While older residences in Cragin already stood close to the manufacturing district, new one-family bungalows and two-flats were built to the north and west. Belmont Park developed rapidly during the 1920s with modern brick one- and two-story units. Although by 1930 much of the land north of Fullerton and to the west was still open, the overall result of this decade's extensive residential development was the expansion of the separate communities and their fusion into one community area called Belmont Cragin. By the close of the decade, the community's present residential housing mix already was well-established.

Thirdly, Belmont Cragin's population increased dramatically from 13,492 in 1920 to 60,221 in 1930. Compared to later years, the 1930 population was very young, with a median age of 25 years. The new residents continued to be predominantly of either Polish or German stock, yet Italians were moving into the community in increasing numbers. By 1930, one-third of the community's population was foreign-born.

Since 1930, growth in Belmont Cragin has decelerated. The population increased by only 5 percent during the 1930s, which was nowhere near the increment of the previous decade. By 1950 the total population reached its peak figure of 63,546. The proportionate loss of population has increased each decade since then, with a total decline of 16 percent between 1950 and 1980. The predominance of Poles, Italians, and Germans continued over the years, although there has been a recent influx of Spanish-Americans across the southern boundary. In 1940, the Belmont Cragin population began to show a higher than average proportion of residents older than 65. Today, almost 19 percent are 65 and older, and more than 10 percent are in their 70s. Migration into the area increased considerably during the 1960s. such that by 1970, 58 percent of the residents reported moving into Belmont Cragin in the previous 10 years.

Residential, commercial, and industrial development continued into the 1930s, but at a reduced pace. Construction of single-family dwellings in the more sparsely settled northern and western sections continued through the 1950s, but the proportion of dwellings that are single-family units has gone down since 1960. Also by 1960, more than 80 percent of land use in Belmont Cragin was classified as residential. Although there has been some deterioration of housing in the southeastern section along the industrial district, the median value of owner-occupied single-family units is in the top third in the city. Industrial development, on the other hand, continued at a moderate pace after the 1920s. Much of the development occurred west of Central Avenue along the tracks. Moderate industrial expansion has occurred since 1960 as the Galewood industrial district continued to develop between Austin and Oak Park Avenue.

Although retail areas already were well-established along Belmont Cragin 's older streets by 1930, the next two decades saw the rapid development of the Belmont-Central retail area, which became a major retail center, overlapping with neighboring Portage Park. The opening of the Brickyard Shopping Mall in 1978 on the far west side of the community has led to the daily influx of many shoppers into Belmont Cragin. The opening of 100 additional stores is planned at the Brickyard, a major retail center, currently housing 170 stores.

Peter Vukosavich

Community Area 19 -- Belmont Cragin
Population and Housing Characteristics, 1930-1980

	1980	1970	1960	1950	1940	1930
Total Population.......	53,371	57,399	60,883	63,546	63,302	60,221
% Male..................	47.0	47.0	48.4	49.4	50.4	51.0
% Female................	53.0	53.0	51.6	50.6	49.6	49.0
% White.................	96.3	99.7	99.9	99.9	100.0	100.0
% Black.................	0.1	0.0	0.0	0.1	0.0	0.0
% Other Nonwhite Races...	3.6	0.3	0.1	0.0	0.0	0.0
% Under 5 Years Old......	5.2	6.1	8.4	9.0	6.6	9.4
% 5-19 Years Old.........	17.8	20.7	20.2	18.4	23.5	30.6
% 20-44 Years Old........	31.7	28.4	32.3	40.8	44.3	44.2
% 45-64 Years Old........	26.5	30.0	27.0	25.5	21.9	13.3
% 65 Years and Older.....	18.8	14.8	12.1	6.3	3.7	2.5
Median School Years....	11.9	10.3	9.6	8.9	8.3	*
Total Housing Units....	22,183	21,177	20,405	18,722	17,015	*
% In One-Unit Structures.	34.7	35.3	41.8	*	*	*
% Owner Occupied........	53.0	54.4	55.6	53.2	44.2	*
% Renter Occupied........	42.0	43.5	42.3	46.0	54.4	*
% Vacant.................	5.0	2.1	2.1	0.8	1.4	*
% 1+ Persons per Room....	3.0	4.2	5.3	11.0	*	*

Community Area 19 -- Belmont Cragin
Selected Characteristics of Census Tracts: 1980

Tract Number	Total	1901	1902	1903	1904	1905	1906	1907	1908	1909	1910
Total Population.............	53371	1757	4315	4209	7276	1722	6631	5010	4520	1488	1630
% Male..........................	47.0	48.4	47.0	44.6	46.1	46.0	47.2	47.5	46.3	46.8	47.5
% Black.........................	0.1	0.0	0.1	0.0	0.0	0.0	0.3	0.0	0.2	0.2	0.0
% Other Nonwhite................	3.7	7.6	3.2	1.1	2.3	1.3	2.5	2.3	2.6	9.1	9.4
% Of Spanish Origin.............	5.8	11.1	5.4	1.8	2.0	1.0	3.1	2.9	4.3	14.5	16.7
% Foreign Born..................	21.9	27.9	15.6	18.6	19.5	22.1	23.0	26.3	17.7	21.2	12.4
% Living In Group Quarters......	0.6	0.0	0.0	0.0	0.3	0.0	3.6	0.0	0.2	0.0	0.0
% 13 Years Old And Under........	14.7	14.8	14.3	11.5	12.5	11.2	13.6	13.9	14.6	16.1	18.5
% 14-20 Years Old...............	9.8	9.2	10.6	8.1	9.4	8.4	9.8	8.9	9.6	11.2	12.2
% 21-64 Years Old...............	56.6	59.0	56.3	54.2	56.3	58.1	55.7	59.3	56.1	59.9	52.5
% 65-74 Years Old...............	11.8	10.5	11.7	15.4	13.6	13.7	12.3	11.6	12.8	8.3	10.7
% 75 Years Old And Over.........	7.0	6.5	7.0	10.8	8.2	8.5	8.6	6.4	6.9	4.6	6.1
% In Different House............	37.2	39.7	35.1	36.3	33.0	19.2	34.5	34.3	42.1	34.2	44.8
% Families With Female Head.....	15.5	12.1	13.6	11.8	8.5	16.0	10.9	17.7	16.4	12.8	20.8
Median School Years Completed....	11.9	12.2	12.2	12.0	12.1	12.1	11.9	11.4	12.0	12.1	11.6
Median Family Income, 1979.....$$	22246	20649	21973	22972	23227	25833	23603	23306	22341	22847	21595
% Income Below Poverty Level.....	4.0	6.0	1.5	4.8	1.0	3.6	2.6	3.5	7.7	0.0	2.8
% Income Of $30,000 Or More.....	27.1	22.9	30.9	32.5	32.3	37.8	32.2	30.0	25.6	28.4	21.3
% White Collar Workers..........	48.4	50.7	49.0	57.5	55.8	44.5	50.6	47.9	48.3	47.1	48.8
% Civilian Labor Force Unemployed.	6.0	2.5	5.2	3.9	5.5	5.7	4.9	6.5	6.8	2.5	4.9
% Riding To Work By Automobile...	65.4	66.2	65.2	64.9	65.7	67.6	65.3	65.1	63.5	70.7	57.0
Mean Commuting Time - Minutes...	30.4	35.4	27.5	31.1	33.4	31.7	32.1	31.4	30.4	28.9	25.3
Population Per Household..........	2.5	2.5	2.6	2.2	2.5	2.4	2.6	2.4	2.4	2.9	2.6
Total Housing Units..........	22183	724	1742	2002	2941	741	2621	2210	1960	556	677
% Condominiums...................	0.2	0.0	0.0	0.0	0.0	3.8	0.5	0.0	0.0	0.0	0.0
% Built 1970 Or Later............	1.6	0.0	0.6	0.7	2.0	5.1	2.8	0.0	1.9	1.7	1.3
% Owner Occupied.................	53.0	44.8	56.2	48.6	64.3	66.4	59.4	42.5	45.9	59.4	53.8
% With 1+ Persons Per Room.......	3.0	2.7	1.9	1.4	2.0	2.2	3.1	3.5	2.1	2.9	4.8
Median Value: Owner Units.......$$	55800	58600	59200	59800	61900	60100	57600	54900	53400	51100	41000
Median Rent: Rental Units....$$	199	212	209	209	226	265	204	191	202	206	177
Median Number Of Rooms: All Units.	4.9	5.0	5.2	4.7	5.1	4.8	5.0	4.6	4.8	5.2	4.9

Tract Number	1911	1912	1913	1914
Total Population.............	5584	2553	7677	790
% Male..........................	47.5	47.9	47.9	48.4
% Black.........................	0.0	0.0	0.0	0.0
% Other Nonwhite................	0.1	0.2	0.4	0.5
% Of Spanish Language...........	0.9	2.9	0.9	0.0
% Foreign Born..................	13.6	17.8	23.4	18.5
% Living In Group Quarters......	0.0	1.4	0.0	0.0
% 13 Years Old And Under........	20.8	18.4	20.4	20.9
% 14-20 Years Old...............	9.8	11.5	10.8	10.3
% 21-64 Years Old...............	56.8	57.3	57.8	56.3
% 65-74 Years Old...............	7.9	7.4	6.6	8.1
% 75 Years Old And Over.........	4.7	5.3	4.4	4.4
% In Different House............	59.0	62.5	62.8	69.2
% Families With Female Head.....	13.9	17.1	11.9	15.4
Median School Years Completed....	10.2	9.4	9.7	10.1
Median Family Income, 1969.....$$	11037	10358	11334	10712
% Income Below Poverty Level.....	6.4	8.6	3.7	4.0
% Income of $15,000 or More.....	22.0	25.2	27.9	17.5
% White Collar Workers..........	18.0	21.2	15.0	17.8
% Civilian Labor Force Unemployed.	2.0	3.7	3.1	0.0
% Riding To Work By Automobile...	55.3	56.5	57.8	62.0
Population Per Household..........	2.8	2.8	3.0	3.0
Total Housing Units..........	2086	944	2678	263
% Condominiums & Cooperatives.....	0.8	0.0	0.4	0.0
% Built 1960 Or Later............	2.6	1.8	10.1	5.3
% Owner Occupied.................	44.6	47.1	52.7	70.0
% With 1+ Persons Per Room.......	4.7	6.9	7.0	4.6
Median Value: Owner Units.......$$	20800	20100	20500	20800
Median Rent: Rental Units....$$	103	82	104	109
Median Number Of Rooms: All Units.	4.8	4.4	4.7	4.8

Community Area 19 — Belmont Cragin
Selected Characteristics of Census Tracts: 1970

Tract Number	TOTAL	1901	1902	1903	1904	1905	1906	1907	1908	1909	1910
Total Population	57399	1611	4437	4521	7837	1701	7033	5327	4906	1558	1864
% Male	47.0	49.0	47.0	45.0	45.9	46.8	48.0	46.7	46.7	46.9	46.7
% Black	0.0	0.1	0.0	0.0	0.0	0.1	0.0	0.0	0.0	0.0	0.0
% Other Nonwhite	0.3	1.1	0.3	0.3	0.3	0.1	0.2	0.3	0.2	0.6	0.4
% Of Spanish Language	1.2	0.0	1.6	0.6	2.1	0.0	0.9	1.7	0.3	3.0	0.1
% Foreign Born	18.6	15.6	17.2	22.3	15.8	22.2	18.5	23.7	19.1	11.2	10.3
% Living In Group Quarters	0.2	0.7	0.2	0.0	0.6	0.0	0.1	0.0	0.5	0.0	0.0
% 13 Years Old And Under	18.1	16.9	18.8	13.8	15.7	15.7	18.3	16.9	17.5	19.1	22.6
% 14-20 Years Old	10.2	11.7	10.5	8.6	10.0	11.2	11.2	9.4	9.4	11.2	10.6
% 21-64 Years Old	57.0	57.2	54.5	56.6	57.8	59.0	56.2	58.7	57.2	55.1	54.1
% 65-74 Years Old	9.1	8.9	10.5	12.9	10.7	10.3	8.5	8.7	9.6	8.3	8.6
% 75 Years Old And Over	5.6	5.3	5.7	8.1	5.7	3.8	5.7	6.8	6.3	6.4	4.1
% In Different House	63.3	57.1	60.5	64.3	67.9	67.6	66.6	59.6	62.6	60.7	64.9
% Families With Female Head	12.3	14.0	11.5	13.0	11.0	9.4	12.2	12.1	11.7	10.8	13.2
Median School Years Completed	10.3	10.7	10.9	10.3	10.3	11.3	10.6	10.2	9.5	10.7	10.5
Median Family Income, 1969 $$	11403	11207	11463	11435	12513	12239	11561	10843	11818	11348	10136
% Income Below Poverty Level	4.7	3.8	5.3	3.2	3.6	6.7	3.8	3.8	2.2	4.0	
% Income of $15,000 or More	27.1	27.6	28.1	24.0	34.9	29.9	27.6	21.7	28.2	29.3	22.5
% White Collar Workers	19.3	15.4	18.3	21.3	25.3	19.9	19.2	19.5	19.8	17.4	14.2
% Civilian Labor Force Unemployed	3.0	3.9	3.0	2.3	1.5	3.0	3.6	5.2	1.9	5.3	4.0
% Riding To Work By Automobile	58.2	53.6	62.5	60.8	57.4	59.9	57.8	59.4	59.3	53.8	56.1
Population Per Household	2.8	2.6	2.8	2.4	2.8	2.8	2.9	2.6	2.6	2.9	2.8
Total Housing Units	21185	624	1622	1870	2825	615	2443	2110	1896	538	671
% Condominiums & Cooperatives	0.6	0.0	0.7	1.4	0.9	0.0	0.0	0.8	0.8	0.9	0.0
% Built 1960 Or Later	5.3	1.6	1.8	4.4	4.8	12.4	7.6	3.6	4.7	1.8	4.5
% Owner Occupied	53.6	44.6	57.7	49.7	64.6	74.8	63.1	41.8	45.1	60.2	54.1
% With 1+ Persons Per Room	4.4	3.4	3.2	2.4	3.2	3.6	5.4	4.1	3.4	4.5	5.6
Median Value: Owner Units $$	23400	23000	23300	24800	26400	26700	23500	22900	22900	22100	20100
Median Rent: Rental Units $$	111	116	115	117	128	116	114	109	113	111	99
Median Number Of Rooms: All Units	4.8	5.0	5.1	4.7	5.0	4.9	5.0	4.6	4.8	5.1	4.9

Tract Number	1911	1912	1913	1914
Total Population	5009	2290	6811	703
% Male	48.3	47.5	47.7	47.8
% Black	0.2	0.0	0.0	0.0
% Other Nonwhite	6.9	3.3	4.3	4.8
% Of Spanish Origin	14.4	5.7	7.2	4.3
% Foreign Born	23.1	31.3	25.4	22.0
% Living In Group Quarters	0.0	0.6	0.1	0.0
% 13 Years Old And Under	18.9	16.2	17.3	14.2
% 14-20 Years Old	10.5	9.3	10.8	12.4
% 21-64 Years Old	56.7	57.8	56.7	58.6
% 65-74 Years Old	9.1	11.6	10.2	9.0
% 75 Years Old And Over	4.7	5.0	5.0	5.8
% In Different House	40.3	35.5	46.9	31.0
% Families With Female Head	20.2	25.4	19.1	18.8
Median School Years Completed	11.3	10.7	10.8	10.7
Median Family Income, 1979 $$	19859	17917	21378	23625
% Income Below Poverty Level	6.5	7.2	6.3	0.0
% Income Of $30,000 Or More	15.2	18.7	20.8	20.0
% White Collar Workers	39.0	37.4	42.9	49.5
% Civilian Labor Force Unemployed	6.6	8.3	9.1	5.7
% Riding To Work By Automobile	67.6	61.9	67.0	65.5
Mean Commuting Time – Minutes	27.2	29.6	28.5	29.8
Population Per Household	2.6	2.5	2.7	2.7
Total Housing Units	2120	958	2660	271
% Condominiums	0.0	0.0	0.0	0.0
% Built 1970 Or Later	0.9	0.5	2.6	1.4
% Owner Occupied	44.4	47.9	53.2	70.8
% With 1+ Persons Per Room	3.9		4.7	1.9
Median Value: Owner Units $$	43200	44400	47400	49700
Median Rent: Rental Units $$	182	157	200	197
Median Number Of Rooms: All Units	4.8	4.5	4.8	4.9

Community Area 20

Hermosa

The Hermosa community originated as one of the suburban developments in Jefferson Township during the 1870s and 1880s. Although various sections were subdivided during the 1870s, the first actual settlement in the prairie territory later to be named Hermosa occurred in the 1880s. Scotch immigrants built homes in the area, and named it Kelvyn Grove after the eighth Lord Kelvyn. They were joined by Germans and Scandinavians who built frame homes in the vicinity of present-day Kelvyn Park in the northwestern section of the community. Settlements also appeared in southern Hermosa, extending into what is now the community of Humboldt Park. Most of these settlers were Germans and Swedes. When the various settlements in the territory, along with the rest of Jefferson Township, were annexed to Chicago in 1889, the new community was given the name Hermosa at the request of the city.

Community Area 20 -- Hermosa
Population and Housing Characteristics, 1930-1980

	1980	1970	1960	1950	1940	1930
Total Population.......	19,547	19,838	21,429	22,805	22,894	23,518
% Male...................	48.5	47.2	48.0	48.9	49.9	50.6
% Female.................	51.5	52.8	52.0	51.1	50.1	49.4
% White..................	80.8	99.5	99.9	99.9	100.0	100.0
% Black..................	0.4	0.0	-	0.0	-	0.0
% Other Nonwhite Races...	18.8	0.5	0.1	0.1	0.0	0.0
% Under 5 Years Old......	7.7	7.3	9.4	8.8	5.9	8.0
% 5-19 Years Old.........	22.8	22.9	20.1	17.8	20.7	24.7
% 20-44 Years Old........	36.1	29.6	31.9	38.5	44.2	46.2
% 45-64 Years Old........	20.5	26.6	26.7	26.8	22.7	16.8
% 65 Years and Older.....	12.9	13.6	11.9	8.1	6.5	4.3
Median School Years......	11.4	10.5	9.7	9.2	8.5	*
Total Housing Units......	7,372	7,270	7,397	7,138	6,680	*
% In One-Unit Structures.	25.2	23.4	21.5	*	*	*
% Owner Occupied.........	44.3	43.4	44.4	44.1	36.4	*
% Renter Occupied........	51.4	54.2	52.7	54.9	62.3	*
% Vacant.................	4.3	2.4	2.9	1.0	1.3	*
% 1+ Persons per Room....	5.2	4.9	4.9	7.0	*	*

Community Area 20 -- Hermosa
Selected Characteristics of Census Tracts: 1980

Tract Number	Total	2001	2002	2003	2004	2005	2006
Total Population.............	19547	3154	4074	1621	6493	3448	757
% Male.......................	48.5	45.8	48.3	48.2	50.2	49.0	46.4
% Black......................	0.4	0.0	0.1	0.6	0.4	0.7	1.3
% Other Nonwhite.............	18.8	7.2	10.5	13.3	24.0	26.7	42.5
% Of Spanish Origin..........	31.2	6.8	19.3	25.0	40.8	46.8	56.1
% Foreign Born...............	20.1	20.4	23.8	22.2	17.8	19.8	14.6
% Living In Group Quarters...	0.4	0.2	0.1	0.1	0.1	1.7	0.1
% 13 Years Old And Under.....	20.6	13.2	17.9	20.5	24.3	23.8	20.2
% 14-20 Years Old............	11.8	8.3	11.2	12.0	12.9	13.1	14.0
% 21-64 Years Old............	54.7	56.7	57.7	54.1	53.1	52.3	55.9
% 65-74 Years Old............	7.7	12.8	8.1	8.5	5.9	6.0	6.5
% 75 Years Old And Over......	5.1	8.9	5.1	4.9	3.7	4.8	3.4
% In Different House.........	46.7	38.0	46.4	45.2	55.8	40.0	44.0
% Families With Female Head..	20.9	14.6	19.2	20.2	24.5	19.3	21.3
Median School Years Completed	11.4	12.2	12.1	10.6	10.6	11.0	9.4
Median Family Income, 1979...$$	19118	23684	18098	20156	18839	19671	10733
% Income Below Poverty Level	10.0	4.1	10.3	4.6	14.4	5.3	27.6
% Income Of $30,000 Or More.	20.3	33.0	20.8	20.3	15.3	19.3	6.9
% White Collar Workers.......	42.9	53.7	46.5	40.4	34.5	42.1	41.4
% Civilian Labor Force Unemployed.	7.8	5.7	8.2	6.6	7.9	9.5	9.7
% Riding To Work By Automobile....	66.2	64.7	63.6	59.0	68.1	68.4	81.2
Mean Commuting Time - Minutes.	28.7	29.9	29.1	27.7	27.7	29.3	28.8
Population Per Household..........	2.8	2.3	2.6	2.7	2.9	3.2	2.8
Total Housing Units...........	7372	1413	1584	610	2367	1110	288
% Condominiums................	0.0	0.0	0.0	0.0	0.0	0.0	0.0
% Built 1970 Or Later.........	1.2	0.0	3.9	0.0	0.7	0.0	2.4
% Owner Occupied..............	44.3	50.9	42.4	46.4	42.7	43.2	35.8
% With 1+ Persons Per Room....	5.2	1.5	4.0	4.7	6.6	8.1	8.5
Median Value: Owner Units....$$	43000	56500	49600	33800	34200	31100	-
Median Rent: Rental Units....$$	187	217	205	185	172	173	160
Median Number Of Rooms: All Units.	5.0	4.8	5.0	5.1	5.0	5.2	4.6

Community Area 20 -- Hermosa
Selected Characteristics of Census Tracts: 1970

Tract Number	TOTAL	2001	2002	2003	2004	2005	2006
Total Population.............	19838	3362	4152	1549	6671	3419	685
% Male.......................	47.2	46.1	46.9	46.5	48.2	47.0	47.4
% Black......................	0.0	0.0	0.0	0.0	0.0	0.2	0.0
% Other Nonwhite.............	0.5	0.2	0.5	0.6	0.7	0.4	0.1
% Of Spanish Language........	3.9	0.9	5.8	0.6	4.5	4.8	5.5
% Foreign Born...............	13.6	13.2	15.5	16.6	12.3	13.7	10.8
% Living In Group Quarters...	0.3	0.0	0.0	0.0	0.0	1.6	0.0
% 13 Years Old And Under.....	21.5	14.5	19.5	19.5	25.1	24.9	21.9
% 14-20 Years Old............	10.2	9.1	9.4	11.2	10.7	10.9	8.2
% 21-64 Years Old............	54.7	57.5	56.4	54.0	53.4	52.0	57.2
% 65-74 Years Old............	8.5	11.2	9.3	9.2	6.7	7.8	8.8
% 75 Years Old And Over......	5.2	7.6	5.4	6.1	4.1	4.4	3.9
% In Different House.........	58.1	70.5	52.7	51.8	58.5	54.1	56.7
% Families With Female Head..	12.7	10.9	12.2	12.1	12.3	15.7	15.9
Median School Years Completed	10.5	11.2	11.0	10.9	10.2	9.9	8.9
Median Family Income, 1969...$$	10799	11777	11639	11127	9943	10671	8844
% Income Below Poverty Level	4.8	3.7	3.0	7.0	6.5	3.0	9.6
% Income of $15,000 or More.	22.2	29.7	24.6	28.7	17.7	18.6	13.5
% White Collar Workers.......	18.0	24.4	19.9	12.9	16.4	15.1	11.0
% Civilian Labor Force Unemployed.	3.2	2.5	3.2	3.6	3.6	3.2	2.8
% Riding To Work By Automobile....	58.1	59.8	56.3	61.2	59.5	56.4	47.2
Population Per Household..........	2.8	2.5	2.7	2.8	2.9	3.0	2.7
Total Housing Units...........	7275	1344	1572	572	2351	1175	261
% Condominiums & Cooperatives.....	0.4	0.0	1.0	0.0	0.3	0.4	0.0
% Built 1960 Or Later.........	1.8	0.7	2.6	0.0	2.2	2.0	2.0
% Owner Occupied..............	43.2	52.4	40.1	44.9	40.9	42.0	37.2
% With 1+ Persons Per Room....	4.5	2.5	3.5	4.1	5.6	6.5	2.7
Median Value: Owner Units....$$	20600	23700	21700	17700	18000	17300	-
Median Rent: Rental Units....$$	102	115	110	102	95	90	92
Median Number Of Rooms: All Units.	4.9	4.8	4.9	5.0	5.0	5.1	4.8

After annexation the community benefited from the expansion of the city's transportation system to the northwest side. Streetcar lines were extended to Grand, Belmont, and Fullerton avenues, and a new streetcar line was installed on Pulaski Road. Industries sprung up along the tracks of the Chicago, Milwaukee, and St. Paul Railroad in the southeastern section of the community. The industrialization of southern Hermosa had begun in 1884 when the Laminated Wood Company had purchased a vacated locomotive factory in the area. The population was 15,152 in 1920.

By 1930, Hermosa's population had grown to more than 23,000. While Germans and Scandinavians remained the predominant foreign stock, numerous Poles and Austrians had appeared in the community. This population growth led to a building boom in Hermosa in the 1920s. The once sparsely-inhabited area north of Fullerton Avenue and east of Kilbourn Avenue had developed into a neighborhood of brick bungalows and two-flats. This became known as Kelvyn Park, after the city park which had opened in 1920. South of Kelvyn Park, new residential construction had also appeared, especially in the area bounded by the tracks of the Chicago and North Western, Pulaski Road, Belden and Armitage avenues. That area was filled with brick bungalows, two-deckers and three-deckers, along with some small apartment buildings.

Since the expansive decade of the 1920s Hermosa has experienced some decline in population, mostly during the 1950s and the 1960s. By 1980, the population of the community had decreased to fewer than 20,000 residents. Hispanics now comprise nearly a third of the population, and Puerto Ricans are the largest of the Spanish-speaking groups. The area is generally white, although some blacks have moved in during the most recent decade. The European whites are principally of Polish, German and Irish ancestry.

Housing construction in Hermosa has also diminished. Most of the present-day housing structures are at least 40 years old, and less than 3 percent of the housing units were built after 1950. Nevertheless, 79 percent of the housing structures in the area were judged to be architecturally sound in a 1970 survey commissioned by the Department of Planning. There has been some concern, however, about the lack of home improvements in Hermosa since then. The number of housing repairs during the 1970s was the second lowest among the city's 77 community areas, while the overall level of housing rehabilitation was disproportional to the existing volume of aging housing. It may be that since such a high percentage of the community's housing received a favorable rating in 1970, much rehabilitation occurred prior to that time. Seventy percent of all housing units are in two- to nine-unit structures, 27 percent is in single-family dwellings. The median value of single-family units is somewhat less than the city median.

Outside of the housing situation, the residents of Hermosa are concerned about crime. Although Hermosa had a rate of 21 reported crimes per 1,000 population during the late 1970's — slightly higher than many of the other northwest side communities — the area was below the city median of 22 reported crimes per 1,000. Nevertheless, area residents are disturbed by perceived increases in criminal activity, and have resorted to forming surveillance groups and other anti-crime programs. The programs seem to have met with some success, and affirm the residents' desire to make Hermosa a better place to live.

Winston McDowell

Avondale

Avondale is one of several northwest side communities that grew with the development of Milwaukee Avenue and the railroads running northwest. But at the beginning of the 19th century the land was low-lying virgin prairie; its only man-made feature was a crooked Indian trail which became Milwaukee Avenue. By 1840 a few farming families had settled in the area including the Sweeneys at Milwaukee and Belmont avenues and Major Mark Noble who lived in the vicinity of Elston Avenue and Roscoe Street. The meandering Indian trail was straightened and planked in 1848 and 1849 so that farmers could bring their produce more easily to the Chicago Randolph Street Market. In the mid-1850s the Chicago, Milwaukee and St. Paul Railroad, which forms the western boundary of Avondale, and the Chicago and North Western Railroad, which cuts diagonally through the center of Avondale, were constructed. However, the population remained sparse until 1870 when the Chicago, Milwaukee and St. Paul railroad was extended to Milwaukee and about a dozen families purchased some recently-subdivided tracts of land. By 1873 Avondale warranted a post office which was built at Belmont and Troy, a stop on the Chicago and North Western line. By 1880 about 20 black families lived east of Milwaukee Avenue and built the first church in Avondale, Allen Church. In 1881 there were about 60 houses in an area that included the western end of Avondale and was bounded by Belmont, California, Fullerton and Pulaski.

Chicago city dwellers were attracted to suburban villages like Avondale for its cheaper housing and cleaner air. The railroads and horsecars on Milwaukee Avenue, which crosses the center of Avon-

dale, provided feasible if not pleasant transportation to city jobs. The village of Maplewood, which at that time included the southern part of Avondale and most of present day Logan Square, immediately to the south, had a population of about 6,000 in 1884. It wasn't until 1889, however, when the Township of Jefferson (including Avondale) was annexed to the city of Chicago and the amenities of city life such as sewers, water and sidewalks were added, that rapid growth occurred.

Although the Milwaukee Avenue Plank road was the main highway through the Northwest Side it was a rather uncertain one. The oak planks that were laid remained in place only a short time, some of them warped in the heat, others broke under heavy loads and what remained was finally carried away in the spring floods or by people who needed firewood. Despite the deteriorating condition of the road, tollgates

Community Area 21 -- Avondale
Population and Housing Characteristics, 1930-1980

	1980	1970	1960	1950	1940	1930
Total Population.......	33,527	35,806	39,748	45,313	47,684	48,433
% Male...................	48.4	47.8	48.5	49.0	49.6	49.8
% Female.................	51.6	52.2	51.5	51.0	50.4	50.2
% White..................	86.8	99.1	99.7	99.9	100.0	100.0
% Black..................	0.2	0.0	0.0	0.0	0.0	0.0
% Other Nonwhite Races...	13.0	0.9	0.3	0.1	0.0	0.0
% Under 5 Years Old......	7.0	7.5	9.9	9.3	6.6	8.2
% 5-19 Years Old.........	19.4	22.5	20.8	18.0	21.8	27.0
% 20-44 Years Old........	37.1	30.6	33.4	41.4	45.2	46.0
% 45-64 Years Old........	22.9	26.5	24.9	24.4	21.1	14.8
% 65 Years and Older.....	13.6	12.9	11.0	6.9	5.3	4.0
Median School Years....	11.6	10.0	9.2	8.9	8.2	*
Total Housing Units....	13,986	13,932	13,798	14,151	13,743	*
% In One-Unit Structures.	13.5	12.2	11.2	*	*	*
% Owner Occupied.........	35.4	33.4	36.8	35.6	29.2	*
% Renter Occupied........	59.1	62.2	60.8	63.5	69.0	*
% Vacant.................	5.5	4.4	2.4	1.9	1.8	*
% 1+ Persons per Room....	5.1	5.8	6.6	9.5	*	*

Community Area 21 -- Avondale
Selected Characteristics of Census Tracts: 1980

Tract Number	Total	2101	2102	2103	2104	2105	2106	2107	2108	2109
Total Population.............	33527	3154	990	5196	2098	6256	6966	4687	1318	2862
% Male.......................	48.4	48.0	46.6	46.5	45.7	48.1	50.0	50.2	49.2	48.3
% Black......................	0.2	0.0	0.1	0.0	0.0	0.0	0.5	0.4	0.1	0.2
% Other Nonwhite.............	13.0	13.4	11.0	6.0	6.1	4.5	13.4	25.2	27.9	21.5
% Of Spanish Origin..........	20.5	18.2	7.9	5.7	7.7	5.9	26.4	40.9	43.6	36.8
% Foreign Born...............	27.2	19.0	24.2	27.7	34.0	40.4	26.3	18.9	22.0	21.0
% Living In Group Quarters...	0.2	0.0	0.0	0.0	1.3	0.0	0.0	0.2	0.0	0.3
% 13 Years Old And Under.....	17.7	19.8	17.2	14.6	12.5	13.4	18.0	23.6	26.3	20.8
% 14-20 Years Old............	10.3	12.5	10.1	9.5	8.6	7.7	10.8	11.8	12.2	11.9
% 21-64 Years Old............	58.3	56.4	60.2	59.6	59.9	63.6	58.4	54.6	52.2	53.6
% 65-74 Years Old............	8.7	7.2	8.9	10.3	12.3	9.7	8.6	6.2	6.4	8.5
% 75 Years Old And Over......	4.9	4.2	3.6	6.0	6.7	5.6	4.2	3.8	2.8	5.1
% In Different House.........	46.0	42.5	25.4	47.9	43.4	51.1	51.6	45.8	46.0	33.2
% Families With Female Head..	21.7	22.7	18.8	23.9	14.4	23.0	20.0	22.3	27.2	19.4
Median School Years Completed..	11.6	11.7	11.8	12.1	11.4	11.1	11.5	11.7	12.1	11.1
Median Family Income, 1979...$$	19144	19411	19219	20920	25000	19348	17654	16734	14457	20625
% Income Below Poverty Level....	8.7	10.0	3.0	5.5	3.6	10.1	7.6	10.7	23.1	9.6
% Income Of $30,000 Or More....	19.1	14.6	15.2	22.1	32.4	18.4	15.8	16.7	8.5	28.6
% White Collar Workers.......	40.4	46.5	44.5	44.6	36.7	35.8	37.1	41.2	44.0	44.0
% Civilian Labor Force Unemployed.	8.3	10.6	4.7	7.2	6.3	9.5	7.7	8.8	10.9	7.4
% Riding To Work By Automobile....	54.8	51.1	62.5	51.2	48.2	57.2	53.6	61.6	55.2	56.0
Mean Commuting Time - Minutes...	28.8	26.9	26.9	29.3	30.8	29.7	30.0	28.3	25.2	25.9
Population Per Household..........	2.5	2.6	2.5	2.4	2.4	2.4	2.6	2.8	2.9	2.6
Total Housing Units..........	13986	1258	427	2267	916	2785	2909	1775	486	1163
% Condominiums...............	0.0	0.0	0.0	0.0	0.0	0.0	0.0	0.0	0.0	0.0
% Built 1970 Or Later........	0.4	0.0	0.1	0.0	0.0	0.9	0.9	0.6	0.0	0.0
% Owner Occupied.............	35.4	38.4	37.5	35.9	41.5	32.3	34.4	32.6	31.1	41.8
% With 1+ Persons Per Room...$$	5.1	3.8	5.2	2.7	2.0	4.3	6.9	7.7	9.7	5.8
Median Value: Owner Units....$$	39500	41300	-	47000	55400	39200	35200	36400	-	33600
Median Rent: Rental Units....$$	176	175	158	191	193	165	173	179	176	163
Median Number Of Rooms: All Units.	4.6	4.9	4.2	4.7	4.9	4.4	4.4	4.8	4.9	4.9

Community Area 21 -- Avondale
Selected Characteristics of Census Tracts: 1970

Tract Number	TOTAL	2101	2102	2103	2104	2105	2106	2107	2108	2109
Total Population.............	35806	3727	1133	5888	2300	6935	6864	4558	1214	3187
% Male.......................	47.8	47.8	49.0	47.1	46.5	47.4	48.3	48.2	46.7	48.5
% Black......................	0.0	0.0	0.0	0.0	0.0	0.0	0.0	0.0	0.5	0.1
% Other Nonwhite.............	0.9	1.2	0.5	0.8	1.0	0.5	0.6	1.5	1.7	0.9
% Of Spanish Language........	4.6	2.8	4.1	1.2	4.8	1.1	5.2	5.4	3.0	18.2
% Foreign Born...............	16.1	8.3	15.5	18.8	16.0	22.9	16.2	10.2	8.4	16.2
% Living In Group Quarters...	0.3	0.2	0.0	0.3	1.8	0.4	0.3	0.0	0.0	0.0
% 13 Years Old And Under.....	21.0	24.5	21.7	18.5	16.9	18.6	20.9	24.6	21.3	24.4
% 14-20 Years Old............	10.7	12.0	12.5	10.4	9.6	10.5	10.3	10.5	10.4	11.4
% 21-64 Years Old............	55.4	52.5	55.3	57.2	58.3	56.7	55.8	53.4	56.1	52.7
% 65-74 Years Old............	8.1	7.5	6.8	8.3	9.9	8.5	8.3	7.4	6.7	7.7
% 75 Years Old And Over......	4.8	3.6	3.7	5.6	5.3	5.8	4.6	4.1	5.5	3.8
% In Different House.........	58.6	58.8	60.4	64.1	58.0	54.4	60.3	58.1	59.6	54.0
% Families With Female Head..	14.1	12.2	16.3	13.1	11.7	15.3	14.9	14.7	18.7	12.8
Median School Years Completed...	10.0	10.5	9.8	10.6	11.0	9.6	9.5	10.0	9.8	10.2
Median Family Income, 1969...$$	10495	10466	9969	11586	11580	10411	9861	10214	8865	10455
% Income Below Poverty Level....	6.4	7.6	6.1	4.3	5.6	6.8	6.0	9.1	1.3	7.5
% Income of $15,000 or More.....	21.6	22.3	21.0	26.5	24.1	20.8	20.2	18.4	18.8	19.4
% White Collar Workers.......	16.1	13.9	17.7	21.2	20.4	16.2	14.3	12.9	15.6	12.7
% Civilian Labor Force Unemployed.	3.3	2.6	0.0	3.0	3.1	4.1	3.9	4.3	1.4	1.8
% Riding To Work By Automobile....	51.4	49.8	60.6	49.3	51.4	49.8	49.7	58.1	45.7	54.6
Population Per Household..........	2.7	3.0	2.7	2.7	2.7	2.6	2.7	2.8	2.7	2.9
Total Housing Units..........	13751	1328	429	2249	876	2774	2703	1741	486	1165
% Condominiums & Cooperatives.....	0.4	0.0	0.0	0.7	0.0	0.6	0.0	1.0	0.0	0.0
% Built 1960 Or Later........	1.3	1.0	2.6	1.0	1.7	1.4	1.2	1.0	1.0	1.4
% Owner Occupied.............	34.5	38.5	41.0	35.2	41.3	29.8	34.1	32.2	30.0	38.6
% With 1+ Persons Per Room...$$	5.7	7.5	7.2	4.3	3.8	5.1	6.2	6.3	4.5	7.7
Median Value: Owner Units...$$	18200	17600	-	21400	22100	18400	17200	17800	16300	15700
Median Rent: Rental Units...$$	92	92	81	101	112	86	88	93	88	90
Median Number Of Rooms: All Units.	4.6	4.9	4.1	4.7	4.9	4.3	4.3	4.7	4.6	4.8

existed along Milwaukee Avenue as late as annexation. One tollgate was burned down in 1889 by the enraged citizens of Avondale who dressed up as Indians one night and staged a riot to protest the "no-good" road. The owner of the tollgate, Amos Snell, was killed in the riot and the gate was never replaced. The city resurfaced the road in the early 1890s.

The next several decades, from 1890 to 1920, were a period of great development for Avondale. Avondale School was built in 1894 and 1895 and stands today with several additions. The improvements in surface transit facilities — the electrification and extension of the Elston and Milwaukee Avenue car lines in 1894 — led to the more intensive settlement of the community south of Belmont Avenue. The Logan Square branch of the elevated line, when completed to Logan Square in 1895, offered a terminal a short distance south of the southern boundary of the community. In addition, factories which were constructed along both railroad tracks and along the west bank of the North Branch of the Chicago River, as well as the brickyards in the vicinity of Belmont and California avenues, attracted workers who sought living quarters near their work. Most of their frame cottages were clustered around the factories and railroad yards. A majority of the residents east of Kedzie Avenue were Germans and Scandinavians, while those residing between Kedzie and Milwaukee avenues were a mixture of Germans and Poles. The latter began moving into Avondale in the early 1890s.

The community continued to increase until it reached a population of 38,192 by 1920. More than one-fourth of the 1920 population was foreign-born, mostly Germans and Poles, with a lesser proportion of Swedes and Austrians. During the next decade the population of the community increased by 10,000. There was a large increase in the number of Poles who became the predominant foreign stock in Avondale, comprising 33 percent of the population in 1930. With the influx of Poles, some of the Germans and Swedes moved to communities or suburbs to the north and northwest. In the latter part of the 1920s, even some of the Poles, earlier residents or their descendants, were moving north and northwest to communities like Portage Park. Other Poles, however, chiefly from the overcrowded and deteriorating areas west of the Loop, were moving into Avondale.

Residential construction in Avondale entered a boom period during the 1920s. The installation of new transit lines on Kedzie Avenue and Pulaski Road and the extension of the Belmont Avenue line provided better transportation facilities for many neighborhoods and sped their development. The newer areas in the northern and western parts of the community were built up with brick bungalows, two- and three-flats, and some small apartment buildings. In the older sections of the community where frame structures predominated, new construction of brick bungalows, two- and three-flats was common. By the mid-1920s, Avondale was a well-settled, residentially mature community. In the general section east of Milwaukee Avenue, the diagonal streets, Avondale and Elston avenues, and the curves of the river left many odd-shaped patches of vacant land. Under the zoning ordinances, all land east of Elston Avenue, except for a few blocks facing Addison Street, were zoned for business and industry, most of it for heavy industry. The triangular piece of land bounded by the Chicago and North Western tracks, Kedzie Avenue, and Addison Street was also zoned for heavy industry. This industrial district extended south to the

intersection of Belmont and Kimball avenues. The northern part of this industrial area constituted the forerunner of the present-day Addison Kedzie Industrial District. Factories producing a variety of products were built through the industrial areas. By 1930, Avondale appeared to be a relatively stable "rental area" community, most of whose dwelling units were in brick two- and three-flats and small apartment buildings, although there were also a good many frame and brick bungalows.

The population of Avondale has declined steadily from its peak of more than 48,000 in 1930 to about 33,500 in 1980. During the most recent decade the population declined about 6 percent while the city as a whole lost almost 11 percent. Poles have remained the dominant descent group still comprising almost one-third of the total population. Since 1930, there has been an influx of Italians into the community and beginning in 1970, Hispanics have also begun to move in. The Hispanic population which has increased from about 1,600 in 1970 to almost 7,000 in 1980, accounts for more than 20 percent of the total followed by the German descent group which is less than 10 percent. The remaining portion is made up of mixed European ancestry with a scattering of Asiatics, mostly Filipino. The 1979 median income of about $19,000 is slightly above that for the city as a whole, the unemployment rate, about 8 percent, is below the city median.

There has been little residential construction in the community since 1930. In the 1950s there was extensive demolition of old frame houses in the eastern section to make room for the Kennedy Expressway. Despite this, the number of housing units has remained stable, the result of conversion to apatments. However, as the small frame homes that had been built near the industrial areas began to age, people began leaving the area in search of newer homes in the suburbs and the area started to deteriorate. Absentee landlords failed to maintain aging buildings and businessmen worried about the declining value of once prime real estate. Avondale began to face problems similar to those of other urban areas around the country in the 1960s and 1970s. Today, most residents live in low-rise (two- to nine-unit) apartment buildings, and almost 30 percent of these units are overcrowded, compared to less than 7 percent in 1960. Many landlords live on the premises, and more than one-third of all units are owner-occupied. Only 15 percent of all units are single-family dwellings, and their median value is less than that of the city.

Several community organizations have attempted efforts at economic revitalization, rehabilitation of abandoned homes and the development and coordination of social services. The vacancy rate has increased about one percentage point from 1970 to 1980. Construction of the Kennedy Plaza shopping area at Kimball, Belmont and the Kennedy Expressway, the commercial rehabilitation of some sections of Milwaukee and Fullerton avenues, and the redevelopment of a large vacant factory building are all viewed as positive signs in the community. The Logan Square elevated train, now called the Jefferson line, links the community with O'Hare Airport. Because of its easy access to downtown Chicago, some people have "rediscovered" Avondale for its convenient location and as a relatively inexpensive place to live. In addition, the ethnically diverse population of Avondale provides a cultural and commercial mix that some area residents identify as an attractive feature in city life.

Elfriede Wedam

Logan Square

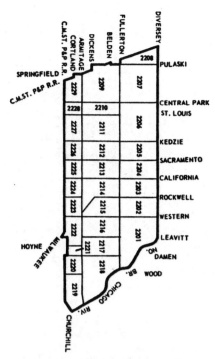

Logan Square, at Milwaukee Avenue and the west end of Logan Boulevard, has provided the name of a large community area, parts of which were in existence before the Square itself. The Square was named for John A. Logan, Illinois politician and Civil War general. In 1836, Martin Kimbell claimed a 160-acre tract bounded by the present Kimball, Diversey, Hamlin and Fullerton avenues. Through the 1840s, this area was prairie and then farmland, as Kimbell's property was gradually sold to farmers. After the Northwest Plank Road (Milwaukee Avenue) was laid in 1849 and 1850, some stores appeared. G.M. Powell established the Powell House Hotel at the present intersection of Armitage and Milwaukee avenues. The hotel served as the terminus of a horse-drawn omnibus line which came up the Plank Road, and housed the area's first post office. The Chicago and North Western Railroad began operating in the area in 1854, along the eastern boundary parallel to the North Branch of the Chicago River.

In the early 1860s, few families resided north of North Avenue, but a gradual expansion began along Milwaukee Avenue in 1863, when the city limits were extended to Western and Fullerton avenues. The area between the river, Diversey and Western avenues was added by another annexation in 1869. In that year, a suburban settlement developed to the south and west of the present Maplewood station of the Chicago and North Western Railroad. The railroad station and the first frame house were built in 1870, followed by more frame houses and a toy factory in 1871.

The 1869 annexation had also added to the city the land which was to become Humbolt Park, which the newly-created West Side Board proposed to develop immediately. This set off a wave of speculation which quickly drove the value of what had been farmland near the park site up from $250 to $5,000 an acre. Humboldt Boulevard was built and a Humboldt suburban subdivision followed in 1870. The Milwaukee Railroad built a Humboldt station at Bloomingdale and California avenues, and this development (in Census Tract 2225) grew rapidly.

However, most of the land in the Logan Square area remained undeveloped until after the Fire of 1871. The city fire limits, prohibiting the construction of frame houses within its boundaries, did not extend into Logan Square. This motivated many families to rebuild in the eastern section of the community area, principally along Milwaukee Avenue and in Maplewood, because of access to transportation facilities. By 1884, Maplewood had a population of 6,000, including many who had wished to live close to the factories that were already going up along the railroad tracks and the river. By the mid-1880s, a considerable number of Swedes began to settle between Diversey and Fullerton avenues from Western to Kimball Avenue, and Norwegians began to move into an area south of there In 1889. The remainder of the present community area was annexed to Chicago as part of the Town of Jefferson.

With the coming of the elevated line to Logan Square and the extension of the surface lines and the boulevards in the 1890s, the community began to develop rapidly. Many residents built homes near the elevated station at Fullerton and Milwaukee avenues. The area west of the station was settled by Swedes, who were followed into the area by Germans. An increasing number of Norwegians settled east of the station. In the northwest corner, Homer Pennock began construction of a large stove factory and frame houses for prospective workers around 1895. The factory burned down prior to completion, however, and Pennock pulled out, leaving his prospective workers holding the lots he had sold them. Lyon and Healy later erected their piano factory in the vicinity. The local railroad station was named for Healy as well as the Healy Industrial District.

During the first two decades of the 20th century, Logan Square flourished as a commercial center. Milwaukee and Fullerton avenues were already shopping areas, with many stores at Milwaukee and Armitage avenues. The population increased steadily, reaching 108,685 by 1920. Germans and Norwegians constituted the area's largest foreign-born groups. Around this time, Poles began to settle in large numbers, principally near the factory area in the northwest corner and the growing industrial area between the North Western tracks and the river. Russian Jews began to in-migrate after 1912, tending to settle along Logan Boulevard and the streets nearby. The growth in population led to the construction of the first large apartment building along Kedzie Boulevard.

During the 1920s Logan Square achieved full development and residential maturity. Poles had moved into the community area in such numbers as to become the most numerous foreign-stock group, far surpassing the Germans and Scandinavians, who were beginning to move out. The largest influx of Russian Jews took place after World War I, and by 1930 this group had become one of the area's largest. The community experienced a building boom, especially after 1924, when Ada Sawyer Garrett sold the Logan Square Ball Park for $650,000, providing land for what became a $12 million development. East of Healy Industrial District and Pulaski Road were small frame homes of Polish and Scandinavian workers, and farther east new brick homes, two-flats and smaller apartment buildings. The section around Kedzie and Humboldt Boulevards and Palmer Square was a higher class residential district where many Russian Jews and Germans lived in brick residences and apartment buildings. Another distinct Polish settlement was located east of Western Avenue, where they replaced the reduced German population. The Swedish population center was still east of Palmer Square, while the central portion of the community area was principally Norwegian, Swedish and German. Russian Jews still tended to reside on the boulevards. Opposite Logan Square on Milwaukee Avenue, between Sawyer and Kimball avenues, a syndicate of developers built the Harding Theatre and surrounded it with retail outlets, apartments and offices. In 1930, the population of Logan Square reached a peak of 114,174, through "doubling-up" and the the compartmentalizing of once-fancy apartment buildings during the Depression.

From 1930 to 1960, the population of Logan Square declined at a steady, gradual rate, to less than 95,000 at the latter date. Poles were still the dominant group among the foreign stock in 1960, followed by

Community Area 22 -- Logan Square
Population and Housing Characteristics, 1930-1980

	1980	1970	1960	1950	1940	1930
Total Population.......	84,768	88,555	94,799	106,763	110,010	114,174
% Male..................	49.8	49.0	49.1	48.8	49.1	50.2
% Female................	50.2	51.0	50.9	51.2	50.9	49.8
% White.................	71.2	97.6	99.2	99.7	100.0	99.9
% Black.................	2.7	0.7	0.4	0.2	0.0	0.0
% Other Nonwhite Races...	26.1	1.7	0.4	0.1	0.0	0.1
% Under 5 Years Old.....	9.8	9.1	10.1	9.0	6.1	7.6
% 5-19 Years Old.........	25.3	25.7	22.0	18.3	21.6	27.1
% 20-44 Years Old........	37.9	32.2	33.8	41.1	43.8	44.1
% 45-64 Years Old........	17.6	22.6	23.5	23.7	22.4	16.5
% 65 Years and Older.....	9.4	10.4	10.6	7.9	6.1	4.7
Median School Years....	10.5	9.8	9.1	8.9	8.2	*
Total Housing Units....	32,514	32,276	33,589	33,529	32,254	*
% In One-Unit Structures.	9.9	9.8	9.7	*	*	*
% Owner Occupied.........	25.6	26.5	27.7	27.9	22.1	*
% Renter Occupied........	65.1	68.0	67.9	70.9	75.1	*
% Vacant.................	9.3	5.5	4.4	1.2	2.8	*
% 1+ Persons per Room....	10.8	8.3	8.1	10.4	*	*

Community Area 22 -- Logan Square
Selected Characteristics of Census Tracts: 1980

Tract Number	Total	2201	2202	2203	2204	2205	2206	2207	2208	2209	2210
Total Population.............	84768	609	2147	3025	3218	3757	9345	7128	85	6261	3233
% Male......................	49.8	48.8	49.3	49.4	48.9	53.1	51.8	48.4	-	48.6	50.4
% Black.....................	2.6	2.5	1.6	1.0	1.1	1.6	2.1	0.1	-	1.4	2.3
% Other Nonwhite.............	26.1	34.0	28.9	30.4	19.7	20.0	25.8	12.4	-	15.9	29.2
% Of Spanish Origin..........	51.7	55.7	50.3	44.5	39.2	52.7	47.2	24.9	-	46.4	64.2
% Foreign Born..............	23.3	10.8	30.9	21.0	21.0	25.9	28.3	23.8	-	20.2	20.6
% Living In Group Quarters...	1.1	0.0	0.0	1.0	0.0	2.4	1.0	2.8	-	0.2	0.4
% 13 Years Old And Under.....	24.9	26.1	24.7	24.8	17.7	20.6	20.6	19.0	-	23.9	30.2
% 14-20 Years Old............	12.3	14.3	12.5	12.3	11.1	12.2	11.7	9.5	-	12.9	13.8
% 21-64 Years Old............	53.4	48.6	54.2	55.3	58.4	57.1	56.2	56.6	-	53.1	50.1
% 65-74 Years Old............	6.0	7.9	5.8	5.0	8.0	6.1	7.3	8.4	-	7.0	3.8
% 75 Years Old And Over......	3.4	3.1	2.8	2.6	4.8	4.0	4.2	6.4	-	3.1	2.1
% In Different House.........	52.5	62.5	53.1	52.5	32.9	57.2	55.3	45.3	-	48.1	76.2
% Families With Female Head...	28.3	30.5	27.7	26.5	16.8	23.3	25.9	21.4	-	27.5	31.9
Median School Years Completed.	10.5	9.5	9.9	12.0	11.9	11.6	11.2	11.9	-	11.3	9.5
Median Family Income, 1979...$$	16224	12647	17750	18542	21438	19147	18327	19732	-	18206	12708
% Income Below Poverty Level....	18.7	20.1	13.7	12.8	10.1	9.5	15.9	7.9	-	15.0	26.5
% Income Of $30,000 Or More....	14.6	20.8	9.8	17.5	28.9	19.6	16.2	17.5	-	21.7	9.1
% White Collar Workers.......	38.3	28.0	39.4	44.0	51.0	44.0	39.8	40.1	-	39.1	29.0
% Civilian Labor Force Unemployed.	9.4	6.6	8.5	10.8	9.5	9.0	8.1	6.7	-	7.6	9.4
% Riding To Work By Automobile....	58.2	49.4	66.0	64.6	62.2	55.4	41.8	58.9	-	65.8	67.3
Mean Commuting Time - Minutes...	28.7	22.0	28.1	27.2	27.3	25.9	29.4	29.5	-	32.1	29.4
Population Per Household...	2.8	2.9	2.9	3.0	2.6	2.6	2.5	2.6	-	2.9	3.0
Total Housing Units..........	32514	240	808	1093	1291	1499	3847	2907	30	2398	1139
% Condominiums...............	0.0	0.0	0.0	0.0	0.0	0.0	0.0	0.0	-	0.0	0.0
% Built 1970 Or Later........	1.3	0.0	0.9	3.2	1.3	1.3	0.6	0.8	-	1.4	1.1
% Owner Occupied.............	25.6	27.9	31.3	28.6	37.3	23.7	19.3	30.6	-	33.9	24.3
% With 1+ Persons Per Room......	10.8	11.6	9.9	11.1	5.7	11.3	10.4	4.8	-	8.2	9.9
Median Value: Owner Units......$$	30500	-	31400	32100	34600	39600	38300	36300	-	32300	31500
Median Rent: Rental Units......$$	168	169	178	189	198	185	187	185	-	176	170
Median Number Of Rooms: All Units.	4.7	4.8	4.7	5.1	5.6	4.8	4.3	4.8	-	5.0	4.8

Tract Number	2211	2212	2213	2214	2215	2216	2217	2218	2219	2220	2221
Total Population.............	5745	3404	4184	3238	3335	3866	3225	1418	692	1629	1014
% Male......................	47.8	49.8	51.7	49.4	50.8	48.8	50.0	50.6	48.4	51.2	48.3
% Black.....................	4.9	4.7	1.6	0.9	1.6	1.6	2.0	4.1	0.2	0.2	1.1
% Other Nonwhite.............	30.2	34.7	28.0	27.9	29.1	25.7	34.9	41.7	13.3	18.4	37.2
% Of Spanish Origin..........	57.3	72.1	64.4	64.6	56.2	45.1	48.3	54.7	19.8	37.5	57.5
% Foreign Born..............	20.5	26.5	25.7	19.8	31.7	18.8	28.6	36.0	19.6	21.9	20.2
% Living In Group Quarters...	3.7	0.1	4.2	0.1	0.0	0.0	0.0	0.0	0.0	0.0	0.0
% 13 Years Old And Under.....	25.7	30.9	25.5	28.3	27.6	23.4	24.5	26.1	18.6	22.7	27.9
% 14-20 Years Old............	11.2	12.5	11.3	14.5	12.3	12.5	12.3	13.3	13.4	11.2	12.1
% 21-64 Years Old............	51.1	50.3	55.9	50.4	51.8	53.8	52.6	52.8	56.4	57.2	54.2
% 65-74 Years Old............	6.5	4.4	4.5	4.8	5.1	7.1	7.3	5.3	8.4	6.8	3.5
% 75 Years Old And Over......	5.5	1.9	2.8	2.0	3.2	3.2	3.3	2.5	3.2	2.1	2.3
% In Different House.........	68.9	56.6	58.4	47.4	53.5	41.7	53.6	72.4	29.3	51.2	54.1
% Families With Female Head...	35.8	33.9	26.3	28.3	29.0	24.7	27.3	31.7	29.8	20.7	28.2
Median School Years Completed....	10.7	10.1	10.3	9.5	9.9	10.8	7.9	7.9	10.6	10.3	7.9
Median Family Income, 1979...$$	14795	15332	16094	13764	14904	12464	12168	14352	18500	17241	14167
% Income Below Poverty Level.....	19.9	24.4	20.3	26.7	17.8	21.7	28.8	27.5	12.2	8.1	19.3
% Income Of $30,000 Or More.....	12.3	9.1	15.3	9.1	11.8	10.9	7.5	15.0	16.3	10.7	12.3
% White Collar Workers.......	44.7	32.9	34.3	32.4	32.1	39.2	37.6	19.4	54.3	35.7	33.1
% Civilian Labor Force Unemployed.	13.2	10.2	6.2	13.4	13.4	11.8	5.4	8.0	8.3	8.2	10.0
% Riding To Work By Automobile....	60.2	65.9	60.5	55.0	57.2	56.4	60.8	54.5	59.2	57.0	46.5
Mean Commuting Time - Minutes...	29.2	29.1	27.4	24.2	29.9	26.8	29.0	35.1	21.1	24.0	33.9
Population Per Household...	2.7	3.3	2.9	3.2	3.0	2.7	2.7	3.1	2.5	2.7	3.0
Total Housing Units..........	2271	1173	1489	1199	1186	1604	1387	508	323	686	392
% Condominiums...............	0.0	0.0	0.0	0.0	0.0	0.0	0.0	0.0	0.0	0.0	0.0
% Built 1970 Or Later........	1.2	0.4	0.4	4.1	2.2	2.2	1.0	0.0	2.4	1.4	2.3
% Owner Occupied.............	18.9	19.4	17.5	27.5	26.5	28.4	23.5	28.3	29.7	29.9	28.3
% With 1+ Persons Per Room......	8.5	13.7	17.2	15.8	13.3	11.5	10.0	16.7	5.1	7.0	11.5
Median Value: Owner Units......$$	30400	-	27400	19900	31100	26100	23600	-	-	-	-
Median Rent: Rental Units......$$	177	183	161	155	161	150	135	130	128	138	145
Median Number Of Rooms: All Units.	4.8	4.8	4.3	4.7	4.9	4.4	4.2	4.3	4.6	4.3	4.5

Community Area 22 -- Logan Square
Selected Characteristics of Census Tracts: 1980

Tract Number	2222	2223	2224	2225	2226	2227	2228	2229
Total Population.............	2190	1131	2008	2007	2553	2172	934	1215
% Male.........................	50.2	52.6	48.4	48.1	49.4	46.4	51.3	50.5
% Black........................	8.9	2.6	3.6	3.2	14.1	5.0	4.4	1.7
% Other Nonwhite...............	35.6	15.5	22.9	24.6	41.5	42.3	24.0	18.8
% Of Spanish Origin............	57.7	45.2	64.6	72.4	62.6	67.3	60.4	56.0
% Foreign Born.................	24.6	8.0	21.6	13.3	13.3	29.5	23.5	20.2
% Living In Group Quarters.....	0.0	0.0	0.2	1.1	0.8	2.6	0.0	0.0
% 13 Years Old And Under.......	26.0	27.4	29.5	34.7	31.4	31.6	28.9	29.0
% 14-20 Years Old..............	15.2	13.1	13.6	13.9	13.4	14.0	13.5	14.7
% 21-64 Years Old..............	51.1	52.5	51.4	46.5	49.9	47.1	51.3	50.1
% 65-74 Years Old..............	4.9	4.7	3.5	3.4	3.4	4.7	3.9	4.3
% 75 Years Old And Over........	2.8	2.3	1.9	1.5	2.0	2.7	2.5	2.0
% In Different House...........	41.6	34.3	49.7	42.5	48.0	47.8	65.9	58.5
% Families With Female Head....	35.6	26.5	26.4	32.3	40.0	36.2	27.0	29.9
Median School Years Completed....	7.9	9.8	9.3	9.3	7.9	7.9	7.9	11.0
Median Family Income, 1979....$$	17656	14258	16375	11619	9952	14572	12188	17381
% Income Below Poverty Level.....	27.3	24.2	16.2	29.4	36.1	23.7	33.2	21.8
% Income Of $30,000 Or More.....	19.2	7.2	9.8	11.3	12.2	12.6	2.3	16.0
% White Collar Workers.........	37.8	35.6	39.6	37.5	30.6	29.3	33.9	43.3
% Civilian Labor Force Unemployed.	8.5	20.7	15.2	6.5	8.9	10.0	20.5	8.7
% Riding To Work By Automobile....	54.5	51.1	65.8	67.5	64.6	58.0	68.1	72.4
Mean Commuting Time - Minutes...	34.0	31.5	28.0	30.4	29.2	23.2	25.3	31.2
Population Per Household.......	3.2	3.0	3.2	3.4	2.9	3.4	2.8	3.4
Total Housing Units...........	810	416	677	629	985	749	363	415
% Condominiums.................	0.0	0.0	0.0	0.0	0.0	0.0	0.0	0.0
% Built 1970 Or Later..........	1.1	0.0	2.9	2.5	0.0	1.5	0.0	0.0
% Owner Occupied...............	28.0	29.1	24.5	26.2	15.7	20.3	22.3	33.7
% With 1+ Persons Per Room.....	14.0	11.5	13.5	19.0	12.2	20.1	11.7	8.8
Median Value: Owner Units......$$	26900	-	-	-	-	-	-	32500
Median Rent: Rental Units......$$	149	142	146	161	154	162	158	164
Median Number Of Rooms: All Units.	4.9	4.7	4.9	4.9	4.4	4.5	4.4	5.0

Community Area 22 -- Logan Square
Selected Characteristics of Census Tracts: 1970

Tract Number	TOTAL	2201	2202	2203	2204	2205	2206	2207	2208	2209	2210
Total Population.............	88555	659	2068	3141	3407	3644	8310	7237	51	5942	3504
% Male.........................	49.0	52.4	48.6	48.4	49.0	50.1	48.8	47.4	-	49.3	50.0
% Black........................	0.7	0.9	0.4	0.1	0.1	0.0	0.1	0.1	-	0.1	0.0
% Other Nonwhite...............	1.7	4.1	2.4	4.4	1.0	1.2	1.1	0.9	-	0.6	1.0
% Of Spanish Language..........	17.8	16.5	13.4	10.9	11.2	19.2	8.1	3.2	-	6.6	19.3
% Foreign Born.................	18.1	13.9	12.9	13.9	20.9	23.7	26.3	19.8	-	15.8	18.7
% Living In Group Quarters.....	0.7	0.0	0.0	0.0	0.0	0.0	0.0	0.0	-	0.1	0.3
% 13 Years Old And Under.......	25.2	21.7	24.0	26.8	20.8	20.2	17.7	20.9	-	22.7	29.7
% 14-20 Years Old..............	11.2	11.5	11.0	12.1	12.4	10.3	10.3	10.8	-	10.8	11.5
% 21-64 Years Old..............	53.2	56.1	55.2	52.7	55.7	56.9	57.0	54.5	-	55.1	50.3
% 65-74 Years Old..............	6.4	5.0	6.5	5.3	7.1	7.2	9.8	7.4	-	7.4	5.4
% 75 Years Old And Over........	4.0	4.9	3.1	4.0	4.1	5.3	5.2	3.9	-	3.9	3.2
% In Different House...........	48.6	50.9	53.7	41.9	59.7	42.9	48.9	54.3	-	53.6	39.8
% Families With Female Head....	14.7	17.6	13.2	13.1	11.7	14.4	13.6	13.1	-	11.3	14.3
Median School Years Completed....$$	9.8	10.0	9.6	10.6	10.6	9.9	10.3	10.1	-	10.3	9.7
Median Family Income, 1969....$$	9915	9867	10342	11013	11151	9798	10254	11360	-	10434	9102
% Income Below Poverty Level.....	10.0	14.8	12.2	6.3	6.1	10.3	6.4	4.2	-	5.9	9.6
% Income of $15,000 or More.....	17.9	38.3	14.1	23.0	19.9	19.4	20.4	23.3	-	21.2	12.4
% White Collar Workers.........	15.1	2.0	15.8	21.7	18.8	15.2	20.4	19.2	-	16.2	10.7
% Civilian Labor Force Unemployed.	4.9	2.9	4.8	4.6	3.8	6.4	3.9	3.0	-	2.7	4.8
% Riding To Work By Automobile....	50.6	56.5	43.7	55.3	51.8	51.7	42.2	49.8	-	54.9	56.5
Population Per Household.......	2.9	2.8	2.7	3.0	2.9	2.6	2.4	2.8	-	2.9	3.2
Total Housing Units...........	32301	243	799	1076	1216	1470	3656	2620	21	2158	1141
% Condominiums & Cooperatives.....	0.3	0.0	1.1	0.0	0.7	0.3	0.4	0.7	-	0.6	0.0
% Built 1960 Or Later..........	0.8	0.0	0.8	3.7	0.5	0.0	0.2	0.8	-	1.7	0.9
% Owner Occupied...............	26.2	37.0	29.4	27.2	35.4	21.4	19.2	31.5	-	36.0	25.4
% With 1+ Persons Per Room.....	8.4	6.8	6.0	10.0	4.3	6.0	5.5	5.2	-	5.1	10.8
Median Value: Owner Units......$$	15300	-	15900	15600	16900	17600	18100	17800	-	16200	15800
Median Rent: Rental Units......$$	91	84	85	100	103	98	102	99	-	98	98
Median Number Of Rooms: All Units.	4.6	4.9	4.5	4.8	5.5	4.6	4.1	4.8	-	5.0	4.7

Tract Number	2211	2212	2213	2214	2215	2216	2217	2218	2219	2220	2221
Total Population.............	5918	3976	4118	3489	3482	4354	3659	1804	815	2049	1071
% Male.........................	48.7	49.4	48.2	51.2	48.0	48.3	48.8	48.2	50.3	49.7	47.3
% Black........................	0.6	0.1	0.2	0.5	0.5	0.2	0.2	7.6	1.0	0.0	0.0
% Other Nonwhite...............	1.8	2.1	1.7	1.7	3.6	2.6	1.0	1.8	2.5	1.6	0.5
% Of Spanish Language..........	19.1	25.4	31.6	26.1	23.2	21.3	16.5	14.0	4.6	11.1	3.4
% Foreign Born.................	21.2	27.0	18.9	11.7	10.3	19.8	16.8	14.6	14.7	19.2	15.8
% Living In Group Quarters.....	0.1	0.6	1.5	0.5	0.1	0.0	0.9	0.0	4.8	0.3	0.0
% 13 Years Old And Under.......	25.9	29.4	26.2	29.3	25.9	25.9	25.3	27.1	18.8	25.3	27.5
% 14-20 Years Old..............	11.2	11.0	10.5	12.4	11.3	11.3	10.2	9.8	12.3	12.4	9.4
% 21-64 Years Old..............	52.4	51.6	51.1	49.7	52.4	54.8	55.3	52.1	57.2	54.1	51.9
% 65-74 Years Old..............	6.8	5.2	6.9	5.1	6.5	5.4	5.9	5.2	7.7	5.2	5.2
% 75 Years Old And Over........	3.7	2.8	5.2	3.5	3.8	3.7	3.8	4.0	4.0	3.0	5.9
% In Different House...........	46.8	41.5	41.0	43.8	52.0	56.3	56.1	57.8	45.6	54.3	53.8
% Families With Female Head....	17.3	15.7	16.2	16.0	15.6	15.4	14.3	18.3	13.6	12.7	21.5
Median School Years Completed....	10.4	10.4	9.9	8.9	9.6	9.6	9.0	8.7	9.8	9.4	9.8
Median Family Income, 1969......$$	10046	8506	8922	8886	9469	10413	9152	9403	9594	9947	9625
% Income Below Poverty Level....	11.8	10.8	10.6	13.4	10.7	12.1	15.7	11.6	10.1	7.0	13.5
% Income of $15,000 or More.....	20.3	15.4	18.3	13.7	12.8	13.9	13.6	14.4	21.6	16.0	16.6
% White Collar Workers.........	16.6	13.7	17.0	11.9	12.6	10.6	11.4	7.6	17.1	16.1	10.6
% Civilian Labor Force Unemployed.	3.4	7.5	4.3	5.0	3.8	4.3	4.3	6.4	2.6	5.0	18.8
% Riding To Work By Automobile....	50.1	51.4	51.0	49.2	51.8	57.3	51.0	45.6	63.6	51.3	42.5
Population Per Household.......	2.9	3.2	2.8	3.1	2.9	2.9	2.8	2.8	2.8	2.9	2.9
Total Housing Units...........	2162	1286	1502	1235	1251	1565	1364	685	296	732	419
% Condominiums & Cooperatives.....	0.0	0.7	0.5	0.5	0.0	0.0	0.0	0.0	0.0	0.0	0.0
% Built 1960 Or Later..........	0.6	1.0	0.6	0.5	0.0	0.3	1.5	0.6	1.9	3.1	0.0
% Owner Occupied...............	20.7	21.7	18.3	25.7	26.7	31.1	26.0	26.6	32.8	29.0	31.0
% With 1+ Persons Per Room.....	7.9	10.5	7.7	11.5	7.7	11.7	11.7	10.3	5.4	9.3	7.8
Median Value: Owner Units......$$	15700	15000	14200	12600	15200	13500	13700	11300	-	13600	-
Median Rent: Rental Units......$$	99	105	90	77	85	71	67	64	60	67	71
Median Number Of Rooms: All Units.	4.5	4.8	4.5	4.5	4.7	4.3	4.2	4.2	4.5	4.3	4.4

Community Area 22 -- Logan Square
Selected Characteristics of Census Tracts: 1970

Tract Number	2222	2223	2224	2225	2226	2227	2228	2229
Total Population............	2835	1504	2254	2083	2492	2441	1033	1215
% Male...........................	50.1	50.1	49.8	49.2	50.9	48.9	47.8	48.2
% Black..........................	10.3	0.2	0.4	0.6	0.5	0.2	0.5	0.0
% Other Nonwhite.................	1.9	0.9	1.3	1.1	1.8	2.1	4.5	1.2
% Of Spanish Language............	35.0	22.4	29.2	44.4	24.0	25.7	36.3	18.1
% Foreign Born...................	16.8	5.6	12.1	12.2	12.8	20.3	18.5	6.0
% Living In Group Quarters.......	0.3	0.0	0.0	0.0	0.0	0.3	0.0	0.0
% 13 Years Old And Under.........	32.5	32.4	31.2	32.2	29.0	29.5	27.0	27.4
% 14-20 Years Old................	12.7	11.6	12.7	12.5	11.6	10.6	10.2	12.8
% 21-64 Years Old................	47.7	49.5	49.9	48.2	50.7	50.6	54.3	51.0
% 65-74 Years Old...............	4.2	4.3	3.9	4.6	5.4	6.0	5.6	5.4
% 75 Years Old And Over.........	3.0	2.3	2.3	2.5	3.3	3.3	2.9	3.3
% In Different House............	49.8	39.6	46.9	45.5	33.9	40.4	37.1	61.6
% Families With Female Head......	18.0	19.7	18.0	13.5	14.8	16.8	14.7	12.7
Median School Years Completed....	9.0	9.4	9.1	8.7	9.9	9.3	9.4	10.6
Median Family Income, 1969......$$	9233	8524	8845	9000	9064	9694	10095	10568
% Income Below Poverty Level.....	19.0	16.9	12.6	9.2	16.9	10.1	10.2	8.7
% Income of $15,000 or More.....	20.8	22.0	12.5	16.4	15.1	14.8	5.8	17.0
% White Collar Workers...........	10.0	13.1	13.1	9.8	13.7	12.5	10.1	11.3
% Civilian Labor Force Unemployed.	9.8	8.6	4.2	8.9	8.2	5.0	3.6	5.2
% Riding To Work By Automobile....	46.6	34.3	55.7	48.9	51.6	54.5	53.1	59.0
Population Per Household..........	3.4	3.3	3.3	3.4	2.9	3.1	2.8	3.2
Total Housing Units..........	944	510	750	667	943	809	380	401
% Condominiums & Cooperatives.....	0.0	0.0	0.0	0.0	0.0	0.0	0.0	0.0
% Built 1960 Or Later............	0.0	0.0	0.5	0.9	1.2	0.6	1.6	.5
% Owner Occupied.................	28.7	22.7	26.3	26.2	18.3	24.2	23.9	37.7
% With 1+ Persons Per Room.......	14.2	14.1	11.8	14.0	13.2	10.8	7.4	9.0
Median Value: Owner Units.......$$	12800	-	-	-	-	-	-	16800
Median Rent: Rental Units.......$$	75	70	79	88	87	86	86	88
Median Number Of Rooms: All Units.	4.7	4.6	4.9	4.8	4.3	4.8	4.3	5.0

Germans, Scandinavians, Italians and Russian Jews. A growing Puerto Rican population had moved in, originally concentrated in the southeastern portion. Residential construction was negligible in that 30-year period. The eastern third of the community area, adjacent to the industrial areas along the river and the railroad tracks, deteriorated steadily. In 1957, the Community Conservation Board included the southeastern third of Logan Square, bounded by Fullerton and California avenues, in the "East Humboldt Park-Near North West" renewal area. Construction of the Northwest (Kennedy) Expressway, which cut through the community area near its eastern boundary, began in 1957, and contributed to a mass migration. More than 22,000 people left the Logan Square area between 1950 and 1960. Many businesses closed, and "For Rent" signs became common in Fullerton, Milwaukee and Diversey Avenue storefronts. By 1963, however, Logan Square was showing signs of rejuvenation: an influx of retail franchises, construction of several new buildings, and the renovation of older business and residential structures. The Logan Square Neighborhood Association, a community organization incorporated in 1963, has worked for improvement of existing housing and development of a more cohesive community spirit among residents.

However, the number of inhabitants has continued to drop. It now stands at slightly less than 85,000, less than 75 percent of the peak figure of a half century ago. The fact that Logan Square has not lost population as rapidly as the total city is attributable to a massive influx of Hispanics. In 1960, 569 persons of Spanish origin lived in the community. This grew to almost 16,000 in 10 years and to almost 44,000, more than half the area total, in 1980. Today, the Hispanic population exceeds 50 percent in 18 of the 29 census tracts comprising Logan Square, is greater than 45 percent in six others, and approaches 40 percent in two of those remaining. Among the Spanish-origin residents of Logan Square, the principal subgroups are Puerto Rican (55 percent), Mexican (34 percent) and Cuban (4 percent).

The relation between people and housing in Logan Square has changed very little in the last 20 years. The area has about 1,000 fewer housing units than in 1960, and almost three-fourths of the units are still in the hands of absentee owners. More than a fifth (21.9 percent) of the community population live in overcrowded housing units — those with a ratio of more than one person per room. Of all housing units, only 12.4 percent are single-family structures. The median value of single-family owner-occupied homes was $30,460 in 1980, roughly one-third less than the city average.

Despite a 25 percent numerical loss in the last half century, Logan Square continues to perform a function in much the same way it has carried on for more than a century thus far — it is home to a foreign language ethnic working class population. The Scandinavians and the Germans who settled the area are gone, and the Poles and Russian Jews who succeeded them are leaving. Hispanic Americans now occupy the community area. Subsequent editions of the *Fact Book* will probably trace their progress and eventual mobility to other places, perhaps to be succeeded in Logan Square by another group in similar circumstances.

Will Hogan

Humboldt Park

The Humboldt Park community area gets its name from the 207-acre city park which lies just outside its eastern boundary. Most of the land was annexed to the city in 1869, when an act of the state legislature extended the city limits to North Avenue and the present Pulaski Road. At that time, the area was sparsely-settled prairie and farmland, although it was traversed by Whiskey Point Road (Grand Avenue), which had existed since the 1840s. The park was named for the German naturalist, Alexander von Humboldt, and its establishment, also in 1869, was a key factor in the settlement of the community, although the first Humboldt land development occurred north and east of the park, in the Logan Square and West Town community areas. However, in the early 1870s another settlement, Pacific Junction, so called because of its location near the junction of two lines of the Chicago (Milwaukee, St. Paul) and Pacific Railroad, appeared around Bloomingdale Avenue, from Hamlin to Springfield avenues, along the northern boundary. Another development, Simon's Subdivision (present Census Tracts 2302 and 2303), was named for Edward Simon, who had farmed the land. This northeastern area was settled largely by Germans and did not develop extensively until the Armitage Avenue streetcar line came in, after the turn of the century.

The creation of the West Side parks and the area's location just beyond the city fire code limits encouraged settlement after the Great Fire. Those who came were workingmen seeking inexpensive frame houses to replace those lost in the Fire. The new car shops of the Chicago and North Western Railroad, between Pulaski Road and Kinzie Street, covering almost the entire southwestern corner of the community area, attracted many workers and led to further subdivision along the southern periphery. Humboldt Park was developed along the railroads, close to the new parks, along Division Street, North and Grand avenues. New construction tended to radiate from these foci, interspersed with stretches of undeveloped land.

By 1889, the present Humboldt Park community area had come entirely within the city limits through annexation of the Town of Jefferson, which included the Pacific Junction and Simon's Subdivision settlements, and the northwestern corner Tract 2305, which was ceded to Chicago by Cook County. The northeastern Census Tract 2301 had been added by agreement between Chicago and the then-Village of Jefferson in 1887.

Inadequate transportation facilities retarded further settlement until the late 1890s. Before that time, the horse-drawn car lines on every major east-west thoroughfare between North Avenue and Kinzie Street reached only to California Avenue. During the 1880s and 1890s, Germans and Scandinavians continued to settle in Humboldt Park, the Scandinavians moving in from the West Town area as more Poles settled there. More in-migrants followed improvements in transit facilities at the turn of the century. The Humboldt Park branch of the Metropolitan elevated line was built to Lawndale Avenue by 1895, providing northern Humboldt Park with rapid transit service to the Loop. Residents of the southern portion of the community area availed themselves of similar service via the Lake Street branch of the elevated line, located a few blocks beyond the southern community boundary. Electric surface lines ran along Grand and North avenues. New brick bungalows and two-flats were erected alongside the older frame structures before 1900.

The population of Humboldt Park grew rapidly during the first two decades of the 20th century, reaching 65,095 by 1920. At that point, 28 percent of the population were foreign born, chiefly German and Norwegian. An influx of Italians and Poles from West Town and the Near North Side stimulated residential construction from 1900 to 1920. Along the earlier-settled northern boundary there were many one- and

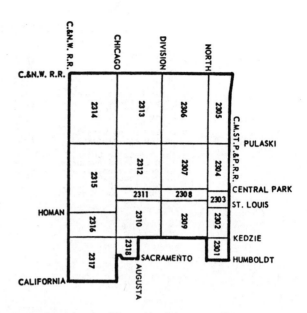

two-story frame houses. The residential pattern of Humboldt Park had been established by 1919.

North Avenue was the leading business strip from 1900 to 1920, but most Humboldt Park residents took their business to the area between Western and California in West Town, where greater shopping opportunities existed. There were also shops on Pulaski Road and Chicago and Grand avenues, and Division Street was developing into a strip of Russian-Jewish shops. Humboldt Park had industry from its earliest days. Manufacturing establishments located near the railroad along the western and northern peripheries, and in the southeastern section.

The population of Humboldt Park increased to more than 80,000 by 1930, of which 31 percent were foreign-born. Italians moved in steadily from areas to the east. They and the Germans became the most numerous foreign stock groups, followed by Poles and Russian Jews. Italians and Poles spread throughout the area, while Russian Jews moved from farther east to the west side of the park. These in-migrants replaced many older German, Scandinavian and Irish residents and their descendants, who had moved to areas farther north and northwest. Considerable residential construction was undertaken during the '20s, including many brick two- and three-flats and some small apartment buildings, tending to reinforce the existing residential pattern. The manufacturing areas expanded along the western, southern and northern boundaries, and factories began to appear in more scattered locations.

The population of Humboldt Park has been declining since 1930. By 1960, Italians had become the largest foreign stock group, followed by Poles, Germans and Russian Jews. In the 1950s, small black and Hispanic populations settled in the community, with blacks concentrated in the extreme southeastern sectors. Between 1930 and 1960, industry expanded along the Chicago and North Western tracks at the western and southern boundaries.

The numerical decrease has tended to level off since 1960. The decade after that produced a small increase in population, but the total fell off again in the 1970s to just under 71,000, a drop of about 12 percent from the 1930 peak. As in other northwest side community areas, a mass out-migration of European-descended whites has been balanced by an influx of Latins and blacks. In 1960, Humboldt Park was 99 percent white. Almost 71,000 whites and 400 blacks lived in the community. Today slightly more than 25,000 blacks live there, slightly fewer than 25,000 whites. Twenty years ago, fewer than 300 Puerto Ricans, plus a few others of Spanish origin, lived in Humboldt Park, today almost 29,000 Latinos live there. The area population is now 41 percent Hispanic. Geographically, the largest subgroup remains Puerto Ricans, who are more than 60 percent of the Latins, twice as numerous

Community Area 23 — Humboldt Park
Population and Housing Characteristics, 1930-1980

	1980	1970	1960	1950	1940	1930
Total Population.......	70,866	71,726	71,609	76,199	79,329	80,835
% Male..................	48.4	48.3	49.2	49.3	50.1	51.1
% Female................	51.6	51.7	50.8	50.7	49.9	48.9
% White.................	35.0	79.2	99.1	99.8	100.0	99.9
% Black.................	35.6	19.4	0.6	0.1	0.0	0.1
% Other Nonwhite Races...	29.4	1.4	0.3	0.1	0.0	0.0
% Under 5 Years Old......	11.0	10.3	10.5	9.3	6.4	7.9
% 5-19 Years Old.........	31.6	28.9	21.9	18.8	22.6	27.4
% 20-44 Years Old........	36.0	32.2	34.6	41.6	44.0	44.2
% 45-64 Years Old........	14.9	19.9	23.1	23.1	21.6	16.5
% 65 Years and Older.....	6.5	8.7	9.9	7.2	5.4	4.0
Median School Years....	10.3	9.2	9.0	8.9	8.1	*
Total Housing Units....	23,746	23,360	23,919	22,633	21,957	*
% In One-Unit Structures.	16.4	14.5	12.8	*	*	*
% Owner Occupied.........	32.1	33.5	35.3	35.8	28.6	*
% Renter Occupied........	58.0	60.7	61.0	63.2	69.3	*
% Vacant................	9.9	5.8	3.7	1.0	2.1	*
% 1+ Persons per Room....	12.9	12.1	7.7	9.8	*	*

Community Area 23 — Humboldt Park
Selected Characteristics of Census Tracts: 1980

Tract Number	Total	2301	2302	2303	2304	2305	2306	2307	2308	2309	2310
Total Population.............	70879	2080	2523	1236	2658	3137	7191	6606	1353	6797	3995
% Male.......................	48.4	48.7	51.3	50.3	48.8	50.8	49.9	49.0	50.4	47.9	48.9
% Black......................	35.6	13.8	4.7	2.8	1.4	2.8	2.4	3.6	6.5	13.3	41.8
% Other Nonwhite.............	29.4	50.4	61.2	72.0	23.4	41.7	40.0	49.3	47.2	46.7	33.5
% Of Spanish Origin..........	40.7	65.4	73.5	72.4	60.1	63.2	51.7	61.8	63.1	69.8	46.2
% Foreign Born...............	14.6	13.9	24.5	28.6	13.1	22.0	24.1	18.4	18.0	13.9	9.9
% Living In Group Quarters...	0.7	1.7	3.8	0.2	0.0	0.0	0.2	0.2	0.0	0.2	1.5
% 13 Years Old And Under.....	29.8	33.6	33.5	34.1	27.5	28.4	25.4	29.0	26.5	31.6	31.4
% 14-20 Years Old............	14.8	16.6	15.8	14.0	13.1	12.0	12.3	13.2	14.9	15.4	16.3
% 21-64 Years Old............	48.9	44.7	47.1	45.8	51.0	50.5	52.7	50.2	49.2	48.0	48.3
% 65-74 Years Old............	4.2	3.7	2.5	3.4	5.3	6.2	6.0	5.0	7.0	3.2	2.7
% 75 Years Old And Over......	2.2	1.4	1.1	2.7	3.2	2.8	3.5	2.6	2.4	1.9	1.3
% In Different House.........	48.9	47.8	52.8	63.9	42.3	60.2	52.2	56.1	46.9	46.6	46.2
% Families With Female Head..	37.1	46.0	28.0	27.0	27.6	22.8	27.5	25.6	24.6	38.7	38.2
Median School Years Completed...	10.3	9.0	7.9	7.9	9.8	10.2	10.7	10.4	10.3	9.5	10.0
Median Family Income, 1979...$$	14462	9826	11467	16731	14604	16317	16575	16176	16167	12343	12943
% Income Below Poverty Level..	25.9	47.7	32.5	32.1	24.6	9.0	18.4	21.3	16.9	30.7	31.5
% Income Of $30,000 Or More...	13.4	11.8	7.3	14.2	10.6	17.7	13.7	11.8	19.9	9.8	15.2
% White Collar Workers.......	33.0	27.7	24.3	19.5	33.6	28.6	32.9	34.9	42.2	35.9	37.9
% Civilian Labor Force Unemployed.	12.9	5.9	7.5	15.5	5.8	12.5	11.5	13.8	10.4	14.3	15.8
% Riding To Work By Automobile....	62.4	48.6	69.6	72.1	68.0	64.6	58.6	69.6	61.0	62.6	54.7
Mean Commuting Time - Minutes...	30.2	40.7	28.4	26.6	32.6	29.1	30.1	28.2	32.9	29.5	30.3
Population Per Household.........	3.3	3.2	3.6	4.0	3.2	3.0	2.9	3.1	3.5	3.3	3.6
Total Housing Units..........	23746	1090	773	338	842	1139	2674	2283	406	2307	1264
% Condominiums...............	0.0	0.0	0.0	0.0	0.0	0.0	0.0	0.0	0.0	0.0	0.0
% Built 1970 Or Later........	1.6	0.6	1.0	0.0	1.3	0.0	1.6	0.7	2.0	0.0	4.1
% Owner Occupied.............	32.1	14.1	23.0	26.6	47.3	31.3	30.0	38.0	54.7	24.8	33.9
% With 1+ Persons Per Room...	12.9	13.2	16.7	23.5	7.6	13.3	9.7	10.9	9.5	11.2	16.0
Median Value: Owner Units......$$	27400	18900	-	-	25900	27500	33100	24700	24700	24600	27500
Median Rent: Rental Units......$$	167	168	156	151	164	166	169	162	165	168	168
Median Number Of Rooms: All Units.	5.0	4.6	5.0	5.0	5.2	4.8	4.8	5.0	5.6	5.2	5.1

Tract Number	2311	2312	2313	2314	2315	2316	2317	2318
Total Population.............	1897	9126	6547	13	11173	2635	1476	436
% Male.......................	47.4	47.8	49.2	-	46.3	45.5	44.8	50.5
% Black......................	73.2	53.0	5.8	-	97.8	96.4	97.8	7.8
% Other Nonwhite.............	17.7	20.4	24.2	-	0.6	0.7	0.6	62.4
% Of Spanish Origin..........	19.2	33.8	29.9	-	1.2	0.7	0.9	80.5
% Foreign Born...............	8.3	11.9	31.3	-	1.3	0.0	1.3	16.0
% Living In Group Quarters...	0.4	0.2	0.2	-	1.4	2.5	0.0	0.0
% 13 Years Old And Under.....	34.4	32.9	21.9	-	31.9	29.1	33.1	31.2
% 14-20 Years Old............	17.4	15.1	10.7	-	17.8	18.0	18.6	12.8
% 21-64 Years Old............	45.2	48.0	54.8	-	45.6	49.0	44.2	50.0
% 65-74 Years Old............	2.3	2.6	8.1	-	2.9	3.0	3.4	4.8
% 75 Years Old And Over......	0.7	1.4	4.6	-	1.8	0.9	0.7	1.1
% In Different House.........	46.9	62.0	49.7	-	35.9	30.0	38.2	76.8
% Families With Female Head..	38.4	40.7	20.1	-	54.0	55.0	60.4	34.1
Median School Years Completed...	11.2	10.7	10.6	-	10.8	10.7	10.8	9.2
Median Family Income, 1979...$$	14948	14093	20621	-	10844	13594	11281	11696
% Income Below Poverty Level..	25.4	29.7	9.5	-	36.6	25.6	33.3	31.3
% Income Of $30,000 Or More...	15.3	10.8	24.2	-	12.0	7.0	15.9	5.7
% White Collar Workers.......	37.5	32.1	36.8	-	29.3	28.0	38.1	25.3
% Civilian Labor Force Unemployed.	11.1	15.8	7.2	-	17.3	18.8	9.4	15.0
% Riding To Work By Automobile....	74.6	61.8	64.4	-	63.4	50.9	38.6	73.6
Mean Commuting Time - Minutes...	30.6	30.4	29.7	-	32.2	26.9	28.4	21.8
Population Per Household.........	3.8	3.3	3.4	-	3.7	3.7	3.6	3.2
Total Housing Units..........	543	3023	2539	0	3174	748	444	159
% Condominiums...............	0.0	0.0	0.0	-	0.0	0.0	0.0	0.0
% Built 1970 Or Later........	0.0	1.4	1.3	-	3.6	1.7	8.8	0.0
% Owner Occupied.............	42.5	30.5	47.2	-	27.8	24.3	23.0	17.6
% With 1+ Persons Per Room...	13.8	12.9	7.8	-	18.3	17.5	21.4	13.2
Median Value: Owner Units......$$	29400	27700	31300	-	27200	24800	-	-
Median Rent: Rental Units......$$	179	175	157	-	168	173	159	164
Median Number Of Rooms: All Units.	5.5	5.0	4.8	-	4.9	5.2	5.0	4.6

Community Area 23 — Humboldt Park
Selected Characteristics of Census Tracts: 1970

Tract Number	TOTAL	2301	2302	2303	2304	2305	2306	2307	2308	2309	2310
Total Population	71726	2702	2623	1327	2325	1468	8099	5912	1286	8142	4099
% Male	48.3	50.8	49.4	49.4	48.6	52.1	48.1	48.2	50.0	49.0	49.1
% Black	19.4	0.4	0.1	0.0	0.0	2.3	0.1	0.2	1.1	1.8	2.5
% Other Nonwhite	1.4	2.4	1.4	3.1	1.1	1.2	1.1	1.7	1.3	2.5	4.6
% Of Spanish Language	15.6	27.3	34.7	22.4	8.0	5.8	5.5	13.2	30.3	52.5	32.4
% Foreign Born	18.2	20.6	14.1	12.3	11.7	23.3	18.1	22.5	17.1	16.2	25.6
% Living In Group Quarters	0.7	0.5	2.5	0.0	0.0	8.0	0.1	0.2	0.2	0.4	0.7
% 13 Years Old And Under	28.9	29.5	28.2	32.3	23.1	20.1	23.3	25.3	24.4	31.8	29.9
% 14-20 Years Old	11.9	11.7	14.1	14.9	12.0	9.9	10.5	10.9	10.9	12.6	12.0
% 21-64 Years Old	50.5	50.4	50.2	47.1	53.0	54.0	55.4	53.5	54.3	48.5	51.3
% 65-74 Years Old	5.3	5.5	4.6	3.3	7.1	8.9	6.8	6.5	6.2	4.5	4.5
% 75 Years Old And Over	3.4	2.8	2.8	2.3	4.9	7.2	4.0	3.9	4.2	2.6	2.3
% In Different House	45.3	30.3	41.7	44.1	54.2	53.8	57.6	57.0	60.6	42.4	44.5
% Families With Female Head	15.7	14.7	13.4	14.6	14.8	12.0	13.5	12.1	9.9	14.9	14.4
Median School Years Completed	9.2	9.2	8.9	8.8	9.6	8.9	9.7	9.4	9.9	9.0	8.9
Median Family Income, 1969$$	9472	8250	8237	9731	11279	9857	10265	10190	10594	8510	8654
% Income Below Poverty Level	13.0	17.6	12.6	17.9	4.1	5.6	6.4	10.3	20.1	16.8	12.7
% Income of $15,000 or More	16.1	7.8	14.6	19.3	10.4	20.7	20.4	19.6	19.0	15.1	14.3
% White Collar Workers	12.0	13.4	11.2	8.7	10.5	10.8	12.0	13.5	21.9	11.7	12.6
% Civilian Labor Force Unemployed	4.8	8.5	1.9	5.6	3.2	2.0	3.7	4.1	4.7	6.6	3.1
% Riding To Work By Automobile	54.0	51.2	47.0	48.6	63.6	52.9	53.9	57.8	62.3	55.4	49.7
Population Per Household	3.2	3.0	3.2	3.6	3.0	2.7	2.8	2.8	3.1	3.4	3.5
Total Housing Units	23323	955	861	393	808	524	2991	2004	427	2496	1264
% Condominiums & Cooperatives	0.4	0.0	0.0	0.0	0.0	0.0	0.2	0.5	0.0	0.4	0.6
% Built 1960 Or Later	2.3	0.9	0.0	0.9	1.1	3.2	2.1	2.8	0.0	0.4	0.7
% Owner Occupied	33.1	22.4	25.2	23.2	48.4	29.8	31.4	38.6	53.9	24.8	33.9
% With 1+ Persons Per Room	11.9	14.3	12.0	17.2	6.9	6.1	6.4	8.6	7.4	15.4	14.3
Median Value: Owner Units$$	15500	13600			15100		17400	15000	14900	14000	14900
Median Rent: Rental Units$$	96	91	81	82	90	85	94	92	89	99	99
Median Number Of Rooms: All Units	4.8	4.2	4.8	4.8	5.1	4.8	4.7	4.9	5.3	4.9	4.9

Tract Number	2311	2312	2313	2315	2316	2317	2318
Total Population	1418	7675	6195	12481	3638	2114	222
% Male	49.6	47.7	47.7	46.9	47.5	47.9	53.6
% Black	0.0	0.1	0.0	69.8	82.8	88.1	0.0
% Other Nonwhite	0.3	0.4	0.4	0.8	1.5	1.0	7.7
% Of Spanish Language	5.4	1.8	1.8	5.0	7.9	1.4	26.1
% Foreign Born	33.4	36.5	25.0	7.3	3.5	0.6	33.8
% Living In Group Quarters	0.0	0.4	0.1	1.1	0.4	0.0	0.0
% 13 Years Old And Under	23.2	22.6	19.3	37.0	42.1	43.1	31.1
% 14-20 Years Old	10.2	10.9	11.8	12.7	13.3	13.9	14.9
% 21-64 Years Old	55.1	55.0	56.9	44.0	42.1	40.1	50.5
% 65-74 Years Old	6.8	6.9	7.0	3.8	1.7	1.9	1.4
% 75 Years Old And Over	4.7	4.6	4.9	2.5	0.9	1.0	2.3
% In Different House	58.2	52.0	64.5	25.4	23.0	36.6	17.1
% Families With Female Head	7.1	11.5	12.2	24.5	25.5	29.4	16.0
Median School Years Completed	8.7	8.8	9.0	9.7	10.0	9.6	12.2
Median Family Income, 1969$$	9500	10216	10709	8439	8370	6194	8429
% Income Below Poverty Level	4.6	7.4	5.9	19.8	26.9	24.7	0.0
% Income of $15,000 or More	26.8	15.9	22.3	12.6	9.2	4.7	0.0
% White Collar Workers	13.5	11.5	12.7	9.4	12.9	14.3	6.5
% Civilian Labor Force Unemployed	3.2	3.3	3.8	6.4	10.9	7.2	0.0
% Riding To Work By Automobile	54.6	55.6	49.3	55.3	53.7	42.7	54.7
Population Per Household	3.1	3.0	2.8	3.7	4.3	4.3	3.4
Total Housing Units	478	2630	2291	3712	890	523	76
% Condominiums & Cooperatives	0.0	0.6	0.4	0.5	0.8	0.0	0.0
% Built 1960 Or Later	0.0	1.2	1.8	6.9	0.7	4.9	0.0
% Owner Occupied	46.0	35.7	49.0	26.7	27.2	25.8	19.7
% With 1+ Persons Per Room	6.3	7.0	5.6	18.8	24.6	31.0	15.2
Median Value: Owner Units$$	15300	14900	18500	13900		16300	
Median Rent: Rental Units$$	89	95	88	106	110	109	94
Median Number Of Rooms: All Units	5.1	4.9	4.7	4.8	5.0	4.9	4.6

as Mexicans. Humboldt Park has very distinct Hispanic and black areas. Nearly three-quarters of the Hispanic residents live in the nine census tracts north of Division Street, while nearly 60 percent of the area's black population is located in three tracts south of Chicago Avenue and east of Pulaski Road.

The last decade has produced numerous problems for Humboldt Park. During the middle to late 1970s, the community area was the scene of numerous fires, many attributed to arson. From January to November in 1978 alone, of 3,000 fires reported, 1,200 were determined to have been set. In July, 1980, Neighborhood Housing Services Incorporated designated the area between Pulaski, Chicago, and the Milwaukee Road tracks for financial and technical assistance in badly-needed home rehabilitation. During the mid-1970s, rioting broke out and many area businesses were looted following a Puerto Rican Day parade. In July, 1981, two people were killed and nine wounded in gang-related shootings, prompting city officials to crack down on local taverns where illegal activities were alleged to have taken place.

In spite of the fires, there were only 173 fewer housing units in 1980 than there had been 20 years before. Overcrowding has increased. Thirteen percent of all 1980 units had more than one person per room, compared with 7.7 percent in 1960. The 1980 rate of housing units vacancy was 10 percent. Of all 1980 housing units, 18 percent were single-family dwellings, and 3.4 percent were located in buildings with 10 or more units. The median value of single-family, owner-occupied units in Humboldt Park was $27,403 in 1980, about 60 percent of the city average.

Throughout its history, the Humboldt Park community area has contained a rich mix of peoples, many of whom moved into the area having accumulated their initial money after immigrating to the United States. Within the last 20 years, this process has slowed somewhat especially for blacks who are indeed not new at all to this country—and yet has remained the same for many Hispanics who are beginning to gain a financial foothold.

Will Hogan

West Town

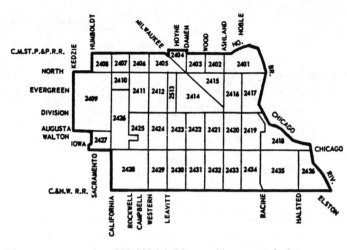

Much of the portion of the West Town community area east of Wood Street was within the limits of the City of Chicago as incorporated in March, 1837. Several old Indian trails passing through the near North west Side later became important thoroughfares — Whiskey Point Road (Grand Avenue), the portage trail along the present Ogden Avenue, and two trails heading northwest (now Milwaukee and Elston avenues). Although Mark Noble had bought land and farmed there in 1830, the North west Side was largely unsettled through the 1840s.

The Southwest (Ogden Avenue) and Northwest (Milwaukee Avenue) Plank Roads were completed in 1849. The Galena and Chicago Union was the first railroad leading into Chicago, the tracks running along Kinzie to State Street by 1851. In that year, the city limits were extended to Western and North avenues. The Chicago and North Western built its west and northwest lines shortly thereafter. Workingmen moved into the vicinity of Kinzie Street, near Milwaukee and Grand avenues, in order to be close to the Galena and Northwestern car repair shops at those intersections. Many of the residential structures built in that neighborhood were wood-frame shacks which deteriorated quickly into slums.

By 1857, the built-up area of Chicago reached about as far west as Racine Avenue and as far north as Division Street. The Milwaukee Avenue horse-drawn streetcar line encouraged other patches of settlement from its inception in 1859, running northwest from Halsted Street. In 1863, the state legislature extended the city limits to Bloomingdale and Western avenues to the northwest, and farther west beyond Kedzie Avenue in 1869. The area developed slowly during the 1860s. Homes were built near the railroad shops and yards and also near the newly-constructed factories by the river and along Milwaukee Avenue. Poles had already begun to settle the area, especially near the factories and the present Pulaski Park at Noble Street and Potomac Avenue. The establishment, in 1869, of the 207-acre Humboldt Park in West Town's northwest corner, and the construction of a Humboldt station by the Milwaukee Railroad, led to a settlement, principally German and Scandinavian, just north of the park.

After the Great Fire, the near Northwest Side became a refuge for many workers who wished to build cheap frame homes, but could not do so within the recently established city fire limits. In the decades that followed, the trickle of Polish immigration became a flood, as West Town became also a refuge for thousands fleeing Old World poverty and persecution. The area around Division Street and Ashland Avenue became known as Polish Downtown and before 1900 almost 25,000 Poles lived within a half-mile radius of this intersection. A significant number of the Polish immigrants were Jews, and they were joined by many Russian Jews, who were moving from the Near West Side to the area east of Humboldt Park. Early in the 1900s about a fourth of Chicago's Jewish population lived there. Italians settled near Grand Avenue and, in the 1880s, Ukrainian immigrants also began to locate in the southeast. Affluent German businessmen constructed mansions on Hoyne Street, north of Division. New factories located along the northern, southern and eastern edges of West Town in the 1870s and 1880s. A shopping area developed at North and California avenues, and Milwaukee Avenue became a retail strip. Census Tracts 2406 through 2408, which completed the West Town community area, were annexed from the Village of Jefferson in 1889. West Town's residential development was accelerated by the completion of branches of the elevated train line to Logan Square and Humboldt Park in 1895, and the area achieved residential maturity by the early 1900s. The Polish population began to move northwest, along Milwaukee Avenue.

The population of West Town evidently peaked in 1910, at which time density was very high, and has been declining since. In 1920,

there were more than 218,000 inhabitants, 44 percent of whom were foreign-born. Poles were the largest foreign-born faction, followed by Russian Jews, residing primarily near Humboldt Park, and Italians, who tended to live in the older southeastern portion. During the 1920s, the earlier German and Scandinavian settlers, and even some Poles, began to leave West Town. The area population dropped by more than 30,000 during that decade. The Russian Jews began to relocate on the western side of the park in the Humboldt Park community area and in places farther north, such as Albany Park and Rogers Park. Persons of Polish ancestry comprised 49 percent of those remaining in West Town in 1930, and the next largest foreign-born groups, the Italians and Russian Jews, each made up about 10 percent of the total.

The decades since 1930 have marked the progressive thinning out of West Town's population — less than 170,000 in 1940; less than 140,000 in 1960; less than 100,000 today. Numerical losses from the West Town population account for more than 10 percent of the total loss incurred by the city as a whole over the last 30 years. The area population has dropped by 40 percent since 1950, and it is today little more than 40 percent of what it was in the early part of the century.

The area's ethnic makeup has changed dramatically since 1960. Then, Poles were still the largest foreign-stock group, followed by Russian Jews, Italians and Germans. At that time, a Spanish-origin population nucleus had formed. The 1960 census revealed that 25 percent (7,948) of the city's Puerto Rican population lived in West Town, with the heaviest concentration in the northwestern and southeastern corners. By 1970, Hispanics comprised 39 percent of the total population, and in 1980 that figure reached 57 percent, almost 55,000 people. West Town had the largest concentration of Puerto Ricans of any Chicago community area — almost 28,500 — in 1980. Mexicans numbered nearly 23,500, and Cubans and other persons of Spanish origin about 2,700. Two-thirds of the area's 36 census tracts are predominantly Hispanic. Blacks first lived in West Town around 1930, and in 1980 comprised 9 percent of the total population.

The area housing stock has been decimated in recent years. There had been new construction through the 1920s, but very little since 1930. According to the 1940 census, 58 percent of the dwelling units in use at that time were in structures built before 1900. Unlike nearby Northwest Side community areas, most of West Town's housing has not aged gracefully. The construction of the Kennedy (Northwest) Expressway during the late 1950s contributed to the net loss of nearly 1,600 housing units in the decade ending in 1960. The problem of deteriorating housing was exacerbated by a high incidence of fires, including many arsons, during the 1970s, which prompted the mayor to form the West Town Arson Task Force in 1976, and the creation of the Arson Committee of the Northwest Community Organization to patrol the streets. Between 1960 and 1980, West Town lost more than 22 percent, close to 10,600 units, of its housing. Of the existing units,

Community Area 24 — West Town
Population and Housing Characteristics, 1930-1980

	1980	1970	1960	1950	1940	1930
Total Population.......	96,428	124,800	139,657	161,620	169,924	187,292
% Male...................	50.1	50.1	50.9	50.8	51.4	51.9
% Female.................	49.9	49.9	49.1	49.2	48.6	48.1
% White..................	55.1	92.1	97.7	98.3	99.6	99.5
% Black..................	9.0	4.4	1.7	1.4	0.4	0.4
% Other Nonwhite Races...	35.9	3.5	0.6	0.3	0.0	0.1
% Under 5 Years Old......	10.5	11.0	10.9	10.0	6.5	8.3
% 5-19 Years Old.........	28.3	29.2	25.6	20.1	25.5	34.4
% 20-44 Years Old........	36.0	32.3	34.8	42.7	42.0	40.4
% 45-64 Years Old........	16.6	19.6	19.9	20.8	21.9	14.0
% 65 Years and Older.....	8.6	7.9	8.8	6.4	4.1	2.9
Median School Years....	9.2	8.6	8.6	8.5	7.4	*
Total Housing Units....	36,790	43,188	47,414	49,005	47,910	*
% In One-Unit Structures.	5.3	6.1	6.0	*	*	*
% Owner Occupied.........	18.7	19.5	20.6	20.6	15.4	*
% Renter Occupied........	68.6	71.4	73.0	77.6	80.5	*
% Vacant.................	12.7	9.1	6.4	1.8	4.1	*
% 1+ Persons per Room....	12.8	13.6	14.4	14.1	*	*

Community Area 24 — West Town
Selected Characteristics of Census Tracts: 1980

Tract Number	Total	2401	2402	2403	2404	2405	2406	2407	2408	2409	2410
Total Population.............	96428	208	1478	1773	435	1253	1443	1719	2104	2513	2538
% Male.......................	50.1	52.9	52.2	50.3	50.1	52.3	51.4	49.9	49.1	49.0	48.7
% Black......................	9.0	5.3	0.6	0.9	0.5	6.6	8.0	3.6	3.6	21.9	18.5
% Other Nonwhite.............	35.9	26.4	21.2	30.1	34.9	51.9	47.1	46.4	40.5	43.0	45.7
% Of Spanish Origin..........	56.7	63.0	64.0	49.3	47.8	69.0	64.2	69.3	71.2	59.2	62.3
% Foreign Born...............	27.5	7.6	39.1	27.7	19.5	19.9	33.9	12.8	19.6	17.4	17.4
% Living In Group Quarters...	0.9	0.0	0.0	0.0	0.0	0.0	0.4	1.2	0.0	0.2	4.8
% 13 Years Old And Under.....	27.1	28.8	32.3	25.1	24.6	25.9	31.0	31.4	33.1	36.1	29.7
% 14-20 Years Old............	13.7	10.1	14.7	11.0	9.9	11.8	15.0	17.7	15.5	13.6	15.4
% 21-64 Years Old............	50.6	48.6	47.8	54.4	57.5	54.4	49.1	45.6	45.3	44.9	45.4
% 65-74 Years Old............	5.6	8.2	3.5	6.9	3.9	5.5	3.0	4.2	2.8	3.8	4.1
% 75 Years Old And Over......	3.0	4.3	1.8	2.6	4.1	2.4	1.9	1.0	3.2	1.7	5.4
% In Different House.........	47.9	59.4	63.9	45.1	39.2	36.5	43.9	49.6	60.9	81.2	31.4
% Families With Female Head..	34.3	32.3	27.4	23.0	21.1	37.5	44.2	36.2	38.3	46.9	43.6
Median School Years Completed.	9.2	7.9	7.9	10.0	7.9	10.0	7.9	7.9	9.0	11.0	9.4
Median Family Income, 1979.....$$	12974	6541	15263	13250	20341	13378	8370	11196	12071	10953	10625
% Income Below Poverty Level....	27.2	60.4	17.7	22.6	17.5	30.5	50.6	39.8	35.3	35.5	38.3
% Income Of $30,000 Or More.....	10.2	0.0	10.0	13.6	10.3	10.3	8.3	3.3	4.8	3.9	8.3
% White Collar Workers..........	34.7	24.1	36.0	35.0	19.2	41.0	38.2	26.8	30.6	32.0	23.7
% Civilian Labor Force Unemployed.	10.9	30.8	12.2	11.7	13.6	19.1	22.2	16.0	13.6	10.0	12.8
% Riding To Work By Automobile....	53.9	42.6	56.8	58.5	55.8	55.3	60.3	70.4	56.8	57.6	53.6
Mean Commuting Time - Minutes...	28.1	47.8	29.4	30.6	24.7	29.7	18.3	27.7	31.0	28.2	29.4
Population Per Household..........	3.0	2.8	3.4	2.9	2.6	2.9	3.1	3.5	3.1	3.4	3.3
Total Housing Units..........	36790	97	513	692	188	583	570	630	855	903	830
% Condominiums...............	0.2	0.0	0.0	0.0	0.0	0.0	0.0	0.0	0.0	0.0	0.0
% Built 1970 Or Later........	2.5	0.0	0.0	3.1	3.3	0.5	0.0	2.3	0.0	0.8	4.6
% Owner Occupied.............	18.7	28.9	20.5	26.0	26.1	19.2	16.7	20.6	19.6	12.6	12.4
% With 1+ Persons Per Room...	12.8	14.9	20.5	14.1	8.5	9.0	13.7	15.5	13.6	16.5	14.0
Median Value: Owner Units.......$$	23500	—	—	—	—	—	—	—	—	—	—
Median Rent: Rental Units.......$$	138	112	133	124	134	162	158	148	150	154	153
Median Number Of Rooms: All Units.	4.6	4.6	4.2	4.3	4.3	5.1	5.1	4.9	4.9	4.6	4.9

Tract Number	2411	2412	2413	2414	2415	2416	2417	2418	2419	2420	2421
Total Population.............	4802	2463	1954	4551	3792	4960	315	666	1291	4984	3865
% Male.......................	47.9	49.3	53.0	49.5	50.9	51.8	49.8	50.3	49.6	49.0	53.1
% Black......................	15.7	18.7	27.9	19.9	1.7	1.3	6.0	44.3	49.1	20.8	3.5
% Other Nonwhite.............	45.5	49.3	23.5	36.8	20.4	34.1	14.9	11.1	18.9	26.7	35.3
% Of Spanish Origin..........	69.7	62.6	38.6	55.1	69.2	65.7	22.9	24.5	25.6	53.7	50.6
% Foreign Born...............	17.2	15.2	11.3	23.9	32.6	39.8	10.8	9.8	2.7	32.4	37.9
% Living In Group Quarters...	0.1	2.4	10.6	0.0	0.0	0.5	0.0	0.8	0.0	1.1	0.9
% 13 Years Old And Under.....	32.7	30.4	24.5	28.3	27.4	30.9	14.6	24.2	27.7	27.1	22.5
% 14-20 Years Old............	17.0	15.1	13.2	15.0	12.7	14.8	17.8	15.0	16.1	11.5	11.7
% 21-64 Years Old............	45.8	48.7	50.4	45.8	51.6	48.7	57.5	50.8	50.8	47.8	55.5
% 65-74 Years Old............	2.5	3.5	7.1	5.9	6.4	3.9	7.3	6.9	4.0	7.3	7.7
% 75 Years Old And Over......	1.9	2.3	4.8	5.0	1.9	1.7	2.9	3.2	1.4	6.3	2.7
% In Different House.........	61.5	47.1	37.9	55.6	42.2	55.4	30.2	51.8	49.6	49.3	47.3
% Families With Female Head..	46.8	38.9	38.9	43.8	30.2	26.9	27.0	41.2	31.7	33.1	30.9
Median School Years Completed....	7.9	10.6	11.0	9.1	7.9	7.9	9.9	12.0	10.9	7.9	7.9
Median Family Income, 1979.....$$	6958	13482	12167	10263	13948	15907	13611	14097	15795	14966	12013
% Income Below Poverty Level....	47.4	32.2	31.6	39.3	26.9	23.4	0.0	19.9	19.3	20.6	25.4
% Income Of $30,000 Or More.....	7.6	11.7	17.2	8.0	8.1	8.9	12.8	5.3	15.9	13.3	10.5
% White Collar Workers..........	23.6	40.5	40.1	38.2	29.6	31.2	33.3	35.0	48.8	35.3	23.1
% Civilian Labor Force Unemployed.	19.3	15.0	11.1	7.5	8.5	10.0	24.3	9.7	13.6	15.7	15.4
% Riding To Work By Automobile....	58.2	53.6	60.3	54.0	56.5	47.5	53.6	48.1	50.7	56.1	52.3
Mean Commuting Time - Minutes...	27.5	19.7	25.5	25.7	30.6	22.6	22.9	28.6	27.0	31.2	30.6
Population Per Household..........	3.5	3.3	2.8	2.8	3.0	3.3	2.5	2.8	2.8	3.4	2.4
Total Housing Units..........	1598	785	836	2042	1388	1780	142	268	439	1954	1836
% Condominiums...............	0.0	0.0	0.0	0.0	0.0	0.0	0.0	0.0	0.0	1.3	0.0
% Built 1970 Or Later........	1.0	3.1	0.0	5.8	3.7	0.6	0.0	0.9	5.1	17.8	0.0
% Owner Occupied.............	17.8	25.6	14.8	10.9	19.4	10.1	13.4	17.9	13.2	14.9	15.8
% With 1+ Persons Per Room...	16.5	14.3	13.2	13.8	14.8	22.9	9.7	13.9	13.3	12.3	10.9
Median Value: Owner Units.......$$	—	—	—	—	21700	—	—	—	—	—	—
Median Rent: Rental Units.......$$	151	155	148	144	134	131	124	114	152	127	115
Median Number Of Rooms: All Units.	4.9	5.3	5.1	4.4	4.3	4.1	4.4	4.3	4.9	3.9	4.1

Tract Number	2422	2423	2424	2425	2426	2427	2428	2429	2430	2431	2432
Total Population.............	4280	4091	3804	3763	7281	2686	1623	2293	2973	2766	2771
% Male.......................	50.2	51.5	45.8	49.9	49.4	49.6	47.9	50.5	50.3	49.4	49.5
% Black......................	1.6	1.6	1.2	2.6	7.9	23.9	2.8	2.1	3.1	1.4	1.6
% Other Nonwhite.............	38.0	28.4	31.3	39.1	45.3	40.2	19.8	20.1	31.5	37.3	34.0
% Of Spanish Origin..........	52.3	39.2	21.7	56.8	73.0	61.2	22.5	45.1	53.0	59.8	66.7
% Foreign Born...............	39.9	31.9	44.1	33.5	18.1	20.1	20.8	27.3	29.7	26.1	23.5
% Living In Group Quarters...	0.0	0.0	3.8	0.2	0.5	0.0	0.0	0.2	0.0	0.0	0.0
% 13 Years Old And Under.....	23.9	20.9	13.9	23.3	31.0	31.9	18.8	24.9	25.3	24.1	28.9
% 14-20 Years Old............	11.8	10.2	9.4	12.2	15.4	14.9	11.6	12.1	15.1	14.6	14.5
% 21-64 Years Old............	54.1	57.0	59.9	53.4	47.7	48.2	53.9	52.8	52.2	53.6	50.2
% 65-74 Years Old............	7.2	7.8	11.2	7.6	4.0	3.4	10.4	7.1	4.7	5.7	4.3
% 75 Years Old And Over......	3.0	4.0	5.4	3.4	1.9	1.6	5.3	3.2	2.7	2.0	2.1
% In Different House.........	48.0	47.6	44.3	31.5	38.9	31.2	41.3	41.9	44.6	52.4	57.2
% Families With Female Head..	31.9	29.1	26.7	29.2	38.6	44.5	25.7	32.0	31.1	29.4	28.7
Median School Years Completed.	7.9	9.4	12.3	10.4	9.1	9.5	10.4	9.8	7.9	7.9	7.9
Median Family Income, 1979.....$$	13446	16662	18294	16324	9579	12156	16468	14200	13622	16047	14718
% Income Below Poverty Level....	22.8	16.5	12.8	16.4	41.7	31.9	14.7	22.5	25.1	10.6	27.8
% Income Of $30,000 Or More....	9.3	10.6	21.2	16.2	6.5	14.1	14.7	16.9	10.7	13.2	5.9
% White Collar Workers........	35.1	44.3	49.9	37.8	25.1	32.1	40.3	41.5	35.3	31.3	31.0
% Civilian Labor Force Unemployed.	8.7	6.4	6.0	10.7	13.0	11.3	4.2	4.0	6.3	6.9	8.5
% Riding To Work By Automobile..	53.3	53.5	46.2	56.1	60.2	60.8	60.1	49.0	59.8	60.1	49.9
Mean Commuting Time – Minutes...	28.7	29.7	25.1	31.3	31.2	33.7	22.7	27.4	30.1	29.4	30.2
Population Per Household.........	2.7	2.6	2.3	2.8	3.2	3.4	2.6	2.8	3.2	3.0	3.4
Total Housing Units..........	1764	1719	1676	1463	2484	817	673	894	1068	1000	1010
% Condominiums...............	0.0	1.4	0.0	0.0	0.0	0.0	0.0	0.0	0.0	0.0	0.0
% Built 1970 Or Later........	1.1	0.5	0.7	2.6	1.1	0.0	1.6	0.7	0.0	0.9	0.0
% Owner Occupied.............	21.4	25.8	18.6	23.7	18.3	18.5	41.8	22.9	24.3	28.8	20.7
% With 1+ Persons Per Room...$$	9.9	6.9	3.7	9.1	14.2	16.3	5.0	9.8	13.2	10.0	15.2
Median Value: Owner Units......$$	–	34600	–	21900	20800	–	27600	–	22500	22000	–
Median Rent: Rental Units...$$	124	141	146	137	152	161	126	135	134	128	135
Median Number Of Rooms: All Units.	4.4	4.6	4.8	4.7	4.8	4.8	5.0	4.7	4.9	5.0	5.0

Tract Number	2433	2434	2435	2436
Total Population.............	3052	3734	1934	270
% Male.......................	50.5	52.3	49.8	85.2
% Black......................	0.5	0.8	26.6	13.0
% Other Nonwhite.............	38.8	50.9	33.9	13.3
% Of Spanish Origin..........	58.5	73.4	47.2	26.7
% Foreign Born...............	31.8	34.8	41.2	18.0
% Living In Group Quarters...	0.0	0.0	1.6	49.3
% 13 Years Old And Under.....	26.0	30.9	27.1	4.1
% 14-20 Years Old............	13.0	15.6	13.7	7.0
% 21-64 Years Old............	51.0	48.7	53.1	85.2
% 65-74 Years Old............	7.1	3.1	4.4	3.3
% 75 Years Old And Over......	2.9	1.8	1.8	0.4
% In Different House.........	40.9	59.8	46.2	74.9
% Families With Female Head..	30.1	23.8	32.5	30.0
Median School Years Completed.	7.9	7.9	7.9	12.2
Median Family Income, 1979.....$$	12442	12458	13923	17639
% Income Below Poverty Level....	27.9	26.6	9.5	0.0
% Income Of $30,000 Or More....	9.3	8.7	5.7	0.0
% White Collar Workers........	29.7	29.5	42.1	49.7
% Civilian Labor Force Unemployed.	4.2	12.3	12.2	12.8
% Riding To Work By Automobile..	50.7	43.9	43.5	0.0
Mean Commuting Time – Minutes...	28.5	25.1	28.4	8.4
Population Per Household.........	2.9	3.6	2.9	2.1
Total Housing Units..........	1219	1211	775	88
% Condominiums...............	0.0	0.0	0.0	0.0
% Built 1970 Or Later........	0.0	1.5	12.5	0.0
% Owner Occupied.............	17.3	15.6	9.3	5.7
% With 1+ Persons Per Room...	11.2	19.8	13.6	9.4
Median Value: Owner Units......$$	–	–	–	–
Median Rent: Rental Units...$$	126	125	134	170
Median Number Of Rooms: All Units.	4.4	4.7	4.4	4.3

Community Area 24 — West Town
Selected Characteristics of Census Tracts: 1970

Tract Number	TOTAL	2401	2402	2403	2404	2405	2406	2407	2408	2409	2410
Total Population.............	124800	393	1947	2035	583	1714	1972	2171	2670	3564	3939
% Male.......................	50.1	49.6	51.0	50.3	47.5	50.6	49.3	51.2	51.8	49.3	52.0
% Black......................	4.4	5.6	5.8	0.0	0.7	2.6	0.1	0.5	1.8	4.2	1.2
% Other Nonwhite.............	3.5	4.6	1.9	3.5	1.4	2.3	10.3	2.9	2.8	10.8	4.7
% Of Spanish Language........	39.1	16.6	24.5	24.3	31.5	46.3	29.1	44.3	33.4	52.3	60.7
% Foreign Born...............	19.1	19.3	8.5	20.7	17.5	16.8	6.0	13.6	20.0	20.9	21.2
% Living In Group Quarters...	1.2	0.0	0.4	0.1	0.2	0.0	0.2	0.0	1.4	1.0	4.0
% 13 Years Old And Under.....	29.5	19.3	33.0	27.3	28.8	28.4	33.6	31.9	28.4	31.7	31.9
% 14-20 Years Old............	12.5	13.5	12.9	12.8	11.7	13.9	13.0	14.6	12.3	11.1	12.6
% 21-64 Years Old............	50.1	57.0	47.4	52.0	52.1	49.2	46.7	47.2	51.2	50.5	46.4
% 65-74 Years Old............	4.6	8.7	4.5	4.7	3.3	5.4	4.4	4.0	4.8	3.8	4.2
% 75 Years Old And Over......	3.3	1.5	2.3	2.3	4.1	3.0	2.2	2.3	3.3	2.9	4.9
% In Different House.........	46.3	66.4	40.9	58.3	50.8	42.1	42.8	38.3	43.8	39.2	34.2
% Families With Female Head..	18.0	24.5	17.7	16.2	11.5	15.8	16.7	15.5	17.1	16.6	18.4
Median School Years Completed.	8.6	8.6	9.0	8.7	8.8	8.7	9.0	8.7	9.1	8.6	8.3
Median Family Income, 1969.....$$	8021	6107	8205	9286	8323	8103	9171	7622	7891	8069	7636
% Income Below Poverty Level....	19.4	16.1	22.5	17.0	20.2	21.3	23.5	12.4	15.6	23.8	29.6
% Income of $15,000 or More....	12.2	8.4	17.3	11.6	7.1	7.2	12.5	11.5	15.6	10.9	10.0
% White Collar Workers........	10.9	19.6	16.1	10.5	11.8	7.9	11.5	8.5	9.9	16.3	5.3
% Civilian Labor Force Unemployed.	6.0	34.8	9.2	2.0	7.3	9.9	7.7	11.1	7.1	8.1	11.3
% Riding To Work By Automobile....	46.7	29.6	62.3	58.4	41.9	50.6	65.1	51.7	62.0	45.0	52.5
Population Per Household.........	3.1	2.6	3.5	3.0	3.0	3.2	3.4	3.5	3.0	3.3	3.3
Total Housing Units..........	43188	157	600	753	201	569	663	691	950	1101	1279
% Condominiums & Cooperatives.....	0.5	0.0	0.0	0.0	0.0	0.0	0.0	0.9	0.0	0.5	0.0
% Built 1960 Or Later........	3.3	0.0	0.0	0.0	2.6	3.8	0.6	0.0	0.6	1.6	2.5
% Owner Occupied.............	18.9	15.3	17.8	25.2	26.4	21.8	24.7	24.3	18.9	16.9	16.2
% With 1+ Persons Per Room...	14.2	6.7	15.0	12.9	11.5	12.9	15.4	15.7	14.6	17.0	17.3
Median Value: Owner Units......$$	12400	–	–	–	–	–	–	–	–	–	–
Median Rent: Rental Units...$$	72	81	69	63	68	85	76	77	88	88	86
Median Number Of Rooms: All Units.	4.3	4.5	4.3	4.2	4.5	4.8	4.5	4.8	4.3	4.5	4.3

Community Area 24 — West Town
Selected Characteristics of Census Tracts: 1970

Tract Number	2411	2412	2413	2414	2415	2416	2417	2418	2419	2420	2421
Total Population..............	6995	5221	3840	7269	4151	5203	520	822	1622	5167	4760
% Male.......................	50.9	49.4	50.9	52.4	49.3	49.1	48.7	47.6	49.4	49.3	52.0
% Black......................	3.6	16.6	10.4	9.5	0.8	0.5	7.3	52.7	34.8	6.8	0.7
% Other Nonwhite.............	10.3	2.8	1.4	2.6	4.2	1.4	4.2	0.0	1.9	1.1	2.2
% Of Spanish Language........	68.4	60.1	49.5	45.0	35.9	27.0	7.0	21.3	17.0	33.9	24.4
% Foreign Born...............	17.2	9.4	12.2	14.5	17.2	17.0	9.6	4.4	6.1	20.5	20.9
% Living In Group Quarters...	0.2	1.8	4.9	0.9	0.1	0.7	3.8	1.5	0.4	1.3	1.0
% 13 Years Old And Under.....	37.0	37.0	36.9	31.5	27.5	30.4	25.0	27.1	32.2	24.9	21.2
% 14-20 Years Old............	13.4	14.2	11.6	12.5	11.8	12.0	12.1	17.3	15.8	11.6	11.4
% 21-64 Years Old............	45.1	43.8	42.5	47.8	52.3	50.0	52.5	48.3	47.3	49.5	57.7
% 65-74 Years Old............	2.9	3.0	3.9	5.0	5.3	4.6	6.3	4.6	2.2	7.5	5.7
% 75 Years Old And Over......	1.6	1.9	5.1	3.2	3.1	3.1	4.0	2.7	2.6	6.5	3.9
% In Different House.........	36.4	37.8	33.6	48.7	51.7	48.8	51.3	59.1	26.7	54.5	56.2
% Families With Female Head..	18.9	21.4	25.9	18.9	17.5	17.5	16.7	35.0	19.6	18.1	18.1
Median School Years Completed...$$	8.4	8.1	8.0	8.3	8.6	8.5	9.4	9.1	8.9	8.7	8.6
Median Family Income, 1969......$$	7012	6106	5420	6759	8075	7933	7300	6639	9390	7445	7969
% Income Below Poverty Level...	24.8	28.2	37.2	25.7	15.9	21.9	23.6	33.6	17.4	19.5	9.5
% Income of $15,000 or More....	8.9	6.6	7.2	8.8	12.4	10.6	2.5	10.2	12.6	8.7	11.3
% White Collar Workers.........	10.2	9.4	6.2	6.8	9.9	9.7	12.9	13.3	10.1	10.6	11.7
% Civilian Labor Force Unemployed.	8.8	4.9	5.7	7.7	3.7	4.5	7.8	5.5	3.5	4.9	4.0
% Riding To Work By Automobile....	48.9	48.7	41.6	44.4	47.4	39.7	20.3	29.8	53.7	32.8	44.7
Population Per Household..........	3.7	3.9	3.5	3.1	3.0	3.1	2.7	2.7	3.0	2.6	2.5
Total Housing Units..........	2117	1417	1190	2652	1571	1839	232	344	524	2536	2034
% Condominiums & Cooperatives.....	0.0	0.4	0.0	0.0	0.3	0.0	0.0	0.0	0.0	0.0	0.0
% Built 1960 Or Later.............	3.8	0.3	2.9	5.3	0.0	0.8	0.0	1.7	16.2	2.9	0.0
% Owner Occupied..................	19.3	16.9	13.2	12.3	23.7	13.7	14.7	0.9	26.0	29.0	0.0
% With 1+ Persons Per Room........	19.5	21.0	21.6	14.9	12.4	17.2	12.0	11.3	12.2	12.0	17.0
Median Value: Owner Units......$$	-	-	-	-	11700	-	-	15.4	16.2	11.1	9.3
Median Rent: Rental Units......$$	83	84	84	81	63	57	50	69	64	59	61
Median Number Of Rooms: All Units.	4.5	5.0	4.3	4.2	4.2	4.1	4.1	4.2	4.6	3.8	4.0

Tract Number	2422	2423	2424	2425	2426	2427	2428	2429	2430	2431	2432
Total Population..............	4957	4794	4590	4510	10334	2838	1916	2968	3568	3298	3502
% Male.......................	50.9	49.0	44.9	48.6	49.0	50.7	48.8	50.7	49.9	49.3	50.7
% Black......................	0.4	0.4	0.3	0.7	1.7	2.1	2.4	3.1	5.0	1.0	0.7
% Other Nonwhite.............	1.5	6.5	4.2	2.3	3.0	2.3	1.9	1.5	5.5	1.8	2.8
% Of Spanish Language........	27.3	18.3	10.3	32.5	58.4	40.5	10.4	34.6	29.3	32.7	46.0
% Foreign Born...............	26.7	34.6	40.1	27.1	18.8	24.4	19.4	21.0	20.9	12.1	14.7
% Living In Group Quarters...	0.2	0.3	5.3	0.4	0.1	0.9	0.0	0.2	0.3	0.0	0.3
% 13 Years Old And Under.....	24.5	21.6	16.4	24.6	33.3	31.6	24.6	29.2	30.5	28.0	30.8
% 14-20 Years Old............	11.8	12.2	13.0	12.2	12.8	11.3	11.7	12.5	12.2	12.2	12.7
% 21-64 Years Old............	53.5	57.3	59.1	54.3	47.9	50.8	52.6	50.6	49.6	51.7	50.3
% 65-74 Years Old............	5.3	5.3	6.9	5.4	3.5	3.6	6.6	4.6	5.3	5.0	3.9
% 75 Years Old And Over......	4.8	3.7	4.5	3.5	2.5	2.7	4.5	3.1	2.5	3.0	2.4
% In Different House.........	53.2	57.9	52.4	53.3	36.3	37.0	63.4	42.6	50.7	53.1	40.2
% Families With Female Head..	16.3	16.0	13.6	18.7	20.3	17.3	17.9	18.5	16.9	16.2	16.9
Median School Years Completed...$$	8.6	8.7	10.4	8.6	8.4	9.4	8.9	8.6	8.5	8.7	8.8
Median Family Income, 1969......$$	8725	9635	11455	8780	7581	8054	9097	8533	9318	8774	8461
% Income Below Poverty Level...	10.4	12.6	5.4	14.7	22.7	12.7	12.1	21.3	14.6	17.9	15.8
% Income of $15,000 or More....	13.3	18.0	25.7	15.6	10.7	18.0	14.3	17.3	12.7	9.8	15.4
% White Collar Workers.........	10.4	11.4	22.0	11.9	10.2	11.3	10.4	14.3	11.3	9.9	9.0
% Civilian Labor Force Unemployed.	2.4	5.0	5.4	3.8	8.0	3.4	2.6	8.3	5.2	4.3	9.0
% Riding To Work By Automobile....	44.1	43.3	40.3	51.9	49.3	58.6	52.3	51.5	38.6	52.9	51.1
Population Per Household..........	2.8	2.9	2.8	2.9	3.4	3.2	3.0	3.2	3.3	3.1	3.2
Total Housing Units..........	1913	1755	1597	1611	3224	918	666	1007	1155	1137	1197
% Condominiums & Cooperatives.....	0.0	0.4	0.8	0.0	0.3	0.0	0.0	0.7	0.0	0.0	0.0
% Built 1960 Or Later.............	0.8	0.0	0.0	1.7	0.7	0.8	0.8	0.7	1.0	0.0	1.2
% Owner Occupied..................	21.1	26.1	19.8	23.8	20.1	21.6	39.0	21.3	27.4	24.9	19.0
% With 1+ Persons Per Room........	10.8	8.9	6.2	6.9	16.8	15.1	6.9	14.2	15.8	11.3	15.6
Median Value: Owner Units......$$	-	16500	-	12800	12300	-	14000	-	11000	11200	-
Median Rent: Rental Units......$$	60	69	78	73	80	92	71	75	73	66	69
Median Number Of Rooms: All Units.	4.2	4.5	4.6	4.4	4.5	4.5	4.8	4.4	4.6	4.7	4.4

Tract Number	2433	2434	2435	2436
Total Population..............	3978	4448	2182	359
% Male.......................	50.5	49.8	52.2	76.6
% Black......................	1.0	2.1	25.8	3.9
% Other Nonwhite.............	1.9	1.5	2.0	7.8
% Of Spanish Language........	38.3	50.4	26.9	19.0
% Foreign Born...............	19.7	18.5	13.7	2.4
% Living In Group Quarters...	0.4	0.5	4.9	49.3
% 13 Years Old And Under.....	29.8	33.2	32.2	8.6
% 14-20 Years Old............	12.6	14.0	12.0	4.2
% 21-64 Years Old............	49.9	47.3	48.4	77.4
% 65-74 Years Old............	4.9	3.4	4.6	5.6
% 75 Years Old And Over......	2.9	2.1	2.8	4.2
% In Different House.........	56.8	54.0	30.6	27.8
% Families With Female Head..	13.9	17.0	21.9	12.8
Median School Years Completed...$$	8.8	8.5	8.2	10.9
Median Family Income, 1969......$$	8494	7952	7645	7500
% Income Below Poverty Level...	12.8	28.5	19.5	0.0
% Income of $15,000 or More....	12.5	10.5	9.3	0.0
% White Collar Workers.........	12.8	9.4	4.4	5.9
% Civilian Labor Force Unemployed.	3.7	5.0	7.4	2.3
% Riding To Work By Automobile....	44.4	48.3	33.1	13.2
Population Per Household..........	3.2	3.6	3.3	2.2
Total Housing Units..........	1370	1414	711	93
% Condominiums & Cooperatives.....	0.0	0.6	0.0	0.0
% Built 1960 Or Later.............	0.7	0.3	1.4	22.3
% Owner Occupied..................	16.1	15.6	11.3	5.4
% With 1+ Persons Per Room........	14.4	20.2	16.4	8.3
Median Value: Owner Units......$$	-	-	-	-
Median Rent: Rental Units......$$	59	63	66	74
Median Number Of Rooms: All Units.	4.3	4.4	4.4	3.9

almost 13 percent were vacant in 1980, and a similar percentage was overcrowded (more than one person per room). Twenty-six percent of West Town's population lived in overcrowded housing units in 1980. Another structural problem for area residents is that the "vaulted" sidewalks, raised about 6 feet from their original levels around the turn of the century by city engineers, are crumbling and collapsing. Buildings with two to nine housing units contain 85 percent of West Town's housing stock, 9 percent are single-family homes, and 6 percent of all housing units are in buildings with 10 or more units. These figures, compared to 1960, show a slight shift away from buildings with the most units. The median value of single-family, owner-occupied homes in West Town was $23,518 in 1980, less than half of the city median.

The oldest and largest of West Town's three main industrial districts is located on the eastern edge along the river. The other two are situated along the Chicago and North Western Railroad at the southern edge, and at the intersection of the Chicago, Milwaukee, and St. Paul tracks and Milwaukee Avenue at the northern boundary. These areas have not expanded much since World War II. A major retail center is located in the eastern section of the area, comprised of the stores on Chicago Avenue from Noble to Wood streets. To the northeast is another area of retail establishments on Milwaukee Avenue between the intersections of Thomas and Cleaver streets and North and Damen avenues. In the general area many stores have been boarded up or converted into churches.

West Town was one of the residential developments that made possible the accelerated industrial expansion of Chicago after the Fire and before the turn of the century. At its population peak, it was incredibly crowded and diverse, a model of the urbanized neighborhood in the industrialized city. Churches, stores, restaurants, landmarks and traces of its polyethnic heritage — Polish, Italian, Ukrainian, Jewish — survive, intermingled with the signs and structures of the new Hispanic culture. Amidst the deterioration of the aged housing is Wicker Park, surrounded by fine old homes, many in various stages of rehabilitation. Industrial and residential decentralization have made the teeming early-century neighborhood unnecessary, and have led away the descendants of those who came to work in the old industrial complex, but the neighborhood survives, and the old houses continue to shelter those who have come to participate in an industrial realignment which will lead to further change for West Town and Chicago.

Will Hogan

Community Area 25

Austin

The community of Austin, an area of 138,026 residents in 1980, is the city's largest, in terms of both geographical size and population. It is located at the edge of the city, about five miles due west of the Loop. To the west of Austin lies suburban Oak Park, directly south is the working-class suburb of Cicero. Until 1960, Austin was virtually an all-white community, various European-descended ethnic groups — Italians, Irish, English, Scots, and European Jews — residing in the brick bungalows, duplexes, and two-flats found there. In the last 20 years, however, the racial composition of Austin has changed dramatically, as the community has become three-fourths black.

Austin was originally part of the poorly-drained prairie west of Chicago. In 1835 Henry L. DeKoven purchased 280 acres of land from the federal government, including an area called Sand Ridge, now Central Austin. In 1842 John Pierson built the Six Mile House, a two-story tavern located on an old Indian trail which was to become the Lake Street turnpike, near what is now Pine Street. The tavern served as a stopover for weary travelers leaving Chicago on their way to the surrounding settlements. In 1848, it became a stop on the Galena and Chicago Union Railroad. The railroad ran parallel to Lake Street, which was planked in 1849. When Cicero township was organized in 1857, Sand Ridge and the area south of it were included. Ten years later Cicero was incorporated as a town.

Henry W. Austin was instrumental in the early development of the community area. In 1865, Austin purchased DeKoven's land. Next, he laid out a subdivision with wide streets along which he planted hundreds of shade trees. He called the development Austinville and this was the name given to the new Chicago and North Western depot opened there in 1866. Austin donated part of his land holdings to entice a New England clock manufacturing establishment to relocate, bringing its employees to settle in the area. However the clock factory was short-lived. It became a shoe factory, and a tannery, before being destroyed by fire. Cicero, of which Austinville was a part, built its town hall there in 1871, near the present intersection of Lake Street and Central Avenue, in Holden Park.

By 1884 the community, now called Austin, had a population of 1,359 persons. English and some native Americans had settled along the community's western border. German, Irish, Scandinavian and Polish settlers lived along the Chicago, Milwaukee and St. Paul railroad tracks at the community's northern boundary. As transportation improved with the introduction of hourly service by the Chicago and North Western, the completion of the Lake Street branch of the elevated lines in 1893, and the extension of the streetcar lines along Madison Street and Chicago Avenue, the area began to grow rapidly. By 1900, Austin's population surpassed 4,000.

During these early years Austin, along with neighboring Oak Park, was still a part of the Town of Cicero. In 1889, however, Austin and

Community Area 25 — Austin
Population and Housing Characteristics, 1930–1980

	1980	1970	1960	1950	1940	1930
Total Population.......	138,026	127,981	125,133	132,180	132,107	131,114
% Male...................	46.7	47.6	47.1	47.3	47.7	48.7
% Female.................	53.3	52.4	52.9	52.7	52.3	51.3
% White..................	20.8	66.3	99.9	99.8	100.0	99.9
% Black..................	73.8	32.5	0.0	0.1	0.0	0.1
% Other Nonwhite Races...	5.4	1.2	0.1	0.1	0.0	0.0
% Under 5 Years Old......	10.1	9.1	8.6	8.4	5.7	7.3
% 5-19 Years Old.........	30.5	25.2	19.4	16.8	19.3	21.3
% 20-44 Years Old........	38.2	34.3	30.6	37.7	43.6	47.2
% 45-64 Years Old........	15.1	20.3	28.3	27.9	24.2	19.3
% 65 Years and Older.....	6.1	11.1	13.1	9.2	7.2	4.9
Median School Years....	12.1	11.2	11.3	11.0	9.1	*
Total Housing Units....	44,682	44,841	44,554	41,451	39,423	*
% In One-Unit Structures..	23.2	21.0	23.1	*	*	*
% Owner Occupied.........	36.6	35.0	37.7	37.2	29.0	*
% Renter Occupied........	56.5	60.7	59.7	61.7	68.6	*
% Vacant.................	6.9	4.3	3.6	1.1	2.4	*
% 1+ Persons per Room....	11.4	7.8	5.4	9.7	*	*

Community Area 25 — Austin
Selected Characteristics of Census Tracts: 1980

Tract Number	Total	2501	2502	2503	2504	2505	2506	2507	2508	2509	2510
Total Population.............	138026	429	2600	4283	5753	7548	5062	7334	3190	917	1700
% Male.......................	46.7	51.3	47.9	48.3	46.7	46.4	48.2	47.3	47.2	49.6	48.9
% Black......................	73.8	1.9	1.7	0.5	0.4	0.0	30.9	58.2	54.8	27.3	88.4
% Other Nonwhite.............	5.5	31.0	25.0	25.4	13.5	2.0	27.7	16.0	19.6	17.9	3.3
% Of Spanish Origin..........	5.9	39.6	28.8	31.3	19.5	1.5	15.9	16.0	15.2	32.3	3.4
% Foreign Born...............	6.6	30.6	26.4	28.9	28.1	10.0	24.5	12.7	15.1	21.1	4.6
% Living In Group Quarters...	1.0	0.0	0.0	0.0	0.0	0.0	0.0	0.1	0.4	0.0	0.0
% 13 Years Old And Under.....	28.3	25.9	21.1	19.5	19.5	14.0	26.8	29.4	29.4	27.8	32.1
% 14-20 Years Old............	14.4	12.4	11.7	12.1	10.1	9.5	14.1	12.4	14.1	12.6	13.2
% 21-64 Years Old............	51.2	51.7	54.0	55.8	54.0	56.9	50.7	51.9	50.6	53.2	51.6
% 65-74 Years Old............	3.9	7.9	8.2	7.8	9.4	12.3	5.1	3.7	3.7	4.6	1.8
% 75 Years Old And Over......	2.2	2.1	4.9	4.9	7.1	7.4	3.3	2.6	2.1	1.7	1.2
% In Different House.........	45.1	11.8	43.8	45.2	41.4	29.0	54.0	76.0	68.8	69.7	44.3
% Families With Female Head..	42.5	21.9	20.9	18.2	14.2	10.4	22.3	34.3	27.3	31.3	47.4
Median School Years Completed..	12.1	11.7	11.6	11.7	11.8	12.4	12.4	12.3	12.3	12.1	11.8
Median Family Income, 1979...$$	16566	10208	21194	19591	19552	26833	24075	19819	22061	18300	19798
% Income Below Poverty Level....	21.8	20.7	10.4	9.2	9.7	1.8	7.9	17.9	11.3	16.5	18.1
% Income Of $30,000 Or More.....	18.9	9.0	28.6	24.1	24.2	40.7	34.3	18.7	30.0	16.0	16.9
% White Collar Workers..........	43.1	44.9	43.1	44.1	47.2	63.1	48.4	50.2	50.5	48.4	40.4
% Civilian Labor Force Unemployed.	13.9	0.0	7.6	8.9	9.3	2.7	8.1	9.1	11.2	5.3	11.8
% Riding To Work By Automobile...	64.2	53.7	72.1	67.6	69.8	74.5	63.4	68.5	62.2	62.0	63.8
Mean Commuting Time - Minutes...	32.9	25.4	31.1	32.1	32.7	28.9	32.7	31.7	29.2	35.6	35.3
Population Per Household.........	3.3	3.0	3.0	2.9	2.7	2.7	3.6	3.1	3.5	3.0	3.0
Total Housing Units...........	44682	155	901	1541	2180	2932	1534	2522	945	336	640
% Condominiums................	1.3	0.0	0.0	0.0	0.0	14.6	0.5	0.0	0.0	0.0	0.0
% Built 1970 Or Later.........	3.6	0.0	0.8	0.5	0.5	16.0	0.7	0.0	0.0	0.0	0.0
% Owner Occupied..............	36.6	38.1	58.2	46.3	51.3	82.2	63.6	40.0	51.1	43.2	27.2
% With 1+ Persons Per Room....	11.4	11.2	6.6	7.4	5.2	1.4	10.3	7.2	11.1	8.3	11.2
Median Value: Owner Units....$$	41600	-	38700	40900	48000	68400	43300	40800	38900	34200	34200
Median Rent: Rental Units....$$	191	161	179	188	201	233	198	218	216	175	174
Median Number Of Rooms: All Units.	5.0	4.9	5.1	5.0	5.0	5.5	5.6	5.2	5.5	5.0	4.7

Tract Number	2511	2512	2513	2514	2515	2516	2517	2518	2519	2520	2521
Total Population.............	6358	5268	6770	6722	7463	6102	2888	9144	10437	9122	12974
% Male.......................	45.9	47.5	46.8	46.0	47.9	46.2	46.4	45.5	47.7	45.8	45.5
% Black......................	89.6	89.4	81.9	92.0	96.6	96.6	88.2	98.3	96.8	98.4	99.1
% Other Nonwhite.............	3.6	2.9	5.8	0.9	0.4	0.8	3.4	0.6	0.7	0.3	0.1
% Of Spanish Origin..........	3.1	3.6	5.9	2.0	0.9	0.9	8.6	1.3	1.5	0.6	0.2
% Foreign Born...............	3.8	2.7	4.8	1.0	0.6	0.6	3.7	1.1	0.7	1.3	0.5
% Living In Group Quarters...	1.5	0.0	0.0	0.5	1.4	0.0	1.4	0.2	2.2	1.7	0.4
% 13 Years Old And Under.....	31.6	31.7	31.5	29.9	30.9	31.0	32.8	32.0	30.1	32.9	30.0
% 14-20 Years Old............	14.8	17.4	12.3	15.1	16.7	18.3	17.4	15.7	15.2	13.2	16.7
% 21-64 Years Old............	51.2	46.8	52.1	49.2	49.6	48.2	46.4	48.8	51.7	50.6	50.0
% 65-74 Years Old............	1.7	2.1	2.6	4.3	1.8	1.9	2.6	2.6	2.3	1.9	2.5
% 75 Years Old And Over......	0.6	2.0	1.6	1.6	1.0	0.7	0.8	0.9	0.7	1.4	0.8
% In Different House.........	53.4	50.9	65.4	41.9	45.7	23.2	23.5	42.0	54.3	53.7	34.4
% Families With Female Head..	43.0	34.1	38.2	49.5	47.6	44.1	46.6	56.0	54.9	58.2	50.5
Median School Years Completed..	12.1	12.1	12.2	12.1	12.1	11.4	11.0	12.0	12.0	12.0	12.1
Median Family Income, 1979......$$	15829	18320	19421	12706	13082	15481	14033	11250	11844	10969	15818
% Income Below Poverty Level....	22.6	20.5	17.8	29.5	27.2	25.0	29.5	34.7	32.2	33.3	24.1
% Income Of $30,000 Or More.....	17.1	20.1	18.4	8.5	13.3	19.3	18.0	9.5	12.5	9.9	17.8
% White Collar Workers..........	37.6	42.6	43.7	46.4	37.9	34.6	34.0	40.0	33.9	37.8	38.3
% Civilian Labor Force Unemployed.	17.1	15.2	11.6	13.7	19.3	13.7	20.2	19.4	19.4	17.1	20.7
% Riding To Work By Automobile...	62.7	66.9	67.2	55.7	53.4	66.3	68.6	60.3	59.2	61.0	65.6
Mean Commuting Time - Minutes...	32.1	36.2	32.8	33.8	37.3	31.5	29.7	32.8	35.4	35.5	32.8
Population Per Household.........	3.6	3.9	3.3	3.2	3.5	3.5	3.9	4.1	3.4	3.2	3.6
Total Housing Units...........	1856	1473	2169	2247	2276	1654	764	2892	3653	3216	3860
% Condominiums................	0.0	0.0	0.0	0.5	0.6	0.0	0.0	0.0	0.4	2.0	0.0
% Built 1970 Or Later.........	2.1	3.2	0.7	8.4	4.6	4.5	10.8	1.6	3.6	3.9	1.2
% Owner Occupied..............	34.6	60.1	40.8	22.9	26.8	44.9	33.8	20.0	16.3	12.4	27.6
% With 1+ Persons Per Room....	11.2	13.4	8.3	10.8	14.9	15.9	18.1	14.3	15.8	16.6	13.8
Median Value: Owner Units.......$$	36300	34200	33700	37100	27600	28100	27700	34300	31200	38200	36500
Median Rent: Rental Units....$$	199	193	195	193	188	175	172	178	191	198	196
Median Number Of Rooms: All Units.	5.2	5.6	5.3	4.6	4.8	5.3	5.4	4.8	4.2	4.0	5.1

Community Area 25 — Austin
Selected Characteristics of Census Tracts: 1980

Tract Number	2522	2523	2524
Total Population............	12073	1376	2513
% Male....................	45.9	45.4	47.2
% Black...................	97.5	96.3	23.1
% Other Nonwhite..........	0.5	1.0	2.9
% Of Spanish Origin.......	0.4	1.9	4.4
% Foreign Born............	1.2	1.3	12.5
% Living In Group Quarters.	2.7	0.0	13.0
% 13 Years Old And Under...	27.8	29.7	17.5
% 14-20 Years Old.........	15.4	18.6	9.0
% 21-64 Years Old.........	53.0	47.4	53.8
% 65-74 Years Old.........	2.8	3.3	11.3
% 75 Years Old And Over...	1.0	1.0	8.5
% In Different House......	32.5	17.4	37.8
% Families With Female Head......	49.6	47.1	24.0
Median School Years Completed...	11.8	11.3	11.6
Median Family Income, 1979.....$$	14387	13661	20383
% Income Below Poverty Level....	29.3	30.6	7.6
% Income Of $30,000 Or More.....	18.3	4.6	16.8
% White Collar Workers...	40.7	37.9	41.5
% Civilian Labor Force Unemployed.	15.9	11.2	9.4
% Riding To Work By Automobile....	61.6	60.2	58.6
Mean Commuting Time - Minutes...	33.0	30.4	35.1
Population Per Household..........	3.4	3.9	2.6
Total Housing Units..........	3648	387	901
% Condominiums...............	0.6	0.0	0.0
% Built 1970 Or Later........	4.0	6.2	0.0
% Owner Occupied.............	29.5	38.0	39.1
% With 1+ Persons Per Room...	13.8	13.0	5.1
Median Value: Owner Units.....$$	36800	30800	40300
Median Rent: Rental Units.....$$	178	172	179
Median Number Of Rooms: All Units.	4.9	5.3	4.9

Community Area 25 — Austin
Selected Characteristics of Census Tracts: 1970

Tract Number	TOTAL	2501	2502	2503	2504	2505	2506	2507	2508	2509	2510
Total Population............	127981	481	2640	4183	5795	7445	4479	6138	2742	941	617
% Male....................	47.6	46.4	49.5	46.9	46.8	47.1	44.9	45.6	47.7	49.4	54.1
% Black...................	32.5	0.0	0.0	0.0	0.0	0.0	0.0	0.0	0.0	0.0	0.0
% Other Nonwhite..........	1.2	0.0	0.7	0.6	0.1	0.3	0.3	0.3	0.3	1.4	1.3
% Of Spanish Language......	3.6	0.0	4.6	2.2	0.6	0.6	0.3	2.0	1.8	17.7	25.2
% Foreign Born............	10.8	6.2	18.8	17.1	23.3	11.4	15.2	22.4	18.0	13.5	26.9
% Living In Group Quarters.	0.6	0.0	0.3	0.1	0.0	0.0	0.6	0.0	0.7	0.0	0.0
% 13 Years Old And Under...	25.1	27.4	20.0	19.1	18.7	16.7	22.3	18.6	20.6	23.2	19.0
% 14-20 Years Old.........	10.9	11.6	10.9	8.7	8.7	10.4	11.5	9.2	11.1	11.5	9.7
% 21-64 Years Old.........	53.0	52.6	54.7	56.6	55.2	56.2	50.1	55.2	53.7	53.7	60.3
% 65-74 Years Old.........	6.8	4.4	8.8	10.2	11.5	11.3	9.5	10.6	9.2	7.7	7.0
% 75 Years Old And Over...	4.2	4.0	5.5	5.4	6.0	5.3	6.5	6.5	5.4	4.0	4.1
% In Different House......	42.9	55.3	62.8	60.3	60.7	69.6	57.0	59.1	62.9	45.7	47.2
% Families With Female Head.....	15.9	19.0	11.4	12.6	12.8	10.4	14.9	13.6	12.2	11.1	13.9
Median School Years Completed.....	11.2	8.8	10.0	10.7	11.4	12.1	11.6	10.3	10.9	9.5	9.9
Median Family Income, 1969.....$$	10631	9667	12048	11529	11610	13853	12640	11014	11360	11750	10520
% Income Below Poverty Level.....	8.1	15.7	3.5	6.6	3.8	2.2	5.4	7.0	4.4	5.6	4.4
% Income of $15,000 or More.....	23.8	23.3	32.2	27.9	26.1	43.6	36.1	25.4	30.5	19.0	24.7
% White Collar Workers.....	19.7	9.9	15.6	19.7	21.3	37.9	22.9	21.0	20.7	9.2	16.7
% Civilian Labor Force Unemployed.	4.1	2.2	2.6	2.5	2.7	2.3	1.5	2.9	2.2	3.4	3.8
% Riding To Work By Automobile.	55.1	65.5	51.1	58.7	58.8	66.8	54.0	54.1	63.2	58.6	38.7
Population Per Household..........	3.0	3.0	3.0	2.7	2.7	3.0	3.2	2.8	3.1	2.9	2.4
Total Housing Units..........	44844	168	890	1554	2145	2485	1438	2251	908	344	263
% Condominiums & Cooperatives.....	0.7	0.0	0.0	1.0	1.4	0.0	0.3	0.8	0.8	0.0	0.0
% Built 1960 Or Later......	3.4	5.3	2.5	3.2	2.9	3.2	0.9	2.4	1.1	0.0	3.4
% Owner Occupied...........	34.4	36.3	57.4	46.5	50.2	81.9	64.7	41.4	53.6	47.7	21.3
% With 1+ Persons Per Room......	8.2	8.9	6.9	4.3	4.6	2.9	5.2	3.9	5.2	6.4	9.5
Median Value: Owner Units.......$$	20900	-	21300	21400	22900	30100	21900	21600	20500	18400	-
Median Rent: Rental Units.......$$	116	88	106	113	122	131	117	119	115	88	107
Median Number Of Rooms: All Units.	4.8	4.9	4.9	4.9	5.0	5.6	5.5	5.0	5.2	4.7	4.2

Tract Number	2511	2512	2513	2514	2515	2516	2517	2518	2519	2520	2521
Total Population............	6143	4557	5750	5645	5375	4823	2844	10887	8905	7229	11817
% Male....................	46.5	46.6	46.5	47.2	49.9	49.3	51.2	47.7	48.5	47.9	47.5
% Black...................	0.1	0.1	0.0	0.4	5.0	1.1	0.8	91.1	73.7	20.4	67.7
% Other Nonwhite..........	2.7	0.4	0.7	1.1	2.5	1.3	1.7	0.5	2.1	4.1	1.8
% Of Spanish Language......	6.1	1.4	5.1	7.1	4.6	9.1	17.2	1.2	3.7	6.4	3.2
% Foreign Born............	15.5	11.7	20.0	16.3	13.5	11.9	7.1	1.5	3.2	11.0	7.0
% Living In Group Quarters.	2.8	0.2	0.1	0.7	0.7	0.0	0.0	0.4	0.2	0.2	0.7
% 13 Years Old And Under...	21.7	23.3	22.2	18.2	21.5	26.9	28.0	35.1	29.1	16.9	30.9
% 14-20 Years Old.........	11.5	11.4	10.4	8.6	10.0	12.0	11.6	12.6	11.8	8.9	11.3
% 21-64 Years Old.........	53.2	50.6	52.5	56.6	54.7	50.4	51.6	50.0	52.0	58.6	50.6
% 65-74 Years Old.........	7.8	8.1	9.1	9.9	8.3	6.9	5.6	1.8	3.5	9.7	4.3
% 75 Years Old And Over...	5.7	6.5	5.9	6.7	5.5	3.7	3.2	1.2	2.6	5.9	2.8
% In Different House......	53.8	61.5	60.3	42.8	41.9	52.3	49.4	16.9	20.0	37.6	25.6
% Families With Female Head.....	13.8	11.5	14.9	16.5	16.1	13.8	14.3	22.0	19.8	16.6	17.7
Median School Years Completed.....	10.7	11.6	10.6	11.7	11.5	10.5	10.2	11.1	11.7	12.3	11.9
Median Family Income, 1969......$$	11115	11613	11264	10670	10647	10989	9984	8251	9609	10218	10927
% Income Below Poverty Level.....	4.3	1.6	2.5	2.5	5.4	2.0	2.4	17.0	14.0	5.2	8.0
% Income of $15,000 or More.....	24.9	30.5	25.5	25.5	26.4	27.0	22.5	8.7	17.3	25.1	19.6
% White Collar Workers.....	20.1	24.1	17.0	23.4	25.0	16.7	9.4	12.0	16.2	29.1	18.3
% Civilian Labor Force Unemployed.	3.1	2.1	5.3	2.3	4.2	5.5	4.7	7.9	5.5	3.2	4.8
% Riding To Work By Automobile....	53.4	56.7	51.3	46.5	53.1	56.9	51.4	55.7	46.8	50.2	57.9
Population Per Household..........	2.9	3.2	2.9	2.3	2.5	3.2	3.2	3.3	3.0	2.2	3.4
Total Housing Units..........	2104	1484	2039	2562	2248	1584	968	3397	3342	3481	3684
% Condominiums & Cooperatives.....	0.7	0.7	1.0	0.2	0.5	0.3	0.0	0.3	1.3	0.8	0.7
% Built 1960 Or Later......	1.1	0.4	0.2	3.0	7.7	0.7	1.7	0.7	5.0	13.4	3.4
% Owner Occupied...........	37.1	58.5	43.1	18.7	27.2	43.6	36.7	17.1	14.3	9.6	27.0
% With 1+ Persons Per Room......	6.3	5.1	5.4	5.0	5.1	8.1	10.4	15.8	10.8	5.6	10.4
Median Value: Owner Units.......$$	18000	19000	18100	18100	16400	15200	13700	15900	18000	19100	18800
Median Rent: Rental Units.......$$	109	110	111	108	110	101	92	115	124	123	125
Median Number Of Rooms: All Units.	4.9	5.6	5.1	3.8	4.3	5.2	5.1	4.5	4.0	3.7	5.0

Oak Park split over the issue of the extension of the Lake Street line to Austin Avenue, which Austin favored. The Austinites prevailed, using political pressure to obtain the extension. Residents of Cicero and Oak Park, angered by these political tactics, used their numerical advantages to pass a joint election proposal which would annex Austin to Chicago. Parallel measures for the annexation of Cicero and Oak Park were defeated. Thus, against the wishes of the inhabitants, the village of Austin became part of Chicago in 1899.

Austin experienced tremendous residential growth in the first three decades following its annexation to Chicago. In North Austin, the extension of the Division Street streetcar line to Austin Boulevard in 1915 led to the building of duplexes, two-flats, and brick bungalows in order to accommodate the influx of first- and second-generation Germans and Swedes. Eastern European Jews poured into the apartment buildings surrounding Columbus Park in South Austin. By 1920, the population of Austin neared 75,000. The southeastern section of Austin was rapidly built up during the 1920s, and settled by Scots, English, Irish, and Germans. By 1930, Austin had achieved residential maturity — a result of the widespread residential construction from 1900 to 1930 — and a population of more than 130,000. The major foreign stocks were Germans, Irish, and Swedes, with a smaller number of Italians and Russian Jews.

The size and composition of Austin's population remained relatively stable through the Depression and World War II. It always had been a white community, but during the 1950s whites began to move out. The number of residents had dropped to 125,000 by 1960, and the baby boom of the preceding decade had masked an out-migration of 18,000. During these decades many Italians had moved into Austin from the Near West Side and East and West Garfield Park, communities that were overcrowded and deteriorating. By 1960, Italians had become the most numerous foreign-stock nationality, followed by Irish, Germans and Poles. During the following decade blacks, who had succeeded the Italians in the poorer community areas to the east, began to move into Austin. The number of blacks rose from 31 in 1960 to 41,583 10 years later. Almost as many whites moved out and by 1970 blacks constituted 32 percent of the total population.

Rapid racial turnover led to a rapidly-developing sequence of problems: racial integration and, later, expansion of the capacities of neighborhood schools; maintenance of the housing stock, particularly those units owned by absentee landlords; the practice of unscrupulous real estate companies, who manipulated racial fears and tensions for profit; increasing crime and lack of understanding between the police and the new residents; the delivery of city services to the rapidly changing and expanding population of Austin. A parade of community organizations, utilizing various philosophies and tactics, came into being to deal with these problems. The United Property Group and the Austin Community Organization were formed in the early 1960s by thousands of white members. Shortly after the middle of the decade, each had disappeared as their following began to migrate from the area. They were succeeded by the Organization for a Better Austin, racially integrated, which used direct-action methods and a confrontational approach, and the Town Hall Assembly, a white group which stressed more traditional community organization.

The racial turnover continued in the 1970s as the incoming black population, at first concentrated in the southeast corner, began to spread north and west. More than 50,000 whites moved out of Austin during the most recent decade, more than 60,000 blacks moved in. By 1980, the population had increased by 10,000 to its current historic high. Blacks filled southern and central Austin, and were now living among whites who had lived in northern Austin for generations, or who had fled to that area from southern Austin or other racially changing neighborhoods on Chicago's West and South Sides.

Community Area 25 — Austin Selected Characteristics of Census Tracts: 1970			
Tract Number	2522	2523	2524
Total Population.............	14616	1426	2503
% Male................................	48.2	49.9	43.9
% Black..............................	95.1	80.2	8.1
% Other Nonwhite..................	0.3	1.5	0.4
% Of Spanish Language..............	0.3	4.6	3.0
% Foreign Born......................	0.7	4.1	10.8
% Living In Group Quarters........	1.0	0.0	4.5
% 13 Years Old And Under..........	33.9	39.6	18.7
% 14-20 Years Old..................	12.6	14.1	8.9
% 21-64 Years Old..................	51.3	42.1	53.2
% 65-74 Years Old..................	1.4	2.9	10.8
% 75 Years Old And Over...........	0.7	1.3	8.4
% In Different House..............	22.9	38.2	47.4
% Families With Female Head.......	19.9	22.7	13.5
Median School Years Completed.....	11.2	10.6	10.9
Median Family Income, 1969......$$	8780	8125	10807
% Income Below Poverty Level.....	15.4	26.4	9.4
% Income of $15,000 or More.....	14.6	11.8	25.8
% White Collar Workers...........	10.8	7.8	21.8
% Civilian Labor Force Unemployed.	6.0	1.0	4.2
% Riding To Work By Automobile....	59.3	44.8	54.1
Population Per Household..........	3.6	4.1	2.8
Total Housing Units..........	4237	362	906
% Condominiums & Cooperatives.....	1.0	0.0	0.0
% Built 1960 Or Later.............	2.4	3.7	1.7
% Owner Occupied..................	21.6	38.4	37.1
% With 1+ Persons Per Room........	18.1	19.4	4.4
Median Value: Owner Units.......$$	19000	17000	20700
Median Rent: Rental Units.......$$	121	105	112
Median Number Of Rooms: All Units.	4.7	5.3	4.8

Today, most whites in Austin live north of North Avenue. The area immediately south is mixed, blacks predominating in the tracts bordering on Laramie Avenue in the center, whites in the majority near the east and west peripheries. Except for the far southwest corner, bordering on suburban Cicero, Austin south of Division Street is now predominantly black. Six percent of the Austin population is Hispanic, and a sizeable group of other non-whites, principally Filipinos, has moved into northern Austin. Among the remaining whites, people claiming Italian, Polish, German and Irish descent are most numerous.

There has been little construction in Austin in the last 20 years. The slight growth in number of units in that time seems principally due to substruction of existing units. About a fourth of the units are single-family dwellings, many of the others are two-flats, about 40 percent of all units being owner-occupied. The median value of single-family owner-occupied units is about average for the city. There are housing problems in Austin. About one in every 15 units is vacant, while 22 percent of the residents live in overcrowded housing. However, there is some housing restoration going on. Central Austin, a racially integrated area, bounded by Augusta Boulevard, West End Street, Pine Street, and Austin Avenue, renamed "Austin Village" by those who live there, has undergone housing rehabilitation. Rehabilitation included a number of mansions designed by architect Frederick R. Schock during the 19th century.

There is a major retail center in the northwest corner of Austin, straddling the city limits at Harlem and Bloomingdale avenues, running along Harlem to North Avenue, and along North Avenue into suburban Oak Park, River Forest and Elmwood Park.

Today, the major problems confronting Austin tend to be concentrated in the southern part of the community. While 31 percent of Austin's residents received public aid in 1979, 83 percent of that assistance went to South Austin. The South Austin Coalition Community Council, an organization which became important in the 1970s, has sponsored projects and pressured local firms to provide jobs for South Austin's more than 5,000 unemployed residents. This neighborhood contains many abandoned buildings — the entire Austin community area had 358 boarded up housing units in 1980, fourth highest in Chicago. High employment, a high crime rate and abandoned buildings have made South Austin a blighted area.

Austin is basically three communities: impoverished South Austin, the revitalized Austin Village area, and North Austin, the last stand for many whites who fear further black relocation. Time will tell which of these neighborhoods will characterize the entire community.

Winston McDowell

West Garfield Park

The West Garfield Park community area was an empty prairie more than three miles outside the city limits when the City of Chicago was incorporated in 1837. In the 1840s the Pennsylvania Avenue (Lake Street) Road was planked and the Galena and Chicago Union Railroad was laid west from the city, but the area was still outside the city limits, and it remained unpopulated until after the Civil War. In 1869, the land east of Pulaski Road was annexed to the city, and the newly formed West Side Park Board announced the establishment of Central Park, just to the east. This produced some speculation in land adjacent to the proposed park. The Galena and Chicago Union Railroad, which had become the Chicago and North Western, set up shops at the present intersection of Pulaski and Kedzie Street in 1873. This produced a settlement of 2,000 Scandinavian, Irish and German workers, which was called Central Park, at Keeler Avenue and Lake Street. The Irish lived on parcels of land called "patches," as they had been in the old country. Agriculture and other rural activities began to develop around the settlement. Charles Voltz, who had a farm at Kostner Avenue and Madison Street, produced milk and vegetables for village residents. Barry Point Road, which became Fifth Avenue, led to an inn operated by the Widow Barry. In 1878 the St. Mel parish was established at Keeler Avenue and Maypole Street, and a number of other churches soon appeared. In 1885, Central Park was renamed for the assassinated President Garfield, and the area surrounding the park had a new identity.

Early in 1889, the rest of the community area was annexed to the city. Garfield Park had become a major recreational area. In the park were a lagoon, a bandstand, an expanding "flower house," a golf course and other amenities. A race track, called the Gentlemen's Trotting and Racing Club, was built at Madison and Pulaski. Here, in addition to the races, John L. Sullivan staged a prize fight and Buffalo Bill presented his Wild West Show. The north side of Madison, immediately south of the track, became a strip of saloons and beer gardens, frequented by jockeys, trainers, and track patrons.

In the 1890s, transportation links to the Loop were established by the construction of the Lake Street and Garfield Park rapid transit elevated lines. Now subdivision and construction began to accelerate, especially near the elevated tracks. Expensive brick two-flats and small apartment buildings went up in the eastern part of the community area, near the Park. In the rest of the neighborhood, stone front two-flats and single-family homes predominated.

Chicago and North Western Railroad tracks became the northern and western boundaries of West Garfield Park and industry began to locate along these lines and along another track which ran just south of Taylor Street, the southern community boundary. After the turn of the century as the Loop filled with other activities and land values there soared, wholesale houses and warehouses began to move out of the center to locations along belt-line railroads. The residential portion of West Garfield Park gradually was surrounded on three sides by industrial activities. In the 1890s, light industry began to locate on Fifth Avenue and along Pulaski Road.

The teeming Near West Side and West Town community areas served as a port of entry for many working-class immigrants. As some prospered, they moved in the areas around the West Side parks, Russian Jews to the west of Garfield Park, Italians more to the east. By 1920 more than 40,000 people, mainly first- and second-generation Irish with a sprinkling of Russian Jews, lived in West Garfield Park. The community area had reached residential maturity in 1919, but construction went on during the 1920s, especially after the introduction of bus lines on Jackson, Independence and Washington Boulevards. By 1930, the number of residents reached what proved to be the

all-time high for West Garfield Park, more than 50,000. The Irish were still most numerous among foreign stock, but more Russian Jews and now Italians were moving in from farther east, replacing some of the Irish. A handful of blacks lived along Lake Street, the oldest industrial section of the community.

With the onset of the Depression, construction came to a virtual halt in 1930. During the decades that followed, the population dropped to 48,000, then less than 46,000 in 1960. By that time 99 percent of the housing in West Garfield Park was at least 30 years old. After the Second World War, the number of housing units was increased by the conversion of larger single-family units and duplexes into multiple units. Further conversions to keep up the housing stock were made necessary by demolitions along the route of the Congress Street (Eisenhower) Expressway. In the 1950s a substantial displacement in the ethnic and racial composition of the population had begun to occur as almost a third of the white population moved out, to be replaced by more than 7,000 blacks. Among the white remainder, Italians had replaced Irish as the most numerous nationality among the foreign stock. Most of the Russian Jews had moved out, migrating to city areas to the north and northwest of West Garfield Park, and 1,600 Mexicans constituted the third largest foreign-stock group.

In the 20 years since 1960, West Garfield Park has become a black community. More than 40,000 blacks moved in during the 1960s, and the black population was almost 47,000 at the end of the decade. During the most recent decade, thousands of blacks as well as most of the remaining whites have moved out of West Garfield Park. Today, the total population is less than 34,000, about two-thirds of the historic high in 1930. Ninety-nine percent of the residents are black, despite the net loss of more than 13,000 blacks in the last 10 years. All but 200 of the Mexicans are gone, and fewer than 100 residents of either Italian or Irish descent remain.

Today, there are fewer than 10,000 housing units in West Garfield Park, compared to more than 14,500 20 years ago. The proportion living in overcrowded housing (more than one person per room) has almost doubled during that time, from 16 to 30 percent. People and houses have disappeared from every sector of West Garfield Park, but especially from the northeast corner, north of Madison Street, east of Pulaski Road, where the number of residents dropped by more than half between 1970 and 1980. Large empty lots, formerly occupied by small- and medium-sized apartment buildings, are mute evidence of the loss of dwelling space caused by the withdrawal of investment, undermaintenance and arson. Attrition among the larger structures has been especially high; 20 years ago there were almost 3,000 housing units in West Garfield Park located in buildings with 10 or more units, today there are barely 700. The median value of owner-occupied single units is slightly more than half the city median.

Community Area 26 -- West Garfield Park
Population and Housing Characteristics, 1930-1980

	1980	1970	1960	1950	1940	1930
Total Population.......	33,865	48,464	45,611	48,443	48,447	50,014
% Male..................	46.1	47.2	49.4	48.7	49.0	49.8
% Female................	53.9	52.8	50.6	51.3	51.0	50.2
% White.................	0.7	2.8	83.6	99.8	99.9	99.8
% Black.................	98.9	96.9	15.8	0.0	0.0	0.1
% Other Nonwhite Races...	0.4	0.3	0.6	0.2	0.1	0.1
% Under 5 Years Old......	10.8	12.3	13.3	8.8	6.0	6.5
% 5-19 Years Old........	34.9	38.6	24.2	18.1	21.0	22.7
% 20-44 Years Old........	33.4	34.4	35.9	40.8	43.9	46.7
% 45-64 Years Old........	15.9	11.0	18.5	24.1	22.5	19.4
% 65 Years and Older.....	5.0	1.6	8.1	8.2	6.6	4.7
Median School Years....	10.9	10.3	9.0	9.6	8.6	*
Total Housing Units....	9,528	13,171	14,590	14,553	13,186	*
% In One-Unit Structures.	7.5	6.5	6.5	*	*	*
% Owner Occupied.........	22.4	17.3	20.5	23.0	18.6	*
% Renter Occupied........	73.0	75.0	73.3	75.4	78.5	*
% Vacant................	4.6	7.7	6.2	1.6	3.9	*
% 1+ Persons per Room....	16.4	20.3	15.9	13.4	*	*

Community Area 26 -- West Garfield Park
Selected Characteristics of Census Tracts: 1980

Tract Number	Total	2601	2602	2603	2604	2605	2606	2607	2608	2609	2610
Total Population.............	33865	1950	2056	3011	2888	3558	4503	4013	4618	2896	4372
% Male.......................	46.1	42.5	47.0	46.2	46.8	44.8	46.5	46.3	46.2	46.3	46.9
% Black......................	98.8	96.9	98.2	97.8	98.6	99.4	99.2	99.1	99.4	99.2	99.C
% Other Nonwhite.............	0.4	1.1	0.8	0.4	0.7	0.3	0.3	0.3	0.4	0.3	0.2
% Of Spanish Origin..........	0.8	0.8	1.3	1.5	0.6	0.8	1.1	0.6	0.6	0.9	0.4
% Foreign Born...............	0.8	0.0	1.8	1.2	1.8	0.0	1.0	0.9	0.2	0.2	1.C
% Living In Group Quarters...	1.3	7.8	4.2	0.6	0.9	0.0	0.3	1.4	2.2	0.0	0.C
% 13 Years Old And Under.....	30.5	26.6	30.8	31.9	31.0	31.4	31.0	30.2	31.2	29.8	29.8
% 14-20 Years Old............	17.6	16.2	16.1	17.3	16.4	17.7	18.1	18.7	17.5	20.0	16.9
% 21-64 Years Old............	46.9	44.1	49.1	46.9	49.7	46.7	47.2	46.3	45.5	44.7	48.7
% 65-74 Years Old............	3.3	6.8	2.6	2.8	2.0	3.0	2.5	3.6	4.3	3.4	3.3
% 75 Years Old And Over......	1.6	6.4	1.4	1.2	0.8	1.3	1.2	1.3	1.5	2.0	1.3
% In Different House.........	40.7	27.6	57.7	52.4	47.7	41.0	43.8	40.8	36.5	28.1	36.C
% Families With Female Head..	57.8	63.2	63.2	63.0	58.5	59.8	52.2	56.9	60.4	62.8	48.6
Median School Years Completed....	10.9	9.2	10.5	10.8	11.3	11.1	10.6	10.4	11.5	11.5	10.9
Median Family Income, 1979......$$	10922	7380	9557	11196	11667	10927	11287	9891	11202	14115	11423
% Income Below Poverty Level..	37.2	51.3	41.0	42.4	36.8	36.8	34.7	36.9	36.9	29.6	36.1
% Income Of $30,000 Or More...	10.8	2.1	6.4	6.2	12.7	9.0	12.4	4.9	10.9	23.2	10.9
% White Collar Workers.......	34.9	36.5	24.0	33.2	39.8	30.9	33.8	31.8	41.1	39.9	33.6
% Civilian Labor Force Unemployed.	20.7	32.3	28.7	17.3	21.0	20.4	17.2	28.0	13.8	19.0	19.3
% Riding To Work By Automobile.	60.2	53.3	39.7	59.3	56.9	60.0	71.5	63.0	61.5	63.7	55.6
Mean Commuting Time - Minutes...	33.4	28.9	43.0	37.8	31.8	33.5	32.1	34.1	32.0	30.8	32.9
Population Per Household..........	3.7	2.7	3.4	3.7	3.5	3.7	3.9	3.9	3.8	3.9	3.7
Total Housing Units..........	9582	694	612	875	871	1004	1184	1060	1265	778	1239
% Condominiums...............	0.0	0.0	0.0	0.0	0.0	0.0	0.0	0.0	0.0	0.0	0.0
% Built 1970 Or Later........	1.8	0.7	3.2	1.2	0.0	1.5	2.0	0.0	5.3	1.3	2.1
% Owner Occupied.............	22.4	10.1	15.8	18.9	17.1	26.3	28.2	25.7	17.5	24.4	31.1
% With 1+ Persons Per Room...	16.4	13.0	17.2	18.8	16.9	14.4	16.0	18.8	17.5	15.5	15.3
Median Value: Owner Units......$$	25400	-	-	-	-	25800	-	31400	-	-	25200
Median Rent: Rental Units....$$	171	146	164	164	180	176	180	170	174	166	171
Median Number Of Rooms: All Units.	5.2	3.6	4.8	5.0	4.7	5.2	5.6	5.6	5.4	5.6	5.2

Community Area 26 -- West Garfield Park
Selected Characteristics of Census Tracts: 1970

Tract Number	TOTAL	2601	2602	2603	2604	2605	2606	2607	2608	2609	2610
Total Population.............	48464	4041	3073	3344	3445	4962	6680	6043	7006	3910	5960
% Male.......................	47.2	48.3	48.2	46.8	47.5	47.2	46.6	47.2	47.1	46.4	47.3
% Black......................	96.9	86.1	94.7	94.8	96.0	98.7	98.7	98.7	98.5	98.5	98.6
% Other Nonwhite.............	0.3	0.2	0.3	0.5	0.3	0.3	0.2	0.4	0.4	0.2	0.3
% Of Spanish Language........	0.7	0.5	5.8	0.5	1.4	0.2	0.3	0.0	0.0	0.3	0.6
% Foreign Born...............	0.5	2.1	0.9	1.4	0.3	0.9	0.2	0.1	0.0	0.3	0.1
% Living In Group Quarters...	1.2	11.0	0.5	0.5	0.7	0.1	0.1	0.1	0.8	0.1	0.1
% 13 Years Old And Under.....	38.2	33.4	31.9	34.7	36.7	40.0	40.2	39.5	37.3	43.4	40.1
% 14-20 Years Old............	14.5	13.0	12.7	13.7	12.6	15.0	14.8	15.0	15.1	16.7	14.6
% 21-64 Years Old............	43.7	39.8	52.8	48.4	48.8	42.3	42.9	43.0	44.2	37.3	42.2
% 65-74 Years Old............	2.4	8.1	1.5	2.3	1.3	1.8	1.4	1.9	2.5	1.7	2.1
% 75 Years Old And Over......	1.3	5.8	1.1	1.0	0.5	0.8	0.8	0.7	0.9	0.9	1.0
% In Different House.........	47.8	36.2	23.9	40.9	40.6	48.7	52.7	46.2	50.4	66.8	56.6
% Families With Female Head..	29.1	36.1	29.0	26.7	24.1	30.1	24.9	28.1	31.2	40.3	25.2
Median School Years Completed....	10.3	9.1	10.4	11.0	11.4	10.0	10.3	10.4	10.4	9.4	10.0
Median Family Income, 1969......$$	7532	6091	6831	7000	8348	8153	7908	7855	7296	6740	7894
% Income Below Poverty Level..	24.5	36.8	26.7	20.4	18.2	21.0	21.0	24.6	28.3	31.8	20.2
% Income Of $15,000 or More...	9.9	5.3	8.1	9.4	8.6	7.0	8.4	11.5	11.1	6.9	18.0
% White Collar Workers.......	8.8	13.4	5.7	9.2	8.0	9.5	7.2	8.8	8.9	10.0	9.1
% Civilian Labor Force Unemployed.	8.0	9.8	5.7	3.4	6.6	8.1	6.6	7.7	11.4	13.6	6.6
% Riding To Work By Automobile....	54.7	52.5	55.9	60.2	64.1	46.7	55.4	54.0	51.5	64.5	50.6
Population Per Household.........	3.9	3.1	3.0	3.4	3.6	4.2	4.3	4.2	4.0	4.7	4.4
Total Housing Units..........	13177	1384	1125	1006	997	1296	1632	1555	1850	888	1444
% Condominiums & Cooperatives.....	0.4	0.0	0.0	0.0	0.0	0.6	0.0	0.4	1.1	0.8	0.5
% Built 1960 Or Later........	2.2	13.5	0.9	1.5	0.4	1.4	0.7	0.3	1.2	1.0	1.0
% Owner Occupied.............	16.9	5.9	11.9	16.4	16.0	22.6	20.5	16.8	12.9	20.7	26.0
% With 1+ Persons Per Room......	22.0	20.1	14.0	15.8	16.1	24.2	22.6	22.2	25.7	29.6	25.8
Median Value: Owner Units.......$$	15700	-	-	17700	-	15500	-	-	-	-	15100
Median Rent: Rental Units....$$	112	94	106	107	118	115	116	116	117	112	111
Median Number Of Rooms: All Units.	4.8	3.1	4.2	4.8	4.6	5.0	5.2	5.1	4.8	5.3	5.0

In 1979, the median family income among residents of West Garfield Park was less than $10,000, constrasted with the city median, which was more than $15,000. Almost 40 percent live below the census poverty level. The general unemployment rate exceeds 20 percent. Among those 16 to 19 years old, the unemployment rate is about 40 percent for those who were graduated from high school, and greater than 60 percent among those who did not. More than one-third of all families draw Aid to Dependent Children. There are no public housing units for families, although there is one public housing structure for the elderly. Industry still exists north of Lake Street, but most of the plants are small and do not employ many local residents.

Elsewhere, factories are shutting down. The business hub of West Garfield Park is a major retail center running along Madison Street from Hamlin to Kilbourn avenues. Stores and shops occupy the south side of Lake Street at the northern boundary of the community area. Although many stores were burned out in the riots of March, 1968, the storefronts are slowly being reoccupied. Several community-based groups have been formed to do something about deteriorating housing conditions and the erosion of the economic base of West Garfield Park. They face an uphill struggle against the results of 50 years of neglect.

Dick Hansis

Community Area 27

East Garfield Park

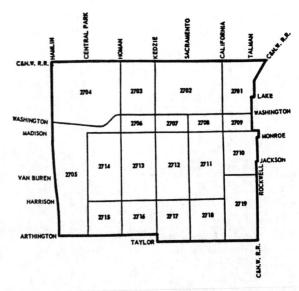

The community of East Garfield Park, like its western neighbor, West Garfield Park, remained undeveloped prairie and farmland until the late 1860s. Residential growth in the region had been hampered by the lack of adequate transportation facilities. In 1869, some public improvements appeared following the annexation of what is now the present community of East Garfield Park to the city of Chicago through an act of the state legislature, and the announcement of the impending creation of a city park in the area by the West Side Park Board. Nevertheless, transportation on the West Side remained poor. Even in the 1880s, the horse-drawn car lines in East Garfield Park were reputed to be the slowest in the city.

From 1885 to 1914, however, East Garfield Park began to grow at a faster pace. The completion of the Lake Street and Garfield Park branches of the elevated lines and the electrification of the surface lines, now made the area more accessible to individuals who wanted to move to "Chicago's nearest suburb." As a consequence, by around 1900, East Garfield Park had become a residential community consisting of primarily brick cottages and two-flats, with some older frame structures in the southern and eastern sections of the community. By 1920, the population of the area had grown to 56,269, characterized by a large Irish population, along with Germans, Russian Jews, and Italians.

The residential growth of East Garfield Park was further aided by the emergence of industry in the community. During the years 1900 to 1914, factories, warehouses, and industrial plants had relocated to the West Side in order to take advantage of lower land values and lower taxes. These industrial areas were generally concentrated along the northern, eastern, and southern boundaries where the tracks of the Chicago and North Western, Pennsylvania, and Baltimore and Ohio Railroads, respectively, provided accessible transportation facilities. Along the tracks of the Pennsylvania Railroad, coal, ice, and building material yards were established, as well as large industrial plants. The development of these industrial areas in East Garfield Park attracted workers who later settled in the community.

Residents of East Garfield Park could enjoy the rustic atmosphere of beautiful Garfield Park, located in the northwestern section of the community. First known as Central Park, the 187-acre park was laid out by Frederick Law Olmstead in 1869 as a part of Chicago's chain of parks and boulevards around the center of the city. Within the park lay a double lake, separated by a narrow penisula of land that served as a carriage route. For many years, recreational life on the West Side revolved around the park.

East Garfield Park continued to grow, as the population exceeded 63,000 in 1930. By 1930, Italians had replaced the Irish as the predominant ethnic group in the region, with Russian Jews comprising the third-largest nationality. A minute black population — approximately 3 percent of the total — was concentrated in the northwestern portion of the community.

After World War II, more than 70,000 people lived in East Garfield Park.

As the years progressed, however, the ethnic composition of East Garfield Park changed dramatically. Whites began moving out in massive numbers and, by 1960, the black population of the community had risen to 62 percent of the total. The region's new black residents had arrived from the South, and from the older, overcrowded, black communities in Chicago. Today, East Garfield Park is virtually an all-black community, with little evidence of the white ethnic groups who once lived there.

The new black inhabitants of East Garfield Park were confronted with many problems. Housing was one of the most serious. In 1969, the city's Department of Urban Renewal declared that two-thirds of the housing structures in the Madison-Kedzie area were either substandard or dilapidated to the point where they warranted clearance. The deteriorated housing conditions in East Garfield Park mirrored the fact that less than 3 percent of the housing units in the community had been built after 1960. The major housing construction in the area had occurred in the southern portion of the community, where the Chicago Housing Authority completed the 126-unit Harrison Courts project in 1950. Although Harrison Courts was occupied primarily by non-

Community Area 27 -- Garfield Park
Population and Housing Characteristics, 1930-1980

	1980	1970	1960	1950	1940	1930
Total Population.......	31,580	52,185	66,871	70,091	65,789	63,353
% Male.................	46.2	46.9	49.6	49.6	49.9	51.1
% Female...............	53.8	53.1	50.4	50.4	50.1	48.9
% White................	0.7	1.7	38.0	82.9	95.4	96.8
% Black................	99.0	98.0	61.5	16.7	4.5	2.9
% Other Nonwhite Races...	0.3	0.3	0.5	0.4	0.1	0.3
% Under 5 Years Old......	10.2	12.9	17.2	9.8	6.8	7.0
% 5-19 Years Old.........	31.9	37.2	27.1	18.2	21.8	23.7
% 20-44 Years Old........	32.0	32.7	38.3	44.3	44.6	46.8
% 45-64 Years Old........	18.1	13.1	12.9	21.0	21.1	18.2
% 65 Years and Older.....	7.8	4.1	4.5	6.7	5.7	4.3
Median School Years.....	10.7	9.8	8.2	9.0	8.3	*
Total Housing Units....	10,933	16,065	20,353	21,509	19,423	*
% In One-Unit Structures.	6.0	6.4	6.8	*	*	*
% Owner Occupied.........	17.8	13.0	13.4	16.2	14.6	*
% Renter Occupied........	71.6	75.9	79.1	81.5	80.8	*
% Vacant.................	10.6	11.1	7.5	2.3	4.6	*
% 1+ Persons per Room....	14.7	20.4	28.7	20.2	*	*

Community Area 27 -- East Garfield Park
Selected Characteristics of Census Tracts: 1980

Tract Number	Total	2701	2702	2703	2704	2705	2706	2707	2708	2709	2710
Total Population.............	31580	508	2127	1950	1592	1951	1085	969	905	562	1707
% Male.......................	46.2	44.7	47.4	47.2	45.9	44.0	46.9	42.2	49.4	49.6	47.0
% Black......................	99.0	93.3	99.5	99.3	99.2	98.9	99.4	99.3	99.1	98.4	99.5
% Other Nonwhite.............	0.3	1.2	0.1	0.1	0.3	0.8	0.3	0.2	0.4	0.0	0.2
% Of Spanish Origin..........	0.8	2.6	0.3	0.9	0.4	0.2	0.2	0.8	0.1	0.5	0.2
% Foreign Born...............	0.6	0.0	0.0	1.8	0.0	0.0	0.0	0.0	1.7	4.4	0.5
% Living In Group Quarters...	0.3	6.3	0.0	0.0	1.1	0.0	0.0	0.3	0.1	0.0	0.0
% 13 Years Old And Under.....	28.3	27.4	20.5	27.7	25.6	30.1	23.7	25.8	20.4	22.2	25.9
% 14-20 Years Old............	16.0	13.8	13.8	14.7	18.1	17.4	13.5	10.2	11.5	11.4	16.4
% 21-64 Years Old............	47.8	46.5	54.0	47.7	48.3	40.7	54.7	55.0	55.8	52.5	48.0
% 65-74 Years Old............	5.3	7.5	7.7	6.9	5.8	5.5	6.1	6.1	8.2	9.1	7.4
% 75 Years Old And Over......	2.5	4.9	4.0	2.9	2.2	6.3	2.0	2.9	4.1	4.8	2.3
% In Different House.........	37.8	27.8	26.5	30.2	38.8	40.1	39.5	47.0	45.4	38.1	48.6
% Families With Female Head..	61.1	59.6	54.7	66.1	60.2	62.4	64.9	59.4	57.7	50.7	57.7
Median School Years Completed..	10.7	12.3	11.7	11.0	11.4	10.2	12.1	10.5	10.6	12.0	10.2
Median Family Income, 1979......$$	9682	7813	12352	6651	12429	7466	11797	10667	14821	16538	9244
% Income Below Poverty Level....	40.3	41.8	23.3	56.2	30.6	45.6	35.0	27.1	28.8	33.9	48.1
% Income Of $30,000 Or More....	7.9	0.0	9.5	11.8	14.8	3.7	0.0	4.2	23.7	15.3	5.7
% White Collar Workers.......	37.5	42.5	41.4	39.7	39.1	34.4	40.9	53.1	37.2	67.5	25.3
% Civilian Labor Force Unemployed.	20.6	12.4	15.5	23.7	20.4	23.6	12.4	16.5	16.3	32.1	9.6
% Riding To Work By Automobile....	51.6	70.8	52.1	58.1	44.2	59.8	55.0	58.1	71.7	60.5	33.1
Mean Commuting Time - Minutes...	30.7	23.5	32.2	31.3	30.5	29.9	33.9	27.2	27.7	26.8	33.7
Population Per Household..........	3.2	3.3	2.9	3.1	3.4	3.1	2.5	2.2	2.5	2.6	3.1
Total Housing Units..........	10933	184	808	692	483	699	465	544	433	262	631
% Condominiums...............	0.0	0.0	0.0	0.0	0.0	0.0	0.0	0.0	0.0	0.0	0.0
% Built 1970 Or Later........	2.3	0.0	0.0	0.0	3.3	8.0	10.1	0.0	2.3	0.0	0.0
% Owner Occupied.............	17.8	26.1	24.4	18.9	27.3	10.6	9.5	11.0	18.9	24.0	18.5
% With 1+ Persons Per Room...	14.7	16.1	9.0	13.7	12.8	15.8	11.4	12.2	7.4	12.1	12.5
Median Value: Owner Units.......$$	22800	-	-	-	-	-	-	-	-	-	-
Median Rent: Rental Units.......$$	155	135	149	154	164	152	171	155	141	148	147
Median Number Of Rooms: All Units.	4.8	4.8	5.0	4.9	5.3	4.5	3.5	4.1	4.3	3.8	5.1

Tract Number	2711	2712	2713	2714	2715	2716	2717	2718	2719
Total Population.............	2552	1850	2346	3925	1542	1396	1818	1788	1007
% Male.......................	47.1	47.0	45.8	45.1	45.8	46.9	45.9	45.9	46.1
% Black......................	98.7	97.2	99.0	99.4	99.2	98.1	99.9	99.4	99.3
% Other Nonwhite.............	0.4	0.9	0.1	0.1	0.5	0.6	0.0	0.1	0.3
% Of Spanish Origin..........	0.5	1.0	2.5	0.7	0.3	1.2	0.9	2.3	0.2
% Foreign Born...............	1.4	0.0	1.3	0.0	0.0	0.0	0.4	0.9	0.8
% Living In Group Quarters...	0.0	0.9	0.8	0.2	0.6	0.0	0.0	0.0	0.1
% 13 Years Old And Under.....	26.2	26.8	32.6	33.4	33.1	28.5	32.6	32.0	25.7
% 14-20 Years Old............	14.3	16.4	18.9	15.3	16.4	15.3	20.0	18.7	21.5
% 21-64 Years Old............	48.9	49.7	44.2	46.9	45.0	49.9	43.3	44.1	46.7
% 65-74 Years Old............	6.7	4.6	3.2	3.4	3.4	4.9	2.6	3.8	4.8
% 75 Years Old And Over......	3.9	2.4	1.2	1.0	1.5	1.4	1.4	1.3	1.3
% In Different House.........	34.9	38.7	42.1	39.6	42.0	43.9	36.9	23.4	44.5
% Families With Female Head..	62.1	60.2	65.1	66.8	61.0	55.7	56.9	57.8	61.3
Median School Years Completed..	10.1	10.3	10.9	11.0	11.2	11.2	9.6	10.9	10.7
Median Family Income, 1979......$$	8457	8953	12415	8474	8068	11071	7220	10556	10909
% Income Below Poverty Level....	41.4	37.8	37.6	46.8	47.6	34.2	55.3	36.8	37.5
% Income Of $30,000 Or More....	4.3	11.7	5.8	4.8	3.0	4.1	9.7	14.2	10.1
% White Collar Workers.......	39.0	31.5	34.0	38.3	38.8	19.5	43.2	33.0	41.1
% Civilian Labor Force Unemployed.	13.8	16.8	24.2	26.2	20.3	21.7	29.7	25.1	22.5
% Riding To Work By Automobile....	46.5	43.3	47.9	50.1	66.8	60.3	46.4	40.4	48.8
Mean Commuting Time - Minutes...	28.7	31.3	34.1	28.4	33.9	32.3	26.5	31.2	33.9
Population Per Household..........	3.1	3.2	3.6	3.3	4.0	3.5	3.9	3.9	4.1
Total Housing Units..........	921	625	704	1357	411	429	539	488	258
% Condominiums...............	0.0	0.0	0.0	0.0	0.0	0.0	0.0	0.0	0.0
% Built 1970 Or Later........	1.3	0.0	10.7	1.3	0.0	0.0	1.3	0.0	0.0
% Owner Occupied.............	19.9	17.6	15.2	9.6	27.7	21.2	24.1	17.4	22.1
% With 1+ Persons Per Room...	13.9	15.4	18.4	16.9	17.1	18.3	18.2	20.5	16.3
Median Value: Owner Units.......$$	-	-	-	-	-	-	-	-	-
Median Rent: Rental Units.......$$	135	150	168	160	171	169	160	151	154
Median Number Of Rooms: All Units.	4.6	4.8	5.0	4.3	5.4	5.2	5.4	5.2	5.6

Community Area 27 — East Garfield Park
Selected Characteristics of Census Tracts: 1970

Tract Number	TOTAL	2701	2702	2703	2704	2705	2706	2707	2708	2709	2710
Total Population	52185	825	3494	3529	2354	3092	1863	1061	1630	955	2889
% Male	46.9	45.2	47.8	45.3	47.1	43.8	48.8	45.7	48.3	48.7	45.4
% Black	98.0	98.8	98.9	96.1	99.0	97.2	97.5	97.5	99.2	99.2	99.1
% Other Nonwhite	0.3	0.0	0.2	0.1	0.2	1.1	0.4	0.5	0.2	0.3	0.3
% Of Spanish Language	1.0	0.0	1.4	0.1	0.0	2.2	2.2	0.5	1.0	0.0	0.4
% Foreign Born	0.3	0.0	0.2	0.9	0.2	0.2	0.0	0.0	0.8	0.0	0.3
% Living In Group Quarters	0.9	3.0	0.6	4.5	0.0	0.7	0.3	1.5	0.0	1.4	0.2
% 13 Years Old And Under	37.2	31.3	32.7	34.4	33.3	37.3	28.3	32.0	28.5	32.0	34.9
% 14-20 Years Old	14.6	13.6	13.9	14.5	14.4	12.7	13.2	10.7	11.2	10.5	14.3
% 21-64 Years Old	44.0	45.7	46.9	43.5	48.0	43.4	55.3	51.9	54.4	51.2	44.9
% 65-74 Years Old	2.9	6.2	4.4	4.0	3.1	4.9	2.4	4.2	4.2	5.3	4.0
% 75 Years Old And Over	1.3	3.3	2.0	3.6	1.1	1.6	0.8	1.0	1.7	0.9	1.9
% In Different House	49.1	81.4	50.8	45.2	57.4	39.9	39.8	56.2	56.7	53.5	66.8
% Families With Female Head	33.8	29.7	30.8	35.3	28.7	36.6	27.1	36.7	26.2	24.6	35.6
Median School Years Completed	9.8	9.1	10.0	9.5	10.1	9.4	11.5	10.3	9.5	9.1	10.0
Median Family Income, 1969 $$	6357	7043	7741	5569	6569	5721	5819	7222	6633	6467	7201
% Income Below Poverty Level	32.4	19.6	21.1	40.7	37.0	33.5	25.2	19.8	25.7	20.3	23.8
% Income of $15,000 or More	7.8	4.3	10.9	9.7	11.6	6.2	7.5	12.6	10.4	3.4	10.9
% White Collar Workers	8.3	4.9	6.1	11.5	7.7	11.6	8.5	10.8	7.7	8.1	7.1
% Civilian Labor Force Unemployed	8.4	9.4	3.7	6.6	10.0	10.6	3.7	10.2	5.1	3.6	3.0
% Riding To Work By Automobile	46.7	47.3	46.1	44.5	57.8	44.9	50.9	34.7	38.5	48.7	45.6
Population Per Household	3.6	3.4	3.4	3.6	3.6	3.2	2.8	2.8	2.6	3.0	3.3
Total Housing Units	16101	265	1193	1074	725	1043	711	410	717	342	973
% Condominiums & Cooperatives	0.2	0.0	0.6	0.7	0.0	0.0	0.0	0.0	0.7	0.0	0.0
% Built 1960 Or Later	2.8	2.1	0.9	0.8	0.0	11.7	1.8	4.6	0.3	3.2	1.7
% Owner Occupied	12.9	21.9	17.4	15.6	19.6	8.5	7.0	8.8	11.9	13.2	14.3
% With 1+ Persons Per Room	22.4	17.9	18.4	23.8	19.9	18.0	16.3	18.4	14.6	19.0	15.6
Median Value: Owner Units $$	13500	–	–	–	–	–	–	–	–	–	–
Median Rent: Rental Units $$	103	95	91	101	108	104	103	95	87	89	98
Median Number Of Rooms: All Units	4.4	4.4	4.4	4.4	4.6	4.1	3.4	3.3	3.0	3.6	4.5

Tract Number	2711	2712	2713	2714	2715	2716	2717	2718	2719
Total Population	3434	3840	2801	6753	2236	2494	3730	3132	2073
% Male	47.0	48.2	48.5	47.9	46.2	47.7	45.2	47.1	45.8
% Black	98.2	97.2	96.9	97.8	99.4	98.0	99.1	96.9	97.7
% Other Nonwhite	0.2	1.0	0.2	0.1	0.0	0.2	0.1	0.7	0.1
% Of Spanish Language	2.1	0.0	0.2	0.0	0.0	2.1	0.7	3.8	3.6
% Foreign Born	0.0	0.0	1.4	0.2	0.0	0.2	0.6	0.1	0.3
% Living In Group Quarters	0.2	0.2	1.0	1.4	0.4	0.0	0.8	0.3	0.4
% 13 Years Old And Under	31.7	39.7	40.8	38.8	42.8	40.2	43.8	43.0	43.4
% 14-20 Years Old	13.8	15.5	15.5	11.9	15.2	15.9	20.4	18.0	18.1
% 21-64 Years Old	49.3	41.4	40.3	47.0	39.7	41.3	33.9	37.3	36.8
% 65-74 Years Old	3.6	2.3	2.0	1.7	1.7	1.9	1.5	1.3	1.4
% 75 Years Old And Over	1.5	1.1	1.4	0.7	0.6	0.7	0.5	0.4	0.3
% In Different House	47.5	43.4	38.2	42.4	47.1	59.6	49.1	60.5	41.3
% Families With Female Head	32.4	36.8	35.6	32.1	40.8	31.4	40.2	36.9	35.1
Median School Years Completed	9.1	9.8	10.5	10.5	10.1	10.0	9.6	9.3	9.4
Median Family Income, 1969 $$	5763	5042	6932	6065	7018	7797	5762	6310	7397
% Income Below Poverty Level	30.1	49.3	28.5	30.4	26.9	30.2	41.9	44.8	29.6
% Income of $15,000 or More	6.5	5.4	8.2	5.4	11.6	7.2	4.4	6.3	9.9
% White Collar Workers	8.9	9.1	8.8	7.1	8.4	7.4	9.5	4.8	8.1
% Civilian Labor Force Unemployed	7.7	9.3	8.0	9.8	10.4	9.7	10.7	18.9	6.3
% Riding To Work By Automobile	38.4	41.6	48.9	43.9	51.8	60.5	47.4	54.1	52.5
Population Per Household	3.2	3.8	4.0	3.5	4.4	3.9	4.9	4.5	4.8
Total Housing Units	1163	1142	770	2186	524	720	853	760	530
% Condominiums & Cooperatives	0.9	0.0	0.0	0.0	0.0	0.0	0.0	0.0	0.0
% Built 1960 Or Later	2.6	0.8	2.3	1.5	7.0	3.3	10.0	0.0	0.8
% Owner Occupied	15.3	13.4	13.6	6.0	16.0	11.5	15.1	15.5	15.3
% With 1+ Persons Per Room	17.3	26.9	28.0	24.4	28.1	27.8	31.8	26.6	32.4
Median Value: Owner Units $$	–	–	–	–	–	–	–	–	–
Median Rent: Rental Units $$	90	104	107	111	111	105	112	101	98
Median Number Of Rooms: All Units	4.3	4.3	4.5	3.9	5.2	4.6	5.2	5.1	5.0

whites, most of the incoming black population lived in the older, multiple-family, rented structures characteristic of East Garfield Park. Many of these structures had been substructed in order to accommodate more people. The housing shortage in East Garfield Park was exacerbated by the turmoil which broke out on the West Side following the murder of Dr. Martin Luther King, Jr. in April, 1968. An estimated 300 East Garfield Park families were left homeless following the riots.

Today there are fewer than 10,000 occupied dwelling units in the community area, less than half the total in 1950. The most serious loss has occurred among rental units, more than 55 percent of which have disappeared during that time. The percentage of units owner-occupied has increased, but the median value of such units has actually gone down in the last 30 years. It now stands at less than one-third of the city median, and East Garfield Park is third from the bottom of the distribution of housing values over 77 Chicago community areas.

The historic Francisco Terrace Apartments, located at 237 North Francisco, were among the decaying housing structures in East Garfield Park. The building was designed in 1895 by Frank Lloyd Wright as one of the city's first housing projects for low-income families. Decay and persistent vandalism virtually ruined the structure. The building was demolished in March 1974, despite the efforts of civic groups to have the structure declared a landmark.

East Garfield Park faces other problems besides housing. In 1980, the community median family income of $9,682 was among the 10 lowest in the city. Forty-three percent of all individuals in the community live below the poverty level, with the highest poverty concentrations in Census Tracts 2712 and 2714. The dismal economic conditions reflected the loss of thousands of jobs from the West Side, as many firms had chosen to relocate to the suburbs. The community's rising crime rate — East Garfield Park had one of Chicago's highest juvenile delinquency rates in the middle 1960s — and the 1968 civil disturbances were the last straws for many industries which chose to leave the area. Given problems of inadequate housing, crime, and unemployment, it is not surprising that large numbers of blacks began to move out in the most recent decade. The population of East Garfield Park decreased from 66,871 in 1960 to 31,580 in 1980, a decline of approximately 53 percent.

The remaining residents have not given up on East Garfield Park. Various community organizations like the Chicago-West Business Association have worked for better housing, law enforcement, and more social services for the area. The persistent demand for affordable housing was probably a factor in the construction of Martin Luther King Jr. Plaza at Madison and Kedzie avenues. This 138-unit combination of townhouses and apartments was the first major construction in an area devastated by the 1968 violence. Community concerns about housing resulted in the construction of the Ike Sims Village Complex in 1982. The federally-subsidized, 4-acre site in the northwestern portion of the community — named for a prominent West Side community leader—provides apartments for the elderly and low-income families.

One of the most active community organizations in East Garfield Park is the Fifth City Human Development Project, located in the southwest section of the community. Originally founded in 1963 by Evanston, Illinois whites affiliated with the Ecumenical Institute, the organization presently is staffed primarily by local residents. It is

involved with a variety of projects, including the rehabilitation of several abandoned buildings — aided by the Federal Housing Administration — construction of a shopping center at Homan and Jackson avenues, creation of a pre-school center, and a community safe streets program. It is possible that community organization will lead to a sequence of events resulting in the restoration of East Garfield Park.

Winston McDowell

Community Area 28

Near West Side

The Near West Side, which served for more than a century as the port of entry for immigrants to Chicago, has undergone dramatic changes in the last 20 years. The history of the neighborhood can be traced back as far as 1828 when Wolf Point Tavern, at the confluence of the North and South Branches of the Chicago River, was the only building around. With the incorporation of Chicago in 1837 the city extended its limits to Wood Street and Cermak Road.

Irish immigrants settled in wooden cottages along the river as the Near West Side developed as a manufacturing center, with lumber yards, foundries and flour mills. In 1848 the Galena and Chicago Union (Chicago and North Western) Railroad built a terminal at Halsted and Kinzie streets. Other railroads used the Union Depot at Canal and Madison streets, which was completed in 1860. The car shops and grain elevators near the Rock Island railroad tracks attracted many workers in the 1850s. In 1851 the land east of Western Avenue, comprising most of the rest of the Near West Side, was annexed to the city, which laid sewers and gas lines and bridged the river at Polk Street. The population began to grow rapidly in the early 1850s. Thousands of small frame cottages, occupied by Germans, Irish and Scandinavians, were built extending to Halsted Street on the west and Roosevelt Road on the south.

Trade and manufacturing developed rapidly in Chicago during the Civil War and the years that followed. The demand for labor increased and, in the decade preceding the Fire of 1871, the population nearly tripled to reach 160,000. The area east of Halsted Street, south of Harrison Street had become a slum, which it was to remain for a century. In 1864 Samuel A. Walker, from Kentucky, began a high-status real estate development along Ashland Avenue, which he named for Henry Clay's home. Ashland remained a fashionable residential area until the 1890s, and the neighborhood spread east toward Halsted Street, between Lake and Van Buren streets. The remainder of the community area west of Western Avenue was annexed to Chicago in 1869. Although the Chicago Fire originated in the Near West Side, near DeKoven Street, it burned north and east, causing minor damage to the neighborhood, while resulting in an increase of business activity and housing construction in the period after the Fire. The population ballooned temporarily to more than 200,000, mainly from refugees from the Fire, and the entire area south of Madison Street, east of Western Avenue, experienced construction.

In the decades that followed, new immigrants from southern and eastern Europe arrived, mostly Italians, and Russian and Polish Jews, displacing the older German and Irish populations. The newcomers settled in the Halsted slum, the Italians between Polk and Taylor streets, the Jews southward to 16th Street. The intersection of Halsted and Maxwell streets became the center of the Jewish business community. By 1900 more Greeks were moving in, settling also east of Halsted between Polk and Harrison streets. The Near West Side was

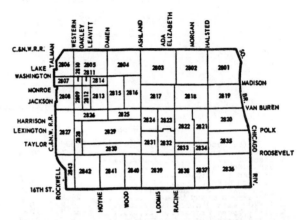

completely built up by 1895. Inhabitants were poorly housed and badly overcrowded. The poverty and deterioration of the area led to the establishment of Hull House, the first settlement house in Chicago, founded in 1889 by Jane Addams and Ellen Gates Starr. By 1910 Hull House was a 13-building complex offering day-care, a music school, a theatre, English and citizenship classes, as well as many other services to thousands of people every week.

After the turn of the century, the Eastern European Jewish community began to break up. As the Jews vacated the Near West Side ghetto, their place was taken by blacks and Mexicans. By 1930, when the population had dropped to 152,000, blacks constituted about a sixth of the total. The number of residents dropped off by another 16,000 during the Depression and, in 1940, almost 26,000 blacks lived on the Near West Side, about a fifth of the total. In 1940, Italians were still most numerous among the foreign born, followed by Mexicans and Greeks.

During this time little private home construction took place in the Near West Side, but numerous public housing projects were sited there. The first project, Jane Addams Homes, was built in 1938, offering 304 low-rise family living units. The 834-unit Robert Brooks Homes were built in 1942. In the 1950s the Chicago Housing Authority built Maplewood Courts, 132 units, Loomis Courts, 126 units, Abbott Homes, 1,218 units, and Governor Henry Horner Homes, 920 high-rise units to which 745 more were added in the early 1960s. Today, the Near West Side has one of the highest concentrations of public housing in the city, exceeding 20 percent of its total housing stock.

In 1941 an act of the state legislature led to the establishment of the Medical Center District, providing a central area for medical institutions, which included Cook County Hospital, a Veterans Administration Hosptial, the Chicago State Tuberculosis Hospital, Presbyterian-St. Luke's Hospital and the Research Hospital and Medical School of the University of Illinois. Extensive construction has since taken place in the area, including the new University of Illinois Hospital and medical library. Manufacturing establishments, railroads yards, wholesale houses and light industry continued to concentrate in the eastern section of the Near West Side. Madison Street was the

Community Area 28 -- Near West Side
Population and Housing Characteristics, 1930-1980

	1980	1970	1960	1950	1940	1930
Total Population.......	57,296	78,703	126,610	160,362	136,518	152,457
% Male..................	47.1	49.0	53.0	53.6	55.1	56.0
% Female................	52.9	51.0	47.0	46.4	44.9	44.0
% White.................	16.3	25.2	45.6	58.5	80.8	78.4
% Black.................	74.7	72.2	53.8	40.9	18.9	16.6
% Other Nonwhite Races....	9.0	2.6	0.6	0.6	0.3	5.0
% Under 5 Years Old.....	10.6	11.0	15.3	10.9	7.1	8.6
% 5-19 Years Old........	32.3	37.0	27.6	21.6	24.0	26.6
% 20-44 Years Old.......	34.0	30.8	34.7	42.0	40.2	43.3
% 45-64 Years Old.......	15.0	14.7	16.6	19.0	22.6	17.7
% 65 Years and Older....	8.1	6.5	5.8	6.5	6.1	3.8
Median School Years....	10.8	9.4	8.3	8.3	7.5	*
Total Housing Units....	20,064	23,706	37,057	41,164	39,735	*
% In One-Unit Structures.	11.3	9.4	13.0	*	*	*
% Owner Occupied.........	10.2	9.2	9.6	11.7	10.6	*
% Renter Occupied........	81.2	82.3	82.5	84.9	83.0	*
% Vacant................	8.6	8.5	7.9	3.4	6.4	*
% 1+ Persons per Room....	18.0	21.3	28.9	32.6	*	*

Community Area 28 -- Near West Side
Selected Characteristics of Census Tracts: 1980

Tract Number	Total	2801	2802	2803	2804	2805	2806	2807	2808	2809	2810
Total Population.............	57305	174	193	342	4347	4621	183	512	5924	1151	145
% Male.......................	47.1	98.3	81.9	65.5	41.9	45.6	46.4	46.5	42.1	48.4	48.3
% Black......................	74.7	1.1	26.9	84.2	99.8	99.7	98.4	99.6	99.4	97.0	98.6
% Other Nonwhite.............	9.0	0.6	13.5	4.1	0.1	0.2	0.0	0.0	0.4	1.4	0.0
% Of Spanish Origin..........	10.0	0.0	18.7	5.0	0.4	1.4	0.0	0.8	0.8	1.0	0.0
% Foreign Born...............	9.0	10.5	12.7	0.0	1.1	1.1	0.0	0.0	3.1	0.7	0.0
% Living In Group Quarters...	3.3	0.0	8.3	27.8	0.2	0.1	0.0	0.0	0.0	1.6	0.0
% 13 Years Old And Under.....	29.8	0.6	10.4	14.6	43.7	41.0	25.7	26.0	41.8	29.8	20.0
% 14-20 Years Old............	15.2	0.6	9.3	7.9	17.0	24.0	26.8	15.2	19.1	10.3	10.3
% 21-64 Years Old............	46.8	60.3	59.1	67.5	37.1	33.1	38.8	45.3	34.3	53.9	55.2
% 65-74 Years Old............	5.2	29.3	17.6	7.0	1.6	1.2	5.5	9.0	3.3	4.3	9.0
% 75 Years Old And Over......	2.9	9.2	3.6	2.9	0.7	0.7	3.3	4.5	1.5	1.7	5.5
% In Different House.........	40.3	67.7	45.2	59.7	30.7	33.0	0.0	43.1	24.5	75.8	10.4
% Families With Female Head..	65.6	0.0	33.3	50.0	80.3	77.7	75.9	56.3	80.9	60.0	77.8
Median School Years Completed	10.8	10.5	10.2	12.2	11.0	9.6	11.2	10.6	10.3	10.8	11.5
Median Family Income, 1979...$$	7535	0	30468	35055	5102	6194	10227	8900	5255	15625	14236
% Income Below Poverty Level....	48.9	0.0	0.0	0.0	68.1	70.5	47.6	39.0	68.1	16.7	0.0
% Income Of $30,000 Or More....	8.2	0.0	100.0	53.8	4.1	2.8	0.0	12.7	1.4	6.3	0.0
% White Collar Workers.......	46.9	15.1	16.0	36.8	32.8	29.0	0.0	21.8	40.3	39.8	39.7
% Civilian Labor Force Unemployed.	15.8	0.0	0.0	6.3	11.0	23.9	0.0	0.0	24.6	13.0	28.4
% Riding To Work By Automobile....	41.2	0.0	44.0	41.2	34.8	37.6	100.0	39.3	35.3	37.4	15.5
Mean Commuting Time - Minutes...	26.9	21.3	17.0	38.1	35.0	31.1	37.2	32.4	33.3	28.2	36.1
Population Per Household.....	3.0	1.0	1.7	2.4	3.9	5.0	3.5	2.8	3.9	2.7	2.4
Total Housing Units..........	20064	177	114	120	1158	934	65	187	1581	438	65
% Condominiums...............	1.1	0.0	0.0	0.0	0.9	1.2	0.0	0.0	0.0	0.0	0.0
% Built 1970 Or Later........	12.1	0.0	0.0	0.0	1.0	0.0	0.0	0.0	0.7	60.7	26.6
% Owner Occupied.............	10.2	2.8	0.9	10.8	4.0	4.2	12.3	19.3	4.6	4.6	26.2
% With 1+ Persons Per Room...	18.0	0.0	7.8	14.7	30.1	44.3	11.3	11.0	28.7	8.3	3.3
Median Value: Owner Units......$$	27900	-	-	-	-	-	-	-	-	-	-
Median Rent: Rental Units......$$	107	78	114	138	81	72	141	125	62	215	135
Median Number Of Rooms: All Units.	4.1	1.1	1.2	3.6	4.2	4.9	5.6	4.8	4.3	4.0	4.6

Tract Number	2811	2812	2813	2814	2815	2816	2817	2818	2819	2820	2821
Total Population.............	384	945	1167	574	1295	1338	772	580	449	5	0
% Male.......................	46.6	45.1	44.2	51.6	50.3	52.6	67.4	86.6	88.4	-	-
% Black......................	99.2	98.3	98.5	94.5	99.1	91.6	28.4	22.1	25.8	-	-
% Other Nonwhite.............	0.0	0.0	0.2	1.6	0.0	1.8	9.6	9.8	8.5	-	-
% Of Spanish Origin..........	0.0	2.0	1.2	3.0	0.0	2.6	13.7	17.8	9.8	-	-
% Foreign Born...............	0.0	0.0	0.7	3.4	0.0	5.8	10.3	18.6	13.7	-	-
% Living In Group Quarters...	0.0	0.0	0.0	5.1	0.0	0.0	49.6	34.5	23.4	-	-
% 13 Years Old And Under.....	17.2	24.9	18.7	17.6	26.6	8.1	10.2	4.3	2.4	-	-
% 14-20 Years Old............	13.8	16.1	14.3	9.1	17.5	8.0	4.1	7.1	3.6	-	-
% 21-64 Years Old............	51.8	47.6	45.2	55.1	48.0	41.3	70.7	74.8	72.2	-	-
% 65-74 Years Old............	10.2	8.9	14.4	12.7	5.9	22.0	9.5	11.4	16.5	-	-
% 75 Years Old And Over......	7.0	2.5	7.5	5.6	1.9	20.6	5.4	2.4	5.3	-	-
% In Different House.........	39.4	38.0	47.9	42.9	40.0	43.2	65.8	56.5	47.1	-	-
% Families With Female Head..	64.9	55.1	54.9	56.4	62.6	64.0	40.5	23.1	30.0	-	-
Median School Years Completed....	7.9	9.9	7.9	7.9	9.7	7.9	11.4	11.5	7.9	-	-
Median Family Income, 1979...$$	10729	7434	8182	4917	13527	6200	12500	28472	2499	-	-
% Income Below Poverty Level....	38.0	24.6	42.7	56.3	32.3	43.8	28.9	39.4	100.0	-	-
% Income Of $30,000 Or More....	0.0	6.3	5.0	0.0	15.5	0.0	31.6	33.3	0.0	-	-
% White Collar Workers.......	51.1	30.3	49.3	25.3	33.9	36.8	38.4	31.0	66.7	-	-
% Civilian Labor Force Unemployed.	18.2	41.3	14.4	38.5	25.7	21.7	19.9	14.3	59.8	-	-
% Riding To Work By Automobile....	48.9	65.5	60.8	59.3	48.3	30.3	17.1	25.1	23.5	-	-
Mean Commuting Time - Minutes...	30.5	20.0	37.0	50.1	31.4	28.2	25.4	20.1	12.4	-	-
Population Per Household.....	2.3	3.1	2.4	2.2	3.0	1.5	2.1	1.3	1.2	-	-
Total Housing Units..........	194	320	599	309	451	999	348	357	363	22	0
% Condominiums...............	0.0	0.0	0.0	0.0	0.0	0.0	0.0	0.0	0.0	-	-
% Built 1970 Or Later........	0.0	0.0	41.0	0.0	1.8	2.6	0.0	5.9	0.0	-	-
% Owner Occupied.............	16.0	31.6	13.2	12.6	14.9	4.8	10.1	2.0	0.8	-	-
% With 1+ Persons Per Room...	10.7	17.6	11.2	10.4	21.2	5.4	9.0	4.2	4.8	-	-
Median Value: Owner Units......$$	-	-	-	-	-	-	-	-	-	-	-
Median Rent: Rental Units......$$	130	137	103	129	130	75	133	131	132	-	-
Median Number Of Rooms: All Units.	3.6	4.3	3.7	3.2	3.7	2.4	2.2	1.3	1.1	-	-

Community Area 28 -- Near West Side
Selected Characteristics of Census Tracts: 1980

Tract Number	2822	2823	2824	2825	2826	2827	2828	2829	2830	2831	2832
Total Population.............	1480	876	1415	784	214	2257	1988	2058	851	1845	3210
% Male..........................	52.0	51.1	50.4	36.1	44.4	49.4	53.3	49.8	60.9	51.7	40.7
% Black.........................	2.1	2.1	13.4	15.7	42.5	42.9	12.6	15.7	30.8	12.0	83.4
% Other Nonwhite................	18.5	19.5	19.7	72.1	48.1	30.0	40.4	38.9	33.6	26.0	5.3
% Of Spanish Origin.............	18.3	17.8	15.8	5.5	55.1	50.4	65.4	30.9	41.7	17.7	6.5
% Foreign Born..................	17.5	10.2	27.5	69.2	18.3	26.5	31.1	39.4	34.3	20.1	5.9
% Living In Group Quarters......	0.0	2.2	0.3	2.2	0.0	0.0	0.0	25.1	49.5	0.0	0.4
% 13 Years Old And Under........	16.1	12.4	10.0	22.2	31.8	31.0	26.3	15.1	19.5	13.2	29.7
% 14-20 Years Old...............	12.0	9.2	5.7	2.6	14.5	16.2	13.6	8.7	32.3	6.8	13.4
% 21-64 Years Old...............	62.5	64.0	76.2	70.2	49.1	48.2	54.8	69.8	44.9	71.7	45.9
% 65-74 Years Old...............	6.7	8.8	5.2	3.1	3.3	3.4	4.1	4.3	2.4	5.1	6.6
% 75 Years Old And Over.........	2.8	5.5	2.8	2.0	1.4	1.2	1.3	2.0	0.9	3.3	4.5
% In Different House............	50.4	43.2	73.0	75.5	23.8	40.0	40.4	66.3	69.0	56.0	48.3
% Families With Female Head.....	17.5	20.0	21.4	20.0	45.5	40.0	24.1	19.9	28.6	20.8	72.0
Median School Years Completed...	13.7	13.8	16.1	16.1	10.8	7.9	7.9	15.9	9.5	15.1	10.1
Median Family Income, 1979...$$	19306	26579	19538	28833	10833	9592	13651	17454	14830	18777	5587
% Income Below Poverty Level....	22.5	1.4	3.3	0.0	39.7	39.3	33.3	15.3	9.5	13.4	52.3
% Income Of $30,000 Or More.....	21.1	31.6	29.0	45.7	0.0	11.2	10.2	12.4	0.0	28.6	4.8
% White Collar Workers..........	58.5	71.5	77.5	90.4	91.4	28.9	31.5	75.0	32.7	59.7	33.8
% Civilian Labor Force Unemployed.	3.0	0.0	7.4	1.7	0.0	16.1	13.8	4.3	19.2	4.1	13.7
% Riding To Work By Automobile...	47.2	38.2	37.7	16.2	72.4	67.1	51.3	39.1	35.3	39.6	25.3
Mean Commuting Time - Minutes...	21.1	18.9	22.8	9.1	31.2	28.8	31.6	19.0	33.6	16.1	25.8
Population Per Household.........	2.6	2.6	2.0	2.3	3.7	3.9	3.7	2.5	4.0	2.1	2.6
Total Housing Units..........	705	341	721	335	62	700	605	652	112	899	1292
% Condominiums..................	7.2	8.2	0.0	3.0	0.0	0.0	0.0	0.0	0.0	2.2	1.2
% Built 1970 Or Later...........	17.5	13.2	67.3	9.2	0.0	1.9	0.0	9.7	0.0	43.9	6.1
% Owner Occupied................	26.0	31.4	10.7	0.6	35.5	22.9	25.3	15.0	9.8	16.1	4.9
% With 1+ Persons Per Room......	6.8	4.6	5.3	23.1	15.5	21.6	19.7	15.4	29.0	5.6	13.8
Median Value: Owner Units.....$$	72100	-	-	-	-	18000	-	-	-	101900	-
Median Rent: Rental Units.....$$	158	196	273	227	134	137	143	197	132	305	74
Median Number Of Rooms: All Units.	4.7	5.4	3.9	2.7	5.5	5.0	5.0	3.4	4.5	3.9	3.6

Tract Number	2833	2834	2835	2836	2837	2838	2839	2840	2841	2842	2843
Total Population.............	479	4	0	62	219	3090	7925	1457	967	962	61
% Male..........................	49.7	-	-	-	57.1	43.5	40.7	49.0	46.8	44.7	-
% Black.........................	6.5	-	-	-	63.5	99.4	99.4	98.4	99.1	99.2	-
% Other Nonwhite................	23.8	-	-	-	11.0	0.6	0.3	1.3	0.3	0.2	-
% Of Spanish Origin.............	39.9	-	-	-	18.3	0.7	0.8	0.3	1.9	1.2	-
% Foreign Born..................	42.5	-	-	-	4.3	0.0	1.1	1.2	C.0	2.8	-
% Living In Group Quarters......	5.8	-	-	-	13.7	0.0	0.0	0.0	0.0	0.0	-
% 13 Years Old And Under........	18.4	-	-	-	16.4	42.7	38.6	26.8	21.9	26.6	-
% 14-20 Years Old...............	12.9	-	-	-	14.2	18.7	16.9	14.1	14.2	17.7	-
% 21-64 Years Old...............	57.2	-	-	-	48.4	36.7	38.7	46.1	49.9	45.4	-
% 65-74 Years Old...............	6.5	-	-	-	11.9	1.3	3.2	8.5	9.9	6.5	-
% 75 Years Old And Over.........	5.0	-	-	-	9.1	0.7	2.5	4.5	4.0	3.7	-
% In Different House............	30.0	-	-	-	52.3	28.5	28.3	41.4	36.0	21.3	-
% Families With Female Head.....	35.8	-	-	-	40.0	72.3	83.7	58.3	62.8	56.5	-
Median School Years Completed...	7.9	-	-	-	10.3	11.8	10.7	10.4	10.3	9.6	-
Median Family Income, 1979...$$	8958	-	-	-	6250	6757	4527	7212	10326	14074	-
% Income Below Poverty Level....	35.1	-	-	-	100.0	59.0	72.9	46.2	28.6	20.0	-
% Income Of $30,000 Or More.....	0.0	-	-	-	0.0	3.3	3.5	11.1	10.0	5.7	-
% White Collar Workers..........	46.2	-	-	-	0.0	46.1	35.6	40.6	33.3	32.1	-
% Civilian Labor Force Unemployed.	0.0	-	-	-	41.4	22.1	38.8	27.4	9.7	7.7	-
% Riding To Work By Automobile...	19.6	-	-	-	0.0	41.8	48.7	31.3	50.6	70.0	-
Mean Commuting Time - Minutes...	2.4	-	-	-	13.8	38.9	32.5	33.3	36.5	30.1	-
Population Per Household.........	2.8	-	-	-	2.3	4.4	3.4	3.0	2.8	3.3	-
Total Housing Units..........	195	0	0	32	95	728	2500	560	391	314	24
% Condominiums..................	0.0	-	-	-	0.0	0.0	2.8	0.0	0.0	0.0	-
% Built 1970 Or Later...........	8.1	-	-	-	0.0	39.2	6.1	0.0	4.8	1.6	-
% Owner Occupied................	20.5	-	-	-	5.3	0.8	1.6	21.6	18.2	21.3	-
% With 1+ Persons Per Room......	11.2	-	-	-	9.8	32.9	23.4	12.5	9.4	12.4	-
Median Value: Owner Units.....$$	-	-	-	-	-	-	-	-	-	-	-
Median Rent: Rental Units.....$$	135	-	-	-	92	84	75	116	120	128	-
Median Number Of Rooms: All Units.	4.8	-	-	-	4.7	4.6	3.9	5.1	4.9	5.1	-

Community Area 28 -- Near West Side
Selected Characteristics of Census Tracts: 1970

Tract Number	TOTAL	2801	2802	2803	2804	2805	2806	2807	2808	2809	2810
Total Population.............	78703	164	428	988	5259	4953	155	518	5806	1059	337
% Male..........................	49.0	98.2	92.1	60.1	44.0	46.0	49.0	47.5	44.0	47.8	47.5
% Black.........................	72.2	0.0	2.8	79.1	99.8	99.4	100.0	98.6	99.5	95.5	99.7
% Other Nonwhite................	2.6	0.6	1.6	0.6	0.2	0.3	0.0	0.0	0.2	0.3	0.0
% Of Spanish Language...........	8.9	4.5	9.3	0.0	1.6	0.5	0.0	0.0	0.4	3.6	0.0
% Foreign Born..................	6.7	11.3	7.6	4.3	0.3	0.0	0.0	1.3	0.0	0.0	0.0
% Living In Group Quarters......	6.1	37.2	21.7	8.2	0.0	0.3	0.0	0.0	0.0	0.7	0.0
% 13 Years Old And Under........	35.0	0.0	1.2	22.5	45.5	49.0	40.6	31.3	49.0	29.8	24.3
% 14-20 Years Old...............	14.7	0.0	1.9	14.8	17.8	21.0	16.1	14.5	15.2	16.0	15.4
% 21-64 Years Old...............	43.8	65.2	79.7	53.3	33.6	28.0	38.7	46.3	31.9	47.2	48.7
% 65-74 Years Old...............	4.3	26.8	11.9	7.0	2.0	1.5	3.9	5.0	2.6	5.0	8.0
% 75 Years Old And Over.........	2.2	7.9	5.4	2.4	1.1	0.6	0.6	2.9	1.3	2.0	3.6
% In Different House............	55.9	46.9	55.8	28.9	53.5	66.2	14.9	23.5	71.0	63.9	67.9
% Families With Female Head.....	36.7	-	38.5	26.6	56.9	48.6	26.7	41.9	49.4	33.6	34.8
Median School Years Completed...	9.4	8.6	10.1	10.0	9.8	10.0	10.1	7.9	9.8	8.3	8.9
Median Family Income, 1969......$$	6012	-	9000	8067	4660	5365	8000	5083	4591	7786	8429
% Income Below Poverty Level....	34.7	-	50.0	36.4	45.8	44.3	18.5	35.8	47.3	38.1	16.4
% Income of $15,000 or More.....	7.1	-	0.0	9.5	2.3	6.0	0.0	12.6	2.0	15.5	25.7
% White Collar Workers..........	16.2	6.0	10.7	11.0	5.1	8.3	29.6	25.7	8.7	12.2	7.6
% Civilian Labor Force Unemployed.	8.0	10.7	4.1	8.5	9.9	6.8	10.0	13.5	4.3	13.9	12.7
% Riding To Work By Automobile...	37.9	0.0	42.6	45.8	35.9	42.2	26.5	15.9	41.4	66.4	38.0
Population Per Household.........	3.4	1.0	1.2	2.6	4.0	5.4	3.9	3.2	4.4	3.2	2.7
Total Housing Units..........	23741	114	316	395	1351	938	49	176	1377	412	146
% Condominiums & Cooperatives.....	0.5	0.0	0.0	0.0	5.7	0.0	-	0.0	0.5	0.0	0.0
% Built 1960 Or Later...........	11.8	0.0	0.0	2.5	10.5	42.6	-	2.6	32.1	3.4	0.0
% Owner Occupied................	8.7	0.0	1.9	4.8	1.3	3.7	-	15.3	3.3	11.4	16.4
% With 1+ Persons Per Room......	22.8	2.0	2.8	16.8	33.7	50.7	-	16.6	34.7	24.7	12.0
Median Value: Owner Units.....$$	12800	-	-	-	-	-	-	-	-	-	-
Median Rent: Rental Units.....$$	76	45	48	76	77	79	-	82	75	86	69
Median Number Of Rooms: All Units.	4.1	1.0	1.1	2.2	4.1	4.9	-	4.2	4.5	3.8	3.5

Community Area 28 — Near West Side
Selected Characteristics of Census Tracts: 1970

Tract Number	2811	2812	2813	2814	2815	2816	2817	2818	2819	2820	2822
Total Population.............	669	1557	2226	1096	2960	2706	2483	1020	793	76	1717
% Male........................	48.1	46.0	47.2	46.7	49.0	48.5	64.0	90.6	93.2	–	51.0
% Black.......................	99.9	96.2	98.0	96.8	97.3	87.2	54.9	13.3	7.1	–	0.3
% Other Nonwhite..............	0.0	0.4	0.4	0.8	0.9	2.9	2.8	3.2	2.9	–	3.1
% Of Spanish Language.........	0.0	0.0	0.8	0.0	0.0	1.0	14.6	5.2	13.0	–	18.2
% Foreign Born................	0.0	0.2	0.0	1.5	0.0	6.2	4.6	9.3	14.2	–	15.1
% Living In Group Quarters....	0.0	1.0	0.4	3.3	0.3	1.3	20.0	72.1	54.7	–	0.4
% 13 Years Old And Under......	29.6	39.5	43.8	32.3	35.2	25.9	20.7	4.1	2.6	–	21.6
% 14-20 Years Old.............	11.7	14.2	13.8	13.7	13.0	10.1	8.1	7.6	1.5	–	15.8
% 21-64 Years Old.............	49.5	42.4	38.2	46.5	47.8	42.9	59.4	65.8	73.6	–	54.5
% 65-74 Years Old.............	6.6	2.8	3.2	5.4	2.6	12.7	7.4	17.0	15.3	–	5.8
% 75 Years Old And Over.......	2.7	1.2	1.0	2.1	1.4	8.4	4.4	5.5	6.9	–	2.4
% In Different House..........	68.7	58.6	50.9	70.0	51.4	43.5	35.8	49.1	42.7	–	56.3
% Families With Female Head...	28.1	36.1	34.1	39.7	36.9	36.7	31.1	21.4	9.1	–	16.5
Median School Years Completed..	9.0	9.5	9.1	8.8	9.0	8.6	9.6	8.9	8.9	–	9.4
Median Family Income, 1969...$$	8019	5258	5694	6000	5652	5529	4692	3421	11571	–	10111
% Income Below Poverty Level..	16.4	38.0	43.4	35.1	35.1	34.1	42.2	18.0	0.0	–	7.1
% Income of $15,000 or More...	9.5	1.7	1.2	10.9	5.7	2.9	3.2	6.0	36.4	–	24.5
% White Collar Workers........	5.8	6.1	12.3	6.4	5.3	15.7	14.0	13.1	6.9	–	18.7
% Civilian Labor Force Unemployed..	7.1	13.4	12.2	6.0	14.6	6.3	9.6	17.8	7.2	–	3.9
% Riding To Work By Automobile....	33.5	41.0	38.3	23.6	35.3	35.1	28.3	6.4	19.8	–	53.4
Population Per Household.......	2.8	4.0	4.2	3.3	3.0	2.1	2.2	1.6	1.2	–	3.0
Total Housing Units..........	261	450	620	366	1184	1397	1128	237	373	24	588
% Condominiums & Cooperatives.....	0.0	0.0	0.0	0.0	0.0	0.4	0.0	0.0	0.0	–	0.9
% Built 1960 Or Later..........	1.4	0.0	1.3	1.1	8.6	30.9	0.5	0.0	0.0	–	2.2
% Owner Occupied...............	12.6	14.2	15.5	13.1	9.2	2.6	5.4	3.0	0.5	–	16.8
% With 1+ Persons Per Room.....	14.3	29.5	32.6	21.2	22.6	13.8	14.1	7.2	1.6	–	8.6
Median Value: Owner Units......$$	–	–	–	–	–	–	–	–	–	–	–
Median Rent: Rental Units......$$	86	94	94	85	82	68	76	54	57	–	72
Median Number Of Rooms: All Units.	3.4	4.2	4.6	4.1	3.6	2.6	1.4	1.3	1.1	–	4.9

Tract Number	2823	2824	2825	2826	2827	2828	2829	2830	2831	2832	2833
Total Population.............	1097	1295	686	1566	3337	2422	4509	1449	1703	3543	624
% Male........................	50.8	47.9	43.4	46.2	50.6	51.6	49.1	56.6	51.8	42.0	48.1
% Black.......................	1.0	0.2	12.5	84.9	30.2	9.4	19.3	32.8	5.1	78.7	0.8
% Other Nonwhite..............	6.7	5.7	27.6	4.5	4.9	5.1	14.1	10.3	3.7	1.2	7.7
% Of Spanish Language.........	12.9	17.1	2.4	5.8	55.7	52.8	15.6	17.1	29.9	8.1	53.3
% Foreign Born................	18.5	24.4	44.4	5.8	29.0	27.1	20.0	3.8	26.4	5.3	20.1
% Living In Group Quarters....	4.7	0.0	0.0	0.0	0.6	0.5	34.7	65.6	0.8	0.9	5.4
% 13 Years Old And Under......	17.8	24.0	21.1	45.5	32.6	30.4	19.4	30.2	25.2	34.2	30.0
% 14-20 Years Old.............	12.2	11.4	3.1	17.8	12.4	14.5	11.7	26.9	13.0	14.1	13.8
% 21-64 Years Old.............	60.0	56.1	73.8	34.1	51.1	50.1	65.2	39.9	53.4	40.2	49.5
% 65-74 Years Old.............	6.8	5.4	1.6	1.5	2.4	3.6	2.2	1.7	5.6	6.5	5.0
% 75 Years Old And Over.......	3.2	3.0	0.4	1.1	1.5	1.4	1.5	1.4	2.8	4.9	1.8
% In Different House..........	51.3	50.2	18.8	37.2	48.9	62.2	35.8	29.8	57.6	60.6	48.7
% Families With Female Head...	16.4	14.0	13.8	43.9	15.9	10.5	11.9	25.5	13.9	48.6	24.3
Median School Years Completed..	11.9	11.1	16.0	8.9	9.3	8.8	12.3	8.9	8.8	9.1	9.9
Median Family Income, 1969....$$	10731	9464	10791	5059	7730	8331	9098	8250	9472	4721	7083
% Income Below Poverty Level..	9.8	7.0	1.6	47.0	13.6	10.9	9.2	21.5	16.3	39.5	14.9
% Income of $15,000 or More...	30.0	21.6	20.4	7.6	9.9	10.3	11.8	3.6	13.4	4.7	15.8
% White Collar Workers........	30.9	29.8	71.1	4.7	9.3	14.6	41.0	16.2	17.5	13.9	25.7
% Civilian Labor Force Unemployed.	2.1	5.4	0.0	9.9	6.1	4.1	2.3	6.4	4.9	6.7	8.0
% Riding To Work By Automobile....	34.1	56.6	21.5	46.1	41.1	52.3	28.5	28.3	48.4	27.3	25.8
Population Per Household.......	3.2	2.9	2.2	4.4	3.7	3.7	2.8	4.0	3.3	2.9	3.5
Total Housing Units..........	333	476	318	399	976	687	1064	146	543	1250	182
% Condominiums & Cooperatives.....	1.8	1.1	0.0	0.0	0.0	0.0	0.0	0.0	0.0	0.0	0.0
% Built 1960 Or Later..........	16.3	5.7	83.5	24.0	0.5	0.0	6.1	3.3	0.0	5.3	0.0
% Owner Occupied...............	27.6	16.0	0.3	9.5	19.9	20.8	13.3	7.5	16.4	5.1	19.8
% With 1+ Persons Per Room.....	6.7	9.1	12.0	35.9	18.2	17.4	15.4	22.4	14.8	16.4	12.9
Median Value: Owner Units......$$	–	–	–	–	10500	–	10900	–	–	–	–
Median Rent: Rental Units......$$	83	75	137	78	76	77	91	67	69	70	65
Median Number Of Rooms: All Units.	5.4	4.6	3.0	4.6	4.8	5.0	4.4	4.4	4.8	3.7	4.9

Tract Number	2834	2835	2836	2837	2838	2839	2840	2841	2842	2843
Total Population.............	17	76	206	1070	2543	8703	2722	2227	1750	188
% Male........................	–	–	48.1	49.9	47.7	42.7	48.2	47.0	46.5	44.7
% Black.......................	–	–	80.1	94.1	96.7	99.5	97.1	99.5	95.8	82.4
% Other Nonwhite..............	–	–	0.0	1.1	0.3	0.1	0.4	0.0	0.1	2.1
% Of Spanish Language.........	–	–	6.1	4.8	2.2	0.1	1.1	0.0	0.0	0.0
% Foreign Born................	–	–	6.1	5.4	0.0	0.1	0.4	0.0	0.0	0.0
% Living In Group Quarters....	–	–	0.0	0.0	2.2	0.2	0.0	0.4	1.1	0.0
% 13 Years Old And Under......	–	–	22.3	34.3	49.5	42.3	34.8	35.1	38.1	50.0
% 14-20 Years Old.............	–	–	5.8	13.9	18.5	16.8	15.1	16.1	15.4	19.1
% 21-64 Years Old.............	–	–	52.4	45.7	30.3	35.1	43.5	42.8	41.0	28.7
% 65-74 Years Old.............	–	–	17.0	5.1	1.3	3.8	4.8	4.4	4.1	0.5
% 75 Years Old And Over.......	–	–	2.4	0.9	0.4	2.0	1.8	1.6	1.4	1.6
% In Different House..........	–	–	46.8	64.2	76.7	66.9	70.1	60.3	49.4	48.8
% Families With Female Head...	–	–	32.5	32.5	57.3	54.3	30.0	33.1	31.8	27.6
Median School Years Completed..	–	–	4.5	7.0	9.7	9.1	8.3	8.9	8.2	7.8
Median Family Income, 1969....$$	–	–	4333	5341	4160	4444	6088	5638	6019	6500
% Income Below Poverty Level..	–	–	41.9	43.8	61.0	44.5	40.0	36.7	36.7	28.6
% Income of $15,000 or More...	–	–	0.0	3.5	1.8	2.7	7.6	1.0	10.4	0.0
% White Collar Workers........	–	–	14.3	15.8	24.1	8.9	4.2	3.2	13.7	0.0
% Civilian Labor Force Unemployed.	–	–	12.5	6.3	16.7	11.7	7.1	21.6	12.1	0.0
% Riding To Work By Automobile....	–	–	0.0	33.2	25.8	35.2	54.8	44.1	51.6	100.0
Population Per Household.......	–	–	2.5	3.3	4.8	3.7	3.9	3.8	4.0	5.9
Total Housing Units..........	11	26	105	397	549	2498	752	641	453	33
% Condominiums & Cooperatives.....	–	–	0.0	0.0	0.0	0.0	0.0	0.9	0.0	–
% Built 1960 Or Later..........	–	–	0.0	0.0	55.6	12.1	0.0	0.0	1.0	–
% Owner Occupied...............	–	–	7.6	1.3	0.5	1.3	17.6	14.7	18.8	–
% With 1+ Persons Per Room.....	–	–	8.5	25.2	45.7	29.6	20.5	22.8	26.6	–
Median Value: Owner Units......$$	–	–	–	–	–	–	–	–	–	–
Median Rent: Rental Units......$$	–	–	66	64	75	76	76	77	86	–
Median Number Of Rooms: All Units.	–	–	4.3	3.9	4.3	4.0	4.9	4.5	4.7	–

location of major commerical centers at its intersections with Halsted Street and Ashland Avenue. The mile between these two was the site of Skid Row, a strip of cubicle hotels, cheap restaurants, religious missions and bars that provided for the needs of homeless, indigent, alcoholic men. The aging mansions on Ashland Avenue were converted to rooming houses, businesses, fraternity houses and labor union headquarters.

A massive black influx, fed by the migration of blacks from the South that began during the 1940s, brought the population back up to 160,000, 40 percent of whom were black, at the end of that decade. In the three decades since, the physical layout of the Near West Side has been subject to continuous and major alteration. In the 1950s the Chicago Land Clearance Commission commenced eight different urban renewal projects in the community area, most of them designed for light industrial, commercial or institutional redevelopment. The construction of the Northwest (Kennedy) and Dan Ryan Expressways, which met at Congress Street, and were connected to that expressway and to the downtown area by the large and elaborate Congress Street Circle interchange, wiped out most of the Greek settlement. The construction of the University of Illinois Chicago campus, beginning in the early 1960s in the Harrison-Halsted redevelopment district, resulted in the demolition of nearly all the Hull House complex, as well as much of the historic Italian neighborhood which it served. Elsewhere in the Harrison-Halsted area, as well as in the adjacent Racine-Congress redevelopment district, land was cleared for the construction of new apartments, town houses and shopping facilities.

Today there are fewer than half the number of housing units there were in the Near West Side in 1950, and not many more than one-third the people. The southeastern corner of the community, bounded by Van Buren on the north, Morgan Street on the west is now inhabited by fewer than 300 residents. Blacks continue to live in the northwest corner, bounded by Ashland on the east and Van Buren on the south. Although the number of blacks has declined dramatically over the last two decades, they comprise three-fourths of the population of the Near West Side. Whites have moved out in massive numbers since 1950; today 9,350 live there, compared to 10 times that number 30 years ago. Most whites live in the central area, between the University of Illinois

campus and the Medical Center District. This includes the small residual Italian ethnic neighborhood along Taylor Street. Most of the Hispanics live in the west-central part of the community, west of Ashland between Van Buren Street and Roosevelt Road. They comprise 10 percent of the population, and the great majority of them are Mexicans.

The development of the University campus and the other urban renewal activities in the center of the area set off a wave of housing renovation and rehabilitation nearby. The Jackson Boulevard Historic District, a strip of deteriorated mansions from the old Ashland Avenue days, is being recreated as a fashionalbe neighborhood. The Westgate Mill district, a 110-acre area immediately north of the University of Illinois bounded by Racine Avenue, Monroe Street and the Eisenhower and Kennedy Expressways, was the city's largest garment district in the 1920s, and is the location of a million square feet of loft space, much of which is to be converted for residential and commercial use.

The old Skid Row area on Madison Street has been torn down to make way for new construction, including the Presidential Towers, a 49-story housing development that will add 2,346 rental housing units. More than two million square feet of office space will be provided by the con-c struction of the Gateway IV complex and the building at 525 Monroe Street. Land has been cleared south of the University for the development of a technological park. West of the University the Tri Taylor Home neighborhood, located between Western and Ogden avenues, has attained historic landmark status, and a joint private-city-state-federal program has been proposed that would provide low interest mortgages for those interested in renovating the 100-year old box-like brick structures.

During the next 10 years, it would appear that the eastern half of the Near West Side will become a neighborhood of office buildings and upper-middle-class homes, surrounding a core of medical, educational aand technological institutions. The western half, currently a black and Hispanic blue-collar residential area, should survive in that form, anchored by the large public housing projects in the area.

M.W.H.
Sibylle Allendorf

Community Area 29

North Lawndale

The North Lawndale community area was an undeveloped prairie west of Chicago in the 1830s. Like several west side communities, it was originally included in the township of Cicero when that township was organized in 1857. North Lawndale was crossed by a road which had been used by Indians and subsequent white settlers in the region as a portage trail between Lake Michigan and the Des Plaines River. This became the Southwestern Plank Road, presently known as Ogden Avenue. In 1863 Crawford, a small unincorporated village, appeared following the construction of the tracks of the Chicago, Burlington, and Quincy Railroad in the area. The village which was named after Peter Crawford, who had purchased 160 acres of land and built a home on Ogden Avenue, developed around the railroad station and the local store in the southwestern border of the territory. Crawford, comprised of native Americans, Germans, and Dutch, gradually emerged as a residential suburb of Chicago.

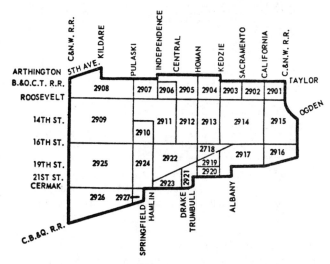

In 1869, the eastern section of North Lawndale to Pulaski Road was annexed to Chicago by an act of the state legislature. Consequently, streets were platted and drainage ditches were installed between Western Avenue — formerly the city limits — and Crawford Avenue

Community Area 29 -- North Lawndale
Population and Housing Characteristics, 1930-1980

	1980	1970	1960	1950	1940	1930
Total Population.......	61,523	94,772	124,937	100,489	102,470	112,261
% Male..................	45.9	46.6	48.1	49.7	50.5	50.9
% Female................	54.1	53.4	51.9	50.3	49.5	49.1
% White.................	1.7	3.1	8.6	86.7	99.6	99.6
% Black.................	96.5	96.4	91.1	13.1	0.4	0.3
% Other Nonwhite Races...	1.8	0.5	0.3	0.2	0.0	0.0
% Under 5 Years Old......	10.3	12.7	18.5	9.6	6.2	7.3
% 5-19 Years Old........	34.9	40.3	30.3	20.1	23.7	30.1
% 20-44 Years Old.......	32.1	30.7	36.0	40.9	42.6	42.8
% 45-64 Years Old.......	16.2	12.4	11.9	22.0	21.8	16.3
% 65 Years and Older.....	6.5	3.9	3.3	7.4	5.7	3.5
Median School Years....	10.8	10.0	8.7	8.7	7.7	*
Total Housing...........	18,592	25,342	30,243	20,009	26,182	*
% In One-Unit Structures.	6.3	6.2	7.4	*	*	*
% Owner Occupied........	19.9	16.0	17.9	21.7	15.6	*
% Renter Occupied........	72.5	73.2	77.6	76.9	80.7	*
% Vacant................	7.6	10.8	4.5	1.4	3.7	*
% 1+ Persons per Room....	16.8	26.1	32.5	15.9	*	*

Community Area 29 -- North Lawndale
Selected Characteristics of Census Tracts: 1980

Tract Number	Total	2901	2902	2903	2904	2905	2906	2907	2908	2909	2910
Total Population.............	61534	11	1695	682	0	1340	646	1260	1227	7628	2040
% Male.......................	45.9	-	45.1	43.8	-	45.1	46.6	47.7	48.4	45.3	44.5
% Black......................	96.5	-	99.8	100.0	-	99.6	98.5	99.8	99.4	98.8	99.4
% Other Nonwhite.............	1.8	-	0.0	0.0	-	0.0	1.1	0.1	0.5	0.4	0.3
% Of Spanish Origin..........	2.7	-	0.3	0.1	-	0.0	1.1	1.4	0.6	0.9	0.3
% Foreign Born...............	2.0	-	2.2	1.4	-	0.4	2.5	0.6	2.2	0.4	0.0
% Living In Group Quarters...	1.0	-	0.0	0.0	-	0.0	3.3	0.0	0.0	0.4	0.0
% 13 Years Old And Under.....	30.4	-	33.2	34.8	-	31.9	22.9	29.9	28.9	33.2	32.8
% 14-20 Years Old............	17.0	-	17.0	15.4	-	19.3	17.3	18.1	16.6	15.7	17.0
% 21-64 Years Old............	46.0	-	44.0	42.4	-	43.0	52.6	44.8	48.3	45.5	43.5
% 65-74 Years Old............	4.6	-	4.1	5.7	-	4.2	5.6	5.2	4.4	3.9	5.3
% 75 Years Old And Over......	2.0	-	1.7	1.8	-	1.6	1.5	2.0	1.7	1.7	1.4
% In Different House.........	34.1	-	46.2	50.3	-	32.3	35.4	34.6	50.5	37.9	39.1
% Families With Female Head..	60.9	-	73.3	75.0	-	71.8	68.8	63.7	59.3	61.3	68.3
Median School Years Completed....	10.8	-	10.2	9.3	-	7.9	10.3	12.1	10.8	10.6	11.1
Median Family Income, 1979......$$	9902	-	7364	5406	-	9258	7500	10667	11492	9981	7730
% Income Below Poverty Level....	39.9	-	47.5	70.1	-	43.3	47.4	39.1	34.7	42.6	50.3
% Income Of $30,000 Or More....	8.3	-	8.1	0.0	-	3.6	3.3	10.0	2.6	5.3	5.3
% White Collar Workers.......	37.8	-	32.0	42.4	-	20.5	6.7	38.6	42.3	33.8	38.7
% Civilian Labor Force Unemployed.	20.4	-	28.3	39.8	-	25.4	31.0	26.3	22.8	23.5	24.1
% Riding To Work By Automobile....	58.0	-	38.6	64.4	-	49.6	47.0	61.8	41.2	58.0	58.2
Mean Commuting Time - Minutes.	33.1	-	31.0	25.8	-	35.1	27.4	33.1	39.2	42.1	39.2
Population Per Household..........	3.5	-	3.6	3.6	-	3.7	3.4	3.6	3.2	3.5	3.5
Total Housing Units...........	18592	3	509	209	0	434	200	391	440	2314	628
% Condominiums...............	0.0	-	0.0	0.0	-	0.0	0.0	0.0	0.0	0.0	0.0
% Built 1970 Or Later........	2.8	-	3.6	6.0	-	0.9	4.1	1.3	3.4	2.0	0.0
% Owner Occupied.............	19.9	-	9.8	17.2	-	9.4	20.5	26.1	16.4	18.8	17.5
% With 1+ Persons Per Room...	16.8	-	18.8	16.8	-	23.0	11.9	14.7	15.4	18.0	17.7
Median Value: Owner Units......$$	25200	-	-	-	-	-	-	-	-	22100	-
Median Rent: Rental Units....$$	156	-	153	143	-	153	159	156	159	159	158
Median Number Of Rooms: All Units.	5.0	-	4.8	4.9	-	4.7	5.2	5.2	4.9	4.7	4.9

Tract Number	2911	2912	2913	2914	2915	2916	2917	2918	2919	2920	2921
Total Population.............	6491	3921	4375	2515	3413	1187	973	888	631	1174	1081
% Male.......................	45.2	45.1	44.6	47.0	45.0	52.0	47.4	44.4	47.5	45.4	47.0
% Black......................	99.5	99.5	99.4	95.8	84.2	14.0	97.5	98.4	98.9	98.7	98.9
% Other Nonwhite.............	0.2	0.4	0.2	0.8	8.1	53.1	1.8	1.5	0.6	0.2	0.8
% Of Spanish Origin..........	0.5	0.9	0.6	1.3	10.8	71.2	0.4	2.1	0.0	0.3	1.9
% Foreign Born...............	0.2	0.1	0.0	1.6	7.6	47.6	0.0	6.3	1.0	0.5	0.6
% Living In Group Quarters...	0.3	2.9	1.1	6.1	4.0	0.0	0.0	0.0	0.0	0.0	0.0
% 13 Years Old And Under.....	31.9	31.7	31.9	30.4	32.6	33.2	25.8	32.4	25.8	27.1	27.1
% 14-20 Years Old............	18.6	19.7	19.6	16.8	20.7	14.2	12.6	16.8	18.1	17.5	16.1
% 21-64 Years Old............	44.0	42.9	41.5	45.8	41.8	47.7	52.5	43.8	47.2	46.2	46.8
% 65-74 Years Old............	3.8	4.5	4.5	4.7	3.1	3.5	5.1	4.2	7.3	6.5	7.0
% 75 Years Old And Over......	1.7	1.3	2.6	2.4	1.7	1.4	3.9	2.8	1.6	2.8	3.0
% In Different House.........	36.9	37.2	33.0	30.2	28.1	38.3	18.7	46.9	20.9	17.3	54.1
% Families With Female Head..	65.2	69.5	69.8	65.2	65.3	23.7	51.4	67.7	58.1	59.3	51.9
Median School Years Completed....	10.6	10.5	10.5	11.1	10.3	7.9	12.0	10.9	9.3	10.7	11.3
Median Family Income, 1979......$$	9164	8419	8624	7757	6063	16198	9345	10250	8871	11083	9946
% Income Below Poverty Level....	43.2	45.4	43.5	47.7	54.4	29.0	30.3	32.8	45.9	40.6	37.5
% Income Of $30,000 Or More.....	6.3	5.9	4.9	7.3	2.4	15.0	8.0	6.2	0.0	13.5	11.2
% White Collar Workers.......	37.5	38.5	40.8	40.7	39.9	36.8	32.3	39.2	27.0	37.4	49.3
% Civilian Labor Force Unemployed.	18.6	16.2	20.6	16.9	31.2	23.3	15.0	38.7	34.6	16.5	19.9
% Riding To Work By Automobile....	46.1	56.2	54.1	63.6	51.4	57.2	73.3	70.3	47.3	57.6	55.6
Mean Commuting Time - Minutes...	32.1	31.2	31.9	29.9	29.1	28.9	38.3	30.3	24.4	22.7	31.5
Population Per Household..........	3.7	3.7	3.8	3.6	4.0	3.6	3.2	3.7	3.5	3.5	3.5
Total Housing Units...........	1945	1103	1201	695	850	385	345	266	187	346	329
% Condominiums...............	0.0	0.0	0.0	0.0	0.0	0.0	0.0	0.0	0.0	0.0	0.0
% Built 1970 Or Later........	4.3	1.7	1.7	1.8	6.3	7.2	0.0	0.0	0.0	3.7	0.0
% Owner Occupied.............	12.2	14.5	15.1	9.6	14.9	20.8	23.5	15.4	26.7	28.9	29.8
% With 1+ Persons Per Room...	20.1	19.4	18.8	20.0	29.4	21.4	9.9	14.4	13.5	9.6	12.6
Median Value: Owner Units......$$	-	-	-	-	-	-	-	-	-	-	-
Median Rent: Rental Units....$$	156	154	157	153	111	139	151	157	159	155	159
Median Number Of Rooms: All Units.	4.9	5.0	5.1	4.9	4.8	4.5	5.6	5.1	5.3	5.5	5.4

(Pulaski Road). In the same year, the legislature created the West Park Board and provided for the creation of three parks on the West Side. One of the three, Douglas Park — named after Illinois Senator Stephen A. Douglas — was established in the eastern section of the North Lawndale community area. The name "Lawndale" was supplied by Millard and Deeker, a real estate firm which subdivided the area in 1870. In 1871, after the Fire, the McCormick Reaper Company (International Harvester) built a large plant in the nearby Lower West Side neighborhood. As a result, many plant workers moved to eastern North Lawndale, with some employees choosing to build their own frame homes and cottages.

Although North Lawndale experienced little further growth during the 1880s, the end of the decade saw a resurgence of activity. In 1889, the remaining area west of Pulaski Road was annexed by a resolution of the Cook County Commissioners. This completed the land area of North Lawndale, which included the portion of the yet unincorporated village of Crawford north of the Burlington tracks. The section south of the tracks became part of South Lawndale.

Transportation played a key role in the growth of North Lawndale. The construction of the Garfield Park branch of the elevated tracks during the 1890s spurred the development of the area along the northern boundary of the community. Conversely, the southern section

Community Area 29 — North Lawndale
Selected Characteristics of Census Tracts: 1980

Tract Number	2922	2923	2924	2925	2926	2927
Total Population	4551	1243	3963	6478	2121	0
% Male	47.4	45.2	47.1	45.4	47.9	—
% Black	99.2	98.8	98.4	98.8	98.6	—
% Other Nonwhite	0.3	0.1	0.3	0.5	0.3	—
% Of Spanish Origin	0.8	0.1	0.8	1.2	0.3	—
% Foreign Born	2.6	0.0	1.6	0.2	0.0	—
% Living In Group Quarters	0.7	0.2	0.7	0.1	0.0	—
% 13 Years Old And Under	28.2	30.7	30.4	26.4	24.4	—
% 14-20 Years Old	16.1	16.7	14.4	15.2	15.7	—
% 21-64 Years Old	47.0	46.4	47.7	52.1	53.9	—
% 65-74 Years Old	5.7	4.7	5.3	4.6	4.3	—
% 75 Years Old And Over	3.0	1.5	2.2	1.7	1.7	—
% In Different House	36.2	25.2	32.1	28.7	21.7	—
% Families With Female Head	59.6	61.9	53.6	51.6	39.6	—
Median School Years Completed	10.7	11.0	11.3	11.7	11.7	—
Median Family Income, 1979 $$	11334	11250	12026	12727	16603	—
% Income Below Poverty Level	34.0	36.7	31.6	27.9	30.0	—
% Income Of $30,000 Or More	11.1	11.4	12.4	14.0	19.3	—
% White Collar Workers	42.4	26.3	37.1	40.5	39.9	—
% Civilian Labor Force Unemployed	18.8	13.8	17.1	15.4	16.8	—
% Riding To Work By Automobile	57.1	51.4	76.3	60.6	72.7	—
Mean Commuting Time - Minutes	33.9	42.9	39.6	28.3	28.8	—
Population Per Household	3.5	3.4	3.3	3.3	3.4	—
Total Housing Units	1432	374	1268	2087	651	0
% Condominiums	0.0	0.0	0.0	0.0	0.0	—
% Built 1970 Or Later	2.1	0.0	2.3	5.9	1.2	—
% Owner Occupied	23.2	27.3	23.3	29.7	35.9	—
% With 1+ Persons Per Room	14.0	15.0	12.6	12.4	10.5	—
Median Value: Owner Units $$	—	—	—	30500	23900	—
Median Rent: Rental Units $$	160	157	166	161	154	—
Median Number Of Rooms: All Units	5.6	5.2	5.1	5.1	4.7	—

Community Area 29 — North Lawndale
Selected Characteristics of Census Tracts: 1970

Tract Number	TOTAL	2901	2902	2903	2904	2905	2906	2907	2908	2909	2910
Total Population	94772	71	2393	1482	723	1987	916	1862	2165	13699	3337
% Male	46.6	—	48.0	48.7	48.4	46.1	46.4	46.1	47.3	45.6	47.6
% Black	96.3	—	99.5	99.5	98.9	99.5	100.0	98.7	98.8	98.6	99.6
% Other Nonwhite	0.5	—	0.2	0.0	0.7	0.5	0.0	0.7	0.6	0.3	0.2
% Of Spanish Language	1.6	—	0.0	2.0	0.0	0.0	6.1	1.7	0.0	0.4	0.0
% Foreign Born	0.8	—	0.0	0.5	0.0	0.9	0.0	0.3	0.2	0.1	0.0
% Living In Group Quarters	1.2	—	0.3	0.0	0.0	0.0	0.0	0.0	0.5	0.3	0.6
% 13 Years Old And Under	39.5	—	41.3	37.8	42.9	42.2	38.3	36.9	43.1	43.0	42.9
% 14-20 Years Old	15.4	—	15.2	18.4	14.7	14.1	17.0	15.0	14.5	15.1	15.0
% 21-64 Years Old	41.3	—	39.9	40.3	38.0	40.8	42.8	44.5	40.0	39.3	38.8
% 65-74 Years Old	2.5	—	2.7	2.7	3.2	2.2	1.3	2.5	1.7	2.0	2.3
% 75 Years Old And Over	1.3	—	1.0	0.9	1.2	0.8	0.5	1.1	0.6	0.6	0.9
% In Different House	55.6	—	60.3	63.1	62.1	53.8	65.8	56.3	34.2	55.1	53.3
% Families With Female Head	33.3	—	40.0	39.3	45.2	38.6	30.6	38.5	38.5	36.0	33.7
Median School Years Completed	10.0	—	10.0	10.2	8.6	8.8	10.2	10.1	9.8	9.5	9.2
Median Family Income, 1969 $$	6972	—	6375	5295	5679	6125	7660	6135	6707	6507	7565
% Income Below Poverty Level	30.0	—	38.2	41.0	45.2	33.4	16.2	33.3	35.3	36.1	26.3
% Income of $15,000 or More	10.5	—	6.4	6.3	10.6	3.1	10.2	8.9	8.4	7.8	11.7
% White Collar Workers	9.4	—	7.5	10.4	13.0	9.4	17.3	2.9	8.2	6.9	7.6
% Civilian Labor Force Unemployed	8.6	—	9.8	12.2	15.7	8.4	9.8	8.5	11.4	8.3	4.5
% Riding To Work By Automobile	49.1	—	51.8	56.6	37.4	57.5	47.7	53.7	47.8	41.9	61.5
Population Per Household	4.1	—	4.0	4.1	3.9	4.0	4.2	4.0	4.1	4.3	4.4
Total Housing Units	25328	12	658	397	219	555	252	518	594	3498	897
% Condominiums & Cooperatives	0.4	—	0.0	0.0	0.0	0.0	0.0	0.0	0.0	0.7	0.0
% Built 1960 Or Later	3.8	—	1.2	0.0	2.7	6.6	0.0	2.1	0.9	1.3	2.2
% Owner Occupied	15.5	—	7.1	16.1	11.0	5.9	15.9	19.3	15.7	15.2	11.7
% With 1+ Persons Per Room	27.1	—	23.3	25.4	29.4	27.6	29.4	24.1	32.4	33.1	33.0
Median Value: Owner Units $$	15500	—	—	—	—	—	—	—	—	12100	—
Median Rent: Rental Units $$	105	—	104	109	99	102	102	107	103	103	107
Median Number Of Rooms: All Units	4.8	—	4.7	5.1	4.4	4.4	4.9	5.1	4.5	4.4	4.7

Tract Number	2911	2912	2913	2914	2915	2916	2917	2918	2919	2920	2921
Total Population	9995	6291	7022	3609	4776	1279	1892	1579	1283	1694	1551
% Male	46.6	45.5	46.2	45.3	45.7	48.6	42.8	46.5	46.0	46.8	47.3
% Black	99.5	99.4	99.3	95.4	83.4	2.2	86.5	99.3	99.3	97.3	98.5
% Other Nonwhite	0.2	0.3	0.3	0.1	1.7	15.5	0.1	0.1	0.0	0.1	0.6
% Of Spanish Language	0.0	0.9	0.0	0.0	5.5	64.1	0.0	1.1	0.0	1.0	0.0
% Foreign Born	0.0	0.1	0.1	0.4	3.0	35.4	0.0	0.0	0.0	0.5	0.3
% Living In Group Quarters	0.3	0.2	1.7	4.5	5.9	2.0	13.4	0.5	0.0	2.4	0.6
% 13 Years Old And Under	43.7	42.1	42.3	38.8	37.1	26.3	31.3	42.0	39.2	37.6	38.3
% 14-20 Years Old	16.2	16.3	14.5	15.7	18.4	13.4	15.4	17.0	20.4	15.6	15.0
% 21-64 Years Old	37.4	38.3	38.9	38.8	40.6	53.8	37.2	38.2	37.8	41.1	42.5
% 65-74 Years Old	2.0	2.5	3.0	2.9	2.4	4.0	4.2	2.2	1.9	4.0	3.1
% 75 Years Old And Over	0.7	0.8	1.2	3.9	1.5	2.5	11.9	0.7	0.6	1.7	1.2
% In Different House	53.0	59.9	57.5	49.6	48.9	47.6	52.9	53.6	47.4	58.6	55.9
% Families With Female Head	41.1	41.9	35.3	35.6	27.9	12.6	33.9	40.3	38.8	31.1	31.5
Median School Years Completed	9.8	9.9	9.7	9.3	11.0	10.7	11.4	9.6	9.4	9.4	9.2
Median Family Income, 1969 $$	6083	5601	5928	6354	6879	8500	7929	7174	6933	6610	6878
% Income Below Poverty Level	39.8	38.7	39.7	31.2	22.4	13.8	26.4	36.3	34.2	18.4	33.2
% Income of $15,000 or More	7.9	5.4	10.0	8.4	4.9	19.0	11.5	7.6	6.7	5.4	15.6
% White Collar Workers	7.0	12.2	6.9	12.9	16.7	26.0	8.6	2.6	11.8	5.4	6.4
% Civilian Labor Force Unemployed	11.5	12.2	9.1	15.7	7.4	10.0	8.1	10.3	7.9	13.0	11.2
% Riding To Work By Automobile	45.4	43.3	49.6	42.3	35.2	60.0	61.7	48.3	29.7	52.8	44.7
Population Per Household	4.5	4.2	4.4	4.2	4.4	3.3	4.2	4.5	4.4	4.2	4.3
Total Housing Units	2693	1781	1850	937	1085	405	422	399	322	444	402
% Condominiums & Cooperatives	0.5	0.0	0.4	0.5	0.0	0.0	0.0	0.0	0.0	1.8	1.5
% Built 1960 Or Later	1.9	3.8	4.6	4.8	19.6	3.4	0.0	0.0	0.0	1.0	1.2
% Owner Occupied	10.4	10.3	9.7	8.9	12.0	21.0	18.0	11.8	12.7	20.5	23.6
% With 1+ Persons Per Room	34.0	30.4	29.5	26.5	30.7	16.0	23.5	32.4	29.1	28.7	27.7
Median Value: Owner Units $$	—	—	—	—	—	—	—	—	—	—	—
Median Rent: Rental Units $$	107	102	110	107	91	77	109	103	110	107	100
Median Number Of Rooms: All Units	4.8	4.9	5.0	5.0	4.5	4.5	5.1	4.9	5.2	4.8	5.1

Community Area 29 -- North Lawndale
Selected Characteristics of Census Tracts: 1970

Tract Number	2922	2923	2924	2925	2926	2927
Total Population	7973	1496	5804	7162	2640	91
% Male	47.4	49.0	47.3	47.5	48.9	—
% Black	99.0	99.2	99.3	97.9	92.5	—
% Other Nonwhite	0.3	0.1	0.1	0.3	0.5	—
% Of Spanish Language	0.0	0.0	0.5	0.0	2.0	—
% Foreign Born	0.0	0.4	0.3	0.0	0.7	—
% Living In Group Quarters	0.5	0.0	0.0	0.7	0.3	—
% 13 Years Old And Under	37.7	33.4	36.3	34.1	32.8	—
% 14-20 Years Old	15.0	11.9	14.9	14.0	14.5	—
% 21-64 Years Old	43.0	51.0	45.1	48.7	49.9	—
% 65-74 Years Old	3.1	2.6	2.7	2.3	1.8	—
% 75 Years Old And Over	1.2	1.1	1.0	0.9	1.0	—
% In Different House	58.6	69.1	64.3	55.8	54.4	—
% Families With Female Head	34.7	29.1	24.3	20.4	16.6	—
Median School Years Completed	10.2	10.3	10.6	10.8	11.1	—
Median Family Income, 1969...$$	7379	8250	8385	9088	9364	—
% Income Below Poverty Level	27.2	20.4	18.9	13.8	10.1	—
% Income of $15,000 or More	10.7	6.3	23.9	18.2	14.6	—
% White Collar Workers	5.5	6.8	14.4	11.3	8.0	—
% Civilian Labor Force Unemployed	8.1	3.1	6.2	4.4	4.1	—
% Riding To Work By Automobile	54.5	57.4	52.4	54.7	53.7	—
Population Per Household	4.1	3.3	3.8	3.8	3.7	—
Total Housing Units	2136	480	1635	1941	752	44
% Condominiums & Cooperatives	0.3	0.0	0.5	0.7	0.9	—
% Built 1960 Or Later	1.9	1.9	1.0	13.3	1.3	—
% Owner Occupied	17.6	19.6	15.0	32.1	35.9	—
% With 1+ Persons Per Room	23.6	11.3	21.4	17.3	16.2	—
Median Value: Owner Units...$$	15300	—	—	17900	16300	—
Median Rent: Rental Units...$$	108	104	109	111	102	—
Median Number Of Rooms: All Units	5.0	4.9	4.8	5.1	4.8	—

of North Lawndale lagged behind its northern counterpart until the Douglas Park line, previously built only to Western Avenue, was extended to Pulaski Road in 1902, and to Cicero Avenue in 1907. Transportation also played a part in North Lawndale's development when many industrial plants relocated along the belt-line railroads. In 1903 the Western Electric Company plant was built in nearby Cicero. Western Electric and other factories attracted hundreds of new residents to North Lawndale.

In the early 20th century North Lawndale experienced a tremendous population surge. Between 1910 and 1920, the population of the community doubled from 46,226 to 93,750. By 1920 Russian Jews were the dominant foreign-born group in the community, surpassing the Polish and Czechoslovakian nationalities, some of whom were also Jewish. By 1930, Russian Jews comprised 46 percent of the population of North Lawndale, which had surpassed 112,000. Many of them had moved to North Lawndale from the Near West Side. Roosevelt Road became the best known Jewish commercial street in Chicago.

The population of North Lawndale dropped to approximately 100,000 between 1930 and 1950. In part, this decline was due to the fact that some of the area's Jewish population had moved northward to communities like Albany Park and Rogers Park. Beginning in the 1940s and continuing into the 1950s, blacks had begun to replace the relocated Jews. Most of these newly arrived blacks — approximately 13,000 in 1950 — lived near the northern boundary of North Lawndale. While the new residents were confined to the northern section of the community, the influx of blacks seemingly enhanced the ethnic diversity of North Lawndale. This led a local newspaper to proclaim in 1955 that in North Lawndale "new people are mingling with the old. The melting pot is bubbling again."

The ethnic diversity of North Lawndale was short-lived. Whites fled North Lawndale in droves, many succumbing to racial fears which were easily manipulated by unscrupulous realtors. The white population of North Lawndale dropped from 87,000 in 1950 to less than 11,000 in 1960. The whites that remained in the community were located primarily south of Cermak Road. During the 1950s North Lawndale's black population increased from 13,000 to more than 113,000. As the incoming blacks saturated residential areas in the community the population rose to an all-time high, nearly 125,000 in 1960, of whom more than 90 percent were black.

The new residents of North Lawndale encountered economic difficulties. As a result of the riots which struck several West Side communities in 1968, many storeowners were forced to move when insurance companies either canceled their policies or increased their premiums. It has been estimated that the effects of the riots, coupled with the racial turnover in North Lawndale between 1960 and 1970, have resulted in the loss of 75 percent of the business establishments and 25 percent of the jobs in the community area. North Lawndale suffered another severe blow when the International Harvester Company tractor works closed in 1969, with the loss of an estimated 3,400 jobs. The depressed economic conditions have lingered; according to the 1980 Census, more than one-fifth of the labor force was unemployed and North Lawndale's median family income was among the 10 lowest of Chicago's 77 community areas.

The population of North Lawndale has decreased by approximately 30,000 in each decade since 1960, and the great majority of the outmigrants has been black. Today blacks comprise 96 percent of the 60,000 who remain. There are about 1,000 whites and 1,000 other non-whites living in the area. Three percent of all residents are Hispanic. The population of North Lawndale is very young — the median age is a little over 22 years and 30 percent are less than 18 years old. More than 60 percent of all households with children under 18 are headed by females. The great majority of all housing units is in small (two to nine unit) apartment buildings.

The most serious problem confronting North Lawndale is inadequate housing. Although the population has dropped by more than 50 percent in the last 20 years, the number of housing units has dropped more than 40 percent during the same time to 18,595, almost all of which are overcrowded. During one period between January, 1970 and June, 1973, only 91 new units were built while 2,714 were demolished. One recent survey estimated that only 8 percent of the structures in one section of North Lawndale were architecturally sound. The deteriorated conditions are the legacy of antiquated housing, real estate speculation during the years of racial transition, inadequate building inspection, lax enforcement of building code violations, and the disregard of property by the tenants.

There have been some limited attempts to address the housing problem in North Lawndale. In 1954, the Chicago Housing Authority opened Ogden Courts, a 136-unit complex in the eastern section of the community. Fourteen years later Kedvale Square, located at 19th and Kedvale streets, was completed. The project was financed through the Federal Housing Administration, in conjunction with the Community Renewal Foundation and business organizations like Sears, Roebuck, and Company. At 19th and Kostner streets a group of businessmen and a minority-owned bank acquired property from the Coca-Cola Company in order to build Lawndale Manor. Completed in 1971, Lawndale Manor consisted of three buildings containing 192 units for low-income persons. Finally, a housing rehabilitation program had been proposed in 1982 for the Douglas Park area. The program's coordinators — Joseph T. Ryerson and Sons Steel Corporation, Mount Sinai hospital, and community residents, needed to raise approximately $500,000 over the following five years for the project.

The minority-owned Pyramidwest Development Corporation sponsored the construction in 1981 of the federally-subsidized Lawndale Terrace, which is located at Roosevelt Road and Kedzie Avenue. The $7 million complex was part of the economic development corporation's five-year plan to bring more than 2,000 new residential units

to the community. In addition to its housing program, Pyramidwest has developed two other projects: the Lawndale Plaza Shopping Center at Roosevelt and Kedzie, and the creation of an industrial park at the former International Harvester site at 26th Street and California Avenue. Neither endeavor has met with much success: Pyramidwest has been unable to attract either a major retailer to the shopping center, or any industries to the industrial park. Unless some sort of commercial or industrial development takes place in the community area or nearby, it would appear that North Lawndale faces a future of further deterioration and greater poverty.

Winston McDowell

South Lawndale

However they may differ today, the origins of South Lawndale and North Lawndale are quite similar. The area, which was largely prairie and swampland, benefited from the land boom that accompanied construction of the Illinois-Michigan Canal, which served as a community area boundary for many years, in 1848. Today, the Stevenson Expressway, built over the old Illinois-Michigan canal bed, is the southern limit. The Chicago, Burlington, and Quincy Railroad was laid in 1863, giving rise to Crawford, a small unincorporated village at the northwestern boundary of the area. Native-born Americans, German and Dutch immigrants were the original settlers of Crawford.

Aside from Crawford, most of the area was farmland. The eastern two-thirds of the community (from Western Avenue to Pulaski Road) was annexed to Chicago via state legislation in 1869, and this area was initially subdivided in 1871. The McCormick reaper plant, built on Western Avenue at 22nd Street after the Fire destroyed the lakefront facility, provided employment to blue-collar workers, and its location east of South Lawndale made it convenient for workers to settle in the area's northeastern portion. Apart from this settlement, South Lawndale did not experience development until the general westward expansion of the city began to bring residents into the eastern part of the area around 1885. Germans and Czechoslovakians gradually moved westward on 22nd Street (which was to become Cermak Road). The remainder of South Lawndale, west of Pulaski Road, was annexed to the city in 1889. South Lawndale began to develop rapidly, but transportation to the central business district was as yet inadequate, with service provided only by the Chicago, Burlington and Quincy and the horse-drawn omnibus service along Ogden Avenue. The Douglas Park branch of the elevated, which came to the general area in the 1890s, was not extended to Crawford Avenue (Pulaski Road) until 1902, and did not reach Cicero until 1907. The elevated trains were easily accessible only to those living in the northern section of South Lawndale.

Meanwhile, the outward movement of industry to sites along the beltline railroads on the western boundary, and along the railroads close to the northern, eastern and southern boundaries induced many workingmen's families to settle in South Lawndale. The construction of the International Harvester Company plant near the southeast corner of South Lawndale, and the Western Electric Company's Hawthorne Works in Cicero, just northwest of the area, drew more settlers. The highly visible Czech and German colonies encouraged more of these peoples, including recent immigrants, to move in. Many new residences were constructed after 1908 and, by 1914, South Lawndale had achieved residential maturity, only a few vacant lots remaining in the southwestern part of the area.

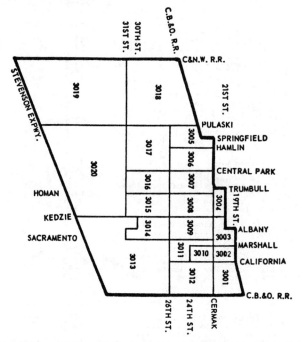

South Lawndale's rapid development during the first two decades of the 20th century brought its population to more than 84,000 in 1920. At this time, Czechoslovakians were by far the largest foreign-born group in South Lawndale, followed by Germans. The foreign-born, plus those of Czechoslovakian and German descent, made up the bulk of the area's total population.

After 1910, Poles began to move in, mostly into the northeastern corner, from the 18th Street and Ashland Avenue vicinity, and replaced former residents that had moved westward to settle the newer communities of Berwyn, Oak Park, and Austin. By 1930, Poles became the most numerous nationality group in the area.

The portion of South Lawndale east of Kedzie Avenue had been the center of earlier settlement, but by 1920, that area was deteriorating, due in part to expanding industrial land use in the southern section and along the eastern boundary. There was still some vacant land south of 31st Street, and to the west a few factories stood amid much undeveloped land.

Between 1920 and 1960, South Lawndale did not change substantially. While the streetcar lines provided more transit facilities, service to the Loop had yet to be initiated. Most residents worked in the area establishments and, by the end of that period, in the western suburbs. The population of South Lawndale declined steadily from 1920 to 1960, by which time it had fallen below 61,000. In 1960, the largest nationality group was Polish, followed by Czechoslovakians and Germans. In 1960, nearly one-fifth of the city's Czechoslovakian population resided in South Lawndale. Blacks moved in slowly during

Community Area 30 -- South Lawndale
Population and Housing Characteristics, 1930-1980

	1980	1970	1960	1950	1940	1930
Total Population.......	75,204	62,895	60,940	66,977	70,915	76,749
% Male...................	53.3	51.3	50.4	51.4	51.9	51.7
% Female.................	46.7	48.7	49.6	48.6	48.1	48.3
% White..................	44.6	86.1	93.9	97.9	98.9	98.9
% Black..................	8.6	10.3	5.9	2.0	1.1	0.9
% Other Nonwhite Races...	46.8	3.6	0.2	0.1	0.0	0.2
% Under 5 Years Old......	12.1	9.9	9.8	8.6	5.9	7.8
% 5-19 Years Old.........	28.4	27.1	21.7	17.5	21.3	29.7
% 20-44 Years Old........	40.4	34.5	34.7	43.6	46.6	45.1
% 45-64 Years Old........	12.7	19.6	23.5	23.4	21.7	14.5
% 65 Years and Older.....	6.4	8.9	10.3	6.9	4.5	2.9
Median School Years	7.9	9.2	8.9	8.8	8.0	*
Total Housing Units....	20,899	20,187	20,308	20,495	19,873	*
% In One-Unit Structures.	12.3	15.3	15.6	*	*	*
% Owner Occupied.........	34.2	35.2	39.8	39.2	35.5	*
% Renter Occupied........	58.3	59.2	56.5	59.6	63.3	*
% Vacant.................	7.5	5.6	3.7	1.2	1.2	*
% 1+ Persons per Room....	24.7	13.3	9.8	9.7	*	*

Community Area 30 -- South Lawndale
Selected Characteristics of Census Tracts: 1980

Tract Number	Total	3001	3002	3003	3004	3005	3006	3007	3008	3009	3010
Total Population.............	75204	2347	1225	1905	558	3636	3354	5443	5083	5507	1490
% Male...................	53.3	53.6	54.4	46.5	46.2	50.5	49.5	51.6	54.2	51.5	52.6
% Black..................	8.6	0.8	0.2	45.4	98.6	12.2	19.0	2.6	1.3	1.1	0.0
% Other Nonwhite.........	46.8	68.5	71.9	38.8	0.0	48.2	39.0	60.6	52.3	56.0	80.8
% Of Spanish Origin......	74.1	84.6	88.7	46.7	0.0	76.0	69.9	89.1	90.2	86.7	89.0
% Foreign Born...........	42.2	50.8	62.7	29.7	0.0	41.6	35.2	50.5	57.8	51.9	53.4
% Living In Group Quarters..	6.3	0.0	1.7	0.0	0.0	0.1	2.5	0.7	0.0	0.0	0.0
% 13 Years Old And Under...	29.1	33.4	33.8	25.8	23.8	32.1	29.1	35.1	33.4	33.2	32.8
% 14-20 Years Old........	13.8	13.4	13.6	11.5	18.6	12.3	14.9	13.7	14.7	13.4	13.6
% 21-64 Years Old........	50.6	48.6	49.3	41.2	50.0	49.6	48.4	46.6	48.4	49.0	48.3
% 65-74 Years Old........	4.1	3.2	2.4	14.3	5.2	3.7	4.9	3.0	2.1	2.6	3.4
% 75 Years Old And Over...	2.4	1.4	1.0	7.1	2.3	2.3	2.7	1.5	1.4	1.7	1.9
% In Different House......	53.6	51.4	77.9	44.8	28.5	51.7	44.3	51.7	49.1	54.8	53.4
% Families With Female Head...	17.5	18.0	22.8	35.3	43.4	19.5	27.1	20.6	15.2	16.3	13.0
Median School Years Completed....	7.9	7.9	7.9	7.9	10.4	7.9	9.2	7.9	7.9	7.9	7.9
Median Family Income, 1979...$$	16410	15890	10458	14323	16154	16265	15079	14371	16308	12169	16433
% Income Below Poverty Level.	19.5	21.3	40.4	31.1	31.3	16.9	23.8	21.9	18.4	24.8	26.0
% Income Of $30,000 Or More.....	14.0	9.8	4.4	10.4	17.0	8.7	15.0	8.5	15.9	9.8	18.8
% White Collar Workers.	25.7	18.4	18.2	26.0	22.9	24.4	28.1	24.8	22.1	25.1	27.9
% Civilian Labor Force Unemployed.	13.7	16.5	18.4	15.7	27.2	12.8	8.0	15.1	18.4	24.3	14.9
% Riding To Work By Automobile....	64.4	50.1	52.2	61.9	77.7	73.0	73.9	61.6	67.3	57.7	78.7
Mean Commuting Time - Minutes...	30.8	29.2	29.9	29.5	37.5	31.7	26.5	32.2	37.0	29.7	25.9
Population Per Household..........	3.6	3.7	4.1	2.5	3.7	3.7	3.8	4.0	4.0	3.8	3.9
Total Housing Units..........	20899	730	309	791	158	1053	925	1450	1421	1620	413
% Condominiums.................	0.2	0.0	0.0	0.0	0.0	0.0	0.0	0.0	3.5	0.0	0.0
% Built 1970 Or Later...........	3.2	0.0	0.0	42.4	0.0	2.2	0.6	3.0	3.4	0.7	3.3
% Owner Occupied.............	34.2	22.5	22.7	10.0	43.0	28.0	35.7	25.4	24.9	23.1	32.9
% With 1+ Persons Per Room.......	24.7	25.8	43.2	16.2	15.9	23.8	21.0	29.4	33.3	30.8	32.6
Median Value: Owner Units.......$$	27700	–	–	–	–	–	28800	23600	20300	18300	–
Median Rent: Rental Units.......$$	150	133	150	86	161	155	157	155	147	137	142
Median Number Of Rooms: All Units.	4.3	4.2	3.9	3.4	5.3	4.3	5.0	4.4	4.2	4.1	4.3

Tract Number	3011	3012	3013	3014	3015	3016	3017	3018	3019	3020
Total Population.............	2653	4440	4763	967	3501	4811	7657	12103	1439	2322
% Male...................	53.2	50.8	87.1	51.4	50.2	50.6	52.0	49.8	47.9	49.5
% Black..................	0.3	3.2	69.1	1.1	0.5	0.7	0.4	1.1	1.0	0.6
% Other Nonwhite.........	61.7	44.6	10.8	54.6	44.6	52.6	42.8	44.1	37.7	33.2
% Of Spanish Origin......	82.8	74.8	11.5	82.2	84.1	81.9	76.9	74.1	68.9	64.4
% Foreign Born...........	47.0	41.8	4.2	1.2	50.9	50.2	46.7	40.6	35.4	29.0
% Living In Group Quarters..	0.0	0.0	95.5	0.4	0.3	0.0	0.3	0.1	0.0	0.0
% 13 Years Old And Under...	30.0	30.9	1.2	32.5	31.7	31.5	29.3	29.6	27.2	26.7
% 14-20 Years Old........	13.4	14.1	20.4	13.4	13.7	14.2	12.1	12.1	15.2	12.4
% 21-64 Years Old........	52.0	49.8	74.8	50.5	48.3	48.4	50.4	49.9	50.1	48.6
% 65-74 Years Old........	2.7	3.6	1.2	2.1	3.8	3.7	5.1	4.9	5.4	8.9
% 75 Years Old And Over...	1.8	1.7	2.4	1.6	2.5	2.2	3.1	3.0	2.0	3.4
% In Different House......	61.5	44.2	59.3	49.2	56.7	60.0	57.1	56.5	46.9	41.4
% Families With Female Head......	16.2	25.6	14.8	22.1	12.2	15.0	11.5	16.1	7.9	12.4
Median School Years Completed....	7.9	9.1	11.5	7.9	7.9	7.9	7.9	9.3	10.9	10.2
Median Family Income, 1979...$$	16209	14821	14107	9432	15300	18781	18686	18012	21827	20931
% Income Below Poverty Level.	19.2	23.0	14.8	40.0	20.9	18.8	12.4	14.9	18.1	3.7
% Income Of $30,000 Or More.....	15.0	10.8	9.3	15.8	11.3	17.8	13.0	16.3	37.7	24.8
% White Collar Workers.	22.3	28.4	0.0	26.7	20.0	22.4	24.3	29.3	34.1	40.7
% Civilian Labor Force Unemployed.	14.6	16.2	0.0	10.6	14.1	13.4	7.1	10.1	9.0	10.9
% Riding To Work By Automobile....	64.5	58.9	67.1	49.0	62.3	66.8	68.3	64.2	75.2	60.3
Mean Commuting Time - Minutes...	27.7	28.9	26.9	29.1	30.0	31.1	33.3	30.5	25.1	31.7
Population Per Household..........	3.6	3.6	3.5	3.9	3.8	3.8	3.8	3.4	3.5	3.3
Total Housing Units..........	804	1349	65	293	998	1400	2352	3617	415	736
% Condominiums.................	0.0	0.0	0.0	0.0	0.0	0.0	0.0	0.0	0.0	0.0
% Built 1970 Or Later...........	0.0	0.0	0.0	1.9	0.0	2.2	0.0	3.3	0.0	2.2
% Owner Occupied.............	23.3	27.1	41.5	29.7	36.7	39.2	42.3	43.5	64.1	65.9
% With 1+ Persons Per Room.......	27.5	22.7	16.1	32.4	28.6	26.4	21.5	20.2	20.0	17.5
Median Value: Owner Units.......$$	–	20900	–	–	22900	26300	29800	30400	34500	28800
Median Rent: Rental Units.......$$	140	137	161	148	152	154	159	159	159	158
Median Number Of Rooms: All Units.	4.2	4.4	4.4	4.2	4.2	4.2	4.3	4.5	4.5	4.3

this period, and by 1960 comprised almost 6 percent of the area's population, residing predominantly near the northern industrial area, adjacent to the growing black settlement in North Lawndale.

Since 1960, however, South Lawndale has become predominantly Hispanic. The 1960 Census counted 258 Puerto Ricans (four-tenths of 1 percent of the area's population). In 1970, about a third of the population was of Spanish origin, and today more than 74 percent is Hispanic. The total population of South Lawndale increased by more than 23 percent from 1960 to 1980, as the influx of Hispanics was much greater than the out-migration of Poles, Czechoslovakians and Ger-

mans in that period. Today, more than 50,000 Mexicans live in South Lawndale, two-thirds of the community total. The area is home to 20 percent of all Mexicans in the city, and this is the greatest community concentration of Mexicans in Chicago. The black area population peaked at 10 percent in 1970, and dropped to just under 9 percent in 1980. In 1980, more than half of South Lawndale's nearly 6,500 blacks lived in the southeastern corner (Tract 3013).

Very few new units have been added to South Lawndale's housing stock since 1920. Most new residential construction in the twenties took place in the western portion of the area. Only 2 percent of the 1960

Community Area 30 -- South Lawndale
Selected Characteristics of Census Tracts: 1970

Tract Number	TOTAL	3001	3002	3003	3004	3005	3006	3007	3008	3009	3010
Total Population	62895	2121	999	1707	680	3062	3358	4490	4517	4820	1268
% Male	51.3	50.0	52.6	49.3	49.3	46.9	50.5	49.1	49.3	49.9	48.6
% Black	10.3	6.2	2.7	35.6	98.1	21.0	28.3	1.5	8.4	4.2	0.2
% Other Nonwhite	3.7	10.7	7.3	3.0	0.0	2.4	6.8	7.6	4.2	6.9	5.1
% Of Spanish Language	31.9	65.3	62.4	35.0	0.9	27.5	37.8	49.2	50.5	50.1	57.9
% Foreign Born	22.4	27.9	29.3	23.1	0.0	19.5	15.6	31.2	30.3	28.3	28.4
% Living In Group Quarters	5.6	0.4	0.6	0.4	0.7	0.7	3.5	0.7	0.2	0.6	0.0
% 13 Years Old And Under	26.6	30.6	30.6	35.6	36.5	29.5	27.7	30.8	31.0	30.2	32.1
% 14-20 Years Old	12.3	13.2	13.6	13.1	15.4	12.1	13.1	11.8	12.6	11.2	15.1
% 21-64 Years Old	52.2	49.7	50.6	46.7	44.7	48.9	49.7	49.9	48.6	50.9	46.5
% 65-74 Years Old	5.4	3.9	3.0	3.2	2.4	5.8	5.4	4.5	4.4	4.3	4.2
% 75 Years Old And Over	3.5	2.6	2.2	1.3	1.0	3.7	4.2	2.9	3.4	3.4	2.1
% In Different House	49.5	48.9	27.0	41.0	60.8	55.8	52.4	52.2	44.6	56.2	45.4
% Families With Female Head	14.9	16.4	10.2	16.7	20.8	18.4	14.2	14.0	16.6	16.3	15.0
Median School Years Completed	9.1	8.9	9.0	8.9	9.5	9.8	10.9	8.6	8.8	8.6	8.7
Median Family Income, 1969.....$$	9044	7567	6940	7551	6944	8106	11690	8500	7611	7923	8418
% Income Below Poverty Level	11.7	11.7	9.7	15.3	17.3	21.2	4.4	10.9	20.7	16.2	13.5
% Income of $15,000 or More	15.8	16.9	21.7	7.5	11.2	6.0	38.5	12.2	12.7	12.7	12.1
% White Collar Workers	12.1	9.7	14.5	12.8	6.6	14.5	19.0	7.3	10.0	12.7	10.9
% Civilian Labor Force Unemployed	3.9	3.5	6.5	4.9	5.8	6.0	2.4	2.0	2.8	5.4	3.6
% Riding To Work By Automobile	54.3	38.8	48.7	54.1	59.8	55.4	52.5	52.8	50.6	51.9	56.9
Population Per Household	3.1	3.3	3.2	3.6	4.1	3.1	3.3	3.3	3.4	3.2	3.6
Total Housing Units	20220	693	347	540	185	1023	1020	1436	1465	1584	372
% Condominiums & Cooperatives	0.3	0.0	0.0	0.0	0.0	0.0	0.0	0.5	0.0	0.5	0.0
% Built 1960 Or Later	0.9	0.0	0.0	0.0	0.0	0.6	2.3	0.0	0.0	0.4	0.0
% Owner Occupied	35.1	24.0	22.8	16.3	34.6	26.1	32.5	29.1	28.2	25.6	28.2
% With 1+ Persons Per Room	14.0	22.5	14.5	21.5	23.3	13.1	13.1	16.9	19.3	17.3	20.0
Median Value: Owner Units......$$	12600	–	–	–	–	–	14400	11700	10700	9300	–
Median Rent: Rental Units......$$	75	66	71	88	104	84	93	76	78	67	69
Median Number Of Rooms: All Units	4.3	4.2	4.1	4.4	5.1	4.4	4.9	4.4	4.3	4.2	4.5

Tract Number	3011	3012	3013	3014	3015	3016	3017	3018	3019	3020
Total Population	2211	4652	3370	904	2664	3549	6062	9395	1106	1960
% Male	49.5	50.0	91.6	50.9	48.8	47.4	47.9	48.2	49.1	50.1
% Black	0.7	7.4	71.2	0.4	0.0	0.0	0.0	0.1	0.0	0.0
% Other Nonwhite	6.7	5.3	1.2	0.1	2.7	1.5	1.4	0.6	1.2	0.4
% Of Spanish Language	48.9	30.2	2.3	29.0	42.4	30.9	19.1	14.3	7.1	5.7
% Foreign Born	25.6	20.1	1.2	19.8	24.1	27.8	28.1	17.9	18.0	14.7
% Living In Group Quarters	0.4	0.4	93.9	0.0	0.0	0.6	0.1	0.5	0.0	0.0
% 13 Years Old And Under	31.6	29.2	2.3	29.4	28.9	25.9	22.2	24.9	23.2	21.8
% 14-20 Years Old	12.2	14.7	25.0	13.3	9.6	9.6	9.7	10.1	10.3	9.2
% 21-64 Years Old	49.3	50.2	71.6	49.3	51.1	52.2	55.2	52.6	54.6	57.6
% 65-74 Years Old	3.8	3.3	0.8	5.0	6.5	7.0	8.3	7.7	6.3	7.2
% 75 Years Old And Over	3.2	2.6	0.3	3.0	3.9	5.2	4.7	4.7	5.5	4.1
% In Different House	43.8	59.6	4.3	46.7	49.2	44.7	52.3	57.3	63.5	66.0
% Families With Female Head	13.6	19.9	20.0	13.8	15.1	14.1	12.2	13.8	12.0	11.7
Median School Years Completed	8.6	10.0	9.7	8.8	9.0	8.9	9.0	9.7	9.3	9.2
Median Family Income, 1969.....$$	8092	8433	8364	8833	8400	9660	9967	9694	12097	10170
% Income Below Poverty Level	10.8	13.6	16.7	16.1	13.6	12.6	6.3	6.9	1.7	7.6
% Income of $15,000 or More	12.8	12.8	0.0	11.6	10.4	18.0	18.8	17.5	24.0	17.9
% White Collar Workers	11.5	14.5	17.2	7.9	12.0	9.4	12.8	14.1	6.6	7.7
% Civilian Labor Force Unemployed	5.9	3.6	0.0	8.1	5.0	4.0	4.2	2.6	5.2	2.9
% Riding To Work By Automobile	49.9	48.6	38.2	60.4	63.1	60.0	52.0	58.1	63.5	60.4
Population Per Household	3.3	3.4	3.4	3.3	3.0	2.9	2.7	2.9	2.9	2.8
Total Housing Units	703	1405	63	294	953	1302	2303	3403	403	726
% Condominiums & Cooperatives	0.9	0.7	0.0	0.0	0.0	0.0	0.2	0.5	0.0	0.0
% Built 1960 Or Later	0.7	6.2	0.0	0.0	0.0	0.3	0.0	0.9	1.0	2.0
% Owner Occupied	24.3	24.4	49.2	37.8	40.1	41.6	43.4	43.2	65.3	62.0
% With 1+ Persons Per Room	18.9	16.9	15.0	19.1	14.3	10.9	9.9	8.9	8.5	9.1
Median Value: Owner Units......$$	–	10500	–	–	11400	11600	12300	13400	14000	12700
Median Rent: Rental Units......$$	67	75	85	74	68	70	74	76	74	76
Median Number Of Rooms: All Units	4.2	4.4	4.6	4.3	4.2	4.2	4.2	4.4	4.3	4.1

housing units were in structures built since 1940, and fewer than 600 units were added between 1960 and 1980. Nearly one-fourth of the housing units in South Lawndale are overcrowded (contain more than one person per room). More than 39 percent of all South Lawndale residents live in overcrowded units — more than twice the city percentage. Most housing units in the area are in two-, three- and four-unit structures, 15 percent are single-family homes, and about 2.5 percent are located in buildings with 10 or more units. Thirty-four percent of all 1980 housing units were owner-occupied, and Hispanics inhabited 57 percent of all owner-occupied units. In 1941-42, the Chicago Housing Authority erected the Lawndale Gardens project, row-houses containing 128 units, in Tract 3012. The median value of single-family, owner-occupied homes in South Lawndale was $27,706 in 1980, less than 60 percent of the city median. Cook County Jail, the Criminal Court House, the House of Correction, and the Municipal Contagious Disease Hospital are all located in Tract 3013.

Industrial areas developed between 1920 and 1960 to a point where they and the large railroad yards virtually surrounded the residential area of South Lawndale. Considerable industrial development took place along the western boundary on previously undeveloped land. Also, along the Sanitary and Ship Canal, to the south, large industrial and public utility plants were built. Prior to the late 1960s, the huge International Harvester plant dominated the industrial area along the eastern border. At that time, however, Harvester and other industrial employers began to relocate, leaving unemployment in their wake. A major retail center is located in the middle of South Lawndale, including stores on 26th Street from Kedzie to Karlov avenues.

In recent years, there has been a tendency to refer to North Lawndale simply as "Lawndale," which started about the time the North Lawndale urban renewal project of the 1960s was given that name. Perhaps to avoid identification with North Lawndale, perhaps to assert an independent identity, there has been a movement in South Lawndale to rename that community area "Little Village." Large signs with that name have been painted on railroad overpasses. A Little Village Community Council and a Little Village Chamber of Commerce share headquarters on West 26th Street.

Will Hogan

Lower West Side

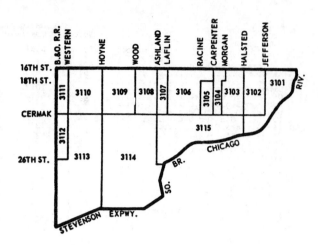

During the early days of Chicago, a region of swamps and truck farms lay south and west of the growing settlement, near the South Branch of the Chicago River. The territory, located at the eastern end of the portage which connected the Des Plaines River with Lake Michigan, was called the Southwest Side, later the Lower West Side. The northeastern third of the Lower West Side was included within the city limits at the time of the incorporation of the City of Chicago in 1837. Much of the land in the area was owned by John Welsh or the Illinois-Michigan Canal Commission. As the canal neared completion, however, the land in its vicinity rose in value and was sold. By 1845, all of the land in the area had been claimed, but there was little settlement except by truck farmers. These farmers used two main roads, presently Halsted Street and Blue Island Avenue, respectively, to bring their produce to the city.

Initial industrial development along the South Branch of the Chicago River took place as the canal was completed in 1848, and as the Chicago and Alton Railroad entered the area in the early 1850s. In 1853, state legislation annexed the remaining sections of the Lower West Side to the city. Although the area had been thoroughly subdivided, the population consisted of truck farmers along with a scattering of workingmen who lived close to the river. Extensive settlement did not take place until after 1857. No houses had been constructed west of Ashland Avenue through the 1860s. Blue Island Avenue was known as Black Road at the time due to its black cinder constitution. Lumber yards, brickyards, and a limestone quarry could be found along the river bank. Original settlers of the area were native Americans, Irish and Germans.

The Lower West Side was an area of rapid growth during the 1870s, especially east of Ashland Avenue. Though the Fire did not touch the area, it did encourage development, particularly west of Ashland, due to the Lower West Side's proximity beyond the fire limits, enabling workingmen to rebuild their inexpensive frame homes. The industrial district expanded as industries relocated after the Fire. After 1871, slips were dredged out along the river and dock frontage and private railroad sidings provided for prospective tenants. Several industries moved in along the river between Ashland and Western avenues. The McCormick Reaper Company built a new plant at 27th Street and Western Avenue, which opened in 1873, and a facility at 22nd Street and Western Avenue in 1903. The McCormick Company also donated land for the construction of churches and built homes to sell to its employees. More lumber yards located by the river, and wood-product industries were established nearby.

By 1875, the first public improvements were introduced to the Lower West Side. This and industrial expansion triggered rapid residential growth. To make room for the improved drainage and sewer system, vaulted streets and sidewalks were installed 8 to 10 feet above original levels, leaving the first floors of many homes below street level. Germans and Irish were still moving in during this time, but Poles and Czechoslovakians had begun to move in as well.

The Lower West Side continued to develop rapidly through the final decades of the 19th century. Residential growth was encouraged by further industrial expansion and improved public transportation. The Polish and Czechoslovakian communities continued to expand. The Lower West Side achieved residential maturity by 1895, at which time some of the older frame structures in the southeastern area of initial settlement began to display signs of deterioration, due in part to the expansion of industry into what had previously been strictly residential areas.

The early years of the 20th century witnessed further expansion of industry and of railroads in the Lower West Side. The Illinois-

Michigan Canal had silted up by the turn of the century, and so industry welcomed the completion of the new Chicago Sanitary and Ship Canal, parallel to and north of the older waterway, in 1900. Czechoslovakians continued to move in, replacing the rapidly migrating Irish and German populations. Lithuanians, attracted by the prospects for industrial employment, began to move in around the turn of the century also, and a small Italian community developed, composed of about 1,200 migrants from Tuscany. The Lower West Side reached its historic population peak at 85,680 in 1920. The influence of the Czech immigrants, many of whom came from Bohemia, became so pervasive that the central part of the community area, around 22nd Street, began to be called "Pilsen," after one of the principal Bohemian cities. In 1932, after the sudden death of the popular Czech-descended Mayor of Chicago, Anton Cermak, the name of 22nd Street was changed to Cermak Road. After 1920, the Czech population began to move west, along Cermak Road. By 1930, the largest nationalities of the Lower West Side were Poles, Czechoslovakians, Yugoslavians, Lithuanians, Germans and Italians.

The area population dropped precipitously, by almost 20,000, in the 1920s. The following decade brought the Depression and another loss of more than 8,000. Losses in the 30 years after that averaged about 4,500 per decade so that, in 1970, the total population stood at less than 45,000, a decline approaching 50 percent over five decades. In the last 20 years, a Hispanic influx has stabilized the population total. Mexicans began moving in in the early 1950s, and by 1960 had become so numerous that only Polish foreign stock outnumbered them. By 1960 Puerto Ricans had begun to move in. In 1970, more than half of the residents of the Lower West Side were Spanish speaking. Since 1970, the total population has grown by 1 percent, the first increase in 60 years.

In 1980, almost 78 percent of the area population was Hispanic. More than 32,000 Mexicans, 72 percent of the total, reside in the Lower West Side, making this the second highest concentration of Mexicans of all community areas in the city of Chicago. In 1980, only the area's southeastern (Tract 3115) and southwestern (Tracts 3112, 3113, which are still the Italian district) corners, contained non-Hispanic majorities. Although the four tracts south of Cermak Road comprise around half of the acreage of the area, they are inhabited by less than 18 percent of all residents, due to their industrial nature. All tracts north of Cermak Road are more than two-thirds Mexican. Almost one-third of Chicago's Mexican population resided in the contiguous South Lawndale-Lower West Side area in 1980.

The volume of housing stock in the Lower West Side has declined steadily since 1940, and little new residential construction has taken place in the area since 1930. Nearly 1,300 units of housing were lost between 1940 and 1960, and by 1980 another 1,939 housing units had disappeared. In 1980 one in every five housing units was overcrowded,

Community Area 31 -- Lower West Side
Population and Housing Characteristics, 1930-1980

	1980	1970	1960	1950	1940	1930
Total Population	44,951	44,498	48,448	53,991	57,908	66,198
% Male	52.2	50.8	51.0	50.8	52.1	52.7
%Female	47.8	49.2	49.0	49.2	47.9	47.3
% White	46.2	93.8	98.6	99.7	100.0	99.3
% Black	1.1	2.4	1.1	0.3	0.0	0.0
% Other Nonwhite Races	52.7	3.8	0.3	0.0	0.0	0.7
% Under 5 Years Old	12.1	10.8	12.0	9.6	6.6	7.9
% 5-19 Years Old	28.3	31.3	25.6	20.2	23.8	34.2
% 20-44 Years Old	37.5	32.5	34.5	42.6	42.1	39.5
% 45-64 Years Old	15.1	18.6	19.0	20.3	23.2	15.5
% 65 Years and Older	7.0	6.8	8.9	7.3	4.3	2.9
Median School Years	7.9	8.5	8.5	8.5	7.4	*
Total Housing Units	14,673	14,509	16,612	17,242	17,907	*
% In One-Unit Structures	7.0	8.5	9.2	*	*	*
% Owner Occupied	22.0	23.4	23.2	23.6	20.0	*
% Renter Occupied	66.3	66.7	68.7	74.0	74.4	*
% Vacant	11.7	9.9	8.1	2.4	5.6	*
% 1+ Persons per Room	22.7	18.1	14.8	11.9	*	*

Community Area 31 -- Lower West Side
Selected Characteristics of Census Tracts: 1980

Tract Number	Total	3101	3102	3103	3104	3105	3106	3107	3108	3109	3110
Total Population	44951	411	2027	2244	1936	2099	8207	2388	5927	5859	6423
% Male	52.2	56.2	52.8	51.6	51.9	53.0	52.8	53.0	52.3	51.4	52.1
% Black	1.1	0.0	0.3	1.5	3.3	0.3	2.4	1.1	0.6	0.3	0.1
% Other Nonwhite	52.8	74.5	53.0	52.4	63.4	61.5	58.7	68.6	56.3	46.1	51.3
% Of Spanish Origin	77.6	78.6	74.5	84.5	86.9	90.3	89.5	90.1	83.6	74.5	75.1
% Foreign Born	44.7	49.4	41.4	49.2	48.9	42.2	52.4	54.8	39.9	42.5	44.0
% Living In Group Quarters	0.4	0.0	0.0	0.0	0.0	0.0	0.0	2.8	0.7	0.0	0.0
% 13 Years Old And Under	29.0	24.8	26.8	29.4	31.6	33.5	32.2	28.6	29.8	28.0	30.0
% 14-20 Years Old	13.6	13.1	13.2	15.0	15.3	13.7	14.4	15.7	13.7	13.8	13.7
% 21-64 Years Old	50.3	55.0	52.9	50.8	47.7	48.4	45.8	51.4	50.8	51.8	49.8
% 65-74 Years Old	4.7	5.8	4.8	3.2	3.6	3.0	5.0	2.9	4.0	4.4	4.3
% 75 Years Old And Over	2.3	1.2	2.3	1.6	1.7	1.4	2.6	1.4	1.7	2.0	2.2
% In Different House	48.1	68.6	40.6	49.9	40.2	55.5	52.0	44.1	48.5	47.0	54.4
% Families With Female Head	19.3	29.8	20.3	18.0	20.6	19.3	20.0	20.7	18.2	19.6	17.3
Median School Years Completed	7.9	7.9	7.9	7.9	7.9	7.9	7.9	7.9	7.9	7.9	7.9
Median Family Income, 1979 $$	14487	11250	16397	18655	13056	11655	12275	15578	13142	14024	15077
% Income Below Poverty Level	23.5	6.6	17.3	27.3	26.3	27.8	28.4	28.0	26.3	23.0	24.0
% Income Of $30,000 Or More	12.5	8.3	11.7	19.1	12.9	7.3	9.2	14.5	11.5	11.8	12.1
% White Collar Workers	27.3	41.9	26.8	26.5	26.3	26.7	21.5	12.5	29.5	28.2	22.1
% Civilian Labor Force Unemployed	16.2	12.4	26.0	11.7	24.2	21.0	12.8	8.6	11.3	17.7	24.2
% Riding To Work By Automobile	57.0	57.6	46.8	65.0	70.1	43.5	58.0	48.9	56.2	57.2	56.5
Mean Commuting Time - Minutes	28.7	32.5	27.3	23.0	33.3	28.8	30.5	27.7	28.5	28.4	29.6
Population Per Household	3.5	3.3	3.3	3.7	3.6	3.8	3.6	3.9	3.4	3.4	3.6
Total Housing Units	14673	138	709	723	644	626	2616	647	1782	1940	2014
% Condominiums	0.1	0.0	0.0	0.0	0.0	0.0	0.5	0.0	0.0	0.0	0.0
% Built 1970 Or Later	3.4	0.0	1.5	1.8	5.4	1.3	11.3	0.0	2.1	0.9	0.3
% Owner Occupied	22.0	20.3	21.7	21.7	22.0	20.6	14.0	16.5	21.9	21.6	27.1
% With 1+ Persons Per Room	22.7	20.6	21.2	23.7	29.2	25.7	27.2	28.6	26.1	22.2	23.1
Median Value: Owner Units $$	21700	-	-	-	-	-	-	-	-	24000	22500
Median Rent: Rental Units $$	129	127	125	133	115	131	124	136	128	130	136
Median Number Of Rooms: All Units	4.3	4.3	4.3	4.7	4.1	4.6	4.1	4.4	4.4	4.3	4.3

Tract Number	3111	3112	3113	3114	3115
Total Population	49	238	4254	2803	86
% Male	-	49.6	49.6	52.8	-
% Black	-	0.0	0.0	0.5	-
% Other Nonwhite	-	10.9	34.5	47.7	-
% Of Spanish Origin	-	43.7	46.2	64.3	-
% Foreign Born	-	43.0	36.0	40.0	-
% Living In Group Quarters	-	0.0	0.0	0.0	-
% 13 Years Old And Under	-	28.2	22.1	26.1	-
% 14-20 Years Old	-	8.0	10.2	12.9	-
% 21-64 Years Old	-	54.2	54.5	52.5	-
% 65-74 Years Old	-	5.5	8.2	6.4	-
% 75 Years Old And Over	-	4.2	5.0	2.1	-
% In Different House	-	36.6	39.4	43.8	-
% Families With Female Head	-	15.2	22.9	16.5	-
Median School Years Completed	-	7.9	11.0	7.9	-
Median Family Income, 1979 $$	-	9079	17258	17618	-
% Income Below Poverty Level	-	41.7	14.2	15.6	-
% Income Of $30,000 Or More	-	0.0	15.8	18.7	-
% White Collar Workers	-	45.3	38.1	40.2	-
% Civilian Labor Force Unemployed	-	20.2	13.7	10.3	-
% Riding To Work By Automobile	-	14.7	61.1	62.5	-
Mean Commuting Time - Minutes	-	29.1	26.7	29.1	-
Population Per Household	-	3.0	2.7	3.3	-
Total Housing Units	14	101	1733	983	3
% Condominiums	-	0.0	0.0	0.0	-
% Built 1970 Or Later	-	0.0	2.3	3.1	-
% Owner Occupied	-	18.8	28.1	28.5	-
% With 1+ Persons Per Room	-	13.7	10.1	18.4	-
Median Value: Owner Units $$	-	-	23900	21600	-
Median Rent: Rental Units $$	-	111	127	137	-
Median Number Of Rooms: All Units	-	4.3	4.4	4.4	-

Community Area 31 -- Lower West Side
Selected Characteristics of Census Tracts: 1970

Tract Number	TOTAL	3101	3102	3103	3104	3105	3106	3107	3108	3109	3110
Total Population	44498	515	2122	2881	2063	2251	8403	2493	5492	5521	5467
% Male	50.8	48.7	51.7	52.7	50.2	52.2	52.3	50.9	49.7	49.8	50.4
% Black	2.4	0.2	0.2	4.3	6.2	0.1	2.9	1.6	4.4	0.5	2.0
% Other Nonwhite	3.8	0.0	3.5	3.4	5.1	3.8	3.9	2.6	6.8	2.7	4.1
% Of Spanish Language	54.9	58.6	59.5	70.2	74.5	81.1	79.5	62.4	58.0	45.9	39.8
% Foreign Born	25.6	11.9	26.1	33.6	32.0	46.8	28.7	24.7	22.7	22.0	18.0
% Living In Group Quarters	0.7	0.0	1.6	0.2	0.0	0.0	1.1	1.7	0.2	0.2	0.6
% 13 Years Old And Under	30.6	30.3	25.3	35.3	33.6	31.9	35.2	32.7	31.1	29.2	30.3
% 14-20 Years Old	13.3	11.3	13.1	14.9	15.5	13.3	13.7	15.6	14.4	13.0	12.8
% 21-64 Years Old	49.3	52.0	52.2	43.9	45.2	47.9	46.4	46.8	48.2	51.5	50.4
% 65-74 Years Old	4.1	4.9	5.4	3.6	3.6	2.8	2.9	3.0	4.0	3.8	4.1
% 75 Years Old And Over	2.6	1.6	3.9	2.3	2.0	2.8	1.7	1.9	2.2	2.5	2.5
% In Different House	54.4	78.6	54.2	43.9	61.4	43.6	53.5	47.5	50.4	53.0	57.8
% Families With Female Head	14.6	10.4	15.3	16.8	14.3	13.1	12.7	16.2	17.1	15.6	15.0
Median School Years Completed	8.5	8.5	8.5	8.0	8.0	7.6	7.5	8.4	8.6	8.7	8.8
Median Family Income, 1969 $$	8557	8603	8705	8479	8783	7090	7746	7177	8552	8689	9326
% Income Below Poverty Level	15.5	10.3	14.0	19.6	13.9	14.0	20.5	23.7	16.4	12.6	15.1
% Income of $15,000 or More	14.2	12.1	16.9	17.2	8.5	13.0	11.3	8.3	13.0	15.7	15.9
% White Collar Workers	10.5	0.0	10.3	9.8	6.0	6.6	9.4	11.8	12.2	11.1	6.8
% Civilian Labor Force Unemployed	6.1	1.8	5.5	4.8	10.9	4.5	7.9	3.3	7.9	3.7	6.8
% Riding To Work By Automobile	46.8	63.4	49.8	44.7	49.8	57.9	41.8	53.0	46.4	44.9	48.3
Population Per Household	3.4	3.2	3.1	3.8	3.7	3.5	3.7	3.6	3.5	3.2	3.3
Total Housing Units	14557	178	778	891	656	709	2562	739	1759	1848	1806
% Condominiums & Cooperatives	0.1	0.0	0.0	0.0	0.0	0.0	0.0	0.0	0.4	0.0	0.4
% Built 1960 Or Later	0.9	3.3	0.0	1.0	1.1	0.7	0.6	0.7	1.0	1.1	2.2
% Owner Occupied	23.1	27.5	22.0	21.1	20.0	19.2	14.6	15.8	23.1	26.8	26.9
% With 1+ Persons Per Room	18.2	16.1	13.8	24.7	25.9	21.6	25.3	21.3	19.4	15.5	17.1
Median Value: Owner Units $$	10500	-	-	-	-	-	9200	-	10000	10900	11400
Median Rent: Rental Units $$	63	57	56	63	57	59	64	65	65	61	65
Median Number Of Rooms: All Units	4.3	4.3	4.4	4.5	4.4	4.3	4.1	4.3	4.4	4.3	4.4

Tract Number	3111	3112	3113	3114
Total Population	64	350	4254	2622
% Male	-	55.1	48.9	49.7
% Black	-	6.3	2.4	0.7
% Other Nonwhite	-	5.1	1.2	3.8
% Of Spanish Language	-	19.6	12.7	27.6
% Foreign Born	-	19.3	25.5	17.1
% Living In Group Quarters	-	2.6	1.4	0.4
% 13 Years Old And Under	-	23.1	20.7	28.6
% 14-20 Years Old	-	14.0	10.1	11.8
% 21-64 Years Old	-	57.4	56.1	52.0
% 65-74 Years Old	-	3.1	7.2	4.8
% 75 Years Old And Over	-	2.3	5.8	2.8
% In Different House	-	63.6	66.8	57.1
% Families With Female Head	-	10.5	12.7	15.0
Median School Years Completed	-	9.0	8.9	9.4
Median Family Income, 1969 $$	-	6964	9729	9387
% Income Below Poverty Level	-	30.3	7.6	9.9
% Income of $15,000 or More	-	5.3	17.1	18.8
% White Collar Workers	-	4.2	18.1	11.1
% Civilian Labor Force Unemployed	-	5.6	4.0	7.7
% Riding To Work By Automobile	-	56.9	46.9	41.7
Population Per Household	-	3.0	2.8	3.2
Total Housing Units	22	117	1607	885
% Condominiums & Cooperatives	-	0.0	0.4	0.0
% Built 1960 Or Later	-	8.3	0.0	0.0
% Owner Occupied	-	17.9	31.5	32.0
% With 1+ Persons Per Room	-	9.7	7.8	13.2
Median Value: Owner Units $$	-	-	11700	11100
Median Rent: Rental Units $$	-	64	64	66
Median Number Of Rooms: All Units	-	4.2	4.4	4.5

having more than one person per room. Nearly 40 percent of all Lower West Side residents lived in overcrowded housing, a figure more than double the city average. Twenty-two percent of all units were owner-occupied in 1980, but despite their numerical majority in the area, less than half of all owner-occupied housing units were owned by Hispanics. The median value of single-family, owner-occupied, non-condominium homes in the Lower West Side was $21,666, less than half of the city median. More than 87 percent of all area housing units were in small apartment buildings with from two to nine total units in 1980, just more than 9 percent in single-family homes.

Today, Mexican restaurants and stores dominate the Pilsen shopping areas on 18th Street and Blue Island Avenue. Bright murals on Blue Island and Racine avenues, 18th and 21st streets, show the cultural heritage of the immigrant Hispanics. The newly-constructed Benito Juarez High School on Ashland Avenue gives evidence of their hope of the future. Yet Czech and Polish stores do business on 18th Street and,

in the southwest corner along Oakley Street, the Italian colony survives intact, closed off by railroad tracks and factories. Thus, while the Hispanics have reoccupied the western Pilsen residential area, some hint of the old ethnic heterogeneity survives.

The Lower West Side is one of the oldest industrial areas in Chicago. The industries located there have used much of the land area, because of the heavy machinery and bulky raw materials they use. Thus, an admixture of residential and industrial uses prevailed in every part of the community area. However, after the riots to the north in 1968, many industrial employers sought to relocate, and several, including the International Harvester Company plant, did so leaving industrial wasteland and unemployment behind. Much discussion regarding the use of deserted industrial sites has been carried on in the community and persists today as plans for revitalizing these areas are developed.

Will Hogan

The Loop

The Loop is Chicago's central business district, built over the site of the original settlement. The name came from the ring of elevated railroad tracks, running along Wells, Van Buren, Wabash and Lake streets, consolidated in 1897 as the Union Loop, which quickly became the name of the downtown area. Plates in the sidewalks near the intersection of Michigan Avenue and Wacker Drive show the location of the original Fort Dearborn. Chicago originated as a village around that fort, which included 12 log cabins by 1830, at which time a town of Chicago from Kinzie to Madison streets, between State and Des Plaines streets, was platted by commissioners of the Illinois-Michigan Canal.

From the beginning, the town grew rapidly. It was the site of the regional government land office, an off-loading point for western migrants, a center of trade for a rapidly developing hinterland populated by white settlers and Indians, and the seat of Cook County. In 1837, the newly incorporated city of Chicago counted a population of 4,179, most of whom lived in the Loop.

As the city grew in the 1840s the residential buildings clustered between Randolph and Madison streets, but the more fashionable ones were located on Michigan and Wabash avenues, south of Van Buren Street. Small frame cottages dominated on Madison and Monroe Street. Lake Street was the most important retail strip, with some development on Wells and State streets, while the wholesale and warehouse district was along South Water Street (later Wacker Drive). Lumber yards which fed the incessant construction activity occupied the area along the South Branch of the Chicago River, all the way to 12th Street (Roosevelt Road). Between 1841 and 1846 the city population grew from 5,000 to 14,000. In 1848 the Illinois-Michigan Canal was completed and railroad construction began. In 1847 the first large convention was held in the Loop, a regional meeting held to organize a response to President Polk's veto of an internal improvement bill. Thousands of visitors crowded hotels and had to be accommodated in private homes for lack of rooms.

The 1850s were marked by economic prosperity and an accelerated increase in the city population, which exceeded 100,000 in 1860. In 1853 the first combined City Hall-County Court House building was opened. A decade of public improvements resulted in the construction of sidewalks, new bridges and sewers and the installation of gaslight. Brick buildings four to five stories high appeared on Lake and Randolph streets and workers' homes were constructed around the car repair shops of the Rock Island Railroad. However, alley lean-to dwellings and wooden shanties could be found interspersed in the business blocks along Clark and State streets. Railroad terminals and grain elevators stretched along the South branch of the Chicago River.

In the latter part of the 1860s a serious problem with proposed street paving became apparent. The downtown area was built on swampy ground, only a few feet above the water level of Lake Michigan. It was difficult to keep streets dry and cellars drained. If the new street surfaces were not to be washed away, the street level would have to be elevated by from four to seven feet. This would also necessitate raising the buildings, many of which were by now several stories high. Property owners fought the plan in court, but lost. The buildings were raised by armies of laborers, operating screw jacks. By 1860, the entire area along the lake and the river had been elevated to the new grade.

The 1860s were marked by shifts of various activity centers in the Loop: retail establishments moved down Clark, Dearborn and State streets toward Madison Street, while manufacturing and wholesaling concentrated north of Randolph Street towards the Chicago River. The latter industry also started to move to locations near waterways and railroads. Coal and lumber yards, stone cutting firms and warehouses

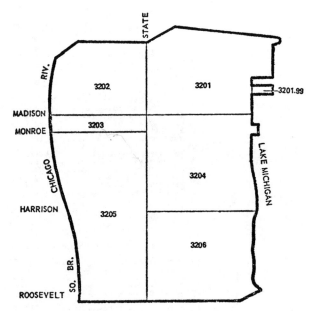

migrated towards locations along the river. When the Board of Trade moved down LaSalle Street from Wacker Drive to a building at LaSalle and Washington streets it brought along other financial institutions as well. The area encompassed by Lake, Wells, Adams and State streets, on which were located the Board of Trade Building and the Court House, became the center of a development which included banks, offices of real estate and insurance agents, attorneys, architects, contractors, and newspapers, telegraph companies, and advertising agencies. Physicians' offices, art and music studios clustered east of this, around Madison, Randolph, Dearborn and Clark streets. The 1860 Republican National Convention held in the Wigwam, a temporary building on Lake Street at Wacker Drive, stimulated hotel construction.

Until the late 1860s State Street was a dirt road lined by cheap residential buildings. Then Potter Palmer, who owned about one mile of land along the street, demolished all the houses on his property and constructed a large store at Randolph and State Street which he leased to Field, Leiter and Company, who relocated from Lake Street, to be followed soon by many retailers. By 1870, 30-40 marble fronted store buildings had been erected on State Street. Wholesale firms took over the buildings on Lake Street which had been left by retail and financial concerns. An elegant hotel, the Palmer House, opened late in 1870.

The 1871 Fire destroyed most of the business section of the Loop, and the homes of 28,000 people downtown. The business buildings were quickly rebuilt, with the help of Eastern capital, but the Loop would never again serve as a residential district to the former extent. The new fire code forbidding the construction of wooden buildings in the Loop reinforced the progressive decline of the residential character of the Loop. In the south part of the Loop converted mansions served as rooming houses or combined office and living quarters, while the central business district was being rebuilt. The retail and financial institutions eventually returned to their former locations. Innovations in building techniques facilitated an increase in the height of buildings, which in general were at least one story higher. Thus, engineer W. LeBaron Jenney's use of cast iron beams in the construction of the Home Insurance Building (completed in 1885) allowed the support of more weight on each floor. Between 1885 and 1894, 21 new skyscrapers between 12 and 16 stories high were built, among them the Rookery on LaSalle and Adams streets, and the Monadnock Building on Jackson Boulevard.

In 1881 the Board of Trade moved south on LaSalle Street again, this time to Jackson Boulevard, causing a shift of the financial center with it. More office buildings were erected on Jackson, VanBuren, Wells

Community Area 32 — The Loop
Population and Housing Characteristics, 1930-1980

	1980	1970	1960	1950	1940	1930
Total Population	6,462	4,933	4,337	7,018	6,221	7,851
% Male	56.0	64.3	83.4	79.3	77.6	79.8
% Female	44.0	35.7	16.6	20.7	22.4	20.2
% White	73.1	86.6	88.5	94.7	98.3	97.3
% Black	19.0	11.9	10.4	3.9	0.2	1.2
% Other Nonwhite Races	7.9	1.5	1.1	1.4	1.5	1.5
% Under 5 Years Old	1.5	1.2	0.6	0.6	0.3	0.6
% 5-19 Years Old	4.0	2.7	2.9	5.4	1.9	4.1
% 20-44 Years Old	40.6	35.0	35.9	44.6	41.5	46.9
% 45-64 Years Old	32.6	41.9	40.7	35.5	44.5	39.5
% 65 Years and Older	21.3	19.2	19.9	13.9	11.8	8.9
Median School Years	12.7	12.4	10.3	10.8	9.5	*
Total Housing Units	4,182	3,090	2,519	150	703	*
% In One-Unit Structures	6.1	1.2	0.9	0.9	*	*
% Owner Occupied	38.9	0.5	0.7	13.3	0.1	*
% Renter Occupied	53.4	93.4	93.3	82.7	64.3	*
% Vacant	7.7	6.1	6.0	4.0	35.6	*
% 1+ Persons per Room	2.7	3.4	6.0	17.7	*	*

Community Area 32 — Loop
Selected Characteristics of Census Tracts: 1980

Tract Number	Total	3201	3201.99	3202	3203	3204	3205	3206
Total Population	6462	2606	18	28	0	437	1888	1485
% Male	56.0	49.7	-	-	-	64.5	65.8	51.3
% Black	19.0	6.8	-	-	-	15.3	28.2	29.8
% Other Nonwhite	7.8	7.5	-	-	-	24.9	7.5	4.2
% Of Spanish Origin	3.4	2.5	-	-	-	3.4	4.9	3.2
% Foreign Born	11.4	10.2	-	-	-	29.1	9.2	11.2
% Living In Group Quarters	17.3	0.7	-	-	-	83.1	33.3	5.3
% 13 Years Old And Under	2.9	3.8	-	-	-	0.5	2.6	2.7
% 14-20 Years Old	3.8	2.3	-	-	-	23.1	2.8	1.3
% 21-64 Years Old	72.0	76.5	-	-	-	70.0	68.7	69.2
% 65-74 Years Old	13.8	11.4	-	-	-	2.1	17.2	17.4
% 75 Years Old And Over	7.4	6.1	-	-	-	4.3	8.7	9.4
% In Different House	52.9	33.9	-	-	-	88.1	76.1	47.5
% Families With Female Head	21.1	19.8	-	-	-	-	15.9	35.0
Median School Years Completed	12.7	12.8	-	-	-	15.4	12.5	12.4
Median Family Income, 1979 $$	26790	31650	-	-	-	-	7639	20313
% Income Below Poverty Level	4.7	0.0	-	-	-	-	14.0	12.6
% Income Of $30,000 Or More	43.9	52.8	-	-	-	-	32.6	23.0
% White Collar Workers	70.4	78.2	-	-	-	69.1	63.1	59.7
% Civilian Labor Force Unemployed	7.0	3.7	-	-	-	2.2	11.1	11.4
% Riding To Work By Automobile	29.3	45.4	-	-	-	10.9	8.9	17.1
Mean Commuting Time - Minutes	22.0	22.8	-	-	-	14.4	25.5	18.4
Population Per Household	1.4	1.5	-	-	-	1.1	1.2	1.3
Total Housing Units	4182	1684	0	12	0	69	1251	1166
% Condominiums	47.0	97.4	-	-	-	11.6	25.1	0.0
% Built 1970 Or Later	33.5	38.3	-	-	-	0.0	52.6	6.8
% Owner Occupied	38.9	81.7	-	-	-	15.9	19.0	0.1
% With 1+ Persons Per Room	2.7	1.5	-	-	-	1.5	4.2	3.4
Median Value: Owner Units $$	-	-	-	-	-	-	-	-
Median Rent: Rental Units $$	249	499	-	-	-	364	119	283
Median Number Of Rooms: All Units	2.9	3.3	-	-	-	2.0	2.5	2.5

Community Area 32 — Loop
Selected Characteristics of Census Tracts: 1970

Tract Number	TOTAL	3201	320199	3202	3203	3204	3205	3206
Total Population	4934	1375	108	225	1	72	1185	1968
% Male	64.3	42.4	100.0	81.8	-	-	88.7	60.8
% Black	11.9	0.8	5.5	16.0	-	-	13.0	19.2
% Other Nonwhite	1.5	0.4	5.5	0.0	-	-	2.3	1.9
% Of Spanish Language	1.7	1.2	0.0	2.9	-	-	0.9	2.4
% Foreign Born	7.4	12.6	0.0	2.9	-	-	3.4	7.1
% Living In Group Quarters	21.8	0.0	98.2	30.7	-	-	66.0	5.5
% 13 Years Old And Under	1.9	0.7	0.9	3.6	-	-	3.7	1.7
% 14-20 Years Old	2.9	1.5	25.5	0.4	-	-	1.5	3.8
% 21-64 Years Old	76.0	74.2	73.6	56.4	-	-	69.6	83.4
% 65-74 Years Old	14.0	17.7	0.0	30.2	-	-	18.1	8.1
% 75 Years Old And Over	5.1	6.0	0.0	9.3	-	-	7.1	3.0
% In Different House	28.1	50.8	0.0	32.3	-	-	24.9	15.6
% Families With Female Head	9.9	10.9	-	25.0	-	-	13.6	7.8
Median School Years Completed	12.5	14.0	12.8	12.8	-	-	10.0	12.5
Median Family Income, 1969 $$	20929	26656	-	7250	-	-	5500	19248
% Income Below Poverty Level	5.0	0.0	-	57.6	-	-	23.8	3.3
% Income of $15,000 or More	70.8	82.1	-	23.1	-	-	0.0	69.8
% White Collar Workers	49.9	73.0	-	40.5	-	-	20.6	46.8
% Civilian Labor Force Unemployed	5.3	2.4	-	2.2	-	-	15.9	2.8
% Riding To Work By Automobile	23.9	33.6	100.0	0.0	-	-	5.5	19.6
Population Per Household	1.3	1.5	2.0	1.1	-	-	1.1	1.3
Total Housing Units	3083	970	0	159	0	72	403	1479
% Condominiums & Cooperatives	0.0	0.0	-	0.0	-	0.0	0.0	0.0
% Built 1960 Or Later	52.0	93.0	-	3.0	-	0.0	0.0	48.1
% Owner Occupied	0.2	0.0	-	1.3	-	0.0	0.2	0.1
% With 1+ Persons Per Room	2.9	1.3	-	5.1	-	0.0	6.0	3.0
Median Value: Owner Units $$	-	-	-	-	-	-	-	-
Median Rent: Rental Units $$	164	269	-	105	-	55	69	130
Median Number Of Rooms: All Units	1.6	2.9	-	1.0	-	1.0	1.1	1.4

and LaSalle. By the mid-1880s the administrative, financial and communications center, clustered around the Court House-City Hall, the Board of Trade, and the Federal Building, covered an area bounded by Randolph, State, VanBuren and Wells streets. By this time, the Loop had become a center of culture as well: clubs, theaters, the Auditorium building on Michigan Avenue and Congress Parkway (1889), later the Art Institute on Michigan and Adams streets (1893), and Orchestra Hall (1904) provided facilities for entertainment and intellectual stimulation. The Congress Hotel (1893) hosted political convention headquarters.

Between 1894 and 1898 the construction of elevated lines which terminated in the Loop brought an influx of shoppers to the area and more retail trade to State Street. The circle of high wooden trestles gave its name to the Loop. After the turn of the century retail shops dominated the ground floors of virtually all buildings in the Loop, the wholesale area expanded down Wells Street, and produce markets sprawled along Wacker Drive. A new Court House-City Hall complex was completed by 1910, as was the palatial Blackstone Hotel.

The land comprising Lakeside Park had been reclaimed from the lake. The Illinois Central tracks, running parallel to and 200 yards east of Michigan Avenue, were laid on trestles in the water in 1852. Landfill occurred on both sides of the tracks, augmented by dumping the debris from the Fire inside the breakwater, and by the 1880s the right-of-way ran through a new land area on the lakefront, nominally dedicated to public use but in practice often used as a dumping ground. A number of attempts were made to secure the land for private development, all stoutly resisted by conservationists led by businessman A. Montgomery Ward, who went to court to protect the park. Construction of the Art Institute, at the time of the Columbian Exposition, went uncontested. In 1902, a year after the park had been renamed for President Grant, the court ruled for Ward. The Park was cleaned up and landscaped, and its role was outlined in the Plan of Chicago, submitted by architect Daniel Burnham in 1909 and adopted by the city a year later. The Lake Front Ordinance of 1919 provided for the preservation and development of the park.

The 1920s brought a building boom in the Loop, during which the downtown area expanded upward and outward. New zoning ordinances encouraged the construction of higher buildings and the use of setback towers. Among the structures built were the 21-story Chicago Temple (1923), the huge Stevens (Conrad Hilton) Hotel (1927), the 41-story Bankers Building (1928) and the 45-story Civic Opera (1929). Construction of the broad two-level Wacker Drive facilitated automobile and truck traffic in the Loop, drove out the produce markets and created a new strip for office buildings. The construction of parking lots and office buildings put pressure on wholesalers to move out. Some warehouses were converted into office buildings. After the Great Depression, in the 1940s, about one-and-a-half million square feet of

floor space was converted to office use. Work on the downtown subway was completed and construction of the 41-story Prudential Insurance Building over the Illinois Central tracks set off a new wave of construction in the Loop area. An underground garage was built under Grant Park.

Between 1957 and 1977 30 million square feet of office space was added to the central area. Buildings rose to unprecedented heights with the construction of the Inland Steel Building (1957), First National Bank (1969) and, tallest of all, the Sears Tower (1975). However, the boom in office building construction caused a change in the atmosphere of the Loop. While in the 1950s activities were around-the-clock, in the 1970s they ended at 5 p.m. The replacement of restaurants, theaters, night clubs and stores with skyscrapers stamped an austere character on the district. Efforts have been made to stem this development. In 1978 the conversion of downtown State Street into a shopping mall started; several new convention hotels have been built; the Printing House Row area, composed of old office and industrial buildings has been converted for residential use; Dearborn Park, a 51-acre site surrounded by Polk, State, 15th and Clark streets, was completed in 1980 with 939 residential units.

In 1960, the number of residents dropped to a historic low, less than 4,500. Since then the population has grown by almost 2,000, with prospects of future growth as housing developments are completed. In 1980 the Loop population was about three-fourths white, one-fifth black. Despite the new housing, it is an aging population, the median age is 47.5; and a poor one, with a median family income less than $12,000.

Despite changes in the last 20 years, the Loop is still Chicago's most important retail district. Sales in 1977 nearly equaled the combined volume of all other major retail areas in the city.

Sibylle Allendorf

Near South Side

Before incorporation of the city of Chicago in 1837 the area just south of 12th Street (now Roosevelt Road) was a sandy wasteland traversed by wagon trails. Its first residents were poor Germans, Irish and a few Scandinavians who came to work on the Illinois and Michigan Canal between 1836 and 1848. They stayed to work in the lumber district along the South Branch of the Chicago River, where they eventually built a shantytown of greenwood cottages and pieced-together shacks which, in recognition of its predominantly Irish character, was called the Patch.

There was little development of this part of the city until the 1850s, when railroads entered Chicago. Several railroads laid their tracks through the South Side of Chicago, enhancing the property values in their vicinity and promoting subdivision. Legislative action by the state in 1853 extended the limits of the city south to 31st Street. The establishment of industrial enterprises within and near the Near South Side, as well as the railroad yards and shops, created a demand for workers who, in turn, sought inexpensive lots and homes near their work. Workingmen's frame homes and boarding houses were constructed on the vacant prairie and wasteland south of Roosevelt Road. A different type of development was stimulated by the opening of the South Side horse-drawn surface car on State Street in 1859. Extended in the early 1860s, this system provided the Near South Side with excellent local transportation and gave further impetus to residential development.

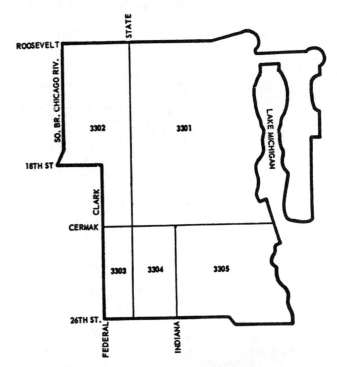

After 1865, the socially-preferred residential section tended to move southward along Wabash and Michigan avenues towards Cermak Road, this being accelerated by the steady encroachment by business upon residential areas within the Loop area. The public transportation facilities of the South Side made its avenues easily accessible to the

Community Area 33 -- Near South Side
Population and Housing Characteristics, 1930-1980

	1980	1970	1960	1950	1940	1930
Total Population.......	7,243	8,767	10,350	11,317	7,306	10,416
% Male...................	41.1	47.4	50.7	49.8	52.9	58.0
% Female.................	58.9	52.6	49.3	50.2	47.1	42.0
% White..................	3.4	11.9	22.7	30.4	73.5	74.4
% Black..................	94.2	85.4	76.8	69.3	25.9	23.8
% Other Nonwhite Races...	2.4	2.7	0.5	0.3	0.6	1.9
% Under 5 Years Old......	12.6	11.7	14.9	11.5	4.7	4.6
% 5-19 Years Old.........	33.4	32.9	30.6	18.4	15.4	14.2
% 20-44 Years Old........	34.7	31.0	31.6	45.4	48.0	53.6
% 45-64 Years Old........	9.9	13.4	14.8	18.7	24.5	23.6
% 65 Years and Older.....	9.4	11.0	8.1	6.0	7.4	4.6
Median School Years....	11.7	10.0	8.6	8.2	8.3	*
Total Housing Units....	2,487	3,223	3,803	2,875	2,341	*
% In One-Unit Structures.	0.0	2.0	8.4	*	*	*
% Owner Occupied.........	0.5	0.6	1.6	3.1	0.7	*
% Renter Occupied........	96.9	89.9	86.6	93.1	81.5	*
% Vacant.................	2.6	9.5	11.8	3.8	17.8	*
% 1+ Persons per Room....	16.1	19.7	30.1	50.5	*	*

Community Area 33 -- Near South Side
Selected Characteristics of Census Tracts: 1980

Tract Number	Total	3301	3302	3303	3304	3305
Total Population.............	7243	1981	1777	3233	56	196
% Male.......................	41.1	43.9	37.1	41.6	-	42.9
% Black......................	94.2	88.4	97.2	99.8	-	33.2
% Other Nonwhite.............	2.4	2.5	2.0	0.2	-	39.3
% Of Spanish Origin..........	1.5	3.7	1.6	0.2	-	0.5
% Foreign Born...............	4.6	6.0	1.6	2.9	-	51.6
% Living In Group Quarters...	3.9	7.3	0.0	0.0	-	65.8
% 13 Years Old And Under.....	33.7	23.4	33.7	42.0	-	2.0
% 14-20 Years Old............	14.3	8.5	14.3	18.5	-	6.1
% 21-64 Years Old............	42.6	60.0	28.5	37.3	-	78.1
% 65-74 Years Old............	4.7	4.7	10.1	1.4	-	9.2
% 75 Years Old And Over......	4.7	3.4	13.4	0.9	-	4.6
% In Different House.........	33.6	38.6	35.1	28.2	-	54.5
% Families With Female Head..	75.5	58.3	78.7	82.9	-	-
Median School Years Completed....	11.7	12.6	9.4	11.0	-	16.1
Median Family Income, 1979....$$	7326	15191	5192	5234	-	-
% Income Below Poverty Level.....	42.7	9.4	55.1	59.2	-	-
% Income Of $30,000 Or More.....	5.8	11.3	0.0	4.8	-	-
% White Collar Workers.......	53.3	56.0	47.2	45.5	-	84.5
% Civilian Labor Force Unemployed.	20.3	11.2	35.2	30.2	-	0.0
% Riding To Work By Automobile....	32.9	41.0	16.2	24.6	-	33.0
Mean Commuting Time - Minutes...	31.3	34.2	30.1	29.9	-	13.6
Population Per Household.........	2.9	2.2	2.5	4.0	-	2.2
Total Housing Units..........	2487	867	733	821	22	44
% Condominiums...............	0.0	0.0	0.0	0.0	-	-
% Built 1970 Or Later........	14.9	36.2	4.5	2.2	-	-
% Owner Occupied.............	0.5	0.6	0.1	0.4	-	-
% With 1+ Persons Per Room...	16.1	5.8	12.6	30.0	-	-
Median Value: Owner Units.......$$	-	-	-	-	-	-
Median Rent: Rental Units....$$	90	241	49	78	-	-
Median Number Of Rooms: All Units.	3.8	3.7	3.3	4.1	-	-

Community Area 33 -- Near South Side
Selected Characteristics of Census Tracts: 1970

Tract Number	TOTAL	3301	3302	3303	3304	3305
Total Population.............	8767	2626	1902	3558	312	369
% Male.......................	47.4	56.1	41.5	43.8	62.5	38.5
% Black......................	85.4	71.8	91.1	97.6	92.9	30.1
% Other Nonwhite.............	2.7	3.1	2.5	0.2	0.0	26.0
% Of Spanish Language........	1.5	2.1	1.4	1.1	3.1	0.0
% Foreign Born...............	2.6	4.8	4.0	0.0	0.0	7.1
% Living In Group Quarters...	6.4	8.7	0.0	3.3	0.0	57.5
% 13 Years Old And Under.....	33.5	20.7	36.2	44.0	16.7	23.3
% 14-20 Years Old............	12.8	8.1	8.7	19.6	8.0	4.3
% 21-64 Years Old............	42.7	61.5	32.2	30.6	65.1	61.0
% 65-74 Years Old............	6.5	5.4	14.7	2.7	6.4	8.7
% 75 Years Old And Over......	4.5	4.2	8.1	3.1	3.8	2.7
% In Different House.........	31.0	17.5	7.9	52.6	29.9	35.2
% Families With Female Head......	40.9	21.6	28.5	64.0	28.3	30.0
Median School Years Completed....	10.0	11.0	8.9	9.8	9.9	10.2
Median Family Income, 1969......$$	5254	8339	4231	4471	4543	9800
% Income Below Poverty Level.....	37.2	16.4	41.9	51.5	23.9	0.0
% Income of $15,000 or More.....	6.1	14.4	3.0	1.2	0.0	41.7
% White Collar Workers.......	16.3	20.5	10.7	9.6	5.9	42.6
% Civilian Labor Force Unemployed.	7.0	1.9	12.0	11.9	11.1	2.3
% Riding To Work By Automobile....	32.7	31.7	43.7	34.8	27.5	12.3
Population Per Household.........	2.8	2.1	2.7	4.4	1.8	1.6
Total Housing Units.........	3240	1346	723	799	274	98
% Condominiums & Cooperatives.....	0.0	0.0	0.0	0.0	0.0	0.0
% Built 1960 Or Later........	39.3	38.1	94.5	3.2	4.1	41.3
% Owner Occupied.............	0.6	1.0	0.1	0.4	0.4	2.0
% With 1+ Persons Per Room.......	20.3	9.4	16.5	41.8	17.5	10.2
Median Value: Owner Units.......$$	-	-	-	-	-	-
Median Rent: Rental Units......$$	81	107	61	79	77	68
Median Number Of Rooms: All Units.	3.3	2.5	3.3	4.1	1.2	2.0

downtown area. Indiana, Prairie, Calumet, and Michigan avenues and Grand Boulevard (now Martin Luther King Jr. Drive) were beginning to be lined with marble-front ornate dwellings. Workingmen were also attracted to the Near South Side by the increased number of manufacturing establishments locating within and near the neighborhood. Their frame houses were scattered in the section west of State Street.

The Fire of 1871, beginning on the west side of the Chicago River, left the Near South Side intact. Business enterprises, burned out of the central business district, set up temporary headquarters in residences on south Wabash Avenue. This ruined Wabash Avenue as a residential street. Its old mansions were converted into rooming houses or structures combining business and residential uses. After another major fire in the near South Side in 1874, which destroyed much of the Patch, the area began to develop rapidly. Most of the Patch area was converted to railroad yards after the fire. The first mansions of the city's wealthy were erected on Prairie Avenue, between 16th and 22nd streets. At the same time many workingmen, burned out of their homes, sought new dwellings near the growing industrial establishments on the South Side. The avenues of the Near South Side continued to flourish, and when Michigan Avenue was made a boulevard in 1880, it became residentially fashionable and desirable. During the 1880s and 1890s, the Prairie Avenue section of the Near South Side, east of Michigan Avenue, reached a height of elegance. Between 16th and 22nd streets, Prairie Avenue was lined with more than fifty mansions, including the homes of George M. Pullman, Marshall Field, Phillip Armour and many others of of the Chicago elite. Although Prairie Avenue was the wealthiest neighborhood in Chicago, the Near South Side held both rich and poor, immigrants as well as American-born. During the 1880s new apartment buildings were built rapidly, especially along car-line streets like Cottage Grove Avenue and State Street, whose horsecar lines were converted into cable lines as far south as 39th Street.

Through the second half of the 19th century, the dominant attraction of the Near South Side was its superior transportation facilities. The establishment of the cross-town horse-car line on 26th Street from 1887 through 1889 was an impetus to development, while the construction of the steam elevated system, the "Alley L," between State Street and Wabash Avenue from Congress Street to 39th in 1890-92 sped development along its route.

As railroad lines entered the city, the North, West and South Sides competed for their terminals, while Loop businessmen fought to keep them from building downtown. The result was that by 1903 there were four major terminals, the Illinois Central's Central Station, the Dearborn Street Station, Chicago Grand Central Depot, and LaSalle Street Station, all located in the south part of the Loop, immediately north of the Near South Side. Although the railroad stations brought thousands of jobs to the area, they brought problems as well. The heavy passenger traffic attracted houses of prostitution, gambling rooms and saloons. The Columbian Exposition of 1893 created a boom in land values all over the South Side and led to the construction of apartment buildings and hotels on the Near South Side in anticipation of crowds of visitors that did not materialize. At the close of the 19th century, the fashionable residential area of the community had lost its prestige, a development accentuated by the migration southward of the Loop vice area along State Street and Wabash Avenue.

The most significant factor in the decline of Prairie Avenue and the adjoining area was the infusion of commercial and industrial enterprises. The first automobile showrooms appeared on Michigan Avenue in 1908.

By 1911 there were 26 automobile outlets between 22nd and 25th streets along Michigan Avenue. At the same time business leaders in pursuit of further development were urging the removal of the railroad yards so that the Loop could expand southward. The opening decades of this century witnessed further relocation of wholesale houses and warehouses forced out of the Loop by the expanding retail area. Print shops began to locate along Cermak Road, in the vicinity of Prairie Avenue. In addition, enterprises such as commercial laundries, tailoring and millinery shops became widespread in the area. As industrial and commercial uses permeated the community, the old mansions were converted into rooming houses or offices or torn down to make room for factories and warehouses. Proximity to the railroad terminals gave the Near South Side access to Chicago's convention trade. The Coliseum at 15th Street and Wabash was the site of Republican national conventions quadrennially from 1904 to 1920, and of the Bull Moose Progressive convention in 1912. In 1860, 600 of the 750 blacks in Chicago resided in the Near South Side, and that number grew slowly during the rest of the 19th Century. Blacks had been confined to the area west of Wabash Avenue but by 1912 the Black Belt began to extend eastward. During and after World War I, there was a great influx of blacks into the city, many of whom sought housing in the

low-rent areas of the South Side. As their numbers increased and they expanded southward and eastward, the older residents, mainly those of Irish and German descent, moved to other communities.

The 1920s and early 1930s brought a series of public buildings and events to the northeast corner of the Near South Side, that part which is adjacent to the southern boundary of Grant Park. In 1921, the Field Museum of Natural History was transferred to a new building just south of the park from the old Columbian Exposition Palace of Fine Arts in Hyde Park. A year later, construction began to the south on Soldier Field, which became the site of many outdoor conventions and sporting events, including the legendary second Dempsey-Tunney prize fight in 1927. The Adler Planetarium was dedicated in 1930, and the Shedd Aquarium opened the following year. The 1920s saw the creation of Burnham Park and the adjoining Northerly Island, 598 acres built out into the lake from sand and debris, which became the site of the Century of Progress Exposition of 1933 and 1934.

The old Tenderloin district had been officially closed in 1912 by a reform administration, but persisted as an entertainment area until the 18th Amendment added a new dimension to organized crime. The area was ruled by a succession of chieftains, culminating in Al Capone, who used bootlegging as the revenue source of a criminal empire in the 1920s. Capone lived and maintained his city headquarters at the Lexington Hotel, Michigan Avenue and Cermak Road.

The Near South Side experienced a decline in population from 1920 until the decade of the 1940s when there was an unprecedented movement of blacks into Chicago. In the 1950s, there was another drop, caused primarily by migration of the white population. The flight of white American-born and those of Irish and German nativity was completed. Since the initial in-movement of blacks around World War I, they have constituted an increasing proportion of the population of the Near South Side, until in 1980 they made up 94 percent of the population. The significant rises in the black count of the Near South Side from the 1940s was not matched by a corresponding growth in housing units. The result was a tremendous concentration of the black community, which was compelled to operate within a segregated housing market. The black area became an overcrowded and deteriorated slum, a center of increasing poverty and crime. There was practically no new construction in the community area until 1955 when the Chicago Housing Authority completed the Harold L. Ickes Homes. Located on an 18-acre site at 22nd and State, the Ickes Homes consist of six 7-story and seven 15-story buildings, containing about 800 housing units, almost wholly occupied by blacks. Otherwise, residential land use has declined steadily as industrial and commercial uses have expanded.

Since 1960 residential areas have declined in the Near South Side, which is now characterized by an admixture of residential and other land uses. In 1966 the Chicago Housing Authority opened the Raymond Hilliard Homes on seven acres of land at Cermak and State, just east of Chinatown. There has been extensive expansion of wholesale facilities along Michigan Boulevard, which is still an area of automobile agencies and of auto accessories dealers. Even more extensive has been the general expansion of industrial and warehouse establishments throughout the community, especially in the industrial area west of the Illinois Central tracks. The gigantic Lakeside Press building stands on the site of the old printing shops on Cermak Road. Just south, at 24th Street and Michigan Avenue, is the plant of the Chicago Daily Defender, one of the most important black newspapers, which has been published in the Near South Side since 1905.

In 1960, the Chicago Land Clearance Commission, later absorbed by the Department of Urban Renewal, designated a 42-acre site in the community for redevelopment for institutional and light industrial use. Most of this project, known as "25th-South Parkway" lies along the southern boundary of the community in Census Tracts 3305 and 3304.

A key component of this project was the construction between 1964 and 1968 of the expanded Mercy Hospital Complex. The public area on the lakefront was expanded by the completion in 1960 of McCormick Place, a major convention center which was destroyed by fire in 1967 and has been since rebuilt. McCormick Inn added hotel facilities to the convention area.

The population of the Near South Side has dropped since 1950, and now stands at just over 7,000, down more than a third from the high 30 years ago, less than what it was at the end of the Depression. Almost all housing units are renter occupied, and the importance of the large projects is shown by the number (83 percent of the total) who live in structures of 10 or more units. Three-fourths of all households with children under 18 are headed by females. The unemployment rate is more than 20 percent. The median family income is second lowest in the city, and more than 40 percent of all residents live below the poverty level.

The Near South Side contains part of the Dearborn Park housing development, built on the site of the old abandoned railroad yards south to 15th Street between State and Clark streets, which will bring hundreds of middle-income owners and renters into the community. The 19th century elite residential area was designated the Prairie Avenue Historic District in 1973. Sponsors are making earnest efforts to restore the lost beauty of that area.

On any given day, the Near South Side is occupied by three populations: visitors to the public structures east of Lake Shore Drive, commuters who work in the industrial facilities, and the impoverished and disorganized residents of the projects. There are rumors about the redevelopment of the community area, but not much has come of them. Residential redevelopment has taken place for the most part north and farther south of the Loop, while the office building area is expanding into the Near West Side. The present pattern of land use appears stable, and the area may endure in its present form for the rest of the 20th century. Proximity to the Loop, accessibility to public transportation and major highways will be important factors in the renovation of the Near South Side, whatever form that may take.

M.W.H.
Robert N. Nartey

Community Area 34

Armour Square

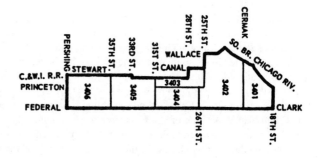

Armour Square is a variegated, polyethnic strip of urban land about two miles south of the center of Chicago. It is a marginal area, comprised of scraps and remainders of land from the surrounding Near South Side, Bridgeport and Douglas neighborhoods. The community area is named for Armour Square Park, itself a land residual from the tract provided for the nearby Armour Institute of Technology. The land became progressively isolated from the rest of the Chicago by the construction of a large railroad yard to the north and by railroad tracks to the east and west which have been raised above street level. Armour Square is highly accessible to the center of the city, traversed north to south by public train tracks and two expressways, yet the space requirements of these facilities have caused half the residents to move away. Originally a section of prairie and low swampy land, Armour Square was crossed in the north by an Indian trail, which became Archer Avenue, and by a trail which crossed the South Branch of the Chicago River at 18th Street. Some businesses were established and a Rock Island Railroad track was laid through northern Armour Square upon completion of the Illinois-Michigan Canal in 1848.

Armour Square's first settlers were Irish, German and Swedish laborers, and the area became a workingmen's residential district. The availability of cheap lots, in close proximity to rapidly developing industrial areas, attracted new residents who settled in scattered fashion in a growing Armour Square. The state legislature extended the city limits to 31st Street in 1853 and, by 1863, the remainder of the community area from 31st Street to Pershing Road (39th Street) had been annexed as well.

In the 1860s, settlement in Armour Square extended a little south of 36th Street. The Union Stock Yards opened in 1865 and stimulated settlement in the southern part of the area. Business streets began to develop along the horsecar routes on Archer and Wentworth avenues. Armour Square was untouched by the Great Fire in 1871, but was nevertheless affected by it. Frame dwellings were still permitted after the Fire in Armour Square, and this made the area ideal for displaced workingmen who sought to rebuild inexpensively. The new trunk-line railroads built during the 1880s hastened the development of the community and motivated the further settlement of workingmen. Some industry developed in Armour Square near the railroad tracks at its eastern and western boundaries. During the 1880s the old horse-drawn streetcar lines were converted to electric drive, while new horsecar lines were built on cross streets such as 26th and 35th streets. Continued rapid development from 1885 to 1895 led to the achievement of residential maturity in 1895.

By the turn of the century, commercial and manufacturing establishments were expanding south of Roosevelt Road and into the northern part of Armour Square. Other business enterprises were to be found scattered through the community. The Chicago White Sox built a ball park at Pershing Road and Wentworth Avenue, which was later taken over by a Negro League team, the American Giants, after the White Sox built Comiskey Park at 35th Street and Shields Avenue. Today, Comiskey Park bisects Armour Square between 33rd and 35th streets. Impetus for the industrial development of southwestern Armour Square was given by the development of the Central Manufacturing District to the west (between 35th Street and Pershing Road from Ashland to Morgan avenues) just after the turn of the century. Gradually, industrial plants located along the river, Archer Avenue, and Pershing Road, and along the Pennsylvania Railroad tracks. Industry began to infiltrate residential areas during this period. The tracks of the Pennsylvania Railroad, and of the Fort Wayne and Indiana Railroad, were elevated above grade in 1906, creating an imposing physical boundary between Armour Square and Bridgeport. streets running to Douglas, on the east, had been closed when the New York Central tracks were raised in 1892.

Community Area 34 -- Armour Square
Population and Housing Characteristics, 1930-1980

	1980	1970	1960	1950	1940	1930
Total Population.......	12,475	13,058	15,783	23,294	18,472	21,450
% Male..................	47.4	48.2	50.7	50.3	51.6	54.9
% Female................	52.6	51.8	49.3	49.7	48.4	45.1
% White.................	32.3	43.0	57.7	47.6	73.2	70.8
% Black.................	25.3	31.6	31.4	46.9	22.0	18.9
% Other Nonwhite Races...	42.4	25.4	10.9	5.5	4.8	10.2
% Under 5 Years Old.....	6.3	8.9	12.8	12.2	7.6	10.2
% 5-19 Years Old........	23.5	30.7	30.0	25.7	29.6	30.7
% 20-44 Years Old.......	34.1	29.8	32.1	39.7	36.9	40.3
% 45-64 Years Old.......	21.3	18.5	16.8	16.9	20.7	15.8
% 65 Years and Older.....	14.8	12.1	8.3	5.5	5.2	3.0
Median school Years.....	10.6	9.0	8.6	8.1	6.4	*
Total Housing Units....	4,679	4,280	4,492	5,927	5,056	*
% In One-Unit Structures.	12.7	12.2	15.0	*	*	*
% Owner Occupied........	20.4	18.6	19.3	19.1	18.5	*
% Renter Occupied........	74.8	75.9	76.4	79.4	76.0	*
% Vacant................	4.8	5.5	9.1	1.5	5.5	*
% 1+ Persons per Room....	13.0	15.0	19.6	26.8	*	*

Community Area 34 -- Armour Square
Selected Characteristics of Census Tracts: 1980

Tract Number	Total	3401	3402	3403	3404	3405	3406
Total Population.............	12475	85	5319	1388	1606	1785	2292
% Male.......................	47.4	-	48.8	49.0	51.0	43.3	43.1
% Black......................	25.3	-	5.3	8.2	6.3	20.6	99.7
% Other Nonwhite.............	42.3	-	76.0	39.8	36.0	2.4	0.0
% Of Spanish Origin..........	4.8	-	2.6	7.9	17.0	4.4	0.2
% Foreign Born...............	34.4	-	57.8	33.6	32.9	5.8	1.2
% Living In Group Quarters...	0.2	-	0.1	0.0	1.6	0.0	0.0
% 13 Years Old And Under.....	19.1	-	17.8	14.8	18.6	12.1	30.6
% 14-20 Years Old............	12.6	-	12.3	11.6	10.6	8.4	18.7
% 21-64 Years Old............	53.6	-	57.2	57.4	60.5	46.6	43.3
% 65-74 Years Old............	8.6	-	8.0	9.2	3.6	17.1	4.2
% 75 Years Old And Over......	6.2	-	4.7	7.0	3.6	15.8	3.2
% In Different House.........	35.8	-	41.6	41.4	44.5	25.9	20.4
% Families With Female Head..	27.8	-	11.0	14.5	13.4	21.0	72.5
Median School Years Completed.	10.6	-	10.4	11.3	11.0	9.7	11.1
Median Family Income, 1979......$$	15211	-	14402	19837	23879	16957	9052
% Income Below Poverty Level....	23.4	-	21.9	22.2	8.3	19.6	45.5
% Income Of $30,000 Or More....	15.0	-	15.0	18.8	29.1	8.0	5.8
% White Collar Workers.......	41.3	-	39.6	42.6	40.7	53.8	37.6
% Civilian Labor Force Unemployed.	7.7	-	2.6	4.4	9.4	12.5	21.8
% Riding To Work By Automobile....	57.9	-	59.1	64.5	66.9	61.5	28.1
Mean Commuting Time - Minutes...	24.7	-	26.0	26.2	21.1	17.4	26.9
Population Per Household......	2.8	-	3.1	2.5	2.8	1.9	3.6
Total Housing Units..........	4679	47	1798	598	621	966	649
% Condominiums...............	0.6	-	1.6	0.0	0.0	0.0	0.0
% Built 1970 Or Later........	12.8	-	19.6	12.1	3.9	14.8	1.3
% Owner Occupied.............	20.3	-	21.6	29.9	23.8	16.6	10.6
% With 1+ Persons Per Room...	13.0	-	18.7	7.0	10.3	2.4	21.2
Median Value: Owner Units.......$$	42200	-	47200	40000	-	-	-
Median Rent: Rental Units....$$	118	-	144	105	137	82	96
Median Number Of Rooms: All Units.	4.3	-	4.0	4.6	4.9	3.7	4.4

Community Area 34 -- Armour Square
Selected Characteristics of Census Tracts: 1970

Tract Number	TOTAL	3401	3402	3403	3404	3405	3406
Total Population.............	13058	95	4375	1391	1867	2133	3197
% Male.......................	48.2	-	50.9	46.9	50.2	47.4	43.6
% Black......................	31.6	-	6.1	10.0	11.7	15.4	99.4
% Other Nonwhite.............	25.4	-	70.9	1.7	2.8	2.0	0.3
% Of Spanish Language........	6.1	-	5.4	6.6	20.6	3.3	0.6
% Foreign Born...............	24.0	-	48.7	19.6	21.6	14.7	0.0
% Living In Group Quarters...	0.5	-	0.5	0.0	0.4	0.3	0.3
% 13 Years Old And Under.....	27.0	-	26.4	23.4	23.6	18.5	37.4
% 14-20 Years Old............	14.4	-	14.9	9.8	15.6	8.4	19.4
% 21-64 Years Old............	46.5	-	49.4	49.0	51.4	49.6	36.5
% 65-74 Years Old............	7.5	-	6.3	9.7	5.1	14.3	4.6
% 75 Years Old And Over......	4.6	-	3.1	8.0	4.3	9.0	2.1
% In Different House.........	59.9	-	52.6	62.4	56.5	60.3	69.2
% Families With Female Head..	22.4	-	10.7	16.5	17.6	14.3	51.4
Median School Years Completed.	8.9	-	8.8	8.8	9.3	9.0	9.3
Median Family Income, 1969......$$	7835	-	8784	9459	8870	8680	4873
% Income Below Poverty Level.....	19.3	-	7.4	9.7	14.1	17.2	42.1
% Income of $15,000 or More.....	13.0	-	16.4	14.3	13.4	18.6	3.7
% White Collar Workers.......	14.3	-	12.4	20.4	13.2	21.7	6.3
% Civilian Labor Force Unemployed.	4.9	-	4.0	3.2	5.1	2.8	10.5
% Riding To Work By Automobile....	45.5	-	33.9	60.9	54.8	52.9	48.3
Population Per Household......	3.2	-	3.5	2.7	3.1	2.4	4.1
Total Housing Units..........	4270	33	1287	541	637	972	800
% Condominiums & Cooperatives.....	0.1	-	0.5	0.0	0.0	0.0	0.0
% Built 1960 Or Later........	13.2	-	10.6	14.8	0.0	36.3	0.0
% Owner Occupied.............	18.4	-	18.6	25.1	20.9	18.6	11.6
% With 1+ Persons Per Room...	15.8	-	24.2	6.7	10.4	4.1	26.6
Median Value: Owner Units.......$$	15500	-	21900	-	-	-	-
Median Rent: Rental Units....$$	68	-	72	55	62	58	82
Median Number Of Rooms: All Units.	4.3	-	4.2	4.4	4.9	3.8	4.5

As the older German, Irish, and Swedish residents began to vacate their frame cottages and two- and three-flats, new immigrant groups seeking low-rent housing moved in. Italians and Yugoslavians began moving into Armour Square in the early 1900s, becoming the first and second most populous foreign-born groups, respectively, by 1920. Prior to World War I, blacks lived primarily in a section east of the Rock Island tracks. The postwar black influx to the city saw black residential settlement even beyond the tracks to the west, and south of Pershing Road. By 1920, nearly one-fourth of Armour Square's population was black. Around 1912, Chinese began to move from the original Chinese settlement on South Clark Street, where rents had been raised significantly, to Cermak Road and Wentworth Avenue. The Chinese influx was made possible by a series of 10-year leases on buildings which were contracted through the H. O. Stone Company by members of the On Leong Businessmen's Association. Cermak Road and Wentworth Avenue soon became the hub of Chicago's Chinatown.

Chinatown has since served as the midwest's residential reception area for new immigrants from mainland China and Taiwan.

Between 1920 and 1960, the only new construction in Armour Square was of two public housing projects. The further encroachment of industry contributed to residential deterioration. In 1946, Wentworth Gardens, a 422-unit Chicago Housing Authority (CHA) development occupying 16 acres, was built at 37th Street and Princeton Avenue, on the site of the former White Sox and American Giants baseball park, covering land once occupied by the splendid C.D. Peacock mansion. In 1952, the CHA completed Archer Courts, which occupies five acres at 23rd Street and Princeton Avenue and contains 148 rental units. Both Wentworth Gardens and Archer Courts have been inhabited almost exclusively by blacks since opening. Despite these CHA additions, the total housing inventory declined sharply during the 1950s, primarily due to land clearance for the Dan Ryan and Stevenson Expressways.

Armour Square's population declined between 1920 and 1940, but increased during the 1940s due to blacks moving in. By 1950, nearly one-half of the total population of Armour Square was black. However, the black population dwindled as a result of the demolition of dwelling units for the expressways. In 1960, blacks comprised less than one-third of the area's total population, after the removal of nearly 6,000 persons. The black population of Armour Square was heavily concentrated in the area's southernmost census tract. Meanwhile the Chinese population increased gradually and, in 1960, concentrated in Armour Square's two northernmost tracts. In 1960, Italians remained the most numerous foreign-stock group. An influx of Mexicans took place between 1930 and 1960, when the Mexican population was second among foreign-stock groups. In 1963, the Raymond Hilliard Homes were opened at Cermak Road and State Street, just east of Chinatown. A 198-unit housing development for the elderly, Armour Square Apartments, was opened in 1965 at 32nd Street and Wentworth Avenue.

Nevertheless, during the 1960s Armour Square's total population decreased by 17 percent. A distinct residential pattern, tending to segregate whites, blacks, and persons of other non-white races — primarily Chinese — began to emerge at this time. The Chinese were the principal inhabitants of the area north of Cermak Road and, by 1970, they constituted two-thirds of the population north of 26th Street. More than a third of the European whites, who had occupied the central area between 26th and 35th streets in 1970, moved out of Armour Square during the decade, while blacks and Latins moved in. The area south of 35th Street, where the large public housing projects were located, became overwhelmingly black.

In the most recent decade, some blacks have moved into the northern area, while Hispanics continued to move into the central section. Whites, despite another new drop of 1,500 persons, still constitute about two-thirds of the population residing between 26th and 35th streets. South of 35th Street, Armour Square is almost exclusively black. The current population is about 12,500, little more than half the number of inhabitants 30 years ago.

Today, Armour Square is a community area of single-family bungalows, two- and three-flat apartment buildings, and large housing projects located in the south. About two-thirds of the housing units are in small multiple structures, two to nine units, while the rest are evenly divided between single-family homes and larger buildings. About 10 percent of the area population lives in some kind of subsidized housing. The exodus of blacks from the area continues, while Latins and Chinese continue to move in. The white remainder is principally Italian. Shopping is restricted to an area of small stores along 31st Street and to Chinatown around Cermak Road and Wentworth Avenue.

The headquarters of On Leong Tong, the Chinese Merchants Association, better known as "Chinese City Hall," Comiskey Park, and Wentworth Gardens are the most imposing and symbolic buildings in Armour Square. As the Asian population grows, finding housing for them continues to be a problem. In the last 20 years, Chinatown businessmen, aided by capital from Hong Kong, have put together not-for-profit residential developments targeted for low-income employed homeseekers, including the $9 million dollar, 132-unit Appleville condominiums at Canal Street and 24th Place, and Chinatown Courts, a five-building, 22-unit development at 26th Street and Shields Avenue. At this writing, more townhouse developments are in construction south of 26th Street, indicating further territorial expansion of the Asian Community in Armour Square.

Will Hogan

Douglas

The Douglas community area was one of the city's earliest settlements. It is named for senator Stephen A. Douglas, who is buried in an ornate tomb at the east end of 35th Street. Prior to 1850, Douglas was a wilderness traversed by two old Indian trails — the current Cottage Grove and Vincennes avenues. Myrick's Tavern, on Cottage Grove at 29th Street was a stopover for cattle drovers. Douglas was incorporated into Chicago via separate acts of the Illinois legislature. The initial annexation added the area north of 31st Street in 1853, while the remainder of the area was added 10 years later.

In 1852, Senator Douglas, who was also a land speculator and developer, purchased 70 acres of lakefront land between 33rd and 35th streets. In 1856 Douglas donated land to the Baptist Church for the establishment of a University of Chicago, which opened in 1860. He also designated land for two residential parks, Groveland and Woodland, across from the University. Douglas called his own estate Oakenwald, and built a summer cottage there in 1856. That year John

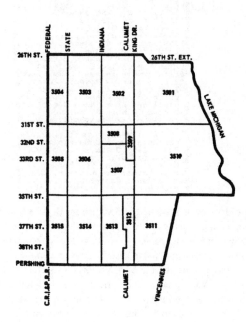

Community Area 35 — Douglas
Population and Housing Characteristics, 1930-1980

	1980	1970	1960	1950	1940	1930
Total population.......	35,700	41,276	52,325	78,745	53,124	50,285
% Male.................	42.4	44.9	47.8	47.7	47.7	50.7
% Female...............	57.6	55.1	52.2	52.3	52.3	49.3
% White................	9.9	12.1	7.4	2.7	6.2	11.1
% Black................	86.6	85.7	91.8	97.1	93.7	88.8
% Other Nonwhite Races...	3.5	2.2	0.8	0.2	0.1	0.3
% Under 5 Years Old....	9.0	10.2	15.1	11.0	7.4	6.5
% 5-19 Years Old........	26.2	33.3	29.9	21.7	22.1	18.0
% 20-44 Years Old........	36.4	32.0	33.0	43.3	44.2	55.7
% 45-64 Years Old........	16.5	16.8	15.9	18.7	21.1	17.4
% 65 Years and Older.....	11.9	7.7	6.1	5.3	5.2	2.4
Median School Years....	12.4	11.4	9.3	8.2	7.4	*
Total Housing Units....	15,168	15,738	15,816	21,474	15,688	*
% In One-Unit Structures.	4.4	5.8	5.6	*	*	*
% Owner-Occupied........	4.7	4.6	5.8	8.3	5.8	*
% Renter Occupied.......	89.9	90.2	90.7	89.9	87.5	*
% Vacant...............	5.4	5.2	3.5	1.8	6.7	*
% 1+ Persons per Room....	10.1	16.2	29.0	43.6	*	*

Community Area 35 — Douglas
Selected Characteristics of Census Tracts: 1980

Tract Number	Total	3501	3502	3503	3504	3505	3506	3507	3508	3509	3510
Total Population.............	35700	2441	3083	1366	2766	518	2702	1237	318	105	3519
% Male.......................	42.4	35.1	41.1	49.6	39.3	82.2	57.8	39.4	47.5	53.3	38.7
% Black......................	86.6	26.8	95.4	87.3	99.5	22.2	31.6	98.7	98.7	100.0	91.9
% Other Nonwhite.............	3.5	17.7	2.0	2.6	0.5	22.4	17.0	0.4	0.0	0.0	1.6
% Of Spanish Origin..........	0.9	1.7	0.7	1.9	0.4	4.1	1.7	0.1	0.0	0.0	0.6
% Foreign Born...............	4.7	19.0	1.6	3.1	0.8	24.5	24.5	3.3	5.3	16.9	3.1
% Living In Group Quarters...	7.0	4.7	0.2	0.2	0.0	-	60.5	0.0	0.0	0.0	0.0
% 13 Years Old And Under.....	24.4	6.5	23.0	14.3	41.8	0.0	5.1	16.2	18.6	14.3	9.3
% 14-20 Years Old............	12.9	4.3	13.0	5.1	16.3	60.0	18.3	9.5	10.7	13.3	5.0
% 21-64 Years Old............	50.7	75.3	47.6	76.8	38.5	40.0	61.3	40.7	50.0	47.6	68.3
% 65-74 Years Old............	6.9	9.0	9.8	2.8	2.4	0.0	5.3	18.0	10.7	11.4	11.3
% 75 Years Old And Over......	5.0	5.0	6.7	1.1	1.1	1.0	10.1	15.5	10.1	13.3	6.1
% In Different House.........	39.8	56.0	30.7	54.8	25.8	83.6	81.3	46.1	51.7	33.3	28.4
% Families With Female Head..	70.0	18.8	64.3	24.2	83.3	-	13.7	62.7	50.0	58.3	46.9
Median School Years Completed....	12.4	16.1	11.7	15.3	11.1	15.7	14.1	10.3	10.5	12.1	14.7
Median Family Income, 1979......$$	8578	23423	9503	29130	4759	-	12660	7917	10795	30285	24297
% Income Below Poverty Level....	42.6	2.6	30.0	2.0	78.1	-	29.4	37.1	34.4	47.8	5.2
% Income Of $30,000 Or More....	11.3	32.3	9.9	46.9	0.0	-	7.9	14.9	18.0	52.2	33.0
% White Collar Workers.......	70.3	88.7	68.9	77.4	48.6	77.9	78.6	60.4	61.4	55.2	85.3
% Civilian Labor Force Unemployed.	11.3	2.4	7.7	2.0	28.3	7.7	9.1	18.3	13.5	0.0	2.0
% Riding To Work By Automobile....	41.8	34.1	51.3	54.0	23.8	9.3	26.5	28.2	65.1	37.9	55.9
Mean Commuting Time - Minutes...	26.5	19.7	27.8	26.3	28.4	11.8	18.3	34.3	31.5	30.5	27.6
Population Per Household.....	2.3	1.4	2.2	2.2	1.7	3.4	1.8	1.9	2.8	2.7	1.6
Total Housing Units.........	15168	1844	1401	807	811	1	617	737	165	96	2219
% Condominiums...............	0.9	0.0	1.0	3.7	1.2	-	0.0	0.0	0.0	53.1	0.5
% Built 1970 Or Later........	8.8	2.2	35.9	19.0	2.1	-	5.2	33.3	0.0	54.1	0.2
% Owner Occupied.............	4.7	0.2	2.0	8.7	0.6	-	2.9	14.7	24.8	18.8	1.8
% With 1+ Persons Per Room...	10.1	2.7	9.8	2.3	26.5	-	21.9	5.8	7.1	15.4	1.6
Median Value: Owner Units......$$	25900	-	-	-	-	-	-	-	-	-	-
Median Rent: Rental Units......$$	155	212	175	338	76	-	181	78	156	144	281
Median Number Of Rooms: All Units.	3.6	2.6	3.1	3.2	3.8	-	1.6	3.4	4.7	4.9	3.3

Tract Number	3511	3512	3513	3514	3515
Total Population.............	7586	939	1827	1863	5430
% Male.......................	38.1	46.1	47.2	50.0	38.6
% Black......................	99.5	98.7	98.8	99.0	99.5
% Other Nonwhite.............	0.4	0.0	0.1	0.9	0.5
% Of Spanish Origin..........	0.7	0.0	0.9	0.1	0.9
% Foreign Born...............	1.2	0.0	0.0	1.0	0.3
% Living In Group Quarters...	0.0	0.0	12.5	0.2	0.0
% 13 Years Old And Under.....	32.9	17.0	16.7	18.9	45.2
% 14-20 Years Old............	14.1	9.6	12.1	11.2	15.8
% 21-64 Years Old............	44.4	53.6	49.8	52.1	36.1
% 65-74 Years Old............	4.9	14.5	10.8	10.8	2.4
% 75 Years Old And Over......	3.7	5.3	10.6	7.0	0.5
% In Different House.........	30.1	16.3	46.7	28.7	37.4
% Families With Female Head...	79.5	44.7	60.1	50.2	84.8
Median School Years Completed....	12.0	11.0	10.5	9.8	10.5
Median Family Income, 1979......$$	6417	9739	8958	9157	4399
% Income Below Poverty Level....	51.7	12.8	36.2	31.3	74.4
% Income Of $30,000 Or More....	3.5	12.8	18.0	6.3	0.9
% White Collar Workers.......	59.7	39.6	44.8	37.4	33.5
% Civilian Labor Force Unemployed.	20.9	33.4	17.9	21.4	21.8
% Riding To Work By Automobile....	38.7	48.1	48.4	38.3	18.6
Mean Commuting Time - Minutes...	33.6	32.7	32.2	27.4	29.4
Population Per Household.....	2.8	2.5	2.7	2.4	3.4
Total Housing Units.........	2842	430	669	902	1627
% Condominiums...............	0.0	0.0	0.0	0.0	1.1
% Built 1970 Or Later........	6.2	0.0	3.5	9.8	0.0
% Owner Occupied.............	1.2	16.0	19.6	15.6	0.6
% With 1+ Persons Per Room...	12.4	9.4	8.5	10.1	19.6
Median Value: Owner Units......$$	-	-	22000	18800	-
Median Rent: Rental Units......$$	91	142	135	152	76
Median Number Of Rooms: All Units.	3.9	4.0	4.7	4.1	4.3

B. Sherman bought the tavern and some adjoining cattle pens and converted the property into a stockyard. Charles Cleaver bought 20 acres extending from 37th to 39th streets between Ellis Avenue and the lake for soap and rendering works. In 1857, Cleaver platted 100 acres for the village of Cleaverville.

Cottage Grove Avenue derived its name from Henry Graves' home, called "Cottage," which was bordered by a grove near 32nd Street and the old Indian trail which became that street.

During the Civil War, about 60 acres of Douglas' land was used as a prison camp for Confederate soldiers. By 1870 much of Groveland and Woodland Parks had been built up. At that time the horse-drawn omnibus line had been installed along Cottage Grove Avenue connecting 39th Street to the Loop, adding to the desirability of Douglas' lakefront location. Douglas developed into an area of greystones and Victorian mansions, becoming a fashionable residential district in the 1870s. In 1880, Michael Reese Hospital was built near the site of the old stockyards at 29th Street and Cottage Grove Avenue. Cottage Grove Avenue was the area's main commercial strip, and in 1896 the businessmen from 26th to 39th streets formed the South Side Businessmen's Association. The Armour Institute of Technology, funded

Community Area 35 — Douglas
Selected Characteristics of Census Tracts: 1970

Tract Number	TOTAL	3501	3502	3503	3504	3505	3506	3507	3508	3509	3510
Total Population	41276	2992	2689	746	2939	705	1828	1561	547	925	3836
% Male	44.9	39.7	42.9	47.6	40.6	88.1	54.7	47.6	66.0	48.4	43.5
% Black	87.6	23.5	79.9	33.6	99.8	4.0	42.3	99.5	64.2	99.4	85.1
% Other Nonwhite	1.9	8.9	4.4	7.9	0.2	15.7	11.3	0.1	1.2	0.5	2.4
% Of Spanish Language	1.3	5.0	0.0	5.2	1.0	0.9	3.8	0.5	0.8	0.0	0.2
% Foreign Born	2.7	17.2	4.6	3.6	0.0	8.6	11.7	0.3	0.7	0.0	3.8
% Living In Group Quarters	3.5	11.0	0.0	1.2	0.0	98.7	11.5	1.5	33.5	1.5	0.3
% 13 Years Old And Under	31.1	10.7	35.4	14.6	44.6	0.1	18.2	25.8	20.3	28.2	13.9
% 14-20 Years Old	14.5	6.2	13.6	3.6	15.8	59.3	9.0	15.1	33.7	12.5	4.0
% 21-64 Years Old	46.7	75.3	42.4	78.7	34.2	40.6	64.4	44.4	34.4	44.2	73.0
% 65-74 Years Old	5.2	5.6	5.6	2.0	3.2	0.0	5.2	9.7	9.3	10.5	7.2
% 75 Years Old And Over	2.4	2.2	2.9	1.1	2.1	0.0	3.2	5.0	2.4	4.5	1.9
% In Different House	53.4	33.5	46.4	0.7	68.1	5.5	41.3	62.1	35.8	84.7	49.5
% Families With Female Head	42.6	9.8	36.1	6.7	6C.8	–	16.6	36.7	42.9	33.7	17.7
Median School Years Completed	11.4	16.2	11.3	16.2	9.8	17.1	12.5	8.7	8.4	8.0	13.8
Median Family Income, 1969 $$	6260	13512	6372	18118	4924	–	7694	7580	4708	6441	13482
% Income Below Poverty Level	30.2	4.6	17.8	0.0	38.0	–	14.7	23.9	43.2	25.5	2.1
% Income of $15,000 or More	11.9	40.5	7.1	65.1	1.3	–	15.3	8.9	2.6	13.1	42.1
% White Collar Workers	33.1	72.9	34.2	68.8	11.2	44.3	48.9	12.9	24.7	0.0	51.8
% Civilian Labor Force Unemployed	5.4	0.9	6.0	3.8	13.0	2.8	1.7	7.1	12.6	9.1	2.3
% Riding To Work By Automobile	42.5	43.6	39.0	57.1	25.8	27.7	28.8	51.0	45.8	52.0	56.7
Population Per Household	2.9	1.6	3.0	1.9	3.7	1.8	2.1	3.2	3.1	2.8	1.8
Total Housing Units	17010	1665	913	404	805	5	648	619	237	398	2109
% Condominiums & Cooperatives	0.0	0.0	0.0	1.7	0.0	–	0.0	0.0	0.0	0.0	0.0
% Built 1960 Or Later	19.8	58.7	46.0	96.8	6.8	–	5.1	0.0	2.2	0.0	15.6
% Owner Occupied	4.1	0.1	0.3	11.1	0.5	–	2.9	16.8	15.6	14.6	2.0
% With 1+ Persons Per Room	17.0	3.7	18.6	2.9	34.2	–	26.0	17.8	17.8	15.2	2.4
Median Value: Owner Units $$	17000	–	–	–	–	–	–	–	–	–	–
Median Rent: Rental Units	96	133	91	177	78	–	98	84	80	68	147
Median Number Of Rooms: All Units	3.7	2.7	3.4	3.1	3.9	–	1.7	4.1	4.2	4.0	3.3

Tract Number	3511	3512	3513	3514	3515
Total Population	7681	1307	2953	3607	6960
% Male	40.7	45.3	45.4	46.9	42.2
% Black	99.2	99.2	99.1	99.4	99.9
% Other Nonwhite	0.5	0.2	0.5	0.2	0.0
% Of Spanish Language	1.4	5.3	1.3	0.9	0.0
% Foreign Born	0.6	3.8	0.2	0.4	0.1
% Living In Group Quarters	0.0	1.9	0.6	0.4	0.3
% 13 Years Old And Under	36.6	21.6	33.8	30.4	47.0
% 14-20 Years Old	15.7	11.6	14.7	15.0	18.0
% 21-64 Years Old	41.0	56.3	43.7	44.9	31.3
% 65-74 Years Old	4.3	7.6	5.3	6.7	2.3
% 75 Years Old And Over	2.3	2.8	2.6	3.0	1.4
% In Different House	54.9	55.2	71.4	53.3	58.3
% Families With Female Head	56.7	31.2	44.0	42.5	66.8
Median School Years Completed	10.8	9.4	10.2	8.9	9.8
Median Family Income, 1969 $$	5513	5871	5402	6403	3476
% Income Below Poverty Level	31.1	21.3	34.1	28.0	60.1
% Income of $15,000 or More	2.8	6.3	4.3	4.9	1.3
% White Collar Workers	14.5	14.1	7.5	10.7	7.5
% Civilian Labor Force Unemployed	6.2	5.5	6.2	7.4	11.0
% Riding To Work By Automobile	36.0	35.4	47.8	34.0	34.3
Population Per Household	3.2	2.4	3.4	3.0	4.2
Total Housing Units	2331	901	1646	2487	1842
% Condominiums & Cooperatives	0.0	0.0	0.0	0.0	0.0
% Built 1960 Or Later	23.7	6.8	5.2	1.9	8.8
% Owner Occupied	1.2	4.6	6.2	1.4	
% With 1+ Persons Per Room	17.9	11.8	18.9	19.3	35.0
Median Value: Owner Units $$	–	–	14200	14400	–
Median Rent: Rental Units	79	112	92	85	80
Median Number Of Rooms: All Units	3.9	3.6	4.1	3.8	4.3

by the prominent meatpacking family, opened a campus on Federal Street between 32nd and 33rd streets in 1891.

By 1900, however, Douglas had already reached residential maturity and had begun to change. Apartment buildings were put up in the area, including some in the two residential parks. The first residents of Groveland and Woodland began to resettle in more freshly-developed areas. An Italian working class area in the Western part of Douglas became the Federal Street slum. Some blacks began to move into the area from the Loop. As the Douglas residential area changed, industry became more prevalent. Light manufacturing establishments were set up from 26th to 29th streets along Indiana and Cottage Grove avenues, and a brewery was established between 26th and 27th streets from Cottage Grove Avenue to the Illinois Central tracks.

Blacks inhabited the residential area on Cottage Grove Avenue to 35th Street by 1916. With the wartime demand for labor, Chicago's black population increased substantially, and many of the new migrants settled in Douglas. By 1920, blacks resided in many of the converted older homes and kitchenette apartments north of 39th Street (Pershing Road) and west of Cottage Grove Avenue. Some middle-class black families were already relocating farther south. Blacks moved into the Federal Street slum. The population of Douglas reached 58,388 in 1920 and was 74 percent black. By 1930, the total population had declined to just over 50,000, while the black proportion of that total increased to 89 percent. At this time Douglas was the center of the black community of Chicago. Business and professional offices converged around the intersection of State and 31st streets.

The area became a center for black institutions as well. The Quinn Chapel African Methodist Episcopal congregation, which originated in the Loop in the 1840s, and had participated in the abolitionist movement and the underground railroad, built the current Quinn Chapel at 24th Street and Wabash Avenue in 1892. The Olivet Baptist Church had moved from the Loop to Douglas in 1893, eventually settling in a building at 31st Street and King Drive. The Olivet Church, which had the largest black congregation in the city, provided facilities for incoming black migrants during World War I. In 1919, an incident at the 29th Street beach touched off a weeklong race riot, the worst in Chicago's history. It spread far beyond the boundaries of Douglas, resulting in 38 deaths and hundreds of injuries. The Olivet Church organized to help victims of the riot and to bring calm to the area in the troubled months that followed. The Frederick Douglas Center, founded in 1904, was a settlement house for blacks, whose outreach activities eventually touched the lives of many South Side blacks.

More than 90 percent of the residences located by the 1939 Land Use Survey had been built prior to 1895, and almost a fourth had been built before 1885. About one-third of the residential structures had been substructed into apartments and furnished rooms, and more than half of these were in need of repair. The population had grown by 3,000 during the 1930s and was now 94 percent black.

New construction in the Douglas area took the form of Chicago Housing Authority projects during the forties. The Ida B. Wells housing project (about 1,000 low-rise units, later expanded) at 37th Street and South Park Way (now Dr. Martin Luther King Jr. Drive) opened in 1941, and nine years later Dearborn Homes (800 units) opened at 27th and State streets. However, further substruction of the remaining mansions was necessary to accommodate another 30,000 blacks who moved into the community area during World War II. In 1950 the population exceeded 76,000, a historic high, almost all black and overcrowded to an unprecedented degree.

After the war, the Illinois Institute of Technology (created by the merger of the Armour and Lewis Institutes) and Michael Reese Hospital combined forces to plan for a future of the Douglas area, forming the South Side Planning Board. This group, along with the Chicago Land Clearance Commission and the Chicago Housing Authority, commenced to reshape the future of Douglas. The Illinois Institute of Technology began a $25 million expansion of its campus, which covered 120 acres of former slum area west of Michigan Avenue between 30th and 35th streets. In 1952, the CHA completed the 326 unit Prairie Avenue Courts project. Stateway Gardens, more than 1,600 units, was built over the Federal Street slum south of 35th Street in 1958, and more than 200 units were added to Prairie Avenue Courts in that year. The 479 unit Clarence Darrow project was built in 1961. Private development also took place, beginning with the Lake Meaddows development near 35th Street and King Drive covering 100 acres and including 10 apartment buildings, more than 2,000 housing units, a

shopping center, school, commercial building, and a park. North of Lake Meadows on the east side of King Drive between 26th and 31st streets, the Prairie Shores complex was opened in 1962. It has grown to five apartment buildings and almost 1,700 housing units. South Commons, on Michigan Avenue south of 26th Street, was completed in the 1960s and covers 30 acres.

The demolition and land clearance of these two decades produced a sharp drop in the community area population, which fell by a third in the 1950s, and by more than a fifth during the following decade. In this time the black population decreased by 35,000, while whites began to move back into the area. The present population of Douglas, just under 36,000, is less than half what is was in the overcrowded 1940s. Blacks are now 87 percent of the population, whites have increased to 12 percent, other races and Latinos remain negligible in number. Eighty-six percent of the white population of Douglas lives in or near the Prairie Shores and South Commons developments.

In 1980, more than one-fifth of Douglas' population still lived in overcrowded housing units. Ninety-five percent of all housing units are rented. The greatest proportion, nearly two-thirds, of all homes are located in structures with 10 or more units. Fewer than 15 percent of all units are single-family homes. Some housing rehabilitation is going on in the area of Calumet and 32nd streets, near Prairie Shores and Lake Meadows, where the restoration of townhouses designed by Frank Lloyd Wright may signal the redevelopment of a stylish neighborhood.

Will Hogan

Oakland

The Oakland community area is a mile-long strip located between Lake Michigan on the east and Vincennes and Cottage Grove avenues on the west, extending south from 35th Street to 43rd Street. In the early days Samuel Ellis operated a tavern, the Ellis Inn, on 35th Street near the intersection of the Vincennes Trail and a road that came up the lakeshore. In 1851, a Loop industrialist named Charles Cleaver established a soap factory and lard rendering works in a swampy area between 37th and 39th streets. This location provided the factory with access to the Sherman and Cottage Grove stockyards in the Douglas area to the northwest. Cleaver envisioned a company town. He built wooden homes for his workers and Oakwood Hall, an elaborate house for himself, located on a large lot at Oakland Boulevard and Ellis Avenue. He established a grocery and general store, and provided a religious meeting house and a town hall. The Oakland community is an outgrowth of the Cleaverville settlement, located south of the factory, platted in 1857.

Politically, Cleaverville became part of the Town of Hyde Park, incorporated in 1861. The area north of 39th Street (Pershing Road) was part of an extension to Chicago legislated in 1863. A big boost to growth in Oakland came as a result of a train station established by the Illinois Central Railroad, and subsidized by Cleaver. In 1871 developers resubdivided the area and the name Oakland was applied to the entire community. In 1867, horsecar service on Cottage Grove Avenue was extended to 39th Street (Pershing Road) which, along with the trains, gave the Oakland community good transportation to the downtown business district. After Hyde Park voted for prohibition, a string of saloons appeared near the car terminal on the north (Chicago) side of 39th Street.

Oakland grew rapidly as a select residential suburb. Among prominent residents were ex-Senator Lyman Trumbull and his brother George, Charles Cleaver, realtor George G. Pope and manufacturer Joseph Bonfield. In 1882, horsecars in Oakland were converted to cable cars. This, in addition to the community's close proximity to Lake Michigan, further acccelerated growth. In 1889, the south half of Oakland became part of Chicago when Hyde Park was annexed to the city. By 1895, Oakland had reached residential maturity.

Oakland began to change from an affluent community as early as the beginning of the 20th century. Irish workers began moving in from the stockyards area and the wealthier residents began to move out. Mass-produced single-family dwellings appeared in the 1890s. Conversion

Community Area 36 -- Oakland
Population and Housing Characteristics, 1930-1980

	1980	1970	1960	1950	1940	1930
Total Population.......	16,748	18,291	24,378	24,464	14,500	14,962
% Male..................	42.6	45.3	46.8	48.1	49.6	51.1
% Female................	57.4	54.7	53.2	51.9	50.4	48.9
% White.................	0.3	0.7	1.3	17.7	76.9	70.0
% Black.................	99.4	98.9	98.2	77.4	22.1	28.9
% Other Nonwhite Races..	0.3	0.4	0.5	4.9	1.0	1.2
% Under 5 Years Old.....	12.1	11.5	18.3	10.7	7.1	5.9
% 5-19 Years Old........	40.9	44.6	30.3	19.1	18.8	15.8
% 20-44 Years Old.......	28.9	24.4	32.3	49.0	42.4	49.8
% 45-64 Years Old.......	11.8	12.8	14.4	15.9	23.6	22.7
% 65 Years and Older....	6.3	6.7	4.7	5.3	8.1	5.8
Median School Years....	11.1	9.6	8.8	9.4	8.7	*
Total Housing Units....	5,209	5,686	7,834	7,869	5,704	*
% In One-Unit Structures.	8.6	8.1	12.2	*	*	*
% Owner Occupied........	3.9	4.3	5.9	6.0	6.0	*
% Renter Occupied.......	89.7	84.0	87.6	91.9	79.8	*
% Vacant................	6.4	11.7	6.5	2.1	4.2	*
% 1+ Persons per Room....	22.4	28.7	38.6	40.2	*	*

Community Area 36 -- Oakland
Selected Characteristics of Census Tracts: 1980

Tract Number	Total	3601	3602	3603	3604	3605
Total Population.............	16748	1034	5543	2586	4169	3416
% Male........................	42.6	41.0	42.6	42.3	40.7	45.7
% Black.......................	99.4	96.0	99.6	100.0	99.2	99.9
% Other Nonwhite..............	0.3	0.9	0.4	0.0	0.4	0.0
% Of Spanish Origin...........	0.6	0.7	0.3	0.5	1.0	0.7
% Foreign Born................	0.7	0.0	0.9	0.6	0.4	1.0
% Living In Group Quarters....	0.5	4.4	0.0	0.0	0.6	0.4
% 13 Years Old And Under......	36.0	37.9	36.1	35.8	35.5	36.2
% 14-20 Years Old.............	19.3	10.3	22.0	21.4	16.5	19.4
% 21-64 Years Old.............	38.4	45.5	37.9	38.1	36.7	39.4
% 65-74 Years Old.............	3.5	4.2	2.5	3.6	4.8	3.2
% 75 Years Old And Over.......	2.8	2.2	1.5	1.0	6.4	1.9
% In Different House..........	37.3	56.4	32.6	36.6	35.2	42.3
% Families With Female Head...	78.5	64.2	80.8	79.6	78.3	78.9
Median School Years Completed...	11.1	12.5	11.2	10.7	10.8	10.6
Median Family Income, 1979.....$$	5555	10931	5583	4548	6550	4306
% Income Below Poverty Level...	60.9	19.9	65.9	68.6	55.8	70.3
% Income Of $30,000 Or More....	3.7	4.8	1.7	5.2	5.3	3.5
% White Collar Workers........	41.6	49.8	42.6	39.7	41.3	35.9
% Civilian Labor Force Unemployed.	29.5	21.6	26.2	21.9	36.2	33.6
% Riding To Work By Automobile...	41.0	44.2	33.5	50.2	41.7	44.3
Mean Commuting Time - Minutes...	33.1	34.9	29.9	34.1	33.2	37.5
Population Per Household..........	3.4	2.8	3.9	3.3	3.1	3.5
Total Housing Units..........	5209	367	1453	873	1414	1102
% Condominiums................	0.0	0.0	0.0	0.0	0.0	0.0
% Built 1970 Or Later.........	19.6	75.3	20.1	34.5	7.2	5.3
% Owner Occupied..............	3.9	2.5	1.0	3.8	5.6	5.9
% With 1+ Persons Per Room.....$$	22.4	7.8	28.2	21.3	18.0	26.5
Median Value: Owner Units.......$$	30400	-	-	-	-	-
Median Rent: Rental Units.......$$	87	208	81	81	81	104
Median Number Of Rooms: All Units.	4.1	4.0	4.2	4.0	3.9	4.0

Community Area 36 -- Oakland
Selected Characteristics of Census Tracts: 1970

Tract Number	TOTAL	3601	3602	3603	3604	3605
Total Population.............	18291	602	5356	1945	7542	2846
% Male........................	45.3	46.8	44.4	48.9	43.8	48.1
% Black.......................	98.9	90.4	99.5	98.8	99.3	98.6
% Other Nonwhite..............	0.4	0.3	0.4	0.2	0.4	0.8
% Of Spanish Language.........	0.7	0.0	1.3	2.9	0.0	0.4
% Foreign Born................	0.3	2.6	0.1	0.3	0.2	0.4
% Living In Group Quarters....	1.2	9.1	0.1	2.0	0.2	3.4
% 13 Years Old And Under......	40.4	38.7	44.6	33.7	44.3	26.9
% 14-20 Years Old.............	17.4	15.0	23.5	12.8	17.0	10.5
% 21-64 Years Old.............	35.6	36.9	28.1	46.3	31.7	52.5
% 65-74 Years Old.............	4.4	6.3	2.1	4.8	4.8	6.9
% 75 Years Old And Over.......	2.3	3.2	1.6	2.5	2.2	3.3
% In Different House..........	58.0	40.2	69.4	49.1	57.1	47.5
% Families With Female Head...	48.3	44.5	55.2	42.9	50.5	36.6
Median School Years Completed...	9.6	8.6	8.9	9.1	9.4	10.0
Median Family Income, 1969.....$$	4879	3661	5079	4559	4439	6345
% Income Below Poverty Level...	44.4	58.0	41.6	40.2	51.2	33.0
% Income of $15,000 or More....	3.2	3.1	2.5	3.2	2.5	5.6
% White Collar Workers........	10.3	9.9	3.9	9.5	11.1	16.5
% Civilian Labor Force Unemployed.	13.4	3.5	14.7	15.6	12.7	13.1
% Riding To Work By Automobile....	31.9	26.7	26.3	27.1	30.0	43.4
Population Per Household..........	3.6	3.5	4.9	2.8	3.9	2.4
Total Housing Units..........	5686	168	1130	1023	2084	1281
% Condominiums & Cooperatives.....	0.2	0.0	0.0	0.0	0.6	0.0
% Built 1960 Or Later.............	28.9	3.2	35.4	31.3	42.4	1.8
% Owner Occupied..............	4.2	.7	1.1	4.2	4.4	6.2
% With 1+ Persons Per Room......$$	30.1	27.4	44.4	20.8	31.9	19.5
Median Value: Owner Units.......$$	15100	-	-	-	-	-
Median Rent: Rental Units.......$$	81	85	79	81	77	90
Median Number Of Rooms: All Units.	3.7	3.5	4.4	3.2	4.0	2.7

of large homes into apartment buildings and rooming houses began. The availability of smaller units attracted many transients into the community. After 1910, apartment buildings were constructed and the Kenwood branch of the elevated line connected Oakland and the stockyards.

Oakland had 16,540 residents by 1920. Blacks then constituted 17 percent of the population. Many early black southern migrants settled in this area when they first came to the city. During the 1920s, blacks lived mainly in the area east of State Street and south from 35th Street. Those of European descent lived mainly in the area east of Cottage Grove Avenue. By 1930, even though the total population of Oakland had declined to less than 15,000, the black population increased to 4,317, 29 percent of the total. Leading nationalities among the foreign stock were the Germans, English, Irish and Canadians. A small Japanese-American community grew up between 35th and 39th streets, on Lake Park Avenue.

During the 1930s, there was no new construction in Oakland and the population declined slightly. Between 1940 and 1950, however, the population increased 70 percent to its historic high, in excess of 24,000. This was due to an increase in the Black American population, which was now more than three-fourths of the total. Construction of the 1,650 unit Ida B. Wells Homes housed many of these new residents. Conversion of large apartment buildings and houses into smaller more numerous apartments served to house the remaining newcomers.

By the end of World War II, the Black American population had moved east of Cottage Grove along 39th Street and occupied most of the community of Oakland. The growing population of Oakland was housed by the conversion of larger homes and the subdivision of large apartments into kitchenettes. In 1953, the Chicago Housing Authority provided the only new construction in Oakland since the Wells project — the Victor Olander Homes. The Olander Homes contained 150 dwelling units. In 1958, a 150-unit extension of this project was completed. Later, the Madden Park project was completed at Pershing Road and Ellis Avenue in 1956, the Chicago Land Clearance Commission (CLCC) authorized the 37th-Cottage Grove Project. The Pershing-Cottage Grove redevelopent was shared by the Oakland and Grand Boulevard community areas.

The population of Oakland has been declining for the last 30 years. In the 1950s, most of the rest of the whites moved out, but almost as many blacks moved in. By 1960, blacks constituted 98 percent of the total population. After that blacks started moving farther south and west as the land clearance demolitions commenced. In the 1960s Oakland lost a fourth of its population and almost the same proportion of its housing.

By 1970, the Oakland community was experiencing serious economic problems. The unemployment and poverty rates were high. By 1980, more than three-fifths of all of Oakland residents lived below the poverty level. Unemployment approached 30 percent. The median family income was less than $6,000, the lowest of any community area in the city. More than a fifth of the residents live in overcrowded housing. The population has dropped almost to its post-Depression level. Despite its lakefront location and transportation connections, Oakland seems likely to remain a poverty area for the balance of this decade.

Annie Ruth Leslie

Community Area 37

Fuller Park

The Fuller Park community area of Chicago is an elongated strip of land, hemmed in on the east and west by railroad tracks, running two miles from Pershing road on the north to Garfield Boulevard on the south. The name comes from the block-and-a-half-long city park, located south of 45th Street between Stewart and Princeton streets. The area is small in size, and much of the land is covered by railroad tracks or by the Dan Ryan Expressway, which traverses it from north to south borders.

Fuller Park was originally part of the northern fringe of the town of Lake, incorporated in 1865. Like other communities near the Loop, the residential development of Fuller Park was spurred by the Chicago Fire of 1871, and the subsequent strict fireproof codes that required expensive building materials. Many Chicagoans could not afford the expenses of fireproofing and Fuller Park was outside the fire code area. In spite of its flexible fireproof codes, Fuller Park remained relatively small throughout the 19th and 20th centuries reaching its maximum growth by 1950 at a population of 17,174 residents. Since the 1950s, when construction of the Dan Ryan Expressway through the heart of the community displaced about a third of its residents, Fuller Park's population has steadily decreased. A good portion of the community is taken up by railroad tracks. Today, the community is a narrow corridor of a neighborhood in the geographic heart of Chicago.

In the 19th century, railroads built facilities in Fuller Park because of its close proximity to downtown Chicago. In 1868, the Rock Island car and locomotive works had been built between 47th and 51st streets. In 1871, the Lake Shore and Michigan Southern Railways built division shops and roundhouses at 42nd and State streets. The shops and engine houses of the Wabash Railroad were at 41st and Stewart streets and the shops of the Pittsburgh and Fort Wayne Railroad were at Stewart and 55th streets. After the Civil War, many who worked in the Union Stock yards, immediately west, settled there. Fuller Park was basically a frame village reaching residential maturity in 1895.

Irish workers were among the first settlers to live in Fuller Park. They worked mainly for the railroads and stockyards. Horsecars on Wentworth Avenue, the main business street, Pershing Road, 43rd and 47th streets provided transportation to downtown Chicago. Austrian and German groups, also railroad and stockyard workers, followed the Irish. In 1889, the Town of Lake including Fuller Park was annexed to Chicago.

Blacks began moving into Fuller Park during the late 1890s and early 1900s. Many of these early residents were also industrial and stockyards workers. By 1920, blacks comprised 12 percent of the community population, which was then 16,541. The population dropped by 2,000 in the 1920s. A disproportionate decline in the black population was partly due to the displacement of black workers by returning World War I veterans, and partly the consequence of racial hostility, which had surfaced after the war.

By 1930, the northern part of the community area became more industrialized. As the housing began to deteriorate and vacant lots appeared, the Irish had begun to move out of Fuller Park. Germans and Austrians were then the most numerous foreign stock. Slavic and Mexican workers were moving in. However blacks were responsible

Community Area 37 -- Fuller Park
Population and Housing Characteristics, 1930-1980

	1980	1970	1960	1950	1940	1930
Total Population.......	5,832	7,372	12,181	17,174	15,094	14,437
% Male...................	45.1	47.8	48.4	48.7	51.2	51.9
% Female.................	54.9	52.2	51.6	51.3	48.8	48.1
% White..................	0.8	2.1	3.9	50.2	90.3	89.0
% Black..................	98.7	96.9	96.0	49.7	9.5	7.6
% Other Nonwhite Races...	0.5	1.0	0.1	0.1	0.2	3.4
% Under 5 Years Old......	7.8	10.6	15.9	12.0	8.9	9.8
% 5-19 Years Old.........	29.9	36.8	31.0	23.7	29.0	31.8
% 20-44 Years Old........	27.9	27.0	32.2	42.3	37.6	38.3
% 45-64 Years Old........	17.5	18.5	16.5	16.7	19.6	16.2
% 65 Years and Older.....	16.9	7.1	4.4	5.3	4.9	3.9
Median School Years......	10.2	9.1	8.5	8.5	7.7	*
Total Housing Units....	2,023	2,287	2,954	4,147	4,119	*
% In One-Unit Structures.	22.1	18.7	11.4	*	*	*
% Owner Occupied.........	27.6	26.8	28.4	29.9	26.4	*
% Renter Occupied........	66.9	56.9	66.3	67.8	67.4	*
% Vacant.................	5.5	16.3	5.3	2.3	6.2	*
% 1+ Persons per Room....	12.1	21.0	31.1	24.3	*	*

Community Area 37 -- Fuller Park
Selected Characteristics of Census Tracts: 1980

Tract Number	Total	3701	3702	3703	3704
Total Population.............	5832	1552	1758	1164	1358
% Male.......................	45.1	39.4	46.9	47.8	47.0
% Black......................	98.7	98.3	97.6	99.8	99.6
% Other Nonwhite.............	0.5	0.5	0.9	0.1	0.3
% Of Spanish Origin..........	1.2	1.2	1.6	0.0	1.2
% Foreign Born...............	0.8	0.4	1.0	0.0	1.8
% Living In Group Quarters...	0.8	1.2	0.4	0.4	1.3
% 13 Years Old And Under.....	24.7	19.8	24.1	29.9	26.7
% 14-20 Years Old............	15.1	14.5	15.1	15.4	15.6
% 21-64 Years Old............	43.3	35.6	46.4	46.0	45.8
% 65-74 Years Old............	9.9	14.5	10.5	5.2	8.1
% 75 Years Old And Over......	6.9	15.7	3.9	3.5	3.8
% In Different House.........	28.7	29.3	32.2	20.4	29.9
% Families With Female Head..	55.5	51.4	54.0	60.6	56.6
Median School Years Completed	10.2	7.9	10.9	10.7	10.9
Median Family Income, 1979......$$	10799	8902	12532	10179	11983
% Income Below Poverty Level.	34.5	31.4	32.6	51.3	26.8
% Income Of $30,000 Or More..	8.1	1.8	15.1	7.5	4.3
% White Collar Workers.......	35.9	31.1	39.4	36.4	33.7
% Civilian Labor Force Unemployed.	22.2	28.1	14.3	22.3	28.0
% Riding To Work By Automobile....	53.6	38.5	54.6	51.1	63.7
Mean Commuting Time - Minutes....	35.9	42.7	39.8	31.8	29.4
Population Per Household..........	3.0	2.3	3.2	3.7	3.4
Total Housing Units..........	2023	683	596	334	410
% Condominiums...............	0.0	0.0	0.0	0.0	0.0
% Built 1970 Or Later........	19.3	40.7	1.7	19.0	7.9
% Owner Occupied.............	27.6	13.0	34.2	40.1	32.0
% With 1+ Persons Per Room...	12.1	9.6	12.6	16.7	12.1
Median Value: Owner Units.......$$	24800	-	25400	23000	28100
Median Rent: Rental Units.......$$	118	66	143	138	144
Median Number Of Rooms: All Units.	4.9	3.4	5.2	5.6	5.4

Community Area 37 -- Fuller Park
Selected Characteristics of Census Tracts: 1970

Tract Number	TOTAL	3701	3702	3703	3704
Total Population.............	7372	1467	2524	1387	1994
% Male.......................	47.8	49.0	46.8	48.4	47.8
% Black......................	96.9	94.9	97.6	99.6	95.7
% Other Nonwhite.............	1.0	3.3	0.7	0.1	0.3
% Of Spanish Language........	0.8	2.2	0.2	1.3	0.3
% Foreign Born...............	0.1	0.9	0.0	0.0	0.0
% Living In Group Quarters...	1.0	0.5	1.1	0.0	2.0
% 13 Years Old And Under.....	34.1	39.1	33.2	31.4	33.6
% 14-20 Years Old............	14.7	11.5	15.8	16.7	14.2
% 21-64 Years Old............	44.1	43.1	44.5	43.2	44.8
% 65-74 Years Old............	5.1	4.2	4.7	6.3	5.7
% 75 Years Old And Over......	2.0	2.2	1.9	2.4	1.7
% In Different House.........	55.8	45.8	53.6	54.2	67.3
% Families With Female Head..	30.2	26.6	30.0	34.2	30.5
Median School Years Completed......	9.0	8.7	9.2	9.3	9.2
Median Family Income, 1969......$$	6492	5837	7142	5667	7056
% Income Below Poverty Level.	27.0	20.1	30.6	35.6	20.3
% Income of $15,000 or More..	8.6	7.5	11.6	6.7	6.4
% White Collar Workers.......	10.3	9.5	10.6	10.2	10.3
% Civilian Labor Force Unemployed.	11.9	11.9	11.8	16.5	8.4
% Riding To Work By Automobile....	46.8	26.9	49.0	48.9	51.8
Population Per Household..........	3.8	4.0	3.7	3.7	3.8
Total Housing Units..........	2293	617	720	399	557
% Condominiums & Cooperatives.	0.6	1.0	1.0	0.0	0.0
% Built 1960 Or Later........	14.7	50.3	5.7	0.0	0.7
% Owner Occupied.............	26.0	13.8	33.5	31.6	25.9
% With 1+ Persons Per Room...	21.1	23.8	20.3	20.0	21.0
Median Value: Owner Units.......$$	12400	-	16000	10500	-
Median Rent: Rental Units.......$$	88	81	86	89	93
Median Number Of Rooms: All Units.	4.8	3.8	4.9	5.1	5.1

for most of a small population increase in the 1940s, and a spurt to an all-time high in 1950, by which time they were 50 percent of the population. Prior to the 1950s, segregated housing practices had forced blacks to live mainly east of Wentworth Avenue. After this period, they moved in large numbers west of Wentworth Avenue. During the 1950s the Dan Ryan Expressway was built through the heart of Fuller Park. Demolitions clearing land for the expressway led to a population decrease of almost one-third. Although construction of the expressway seriously disrupted and displaced residents, very little new housing was built during this period. The only new construction during the 1950s was the West Kenwood Garden Projects, a 52-unit row-house development selling single-family homes, built by the Chicago Dwellings Association in 1956.

By 1960, the population of Fuller Park had decreased to just over 12,000 persons, of which 96 percent were black. Mexican-Americans were the largest non-black group. In the decade that followed, the population dropped to 7,372. Today, fewer than 6,000 live in Fuller Park, of whom 99 percent are black.

In 1980, the unemployment rate in Fuller Park exceeded 20 percent. More than 40 percent of all residents were classified as falling below the poverty line. More than half the households with children under 18 were headed by females. The housing stock has dwindled to fewer than 2,000 units, more than three-fourths of which are overcrowded. Most residents live in small (two to nine unit) apartment buildings.

During the 1980s, various community organizations have sprung up to do something about the deterioration of neighborhood streets and buildings. The efforts of organizations such as the recently-organized Neighbors of Fuller Park have been directed toward the city administration, whom they accuse of having ignored problems in the area. The Fuller Park Community Field House has been identified as a major community facility needing renovation. Perhaps the efforts of the neighborhood organizations will lead to a new vitality in Fuller Park, but redevelopment is clearly dependent on outside resources. Three ordinances were recently approved by the City of Chicago Council on redevelopment projects in and near Fuller Park. These include authorization of the Land Clearance Commission to sell two parcels of land to the Illinois Institute of Technology and to expand the 37th-Cottage Grove Project. Other redevelopment plans await approval.

Annie Ruth Leslie

Community Area 38

Grand Boulevard

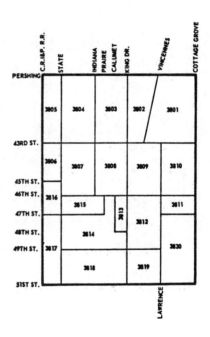

The Grand Boulevard community area is located about four miles directly south of the downtown business district. The name is taken from that of the broad tree-lined street (later called South Park Way, now Dr. Martin Luther King, Jr. Drive) which runs through the center of the neighborhood toward the downtown area. Grand Boulevard was originally a part of the Town of Hyde Park, formed in 1861. At this time, the area was mainly prairie with a few scattered houses. Two Indian roads, which became Cottage Grove and Vincennes avenues, were used by farmers to haul grain and cattle to Chicago.

After the Civil War and the Great Fire, many middle-class families moved to Grand Boulevard in an attempt to get away from the city. The original settlers were mostly native Americans of English, Scotch and Irish descent. The population grew rapidly. In 1871, the Langley Methodist Episcopal Church was erected. In 1881, the Irish organized the parish of St. Elizabeth of Hungary at the corner of 41st Street and Wabash Avenue. In 1873, School District No. 7 was formed to serve the part of Grand Boulevard called Forrestville. The South Park Commission planned the Chicago boulevard system in 1869, and a massive beautification of Grand Boulevard began in 1874. While this was going on, many mansions and single-family homes were built along Grand Boulevard and adjacent streets. So extensive was this beautification and building up of Grand Boulevard that it became a popular route for the carriage-riding public.

Grand Boulevard received a major impetus for growth in 1882 when cable cars started running along Cottage Grove Avenue to 39th Street. In 1887, these cars were extended to 63rd Street. The community's growth continued after the village of Hyde Park was annexed to Chicago in 1889. A half century later, a survey would show that 60 percent of all structures existing in Grand Boulevard in 1939 had been built between 1885 and 1894, and until 1960 housing expansion came about through conversion and substruction of older structures. In 1894, Grand Boulevard was residentially mature, consisting mainly of single-family homes and three-story apartment buildings. By 1896, the

Indiana Avenue and State Street lines were electrified, providing faster transportation to the Loop and making the community even more attractive.

Around the turn of the century, as the first generation of residents began to break up and move away, German Jewish families began moving south into Grand Boulevard. They established the Isaiah Israel Temple at 50th Street and Drexel Boulevard and built a new temple at 46th Street and Grand Boulevard in 1915. Many Jewish families operated businesses along commercial strips like 35th, 47th and 51st streets.

After 1920, the pattern of ethnic residence changed with many black Americans moving into the area. As early as 1890, blacks lived in Grand Boulevard, residing primarily in the 4600 block of Langley and Champlain avenues. Many lived in the area as servants of rich whites. The First World War stepped up migration of blacks from the rural South to Chicago, because there was a need for them as industrial workers. For a short period, the economic success of these workers

Community Area 38 -- Grand Boulevard
Population and Housing Characteristics, 1930-1980

	1980	1970	1960	1950	1940	1930
Total Population.......	53,741	80,150	80,036	114,557	103,256	87,005
% Male..................	45.6	46.2	47.7	47.3	46.5	49.0
% Female................	54.4	53.8	52.3	52.7	53.5	51.0
% White.................	0.3	0.5	0.5	1.0	1.8	5.2
% Black.................	99.4	99.3	99.4	98.9	98.1	94.7
% Other Nonwhite Races...	0.3	0.2	0.1	0.1	0.1	0.1
% Under 5 Years Old......	9.5	9.4	11.7	8.3	6.4	6.4
% 5-19 Years Old........	31.5	36.4	21.3	16.8	20.6	17.8
% 20-44 Years Old.......	27.9	24.8	32.6	45.3	49.9	59.7
% 45-64 Years Old	17.5	18.4	25.0	24.0	19.1	14.0
% 65 Years and Older.....	13.6	11.0	9.4	5.6	4.0	2.1
Median School Years....	10.5	9.4	8.7	8.5	7.9	*
Total Housing Units.....	20,852	25,948	26,486	31,598	29,523	**
% In One-Unit Structures.	3.9	5.4	4.4	*	*	**
% Owner Occupied.........	6.4	6.6	7.6	7.8	5.4	**
% Renter Occupied........	83.3	85.4	88.9	90.9	91.9	**
% Vacant.................	10.3	8.0	3.5	1.3	2.7	**
% 1+ Persons per Room....	13.6	20.8	22.1	38.5	*	**

Community Area 38 -- Grand Boulevard
Selected Characteristics of Census Tracts: 1980

Tract Number	Total	3801	3802	3803	3804	3805	3806	3807	3808	3809	3810
Total Population.............	53741	3151	2020	4755	1780	3029	3694	2070	2453	2349	3105
% Male.......................	45.6	43.4	43.7	47.2	48.8	43.8	42.3	46.8	47.6	47.6	44.6
% Black......................	99.4	98.9	99.4	99.5	98.9	99.9	99.7	99.5	99.2	99.1	99.9
% Other Nonwhite.............	0.3	0.4	0.4	0.1	0.1	0.0	0.2	0.2	0.4	0.5	0.1
% Of Spanish Origin..........	0.7	0.5	0.5	0.4	0.3	1.6	0.9	1.5	0.6	0.6	0.1
% Foreign Born...............	0.8	1.1	1.1	0.9	1.3	1.0	0.9	0.8	0.0	0.3	0.2
% Living In Group Quarters...	1.5	0.7	0.2	0.8	2.2	0.8	0.5	10.6	2.9	0.7	0.6
% 13 Years Old And Under.....	27.7	22.7	10.2	26.3	26.2	42.3	44.6	18.6	16.9	19.3	38.2
% 14-20 Years Old............	15.3	16.2	6.7	15.1	15.6	23.6	22.3	10.3	9.0	12.8	21.7
% 21-64 Years Old............	43.3	38.3	37.5	47.8	45.4	33.2	32.1	47.2	54.8	50.3	34.1
% 65-74 Years Old............	8.0	10.1	26.7	7.3	8.3	0.5	0.6	13.8	12.4	11.7	3.5
% 75 Years Old And Over......	5.6	12.7	18.9	3.6	4.6	0.4	0.4	10.1	6.9	5.8	2.4
% In Different House.........	34.2	37.7	47.5	24.4	16.4	31.0	37.5	43.6	40.8	41.4	24.4
% Families With Female Head..	71.1	63.7	60.8	69.2	60.1	79.4	80.9	55.1	62.4	63.4	76.6
Median School Years Completed..	10.5	9.4	10.2	10.8	10.2	10.9	10.9	10.2	10.2	10.6	10.7
Median Family Income, 1979...$$	6945	7294	8295	5230	5946	6514	5292	9310	8353	8068	6819
% Income Below Poverty Level..	51.4	48.5	27.1	55.9	52.5	67.8	77.4	32.6	33.8	40.8	59.2
% Income Of $30,000 Or More...	4.9	4.6	6.0	8.6	2.5	1.4	0.0	10.9	3.6	8.3	4.3
% White Collar Workers.......	38.0	32.5	48.7	28.9	34.7	25.1	28.5	37.0	26.4	36.5	54.8
% Civilian Labor Force Unemployed.	24.2	25.8	19.5	19.8	35.6	51.5	35.2	22.6	20.7	26.6	23.2
% Riding To Work By Automobile.	36.8	44.2	37.7	27.2	35.8	33.1	37.5	44.7	36.5	34.5	34.6
Mean Commuting Time - Minutes...	36.3	39.4	30.1	35.3	37.2	43.4	37.5	47.3	36.7	35.9	38.2
Population Per Household.........	2.8	2.4	1.7	2.8	2.8	5.0	4.9	2.3	2.2	2.6	4.1
Total Housing Units...........	20852	1510	1274	1896	701	635	790	963	1193	1032	837
% Condominiums................	0.2	0.0	0.0	0.0	1.6	0.0	0.0	0.0	0.0	0.0	0.0
% Built 1970 Or Later........	7.4	13.8	48.0	1.0	0.0	3.2	2.9	1.1	3.8	1.4	7.4
% Owner Occupied.............	6.3	9.1	5.7	9.5	6.4	0.6	1.1	4.5	5.4	13.3	6.1
% With 1+ Persons Per Room...	13.6	8.9	3.9	13.3	12.7	40.4	39.0	9.0	5.6	8.9	27.0
Median Value: Owner Units....$$	23400	17200	–	23800	–	–	–	–	–	23800	–
Median Rent: Rental Units....$$	138	92	149	152	143	65	64	151	156	161	84
Median Number Of Rooms: All Units.	4.3	4.1	3.1	4.4	4.3	4.9	4.9	3.6	4.1	4.6	4.9

Tract Number	3811	3812	3813	3814	3815	3816	3817	3818	3819	3820
Total Population.............	675	2837	416	3098	1826	2180	5681	3090	1819	3713
% Male.......................	46.4	44.0	51.9	48.5	45.5	42.3	42.9	52.9	46.3	44.7
% Black......................	99.3	99.6	100.0	99.2	99.5	99.5	99.9	98.7	98.5	99.3
% Other Nonwhite.............	0.6	0.1	0.0	0.3	0.4	0.4	0.1	0.3	0.8	0.3
% Of Spanish Origin..........	0.6	0.1	0.5	0.9	0.5	1.5	0.7	0.5	0.4	0.2
% Foreign Born...............	0.6	0.6	0.0	1.9	2.2	0.3	0.1	0.5	1.1	1.3
% Living In Group Quarters...	0.1	0.4	3.1	0.7	0.4	0.0	0.5	8.1	1.2	0.7
% 13 Years Old And Under.....	23.0	18.9	14.2	19.5	21.6	44.0	43.7	16.1	20.7	21.6
% 14-20 Years Old............	12.1	8.1	7.5	10.6	9.0	23.3	23.7	7.6	13.3	13.0
% 21-64 Years Old............	49.5	51.4	56.0	50.4	54.1	31.8	31.5	55.9	52.6	47.3
% 65-74 Years Old............	8.4	13.0	14.2	12.5	9.4	0.6	0.8	11.4	8.6	9.4
% 75 Years Old And Over......	7.0	8.6	8.2	7.0	5.9	0.3	0.4	9.0	4.8	8.7
% In Different House.........	24.9	36.5	0.0	29.7	31.7	24.3	33.4	39.2	47.0	42.4
% Families With Female Head..	66.7	59.3	54.3	66.0	66.8	78.0	82.5	62.3	65.7	68.6
Median School Years Completed..	12.1	10.2	9.9	10.1	10.4	11.0	10.7	10.4	11.1	10.7
Median Family Income, 1979...$$	10677	9531	15350	7338	7035	4947	4965	8472	8355	7989
% Income Below Poverty Level..	31.4	33.0	30.8	40.7	38.9	72.0	81.3	40.5	39.7	41.7
% Income Of $30,000 Or More...	5.8	9.3	0.0	4.8	5.7	1.3	1.1	5.4	12.2	5.0
% White Collar Workers.......	47.5	43.9	40.3	35.4	44.1	38.9	38.1	43.6	40.6	38.6
% Civilian Labor Force Unemployed.	14.6	14.5	5.4	16.5	21.7	18.2	27.4	24.8	24.4	25.9
% Riding To Work By Automobile.	37.1	51.5	7.4	40.9	36.8	42.6	19.0	42.3	33.6	36.4
Mean Commuting Time - Minutes...	37.7	33.6	36.8	31.0	31.5	36.5	34.3	41.7	36.2	36.0
Population Per Household.........	2.6	2.2	2.1	2.4	2.1	5.0	4.9	2.0	2.5	2.5
Total Housing Units...........	294	1396	230	1406	930	479	1261	1507	882	1636
% Condominiums................	0.0	0.0	0.0	0.0	0.0	2.1	1.7	0.0	0.0	0.0
% Built 1970 Or Later........	2.4	22.8	0.0	3.1	2.4	2.5	0.6	4.3	0.5	1.3
% Owner Occupied.............	11.9	8.7	2.6	4.8	2.3	0.8	0.7	5.5	9.0	10.0
% With 1+ Persons Per Room...	5.4	4.5	6.3	7.7	7.3	39.7	37.2	6.5	8.5	8.4
Median Value: Owner Units....$$	–	–	–	–	–	–	–	–	–	22200
Median Rent: Rental Units....$$	153	171	137	159	149	59	59	160	162	168
Median Number Of Rooms: All Units.	4.7	4.2	3.7	4.0	3.5	4.9	4.9	3.1	4.2	4.5

Community Area 38 — Grand Boulevard
Selected Characteristics of Census Tracts: 1970

Tract Number	TOTAL	3801	3802	3803	3804	3805	3806	3807	3808	3809	3810
Total Population	80150	6170	3333	5024	2912	3778	4849	2966	5164	4496	4551
% Male	46.2	45.9	47.2	47.9	46.7	44.5	44.5	45.1	47.9	46.8	46.1
% Black	99.3	99.4	99.1	99.6	99.1	99.8	99.8	99.2	99.4	99.6	99.7
% Other Nonwhite	0.2	0.1	0.3	0.1	0.2	0.2	0.2	0.3	0.3	0.2	0.2
% Of Spanish Language	0.6	1.0	0.3	0.0	0.0	0.4	0.1	0.0	0.0	0.0	1.0
% Foreign Born	0.2	0.4	0.0	0.0	0.2	0.0	0.0	0.3	0.2	0.0	0.0
% Living In Group Quarters	1.6	1.9	0.4	1.0	2.6	0.0	0.2	2.6	2.3	1.5	0.5
% 13 Years Old And Under	33.5	33.0	24.5	31.1	31.3	54.0	54.2	21.5	22.4	26.6	44.2
% 14-20 Years Old	13.7	12.7	10.0	13.4	13.3	20.8	21.7	9.2	9.8	12.3	17.6
% 21-64 Years Old	41.8	38.4	50.2	45.4	44.8	24.0	23.5	52.3	51.9	47.9	33.1
% 65-74 Years Old	7.5	10.8	11.2	7.1	7.8	0.6	0.4	12.0	10.4	9.0	3.5
% 75 Years Old And Over	3.5	5.1	4.1	3.0	2.8	0.5	0.1	4.9	5.4	4.2	1.6
% In Different House	58.8	46.2	62.2	63.9	43.0	65.5	70.1	55.3	66.2	58.8	58.9
% Families With Female Head	40.2	37.1	36.9	37.0	34.4	58.4	61.3	29.7	34.1	36.3	44.0
Median School Years Completed	9.4	8.5	9.8	9.3	9.4	9.5	10.1	8.9	9.2	9.1	9.7
Median Family Income, 1969 $$	5644	4761	6325	6122	6074	4414	5177	6073	6525	5052	5643
% Income Below Poverty Level	37.4	37.3	29.1	38.0	33.3	57.5	51.7	32.2	31.9	33.4	40.3
% Income of $15,000 or More	5.6	4.8	4.3	7.2	8.0	3.3	2.0	7.2	6.9	5.8	2.3
% White Collar Workers	9.7	9.9	9.9	13.1	14.4	4.5	7.5	8.5	8.1	13.3	7.2
% Civilian Labor Force Unemployed	9.5	10.7	6.0	8.6	7.6	9.6	15.6	6.5	10.8	13.1	15.9
% Riding To Work By Automobile	34.8	49.7	33.8	30.6	36.7	45.9	20.6	25.7	33.9	33.0	33.2
Population Per Household	3.3	3.2	2.7	3.1	3.4	6.2	6.4	2.5	2.6	2.9	4.6
Total Housing Units	25937	2131	1291	1790	912	633	785	1230	2128	1710	1053
% Condominiums & Cooperatives	0.2	0.0	0.0	0.3	1.5	0.0	0.0	0.0	0.4	0.0	0.0
% Built 1960 Or Later	16.5	25.8	0.6	15.3	11.3	76.5	74.3	4.4	1.6	2.8	31.9
% Owner Occupied	6.5	10.2	11.9	6.7	4.6	0.3	0.3	4.6	6.5	10.8	7.4
% With 1+ Persons Per Room	21.6	19.3	14.5	19.7	20.8	64.3	66.8	11.9	13.1	14.9	36.1
Median Value: Owner Units $$	15700	13500	13400	18500	-	-	-	-	-	16400	-
Median Rent: Rental Units $$	89	83	88	94	97	77	77	92	92	94	80
Median Number Of Rooms: All Units	4.2	4.1	3.6	4.1	4.4	4.9	4.9	3.6	3.8	4.0	4.9

Tract Number	3811	3812	3813	3814	3815	3816	3817	3818	3819	3820
Total Population	1308	3697	941	5385	1900	2777	7619	4070	3530	5680
% Male	44.3	46.7	42.3	48.6	46.3	44.4	45.6	50.0	45.7	43.8
% Black	99.8	96.9	98.9	99.5	99.6	99.9	99.8	98.4	99.4	98.8
% Other Nonwhite	0.1	0.2	0.4	0.2	0.2	0.0	0.1	0.1	0.3	0.2
% Of Spanish Language	0.0	0.7	0.0	0.0	1.0	0.0	2.1	0.2	0.6	1.5
% Foreign Born	0.5	0.2	0.0	0.1	1.4	0.0	0.1	0.4	0.5	0.3
% Living In Group Quarters	0.0	9.6	1.3	2.1	0.4	0.0	0.0	3.0	1.2	0.7
% 13 Years Old And Under	28.9	21.1	19.3	22.3	23.4	53.9	54.2	18.6	25.9	27.1
% 14-20 Years Old	9.5	9.6	8.5	9.2	10.6	19.9	21.4	8.8	11.0	11.3
% 21-64 Years Old	48.5	50.0	53.7	53.2	52.1	25.0	23.3	58.3	48.0	45.6
% 65-74 Years Old	9.7	11.6	12.8	10.8	9.6	0.7	0.7	10.3	10.3	10.5
% 75 Years Old And Over	3.4	7.7	5.7	4.4	4.4	0.5	0.5	4.0	4.7	5.5
% In Different House	51.2	55.6	83.4	58.3	46.4	74.9	62.3	54.1	60.0	49.4
% Families With Female Head	40.8	33.8	32.1	33.3	30.2	56.6	61.4	30.3	34.8	37.9
Median School Years Completed	10.1	9.2	11.9	9.0	9.9	9.9	10.0	10.6	9.5	9.3
Median Family Income, 1969 $$	5880	5661	7278	5819	5909	3731	4807	6595	6303	5826
% Income Below Poverty Level	28.5	29.1	16.5	32.1	20.3	60.7	53.7	22.1	30.2	33.0
% Income of $15,000 or More	8.0	7.9	10.0	8.4	2.9	3.3	1.8	10.3	4.1	6.1
% White Collar Workers	14.1	11.7	12.1	9.3	12.7	3.2	6.9	12.8	4.9	6.5
% Civilian Labor Force Unemployed	12.7	8.1	12.0	5.8	11.0	20.3	11.9	9.5	5.2	5.7
% Riding To Work By Automobile	27.1	33.5	30.3	35.7	39.0	28.6	37.0	32.0	33.9	41.0
Population Per Household	3.0	2.8	2.3	2.7	2.5	6.2	6.3	2.3	2.7	2.9
Total Housing Units	450	1277	430	2186	823	473	1241	1939	1369	2086
% Condominiums & Cooperatives	0.0	0.5	0.0	0.4	0.0	0.0	0.0	0.0	0.0	0.3
% Built 1960 Or Later	2.6	2.1	0.0	1.6	3.1	70.1	88.6	1.9	2.2	8.6
% Owner Occupied	8.7	9.5	2.1	4.7	2.6	0.0	0.5	4.6	7.2	9.4
% With 1+ Persons Per Room	17.9	11.9	8.5	10.4	12.6	65.9	64.2	9.5	14.5	14.4
Median Value: Owner Units $$	-	-	-	-	-	-	-	-	-	15200
Median Rent: Rental Units $$	93	104	103	100	99	77	77	94	102	103
Median Number Of Rooms: All Units	4.1	4.2	3.7	3.9	3.5	4.9	5.0	3.1	3.7	4.3

allowed some black residents to buy homes east of State Street away from the Federal Street slum where newcomers usually settled. Blacks owned homes between 39th and 47th streets, Cottage Grove and State streets. Julius Rosenwald's large-scale housing project, Michigan Boulevard Garden Apartments, built in 1929, facilitated middle-income black settlement in Grand Boulevard. As blacks moved into Grand Boulevard, whites moved farther south to the Kenwood and Hyde Park community areas, where restrictive covenants interdicted black home ownership.

Prior to that, during a serious housing shortage between 1918 and 1920, efforts had been made to keep blacks out of the Grand Boulevard community. However by 1920, they were 32 percent of the community's population, and blacks purchased the Ebenezer Baptist Church on Vincennes Avenue at 45th Street from whites who had moved out. A decade later blacks constituted 95 percent of the population. For the next 20 years, Grand Boulevard, once known chiefly for its rich white families, was the center of "Bronzeville." By 1925, 47th Street was the most important retail trade and entertainment area for black Chicagoans. It was the location of excellent restaurants and hotels. During the decades that followed, the community became world famous for its live entertainment spots and the development of black stars and writers, such as Sarah Vaughn, Joe Williams, Nat Cole, Leontyne Price and Richard Wright. The community was referred to as "the Harlem of Chicago" and the center of the bright light area was the Regal Theatre at 47th and Grand Boulevard.

Between 1920 and 1950, Grand Boulevard experienced a tremendous growth in population. In 1920, the number of residents was 77,000 and this increased by 10,000 in the decade that followed. Population growth was slow in most Chicago communities during the 1930s, due to the Depression, but the 1940 Census found more than 100,000 residents in Grand Boulevard, 98 percent of whom were black. Segregated real estate codes forced blacks to live only in certain communities such as Grand Boulevard. New housing had not kept pace with the population increase and in time, segregation brought about a congested neighborhood characterized by deteriorating streets and buildings. The World War II labor market brought about a further piling up of the community's population, which increased to its historic high, more than 114,000 in 1950.

In 1959 the Chicago Land Clearance Commission authorized the demolition of two one-block projects to make way for commercial use. These projects included the State-51st Street and State-Pershing Road projects. The demolition was completed in 1962. As a result of land clearance and the opening of other community areas to black residents the population dropped from 114,000 to 80,000 in 1960.

The 1960s saw an increase in new housing units. Some 4,289 units were constructed during this decade as compared to only 1,636 in

1950s. This increase in housing resulted primarily from construction of the Robert Taylor Homes, named for the first black chairman of the Chicago Housing Authority, which run along the western part of the community area. Most of the 28 high-rise buildings of the Robert Taylor Homes are located in Grand Boulevard, which has one of the most dense concentrations of public housing in Chicago.

Despite construction of the Taylor projects, the total number of housing units in Grand Boulevard has dropped by more than one-third in the last 30 years. Although the population, currently less than 54,000, is little more than half the 1950 high, more than one-fourth of all residents live in overcrowded housing. There are not many single-family homes in Grand Boulevard, more than half of the housing units are in small apartment buildings, and about a third are in large (10 units or more) structures. The current population is virtually all black and very young; 37 percent of the total is less than 18 years old. Seventy percent of all households with children under 18 are headed by females. The unemployment rate in Grand Boulevard was almost 32 percent in 1980, and more than half the residents were classified as living below the poverty line. The 1979 median family income, less than $7,000, was the lowest median reported in any of the 77 Chicago community areas.

Grand Boulevard has recently received attention from private real estate developers. A $15-million rehabilitation of the historic Michigan Boulevard Garden Apartments is planned as a joint venture between the Capital Associates Development Corporation and the Chicago Urban League. Although the 47th Street area has deteriorated and the Regal Theatre was torn down a decade ago, other monuments endure. Grand Boulevard is the home of the nation's oldest black hospital, Provident, founded by Dr. Daniel Hale Williams in 1891. After experiencing many financial difficulties during the 1970s, the hospital recently cut the ribbon on a new 300-bed $50-million facility at 500 East 51st Street. The community is also the home of the DuSable High School named for Jean Baptiste DuSable, the black American founder of Chicago.

Annie Ruth Leslie

Community Area 39

Kenwood

The first settler of this community area, Dr. John A. Kennicott, built a suburban retreat south of 43rd Street near the tracks of the Illinois Central Railroad in 1856, and named his estate "Kenwood," after his mother's birthplace in Scotland. That name was also used for the 47th Street station of the Illinois Central, opened three years later, and was gradually applied to the entire area. Another early settler, Dr. William B. Egan, built an elaborate garden estate sprawling roughly between 47th and 55th Street, Woodlawn and Cottage Grove avenues, naming it "Egandale." Under economic duress, Dr. Egan opened his gardens to the public and offered the western half of Egandale for sale in 1863. In the meantime, the area had become part of Hyde Park Township, incorporated in 1861. The Great Fire in 1871 provided a major stimulus for further residential development. By 1874, many large homes had been built on spacious lots with rolling lawns. Kenwood became known as "the Lake Forest of the South Side." After the establishment of the South Parks Commission in 1869, the sons of Philadelphia banker Francis Drexel donated Drexel Boulevard to the commissioners, thus significantly improving the desirability of their lots along both sides of the wide Boulevard.

Transportation facilities in Kenwood were improved when the horse drawn railway lines along Cottage Grove Avenue were extended southward to 55th Street between 1870 and 1878. In the last 20 years of the 19th century Kenwood was the fashionable suburb of the South Side, as its population came to include wealthy stock yards executives and fashionable families, some of whom had moved from the wealthy area at 16th Street and Prairie Avenue. Gracious single-family homes were built along Drexel Boulevard, and between 45th and 50th streets from Drexel Boulevard to Blackstone Avenue, and many single-family row houses were built between 43rd and 47th streets. Despite the objections of most residents, Kenwood was annexed to Chicago in 1889, as part of the Village of Hyde Park.

A mixed commercial and residential strip developed along 47th Street between Cottage Grove and Lake Park avenues. The elevated train line was extended to a terminus at 42nd Place and the lake in 1910, adding greatly to the appeal of Kenwood to clerical and sales workers employed in the Loop. The easy commute to and from the Loop encouraged construction of kitchenette apartments along Drexel Boulevard and the conversion of older homes to rooming houses, primarily along the northern edge of the area. At this time Drexel Boulevard north of 47th Street was composed of this sort of housing interspersed with fine homes, while the Kenwood area south of 47th Street maintained its single-family mansions.

During the decades after annexation that area was the residence of many of the commercial, industrial and cultural elite of Chicago, including industrialists Gustavus Swift and Martin Ryerson; John G. Shedd, the Marshall Field executive who donated the city aquarium; Sears Roebuck executive Max Adler, who endowed the planetarium, and Julius Rosenwald, noted for many philanthropic efforts. Architect Louis Sullivan lived in a house designed on Lake Park Avenue, and Edgar Masters wrote much of the Spoon River Anthology in his home on Kenwood Avenue. The affluent residents commissioned Chicago's leading architects to design their homes, and the area became peppered with houses in the Queen Anne and Shingle styles, representative designs from the Renaissance revival and Prairie schools. In the midst

Community Area 39 -- Kenwood
Population and Housing Characteristics, 1930-1980

	1980	1970	1960	1950	1940	1930
Total Population.......	21,974	26,908	41,533	35,705	29,611	26,942
% Male..................	45.9	46.3	47.9	47.6	45.3	45.4
% Female................	54.1	53.7	52.1	52.4	54.7	54.6
% White.................	19.8	20.1	15.1	84.7	99.0	99.2
% Black.................	77.5	78.9	83.9	9.7	0.9	0.7
% Other Nonwhite Races...	2.7	1.0	1.0	5.6	0.1	0.2
% Under 5 Years Old......	7.0	9.5	15.1	8.5	5.2	4.3
% 5-19 Years Old........	19.0	23.7	20.3	12.9	13.9	13.8
% 20-44 Years Old........	40.5	32.9	40.7	45.9	46.9	51.3
% 45-64 Years Old........	20.2	22.9	18.0	23.6	25.1	23.9
% 65 Years and Older....	13.3	11.0	5.9	9.1	8.9	6.7
Median School Years....	12.9	11.9	10.5	12.2	11.6	*
Total Housing Units....	11,256	11,597	15,428	12,771	10,500	*
% In One-Unit Structures.	6.2	7.1	10.8	*	*	*
% Owner Occupied.........	20.1	10.3	8.6	9.5	7.2	*
% Renter Occupied........	69.0	80.8	85.2	87.4	84.5	*
% Vacant.................	10.0	8.9	6.2	3.1	8.3	*
% 1+ Persons per Room....	6.3	13.3	26.3	21.5	*	*

Community Area 39 -- Kenwood
Selected Characteristics of Census Tracts: 1980

Tract Number	Total	3901	3902	3903	3904	3905	3906	3907
Total Population.............	21974	2114	2357	3324	3409	1926	1875	6969
% Male.......................	45.9	45.7	48.0	45.2	46.2	44.2	50.3	44.6
% Black......................	77.5	99.4	98.7	96.9	96.8	79.9	43.8	53.3
% Other Nonwhite.............	2.7	0.4	0.7	0.5	0.6	2.9	7.5	4.9
% Of Spanish Origin..........	1.1	1.1	0.3	0.8	0.9	1.6	1.1	1.5
% Foreign Born...............	5.3	0.0	3.5	2.1	2.1	2.0	13.8	9.2
% Living In Group Quarters...	2.1	0.1	1.0	10.5	1.8	0.8	0.6	0.1
% 13 Years Old And Under.....	18.3	24.5	23.8	20.3	19.2	20.7	20.6	11.8
% 14-20 Years Old............	9.2	16.7	11.1	9.6	9.3	9.4	10.0	5.7
% 21-64 Years Old............	59.2	50.9	52.7	53.6	53.7	59.8	62.3	68.4
% 65-74 Years Old............	8.0	5.6	8.3	8.9	10.3	6.0	4.6	8.6
% 75 Years Old And Over......	5.3	2.3	4.2	7.6	7.5	4.2	2.4	5.4
% In Different House.........	51.6	45.7	32.1	44.3	51.9	57.2	40.2	64.4
% Families With Female Head..	50.1	57.0	63.4	60.8	58.9	43.1	20.7	43.2
Median School Years Completed.	12.9	11.4	11.1	11.0	12.4	14.0	16.1	16.1
Median Family Income, 1979.....$$	16140	8857	6350	8415	11067	19038	30330	23668
% Income Below Poverty Level....	20.2	41.7	46.5	34.4	26.4	8.9	8.5	4.9
% Income Of $30,000 Or More....	23.2	3.0	9.7	1.6	9.1	36.4	50.7	35.8
% White Collar Workers.........	71.3	32.4	38.8	45.6	61.1	73.6	77.5	86.7
% Civilian Labor Force Unemployed.	10.0	18.1	20.4	21.5	14.6	6.2	3.8	5.3
% Riding To Work By Automobile....	53.1	46.1	56.0	43.2	48.9	47.6	52.1	58.0
Mean Commuting Time - Minutes...	32.1	43.1	39.0	40.7	36.8	33.7	23.7	28.8
Population Per Household.........	2.1	2.7	2.5	2.2	2.0	2.4	2.7	1.8
Total Housing Units..........	11256	952	1243	1640	1802	902	727	3990
% Condominiums...............	13.4	0.0	0.0	0.0	6.7	9.4	23.8	28.3
% Built 1970 Or Later........	16.1	4.6	4.3	5.1	5.2	12.6	2.0	35.2
% Owner Occupied.............	20.1	10.4	11.2	3.0	14.8	22.0	46.9	29.3
% With 1+ Persons Per Room...	6.3	15.6	11.2	9.7	8.7	4.2	4.5	1.8
Median Value: Owner Units.....$$	89500	-	30400	-	34200	151000	126700	125000
Median Rent: Rental Units.....$$	203	170	153	180	177	228	244	333
Median Number Of Rooms: All Units.	3.6	3.6	3.4	3.4	3.1	4.1	5.6	3.8

Community Area 39 -- Kenwood
Selected Characteristics of Census Tracts: 1970

Tract Number	TOTAL	3901	3902	3903	3904	3905	3906	3907
Total Population.............	26908	4354	5205	4873	4261	1860	2167	4188
% Male.......................	46.3	47.3	46.0	46.5	45.7	45.6	49.7	44.5
% Black......................	78.9	98.5	98.8	96.0	94.2	72.3	42.4	20.2
% Other Nonwhite.............	1.0	0.4	0.5	0.3	0.9	2.0	3.1	1.9
% Of Spanish Language........	1.0	0.0	1.6	0.2	1.2	1.8	2.3	1.2
% Foreign Born...............	3.6	0.3	0.0	0.8	2.8	3.9	7.2	13.8
% Living In Group Quarters...	2.7	1.5	0.9	5.6	5.4	5.0	0.8	0.0
% 13 Years Old And Under.....	25.1	36.4	33.6	26.7	18.4	20.4	28.0	8.4
% 14-20 Years Old............	9.4	12.7	13.1	9.3	7.8	7.1	8.6	4.8
% 21-64 Years Old............	54.4	45.7	46.7	54.2	56.9	64.6	57.9	64.4
% 65-74 Years Old............	7.4	3.9	4.9	6.1	9.7	5.7	3.5	15.9
% 75 Years Old And Over......	3.7	1.4	1.7	3.6	7.1	2.2	2.0	6.6
% In Different House.........	49.1	54.0	48.1	42.3	54.1	52.1	55.3	44.3
% Families With Female Head..	28.0	41.7	39.1	32.0	27.3	19.8	18.7	11.7
Median School Years Completed..	11.9	9.8	9.9	10.1	11.3	12.7	15.4	13.2
Median Family Income, 1969.....$$	8053	5340	5881	6032	7805	12020	15372	15217
% Income Below Poverty Level....	24.1	38.9	39.7	28.9	12.4	8.9	18.8	5.9
% Income of $15,000 or More.....	20.1	7.4	5.3	3.1	8.6	35.0	50.7	50.6
% White Collar Workers.........	30.9	13.7	8.9	9.8	19.9	43.6	56.1	62.2
% Civilian Labor Force Unemployed.	5.0	5.4	8.0	7.5	3.6	7.3	1.7	2.3
% Riding To Work By Automobile....	48.7	30.7	41.5	34.4	49.6	61.5	52.7	65.1
Population Per Household.........	2.5	3.0	3.1	2.5	2.2	2.4	2.8	1.8
Total Housing Units..........	11602	1637	1915	1958	2090	757	866	2379
% Condominiums & Cooperatives.....	4.0	0.0	0.0	0.0	5.5	6.1	9.1	9.5
% Built 1960 Or Later.............	11.3	1.1	0.8	8.7	15.6	5.1	2.5	29.8
% Owner Occupied.................	6.5	6.1	9.2	2.3	4.2	16.1	21.2	1.5
% With 1+ Persons Per Room.......	13.4	24.6	24.7	17.2	10.5	4.7	4.5	2.2
Median Value: Owner Units......$$	34400	-	16000	-	16700	49800	43800	-
Median Rent: Rental Units......$$	112	102	100	103	105	127	130	171
Median Number Of Rooms: All Units.	3.3	3.2	3.3	3.1	3.1	4.0	4.4	3.3

of this, a cow pasture survived from the 19th century, kept intact by a will covering the old Dunham farm at 49th Street and Blackstone Avenue, ending only with the death of the heir in 1928. During the 1920s Kenwood began to decline as a fashionable neighborhood, but many living south of 47th Street chose to stay because of proximity to the University of Chicago, a mile south in Hyde Park. This was the beginning of the split between north and south Kenwood, divided at 47th Street.

By 1919 Kenwood was a residentially mature area of single-family homes and large apartment buildings. Beginning in 1920, however, conversions of single-family homes accelerated. The commercial area along 43rd Street began to deteriorate. In 1920, the population of Kenwood was just greater than 21,000. Sizable numbers of German Jews were moving in. They built Kehilath Anshe Mayriv (K.A.M.) Temple on 50th Street in 1923.

Kenwood experienced a 28 percent growth in population during the 1920s. This increase was accompanied by considerable construction in the area, including some high-rise apartment buildings. More than 100 existing structures were converted, mostly single-family homes, into multi-family apartment buildings. German Jews, English, and Irish were the most numerous of the nationality groups in 1930.

The population increased only slightly during the following decade. Transient and single persons were attracted to Kenwood by the inexpensive housing, especially in the northern half of the area. Conversion of single-family units south of 47th Street was generally infeasible due to zoning ordinaces and the vigilance of residents desiring to maintain the low population density of their neighborhood. Nevertheless, as the northern half of Kenwood deteriorated, the southern section became less attractive also and homes along Ellis, Drexel, Woodlawn, Kimbark, and Kenwood avenues were offered for sale. By 1940, some of these homes had become private schools, nursing homes, and various other institutions. Meanwhile, the area east of the Illinois Central tracks, which had been built up with high-rise apartment buildings in the previous decade, emerged as one of the most desirable and exclusive residential districts in the city.

Between 1940 and 1960, Kenwood's population increased by 41 percent while construction virtually ceased. Jewish refugees from Nazi Germany settled in the area during World War II, maintaining that group's position as the most numerous. There was an influx of Japanese, settling mostly in the northern part of the area. Most significant for the future of Kenwood, however, was the first movement of blacks into the area. Before the war, Cottage Grove Avenue had served as the boundary between the densely-populated "Black Belt" of the South Side and Kenwood. Beginning in the mid-1940s, blacks began to move into the northern and eastern portions of the area, and by 1950 they comprised 10 percent of the population of Kenwood. Still further conversion of once-spacious dwelling units went on during the late 1940s, in an attempt to accommodate the increased demand in housing after the war.

The racial composition of Kenwood changed dramatically during the fifties. In 1950, the community was almost 85 percent white, but by 1960, it had changed to 84 percent black. The racial turnover of Kenwood resulted in a net increase in the total population of more than 16 percent, to a peak of more than 41,000 persons. Only the area south of 47th Street and east of Ellis Avenue retained whites in substantial numbers. By now, large homes south of 47th Street were being substructed for apartments. The Kenwood branch of the elevated lines was discontinued in 1958, and the community was beginning to deteriorate noticeably.

Organized efforts to renovate Kenwood began to take shape in the 1950s. In 1949, the Hyde Park-Kenwood Community Conference was organized by a group of ministers from the two communities. In the early part of the decade the Kenwood Open House Committee sponsored tours of the large old houses in south Kenwood, organized opposition to changes in zoning ordinances that would have allowed for further conversions, saw to it that such ordinances were enforced on those homeowners who had converted illegally, and provided financial incentives to others who desired to restructure converted homes into single-family units. A Hyde Park-Kenwood conservation area, which included south Kenwood, was designated in 1956. Demolition for urban renewal in the south Kenwood area got under way in 1960, and two years later ground was broken by the Chicago Dwellings Association for a nine-story building containing more than 100 apartments for rental to elderly middle-income families at 51st Street and Cottage Grove Avenue. While urban renewal was going on in the south half of Kenwood, demolition of deteriorated structures without renewal proceeded in the north half.

The number of housing units in Kenwood decreased by more than 4,000 between 1960 and 1980. North of 47th Street there are less than half the units counted 20 years ago. Only the southeast corner of the community, east of Dorchester Avenue, has been extensively redeveloped.

This area is the site of several high-rise developments, including Lake Village, at 47th Street and Lake Park Avenue; Harper Square, between 48th and 49th streets from Dorchester to Lake Park, the Newport, at 48th Street and the lake, the Regents Park, which runs along Lake Shore Drive from 50th Street to East Hyde Park Boulevard (51st Street). The Harper Square complex is co-operative, comprised of two high-rise structures and 22 town homes. It opened in May, 1971 and was constructed through a joint venture of the Amalgamated Clothing Workers Union and the Illinois Housing Development Authority. Lake Village, opened in 1973, consists of a 25-story high-rise building and 18 low-rise units.

The result of these changes in the last 20 years has been a population drop of nearly one-half and a shift in the relative densities of population in the north and south halves of Kenwood. In 1960 more than half of all residents lived north of 47th Street. Today almost two-thirds live south of 47th. All of the net housing loss has occurred in the north. The loss of total population has not changed the racial composition much — the percentage black fell from 84 to 77 during this time, while the percentage white has increased from 15 to 20. About two-thirds of the whites live in the redeveloped southeast corner, which is as densely settled as in 1960. Although there were always socio-economic differences between the north and south halves of Kenwood, these differences have increased in the last two decades. The southern half is an area of expensive homes, typically valued in excess of $100,000, while home values north of 47th Street tend to center on $30,000. The area south of 47th Street has been increasingly identified with Hyde Park, especially since urban renewal, while the north half tends to be associated with the Oakland community area.

Will Hogan

Washington Park

The center of the Washington Park community area is situated about seven miles south and slightly east of downtown Chicago. The name is taken from the large city park that comprises the eastern half of the neighborhood. Washington Park was first developed out of swamp and forest land. Development began in the northwestern section of the community west of State Street and north of 55th Street (Garfield Boulevard). This area was then part of the Town of Lake. The land east of State Street was part of the Village of Hyde Park. When the community was first settled, it grew slowly. The original inhabitants were Irish and Germans, who worked in the Rock Island Railroad yards established north of 51st Street in 1856. It was not until after 1880 that Washington Park experienced rapid development. At least three factors account for this development: the establishment of the South Park Board which purchased acreages for what are now Washington and Jackson Parks; the extensive build-up of elegant homes southward along Grand Boulevard (which became South Park Way and, later, Martin Luther King, Jr. Drive); and the opening of the Washington Park race track in 1884. This race track was located in the Woodlawn community area between 61st and 63rd streets, Cottage Grove Avenue and South Park Way. These developments resulted in a flurry of land speculation in areas facing the proposed parks and a settlement of race track employees along 63rd Street. Although Washington Park developed more rapidly after the South Park Board built up South Park Way and the Midway in neighboring Hyde Park, the area experienced great growth after rumors of the 1893 Columbian Exposition spread across the South Side. By 1893, Washington Park was built up with homes and residences from State Street to South Park Way as far south as Garfield Boulevard.

Good transportation accelerated growth of the community. By 1887, with cable cars running as far as 63rd Street on State Street and 67th Street on Cottage Grove Avenue, Washington Park experienced tremendous growth. The community area was annexed to Chicago in 1889.

The northwestern section of Washington Park developed after the 1890s when the "L" lines were built to 55th Street in 1892. The elevated was completed to its Jackson Park terminus in 1893. During this period, shopping areas grew up around elevated terminals at 51st, 55th, 58th and 61st streets. Despite the buildup of the 1890s, a great deal of Washington Park was still prairie in 1893. However, the area east of Indiana Avenue was built up with small apartments in the decade following 1895. After the Washington Park track was closed in 1905, apartment building in the nearby Washington Park community area was stimulated by subdivision and apartment construction on the land that had been occupied by the track between 1908 and 1912. By 1915, Washington Park was residentially mature, the area west of State Street being occupied mostly by railroad workers, while young clerical and sales workers lived in the east.

Jews and blacks began moving into Washington Park in the 1890s. While Jewish people lived near the elevated, blacks lived in the western working class area on Lafayette Street between Garfield Boulevard and 58th Street. After 1915 more blacks began to move out of the Black Belt to the north into Washington Park, west of State Street and north of Garfield Boulevard. This development set off racial hostility and, eventually, violence. The home of Jesse Binga, the most important black businessman in Chicago, was bombed four times between 1917 and 1920. Nevertheless the wartime migration of blacks into Chicago continued and they occupied most of the old working class area west of State Street. After the South Side race riot of 1919 the black area expanded eastward along Garfield Boulevard to Michigan Avenue. By 1920 the population of Washington Park was 38,076, of which 15

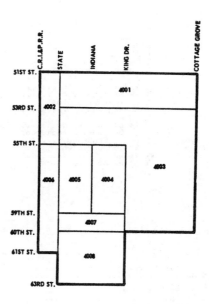

percent was black. Large numbers of whites moved out in the 1920s and, by 1930, blacks accounted for 92 percent of a population which had increased to more than 44,000. In 1940, blacks were 97 percent of the total; by 1950, 99 percent of an all-time high number, nearly 57,000.

During the Depression and World War II, the number of community inhabitants had increased by 29 percent. Very little building occurred during this period. New residents were housed by subdivision of existing apartments, often into kitchenettes. The building of the moderate-income housing project, Midway Gardens, at 60th Street and Langley was almost the only new construction during the 1950s. When urban renewal programs began to demolish buildings and build more expensive housing during the 1960s, many community groups organized local ward-level renewal movements aimed at rehabilitating residential property and preserving older buildings, seeking to make land clearance unnecessary.

Despite these efforts, the number of housing units in Washington Park has decreased by more than 25 percent in the last 30 years. This has happened although Washington Park includes one of the highest concentrations of public housing units in Chicago. Some 2,287 subsidized housing units are located there. Today more than half the units left are in small (two- to nine-unit) apartment buildings, and about a third are in larger structures. Although the number of residents dropped sharply in the 1950s and again in the 1970s to less than 32,000 today, almost 30 percent live in overcrowded housing. More than a third of the population today is under 18 years of age, and almost 70 percent of the households with children under 18 are headed by females. Washington Park is one of Chicago's most distressed areas. The unemployment rate is more than 20 percent. The 1979 median family income, slightly less than $8,200, was one of the five lowest in the city. Almost half of the residents live below the poverty level.

Economic development in Washington Park has been slow, but one major business development has been the South Plant of Interstate Brands Corporation (IBC), one of the largest wholesale bakers in the country. The Arrow Services Project, begun in 1981, involves the rehabilitation of an unused one-story industrial building and the construction of a compatible addition to it for purposes of expanding an industrial laundry located in the Washington Park community.

Annie Ruth Leslie

Community Area 40 -- Washington Park
Population and Housing Characteristics, 1930-1980

	1980	1970	1960	1950	1940	1930
Total Population.......	31,935	46,024	43,690	56,856	52,736	44,016
% Male..................	45.3	47.0	48.0	47.5	46.8	49.0
% Female................	54.7	53.0	52.0	52.5	53.2	51.0
% White.................	0.3	0.5	0.8	1.1	2.7	7.9
% Black.................	99.3	99.2	99.1	98.8	97.5	91.9
% Other Nonwhite Races.....	0.4	0.3	0.1	0.1	0.0	0.2
% Under 5 Years Old......	9.9	9.0	9.7	7.2	5.8	7.1
% 5-19 Years Old........	30.8	31.8	18.1	15.7	19.9	18.5
% 20-44 Years Old........	28.5	28.5	34.9	47.0	51.8	57.8
% 45-64 Years Old........	18.8	20.3	27.6	24.5	18.5	14.3
% 65 Years and Older.....	12.0	10.4	9.4	5.6	4.0	2.3
Median School Years....	11.0	10.0	9.0	9.3	8.5	*
Total Housing Units....	12,085	15,890	15,878	16,477	13,768	*
% In One-Unit Structures.	3.1	4.6	2.9	*	*	*
% Owner Occupied........	5.2	5.0	6.9	6.9	4.9	*
% Renter Occupied........	85.7	87.5	89.3	92.1	92.3	*
% Vacant................	9.1	7.5	3.8	1.0	2.8	*
% 1+ Persons per Room....	13.2	17.0	18.2	33.9	*	*

Community Area 40 -- Washington Park
Selected Characteristics of Census Tracts: 1980

Tract Number	Total	4001	4002	4003	4004	4005	4006	4007	4008
Total Population.............	31935	3262	5958	3424	4534	3560	1264	2277	7656
% Male.......................	45.3	45.3	43.1	46.6	47.4	45.8	45.4	46.2	44.4
% Black......................	99.3	99.1	99.5	99.4	98.9	99.6	99.2	99.5	99.4
% Other Nonwhite.............	0.4	0.3	0.4	0.3	0.6	0.2	0.4	0.1	0.4
% Of Spanish Origin..........	0.6	1.0	0.8	0.4	0.7	0.5	0.2	0.1	0.7
% Foreign Born...............	0.9	1.5	0.5	0.8	0.4	0.4	1.2	0.2	1.7
% Living In Group Quarters........	0.9	0.3	0.4	0.8	1.6	0.9	0.0	3.6	0.4
% 13 Years Old And Under........	27.8	22.6	44.9	19.7	22.4	19.3	26.7	25.2	28.5
% 14-20 Years Old............	14.8	11.7	22.8	11.6	11.2	10.2	14.2	11.5	16.6
% 21-64 Years Old............	45.3	51.0	31.1	50.4	51.6	52.7	45.9	46.7	44.2
% 65-74 Years Old............	7.3	9.0	0.6	10.7	9.1	11.2	7.8	11.2	6.3
% 75 Years Old And Over........	4.7	5.7	0.6	7.6	5.8	6.5	5.3	5.4	4.3
% In Different House.........	39.6	34.0	32.7	43.1	51.1	36.6	24.4	44.6	41.4
% Families With Female Head......	70.0	64.2	85.3	64.8	64.7	59.9	56.7	62.5	69.9
Median School Years Completed....	11.0	9.9	10.7	10.9	10.7	11.2	12.2	11.1	11.5
Median Family Income, 1979......$$	8158	7483	5745	9982	8582	10800	12012	7687	8717
% Income Below Poverty Level....	43.2	41.0	73.7	31.9	41.5	30.8	27.1	38.3	39.7
% Income Of $30,000 Or More.....	6.5	2.8	0.4	4.9	9.5	10.1	19.1	5.9	7.4
% White Collar Workers........	39.8	39.0	38.6	39.3	36.6	42.6	36.1	33.5	43.6
% Civilian Labor Force Unemployed.	21.0	26.5	31.4	17.7	21.5	17.9	11.7	15.9	21.4
% Riding To Work By Automobile....	40.0	48.2	30.0	39.1	39.3	44.9	49.9	41.2	35.5
Mean Commuting Time - Minutes...	39.4	42.8	41.2	36.3	44.0	41.5	36.3	33.4	37.9
Population Per Household........	2.9	2.5	5.0	2.4	2.4	2.5	3.2	2.7	2.9
Total Housing Units..........	12085	1457	1331	1551	2092	1545	448	930	2731
% Condominiums...............	0.6	0.5	1.5	0.9	0.0	0.0	0.0	0.0	1.0
% Built 1970 Or Later........	4.1	6.4	2.6	2.5	2.4	1.3	0.7	0.0	9.3
% Owner Occupied.............	5.2	5.6	1.5	6.0	2.8	7.9	25.4	4.8	3.5
% With 1+ Persons Per Room....	13.2	7.3	35.5	9.0	9.6	7.1	11.7	8.7	15.5
Median Value: Owner Units.......$$	21900	-	-	176	175	187	152	184	-
Median Rent: Rental Units.....$$	169	178	63	176	175	187	152	184	170
Median Number Of Rooms: All Units.	4.4	4.3	5.0	4.3	4.0	4.6	5.3	4.4	4.2

Community Area 40 -- Washington Park
Selected Characteristics of Census Tracts: 1970

Tract Number	TOTAL	4001	4002	4003	4004	4005	4006	4007	4008
Total Population.............	46024	5439	7682	5398	8380	5250	2669	3091	8115
% Male.......................	47.0	47.8	44.8	47.7	48.8	47.6	47.3	46.1	45.9
% Black......................	99.2	98.7	99.9	98.9	99.3	99.3	99.3	98.9	98.9
% Other Nonwhite.............	0.3	0.2	0.0	0.5	0.3	0.3	0.2	0.1	0.7
% Of Spanish Language........	0.4	0.4	0.0	0.3	0.7	0.0	0.0	0.0	1.2
% Foreign Born...............	0.2	1.0	0.0	0.6	0.0	0.2	0.0	0.0	0.1
% Living In Group Quarters........	1.3	3.8	0.0	1.3	1.4	0.6	0.7	3.0	0.6
% 13 Years Old And Under........	29.9	23.1	54.5	21.9	20.9	22.6	32.7	21.9	32.4
% 14-20 Years Old............	12.4	10.5	20.1	8.6	9.9	9.0	13.7	11.5	13.7
% 21-64 Years Old............	47.3	51.4	24.3	56.0	57.4	55.0	43.1	54.1	44.1
% 65-74 Years Old............	7.2	10.1	0.8	9.0	8.2	9.4	6.9	8.8	7.2
% 75 Years Old And Over........	3.2	4.8	0.2	4.5	3.6	3.9	3.6	3.8	2.6
% In Different House.........	56.5	53.1	58.2	60.1	51.0	59.5	52.8	51.2	62.1
% Families With Female Head.......	34.8	30.8	61.6	32.8	28.8	25.8	30.2	35.7	34.4
Median School Years Completed....	10.0	10.0	10.0	9.8	10.1	10.1	9.8	10.2	10.5
Median Family Income, 1969......$$	6547	6914	4092	6235	6369	8106	6250	7672	6924
% Income Below Poverty Level....	28.2	24.4	61.6	24.4	22.3	17.5	32.9	21.5	19.8
% Income of $15,000 or More.....	8.3	12.3	1.4	13.2	9.0	11.0	2.9	5.2	7.5
% White Collar Workers........	8.6	7.8	4.9	8.9	8.3	12.0	5.3	8.0	9.0
% Civilian Labor Force Unemployed.	8.0	7.7	18.6	9.7	6.1	6.3	6.1	5.9	7.7
% Riding To Work By Automobile....	38.7	32.8	33.3	40.3	38.7	41.2	42.0	37.9	41.3
Population Per Household........	3.1	2.8	6.1	2.6	2.5	2.8	3.4	2.7	3.2
Total Housing Units..........	15888	2095	1327	2246	3494	1992	840	1184	2710
% Condominiums & Cooperatives.....	0.4	0.7	0.0	0.5	0.2	0.0	0.0	0.0	1.0
% Built 1960 Or Later........	11.6	6.7	75.6	0.0	1.0	6.0	0.0	0.9	20.0
% Owner Occupied.............	4.6	4.9	1.3	4.0	2.5	5.9	18.8	5.3	3.8
% With 1+ Persons Per Room.......	17.4	12.8	60.6	11.7	12.8	9.3	15.1	10.0	19.7
Median Value: Owner Units.......$$	13300	-	-	-	-	-	10800	-	-
Median Rent: Rental Units.....$$	102	103	77	107	106	113	86	111	100
Median Number Of Rooms: All Units.	4.2	4.1	5.0	3.9	3.6	4.4	4.9	4.2	4.1

Hyde Park

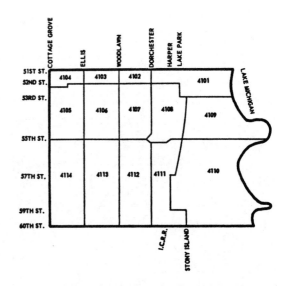

In 1853, Paul Cornell, a young lawyer who had migrated to Chicago from New York, purchased 300 acres of uninhabited land with the intent of building a suburb. He decided to call the area Hyde Park after dignified communities by that name in London and New York state. Cornell persuaded the Illinois Central Railroad to build a station at Oak (later 53rd) Street and Lake Park Avenue in 1856. In 1857, Cornell moved to the area and built the Hyde Park House hotel at 53rd Street near Lake Michigan. In 1861, the town of Hyde Park was incorporated, extending from 39th to 63rd streets, from State Street to Lake Michigan, including the settlements of Oakland, Egandale, Forestville, Kenwood, and South Park. The southern boundary was later extended to 138th Street.

In its early years, Hyde Park developed as a suburb of fine homes built on large estates. This changed, however, as substantial subdivision took place, particularly in the late 1860s. Paul Cornell anticipated that the establishment of a parks commission for the area would aid in its growth, and he led a group of South Siders who lobbied successfully in Springfield for the creation of the South Park Board in 1869. Plans were announced for Washington and Jackson Parks in that year. Growth was also stimulated when residents of the township paid for the construction of Hyde Park High School at 50th Street and Lake Park Avenue in 1870. In 1872, the Village of Hyde Park was incorporated. By now, there was a business center near 53rd Street and Lake Park Avenue, as well as a water works and gas plant. In 1880, the population of the Village of Hyde Park was 15,176. Transportation facilities were improved as the Cottage Grove Avenue cable cars extended to 67th Street by 1887, with a line running along 55th Street to Lake Park Avenue.

The early 1890s were boom years. Hyde Park Township was annexed to Chicago in 1889. By 1890, construction was underway for the World's Columbian Exposition in Jackson Park, and shortly thereafter the Baptist Church built the first structures of the University of Chicago on land donated by Marshall Field at the north edge of the Midway Plaisance. The expectation of the Fair caused a flurry of apartment and hotel building. Many of the structures built to accommodate visitors to the Fair became rooming houses, particularly along Lake Park Avenue from 53rd to 55th streets. After the University of Chicago opened in 1892, a residential area for faculty and staff grew up east of the campus, south of 55th Street between Woodlawn and Harper avenues. As Hyde Park grew, so did the two main business districts at 53rd Street and Lake Park Avenue and along 55th Street. A university-oriented shopping area developed on 57th Street east of Kimbark Avenue.

By 1920, single-family homes, apartment buildings, and rooming houses comprised the housing stock. The general area south of 55th Street was centered around the University of Chicago, while the northern half of the area was more oriented toward the Loop, which was easily accessed by the Illinois Central trains. In 1920, the total population of Hyde Park was 37,523, with the largest ethnic group being Irish, followed by Germans and Russian Jews.

After World War I many Jews, particularly of German ancestry, moved into Hyde Park from Grand Boulevard as blacks began to occupy that area. These newcomers were primarily apartment dwellers, settling along Hyde Park Boulevard and east of the Illinois Central tracks in large hotels and apartment hotels. By 1930, the total population of Hyde Park had increased to 48,017 as Germans and Russians, many of whom were Jews, became more numerous than the Irish. During the 1930s, owners began compartmentalizing once-spacious homes in the University of Chicago area in order to provide housing for students. Other conversions took place around 53rd Street and Lake Park Avenue to house more Loop workers.

From 1930 to 1950, Hyde Park's population increased 15 percent to its historic peak, more than 55,000, while in the same period there was little new construction, save for some new apartments. As even more buildings were converted to smaller but numerous housing units, Hyde Park increasingly became an area of transient occupancy. During the 1940s, many blacks began moving into Hyde Park from the west, settling between Cottage Grove Avenue and Drexel Boulevard north of 55th Street. A small Japanese group also settled in Hyde Park during the 1940s.

During the 1950s, the influx of blacks accelerated, many moving west of Ellis Avenue and, in the central section, from Ellis Avenue to the Illinois Central tracks. While the total population of Hyde Park dropped to 45,000 during the 1950s, the black population increased, to become almost 38 percent of the total in 1960. Germans and Russian Jews were still the largest foreign-stock groups, and a small number of Puerto Ricans had settled in Hyde Park.

By the end of the Second World War, many of the structures that had been built during the Columbian Exposition boom were in considerable disrepair and in need of either substantial rehabilitation or demolition. After the Supreme Court struck down restrictive covenants, which kept blacks out of Hyde Park and many other American residential areas, black ghettoes to the north were cleared to make way for public housing projects, bringing poor blacks into a Hyde Park where many had fought their entrance for 50 years. This compounded the postwar housing shortage and brought racial and socioeconomic tensions to a head. Area residents formed the Hyde Park-Kenwood Community Conference to halt urban decay and encourage racial integration. The University of Chicago underwrote the South East Chicago Commission, which was formed in 1952 to battle crime, eliminate the unlawful substruction of apartments, and to help develop a strong commercial base for the Hyde Park area. The Field Foundation donated $100,000 in 1953 for planning efforts to improve Hyde Park, and the Chicago Land Clearance Commission surveyed the area for redevelopment. In 1955, as part of the "Hyde Park A" project, demolition began on 56th Street from Lake Park Avenue west toward Kenwood Avenue.

In 1956, the Community Conservation Board authorized the Hyde Park-Kenwood conservation area comprised of Hyde Park plus the southern half of Kenwood. A year later the Chicago City Council approved a $20 million redevelopment project for East 55th Street from Dorchester to Lake Park avenues. This project included the University Park condominiums between Dorchester and Harper avenues, townhouses along 55th Street, and the nine-acre Hyde Park Shopping Center at Lake Park Avenue. In 1962, a group of 15 local businessmen built

Community Area 41 -- Hyde Park
Population and Housing Characteristics, 1930-1980

	1980	1970	1960	1950	1940	1930
Total Population.......	31,198	33,559	45,577	55,206	50,550	48,017
% Male..................	50.7	48.5	48.2	46.6	45.2	45.9
% Female................	49.3	51.5	51.8	53.4	54.8	54.1
% White.................	55.6	64.1	59.7	94.9	98.5	98.3
% Black.................	37.2	31.1	37.7	3.2	1.1	1.1
% Other Nonwhite Races...	7.2	4.8	2.6	1.9	0.4	0.6
% Under 5 Years Old......	4.6	6.0	9.4	6.9	4.8	4.8
% 5-19 Years Old........	15.7	17.0	16.6	13.2	14.7	15.4
% 20-44 Years Old........	52.4	47.8	40.6	42.5	47.2	49.6
% 45-64 Years Old........	17.0	17.8	21.8	26.4	24.6	23.5
% 65 Years and Older....	10.3	11.4	11.6	11.0	8.7	6.7
Median School Years....	16.1	15.0	12.5	12.5	12.2	*
Total Housing Units....	15,493	15,717	19,621	19,928	17,013	*
% In One-Unit Structures.	7.9	8.8	7.6	*	*	*
% Owner Occupied.........	23.8	14.0	9.5	9.0	5.7	*
% Renter Occupied........	69.5	76.8	81.0	87.5	86.9	*
% Vacant.............	6.7	9.2	9.5	3.5	8.4	*
% 1+ Persons per Room....	3.5	4.3	9.6	12.9	*	*

Community Area 41 -- Hyde Park
Selected Characteristics of Census Tracts: 1980

Tract Number	Total	4101	4102	4103	4104	4105	4106	4107	4108	4109	4110
Total Population.............	31198	1826	1544	903	660	3105	2527	2463	3565	4031	3465
% Male......................	50.7	50.2	52.1	49.5	44.2	45.4	53.0	51.2	51.9	52.8	48.2
% Black.....................	37.2	41.3	49.7	82.8	93.2	88.3	46.3	31.3	42.3	28.0	17.5
% Other Nonwhite............	7.2	6.8	6.0	3.5	0.6	1.1	5.0	11.6	8.4	7.1	6.6
% Of Spanish Origin.........	2.3	4.7	6.0	1.9	0.6	1.2	1.9	3.4	2.6	2.0	2.2
% Foreign Born..............	12.2	13.9	13.7	6.7	3.0	2.3	7.7	14.4	10.2	13.6	16.7
% Living In Group Quarters..	8.7	0.1	0.1	0.6	1.7	2.5	22.6	2.2	1.8	14.6	7.0
% 13 Years Old And Under....	12.3	11.9	14.2	13.2	16.8	18.9	14.5	12.4	10.9	10.0	7.3
% 14-20 Years Old...........	10.5	4.7	5.8	8.6	7.1	10.4	9.5	8.9	5.5	14.1	4.0
% 21-64 Years Old...........	67.0	72.0	75.5	67.2	61.4	59.2	69.3	73.3	74.1	66.1	64.3
% 65-74 Years Old...........	5.7	6.4	3.3	7.2	9.1	6.9	4.2	3.4	5.8	4.8	11.4
% 75 Years Old And Over.....	4.5	5.1	1.1	3.8	5.6	4.6	2.5	2.1	3.8	4.9	13.1
% In Different House........	59.4	65.2	81.1	43.1	28.5	45.6	69.5	67.4	66.7	60.5	52.7
% Families With Female Head.	34.1	28.0	31.5	38.5	53.1	60.6	43.8	35.2	36.8	23.7	26.8
Median School Years Completed....	16.1	16.1	16.1	14.1	13.7	12.3	16.1	16.1	16.1	16.1	16.1
Median Family Income, 1979...$$	22115	29167	14393	19531	16250	14688	12087	15977	21311	30994	30746
% Income Below Poverty Level.	9.1	6.9	12.1	15.2	23.6	15.0	21.7	8.1	7.9	3.0	1.5
% Income Of $30,000 Or More..	36.0	47.6	16.6	30.0	30.6	12.2	14.4	20.3	31.9	52.2	51.9
% White Collar Workers......	80.0	81.1	75.6	64.2	66.2	64.2	79.6	82.9	78.5	78.9	84.7
% Civilian Labor Force Unemployed.	5.5	5.1	4.1	10.1	3.7	11.0	7.7	4.9	6.1	6.0	3.6
% Riding To Work By Automobile....	38.2	48.9	46.4	35.1	57.6	44.2	38.3	30.4	42.5	41.6	36.2
Mean Commuting Time - Minutes...	25.3	26.4	27.5	38.4	36.5	31.1	28.4	26.0	29.1	23.4	23.9
Population Per Household..........	2.0	1.7	1.9	2.1	2.2	2.4	2.3	2.1	1.7	1.8	1.6
Total Housing Units..........	15493	1166	855	473	353	1356	915	1322	2139	2204	2060
% Condominiums...............	17.7	19.0	5.0	20.5	11.0	6.5	3.2	11.0	28.2	31.7	14.0
% Built 1970 Or Later........	3.4	2.3	0.0	0.0	0.0	1.5	1.7	1.3	2.9	5.6	10.0
% Owner Occupied.............	23.8	19.4	9.7	18.8	18.4	13.2	22.0	20.0	25.8	26.7	21.1
% With 1+ Persons Per Room...	3.5	3.4	5.8	5.3	5.1	5.7	4.2	4.0	3.5	3.3	1.9
Median Value: Owner Units.......$$	98000	-	-	-	-	68400	96600	77700	84000	-	-
Median Rent: Rental Units....$$	243	252	214	249	231	219	227	252	233	230	300
Median Number Of Rooms: All Units.	3.7	3.0	2.9	4.3	4.3	4.1	4.3	4.1	3.0	3.2	3.5

Tract Number	4111	4112	4113	4114
Total Population.............	2451	2374	772	1512
% Male......................	51.4	48.4	65.0	53.1
% Black.....................	5.9	7.8	1.8	30.0
% Other Nonwhite............	8.3	7.5	10.1	17.6
% Of Spanish Origin.........	1.3	1.8	1.6	1.3
% Foreign Born..............	17.4	12.6	14.4	21.2
% Living In Group Quarters........	9.6	16.0	63.0	0.0
% 13 Years Old And Under.........	12.5	12.3	3.2	15.6
% 14-20 Years Old................	14.0	19.4	46.0	8.7
% 21-64 Years Old................	66.1	59.5	46.9	71.3
% 65-74 Years Old................	4.3	5.8	1.4	2.8
% 75 Years Old And Over..........	3.1	3.0	2.5	1.5
% In Different House.............	47.1	54.6	83.6	62.7
% Families With Female Head......	13.7	16.5	23.8	29.2
Median School Years Completed....	16.1	16.1	16.1	16.1
Median Family Income, 1979...$$	40000	40000	25714	14158
% Income Below Poverty Level.....	2.5	3.3	16.1	16.7
% Income Of $30,000 Or More.....	63.4	67.6	41.9	8.4
% White Collar Workers..........	92.2	88.1	65.6	87.7
% Civilian Labor Force Unemployed.	1.5	2.7	2.2	6.5
% Riding To Work By Automobile....	32.9	31.0	8.3	31.6
Mean Commuting Time - Minutes...	20.1	19.0	9.6	18.7
Population Per Household..........	2.3	2.3	2.0	2.4
Total Housing Units..........	975	883	146	646
% Condominiums...............	22.4	24.2	37.0	0.0
% Built 1970 Or Later........	1.6	0.5	8.0	3.0
% Owner Occupied.............	47.8	45.3	58.9	8.5
% With 1+ Persons Per Room.......	0.8	1.6	1.4	4.5
Median Value: Owner Units.......$$	122500	152000	-	-
Median Rent: Rental Units.......$$	303	259	291	253
Median Number Of Rooms: All Units.	5.6	5.3	5.0	4.3

Community Area 41 -- Hyde Park
Selected Characteristics of Census Tracts: 1970

Tract Number	TOTAL	4101	4102	4103	4104	4105	4106	4107	4108	4109	4110
Total Population.............	33559	1836	1736	1196	880	3641	3075	3116	3304	4183	2907
% Male.........................	48.5	47.3	48.2	49.6	44.5	49.1	50.3	49.7	48.4	47.3	45.6
% Black........................	31.1	15.6	40.0	81.6	94.7	88.1	50.2	35.6	18.4	6.6	5.7
% Other Nonwhite...............	4.8	6.0	4.6	0.9	0.2	1.5	5.2	6.3	7.3	2.7	4.3
% Of Spanish Language..........	2.6	3.1	8.7	1.0	1.4	3.1	4.2	2.1	2.1	1.9	0.8
% Foreign Born.................	11.5	15.8	14.2	6.0	3.0	3.7	5.4	11.5	11.9	19.4	12.0
% Living In Group Quarters.....	7.2	0.0	0.0	1.7	0.8	4.0	1.1	1.7	2.6	6.5	
% 13 Years Old And Under.......	15.8	12.9	16.6	16.6	17.8	20.8	21.7	19.8	13.9	10.6	8.6
% 14-20 Years Old..............	9.5	3.8	6.7	11.1	7.6	10.5	9.3	9.2	6.1	5.0	5.5
% 21-64 Years Old..............	63.3	66.0	73.6	63.0	63.5	60.6	62.7	64.2	71.2	61.3	58.7
% 65-74 Years Old..............	6.7	9.6	1.8	6.4	8.6	4.8	4.1	4.3	5.9	12.0	14.8
% 75 Years Old And Over........	4.7	7.8	1.3	2.9	2.4	3.4	2.2	2.6	3.0	11.0	12.4
% In Different House...........	34.4	27.7	18.9	33.5	40.3	35.3	33.5	30.9	37.7	40.6	44.2
% Families With Female Head....	14.4	12.5	10.5	19.4	27.1	26.7	16.9	12.2	13.2	12.0	12.0
Median School Years Completed..	14.8	14.5	15.6	12.6	12.5	12.1	12.1	12.9	14.9	16.4	14.1	14.3
Median Family Income, 1969.....$$	11244	11122	7603	10353	8694	8339	8816	10581	11842	13960	15603
% Income Below Poverty Level....	6.8	3.5	7.6	8.6	8.1	10.9	6.6	12.0	3.3	6.0	4.2
% Income of $15,000 or More....	32.9	30.3	16.4	32.1	14.1	12.2	20.2	20.3	33.9	45.5	51.9
% White Collar Workers.........	56.1	63.9	56.7	33.1	37.1	21.0	46.7	50.9	64.7	66.0	63.0
% Civilian Labor Force Unemployed.	2.7	2.7	1.8	3.4	2.8	3.4	3.1	2.7	1.9	4.4	0.9
% Riding To Work By Automobile....	43.2	55.0	35.2	49.5	40.1	49.0	52.1	39.5	44.1	52.9	43.3
Population Per Household........	2.2	1.8	2.2	2.5	2.4	2.6	2.7	2.4	1.9	1.8	1.8
Total Housing Units..........	15683	1130	836	490	374	1379	1147	1305	2063	2589	1784
% Condominiums & Cooperatives.....	6.5	9.5	0.6	12.0	5.9	0.0	4.4	3.9	2.9	9.0	13.5
% Built 1960 Or Later.........	11.7	15.1	4.0	2.4	7.1	15.4	4.3	3.3	27.4	5.7	18.4
% Owner Occupied..............	7.4	2.2	4.8	6.5	7.2	6.7	11.5	11.3	5.6	1.6	2.6
% With 1+ Persons Per Room....	4.5	3.4	8.7	4.1	5.0	7.1	7.1	7.1	3.4	3.6	2.9
Median Value: Owner Units.......$$	39800					24300	33100	31200	35400		
Median Rent: Rental Units......$$	134	136	120	130	117	122	124	126	140	154	148
Median Number Of Rooms: All Units.	3.6	2.9	2.8	4.2	4.2	4.0	4.2	3.8	3.0	2.6	3.4

Tract Number	4111	4112	4113	4114
Total Population.............	2895	2429	809	1552
% Male.........................	47.8	43.8	72.3	48.8
% Black........................	4.3	3.7	4.1	30.5
% Other Nonwhite...............	6.9	4.3	4.9	11.4
% Of Spanish Language..........	2.0	2.9	1.8	1.8
% Foreign Born.................	16.3	8.4	7.1	18.6
% Living In Group Quarters........	24.4	13.3	66.0	5.5
% 13 Years Old And Under.......	16.1	16.3	2.6	21.9
% 14-20 Years Old..............	12.4	17.0	47.6	8.2
% 21-64 Years Old..............	64.1	58.2	46.5	66.9
% 65-74 Years Old..............	4.8	5.7	2.8	1.8
% 75 Years Old And Over........	2.6	2.8	0.5	1.2
% In Different House...........	31.8	33.2	18.3	34.8
% Families With Female Head......	9.9	8.1	7.3	11.1
Median School Years Completed....	17.1	17.1	16.9	15.7
Median Family Income, 1969......$$	22074	16006	19286	9672
% Income Below Poverty Level....	2.5	5.2	0.0	10.5
% Income of $15,000 or More....	61.8	52.9	73.7	23.8
% White Collar Workers.........	73.9	73.8	53.7	59.3
% Civilian Labor Force Unemployed.	2.3	1.4	6.7	2.1
% Riding To Work By Automobile....	33.2	29.9	23.3	27.5
Population Per Household........	2.5	2.4	2.2	2.6
Total Housing Units..........	952	898	141	595
% Condominiums & Cooperatives.....	9.2	5.3	37.6	0.0
% Built 1960 Or Later.........	13.3	10.7	4.9	4.6
% Owner Occupied.................	22.5	19.6	10.6	8.4
% With 1+ Persons Per Room....	0.7	1.1	0.0	7.1
Median Value: Owner Units.......$$	46300	50100		
Median Rent: Rental Units......$$	163	141	170	130
Median Number Of Rooms: All Units.	5.6	4.8	5.1	4.1

the Kimbark Village shopping center on cleared land along 53rd Street from Kimbark to Woodlawn avenues. The Harper Court Foundation developed a sliding-scale rental complex, on Harper Avenue at 53rd Street, for displaced artisans and merchants who could afford low rents along with restaurateurs who could support the projects with market-rate rental payments. Harper Court opened in 1965.

During the 1960s, the first full decade of urban renewal in Hyde Park, the total population dropped by 12,000, more than half of whom were blacks. Nevertheless, blacks still comprised almost a third of the total in 1970. Housing overcrowding was reduced. In 1960, almost 10 percent of the population of Hyde Park lived in housing units with more than one person per room but 10 years later that figure had fallen to less than 2 percent. The number of housing units decreased by more than 20 percent during the decade and, in 1970, two-thirds of them were situated in buildings with 10 or more units each.

In 1980, 31,000 people lived in Hyde Park, the lowest number in more than 60 years, the total having dropped by more than 40 percent since the 1950 peak. The percentage black has remained greater than 30 for the last three censuses. Although it has been cited as a racially-integrated Chicago community area, sub-areas of Hyde Park are not generally integrated, and two areas are particularly segregated. The immediate vicinity of the University of Chicago, (Tracts 4111, 4112 and 4113) are in sum almost 86 percent white. Taken together, Tracts

4103, 4104 and 4105, in the northeastern corner of Hyde Park, are almost 88 percent black. The northern half of Hyde Park contains four tracts (4101, 4102, 4106 and 4108), comprised of more than 40 percent black and 40 percent white population, making this the most racially balanced part of the neighborhood.

During the 1970s, the number of all housing units that were single-family homes more than doubled, to 19.5 percent, while the percentage in buildings of 10 or more units dropped to 47 percent. The percentage of the population living in overcrowded housing units had crept up to 6.3 in 1980, and there were 1.2 percent fewer housing units than in 1970. The median value of single-family, owner-occupied homes in Hyde Park in 1980 was $98,000, more than double the city-wide median.

In 1980, at the end of the second decade of urban renewal, streets had been widened, schools, parks and playgrounds had been added, and virtually all housing units had been brought up to the city's building codes. In retrospect, the University of Chicago gave the area a galvanizing institutional force, and middle-class blacks, University faculty and young marrieds have kept demand for middle-class housing high in Hyde Park-Kenwood, thus pricing the poor out of the area for the most part and achieving managed integration.

Will Hogan

Woodlawn

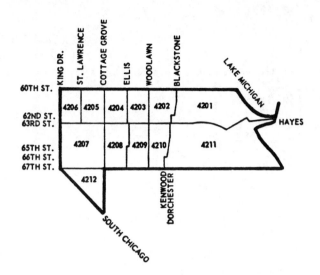

Woodlawn is located on Chicago's South Side about eight miles from the Loop. It is situated just south of the University of Chicago, separated from Lake Michigan by Jackson Park. Comprised first of Dutch, then Irish and German ethnic groups, today Woodlawn is almost entirely black.

During the early 19th century, Woodlawn was part of a swampy wilderness. In the 1850s, a few Dutch farmers reclaimed the area for truck farming. Vegetable growing became the chief means of making a livelihood from the marshy and unproductive land. In 1862, the Illinois Central Railway opened its first Woodlawn train stop at 63rd Street. Although this stimulated the movement of settlers and nearby neighbors, the community remained sparsely settled until the 1890s. In 1884, the first Woodlawn directory reported a population of approximately 500. By 1886, the population had increased to 1,000 inhabitants. After Woodlawn was annexed to Chicago in 1889, the community experienced unprecedented growth. In anticipation of the 1893 Columbian Exposition, to be held in nearby Jackson Park, many hotels, apartment buildings and stores were built in Woodlawn. The Jackson Park elevated train line was completed; 63rd Street and Cottage Grove Avenue became thriving shopping areas. By the time of the Fair, Woodlawn was an established community with 20,000 residents. The population dropped when the Fair ended and Woodlawn's growth pattern slowed considerably. The once-bustling hotels and apartment buildings now stood empty and quiet. Woodlawn resumed growth during the early 20th century when city plans for development in the south lakeshore area began in neighboring communities. Between 1908 and 1912, the area formerly occupied by the old Washington Park track, located in Woodlawn's northwest corner, was built up with many apartments. The neighborhood consisted mainly of single-family homes with an increasing number of two-, three- and four-story buildings.

In decades subsequent to the 1890s, Woodlawn's population growth kept pace with the rest of Chicago. However, between 1934 and 1940 Chicago experienced little increase in population, while Woodlawn's growth was 22 percent. This occurred during a time when there was practically no new construction. Many additional dwelling units were created by subdividing existing structures. These and later conversions began an era of substandard housing in Woodlawn. The neglect of older buildings led to neighborhood decay. By 1940, the shopping area along 63rd Street had deteriorated badly. In the late 1930s the Woodlawn Plan was prepared by the Chicago Plan Commission in collaboration with the Woodlawn Planning Commission. This program aimed at rehabilitation and improvement of the general appearance of the community area.

After 1910 the population, until then dominated by Dutch groups, began to include those of Irish and German origin. Around 63rd Street many of the new residents were transients, or workers who commuted daily to the Loop. As early as 1910, blacks lived in Woodlawn, some relocating from the deteriorating Near South Side. Many of these families lived in servant quarters in affluent areas such as Harper Street. In 1920, Woodlawn's black population was 2 percent of the total. A city-wide housing shortage developed after World War I, when returning veterans and rural southern black migrants came to Chicago in large numbers. As the housing problem grew, blacks moved farther south beyond 47th and 60th streets. By 1930, blacks accounted for 13 percent of Woodlawn's population, by 1940, 17 percent. During this period, blacks were concentrated west of Cottage Grove Avenue, which was a racial boundary. The University of Chicago's close proximity to Woodlawn also influenced the community's population. In 1930, at least half of the faculty lived in Woodlawn. This factor,

coupled with the high cost of property, discouraged an expansion of the campus into Woodlawn at that time.

Between 1930 and 1960, Woodlawn's population increased 23 percent to an all-time high of more than 81,000. This occurred during a time when the only new construction in Woodlawn was Midway Gardens, a 318-unit housing project built in 1953. During this time, blacks moved into Woodlawn east of Cottage Grove Avenue in large numbers. By 1950, blacks were 39 percent of the community's population and by 1960, they constituted 89 percent. During the 1950s there was massive racial turnover in Woodlawn. The white population dropped by 40,000 and the black population grew by the same number.

After World War II, blacks began to replace immigrants as primary sources of unskilled labor. Unlike other immigrant groups who moved out of menial low-paying jobs and into expanding neighborhoods, they were unable to enter into higher-paying jobs and other neighborhoods. These factors, combined with high unemployment, led to widespread poverty in the black community. The continuing poverty of Woodlawn's black residents and the decrease of city services contributed to deteriorating buildings and streets. During the 1970s, a large number of fires destroyed many apartment and business buildings in Woodlawn. Neglect led to the further deterioration of other buildings. Today, the once-busy and prosperous buildings that housed stores along 63rd Street are either empty, burned out or boarded up.

In the early 1960s, Woodlawn became the center of an ongoing controversy between The Woodlawn Organization (TWO) and the University of Chicago. Many residents feared the University's proposed South Campus expansion would extend into Woodlawn, dislocating the local populace. The Woodlawn Organization was founded by Saul Alinsky and the Industrial Areas Foundation, aided by grants from the Schwartzhaupt Foundation in New York, the Roman Catholic Archdiocese in Chicago and the Presbyterian Church nationally and locally. Picketing, mass marches and mass descent on city hall dramatized the controversy between TWO and the University. In the late 1960s TWO, the University of Chicago and city officials reached an agreement that no buildings would be demolished in Woodlawn for the completion of the South Campus until new housing for displaced residents was built in an area designated in Woodlawn. Land was set aside for that purpose. Later, Woodlawn received more national attention when controversy developed between TWO and the gang then called the Blackstone Rangers. The controversy centered around the use of gang members in leadership roles within federally-funded community programs. The growth of the Rangers and the violence that surrounded them led to community and city-wide concern. The implementation of community programs in Woodlawn in the 1960s produced little change; the renovation of Woodlawn did not happen, while poverty and unemployment increased.

Community Area 42 — Woodlawn
Population and Housing Characteristics, 1930-1980

	1980	1970	1960	1950	1940	1930
Total Population.......	36,323	53,814	81,279	80,699	71,685	66,052
% Male.....................	45.8	46.4	48.5	48.9	47.9	49.3
% Female...................	54.2	53.6	51.5	51.1	52.1	50.7
% White....................	3.5	3.6	10.4	60.0	82.9	86.6
% Black....................	95.7	95.8	89.1	38.8	16.9	13.0
% Other Nonwhite Races...	0.8	0.6	0.5	1.2	0.2	0.4
% Under 5 Years Old......	8.2	10.0	13.6	7.2	5.2	4.8
% 5-19 Years Old.........	24.9	27.4	20.6	13.1	16.5	16.7
% 20-44 Years Old........	32.1	33.7	41.1	46.5	45.8	50.5
% 45-64 Years Old........	20.4	19.5	18.4	25.0	24.7	22.3
% 65 Years and Older....	14.4	9.4	6.3	8.2	7.8	5.7
Median School Years....	11.8	10.6	9.9	11.3	10.0	*
Total Housing Units....	15,747	22,255	29,616	27,624	23,444	*
% In One-Unit Structures.	5.2	5.0	7.2	*	*	*
% Owner Occupied........	12.6	10.0	8.8	9.9	7.9	*
% Renter Occupied........	76.8	75.4	84.6	87.7	86.5	*
% Vacant..................	10.6	14.6	6.6	3.4	5.6	*
% 1+ Persons per Room....	9.4	12.8	23.3	21.1	*	*

Community Area 42 — Woodlawn
Selected Characteristics of Census Tracts: 1980

Tract Number	Total	4201	4202	4203	4204	4205	4206	4207	4208	4209	4210
Total Population.............	36323	1075	2343	2240	2310	3756	3339	5808	3555	4036	3192
% Male....................	45.8	43.3	45.6	51.5	44.2	44.1	45.3	45.8	46.7	45.3	48.5
% Black....................	95.7	86.2	89.6	84.9	78.2	98.8	99.6	99.1	99.1	99.2	97.4
% Other Nonwhite............	0.8	3.1	1.7	1.4	3.2	0.8	0.1	0.4	0.3	0.2	0.8
% Of Spanish Origin.........	0.8	1.8	1.0	2.1	1.9	0.6	0.7	0.6	0.4	0.6	0.6
% Foreign Born..............	2.3	8.7	1.5	2.8	10.2	2.8	0.7	0.8	1.4	1.4	0.7
% Living In Group Quarters..	3.2	0.1	13.6	15.1	9.0	0.3	0.2	0.5	1.9	0.5	4.8
% 13 Years Old And Under....	22.5	21.7	21.2	18.6	27.3	20.1	17.2	21.8	24.3	25.3	25.2
% 14-20 Years Old...........	12.4	12.4	10.4	16.1	12.3	12.5	9.3	12.0	13.4	14.0	11.7
% 21-64 Years Old...........	50.6	54.1	53.1	56.4	47.8	50.3	52.4	51.3	51.3	44.7	53.1
% 65-74 Years Old...........	8.5	7.0	8.4	6.2	3.8	10.3	12.1	8.7	7.7	9.6	6.6
% 75 Years Old And Over.....	6.0	4.8	6.9	2.7	8.8	6.7	9.1	6.3	3.4	6.3	3.4
% In Different House........	44.3	42.3	70.0	48.4	59.3	33.4	33.1	45.7	36.8	48.0	53.1
% Families With Female Head.	61.2	59.5	64.0	65.2	58.3	60.9	62.2	61.4	58.8	61.6	63.2
Median School Years Completed.	11.8	12.5	11.1	11.4	12.1	12.1	11.2	11.7	11.6	11.6	11.4
Median Family Income, 1979...$$	10546	14087	7806	6964	12555	11350	9641	10680	16048	7321	8187
% Income Below Poverty Level..	32.3	9.8	46.9	50.0	29.1	28.9	27.3	32.9	20.3	42.6	39.0
% Income Of $30,000 Or More.....	8.3	9.8	2.2	6.0	4.4	6.7	8.1	10.8	16.5	4.7	7.5
% White Collar Workers........	51.8	56.0	49.1	49.4	66.1	63.0	49.8	48.8	47.3	44.6	40.4
% Civilian Labor Force Unemployed.	19.3	9.1	23.1	21.7	24.6	14.2	20.7	19.2	19.5	18.2	25.7
% Riding To Work By Automobile..	45.6	49.9	32.6	40.7	32.9	42.9	49.5	54.0	49.1	45.2	35.2
Mean Commuting Time - Minutes...	36.1	26.5	29.1	33.2	33.5	36.8	43.8	38.2	36.0	38.2	37.6
Population Per Household..........	2.5	2.2	2.2	2.1	2.9	2.4	2.4	2.6	2.7	2.6	2.5
Total Housing Units..........	15747	534	1033	1006	859	1690	1513	2525	1570	1700	1454
% Condominiums...............	0.5	0.0	0.0	0.0	0.0	0.0	0.0	0.0	1.2	2.4	0.0
% Built 1970 Or Later.............	5.9	41.3	0.8	0.7	6.0	8.0	1.8	0.9	2.5	4.2	11.0
% Owner Occupied.................	12.6	0.4	5.4	2.9	3.1	10.2	13.6	22.6	14.4	16.5	7.5
% With 1+ Persons Per Room....$$	9.4	4.9	10.1	8.2	12.2	6.9	4.9	7.4	10.6	12.3	15.9
Median Value: Owner Units....$$	26600	-	-	-	-	-	-	25500	23200	28400	-
Median Rent: Rental Units.....$$	175	238	161	167	193	183	187	165	168	168	169
Median Number Of Rooms: All Units.	4.2	3.5	3.0	3.0	4.2	4.4	4.8	4.8	4.2	4.3	3.1

Tract Number	4211	4212
Total Population.............	2675	1994
% Male....................	44.8	43.2
% Black....................	98.0	99.2
% Other Nonwhite............	0.8	0.3
% Of Spanish Origin.........	0.7	0.6
% Foreign Born..............	1.4	3.6
% Living In Group Quarters..	1.0	0.0
% 13 Years Old And Under....	27.7	18.6
% 14-20 Years Old...........	14.4	11.2
% 21-64 Years Old...........	48.3	48.5
% 65-74 Years Old...........	6.5	11.5
% 75 Years Old And Over.....	3.1	10.2
% In Different House........	34.3	36.4
% Families With Female Head.	64.0	51.9
Median School Years Completed.	12.2	11.7
Median Family Income, 1979.....$$	10942	16397
% Income Below Poverty Level..	34.9	23.0
% Income Of $30,000 Or More.....	5.5	13.1
% White Collar Workers........	53.8	58.5
% Civilian Labor Force Unemployed.	16.5	18.3
% Riding To Work By Automobile..	43.7	53.7
Mean Commuting Time - Minutes...	37.3	31.1
Population Per Household..........	2.8	2.5
Total Housing Units..........	1018	845
% Condominiums...............	1.6	0.0
% Built 1970 Or Later.............	6.9	12.0
% Owner Occupied.................	5.2	30.1
% With 1+ Persons Per Room....$$	13.6	6.2
Median Value: Owner Units....$$	-	26100
Median Rent: Rental Units.....$$	184	165
Median Number Of Rooms: All Units.	4.1	4.8

Community Area 42 -- Woodlawn
Selected Characteristics of Census Tracts: 1970

Tract Number	TOTAL	4201	4202	4203	4204	4205	4206	4207	4208	4209	4210
Total Population	53814	2051	4097	4042	2613	3718	4213	7103	5849	5649	5373
% Male	46.4	49.9	47.8	51.6	44.5	44.3	45.0	45.9	47.4	45.0	45.7
% Black	95.8	86.7	92.3	90.5	74.7	98.5	99.1	99.2	98.9	98.4	97.1
% Other Nonwhite	0.6	0.7	0.5	0.6	3.0	0.7	0.2	0.5	0.5	0.6	0.4
% Of Spanish Language	1.3	2.5	3.4	2.0	0.0	0.8	0.9	1.7	0.1	1.1	2.6
% Foreign Born	1.1	2.5	0.1	1.6	7.7	0.0	2.1	1.0	0.0	1.4	0.1
% Living In Group Quarters	2.4	4.9	3.3	9.2	7.3	0.6	0.3	0.6	0.7	1.6	3.4
% 13 Years Old And Under	28.0	28.4	33.7	27.8	28.0	18.4	18.1	22.6	28.5	29.0	32.6
% 14-20 Years Old	11.0	12.4	11.1	14.0	8.8	9.6	9.1	10.9	11.1	10.7	10.4
% 21-64 Years Old	51.6	52.9	50.7	53.8	51.2	57.0	56.6	53.3	53.9	49.7	50.8
% 65-74 Years Old	6.4	3.6	3.2	3.4	4.7	10.8	11.0	9.1	5.1	7.1	4.0
% 75 Years Old And Over	3.0	2.7	1.3	1.0	7.3	4.2	5.2	4.1	1.5	3.5	2.1
% In Different House	44.7	20.1	27.5	40.5	45.9	56.9	43.6	59.1	53.0	55.8	35.4
% Families With Female Head	34.0	35.0	36.4	33.0	29.9	30.1	28.3	29.0	38.8	35.9	36.1
Median School Years Completed	10.6	10.4	10.8	10.4	11.9	11.0	9.9	10.9	10.4	10.6	10.4
Median Family Income, 1969 $$	6611	5742	5782	5594	7096	8635	7916	7352	6021	6965	6054
% Income Below Poverty Level	26.5	32.2	31.8	29.8	23.6	10.4	9.0	20.2	33.6	26.9	32.9
% Income of $15,000 or More	7.9	4.4	5.2	4.2	15.0	14.3	11.2	7.8	5.1	7.8	4.8
% White Collar Workers	13.0	17.8	10.1	16.4	28.6	15.8	9.4	11.4	10.4	10.9	8.8
% Civilian Labor Force Unemployed	7.1	13.4	9.7	7.7	5.7	4.8	6.1	5.9	7.9	7.2	10.1
% Riding To Work By Automobile	40.1	24.2	48.1	31.4	31.2	41.4	40.6	45.7	40.5	40.7	42.7
Population Per Household	2.8	2.6	2.8	2.7	2.9	2.5	2.6	2.7	2.7	2.8	2.8
Total Housing Units	22261	1045	1595	1595	972	1747	1842	2900	2497	2281	2301
% Condominiums & Cooperatives	0.7	0.0	0.8	0.0	0.0	0.5	0.3	0.2	0.6	3.6	0.3
% Built 1960 Or Later	5.9	0.9	4.5	0.6	9.0	19.7	2.1	4.9	0.8	6.9	4.9
% Owner Occupied	9.1	0.9	2.3	2.5	4.3	10.2	11.1	22.0	8.8	10.3	3.9
% With 1+ Persons Per Room	13.3	20.3	19.5	15.1	14.8	6.9	6.3	8.5	10.4	13.1	18.1
Median Value: Owner Units $$	17300	-	-	-	-	-	-	17000	-	17300	-
Median Rent: Rental Units $$	110	107	112	109	110	117	114	106	109	108	108
Median Number Of Rooms: All Units	3.9	2.3	3.3	3.4	4.2	4.2	4.4	4.5	3.9	4.0	3.0

Tract Number	4211	421199	4212
Total Population	6846	19	2241
% Male	45.9	-	44.4
% Black	98.3	-	98.9
% Other Nonwhite	0.3	-	0.2
% Of Spanish Language	0.7	-	0.0
% Foreign Born	0.2	-	0.0
% Living In Group Quarters	1.1	-	0.3
% 13 Years Old And Under	38.0	-	23.8
% 14-20 Years Old	12.5	-	10.3
% 21-64 Years Old	44.6	-	46.1
% 65-74 Years Old	3.8	-	13.3
% 75 Years Old And Over	1.2	-	6.6
% In Different House	28.7	-	58.0
% Families With Female Head	41.7	-	28.4
Median School Years Completed	10.5	-	10.5
Median Family Income, 1969 $$	6131	-	7946
% Income Below Poverty Level	36.1	-	23.3
% Income of $15,000 or More	4.9	-	17.8
% White Collar Workers	10.8	-	19.8
% Civilian Labor Force Unemployed	5.2	-	6.0
% Riding To Work By Automobile	34.8	-	51.2
Population Per Household	3.3	-	2.7
Total Housing Units	2614	0	872
% Condominiums & Cooperatives	0.2	-	0.9
% Built 1960 Or Later	6.8	-	17.2
% Owner Occupied	3.6	-	28.3
% With 1+ Persons Per Room	21.6	-	8.7
Median Value: Owner Units $$	-	-	17200
Median Rent: Rental Units $$	113	-	100
Median Number Of Rooms: All Units	3.7	-	4.7

In 1960, there were almost 30,000 housing units in Woodlawn. By 1970, the number had dropped to 22,263, and today there are fewer than 16,000. Since 1960, both whites and blacks have been moving out of Woodlawn. Today, the population total is slightly more than 36,000, a drop of 55 percent from the historic high reached 20 years ago. The population is 96 percent black; only about 1,200 whites live there now. Proportions of Hispanics and other races are negligible. Single-family housing units comprise 14 percent of Woodlawn's dwelling units. Less than 15 percent is owner-occupied. This is comparable to 39 percent for Chicago. Woodlawn's median value owner-occupied housing is $26,647 as compared to $47,200 for Chicago. Today, Woodlawn is one of Chicago's poorest communities with an unemployment rate of 16.7 percent, compared to the overall city rate of 10.7. The median family income is $10,545, which puts Woodlawn among the 10 lowest community areas in the city.

Some recent city plans for development include the renovation of the Dr. Deton J. Brooks Jr. Parent Child Center at 69th and Stony Island, renovation of the 68th Street pumping station by the Department of Public Works, and the designation of three streets to be resurfaced. Many other plans for redevelopment of Woodlawn have been proposed by The Woodlawn Organization and other community groups, and await study or execution.

Annie Ruth Leslie

Community Area 43

South Shore

When Chicago became an incorporated place, the South Shore area was part of the swampy land and forest lying south of the new city. German truck farmers began moving into the area in the 1860s and 1870s, but few people lived in South Shore during this time.

In 1881, the Illinois Central Railroad built a South Kenwood station at 71st Street and Jeffrey Boulevard. By 1889 a small settlement had grown up near the station, called Bryn Mawr, a name by which the station itself soon came to be known. The Bryn Mawr area came to include the land from 71st to 73rd streets, between Cregier and Paxton avenues. Northwest of Bryn Mawr was the Parkside area, running from 67th to 71st streets and west to Dorchester Avenue, where a few frame

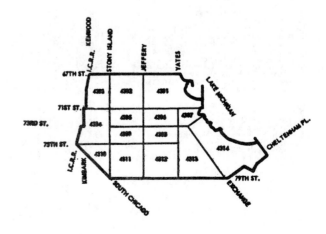

Community Area 43 —South Shore
Population and Housing Characteristics, 1930-1980

	1980	1970	1960	1950	1940	1930
Total Population.......	77,743	80,660	73,086	79,336	79,593	78,755
% Male..................	45.8	46.0	45.3	45.7	46.2	46.6
% Female................	54.2	54.0	54.7	54.3	53.8	53.4
% White.................	3.6	29.9	89.6	99.8	99.7	99.7
% Black.................	95.1	69.0	9.6	0.2	0.3	0.2
% Other Nonwhite Races...	1.3	1.1	0.8	0.0	0.0	0.1
% Under 5 Years Old.....	8.7	7.9	6.7	7.7	5.5	6.5
% 5-19 Years Old.........	24.0	20.3	16.4	15.0	17.0	18.7
% 20-44 Years Old........	43.3	40.0	27.8	36.8	45.0	49.2
% 45-64 Years Old........	17.5	20.3	33.4	30.5	25.1	20.8
% 65 Years and Older.....	6.5	11.5	15.7	10.0	7.4	4.8
Median School Years....	12.6	12.3	12.2	12.3	12.1	*
Total Housing Units....	34,162	33,359	30,001	29,930	26,415	*
% In One-Unit Structures.	10.2	11.8	17.8	*	*	*
% Owner Occupied........	17.7	16.9	21.1	21.9	14.5	*
% Renter Occupied.......:	74.1	79.3	74.9	76.8	80.9	*
% Vacant................	8.2	3.8	4.0	1.3	4.6	*
% 1+ Persons per Room....	6.7	5.5	3.9	8.2	*	*

Community Area 43 — South Shore
Selected Characteristics of Census Tracts: 1980

Tract Number	Total	4301	4302	4303	4304	4305	4306	4307	4308	4309	4310
Total Population.............	77743	12735	7023	4393	4114	5959	2778	2774	2636	2585	1558
% Male.......................	45.8	44.8	45.9	44.7	44.4	47.0	46.8	48.4	47.2	44.4	46.1
% Black......................	95.1	95.4	93.5	99.3	97.6	97.9	93.3	92.2	93.1	97.9	97.9
% Other Nonwhite.............	1.3	0.7	1.1	0.3	1.2	1.0	2.3	1.6	1.8	1.0	0.6
% Of Spanish Origin..........	1.2	0.4	0.8	0.6	1.6	0.5	1.0	1.1	1.3	0.7	1.0
% Foreign Born...............	2.4	1.4	1.7	1.4	0.7	1.6	2.3	3.8	1.7	1.1	0.3
% Living In Group Quarters...	0.4	0.0	0.0	0.0	0.0	0.2	0.4	0.4	0.0	0.0	1.1
% 13 Years Old And Under.....	23.3	21.7	23.5	28.2	24.6	24.8	25.1	19.6	22.3	24.0	25.4
% 14-20 Years Old............	11.1	9.2	11.2	12.9	14.0	9.9	11.8	6.7	12.1	13.3	16.4
% 21-64 Years Old............	59.0	61.0	59.9	50.7	53.0	59.9	57.8	68.8	58.6	57.5	50.7
% 65-74 Years Old............	4.3	4.9	3.6	5.7	5.7	3.9	3.6	3.1	4.7	3.8	4.9
% 75 Years Old And Over......	2.3	3.1	1.8	2.5	2.7	1.6	1.6	1.8	2.3	1.4	2.6
% In Different House.........	48.3	56.4	46.2	41.1	29.5	55.0	54.0	68.2	43.1	36.8	23.4
% Families With Female Head..	49.3	53.6	47.2	63.2	53.3	49.6	42.8	49.5	39.5	47.0	46.1
Median School Years Completed..	12.6	13.0	12.6	11.9	12.1	12.4	12.8	13.4	12.8	12.5	12.0
Median Family Income, 1979.....$$	15969	16199	14210	8770	15605	12178	18631	16875	20931	15979	12788
% Income Below Poverty Level....	20.8	19.9	24.5	41.6	22.2	26.5	14.8	16.3	15.7	25.5	27.0
% Income Of $30,000 Or More.....	19.1	21.4	25.2	6.1	15.5	7.5	25.1	14.7	30.8	24.1	16.2
% White Collar Workers..........	59.0	67.8	58.2	39.5	53.4	46.4	64.5	63.9	66.4	55.7	45.8
% Civilian Labor Force Unemployed.	13.1	11.3	13.4	23.0	16.5	15.0	15.4	9.4	9.9	11.5	12.4
% Riding To Work By Automobile....	56.7	58.8	54.2	52.3	60.6	47.7	53.5	49.8	55.1	49.3	65.4
Mean Commuting Time - Minutes...	40.2	39.5	38.1	42.5	39.4	41.9	35.7	41.8	41.3	41.6	36.2
Population Per Household.........	2.5	2.1	2.5	2.7	3.1	2.3	2.8	1.9	2.8	2.8	3.5
Total Housing Units..........	34162	6543	3481	1826	1374	2736	1110	1506	992	981	470
% Condominiums...............	3.3	6.7	0.4	0.0	0.0	0.0	5.8	2.6	0.0	0.0	0.0
% Built 1970 Or Later........	2.7	2.4	8.1	2.5	0.9	2.4	0.0	3.6	0.8	1.0	1.2
% Owner Occupied.............	17.8	9.9	12.8	9.6	30.2	9.4	26.9	8.2	34.2	24.5	40.6
% With 1+ Persons Per Room....	6.7	4.6	9.7	14.4	8.5	8.4	7.0	3.8	3.5	5.9	11.1
Median Value: Owner Units.......$$	39400	48800	89500	–	31600	33800	58200	–	48200	47700	23800
Median Rent: Rental Units....$$	223	238	205	187	194	210	226	258	230	217	189
Median Number Of Rooms: All Units.	4.3	4.0	4.0	4.2	5.0	3.8	4.9	3.6	5.1	4.5	5.1

Tract Number	4311	4312	4313	4314
Total Population.............	5956	4399	12811	8022
% Male.......................	44.7	46.9	45.8	46.6
% Black......................	97.0	96.4	96.6	86.7
% Other Nonwhite.............	1.9	0.9	1.6	1.8
% Of Spanish Origin..........	0.7	0.7	1.5	3.7
% Foreign Born...............	3.0	2.4	2.9	5.8
% Living In Group Quarters...	0.3	0.0	0.1	2.5
% 13 Years Old And Under.....	20.6	23.1	27.2	17.0
% 14-20 Years Old............	11.7	15.2	11.9	7.6
% 21-64 Years Old............	61.2	55.9	56.0	65.9
% 65-74 Years Old............	4.6	3.6	3.2	5.5
% 75 Years Old And Over......	1.9	2.2	1.6	4.1
% In Different House.........	38.3	25.1	55.7	56.1
% Families With Female Head..	42.0	32.1	53.8	47.8
Median School Years Completed..	12.6	12.6	12.4	13.0
Median Family Income, 1979.....$$	19914	23656	12350	19380
% Income Below Poverty Level....	8.7	8.2	25.1	13.7
% Income Of $30,000 Or More.....	22.4	36.1	12.3	21.9
% White Collar Workers..........	58.6	60.0	54.5	64.1
% Civilian Labor Force Unemployed.	10.3	11.0	17.4	9.6
% Riding To Work By Automobile....	62.6	69.9	51.0	61.8
Mean Commuting Time - Minutes...	40.1	35.3	45.8	38.5
Population Per Household.........	2.7	3.5	2.7	1.9
Total Housing Units..........	2293	1302	5174	4374
% Condominiums...............	0.0	0.0	0.0	13.1
% Built 1970 Or Later........	0.7	2.3	2.1	3.0
% Owner Occupied.............	30.0	69.3	11.8	16.6
% With 1+ Persons Per Room....	5.2	7.2	8.1	3.5
Median Value: Owner Units.......$$	36600	37700	30600	32000
Median Rent: Rental Units....$$	218	224	227	240
Median Number Of Rooms: All Units.	4.9	5.6	4.3	3.6

Community Area 43 -- South Shore
Selected Characteristics of Census Tracts: 1970

Tract Number	TOTAL	4301	4302	4303	4304	4305	4306	4307	4308	4309	4310
Total Population	80660	13388	7838	5383	4538	5958	2968	3346	2493	2457	2193
% Male	46.0	46.0	46.3	46.7	46.3	48.0	45.6	40.9	47.5	46.9	45.9
% Black	69.0	73.6	86.0	98.1	95.0	90.4	47.7	20.9	59.4	84.8	91.5
% Other Nonwhite	1.1	0.8	0.9	0.6	1.9	0.7	1.4	1.6	1.0	0.9	0.3
% Of Spanish Language	1.5	0.6	0.4	1.4	1.3	1.2	2.9	3.0	0.9	3.3	1.6
% Foreign Born	5.7	4.6	3.0	0.6	0.3	1.9	7.1	13.4	6.4	3.1	3.7
% Living In Group Quarters	0.9	0.3	0.9	0.3	0.6	0.1	1.8	5.5	0.3	0.0	5.1
% 13 Years Old And Under	20.8	18.6	21.1	27.3	28.8	22.0	19.2	7.1	22.7	24.5	32.9
% 14-20 Years Old	9.0	7.4	8.9	11.2	13.8	8.6	9.8	5.1	8.9	10.9	13.0
% 21-64 Years Old	58.8	62.9	63.5	55.2	52.2	63.4	55.8	58.1	57.0	59.5	44.5
% 65-74 Years Old	7.3	7.0	4.4	4.7	3.3	4.0	9.0	17.5	7.8	3.2	3.6
% 75 Years Old And Over	4.2	4.1	2.1	1.7	1.9	1.9	6.3	12.3	3.6	1.9	5.9
% In Different House	33.6	25.1	30.8	46.0	57.6	24.8	33.5	37.2	30.2	34.6	44.9
% Families With Female Head	20.5	22.3	20.3	27.0	22.8	22.3	20.5	16.6	15.3	20.6	25.8
Median School Years Completed	12.3	12.5	12.0	10.9	11.4	11.9	12.7	12.5	12.5	12.3	10.6
Median Family Income, 1969 $$	10461	11063	10506	7557	8361	9232	10679	12754	12695	9948	7318
% Income Below Poverty Level	7.8	7.0	10.2	17.6	12.5	9.2	7.3	5.5	0.5	7.2	13.6
% Income of $15,000 or More	24.4	28.2	24.2	10.1	15.3	12.6	37.4	37.0	40.5	17.8	9.4
% White Collar Workers	29.1	33.8	24.6	9.6	16.1	17.5	36.7	48.7	38.2	28.1	15.6
% Civilian Labor Force Unemployed	4.2	3.7	6.5	5.4	5.1	4.3	4.4	2.0	1.5	6.2	5.7
% Riding To Work By Automobile	51.4	52.9	45.1	50.4	44.4	46.4	52.3	54.9	63.4	49.7	53.1
Population Per Household	2.5	2.3	2.4	2.8	3.4	3.4	2.4	1.8	2.8	2.9	3.8
Total Housing Units	33368	6115	3263	1993	1368	2640	1275	1901	909	883	578
% Condominiums & Cooperatives	2.2	5.2	0.6	0.3	0.4	0.5	2.3	4.1	2.4	0.6	1.9
% Built 1960 Or Later	10.8	13.0	4.3	3.1	3.7	1.1	2.3	31.1	2.1	6.0	8.8
% Owner Occupied	14.9	3.9	12.1	8.1	25.8	9.2	19.4	4.1	35.5	27.6	30.4
% With 1+ Persons Per Room	5.7	4.1	7.0	13.2	13.1	7.8	4.5	1.7	3.6	5.7	14.2
Median Value: Owner Units $$	20200	26400	36000	-	16400	18400	25100	-	23000	22700	16000
Median Rent: Rental Units $$	134	142	129	117	126	128	133	157	135	135	117
Median Number Of Rooms: All Units	4.1	3.9	3.8	4.0	4.9	3.7	4.1	3.3	5.1	4.5	5.0

Tract Number	4311	4312	4313	4314
Total Population	6348	4062	12131	7557
% Male	45.8	47.3	46.0	44.0
% Black	88.8	66.3	61.2	8.0
% Other Nonwhite	1.6	1.6	1.2	1.4
% Of Spanish Language	1.7	0.1	1.8	2.7
% Foreign Born	4.9	5.8	7.4	15.8
% Living In Group Quarters	0.4	0.4	0.1	1.7
% 13 Years Old And Under	24.1	26.1	20.7	9.6
% 14-20 Years Old	11.0	11.2	8.5	5.5
% 21-64 Years Old	58.6	53.4	59.5	57.0
% 65-74 Years Old	4.2	5.9	7.2	18.2
% 75 Years Old And Over	2.0	3.4	4.1	9.6
% In Different House	40.3	34.4	22.6	42.4
% Families With Female Head	21.1	12.7	21.3	15.5
Median School Years Completed	12.2	12.5	12.3	12.4
Median Family Income, 1969 $$	10768	12185	10332	12084
% Income Below Poverty Level	5.9	3.7	7.0	3.2
% Income of $15,000 or More	25.3	34.0	21.4	30.5
% White Collar Workers	23.1	34.0	27.5	42.9
% Civilian Labor Force Unemployed	4.7	4.2	4.0	2.6
% Riding To Work By Automobile	57.3	59.8	49.1	52.3
Population Per Household	2.9	3.3	2.5	1.9
Total Housing Units	2238	1239	4924	4042
% Condominiums & Cooperatives	0.8	0.8	0.9	3.7
% Built 1960 Or Later	7.6	6.9	4.9	32.1
% Owner Occupied	30.9	67.7	13.0	8.5
% With 1+ Persons Per Room	6.4	5.3	4.5	2.5
Median Value: Owner Units $$	19500	19600	17700	16800
Median Rent: Rental Units $$	135	140	132	149
Median Number Of Rooms: All Units	4.8	5.8	4.2	3.4

homes were built before 1893. South of Parkside was Essex, stretching from 71st to 75th streets between Stony Island Avenue and the Illinois Central tracks. Essex was an outgrowth of Paul Cornell's 1855 settlement, and the early settlers of the area were primarily British railroad workers. South Shore was still mostly open land when the Village of Hyde Park was annexed to the city of Chicago in 1889. The sale of open lots was stimulated by speculation concerning the impending Columbian Exposition near the end of the century. Only a small amount of construction took place, however, as some frame hotels were built to serve a disappointing turnout of customers.

Around the turn of the century, apartment buildings began to go up in South Shore. Bryn Mawr and Parkside were the areas of earliest development. In 1905, Jackson Park Highlands, covering the area from 67th to 71st streets between Jeffrey Boulevard and Cregier Avenue, was subdivided. The Jackson Park Highlands area, so named because a portion of it lay on a ridge above a lagoon, developed into a high grade residential district. Following the closing of the Washington Park race track, some former members of the Washington Park Club, along with other well-to-do residents, formed the South Shore Country Club, which occupied land along the lakefront from 67th to 71st streets. Transportation was improved in the area when the streetcar lines were consolidated with the Chicago lines in 1910.

By 1920, South Shore was in the midst of a building boom. The land from 75th to 79th streets between Clyde and Oglesby avenues was built up mainly with single-family homes, while other areas were developed with single-flats, two-flats, and apartment hotels. The 1920 population of South Shore was 31,832, with Swedish and English nationality groups claiming the highest proportions. The population of South Shore in 1920 was mostly Protestant, although both English and Irish Catholics lived in the Essex sub-area, and some Jews had settled in Bryn Mawr.

The population of South Shore increased by almost 150 percent during the 1920s, to 78,755. Stimulation for the construction of tall apartment buildings along the lakefront from Hyde Park Boulevard to 79th Street was provided by the completion of the Outer Drive and the development of bathing beaches during the decade. Between 1921 and 1925, the old 80-acre Windsor Park golf course, from 75th to 79th streets between Colfax and Phillips avenues, became solidly built up with apartment buildings. Many Jewish families moved to South Shore from the Washington Park area, and formed the first Jewish congregation in the area. By 1930, the largest nationality groups were German, Irish, and English.

Although much undeveloped land still remained, by 1935 South Shore had achieved residential maturity. Frame homes, bungalows, and elaborate single-family homes were most visible at this point, interspersed with apartment districts covering whole blocks. Seventy-first Street was the leading commercial strip in South Shore, with some businesses along Stony Island Avenue as well.

While the total number of persons in South Shore had not grown considerably in the 1930s, its constituent subpopulations transformed substantially. Russian Jews became the most populous nationality group, followed by Swedish, German, Irish, and English. In 1940, 40 percent of all South Shore housing units were located in structures with 20 or more total units. The population was stable during the 1940s.

Although the population of South Shore declined by 8 percent during the 1950s, new construction accelerated. After World War II, apartment buildings were constructed on lots that long had been vacant along South Shore Drive, as well as in newly-cleared lots where frame homes once stood. Other vacant lots were used for the construction of single-family homes and two-flats.

In 1950, blacks comprised less than 1 percent of the population of South Shore. By 1960, however, South Shore was 10 percent black, and a rapid racial transformation of the area was under way. In 1960, virtually all black residents lived in the sub-area north of 75th Street and west of Stony Island Avenue. During the 1960s the racial composition of South Shore changed to 69 percent black and less than 30 percent white. The sub-area west of Jeffrey Boulevard was nearly 91 percent black, while 88 percent of South Shore's white population lived between Jeffrey Boulevard and Lake Michigan in 1970. The total population reached its historic high, just under 81,000. The total dropped to less than 78,000 in the most recent decade, as almost all of the remaining whites moved out. The population of South Shore is 95 percent black now, and there is no discernible white enclave.

In 1980, almost 7 percent of South Shore's total population resided in overcrowded housing units (units with more than one person per room). Eight percent of the total housing units were vacant, and more than 80 percent of all units were rental properties. Fifty-five percent of all housing units in South Shore were located in structures with from two to nine units, and about 15 percent of all units were single-family homes. The median value of single-family owner-occupied homes in

South Shore is $39,400, less than the city-wide median, but comparable to values in neighboring Chatham and Avalon Park.

The last 30 years have brought deterioration to the once exclusive South Shore community area. However, the new residents have become conscious of the threat, and efforts have been undertaken to prevent further decline. The South Shore National Bank, which had been moribund in the community, was sold to a new group of investors, who have been able to attract new deposits and to involve the bank in community renovation. An organized effort, originating within South Shore but involving groups from all over the city, resulted in the preservation of the elegant buildings and golf course of the old South Shore Country Club, which had been sold to the Chicago Park District. The Park District had planned a park of more modest facilities.

Some important housing improvements in South Shore began after the Chicago Area Renewal Effort Service Corporation (RESCORP), a group of 50 to 60 savings and loan associations, took an interest in the area. A $4 million program was conceived and executed by RESCORP and the Illinois Housing Development Authority. This program, called New Vistas, began in February, 1975 and involved the upgrading of about 150 housing units in five buildings between Jeffrey Boulevard and South Shore Drive from 67th to 71st streets. With the successful completion of this program, the group, spearheaded by the efforts of the South Shore Bank's City Lands Corporation, embarked on the New Vistas II program to upgrade 154 housing units near 69th Street and Paxton Avenue to a cost of $4.2 million. South Shore is an area where community interest is coalescing to fight urban decay and its ramifications.

Will Hogan

Chatham

Chatham is a South Side community area located nine miles from the Loop. In 1860, this land was a part of a low-lying swamp south of Chicago. The first buildings in Chatham were corn cribs built in that year by the Illinois Central Railway along its tracks from 75th to 95th streets. The curiously-named Avalon Highlands was the first residential area. It was in fact a deep swamp used mainly for duck hunting, but it was settled between 1884 and 1895 by some Italian stonemasons, who built frame houses there. Other frame houses were built by railroad workers in the northwestern section of Chatham during the 1880s.

The subdivision of Dauphin Park, located between 87th and 93rd streets, South Park Avenue and the Illinois Central tracks, was laid out in 1889 after Chatham was annexed to Chicago as a part of the Village of Hyde Park and the Town of Lake. Dauphin Park, which was later called Chesterfield, was settled by Hungarian and Irish railroad workers.

Most of Chatham remained grassland and swamp until the 1880s. The section between 79th and 83rd streets, Cottage Grove and South Park Avenue was known as Chatham Fields. These fields were used mainly as a picnic area. In 1891, the Cottage Grove Avenue cable car ran to 71st Street and a horsecar ran to 75th Street. By 1892, the Calumet Electric Company ran cars on Cottage Grove Avenue to Pullman. The community area was still very sparsely settled.

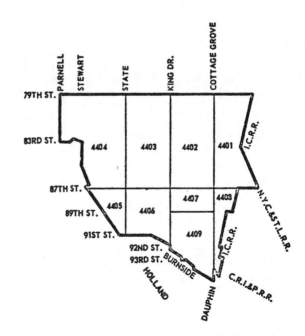

Decades later, the Avalon Highlands section of Chatham began to develop. Between 1911 and 1915, more than 150 houses were built in this area. In 1918 and 1919, bungalows were built at 79th Street and Maryland Avenue and a new community called "Garden Homes" was developed between Indiana Avenue and State Street from 87th to 89th streets. In 1920, the 79th Street station on the main line of the Illinois Central was opened. By now 9,774 people lived in Chatham, many of

Community Area 44 — Chatham
Population and Housing Characteristics, 1930, 1980

	1980	1970	1960	1950	1940	1930
Total Population......	40,725	47,287	41,962	40,845	37,788	36,228
% Male.................	44.9	46.4	47.5	47.7	48.6	49.5
% Female...............	55.1	53.6	52.5	52.3	51.4	50.5
% White................	0.8	0.2	36.0	99.1	99.9	99.7
% Black................	98.5	97.5	63.7	0.8	0.1	0.0
% Other Nonwhite Races...	0.7	0.5	0.3	0.1	0.0	0.3
% Under 5 Years Old......	6.4	6.8	9.4	8.8	6.7	8.8
% 5-19 Years Old........	19.1	24.32	19.4	17.4	19.9	21.8
% 20-44 Years Old........	34.9	36.7	37.8	37.4	46.4	49.5
% 45-64 Years Old........	27.7	25.0	24.7	28.7	22.0	16.4
% 65 Years and Older.....	11.9	7.2	8.7	7.7	5.0	3.5
Median School Years....	12.5	12.2	11.8	12.1	10.4	*
Total Housing Units....	17,138	16,900	14,378	13,162	11,643	*
% In One-Unit Structures.	31.3	31.7	34.1	*	*	*
% Owner Occupied.........	37.8	39.3	36.9	34.5	24.1	*
% Renter Occupied........	58.0	58.0	58.3	64.4	72.4	*
% Vacant................	4.2	2.7	4.8	1.1	3.5	*
% 1+ Persons per Room....	4.4	6.3	6.8	8.2	*	*

Community Area 44 — Chatham
Selected Characteristics of Census Tracts: 1980

Tract Number	Total	4401	4402	4403	4404	4405	4406	4407	4408	4409
Total Population.............	40725	10463	10160	5640	4454	0	2093	1937	2252	3726
% Male........................	44.9	44.8	43.4	44.5	46.6	-	46.8	46.9	47.1	44.8
% Black.......................	98.5	98.9	99.0	97.9	98.5	-	97.1	97.7	98.0	98.5
% Other Nonwhite.............	0.7	0.7	0.5	0.8	0.6	-	1.4	0.6	0.8	0.5
% Of Spanish Origin..........	0.7	0.6	0.8	0.9	0.2	-	0.9	0.7	0.3	0.6
% Foreign Born...............	1.8	2.5	1.0	1.2	1.0	-	0.9	3.6	3.5	1.9
% Living In Group Quarters....	0.1	0.0	0.0	0.4	0.2	-	0.1	0.0	0.3	0.0
% 13 Years Old And Under.....	17.1	21.0	14.6	12.7	17.9	*	14.9	13.4	21.7	19.2
% 14-20 Years Old...........	10.1	8.5	8.5	9.4	14.7	*	12.1	10.7	9.3	13.4
% 21-64 Years Old...........	60.8	62.5	62.1	62.1	58.0	-	60.1	59.7	60.2	55.4
% 65-74 Years Old...........	8.2	5.4	9.8	11.1	7.0	-	9.1	10.3	6.4	8.1
% 75 Years Old And Over.....	3.8	2.6	4.9	4.7	2.4	-	3.8	5.9	2.4	3.9
% In Different House........	32.8	45.2	34.2	24.3	23.8	-	6.5	17.3	47.3	33.3
% Families With Female Head..	45.2	55.3	47.1	35.1	35.7	-	28.0	33.6	47.9	44.8
Median School Years Completed..	12.5	12.5	12.6	12.7	12.4	-	12.6	12.2	12.2	12.3
Median Family Income, 1979......$$	18797	12885	18070	24771	22302	-	25573	20893	17552	16930
% Income Below Poverty Level...	12.6	22.2	10.9	4.1	9.2	-	4.3	8.7	11.3	15.4
% Income Of $30,000 Or More.....	23.4	17.3	19.5	37.3	28.1	-	36.9	22.5	24.4	15.3
% White Collar Workers........	56.2	52.3	57.5	64.1	57.9	-	54.2	56.1	50.5	51.0
% Civilian Labor Force Unemployed.	11.2	13.7	9.6	6.6	12.6	-	11.4	7.9	10.6	16.1
% Riding To Work By Automobile...	58.7	53.3	60.8	61.0	60.4	-	74.5	56.8	49.0	59.3
Mean Commuting Time - Minutes...	39.8	41.5	39.6	37.9	37.5	-	37.9	43.4	38.7	42.0
Population Per Household.........	2.5	2.2	2.2	2.5	3.0	-	3.0	2.8	2.5	3.1
Total Housing Units..........	17138	4964	4732	2337	1494	0	714	713	931	1253
% Condominiums...............	1.1	0.8	3.1	0.0	0.0	-	0.0	0.0	0.0	0.0
% Built 1970 Or Later........	1.6	2.1	0.2	0.6	2.6	-	4.1	3.2	2.2	2.5
% Owner Occupied.............	37.8	13.6	30.1	55.1	64.7	-	89.9	69.4	27.3	58.3
% With 1+ Persons Per Room......	4.4	5.5	3.1	2.9	5.8	-	3.4	2.4	4.6	7.2
Median Value: Owner Units.......$$	39200	31400	40100	46500	39100	-	40000	37000	36500	32900
Median Rent: Rental Units.......$$	213	215	217	212	190	-	212	189	227	187
Median Number Of Rooms: All Units.	4.7	4.0	4.5	5.2	5.4	-	5.6	5.4	4.4	5.3

Community Area 44 — Chatham
Selected Characteristics of Census Tracts: 1970

Tract Number	TOTAL	4401	4402	4403	4404	4406	4407	4408	4409
Total Population.............	47287	11492	12079	6533	5429	2275	2316	2511	4652
% Male........................	46.4	46.8	45.0	46.5	47.5	48.4	46.4	46.3	46.6
% Black.......................	97.5	98.2	98.6	97.2	97.3	96.9	94.7	96.6	96.5
% Other Nonwhite.............	0.5	0.3	0.4	0.7	0.7	0.5	0.6	0.1	0.8
% Of Spanish Language........	1.1	1.0	0.9	0.9	0.8	0.6	4.0	0.6	1.7
% Foreign Born...............	0.8	1.6	0.6	0.6	0.8	0.0	1.0	0.2	0.5
% Living In Group Quarters....	0.3	0.1	0.1	0.9	0.2	0.0	0.1	0.0	0.9
% 13 Years Old And Under.....	21.2	20.9	17.6	18.0	28.0	21.8	22.2	23.5	25.6
% 14-20 Years Old...........	11.4	8.8	10.2	11.4	14.1	15.3	12.2	10.3	16.2
% 21-64 Years Old...........	60.2	65.3	62.7	61.9	52.8	56.4	56.7	60.9	50.3
% 65-74 Years Old...........	5.3	3.9	7.1	6.4	3.6	4.7	5.7	3.3	5.5
% 75 Years Old And Over.....	2.0	1.1	2.4	2.4	1.6	1.8	3.2	2.0	2.4
% In Different House........	61.8	50.8	59.5	76.5	67.0	81.0	75.8	44.6	60.5
% Families With Female Head....	19.7	23.0	21.8	14.1	15.1	11.7	17.4	23.8	20.8
Median School Years Completed....	12.2	12.2	12.3	12.3	12.1	12.2	11.8	12.0	11.7
Median Family Income, 1969......$$	10772	10023	10798	11648	10581	13753	11360	10645	10089
% Income Below Poverty Level....	7.7	9.5	5.1	5.3	8.4	0.6	14.0	11.7	10.2
% Income of $15,000 or More.....	25.1	20.0	22.6	32.6	26.2	39.3	26.8	25.7	25.5
% White Collar Workers........	22.5	19.4	22.0	30.1	19.3	30.7	20.2	28.1	18.8
% Civilian Labor Force Unemployed.	3.5	4.0	3.4	2.8	3.6	3.4	1.8	3.9	4.8
% Riding To Work By Automobile....	60.5	59.3	57.8	64.8	61.6	70.1	67.8	62.3	54.8
Population Per Household...........	2.9	2.5	2.6	2.9	3.6	3.5	3.3	2.9	3.6
Total Housing Units..........	16912	4763	4712	2297	1547	666	726	872	1329
% Condominiums & Cooperatives.....	3.2	0.8	10.0	0.4	0.5	1.5	0.0	0.0	0.0
% Built 1960 Or Later...........	13.4	10.1	7.3	16.9	18.2	18.3	18.6	42.9	10.5
% Owner Occupied..................	35.8	12.1	24.8	55.1	60.6	90.8	69.6	28.3	55.9
% With 1+ Persons Per Room........	6.4	5.6	4.3	3.5	12.0	7.2	7.5	9.1	12.9
Median Value: Owner Units.......$$	21300	19400	22500	24500	20500	21300	20200	19100	18800
Median Rent: Rental Units.......$$	133	134	135	134	116	121	125	141	123
Median Number Of Rooms: All Units.	4.7	4.0	4.5	5.2	5.2	5.6	5.3	4.3	5.2

whom were foreign born. Hungarians were the most numerous nationality group.

The 1920s were prosperous years for Chatham residents and this community, like many others on the South Side, witnessed a building boom and manufacturing growth that increased Chatham's population to more than 36,000 in 1930. German, Irish and Swedish groups were the predominant foreign-born groups. Despite the growth of Chatham, there were large vacant land areas south of 85th Street and in the southwestern section of the community. Nevertheless Chatham was

residentially mature by 1930. Most of the manufacturing had developed in the district between 83rd and 87th streets and along the railroads. Chatham was a middle-class community of professionals, semi-professionals and service workers that had experienced growth despite poor transportation to the Loop and limited shopping facilities. The population increased by 1,500 during the Depression years.

Chatham's growth was partly arrested because of a 100-year mixup. In 1836, when Chatham had been a water puddle area far from the city limits, many speculators saw in it a potentially attractive suburban settlement. When John Wilson purchased an 80-acre tract of land in Chatham — bounded by 83rd and 87th streets, Cottage Grove Avenue and St. Lawrence, the receipt for this purchase was issued to his agent, Issac Palmer. This led to a century of litigation involving Wilson's heirs and the City of Chicago, while much of this area remained vacant. Within two years of the settlement, a 550-unit Chatham Fields Housing Project was built by private developers. This development stimulated Chatham's growth through the 1940s and into the 1950s. The population increased about 8 percent between 1940 and 1950 to more than 40,000 people. By the 1950s, Chatham had a new shopping center on Cottage Grove and a light manufacturing district along 87th Street.

During the 1950s, Chatham changed from immigrant-origin white to black residents. The post-World War II growth of the black population in Chicago accounted for their increasing numbers in communities like Chatham. The Black Belt, to the north, was badly overcrowded and housing discrimination kept blacks out of many other communities south of 63rd Street. As blacks moved into Chatham, large numbers of whites moved out to other South Side communities.

By 1960, the black population was 64 percent of the total. They increased to almost 98 percent by 1970, when the total population was more than 47,000.

Chatham remained a middle-class community with little change in neighborhood appearance after blacks moved there. Unlike some other South Side neighborhoods where a major effort had to be undertaken during the 1970s to salvage aging apartment buildings, Chatham remained a community of well-maintained apartment buildings with many blocks of single-family homes.

During the last decade, the population declined by about 6,500, and is now slightly smaller than the population in 1950. Most of those who left apparently were blacks, since the white exodus was almost complete in 1970 and only small numbers of the other non-white races have ever lived in Chatham. The decrease may be due to the migration of grown children; the population of Chatham is older than that of most black areas. The median age is more than 30 and nearly 12 percent of all residents are 65 or older. The majority of residents live in rented apartments, but almost 35 percent live in single-family homes, and more than 39 percent of all units are owner-occupied. The median value of single-family dwelling units is similar to those of the neighboring South Shore and Avalon Park community areas, higher than most medians on the South Side, but lower than that of the city as a whole.

Headquarters of several of the city's and the nation's largest black-owned businesses and financial institutions are located in Chatham. These businesses include Johnson Products, Ultra Sheen Hair Products, Independence Bank of Chicago and Seaway National Bank of Chicago. Black businessmen formed various business associations during the 1970s and 80s to improve the business section of Chatham. The main shopping strips, on Cottage Grove Avenue, East 79th and East 87th streets have lost business to outside malls and shopping centers such as Ford City and Evergreen Park but some retailers have moved into the Chatham community. The May Company's Venture operation bought the Turn Style store at 87th and Lafayette in 1978 and the Zayre Corporation opened a store at 7538 Stony Island Avenue in 1978. High interest rates partly explain the limited development of small businesses in Chatham. Groups like the 200-member Chatham Business Association hope to replace marginal retail strips with "mini malls."

One of the largest black housing cooperatives in the United States is the Chatham Park Village Cooperative. The area — the first rental property in Illinois to convert to cooperative ownership — is bound on the north by 83rd Street, the south by 84th Street, the east by Evans Avenue, and the west by St. Lawrence Avenue. Chatham Park served as a pattern for the establishment of other cooperative housing developments in Park Forest and Detroit.

Annie Ruth Leslie

Community Area 45

Avalon Park

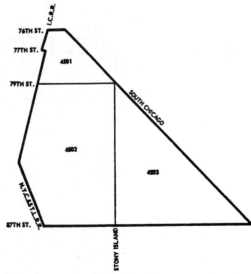

The Avalon Park community area is located on Chicago's South Side, about 10 miles from the Loop. Situated on high ground, it is part of a triangle formed by the present community areas of Avalon Park, Burnside and Calumet Heights. Avalon Park is a modestly-affluent residential plateau, surrounded on three sides by manufacturing and railroad tracks. Although the land was covered by swamps during the 19th century, it grew out of the shores of the prehistoric Stony Island. When all of the Chicago area was a lake, that island's rocky ridge protruded above the water line from the current Stony Island Avenue to Kingston Street, between 92nd and 93rd streets. Unlike surrounding communities like Burnside and Greater Grand Crossing, Avalon Park remained a swamp infested with mosquitoes until the early 20th century. The first settlers were railroad workers who located in the northern periphery, near Grand Crossing.

Because early Avalon Park was mainly swampland, it did not attract truck farmers. Early settlers were few in numbers. The area was not an attractive home site: Houses had to be built on posts; there was a garbage dump along 83rd Street and the Village of Hyde Park had a contagious disease hospital in the area. The section of Avalon Park between 81st and 83rd streets and Woodlawn and Dorchester avenues was subdivided by Jonathan Pierce in 1888. It was called Pierce's Park but early settlers called it Pennytown for an old man named Penny who owned a general store and sold settlers homemade popcorn balls near 79th Street and Avalon Avenue. Another area belonging to J. Ogden Armour was called Hog Island. Avalon Park was annexed to Chicago in 1889 as a part of the Village of Hyde Park. In 1890 the city designated land at 83rd Street and Woodlawn Avenue, covered by Mud Lake, which was a popular fishing, duck hunting and rabbit shooting area, as the site of a park to be called Avalon Park.

Community Area 45 — Avalon Park
Population and Housing Characteristic, 1930, 1980

	1980	1970	1960	1950	1940	1930
Total Population.......	13,792	14,412	12,710	11,358	10,464	10,023
% Male.................	46.5	47.1	48.5	48.8	49.4	50.2
% Female...............	53.5	52.9	51.5	51.2	50.6	49.8
% White................	2.7	16.3	99.7	99.9	100.0	100.0
% Black................	96.2	82.7	0.0	0.1	0.0	0.0
% Other Nonwhite Races...	1.1	1.0	0.3	0.0	0.0	0.0
% Under 5 Years Old......	6.0	8.3	9.1	8.5	6.2	9.1
% 5-19 Years Old.........	27.5	31.0	23.8	21.2	23.7	24.9
% 20-44 Years Old........	37.0	36.1	28.1	35.2	41.0	46.2
% 45-64 Years Old........	23.4	18.0	27.7	27.5	23.9	16.0
% 65 Years and Older.....	6.1	6.6	11.3	7.6	5.2	3.8
Median School Years......	12.6	12.4	12.1	12.1	10.4	*
Total Housing Units....	4,302	4,206	3,913	3,335	2,926	*
% In One-Unit Structures.	67.1	70.9	70.0	*	*	*
% Owner Occupied.........	71.3	70.3	74.2	67.4	54.5	*
% Renter Occupied........	26.9	27.7	23.7	31.9	44.1	*
% Vacant................	1.8	2.0	2.1	0.7	1.4	*
% 1+ Persons per Room....	5.4	6.5	4.3	7.2	*	*

Community Area 45 — Avalon Park
Selected Characteristics of Census Tracts: 1980

Tract Number	Total	4501	4502	4503
Total Population.............	13792	555	8189	5048
% Male........................	46.5	42.2	46.5	47.0
% Black.......................	96.1	97.8	95.7	96.6
% Other Nonwhite..............	1.1	0.9	1.4	0.8
% Of Spanish Origin...........	0.8	0.4	1.1	0.4
% Foreign Born................	1.4	5.8	1.5	0.9
% Living In Group Quarters....	0.2	0.0	0.2	0.1
% 13 Years Old And Under......	20.3	22.3	20.2	20.3
% 14-20 Years Old.............	15.2	14.6	15.6	14.7
% 21-64 Years Old.............	58.4	58.4	58.1	58.8
% 65-74 Years Old.............	4.3	3.2	4.3	4.3
% 75 Years Old And Over.......	1.9	1.4	1.8	1.9
% In Different House..........	23.5	29.7	20.2	28.0
% Families With Female Head...	32.0	51.1	31.9	30.0
Median School Years Completed...	12.6	12.5	12.7	12.6
Median Family Income, 1979......$$	24209	26250	24756	23225
% Income Below Poverty Level...	9.7	25.4	8.7	9.8
% Income Of $30,000 Or More....	37.5	40.2	39.8	33.7
% White Collar Workers........	59.0	41.2	62.5	55.5
% Civilian Labor Force Unemployed.	9.3	0.0	9.2	10.3
% Riding To Work By Automobile....	66.6	66.5	67.5	65.2
Mean Commuting Time - Minutes...	41.8	44.0	41.2	42.7
Population Per Household..........	3.3	2.8	3.4	3.1
Total Housing Units..........	4302	199	2459	1644
% Condominiums................	0.3	0.0	0.6	0.0
% Built 1970 Or Later.........	1.7	9.0	0.9	1.8
% Owner Occupied..............	71.2	50.3	77.2	64.8
% With 1+ Persons Per Room....	5.4	5.6	5.5	5.4
Median Value: Owner Units.....$$	38400	30200	39500	37100
Median Rent: Rental Units......$$	212	182	207	219
Median Number Of Rooms: All Units.	5.6	4.8	5.6	5.5

Community Area 45 — Avalon Park
Selected Characteristics of Census Tracts: 1970

Tract Number	TOTAL	4501	4502	4503
Total Population.............	14412	645	8776	4991
% Male........................	47.1	47.1	47.2	47.0
% Black.......................	82.7	90.1	85.1	77.3
% Other Nonwhite..............	1.0	0.9	1.2	0.7
% Of Spanish Language.........	2.0	0.0	1.8	2.5
% Foreign Born................	2.9	0.0	2.8	3.5
% Living In Group Quarters....	0.2	0.3	0.3	0.0
% 13 Years Old And Under......	28.2	29.6	28.4	27.5
% 14-20 Years Old.............	12.5	12.6	13.1	11.3
% 21-64 Years Old.............	52.7	51.5	52.3	53.6
% 65-74 Years Old.............	4.2	4.7	4.0	4.4
% 75 Years Old And Over.......	2.4	1.7	2.1	3.2
% In Different House..........	38.8	48.0	43.6	29.5
% Families With Female Head......	14.5	18.6	13.3	16.0
Median School Years Completed...	12.4	12.1	12.4	12.3
Median Family Income, 1969......$$	12434	8147	12780	12391
% Income Below Poverty Level....	5.1	12.4	5.7	3.4
% Income of $15,000 or More....	34.1	9.7	35.7	34.2
% White Collar Workers........	25.8	17.2	25.8	26.6
% Civilian Labor Force Unemployed.	4.0	9.2	3.4	4.3
% Riding To Work By Automobile....	60.2	68.3	63.5	53.9
Population Per Household..........	3.5	3.1	3.6	3.3
Total Housing Units..........	4206	211	2453	1542
% Condominiums & Cooperatives.....	1.1	0.0	1.4	0.7
% Built 1960 Or Later.........	7.8	9.0	9.6	4.7
% Owner Occupied..............	69.2	46.9	72.8	66.5
% With 1+ Persons Per Room....	7.7	6.3	8.5	6.5
Median Value: Owner Units.......$$	19900	16600	20400	19700
Median Rent: Rental Units......$$	133	117	134	135
Median Number Of Rooms: All Units.	5.5	5.0	5.6	5.3

More settlers arrived at the time of the Columbian Exposition in 1893. Many of them were skilled German mechanics, who worked in the Pullman shops or in the Burnside shops of the Illinois Central Railroad. In 1900, the 79th Street sewer was installed. This provided for drainage of the swamp. Houses no longer had to be built on posts. After the sewer came gas and water mains, paved streets and sidewalks. Between 1900 and 1910, many single-family homes were built between Stony Island and Creiger avenues, 80th and 83rd streets. The early community of Pennytown was renamed Avalon Park in 1910 under the leadership of the Reverend Lee Anna Starr, pastor of the Avalon Park Community Church during the early 1900s. She also led the movement for purchase of the present site of the community church at 8100 Dante Avenue.

From 1910 to 1918, many brick homes were constructed along Avalon Avenue. The real estate boom of the 1920s settled the community. By 1925, Avalon Park residentially matured. The population grew from 2,911 in 1920 to more than 10,000 in 1930. In 1920, Avalon Park's population consisted of groups of European-born residents of whom about 10 percent were of Swedish extraction. Irish and Germans, many descended from the original settlers, were still among the leading nationalities.

While there was some building during the 1930s, primarily of single-family homes, the community remained largely unchanged. There was considerable building after World War II, which accounted for 27 percent of the 1960 housing units. The population grew slowly through the Depression and World War II, topping 11,000 in 1950 and 12,000 in 1960. Blacks began to move into Avalon Park in the 1960s, part of a black residential expansion which included the neighboring South Shore, Chatham, South Chicago and Calumet Heights community areas. By 1970 the number of residents had reached an all-time high, in excess of 14,000, 83 percent of whom were black. In the most recent decade the population declined slightly, as the remaining whites moved out. Today blacks comprise 96 percent of all residents of Avalon Park.

Avalon Park is a middle-class black community. The atmosphere is suburban, with almost 70 percent of all housing units in single-family dwellings, more than 70 percent owner-occupied. The median esti-

mated value of single-family homes is $38,400, comparable to the medians in South Shore and Chatham, higher than most South Side community medians. The Chicago Vocational School, one of the finest vocational schools in the state, is located in Avalon Park, as is Southeast Community Junior College. In 1978, a block club located at 8500 South Dante founded the Fashion Avenue School of Modeling, Inc., a non-profit institution organized to develop the poise and confidence of their children.

Avalon Park is a relatively stable community economically. Unlike nearby South Side communities where one-half the population is living below the poverty level, Avalon Park reported a median family income greater than $24,000 in 1979. Homeowners in middle-class black neighborhoods depend to a large extent on government and manufacturing for their jobs. Current administration cutbacks in government jobs, coupled with the recession in manufacturing, makes neighborhoods like Avalon Park vulnerable to house abandonment and foreclosure.

Annie Ruth Leslie

Community Area 46

South Chicago

In 1800, the Callimink, as the Calumet River basin was called, served as a hunting ground for the Pottawatomie Indians. Legend has it that the mouth of the Calumet River had been considered as a site for Fort Dearborn, but rejected. In 1833, Lieutenant Jefferson Davis led a government survey party through the Calumet River region. Favorable reports by government engineers and the anticipation of the building of the Illinois and Michigan Canal led to a land boom. By 1835, there were almost 100 white settlers in the Calumet Region. Lewis Benton established the first general store, built 10 homes and the first hotel, The Eagle, in 1837. From the government, he acquired land between 87th and 93rd streets, bounded on the west by the present Commercial Avenue, and on the east by Calumet River and Lake Michigan. In June, 1836, Benton platted his tracts into town lots, in what was called the "City of Calumet." When the canal was located elsewhere, the area reverted to use by hunters and fishermen.

Growth was very slow after that. In 1839, a toll bridge was constructed across the Calumet River near the present site of the 92nd Street bridge. The first railroad, the Lake Shore and Michigan Southern, came in 1848. It was built on trestle work from Calumet to Englewood, a remarkable engineering feat for the time. By 1851, a road had been completed to Chicago. In 1856, a post office was established and, in 1857, the Ainsworth railroad station was opened.

Industrial development of the area began after the Civil War, when the Northwest Fertilizing Company began operation in 1867. Two lumber yards and a small grain elevator soon followed. At the same time, workers arrived to meet the demand for labor. They were mostly Irish but some Swedish families also settled there. On March 5, 1867, by amendment to its charter, the village of Hyde Park extended its southern boundary from what is presently 87th Street to 95th Street, thus including the settlement around Ainsworth station within its boundaries. By 1874, there were four railroad trunk lines in the area and the name of Ainsworth station was changed to South Chicago.

In 1869, the Calumet and the Chicago Canal and Dock Company, a corporation founded by James R. Bowen, was formed to operate a canal and develop the harbor facilities of the Calumet River. This

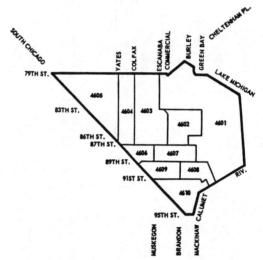

company brought about the construction of piers, docks, bridges and other improvements. The following year, Congress appropriated $362,000 to deepen the river and generally improve the port. In 1873, South Chicago was made a port of entry. In the early days, the lumber industry was most important, but there were also grain elevators, grist mills and a woodworking company. The Illinois Steam Forge Works, the Chicago Iron and Steel Works, the Silicon Steel Company and the Baltimore and Ohio shops were located in South Chicago in the 1870s.

The industrial activity began to attract workers and in 1874 the Calumet and Chicago Canal and Dock Company subdivided 6,000 acres of land and platted a new town on the site of the old Calumet subdivision. In March, 1881, the newly-erected South Works of the North Chicago Rolling Mill Company began to produce steel. At the end of the decade, the North Chicago Rolling Mill Company had grown into the Illinois Steel Company and, with the help of Bowen and the Canal and Dock Company, built a huge new steel mill in South Chicago. This plant eventually became the Carnegie Illinois Steel Company, and later became part of the South Works of the United States Steel Corporation when that corporation was formed in 1901. By this time, South Chicago had become one of the great steel producing areas of the world. In 1883, the Illinois Central Railroad began operating suburban trains through the community. This resulted in

Community Area 46 -- South Chicago
Population and Housing Characteristics, 1930-1980

	1980	1970	1960	1950	1940	1930
Total Population.......	46,422	45,655	49,913	55,715	55,090	56,683
% Male..................	48.2	48l6	49.4	51.0	51.4	53.4
% Female................	51.8	51.4	50.6	49.0	48.6	46.6
% White.................	27.5	76.1	94.8	95.2	98.4	91.2
% Black.................	47.8	22.4	4.9	4.7	1.6	1.3
% Other Nonwhite Races...	24.7	1.5	0.3	0.1	0.0	7.6
% Under 5 Years Old......	9.5	8.6	10.3	10.0	7.8	9.8
% 5-19 Years Old........	28.9	27.5	24.0	21.7	26.4	31.2
% 20-44 Years Old........	36.8	31.2	32.0	41.1	42.3	42.6
% 45-64 Years Old........	17.3	23.2	24.3	21.3	19.6	13.7
% 65 Years and Older....	7.5	9.5	9.4	5.9	3.9	2.7
Median School Years....	11.8	10.3	9.0	9.8	8.0	*
Total Housing Units....	15,616	15,759	15,622	14,931	13,855	*
% In One-Unit Structures.	26.8	26.4	28.2	*	*	*
% Owner Occupied.........	39.0	38.2	41.0	38.6	33.0	*
% Renter Occupied........	53.7	55.4	55.9	60.1	65.0	*
% Vacant.................	7.3	6.4	3.1	1.3	2.0	*
% 1+ Persons per Room....	12.0	9.9	11.8	16.5	*	*

Community Area 46 -- South Chicago
Selected Characteristics of Census Tracts: 1980

Tract Number	Total	4601	4602	4603	4604	4605	4606	4607	4608	4609	4610
Total Population.............	46422	5607	4164	10285	4740	8141	1725	5128	1265	2983	2384
% Male..................	48.2	48.0	49.7	48.0	47.7	46.4	50.0	48.0	48.5	50.4	49.8
% Black.................	47.8	30.2	0.3	48.6	88.0	95.2	19.9	23.7	71.1	9.5	34.1
% Other Nonwhite........	24.7	20.5	48.4	17.6	3.8	1.2	43.1	50.0	22.3	56.4	40.3
% Of Spanish Origin......	39.3	41.7	77.5	34.6	4.5	1.1	62.6	67.6	31.7	82.0	59.1
% Foreign Born..........	16.9	18.4	28.6	16.6	3.0	2.2	33.9	28.2	10.8	33.2	17.7
% Living In Group Quarters........	0.3	0.5	0.0	0.1	0.0	0.2	0.9	0.4	0.0	0.2	1.1
% 13 Years Old And Under....	26.5	26.0	30.1	26.4	24.7	21.3	27.5	34.1	30.4	28.7	21.7
% 14-20 Years Old.......	13.9	10.8	14.1	13.6	14.2	15.2	12.7	14.1	17.4	15.8	13.7
% 21-64 Years Old.......	52.1	53.7	47.8	52.8	55.7	57.0	53.0	47.0	46.4	49.3	45.6
% 65-74 Years Old.......	4.9	6.3	5.4	4.8	3.8	4.2	4.5	2.7	4.3	3.6	12.7
% 75 Years Old And Over....	2.6	3.2	2.6	2.4	1.6	2.3	2.3	2.1	1.5	2.6	6.3
% In Different House......	36.2	42.3	43.6	36.3	35.6	23.3	48.1	44.6	28.8	40.2	29.9
% Families With Female Head....	29.8	24.0	17.8	31.3	32.2	34.6	14.4	32.9	44.7	29.2	33.3
Median School Years Completed....	11.8	12.0	7.9	11.8	12.5	12.6	11.0	7.9	10.4	7.9	9.3
Median Family Income, 1979......$$	20015	20630	19975	20116	20140	23389	23036	13512	14826	17553	17500
% Income Below Poverty Level....	15.0	7.5	14.4	11.9	9.5	10.9	7.6	30.7	25.0	29.4	26.9
% Income Of $30,000 Or More....	22.9	21.8	18.8	22.6	26.4	32.6	30.0	11.6	4.5	20.0	21.8
% White Collar Workers....	43.5	45.3	28.4	42.6	51.6	57.2	30.5	29.1	25.5	30.9	33.6
% Civilian Labor Force Unemployed.	11.4	8.2	13.8	10.3	12.5	9.4	13.4	17.2	13.6	9.7	16.9
% Riding To Work By Automobile....	61.3	52.0	60.4	63.0	59.6	63.4	69.9	62.1	53.5	65.5	63.1
Mean Commuting Time - Minutes....	35.5	35.5	31.3	35.4	40.0	39.9	30.0	30.2	27.2	28.5	33.8
Population Per Household..........	3.2	2.9	3.4	3.2	3.1	3.2	3.4	3.6	3.8	3.4	2.5
Total Housing Units..........	15616	2039	1378	3464	1656	2600	553	1528	386	971	1041
% Condominiums..............	0.5	2.5	0.0	0.0	0.0	1.1	0.0	0.0	0.0	0.0	0.0
% Built 1970 Or Later..............	6.0	1.8	0.5	2.5	1.8	1.3	1.5	20.5	2.1	6.4	32.7
% Owner Occupied................	39.0	40.1	31.3	44.1	48.6	61.3	43.6	19.7	15.3	21.3	10.5
% With 1+ Persons Per Room......	12.0	12.2	18.9	11.5	6.3	5.4	14.5	18.9	18.0	17.6	11.7
Median Value: Owner Units.......$$	32400	28000	21400	27900	36300	37500	28300	23800	-	26800	-
Median Rent: Rental Units.......$$	160	176	122	17C	213	223	161	139	130	151	101
Median Number Of Rooms: All Units.	4.8	4.6	4.3	4.8	5.3	5.6	5.1	4.5	5.5	4.8	3.3

Community Area 46 -- South Chicago
Selected Characteristics of Census Tracts: 1970

Tract Number	TOTAL	4601	4602	4603	4604	4605	4606	4607	4608	4609	4610
Total Population.............	45655	4960	4875	8885	4718	7974	1423	4680	2093	3307	2740
% Male..................	48.6	47.3	49.1	47.8	48.2	47.1	48.8	50.2	47.2	50.3	54.5
% Black.................	22.4	0.8	0.1	6.0	40.4	64.1	0.0	9.5	72.5	1.5	22.6
% Other Nonwhite........	1.5	1.7	2.7	0.6	0.4	1.1	0.4	2.8	1.4	1.9	2.5
% Of Spanish Language......	26.1	15.8	44.1	8.3	4.7	2.0	5.9	66.9	25.3	77.5	55.6
% Foreign Born..........	12.8	11.0	14.1	9.8	9.1	5.8	7.6	22.2	6.1	27.6	24.7
% Living In Group Quarters........	0.5	0.3	0.0	0.2	0.0	0.6	0.6	0.8	1.9	0.5	1.4
% 13 Years Old And Under........	25.3	19.9	30.7	18.5	22.9	24.1	19.3	33.6	36.8	29.2	30.2
% 14-20 Years Old.......	12.5	11.6	13.8	10.8	11.4	11.0	10.5	14.9	16.0	14.6	14.5
% 21-64 Years Old.......	52.8	57.4	48.7	57.0	56.4	55.5	58.0	45.1	41.7	48.6	48.0
% 65-74 Years Old.......	6.0	6.8	4.2	8.4	5.6	6.0	7.6	4.3	3.7	5.6	5.3
% 75 Years Old And Over....	3.4	4.3	2.6	5.3	3.7	4.3	4.6	2.1	1.8	2.1	2.1
% In Different House......	52.0	62.4	63.2	59.0	46.4	33.7	66.8	51.6	51.4	50.8	48.8
% Families With Female Head....	15.2	14.1	14.5	14.0	14.2	13.1	11.6	18.4	29.8	14.3	23.8
Median School Years Completed....	10.3	10.4	8.9	10.1	11.8	12.3	9.7	8.3	8.5	8.8	8.4
Median Family Income, 1969.....$$	9970	10335	8757	9767	10660	11881	11796	8835	7059	9150	8795
% Income Below Poverty Level....	9.7	7.3	13.1	7.2	3.3	5.6	4.7	18.0	33.0	8.1	19.3
% Income of $15,000 Or More....	20.5	20.4	10.9	19.8	27.1	28.7	25.0	14.0	13.5	14.7	16.2
% White Collar Workers....	18.8	21.3	10.7	19.0	25.1	28.4	21.3	8.2	12.0	6.7	9.9
% Civilian Labor Force Unemployed.	4.2	3.4	4.3	3.7	2.0	2.1	0.8	4.6	16.7	6.7	9.4
% Riding To Work By Automobile....	53.2	44.4	44.4	54.9	63.5	62.4	67.3	45.8	41.4	48.0	39.6
Population Per Household..........	3.1	2.7	3.4	2.7	3.0	3.1	2.9	3.7	4.2	3.3	3.0
Total Housing Units..........	15756	1946	1590	3371	1621	2628	516	1360	538	1061	1125
% Condominiums & Cooperatives.....	0.5	0.4	0.5	0.7	0.5	0.9	0.0	0.4	0.0	0.0	0.0
% Built 1960 Or Later..............	4.3	13.7	0.4	1.6	5.7	5.2	1.6	2.4	3.8	3.1	2.8
% Owner Occupied................	37.7	34.7	30.1	44.6	48.4	58.6	42.1	22.2	17.3	20.8	10.9
% With 1+ Persons Per Room......	10.4	7.1	17.9	5.4	6.2	4.7	6.1	20.6	26.2	16.3	19.3
Median Value: Owner Units.......$$	18400	15400	11700	15700	20200	20700	15300	11600	-	-	-
Median Rent: Rental Units.......$$	86	94	64	93	132	135	85	67	71	76	70
Median Number Of Rooms: All Units.	4.7	4.4	4.3	4.6	5.0	5.4	4.9	4.4	5.1	4.4	2.5

many through streets being opened, and provided a direct link with downtown Chicago.

On July 16, 1889, South Chicago became part of the city of Chicago, through annexation of the Village of Hyde Park. Steel mills provided employment for English, Welsh, Irish, Swedish, Polish and German workers. In 1890, a year after annexation, the Calumet area, centered in South Chicago, had a population of 24,495, of which 13,083 were foreign born. As the steel industry grew, three neighborhoods began to emerge, identified by their proximity to the steel mills.

The Bush is bounded by U.S. Steel on the east and South Shore Drive on the west, between 83rd Street and 86th Street. It was called the Bush because in the early days it consisted of nothing more than a strip of sandy beach with some shrubbery. Millgate is south of the Bush area between the mills and is the oldest section of South Chicago. It was so named because all of the steel mills could be approached from there. The third neighborhood, known as South Works, begins at 79th Street and extends south to 83rd Street along Lake Michigan and the Calumet River. It was named after the adjacent U.S. Steel South Works.

The land in these areas was low and flat, subject to flooding and difficult to drain. Throughout there were pools of water, ditches clogged with soot, garbage and industrial debris. Decomposed animals, garbage, and shrubbery littered the roadways, alleys, vacant lots and yards. The mill neighborhoods had the worst housing conditions in South Chicago. The Bush was known for the worst sanitation. According to a report of the Chicago City Homes Association in 1901, the three mill neighborhoods had the most "abominable" housing environment in Chicago. In 1902, 95 percent of the area homes were wood frame. These houses could not meet the fire code restrictions of Chicago, but the Bush, Millgate, and South Works neighborhoods were partially exempted from enforcement of the codes. Because of the growing population and the immediate need for housing, the neighborhoods were divided into "shoe string" lots, 25 feet by 140 feet. The narrow courtways resulted in poor ventilation. All three of the mill neighborhoods had problems with drainage, and this caused very high rates of pneumonia and typhoid fever.

The immigration process began with Swedes, Germans and Poles. Slovenians, Croatians, Lithuanians, Bohemians, Hungarians, and Serbians followed. A mobility pattern that was to continue for decades took shape as Polish immigrants took over unskilled jobs while Swedes and Germans moved to higher-skilled positions. Then the Poles moved up, to be replaced by the Yugoslavians. Mexicans began arriving before the First World War and settled along Commercial Avenue, south of 78th Street.

By 1914, the residential pattern consisted of single-family housing and two-family, two-flat buildings. World War I required an increase in the work force, and the remaining available vacant land was built up. By 1920, South Chicago was residentially mature. By that time, the population was 40,347, with large foreign-born components of Poles, Swedes and Germans. Many Hungarians, Italians and Croatians lived in the Bush, while Mexicans and blacks began to move into Millgate.

The community attained its population peak in 1930 when it had a total of 56,583 inhabitants, a 40 percent increase. Although the number of residents had declined steadily in the ensuing half century, even during World War II, to 46,442 in 1980, the current population is still greater than it was before the great influx of the 1920s.

In the years since 1930, there has been a decline of European nationalities in the area, especially foreign-born and first-generation American. These groups have been reduced by mortality and migration, and an increase in Mexicans, other Spanish-origin nationalities and blacks. The number of foreign born dropped from 11,454 in 1940 to 1,169 in 1970. The foreign stock dropped to less than half the population in 1970 and this included numerous Mexican Americans. The number of people of Spanish origin grew from 11,906 in 1970, when they were 26 percent of the population, to 18,229, 39 percent of the 1980 population. There were 907 blacks in South Chicago in 1940; this grew to more than 10,000 in 1970 and to more than 22,000 in 1980. Blacks are now 48 percent of the area population.

The white population has dropped. In 1940, whites numbered more than 54,000, 98 percent of the number of residents. By 1970, this had fallen to less than 35,000, and today the white population is less than 13,000. Whites now constitute 27 percent of the population of South Chicago. Some who no longer reside in South Chicago still work in the steel mills, commuting from more distant residential locations, but many of the younger whites have simply left the steel mills and the South Chicago milieu behind for white-collar jobs and suburban residences. South Chicago is the location of a major retail center, the area surrounding the intersection of 91st Street and Commercial Avenue.

The number of housing units continued to grow between 1930 and 1960, despite a drop in the local population, but in the last 20 years construction activity has come to a halt. There is little residential or economic development in South Chicago today. The local economy is overcentralized in steel, and payrolls have been cut back more than 80 percent at the South Works in the last decade. The result has been unemployment in excess of 35 percent, and widespread closing of businesses dependent on the plant or the workers. It is apparent that the obsolescent steel plant will not be renovated. The industrial mix of South Chicago will have to become more diversified in order to support the present working population.

James Walker

Burnside

Burnside is the smallest community area in Chicago, a triangular enclave covering only about a five-eighths-square-mile area. The land was originally a marsh and swamp area south of the old city of Chicago. It became part of the Village of Hyde Park, attractive to settlers only after three railroad lines — the Ilinois Central Gulf to the west, the New York Central and St. Louis to the east, and the Chicago, Rhode Island and Pacific to the south — were built around the area.

Colonel W.W. Jacobs owned the property where Burnside is situated, and subdivided it in 1887. He named the area for Civil War General Ambrose E. Burnside. In 1889, the barren, swampy area was annexed to the city of Chicago with the rest of Hyde Park. Burnside had drainage problems with each spring rain. Children went canoeing in the flooded streets. An effort was made to stem the floodtides by the construction of dikes along 87th and 91st streets, but that effort was unsuccessful.

Burnside's development began with the establishment of the Illinois Central Railroad's Burnside shops at 95th Street and Cottage Grove Avenue. In 1889, the first store and post office were opened. Some

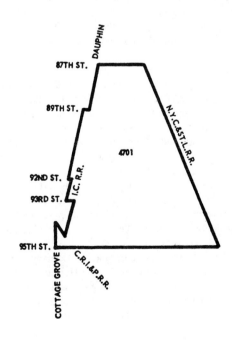

Community Area 47 — Burnside
Population and Housing Characteristics, 1930-1980

	1980	1970	1960	1950	1940	1930
Total Population.......	3,942	3,181	3,463	3,551	3,567	3,483
% Male..................	46.8	48.9	51.4	50.9	52.6	52.2
% Female................	53.2	51.1	48.6	49.1	47.4	47.8
% White.................	9.2	95.8	99.7	99.8	99.8	99.9
% Black.................	88.6	2.9	-	0.2	0.1	-
% Other Nonwhite Races...	2.2	1.3	0.3	-	0.1	0.1
% Under 5 Years Old......	9.1	6.1	9.9	9.9	8.2	10.1
% 5-19 Years Old.........	35.1	26.6	25.0	24.3	29.7	40.9
% 2 Years Old...........	36.9	27.6	33.6	41.1	39.1	35.9
% 45-64 Years Old.......	13.8	27.5	21.5	18.6	20.0	12.1
% 65 Years and Older.....	5.1	12.2	10.0	6.1	3.0	1.0
Median School Years....	12.2	9.4	9.1	8.5	7.5	*
Total Housing Units....	1,114	1,036	1,057	869	821	*
% In One-Unit Structures.	60.6	60.8	55.8	*	*	*
% Owner Occupied.........	64.8	62.8	63.5	59.9	49.3	*
% Renter Occupied........	28.5	35.4	33.6	38.9	49.8	*
% Vacant................	6.7	1.8	2.9	1.2	0.9	*
% 1+ Persons per Room....	13.5	8.8	9.7	15.8	*	*

Community Area 47 — Burnside
Selected Characteristics of Census Tracts: 1980

Tract Number	Total	4701
Total Population.............	3942	3942
% Male...............................	46.8	46.8
% Black..............................	88.6	88.6
% Other Nonwhite...............	2.2	2.2
% Of Spanish Origin...........	2.5	2.5
% Foreign Born..................	6.1	6.1
% Living In Group Quarters....	0.3	0.3
% 13 Years Old And Under......	29.3	29.3
% 14-20 Years Old..............	17.1	17.1
% 21-64 Years Old..............	48.6	48.6
% 65-74 Years Old..............	3.3	3.3
% 75 Years Old And Over.......	1.8	1.8
% In Different House...........	48.1	48.1
% Families With Female Head....	40.2	40.2
Median School Years Completed.	12.2	12.2
Median Family Income, 1979...$$	20625	20625
% Income Below Poverty Level..	15.1	15.1
% Income Of $30,000 Or More...	19.0	19.0
% White Collar Workers.........	41.3	41.3
% Civilian Labor Force Unemployed.	15.2	15.2
% Riding To Work By Automobile.	61.2	61.2
Mean Commuting Time - Minutes...	40.0	40.0
Population Per Household.........	3.8	3.8
Total Housing Units...........	1114	1114
% Condominiums.................	0.0	0.0
% Built 1970 Or Later..........	4.6	4.6
% Owner Occupied...............	64.8	64.8
% With 1+ Persons Per Room.....	13.5	13.5
Median Value: Owner Units.....$$	30200	30200
Median Rent: Rental Units.....$$	183	183
Median Number Of Rooms: All Units.	5.3	5.3

Community Area 47 — Burnside
Selected Characteristics of Census Tracts: 1970

Tract Number	TOTAL	4701
Total Population.............	3181	3181
% Male...............................	48.9	48.9
% Black..............................	2.9	2.9
% Other Nonwhite...............	1.4	1.4
% Of Spanish Language..........	7.9	7.9
% Foreign Born..................	20.2	20.2
% Living In Group Quarters....	0.4	0.4
% 13 Years Old And Under......	22.0	22.0
% 14-20 Years Old..............	12.2	12.2
% 21-64 Years Old..............	53.6	53.6
% 65-74 Years Old..............	7.4	7.4
% 75 Years Old And Over.......	4.7	4.7
% In Different House...........	74.9	74.9
% Families With Female Head....	13.2	13.2
Median School Years Completed.	9.4	9.4
Median Family Income, 1969.....$$	9740	9740
% Income Below Poverty Level..	6.1	6.1
% Income of $15,000 or More...	19.8	19.8
% White Collar Workers.........	12.1	12.1
% Civilian Labor Force Unemployed.	2.7	2.7
% Riding To Work By Automobile.	65.9	65.9
Population Per Household.........	3.1	3.1
Total Housing Units...........	1036	1036
% Condominiums & Cooperatives.....	0.5	0.5
% Built 1960 Or Later..........	6.3	6.3
% Owner Occupied...............	62.4	62.4
% With 1+ Persons Per Room.....	8.3	8.3
Median Value: Owner Units.....$$	15700	15700
Median Rent: Rental Units.....$$	90	90
Median Number Of Rooms: All Units.	4.9	4.9

single-family homes and two-family two deckers were built during the 1890s. The new residents of these freshly-completed homes were primarily Hungarians who came to Burnside to work in the shops and on the railroads. The community grew slowly. Its streets were paved with flagstone and its sidewalks were plank. In 1891, a car line was installed on 93rd Street from the tracks of the Illinois Central to Stony Island Avenue.

Burnside was residentially mature by 1915, its housing stock consisting almost exclusively of small frame homes and some brick or frame two-flats. It was in effect a semi-rural island, isolated from the rest of the city by the surrounding railroad tracks and their adjoining industries. In 1920, the population of Burnside was 1,048, including 38 percent foreign-born and 44 percent first-generation American-born. Poles, Hungarians, and Italians were the most prominent nationality groups at that time.

Burnside's population tripled during the 1920s, as the railroad, steel, and other area industries demanded more laborers. Many homes between 91st and 95th streets east of the Illinois Central tracks served as boarding houses for immigrants who had left their families behind in order to work.

Between 1930 and 1960, the population of Burnside remained relatively stable. At the end of that period the Hungarians and Poles were still the most numerous foreign-stock groups. A sizable number of Russians, including many Ukrainians, settled in Burnside, having found work in the mills and railroad shops. Virtually no new residential

construction took place in Burnside until the 1950s, when primarily single-family homes were built.

Between 1960 and 1970, a few blacks and more Latinos moved into Burnside. The total area population in 1970 was 3,181, an 8 percent decline through the 1960s. By 1970, Latinos comprised 8 percent, and blacks 3 percent of Burnside's total population. The housing stock decreased by 21 units net during the 1960s.

During the most recent decade Burnside's population composition changed from 96 percent white in 1970 to 89 percent black in 1980. Many white residents moved to southern suburbs. This shift in population composition was accompanied by a 24 percent increase in total population to 3,942 persons, Burnside's highest ever. The Latino population began to move out during the 1970s. The population of Burnside is very young, and 40 percent of all families with children under 18 are headed by females. While the total population increased by almost one-fourth, the housing stock grew by only 7.5 percent. The proportion of owner-occupied housing units has increased with every census since 1940, and in 1980 was nearly 70 percent. The vacancy rate is just below the city rate at 6.7 percent. Of the 1,114, total housing units in Burnside in 1980, almost two-thirds were single-family homes, and almost all the remainder were situated in structures with two to nine units. The median value of single-family, owner-occupied housing units in Burnside in 1980 was $30,205, about two-thirds of the city median.

Will Hogan

126

Calumet Heights

Calumet Heights is a South Side Chicago community about a 20-minute drive from the Loop on the Skyway or on Lake Shore Drive. Like the neighboring Avalon Park and Burnside community areas, Calumet Heights is situated on the old Stony Island ridge, outcroppings of which reveal Niagara limestone, the bedrock of the Chicago region. In the 19th century the ridge was thickly covered by burr oaks and wild flowers. The rest of the community area was swampland, isolated from the surrounding city by railroad tracks. During the 1850s and the 1860s, the only human occupation of the area was by a few travelers who used the community's two major roads: the Chicago-Michigan Post Road and another road built near 92nd Street during the 1850s. The Stony Island ridge, including present day Calumet Heights, came into possession of the Calumet and Chicago Canal and Dock Company in the 1870s, and the community began to attract settlers in the 1880s. The first residents lived in the western section of the community around the yards built by the New York Central and St. Louis Railroad. That settlement was named Judd, after the prominent Chicago attorney and politician, Norman P. Judd. A later settlement was built along Stony Island ridge, adjacent to a quarry near 92nd Street.

The Stony Island region was annexed to Chicago in 1889 as a part of the Village of Hyde Park. Between 1890 and 1920, the community grew slowly. Most of the trees were cut down by the new settlers, and the Calumet Heights name came gradually into use. The southeast section was occupied by South Chicago businessmen and the more prosperous steel mill workers, who built frame buildings, cottages and two-deckers. By 1920, there were 3,248 people in Calumet Heights. Many of these residents were foreign-born, Poles being most numerous. Much of the land was still vacant. The quarry at 92nd Street and its machinery had to be abandoned when it flooded one night, and it became a swimming hole for the children.

A post World War I building boom resulted in a large increase in single frame and brick homes and apartment buildings. While most of the new building was of single-family structures, an apartment building area arose west of Stony Island Avenue between 87th and 91st streets. Between 1920 and 1930, the population more than doubled to 7,343. The leading foreign-stock nationalities were Poles, Italians and Irish.

Prosperity and growth slowed down in Calumet Heights as elsewhere in the city of Chicago during the Depression. Between 1930 and 1940, there was a negligible population increase. The community had not yet reached residential maturity since much of the land was vacant. The area between 87th and 91st streets, Stony Island and Yates avenues was unoccupied. The newer apartment area near 87th Street and Stony Island Avenue was surrounded by vacant land. The old flooded quarry remained a popular but dangerous recreation site.

However, after World War II people began moving in and construction accelerated and Calumet Heights experienced a second building boom beginning in the late 1940s. This led to a 26 percent population increase. With a population of 9,349, the community reached residential maturity shortly after 1950.

During the 1950s, the population doubled to more than 19,000. Polish, Russian and German nationalities predominated among the foreign stock. Residential construction continued, and the number of housing units doubled also. By 1960, almost two-thirds of the housing units were in relatively new structures built since the war. The housing units were about three-fourths single-family dwellings, and about three-fourths owner-occupied.

The population of Calumet Heights has increased slightly since 1960, but only a few hundred remain of those who lived there 20 years ago. Blacks began to move into the area in the early 1960s and by the end of the decade they constituted more than half the number of residents. Today blacks are 87 percent of the population. Although early black migrants experienced physical and social hostility from white residents, the transition from an all-white community was gradual, with few major problems. Most of the black newcomers were middle-class professionals from varying income groups, who located in well-kept brick homes on the quiet streets.

Calumet Heights is divided into two major areas: "Stony Island Heights" which comprises the eastern two-thirds of the community and the "Pill Hill" area comprising the remaining western one-third. With the highest concentration, except for Hyde Park, of white-collar residents on the South Side, the community is inhabited mainly by city officials, lawyers, physicians, dentists, business executives, educators, sales and clerical workers. In the Stony Island Heights area smaller brick homes are most numerous and sell for $30,000 to $60,000. On Pill Hill spacious split-level and ranch style homes sell for up to $250,000. Except for Hyde Park and Kenwood, the median value of single-family homes in Calumet Heights is the highest of any South Side community area. Three-fourths of all housing units are owner-occupied.

There is very little industry in either Stony Island Heights or Pill Hill. Some residents work at industrial facilities in nearby neighborhoods. The South Shore Community Hospital is in the Stony Island Heights area and employs many who live in Calumet Heights. The nearest major retail center is in the South Chicago community area a few blocks east on Commercial Avenue between 85th and 93rd streets. There are smaller shopping areas on 87th Street and on Stony Island Avenue.

In 1980 median family income in Calumet Heights ranked seventh among Chicago community areas. By Chicago standards, Calumet Heights is a relatively new neighborhood where most of its residents are homeowners. The crime rate is relatively low and the neighborhood is stable.

Annie Ruth Lesle

Community Area 48 -- Calumet Heights
Population and Housing Characteristics, 1930-1980

	1980	1970	1960	1950	1940	1930
Total population.......	20,505	20,123	19,352	9,349	7,417	7,343
% Male.................	47.1	48.1	49.6	50.0	50.6	52.6
% Female...............	52.9	51.9	50.4	50.0	49.4	47.4
% White................	7.7	53.5	99.8	99.9	99.9	97.6
% Black................	86.8	45.0	0.0	0.1	0.1	0.3
% Other Nonwhite Races.	5.5	1.5	0.2	0.0	0.0	2.1
% Under 5 Years Old......	6.0	7.4	10.4	10.2	8.1	10.3
% 5-19 Years Old..........	28.7	28.7	25.6	21.2	26.5	29.8
% 20-44 Years Old.........	38.1	34.2	33.9	41.4	41.6	42.4
% 45-64 Years Old.........	22.0	23.1	22.9	21.6	19.5	14.5
% 65 Years and Older.....	5.2	6.6	7.2	5.6	4.3	3.0
Median School Years.....	12.7	12.3	11.9	10.1	8.5	*
Total Housing Units....	6,321	6,108	5,677	2,651	1,906	*
% In One-Unit Structures.	71.2	72.1	73.0	*	*	*
% Owner Occupied.........	75.2	76.1	77.2	63.3	41.2	*
% Renter Occupied........	22.8	21.9	20.2	33.8	56.1	*
% Vacant.................	2.0	2.0	2.6	2.9	2.7	*
% 1+ Persons per Room....	6.1	6.8	5.3	10.2	*	*

Community Area 48 -- Calumet Heights
Selected Characteristics of Census Tracts: 1980

Tract Number	Total	4801	4802	4803	4804	4805
Total Population..............	20505	3097	1694	2332	8657	4725
% Male........................	47.1	47.0	46.2	46.0	46.6	49.1
% Black.......................	86.8	95.8	96.6	93.7	91.8	64.8
% Other Nonwhite..............	5.5	0.8	1.9	1.4	3.3	16.0
% Of Spanish Origin...........	7.2	1.1	2.4	2.9	2.3	24.1
% Foreign Born................	4.9	0.0	0.4	2.4	5.0	10.7
% Living In Group Quarters....	0.2	0.1	0.0	0.0	0.3	0.2
% 13 Years Old And Under......	21.7	21.7	16.4	20.6	20.7	25.9
% 14-20 Years Old.............	14.9	14.4	12.0	14.7	15.3	15.6
% 21-64 Years Old.............	58.2	59.2	64.0	59.3	59.4	52.8
% 65-74 Years Old.............	3.2	2.8	4.7	4.2	2.9	3.2
% 75 Years Old And Over.......	2.0	1.9	3.0	1.2	1.7	2.5
% In Different House..........	22.0	14.9	22.4	27.7	17.2	32.6
% Families With Female Head...	25.2	25.5	31.0	34.0	23.5	22.5
Median School Years Completed.	12.7	12.8	12.8	12.8	12.9	12.4
Median Family Income, 1979......$$	26550	26038	26149	27063	28385	24007
% Income Below Poverty Level....	5.5	7.0	4.8	6.9	4.1	7.0
% Income Of $30,000 Or More.....	40.9	40.3	34.4	39.1	45.6	35.3
% White Collar Workers..........	61.4	64.8	59.3	62.7	65.5	50.4
% Civilian Labor Force Unemployed.	7.8	11.4	3.7	6.6	7.8	7.6
% Riding To Work By Automobile....	72.8	80.2	73.2	65.7	73.8	68.7
Mean Commuting Time - Minutes...	38.3	37.2	38.7	41.6	38.4	36.7
Population Per Household..........	3.3	3.2	2.7	3.4	3.4	3.5
Total Housing Units...........	6321	970	636	712	2622	1381
% Condominiums................	0.0	0.0	0.0	0.0	0.0	0.0
% Built 1970 Or Later.........	1.6	2.9	0.8	2.2	1.3	1.2
% Owner Occupied..............	75.2	80.5	54.6	63.3	86.2	66.3
% With 1+ Persons Per Room....	6.1	4.5	1.9	9.2	4.8	10.2
Median Value: Owner Units.....$$	43600	45100	42700	36700	46500	38300
Median Rent: Rental Units......$$	214	252	232	218	214	181
Median Number Of Rooms: All Units.	5.6	5.6	5.3	5.4	5.6	5.4

Community Area 48 -- Calumet Heights
Selected Characteristics of Census Tracts: 1970

Tract Number	TOTAL	4801	4802	4803	4804	4805
Total Population..............	20123	3094	1300	2656	8781	4292
% Male........................	48.1	48.0	47.8	47.6	48.6	47.4
% Black.......................	44.9	63.0	87.4	76.3	41.4	6.8
% Other Nonwhite..............	1.5	1.1	0.3	1.1	2.0	1.7
% Of Spanish Language.........	8.1	2.4	3.8	7.8	6.0	18.1
% Foreign Born................	9.7	6.8	3.2	3.1	8.5	20.2
% Living In Group Quarters....	0.5	0.0	0.0	0.5	0.1	1.7
% 13 Years Old And Under......	25.3	25.1	24.1	29.8	25.9	21.9
% 14-20 Years Old.............	12.1	10.4	10.8	11.6	11.9	14.5
% 21-64 Years Old.............	55.9	57.1	59.8	54.1	56.2	54.4
% 65-74 Years Old.............	4.4	4.7	4.1	2.8	4.1	5.8
% 75 Years Old And Over.......	2.2	2.7	1.3	1.6	1.8	3.4
% In Different House..........	46.7	31.3	54.9	40.2	45.0	62.4
% Families With Female Head...	9.8	8.2	12.8	14.4	8.5	10.1
Median School Years Completed...	12.3	12.4	12.6	12.4	12.4	10.9
Median Family Income, 1969......$$	13319	13372	12352	13951	14089	11621
% Income Below Poverty Level....	3.8	1.6	2.4	5.0	3.9	4.8
% Income of $15,000 or More.....	39.3	37.3	35.1	44.7	44.0	29.3
% White Collar Workers..........	32.8	33.6	43.5	33.8	36.9	19.6
% Civilian Labor Force Unemployed.	2.8	4.1	5.4	3.3	2.3	1.8
% Riding To Work By Automobile....	65.6	69.6	62.5	55.2	69.4	62.8
Population Per Household..........	3.3	3.3	3.8	3.5	3.4	3.2
Total Housing Units...........	6108	945	422	805	2590	1346
% Condominiums & Cooperatives.....	0.1	0.0	0.0	0.7	0.0	0.0
% Built 1960 Or Later.............	14.7	13.4	16.0	11.2	19.3	8.3
% Owner Occupied.................	76.0	84.7	57.1	57.1	85.2	69.3
% With 1+ Persons Per Room.......	6.3	3.9	4.1	8.1	6.3	7.6
Median Value: Owner Units.......$$	22700	23600	21700	19700	23800	19400
Median Rent: Rental Units.......$$	125	153	146	138	117	91
Median Number Of Rooms: All Units.	5.4	5.5	5.3	5.3	5.6	5.2

Roseland

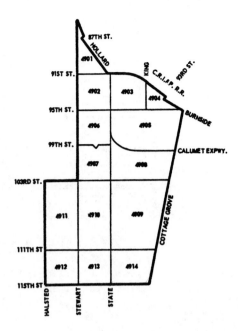

The Roseland community area is located on the far South Side of Chicago, about 11 miles straight south of the Loop. In the middle of the 19th century, the area was mostly swampland with occasional patches of dry prairie. It was traversed by a high ridge on which ran the Thornton Road (now Michigan Avenue), which was also called the Michigan City Road. In 1848 a group of North Hollanders came to the Calumet region in search of suitable land for truck farming, not too far from a market. They settled along the ridge, then called High Prairie, between 103rd and 111th streets. The settlers built frame houses along Thornton Road, which was used to haul their produce to Chicago. A meeting house was built by the Reformed Church in America Society in 1849. In 1852 two railroads were laid through the area — the Illinois Central in the east (along Cottage Grove Avenue) and the Rock Island to the northwest. More Dutch immigrants settled the low prairie land between the ridge and Lake Calumet, to the east. Some of the Dutch worked on the construction of the new railroads. The community area was part of the Town of Lake but, in 1867, the area east of State Street became part of the newly-incorporated Village of Hyde Park.

The village was called Hope at the time of the establishment of the first post office in 1861. The name was changed to Roseland in the early 1870s by the local residents. The farmers planted flowers as well as truck crops, and each cottage produced an annual display of brilliant red roses. In 1880 Roseland was a quiet pastoral village of 772 inhabitants, retaining Old World language and customs on the high prairie of the New World. During the decade that followed the entrance of seven new trunk-line railroads into the Soth Side and the establishment of the Pullman factory village to the east began to change the environment. Swedish, German, English and Irish workers moved into the Roseland area, while some of the Dutch went to work for the railroad or at the Pullman shops. The annexation of both the Town of Lake and the Village of Hyde Park to Chicago in 1889 brought the entire Roseland community area inside the city limits.

In the years that followed the Calumet region became steadily industrialized. The Illinois Central Railroad built its Burnside shops in the northeast section of the community. For many years this was the only industrial development in Roseland, although some workers from nearby industries chose to locate there residentially. The area remained mostly agricultural. Dutch and Swedish remained the predominant nationalities, and some Lithuanians moved in during the decade before World War I.

The ethnic make-up of Roseland began to change after the war. The new immigrants were increasingly Polish and Italian. A handful of blacks moved into the northern area. By 1920, Roseland's population was 28,241. There was still a lot of vacant land all over the community, a large portion belonging to the railroads.

Between 1920 and 1930, Roseland's population increased 53 percent. Lithuanians, Italians, Germans and blacks gained steadily in numbers. The building boom of the 1920s changed the Roseland community. Modern brick bungalows, two-story single-family residences, some two-flats and small apartment buildings were erected. By 1929, the residential pattern of the community was fairly well established, although there were still significant parcels of undeveloped land in the north.

Roseland's growth slowed during the 1930s and picked up during the 1940s when the population increased by 29 percent. Blacks constituted a large portion of this increase, as the northern part of the community began to be built up. Whites began to move out in the 1950s. In 1950, blacks were 18 percent of the community population, which now had passed 50,000. By 1960, they were 23 percent of the total. In 1954, the Chicago Housing Authority completed the Governor Frank O. Lowden

Homes, a 128-unit housing project located north of 95th Street. These units were largely inhabited by blacks.

The last 20 years have brought about a racial turnover in Roseland, while the total population continued to grow. In 1970 blacks constituted 55 percent of the population. The most recent count shows blacks to be 97 percent of an all-time high number of residents, in excess of 64,000.

During the 1960s and 1970s, Roseland was a community where blacks escaping the overcrowded areas to the north could buy a home and build a future. During this period, large numbers of Euro-Americans left Roseland as blacks came into the area. However, large numbers of businesses and industries began to relocate in southern suburbs with the outgoing white populace. By the mid-1970s, Roseland was experiencing a variety of neighborhood ills — unemployment, inflation, mortgage defaults, business failures and gang-related problems. During the 1970s, over 900 mortgages were foreclosed. More than 500 families are in default on mortgages insured by the Federal Housing Administration. The Roseland community was the center of "HUD house" controversy during the 1970s. A HUD house is a boarded-up house displaying a sign indicating repossession by the Department of Housing and Urban Development (HUD). In 1979 HUD announced the beginning of a repair-and-sell program of repossessed houses in the Roseland area.

The quality of life in Roseland is declining in other ways. The infant mortality rate there is 26 per 1,000, one of the worst in the city of Chicago. Roseland's only public health clinic for babies was destroyed by fire in 1980 and never replaced. Eleven physicians serve a community of 64,000 residents compared to 58 physicians in 1960 and 31 in 1970. The business district on Michigan Avenue between 103rd and 115th streets began to decline in the 1960s. This area once housed Robert Hall, Sears Roebuck, and Gately's Peoples stores. These, along with many smaller stores and shops, are now closed. Roseland's economic setbacks are partly caused by the South Side's dwindling industrial base. The nearby Wisconsin Steel plant closed and International Harvester laid off thousands of workers. Unemployment stood at 14 percent in 1980 and has grown since.

By 1980, Roseland's prospects for rising joblessness promise to aggravate already-severe problems with mortgage delinquencies and foreclosure, truancy and gang violence. Roseland had a median household income of $18,539.85.

The economic profile of Roseland residents is mixed. The median family income is more than $20,000, relatively high on the South Side. More than half of those employed work in white-collar occupations.

Community Area 49 — Roseland
Population and Housing Characteristics, 1930-1980

	1980	1970	1960	1950	1940	1930
Total Population.......	64,372	62,512	58,750	56,705	44,009	43,206
% Male.................	47.0	47.5	48.4	49.4	50.6	51.5
% Female...............	53.0	52.5	51.6	50.6	49.4	48.5
% White................	1.9	44.4	72.2	81.6	95.8	97.0
% Black................	97.5	55.1	22.6	18.4	4.2	2.9
% Other Nonwhite Races...	0.6	0.5	0.2	0.0	0.0	0.1
% Under 5 Years Old......	7.5	7.8	9.3	10.3	7.0	8.5
% 5-19 Years Old.........	31.2	29.5	24.1	20.1	22.5	28.0
% 20-44 Years Old........	35.6	30.0	29.6	39.9	42.1	43.3
% 45-64 Years Old........	19.3	22.4	26.4	22.5	22.8	16.3
% 65 Years and Older....	6.4	10.3	10.6	7.2	5.6	3.9
Median School Years.....	12.4	12.0	10.8	10.2	8.6	*
Total Housing Units....	18,771	19,557	18,328	16,066	12,057	*
% In One-Unit Structures.	64.8	60.5	64.6	*	*	*
% Owner Occupied........	62.2	62.1	61.3	56.9	46.4	*
% Renter Occupied........	34.3	35.0	36.8	41.9	52.3	*
% Vacant................	3.5	2.9	1.9	1.2	1.3	*
% 1+ Persons per Room....	8.9	7.6	6.9	9.4	*	*

Community Area 49 — Roseland
Selected Characteristics of Census Tracts: 1980

Tract Number	Total	4901	4902	4903	4904	4905	4906	4907	4908	4909	4910
Total Population.............	64372	763	4059	2645	1252	2381	2128	4362	5367	12661	8972
% Male.................	47.0	47.3	45.1	45.9	44.7	47.8	47.5	47.2	47.1	48.1	46.6
% Black................	97.5	98.3	99.7	98.9	99.3	98.6	98.7	98.8	97.4	97.4	97.9
% Other Nonwhite.......	0.6	0.9	0.2	0.6	0.1	0.6	0.7	0.3	0.3	0.7	0.6
% Of Spanish Origin......	0.9	0.8	0.6	0.3	0.3	0.7	0.7	0.3	0.3	0.7	1.1
% Foreign Born..........	1.9	1.0	1.4	1.6	0.0	0.9	0.8	0.4	1.4	2.4	1.0
% Living In Group Quarters.	0.7	0.0	0.0	0.0	0.0	0.3	0.0	0.0	0.0	0.1	0.1
% 13 Years Old And Under..	24.3	24.4	22.7	15.1	15.3	13.4	16.3	23.1	21.5	24.4	30.0
% 14-20 Years Old........	16.6	17.2	14.5	9.9	12.4	10.5	14.2	20.2	17.4	15.2	20.6
% 21-64 Years Old........	52.7	51.2	51.4	55.7	54.7	61.8	58.1	52.2	56.0	55.7	46.3
% 65-74 Years Old........	4.3	5.5	8.1	12.1	12.1	10.6	7.5	3.0	3.6	3.2	2.0
% 75 Years Old And Over..	2.2	1.7	3.3	7.3	5.6	3.8	3.9	1.4	1.4	1.6	1.0
% In Different House.....	26.0	17.0	23.0	21.6	18.4	18.8	17.4	13.9	17.3	35.9	28.6
% Families With Female Head.	36.0	49.2	48.4	34.8	35.4	28.0	26.0	28.0	30.4	36.3	42.7
Median School Years Completed.	12.4	12.6	12.4	12.8	12.8	12.6	12.3	12.3	12.5	12.5	12.0
Median Family Income, 1979...$$	20189	16705	17734	23615	25549	25673	20000	23562	22966	19063	17041
% Income Below Poverty Level...	15.2	8.7	15.3	5.7	6.7	5.3	12.8	11.2	14.6	18.2	23.1
% Income Of $30,000 Or More.....	27.2	11.4	21.2	39.2	38.9	40.9	32.4	31.0	29.1	24.5	21.2
% White Collar Workers...	52.1	45.9	50.2	68.8	60.5	62.1	46.9	41.9	48.9	58.1	44.2
% Civilian Labor Force Unemployed.	13.6	13.4	15.1	10.4	6.3	7.5	15.3	12.3	11.6	13.4	19.0
% Riding To Work By Automobile....	64.1	41.3	62.7	61.1	71.3	60.1	67.6	70.1	63.3	65.7	61.8
Mean Commuting Time - Minutes..	40.3	44.8	36.7	37.7	31.6	37.8	40.7	39.3	40.2	40.4	41.1
Population Per Household..........	3.5	3.5	3.1	2.8	2.8	2.9	3.4	4.0	3.5	3.2	4.4
Total Housing Units..........	18771	228	1319	964	464	828	647	1101	1567	4174	2173
% Condominiums................	0.0	0.0	0.0	0.0	0.0	0.0	0.0	0.0	0.0	0.0	0.0
% Built 1970 Or Later........	2.9	10.5	0.4	0.0	0.0	2.7	10.2	5.2	2.2	3.3	3.0
% Owner Occupied.............	62.2	24.6	21.3	83.5	69.8	81.8	85.6	88.2	77.5	52.3	64.3
% With 1+ Persons Per Room...	8.9	8.7	8.3	3.6	3.2	2.7	7.9	11.2	7.0	7.0	15.3
Median Value: Owner Units.......$$	36500	-	35800	37000	39200	43300	43600	35400	36900	37900	26800
Median Rent: Rental Units.......$$	183	145	140	187	181	199	158	187	199	202	177
Median Number Of Rooms: All Units.	5.5	5.6	5.2	5.4	5.4	5.6	5.6	5.6	5.6	5.1	5.6

Tract Number	4911	4912	4913	4914
Total Population.............	6857	3388	4721	4816
% Male.................	47.2	47.3	45.9	46.7
% Black................	97.9	98.2	95.5	92.3
% Other Nonwhite.......	0.3	0.2	1.5	1.7
% Of Spanish Origin......	0.5	0.4	1.1	3.2
% Foreign Born..........	4.4	0.4	2.9	2.9
% Living In Group Quarters.	4.3	0.0	2.0	0.6
% 13 Years Old And Under..	23.9	25.5	29.3	29.5
% 14-20 Years Old........	18.4	20.5	17.8	13.2
% 21-64 Years Old........	51.2	50.5	49.1	52.3
% 65-74 Years Old........	3.2	2.4	2.4	3.5
% 75 Years Old And Over..	3.3	1.1	1.4	1.5
% In Different House.....	14.4	19.4	29.6	50.7
% Families With Female Head.	23.8	27.8	44.3	45.4
Median School Years Completed.	12.6	12.4	12.2	12.2
Median Family Income, 1979....$$	24484	23787	17656	13036
% Income Below Poverty Level...	8.7	10.2	23.0	21.0
% Income Of $30,000 Or More.....	38.7	30.7	21.6	11.6
% White Collar Workers...	54.3	52.6	46.6	48.0
% Civilian Labor Force Unemployed.	11.7	16.0	12.1	16.6
% Riding To Work By Automobile....	73.0	73.9	57.6	49.2
Mean Commuting Time - Minutes...	40.3	40.4	43.5	44.9
Population Per Household..........	4.1	4.2	4.0	3.1
Total Housing Units..........	1613	831	1243	1619
% Condominiums................	0.0	0.0	0.0	0.0
% Built 1970 Or Later........	1.1	4.3	1.5	2.2
% Owner Occupied.............	88.4	81.0	52.6	28.5
% With 1+ Persons Per Room...	10.9	10.5	12.6	9.2
Median Value: Owner Units.......$$	41600	39800	28800	31600
Median Rent: Rental Units.......$$	200	222	184	196
Median Number Of Rooms: All Units.	5.6	5.6	5.6	5.0

Twenty-seven percent of all families earned more than $30,000 in 1979, and yet more than 15 percent of all residents lived in poverty. Despite the defaults, 62 percent of housing units are owner-occupied, and about two-thirds of all units are single-family dwellings. Roseland Plaza, a major retail center in the southwest section of the community area, ranked just behind the South Chicago major retail center in sales volume in 1977. Roseland is a community with resources but many problems. A healthy revival of the South Side industrial base would probably save the community from widespread deterioration.

Annie Ruth Leslie

Community Area 49 — Roseland
Selected Characteristics of Census Tracts: 1970

Tract Number	TOTAL	4901	4902	4903	4904	4905	4906	4907	4908	4909	4910
Total Population.............	62512	729	4762	3079	1690	2725	2311	4499	5601	12243	8419
% Male.......................	47.5	46.9	46.3	46.9	44.7	47.6	47.8	49.7	47.8	47.7	47.9
% Black......................	55.1	94.9	99.0	98.6	96.4	98.1	99.4	88.8	78.6	34.0	38.3
% Other Nonwhite.............	0.5	0.4	0.5	0.4	0.7	0.9	0.4	0.3	0.7	0.4	0.3
% Of Spanish Language........	1.9	0.0	0.1	2.4	0.9	0.3	1.7	1.2	2.9	2.6	2.9
% Foreign Born...............	5.6	0.9	0.2	0.7	0.3	0.5	2.1	2.1	4.4	7.9	8.5
% Living In Group Quarters...	0.7	0.0	0.4	0.2	3.4	0.3	0.3	0.0	0.5	0.3	1.8
% 13 Years Old And Under.....	26.2	31.0	27.3	19.7	24.3	20.3	24.2	34.9	30.3	23.7	29.7
% 14-20 Years Old............	12.5	12.5	15.5	12.8	13.1	14.1	14.9	14.3	12.0	10.7	12.9
% 21-64 Years Old............	51.0	51.3	50.7	56.3	50.9	59.2	52.9	46.5	51.0	53.6	45.6
% 65-74 Years Old............	6.2	3.6	4.5	7.3	7.9	4.3	5.4	2.6	4.0	7.2	6.2
% 75 Years Old And Over......	4.0	1.6	1.9	3.8	3.8	2.0	2.6	1.8	2.6	4.9	5.6
% In Different House.........	53.2	67.2	75.4	77.3	74.9	73.3	77.0	25.8	20.2	47.5	51.6
% Families With Female Head..	13.6	17.3	24.6	17.5	18.3	13.0	15.1	9.4	12.0	11.9	15.9
Median School Years Completed	12.0	12.1	12.1	12.4	12.2	12.3	11.5	12.1	12.2	12.0	10.7
Median Family Income, 1969...$$	11193	9682	9026	10577	10769	13290	11685	11696	11935	11266	10094
% Income Below Poverty Level.	5.7	6.8	9.6	7.6	5.2	4.5	1.2	2.3	6.0	6.1	5.4
% Income of $15,000 or More..	26.8	11.4	15.0	26.6	32.5	42.2	33.6	29.7	27.3	25.9	18.7
% White Collar Workers.......	22.1	21.3	13.2	29.5	30.4	31.2	26.0	13.6	20.5	22.8	15.2
% Civilian Labor Force Unemployed.	4.0	6.6	4.0	4.1	2.7	5.1	4.1	7.2	5.2	3.2	2.8
% Riding To Work By Automobile.	62.3	58.1	54.2	60.7	57.9	76.2	69.7	61.9	57.4	59.7	63.2
Population Per Household.....	3.3	3.6	3.7	3.2	3.5	3.4	3.7	4.2	3.5	2.9	3.3
Total Housing Units.........	19533	200	1312	964	473	811	640	1094	1620	4345	2597
% Condominiums & Cooperatives	0.3	0.0	0.0	0.0	0.0	0.0	0.0	0.5	0.6	0.5	0.3
% Built 1960 Or Later.......	9.1	2.7	5.7	14.7	16.4	18.6	47.7	26.3	7.4	7.4	2.2
% Owner Occupied............	61.8	27.0	21.8	83.2	67.2	81.8	85.3	88.2	75.4	53.6	61.0
% With 1+ Persons Per Room..	7.9	11.5	14.6	6.1	9.7	5.6	9.7	15.3	8.7	5.9	9.9
Median Value: Owner Units...$$	19200	–	19700	19600	19700	23800	22400	18300	19400	19700	15400
Median Rent: Rental Units....$$	105	106	100	117	116	128	101	116	119	110	89
Median Number Of Rooms: All Units.	5.3	5.3	5.2	5.4	5.3	5.5	5.4	5.6	5.3	5.0	5.2

Tract Number	4911	4912	4913	4914
Total Population.............	5684	2761	4016	3993
% Male.......................	48.6	47.2	47.2	45.4
% Black......................	61.3	4.1	0.3	0.3
% Other Nonwhite.............	0.3	0.1	0.6	1.0
% Of Spanish Language........	0.7	0.5	2.9	3.0
% Foreign Born...............	3.4	8.8	7.8	16.6
% Living In Group Quarters...	0.4	0.0	0.3	1.8
% 13 Years Old And Under.....	30.4	22.3	23.3	19.3
% 14-20 Years Old............	12.9	12.8	11.9	9.9
% 21-64 Years Old............	49.5	50.0	50.7	52.5
% 65-74 Years Old............	4.6	9.1	8.7	10.9
% 75 Years Old And Over......	2.6	5.8	5.5	7.4
% In Different House.........	34.7	74.5	68.2	59.2
% Families With Female Head..	7.5	9.2	12.9	14.5
Median School Years Completed	12.2	12.1	11.3	11.4
Median Family Income, 1969...$$	12473	12556	10892	10790
% Income Below Poverty Level.	4.3	4.9	5.5	8.8
% Income of $15,000 or More..	32.0	37.2	25.2	26.9
% White Collar Workers.......	23.6	33.2	21.1	25.8
% Civilian Labor Force Unemployed.	4.3	2.3	5.4	1.7
% Riding To Work By Automobile.	77.1	72.8	63.5	46.9
Population Per Household.....	3.7	3.2	2.9	2.5
Total Housing Units.........	1577	884	1413	1603
% Condominiums & Cooperatives	0.3	0.0	0.0	0.6
% Built 1960 Or Later.......	8.9	2.6	1.0	2.8
% Owner Occupied............	89.8	78.3	51.5	29.3
% With 1+ Persons Per Room..	8.5	3.9	5.3	3.3
Median Value: Owner Units...$$	21600	19800	14200	16800
Median Rent: Rental Units....$$	131	114	95	106
Median Number Of Rooms: All Units.	5.6	5.7	5.1	4.8

Community Area 50

Pullman

Pullman originated as a planned model industrial town, conceived and built by the railroad car manufacturer, George M. Pullman. The land was vacant and undeveloped prairie, part of the Village of Hyde Park. In 1877, Pullman designated a tract of 3,500 acres on the western shore of Lake Calumet, from the present 103rd to 115th streets, to be the site of the Pullman Palace Car Company shops. The property was secretly and gradually purchased by the Pullman Land Association and the Palace Car Company and, in 1880, work began on the plants, public facilities and 1,750 residential units. Pullman hired two young architects who had assisted in the renovation of his own residences; Solon S. Beman designed the buildings and Nathan F. Barrett landscaped the village. Workers began to move into the new homes in January, 1881 and, by summer of that year, the new factory began to produce railroad sleeping cars.

The Pullman village was located between 111th and 115th streets from Cottage Grove to Langley avenues. The town and all its facilities were owned and operated by the company. It was served by an Illinois

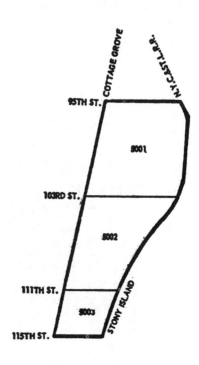

Community Area 50 -- Pullman
Population and Housing Characteristics, 1930-1980

	1980	1970	1960	1950	1940	1930
Total Population.......	10,341	10,893	8,412	8,899	6,523	6,705
% Male..................	46.9	48.2	50.1	51.7	53.5	55.2
% Female................	53.1	51.8	49.9	48.3	46.5	44.8
% White.................	19.2	51.2	99.9	100.0	100.0	99.0
% Black.................	76.4	48.1	-	0.0	0.0	-
% Other Nonwhite Races...	4.4	0.7	0.1	0.0	-	1.0
% Under 5 Years Old......	7.3	9.6	9.6	11.1	7.9	8.8
% 5-19 Years Old.........	29.0	27.3	24.5	20.9	24.7	30.6
% 20-44 Years Old........	37.0	34.6	31.9	41.5	41.5	40.8
% 45-64 Years Old........	18.5	20.5	25.0	20.6	21.4	16.3
% 65 Years and Older.....	8.2	8.0	9.0	5.9	4.5	3.5
Median School Years....	12.4	11.6	9.6	9.0	7.8	*
Total Housing Units....	3,525	3,685	2,795	2,430	1,670	*
% In One-Unit Structures.	69.4	66.0	59.9	*	*	*
% Owner Occupied.........	53.5	63.2	60.5	62.5	41.7	*
% Renter Occupied........	42.0	32.6	33.7	36.2	55.8	*
% Vacant.................	4.5	4.2	5.8	1.3	2.5	*
% 1+ Persons per Room....	8.0	7.8	8.3	11.9	*	*

Community Area 50 -- Pullman
Selected Characteristics of Census Tracts: 1980

Tract Number	Total	5001	5002	5003
Total Population.............	10341	5800	2457	2084
% Male.......................	46.9	46.3	45.6	49.8
% Black......................	76.4	97.0	92.1	0.2
% Other Nonwhite.............	4.5	0.7	2.4	17.4
% Of Spanish Origin..........	6.2	0.5	3.2	25.5
% Foreign Born...............	6.9	1.7	3.3	26.1
% Living In Group Quarters...	0.4	0.4	0.1	0.5
% 13 Years Old And Under.....	23.5	22.8	32.2	15.2
% 14-20 Years Old............	14.6	17.4	13.6	8.2
% 21-64 Years Old............	53.7	54.3	49.4	57.2
% 65-74 Years Old............	5.6	4.1	3.5	12.3
% 75 Years Old And Over......	2.6	1.5	1.4	7.1
% In Different House.........	30.0	14.6	52.8	48.8
% Families With Female Head..	37.1	37.1	45.8	18.1
Median School Years Completed...	12.4	12.6	12.2	12.1
Median Family Income, 1979......$$	21388	22405	17708	23958
% Income Below Poverty Level....	13.4	10.7	26.3	7.4
% Income Of $30,000 Or More....	26.4	27.9	14.6	35.0
% White Collar Workers.......	51.6	53.6	53.1	45.4
% Civilian Labor Force Unemployed.	12.9	12.1	19.5	9.2
% Riding To Work By Automobile....	64.8	71.0	49.7	60.6
Mean Commuting Time - Minutes...	38.5	40.9	45.4	24.3
Population Per Household.........	3.1	3.4	3.6	2.1
Total Housing Units...........	3525	1713	752	1060
% Condominiums...............	1.5	3.0	0.0	0.0
% Built 1970 Or Later........	0.8	0.8	2.0	0.0
% Owner Occupied.............	53.5	59.6	57.3	40.9
% With 1+ Persons Per Room...	8.0	7.7	12.3	5.5
Median Value: Owner Units...$$	30400	37100	24600	24500
Median Rent: Rental Units.....$$	169	181	164	146
Median Number Of Rooms: All Units.	5.0	5.3	4.9	4.5

Community Area 50 -- Pullman
Selected Characteristics of Census Tracts: 1970

Tract Number	TOTAL	5001	5002	5003
Total Population.............	10893	5887	2250	2756
% Male.......................	48.2	47.7	47.9	49.5
% Black......................	48.1	80.2	22.5	0.6
% Other Nonwhite.............	0.7	0.9	0.4	0.5
% Of Spanish Language........	2.7	3.1	1.5	2.5
% Foreign Born...............	7.8	2.9	5.4	19.9
% Living In Group Quarters...	0.7	0.3	0.8	1.5
% 13 Years Old And Under.....	28.5	33.0	26.5	20.2
% 14-20 Years Old............	9.6	9.9	10.0	8.8
% 21-64 Years Old............	53.9	52.2	54.5	57.1
% 65-74 Years Old............	5.4	3.7	6.0	8.7
% 75 Years Old And Over......	2.6	1.2	3.0	5.2
% In Different House.........	42.2	27.3	55.0	62.2
% Families With Female Head..	16.3	15.1	17.9	17.4
Median School Years Completed...	11.6	12.2	10.9	10.3
Median Family Income, 1969......$$	10549	11012	10208	9983
% Income Below Poverty Level....	6.0	5.7	9.4	4.1
% Income of $15,000 or More.....	21.2	23.4	20.0	17.2
% White Collar Workers.......	23.3	24.4	17.7	25.6
% Civilian Labor Force Unemployed.	4.0	3.5	5.3	4.1
% Riding To Work By Automobile....	59.8	65.9	59.4	48.9
Population Per Household.........	3.1	3.5	3.0	2.4
Total Housing Units...........	3683	1675	793	1215
% Condominiums & Cooperatives.....	15.9	34.6	0.9	0.0
% Built 1960 Or Later........	24.6	48.1	7.2	3.7
% Owner Occupied.............	46.9	50.8	54.2	36.9
% With 1+ Persons Per Room...	8.2	9.2	10.6	5.2
Median Value: Owner Units.......$$	17200	19100	14200	11800
Median Rent: Rental Units.....$$	83	124	81	76
Median Number Of Rooms: All Units.	4.8	5.1	4.6	4.4

Central depot at 111th Street and Cottage Grove, just south of the landmark administration building and clock tower. Located south and east of the depot were the Florence Hotel, the Green Stone Church, a school, the Arcade Building (which housed stores, a theater, a bank, offices, a library, and the post office), and the Market House, where fresh, company-inspected produce was sold. The town quickly became a showplace. Visitors were attracted, from Chicago and the rest of the World, to see the snug little workers' homes, the solid clean streets, the stylish public buildings, the fountains, reflecting pool and gardens. North of 111th Street were the manufacturing plants of the Pullman Palace Car Company and its affiliates. Workingmen's homes similar to those in the village were constructed east of Cottage Grove Avenue from 103rd to 106th streets. This northern settlement was known as North Pullman but was considered an integral part of the town of Pullman.

The housing stock of Pullman consisted primarily of two-story single-family row houses, with some single-family detached residences for company executives. Lower-salaried workers were housed in brick "block house" tenements. The residential structures were mostly brick, manufactured in Pullman from clay dredged from the bottom of Lake Calumet. Most of the earlier residents were either German, Irish, Scandinavian, Scottish, or English. By 1884, the village population was estimated by a visitor at about 8,000 persons, most residing between 111th and 115th streets.

After a few years, many employee-residents of Pullman became discontented as a result of their inability to buy homes in the area and the high prices charged by company-owned stores. In 1889, contrary to the wishes of George Pullman, they voted for annexation of Hyde Park to the city of Chicago. For the time being, however, Pullman remained a virtually independent enclave within the city limits of Chicago. More workers were attracted to the area as the plants increased production. By 1892, there was a large foreign-born population in Pullman including more than 20 nationalities. An increasing number of workers were southern and eastern European immigrants.

During the depression years of 1893 and 1894, all Pullman workers took substantial pay cuts, while the Pullman Land Association maintained rents at their previous level. Pullman would negotiate neither the pay-scale nor the rents with an employees' committee, and abruptly terminated several committee members. A strike by the Pullman workers in May, 1894, quickly spread through the American Railway Union of which many were members, to the railroads. Pullman village became again the object of world attention, as observers began to investigate conditions in what once had seemed such an ideal industrial community. The strike had historic consequences, mostly as the result of litigation following Federal intervention and violence in July, 1894. As a result of one suit brought by the workers against Pullman, the Illinois Supreme Court ruled, following his death a few years after the strike, that the charter of the Pullman Company did not authorize it to own or manage a town. Residents henceforth could own homes in Pullman, but the neighborhood declined following the loss of company support.

During the next three decades, as the South Side working-class neighborhoods expanded, Pullman was absorbed into the contiguous city. While large tracts of vacant and undeveloped land remained, and still virtually no settlement north of 103rd Street, Pullman's residential pattern was set by 1895. As production techniques changed in the transition from wood to steel cars, demand for lower-skilled workers increased. The foreign-born population was increased by Polish, Italian, and Greek workers, as older residents began to move out of Pullman. In 1920, foreign-born whites constituted 42 percent of the area's population, the most numerous nationalities were Polish, Italian, and Scandinavian. Other foreign-born groups included Irish, Dutch, Greek, Hungarian, and Czechoslovakian migrants.

During the 1920s, while Pullman industries grew and the community area population continued to decline, Italians moved into the area in increasing numbers, replacing Poles as the largest foreign-stock group in Pullman by 1930. Some Mexicans settled on Langley Avenue between 111th and 115th streets. Very few new residences were built during the 1920s in the village area, but residential growth was just beginning on the vacant land between 95th and 99th streets. Most homes in Pullman proper began to show signs of deterioration, particularly on the southern and eastern fringe between 111th and 115th streets. An occasional modern home was built between older dwellings in the residential area south of 103rd Street. Public buildings as well displayed signs of decay. Transients became common in the area. The number of residents in Pullman changed little in the 1930s, despite the Depression, and increased by more than one-third during and after World War II. In 1950, the community total approached 9,000, as large as that of the old days. During the 1950s, people began to move out of Pullman. Although the 1960 census indicated a decrease of less than 500, there was in fact a net loss of more than 15 percent during the decade, which was covered up by the high birth rates of the postwar era. In 1960 Italians were the largest foreign-stock group, followed by those of Polish descent.

Between 1930 and 1960, most new residential development took place in the northern section of the area between 95th and 99th streets. The remainder of northern Pullman was either industrial or vacant railroad property. Most residential construction during this period was single-family homes. In 1960, 60 percent of the housing units in Pullman were owner-occupied, and an equivalent proportion was in single-family structures. One-third of all 1960 units had been built after 1940.

In the last 20 years, the population composition of Pullman has changed considerably. During the 1960s, at least 3,000 more whites moved out, but more than 5,000 blacks moved in, and the total population reached a historic peak, almost 11,000 in 1970, about equally divided between whites and blacks. The population north of 103rd Street changed from virtually all white to four-fifths black between 1960 and 1970. The central area, from 103rd to 111th streets, had become one-fifth black by 1970. The area south of 111th Street, containing Pullman proper, remained almost entirely white.

Blacks continued to move into Pullman during the last 10 years but the number of residents has dropped, due to the removal of most of the rest of the whites. The population of Pullman north of 111th Street is more than 90 percent black. Ninety percent of Pullman's remaining white population lives in the old Pullman village, south of 111th. Some Latinos have moved in, and they comprise about a fourth of the inhabitants of the southernmost tract.

More than 70 percent of all housing units in Pullman are single-family homes, about one-fourth are in structures containing two to nine units, and less than 3 percent are in larger buildings. The median value of single-family, owner-occupied homes in Pullman is about one-third less than the city-wide median.

Pullman was designated a national landmark in 1970, and the south Pullman District was granted Chicago landmark status two years later. The Historic Pullman Foundation oversees restoration of the area. In 1975, the Foundation purchased the Hotel Florence and many of its original furnishings, and a restoration was planned. Market Hall was scheduled to be renovated in 1981. Individual owners have rehabilitated many of the one-time Pullman executive residences along 111th Street. The Pullman Company, whose fortunes had declined with those of the transcontinental railroads, was sold in 1980 to an eastern conglomerate, which determined to close the Chicago plant. The last Pullman car was manufactured in 1981. Today, the village restoration faces a row of empty and boarded up factory buildings.

M.W.H.
Will Hogan

South Deering

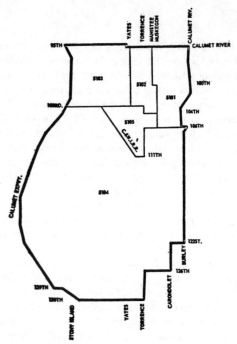

South Deering, which nearly surrounds Lake Calumet, is a large community area on the far South Side that still contains much vacant land. In 1840, it was dotted by shallow swamps and marshes. The first settlers arrived in 1845. Within two years came the construction of the Chittenden Road, which extended east along the Calumet River. By 1848, eight railroad lines ran through the area, including the Illinois Central and Rock Island.

The industrial developent of South Deering began after the Civil War. In 1870, Lake Calumet was dredged and pilings were installed to construct docks and slips which would allow for the landing of freight ships. At this time, Congress had appropriated funds for work on the Calumet Harbor, and a channel was constructed between the Calumet River and Lake Michigan. The Calumet and Chicago Canal Docking Company then constructed docks and artificial harbors. The development of transportation facilities encouraged the location of industries in the area, several of which moved from the banks of the North Branch of the Chicago River to South Deering. In 1875, the Joseph H. Brown Iron and Steel Company constructed a plant on the west bank of the Calumet River at 109th Street. J.T. Torrence, for whom a major street was named, was a large shareholder in the corporation. People began to call the neighborhood "Irondale."

The first post office, known as Brown's Mill, was established in 1878. The steel mill employed 926 workers, primarily Germans, Irish, and Scandanavians. The houses in which these workers and their families lived were owned by the Brown Steel Company, and were located between 106th and 109th streets on the east side of Torrence Avenue. The business district ran along 106th Street between Muskegon and Torrence avenues. It consisted primarily of stores which were interspersed with company houses and boarding houses for the single workers. In 1883, the Ewing Horse Railroad Company was issued a permit to build a line in Brown's Mill, which marked the beginning of public transportation.

In 1882 Brown and Torrence sold their shares in the mill to the Calumet Iron and Steel Company, owned by J.C. Cummings, president of the New York Central Railroad. The name of the post office was changed to Cummings. A year later, there was a major strike. The mill never recovered from the loss of business during the strike. It also faced increasingly stiff competition from other steel mills outside the Cummings community. In 1889, the Cummings area was annexed to the city of Chicago as part of the Village of Hyde Park. Throughout the 1880s and the 1890s, the community experienced increasingly severe economic distress. Many families were forced to leave the area and, in 1891, a community newspaper described Cummings as "almost deserted."

At the end of the decade, the Calumet Iron and Steel Company sold out to the South Chicago Furnace Company, and the area acquired both a new name and a solid industrial base when, in 1900, the Deering Harvester Company bought a controlling interest in that firm. With the formation of International Harvester Company, brought about through the merger of the McCormick and Deering Harvester companies, the industrial development of South Deering was assured. New industries located in the area including the Calumet Coal Company; Peoples Gas, Light, and Coke Company; Illinois Slag and Ballast Company; Chicago Steel and Wire Company; Gold Medal Flour Mill; National Cylinder Gas Company and the Chicago Iron and Coal Company. These were all located along Torrence Avenue, extending south from 105th to 130th streets. In 1905, the name of the mill owned by International Harvester was changed to the Wisconsin Steel Company.

The first immigrants in the period from 1900 to 1913 were Yugoslavians. They were followed by Poles, Italians, Austrians, and Bul-

garians. European immigration was seriously curtailed during World War I, but resumed briefly in the 1920s, with the settlement of the Armenians. The first Mexicans settled in the community as early as 1926, and the first blacks in 1940. Ethnicity determined residential patterns in the South Deering community. Prior to 1900, the Welsh, English and Irish lived along Torrence Avenue from 108th to 111th streets. After 1900, these groups moved to the newer housing areas on 104th and 105th streets. Yugoslavians, Poles, and Italians replaced them in the older housing areas. In 1920, 37 percent of the residents of South Deering were foreign-born, principally Croatians, Serbians, Italians and Mexicans. By 1930, Yugoslavians made up 51 percent of the foreign-born in South Deering.

The residential section east of Torrence Avenue between 95th and 105th streets in South Deering is known as Memorial Park or Slag Valley. This is the oldest and poorest part of South Deering and in the early 20th century was occupied by Poles, Lithuanians, Italians, and Mexicans. Before 1930 the streets remained unpaved and the houses were mostly frame shacks. Slag Valley was gradually surrounded by industries such as Wisconsin Steel, the Gold Medal Flour Mill, and the Chicago Steel and Wire Company. the area adjacent to Lake Calumet between 110th and 116th streets was known as the "South Pole," where the Polish community lived.

In the early 1930s, the South Deering residential area consisted of only one-half square mile of the community's 6-square-mile area. Later in the decade, New Deal federal measures supported municipal improvements and by 1938, 103rd Street was paved and widened to become a major thoroughfare. the improvement of this street also encouraged new residential construction north of 103rd where the Calumet Gardens housing development — later called Jeffrey Manor — was built. In 1938, a Chicago Housing Authority project named Trumbull Park Homes was constructed. Jeffrey Manor became the most populous residential area in South Deering. It is where the newer and more expensive single-family brick houses are located. In 1950, the Chicago Housing Authority attempted to purchase 21 acres of land in Irondale to add 300 units to Trumbull Park Homes, but the project was discontinued because there was too much community opposition.

In 1930, 7,911 people lived in South Deering. In 1940, the population had reached 9,662 and by 1950, it almost doubled to 17,746. This growth was attributable to the continued residential growth of Jeffrey Manor and Trumbull Park. These two developments brought thousands of people who did not work in the area to South Deering. Many were native Americans and the foreign-born percentage was cut

Community Area 51 -- South Deering
Population and Housing Characteristics, 1930-1980

	1980	1970	1960	1950	1940	1930
Total Population.......	19,400	19,405	18,794	17,476	9,662	7,898
% Male.................	47.2	48.6	50.3	51.4	52.6	55.6
% Female...............	52.8	51.4	49.7	48.6	47.4	44.4
% White................	31.2	82.5	99.1	99.9	100.0	87.3
% Black................	54.8	15.9	0.7	0.1	-	-
% Other Nonwhite Races...	14.0	1.6	0.2	0.0	-	12.7
% Under 5 Years Old......	7.6	8.8	11.4	14.8	10.4	10.8
% 5-19 Years Old........	31.3	31.2	30.1	24.6	30.7	35.5
% 20-44 Years Old.......	36.9	30.8	33.9	44.0	39.1	39.6
% 45-64 Years Old.......	17.9	22.1	18.3	13.1	17.0	12.4
% 65 Years and Older....	6.3	7.1	6.3	3.5	2.8	1.7
Median School Years....	12.2	11.6	11.2	10.7	7.7	*
Total Housing Units....	5,804	5,687	5,105	4,488	2,170	*
% In One-Unit Structures.	72.3	72.9	79.1	*	*	*
% Owner Occupied........	68.3	69.6	72.2	68.7	35.8	*
% Renter Occupied.......	28.6	27.8	25.3	30.2	62.5	*
% Vacant...............	3.1	2.6	2.5	1.1	1.7	*
% 1+ Persons per Room...	10.8	10.5	10.8	14.2	*	*

Community Area 51 -- South Deering
Selected Characteristics of Census Tracts: 1980

Tract Number	Total	5101	5102	5103	5104	5104.99	5105
Total Population.............	19400	3673	4250	6903	73	51	4450
% Male.......................	47.2	48.6	47.6	46.1	-	-	47.0
% Black......................	54.8	0.0	77.6	96.1	-	-	15.6
% Other Nonwhite.............	14.1	21.3	4.0	1.3	-	-	37.6
% Of Spanish Origin..........	24.6	41.3	7.5	1.9	-	-	62.2
% Foreign Born...............	11.4	22.6	4.8	2.0	-	-	23.0
% Living In Group Quarters...	0.4	0.0	0.0	0.1	-	-	0.2
% 13 Years Old And Under.....	25.5	19.6	27.2	25.9	-	-	28.4
% 14-20 Years Old............	15.5	13.0	15.7	16.6	-	-	15.8
% 21-64 Years Old............	52.7	55.8	53.2	54.3	-	-	47.1
% 65-74 Years Old............	4.2	7.8	3.2	2.4	-	-	4.9
% 75 Years Old And Over......	2.1	3.9	0.7	0.9	-	-	3.8
% In Different House.........	28.9	32.3	23.6	23.2	-	-	40.5
% Families With Female Head...	31.2	13.5	28.5	36.8	-	-	36.8
Median School Years Completed.	12.2	10.9	12.4	12.6	-	-	10.3
Median Family Income, 1979.....$$	21471	22431	22967	21380	-	-	18621
% Income Below Poverty Level....	11.5	10.3	8.8	7.9	-	-	21.4
% Income Of $30,000 Or More.....	27.7	28.3	30.3	28.3	-	-	22.9
% White Collar Workers..........	50.7	39.2	56.9	60.0	-	-	33.7
% Civilian Labor Force Unemployed.	12.7	12.3	9.7	13.0	-	-	16.1
% Riding To Work By Automobile....	65.0	73.2	63.0	65.5	-	-	56.7
Mean Commuting Time - Minutes...	37.2	25.1	42.0	44.2	-	-	27.5
Population Per Household........	3.4	3.1	3.7	3.5	-	-	3.4
Total Housing Units..........	5804	1236	1176	2018	27	0	1347
% Condominiums...............	0.0	0.0	0.0	0.0	-	-	0.0
% Built 1970 Or Later........	2.8	2.7	1.3	3.3	-	-	3.5
% Owner Occupied.............	68.4	60.8	82.0	85.8	-	-	37.5
% With 1+ Persons Per Room...	10.8	8.1	11.1	9.3	-	-	15.0
Median Value: Owner Units.......$$	30100	33300	32400	28400	-	-	29900
Median Rent: Rental Units.......$$	137	148	244	223	-	-	94
Median Number Of Rooms: All Units.	5.2	5.1	5.3	5.4	-	-	4.6

Community Area 51 -- South Deering
Selected Characteristics of Census Tracts: 1970

Tract Number	TOTAL	5101	5102	5103	5104	5105
Total Population.............	19271	3923	3994	6908	51	4395
% Male.......................	48.6	49.3	49.7	47.9	-	47.9
% Black......................	15.9	0.1	14.7	33.4	-	3.9
% Other Nonwhite.............	1.6	0.8	1.2	1.1	-	3.7
% Of Spanish Language........	16.7	13.1	6.7	5.8	-	45.8
% Foreign Born...............	12.7	21.8	8.1	6.9	-	17.9
% Living In Group Quarters...	0.3	0.7	0.0	0.1	-	0.4
% 13 Years Old And Under.....	28.5	23.9	28.0	28.7	-	32.6
% 14-20 Years Old............	13.0	13.5	12.8	12.4	-	13.4
% 21-64 Years Old............	51.5	54.0	54.0	53.6	-	43.8
% 65-74 Years Old............	4.4	4.8	3.7	3.6	-	5.8
% 75 Years Old And Over......	2.7	3.7	1.5	1.6	-	4.5
% In Different House.........	55.8	74.7	57.8	43.4	-	56.3
% Families With Female Head.......	13.8	11.7	9.7	13.0	-	21.9
Median School Years Completed.......	11.6	9.6	12.1	12.4	-	8.9
Median Family Income, 1969......$$	11152	10426	12213	11881	-	8424
% Income Below Poverty Level....	5.4	2.1	3.1	2.9	-	14.6
% Income of $15,000 or More.....	23.8	24.1	31.4	26.7	-	10.7
% White Collar Workers..........	24.0	11.6	28.9	33.2	-	11.8
% Civilian Labor Force Unemployed.	3.3	3.8	3.5	2.5	-	4.1
% Riding To Work By Automobile....	61.5	61.4	61.0	68.8	-	46.4
Population Per Household........	3.5	3.4	3.5	3.5	-	3.4
Total Housing Units..........	5699	1199	1158	1992	18	1332
% Condominiums & Cooperatives.....	0.1	0.0	0.0	0.4	-	0.0
% Built 1960 Or Later........	10.6	11.4	25.1	4.4	-	6.6
% Owner Occupied.............	69.6	58.5	86.6	89.1	-	36.3
% With 1+ Persons Per Room...	10.5	10.2	9.9	7.2	-	16.2
Median Value: Owner Units.......$$	17300	17300	17800	17200	-	16400
Median Rent: Rental Units.......$$	78	78	147	157	-	73
Median Number Of Rooms: All Units.	5.1	5.0	5.1	5.3	-	4.5

in half. After the spurt in the 1940s, the population in South Deering increased only slightly to 18,794 in 1960 and 19,271 in 1970. Of the total, 3 percent were foreign stock, compared to 47 percent in 1960. In 1960, these were mostly Yugoslavians, Russians and Poles. By 1970, Mexicans had moved into Irondale and Memorial Park. During the 1960s, blacks began to move into Jeffrey Manor and Irondale. By 1970, more than 3,000 blacks lived in South Deering.

The 1970s brought major changes to South Deering, but despite them, the number of residents remained virtually stable, at 19,400 in 1980. The number of whites dropped to 6,044, and they are now less that a third of the total. The decline in high-skill jobs, deteriorating housing, and increasing competition from black and Spanish workers may account for the decrease. Blacks totaled 10,630 in 1980, and they constituted more than half the community total. The Hispanic population increased in 1980 to 4,763. Largely Mexicans, they account for a fourth of the population.

While the population composition changed, the growth of the community was halted by an economic catastrophe. In the late 1970s, a finacially-troubled International Harvester Corporation divested itself of the Wisconsin Steel Works, although the plant stayed open and the giant equipment company remained its principal customer. In late 1979, a long strike closed International Harvester. With its market cut off, Wisconsin Steel in turn shut its doors early in 1980. This meant massive unemployment in South Deering and threatened to lead to an exodus comparable to the one following the Cummings strike, nearly a century ago.

South Deering may be characterized as an area of one-story frame single-family structures. A large proportion of the land is given over to industrial use, and there is also a large amount of unused marshland. Residents of South Deering are currently in conflict over the future development of the vacant marshy area. At 95th and Constance Avenue extending south to 103rd Street is a 15-acre pond-filled field, which residents call the "Prairie." The marshland is one of the last resting places for migratory fowl along the Illinois shoreline of Lake Michigan, and is said to be nesting ground for nearly half of the Audubon Society's list of 200 endangered species of birds. Those South Deering residents who want to make the "Prairie" the city's first ecological park

are supported by ecologists and environmentalists, other nearby communities, and the U.S. Environmental Protection Agency. Others, organizing around the Christ Universal Temple, want to develop a $12 million dollar, 160-unit housing development on the most northerly 7.5 acres. This federally-subsidized housing development has been approved by the city government and the U.S. Department of Housing and Urban Development. The proponents of the housing development believe this would bring new life to the community. This conflict will lead to a decision of major consequence to the community, whatever course is taken.

South Deering has been undergoing change that has altered not only the physical structure of the community but, as in so many other places, the cultural structure as well. The European ethnic groups, the Serbians, Croatians, Poles, Italians, Scandinavians, and Germans are moving out, and they are being succeeded by a growing black and Mexican population. The community has been an industrial center, but the closing of Wisconsin Steel and the decline of opportunities for less-skilled workers in other industries may result in the conversion of a port of industrial entry for minorities into a bird sanctuary. South Deering is a community area with a great industrial history, but the land, plant facilities and housing may not prove adaptable to an industrial future.

James Walker

Community Area 52

East Side

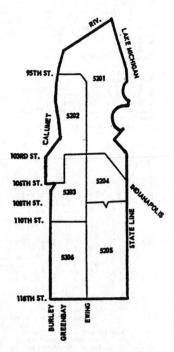

East Side is a virtual island, nearly surrounded by water. Bounded on the north and west by the Calumet River and by Lake Michigan and the Illinois-Indiana state line on the east, the community area can be accessed only by drawbridge from the rest of Chicago. It is traversed by the massive Chicago Skyway Bridge. The East Side extends to addresses more than 4000 east.

Travel to and from East Side in the early 1800s was the business of William See, who had a ferry across the Callimink (Calumet) River at the head of Lake Michigan. In 1839 a pontoon toll bridge was built near the site of the present 92nd Street Bridge. The bridge was a financial success and lasted until 1843 when a freshet from the river destroyed it. A land boom was anticipated in the area after Jefferson Davis, then a young army lieutenant, wrote a report to Washington in 1833, urgently recommending the improvement of the Calumet River and the establishment of a harbor. Stephen A. Douglas, John Wentworth and Elijah K. Hubbard were among those interested in the new developments. The boom never came because the government chose to develop Fort Dearborn at the mouth of the Chicago River instead and the land reverted to the state for nonpayment of taxes. Land on which multimillion dollar industries now stand was auctioned at the Tremont House in Chicago in lots selling for 15, 25 and 30 cents each. Most of the lots were bought by Elliot Anthony who, years later, established the Calumet and Chicago Canal and Dock Company.

The area became Chicago's front door for surface travel. The nearest land route to Eastern cities had to pass through this section in order to skirt the southern shore of Lake Michigan and the northern end of Wolf Lake. The Lake Shore and Michigan Railroad (later the New York Central) extended its tracks through East Side in 1848. The Pennsylvania and Fort Wayne, Elgin and Joliet and Eastern Lines followed. In 1865 there were about a half dozen families living in the wooded area. They were engaged in hunting, fishing and farming. East Side

was originally part of the Village of Hyde Park which extended from 39th Street to 138th Street. Around 1873 it became part of the abortive "City of Calumet." The first recorded name of East Side was "Iron Workers Addition." In 1873, Charles Colehour and Douglas Taylor, two real estate investors, anticipating and influx of mill workers, opened two subdivisions. The Colehour section was south of the railroad tracks and the Taylor section was north of the tracks. For many years there were two different neighborhoods. In 1873 a railroad station named Colehour was opened at 100th Street and Ewing Avenue, and Taylor built the Ewing House Hotel across the street. Germans located in the southern division, Swedes north of the tracks. Both groups built churches, around which their social life centered. Each had its own schools and stores and a rivalry between neighborhoods developed.

Community Area 52 — East Side
Population and Housing Characteristics, 1930-1980

	1980	1970	1960	1950	1940	1930
Total Population.......	21,331	24,649	23,214	21,619	16,513	16,839
% Male.................	48.9	48.9	50.7	51.5	51.9	52.9
% Female...............	51.1	51.1	49.3	48.5	48.1	47.1
% White................	94.2	99.6	99.9	99.9	100.0	99.7
% Black................	0.1	0.1	0.0	0.1	–	–
% Other Nonwhite Races..	5.7	0.3	0.1	0.0	0.0	0.3
% Under 5 Years Old.....	5.8	7.4	10.2	10.1	7.3	9.2
% 5-19 Years Old........	22.3	27.1	24.8	22.4	26.3	30.2
% 20-44 Years Old.......	32.2	29.6	32.8	41.7	41.1	41.2
% 45-64 Years Old.......	26.4	26.6	24.2	20.4	20.8	16.1
% 65 Years and Older....	13.3	9.3	8.0	5.4	4.5	3.3
Median School Years....	11.9	10.8	9.5	9.0	8.1	*
Total Housing Units....	7,754	7,944	6,951	5,909	4,190	*
% In One-Unit Structures.	59.4	54.8	53.3	*	*	*
% Owner Occupied........	67.6	68.6	64.6	61.4	46.3	*
% Renter Occupied.......	28.6	29.1	32.2	37.4	52.0	*
% Vacant...............	3.8	2.3	3.2	1.2	1.7	*
% 1+ Persons per Room...	3.9	7.3	8.4	10.2	*	*

Community Area 52 — East Side
Selected Characteristics of Census Tracts: 1980

Tract Number	Total	5201	5202	5202.99	5203	5204	5205	5206
Total Population.............	21331	1807	3464	90	5423	3706	4263	2578
% Male.......................	48.9	47.9	49.4	–	48.7	47.7	49.4	48.8
% Black......................	0.1	0.2	0.0	–	0.1	0.1	0.0	0.0
% Other Nonwhite.............	5.7	10.5	13.4	–	6.1	2.7	1.5	2.9
% Of Spanish Origin..........	12.6	22.6	27.5	–	14.3	5.3	4.0	6.8
% Foreign Born...............	14.1	14.5	19.6	–	16.0	9.7	11.3	13.9
% Living In Group Quarters...	0.5	0.8	0.1	–	0.0	0.0	0.0	0.0
% 13 Years Old And Under.....	17.1	20.0	20.7	–	17.9	14.4	15.5	15.4
% 14-20 Years Old............	13.1	13.1	12.9	–	13.0	13.0	13.5	13.0
% 21-64 Years Old............	56.5	54.0	55.0	–	55.4	56.4	58.3	59.7
% 65-74 Years Old............	8.9	7.7	7.8	–	9.1	10.4	9.0	8.7
% 75 Years Old And Over......	4.4	5.1	3.6	–	4.6	5.9	3.6	3.2
% In Different House.........	31.0	40.8	38.2	–	31.1	30.9	26.5	21.5
% Families With Female Head..	14.1	16.6	22.5	–	12.6	15.0	9.3	9.1
Median School Years Completed.	11.9	11.0	10.8	–	11.1	12.1	12.2	12.0
Median Family Income, 1979....$$	24582	22826	21133	–	24519	25844	27500	25306
% Income Below Poverty Level....	5.1	17.3	6.5	–	3.3	3.3	5.1	2.2
% Income Of $30,000 Or More.....	36.3	33.4	25.9	–	34.3	40.1	43.0	38.0
% White Collar Workers..........	39.7	41.4	33.9	–	32.7	36.6	48.3	48.5
% Civilian Labor Force Unemployed.	7.3	9.2	6.8	–	8.7	9.0	5.6	3.8
% Riding To Work By Automobile....	75.2	75.8	67.8	–	79.6	75.2	78.0	72.7
Mean Commuting Time – Minutes...	24.9	24.5	24.3	–	21.3	25.1	26.5	29.6
Population Per Household..........	2.8	2.9	2.7	–	2.9	2.7	3.0	3.0
Total Housing Units...........	7754	654	1363	0	1989	1426	1450	872
% Condominiums................	0.0	0.0	0.0	–	0.0	0.0	0.0	0.0
% Built 1970 Or Later.........	3.6	1.0	0.3	–	1.5	0.4	10.9	7.6
% Owner Occupied..............	67.6	49.2	41.9	–	67.9	65.5	88.3	90.0
% With 1+ Persons Per Room....	3.9	6.0	5.3	–	3.9	2.2	3.7	3.2
Median Value: Owner Units......$$	38800	32500	31800	–	36100	39200	42300	39800
Median Rent: Rental Units......$$	166	161	160	–	162	183	182	192
Median Number Of Rooms: All Units.	5.2	5.3	5.1	–	5.1	5.4	5.1	5.1

Community Area 52 — East Side
Selected Characteristics of Census Tracts: 1970

Tract Number	TOTAL	5201	5202	5203	5204	5205	5206
Total Population.............	24649	1961	4332	5601	4259	5878	2618
% Male.......................	48.9	48.1	49.2	48.0	48.6	49.6	49.5
% Black......................	0.1	0.2	0.1	0.1	0.0	0.0	0.3
% Other Nonwhite.............	0.3	1.1	0.5	0.2	0.1	0.0	0.0
% Of Spanish Language........	3.3	5.9	6.3	4.2	1.9	1.3	0.9
% Foreign Born...............	8.8	13.7	12.6	9.1	9.0	3.9	8.9
% Living In Group Quarters...	0.4	2.5	0.6	0.0	0.0	0.1	0.3
% 13 Years Old And Under.....	24.2	22.7	25.8	25.0	22.4	24.1	24.7
% 14-20 Years Old............	11.7	10.1	11.4	10.7	10.8	12.7	14.5
% 21-64 Years Old............	54.8	55.1	54.2	54.2	53.2	56.7	55.3
% 65-74 Years Old............	6.0	8.0	5.2	6.4	8.9	4.5	4.2
% 75 Years Old And Over......	3.2	4.0	3.4	3.7	3.8	2.0	1.3
% In Different House.........	65.3	55.0	59.2	65.5	70.1	68.8	67.3
% Families With Female Head..	9.5	12.5	11.0	11.2	8.4	7.7	6.9
Median School Years Completed...	10.8	10.1	10.3	10.3	11.0	11.8	11.1
Median Family Income, 1969......$$	11509	10379	10018	11173	11912	12272	12874
% Income Below Poverty Level.....	4.4	6.3	6.6	5.7	3.1	3.6	1.3
% Income Of $15,000 or More.....	26.0	22.8	18.3	21.8	28.4	31.6	32.1
% White Collar Workers..........	15.9	19.4	13.5	15.8	13.8	17.4	16.6
% Civilian Labor Force Unemployed.	2.8	1.3	4.8	1.6	2.3	3.6	2.1
% Riding To Work By Automobile....	70.2	54.9	67.8	71.4	68.3	75.6	73.9
Population Per Household..........	3.2	3.0	3.2	3.1	3.0	3.2	3.5
Total Housing Units...........	7945	680	1430	1830	1428	1824	753
% Condominiums & Cooperatives....	0.1	0.0	0.3	0.3	0.0	0.0	0.0
% Built 1960 Or Later.........	14.7	6.3	7.1	13.9	5.8	29.2	20.2
% Owner Occupied..............	68.4	49.4	43.8	67.2	67.4	89.3	86.5
% With 1+ Persons Per Room....	7.7	7.6	7.9	7.0	6.5	8.6	9.3
Median Value: Owner Units......$$	17800	15500	15100	17100	18200	18500	18200
Median Rent: Rental Units......$$	87	82	79	85	100	102	114
Median Number Of Rooms: All Units.	5.0	5.1	5.1	5.0	5.2	4.8	5.0

Good land transportation facilities and possibilities of the Calumet River for harbor and dock frontage early attracted attention to the East Side as a desirable manufacturing center. In 1871 the Silicon Steel Company purchased 52 acres on both sides of the river for an industrial site. Men came looking for work at this mill. The Silicon Steel Company was not successful, but its land sold quickly to other industries and by 1884 a tin plate and steel tool works, a brewery, a bottling plant, a planing and sash mill and a stocking factory had located there. This industrial development led to settlement. In 1880 the East Side had a population of 1,098 residents comprised mainly of German, Irish and Swedish families. In 1889 East Side was added to Chicago with the rest of the Village of Hyde Park.

In the 1890s the steel industry expanded, the harbor was improved and new railroads came into the area. Grain elevators, coal yards, small steel plants and foundries located in the East Side. The Iroquois Steel Company opened a new plant on 95th Street at the Calumet River which became a major employer. The Chicago Shipbuilding Company produced steel freighters. The ship yards are still part of the industrial complex, rebuilding and maintaining ore boats. Iroquois evolved into Youngstown Sheet and Tube Company, which has since left the area. The site is now the location of the massive Iroquois Landing port on Lake Michigan at 92nd Street. In 1891 the Chicago Tack Company built a plant at 118th Street and the river. This became Republic Steel, which remains a major local employer.

Between 1890 and 1920 the Calumet Region became one of the great industrial areas of the world. As industrial establishments sought locations along the Calumet River, or near the railroad tracks in the decades that followed, heavy industries came to predominate in East Side. along the river a succession of foundries, coal yards, grain elevators, lumber yards and small steel plants emerged. As the lakefront filled in, industries located east of the Pennsylvania and New York Central tracks. The area attracted more Irish, Slovak, Italians, Slovenian, Croatian and Serbian families. The community area was settled by ethnic background and there was much rivalry between the neighborhoods. The 1920 census found that 45 percent of the population was foreign-born. By 1920 the portion of the community between 95th and 109th streets from Ewing west to Burley Avenue was built up and residential settlement began to move southward.

The industrial development of the community continued during the 1920s, with the construction of new plants along the eastern bank of the river and the railroad tracks. These included the Republic Steel Works at 116th Street and Burley Avenue and the Chicago Shipbuilding Company on the Calumet River near 100th Street. By 1930 Germans, Swedes, Italians, Serbians and Croatians composed the bulk of the foreign-born population. Much residential construction took place in the 1920s in the area east of Ewing Avenue between 103rd and 108th streets. This was predominantly single-family homes with some two-family buildings and a few small apartment buildings. North of 108th Street a better section of brick bungalows arose. In 1930, nearly 17,000 people lived in East Side. The creation of Calumet Park on filled-in lakefront further enhanced the desirability of home sites in the eastern portion of the community. The fieldhouse was built where Douglas Taylor's mansion once stood.

The decade of the 1930s brought the Depression and turbulence. The population dropped slightly. In 1937 the CIO, which had organized the Republic Steel mill, called a strike at that plant. On Memorial Day, 1937, the striking workers were picnicking and decided to march to the mill gate as a protest and show of strength. The steelworkers were met by the Chicago police. The confrontation became violent and the police started shooting. Ten people, either steelworkers or sympathizers, were killed. This broke the strike. The event has become known as the "Memorial Day Massacre."

During the 1940s the East Side experienced its greatest decennial population growth, emerging from that period with nearly 22,000 residents. During World War II, the industrial district had operated at full capacity, and there were many jobs available. When a housing shortage developed on the far South Side after the war, there were ample vacant lands in East Side for construction sites. The community grew slowly after 1950 to its highest population, approaching 25,000, in 1970. East of Ewing Avenue and south of 95th Street the lake was gradually filled in. The newer residential area south of 106th Street continued to be built up. Republic Steel built a new plant and other industrial additions occurred along the Pennsylvania Railroad tracks and in the southeastern and northwestern corners of East Side.

In the last 10 years, the population has dropped by about 3,000. People of Polish, Serbian and Croatian descent are most numerous, with significant German, Italian and Irish contingents. Many descendants of original residents still live there. About a fourth of the population have lived there all their lives. Homes are handed down from generation to generation and people have no desire to move away. The old rivalries between nationality groups have given way to a strong sense of community in East Side today, where residents are now more concerned about the possibility of outsiders moving in. East Side is like a small mining town built up around industries, mills and shipyards. The residents are white working-class people, many of whom work in the steel mills of Chicago's South Side or in northwestern Indiana. There are still very few blacks in the area though Hispanics (mostly Mexicans) have recently started moving into the northern part of the East Side just across the bridge from the South Chicago neighborhood. Residential property values are stable, though lower than those of several South Side neighborhoods. There are approximately 21,000 people in four square miles, with 14 churches and two high schools.

A shift in the center of population from Avenue M to Ewing Avenue caused the small neighborhood stores on Avenue M, at one time the main business street, to remain storefront residences. The main business district today is the intersection of 106th Street and Ewing Avenue. A new shopping center has also been added at 117th and Avenue O.

Surrounded by industry, East Side has had a long-term problem with air pollution. Twenty years ago graphite in the air would turn the snow black before it hit the ground. Since then the industries have spent millions of dollars to clean up the air.

M.W.H.
Patt Quinn

West Pullman

The West Pullman community area extends from 115th Street on the north to the irregular far south city limits at or near the Little Calumet River. The name is taken from that of a 19th century speculative subdivision which sought to capitalize on the fame of the Pullman Village located in community area 50, to the northeast. The early history of the area centers around the settlement of Kensington and the later development of Gano and West Pullman. During the period of earliest settlement, the Holland Michigan Avenue Road was the only road connecting the isolated prairie to Chicago. A few German farmers settled there.

The first settler of West Pullman was David Andrews, who in 1840 acquired 360 acres of land between what is now State Street, Lowe Avenue, 123rd and 127th Street. During the 1850s, a settlement arose near the Calumet station established in 1852 by the Illinois Central and Michigan Central Railroads at Cottage Grove Avenue and 115th Street. The community grew slowly. In 1878, there were only about 20 houses in the entire settlement. The Kensington village, which had a a population of 250 in 1880, grew to 1,278 in 1883. This area extended to the east of the Illinois Central tracks between 115th and 125th streets, located at that time within the Village of Hyde Park. The sudden growth is attributed to the development of the Illinois Central and Michigan Central Railroads and the establishment of the Pullman Palace Car works as well as other industry in the area, such as the Chicago Forgon Company's Works on 116th Street.

The remaining part of West Pullman was a part of Hyde Park township until 1867 when the area west of State Street was included in the newly-organized Calumet township. In 1881 the Gano subdivision appeared, extending from 115th Street to 119th Street between State Street and Wentworth Avenue. This settlement, which was controlled by the Gano Company of Cincinnati through their agent Thomas Scanlan, consisted mainly of German and Dutch Americans, who had overflowed from the Roseland area. By 1888, the village of Gano was organized and withdrawn from control of Calumet Township. The new village extended from 115th Street to the Little Calumet river, State and Halsted streets, including what would become the West Pullman residential district. In 1889, the Kensington portion of the present West Pullman community area was annexed to Chicago. Gano opposed annexation but due to fiscal problems voted for it in 1890. The industrial development of West Pullman began with the establishment of the West Pullman Land Association, a Minneapolis-financed concern, that purchased open prairie and farm land between 119th and 123rd streets from Wentworth Avenue to Halsted Street. Before this time, most West Pullman residents worked in the Roseland or Pullman communities. However, within a few years attractive offers made by the West Pullman Land Association to industries to locate in the community had led to the construction of many plants and factories in this new manufacturing district.

Improvement in transportation contributed to growth in West Pullman. The Illinois Central was extended to Blue Island and a station was built at 121st street and Stewart Avenue. other suburban services were provided by the Pennsylvania Railroad. On Michigan Avenue, streetcar lines were extended from 115th Street to 119th Street. Tracks were also laid on 119th Street in 1892.

A real estate boom began in West Pullman in 1890. This led to the building of some 600 houses over a four-year period. This boom was attributed to the real estate promotion of the West Pullman Land Association and the speculation encouraged by the 1893 Columbian World Fair. The flourishing industrial district located in the area west of Halsted Street to Ashland Avenue, between 115th and 123rd streets, was annexed to Chicago in 1895. This completed the land area of the present West Pullman community area, except for two small parcels annexed in 1927 and 1928. The depression of 1893 and the Pullman strike brought West Pullman's rapid development to a halt. In 1908, during another depression, the West Pullman Land Association went bankrupt, along with several local industries.

During the early 1900s, the ethnic composition of West Pullman changed. Gradually, Lithuanian, Polish and Hungarian groups replaced the German, Dutch and Irish. Armenians, Czechoslovakians and Norwegians also moved in. After World War I, many Italian Americans moved into areas formerly occupied by pioneer German, Dutch and French residents. Although large areas of West Pullman remained vacant and undeveloped, the community reached residential maturity by 1919. the war was followed by a short depression and the real estate boom of the 1920s. During this period, the population increased from 23,019 in 1920 to 28,000 10 years later.

During the Depression the population of West Pullman declined slightly and much poverty was apparent, especially in the foreign sections. Observers were struck by the contrasts between rich and poor neighborhoods. The population rose to more than 29,000 in 1950, and to 35,000 in 1960. In 1960, Polish, Italian and German groups predominated among the foreign stock of West Pullman. In the decade that followed blacks began to move into West Pullman and by 1970 they constituted one-sixth of a population now in excess of 40,000. Racial turnover in West Pullman led to social unrest. Whites demonstrated and physically harassed the black newcomers. In the 1970s, 30,000 whites moved out of West Pullman, leaving it 91 percent black. Unlike most other Chicago community areas, the population of West Pullman has been growing steadily since World War II and today stands at its historic high, almost 45,000. The number of housing units has increased by 20 percent since 1960, most having been constructed before 1970. The population per household has increased from 3.4 to 3.8 in the last 20 years, and the percentage of the population age 20 or less is now 46, compared to 37 percent in 1960. Most homes in West Pullman are single-family brick bungalows and wood-framed houses. Larger houses surround the West Pulman Park area. The percentage of homes owner-occupied is very high, comparable to such rates in the suburbs. The median value of homes in West Pullman is lower than the general median, but higher than those of adjacent communities, such as Roseland, Pullman and Riverdale.

Layoffs and plant shutdowns of nearby steel mills where many West Pullman residents worked made it difficult for many West Pullman black residents to keep their homes, which had been acquired through loans from the Department of Housing and Urban Devolpment. After owners defaulted, many Hud homes were foreclosed. By 1982, the Greater Roseland Organization began rehabilitating HUD homes.

Annie Ruth Leslie

Community Area 53 -- West Pullman
Population and Housing Characteristics, 1930-1980

	1980	1970	1960	1950	1940	1930
Total Population......	44,904	40,318	35,397	29,265	27,834	28,474
% Male...................	47.6	48.6	49.3	50.3	51.6	52.7
% Female.................	52.4	51.4	50.7	49.7	48.4	47.3
% White..................	5.8	83.1	99.8	99.7	99.6	98.4
% Black..................	90.6	16.5	0.2	0.3	0.4	0.6
% Other Nonwhite Races...	3.6	0.4	0.0	0.0	0.0	1.0
% Under 5 Years Old......	9.9	7.4	11.1	10.5	7.2	9.1
% 5-19 Years Old.........	34.9	30.0	25.2	20.8	25.6	33.0
% 20-44 Years Old........	38.2	28.9	33.0	41.8	41.2	39.8
% 45-64 Years Old........	13.5	24.7	21.8	20.1	21.4	15.1
% 65 Years and Older.....	3.5	9.0	8.9	6.8	4.5	3.0
Median School Years....	12.3	11.5	10.3	9.0	8.0	*
Total Housing Units....	12,281	12,496	10,613	8,285	6,943	*
% In One-Unit Structures.	66.8	63.0	93.0	*	*	*
% Owner Occupied.........	68.4	69.0	66.6	56.4	45.5	*
% Renter Occupied........	27.2	28.5	30.9	41.4	53.4	*
% Vacant.................	4.4	2.5	2.5	2.2	1.1	*
% 1+ Persons per Room....	11.9	9.0	8.2	10.5	*	*

Community Area 53 -- West Pullman
Selected Characteristics of Census Tracts: 1980

Tract Number	Total	5301	5302	5303	5304	5305	5306
Total Population.............	44904	3925	8881	6393	2740	18125	4840
% Male........................	47.6	50.4	46.7	47.4	47.9	47.5	47.4
% Black.......................	90.6	45.8	95.8	98.9	81.8	95.4	93.6
% Other Nonwhite..............	3.6	28.7	0.9	0.3	5.6	0.8	1.9
% Of Spanish Origin...........	5.1	39.8	1.6	0.6	6.2	1.2	3.8
% Foreign Born................	3.5	21.4	1.4	0.2	5.1	1.8	2.4
% Living In Group Quarters....	0.1	0.5	0.1	0.1	0.7	0.0	0.0
% 13 Years Old And Under......	30.9	32.3	32.1	22.0	34.3	32.4	31.9
% 14-20 Years Old.............	15.8	12.8	17.7	19.1	13.0	15.7	12.9
% 21-64 Years Old.............	49.8	48.0	46.9	55.9	48.4	49.1	52.0
% 65-74 Years Old.............	2.4	4.9	2.3	2.0	3.2	1.9	2.1
% 75 Years Old And Over.......	1.1	2.0	1.0	1.0	1.1	0.9	1.0
% In Different House..........	30.4	50.1	28.0	17.9	43.6	26.0	46.2
% Families With Female Head...	30.9	25.9	40.9	29.2	23.7	27.7	34.8
Median School Years Completed..	12.3	10.9	12.1	12.4	12.4	12.5	12.4
Median Family Income, 1979......$$	21247	17393	18226	24508	22273	22010	21662
% Income Below Poverty Level....	13.5	14.4	19.1	12.3	9.3	12.1	12.5
% Income Of $30,000 Or More....	25.9	17.0	15.9	35.5	28.6	28.8	24.2
% White Collar Workers..........	45.9	31.2	42.2	51.4	48.0	47.2	48.2
% Civilian Labor Force Unemployed.	13.5	10.9	18.6	12.8	7.8	12.6	14.2
% Riding To Work By Automobile....	68.6	68.0	65.2	74.0	72.2	67.4	68.8
Mean Commuting Time - Minutes...	42.4	34.5	43.9	41.9	41.1	43.4	42.5
Population Per Household..........	3.8	3.6	4.0	3.8	3.6	3.9	3.4
Total Housing Units..........	12281	1160	2324	1693	786	4826	1492
% Condominiums................	0.0	0.0	0.0	0.0	0.0	0.0	0.0
% Built 1970 Or Later.........	4.3	1.1	3.1	3.2	15.8	2.8	8.6
% Owner Occupied..............	68.4	38.8	59.5	88.0	79.5	76.3	51.5
% With 1+ Persons Per Room......	11.9	18.4	12.8	11.0	9.7	11.1	10.4
Median Value: Owner Units......$$	38700	25200	30200	42200	39500	40600	39100
Median Rent: Rental Units......$$	191	162	190	196	169	197	222
Median Number Of Rooms: All Units.	5.4	4.8	5.6	5.6	5.5	5.5	4.9

Community Area 53 -- West Pullman
Selected Characteristics of Census Tracts: 1970

Tract Number	TOTAL	5301	5302	5303	5304	5305	5306
Total Population.............	40318	3444	7353	7097	2549	16194	3681
% Male........................	48.6	48.1	47.5	48.9	48.8	48.8	49.5
% Black.......................	16.5	0.0	0.2	93.5	0.2	0.2	0.2
% Other Nonwhite..............	0.3	0.8	0.4	0.2	0.5	0.3	0.1
% Of Spanish Language.........	3.7	11.4	6.1	0.9	11.5	1.2	1.9
% Foreign Born................	8.3	13.2	12.0	1.0	7.5	8.4	10.3
% Living In Group Quarters....	0.2	0.9	0.2	0.0	0.0	0.2	0.0
% 13 Years Old And Under......	25.8	23.3	23.5	35.7	28.5	23.6	21.8
% 14-20 Years Old.............	13.1	12.0	11.2	16.1	16.7	12.7	11.3
% 21-64 Years Old.............	52.1	54.1	51.9	46.2	49.9	53.4	57.9
% 65-74 Years Old.............	5.5	6.5	7.9	1.4	2.8	6.4	5.3
% 75 Years Old And Over.......	3.5	4.2	5.5	0.6	2.0	3.9	3.6
% In Different House..........	67.8	58.5	62.9	63.3	74.4	72.8	68.3
% Families With Female Head...	10.7	16.3	12.4	9.4	8.4	9.6	10.8
Median School Years Completed..	11.5	10.5	10.9	12.4	12.2	11.8	11.1
Median Family Income, 1969......$$	11507	9250	10528	12926	11740	11982	11295
% Income Below Poverty Level....	5.6	7.5	5.5	5.7	6.3	5.5	4.1
% Income of $15,000 or More....	28.1	17.0	23.6	34.2	30.3	30.9	24.6
% White Collar Workers..........	20.2	17.1	19.8	16.0	19.0	21.9	24.3
% Civilian Labor Force Unemployed.	3.2	4.6	3.1	5.2	1.5	2.6	1.9
% Riding To Work By Automobile....	63.9	47.6	65.2	66.6	63.3	65.6	64.1
Population Per Household..........	3.3	2.9	3.0	3.0	4.4	3.2	2.9
Total Housing Units..........	12507	1252	2507	1634	686	5121	1307
% Condominiums & Cooperatives.....	0.3	1.0	0.0	1.0	0.0	0.1	0.0
% Built 1960 Or Later.........	17.8	3.7	5.1	84.4	7.0	4.6	29.7
% Owner Occupied..............	68.6	38.5	58.8	86.7	82.8	75.6	59.4
% With 1+ Persons Per Room......	9.3	4.8	8.8	6.4	20.1	14.0	7.5
Median Value: Owner Units......$$	18700	13600	15500	21400	17300	18900	19200
Median Rent: Rental Units......$$	92	79	93	104	90	96	109
Median Number Of Rooms: All Units.	5.1	4.7	5.2	5.5	5.0	5.1	4.8

Riverdale

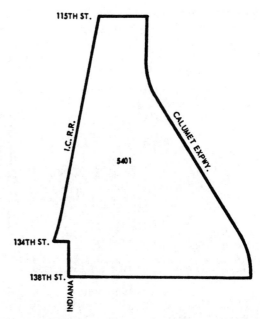

The Chicago community of Riverdale is located at the far south city limits just northeast of the suburb of the same name. It is bounded by the Pullman community area on the north, Interstate Highway 94 (the Calumet Expressway) on the east, the city limits (138th Street) on the south, and the Illinois Central Gulf railroad tracks on the west. Most of the land in the northern two-thirds of the community is non-residential, occupied by railyards, industry and the Calumet sewage treatment plant. Most of the residents live south of 130th Street, east of Indiana Avenue.

The first settler was George Dolton, for whom the suburb adjoining Riverdale is named, who brought his wife and seven children there in 1836. He was shortly joined by J.C. Mathews, with whom he operated a ferry across the Little Calumet River. Six years later Dolton and another settler, Levi Osterhoudt, built a toll bridge across the river which they operated until 1856, when it was purchased by Cook County.

Early German and Dutch settlers arrived in Riverdale during the 1840s and 1850s. They were largely farmers and lumberers. Some worked the railroads. The Illinois Central came through the area in 1852, building the first railroad station at 137th and Ilinois Street in what is now suburban Riverdale. Between 1852 and 1880, six different railroads were built in the Riverdale region. Development of the railroads and the population growth of the city led to widespread truck farming which in turn gave rise to establishments that processed foods. In 1865, a sugar beet refinery and a lumber yard were built. in 1867 the first school was built and Riverdale became part of Hyde Park township. The following year Dolton commissioned David Andrews, the pioneer resident of West Pullman, to survey and and plat the Riverdale area. In 1873, the first post office was opened and the name Riverdale came into general use for the community area, which had been called Dolton or Dolton Junction. The Riverdale settlement, which had a population of 635 in 1880, centered about the railroad station and post office on West 137th Street. When the Village of Hyde Park was annexed to Chicago in 1889, the present Riverdale community area came inside the city limits. Not long after this, the settlements to the south and southwest were incorporated as the suburban villages of Dolton and Riverdale, respectively.

The population of Riverdale became more mixed as Swedish and Irish groups moved into the area to work on the railroads and in the factories. A group of Russians of German descent (Volga Germans) settled north of the Calumet River between 133rd and 136th Streets. They had come to work at the sugar beet refinery.

Industrialization of the Calumet area forced agriculture to give way to industry. Riverdale's population, however, grew slowly. Remoteness from the heart of the city combined with its inadequate transit facilities made Riverdale unattractive to settlers. Those who did locate there worked mostly in steel manufacturing and processing in nearby communities.

The northern section of Riverdale had been the site of a brickyard and sewage farm for Pullman. This section came to be occupied largely by industrial plants. Some industry was located along the railroad tracks. A business section had developed along Indiana Avenue. The dredging and widening of the Little Calumet River by the sanitary district to make it navigable for barges and the building of the Calumet Sag Channel (1911-1922) was a further impetus to industrialization of the Calumet area during the first decades of the 20th century.

In 1920, Riverdale had a population of 1,207. It consisted largely of vacant acreage crossed by many railroad tracks. Residential settlement was confined to the southwestern corner of the community, between 133rd and 138th streets from Indiana Avenue and the city limits east to the Chicago and Western Indiana tracks. A large tract of land in the southeast corner was occupied by the Beaubien Forest Preserve. By 1940, there were 1,500 residents. The older frame housing began to deteriorate.

World War II stimulated growth in Riverdale. Increased industrial activity and expansion produced a demand for low-priced housing. Between 1943 and 1944, the Chicago Housing Authority constructed Altgeld Gardens on vacant land between 130th and 133rd streets from Langley Avenue to Greenwood Avenue. This low-cost housing project provided 1,500 apartments in 162 two-story row houses. Altgeld Gardens revolutionized life in Riverdale. It quadrupled the housing stock and brought rapid expansion and change in the composition of the population as blacks moved into the Altgeld apartments. By 1950 the community's population had increased to 9,790 and 84 percent of this total was black. In 1954, the Chicago Housing Authority completed the Philip Murray Homes, an extension of Altgeld Gardens. the Murray Homes provided 500 new dwelling units. Largely because of this the population grew to more than 11,000 in 1960, 90 percent of whom were black. Locating these housing projects in such a remote area required the construction of many other facilities — a Board of Health station, a public library, school facilities from a nursery school to Carver High School — that Riverdale had lacked.

The population of Riverdale continued to grow in the 1960s, topping 15,000 at the end of that period, despite the fact that several hundred whites moved out. In the most recent decade the number of residents dropped by 10 percent, about the same as the total drop in population of Chicago. Ninety-seven percent of current residents are black. Today, Riverdale has a higher concentration of subsidized housing than most Chicago neighborhoods. It is a poor comunity; 45 percent live in poverty and the median family income is among the 10 lowest of all Chicago community areas. About a fourth of all workers living in Riverdale are unemployed. There are many children — almost 40 percent are of middle-school years or younger, and almost two-thirds of families with children are headed by females.

The small stock of private housing includes many single-family frame homes and bungalows. About one-sixth of all units are owner-occupied and this has gone up in the last 30 years. Eden Greens, an 800-unit townhouse and apartment complex for low- and moderate-income families, is located at 130th Street and Indiana Avenue. The federally-financed project was the the nation's first and largest black-owned and operated development when it began in 1968. Riverdale still lacks urban facilities. Most residents shop in retail areas in West Pullman and Roseland. Roseland Community Hospital on 111th Street is the nearest major medical facility.

Annie Ruth Leslie

Community Area 54 — Riverdale
Population and Housing Characteristics, 1930-1980

	1980	1970	1960	1950	1940	1930
Total Population.......	13,539	15,018	11,448	9,790	1,509	1,486
% Male.................	43.2	45.7	46.7	47.0	49.8	52.4
% Female...............	56.8	54.3	53.3	53.0	50.2	47.6
% White................	2.6	5.0	9.8	15.8	99.6	100.0
% Black................	96.7	94.8	90.1	84.1	0.4	-
% Other Nonwhite Races...	0.7	0.2	0.1	0.1	-	0.0
% Under 5 Years Old......	11.7	12.8	20.1	16.4	8.4	10.5
% 5-19 Years Old.........	42.3	47.4	45.4	41.3	29.9	35.5
% 20-44 Years Old........	32.5	27.9	25.0	32.2	36.2	35.2
% 45-64 Years Old........	10.8	9.3	6.8	7.9	19.1	15.6
% 65 Years and Older.....	2.7	2.6	2.7	2.2	6.4	3.2
Median School Years....	12.1	10.7	10.1	9.0	7.9	*
Total Housing Units....	3,505	3,471	2,295	2,017	378	*
% In One-Unit Structures.	57.4	64.3	93.0	*	*	*
% Owner Occupied.........	16.5	26.6	11.2	14.1	44.4	*
% Renter Occupied........	80.4	70.7	87.9	85.2	53.7	*
% Vacant................	3.1	2.7	0.9	0.7	1.9	*
% 1+ Persons per Room....	25.3	33.0	48.2	43.3	*	*

Community Area 54 — Riverdale
Selected Characteristics of Census Tracts: 1980

Tract Number	Total	5401
Total Population.............	13539	13539
% Male.......................	43.2	43.2
% Black......................	96.7	96.7
% Other Nonwhite.............	0.7	0.7
% Of Spanish Origin..........	1.3	1.3
% Foreign Born...............	1.2	1.2
% Living In Group Quarters...	0.3	0.3
% 13 Years Old And Under.....	37.3	37.3
% 14-20 Years Old............	18.9	18.9
% 21-64 Years Old............	41.2	41.2
% 65-74 Years Old............	2.0	2.0
% 75 Years Old And Over......	0.7	0.7
% In Different House.........	34.0	34.0
% Families With Female Head..	65.1	65.1
Median School Years Completed..	12.1	12.1
Median Family Income, 1979......$$	9434	9434
% Income Below Poverty Level....	44.8	44.8
% Income Of $30,000 Or More.....	7.3	7.3
% White Collar Workers........	43.2	43.2
% Civilian Labor Force Unemployed.	25.3	25.3
% Riding To Work By Automobile..	63.1	63.1
Mean Commuting Time - Minutes...	44.1	44.1
Population Per Household..........	4.0	4.0
Total Housing Units..........	3505	3505
% Condominiums................	0.5	0.5
% Built 1970 Or Later.........	5.8	5.8
% Owner Occupied..............	16.5	16.5
% With 1+ Persons Per Room....	25.3	25.3
Median Value: Owner Units......$$	29300	29300
Median Rent: Rental Units......$$	96	96
Median Number Of Rooms: All Units.	4.6	4.6

Community Area 54 — Riverdale
Selected Characteristics of Census Tracts: 1970

Tract Number	TOTAL	5401
Total Population.............	15018	15018
% Male.......................	45.7	45.7
% Black......................	94.8	94.8
% Other Nonwhite.............	0.2	0.2
% Of Spanish Language........	1.0	1.0
% Foreign Born...............	0.5	0.5
% Living In Group Quarters...	0.3	0.3
% 13 Years Old And Under.....	43.4	43.4
% 14-20 Years Old............	18.6	18.6
% 21-64 Years Old............	35.4	35.4
% 65-74 Years Old............	1.8	1.8
% 75 Years Old And Over......	0.8	0.8
% In Different House.........	50.0	50.0
% Families With Female Head..	44.2	44.2
Median School Years Completed...	10.7	10.7
Median Family Income, 1969......$$	6273	6273
% Income Below Poverty Level....	37.8	37.8
% Income of $15,000 or More.....	5.6	5.6
% White Collar Workers........	12.1	12.1
% Civilian Labor Force Unemployed.	12.1	12.1
% Riding To Work By Automobile....	53.1	53.1
Population Per Household..........	4.4	4.4
Total Housing Units..........	3470	3470
% Condominiums & Cooperatives.....	10.7	10.7
% Built 1960 Or Later.............	33.1	33.1
% Owner Occupied..............	15.9	15.9
% With 1+ Persons Per Room......	33.8	33.8
Median Value: Owner Units......$$	17600	17600
Median Rent: Rental Units......$$	85	85
Median Number Of Rooms: All Units.	4.5	4.5

Community Area 55

Hegewisch

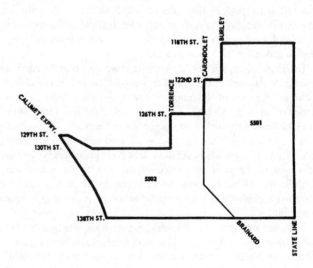

Hegewisch is Chicago's most southeastern community area, separated from neighboring areas by stretches of vacant and undeveloped land and by landfill. Originally the whole territory was an extensive marshland circumvented by the railroads built in the late 1840s and early 1850s. In 1867, the land became part of the Township of Hyde Park. Although the South Chicago and Calumet regions developed during the late 1860s and 1870s promoting the settlement of nearby areas and stimulating speculation in Hegewisch land tracts, no settlement occurred until the 1880s. New railroads cut through the area, industrial development took place at Calumet Harbor and along the Calumet River, and the industrial town of Pullman, founded in 1880 and 1881, gave rise to the town of Hegewisch.

A man named Adolph Hegewisch had hopes for an industrial community emulating the Pullman idea. Hegewisch became president of the United States Rolling Stock Company, then located 15 miles west, on Blue Island Ridge, in 1882. In 1883, the company bought 100 acres of land southwest of the current 135th Street and Brandon Avenue along the railroad tracks, upon which plants and shops were constructed in 1883. An additional 1,500 acres were purchased by a

syndicate representing Hegewisch, the company and other Chicago investors, to accommodate the envisioned workingmen's community as well as other foreseeable industrial enterprises. The business and residential units which were to make up the town were to be located north and northeast of the U.S. Rolling Stock Shops. Some of the land was subdivided and streets were laid out in 1883 and 1884. The Chicago and Western Indiana and Pennsylvania railroads opened Hegewisch stations. A small business center, surrounded by a few

Community Area 55 -- Hegewisch
Population and Housing Characteristics, 1930-1980

	1980	1970	1960	1950	1940	1930
Total Population.......	11,572	11,346	8,936	7,142	7,509	7,890
% Male..................	49.9	50.3	51.5	52.4	53.6	55.1
% Female................	50.1	49.7	48.5	47.6	46.4	44.9
% White.................	97.1	99.6	99.6	100.0	100.0	98.8
% Black.................	0.3	0.2	0.4	0.0	-	-
% Other Nonwhite Races...	2.6	0.2	0.0	0.0	-	1.2
% Under 5 Years Old......	4.8	9.5	11.3	10.5	8.9	9.0
% 5-19 Years Old.........	23.8	30.2	25.6	21.1	26.2	37.5
% 20-44 Years Old........	33.4	31.2	36.3	43.4	42.4	38.8
% 45-64 Years...........	26.8	32.1	19.3	19.0	19.8	12.8
% 65 Years and Older....	11.2	6.0	7.5	6.0	2.7	1.9
Median School Years....	12.1	10.8	8.9	8.6	7.5	*
Total Housing Units....	4,364	3,393	2,631	1,899	1,809	*
% In One-Unit Structures.	56.8	68.3	62.3	*	*	*
% Owner Occupied.........	73.2	72.5	66.9	54.4	43.3	*
% Renter Occupied........	21.4	25.2	29.9	44.8	53.4	*
% Vacant.................	5.4	2.3	3.2	0.8	3.3	*
% 1+ Persons per Room....	4.8	9.9	11.9	13.0	*	*

Community Area 55 -- Hegewisch
Selected Characteristics of Census Tracts: 1980

Tract Number	Total	5501	5502
Total Population.............	11572	7919	3653
% Male.......................	49.9	49.9	50.0
% Black......................	0.3	0.1	0.6
% Other Nonwhite.............	2.7	2.6	2.8
% Of Spanish Origin..........	6.2	5.0	8.8
% Foreign Born...............	8.3	10.1	4.4
% Living In Group Quarters...	0.0	0.1	0.0
% 13 Years Old And Under.....	17.1	16.8	17.7
% 14-20 Years Old............	13.5	11.5	17.9
% 21-64 Years Old............	58.2	58.8	56.9
% 65-74 Years Old............	8.1	9.3	5.5
% 75 Years Old And Over......	3.1	3.5	2.1
% In Different House.........	23.4	29.3	10.6
% Families With Female Head..	12.4	14.8	8.1
Median School Years Completed	12.1	11.9	12.3
Median Family Income, 1979..$$	25681	24313	28820
% Income Below Poverty Level....	4.1	5.3	1.6
% Income Of $30,000 Or More....	35.4	31.1	44.9
% White Collar Workers.........	43.6	41.6	47.4
% Civilian Labor Force Unemployed.	6.9	7.7	5.5
% Riding To Work By Automobile....	75.4	72.9	79.8
Mean Commuting Time - Minutes....	28.6	28.4	28.9
Population Per Household..........	2.8	2.6	3.3
Total Housing Units..........	4364	3240	1124
% Condominiums...............	0.0	0.0	0.0
% Built 1970 Or Later........	13.2	16.5	3.4
% Owner Occupied.............	73.1	67.7	88.7
% With 1+ Persons Per Room...$$	4.8	4.2	6.7
Median Value: Owner Units....	41600	38400	44600
Median Rent: Rental Units....$$	151	148	173
Median Number Of Rooms: All Units.	4.9	4.7	5.2

Community Area 55 -- Hegewisch
Selected Characteristics of Census Tracts: 1970

Tract Number	TOTAL	5501	5502
Total Population.............	11346	7133	4213
% Male.......................	50.3	50.8	49.5
% Black......................	0.2	0.1	0.3
% Other Nonwhite.............	0.2	0.2	0.3
% Of Spanish Language........	3.5	3.4	3.6
% Foreign Born...............	8.4	10.5	5.0
% Living In Group Quarters...	0.2	0.3	0.0
% 13 Years Old And Under.....	30.1	25.4	38.0
% 14-20 Years Old............	10.7	11.4	9.5
% 21-64 Years Old............	53.2	55.7	48.9
% 65-74 Years Old............	3.5	4.1	2.5
% 75 Years Old And Over......	2.5	3.4	1.0
% In Different House.........	72.4	67.4	81.1
% Families With Female Head..	8.1	9.1	6.2
Median School Years Completed	10.8	10.0	12.1
Median Family Income, 1969..$$	11433	11075	11927
% Income Below Poverty Level....	3.6	3.8	3.4
% Income Of $15,000 or More.....	22.2	21.1	24.4
% White Collar Workers.........	17.2	17.0	17.7
% Civilian Labor Force Unemployed.	2.8	3.2	2.0
% Riding To Work By Automobile....	64.0	60.6	70.6
Population Per Household..........	3.4	3.2	3.9
Total Housing Units..........	3395	2316	1079
% Condominiums & Cooperatives.....	0.0	0.0	0.0
% Built 1970 Or Later........	29.9	14.9	62.2
% Owner Occupied.............	72.4	63.9	90.6
% With 1+ Persons Per Room...	9.8	7.4	15.0
Median Value: Owner Units....$$	19100	17700	20500
Median Rent: Rental Units....$$	79	78	90
Median Number Of Rooms: All Units.	5.0	4.9	5.2

blocks of residential structures, was established across the railroad tracks and just north of the company plants.

Hegewisch became part of the city of Chicago when the Village of Hyde Park was annexed in 1889. The population of the area was far short of the 10,000 anticipated by 1885. At its emergence, Hegewisch was populated largely by foreign-born whites including Poles, Swedes, Yugoslavians, Czechoslovakians, and Irish. An industrial boom had been envisioned, but never took place, as proposed canals to Wolf Lake and from Wolf Lake to Lake Michigan were never built. These canals could have led to industrial expansion in the area, but industrialists preferred sites closer to the harbor and Lake Mighigan.

The residential section of Hegewisch grew slowly, gradually fanning out from the originally-settled area but still covering only a few blocks. Further industrial development occurred and more was anticipated when work began on the Calumet Sag Channel in 1911. The Channel had been intended as a drain for sewage but became a boom for commerce upon the Little Calumet and Grand Calumet Rivers, and stimulated industrial growth in the region. The inhabited section of Hegewisch was a small part of the extensive territory now included in the area, and few housing units were added between 1920 and 1950. The residential pattern established by 1920 was neither altered nor substantially expanded during the subsequent 30 years. In 1920, the population of Hegewisch was 47 percent foreign born, of which the largest group was Polish, with some Yugoslavians, Czechoslovakians, Greeks and Swedes.

The population of Hegewisch increased during the 1920s, and by 1930, 55 percent were of Polish stock. The population declined between 1930 and 1950 in spite of the war and postwar industrial boom

in the South Chicago and Calumet region and the postwar housing shortage. During this period, the distance of Hegewisch from the heart of the city and its industrial character probably counterbalanced its appealingly ample supply of residential land.

Population and housing growth began in Hegewisch during the 1950s and has yet to subside. In that decade, the number of housing units in the area increased by 39 percent, and the population by 25 percent. During the 1960s, the housing stock was increased by another 29 percent, to 3,395 units, and the population grew to over 11,000 for the first time. During the 1970s, nearly 1,000 new housing units (almost 29 percent of the 1970 total) were added, most of them single-family units. The population of Hegewisch reached an all-time high of 11,572 in 1980. In 1980, nearly 73 percent of all housing units in Hegewisch were single-family homes, and most of the rest were situated in buildings with fewer than nine units. Of Hegewisch's 4,127 households, more than 77 percent were located in owner-occupied housing units. The median value of single-family, owner-occupied homes in the area in 1980 was $41,607 less than the city median. Nearly 11 percent of the total population of Hegewisch lives in overcrowded housing units.

Hegewisch remained as of 1980 a virtually all-white enclave. some people of Spanish origin have moved in since 1960. In 1980, Hispanics comprised more than 6 percent of the area's total population. Hegwisch also has remained a predominantly blue-collar area. Many residents are municipal employees — policemen and firemen — and many are steelworkers, or labor in steel-related industries. More than a third of all families reported a 1979 income in excess of $30,000. Hegewisch residents have felt the recent and more general economic hard times.

Wisconsin Steel, just north of the area, closed down early in 1980. Other large steel firms and the Ford Motor Company, which operated an assembly plant at 126th Street and Torrence Avenue, have had to make either temporary or permanent layoffs of workers, and have shortened work weeks. There was a good deal of community activism during the 1970s directed towards staving off further landfill operations by both private operators and the city in Hegewisch, where many residents feel that the area already has more than its share of garbage dumps.

The major commercial strip of Hegewisch is along South Baltimore Avenue from 132nd to 134th streets, although many residents do their shopping at the River Oaks Shopping Center in Calumet City to the south, or in the East Side shopping area to the north. Federal funding was obtained through the City of Chicago Department of Planning for a Community Development Block Grant of $300,000, aimed at making the South Baltimore Avenue shopping area more attractive to potential consumers. This project was underway in September, 1981.

Will Hogan

Community Area 56

Garfield Ridge

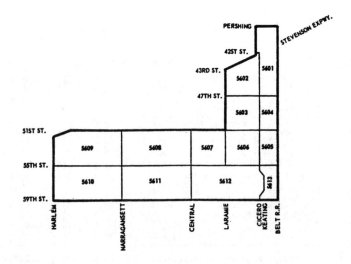

Garfield Ridge is an L-shaped community located on city's far southwest side. It is bounded on the north and west by the Chicago city limits, on the east by the Belt Railway. It is divided from the Clearing community on the south by 59th Street. As late as the 1920s, the area was known as "Archer Limits" because it was the end of the Archer Avenue streetcar line. The central location of Garfield Boulevard (55th Street), plus the fact that the western portion of the community lies on a beach ridge made during various stages of Lake Chicago, later gave rise to the name Garfield Ridge.

The Garfield Ridge community is one of the newer in Chicago, and the area is almost entirely situated on discrete parcels of land annexed to the city after 1900. Only a strip along the east side between Cicero Avenue and the belt line railroad date back to annexation of the Town of Lake in 1889. The land now occupied by Midway Airport was the old Village of Clearing, annexed in April, 1915. The western, central and northeastern residential areas are composed of three separate annexations from the Town of Stickney in 1915 and 1921.

Before 1900 much of the terrain was prairie or swampland, and only sparsely-populated by Dutch truck-farmers. Because of poor transportation to Chicago they transacted most of their business in Joliet. Eventually, roads were extended westward as Chicago's need for food supplies grew. Archer Avenue was extended in a southwestern diagonal reportedly because it followed a short-cut farmers took over real estate magnate "Long John" Wentworth's land. Sulky and running races were held along the road. There were neither stands nor stables and spectators stood on either side of the road. One such gathering spot located along 55th and Archer was known as the "turn o' the road".

The earliest-settled neighborhood in Garfield Ridge, later known as "Sleepy Hollow", was located between Cicero Avenue and the belt-line tracks from the Sanitary and Ship Canal to 47th Street. In 1911 the Bartlett Realty Company purchased over 600 acres of land and subdivided it for resale mostly to Germans, Poles, and Irish. The area, however, remained relatively undeveloped with few paved streets and no utilities. In 1920, the area population was 2,472. There was virtually no industrial development within the community but the need for homesites grew with the expansion of the nearby Clearing and Argo industrial sites to the south and west, respectively. In addition, the location of the Chicago and Alton and Santa Fe yards to the northeast contributed to the development of Garfield Ridge as a community of workingmen's homes.

In 1921, when a part of nearby Stickney Township was annexed to Chicago, a small retail area developed at Archer and Cicero Avenues. Lithuanians, Yugoslovians, and Czechoslovakians had moved into the area, but residential development remained slow. The Chicago Midway Airport was constructed on vacant school property between 55th

and 63rd streets from Cicero to Central avenues. Pre-1920 structures were usually inexpensive frame or brick cottages but most later dwellings were constructed with brick.

By 1930 the number of residents had more than doubled to 6,050. A significant number of Italians had moved into the area but the Poles maintained their dominant position among the foreign-born. They made up more than one-third of the population in 1940, followed by Czechoslovakians, Italians, Lithuanians, and Yugoslavians. World War II and the post-war years brought an expansion of the Clearing and Argo Industrial Districts and other adjacent areas. Several large plants were built in the northeastern sector and along the northern boundary between Narragansett and Harlem. This resulted in a residential boom for Garfield Ridge. The population grew between 1940 and 1950 from 6,813 to 12,900, and tripled in the next decade to 40,449. In 1960, approximately 40 percent of the population was foreign stock with Poles, Italians, and Czechs still the dominant ethnic groups. Many of the residents were employed in blue-collar occupations. The Clearing and Argo industrial sites and Alton and Santa Fe rail yards employed much of the community's labor force.

No blacks lived in Garfield Ridge until 1950, when the Chicago Housing Authority completed construction of 316-unit series of two-story apartment rowhouses in the northeastern sector known as LeClaire Courts. A 300-unit extension was added in 1954. In 1960 blacks were 6 percent of the population and confined exclusively to the housing project area. Between 1960 and 1970, the total population increased to 42,998, the historic high for the community. The 6 percent increase occurred while Chicago, overall, lost 5 percent of its population.

As the area became built up the number of housing units increased from 10,866 to 12,359. Approximately 15 percent of the 1970 total housing units were built after 1960. Eighty percent of all housing units were owner-occupied, compared to an overall Chicago rate of 34 percent.

Community Area 56 -- Garfield Park
Population and Housing Characteristics, 1930-1980

	1980	1970	1960	1950	1940	1930
Total Population.......	37,929	42,998	40,449	12,900	6,813	6,050
% Male.................	47.9	49.2	49.6	50.2	52.4	52.4
% Female...............	52.1	50.8	50.4	49.8	47.6	47.6
% White................	84.2	91.3	93.2	100.0	100.0	99.4
% Black................	13.5	8.2	6.6	0.0	0.0	-
% Other Nonwhite Races..	2.3	0.5	0.2	-	-	0.6
% Under 5 Years Old......	5.0	6.8	12.8	11.3	7.5	10.0
% 5-19 Years Old........	23.0	31.4	29.1	22.0	27.8	42.6
% 20-44 Years Old........	31.2	28.5	36.5	45.4	41.7	33.4
% 45-64 Years Old........	29.0	27.5	16.9	17.6	20.3	12.0
% 65 Years and Older....	11.8	5.8	4.7	3.7	2.7	2.0
Median School Years....	12.1	11.2	10.2	8.8	7.7	*
Total Housing Units....	12,748	12,361	10,866	3,545	1,664	*
% In One-Unit Structures.	83.4	82.8	83.4	*	*	*
% Owner Occupied.........	79.4	80.0	82.1	77.0	63.9	*
% Renter Occupied........	19.6	18.8	15.5	20.6	24.4	*
% Vacant................	0.1	1.2	2.4	2.4	2.7	*
% 1+ Persons per Room....	6.6	11.5	14.0	13.7	*	*

Community Area 56 -- Garfield Park
Selected Characteristics of Census Tracts: 1980

Tract Number	Total	5601	5602	5603	5604	5605	5606	5607	5608	5609	5610
Total Population.............	37935	1058	5107	3125	1338	694	1201	3154	5417	5664	5553
% Male.................	47.9	51.2	45.6	47.9	48.7	49.3	48.4	47.8	46.9	48.4	48.6
% Black................	13.5	4.4	98.4	0.2	0.2	2.2	0.0	0.1	0.1	0.0	0.1
% Other Nonwhite..........	2.3	24.9	0.4	3.1	7.2	6.1	7.4	2.2	1.4	0.5	1.0
% Of Spanish Origin........	4.1	25.3	1.1	9.6	11.9	7.2	4.8	4.1	3.2	2.0	2.1
% Foreign Born...........	8.1	21.3	0.8	9.6	16.3	11.1	6.5	12.6	10.0	5.2	8.2
% Living In Group Quarters.......	0.1	0.0	0.0	0.3	0.0	4.5	0.0	0.1	0.0	0.1	0.0
% 13 Years Old And Under........	16.6	19.8	31.7	16.3	19.1	14.7	13.1	14.1	13.2	13.9	13.7
% 14-20 Years Old........	13.3	12.7	22.8	14.3	11.7	12.2	10.4	10.5	10.8	12.1	11.4
% 21-64 Years Old............	58.4	56.3	43.8	59.2	59.9	61.2	64.6	63.0	61.0	60.2	59.3
% 65-74 Years Old............	8.8	8.3	1.2	7.8	7.5	8.4	8.4	9.4	10.9	10.5	11.7
% 75 Years Old And Over........	3.0	2.9	0.6	2.3	1.9	3.5	3.5	3.1	4.2	3.4	3.9
% In Different House.........	22.5	30.2	20.2	22.0	27.5	39.5	30.2	26.7	26.1	21.2	18.9
% Families With Female Head....	19.1	19.0	50.3	13.2	10.1	14.9	16.4	12.6	11.5	11.7	7.4
Median School Years Completed.....	12.1	12.2	12.0	12.1	11.8	10.7	12.1	12.1	12.1	12.2	12.1
Median Family Income, 1979......$$	24677	22614	15437	27109	26414	26406	23389	25159	24891	26626	25922
% Income Below Poverty Level....	5.7	7.9	32.5	3.9	3.5	13.1	2.4	1.9	2.1	1.1	2.9
% Income Of $30,000 Or More....	34.8	30.6	19.9	44.3	40.9	48.2	32.8	32.0	34.1	39.6	37.3
% White Collar Workers.....	49.9	60.7	44.4	48.6	43.2	45.8	49.4	48.6	50.5	52.6	52.3
% Civilian Labor Force Unemployed.	7.8	13.7	15.7	9.3	8.1	7.5	10.7	7.3	6.7	2.9	7.0
% Riding To Work By Automobile....	70.3	69.5	72.6	77.3	63.5	70.8	61.0	61.3	68.4	72.9	72.3
Mean Commuting Time - Minutes...	31.5	29.9	35.0	29.2	27.1	23.8	33.0	30.0	31.6	31.9	33.9
Population Per Household..........	3.0	3.2	4.4	3.2	3.3	2.8	2.4	2.7	2.7	2.9	2.8
Total Housing Units..........	12748	336	1162	960	406	240	516	1184	2042	1964	1973
% Condominiums.................	0.0	0.0	0.0	0.0	0.0	0.0	0.0	0.0	0.0	0.0	0.0
% Built 1970 Or Later..............	4.6	3.8	2.6	0.0	0.0	0.0	7.9	8.6	13.6	1.6	2.9
% Owner Occupied.............	79.4	66.7	42.0	94.9	97.3	65.8	49.2	68.6	75.0	91.6	89.3
% With 1+ Persons Per Room......	6.6	13.0	27.4	6.8	8.4	6.3	6.0	4.9	2.8	3.9	3.3
Median Value: Owner Units....$$	53200	45200	39400	48300	48400	45600	51300	49300	54000	56600	57400
Median Rent: Rental Units......$$	211	219	51	228	200	164	259	228	254	187	208
Median Number Of Rooms: All Units.	5.0	4.9	4.9	5.2	5.1	4.8	4.4	4.8	5.0	5.1	5.1

Tract Number	5611	5612	5613
Total Population.............	5618	0	6
% Male.................	48.9	-	-
% Black................	0.0	-	-
% Other Nonwhite.........	0.8	-	-
% Of Spanish Origin.........	2.5	-	-
% Foreign Born............	8.4	-	-
% Living In Group Quarters........	0.0	-	-
% 13 Years Old And Under.........	13.2	-	-
% 14-20 Years Old.............	12.2	-	-
% 21-64 Years Old.............	61.6	-	-
% 65-74 Years Old.............	9.8	-	-
% 75 Years Old And Over.........	3.2	-	-
% In Different House...........	17.7	-	-
% Families With Female Head.......	10.4	-	-
Median School Years Completed.....	12.2	-	-
Median Family Income, 1979......$$	24645	-	-
% Income Below Poverty Level....	2.4	-	-
% Income Of $30,000 Or More....	32.9	-	-
% White Collar Workers.........	48.9	-	-
% Civilian Labor Force Unemployed.	7.4	-	-
% Riding To Work By Automobile....	72.1	-	-
Mean Commuting Time - Minutes...	30.8	-	-
Population Per Household..........	2.9	-	-
Total Housing Units..........	1959	0	6
% Condominiums.................	0.0	-	-
% Built 1970 Or Later.............	1.7	-	-
% Owner Occupied.............	91.0	-	-
% With 1+ Persons Per Room......	4.2	-	-
Median Value: Owner Units....$$	56800	-	-
Median Rent: Rental Units......$$	204	-	-
Median Number Of Rooms: All Units.	5.0	-	-

Community Area 56 — Garfield Park
Selected Characteristics of Census Tracts: 1970

Tract Number	TOTAL	5601	5602	5603	5604	5605	5606	5607	5608	5609	5610
Total Population.............	42998	1204	5451	3576	1526	731	1301	3329	5885	6632	6475
% Male.......................	49.2	50.2	49.0	49.4	50.6	48.2	48.7	48.7	49.3	49.2	49.1
% Black......................	8.2	0.2	64.2	0.2	0.0	0.0	0.0	0.0	0.0	0.0	0.0
% Other Nonwhite.............	0.5	8.9	1.0	0.2	0.5	0.3	0.5	0.2	0.1	0.1	0.2
% Of Spanish Language........	2.3	2.2	5.7	1.7	9.0	2.7	1.7	0.4	1.8	1.1	0.6
% Foreign Born...............	7.2	22.8	2.4	6.7	5.5	14.0	8.9	10.2	6.2	5.7	8.8
% Living In Group Quarters...	0.1	0.0	0.3	0.2	0.0	0.0	0.0	0.3	0.0	0.3	0.0
% 13 Years Old And Under.....	25.5	24.0	42.0	26.0	27.7	22.6	19.8	22.1	22.2	23.4	21.0
% 14-20 Years Old............	14.1	13.2	17.6	14.8	13.1	10.8	12.1	12.5	13.6	14.0	13.3
% 21-64 Years Old............	54.5	56.0	38.5	54.1	55.8	57.2	61.4	58.5	57.2	56.1	57.9
% 65-74 Years Old............	3.6	4.3	1.0	3.5	2.3	5.7	4.8	3.6	4.4	4.0	5.0
% 75 Years Old And Over......	2.2	2.5	0.8	1.7	1.0	3.7	1.9	3.2	2.7	2.4	2.9
% In Different House.........	73.7	53.4	66.6	75.1	78.4	65.4	71.5	69.7	72.7	79.0	76.1
% Families With Female Head..	9.0	8.0	19.4	7.8	8.3	10.3	6.9	8.2	8.1	8.0	7.4
Median School Years Completed	11.2	11.0	11.1	11.1	11.4	9.5	10.9	10.0	10.7	11.7	11.5
Median Family Income, 1969...$$	12454	12028	9892	12825	13618	10027	13472	12406	12364	12745	12733
% Income Below Poverty Level.	4.3	4.4	14.5	2.3	0.0	6.1	3.6	2.7	3.6	3.1	3.1
% Income of $15,000 or More..	31.9	30.9	18.4	33.1	39.5	15.7	41.4	32.3	30.4	32.4	34.8
% White Collar Workers.......	17.0	16.9	15.1	18.6	12.1	15.5	19.8	12.3	17.6	21.1	19.7
% Civilian Labor Force Unemployed.	3.3	1.6	7.7	2.7	5.7	3.4	0.0	2.5	2.7	3.6	2.1
% Riding To Work By Automobile....	66.3	67.3	63.5	61.6	67.3	47.4	49.2	65.0	66.7	68.3	66.8
Population Per Household......	3.5	3.4	4.9	3.7	3.8	2.9	2.9	3.2	3.3	3.5	3.3
Total Housing Units.........	12359	363	1125	983	404	261	452	1067	1819	1931	2002
% Condominiums & Cooperatives	0.2	1.4	1.5	0.0	0.0	0.0	0.0	0.7	0.0	0.0	0.0
% Built 1960 Or Later........	14.6	33.1	8.5	9.8	10.6	21.1	28.9	24.6	14.4	11.1	10.6
% Owner Occupied.............	79.7	62.5	40.4	88.5	95.8	59.0	64.2	68.8	81.4	90.7	86.5
% With 1+ Persons Per Room...$$	12.2	12.4	38.8	13.7	13.2	8.0	5.6	9.7	8.9	9.4	7.3
Median Value: Owner Units...$$	22100	21700	19500	22000	22200	20700	22400	21200	21000	22600	22500
Median Rent: Rental Units....$$	111	142	66	140	161	102	146	127	126	103	113
Median Number Of Rooms: All Units.	4.9	4.7	4.8	5.1	5.0	4.6	4.6	4.7	5.0	5.0	4.9

Tract Number	5611
Total Population.............	6888
% Male.......................	49.3
% Black......................	0.0
% Other Nonwhite.............	0.1
% Of Spanish Language........	2.3
% Foreign Born...............	7.5
% Living In Group Quarters...	0.0
% 13 Years Old And Under.....	24.3
% 14-20 Years Old............	14.3
% 21-64 Years Old............	56.1
% 65-74 Years Old............	3.1
% 75 Years Old And Over......	2.1
% In Different House.........	77.4
% Families With Female Head..	7.6
Median School Years Completed	11.4
Median Family Income, 1969...$$	13230
% Income Below Poverty Level.	2.5
% Income of $15,000 or More..	36.5
% White Collar Workers.......	13.6
% Civilian Labor Force Unemployed.	3.4
% Riding To Work By Automobile....	73.8
Population Per Household......	3.6
Total Housing Units.........	1952
% Condominiums & Cooperatives	0.0
% Built 1960 Or Later........	16.2
% Owner Occupied.............	90.8
% With 1+ Persons Per Room...$$	10.3
Median Value: Owner Units...$$	23100
Median Rent: Rental Units....$$	124
Median Number Of Rooms: All Units.	5.0

The population of Garfield Ridge dropped to 37,935 in 1980. This loss (11.8 percent) is greater than that of the city as a whole during the decade. The black population increased by 46.4 percent to 5,116. They now comprise 13.5 percent of the population. Virtually all of the black residents of Garfield Ridge live in Census Tract 5602, in the vicinity of LeClaire Courts.

Garfield Ridge has remained a stable community of predominantly single-family, owner-occupied homes. More than half of the total number of housing units were constructed during the 1950s. Thirty percent were built before then and the remainder since 1960. Only 19 percent of all housing units are renter-occupied and a majority of these are located east of Central Avenue. Most dwellings are made of brick and ample front lawns face the sidewalks and streets. The median value of owner-occupied houses is $6,000 higher than the city median. The western section, by the city limits, has a suburban atmosphere. It is estimated that from 2,500 to 3,000 City of Chicago policemen and firemen live in Garfield Ridge.

Most of the affluent sections of Garfield Ridge, as measured by average housing value, are located west of Central Avenue. The least affluent sections are generally located east of Narragansett. In the eastern section, older buildings and two-story apartment houses are seen more frequently. Rail lines and small businesses encroach on residential areas.

The main commercial strip is Archer Avenue. It bisects the comunity on a diagonal from the northeast to southwest. Specialty shops, food and department stores, doctors' offices, restaurants, banks, and other commercial enterprises line both sides of the street. Another small retail area lies along Cicero Avenue between 47th and 55th streets and most other main streets are dotted with small businesses.

Midway Airport, once the world's busiest, lies in the southeastern part of the community and the businesses in the area immediately surrounding are aviation-related, such as flying schools, airline parts industries and motels. Industrial areas are located along the rail lines, or south of the Stevenson Expressway and the Sanitary and Ship Canal. Some industry exists south of Archer between Cicero and Laramie avenues and in pockets along 51st and 58th streets. There are few vacant parcels of land and no blighted areas.

Antoinette LoBosco

Archer Heights

The southwestern community of Archer Heights is bounded by the Stevenson Expressway on the north, the Belt Line Railroad on the south and west, and the Santa Fe Railroad on the east. The area was once known as the Archer Road district after Archer Avenue, which was named for Colonel William B. Archer, an Illinois and Michigan Canal commissioner. It was under the jurisdiction of the townships of Lake and Cicero until 1889 when the district was annexed to Chicago in two stages. The present name of Archer Heights is somewhat of a misnomer since neither hill nor high ground exist within the community area. The name was taken from a subdivision opened by a real estate company in 1912.

Pottawatomie Indians are believed to have passed through this territory In the early 19th century on their journeys between Lake Michigan and the Desplaines River. Otherwise, huge areas of undrained swampland effectively delayed settlement until well after the turn of the century. As in other southwestern communities, the railroads with attendant industries and real estate speculation eventually provided the impetus for an influx of factory workers to the area.

At one time Patrick Murphy owned much of the land in the southwestern section of the community but his heirs lost it in the early 1900s when they neglected to pay the real estate taxes. The Bartlett Realty Company acquired the land south of 47th Street and west of Pulaski Road when it was sold for back taxes and promptly subdivided it for resale. Land sales remained slow, however, as the marshy land was still undrained, had no water mains, electric lines, paved streets or shops. After 1912 many Polish families moved in, attracted by the large lots and their gardening potential. Other real estate companies soon began to develop the area and it experienced a small boom from 1912 to 1915, and again between 1920 and 1925. This precipitated the installation of public amenities. Most of the early structures were inexpensive frame cottages until after 1916 when brick homes became popular. Vacant lots owned by the railroads surrounded the small residential settlements.

Between 1920 and 1930 the population almost tripled from 2,863 to 8,120 reflective of the continued upgrading of the land for residential use. Poles have remained the dominant ethnic group, comprising over half of the total population since 1930, followed by Italians, Lithuanians, Czechoslovakians, and Russian Jews. Few blacks reside in Archer Heights and a very small but growing number of Spanish Americans have moved in.

Population growth between 1930 and 1950 was modest despite a substantial industrial expansion in the 1940s, brought on partly by the industrial development of neighboring communities and western suburbs during World War II and the post-war period. Several factors may have accounted for this. Railroads nearly ring the community and a significant amount of land was held in reserve for industrial growth. This probably deterred some potential buyers. The automobile had reduced the workers' dependence on proximity to their place of employment. The lack of good public transportation to the central city, coupled with the paucity of local shops detracted even further from its appeal as a residential community.

The last major growth occurred between 1950 and 1960 when the population rose from 8,675 to 10,584, primarily in the southwestern part of the community. Most of the homes built were one- and two-family brick dwellings. Residents were employed primarily in manufacturing occupations and as clerical workers.

The present population is less than 10,000, more than 95 percent of whom are whites of European descent. Almost 18 percent of current residents are foreign-born, the most common nationality being Polish. Sixteen percent are at least 65 years old. Archer Heights is a stable community despite a population loss of almost 13 percent between 1970 and 1980. Sixty-five percent of the homes were owner-occupied in 1980 compared to the Chicago average of 39 percent. More than two-thirds of the residents had lived in their homes at least five years. The current median value of owner-occupied homes is $46,646, which is close to the city median.

The development of a proposed major mail processing facility in the northwest part of the community was successfully opposed by a coalition of Archer Heights civic associations with the support of city administrators in 1978. Residents were afraid the proposed center would increase the traffic congestion, parking problems, noise and air pollution. In another expression of community unity, residents have been active in cleaning up the litter along the Stevenson Expressway Cicero exit ramp, which they consider a gateway into their community.

Much of the northern part of Archer Heights and the land adjacent to the railroads is still occupied by industry and rail yards. Transportation to the downtown area is still a major problem. Commercial businesses are located along Archer Avenue, Pulaski Road, and 47th Street, with scattered establishments along other main arteries. Older frame and newer brick bungalows are interspersed throughout Archer Heights but the main residential district is in the southern part. Here, block after block of quiet streets lined with brick bungalows and neat lawns can be found.

Antoinette LoBosco

Community Area 57 -- Archer Heights
Population and Housing Characteristics, 1930-1980

	1980	1970	1960	1950	1940	1930
Total Population.......	9,708	11,134	10,584	8,675	8,216	8,120
% Male...................	47.9	48.6	49.1	50.5	51.3	52.4
% Female.................	52.1	51.4	50.9	49.5	48.7	47.6
% White..................	97.5	99.7	100.0	99.9	100.0	99.4
% Black..................	0.1	0.0	0.0	0.1	0.0	0.1
% Other Nonwhite Races...	2.4	0.3	–	0.0	–	0.5
% Under 5 Years Old......	4.8	5.9	9.5	10.0	6.3	9.2
% 5-19 Years Old.........	17.0	23.8	23.0	18.1	25.4	40.5
% 20-44 Years Old........	31.9	29.1	36.3	45.5	45.3	37.5
% 45-64 Years Old........	31.1	31.2	20.8	21.4	21.1	11.6
% 65 Years and Older.....	15.2	10.0	10.4	5.0	1.9	1.2
Median School Years....	11.5	10.1	9.0	8.6	7.7	*
Total Housing Units....	3,786	3,869	3,309	2,467	2,044	*
% In One-Unit Structures.	47.5	45.8	49.3	*	*	*
% Owner Occupied.........	63.3	62.2	64.5	57.9	51.9	*
% Renter Occupied........	34.7	35.0	32.7	41.1	47.2	*
% Vacant.................	2.0	2.8	2.8	1.0	0.9	*
% 1+ Persons per Room....	4.0	6.2	8.7	14.5	*	*

Community Area 57 -- Archer Heights
Selected Characteristics of Census Tracts: 1980

Tract Number	Total	5701	5702	5703	5704	5705
Total Population.............	9708	896	1555	4260	1380	1617
% Male.......................	47.9	50.0	50.8	45.8	49.9	47.6
% Black......................	0.1	0.3	0.1	0.0	0.0	0.1
% Other Nonwhite.............	2.4	3.5	2.4	1.9	2.3	3.3
% Of Spanish Origin..........	3.6	4.4	2.4	2.9	5.0	5.3
% Foreign Born...............	17.8	18.0	13.6	20.7	18.7	13.5
% Living In Group Quarters...	0.1	0.0	0.0	0.1	0.3	0.0
% 13 Years Old And Under.....	13.2	11.4	14.3	12.8	9.9	16.7
% 14-20 Years Old............	10.5	11.6	10.5	9.2	10.7	13.0
% 21-64 Years Old............	61.2	61.4	62.3	60.7	65.3	57.6
% 65-74 Years Old............	10.6	11.8	8.6	11.6	10.2	9.8
% 75 Years Old And Over......	4.5	3.8	4.4	5.6	4.0	2.8
% In Different House.........	26.9	23.2	23.7	24.7	35.0	30.9
% Families With Female Head...	13.3	18.5	9.4	14.1	17.4	9.8
Median School Years Completed..	11.5	11.8	12.0	11.1	11.4	12.0
Median Family Income, 1979......$$	23230	20372	24537	23316	22530	27687
% Income Below Poverty Level....	4.8	3.0	0.0	6.6	5.5	4.8
% Income Of $30,000 Or More.....	32.0	18.1	30.2	33.6	27.5	41.5
% White Collar Workers..........	46.6	39.9	47.9	48.9	50.1	39.0
% Civilian Labor Force Unemployed.	6.0	4.7	4.6	6.0	6.9	7.1
% Riding To Work By Automobile....	63.8	60.7	69.8	60.4	62.7	70.1
Mean Commuting Time - Minutes...	29.6	28.4	27.9	29.6	32.2	29.2
Population Per Household.........	2.6	2.6	2.8	2.5	2.4	2.9
Total Housing Units..........	3786	352	566	1706	585	577
% Condominiums...............	0.0	0.0	0.0	0.0	0.0	0.0
% Built 1970 Or Later........	5.7	8.6	3.2	0.9	16.0	9.8
% Owner Occupied.............	63.3	60.2	78.3	64.8	44.3	65.2
% With 1+ Persons Per Room......	4.0	5.1	4.5	3.5	3.4	4.8
Median Value: Owner Units......$$	46600	43300	49700	46400	43400	47900
Median Rent: Rental Units.......$$	199	223	196	186	211	206
Median Number Of Rooms: All Units.	4.8	4.5	4.9	4.9	4.4	4.9

Community Area 57 -- Archer Heights
Selected Characteristics of Census Tracts: 1970

Tract Number	TOTAL	5701	5702	5703	5704	5705
Total Population.............	11134	1038	1714	5273	1525	1584
% Male.......................	48.6	48.5	49.6	48.4	48.4	48.6
% Black......................	0.0	0.0	0.1	0.0	0.0	0.0
% Other Nonwhite.............	0.3	0.7	0.1	0.2	0.7	0.6
% Of Spanish Language........	1.6	8.2	2.2	0.7	0.0	1.2
% Foreign Born...............	14.1	10.4	13.8	15.2	13.6	13.5
% Living In Group Quarters...	0.2	0.0	0.0	0.2	0.8	0.0
% 13 Years Old And Under.....	19.1	18.7	18.4	18.1	18.2	24.3
% 14-20 Years Old............	12.3	12.7	12.6	12.1	12.3	12.2
% 21-64 Years Old............	58.6	61.7	59.4	58.3	59.7	55.8
% 65-74 Years Old............	5.4	3.9	5.3	6.4	5.0	3.9
% 75 Years Old And Over......	4.6	3.1	4.4	5.1	4.8	3.8
% In Different House.........	68.2	60.5	76.4	69.1	65.9	61.9
% Families With Female Head...	11.3	11.5	8.9	11.9	13.9	9.4
Median School Years Completed..	10.1	10.3	10.0	10.1	10.3	10.4
Median Family Income, 1969......$$	12129	11942	12705	11868	12435	12180
% Income Below Poverty Level....	2.9	0.0	1.1	3.7	3.4	3.7
% Income of $15,000 or More.....	28.8	29.7	31.8	26.9	26.5	33.3
% White Collar Workers..........	17.4	18.5	15.3	17.0	23.3	14.3
% Civilian Labor Force Unemployed.	3.4	1.1	5.2	3.2	0.9	5.1
% Riding To Work By Automobile....	59.0	63.0	61.1	62.1	46.4	55.2
Population Per Household.........	3.0	3.0	3.1	2.9	2.8	3.1
Total Housing Units..........	3862	357	567	1865	561	512
% Condominiums & Cooperatives.....	0.3	0.0	0.0	0.6	0.0	0.0
% Built 1960 Or Later............	13.4	18.8	11.9	7.7	20.3	25.0
% Owner Occupied.................	61.9	59.4	77.8	60.6	48.8	64.8
% With 1+ Persons Per Room.......	7.4	8.6	6.7	7.0	6.7	9.3
Median Value: Owner Units.......$$	21000	20200	22000	20800	19800	21200
Median Rent: Rental Units....$$	103	141	102	99	107	99
Median Number Of Rooms: All Units.	4.6	4.3	4.7	4.7	4.3	4.8

Brighton Park

Brighton Park is one of Chicago's earlier-settled southwestern communities. It takes its name from a race track built by "Long John" Wentworth in the 1850s near Archer and Western avenues on the land that is today McKinley Park. Much of the area originally consisted of marsh and swampland, with clay holes and prairie, which were flooded during rainy seasons. Construction of the Illinois and Michigan Canal and Archer Avenue in the 1830s first drew attention to the land. In 1835 Henry Seymour purchased 80 acres north of Pershing Road between Kedzie and California Avenues for subdivision. It included scattered farms that grew hay, cabbage, and garden produce. A town named Brighton was established southeast of the original subdivision in 1840.

The Village of Brighton Park was incorporated in 1851 through the organizational efforts of John Caffery. His company built the Blue Island Plank Road (now Western Avenue) and acquired a 10- to 12-mile stretch of land adjacent to it, along with the area north of 35th Street between Western and California which was subdivided for resale. Early settlers were native-born American, German and Irish immigrants. In 1857 land north of Pershing Road was included in the Town of Cicero, that south of Pershing became part of the the Town of Lake. Brighton had become a livestock trading center, and a stockyard was built at the corner of Archer and Western Avenue. The plank Road was ideal for cattle runs into the city but was not used by drovers after completion of the Union Stockyards in 1865. In the 1860s the Northwestern Horse Nail Company built a factory in town, and the United States Brick Company established a brickyard, near Kedzie by the canal, which it abandoned after the depression of 1873. After the Civil War, the Laflin and Rand company built a blasting powder mill in Brighton. Residents demanded its removal, however, in 1886 after lightning struck one of the warehouses at 46th and Archer. The explosion overturned the house of a prominent citizen and damaged property for miles.

The expansion that followed the Chicago Fire brought the Brighton Cotton Mill, the Brighton Silver Smelting and Refining Company, and the Chicago and Alton Railroad roundhouses and freight yards into the community. Industrial expansion in and near the area attracted more German and Irish workmen. Farms were still scattered south of Pershing, west of California, and along the canal banks. A small community known as South Brighton developed west of Western Avenue between Pershing and 43rd streets.

In 1889 Brighton Park was annexed to Chicago, the area north of Pershing by resolution, and the remainder as part of the Town of Lake. Extensive real estate speculation followed. Building of the Sanfa Fe and other rail lines in the 1880s and 1890s further stimulated industrial development, which in turn required labor. Local improvements were accelerated by the West End Improvement Club. These included sidewalks, a sewer system for Western Avenue, the California Avenue bridge, elevation of road crossings, and the removal of Gypsy camps near 47th and Western. Streetcars along Archer, Kedzie and Western Avenues, and on 38th and 47th streets, soon connected the community to the downtown area.

In the 1890s French migrants from France, Canada, and Bourbonnais, Illinois settled between Western and California from 38th to Pershing Road. To the south, east, and north remained the settlements of German and Irish residents. East European Jews and West Side migrants briefly occupied the northwestern corner of the community, known as Corwith, after the large Crane Company plant there. Most homes were one- and two-story frame dwellings. Streets were still not paved and flooding was common.

Between 1900 and 1925 Brighton Park experienced great industrial and residential growth due to the growth of the Stockyards, neighbor-

ing manufacturing areas such as the Kenwood District, and industries in the community proper. One-story brick homes and small apartment houses began to predominate in this working-class community. Poles, Lithuanians, and Italians settled north of Pershing, German and Irish residents moved south or out of the community, Jews moved north to Lawndale. During World War I Mexicans moved into the area adjacent to the Santa Fe tracks and rented older frame homes or improvised with box cars. In 1930, 37 percent of the population was foreign-born with Poles predominating.

Residential maturity was reached before 1930 when the population peaked at 46,552. It has declined steadily since, by 3,000 to 4,000 per decade, perhaps correlated with the decline and eventual closing of the Stock Yard. Thearea lost almost 5,000 residents (13.5 percent) between 1970 and 1980. The population is now just under 31,000, about a third less than 50 years ago. Today, Brighton Park is predominantly white, with the highest proportion of Polish-descended residents of any community area in the city, It has a sizeable and growing Spanish-origin population (15 percent) residing primarily in the northwestern tract. Twenty-one percent of all current residents are foreign-born. Residents work chiefly in manufacturing. Most are employed in middle-level occupations, 25 percent as clerical workers, 20 percent as operatives, and 16 percent as craftsmen, foremen, and kindred workers. Major manufacturing districts remain all along the canal and rail lines, between Kedzie and the Santa Fe Railroad from Pershing Road south to 43rd Street. Railroads and industries occupy about a third of the land area of the community. The main retail business area has shifted from 38th Street in the early 1900s to Archer Avenue, which bisects the community on a diagonal. Most of the stores are east of Kedzie to about California Avenue.

Virtually all of the housing (95.6 percent) was built before 1940. This in part explains why some of the homes are in need of repair, especially in the older sections of Brighton Park. Thirty-seven percent of all residents reporting in 1980 had moved within the last five years. Two-family brick and frame dwellings predominate throughout the community. Their median value has consistently remained below citywide averages, and is today about $13,000 less than the city median. However, almost half the homes are owner-occupied. In 1979 residents of Brighton park were honored to receive Pope John Paul II at an outdoor Polish-language mass said at Five Holy Martyrs Church. The community was so proud to have hosted this visit that 43rd Street between Western and Kedzie Avenues has since been renamed Pope John II Drive. Still known for its ethnic diversity, Brighton Park is a stable community of lower middle- and working-class residents, whose declining numbers reflect the shrinking industrial base of Chicago.

Antoinette LoBosco

Community Area 58 -- Brighton Park
Population and Housing Characteristics, 1930-1980

	1980	1970	1960	1950	1940	1930
Total Population.......	30,770	35,618	38,019	41,345	45,030	46,552
% Male...................	47.9	48.3	49.8	50.7	51.5	52.0
% Female.................	52.1	51.7	50.2	49.3	48.5	48.0
% White..................	91.7	99.3	99.8	99.9	99.9	98.9
% Black..................	0.1	0.1	0.1	0.1	0.1	0.1
% Other Nonwhite Races...	8.2	0.6	0.1	0.0	0.0	1.0
% Under 5 years Old......	6.2	7.9	9.9	10.0	6.5	9.2
% 5-19 Years Old.........	19.6	23.2	22.5	19.0	24.7	34.9
% 20-44 Years Old........	33.2	30.0	35.4	44.3	44.4	41.5
% 45-64 Years Old........	25.8	28.3	21.9	20.9	21.4	12.5
% 65 Years and Older.....	15.2	10.6	10.3	5.8	3.0	1.9
Median School Years....	11.7	10.0	8.9	8.6	7.6	*
Total housing Units....	12,766	12,962	12,499	12,133	11,566	*
% In One-Unit Structures.	21.4	20.9	18.5	*	*	*
% Owner Occupied.........	46.5	45.2	45.3	43.9	39.8	*
% Renter Occupied........	49.0	50.9	51.8	55.1	58.8	*
% Vacant.................	4.5	3.9	2.9	1.0	1.4	*
% 1+ Persons per Room....	4.9	7.6	9.0	12.4	*	*

Community Area 58 -- Brighton Park
Selected Characteristics of Census Tracts: 1980

Tract Number	Total	5801	5802	5803	5804	5805	5806	5807	5808	5809	5811
Total Population.............	30770	2306	2859	2047	3177	7107	3594	3725	1256	4011	688
% Male........................	47.9	50.2	48.5	49.7	47.3	47.1	46.4	48.5	46.4	48.4	49.7
% Black.......................	0.1	0.0	0.0	0.0	0.0	0.1	0.0	0.0	0.2	0.0	0.0
% Other Nonwhite..............	8.2	11.4	15.0	34.1	2.9	5.3	5.5	4.4	7.1	4.5	4.2
% Of Spanish Origin...........	14.8	25.8	25.4	57.4	6.4	9.9	10.0	9.8	9.3	5.9	8.7
% Foreign Born................	20.6	12.7	15.5	31.7	18.9	19.7	19.4	26.5	22.5	22.2	11.9
% Living In Group Quarters....	0.5	0.0	0.0	0.0	0.0	0.5	0.0	0.0	1.2	2.9	0.0
% 13 Years Old And Under......	16.9	21.3	22.4	23.6	12.2	15.0	14.9	15.0	16.6	17.7	16.6
% 14-20 Years Old.............	10.6	13.5	13.6	14.4	8.2	10.0	9.0	10.5	10.9	9.6	9.6
% 21-64 Years Old.............	57.3	55.0	54.5	54.5	58.6	58.5	58.5	57.4	57.6	57.3	57.4
% 65-74 Years Old.............	10.5	7.3	6.9	5.4	14.6	11.5	11.5	11.7	10.8	10.4	12.1
% 75 Years Old And Over.......	4.7	2.9	2.7	2.1	6.4	6.1	6.1	5.4	4.0	5.0	4.4
% In Different House..........	37.3	46.5	38.8	36.8	25.9	32.8	34.8	34.1	43.8	52.7	33.3
% Families With Female Head...	20.0	20.8	21.3	13.8	13.8	19.9	21.0	22.6	25.9	21.5	20.3
Median School Years Completed.	11.7	11.6	11.8	9.1	11.5	11.6	12.1	12.1	12.2	11.3	11.7
Median Family Income, 1979......$$	20508	20518	20091	19213	22091	20474	20588	17755	21818	21134	18654
% Income Below Poverty Level....	8.0	7.9	12.5	12.1	5.8	7.5	6.2	8.6	12.4	7.3	0.0
% Income Of $30,000 Or More.....	23.8	35.9	29.7	18.2	26.0	23.8	24.6	19.0	18.8	20.7	19.3
% White Collar Workers..........	45.2	45.0	44.1	26.7	54.8	45.9	52.3	47.2	42.3	37.9	39.3
% Civilian Labor Force Unemployed.	7.7	5.1	10.8	8.7	8.6	5.9	7.6	9.3	7.6	7.9	7.5
% Riding To Work By Automobile....	61.2	66.3	70.8	67.3	57.0	56.9	58.6	64.4	59.2	61.2	63.0
Mean Commuting Time - Minutes...	28.5	27.4	23.9	25.3	32.0	29.6	28.4	28.5	30.9	27.3	30.9
Population Per Household..........	2.5	3.0	3.1	3.3	2.3	2.4	2.3	2.4	2.3	2.4	2.3
Total Housing Units..........	12766	805	960	655	1384	3065	1629	1659	566	1730	313
% Condominiums...............	0.0	0.0	0.0	0.0	0.0	0.0	0.0	0.0	0.0	0.0	0.0
% Built 1970 Or Later........	1.0	3.5	1.6	1.9	0.5	0.6	0.0	1.7	0.0	1.0	0.0
% Owner Occupied.............	46.5	47.5	51.0	56.5	56.4	41.5	43.5	48.0	41.3	44.4	42.8
% With 1+ Persons Per Room...	4.9	5.8	8.4	17.1	3.2	4.0	4.4	3.0	4.1	3.3	5.4
Median Value: Owner Units.......$$	34300	31200	31000	35400	42800	33800	32300	32300	29200	32900	31500
Median Rent: Rental Units........$$	153	155	153	137	180	152	152	149	141	152	140
Median Number Of Rooms: All Units.	4.5	5.2	5.2	4.7	4.7	4.4	4.5	4.6	4.2	4.3	4.2

Community Area 58 -- Brighton Park
Selected Characteristics of Census Tracts: 1970

Tract Number	TOTAL	5801	5802	5803	5804	5805	5806	5807	5808	5809	5811
Total Population.............	35618	2752	3085	2199	3575	8385	4038	4363	1562	4816	843
% Male........................	48.3	49.7	47.9	48.7	48.1	48.2	46.9	48.7	48.5	48.5	49.8
% Black.......................	0.1	0.0	0.0	0.0	0.0	0.1	0.0	0.2	0.0	0.4	0.0
% Other Nonwhite..............	0.6	0.4	1.8	0.8	0.5	0.5	0.4	0.5	0.1	0.5	0.4
% Of Spanish Language.........	6.5	7.6	9.3	44.3	5.5	3.9	1.9	1.9	4.5	1.3	0.0
% Foreign Born................	17.5	9.7	11.4	21.4	12.1	18.1	22.8	21.5	21.5	19.6	6.1
% Living In Group Quarters....	0.9	1.7	0.4	0.3	0.0	0.5	0.3	0.3	0.0	3.8	0.7
% 13 Years Old And Under......	21.4	28.4	25.2	29.8	16.5	19.5	18.8	19.2	20.3	22.8	20.5
% 14-20 Years Old.............	11.3	13.0	13.9	14.4	9.5	10.9	10.2	10.8	9.6	10.7	12.7
% 21-64 Years Old.............	56.7	50.6	52.6	49.7	62.2	58.3	58.4	57.7	60.3	55.4	58.5
% 65-74 Years Old.............	6.2	5.0	5.1	3.7	7.6	6.6	7.0	6.9	5.2	6.0	5.6
% 75 Years Old And Over.......	4.4	3.0	3.2	2.4	4.2	4.7	5.6	5.3	4.6	5.0	2.7
% In Different house..........	64.6	52.6	67.1	59.7	68.6	64.9	66.8	69.2	65.6	63.4	53.9
% Families With Female Head...	13.8	16.2	17.6	14.3	10.7	13.7	13.2	13.0	14.4	13.9	12.5
Median School Years Completed.	10.3	9.9	9.7	9.5	10.3	10.0	10.2	10.0	10.4	9.3	9.8
Median Family Income, 1969......$$	10626	10049	10976	11284	11107	10791	10370	10401	9538	10442	10133
% Income Below Poverty Level....	5.8	8.1	6.0	4.7	3.5	5.6	6.7	4.2	8.4	7.4	3.4
% Income of $15,000 or More.....	21.1	19.5	21.6	28.7	22.4	23.1	19.5	19.1	24.9	17.1	14.4
% White Collar Workers..........	14.3	14.4	13.3	8.2	16.4	13.7	17.3	16.4	10.2	13.3	12.5
% Civilian Labor Force Unemployed.	3.6	5.0	4.5	4.6	2.6	2.4	3.6	3.2	9.8	2.8	3.8
% Riding To Work By Automobile....	55.9	51.6	56.9	57.8	59.9	54.8	56.9	56.0	52.8	55.3	58.4
Population Per Household..........	2.8	3.3	3.3	3.6	2.7	2.7	2.7	2.8	2.7	2.7	2.8
Total Housing Units..........	12952	873	990	646	1373	3191	1560	1637	597	1763	322
% Condominiums & Cooperatives.....	0.4	0.6	0.0	0.0	0.4	0.4	0.3	0.3	0.0	0.7	0.0
% Built 1960 Or Later........	4.2	7.0	6.3	18.5	3.6	2.0	2.4	5.8	0.0	2.3	4.1
% Owner Occupied.............	44.8	43.5	50.3	51.4	52.1	39.8	43.4	48.8	42.9	42.3	41.6
% With 1+ Persons Per Room...	7.6	10.9	10.1	19.4	5.2	6.9	5.8	5.6	6.5	7.7	6.8
Median Value: Owner Units.......$$	16800	15100	15000	18500	19400	16500	17100	15400	14300	16600	15600
Median Rent: Rental Units........$$	81	83	77	68	97	80	84	81	76	79	82
Median Number Of Rooms: All Units.	4.4	5.2	4.9	4.7	4.6	4.3	4.4	4.6	4.2	4.3	4.1

McKinley Park

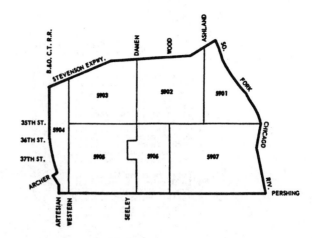

McKinley Park is a working-class community located about four miles southwest of the Loop. Some farmers, mostly New Englanders, came to the area in the early 1840s, finding only a few Irish squatters on the land. An earlier attempt had been made to settle in the area between Ashland and Damen avenues, in a town called Canalport. It was soon vacated. Interest was stimulated in the area with the completion of the Ilinois-Michigan Canal in 1848, and many of the Irish who had worked on it settled in the vicinity of Archer and Ashland avenues in what is now called Bridgeport. In the 1850s most of the area was still open prairie and swampland with a few scattered truck farms and cabbage patches. In 1840 a town called Brighton was laid out in the vicinity of Western Avenue and 35th Street, but it was not incorporated until 1851. It derived its name from the race track located at the site currently occupied by McKinley Park. It operated until 1866 after which the land was rented out as a cabbage farm. The completion of the Chicago and Alton Railroad in 1857 stimulated more interest in the area.

In 1863 the city limits were extended to Pershing Road on the south and Western Avenue on the west, bringing the present area of Mc-Kinley Park, with the exception of a small strip of land between Western and the Pennsylvania tracks, inside the city limits. This signaled the beginning of a period of rapid development. In 1865 a steel mill was constructed at Archer and Ashland Avenues. After the Civil War, the Union Stock Yards and other industries were developed to the southwest of the community. The meat packing industries attracted many workers, mainly German and Irish immigrants, into the community.

After the Fire in 1871 the area continued to develop. Within a few years 11 new plants had opened in the McKinley Park area, mostly foundries and steel mills, along with 27 new brickyards. However, there were still numerous difficulties to be overcome before the area could truly be considered suitable for residence. There were floods in the spring due to the lack of proper drainage. Consequently, many of the early frame houses were built on stilts to protect them from water damage. The uneven land was leveled out by dumping ashes and other refuse which for a while made McKinley Park a malodorous district. It also lacked good transportation.

The 1880s and 1890s were decades of rapid growth and prosperity. Transit facilities were improved as the car line on Archer was extended through the community and a new line on 35th Street was established. Many rows of brick houses and two-flats were built by large real estate companies. In the 1890s, with the construction of the Sanitary and Ship Canal north of the Illinois-Michigan Canal, the streets were packed down and sewers installed. A better residential area, Mt. Pleasant, developed in the triangle formed by 35th Street, Archer and Ashland avenues, where the population was mainly Irish.

The steel mill at Archer and Ashland failed in 1883 and remained closed for two years before it was bought by the Illinois Steel Company. It closed permanently in 1896 and many residents were forced to follow the mill to south Chicago or move elsewhere. This caused an economic crisis in the community marked by the closing of many shops.

Following years of demands by South Side residents for a park in the area, Dan Crilly, contractor, Philip Armour, packer, and Dave Shanahan, legislator, were the men responsible for the laying out of McKinley Park in 1901, shortly after the assassination of President McKinley. It was named in his honor and the surrounding community began to be called the same name.

In 1902 developers began to buy 260 acres of land on either side of the South Fork of the Chicago River between Ashland avenue and Morgan Street, 35th Street and Pershing Road. By 1908 all the land had been purchased and the Central Manufacturing District was formed. New industrial plants were built along the canal and the river, along Western Avenue and the Pennsylvania and Baltimore and Ohio tracks, and along Archer Avenue as well as in the Central Manufacturing District.

By 1920 McKinley Park had reached residential maturity, with 22,016 residents. There had been a turnover in the composition of the population with the southward migration of the Germans and Irish. Polish and Lithuanian immigrants began to establish themselves in the community. The number of residents remained the same in the 1920s but began to decline after 1930. By 1950 the McKinley Park area was comprised mostly of Poles and those of Polish descent. In 1960 its population was almost 100 percent white and, despite the increase in the black population of the city, in 1980 only five blacks lived in the community area. Among the whites, those of Polish, German and Irish descent were most numerous in 1980. However, the Hispanic population, concentrated on the eastern and western boundaries of the community, rose from 6 percent in 1970 to 16 percent in 1980, possibly due to the relatively low cost of housing available there. The median rent is in the neighborhood of $160. The median value of single-family homes is almost $20,000 below the city median.

Housing is fairly evenly distributed between owner-occupied and renter-occupied units, but there has been an overall decrease in the total number of occupied units since 1970. The median family income is just under $20,000. The total number of people living below the poverty level has risen from 7 percent in 1970 to 12 percent in 1980.

There has been a steady decrease in the population of McKinley Park, partly due to the gradual decline of activities at the stockyards. It has drropped from about 22,000 persons in 1920 to 13,000 in 1980. The population of those under 18 years of age has fallen by more than a fourth since 1970. One of the results of this was the closing of the Longfellow Elementary School in 1981. The commmunity is now served by two public and five parochial schools. There are also nine churches in the area. The McKinley Park Civic Association meets once a month to address local problems as well as sponsoring an annual Memorial Day parade.

Despite the decrease in the population a new grocery and drugstore was built at Western and Archer in 1982, also the site of a proposed rapid transit station for the city's planned southwest line. A new restaurant was also built at the corner of Archer and Damen.

The community's most prized property is its namesake, the 69-acre McKinley Park. The city recently completed a $2.5 million renovation and restocking of the park's lagoon, where area residents gather each autumn for a fishing tournament. Other activities sponsored by the park include a day camp for young children and one of the Park District's best gymnastics programs. The park is a favorite place for families to picnic on spring and summer weekends.

Vincent Parker

Community Area 59 --McKinley Park
Population and Housing Characteristics, 1930-1980

	1980	1970	1960	1950	1940	1930
Total Population.......	13,248	15,632	16,908	18,813	20,429	22,032
% Male..................	48.2	48.7	49.4	50.3	51.3	51.6
% Female................	51.8	51.3	50.6	49.7	48.7	48.4
% White.................	92.4	99.6	99.9	100.0	100.0	100.0
% Black.................	0.0	0.0	-	0.0	0.0	0.0
% Other Nonwhite Races...	7.6	0.4	0.1	0.0	0.0	0.0
% Under 5 Years Old......	7.3	8.3	10.1	9.8	7.2	8.9
% 5-19 Years Old.........	22.6	26.4	25.1	21.3	26.7	34.8
% 20-44 Years Old........	34.7	29.8	33.7	41.8	41.8	39.5
% 45-64 Years Old........	23.0	25.9	21.6	21.0	19.8	13.4
% 65 Years and Older.....	12.4	9.6	9.5	6.1	4.5	3.4
Median School Years....	11.6	10.0	8.8	8.6	7.8	*
Total Housing Units....	5,232	5,384	5,422	5,348	5,228	*
% In One-Unit Structures.	26.5	26.3	22.3	*	*	*
% Owner Occupied.........	45.4	43.6	43.6	43.7	38.7	*
% Renter Occupied........	47.6	51.4	52.3	54.8	59.3	*
% Vacant................	7.0	5.0	4.1	2.5	2.0	*
% 1+ Persons per Room....	5.0	8.4	9.8	13.2	*	*

Community Area 59 — McKinley Park
Selected Characteristics of Census Tracts: 1980

Tract Number	Total	5901	5902	5903	5904	5905	5906	5907
Total Population.............	13248	183	2592	2369	930	1581	3297	2296
% Male..................	48.2	49.7	48.3	48.5	48.1	48.3	47.5	49.0
% Black.................	0.0	0.0	0.1	0.0	0.0	0.1	0.0	0.0
% Other Nonwhite........	7.6	8.2	9.4	8.2	8.3	8.7	6.0	5.9
% Of Spanish Origin.....	16.1	49.2	16.9	16.7	19.2	22.0	10.7	14.3
% Foreign Born..........	9.7	4.1	9.9	9.2	6.8	11.6	8.6	11.7
% Living In Group Quarters..	0.1	0.0	0.5	0.0	0.0	0.0	0.0	0.0
% 13 Years Old And Under.....	20.1	27.9	20.9	21.6	24.3	18.4	19.9	16.9
% 14-20 Years Old...........	11.7	11.5	12.0	13.6	14.2	11.2	11.0	9.7
% 21-64 Years Old...........	55.8	50.3	55.3	54.5	52.7	57.2	56.0	58.1
% 65-74 Years Old...........	8.4	6.6	7.5	7.0	5.4	9.6	8.7	10.9
% 75 Years Old And Over.....	4.0	3.8	4.3	3.3	3.3	3.6	4.4	4.3
% In Different House.........	34.4	4.7	39.6	29.3	48.4	29.0	36.9	30.4
% Families With Female Head..	23.1	30.8	22.1	20.4	30.3	24.1	21.1	26.0
Median School Years Completed..	11.6	12.5	12.0	11.0	11.3	12.1	11.0	11.9
Median Family Income, 1979...$$	19989	20208	21151	18816	19152	22708	15698	22708
% Income Below Poverty Level....	9.2	15.2	14.0	6.5	11.3	1.8	12.2	5.7
% Income Of $30,000 Or More.....	23.0	26.1	26.0	24.6	17.0	25.4	19.5	23.3
% White Collar Workers..........	51.0	35.7	49.1	48.2	49.0	54.4	55.9	48.1
% Civilian Labor Force Unemployed.	8.0	12.5	8.2	6.7	13.0	6.6	7.2	8.8
% Riding To Work By Automobile..	58.9	87.5	56.8	57.8	51.1	60.4	64.0	55.2
Mean Commuting Time - Minutes...	26.9	11.8	26.1	27.6	26.8	28.2	27.1	26.7
Population Per Household..........	2.7	3.0	2.8	2.9	3.0	2.7	2.6	2.5
Total Housing Units..........	5232	65	994	905	346	648	1317	957
% Condominiums...............	0.0	0.0	0.0	0.0	0.0	0.0	0.0	0.0
% Built 1970 Or Later........	0.9	0.0	1.6	0.0	0.0	1.7	0.4	1.4
% Owner Occupied.............	45.4	49.2	50.5	53.6	35.8	38.1	43.8	42.7
% With 1+ Persons Per Room....	5.0	8.2	5.2	6.0	6.1	4.2	4.5	4.5
Median Value: Owner Units......$$	27900	-	30400	26200	-	31600	26800	25100
Median Rent: Rental Units......$$	144	148	142	156	160	159	137	130
Median Number Of Rooms: All Units.	4.9	5.1	5.0	5.0	5.2	5.1	4.6	4.7

Community Area 59 — McKinley Park
Selected Characteristics of Census Tracts: 1970

Tract Number	TOTAL	5901	5902	5903	5904	5905	5906	5907
Total Population.............	15632	170	3252	2695	1081	1834	3664	2936
% Male..................	48.7	50.0	48.9	49.3	50.2	47.3	48.6	48.4
% Black.................	0.0	0.0	0.0	0.0	0.0	0.0	0.0	0.1
% Other Nonwhite........	0.4	0.6	0.6	0.3	0.0	0.2	0.4	0.3
% Of Spanish Language...	6.2	29.9	6.5	5.2	9.9	4.8	7.7	3.0
% Foreign Born..........	8.2	16.7	8.5	7.3	12.4	5.5	9.5	6.6
% Living In Group Quarters...	0.7	0.0	0.6	0.0	0.6	0.4	0.1	2.3
% 13 Years Old And Under.....	23.9	24.1	25.7	25.6	31.5	21.9	22.2	20.8
% 14-20 Years Old...........	12.4	12.4	13.2	14.3	10.9	11.8	11.2	12.3
% 21-64 Years Old...........	54.1	50.0	51.9	50.5	48.2	56.4	56.1	58.5
% 65-74 Years Old...........	5.7	7.6	5.6	5.9	6.2	6.6	6.3	4.4
% 75 Years Old And Over.....	3.8	5.9	3.6	3.7	3.2	3.3	4.3	4.0
% In Different House.........	65.7	70.2	59.5	58.4	65.6	61.6	71.4	75.0
% Families With Female Head..	15.6	17.8	16.0	15.0	15.4	12.9	16.4	16.1
Median School Years Completed..	10.0	8.6	9.9	10.4	9.8	10.4	9.7	9.9
Median Family Income, 1969...$$	10662	8688	10656	11100	10878	9911	10649	10624
% Income Below Poverty Level....	7.8	8.9	7.3	9.3	9.4	2.0	8.2	9.3
% Income of $15,000 or More.....	22.1	23.1	24.3	23.0	26.0	17.3	20.3	23.2
% White Collar Workers..........	14.6	0.0	13.5	12.1	21.4	19.4	12.7	15.4
% Civilian Labor Force Unemployed.	3.7	0.0	4.7	5.0	0.8	3.6	2.9	3.8
% Riding To Work By Automobile....	53.0	52.9	49.3	52.1	61.5	51.1	56.0	51.3
Population Per Household.........	3.0	2.8	3.2	3.2	3.3	3.0	2.8	2.9
Total Housing Units..........	5381	61	1075	884	345	639	1348	1029
% Condominiums & Cooperatives.....	0.4	0.0	0.5	0.0	0.0	0.9	0.0	0.9
% Built 1960 Or Later........	3.9	0.0	4.1	6.9	5.2	7.4	0.8	2.6
% Owner Occupied.............	43.3	59.0	45.7	54.6	35.7	37.9	41.9	37.8
% With 1+ Persons Per Room....	8.5	1.7	11.1	10.4	9.8	8.1	6.7	6.8
Median Value: Owner Units......$$	13200	-	13600	12200	12400	15800	13700	12700
Median Rent: Rental Units......$$	75	66	71	80	86	89	74	67
Median Number Of Rooms: All Units.	4.7	5.1	4.9	5.0	5.2	4.9	4.4	4.4

Bridgeport

Bridgeport's early history goes back to the time before the Fort Dearborn massacre, when a farm owned by early settler Charles Lee stretched out on both sides of the Chicago River. The buildings were left abandoned for several years after an Indian attack. Later the converted structures plus some new ones served as a trading post in the area. The area around the river was marshy, turning into higher prairie and farmland around 35th Street, with swampy sites here and there. The first good farm road, known today as Archer Avenue, was constructed in 1831. In 1836 the State of Illinois gave the go-ahead for the construction of the Illinois-Michigan Canal, which was designed to connect the City of Chicago with the Mississippi River. Most of the early settlers, attracted by the job opportunities on the canal construction, were Irish or German immigrants. The bulk of settlements clustered in the northwest, on the old Lee Farm, called "Hardscrabble" by the local population. The Irish population provided the majority of workers, building their shanties and frame cottages along the South Branch of the river. The river exuded unpleasant odors from the blood of animals dumped into it by the various slaughterhouses located there. The area was mainly inhabited by low-income groups and acquired a bad reputation. Besides slaughterhouses and packing firms, a glue factory and rendering establishments had settled in the community.

The construction of the Illinois-Michigan Canal was temporarily halted when the panic of a depression struck in 1837. The population remained relatively small until 1842. With the recovery work resumed on the canal the area experienced an influx of workers, mainly Irish fleeing the potato famine in their country.

Bridgeport acquired its name through the fact that the heavily-laden barges going down the river had to unload at the location where a low bridge spanned the river near Ashland Avenue. This made the bridge area a port, in effect the head of navigation on the river. In 1848 the Illinois-Michigan Canal was completed and Bridgeport became a boomtown, attracting canal-related industries and business establishments to the area. The chief industry was meat-slaughtering which utilized the ready supply of water in the slaughtering process. The most famous stockyard, Brighton yards, was located on the corner of Archer and 39th Street. Other yards were distributed throughout the south side. A large steel mill was near Archer and Ashland avenues. The residential settlements grew mainly north of Archer Avenue. Along Archer Avenue, which ran parallel to the river and the canal, a tavern, stores and hotels sprang up to accommodate cattle drovers herding their animals to the city and to serve travelers from the Southwest.

The Irish continued to move into the area in large numbers through the 1850s, being the predominant ethnic group followed by Germans and native Americans. In the 1850s legendary pitched battles took place between the Irish and the Germans. In 1853 the City of Chicago incorporated the area east of Halsted Street and north of 31st Street into its boundaries. In 1863 the rest of the community was included as well.

In 1865 several yards consolidated in the Union Stock Yards and the independent packers moved to the south and west of the yards. Improved railroad facilities encouraged these changes, since both packers and stockyards depended to an increasing amount on the transportation provided. The cattle drives along Archer Avenue stopped, leaving the road as a major corridor for travelers to the Loop. The area north and east of the yards consisted of truck farms and prairie. By 1869 nine frame shacks had been built. Streets were not paved yet and there was no sewage system.

After the Fire in 1871 industry expanded towards Bridgeport, giving impetus to further development. Breweries, foundries, steel mills and brickyards clustered around the community. In the 1880s and 1890s internal transportation improved greatly. Horsecar lines ran down 26th

to Halsted and on 35th to the south fork of the river and establishments opened along the major throughfares. On 35th and Halsted streets a small shopping center developed. New railroad facilities and belt roads further encouraged the growth of business. While the Irish still dominated, Lithuanians, Czechoslovakians, Poles and Ukrainians started to move in. The neighborhood was dominated by one-story single-family brick houses, two-flats, frame dwellings and small multiple-family houses. At the end of the 19th century, an electric trolley system was introduced in the area, streets were paved and other public improvements made. In 1908 the Central Manufacturing District was opened, a 260-acre site between 35th and Pershing Road, Morgan Street and Ashland Avenue. The east portion of the center was located in Bridgeport. The area attracted a variety of industries and benefited from public improvements. Most business establishments settled along Archer Avenue and on Pershing Road east of Halsted.

In 1919 racial hostility surfaced when some of the members of the local street gangs (the Shields, the Dukies, the Hamburgers and the Hagen Colts, for example) took part in the riots. By 1920 the Irish and Germans had moved to communities such as Englewood and Chicago Lawn and they were replaced by the Poles, Lithuanians, and Italians. The Poles centered around 30th and Ashland Avenue. The population counted 60,443 with 36 percent foreign-born. In 1940 more Lithuanians moved in and became the predominant group, printing their newspaper "Vilnis" in the community. By 1950 the Lithuanians and those of Lithuanian descent constituted the major ethnic group in the area east of Halsted and north of 31st Street, while the Polish population lived west of Halsted and south of 33rd Street.

Since 1920 residential construction has stagnated. In the late 1930s most buildings were of the small-family type; 12 percent of the houses combined business and residential use. Most structures were in good condition, but 14 percent required repair or were unfit for use, and almost the whole area had been declared as near-blighted or blighted. In 1942 Bridgeport Homes was constructed on 31st and Lituanica Avenue, a public housing project with 141 dwelling units in 18 two-story row houses.

Between 1941 and 1948 more plants and industrial constructions were added to the Central Manufacturing District, around the South Fork of the river and Racine, and north of 31st and east of Halsted. Halsted and Archer Avenue remained major business streets.

The community of Bridgeport is located in the 11th ward and has been known for political activity and leadership since its early history. Four recent mayors of Chicago have come from the neighborhood. The first Bridgeport resident to be elected Mayor of Chicago was Edward Kelly in 1935, being followed by Martin Kennelly in 1947. Richard J. Daley, elected in 1955, won six mayoral victories and was replaced by Michael Bilandic after his death in 1977. The mayoral connection to

Community Area 60 -- Bridgeport
Population and Housing Characteristics, 1930-1980

	1980	1970	1960	1950	1940	1930
Total Population.......	30,923	35,167	41,560	46,070	49,109	53,553
% Male..................	48.5	48.2	49.8	50.5	51.6	52.0
% Female................	51.5	51.8	50.2	49.5	48.4	48.0
% White.................	88.7	98.6	99.7	100.0	100.0	99.1
% Black.................	0.1	0.1	0.2	0.0	0.0	0.0
% Other Nonwhite Races...	11.2	1.3	0.1	0.0	0.0	0.9
% Under 5 Years Old......	7.2	9.0	11.1	10.3	7.4	8.5
% 5-19 Years Old.........	23.4	27.6	26.0	22.1	25.6	34.4
% 20-44 Years Old........	35.5	30.0	33.3	41.2	41.4	38.7
% 45-64 Years Old........	22.2	24.1	20.2	19.8	21.0	15.1
% 65 Years and Older.....	11.7	9.3	9.4	6.6	4.6	3.3
Median School Years....	11.0	9.7	8.8	8.5	7.5	*
Total Housing Units....	12,281	12,308	12,314	13,469	13,616	*
% In One-Unit Structures.	19.8	18.0	21.7	*	*	*
% Owner Occupied.........	36.2	34.2	32.8	31.9	28.5	*
% Renter Occupied........	56.1	59.6	62.6	66.4	67.1	*
% Vacant.................	7.7	6.2	4.6	1.7	4.4	*
% 1+ Persons per Room....	6.3	9.5	11.3	12.6	*	*

Community Area 60 -- Bridgeport
Selected Characteristics of Census Tracts: 1980

Tract Number	Total	6001	6002	6003	6004	6005	6006	6007	6008	6009	6010
Total Population.............	30923	265	920	1810	4004	1300	2579	2223	4136	3900	2080
% Male........................	48.5	51.7	50.1	48.2	49.0	46.7	47.9	48.1	48.0	48.8	48.9
% Black.......................	0.1	0.0	0.0	0.0	0.1	0.0	0.2	0.0	0.0	0.1	0.0
% Other Nonwhite..............	11.2	10.9	25.2	13.7	10.4	15.8	7.0	10.3	9.4	16.1	13.7
% Of Spanish Origin...........	21.3	24.5	37.9	21.3	22.2	19.8	16.5	17.5	21.4	26.9	18.9
% Foreign Born................	14.5	26.7	25.6	14.2	23.5	14.3	12.9	11.2	13.7	15.1	14.7
% Living In Group Quarters....	0.2	0.0	0.0	0.0	0.0	1.7	0.0	1.3	0.2	0.2	0.0
% 13 Years Old And Under......	20.1	23.0	21.7	19.6	21.5	19.2	17.3	16.8	20.5	23.6	18.3
% 14-20 Years Old.............	12.3	15.1	13.6	14.9	11.8	11.1	13.6	12.9	9.4	13.2	13.1
% 21-64 Years Old.............	55.8	54.7	53.8	53.6	56.4	55.5	56.6	56.5	57.9	52.3	56.5
% 65-74 Years Old.............	8.2	6.0	6.8	7.7	7.0	10.7	9.0	10.3	8.7	7.2	8.4
% 75 Years Old And Over.......	3.5	1.1	4.0	4.3	3.2	3.5	3.6	3.5	3.5	3.8	3.7
% In Different House..........	36.8	51.6	28.4	35.0	41.0	33.5	39.9	34.4	39.4	37.9	49.1
% Families With Female Head...	23.8	31.0	22.7	19.4	18.3	18.8	24.1	21.9	23.7	39.1	22.8
Median School Years Completed.	11.0	10.2	10.7	11.1	10.6	10.6	10.8	10.6	11.2	10.3	12.0
Median Family Income, 1979.....$$	18999	16875	20170	17522	19029	20120	19173	25000	18319	13652	21767
% Income Below Poverty Level....	12.6	0.0	10.2	11.8	11.4	9.6	11.8	11.5	14.4	23.2	8.1
% Income Of $30,000 Or More.....	20.5	33.3	22.0	19.3	19.4	22.9	20.3	24.8	21.1	13.5	23.6
% White Collar Workers..........	47.3	47.6	38.9	50.3	41.2	52.0	54.2	48.0	44.2	43.2	45.0
% Civilian Labor Force Unemployed.	8.9	0.0	17.2	10.7	11.3	6.3	7.2	5.4	4.3	7.6	7.6
% Riding To Work By Automobile...	56.8	35.6	59.0	60.7	56.8	66.7	55.8	52.4	52.1	58.4	56.0
Mean Commuting Time - Minutes...	25.8	28.6	28.5	24.1	24.6	31.9	25.0	25.6	26.4	25.7	27.1
Population Per Household..........	2.7	2.8	3.1	2.9	2.8	2.6	2.6	2.6	2.5	2.7	2.7
Total Housing Units...........	12281	107	351	685	1504	518	1063	893	1802	1626	819
% Condominiums................	0.0	0.0	0.0	0.0	0.0	0.0	0.0	0.0	0.0	0.0	0.0
% Built 1970 Or Later.........	2.9	0.0	0.0	2.1	1.2	6.2	1.3	4.1	1.6	1.2	2.7
% Owner Occupied..............	36.2	20.6	25.9	34.7	33.1	48.8	43.0	45.7	34.2	25.1	33.5
% With 1+ Persons Per Room....	6.3	7.4	11.0	7.4	5.6	6.2	5.5	4.1	6.6	7.6	6.4
Median Value: Owner Units.......$$	29500			35300	33800	30600	26300	28500	29200	23100	35000
Median Rent: Rental Units....$$	135	155	147	128	139	128	126	126	130	126	141
Median Number Of Rooms: All Units.	4.8	4.9	5.0	5.0	4.8	4.8	5.0	4.9	4.4	4.3	5.0

Tract Number	6011	6012	6013	6014	6015	6016
Total Population.............	1532	1056	235	864	3503	516
% Male........................	48.0	48.0	47.7	51.0	48.4	49.8
% Black.......................	0.0	0.0	0.0	0.1	0.4	3.1
% Other Nonwhite..............	9.3	8.3	17.4	6.9	7.1	10.5
% Of Spanish Origin...........	22.7	14.2	20.9	27.0	17.4	20.7
% Foreign Born................	12.0	9.3	18.3	25.0	5.5	0.0
% Living In Group Quarters....	0.0	0.0	0.0	0.0	0.0	0.0
% 13 Years Old And Under......	21.9	16.7	18.7	20.0	19.6	23.4
% 14-20 Years Old.............	11.5	9.9	13.0	13.5	14.9
% 21-64 Years Old.............	56.0	60.5	54.9	56.4	54.9	55.4
% 65-74 Years Old.............	7.2	8.9	11.1	6.7	9.2	4.1
% 75 Years Old And Over.......	3.4	5.0	6.0	3.9	2.8	2.1
% In Different House..........	36.5	28.9	39.4	34.7	27.1	25.7
% Families With Female Head...	20.2	14.7	32.1	25.0	21.4	17.8
Median School Years Completed....	10.8	12.2	11.9	10.9	11.3	11.0
Median Family Income, 1979......$$	21268	19082	26161	12460	20506	20125
% Income Below Poverty Level....	7.7	8.1	14.0	13.8	10.1	16.8
% Income Of $30,000 Or More.....	15.6	21.8	7.0	12.8	26.2	32.8
% White Collar Workers..........	44.0	65.1	59.6	40.2	52.1	49.6
% Civilian Labor Force Unemployed.	14.1	7.0	10.0	18.6	12.2	8.4
% Riding To Work By Automobile....	65.4	68.0	18.8	47.1	56.8	69.6
Mean Commuting Time - Minutes...	24.9	24.3	33.5	24.5	24.5	23.9
Population Per Household..........	2.9	2.6	2.5	2.7	2.8	3.4
Total Housing Units...........	552	432	113	339	1321	156
% Condominiums................	0.0	0.0	0.0	0.0	0.0	0.0
% Built 1970 Or Later.........	4.7	2.8	13.2	0.8	6.8	17.4
% Owner Occupied..............	39.7	35.0	29.2	33.9	43.5	57.1
% With 1+ Persons Per Room....	7.6	4.7	1.1	6.9	5.4	6.7
Median Value: Owner Units.......$$	33300	-	-	31500	29700	27800
Median Rent: Rental Units....$$	152	143	152	144	138	138
Median Number Of Rooms: All Units.	5.1	5.1	5.0	4.4	5.2	5.6

Community Area 60 -- Bridgeport
Selected Characteristics of Census Tracts: 1970

Tract Number	TOTAL	6001	6002	6003	6004	6005	6006	6007	6008	6009	6010
Total Population	35167	383	1339	2139	4464	1593	3106	2555	4507	4495	2162
% Male	48.2	49.1	48.6	47.3	48.0	47.5	49.0	48.9	48.5	47.9	47.9
% Black	0.1	0.0	0.0	0.3	0.0	0.0	0.0	0.0	0.0	0.0	0.3
% Other Nonwhite	1.3	2.6	2.9	3.0	1.5	0.3	1.5	0.9	1.1	0.7	1.2
% Of Spanish Language	12.6	31.2	40.0	19.2	17.4	5.8	6.4	15.1	6.8	11.0	11.4
% Foreign Born	9.6	25.5	10.0	8.9	12.8	5.5	5.0	5.8	10.6	7.4	14.6
% Living In Group Quarters	0.3	2.1	0.9	0.0	0.1	0.9	0.2	0.2	0.0	0.7	0.4
% 13 Years Old And Under	26.0	30.3	36.4	29.0	27.0	24.7	22.5	22.8	24.3	26.5	23.6
% 14-20 Years Old	12.3	12.5	13.4	13.1	12.0	9.9	12.8	12.2	11.7	11.4	10.3
% 21-64 Years Old	52.5	50.4	45.3	49.3	53.0	55.3	54.8	54.8	54.1	51.1	54.4
% 65-74 Years Old	5.6	3.9	3.1	5.3	4.7	6.3	5.9	6.8	5.7	6.5	6.4
% 75 Years Old And Over	3.7	2.9	1.7	3.4	3.2	3.8	3.9	3.4	4.2	4.4	5.2
% In Different House	62.3	56.7	46.6	59.7	59.9	65.3	63.8	69.7	67.0	51.4	64.7
% Families With Female Head	15.8	9.5	12.5	15.2	15.5	16.7	14.6	14.4	16.5	21.4	12.9
Median School Years Completed	9.7	8.5	9.7	10.0	9.6	9.2	10.1	9.2	9.9	9.2	9.5
Median Family Income, 1969 $$	9823	8529	8854	10282	10078	10615	11325	10478	9637	9042	9813
% Income Below Poverty Level	9.9	7.9	15.3	6.6	13.1	5.7	4.4	9.4	6.5	11.7	11.8
% Income of $15,000 or More	18.0	8.9	9.5	18.8	22.6	14.7	25.5	18.6	17.3	11.7	11.9
% White Collar Workers	13.9	14.8	15.3	7.9	12.5	12.9	14.9	10.9	15.3	15.7	18.7
% Civilian Labor Force Unemployed	4.8	17.7	4.1	4.6	5.5	8.2	4.6	4.5	1.8	5.5	5.4
% Riding To Work By Automobile	49.7	55.3	52.2	48.7	50.7	41.4	55.3	53.7	45.8	48.0	43.0
Population Per Household	3.0	3.2	3.9	3.3	3.1	2.9	3.0	2.9	2.8	2.8	2.9
Total Housing Units	12312	120	358	679	1495	583	1116	934	1760	1683	783
% Condominiums & Cooperatives	0.3	0.0	0.0	0.0	0.5	0.0	0.0	1.0	0.4	0.0	0.0
% Built 1960 Or Later	1.5	0.0	2.7	0.7	2.0	0.7	0.4	0.7	2.3	1.0	0.5
% Owner Occupied	33.7	21.7	25.7	32.0	31.2	41.3	39.3	38.5	32.9	26.7	32.8
% With 1+ Persons Per Room	9.6	12.7	19.2	10.8	8.9	7.6	7.6	8.6	9.8	8.9	
Median Value: Owner Units $$	12400	–	–	–	13800	11600	11600	11900	13000	11600	14500
Median Rent: Rental Units $$	66	73	66	67	66	61	63	62	61	65	70
Median Number Of Rooms: All Units	4.6	4.9	5.0	5.0	4.7	4.6	4.7	4.7	4.4	4.3	4.8

Tract Number	6011	6012	6013	6014	6015	6016
Total Population	1706	973	359	993	3871	522
% Male	48.4	47.7	48.2	49.8	48.0	47.9
% Black	0.2	0.8	0.0	0.0	0.2	1.9
% Other Nonwhite	1.8	0.5	1.9	1.6	1.0	1.5
% Of Spanish Language	16.2	2.4	10.2	6.8	10.7	5.5
% Foreign Born	9.9	15.1	33.4	8.9	7.3	7.1
% Living In Group Quarters	0.0	0.0	0.0	0.0	0.6	0.0
% 13 Years Old And Under	28.8	18.9	22.8	29.7	25.9	36.2
% 14-20 Years Old	14.8	11.2	12.8	12.2	13.6	14.8
% 21-64 Years Old	48.0	56.6	54.9	51.4	52.2	45.0
% 65-74 Years Old	5.6	6.5	5.3	4.9	5.2	2.7
% 75 Years Old And Over	2.8	6.8	4.2	1.8	3.0	1.3
% In Different House	72.2	77.4	46.1	49.2	67.1	60.1
% Families With Female Head	12.4	17.8	15.5	17.1	15.1	13.6
Median School Years Completed	8.9	10.7	8.9	9.9	10.4	10.0
Median Family Income, 1969 $$	9061	9905	7206	8574	10119	8083
% Income Below Poverty Level	11.9	4.0	4.0	16.7	12.4	17.3
% Income of $15,000 or More	11.8	30.1	6.6	12.1	22.5	20.0
% White Collar Workers	5.1	17.5	21.0	20.5	13.4	22.5
% Civilian Labor Force Unemployed	5.9	0.0	0.0	6.2	3.7	12.6
% Riding To Work By Automobile	59.5	49.2	32.3	49.7	49.3	67.9
Population Per Household	3.4	2.8	3.0	3.0	3.2	4.2
Total Housing Units	550	381	123	340	1265	142
% Condominiums & Cooperatives	0.0	1.8	0.0	0.0	0.4	0.0
% Built 1960 Or Later	2.8	0.0	0.0	1.5	3.5	0.0
% Owner Occupied	33.6	29.9	24.4	33.5	41.6	37.3
% With 1+ Persons Per Room	13.6	6.3	10.1	10.6	9.9	20.3
Median Value: Owner Units $$	12900	–	–	–	12400	–
Median Rent: Rental Units $$	69	73	69	66	67	75
Median Number Of Rooms: All Units	4.8	4.9	4.9	4.3	5.1	5.6

the neighborhood helped to bring jobs to the local population. In 1970 13 percent of the employed worked at governmental jobs.

A reminder of racial hostilities exchanged during the open housing marches in the 1960s, an iron gate separating the prevalently-white Bridgeport community from the all-black Princeton-Root public housing project in Fuller Park, was finally taken down in 1982. Similar gates were targeted for dismantling in the same year.

Since 1920 the community has experienced a steady decrease in population, and there has been little new housing construction. The number of residents dropped by 42 percent from 53,553 in 1930 to 30,923 in 1980. The racial background of Bridgeport is mostly white, with a growing minority of Chinese, American Indians, blacks and others. Among the whites, those of Irish, Polish, Italian and German descent are most numerous. About one in eight Bridgeport families live in poverty, but about one in five families reported income in excess of $30,000 in 1979. In 1980 the median value of single-family housing was average for the South Side but below average for the city. The main economic activities are retail trade and manufacturing; clerical and blue-collar occupations are most prevalent in the local labor force.

Sibylle Allendorff

New City

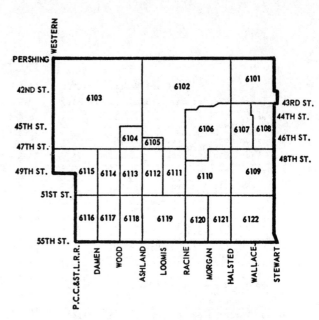

New City is in the old Town of Lake, whose name was derived from the ponds and rivers that dotted the marshlands, only a few feet above the level of Lake Michigan. The name New City referred to a more affluent residential section south of 47th Street, and was applied to the entire neighborhood in earlier editions of the *Fact Book,* although in recent decades it has been more generally called Back of the Yards.

In 1860, there were only a few scattered farms in the area. When the Town of Lake was incorporated in February, 1865, there were fewer than 700 inhabitants. The first post office was privately run, and until 1868 the police force consisted of three volunteers and the fire department consisted of four men and two houses. The first settlements of workers came in the 1870s when Phillip Armour allowed approximately 20 of his old hands to build cottages on company land at 43rd Street and Packers Avenue. The Hutchinson Packing Company erected seven houses for foremen two blocks south. Eventually factories displaced these communities.

The dominant institution in the area was the Union Stock Yards. Opened on Christmas Day, 1865, the yards replaced eight separate livestock centers dispersed around the city. The Union Stockyards and Transit Company purchased 320 acres of vacant land to the south of Pershing Road and west of Halsted Street and constructed the stockyards into which each of nine participating railroads extended a spur line. With the development of the refrigerated railroad car in the 1870s, mass commercial slaughtering became possible and factories bloomed in the western section of the Yards, the eastern portion being devoted to pens. Armour and Company opened its plant in 1867. By 1884, there were more than 30 large packing houses west of the Yards in the section which became known as Packingtown. A belt-line railroad was established to provide rail connections into the Yards for all the trunk railroad lines then coming into Chicago.

The Town of Lake was annexed to Chicago in 1889. Although there were as yet no paved streets, sewers, public utilities, or transportation facilities to the city, residential areas built up quickly during the 1870s and 1880s around the stockyards and Packingtown. The community was settled through necessity, the workers having to live in the vicinity of the plants because of the lack of transportation. The neighborhood was famous for its smell, noticeable for miles depending on the wind. This came from the amassed animals, the factories, particularly those engaged in fertilizer production and tanning, a city garbage dump at 47th Street and Damen Avenue, and an arm of the South Branch of the Chicago River, know as "Bubbly Creek." Packers used this to dump their sewage, and a thick scummy foam resulted. Housing was mostly wooden frame one-and-a-half- or two-story buildings. After 1905, Packingtown gained worldwide notoriety as the site of Upton Sinclair's novel, "The Jungle."

The orginal inhabitants were mostly Irish with some Germans, the latter from Prussia and the Rhineland. Bohemians began to arrive later in the 1870s and 1880s and the first Polish residents, the Zulawski family, settled in 1877. Large numbers of Poles did not appear, however, until after 1886, when the packers imported them as strikebreakers. Slovaks, Lithuanians, Ukrainians and Russians came en masse in the 1890s and early 1900s. With the influx of the new foreign-born groups, many of the older Irish and German families moved south of 49th Street and west of Halsted Street. There were some improvements in local transit facilities—a horsecar line on 47th Street to Ashland Avenue and the Stock Yards branch of the elevated. But the community still had only a few paved streets, and there were as yet no sewers and no electric lights.

During the first two decades of the 20th century, manufacturing areas appeared along the railroad tracks in the western, southern, and eastern portions of New City. The center of industrial activity was an area developed by the Central Manufacturing District. Its first venture, located north and east of the Yards, was so successful by 1915 that it began a second on the south side of Pershing Road between Ashland and Western avenues — the Pershing Road Development.

Activities in the stockyards required the construction of a bank, a hotel and other facilities for stock drovers. Next to the Yards itself, the most familiar feature of the neighborhood to non-residents has been the International Amphitheatre at 43rd and Halsted streets, built in 1900 to house the International Livestock Exposition. It was rebuilt after a fire in 1934, and was the site of Republican and Democratic national conventions in 1952, and the Democratic convention of 1968.

The population reached its peak, 92,659, in 1920. Thirty-seven percent were foreign-born. The sustained immigration of Poles made them the largest foreign-born group, followed by the Irish, Czechoslovakians, Germans, and and Lithuanians. The improved transit facilities of the early 1900s, the installation of sewers, the rehabilitation effort that followed government investigations, and a steady influx of new residents enabled New City to reach residential and industrial maturity by 1914.

The neighborhood was, and remains, heavily Roman Catholic. There are 14 Roman Catholic churches, plus a Polish National, a Byzantine and Ukrainian Catholic, a Methodist and a Lutheran church. In earlier years, there was another Lutheran church for Slovaks, a synagogue and a Russian Orthodox church. There is at present a Moslem center on Ashland Avenue. The Catholic churches tend to be huge structures, several seating 1,800 parishoners. Each became indentified with a specific ethnic group. Almost every church maintained a school and some enrollments reached 1,000. Many of the schools no longer function, but the churches remain the setting for much of the organized activity in the area.

Mary McDowell founded the University of Chicago Settlement House in 1894 and stayed until her death in 1936. The Settlement provided meeting halls, recreational and sports facilities, a day-care center and organized many clubs. Reaction among immigrants was mixed because of opposition from the church and political leaders. The greatest support for the Settlement came from Mexicans, who lived closest and found the neighborhood's warmest welcome there. The Back of the Yards Neighborhood Council was founded by Saul Alinsky and Joseph Meegan in 1939. The Council concentrates on conservation efforts, youth welfare and liaison with government agencies. In the 1950s and 1960s, it dominated the neighborhood; a home improvement drive started in 1953 resulted in 9,000 of 11,000 houses being improved or repaired within 10 years. Blacks moving into the community in the 1970s created the Organization for New City.

Community Area 61 -- New City
Population and Housing Characteristics, 1930-1980

	1980	1970	1960	1950	1940	1930
Total Population	55,860	60,817	67,428	75,917	80,725	87,103
% Male	49.7	48.7	49.7	50.5	51.1	52.4
% Female	50.3	51.3	50.3	49.5	48.9	47.6
% White	57.5	95.6	99.7	99.9	99.9	97.5
% Black	21.9	3.5	0.2	0.1	0.1	0.1
% Other Nonwhite Races	20.6	0.9	0.1	0.0	0.0	2.4
% Under 5 Years Old	11.1	9.7	11.6	10.5	7.8	9.2
% 5-19 Years Old	29.0	27.9	25.4	22.8	27.1	34.5
% 20-44 Years Old	35.1	30.2	34.5	41.7	41.3	39.9
% 45-64 Years Old	17.3	23.2	19.7	19.1	19.8	13.7
% 65 Years and Older	7.5	9.0	8.8	5.9	4.0	2.7
Median School Years	9.9	9.2	8.8	8.6	7.7	*
Total Housing Units	18,603	20,769	21,385	21,116	20,966	*
% In One-Unit Structures	18.1	16.8	14.1	*	*	*
% Owner Occupied	35.2	34.8	35.3	35.3	30.5	*
% Renter Occupied	56.2	58.1	60.1	63.3	66.9	*
% Vacant	8.6	7.1	4.6	1.4	2.6	*
% 1+ Persons per Room	13.9	11.2	12.8	16.5	*	*

Community Area 61 -- New City
Selected Characteristics of Census Tracts: 1980

Tract Number	Total	6101	6102	6103	6104	6105	6106	6107	6108	6109	6110
Total Population	55860	1220	772	4654	2460	183	231	2515	1939	1472	1700
% Male	49.7	49.1	52.7	51.5	54.1	48.6	49.8	51.1	49.3	50.0	48.4
% Black	21.9	6.1	0.0	0.1	0.4	2.2	0.0	1.0	0.2	20.5	62.0
% Other Nonwhite	20.6	5.6	32.9	40.8	47.0	33.9	33.3	4.8	1.6	8.3	18.2
% Of Spanish Origin	35.7	14.6	78.9	61.0	79.5	68.3	30.3	9.5	7.2	12.5	23.2
% Foreign Born	23.9	4.5	58.8	36.8	54.4	8.5	42.8	4.1	2.5	1.2	12.1
% Living In Group Quarters	0.4	0.0	0.0	0.0	0.0	13.7	0.0	3.1	0.2	0.1	0.0
% 13 Years Old And Under	28.2	26.6	25.0	27.1	30.8	21.3	28.1	24.1	26.1	29.4	34.2
% 14-20 Years Old	14.1	16.4	16.1	13.3	13.3	15.3	6.9	15.3	15.4	16.4	16.3
% 21-64 Years Old	50.2	49.3	49.6	51.9	50.7	57.4	49.8	52.6	50.4	46.9	45.2
% 65-74 Years Old	5.1	5.7	6.5	5.2	3.7	3.3	10.4	5.6	5.8	5.0	3.1
% 75 Years Old And Over	2.4	2.0	2.8	2.6	1.5	2.7	4.8	2.5	2.2	2.2	1.2
% In Different House	49.2	47.7	40.9	49.6	59.2	36.3	74.2	37.8	34.0	39.8	67.9
% Families With Female Head	29.3	21.8	23.1	20.0	17.2	25.0	29.6	27.0	18.4	31.0	43.5
Median School Years Completed	9.9	11.2	7.9	7.9	7.9	10.8	7.9	11.5	11.8	10.7	9.9
Median Family Income, 1979 $$	15427	14375	15982	16441	12576	21944	12206	18668	19427	15843	18160
% Income Below Poverty Level	21.9	33.6	14.5	17.6	34.0	6.8	12.5	19.5	14.6	19.9	32.8
% Income Of $30,000 Or More	15.5	9.4	26.9	18.9	7.1	27.3	0.0	19.7	20.5	12.0	9.7
% White Collar Workers	34.4	35.5	27.4	25.6	19.6	26.4	34.4	47.9	40.7	41.7	33.8
% Civilian Labor Force Unemployed	12.4	16.0	9.9	17.2	10.7	0.0	19.0	13.5	7.5	12.4	12.5
% Riding To Work By Automobile	61.4	63.7	44.6	64.4	49.3	67.8	37.5	64.8	69.9	64.9	58.2
Mean Commuting Time - Minutes	31.6	30.7	25.9	30.0	26.0	39.4	33.9	28.0	21.9	26.8	47.0
Population Per Household	3.3	3.4	3.4	3.1	3.7	3.7	3.2	3.3	3.3	3.5	3.7
Total Housing Units	18603	412	253	1667	719	53	89	785	619	442	527
% Condominiums	0.0	0.0	0.0	0.0	0.0	0.0	0.0	0.0	0.0	0.0	0.0
% Built 1970 Or Later	3.4	4.1	4.8	1.6	0.7	0.0	0.0	4.8	5.9	0.0	7.5
% Owner Occupied	35.2	44.2	28.5	23.8	18.6	32.1	55.1	44.7	50.7	41.4	32.1
% With 1+ Persons Per Room	13.9	9.9	20.1	14.9	23.7	14.3	11.8	6.5	9.3	11.6	18.6
Median Value: Owner Units $$	23600	24900	-	27500	-	-	-	26400	22600	20500	21600
Median Rent: Rental Units $$	136	131	116	127	129	113	150	136	131	138	143
Median Number Of Rooms: All Units	4.6	5.5	4.3	4.3	4.3	4.3	5.2	5.6	5.6	5.6	4.8

Tract Number	6111	6112	6113	6114	6115	6116	6117	6118	6119	6120	6121
Total Population	3935	3150	3142	3289	2372	2157	3585	3620	4791	3427	2719
% Male	51.6	52.3	49.7	49.8	47.3	48.7	48.7	48.8	50.0	47.7	46.5
% Black	0.6	0.0	0.1	0.0	0.1	4.7	4.4	15.8	36.0	93.2	92.8
% Other Nonwhite	37.5	25.5	19.3	12.6	11.3	26.1	26.8	21.7	26.9	3.6	3.4
% Of Spanish Origin	57.2	46.5	37.9	34.1	24.2	38.0	48.8	46.2	41.7	4.8	5.1
% Foreign Born	36.7	36.4	32.7	37.1	24.8	22.5	29.7	35.2	19.5	1.4	0.3
% Living In Group Quarters	0.0	1.3	2.1	0.0	0.0	0.0	0.4	0.0	0.0	0.0	10.8
% 13 Years Old And Under	29.7	24.5	21.8	23.7	19.8	24.5	29.1	28.9	31.7	34.0	33.7
% 14-20 Years Old	12.9	11.7	11.3	10.7	11.0	11.9	12.5	12.7	15.1	17.4	19.3
% 21-64 Years Old	50.5	54.3	55.3	55.9	55.1	53.1	50.6	51.2	47.2	45.1	43.8
% 65-74 Years Old	4.9	6.3	8.2	6.8	10.5	6.8	4.8	4.5	3.9	2.7	2.2
% 75 Years Old And Over	2.1	3.2	3.4	2.9	3.3	3.7	3.0	2.7	2.1	0.8	1.0
% In Different House	57.0	57.4	45.3	46.2	50.0	47.3	65.0	61.0	58.7	31.2	36.9
% Families With Female Head	18.5	21.5	23.2	21.0	24.2	19.6	23.9	24.1	32.7	51.5	54.4
Median School Years Completed	7.9	7.9	9.4	9.3	10.1	10.8	9.5	9.9	10.9	11.1	11.5
Median Family Income, 1979 $$	15547	16437	16667	17775	17500	19611	16380	16707	12215	8852	10040
% Income Below Poverty Level	21.3	13.1	11.9	14.2	8.7	7.6	21.5	19.3	23.6	43.0	43.3
% Income Of $30,000 Or More	13.2	14.1	17.2	18.5	12.6	27.3	17.2	12.5	16.4	10.0	17.4
% White Collar Workers	27.3	31.0	36.5	33.4	36.7	37.1	38.4	34.7	43.5	39.0	32.7
% Civilian Labor Force Unemployed	11.8	9.0	11.1	6.4	8.1	13.6	11.8	9.4	16.4	23.0	16.4
% Riding To Work By Automobile	68.7	53.9	54.5	66.4	65.1	65.4	68.5	63.8	53.6	59.0	55.3
Mean Commuting Time - Minutes	27.6	27.3	29.4	28.0	31.1	36.0	28.2	33.3	35.3	38.9	51.0
Population Per Household	3.2	2.9	2.8	2.8	2.6	3.0	3.2	3.3	3.4	4.0	3.9
Total Housing Units	1336	1158	1203	1263	976	768	1190	1193	1538	971	774
% Condominiums	0.0	0.0	0.0	0.0	0.0	0.0	0.0	0.0	0.0	0.0	0.0
% Built 1970 Or Later	4.5	0.9	3.0	2.3	1.0	1.8	1.8	1.3	0.4	0.0	8.0
% Owner Occupied	33.3	31.8	33.5	33.7	43.6	53.3	38.9	40.0	29.5	34.3	30.9
% With 1+ Persons Per Room	15.4	11.4	9.2	10.8	7.7	12.2	15.6	14.1	11.6	18.4	17.6
Median Value: Owner Units $$	19100	18400	22900	23000	24500	28400	23100	23600	23400	22900	26600
Median Rent: Rental Units $$	126	124	123	127	125	141	145	146	154	175	168
Median Number Of Rooms: All Units	4.4	4.4	4.3	4.2	4.3	4.6	4.5	4.7	4.8	5.5	5.3

Community Area 61 -- New City
Selected Characteristics of Census Tracts: 1980

	Tract Number	6122
Total Population.............		2527
% Male...........................		46.7
% Black..........................		97.2
% Other Nonwhite.................		1.7
% Of Spanish Origin..............		2.5
% Foreign Born...................		0.8
% Living In Group Quarters.......		0.5
% 13 Years Old And Under.........		34.6
% 14-20 Years Old................		20.2
% 21-64 Years Old................		41.5
% 65-74 Years Old................		2.8
% 75 Years Old And Over..........		0.9
% In Different House.............		25.3
% Families With Female Head......		60.7
Median School Years Completed....		10.3
Median Family Income, 1979......$$		9011
% Income Below Poverty Level.....		46.0
% Income Of $30,000 Or More......		8.3
% White Collar Workers...........		33.6
% Civilian Labor Force Unemployed.		10.5
% Riding To Work By Automobile....		63.9
Mean Commuting Time - Minutes....		44.4
Population Per Household..........		4.3
Total Housing Units..........		667
% Condominiums...................		0.0
% Built 1970 Or Later............		11.6
% Owner Occupied.................		35.5
% With 1+ Persons Per Room.......		19.9
Median Value: Owner Units.......$$		26800
Median Rent: Rental Units.....$$		169
Median Number Of Rooms: All Units.		5.6

Since its numerical high in 1920, the population of New City has declined in constant decrements of approximately 6,000 per decade. By 1940, the number of inhabitants had dropped to 80,725, by 1960 to 67,428, and by 1980 to 55,860. The latest figure marks a population decrease of 40 percent in 60 years. At present, the older European-descended population is aging and their children are leaving the area. To some extent, they have been replaced by Mexicans, the most recent wave of newcomers, who began to arrive during the First World War and after, when European immigration ended. These people came from the Central Highland region of Mexico. Their original settlement was north of 47th Street and east of Ashland Avenue. Persons of Polish and Mexican descent are now most numerous in the area. In 1980 almost 20,000 persons of Spanish origin lived there, 36 percent of the total population. New City was virtually an all-white neighborhood until 1960. In the decade that followed, 2,000 blacks moved in, and by 1980 the number of blacks exceeded 12,000, 22 percent of the area population. Blacks are presently concentrated east of Ashland Avenue, south of 51st Street, in an area adjacent to heavily-black Englewood.

There has been little housing construction in New City in the last half-century. The total number of units decreased by almost 3,000, 13

Community Area 61 -- New City
Selected Characteristics of Census Tracts: 1970

Tract Number	TOTAL	6101	6102	6103	6104	6105	6106	6107	6108	6109	6110
Total Population.............	60817	1790	853	5458	2390	309	308	3673	2333	1859	1754
% Male..........................	48.7	49.8	54.2	51.0	51.7	43.7	53.9	49.8	49.0	48.0	48.9
% Black.........................	3.5	10.9	0.0	0.2	0.0	0.0	0.0	0.1	0.3	1.9	0.0
% Other Nonwhite................	0.9	1.0	2.1	1.4	1.7	3.9	1.3	0.3	0.5	1.5	0.9
% Of Spanish Language...........	12.9	10.4	80.2	27.8	56.5	56.8	27.1	3.4	9.8	12.7	4.3
% Foreign Born..................	14.2	3.8	36.8	24.3	33.9	7.4	20.6	5.2	4.0	6.2	7.0
% Living In Group Quarters......	0.8	0.2	1.1	2.2	0.4	9.4	0.0	1.1	0.1	0.4	0.4
% 13 Years Old And Under........	27.1	36.4	31.7	29.2	30.7	24.6	27.6	32.1	33.9	34.3	26.2
% 14-20 Years Old...............	12.2	15.8	11.6	12.5	12.4	14.9	14.3	13.1	13.0	11.6	12.8
% 21-64 Years Old...............	51.8	42.8	49.6	52.0	50.0	52.4	51.0	46.4	46.9	46.2	52.5
% 65-74 Years Old...............	5.4	3.1	4.9	3.8	3.8	5.8	5.2	5.4	3.9	5.3	5.1
% 75 Years Old And Over.........	3.5	1.8	2.2	2.5	3.1	2.3	1.9	3.0	2.3	2.6	3.5
% In Different House............	58.6	54.6	54.2	57.2	53.1	83.9	51.0	53.9	61.7	51.3	59.5
% Families With Female Head.....	16.2	15.9	11.0	16.5	12.7	20.0	11.1	19.5	14.3	17.0	18.7
Median School Years Completed....	9.2	9.0	8.4	8.6	8.7	9.5	10.0	10.1	9.7	10.0	9.7
Median Family Income, 1969......$$	9808	8106	8737	9781	8919	9950	11000	10600	10352	10048	10341
% Income Below Poverty Level....	10.2	23.2	5.6	12.1	11.0	11.4	4.7	10.5	11.9	9.4	9.0
% Income of $15,000 or More.....	16.1	10.0	7.6	16.0	15.7	16.5	10.1	19.4	13.1	18.1	18.9
% White Collar Workers..........	12.6	14.3	6.0	13.1	14.1	0.0	21.8	11.1	13.3	15.7	8.7
% Civilian Labor Force Unemployed.	4.8	7.9	9.3	4.9	6.8	5.9	7.0	5.2	11.3	5.5	5.4
% Riding To Work By Automobile....	55.4	54.5	49.3	54.5	53.6	62.5	73.8	52.6	63.2	56.3	61.5
Population Per Household..........	3.1	4.1	3.4	3.3	3.4	3.4	3.5	3.4	3.7	3.7	3.1
Total Housing Units..........	20784	471	267	1733	765	90	97	1197	678	552	589
% Condominiums & Cooperatives.....	0.2	0.0	0.0	0.4	0.0	0.0	0.0	0.0	0.7	0.0	0.0
% Built 1960 Or Later............	1.8	9.0	0.0	1.1	0.0	0.0	0.0	1.9	2.9	2.8	0.7
% Owner Occupied.................	34.6	39.1	25.5	25.7	20.1	24.4	61.9	31.2	44.2	38.4	40.7
% With 1+ Persons Per Room.......	11.4	22.9	21.6	17.5	17.5	19.5	18.4	13.3	14.1	14.9	9.2
Median Value: Owner Units.......$$	12700	11200	-	12400	-	-	-	11800	11100	10800	11600
Median Rent: Rental Units.....$$	69	68	55	62	62	59	57	71	68	70	68
Median Number Of Rooms: All Units.	4.4	5.2	4.1	4.2	4.2	4.3	5.3	5.0	5.4	5.6	4.5

Tract Number	6111	6112	6113	6114	6115	6116	6117	6118	6119	6120	6121
Total Population.............	3963	3419	3405	3453	2612	2126	3429	3409	4424	3224	3379
% Male..........................	49.2	49.3	47.5	47.8	48.3	48.4	47.1	46.8	47.1	48.7	48.9
% Black.........................	0.0	0.0	0.0	0.0	0.0	0.0	0.0	0.0	0.0	4.9	4.8
% Other Nonwhite................	0.6	0.6	0.3	0.9	0.3	0.6	0.5	0.4	0.5	1.2	2.2
% Of Spanish Language...........	11.8	7.9	8.6	3.7	5.3	1.2	5.8	3.9	7.7	8.2	19.0
% Foreign Born..................	12.0	13.6	17.9	17.2	21.2	10.8	13.3	14.9	13.1	11.4	14.9
% Living In Group Quarters......	0.0	1.5	1.0	0.2	0.0	0.0	0.7	0.0	0.4	0.0	1.3
% 13 Years Old And Under........	25.9	22.5	21.2	23.0	22.3	23.3	23.1	22.1	23.1	25.4	27.7
% 14-20 Years Old...............	11.7	12.2	12.2	11.6	10.7	10.2	11.7	12.3	12.5	10.9	12.2
% 21-64 Years Old...............	54.6	55.3	55.6	56.4	58.1	56.0	53.2	54.1	52.7	52.9	49.9
% 65-74 Years Old...............	4.7	5.5	6.7	5.5	5.3	6.1	7.3	6.3	7.0	6.2	6.6
% 75 Years Old And Over.........	3.1	4.5	4.2	3.5	3.6	4.4	4.7	5.1	4.7	4.6	3.6
% In Different House............	63.3	59.8	57.2	58.1	59.2	72.0	61.2	61.7	61.2	60.3	50.6
% Families With Female Head.....	16.9	15.9	16.8	13.8	14.7	14.9	15.4	15.8	15.5	17.2	15.0
Median School Years Completed....	8.9	9.1	8.9	8.9	8.8	9.5	9.6	9.0	9.7	9.9	9.6
Median Family Income, 1969......$$	9150	9004	9493	10035	10202	9929	9261	10511	10402	10144	10246
% Income Below Poverty Level....	11.6	9.3	6.8	6.6	9.7	5.6	10.7	7.4	6.1	9.4	11.8
% Income of $15,000 or More.....	13.8	12.5	18.4	16.8	15.4	16.2	15.7	21.4	17.3	18.0	15.5
% White Collar Workers..........	9.5	13.8	13.4	10.9	11.3	17.3	16.5	14.3	11.1	14.8	12.8
% Civilian Labor Force Unemployed.	5.1	3.6	2.8	5.2	2.7	1.4	4.8	2.7	3.4	4.8	5.8
% Riding To Work By Automobile....	54.2	46.0	46.0	61.4	55.4	67.4	55.5	54.4	54.9	59.1	53.5
Population Per Household..........	3.0	2.8	2.8	2.9	2.9	2.9	2.8	2.9	2.9	3.0	3.3
Total Housing Units..........	1455	1299	1272	1276	980	748	1251	1225	1619	1129	1119
% Condominiums & Cooperatives.....	0.0	0.4	0.0	1.2	0.8	0.7	0.0	0.0	0.4	0.0	0.0
% Built 1960 Or Later............	1.9	0.3	2.9	2.7	2.6	1.9	2.0	1.3	1.3	1.8	0.4
% Owner Occupied.................	31.8	29.1	31.6	33.5	40.7	55.1	41.0	41.3	32.4	40.9	33.3
% With 1+ Persons Per Room.......	11.2	8.6	8.3	8.7	8.7	7.8	8.4	7.0	7.6	7.0	11.4
Median Value: Owner Units.......$$	11300	12000	12500	13800	15600	16700	14400	14400	13900	12400	12500
Median Rent: Rental Units.....$$	65	66	62	67	67	71	72	78	76	86	80
Median Number Of Rooms: All Units.	4.2	4.2	4.2	4.2	4.4	4.5	4.4	4.6	4.5	5.1	4.9

Community Area 61   -- New City
Selected Characteristics of Census Tracts: 1970

	Tract Number	6122
Total Population.............		3247
% Male...............................		47.2
% Black..............................		48.5
% Other Nonwhite....................		1.1
% Of Spanish Language...............		7.8
% Foreign Born......................		4.7
% Living In Group Quarters..........		1.5
% 13 Years Old And Under............		38.7
% 14-20 Years Old...................		13.4
% 21-64 Years Old...................		41.9
% 65-74 Years Old...................		3.8
% 75 Years Old And Over.............		2.2
% In Different House................		56.4
% Families With Female Head.........		23.8
Median School Years Completed......		11.3
Median Family Income, 1969......$$		9481
% Income Below Poverty Level.....		18.6
% Income of $15,000 or More.....		13.4
% White Collar Workers..............		8.0
% Civilian Labor Force Unemployed...		5.3
% Riding To Work By Automobile....		58.7
Population Per Household...........		4.0
Total Housing Units.........		972
% Condominiums & Cooperatives.....		0.0
% Built 1960 Or Later.............		1.5
% Owner Occupied..................		28.1
% With 1+ Persons Per Room.......		21.5
Median Value: Owner Units.......$$		12300
Median Rent: Rental Units.......$$		90
Median Number Of Rooms: All Units.		5.3

percent, between 1960 and 1980. Today, about 20 percent of all units are single-family dwellings. Of these, 38 percent are owner-occupied. The median value of owner-occupied units is slightly less than half the city median. As in 1960, the small apartment building (two- to nine-unit) is the most common form of housing, with more than three-fourths of all New City units being located in such buildings.

The biggest change in recent years was the closing of the Stock Yards in 1971. At its height, the Yards had employed 40,000, but payrolls declined steadily after 1920. Swift and Company ended hog dressing in 1952, the entire pork operation on April 29, 1957; Wilson and Company closed its Chicago plants in 1955. Through the Back of the Yards Council many workers found other employment and no mass exodus resulted. In the later 1970s the Yards area became an industrial park, the city assisting by improving services and facilities and with loan assurances. As a result, almost a dozen companies have relocated there. Most of this, however, is warehousing and other non-labor-intensive work, so it is not expected that it will draw many workers back to the area. Today, the unemployment rate is more than 12 percent, and more than one-fifth of the families in New City live in poverty. There is a major retail center around the intersection of 47th Street and Ashland Avenue.

Robert A. Slayton

Community Area 62

West Elsdon

West Elsdon is a quiet, almost entirely-residential community on Chicago's southwest side. As is true for other neighboring areas, its growth was tied to the railroads. The community became known as West Elsdon because of its proximity to the railroad town of Elsdon at 51st Street and Kedzie (now Gage Park). In 1865 the area became part of the newly-formed Town of Lake. It consisted mostly of vast stretches of prairie, swamp, and some farmland, with a few small frame shacks. Speculation that rail lines would be built along Central Park Avenue brought a real estate promotion in the 1870s. James A. Campbell subdivided the land for resale between 55th and 59th Street, Central Park and Pulaski Road, but residential construction was slow due to its general inaccessability and lack of improvements.

West Elsdon was annexed to Chicago as part of the Town of Lake in 1889. Area-wide speculation followed and lots were sold at inflated prices, until the Panic of 1893 when they dropped sharply. In 1894 only 38 residential structures existed in the entire community. They were mostly frame dwellings inhabited by Irish workers employed at the nearby car shops of the Grand Trunk Railroad. Some residents were truck farmers. Poles and Czechs settled in the southeastern sector in small numbers. Development of the Belt Railroad brought some industrial expansion. Passenger depots for suburban trains were opened by the Grand Trunk Railroad at 51st and 55th streets, but lack of sewers, paved streets, and other improvements kept growth to a minimum.

The availability of cheap land, World War I, and the development of neighboring Clearing, Central, and Kenwood industrial districts attracted more residents in the early 1900s. By 1916 a real estate subdivision called Lawnvue developed between 55th and 59th from the Trunk lines to Pulaski and population rose to 855 by 1920. One-fourth of the residents were foreign-born with Poles, Czechs, and Italians predominating.

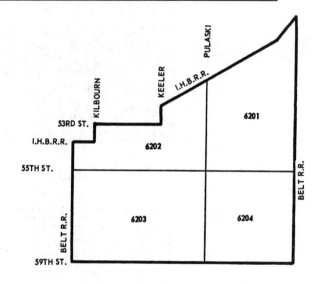

The Southwest Side building boom of the 1920s provided some new housing, mostly east of Pulaski Road. the population grew by 234 percent between 1920 and 1930. Poles were still the major ethnic group with settlements of Czechs, Yugoslavs, Lithuanians, Italians, and Irish. Residential construction after 1930 consisted primarily of single-family brick homes. The Depression slowed growth, but the population increased by 13 percent between 1930 and 1940 when more than 3,000 lived there. In those years West Elsdon still had a rural look. Many of the frame homes were built of second hand wood from the Elsdon car shops. Goats and cows grazed in pastures along 55th Street, as they had on the farms 50 years before.

A significant demand for housing was created by World War II and the postwar industrial boom of the Southwest Side, though there was no real industrial growth within the community proper. However, the residential community grew rapidly. Automobiles provided solutions to the problems of poor transporation and the lack of a major retail business center. The population more than doubled between 1940 and 1950 and increased again by 84 percent between 1950 and 1960, when it peaked at 14,000. About half of the residents were foreign-born. Since then the population has declined by 200 between 1960 and 1970,

Community Area 62 -- West Elsdon
Population and Housing Characteristics, 1930-1980

	1980	1970	1960	1950	1940	1930
Total Population.......	12,797	14,059	14,215	7,728	3,255	2,861
% Male..................	46.6	47.5	48.7	49.6	50.6	53.2
% Female................	53.4	52.5	51.3	50.4	49.4	46.8
% White.................	98.4	99.8	100.0	99.9	100.0	98.1
% Black.................	0.0	0.0	–	0.1	–	–
% Other Nonwhite Races..	1.6	0.2	0.0	0.0	–	1.9
% Under 5 Years Old.....	4.4	5.4	8.4	11.5	6.7	11.7
% 5-19 Years Old........	16.9	23.4	25.5	21.4	30.7	39.8
% 20-44 Years Old.......	29.5	26.8	34.9	45.9	41.4	36.0
% 45-64 Years Old.......	31.2	34.1	24.0	18.1	18.7	10.8
% 65 Years and Older....	18.0	10.2	7.2	3.1	2.5	1.7
Median School Years....	12.1	10.6	9.7	8.9	7.7	*
Total Housing Units....	4,910	4,626	4,177	2,117	739	*
% In One-Unit Structures.	72.1	74.7	80.8	*	*	*
% Owner Occupied........	79.7	80.4	84.2	80.7	59.7	*
% Renter Occupied.......	19.3	18.2	14.1	16.7	38.8	*
% Vacant................	1.0	1.4	1.7	3.6	1.5	*
% 1+ Persons per Room....	2.9	6.6	8.3	12.1	*	*

Community Area 62 -- West Elsdon
Selected Characteristics of Census Tracts: 1980

Tract Number	Total	6201	6202	6203	6204
Total Population..............	12797	2907	1773	4952	3165
% Male.........................	46.6	48.6	46.0	45.8	46.6
% Black........................	0.1	0.1	0.2	0.0	0.0
% Other Nonwhite...............	1.6	1.9	1.7	1.1	2.1
% Of Spanish Origin............	2.3	3.1	2.4	1.6	2.7
% Foreign Born.................	11.9	11.4	14.0	9.3	15.4
% Living In Group Quarters.....	0.3	0.0	0.0	0.7	0.0
% 13 Years Old And Under.......	12.6	13.6	12.5	11.9	12.7
% 14-20 Years Old..............	10.3	11.7	10.2	9.4	10.4
% 21-64 Years Old..............	59.2	59.6	61.7	60.0	56.0
% 65-74 Years Old..............	12.7	10.6	11.3	13.4	14.4
% 75 Years Old And Over........	5.3	4.5	4.3	5.3	6.4
% In Different House...........	30.4	26.9	35.4	27.4	35.7
% Families With Female Head....	13.8	10.6	15.8	15.1	14.2
Median School Years Completed....	12.1	12.1	10.8	12.2	11.4
Median Family Income, 1979......$$	23560	23438	25962	25175	20922
% Income Below Poverty Level....	3.7	4.3	1.1	4.5	3.4
% Income Of $30,000 Or More.....	32.1	34.9	39.0	32.7	24.2
% White Collar Workers.........	49.3	47.1	45.5	55.4	43.2
% Civilian Labor Force Unemployed.	5.1	4.6	11.0	2.0	7.1
% Riding To Work By Automobile....	72.5	64.1	70.9	77.0	74.0
Mean Commuting Time – Minutes...	29.8	31.7	30.6	27.7	31.3
Population Per Household..........	2.6	2.8	2.6	2.5	2.6
Total Housing Units..........	4910	1046	678	1952	1234
% Condominiums.................	2.5	0.0	0.0	6.4	0.0
% Built 1970 Or Later..........	7.9	5.6	7.0	11.6	4.6
% Owner Occupied...............	79.7	91.1	65.0	78.2	80.4
% With 1+ Persons Per Room.....	2.9	3.7	3.1	2.5	2.7
Median Value: Owner Units......$$	48200	47700	53800	48200	47200
Median Rent: Rental Units.....$$	229	199	249	238	188
Median Number Of Rooms: All Units.	4.9	5.0	4.8	4.8	4.9

Community Area 62 -- West Elsdon
Selected Characteristics of Census Tracts: 1970

Tract Number	TOTAL	6201	6202	6203	6204
Total Population.............	14059	3192	1822	5418	3627
% Male.........................	47.5	48.2	47.5	47.0	47.7
% Black........................	0.0	0.0	0.0	0.0	0.1
% Other Nonwhite...............	0.2	0.2	0.1	0.1	0.6
% Of Spanish Language..........	2.0	1.0	4.4	1.5	2.5
% Foreign Born.................	11.3	11.5	13.8	9.4	12.5
% Living In Group Quarters.....	0.4	0.0	0.0	1.2	0.0
% 13 Years Old And Under........	18.6	21.9	18.9	17.2	17.8
% 14-20 Years Old..............	11.7	11.2	11.6	12.3	11.3
% 21-64 Years Old..............	59.5	57.6	60.8	60.4	59.1
% 65-74 Years Old..............	6.8	6.3	5.8	6.7	7.8
% 75 Years Old And Over........	3.4	3.0	2.9	3.5	4.1
% In Different House...........	73.4	76.4	62.5	75.9	72.7
% Families With Female Head.....	10.6	9.6	9.8	11.1	10.9
Median School Years Completed...	10.6	10.7	10.4	10.7	10.4
Median Family Income, 1969......$$	12089	12656	12383	11862	11734
% Income Below Poverty Level....	3.1	2.3	0.0	3.2	5.2
% Income of $15,000 or More.....	31.8	29.7	34.1	30.6	34.1
% White Collar Workers.........	19.6	15.9	19.1	23.3	17.5
% Civilian Labor Force Unemployed.	3.9	4.1	5.1	3.2	4.0
% Riding To Work By Automobile....	67.9	70.1	59.4	70.3	67.1
Population Per Household..........	3.1	3.2	3.0	3.1	3.0
Total Housing Units..........	4631	1006	604	1774	1247
% Condominiums & Cooperatives.....	0.2	0.0	0.0	0.6	0.0
% Built 1960 Or Later..........	13.8	13.5	33.8	9.2	11.2
% Owner Occupied...............	80.2	93.2	66.2	78.5	79.0
% With 1+ Persons Per Room......	6.8	8.4	7.7	6.8	5.2
Median Value: Owner Units......$$	21500	21200	22600	21000	22000
Median Rent: Rental Units......$$	127	92	147	136	106
Median Number Of Rooms: All Units.	4.8	5.0	4.8	4.8	4.8

and by more than a thousand in the most recent decade. A very small number of residents are of Spanish origin and only seven blacks reside in the area. The population of West Elsdon is aging. A fairly large proportion of residents (18 percent) are 65 years of age or older, compared to the citywide average of 11 percent. The median age, 44 years, is well above the Chicago median of 29.

Light manufacturing is found along the tracks. Pulaski Road is the main business strip but there is major retail shopping center in the community. The housing is relatively new, with about 60 percent of all units having been built since 1950. Eighty percent of all housing units are owner-occupied, more than twice the citywide average. The median value of homes is $48,237, which is higher than several surrounding communities.

The number of clerical workers has grown over the years, while the number of operatives and craftsmen has declined. This reflects the national trend in most large urban areas.

Antoinette LoBosco

Gage Park

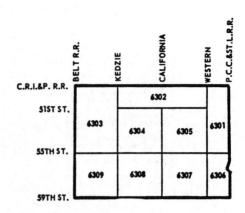

At one time most of southwest Chicago was prairie and swampland inhabited by isolated settlements of immigrants. The first residents of present-day Gage Park were German farmers who arrived in the 1840s and 1850s. The Gages were early property owners. George W. Gage, after whom the community was named, was a political activist and one of the orginal members of the South Park Commission, organized to institute a system of parks and boulevards for the South Side.

The Town of Lake was organized in 1865 and included all of Gage Park. Land values rose soon after when a rumor circulated that the South Park Commission would build a boulevard along Western Avenue. The community drainage system consisted of two ditches along either side of Western Avenue that emptied into "Bubbly Creek." Residents referred to the area as "Little Venice" because wooden sidewalks floated down the street after heavy rains. Land for a park was finally purchased in 1873 at Garfield Boulevard (once known as Pavillion) and Western Avenue. It was named for the Gage family. Later, heirs defaulted on a loan for which land south of the park was held as collateral. Multi-millionaire real estate tycoon Hetty Green foreclosed and took title in 1877. She fought to keep it unimproved until 1911 when her son sold the land to the Bartlett Realty Company, which promptly resold it for subdivision. Another rumor that rail lines were to be laid along Central Park Avenue further raised land values and stimulated speculation in acre tracts. The Grand Trunk Western rail line entered Chicago along this route in 1880 and a small railroad community called Elsdon grew up at 51st and Kedzie. The area between Western and Kedzie avenues was alternately known as Mexico, New Mexico, Oklahoma, and Cabbageville. It consisted of 30 residential structures, some farmhouses and was mostly swampy prairie.

In 1889 Gage Park was annexed to Chicago as part of the Town of Lake. There had been a little growth outside of Elsdon, mostly in the northern part of the community around St. Gall's Mission where persons of German and Irish descent moved in. The nearest streetcar was three miles away and in 1902 two electric surface lines were installed on Western and Kedzie avenues. Some of the land in the southern section was used by packing companies for hair-drying fields.

Gage Park experienced its main construction spurt between 1905 and 1919 when hundreds of brick bungalows and two-flats where built, mostly on the subdivided lands once owned by Hetty Green. The railroads encouraged development of various industrial districts. The belt railroads stimulated development of industry all along their tracks. southwest of Gage Park the Clearing Industrial District, and Kenwood manufacturing site (part of which is located in the community proper) attracted more workers. Czechs and Poles moved in from New City, McKinley Park, and Bridgeport to work in the plants, eventually replacing the Germans as the predominant ethnic groups. By 1920 the population had reached 13,692.

Residential growth accelerated during the 1920s when the population more than doubled, to a high of 31,500 and the community reached residential maturity. Austrians, Italians, and lesser numbers of Lithuanians, Irish and Swedes moved in, in addition to more Czechs, Poles, and Germans. Several neighborhoods developed within the orginal Elsdon settlement. Glendale extended from Homan Avenue west to the tracks between 51st and 53rd streets, Garfield Manor or Garfield Heights grew between Homan and Kedzie from 53rd to 55th, and Burr Ellyn, which extended into Chicago Lawn, grew up between 55th and 59th streets. Inexpensive brick bungalows and two-flats predominated. Most streets were paved and public improvements installed. In 1930 the only area actually called Gage Park was east of

Kedzie, except for a strip between 55th and 59th Street, also referred to as Marquette Manor, the main part of which is in neighboring Chicago Lawn. Residents worked for the Grand Trunk Western Railroad, the Crane Company in Brighton Park, the Stock Yards and other nearby factories. Industries dveloped along all the tracks and most businesses were located along Western and Kedzie avenues, 51st, 55th, and 59th streets, with a small retail area at 59th and Kedzie.

Residential construction fell off sharply during the Depression and the population of Gage Park dropped by 4 percent. It has continued to decline each decade since, the largest loss coming in the 1970s. In 1970, 48 percent of the residents were of foreign stock with Poles, Czechs, Irish, and Lithuanians predominating. The Hispanic population, mostly Mexican, has grown from 1 to 11 percent in the last decade. Virtually all of the 163 resident blacks live in Tract 6307 but those of Spanish origin are dispersed throughout the community. Half of the women working in 1970 and 12 percent of the men were employed as clerical workers. Another fourth of the males worked as craftsmen or other elite blue-collar occupations. A third of the working population was employed in manufacturing.

Business areas are established along 59th Street, 55th Street west of Kedzie and in scattered areas on 51st Street. Western Avenue is a boulevard north of 55th Street; the boulevard dissembles the presence of light industry. The major industrial areas are north of 51st Street between California Avenue and the Sante Fe tracks, and along all the other rail lines. Older two-story frame dwellings predominate north of 51st, with newer brick homes to the south. Sixty-two percent of all units are owner-occupied and just more than half of the structures are multiple-family dwellings. The median value of owner-occupied units is about $10,000 less than the city median but homes and lawns are well-kept throughout the community.

In the mid-1960s, Gage Park was the scene of racial "testing" as a civil rights coalition movement began making inquiries into available housing. Later, Gage Park High School became a center of protests and boycotts when the Chicago Board of Education's redistricting policy permitted blacks and Latinos to enroll. The community has since stabilized. Most recently a coalition of community groups has worked to help rehabilitate community properties.

Antoinette LoBosco

Community Area 63 — Gage Park

Community Area 63 — Gage Park
Population and Housing Characteristics, 1930-1980

	1980	1970	1960	1950	1940	1930
Total Population	24,445	26,698	28,244	30,149	30,343	31,535
% Male	47.3	47.1	48.2	49.3	50.3	51.3
% Female	52.7	52.9	51.8	50.7	49.7	48.7
% White	93.0	99.7	99.9	100.0	100.0	100.0
% Black	0.7	0.0	0.0	0.0	0.0	—
% Other Nonwhite Races	6.3	0.3	0.1	0.0	0.0	0.0
% Under 5 Years Old	6.4	6.2	7.8	8.5	6.1	8.6
% 5-19 Years Old	19.6	22.0	21.0	18.7	23.5	31.3
% 20-44 Years Old	31.7	27.5	32.0	41.3	44.5	44.0
% 45-64 Years Old	24.4	29.4	27.2	25.3	21.9	14.0
% 65 Years and Older	17.9	14.9	12.0	6.2	4.0	2.1
Median School years	12.0	10.6	9.2	8.8	8.2	*
Total Housing Units	9,603	9,631	9,309	8,645	7,874	*
% In One-Unit Structures	46.7	45.7	45.1	*	*	*
% Owner Occupied	60.3	60.1	62.1	60.9	55.8	*
% Renter Occupied	36.6	37.7	36.0	38.3	43.3	*
% Vacant	3.1	2.2	1.9	1.8	0.9	*
% 1+ Persons per Room	4.1	5.2	6.0	10.7	*	*

Community Area 63 — Gage Park
Selected Characteristics of Census Tracts: 1980

Tract Number	Total	6301	6302	6303	6304	6305	6306	6307	6308	6309
Total Population	24445	857	1237	3111	4004	3828	401	3737	4090	3180
% Male	47.3	47.7	49.1	47.2	47.0	47.9	52.9	48.0	45.9	46.1
% Black	0.7	0.6	0.1	0.0	0.0	0.1	38.4	0.0	0.0	0.0
% Other Nonwhite	6.3	13.8	5.1	2.6	3.4	6.0	17.2	15.8	3.1	4.0
% Of Spanish Origin	11.0	29.1	10.6	4.8	6.7	12.0	23.4	22.9	7.3	6.0
% Foreign Born	15.5	17.4	18.5	15.5	16.4	12.3	11.2	13.8	20.2	13.1
% Living In Group Quarters	0.1	0.0	0.0	0.4	0.0	0.0	3.7	0.0	0.0	0.0
% 13 Years Old And Under	17.0	20.8	16.8	14.1	14.8	19.5	26.7	22.3	14.4	14.6
% 14-20 Years Old	10.6	12.0	9.6	10.8	9.9	10.1	10.7	12.0	9.7	11.6
% 21-64 Years Old	54.5	55.5	56.8	55.8	55.7	55.5	52.1	52.4	53.3	53.4
% 65-74 Years Old	11.4	7.1	10.8	12.4	12.2	9.9	8.2	8.6	14.0	12.9
% 75 Years Old And Over	6.5	4.6	6.1	6.9	7.4	5.1	2.2	4.7	8.5	7.6
% In Different House	33.7	43.9	42.4	30.3	41.9	36.5	53.8	34.9	23.6	26.7
% Families With Female Head	14.8	20.4	22.2	13.9	12.7	17.5	35.2	12.7	13.5	11.1
Median School Years Completed	12.0	12.0	12.0	11.2	11.3	11.6	12.2	12.2	12.2	12.1
Median Family Income, 1979 $$	21866	16774	19167	24043	21609	20780	17177	20924	23226	23000
% Income Below Poverty Level	5.1	11.8	9.6	3.4	4.4	7.1	9.4	6.7	3.4	2.8
% Income Of $30,000 Or More	26.1	18.2	26.0	31.2	24.4	20.4	19.8	26.3	31.0	26.2
% White Collar Workers	49.2	42.8	38.1	47.7	48.0	46.8	54.0	49.2	57.1	50.4
% Civilian Labor Force Unemployed	7.8	11.7	8.3	13.4	6.4	9.8	0.0	6.6	6.5	4.4
% Riding To Work By Automobile	68.2	76.6	64.9	64.0	69.6	67.1	48.0	72.0	71.4	66.0
Mean Commuting Time - Minutes	29.9	32.6	30.8	30.2	31.7	24.0	37.7	34.1	30.5	27.2
Population Per Household	2.6	2.6	2.4	2.6	2.5	2.7	2.9	2.9	2.5	2.6
Total Housing Units	9603	364	546	1197	1647	1505	137	1311	1669	1227
% Condominiums	0.0	0.0	0.0	0.0	0.0	0.0	0.0	0.0	0.0	0.0
% Built 1970 Or Later	1.1	0.0	3.9	3.5	0.7	0.1	0.0	0.7	0.0	1.7
% Owner Occupied	60.3	40.9	50.7	64.2	61.1	55.2	43.8	63.5	61.2	68.9
% With 1+ Persons Per Room	4.1	6.0	4.2	3.3	3.7	6.3	5.3	5.8	2.0	3.1
Median Value: Owner Units $$	37100	31100	30000	39500	36200	33400		36300	38000	39900
Median Rent: Rental Units $$	179	167	156	183	170	161	178	193	193	196
Median Number Of Rooms: All Units	4.9	4.5	4.3	5.0	4.7	4.6	5.0	5.2	5.1	5.1

Community Area 63 — Gage Park
Selected Characteristics of Census Tracts: 1970

Tract Number	TOTAL	6301	6302	6303	6304	6305	6306	6307	6308	6309
Total Population	26698	927	1499	3526	4582	4109	417	3611	4502	3525
% Male	47.1	48.3	48.7	46.6	46.7	47.6	51.6	47.9	45.9	46.6
% Black	0.0	0.0	0.0	0.0	0.0	0.0	0.0	0.0	0.0	0.0
% Other Nonwhite	0.3	0.6	0.0	0.3	0.3	0.3	0.2	0.1	0.2	0.4
% Of Spanish Language	1.4	0.0	0.0	0.0	1.9	1.9	0.0	1.0	1.5	3.1
% Foreign Born	15.0	12.0	16.9	10.4	18.2	14.9	23.3	17.5	15.2	11.8
% Living In Group Quarters	0.3	0.0	0.0	0.0	0.0	1.0	5.8	0.0	0.0	0.5
% 13 Years Old And Under	19.1	21.6	20.1	21.2	18.5	20.9	17.7	18.2	16.2	19.3
% 14-20 Years Old	10.6	9.6	10.3	11.5	10.0	10.2	8.6	11.7	10.2	10.7
% 21-64 Years Old	55.5	59.0	57.8	54.2	55.3	55.3	62.4	55.1	55.8	54.5
% 65-74 Years Old	9.3	7.1	6.3	8.1	10.3	8.4	8.4	9.0	11.0	10.0
% 75 Years Old And Over	5.6	2.7	5.5	4.9	6.0	5.1	2.9	5.9	6.7	5.5
% In Different House	65.0	62.2	55.8	71.6	61.8	67.7	68.2	60.7	67.7	63.4
% Families With Female Head	13.4	12.0	13.1	12.5	13.1	14.1	15.5	13.6	12.6	14.9
Median School Years Completed	10.6	10.2	9.8	10.8	9.9	10.3	10.5	10.5	11.3	11.4
Median Family Income, 1969 $$	11479	11280	10577	11862	10659	11526	10476	10658	12877	12187
% Income Below Poverty Level	3.3	2.3	0.6	2.4	2.4	3.7	4.7	3.8	3.1	3.3
% Income of $15,000 or More	28.1	17.6	26.3	33.1	23.4	27.5	24.6	23.3	36.1	28.4
% White Collar Workers	19.6	22.9	15.4	20.4	15.2	20.1	22.4	20.6	22.4	19.5
% Civilian Labor Force Unemployed	2.7	4.7	5.2	3.2	3.3	1.3	2.2	1.6	2.7	2.9
% Riding To Work By Automobile	59.8	49.5	56.0	64.6	55.5	57.3	51.6	67.0	62.3	57.4
Population Per Household	2.8	2.7	2.9	2.9	2.8	2.8	2.6	2.8	2.7	2.9
Total Housing Units	9630	365	537	1237	1663	1477	158	1305	1664	1224
% Condominiums & Cooperatives	0.2	0.0	0.0	0.6	0.4	0.4	0.0	0.0	0.0	0.0
% Built 1960 Or Later	6.9	13.1	8.1	12.5	4.9	4.6	17.9	2.5	6.7	7.5
% Owner Occupied	60.0	41.6	52.7	60.5	61.5	54.6	44.3	62.4	61.4	70.2
% With 1+ Persons Per Room	5.7	4.1	9.2	6.5	6.3	8.2	5.3	4.0	3.5	4.8
Median Value: Owner Units $$	18400	15800	17100	18600	18400	17400	-	18400	18900	18200
Median Rent: Rental Units $$	104	102	84	105	98	88	114	112	116	115
Median Number Of Rooms: All Units	4.8	4.4	4.3	4.9	4.6	4.5	4.5	5.1	5.1	5.1

Clearing

Clearing is one of Chicago's newer communities on the city's far southwest side. It extends along 59th and 65th Street between the Belt Railroad and Harlem Avenue, and includes a smaller section south of 65th to 67th Street from Cicero Avenue east to the tracks. The area between Cicero Avenue and the Belt Railroad from 59th Street to Marquette Road was annexed by election to Chicago as part of the Town of Lake in 1889. The present boundaries reflect a series of annexations through 1923.

The name of the community area comes from the use for which the land was originally intended. A railroad freight clearing yard is a track area where out-going trains are made up and incoming trains broken down to facilitate movement to specific locations. In the 1890s A.B. Stickney, president of the Chicago Great Western Railroad, purchased the land west of Cicero to Harlem Avenue, between 63rd and 79th Street, to build a clearing yard, forseeing that Chicago would become a transcontinental railroad hub. He had track laid in the form of the huge Stickney Circle, south of 65th Street where 13 trunk lines converged. The enterprise failed in the Panic of 1893 and was dubbed "Stickney's Folly." Henry H. Porter bought the property for the Chicago Union Transfer Company in 1898. The yards began operation in 1901, the year in which a Village of Clearing was incorporated, with boundaries at 55th and 65th Street, Cicero and Austin avenues. The yards were sold in 1912, and the company began to develop the Clearing Industrial District on the remainder of Stickney's land. This attracted many factories through the early 1920s, and became a key to settlement of the far Southwest Side.

Before 1900 only a few German and Dutch farmers lived in the area. By 1905 just 10 houses, some of them empty, existed. Italians, Poles, and Lithuanians began settling around 63rd and Central to work in the early industries. "Silk Stocking Boulevard" on 63rd Place east of Central Avenue was home to railroad and factory officials, in contrast to "Moonshine Alley" along 64th Place, where working class arrivals were known to manufacture their own liquor. The Bartlett Realty Company purchased land west of Austin between 63rd and 65th Street in 1911 and subdivided it for resale. The Clearing Company also built some houses and sold lots to workers east of Austin. In 1915 the Village of Clearing was annexed to Chicago by election. The area between 59th and 65th from Austin to Narragansett, part of the Town of Stickney, was added two years later, and territory west of Narragansett in Stickney was annexed in 1923. Property bounded by Central and Cicero, 55th and 63rd remained vacant until the School Board leased it for the construction of Midway Airport in 1926.

By 1920 the population of Clearing was 2,011. Clusters of brick bungalows and frame cottages dotted the area with an occasional two-flat or small farm to be seen. Much of the rest remained prairie. Italians and Poles predominated, with some Lithuanians and Germans. The community was inhabited chiefly by workers employed in the factories just south of the city limits along 65th, with an affluent section remaining east of Central and south of 63rd Street.

A 120 percent increase in population between 1920 and 1930 was accompanied by a construction boom. Most of this can be attributed to the continuing influence of the growing Clearing Industrial District and to the expansion of industrial areas in neighboring communities and suburbs. The last parcel of land west of Narragansett was the scene of an intense real estate promotion. Streets were finally paved and public amenities provided. Completion of Midway Airport, which was to develop the heaviest traffic volume of any airport in the world both attracted and repelled prospective residents.

The 1930s brought a 12 percent increase in population to 6,068 by 1940 but construction dropped off sharply. The total foreign-born

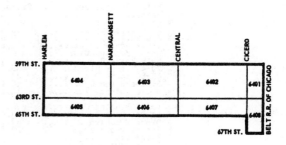

population decreased by half, with Italians, Poles, Lithuanians, and Germans still the dominant ethnic groups. residential areas were scattered and vacant lots remained in the far western part of Clearing. Considerable construction took place between 1940 and 1950 in the eastern part of the community and some in the west as the population grew by almost 75 percent during these years. Much of this growth was linked to wartime and post-war industrial expansion of the Southwest Side and the western suburbs.

In 1960 the population numbered 18,787, a 56 percent increase from 1950 and this number had increased again by 77 percent in 1970, when it peaked at 24,560. Few blacks have ever lived in Clearing and while the number of Hispanics is growing, in 1980 they constituted only 4 percent of the total population. Male residents continue to be employed chiefly in manufacturing and in 1970 almost half of the employed females were clerical workers. Almost 70 percent of dwellings were owned-occupied in 1980, well above the city average of 39 percent. The median value of owner-occupied homes is $54,101, almost $7,000 above the city median. More than 65 percent of the residents have lived in their homes for at least five years, an indicator or the stability of the Clearing community. Nearly two-thirds of the housing in Clearing is in single units and only 3 percent is located in buildings with 10 or more units. The western part, especially along 59th Street, consists of small single-family brick homes. Much of the area is bisected by the Belt Railroad tracks along 64th. Residential land use is more mixed in the eastern part of Clearing with older brick homes, two- and three-flats, and some apartment complexes visible. Picturesque rows of duplex and quadro-homes in the vicinity between Central and Laramie along 63rd and 64th Place follow winding tree-lined streets.

The chief business strip is along 63rd Street west of the airport to Harlem, and retail establishments are scattered along all the main north and south streets. Parking lots line 65th Street from Harlem to about Laramie, accommodating the numerous factories that are part of the suburban Bedford Park industrial site. A small industrial park is located between Oak Park and Harlem avenues, 59th and 63rd streets.

Clearing's population declined for the first time in the 1970s by almost 2,000 residents. The 22,000 who remain are virtually all whites of European descent, Principally Polish, Irish, German and Italian. There is no evidence of any physical deterioration in the general appearance of this quiet Chicago neighborhood. The drop is more likely the result of general migration from the city itself.

Antoinette LoBosco

Community Area 64 — Clearing
Population and Housing Characteristics, 1930-1980

	1980	1970	1960	1950	1940	1930
Total Population.......	22,584	24,911	18,797	10,591	6,068	5,434
% Male.................	49.4	49.8	50.6	52.2	53.0	55.1
% Female...............	50.6	50.2	49.4	47.8	47.0	44.9
% White................	98.4	99.7	99.9	99.9	99.9	99.7
% Black................	0.0	0.0	0.0	0.0	0.1	-
% Other Nonwhite Races...	1.6	0.3	0.1	0.1	0.0	0.3
% Under 5 Years Old......	5.4	8.0	12.1	11.8	7.9	10.9
% 5-19 Years Old........	22.2	29.5	26.9	22.0	24.2	29.5
% 20-44 Years Old........	35.0	33.2	38.4	45.4	46.6	45.1
% 45-64 Years Old.......	27.0	23.6	17.8	16.8	18.5	12.8
% 65 Years and Older....	10.4	5.7	4.8	4.0	2.8	1.7
Median School Years....	12.1	11.5	10.2	9.5	5.0	*
Total Housing Units.....	8,297	7,386	5,465	2,910	1,609	*
% In One-Unit Structures.	63.0	67.2	82.9	*	*	*
% Owner Occupied.........	67.7	#	74.6	63.6	40.7	*
% Renter Occupied........	29.2	#	19.9	35.2	57.2	*
% Vacant................	3.1	#	5.5	1.2	2.1	*
% 1+ Persons per Room....	4.8	10.1	11.6	14.7	*	*

Community Area 64 — Clearing
Selected Characteristics of Census Tracts: 1980

Tract Number	Total	6401	6402	6403	6404	6405	6406	6407	6408
Total Population.............	22584	943	0	6216	3147	3667	3956	3199	1456
% Male.......................	49.4	45.9	—	49.0	49.3	49.5	49.6	51.4	48.1
% Black......................	0.0	0.0	—	0.0	0.0	0.0	0.0	0.0	0.1
% Other Nonwhite.............	1.6	1.4	—	1.3	1.4	1.4	2.3	1.9	0.4
% Of Spanish Origin..........	4.1	5.0	—	3.1	3.6	5.0	3.7	6.1	2.9
% Foreign Born...............	9.2	14.1	—	6.9	7.5	7.5	13.3	9.6	11.2
% Living In Group Quarters...	0.2	0.0	—	0.0	0.0	0.0	0.4	0.7	0.0
% 13 Years Old And Under.....	16.6	17.3	—	16.0	16.5	16.6	14.6	21.2	14.7
% 14-20 Years Old............	13.0	10.7	—	13.7	14.1	14.5	11.1	11.5	13.5
% 21-64 Years Old............	60.0	59.8	—	59.4	61.4	60.6	63.4	56.2	57.0
% 65-74 Years Old............	7.2	8.3	—	7.4	5.5	5.7	7.7	8.0	9.5
% 75 Years Old And Over......	3.2	3.9	—	3.5	2.6	2.5	3.2	3.1	5.4
% In Different House.........	34.5	32.9	—	27.2	37.1	35.2	47.9	29.4	35.8
% Families With Female Head......	11.7	17.1	—	11.1	7.8	9.7	14.0	14.3	12.6
Median School Years Completed....	12.2	12.1	—	12.2	12.2	12.3	12.1	12.0	12.2
Median Family Income, 1979......$$	25176	24625	—	26000	27517	26510	22397	21486	26891
% Income Below Poverty Level....	4.4	9.6	—	1.8	5.0	2.8	5.5	7.2	5.6
% Income Of $30,000 Or More....	34.7	35.3	—	37.9	41.4	34.5	28.1	24.3	47.6
% White Collar Workers..........	47.4	48.7	—	45.7	46.7	49.7	48.5	46.5	46.7
% Civilian Labor Force Unemployed.	6.3	8.1	—	6.4	5.4	5.1	6.4	8.9	3.8
% Riding To Work By Automobile....	77.3	76.1	—	77.2	80.1	79.5	72.0	78.3	80.8
Mean Commuting Time - Minutes...	31.2	29.9	—	32.6	32.0	29.5	31.8	30.1	28.5
Population Per Household..........	2.8	2.6	—	2.9	3.0	2.9	2.4	2.9	2.8
Total Housing Units..........	8297	392	0	2209	1066	1300	1667	1128	535
% Condominiums...............	1.9	0.0	—	0.0	0.0	12.2	0.0	0.0	0.0
% Built 1970 Or Later........	10.9	8.2	—	3.9	6.2	25.7	21.0	1.0	2.9
% Owner Occupied.............	67.8	51.5	—	74.7	83.0	65.8	44.8	79.3	72.3
% With 1+ Persons Per Room......	4.8	3.0	—	5.3	5.0	5.4	3.8	5.6	4.2
Median Value: Owner Units.......$$	54100	47500	—	55900	56900	61000	58100	40100	50000
Median Rent: Rental Units.......$$	235	223	—	214	242	249	244	225	207
Median Number Of Rooms: All Units.	4.9	4.8	—	5.0	5.0	4.8	4.5	5.1	5.2

Community Area 64 — Clearing
Selected Characteristics of Census Tracts: 1970

Tract Number	TOTAL	6401	6403	6404	6405	6406	6407	6408
Total Population.............	24911	1116	7223	3553	3788	3969	3588	1674
% Male.......................	49.8	47.8	49.9	49.8	49.0	50.4	51.5	47.2
% Black......................	0.0	0.0	0.0	0.0	0.0	0.0	0.0	0.0
% Other Nonwhite.............	0.3	0.7	0.2	0.2	0.2	0.5	0.4	0.2
% Of Spanish Language........	2.7	0.0	2.4	2.7	3.2	3.6	3.1	2.3
% Foreign Born...............	8.7	14.2	6.9	7.6	9.2	10.0	7.7	14.3
% Living In Group Quarters...	0.3	0.0	0.3	0.4	0.2	0.0	0.2	0.0
% 13 Years Old And Under.....	26.4	25.5	25.3	27.7	32.0	23.7	26.3	21.8
% 14-20 Years Old............	12.5	9.9	14.1	14.3	12.0	11.4	10.3	12.0
% 21-64 Years Old............	55.4	56.0	54.4	54.4	52.7	59.2	56.6	55.4
% 65-74 Years Old............	3.9	5.6	4.1	2.4	2.2	3.9	5.0	7.8
% 75 Years Old And Over......	1.8	2.9	2.1	1.2	1.1	1.8	1.8	3.0
% In Different House.........	65.1	47.3	71.2	70.2	60.9	54.9	71.6	58.1
% Families With Female Head......	7.8	11.0	7.7	4.8	6.5	7.8	9.8	12.0
Median School Years Completed....	11.5	10.8	11.6	11.5	12.0	11.4	11.0	11.3
Median Family Income, 1969......$$	12280	12846	11966	13402	13045	11815	11330	11514
% Income Below Poverty Level....	2.9	1.4	3.0	1.4	3.0	2.8	2.9	8.9
% Income of $15,000 or More....	29.8	30.7	30.3	35.3	29.4	27.7	24.3	34.4
% White Collar Workers..........	18.3	13.3	20.0	16.9	18.2	18.3	16.4	22.3
% Civilian Labor Force Unemployed.	3.3	7.4	2.1	2.7	1.8	4.8	4.3	3.3
% Riding To Work By Automobile....	69.3	54.8	71.4	72.2	68.6	65.6	70.8	74.5
Population Per Household..........	3.4	3.1	3.4	3.7	3.8	3.0	3.2	3.2
Total Housing Units..........	7397	366	2149	984	1020	1343	1140	395
% Condominiums & Cooperatives.....	0.2	0.0	0.2	0.0	0.0	0.0	0.9	0.0
% Built 1960 Or Later........	31.9	24.5	18.0	40.7	69.3	46.8	7.5	14.3
% Owner Occupied.............	70.8	56.8	75.0	84.0	69.8	52.6	77.5	72.4
% With 1+ Persons Per Room......	10.7	8.1	10.1	13.6	16.1	9.1	8.8	5.4
Median Value: Owner Units.......$$	21900	19500	22000	22100	23700	23500	16800	22000
Median Rent: Rental Units.......$$	133	129	115	150	155	138	111	125
Median Number Of Rooms: All Units.	4.8	4.8	4.9	4.9	4.8	4.5	5.0	5.0

West Lawn

West Lawn's history is inextricably intertwined with the two southwestern communities it lies between — Chicago Lawn and Clearing. In 1876 John Eberhart and James Webb platted a subdivision called Chicago Lawn which included a few blocks west of Central Park Avenue, the present eastern boundary between 59th and 67th. It became known as "West Lawn." The completion of the Grand Trunk Western Railroad in 1880 with suburban service brought more residents to the area. For a few years this part of West Lawn grew with Chicago Lawn. Early settlers were Germans and Swedes who lived mostly east of Hamlin Avenue. The rest of the community was open prairie, swamp and marshland. The elevated terrain west and south drained into West Lawn regularly. Streets became ice skating rinks in winter for local residents but washed out plank sidewalks in spring. Gentlemen would put on hip boots and carry their ladies about. Understandably, settlement remained slow, most preferring to live east of the tracks in Chicago Lawn. West Lawn was annexed to Chicago as part the Town of Lake in 1889. By 1902 only a few dozen frame homes had been erected south of the original settlement. The development of the Clearing Industrial District after the turn of the century soon attracted immigrant laborers who trecked through West Lawn on their way to the factories. Small businesses sprang up at 63rd Street and Central Park Avenue to accommodate them and transit lines were built to this point. By 1910 the need for more housing spurred the development of an area west of Pulaski called West Chicago Lawn. Streetcar lines were extended to Clearing. Real estate promoters acquired the land cheap and resold it at high profits.

The population rose to 2,544 by 1920. Unlike other southwestern communities, only 11 percent of residents were foreign-born. Among these, Germans, Lithuanians and Italians predominated. Residential settlement was still primarily in the northeastern part of the community adjacent to Chicago Lawn. Modest brick bungalows were mixed with older frame homes and it is estimated there were as many real estate offices as grocery stores along 63rd Street. A spring-fed lake at 66th Street and Lawndale Avenue that had once been a brickyard was filled in by ambitious realtors and subdivided for sale.

The first sidewalks were laid in the mid-1920s north of 63rd Street and east of Pulaski Road and work commenced on other streets. Between 1920 and 1930 the immigrant population grew from 282 to 1,782. Germans, Lithuanians, and Italians were still the major ethnic groups, with smaller settlements of Poles and Czechs. Residential construction continued, though at a slower rate, throughout the 1930s despite the Depression. Public improvements were made west of Pulaski..

By 1940 West Lawn was a community of predominantly single-family brick dwellings with some two-flats and older structures in the northeastern sector. For a time, there were improved areas without homes and residential areas without improvements. This situation was brought on by the accruement of delinquent taxes and special assessments to vacant lots where improvements were made. Owners could not afford to build on them. The area at 63rd Street and Pulaski Road developed into a small local shopping corner. Most residents continued to shop at established retail centers in Chicago Lawn.

The population increased by 162 percent between 1940 and 1960, the result of growing industry both within the community and in neighboring areas during World War II and the post-war years. Rows of inexpensive brick homes were built. Poles replaced the Germans as the dominant ethnic group, followed by Italians, Lithuanians, Germans, and Czechs.

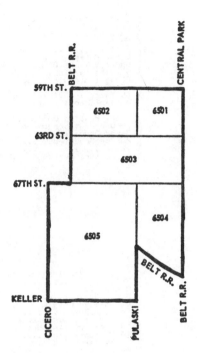

Unlike other southwestern communities, the population grew in the decade between 1960 and 1970 by about 3 percent. West Lawn experienced its first population decline of 2,896 residents between 1970 and 1980. This represents a 10.5 percent decrease, which is slightly lower than the average citywide population loss. The population is predominantly white, including less than 1 percent black and only about 2 percent of Spanish origin. residents are typically in the older age brackets. The median age of 40 is well above the city median.

The northern and eastern portions of the community are almost entirely residential. Brick single-family homes predominate and 79 percent of the units are owner-occupied. Their median value is $50,224. Most blocks have a quiet suburban atmosphere, even along the rail lines on the east and west borders. Small industries can be found along the tracks, especially south of 63rd Street to Marquette Road and on a diagonal following the Belt Railroad.

Pulaski Road is a major thoroughfare and a variety of businesses are located along this north-south street. The major retail center is Ford City, which dominates the southern part of the community. Here, numerous large and small retail establishments and a theater complex attract shoppers from other nearby city and suburban communities. In 1977 Ford City had the highest sales volume of any retail center outside the Loop in Chicago. In addition, other land uses within this area include Daley College, an Army Reserve Base, a multi-storied office building, and a massive apartment complex. West Lawn is a stable community that provides its residents with a variety of services.

Antoinette LoBosco

Community Area 65 -- West Lawn
Population and Housing Characteristics, 1930-1980

	1980	1970	1960	1950	1940	1930
Total Population.......	24,748	27,644	26,910	14,460	10,289	8,919
% Male...................	47.6	48.5	49.1	49.4	50.3	51.1
% Female.................	52.4	51.5	50.9	50.6	49.7	48.9
% White..................	98.4	97.5	100.0	99.9	100.0	100.0
% Black..................	0.2	0.1	0.0	0.1	0.0	0.0
% Other Nonwhite Races...	1.4	0.4	0.0	0.0	-	0.0
% Under 5 Years Old......	4.6	6.0	9.5	10.2	7.6	10.2
% 5-19 Years Old.........	20.1	24.7	25.3	20.2	25.8	33.4
% 20-44 Years Old........	29.6	27.3	34.4	42.3	41.7	40.6
% 45-65 Years Old........	29.3	30.7	23.3	22.0	21.3	13.4
% 65 Years and Older.....	16.4	11.3	7.5	5.3	3.6	2.4
Median School Years....	12.2	11.1	10.3	9.0	8.3	*
Total Housing Units....	9,152	6,267	7,922	4,004	2,623	*
% In One-Unit Structures.	69.2	62.3	79.2	*	*	*
% Owner Occupied.........	77.8	70.2	82.6	73.2	68.3	*
% Renter Occupied........	20.4	25.1	15.6	25.9	29.8	*
% Vacant.................	1.8	4.7	1.8	0.9	1.9	*
% 1+ Persons per Room....	3.3	7.1	7.6	11.7	*	*

Community Area 65 -- West Lawn
Selected Characteristics of Census Tracts: 1980

Tract Number	Total	6501	6502	6503	6504	6505
Total Population.............	24748	3486	5340	7676	4883	3363
% Male........................	47.6	48.3	46.1	47.9	47.2	48.9
% Black.......................	0.2	0.1	0.0	0.0	0.0	1.4
% Other Nonwhite..............	1.4	1.4	1.2	1.4	1.8	1.2
% Of Spanish Origin...........	2.4	3.3	2.1	2.8	1.9	1.8
% Foreign Born................	11.1	10.9	13.8	9.5	10.8	10.9
% Living In Group Quarters....	0.1	0.0	0.0	0.3	0.0	0.0
% 13 Years Old And Under......	14.3	14.9	14.1	14.7	13.6	14.2
% 14-20 Years Old.............	12.3	12.7	10.6	13.1	12.9	11.8
% 21-64 Years Old.............	57.0	53.8	57.6	55.9	59.1	58.7
% 65-74 Years Old.............	11.2	12.6	11.9	11.2	10.0	10.2
% 75 Years Old And Over.......	5.3	6.1	5.8	5.1	4.4	5.1
% In Different House..........	26.3	26.6	24.2	26.6	26.0	29.2
% Families With Female Head...	10.8	11.8	11.3	11.3	8.7	10.9
Median School Years Completed.	12.2	12.2	12.1	12.3	12.2	12.3
Median Family Income, 1979.....$$	25733	22831	24598	27321	25567	26331
% Income Below Poverty Level..	2.7	5.1	2.2	3.0	1.4	2.3
% Income Of $30,000 Or More...	35.5	26.4	31.3	42.4	32.6	40.1
% White Collar Workers........	51.5	46.8	49.8	50.2	53.4	58.5
% Civilian Labor Force Unemployed.	5.4	8.7	7.8	3.9	3.5	4.5
% Riding To Work By Automobile....	72.9	68.1	73.0	69.9	78.4	76.0
Mean Commuting Time - Minutes...	29.9	27.6	29.9	30.8	30.0	29.7
Population Per Household.......	2.7	2.7	2.6	2.8	2.9	2.7
Total Housing Units...........	9152	1318	2104	2752	1692	1286
% Condominiums................	3.4	0.0	0.0	0.0	0.0	24.0
% Built 1970 Or Later.........	4.3	1.7	0.5	2.6	3.0	8.7
% Owner Occupied..............	77.9	69.4	68.9	81.0	88.7	80.3
% With 1+ Persons Per Room....	3.3	3.9	2.6	4.0	3.4	3.4
Median Value: Owner Units.....$$	50200	44600	48300	51500	53900	51500
Median Rent: Rental Units.....$$	218	198	215	212	242	294
Median Number Of Rooms: All Units.	5.0	5.1	4.9	5.1	5.2	4.9

Community Area 65 -- West Lawn
Selected Characteristics of Census Tracts: 1970

Tract Number	TOTAL	6501	6502	6503	6504	6505
Total Population.............	27644	3980	5943	8588	5785	3348
% Male........................	48.5	48.4	47.7	47.6	100.0	49.3
% Black.......................	0.1	0.2	0.0	0.0	1.6	0.0
% Other Nonwhite..............	0.4	0.5	0.2	0.4	2.2	1.1
% Of Spanish Language.........	0.8	0.0	0.0	1.2	0.0	0.0
% Foreign Born................	12.0	11.3	14.5	11.1	14.4	8.4
% Living In Group Quarters....	1.3	0.5	0.0	0.5	100.0	0.0
% 13 Years Old And Under......	20.3	20.5	19.8	21.1	1.1	20.6
% 14-20 Years Old.............	12.0	11.8	10.9	12.5	3.2	14.7
% 21-64 Years Old.............	56.3	55.4	57.3	54.9	95.1	56.2
% 65-74 Years Old.............	7.4	8.2	7.7	7.3	0.5	5.8
% 75 Years Old And Over.......	4.0	4.0	4.3	4.1	0.0	2.5
% In Different House..........	68.5	68.7	65.5	72.1	40.4	68.2
% Families With Female Head...	10.8	10.7	11.3	11.2	-	7.7
Median School Years Completed....	11.2	11.6	10.7	11.2	11.6	11.3
Median Family Income, 1969.....$$	12467	12399	11901	12772	-	13653
% Income Below Poverty Level..	3.0	2.1	3.6	3.5	-	1.0
% Income of $15,000 or More...	32.0	31.7	26.7	34.2	-	41.9
% White Collar Workers........	22.3	25.1	18.3	25.4	0.0	19.6
% Civilian Labor Force Unemployed.	2.5	3.1	3.8	1.4	0.0	1.6
% Riding To Work By Automobile....	66.2	68.2	69.7	64.2	10.1	70.7
Population Per Household.......	3.1	3.1	3.0	3.1	-	3.3
Total Housing Units...........	6276	1308	2031	2103	0	834
% Condominiums & Cooperatives.	0.2	0.4	0.3	0.0	-	0.0
% Built 1960 Or Later.........	13.1	9.1	11.2	8.5	-	36.5
% Owner Occupied..............	70.4	68.7	69.8	77.5	-	57.0
% With 1+ Persons Per Room....	7.0	6.3	6.2	6.9	-	10.9
Median Value: Owner Units.....$$	21100	19600	20900	21700	-	22100
Median Rent: Rental Units.....$$	126	120	121	125	-	222
Median Number Of Rooms: All Units.	4.9	5.0	4.8	5.0	-	4.4

Chicago Lawn

The community of Chicago Lawn grew from two separate settlements, Marquette Manor east of California Avenue and north of Marquette Road, and another area called Chicago Lawn, originally west of Kedzie Avenue and north of Marquette Road. It is located southwest of the Loop and was part of the vast prairie and swampland that covered this part of Chicago. Chicago Lawn was under the jurisdiction of the Town of Lake after 1865 and the only access to it then was Blue Island Road (Western Avenue).

Pioneer land developers James Webb and John Eberhart established a model community in 1876 at 63rd and Central Park Avenue, which they named Chicago Lawn. Buyers were given three-year passes on the Chicago and Southern Railroad, which later became the Grand Trunk Western Railroad. Lithuanians Swedes, Germans, and Jews were among the Early settlers. Henry Gage owned much of the property to the east of this area from 59th to 63rd streets between Western and Kedzie, and a narrower strip from 63rd Street south to Marquette Road between Western and Rockwell. His heirs lost the land in 1877 to real estate magnate Hetty Green when they defaulted on the interest payments of a loan for which the land was collateral. It remained open prairie with some cabbage patches until 1911 when Green sold it to a developing company. A narrow parcel to the east of the Green land around Oakley and 65th was known as South Lynn or Vail's subdivision, platted but not settled until 1884. Some settlers were attracted to the Chicago Lawn subdivision after the Grand Trunk Western extended its service into the community, but this was the only public means of transportation and residential growth remained slow. By 1885, only 40 structures existed, almost all of which were in the original settlement.

Annexation to Chicago came in 1889 as part of the Town of Lake. By 1900 electric surface lines ran on Kedzie south to 63rd, on Western south to 71st, and on 63rd between Ashland and Central avenues. This did not bring settlement to the area, however, since large tracts of farmland surrounded Chicago Lawn. Much of the development of the eastern sector came after the Green land was sold and developed into a subdivision called Marquette Manor. Some two- and three-unit dwellings were built but real growth came after World War I when the neighborhood was intensely promoted. French, German and Irish moved in from Brighton Park and McKinley Park, and Lithuanians settled at Marquette Road and Washtenaw. Most of the land south of 71st Street remained in the hands of the railroads.

The greatest growth period came in the 1920s. The Chicago Lawn and Marquette Manor subdivisions merged as residents moved eastward and westward, respectively. The population grew from 14,000 to 47,000 between 1920 and 1930, as new settlers continued to migrate in from neighboring communities. In 1930 about a fourth of the residents were foreign-born. Poles and Italians had joined the older ethnic groups. Most of the new structures were one-story single-family dwellings. Many apartment buildings were constructed, especially between 63rd and Marquette Road from Western to Kedzie. Although Chicago Lawn is not an industrial community, its residents were mainly employed in nearby manufacturing areas as skilled workers, mechanics, and in supervisory positions. Marquette Manor was renovated in 1937 but otherwise Chicago Lawn experienced little residential growth in the 1930s. It was changed to a limited extent by World War II amd the post-war housing boom on the Southwest Side. The population of Chicago Lawn peaked in 1960 at 51,347 and has declined in each decade since, although more slowly than the city as a whole. In 1970 about 53 percent of the population was of foreign stock, led by Lithuanians, Irish, Poles, Germans, and Italians.

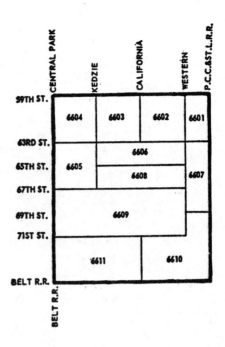

Many activities center around the Lithuanian community. The area around Marquette Park includes a hospital-church-school complex run by the Sisters of St. Casimir, a Lithuanian order. Maria High School, a girls' school, is located at 67th and California Avenue. Directly south of Maria is Holy Cross Hospital. Chicago Lawn has been called the "Lithuanian Gold Coast" because living there represented status and success (a house with a garden) to immigrants. A rapid increase in the number of blacks and residents of Spanish origin has occurred in the last 10 years, especially since 1975. Together, they make up 21 percent of the population (about 10.5 percent each) compared to less than 1 percent in 1970. Thus while whites have been moving out for the last 20 years, their loss has been offset to a considerable extent by the growth of the black and Hispanic populations. Almost all of the black residents live east of Western Avenue in Tracts 6601, 6607, and 6610. Those of Spanish origin reside throughout the community.

The rate of owner occupancy has remained relatively stable since 1950 at approximately 54 percent. Over half of all housing in Chicago Lawn is in multiple-unit structures. The median value of single-family homes is almost $8,000 less than that of the city as a whole but properties are in generally good repair. Seventy-four percent were built before 1940 and the oldest frame structures are in the original Chicago Lawn and Marquette Manor subdivisions.

Businesses are located on 63rd Street, Western Avenue, and 71st Street between California and Western, with a major retail center at 63rd and Western and another important area at 63rd and Kedzie Avenue. Land uses on 59th Street are mixed and some light industry is located along the eastern and southern tracks, especially south of 71st. Development of neighboring Ford City and Evergreen Plaza shopping centers has somewhat undermined local retailing. Restaurants and food stores offer a variety of East European, Middle and Far Eastern foodstuffs. These include Lithuanian, Polish, Hispanic, Thai, Arabic, Chinese, Korean, and Filipino fares. German, Irish, Italian, and French restaurants can also be found. Marquette Park takes up the area between Central Park and California avenues from 67th to 71st Street, with Maria High School adjacent to its northeast corner.

About 18 percent of the community's residents are more than 65 years of age, compared to 11 percent citywide, but younger residents also seem attracted to the area. Relatively inexpensive housing and in-town residency requirements for city workers led more than 3,000

```
              Community Area 66 -- Chicago Lawn
          Population and Housing Characteristics, 1930-1980
```

	1980	1970	1960	1950	1940	1930
Total Population.......	46,568	48,435	51,347	50,211	49,291	47,462
% Male.................	47.4	46.7	47.9	49.1	49.6	50.2
% Female...............	52.6	53.3	52.1	50.9	50.4	49.8
% White................	83.0	99.6	99.9	100.0	100.0	100.0
% Black................	10.3	0.0	0.0	0.0	0.0	0.0
% Other Nonwhite Races...	6.7	0.4	0.1	0.0	0.0	0.0
% Under 5 Years Old.....	7.3	5.7	7.3	8.2	6.3	8.5
% 5-19 Years Old........	21.2	19.6	19.4	17.5	20.8	26.0
% 20-44 Years Old.......	32.8	26.2	30.3	40.1	45.4	46.5
% 45-64 Years Old.......	21.0	31.4	30.7	27.1	23.0	16.0
% 65 Years and Older....	17.7	17.0	12.3	7.1	4.5	3.0
Median School Years....	12.2	11.2	10.1	9.8	8.6	*
Total Housing Units....	18,165	18,478	17,480	15,014	13,809	*
% In One-Unit Structures.	40.8	40.0	46.1	*	*	*
% Owner Occupied........	52.2	52.1	54.5	50.3	42.1	*
% Renter Occupied.......	44.7	46.0	43.6	48.5	56.1	*
% Vacant...............	3.1	1.9	1.9	1.2	1.8	*
% 1+ Persons per Room....	4.3	4.0	4.7	9.4	*	*

```
          Community Area 66  -- Chicago Lawn
       Selected Characteristics of Census Tracts: 1980
```

Tract Number	Total	6601	6602	6603	6604	6605	6606	6607	6608	6609	6610
Total Population.............	46568	156	5420	5194	3883	3771	5549	2999	4855	3990	5606
% Male.......................	47.4	47.4	48.0	47.0	47.6	47.6	46.9	49.3	47.1	45.7	48.1
% Black......................	10.3	38.5	0.0	0.0	0.0	0.0	0.0	89.7	0.0	0.0	36.2
% Other Nonwhite.............	6.7	7.7	12.1	6.0	2.7	3.0	7.4	1.6	8.9	10.5	6.0
% Of Spanish Origin..........	10.6	17.9	25.7	9.4	2.5	6.7	15.2	1.7	12.9	9.9	6.5
% Foreign Born...............	15.8	6.8	22.7	13.9	15.0	12.7	19.2	1.5	25.5	36.0	17.5
% Living In Group Quarters...	0.4	0.0	0.0	0.0	0.0	0.0	0.0	0.9	0.0	3.9	0.0
% 13 Years Old And Under.....	19.4	17.3	22.7	18.3	18.4	19.3	19.2	32.6	16.8	11.8	22.3
% 14-20 Years Old............	10.9	9.6	11.9	10.2	12.3	12.5	10.6	15.2	9.2	7.5	11.5
% 21-64 Years Old............	52.1	64.1	51.9	51.4	52.2	52.2	50.9	49.1	53.3	51.1	51.8
% 65-74 Years Old............	10.6	5.8	7.8	11.1	10.2	9.7	11.0	2.1	12.6	16.9	8.7
% 75 Years Old And Over......	7.1	3.2	5.7	9.1	6.8	6.2	8.3	1.0	8.2	12.7	5.6
% In Different House.........	43.1	100.0	47.7	40.3	32.7	37.5	42.0	71.2	34.0	44.1	61.0
% Families With Female Head..	18.4	21.1	16.1	18.4	14.2	12.2	17.8	35.1	17.2	20.2	21.0
Median School Years Completed...	12.2	11.8	12.0	12.1	12.1	12.3	12.1	12.2	12.2	12.3	12.3
Median Family Income, 1979.....$$	21058	12273	21887	21610	20718	21284	19106	16759	20842	19449	21531
% Income Below Poverty Level....	7.8	0.0	8.8	7.5	5.4	7.5	11.2	21.2	5.0	7.0	7.2
% Income Of $30,000 Or More....	24.7	0.0	22.7	30.8	22.0	24.9	21.9	13.9	22.6	20.6	26.5
% White Collar Workers.......	49.3	34.8	45.8	52.0	48.6	54.3	45.1	39.0	52.9	58.3	46.1
% Civilian Labor Force Unemployed.	6.8	19.8	7.4	7.7	8.5	6.3	3.5	11.8	7.7	6.1	5.9
% Riding To Work By Automobile....	68.2	62.9	67.1	69.8	67.1	67.1	68.7	61.5	69.3	59.1	72.7
Mean Commuting Time - Minutes....	33.2	64.6	33.9	31.5	28.2	33.9	30.9	37.8	32.1	30.0	35.9
Population Per Household..........	2.6	2.3	2.8	2.5	2.7	2.9	2.4	3.7	2.4	2.1	2.8
Total Housing Units..........	18164	76	1974	2126	1494	1348	2369	818	2117	1872	2043
% Condominiums...............	0.0	0.0	0.0	0.0	0.0	0.0	0.0	0.0	0.0	0.0	0.0
% Built 1970 Or Later........	1.1	20.6	0.4	0.3	0.7	0.4	0.3	2.2	1.3	0.3	2.6
% Owner Occupied.............	52.2	21.1	44.8	44.4	62.7	63.7	38.5	68.3	42.1	36.4	61.2
% With 1+ Persons Per Room...	4.3	4.3	5.7	3.9	3.3	3.1	4.7	9.5	3.1	3.1	5.0
Median Value: Owner Units.......$$	39300	-	38400	37500	39600	43000	37600	32000	38800	30800	36300
Median Rent: Rental Units.......$$	194	195	197	196	190	205	192	192	197	181	194
Median Number Of Rooms: All Units.	5.0	3.4	5.2	4.9	5.1	5.4	4.7	5.3	4.9	4.5	5.0

Tract Number	6611
Total Population.............	5145
% Male.......................	46.7
% Black......................	0.0
% Other Nonwhite.............	5.5
% Of Spanish Origin..........	5.4
% Foreign Born...............	19.1
% Living In Group Quarters...	0.0
% 13 Years Old And Under.....	15.2
% 14-20 Years Old............	9.5
% 21-64 Years Old............	55.1
% 65-74 Years Old............	14.2
% 75 Years Old And Over......	5.9
% In Different House.........	26.3
% Families With Female Head..	11.8
Median School Years Completed...	12.2
Median Family Income, 1979.....$$	24600
% Income Below Poverty Level....	3.8
% Income Of $30,000 Or More....	33.0
% White Collar Workers.......	55.3
% Civilian Labor Force Unemployed.	5.1
% Riding To Work By Automobile....	73.7
Mean Commuting Time - Minutes....	36.8
Population Per Household..........	2.7
Total Housing Units..........	1927
% Condominiums...............	0.0
% Built 1970 Or Later........	1.1
% Owner Occupied.............	80.6
% With 1+ Persons Per Room...	3.4
Median Value: Owner Units.......$$	45300
Median Rent: Rental Units.......$$	215
Median Number Of Rooms: All Units.	5.1

policemen to move in. The number of workers in professional occupations has also grown.

Part of Chicago Lawn's recent history is tied to that of its northern neighbor, Gage Park. In the 1960s racial conflict erupted over housing on the South Side, and the integration of Gage Park High School. Several factors account for the particularly intense struggle in Chicag Lawn. West Englewood, its neighbor to the east, has changed into an all-black community characterized by deteriorating housing and business structures. Many feared this example as an inevitable consequence of racial integration. Illegal real estate tactics were used to panic white residents after the first black families moved in east of Western Avenue in late 1974, so that within less than two years thousands of whites had left. The American Nazi Party, which has its local headquarters in Chicago Lawn, together with the Ku Klux Klan, helped rally residents against black migration. Today, Western Avenue has become the dividing line between the races. Several coalition groups are working to keep the entire area stable. In 1983, under pressure from community residents, the Chicago Housing Authority sold two buildings it had acquired for scattered-site public housing. Although Chicago Lawn has been a community in turmoil in recent years, it appears to be relatively peaceful at present.

Antoinette LoBosco

Community Area 66 -- Chicago Lawn
Selected Characteristics of Census Tracts: 1970

Tract Number	TOTAL	6601	6602	6603	6604	6605	6606	6607	6608	6609	6610
Total Population.............	48435	166	5501	5501	4277	4029	5632	2408	5359	4289	5558
% Male.........................	46.7	41.0	47.2	45.8	46.7	47.2	45.9	48.2	46.2	46.2	47.1
% Black........................	0.0	0.0	0.0	0.0	0.0	0.0	0.0	0.0	0.0	0.1	0.0
% Other Nonwhite...............	0.4	0.6	0.5	0.3	0.0	0.3	0.4	0.2	0.3	0.9	0.5
% Of Spanish Language..........	1.1	0.0	1.5	1.4	0.8	1.3	0.7	0.8	0.7	1.0	1.6
% Foreign Born.................	20.8	9.4	13.6	17.5	14.3	17.2	20.2	16.7	26.2	40.1	24.7
% Living In Group Quarters.....	0.4	0.0	0.4	0.3	0.0	0.0	0.1	1.5	0.0	2.2	0.1
% 13 Years Old And Under.......	17.1	14.5	20.5	16.9	21.1	20.7	15.3	20.3	14.6	10.5	16.4
% 14-20 Years Old..............	9.5	7.8	9.4	9.6	10.6	10.2	8.5	10.8	8.5	7.5	9.0
% 21-64 Years Old..............	56.4	59.0	54.4	53.4	52.6	55.0	55.8	55.9	58.5	59.5	57.8
% 65-74 Years Old..............	10.8	11.4	10.3	12.4	10.2	9.4	13.7	8.4	11.6	12.9	10.8
% 75 Years Old And Over........	6.2	7.2	5.4	7.7	5.4	4.8	6.7	4.7	6.8	9.5	6.1
% In Different House...........	65.3	29.1	60.7	56.1	68.9	63.3	65.3	75.4	62.3	64.1	65.3
% Families With Female Head....	13.6	18.8	14.9	16.6	12.6	13.5	16.9	13.1	13.6	15.0	11.7
Median School Years Completed...	11.2	12.0	11.4	10.8	11.1	11.6	10.8	10.4	11.7	11.1	10.9
Median Family Income, 1969...$$	11582	8636	11764	10942	11258	11804	10503	11333	11152	11222	12148
% Income Below Poverty Level....	4.2	11.6	6.0	4.2	4.2	4.5	4.5	4.7	3.0	2.2	3.9
% Income of $15,000 or More....	29.2	7.4	28.6	26.7	28.9	32.7	25.8	32.9	29.0	27.1	28.4
% White Collar Workers.........	23.5	31.6	23.1	21.7	21.8	24.5	19.0	20.7	27.3	30.9	23.8
% Civilian Labor Force Unemployed.	3.5	0.0	3.3	5.8	5.3	3.2	3.4	2.9	3.1	1.9	2.6
% Riding To Work By Automobile....	58.4	21.8	57.5	53.3	64.0	65.2	58.4	55.3	61.7	47.0	57.5
Population Per Household........	2.7	1.9	2.8	2.6	2.9	2.9	2.4	2.9	2.5	2.3	2.7
Total Housing Units..........	18450	94	2010	2143	1515	1401	2345	841	2187	1882	2103
% Condominiums & Cooperatives.....	0.2	0.0	0.4	0.5	0.0	0.0	0.0	0.0	0.0	0.6	0.0
% Built 1960 Or Later.............	5.1	0.0	3.1	2.9	7.3	6.0	1.7	12.4	3.5	5.0	8.1
% Owner Occupied.................	52.1	20.2	44.6	45.2	61.5	59.9	39.2	65.0	42.4	37.5	62.1
% With 1+ Persons Per Room.......	4.1	2.3	5.2	3.4	4.7	4.5	3.6	6.6	2.2	3.1	4.1
Median Value: Owner Units.......$$	19200	-	19000	19300	18200	19300	18400	16200	19300	18500	18500
Median Rent: Rental Units.......$$	114	107	113	116	112	111	112	104	117	106	115
Median Number Of Rooms: All Units.	4.9	3.5	5.0	4.9	4.9	5.2	4.7	5.0	4.8	4.4	4.9

Tract Number	6611
Total Population..............	5715
% Male.........................	47.3
% Black........................	0.0
% Other Nonwhite...............	0.2
% Of Spanish Language..........	0.8
% Foreign Born.................	17.8
% Living In Group Quarters.......	0.0
% 13 Years Old And Under.........	17.4
% 14-20 Years Old..............	11.2
% 21-64 Years Old..............	60.2
% 65-74 Years Old..............	7.0
% 75 Years Old And Over........	4.2
% In Different House...........	77.6
% Families With Female Head.......	8.7
Median School Years Completed....	11.8
Median Family Income, 1969......$$	12875
% Income Below Poverty Level....	4.0
% Income of $15,000 or More....	34.6
% White Collar Workers.........	21.7
% Civilian Labor Force Unemployed.	3.7
% Riding To Work By Automobile....	65.2
Population Per Household..........	3.0
Total Housing Units..........	1929
% Condominiums & Cooperatives.....	0.0
% Built 1960 Or Later..........	7.3
% Owner Occupied.................	80.0
% With 1+ Persons Per Room.......	5.2
Median Value: Owner Units.......$$	21800
Median Rent: Rental Units.......$$	136
Median Number Of Rooms: All Units.	4.9

Community Area 67

West Englewood

The West Englewood Community is located about eight miles south and west of the Loop. It was an area of swamp and oak forest until after the Civil War. In 1865, the land was included in the Town of Lake. Much of the early development of West Englewood centered on what is now the intersection of 63rd Street and Ashland Avenue, where J.P. Jensen built a dry goods store and a few houses were erected on Samuel E. Gross's nearby subdivision. After the area around the railroad station to the east was renamed Englewood, this community area came to be called Englewood-on-the-Hill, because of some high ground along Loomis Street near 69th, and along Paulina Street near 64th. In the early days the land from 63rd to 67th streets between Ashland Avenue and the Pennsylvania tracks to the west was owned by the Drexel family of Philadelphia, who donated other land to the east which became Drexel Boulevard. The land in West Englewood was known as the Drexel Estate, or Drexel Park. Drexel Park was absorbed in the 360-acre South Lynn development, platted in 1870.

The community began to develop after the Fire of 1871. It grew slowly. The Town of Lake, including the West Englewood community

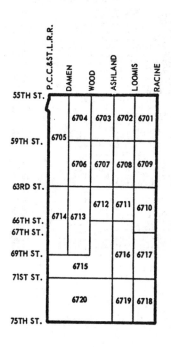

Community Area 67 -- West Englewood
Population and Housing Characteristics, 1930-1980

	1980	1970	1960	1950	1940	1930
Total Popualtion........	62,069	61,910	58,516	62,842	64,171	63,845
% Male.................	46.6	47.7	48.6	49.3	50.0	50.5
% Female...............	53.4	52.4	51.4	50.7	50.0	49.5
% White................	1.3	51.1	88.1	93.9	96.1	96.9
% Black................	98.1	48.3	11.7	6.0	3.9	3.1
% Other Nonwhite Races...	0.6	0.6	0.2	0.1	0.0	0.0
% Under 5 Years Old.....	10.1	9.6	10.7	9.2	6.7	8.7
% 5-19 Years Old........	35.9	33.1	23.4	20.6	24.9	28.2
% 20-44 Years Old.......	35.1	30.3	31.8	39.2	40.9	41.6
% 45-64 Years Old.......	14.8	18.9	23.3	23.3	21.5	17.3
% 65 Years and Older....	4.1	8.1	10.8	8.7	6.0	4.2
Median School Years....	11.8	10.6	9.5	8.9	8.3	*
Total Housing Units.....	16,980	18,511	18,224	17,732	16,778	*
% In One-Unit Structures.	41.3	36.2	38.8	*	*	*
% Owner Occupied........	48.3	47.7	51.0	50.4	44.3	*
% Renter Occupied.......	45.1	46.6	46.3	48.8	54.3	*
% Vacant...............	6.6	5.7	2.7	0.8	1.4	*
% 1+ Persons per Room....	13.9	12.5	8.8	11.0	*	*

Community Area 67 -- West Englewood
Selected Characteristics of Census Tracts: 1980

Tract Number	Total	6701	6702	6703	6704	6705	6706	6707	6708	6709	6710
Total Population.............	62069	2782	3062	2721	3090	2254	3479	2989	2582	2225	692
% Male........................	46.6	47.3	46.8	45.9	44.8	47.1	48.4	45.7	45.4	45.9	43.2
% Black.......................	98.1	98.0	98.3	94.5	95.1	95.4	98.4	98.2	98.9	99.5	99.9
% Other Nonwhite..............	0.6	1.2	0.5	2.7	1.6	1.5	0.3	0.5	0.2	0.2	0.1
% Of Spanish Origin...........	1.1	2.0	1.1	3.5	3.1	2.5	0.4	0.9	0.5	0.2	1.0
% Foreign Born................	1.1	1.6	0.8	2.6	0.6	2.9	0.4	1.6	0.5	0.2	0.0
% Living In Group Quarters....	0.1	0.0	0.0	0.0	0.0	0.0	0.0	0.3	0.2	0.0	0.0
% 13 Years Old And Under......	30.3	30.7	34.8	34.0	32.8	29.8	30.6	32.2	21.6	22.8	22.4
% 14-20 Years Old.............	18.1	20.3	19.0	15.5	16.9	15.6	21.8	19.5	15.3	15.6	8.7
% 21-64 Years Old.............	47.5	46.1	43.7	47.8	47.2	52.6	45.6	44.4	52.7	50.1	55.6
% 65-74 Years Old.............	2.8	2.2	1.6	1.7	2.1	1.5	1.5	2.7	6.5	8.0	9.2
% 75 Years Old And Over.......	1.3	0.7	0.9	1.0	0.9	0.4	0.5	1.2	3.8	3.5	4.0
% In Different House..........	28.5	33.1	38.4	26.1	26.8	50.9	24.2	28.6	28.6	29.1	11.8
% Families With Female Head...	45.9	49.1	55.6	50.0	42.9	37.3	40.8	55.7	48.9	57.2	53.9
Median School Years Completed.	11.8	12.1	10.9	11.3	12.0	11.6	11.4	11.0	12.2	12.1	12.2
Median Family Income, 1979...$$	13909	11023	9627	11109	13882	16791	14159	12827	15608	13326	15179
% Income Below Poverty Level....	29.4	36.6	40.7	38.9	29.2	28.0	36.2	34.0	20.7	32.0	21.2
% Income Of $30,000 Or More....	13.1	17.3	6.7	2.2	13.1	17.0	9.1	10.0	14.5	9.9	14.8
% White Collar Workers........	41.7	34.9	42.6	36.7	34.1	40.4	41.9	44.4	47.5	43.4	39.9
% Civilian Labor Force Unemployed.	20.6	14.7	24.4	15.7	23.1	22.2	30.7	21.5	15.6	16.2	21.8
% Riding To Work By Automobile....	58.8	62.4	55.1	51.9	55.1	59.0	67.4	46.6	60.3	48.8	49.2
Mean Commuting Time - Minutes...	41.5	39.6	38.3	40.8	41.7	48.6	43.1	39.1	38.2	44.5	38.2
Population Per Household.......	3.9	4.1	4.1	3.8	3.8	3.6	4.6	4.3	3.2	3.0	2.5
Total Housing Units..........	16980	776	813	797	875	641	796	779	869	772	285
% Condominiums................	0.0	0.0	0.0	0.0	0.0	0.0	0.0	0.0	0.0	0.0	0.0
% Built 1970 Or Later.........	3.2	2.7	2.8	1.0	0.5	10.1	3.7	0.5	2.7	2.3	0.0
% Owner Occupied..............	48.3	37.0	32.2	34.8	45.6	52.6	55.2	41.5	45.1	40.8	21.4
% With 1+ Persons Per Room....	13.9	15.9	16.6	12.7	12.6	8.2	17.7	20.0	9.6	8.5	4.7
Median Value: Owner Units....$$	27700	27000	23800	25300	28500	28900	27300	25000	25600	29500	-
Median Rent: Rental Units....$$	178	174	180	182	195	233	167	179	177	157	187
Median Number Of Rooms: All Units.	5.4	5.6	5.4	5.3	5.6	5.6	5.6	5.6	5.3	5.2	4.7

Tract Number	6711	6712	6713	6714	6715	6716	6717	6718	6719	6720
Total Population.............	2325	2642	4943	3006	5640	4203	3247	2589	1923	5675
% Male........................	45.9	46.3	46.4	47.3	46.5	46.6	45.5	47.2	46.4	48.0
% Black.......................	98.2	98.7	98.4	98.1	98.1	98.8	99.4	99.3	99.4	98.0
% Other Nonwhite..............	0.9	0.4	0.1	0.2	0.4	0.5	0.1	0.2	0.1	0.6
% Of Spanish Origin...........	0.9	0.8	0.8	0.7	0.7	0.6	0.5	0.2	0.1	1.7
% Foreign Born................	0.6	0.5	0.3	1.3	1.8	1.8	0.7	0.3	0.8	1.7
% Living In Group Quarters....	0.0	0.1	0.0	0.1	0.0	0.1	0.1	0.0	0.0	0.0
% 13 Years Old And Under......	29.0	32.3	31.9	33.7	32.9	29.0	28.9	23.0	23.2	32.5
% 14-20 Years Old.............	16.8	17.9	18.8	19.0	17.3	18.2	19.4	20.5	18.4	18.2
% 21-64 Years Old.............	48.1	45.4	46.3	44.9	47.0	47.9	47.0	51.2	53.0	47.1
% 65-74 Years Old.............	4.4	3.1	1.9	1.5	2.1	3.4	3.4	4.2	4.0	1.4
% 75 Years Old And Over.......	1.7	1.2	1.2	0.9	0.8	1.5	1.4	1.1	1.4	0.8
% In Different House..........	28.4	44.7	24.0	26.2	32.1	26.1	33.8	9.7	11.5	27.2
% Families With Female Head...	52.3	52.0	45.2	42.2	46.1	48.7	52.1	39.5	36.6	32.5
Median School Years Completed.	11.2	11.2	11.0	10.8	12.0	11.6	11.5	12.1	11.9	12.1
Median Family Income, 1979...$$	10313	11250	13244	16402	14031	10536	9897	18696	16360	19918
% Income Below Poverty Level....	35.5	34.0	31.6	18.0	25.7	37.3	38.5	15.1	24.3	13.5
% Income Of $30,000 Or More....	9.3	13.3	9.5	18.2	10.1	9.0	12.9	18.1	29.2	23.6
% White Collar Workers........	33.7	37.4	45.4	45.5	38.2	49.4	39.2	39.8	47.9	43.2
% Civilian Labor Force Unemployed.	31.1	21.3	18.9	19.4	19.0	23.0	22.9	20.9	27.5	16.4
% Riding To Work By Automobile....	58.6	57.6	58.1	69.2	60.6	52.7	62.9	67.5	64.2	61.1
Mean Commuting Time - Minutes...	39.6	41.5	42.7	36.2	43.9	41.9	39.1	36.9	35.4	46.7
Population Per Household.......	3.9	3.7	4.1	4.5	3.9	3.8	3.9	4.0	4.1	4.3
Total Housing Units..........	631	757	1342	707	1543	1178	858	688	491	1382
% Condominiums................	0.0	0.0	0.0	0.0	0.0	0.0	0.0	0.0	0.0	0.0
% Built 1970 Or Later.........	4.2	0.0	3.5	5.0	6.1	2.5	4.1	2.9	0.0	3.9
% Owner Occupied..............	39.6	34.9	49.0	66.8	52.0	39.3	39.6	64.2	68.0	78.8
% With 1+ Persons Per Room....	12.8	14.3	15.0	18.8	14.1	14.2	14.6	12.9	12.9	14.1
Median Value: Owner Units....$$	23500	27600	26000	29200	29100	25400	26000	26600	26700	31200
Median Rent: Rental Units....$$	165	179	181	184	178	177	172	165	183	181
Median Number Of Rooms: All Units.	5.4	5.2	5.5	5.5	5.3	5.4	5.5	5.6	5.6	5.6

Community Area 67 -- West Englewood
Selected Characteristics of Census Tracts: 1970

Tract Number	TOTAL	6701	6702	6703	6704	6705	6706	6707	6708	6709	6710
Total Population	61910	3533	2826	2639	2600	1634	2542	3106	3276	3254	779
% Male	47.6	46.2	49.2	49.7	48.2	46.5	50.4	47.9	46.9	44.7	44.0
% Black	48.3	80.4	33.6	0.0	0.1	0.0	0.9	28.7	96.5	98.8	99.9
% Other Nonwhite	0.6	0.7	1.2	0.7	0.8	0.6	1.2	1.6	0.3	0.5	0.1
% Of Spanish Language	3.2	9.9	8.0	3.7	4.0	4.5	5.5	7.2	0.2	3.0	0.0
% Foreign Born	6.1	3.5	8.7	15.4	14.1	11.3	8.7	8.8	0.9	0.0	0.0
% Living In Group Quarters	0.4	0.2	0.0	0.6	0.7	0.0	0.0	0.5	0.3	0.4	0.0
% 13 Years Old And Under	30.9	40.6	31.9	24.6	25.8	25.0	25.1	30.3	30.7	32.8	18.4
% 14-20 Years Old	13.5	15.4	12.1	11.6	12.0	10.0	12.2	12.7	15.0	14.0	10.1
% 21-64 Years Old	47.5	41.2	47.0	52.7	49.9	53.0	50.5	46.6	48.1	45.7	61.2
% 65-74 Years Old	5.2	1.9	5.8	7.1	7.2	7.7	7.0	6.4	4.2	4.8	7.2
% 75 Years Old And Over	2.9	0.9	3.2	4.0	5.2	4.3	5.2	4.0	1.9	2.7	3.1
% In Different House	51.2	13.5	35.1	62.0	56.9	53.5	71.4	41.4	68.0	58.3	68.4
% Families With Female Head	18.2	26.8	19.0	12.2	15.9	12.3	12.4	16.8	26.6	29.0	24.3
Median School Years Completed	10.7	10.9	10.0	10.0	10.4	9.6	10.3	9.8	11.0	10.9	12.3
Median Family Income, 1969 $$	9654	8353	9921	9701	11732	10524	10072	8157	8000	7889	9615
% Income Below Poverty Level	12.0	17.6	11.5	7.5	10.4	3.7	6.5	16.3	18.4	20.2	1.5
% Income of $15,000 or More	15.9	9.0	16.0	11.7	23.1	21.7	20.1	11.1	14.4	15.4	18.8
% White Collar Workers	14.5	12.2	12.4	19.4	15.0	11.6	16.3	13.7	12.4	15.9	18.1
% Civilian Labor Force Unemployed	6.5	5.9	8.6	3.9	4.8	4.5	7.3	10.3	5.6	5.1	3.7
% Riding To Work By Automobile	56.4	54.7	62.3	54.6	57.1	58.4	55.9	57.4	52.8	51.7	50.6
Population Per Household	3.5	4.3	3.4	3.0	3.3	3.0	3.2	3.2	3.4	3.5	2.8
Total Housing Units	18517	871	952	932	813	564	869	970	949	968	285
% Condominiums & Cooperatives	0.2	0.0	0.0	0.0	0.0	1.1	0.0	0.0	0.6	0.0	0.0
% Built 1960 Or Later	4.3	1.8	0.4	1.5	2.1	6.7	2.5	0.9	2.1	9.3	5.2
% Owner Occupied	47.5	39.0	33.7	37.0	51.7	55.7	51.8	46.0	40.7	33.6	22.8
% With 1+ Persons Per Room	13.6	24.3	12.6	7.3	8.6	7.8	9.0	13.2	15.3	14.7	7.5
Median Value: Owner Units $$	14900	15600	14000	14000	15100	14200	13400	13900	14800	16900	-
Median Rent: Rental Units $$	103	118	95	87	102	98	93	96	109	105	115
Median Number Of Rooms: All Units	5.1	5.3	5.1	4.9	5.4	5.0	5.1	5.1	5.2	5.1	4.6

Tract Number	6711	6712	6713	6714	6715	6716	6717	6718	6719	6720
Total Population	2852	2459	3955	2565	5055	5197	3309	3168	2322	4839
% Male	47.5	47.1	47.2	47.5	47.4	47.6	47.4	47.3	47.7	49.8
% Black	97.1	58.8	2.6	0.0	1.9	97.6	97.8	97.6	96.0	0.4
% Other Nonwhite	0.3	1.5	0.5	0.3	0.3	0.3	0.3	0.1	0.5	0.3
% Of Spanish Language	0.9	5.8	1.6	1.9	0.9	0.9	0.3	0.0	2.2	5.5
% Foreign Born	0.4	6.2	6.6	13.1	13.3	0.5	0.7	1.0	0.3	8.6
% Living In Group Quarters	1.0	0.8	0.2	0.2	0.5	0.2	1.1	0.1	0.0	0.1
% 13 Years Old And Under	35.7	31.4	25.4	25.3	26.3	36.5	36.0	38.6	37.0	27.3
% 14-20 Years Old	15.1	14.2	12.5	12.2	10.8	15.3	16.0	17.1	15.7	11.9
% 21-64 Years Old	45.0	45.8	49.4	51.5	50.7	45.0	44.2	42.0	43.8	49.9
% 65-74 Years Old	2.9	5.3	7.4	7.3	7.9	2.3	2.7	1.4	2.3	7.4
% 75 Years Old And Over	1.3	3.4	5.4	3.7	4.4	0.9	1.1	0.9	1.2	3.5
% In Different House	56.4	22.9	56.8	64.3	62.6	39.9	48.7	40.8	29.1	72.4
% Families With Female Head	23.5	22.9	14.6	9.3	15.6	22.2	24.9	16.0	13.4	11.5
Median School Years Completed	10.8	10.3	10.5	10.7	10.3	11.1	11.3	11.2	11.6	10.6
Median Family Income, 1969 $$	10045	8908	10619	11310	9949	8642	8123	9313	10508	11123
% Income Below Poverty Level	10.3	16.0	12.9	3.1	13.8	14.6	19.6	8.5	4.4	4.8
% Income of $15,000 or More	12.4	13.8	14.3	23.3	15.5	13.2	7.3	17.7	19.6	23.7
% White Collar Workers	11.3	12.0	18.8	20.0	17.9	9.8	14.1	10.8	13.6	14.1
% Civilian Labor Force Unemployed	8.7	8.7	4.3	3.9	3.6	10.8	6.2	5.6	9.3	4.9
% Riding To Work By Automobile	45.9	45.5	57.7	58.1	65.2	53.9	53.8	53.6	57.5	63.4
Population Per Household	4.2	3.2	3.0	3.2	3.1	4.2	4.1	4.8	4.6	3.4
Total Housing Units	745	815	1367	811	1750	1279	904	685	522	1466
% Condominiums & Cooperatives	0.0	2.0	0.0	0.0	0.0	0.5	0.0	0.0	0.0	0.0
% Built 1960 Or Later	3.2	1.5	1.3	9.5	7.9	1.3	4.0	1.9	6.2	11.8
% Owner Occupied	38.5	31.8	49.5	65.7	47.5	39.8	36.4	67.9	69.7	76.6
% With 1+ Persons Per Room	24.9	12.9	8.4	9.3	9.1	20.8	19.1	22.1	20.3	10.8
Median Value: Owner Units $$	14400	15800	13700	15300	14700	14700	14500	14900	15500	16300
Median Rent: Rental Units $$	110	104	97	95	93	112	113	111	119	96
Median Number Of Rooms: All Units	5.2	4.9	5.0	5.0	4.9	5.2	5.2	5.7	5.7	5.1

area, was annexed to Chicago in 1889. With the building boom motivated by the 1893 Columbian Exposition, the area received a major impetus for growth. An electric trolley line was built between Ashland Avenue and the fairground and residents began to refer to the community as West Englewood. By 1896, West Englewood was bound to Chicago by streetcar lines. Sewers were laid in 1901 and other improvements followed soon.

The first settlers were largely working-class people of Swedish and German ethnicity. A small community of blacks lived in West Englewood around Loomis and 63rd streets during the late 19th century.

In 1907, the Englewood elevated train line was extended to Loomis Street. This new access stimulated residential construction in West Englewood. The new structures were mainly single-family frame houses with some two-story flats. The community reached residential maturity about 1914.

Italian-Americans began moving in after 1907. The 1919 race riot, which started on the lakefront, spread to West Englewood, where many black residents were driven out. By 1920, the community totaled 53,276 persons of whom Germans, Irish and Italians were most numerous among the foreign-born. Following World War I, many brick bungalows were built along Garfield Boulevard and Marquette Road. Industry expanded into the community, swelling its population to almost 64,000 in 1930. During the 1920s, the population of West Englewood increased 20 percent. Germans, Irish and Italians were the leading foreign-stock groups, although many of the aging Swedish immigrants remained, and the black colony along Loomis Street had grown to nearly 2,000. During the 1930s local businessmen launched a campaign to change the name of the community to Ogden Hill. The population increased slightly to its historic high in 1940, as more blacks moved in and a few whites moved out. The number of residents dropped noticeably in the 1940s and 1950s as greater numbers of whites moved out. In 1960, blacks were 12 percent of the population of West Englewood, still concentrated near their original settlement at Loomis and 63rd streets. By 1960, Census Tracts 6708 and 6709 had become black neighborhoods.

Although the total was concealed by the high fertility rates of that era, nearly 14,000 whites moved out of West Englewood in the 1950s. The rest have moved out in the last two decades. The total population has grown as even more blacks moved in. The percentage of blacks grew to 48 in 1970 and 98 in 1980, as the expanding black population of Chicago occupied much of the South Side.

There was virtually no residential construction in West Englewood after 1930. In the 1960s. housing began to deteriorate noticeably. The new residents could not afford the upkeep of property. The rapid ethnic turnover of the neighborhood had undermined West Englewood's economy. This coincided with the deterioration of aging buildings brought on by natural decay, overcrowding and the poverty of its new residents.

During 1975, at least 40 buildings were abandoned and 10 demolished. Newly-acquired homes were abandoned by poor families who could not afford to maintain the mortgage payments. The poverty of many homeowners made it difficult for them to get low-interest loans for repairing and upgrading houses.

As a result of large-scale abandonment of homes during the 1970s the West Englewood Community Organization (WECO) was formed in 1970 by a group of three churches in the area. WECO is a community-based research and advocacy group providing assistance to families in West Englewood, ranging from cases of police mistreatment to organizing a community development corporation to spearhead housing rehabilitation efforts. WECO also runs a food co-operative, a state-financed mental health clinic and a summer program of jobs and educational seminars for 100 to 120 youths each year. Many homes and buildings have been rehabilitated and sold through the Neighborhood Housing Service (NHS), which is a national network of more than 90 neighborhood improvement programs through the country, basically concerned with the rehabilitation of abandoned buildings. Various neighborhood oranizations organize block clean-ups and landscaping vacant lots. Downtown and neighborhood banks and savings and loan associations work with community groups by placing representatives on their boards of directors and making loans to low-income residents.

A transitional period of West Englewood's history is over. In 1980. almost three-fourths of the population had been living in the same house for at least five years. The unemployment rate was more than 20 percent and almost 30 percent of all families lived in poverty. Despite this and despite foreclosures nearly half of all housing units were owner-occupied. The houses tend to be small and inexpensive, the median value being $20,000 below the city median. West Englewood is especially vulnerable to cutbacks in government jobs because 14 percent of the community's residents are government employed, mostly with the Postal Service, the Chicago Transit Authority and the School Board.

Annie Ruth Leslie

Community Area 68

Englewood

The Englewood community area is located seven miles south of downtown Chicago. The area was originally swamp and oak forest located on a ridge running southwest from Chicago, now Vincennes Avenue. In the 1840s a station for the Michigan City stage road was built on the ridge.

Englewood developed early because of railroads that located in that area. The first, the Michigan, Southern and Northern Indiana Railway, later part of the New York Central line, ran through the district in 1852. In the same year, the Rock Island and Wabash Railroads were built. In 1854, the Fort Wayne Railroad was built forming a junction around which a settlement called Junction Grove began to develop. The earliest settlers were German and Irish railroad workers and farmers who located around Junction Avenue, now 63rd Street, extending westward from Indiana Avenue to Halsted Street. Most of the area around 63rd and Halsted streets was devoted to truck gardening. Junction Grove became part of the Town of Lake in 1865.

The density of oak trees and forest prompted early settler-realtor Henry B. Lewis to suggest in 1868 that the community's name be changed to Englewood. The name derives from Englewood, New Jersey, then also a forested place and the home of some of the settlers. Developer Lewis thought Englewood gave the place a more prestigious name than Junction Grove, which clearly implied a settlement of railroad workers.

In 1868, the Cook County Normal School (later Chicago State University) was established on 10 acres of land donated by prominent land developer L. W. Beck. After Beck subdivided land near the Normal School, the area attracted middle-class professionals and businessmen, who established a community called Normal Park, or Normalville. Thereafter, local institutional development occurred rapidly. In 1869, the Roman Catholic Parish of St. Anne's was established. Within a decade Baptist, Methodist Episcopalian, Swedish Lutheran, German Evangelical and other churches opened. Englewood High School opened in 1873. In 1872, the area from Wentworth Avenue to Halsted Street south of 55th Street to 71st Street was laid out in streets.

New settlers who were Civil War veterans came to Englewood but the first extensive development of Englewood came after the 1871 Fire when many different groups came into Englewood and built new homes.

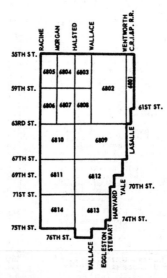

Many settlers were attracted to Englewood because it offered excellent suburban transportation. The schools and churches attracted even more middle-class and professional people. In 1880 the Standard Oil Company constructed works on Michigan Avenue, employing 30 men. The Union Stock Yards, the center of the nation's meat packing industry, was located just north of Englewood. This attracted other residents. Despite these opportunities Englewood was a sparsely-settled area with Irish, German and Scotch residents in 1880. In 1889, the Town of Lake, including Englewood, was annexed to Chicago. Following annexation, the Columbian Exposition occurred, leading to improvement in transportation lines which in turn set off an expansion of Englewood that was to last almost a half century.

Swedish-Americans began moving into Englewood during the pre-Exposition boom of the 1890s. Many German and Irish residents moved farther south. The land west of Halsted Street from 65th to 67th streets, called "Hettie Green's Cabbage Patch," was subdivided and built up with two- and three-story apartment buildings. In 1893, the South Side elevated line was completed to Jackson Park and in 1896, the surface lines on Halsted, 63rd and 59th streets were electrified. By 1905, Englewood was residentially mature with mainly single-family frame dwellings and some two-family and four-family two-deckers.

In 1905 Hamilton Park, located between 72nd and 74th streets on the eastern boundary was opened. The Englwood branch of the elevated line was completed in 1907. In 1920, the population of Englewood was 86,619. One fifth were foreign born with Swedish, Irish and German

Community Area 68 — Englewood
Population and Housing Characteristics, 1930-1980

	1980	1970	1960	1950	1940	1930
Total Population.......	59,075	89,713	97,595	94,134	92,849	89,063
% Male.................	45.5	46.5	48.3	48.7	49.5	50.3
% Female...............	54.5	53.5	51.7	51.3	50.5	49.7
% White................	0.6	3.0	30.8	89.4	97.8	98.7
% Black................	98.9	96.4	68.9	10.5	2.2	1.3
% Other Nonwhite Races...	0.5	0.6	0.3	0.1	0.0	0.0
% Under 5 Years Old......	9.9	11.6	14.9	9.5	6.9	7.1
% 5-19 Years Old........	32.0	36.7	26.9	19.3	22.3	24.0
% 20-44 Years Old........	32.0	31.9	34.33	39.7	41.1	43.4
% 45-64 Years Old........	17.5	14.7	17.2	23.0	22.4	19.9
% 65 Years and Older.....	8.6	5.1	6.7	8.5	7.3	5.6
Median School Years....	11.2	10.5	9.3	9.5	8.5	*
Total Housing Units....	19,301	25,234	27,157	28,059	26,583	*
% In One-Unit Structures.	17.7	15.4	19.2	*	*	*
% Owner Occupied.........	27.1	23.6	26.8	28.3	23.4	*
% Renter Occupied........	64.8	69.4	68.9	70.0	73.4	*
% Vacant................	8.1	7.0	4.3	1.7	3.2	*
% 1+ Persons per Room....	12.3	19.8	22.9	14.5	*	*

Community Area 68 — Englewood
Selected Characteristics of Census Tracts: 1980

Tract Number	Total	6801	6802	6803	6804	6805	6806	6807	6808	6809	6810
Total Population.............	59075	957	6834	2205	2690	3076	3057	2091	2129	6624	6213
% Male.......................	45.5	47.4	45.4	46.3	44.6	45.7	45.1	43.2	46.5	43.9	45.8
% Black......................	98.8	98.3	98.8	99.4	96.7	98.7	99.4	95.7	99.2	98.9	98.9
% Other Nonwhite.............	0.5	0.1	0.3	0.3	1.6	0.8	0.1	3.7	0.3	0.6	0.4
% Of Spanish Origin..........	0.8	0.1	0.7	1.0	3.1	1.5	0.4	1.7	0.9	0.6	0.8
% Foreign Born...............	0.7	0.0	0.6	0.6	0.2	0.2	0.0	3.2	0.0	0.7	0.7
% Living In Group Quarters...	0.5	8.0	0.4	2.1	0.3	0.0	0.0	2.4	0.1	0.4	0.2
% 13 Years Old And Under.....	28.2	23.0	26.2	31.2	31.2	28.9	27.8	25.2	27.3	30.9	25.5
% 14-20 Years Old...........	15.9	14.3	16.4	17.5	18.7	19.1	14.5	14.0	15.7	13.4	14.9
% 21-64 Years Old...........	47.3	47.8	46.4	45.4	45.5	47.0	46.6	50.5	47.9	42.4	49.9
% 65-74 Years Old...........	5.7	9.3	7.3	4.0	3.3	3.8	6.8	6.9	5.9	6.8	6.5
% 75 Years Old And Over......	3.0	5.6	3.7	2.0	1.3	1.1	4.3	3.3	3.2	6.5	3.2
% In Different House.........	36.8	12.0	26.9	49.2	27.8	51.4	44.4	39.5	51.2	45.3	28.0
% Families With Female Head...	57.2	56.9	58.6	61.1	57.8	53.4	59.0	56.3	62.0	61.2	57.5
Median School Years Completed...	11.2	12.1	11.0	10.8	11.5	10.5	10.9	10.6	10.4	10.5	11.0
Median Family Income, 1979......$$	10597	8788	11581	5833	7607	11977	12430	11528	10786	8122	11161
% Income Below Poverty Level....	35.8	50.0	36.6	49.6	48.6	35.6	28.2	35.4	41.4	42.3	29.1
% Income Of $30,000 Or More....	7.7	8.0	10.9	1.4	7.6	7.5	4.6	4.8	5.8	5.8	5.1
% White Collar Workers.......	39.7	44.9	41.2	39.5	36.2	37.6	37.8	48.8	26.2	38.2	40.2
% Civilian Labor Force Unemployed.	18.2	18.5	20.2	14.4	11.4	18.3	19.0	18.2	12.1	23.6	22.9
% Riding To Work By Automobile....	50.6	43.4	48.3	32.7	59.4	54.2	38.4	49.0	52.2	51.9	54.6
Mean Commuting Time - Minutes...	41.3	37.1	38.1	43.7	38.3	40.9	48.7	38.5	43.9	41.0	38.9
Population Per Household.........	3.3	2.9	3.4	3.5	4.0	3.9	3.1	3.1	3.3	2.8	3.2
Total Housing Units...........	19301	328	2192	711	747	874	1034	701	712	2757	2056
% Condominiums...............	0.0	0.0	0.0	0.0	0.0	0.0	0.0	0.0	0.0	0.0	0.0
% Built 1970 Or Later........	4.5	0.0	4.2	1.8	5.4	4.9	1.2	2.4	2.9	13.4	2.3
% Owner Occupied.............	27.1	34.8	32.2	23.6	27.2	30.2	29.3	27.4	26.7	10.0	30.8
% With 1+ Persons Per Room.......	12.3	6.3	12.2	14.9	14.5	13.3	10.6	9.4	12.1	12.6	10.2
Median Value: Owner Units......$$	24700	-	22500	21900	26800	25100	23200	24200	24400	23200	23900
Median Rent: Rental Units......$$	165	145	154	162	176	177	155	159	158	154	166
Median Number Of Rooms: All Units.	5.0	5.5	5.3	5.0	5.6	5.6	5.0	5.2	5.3	3.8	5.2

Tract Number	6811	6812	6813	6814
Total Population.............	6927	6017	4901	5354
% Male.......................	45.3	45.4	46.1	47.1
% Black......................	99.0	99.4	99.4	99.2
% Other Nonwhite.............	0.3	0.2	0.2	0.3
% Of Spanish Origin..........	0.6	0.4	0.9	0.5
% Foreign Born...............	1.6	0.6	0.2	0.2
% Living In Group Quarters...	0.0	0.3	0.7	0.0
% 13 Years Old And Under.....	28.4	30.8	29.2	25.5
% 14-20 Years Old...........	16.7	16.3	15.5	16.8
% 21-64 Years Old...........	48.3	45.9	48.3	51.2
% 65-74 Years Old...........	4.6	5.1	5.1	4.6
% 75 Years Old And Over......	1.9	2.0	1.8	1.9
% In Different House.........	32.7	38.9	44.0	31.6
% Families With Female Head.......	53.9	62.5	58.0	45.6
Median School Years Completed.....	11.3	11.9	11.9	11.8
Median Family Income, 1979......$$	11772	9970	10105	14040
% Income Below Poverty Level.....	30.6	37.0	37.8	27.8
% Income Of $30,000 Or More.....	11.0	1.9	9.5	15.9
% White Collar Workers.......	40.8	38.9	46.0	36.8
% Civilian Labor Force Unemployed.	19.1	12.8	20.3	12.0
% Riding To Work By Automobile...	54.1	44.5	50.3	57.8
Mean Commuting Time - Minutes...	43.2	42.8	43.5	41.3
Population Per Household.........	3.5	3.3	3.3	3.6
Total Housing Units...........	2129	1939	1589	1532
% Condominiums...............	0.0	0.0	0.0	0.0
% Built 1970 Or Later........	2.3	5.7	2.9	1.1
% Owner Occupied.............	29.3	21.1	23.0	51.0
% With 1+ Persons Per Room.......	12.2	15.4	12.3	12.1
Median Value: Owner Units......$$	25200	24500	25900	27300
Median Rent: Rental Units......$$	175	169	184	169
Median Number Of Rooms: All Units.	5.1	4.8	5.0	5.4

Community Area 68 — Englewood
Selected Characteristics of Census Tracts: 1970

Tract Number	TOTAL	6801	6802	6803	6804	6805	6806	6807	6808	6809	6810
Total Population	89713	1607	10946	3647	4688	4959	4833	2931	3327	12843	8158
% Male	46.5	45.7	45.8	47.5	48.6	49.0	46.9	43.4	45.1	45.4	47.3
% Black	96.4	98.5	98.6	93.0	76.5	93.0	98.9	94.1	98.2	97.9	97.4
% Other Nonwhite	0.6	0.1	0.1	0.6	2.2	1.4	0.3	2.6	0.1	0.5	0.5
% Of Spanish Language	1.9	1.0	0.6	4.2	18.2	3.8	0.4	0.9	1.8	1.2	0.0
% Foreign Born	0.6	0.4	0.3	0.3	3.5	0.7	0.0	4.0	0.1	0.8	0.3
% Living In Group Quarters	0.9	1.5	0.5	0.5	1.2	0.5	0.3	3.4	1.1	1.3	1.6
% 13 Years Old And Under	35.6	32.2	34.9	40.5	41.1	42.5	32.5	32.1	34.5	37.2	30.6
% 14-20 Years Old	14.4	12.8	16.2	14.3	14.1	14.5	14.5	13.0	14.8	12.7	14.9
% 21-64 Years Old	44.9	45.4	42.8	41.2	41.1	40.0	44.7	48.6	45.5	44.8	47.7
% 65-74 Years Old	3.6	6.6	4.4	2.6	2.4	2.1	5.7	4.6	3.6	3.6	4.8
% 75 Years Old And Over	1.5	3.0	1.8	1.4	1.4	0.9	2.6	1.7	1.6	1.6	1.9
% In Different House	49.2	82.0	61.0	27.1	23.9	24.7	55.6	59.3	46.9	37.8	50.5
% Families With Female Head	29.7	30.7	31.0	25.4	28.2	26.4	33.4	32.1	31.6	32.0	27.8
Median School Years Completed	10.5	9.6	10.2	10.2	9.9	10.2	10.3	10.3	9.6	10.3	10.4
Median Family Income, 1969 $$	7509	6741	6931	6964	8048	7312	7178	8219	7294	6581	8250
% Income Below Poverty Level	24.3	27.6	28.2	27.4	18.7	24.5	23.2	19.0	28.9	26.7	18.1
% Income of $15,000 or More	11.1	8.4	9.1	9.0	8.9	7.7	11.8	11.1	6.3	7.5	11.6
% White Collar Workers	10.9	17.7	10.6	5.9	9.9	6.6	11.8	21.5	9.8	10.4	10.8
% Civilian Labor Force Unemployed	7.7	5.4	8.8	10.7	10.0	9.5	5.3	4.7	7.5	8.2	6.2
% Riding To Work By Automobile	50.0	52.6	48.9	44.6	56.0	49.8	51.9	39.9	40.6	44.7	54.1
Population Per Household	3.8	3.6	3.8	4.0	4.2	4.5	3.5	3.7	3.8	3.4	3.6
Total Housing Units	25250	473	3013	975	1186	1144	1444	819	945	4244	2406
% Condominiums & Cooperatives	0.5	0.0	0.6	0.5	0.5	0.9	0.0	0.7	0.5	0.3	0.0
% Built 1960 Or Later	5.2	0.0	5.7	4.1	1.0	0.6	0.6	1.3	2.1	14.3	2.7
% Owner Occupied	23.2	27.7	27.2	25.4	20.7	30.1	21.3	25.3	21.6	22.7	26.2
% With 1+ Persons Per Room	20.6	15.5	21.6	23.6	23.5	26.8	17.7	18.7	21.2	22.7	16.4
Median Value: Owner Units $$	15100	-	14000	12700	-	14900	13600	14300	14000	15800	14200
Median Rent: Rental Units $$	110	92	102	106	108	117	102	103	103	108	112
Median Number Of Rooms: All Units	4.8	5.2	5.0	4.9	4.9	5.2	4.9	5.0	4.8	3.8	5.0

Tract Number	6811	6812	6813	6814
Total Population	9321	9232	6396	6825
% Male	46.2	46.9	46.5	47.0
% Black	98.6	97.8	98.3	98.0
% Other Nonwhite	0.3	0.4	0.5	0.2
% Of Spanish Language	0.2	0.7	1.1	0.6
% Foreign Born	0.3	0.1	0.4	0.2
% Living In Group Quarters	0.9	0.0	1.0	0.3
% 13 Years Old And Under	35.4	36.0	33.1	35.7
% 14-20 Years Old	14.3	14.1	13.6	16.1
% 21-64 Years Old	46.1	45.8	49.3	44.3
% 65-74 Years Old	2.9	2.9	3.1	2.8
% 75 Years Old And Over	1.3	1.2	0.9	1.1
% In Different House	54.3	50.7	59.6	60.9
% Families With Female Head	31.3	31.2	26.5	24.6
Median School Years Completed	10.9	11.2	11.9	10.6
Median Family Income, 1969 $$	7423	6915	9505	9159
% Income Below Poverty Level	26.7	27.6	20.5	19.3
% Income of $15,000 or More	12.0	10.1	20.5	18.3
% White Collar Workers	9.8	10.6	13.1	10.3
% Civilian Labor Force Unemployed	9.6	6.4	5.6	7.6
% Riding To Work By Automobile	50.0	51.7	55.5	53.4
Population Per Household	3.9	3.8	3.6	4.2
Total Housing Units	2528	2596	1817	1660
% Condominiums & Cooperatives	0.6	0.9	0.9	0.6
% Built 1960 Or Later	3.0	5.4	6.3	2.4
% Owner Occupied	25.0	19.5	21.4	50.7
% With 1+ Persons Per Room	20.9	21.7	16.6	18.9
Median Value: Owner Units $$	15700	16900	18200	15500
Median Rent: Rental Units $$	114	114	125	111
Median Number Of Rooms: All Units	4.8	4.6	4.9	5.3

the leading nationalities. New construction continued through the 1920s and many new apartment buildings and single-family residences were erected. The population grew to 89,000 in 1930.

Merchandise businesses located at 63rd and Halsted streets in the early 1900s. Because of the elevated and interurban transit lines that moved people across the city, the 63rd and Halsted shopping district was easily accessible. The Becker-Ryan Store building was a vertical shopping center, containing other offices and businesses including a saloon and a Chinese restaurant. Sears Roebuck acquired the Becker-Ryan store in 1929 and closed it in 1934, in the midst of the Depression. However, Sears built a $1.5 million store and leased other properties to create a block-long building. By this time the development of the 63rd and Halsted streets area was so extensive that it was the second busiest commercial area in Chicago. While Englewood's largest businesses thrived during the Depression, small businesses were negatively affected. Several Englewood banks collapsed. Small entertainment enterprises located along 63rd Street east of the shopping area were hurt.

By the late 1930s Englewood had become an area of contrasts. The busy and bustling shopping district expanded and upwardly mobile white-collar households occupied the apartment buildings east of Halsted Street, while working-class families lived in the numerous small homes west of Halsted. Elsewhere housing maintenance and values were in decline. Wentworth Avenue became a street of deteriorating houses, many of them dating back to the 1870s, secondhand stores and bars. Despite the Depression the total population grew to almost 93,000 in 1940. Irish, Germans and Swedes continued to dominate, and there was a pocket of Dutch residents in the southwest corner of the area. Two percent of the Englewood population was black.

Blacks lived in Englewood prior to the Civil War. One small black district (Alden Park at 67th and Racine streets) was once a terminal for the Underground Railroad bringing runaway slaves to safety. By 1885, there were two small black districts in Englewood, one along the western boundary at Racine Avenue and another a mile to the east along Stewart Street. The black population increased steadily in each decade following 1940. By 1950, blacks were 11 percent of the total; then 69 percent in 1960, 96 percent in 1970. By 1980, blacks constituted more than 99 percent of the population. Growth of the black population was brought by different factors, including improved social conditions and steady wages promised by World War II and overcrowding in Black-Belt areas in the decades after the War.

So rapid was the influx of black residents in the 1950s that the total population hit an all-time high, in excess of 97,000, at the end of that decade despite the loss of more than 50,000 whites. In 20 years, the total has dropped by almost 40,000, and this is the result of a black emigration from Englewood. This is probably a direct result of loss of economic opportunity and housing.

The migration of African- and poor Americans into Englewood during and after World War II coincided with a series of events that eventually led to a decline in Englewood's prosperity. New residential construction had ceased after the community filled up in the 1930s and many black residents could not conserve older deteriorating buildings and streets. Racial changes in the neighborhood led to an exodus of white residents who relocated in outlying South and Southwest Side community areas of Chicago. New competitive shopping centers were built after the war in suburban Evergreen Park and in the Chicago Lawn community area which cut into the region served by Englewood's business district. By 1960 the slum area on the periphery of the shopping center had grown to the point where it threatened further commercial development. At the urging of area business leaders the strip was designated an urban renewal district. During the 1960s traffic along Halsted and 63rd streets was diverted around the shopping area, which was converted into a pedestrian mall in the belief, widely held at that time, that this would bring the shoppers back to Englewood. Creation of the mall did not revitalize the retail area. In the mid-1970s, the anchor retail stores like Wieboldts and Sears were closed. Today the Englewood Concourse is the site of small stores, many operated by immigrant Koreans.

Only 2 percent of the 1960 housing units were in structures built since 1940. In addition, considerable demolition of homes in the community took place during the 1950s for various city projects, including the South (Dan Ryan) Expressway, which was built along the eastern boundary of the community. In 1958, the Chicago Land Clearance Commission designated the 69th-Stewart urban renewal area to be redeveloped for institutional, residential and commercial uses in Census Tract 6812, just south of Chicago State University.

Work was completed in the 1960s and a new community college, Kennedy-King was opened in 1971. However, Chicago State University was moved to a new campus in the Roseland community area in 1972.

Today the unemployment rate in Englewood is more than 18 percent. The number of housing units in the area has dropped from 28,000 to 19,000 in the last three decades, and one in eight residents live in overcrowded conditions. The dependency ratio is high, 40 percent are less than 18 years old and more than half the households with children under 18 are headed by females. The median family income is among the lowest in the city and more than a third of all residents live in poverty.

In August of 1980, Mayor Jane Byrne announced a multimillion dollar urban renewal plan for Englewood. This plan has not materialized. The median value of owner-occupied homes in Englewood is among the 10 lowest in the city. Though redevelopment plans stall in Englewood, housing is being improved in the Concourse area. The Antioch Baptist Church at 63rd and Stewart streets heads a housing project of 200 subsidized units that are now under construction. This $11 million development is funded through a tax exempt city housing bond issue. Other housing projects included a $2.4 million 38-townhouse development at 61st and Halsted streets and an 11-story government subsidized apartment building for senior and handicapped citizens under construction at 62nd and Sangamon streets.

Annie Ruth Leslie

Community Area 69

Greater Grand Crossing

Greater Grand Crossing is located approximatley nine miles from the downtown business district. As its name implies, it is comprised of several neighborhoods merged into one community. In its original state, most of the land was under water. The area was in the path of the railroad lines entering Chicago from the south and the east in the early 1850s. Grand Crossing came into existence as the result of an 1853 collision between trains of the Illinois Central and the Michigan Southern Railroads. The historic accident occurred at the intersection of what is now 75th Street and South Chicago Avenue, causing 18 deaths and 40 injuries. Both lines claimed a right-of-way. The management of the Lake Shore and Michigan Southern Railroad had refused to let the Illinois Central cross their tracks, but Roswell B. Mason (later to become mayor of Chicago), then construction chief for the Illinois Central, scoffed at this refusal, kidnapped a guard and built a crossing overnight. The 1853 collision indicated the need for safety and compelled public officials to act. The result was that for many years all trains had to come to a full stop at this junction. Despite this and the installation of signal lights, the crossing remained dangerous, the site of numerous accidents in the decades that followed.

During the mid-19th century, industry developed near railroads. Hyde Park developer Paul Cornell thought the area surrounding the stop would provide an ideal site for subdivision. Although this district was then watery swampland, it had good potential for industrial development because transportation into Chicago was assured. Cornell bought land in this vicinity in 1855, gradually adding to it until 1871. When he held 960 acres, it was subdivided and offered for sale. The result was the Village of Cornell, the name of which was changed to Grand Crossing when it was discovered that another Cornell already existed downstate. Close by was another settlement called Brookline.

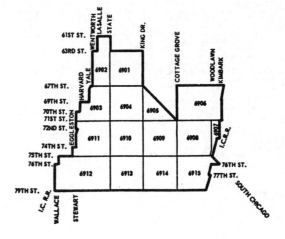

One of the first plants to come to Grand Crossing was the Chicago Tack Company established in 1876 by Orrin L. Bassett, at 75th Street and Woodlawn Avenue. Other new industries included the Cornell Watch Factory, the Patzacak Furniture factory and the Chicago Scale Company. By 1880, Grand Crossing had a furniture factory, a barbed wire factory, a tack company and one or two other small companies.

By 1890 the Brookline neighborhood, which was located between 71st and 75th streets from Cottage Grove to St. Lawrence Avenue, was built up with frame cottages, many of them on blocks or stilts. The earliest settlers of Brookline Crossing were Germans, some of whom were farmers, carpenters and building trade workers.

Another community within Grand Crossing was Park Manor. This developed from truck farming land, east of State Street between Marquette Road and 72nd Street, which was subdivided in 1886. This area remained almost vacant until 1890. The early settlers of Park Manor were of Yankee stock.

The Grand Crossing neighborhood itself lay between 75th and 79th streets from Cottage Grove Avenue on the west to the Illinois Central tracks on the east. By the early 1890s, this area was built up with frame

Community Area 69 -- Greater Grand Crossing

	1980	1970	1960	1950	1940	1930
Total Population.......	45,218	54,414	63,169	61,753	61,554	60,007
% Male..................	45.0	46.0	47.6	48.6	49.0	50.1
% Female................	55.0	54.0	52.4	51.4	51.0	49.9
% White.................	0.6	1.5	13.8	94.1	99.6	99.5
% Black.................	98.8	98.1	85.8	5.8	.0.4	0.4
% Other Nonwhite Races..	0.6	0.4	0.4	0.1	0.0	0.1
% Under 5 Years Old.....	7.2	7.9	11.4	9.0	6.7	7.6
% 5-19 Years Old........	22.6	26.8	22.6	18.9	21.6	22.9
% 20-44 Years Old.......	32.3	32.0	37.1	38.3	41.6	44.5
% 45-64 Years Old.......	23.6	24.4	21.9	24.8	22.8	19.8
% 65 Years and Older....	14.3	8.9	7.0	9.0	7.3	5.2
Median School Years....	12.1	11.4	10.7	10.6	8.9	*
Total Housing Units....	17,671	18,476	18,749	18,786	17,835	*
% In One-Unit Structures.	22.6	21.1	25.2	*	*	*
% Owner Occupied........	31.4	31.7	34.9	35.3	29.0	*
% Renter Occupied.......	64.4	63.9	62.4	63.4	68.4	*
% Vacant................	4.2	4.4	2.7	1.3	2.6	*
% 1+ Persons per Room....	6.5	9.5	14.9	11.7	*	*

Community Area 69 -- Greater Grand Crossing
Selected Characteristics of Census Tracts: 1980

Tract Number	Total	6901	6902	6903	6904	6905	6906	6907	6908	6909	6910
Total Population..............	45218	2673	374	3187	4907	1376	744	459	3269	5918	3025
% Male..........................	45.0	41.9	41.4	44.9	44.3	44.8	46.2	45.1	46.4	44.7	44.4
% Black.........................	98.8	99.3	99.7	99.4	99.2	98.6	98.7	99.8	98.5	98.7	98.1
% Other Nonwhite...............	0.6	0.6	0.3	0.2	0.2	1.2	1.3	0.2	0.5	0.9	0.9
% Of Spanish Origin............	0.6	0.1	0.3	0.6	0.3	0.3	1.6	0.7	0.0	0.8	0.8
% Foreign Born.................	1.2	0.0	0.0	1.9	0.6	0.5	5.3	0.0	0.0	0.8	0.6
% Living In Group Quarters.....	0.2	0.4	0.0	0.0	0.0	0.0	0.0	0.0	0.0	0.0	0.0
% 13 Years Old And Under.......	20.2	23.5	26.2	28.9	18.4	15.6	22.0	20.7	24.8	16.4	12.9
% 14-20 Years Old..............	11.2	13.5	12.0	13.1	9.1	10.0	15.5	19.4	14.6	8.8	6.9
% 21-64 Years Old..............	54.2	48.3	50.0	49.2	53.5	58.1	53.8	51.6	50.7	55.7	56.3
% 65-74 Years Old..............	9.5	8.4	8.3	5.8	12.6	10.0	5.9	6.5	7.1	12.4	15.7
% 75 Years Old And Over........	4.8	6.4	3.5	2.9	6.4	6.4	2.8	1.7	2.8	6.6	8.2
% In Different House...........	31.4	31.2	36.8	49.5	30.3	32.8	13.5	45.4	23.5	29.2	32.2
% Families With Female Head....	52.0	58.7	48.1	60.0	54.1	50.0	37.3	42.4	55.1	47.1	42.8
Median School Years Completed...	12.1	12.2	11.0	12.0	12.0	11.8	10.7	12.1	12.1	11.9	12.5
Median Family Income, 1979......$$	14086	9829	18200	12074	14609	12212	11579	17206	12049	14940	19531
% Income Below Poverty Level...	22.4	32.4	16.3	28.1	24.8	29.7	30.3	30.4	28.7	16.4	5.9
% Income Of $30,000 Or More.....	14.1	12.6	9.3	10.2	13.7	14.1	5.8	8.9	13.3	14.7	15.7
% White Collar Workers.........	49.5	55.4	45.9	38.9	46.4	39.3	36.1	34.0	48.8	44.5	62.5
% Civilian Labor Force Unemployed.	14.2	13.3	19.8	17.2	11.3	16.9	12.4	0.0	12.9	15.1	8.9
% Riding To Work By Automobile....	56.8	44.4	60.3	47.3	58.8	45.9	44.6	56.5	53.6	64.7	65.8
Mean Commuting Time - Minutes...	39.0	33.7	42.0	40.8	35.4	41.9	30.8	52.5	40.7	40.4	32.7
Population Per Household........	2.7	2.8	3.2	3.0	2.4	2.5	3.0	3.6	3.2	2.5	2.3
Total Housing Units...........	17671	982	130	1104	2132	594	269	131	1084	2476	1344
% Condominiums.................	0.0	0.0	0.0	0.0	0.0	0.0	0.0	0.0	0.0	0.0	0.0
% Built 1970 Or Later..........	2.6	2.2	0.0	2.4	2.4	0.0	17.8	0.0	13.7	0.3	2.4
% Owner Occupied...............	31.4	9.0	26.2	14.5	27.2	31.0	31.2	46.6	36.6	31.2	42.6
% With 1+ Persons Per Room.......	6.5	7.3	7.7	12.4	5.6	3.5	6.1	14.1	8.3	4.4	2.2
Median Value: Owner Units......$$	31200	23600	-	26800	29100	27500	-	-	26300	28900	36500
Median Rent: Rental Units......$$	186	182	182	186	192	189	183	194	172	186	197
Median Number Of Rooms: All Units.	4.8	4.8	5.3	4.5	4.6	4.8	5.1	5.4	5.4	4.9	5.0

Tract Number	6911	6912	6913	6914	6915
Total Population..............	5206	3895	2819	4502	2864
% Male..........................	46.1	45.2	44.9	45.6	45.6
% Black.........................	99.4	98.9	98.6	98.7	96.7
% Other Nonwhite...............	0.4	0.4	0.6	0.6	1.4
% Of Spanish Origin............	0.6	0.6	0.7	0.6	1.0
% Foreign Born.................	1.5	0.8	1.9	1.3	3.1
% Living In Group Quarters.....	0.3	0.0	0.0	0.0	0.5
% 13 Years Old And Under.......	26.9	23.2	13.4	14.5	21.5
% 14-20 Years Old..............	12.7	11.8	9.8	10.5	14.0
% 21-64 Years Old..............	50.5	57.2	58.9	57.6	56.7
% 65-74 Years Old..............	6.5	5.8	12.1	11.9	5.7
% 75 Years Old And Over........	3.4	2.1	5.8	5.4	2.2
% In Different House...........	32.3	30.3	23.3	28.3	40.9
% Families With Female Head....	61.9	50.3	38.5	42.9	55.0
Median School Years Completed...	11.8	12.1	12.5	12.4	12.1
Median Family Income, 1979......$$	10307	13650	21641	17118	11059
% Income Below Poverty Level...	33.4	25.3	11.0	11.5	28.7
% Income Of $30,000 Or More.....	12.3	9.3	27.9	19.6	7.1
% White Collar Workers.........	47.8	49.7	57.5	55.1	47.8
% Civilian Labor Force Unemployed.	23.2	16.9	5.6	11.4	20.7
% Riding To Work By Automobile....	52.0	58.3	65.7	59.6	42.6
Mean Commuting Time - Minutes...	46.2	37.8	35.1	40.4	40.4
Population Per Household........	2.9	2.7	2.5	2.6	2.7
Total Housing Units...........	1932	1480	1146	1764	1103
% Condominiums.................	0.0	0.0	0.0	0.0	0.0
% Built 1970 Or Later..........	0.7	0.7	0.6	1.1	6.7
% Owner Occupied...............	21.5	24.4	55.9	50.6	28.5
% With 1+ Persons Per Room.......	11.1	8.8	1.9	4.5	8.4
Median Value: Owner Units......$$	31700	32800	37300	29800	26900
Median Rent: Rental Units......$$	179	193	199	180	187
Median Number Of Rooms: All Units.	4.5	4.6	5.1	5.1	4.6

Community Area 69 -- Greater Grand Crossing
Selected Characteristics of Census Tracts: 1970

Tract Number	TOTAL	6901	6902	6903	6904	6905	6906	6907	6908	6909	6910
Total Population	54414	2694	718	3565	6154	1781	1117	424	3757	6867	3549
% Male	46.0	43.5	43.2	46.5	46.0	46.5	44.4	43.2	46.4	47.3	45.0
% Black	98.1	99.1	99.6	98.9	98.2	98.7	98.7	99.8	96.4	98.6	97.8
% Other Nonwhite	0.5	0.8	0.1	0.3	0.6	0.8	0.2	0.2	0.5	0.5	0.7
% Of Spanish Language	0.9	2.2	4.6	3.4	0.1	0.8	0.6	0.0	1.6	0.6	0.5
% Foreign Born	0.5	0.9	1.0	0.0	0.2	0.4	0.6	0.0	0.0	0.2	0.4
% Living In Group Quarters	0.5	0.3	0.0	0.2	0.2	0.4	0.0	0.0	0.0	0.0	0.0
% 13 Years Old And Under	24.4	23.4	33.6	28.7	22.4	19.5	34.7	30.2	31.3	21.3	13.5
% 14-20 Years Old	11.8	10.4	13.8	12.5	10.6	11.8	14.4	15.3	13.5	10.9	9.0
% 21-64 Years Old	54.8	54.0	47.2	52.5	55.9	58.8	45.0	50.0	48.6	56.4	63.1
% 65-74 Years Old	6.4	8.3	3.6	4.8	7.8	7.1	4.4	2.4	4.6	8.9	10.3
% 75 Years Old And Over	2.5	3.9	1.8	1.4	3.3	2.7	1.4	2.1	2.0	2.5	4.1
% In Different House	63.2	55.2	47.4	46.1	62.6	57.9	58.8	89.9	50.0	69.3	73.4
% Families With Female Head	24.6	30.9	37.9	30.0	24.6	25.4	38.7	17.7	27.7	20.5	17.3
Median School Years Completed	11.4	12.1	10.1	10.3	11.6	10.7	10.2	10.3	10.7	11.6	12.1
Median Family Income, 1969 $$	8667	8896	7000	8364	7858	7896	6655	7833	7950	8531	9109
% Income Below Poverty Level	14.1	9.0	39.6	15.3	13.0	14.0	19.9	22.2	14.6	10.1	11.0
% Income of $15,000 or More	16.5	11.1	20.8	11.0	14.5	12.7	7.4	3.8	12.5	17.1	20.1
% White Collar Workers	15.2	16.4	12.5	11.1	15.2	12.6	7.5	19.6	13.1	15.1	20.5
% Civilian Labor Force Unemployed	5.9	6.3	17.2	4.6	4.8	6.8	13.8	5.5	7.4	7.1	2.9
% Riding To Work By Automobile	54.4	45.6	42.3	56.1	49.2	44.3	53.6	49.0	53.6	59.7	55.9
Population Per Household	3.1	3.0	3.3	3.3	2.9	2.8	3.6	3.5	3.6	2.9	2.7
Total Housing Units	18489	915	254	1147	2229	732	322	136	1111	2452	1352
% Condominiums & Cooperatives	1.3	14.0	0.0	1.3	0.5	1.8	0.0	0.0	0.7	0.5	0.8
% Built 1960 Or Later	5.1	8.5	0.0	15.2	3.2	2.2	0.0	0.0	1.0	1.2	4.6
% Owner Occupied	30.4	9.4	19.7	14.3	27.7	23.1	27.0	37.5	35.2	31.0	40.3
% With 1+ Persons Per Room	9.6	7.8	16.4	13.2	8.0	6.7	21.6	12.3	14.4	7.0	3.4
Median Value: Owner Units $$	17900	-	-	15400	17400	18400	-	-	15300	17900	20000
Median Rent: Rental Units $$	121	163	101	118	122	114	114	115	115	122	126
Median Number Of Rooms: All Units	4.8	5.0	4.2	4.8	4.6	4.4	4.8	4.9	5.2	4.9	5.1

Tract Number	6911	6912	6913	6914	6915
Total Population	7147	4750	3291	5160	3440
% Male	45.9	46.2	46.6	46.5	45.8
% Black	98.6	97.7	97.9	98.2	96.0
% Other Nonwhite	0.4	0.2	0.6	0.3	0.4
% Of Spanish Language	0.5	1.6	1.6	0.0	0.1
% Foreign Born	0.3	0.9	0.6	0.1	0.0
% Living In Group Quarters	1.2	0.2	0.3	0.7	0.9
% 13 Years Old And Under	29.6	27.8	17.0	19.6	29.9
% 14-20 Years Old	12.3	13.8	10.4	11.9	13.1
% 21-64 Years Old	51.5	53.6	61.2	57.8	52.2
% 65-74 Years Old	4.4	3.6	8.0	7.5	3.4
% 75 Years Old And Over	2.2	1.2	3.4	3.2	1.5
% In Different House	58.2	62.3	73.3	75.0	66.4
% Families With Female Head	30.3	25.0	16.3	18.8	29.3
Median School Years Completed	10.5	11.8	12.3	11.3	11.8
Median Family Income, 1969 $$	8121	8676	11542	9996	7610
% Income Below Poverty Level	21.5	16.5	10.1	9.2	15.4
% Income of $15,000 or More	14.4	17.9	31.2	20.4	14.4
% White Collar Workers	8.1	10.1	27.0	19.2	16.6
% Civilian Labor Force Unemployed	8.0	5.6	4.4	4.5	4.2
% Riding To Work By Automobile	52.6	48.1	62.0	60.4	58.3
Population Per Household	3.3	3.3	2.8	3.0	3.1
Total Housing Units	2257	1522	1184	1727	1149
% Condominiums & Cooperatives	0.6	0.0	0.9	0.6	0.6
% Built 1960 Or Later	6.6	8.6	4.2	6.5	5.7
% Owner Occupied	20.0	25.3	53.3	52.8	27.8
% With 1+ Persons Per Room	15.2	13.4	4.2	6.3	10.3
Median Value: Owner Units $$	17300	18000	19700	17400	15600
Median Rent: Rental Units $$	118	123		120	113
Median Number Of Rooms: All Units	4.5	4.5	5.1	5.1	4.6

cottages. First settlers of Grand Crossing were German factory workers.

The Brookdale community was located south and east of the Oakwood Cemetery, extending to the Illinois Central tracks on the east and 71st Street on the South. The first settlers in this area were railroad workers of Irish, English and Scotch backgrounds. Just south was the Essex community, likewise a railroad settlement.

In 1889, all of the neighborhoods that make up Greater Grand Crossing were annexed to Chicago, the section west of State Street as a part of the Town of Lake and the section east of State Street as a part of the Village of Hyde Park. The 1893 Columbian World Farr stimulated the growth of Greater Grand Crossing and buildings sprang up throughout the area. The extension of the Calumet Electric Trolley Line at 63rd Street and South Park Avenue (King Drive) to Cottage Grove Avenue and 93rd streets further stimulated the growth of Greater Grand Crossing. Transit lines were put on 75th and 79th streets along South Chicago Avenue.

Grand Crossing grew steadily between 1895 and 1918. Single-family frame and brick houses, brick two-flats and small apartment buildings were constructed. In 1912 the dangerous crossing was finally removed by elevation of the tracks. By 1920, with a population of 44,538 people, the community was residentially mature. A large settlement of Italians located east of Grand Crossing Park. Blacks settled near the Illinois Central Railroad tracks at Kenwood Avenue and 70th Street.

Between 1920 and 1930, Greater Grand Crossing experienced many changes. The population increased by a third. Blacks moved into the section between 63rd and 67th streets from Wentworth Avenue to the Pennsylvania tracks. By 1930, peoples of Swedish, Irish, German and Italian descent were predominant among the groups of Grand Crossing.

During the Depression and World War II, there were only minor population increases. Blacks began to move in during the war as whites moved out. During the 1950s the percentage black increased from 6 to 86. In 1960 blacks occupied all but the two southeastern census tracts. Mexicans moved in and became the most numerous among the foreign stock, along with the remainders of the Irish and Italian groups. Greater Grand Crossing's ethnic composition changed most drastically during the 1950s. As 50,000 blacks moved into Grand Crossing, 50,000 whites of European ancestry moved farther south and into other suburban communities. By 1980, the black population was 99 percent of the community total. The 1960 total population, 63,000, proved to be an all-time high. The total dropped by 9,000, mostly whites, in the 1960s and another 9,000, mostly blacks, in the most recent decade.

Greater Grand Crossing is an area of small apartments and single-family homes. About two-thirds of all householders are renters. There has been little construction since the community filled up in 1930. The major housing developments have been the construction of the Parkway Garden Homes at 6415 South Calumet Avenue in the 1930s and the Leigh-Johnson Court at 7300 South Dobson Avenue in the 1960s. The latter complex consists of 78 units of eight three-story buildings.

Greater Grand Crossing is a poor community, though not so poor as others on the South Side. Almost a third of all homes are owner-occupied. The median value of owner-occupied homes is slightly less than the median of the South Chicago community area. Although more than a fifth of all residents live in poverty, a large proportion of the community labor force works at white-collar occupations and about one in seven families earned incomes in excess of $30,000 in 1979.

Annie Ruth Leslie

Ashburn

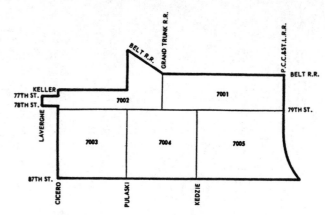

The Ashburn community area came under the jurisdiction of the Town of Lake in 1865. Rumors that a railroad would be tracked through the district led to some land speculation in 1870. By 1880 the Chicago and Grand Trunk Railway (Grand Trunk Western) had entered the city along the anticipated route but when the Town of Lake was annexed to Chicago in 1889 the land had not been subdivided. Shortly before the World's Fair opened in 1893, the real estate firm of Clark and Marsdon opened a subdivision between 79th and 85th streets, Crawford and Central Park avenues. It became known as "Clarkdale," as did the Wabash railroad shop located at the junction of the GTW and the Wabash lines at 83rd Street and Central Park Avenue. These two lines provided the only transportation to the city. Funeral trains ran through the community on their way to the cemeteries south of Chicago.

Later another subdivision was opened by a developer named Mitchell between 83rd and 85th streets, Central Park and Kedzie avenues. The earliest settlers were of Swedish, Dutch, and Irish descent. The first growth was rapid and land became expensive, but this died out quickly and the community sank into obscurity. The area was remote and transportation to the Loop was poor. Whenever there was a fire, the property burned to the ground for lack of equipment. New building virtually stopped and several abandoned structures were taken over by transients. In 1894 there were only 30 residential structures and by 1905 just 18 more had been erected. Ashburn remained part of a seemingly endless prairie without prospect for development at a time when the rest of the city was growing. In 1908 the name of the Wabash property in the area was changed to Ashburn because there was already another Clarkdale on the Wabash line near Decatur, Illinois. The population did not grow even after the Wabash (today part of the Norfolk and Southern Corporation) constructed their Landers Yards at 79th Street and Western Avenue.

During World War I a training field for pilots was constructed between 79th and 83rd streets, Cicero and Pulaski avenues, known as the Ashburn Flying Field. This was Chicago's first airfield and Midway Airport was not opened until several years later. The population reached 1,363 in 1920. Several new homes were built during the war but construction stopped again as people moved to new developments more accessible to the downtown area after the war. Quackenbush and Abbey opened another subdivision between Central Park and Kedzie avenues, 79th to 83rd streets, in 1927. At that time there were about 100 houses in Ashburn, but there were some new apartment buildings along Western Avenue. In 1932 the Western Avenue streetcar extended south as far as 71st Street, still more than a mile north of the built-up area in Ashburn. Some improvements were being made, such as the installation of water mains and sewers, but this made settlement even more difficult. Special assessments were levied to pay for these improvements and many properties became encumbered with delinquent taxes. In addition to that, Ashburn was subject to the new city fire regulations which required that all new construction be brick, and some of the old deeds stipulated that only apartment buildings could be constructed on the lots. As of 1939 all residential structures were south of 79th Street and more than a square mile of the community was not yet subdivided. Between 1930 and 1940 the population remained about 700.

Ashburn did not grow substantially until after World War II. Heavy industrial expansion in the southwest city and suburbs and the postwar housing shortage finally made Ashburn a desirable community. New construction was principally of single-family brick homes for workers in the nearby plants. The number of residents grew from 700 to 7,000 between 1940 and 1950, the number of housing units from 200 to 2,000. By 1950 the number of foreign born had quadrupled and leading nationalities were those of German, Swedish, Italian, Polish, and Lithuanian descent. A smaller number of blacks (390) occupied a veterans' housing project which was torn down in the 1950s.

That decade marked the great population growth period in Ashburn, as the number of residents increased by more than 400 percent to approach 40,000 by 1960. Predominant nationalities among those of foreign stock were the Irish, Polish, Italian, and German. The home construction boom went on to keep pace with population growth. At the end of the decade, 98 percent of all housing units in Ashburn had been built since the end of the war, 98 percent were in single-family dwellings, and 95 percent were owner-occupied.

The Scottsdale subdivision of Ashburn was built on the site of the old airfield and includes a busy shopping mall. This part of Ashburn is also sometimes referred to as "Bogan" (after the high school) or "Wrightwood" or the St. Thomas More Parish area. It encompasses the land from 75th to 87th streets, between Western and Kedzie avenues. The rest of the community is laid out in the familiar Chicago grid pattern and rows and rows of brick houses line the streets.

The population continued to grow until it reached its peak in 1970. At that time, there were only five black residents in the community. By 1980, the population as a whole had declined as it did citywide. The number of black residents grew to more than a thousand, and they now make up about 3 percent of the Ashburn total. All of this growth has been in the southeastern part of the community. Blacks that live in this area have higher median incomes than their white counterparts, though both groups are above the city median. The Ashburn community area median income is one of the top five in the city. Ninety-one percent of all housing units are owner-occupied and the drop from 20 years ago is due to the fact that about one-third of all units added since that time have been in multiple-unit structures. The median value of single-family homes in Ashburn is among the top third of the Chicago community area distribution. Whites are the overwhelming majority, and those of Irish, Polish and German descent are most numerous.

Anti-busing demonstrations and other forms of protest erupted in the 1960s over the intended integration of Bogan High School, located on 79th Street and Pulaski Road. The Chicago Board of Education proposed transfering honor students from nearby black schools to Bogan but had to withdraw the plan after all the opposition. The issue was further exacerbated by a march led by Dr. Martin Luther King into the surrounding area which called national attention to the lack of open housing in Chicago. In the years since, Bogan High School has been sucessfully integrated without major incident.

Ashburn residents have access to several shopping districts. In addition to the Scottsdale Shopping Center, the giant Ford City is just a few blocks north of 75th Street, and suburban Evergreen Plaza is only a mile south of 87th Street. Some manufacturing and light industry are located in the Landers Yards area west of the railroad tracks and north of 75th Street to about Kedzie Avenue, but in general Ashburn has remained a predominantly residential community. More than 90 percent live in single-family units.

Antoinette LoBosco

Community Area 70 -- Ashburn
Population and Housing Characteristics, 1930-1980

	1980	1970	1960	1950	1940	1930
Total Population.......	40,477	47,161	38,638	7,472	731	733
% Male.................	48.5	49.1	49.7	50.4	51.3	57.7
% Female...............	51.5	50.9	50.3	49.6	48.7	42.3
% White................	95.5	98.7	99.9	94.7	100.0	92.3
% Black................	2.7	1.1	0.0	5.2	-	-
% Other Nonwhite Races...	1.8	0.2	0.1	0.1	-	7.6
% Under 5 Years Old......	5.1	6.1	14.7	19.1	10.0	11.2
% 5-19 Years Old........	23.7	33.6	30.3	22.0	19.0	29.5
% 20-44 Years Old.......	30.3	26.4	35.6	45.6	46.5	45.3
% 45-64 Years Old.......	29.1	26.9	15.5	11.0	19.2	12.0
% 65 Years and Older....	11.8	7.0	3.9	2.3	5.3	2.0
Median School Years....	12.4	12.1	12.1	11.9	8.9	*
Total Housing Units....	12,875	12,732	9,793	1,984	210	*
% In One-Unit Structures.	90.8	89.8	97.8	*	*	*
% Owner Occupied.........	90.6	89.9	95.0	66.2	45.2	*
% Renter Occupied........	8.5	9.5	3.1	29.6	50.0	*
% Vacant................	0.9	0.6	0.6	1.9	3.2	*
% 1+ Persons per Room....	4.5	10.8	12.3	23.8	*	*

Community Area 70 -- Ashburn
Selected Characteristics of Census Tracts: 1980

Tract Number	Total	7001	7002	7003	7004	7005	8209
Total Population.............	40477	3283	5493	11564	8975	11162	0
% Male.......................	48.5	48.9	49.1	49.1	48.2	47.7	-
% Black......................	2.7	0.0	0.0	0.0	0.0	9.7	-
% Other Nonwhite.............	1.8	4.1	2.3	1.1	1.6	1.8	-
% Of Spanish Origin..........	2.2	4.6	3.1	1.0	2.1	2.6	-
% Foreign Born...............	7.6	8.8	10.8	7.3	6.6	6.8	-
% Living In Group Quarters...	0.8	0.0	0.0	0.1	0.1	2.8	-
% 13 Years Old And Under.....	16.2	18.5	17.2	14.5	15.0	17.8	-
% 14-20 Years Old............	14.6	12.1	15.7	16.6	14.3	13.0	-
% 21-64 Years Old............	57.3	58.5	58.1	59.2	57.2	54.5	-
% 65-74 Years Old............	7.8	7.4	6.2	6.4	9.2	9.0	-
% 75 Years Old And Over......	4.0	3.5	2.7	3.2	4.3	5.6	-
% In Different House.........	23.6	20.6	30.7	15.8	23.9	28.9	-
% Families With Female Head......	8.5	7.7	8.3	7.8	9.1	9.1	-
Median School Years Completed.....	12.4	12.3	12.4	12.4	12.4	12.5	-
Median Family Income, 1979......$$	27291	25000	27422	27965	26535	27955	-
% Income Below Poverty Level....	2.4	2.8	2.0	1.9	2.1	3.3	-
% Income Of $30,000 Or More.....	42.7	33.9	44.5	44.0	40.3	45.2	-
% White Collar Workers..........	53.2	53.2	50.5	51.9	53.9	55.6	-
% Civilian Labor Force Unemployed.	5.2	5.8	6.0	5.4	4.0	5.5	-
% Riding To Work By Automobile....	78.4	76.6	79.8	81.0	76.7	76.5	-
Mean Commuting Time - Minutes...	31.6	29.5	30.3	31.1	32.1	33.2	-
Population Per Household..........	3.1	3.1	3.2	3.2	3.1	3.1	-
Total Housing Units..........	12875	1079	1716	3606	2962	3512	0
% Condominiums...............	0.4	0.0	0.0	0.0	0.0	1.3	-
% Built 1970 Or Later........	3.1	0.0	2.4	4.7	1.6	5.5	-
% Owner Occupied.............	90.6	83.1	95.5	91.5	91.7	88.6	-
% With 1+ Persons Per Room.......	4.5	3.9	4.9	4.8	4.3	4.7	-
Median Value: Owner Units.......$$	54200	48700	57800	58400	50400	51600	-
Median Rent: Rental Units.......$$	261	259	284	299	240	238	-
Median Number Of Rooms: All Units.	5.3	5.2	5.1	5.3	5.3	5.5	-

Community Area 70 -- Ashburn
Selected Characteristics of Census Tracts: 1970

Tract Number	TOTAL	7001	7002	7003	7004	7005
Total Population.............	47161	3618	6354	14216	10670	12303
% Male.......................	49.1	48.7	49.0	49.9	49.3	48.0
% Black......................	1.1	0.0	0.0	0.0	0.0	4.1
% Other Nonwhite.............	0.2	0.5	0.6	0.1	0.1	0.2
% Of Spanish Language........	1.2	2.0	1.1	0.8	1.4	1.4
% Foreign Born...............	5.9	9.6	5.6	4.6	5.8	6.8
% Living In Group Quarters...	0.2	0.0	0.0	0.2	0.2	0.2
% 13 Years Old And Under.....	25.9	25.8	28.6	28.7	23.9	23.0
% 14-20 Years Old............	15.3	12.8	14.7	16.2	15.7	14.8
% 21-64 Years Old............	51.9	54.9	51.4	49.5	53.1	52.8
% 65-74 Years Old............	4.6	4.5	3.5	3.5	4.8	6.2
% 75 Years Old And Over......	2.4	2.0	1.7	2.1	2.4	3.2
% In Different House.........	71.7	66.8	75.8	69.5	75.3	70.4
% Families With Female Head.......	8.3	8.5	7.0	6.8	7.0	11.7
Median School Years Completed....	12.2	12.2	12.3	12.3	12.2	12.2
Median Family Income, 1969......$$	13848	13212	13763	13933	13660	14222
% Income Below Poverty Level.....	2.2	1.5	2.4	2.9	1.4	2.1
% Income of $15,000 or More.....	41.8	35.5	41.2	41.9	40.7	45.0
% White Collar Workers..........	27.7	23.3	25.2	28.7	24.0	32.4
% Civilian Labor Force Unemployed.	2.7	3.0	2.8	2.5	2.9	2.8
% Riding To Work By Automobile....	73.4	75.7	68.6	78.5	71.7	70.9
Population Per Household..........	3.7	3.5	3.9	4.0	3.6	3.5
Total Housing Units..........	12746	1044	1650	3575	2939	3538
% Condominiums & Cooperatives.....	0.2	0.0	0.0	0.0	0.0	0.7
% Built 1960 Or Later............	24.0	31.3	28.5	29.6	11.1	24.9
% Owner Occupied.................	89.7	82.7	97.3	90.7	93.0	84.5
% With 1+ Persons Per Room.......	11.0	9.1	11.3	13.6	10.6	9.2
Median Value: Owner Units.......$$	23600	22100	23100	24400	22600	24600
Median Rent: Rental Units.......$$	159	169	157	173	148	131
Median Number Of Rooms: All Units.	5.2	5.2	5.1	5.2	5.2	5.4

Auburn Gresham

Auburn Gresham is a community area that developed from several settlements located on Chicago's far South Side. About 1850, a man named Schafer built Ten Mile House, a tavern located at what is now the intersection of 79th Street and Vincennes Avenue. Vincennes was called the State Road, and was a major thoroughfare into Chicago from the south. The area around the tavern was called Cummorn, the name given to the post office which was located at Ten Mile House.

The Auburn section was settled during the 1850s by German and Dutch truck farmers who lived in the area near 83rd Street and Vincennes Avenue. When the Chicago and Western Indiana lines were laid, shops were established there and many railroad workers came to live in this area. In 1872, the Auburn settlement was platted in the vicinity of 76th Street and Wallace Avenue. That area was largely inhabited by railroad workers, three other railroads having been laid through the community area in the meantime.

An area in the western part of Auburn Gresham, which was called "The Grove," was settled after the Civil War and became the subdivision of South Englewood, which was platted in the early 1870s, about the same time as Auburn. That community was later called Gresham. Railroad shops and other industries developed in the area during the 1880s. Some of these early businesses included the Weber Wagon Works at 81st Street, the Abbott Buggy and Carriage Manufacturing Company and the Lee and Fritz grain elevator on the Belt Line.

The subdivision of Brainerd was platted in 1885 by Frank Brainerd. This area was located between Racine and Ashland avenues, 87th and 91st streets. In an effort to attract settlers in 1889, Frank Brainerd donated land and buildings to the Rock Island Railroad for a station at 89th Street. At the turn of the century, this area remained sparsely populated with only a dozen settlers in the area. In 1889, all of Ashburn Gresham north of 87th Street including Auburn, was annexed to Chicago as part of the Town of Lake. In 1890, the section south of 87th Street, including South Englewood and Brainerd, was annexed by ordinance to Chicago.

Much of the community's land remained vacant and was used for truck farming even after the subdivision and annexation of the area. The business district mainly centered in the area near 79th Street at the junction of the Chicago and Rock Island and Chicago and Western Indiana tracks. In 1890, the Vincennes horsecars were extended to 79th Street and along 79th Street to Halsted Street, as a result of the South Side real estate boom associated with the 1893 Columbian Exposition.

Auburn Gresham's growth was steady but slow during the period between 1905 and 1913. The areas of Auburn Gresham east of Halsted Street and between Halsted and Racine Avenue from 75th Street to about 80th Street were built up with single-family bungalows and two-family two-deckers, and the remaining area remained largely vacant. Between 1913 and 1918, car lines on Halsted Street were extended to 119th Street and those on Racine and Ashland avenues to 87th Street. By 1920, the community's population was 19,558. The most numerous among the foreign born were Irish, German and Swedish immigrants. Some Polish and Mexican people lived in the area, working largely at unskilled jobs on the railroads.

During the 1920s, Auburn Gresham, like other South Side communities, experienced considerable growth. During this period, many new buildings, largely brick bungalows, were erected. The northern and eastern parts of the community were highly industrialized. Business sections developed along Vincennes Avenue, Halsted, 79th and 87th streets. Much of the land, however, remained undeveloped and vacant.

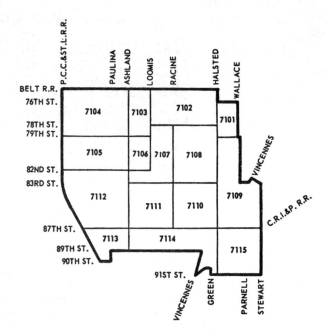

Between 1920 and 1930, Auburn Gresham's population tripled to more than 57,000. The community was primarily a residential area of old frame cottages in the area southeast of 79th and Halsted streets, frame houses near the tracks and brick houses and two-flat apartments in other parts of the community.

Between 1930 and 1960, the population remained relatively stable, increasing to 59,000 by 1960. Irish and German groups predominated among the foreign born. Some new residential construction occurred in the old Brainerd section south of 87th Street. An important commercial center developed near the intersection of 79th and Halsted streets.

The population decreased slightly during the 1950s as 6,000 whites moved out of Auburn Gresham. In the decade that followed 40,000 whites moved out while more than 47,000 blacks moved in. This migration increased the total population to an all-time high, almost 69,000, in 1970. The number of residents dropped in the most recent decade, as the rest of the whites moved out, leaving Auburn Gresham a virtually all-black community area.

This turnover was largely due to the expansion of the black population of Chicago and movement away from the overcrowded Black Belt, while whites moved to more attractive community areas and suburbs, many of them driven by fear of black growth in nearby communities. Many of the new black residents were middle-class homeowners employed by government. Public institutions provide about one-third of the jobs for wage earners in the community. Most of these come from the postal service, the school board and the Chicago Transit Authority. Manufacturing accounts for another third of the jobs. Service and retail trade occupations are underrepresented.

In 1980 Auburn Gresham was an area of single-family homes and small apartment buildings. About half of all housing units were owner-occupied. The median value of single-family units is less than the city median and less than most medians on the southwest side. The unemployment rate was 13 percent, high perhaps because of cutbacks in government employment. While 13 percent of all families lived in poverty in 1979, twice as many lived in relative affluence, with annual incomes in excess of $30,000. Auburn Gresham has a very young population: almost one fourth are 13 years of age or younger, while only 5 percent are 65 and over.

Annie Ruth Leslie

Community Area 71 – Auburn Gresham
Population and Housing Characteristics, 1930-1980

	1980	1970	1960	1950	1940	1930
Total population.......	65,132	68,854	59,484	60,978	57,293	57,381
% Male.................	46.7	47.2	46.9	47.7	48.5	49.5
% Female...............	53.3	51.8	53.1	52.3	51.5	50.5
% White................	1.2	30.9	99.7	100.0	100.0	100.0
% Black................	98.4	68.7	0.2	0.0	0.0	0.0
% Other Nonwhite Races...	0.4	0.4	0.1	0.0	0.0	0.0
% Under 5 Years Old......	8.2	9.0	7.8	8.5	6.3	8.7
% 5-19 Years Old........	29.2	30.1	20.7	19.6	22.4	23.8
% 20-44 Years Old........	38.4	34.4	27.0	36.0	41.8	46.2
% 45-64 Years Old........	19.1	18.3	30.4	27.6	23.0	17.1
% 65 Years and Older.....	5.1	8.2	14.1	8.3	6.5	4.2
Median School Years....	12.3	12.0	10.7	10.6	8.9	*
Total Housing Units....	20,122	20,663	19,448	17,758	15,718	**
% In One-Unit Structures.	40.6	40.7	43.6	*	*	**
% Owner Occupied........	49.7	50.1	53.1	49.7	39.7	**
% Renter Occupied........	46.5	47.0	45.2	49.4	58.4	**
% Vacant................	3.8	2.9	1.7	0.9	1.9	**
% 1+ Persons per Room....	8.5	10.0	5.9	9.6	*	**

Community Area 71 — Auburn Gresham
Selected Characteristics of Census Tracts: 1980

Tract Number	Total	7101	7102	7103	7104	7105	7106	7107	7108	7109	7110
Total Population.............	65132	1854	5899	2032	7888	5699	2603	4869	6892	3098	4707
% Male.......................	46.7	46.5	46.6	46.0	46.9	46.3	45.4	46.8	45.7	46.9	46.4
% Black......................	98.4	98.7	98.8	98.8	98.4	98.4	99.2	98.4	98.9	98.5	98.8
% Other Nonwhite.............	0.4	0.3	0.4	0.8	0.3	0.5	0.4	0.6	0.6	0.3	0.3
% Of Spanish Origin..........	0.7	0.7	0.6	1.0	0.8	0.4	0.2	0.5	0.9	1.0	0.9
% Foreign Born...............	1.1	0.9	0.9	0.0	0.6	0.8	0.6	2.0	0.8	0.4	0.7
% Living In Group Quarters.......	0.2	0.3	0.0	0.0	0.0	0.0	0.0	0.0	0.2	0.0	0.0
% 13 Years Old And Under.....	24.5	25.0	24.4	25.0	28.2	26.2	26.4	23.2	22.0	28.1	23.0
% 14-20 Years Old............	14.9	15.2	14.3	14.1	15.7	12.7	13.6	13.4	13.1	16.6	16.3
% 21-64 Years Old............	55.5	52.8	55.0	56.2	53.1	57.2	54.7	58.2	56.6	50.8	55.0
% 65-74 Years Old............	3.5	4.9	4.4	3.6	2.2	2.8	3.9	3.5	5.6	2.8	4.0
% 75 Years Old And Over......	1.6	2.2	1.9	1.0	0.8	1.1	1.5	1.7	2.7	1.6	1.7
% In Different House.........	27.2	37.6	35.6	31.2	29.0	32.6	38.5	26.1	28.3	37.6	21.2
% Families With Female Head......	35.9	51.6	42.9	41.2	30.5	39.0	39.8	39.5	40.7	45.8	34.3
Median School Years Completed....	12.3	12.1	12.1	12.1	12.3	12.4	12.3	12.4	12.3	12.0	12.3
Median Family Income, 1979.....$$	20531	12125	17191	18449	21388	19903	16114	20095	20637	14123	19674
% Income Below Poverty Level...	13.3	29.3	18.3	18.7	11.4	9.9	9.8	10.9	16.3	21.9	17.2
% Income Of $30,000 Or More.....	27.1	14.4	20.9	30.2	26.0	26.1	19.1	25.6	31.1	14.5	25.5
% White Collar Workers.......	48.3	57.9	40.6	40.9	44.3	48.1	46.1	42.8	51.9	41.5	49.1
% Civilian Labor Force Unemployed.	13.2	15.6	14.2	14.1	10.3	12.6	12.2	13.4	15.0	15.6	13.0
% Riding To Work By Automobile....	62.8	56.5	59.1	58.4	64.8	63.8	64.9	63.0	63.6	52.4	61.7
Mean Commuting Time - Minutes...	41.6	39.9	42.0	45.5	42.8	43.3	40.5	42.5	38.4	39.7	41.5
Population Per Household.........	3.4	3.3	3.2	3.1	3.7	3.1	3.1	3.0	3.1	3.7	3.4
Total Housing Units..........	20122	608	1882	681	2208	1940	856	1701	2274	880	1454
% Condominiums...............	0.4	2.1	0.0	0.0	0.9	1.1	0.0	0.0	0.0	0.0	0.0
% Built 1970 Or Later........	2.0	3.9	0.9	3.6	1.3	0.7	0.0	0.4	0.0	5.6	3.4
% Owner Occupied.............	49.7	29.1	35.6	33.3	63.0	34.4	32.5	35.3	38.5	44.7	53.2
% With 1+ Persons Per Room...	8.5	9.8	7.4	11.5	8.1	6.8	9.3	8.1	7.7	13.0	8.6
Median Value: Owner Units.......$$	39300	35600	34800	36300	40600	43000	40600	38300	41300	30200	33200
Median Rent: Rental Units.....$$	203	184	195	188	207	220	205	210	203	198	189
Median Number Of Rooms: All Units.	5.3	5.1	5.0	4.4	5.6	5.0	4.7	4.9	5.6	5.2	5.3

Tract Number	7111	7112	7113	7114	7115
Total Population.............	3843	6835	1865	3654	3394
% Male.......................	47.4	47.5	47.3	46.4	47.9
% Black......................	98.4	97.2	96.4	98.9	98.1
% Other Nonwhite.............	0.3	0.5	0.5	0.1	0.8
% Of Spanish Origin..........	0.7	0.8	1.0	0.7	0.6
% Foreign Born...............	1.3	2.5	0.8	0.3	1.8
% Living In Group Quarters........	0.0	0.0	0.0	2.0	0.0
% 13 Years Old And Under.....	22.2	26.2	24.3	21.1	19.5
% 14-20 Years Old............	15.7	15.2	14.8	17.0	18.1
% 21-64 Years Old............	56.5	54.9	58.1	56.1	56.9
% 65-74 Years Old............	3.9	2.3	2.0	3.3	3.9
% 75 Years Old And Over......	1.6	1.3	0.8	2.5	1.6
% In Different House.........	22.1	21.4	31.3	10.8	14.1
% Families With Female Head.......	29.8	26.9	29.2	29.6	30.7
Median School Years Completed....$	12.3	12.5	12.7	12.4	12.4
Median Family Income, 1979......$$	22519	23750	28690	22849	23956
% Income Below Poverty Level...	9.2	8.9	8.0	11.3	6.4
% Income Of $30,000 Or More.....	30.7	34.2	47.1	27.4	33.7
% White Collar Workers.......	53.1	54.6	57.1	48.8	53.5
% Civilian Labor Force Unemployed.	15.4	11.4	11.3	12.9	14.3
% Riding To Work By Automobile....	66.6	69.0	55.8	59.5	64.2
Mean Commuting Time - Minutes...	42.7	42.5	44.5	42.7	36.9
Population Per Household.........	3.4	3.5	3.2	3.8	3.8
Total Housing Units..........	1171	1993	602	960	912
% Condominiums...............	0.0	0.0	5.8	0.0	0.0
% Built 1970 Or Later........	6.2	0.0	5.1	5.4	4.2
% Owner Occupied.............	56.4	72.3	65.4	73.0	83.2
% With 1+ Persons Per Room...	8.8	4.7	7.0	10.3	9.6
Median Value: Owner Units.......$$	40100	44500	41400	36500	37200
Median Rent: Rental Units.....$$	208	211	227	199	186
Median Number Of Rooms: All Units.	5.2	5.5	5.1	5.6	5.6

Community Area 71 — Auburn Gresham
Selected Characteristics of Census Tracts: 1970

Tract Number	TOTAL	7101	7102	7103	7104	7105	7106	7107	7108	7109	7110
Total Population	68854	2439	7168	2174	6749	5183	2544	5622	8382	3363	5708
% Male	47.2	46.9	47.1	50.0	47.1	44.1	48.2	48.2	46.5	49.2	47.7
% Black	68.7	97.3	97.4	92.9	3.5	5.8	94.9	94.1	97.1	96.9	95.6
% Other Nonwhite	0.4	0.4	0.3	0.8	0.2	0.3	0.0	0.3	0.5	0.5	0.6
% Of Spanish Language	1.3	2.2	1.9	0.8	1.7	0.2	0.0	1.0	3.0	0.5	0.0
% Foreign Born	4.2	0.6	0.3	1.1	11.3	12.1	0.6	1.3	2.4	0.3	1.8
% Living In Group Quarters	0.4	0.0	0.2	0.0	0.1	0.7	0.0	0.6	0.2	0.5	0.1
% 13 Years Old And Under	28.1	35.1	32.5	31.0	22.4	17.1	27.4	29.3	28.5	34.9	34.4
% 14-20 Years Old	12.6	13.8	12.8	11.6	11.3	10.4	12.4	11.7	12.5	14.5	13.4
% 21-64 Years Old	51.1	46.8	50.9	53.9	51.1	50.1	55.7	54.8	54.1	47.8	48.3
% 65-74 Years Old	5.4	3.6	2.6	2.2	9.9	15.0	2.8	2.7	3.2	2.2	2.6
% 75 Years Old And Over	2.8	0.8	1.2	1.3	5.3	7.4	1.7	1.5	1.7	0.6	1.3
% In Different House	42.3	50.4	47.1	14.7	64.8	61.7	16.8	19.4	43.1	38.1	19.5
% Families With Female Head	16.9	28.6	20.1	16.7	15.7	18.9	17.1	14.5	19.3	19.4	19.4
Median School Years Completed	12.0	11.7	12.0	11.1	12.0	12.0	12.2	12.2	12.0	12.0	12.1
Median Family Income, 1969 $$	10860	7636	10563	10164	12394	10966	9204	10218	11241	8950	10603
% Income Below Poverty Level	8.3	27.4	9.6	7.5	4.9	6.5	9.2	8.8	4.9	13.0	11.3
% Income of $15,000 or More	24.6	11.0	22.8	11.6	33.5	28.4	11.5	18.0	26.8	12.3	19.9
% White Collar Workers	17.8	17.5	10.9	11.9	28.0	31.0	14.5	14.2	13.5	11.1	12.6
% Civilian Labor Force Unemployed	4.6	6.8	5.3	5.3	2.0	3.9	4.2	4.3	5.4	5.4	6.9
% Riding To Work By Automobile	60.4	52.7	59.4	54.7	66.9	55.3	61.9	62.8	58.0	56.8	59.8
Population Per Household	3.4	3.7	3.8	3.3	3.1	2.7	3.1	3.4	3.5	3.9	3.9
Total Housing Units	20658	688	1928	676	2262	1982	872	1667	2425	886	1522
% Condominiums & Cooperatives	0.5	0.7	0.0	0.0	0.9	0.9	1.0	0.4	0.7	0.7	0.4
% Built 1960 Or Later	6.3	1.1	1.2	3.9	4.0	3.6	1.7	1.0	1.0	28.7	7.1
% Owner Occupied	49.6	28.9	39.1	33.9	61.8	34.5	32.0	36.4	38.8	44.7	55.0
% With 1+ Persons Per Room	10.1	15.3	14.6	11.2	6.1	4.5	8.1	10.8	9.6	14.3	14.4
Median Value: Owner Units $$	18900	16800	17800	18900	17900	19600	19600	19100	20600	16600	17700
Median Rent: Rental Units $$	128	118	129	127	123	128	126	131	130	127	125
Median Number Of Rooms: All Units	5.1	4.9	5.0	4.4	5.3	4.9	4.6	4.9	5.5	5.2	5.2

Tract Number	7111	7112	7113	7114	7115
Total Population	4097	6004	1705	3943	3773
% Male	47.5	47.2	45.2	46.6	48.8
% Black	91.3	1.1	1.1	86.7	95.4
% Other Nonwhite	0.4	0.4	0.4	0.2	0.3
% Of Spanish Language	0.6	0.4	0.4	3.0	2.0
% Foreign Born	1.1	9.9	16.7	1.6	1.3
% Living In Group Quarters	0.2	0.0	0.9	2.2	0.2
% 13 Years Old And Under	29.9	18.6	19.3	34.1	31.7
% 14-20 Years Old	13.6	11.6	11.5	14.8	14.5
% 21-64 Years Old	52.2	52.3	51.8	44.6	49.9
% 65-74 Years Old	2.5	12.0	10.3	3.3	2.4
% 75 Years Old And Over	1.8	5.4	7.1	3.2	1.5
% In Different House	11.7	69.0	64.6	22.0	62.5
% Families With Female Head	12.5	13.5	14.6	13.3	11.7
Median School Years Completed	12.1	12.0	11.9	11.8	12.0
Median Family Income, 1969 $$	10837	12026	11949	10892	11532
% Income Below Poverty Level	4.7	6.0	6.7	6.8	8.1
% Income of $15,000 or More	25.4	36.1	33.1	20.6	29.7
% White Collar Workers	12.3	27.7	33.1	11.3	16.0
% Civilian Labor Force Unemployed	5.3	4.8	1.7	4.5	2.7
% Riding To Work By Automobile	56.5	66.0	59.1	55.3	69.8
Population Per Household	3.6	2.9	2.9	4.2	4.1
Total Housing Units	1139	2095	620	944	952
% Condominiums & Cooperatives	0.0	0.3	0.0	0.8	0.5
% Built 1960 Or Later	6.2	3.2	28.8	3.9	32.2
% Owner Occupied	60.0	67.4	56.8	73.8	81.8
% With 1+ Persons Per Room	11.6	5.8	7.3	14.3	14.6
Median Value: Owner Units $$	19900	19700	18500	19100	19400
Median Rent: Rental Units $$	135	119	135	129	116
Median Number Of Rooms: All Units	5.3	5.2	4.9	5.7	5.4

Community Area 72

Beverly

Beverly, located on the Southwest Side, lies some 30 to 40 feet above the the rest of the city on a ridge formed by glaciers thousands of years ago. According to legend, the name was first suggested by an early settler after her childhood home in Massachusetts. Much of the surrounding area was marsh and the ridge became the site of several old Indian trails. One of these was the Vincennes trail, which ran long the top and extended to Fort Dearborn. Farmers living south of the city used it to haul their produce to market. There was also a stagecoach service along this road linking the Village of Blue Island, at the southern end of the ridge, to Chicago. The area was covered by timbered ridges and meadows, populated by bears, wolves, deer, mink, and muskrats.

French-Canadian fur trader Joseph Bailly is believed to have built the first home in the area after he married a Pottawatomie chieftain's daughter in 1822. Ten years later the Indians ceded the land to the government. Dewitt Lane was one of the first settlers. He built a log cabin at 103rd Street and Seeley Avenue on the ridge. John Blackstone bought 3,000 acres of land from the government in 1839 but sold most

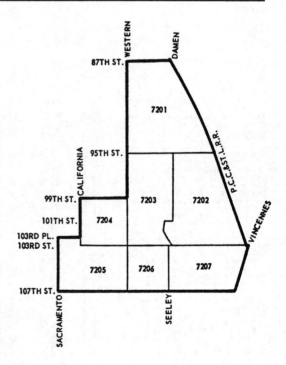

Community Area 72 -- Beverly
Population and Housing Characteristics, 1930-1980

	1980	1970	1960	1950	1940	1930
Total Population.......	23,360	26,771	24,814	20,186	15,910	13,793
% Male....................	47.7	45.9	46.9	47.9	47.2	47.2
% Female..................	52.3	54.1	53.1	52.1	52.8	52.8
% White...................	85.4	99.6	99.9	99.9	99.6	99.6
% Black...................	13.6	0.1	0.1	0.1	0.0	0.0
% Other Nonwhite Races...	1.0	0.3	0.0	0.0	0.4	0.4
% Under 5 Years Old......	7.3	6.3	7.8	7.9	5.3	7.4
% 5-19 Years Old.........	24.5	29.4	26.5	21.7	24.8	26.5
% 20-44 Years Old........	33.0	22.3	22.8	30.8	36.2	40.0
% 45-64 Years Old........	19.8	25.8	30.9	30.2	26.6	20.8
% 65 Years and Older.....	15.4	16.1	12.0	9.4	7.1	5.3
Median School Years....	13.7	12.8	12.6	12.6	12.3	*
Total Housing Units....	7,885	8,190	7,527	5,808	4,272	*
% In One-Unit Structures.	79.1	79.1	86.2	*	*	*
% Owner Occupied.........	79.1	78.4	81.9	82.5	71.8	*
% Renter Occupied........	19.2	20.1	16.3	16.1	25.9	*
% Vacant.................	1.7	1.5	1.8	1.4	2.3	*
% 1+ Persons per Room....	1.9	4.6	4.0	3.3	*	*

Community Area 72 -- Beverly
Selected Characteristics of Census Tracts: 1980

Tract Number	Total	7201	7202	7203	7204	7205	7206	7207
Total Population.............	23360	4104	4886	4352	2186	2304	1976	3552
% Male.......................	47.7	49.2	48.0	48.2	47.8	46.3	48.5	45.2
% Black......................	13.6	12.7	28.9	4.8	0.5	0.1	1.7	27.8
% Other Nonwhite.............	1.0	1.0	1.7	0.9	0.7	0.3	0.7	1.1
% Of Spanish Origin..........	1.3	0.9	1.6	1.6	1.3	0.4	1.4	1.6
% Foreign Born...............	3.2	3.1	2.1	4.2	6.2	2.3	2.9	2.4
% Living In Group Quarters...	0.1	0.0	0.2	0.0	0.0	0.0	0.0	0.0
% 13 Years Old And Under.....	21.2	23.4	22.9	22.1	16.8	18.8	23.0	18.6
% 14-20 Years Old............	12.0	12.9	13.9	11.9	10.9	10.1	11.9	10.2
% 21-64 Years Old............	51.4	51.0	51.4	50.9	53.7	50.5	50.4	52.1
% 65-74 Years Old............	9.0	8.0	6.9	8.9	12.4	11.8	8.7	9.3
% 75 Years Old And Over......	6.5	4.8	4.9	6.3	6.2	8.7	6.0	9.7
% In Different House.........	34.6	32.7	45.0	21.0	26.8	33.6	25.7	50.0
% Families With Female Head..	12.3	8.4	18.1	9.1	12.7	7.5	8.7	17.8
Median School Years Completed..	13.7	15.5	13.5	14.4	12.7	13.0	15.0	12.9
Median Family Income, 1979......$$	29756	33234	27301	31708	25719	31237	34432	25344
% Income Below Poverty Level....	2.7	1.9	4.6	1.5	2.7	1.2	2.4	4.2
% Income Of $30,000 Or More.....	49.5	55.9	45.3	56.1	34.2	55.4	60.3	39.0
% White Collar Workers..........	71.1	80.9	65.7	73.4	64.0	69.4	80.7	64.9
% Civilian Labor Force Unemployed.	4.1	4.4	5.4	3.0	2.8	4.6	5.7	2.7
% Riding To Work By Automobile....	69.5	67.6	66.3	73.8	72.0	73.6	68.3	67.3
Mean Commuting Time - Minutes...	32.9	31.0	32.7	34.3	32.9	34.4	30.1	33.9
Population Per Household..........	3.0	3.3	3.1	3.2	3.0	2.8	3.2	2.5
Total Housing Units..........	7885	1245	1625	1354	742	817	635	1467
% Condominiums...............	1.2	0.0	3.6	0.0	0.0	0.0	0.0	2.5
% Built 1970 Or Later........	0.5	0.0	0.4	0.4	0.0	0.0	0.0	1.8
% Owner Occupied.............	79.1	90.8	72.2	93.6	96.0	84.1	87.4	48.3
% With 1+ Persons Per Room......	1.9	1.3	2.9	1.4	2.6	1.8	1.0	2.0
Median Value: Owner Units....$$	60600	69600	50700	65800	50300	58600	70700	49200
Median Rent: Rental Units.......$$	246	217	234	229	235	241	285	254
Median Number Of Rooms: All Units.	5.6	5.6	5.6	5.6	5.6	5.6	5.6	5.0

Community Area 72 -- Beverly
Selected Characteristics of Census Tracts: 1970

Tract Number	TOTAL	7201	7202	7203	7204	7205	7206	7207
Total Population.............	26771	5009	5692	4740	2757	2582	2085	3906
% Male.......................	45.9	47.5	45.7	47.3	46.1	44.2	47.4	42.7
% Black......................	0.1	0.2	0.2	0.0	0.0	0.0	0.0	0.2
% Other Nonwhite.............	0.3	0.5	0.4	0.3	0.1	0.1	0.2	0.5
% Of Spanish Language........	0.5	0.5	0.5	0.8	0.6	0.3	0.0	0.0
% Foreign Born...............	4.8	6.4	3.7	4.6	2.6	6.1	6.0	4.5
% Living In Group Quarters...	0.3	0.3	0.5	0.0	0.4	0.0	0.0	0.7
% 13 Years Old And Under.....	24.1	26.5	25.9	25.8	24.4	20.1	24.2	18.8
% 14-20 Years Old............	13.0	14.3	12.4	11.8	16.1	13.5	12.9	11.0
% 21-64 Years Old............	46.8	46.3	45.2	47.8	49.3	47.9	47.1	46.0
% 65-74 Years Old............	10.3	8.7	10.2	9.1	7.1	12.2	9.8	15.4
% 75 Years Old And Over......	5.8	4.3	6.3	5.5	3.0	6.3	6.0	8.8
% In Different House.........	64.0	65.3	63.2	63.9	80.1	64.5	52.8	58.2
% Families With Female Head.......	12.1	9.2	12.8	10.6	11.2	14.9	7.4	17.7
Median School Years Completed......	12.7	13.5	12.8	12.9	12.5	12.5	13.7	12.5
Median Family Income, 1969......$$	15750	18950	13880	17614	14698	13901	20625	14220
% Income Below Poverty Level....	2.1	1.5	2.5	1.1	1.3	2.8	1.6	3.5
% Income of $15,000 or More.....	52.4	64.2	43.4	59.3	47.8	42.5	67.7	45.7
% White Collar Workers..........	53.5	60.9	50.4	62.7	47.0	40.6	64.3	46.4
% Civilian Labor Force Unemployed.	2.6	1.3	3.0	2.6	1.1	1.6	2.7	3.0
% Riding To Work By Automobile....	66.5	68.4	58.0	71.8	69.2	72.4	69.2	63.8
Population Per Household..........	3.3	3.7	3.3	3.5	3.7	3.2	3.3	2.7
Total Housing Units..........	8199	1384	1777	1363	743	818	637	1477
% Condominiums & Cooperatives.....	0.7	0.0	1.6	0.0	0.0	0.0	0.0	2.0
% Built 1960 Or Later........	6.4	3.1	8.0	4.4	2.3	4.3	0.8	15.1
% Owner Occupied.............	77.6	92.2	66.0	93.7	97.0	85.9	86.8	44.8
% With 1+ Persons Per Room......	4.9	4.2	4.8	3.9	11.5	6.4	2.7	3.2
Median Value: Owner Units.......$$	27600	34000	22700	30400	24000	25500	31300	21700
Median Rent: Rental Units.......$$	162	117	159	139	165	165	197	165
Median Number Of Rooms: All Units.	6.0	6.8	5.9	6.4	5.6	5.5	6.3	4.8

of it to Thomas Morgan in 1844. Morgan developed the area fom 91st to 115th streets, between Vincennes and California Avenue as a cattle and sheep ranch. By 1860 much of the Beverly area was fenced-in farmland.

In 1852 the Chicago, Rock Island, and Pacific Railroad laid tracks through the region but offered no service to Chicago for residents. In 1859 another railway, the Pittsburgh, Cleveland, Chicago, and St. Louis (later known as the Panhandle and still later part of the Pennsylvania system) laid tracks which crossed the Rock Island at 103rd Street. A small settlement of railroad workers and farmers, mostly German, developed at "the Crossing," which became the nucleus for the community of Washington Heights. In 1864 the Panhandle opened stations at 91st and 103rd streets to accommodate residents. The Rock Island countered by setting up a dummy line to run from its main line at 97th Street south to 99th and Wood streets. Residents began to call the area "Dummy Junction."

After the Civil War the children of Thomas Morgan sold the land and it was acquired by the Blue Island Land and Building Company. Active real estate development began as they subdivided and sold lots. The area north of 107th Street was referred to as the Washington Heights subdivision; the area to the south as Morgan Park. Some of the early settlers were prosperous New Englanders who worked as executives in the stockyards and later the steel mills. As suburban service on the Rock Island and Pennsylvannia Railroads was extended, people moved in from Englewood and Normal Park. The area around 99th Street and Prospect Avenue was known as Walden and that around 103rd and Wood streets as Tracey. The community of Washington Heights was incorported as a village in 1874.

A station at the northern end of the ridge, called North End, was opened for suburban service by the Rock Island and the 91st Street station was called Beverly Hills. The Beverly community developed as a cultural center through the influence of the Director of the Art Institute, W.M.R. French, and his protege, John Vanderpoel. In 1890 the part of Beverly north of 95th Street was annexed to Chicago by ordinance as part of South Englewood. A month later the area east of Western Avenue between 95th and 107th streets was also annexed by election as part of the Village of Washington Heights. A third parcel that makes up Beverly south of 99th Street between Western and California Avenue was annexed to the city in 1914, with the rest of the Village of Morgan Park.

By 1914, however, residents were beginning to feel separate from those communities. They persuaded the Bell Telephone Company to unify three of its exchanges in the one "Beverly." Later, the Rock Island Line was successfully petitioned to designate all stops between 91st and 103rd streets as Beverly Hills stations.

In 1920 the population of Beverly was 7,684, mostly of native white stock. The leading nationalities among the foreign born were those of German and Swedish descent. A post-World War I building boom led to the development of a Beverly Hills subdivision around 100th Street and Damen Avenue. Apartment houses appeared along the tracks and the area around Ashland Avenue and 95th (just east of the community) grew as a business center. The last part of present-day Beverly between 103rd and 107th streets, California and Sacramento avenues, was annexed to Chicago by election in 1927 as part of the Village of Mount Greenwood. At that time there was still much vacant land and prairie on either side of Western Avenue.

The population of Beverly increased by almost 80 percent between 1920 and 1930. The more elaborate homes were built between the hills and Western Avenue, the more modest dwellings in the eastern part of the comunity between the Rock Island and Pennsylvania tracks. The foreign born were still a small minority and the community was developing as a predominantly middle- and upper-class neighborhood. Unlike many other Chicago communities, the population in Beverly grew during the Depression to almost 16,000 in 1940.

After World War ii the vacant land in the western section began to be built up, stimulated by a general post-war building boom and the proximity of suburban Evergreen Plaza shopping mall at 95th Street and Western Avenue. The population passed 20,000 in 1950 and had grown to almost 25,000 by 1960. Most of the housing units were single-family dwellings and owner-occupied. People of Irish descent began to move into the community and became the leading nationality among the foreign stock. Today they are still the predominate group of those that identify a European ancestry, followed by those of German and Swedish descent.

In 1970 the population of Beverly peaked at 26,771. Early in the following decade the racial composition of several South Side communities, especialy Morgan Park, began to change. By 1980 the population of Beverly had declined, as it had citywide, but the black population had grown from 21 residents in 1970 to about 14 percent of the total population in 1980. While much of Beverly is partially integrated, most of the black growth has taken place in the southeastern corner of the community.

The Beverly area planning association (BAPA) is a coalition of groups organized to work for racial stability in the Beverly-Morgan Park area. Many residents credit that organization with the prevention of wholesale white flight and black resegregation. Nevertheless, Beverly has been through some turbulent times in its effort to remain a highly desirable South Side community.

The Beverly Art Center, which contains a museum and a theatre, was opened in the 1960s. Later, part of the area was designated a National Historic District. The heavily-wooded area stretching from the Dan Ryan Woods at 87th Street to 115th Street in Morgan Park, between Prospect Avenue and Hoyne and Seeley avenues, has been preserved for its architectural, historic and natural beauty. For example, the largest set of homes designed by Walter Burley Griffin, who created the standard for the Chicago Bungalow, is located in the 104th Street area. BAPA sponsors Beverly house tours, which exhibit local architecture and life style. The homes and mansions of Longwood Drive are particularly impressive and a visitor tends to lose all sense of the city when in this part of Beverly.

Residents rank second in family income among all community areas in the city. Almost half the families in Beverly reported incomes of $30,000 or more in 1979, and less than 3 percent live in poverty. Eighty percent of all housing units are single-family dwellings, and almost 80 percent are owner-occupied. The median value of owner-occupied single-family units ranks among the city's top twenty. Among community residents is a relatively large concentration of middle- and upper-level city officials. The most important shopping area is on 95th Street. Beverly remains an affluent residential community that has managed successfully to integrate its residents. As for the future, this decade will perhaps be most crucial.

Antoinette LoBosco

Washington Heights

Washington Heights is located on Chicago's Southwest Side between 89th and 107th streets. The present community area is only a small section of the original Village of Washington Heights, which included a large part of the present area of Beverly. Most of the high ground for which Washington Heights is named became part of Beverly. Washington Heights also includes parts of the old Fernwood and Brainerd settlements.

Among early settlers was Norman Rexford, whose home and tavern at 91st Street and Vincennes Road were built in 1834. More settlers came into the area between 1840 and the Civil War. In the 1860s, the land in the vicinity of 103rd Street and Vincennes Avenue became inhabited by a transient population of Irish and German railroad workers, who lived near "The Crossing" of the Rock Island Railroad and the Pittsburgh, Cincinnati and St. Louis Railroad, called the Panhandle line. The coming of the railroads hastened the drainage of the swampy flatlands, thus encouraging settlement.

Having noted the excellent rail transportation and vacant land in the area, a Kansas city bridge builder named Horace Horton built the Chicago Bridge and Iron Company at the Crossing. This company provided jobs and a way of life to Washington Heights residents for more than 80 years. The Chicago Bridge and Iron Company is credited with establishing the Beverly Bank in Washington Heights. The Beverly Bank provided necessary loans for homes to many workmen of the Chicago Bridge and Iron Company.

Subdivision started in the present Washington Heights in 1866 when the area between 103rd and 107th streets from Loomis Street to Racine Avenue was purchased from farmers. A settlement grew up at 103rd and Loomis streets. In 1869, the Blue Island Land and Building Company bought land and divided it into lots. These developers put in sewers, planted trees, built the "dummy line" to the Rock Island tracks, and extended credit to the home buyers. The suburb grew quickly around the new Washington Heights railroad station. The post office opened in 1872 in the cobbler's shop of A.S. Dittman at 1255 West Tracy (103rd) Street and the school building, erected in 1870, was east of it. Although the real estate boom was ended by the Panic of 1873, the Village of Washington Heights was incorporated in 1874. The village stretched westward from Halsted Street to Western Avenue.

To the east of Washington Heights was a district called Fernwood. Fernwood grew rapidly in the section along 103rd Street. By 1885, there were reportedly 180 homes in the community. These settlers were largely Americans of Yankee stock and some Dutch. A third area included in Washington Heights is the old Brainerd subdivision which extended from 87th to 91st streets between Racine and Ashland avenues. The area was subdivided in 1885 and a station of the Rock Island Railroad opened at 89th and Loomis streets in 1889. There were only six houses in all of Brainerd in 1890.

In 1890, most of the present community of Washington Heights came into Chicago when the area north of 95th Street was annexed by ordinance as part of South Englewood, and the Village of Washington Heights, including all of the present community except a small section in the southeast corner, was annexed by election. In the following year Fernwood, too, was annexed to Chicago. By 1891, all of the present community was within the city limits. Except for the developments on 103rd Street and north of the Crossing, the area was mostly vacant land.

After annexation, the Heights (Beverly) and the flat land (Washington Heights) sections began to grow apart. The Washington Heights community area grew very slowly, because of poor transportation to the downtown area. Between 1910 and 1920, transportation improved as the Halsted Street and Racine and Ashland Avenue car lines were

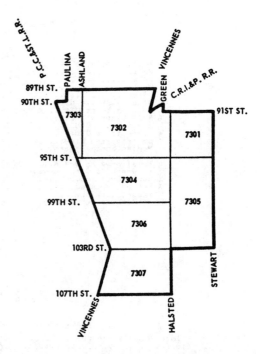

extended south into the Washington Heights community. By 1920, the population was 8,024. The most numerous foreign-born groups were German and Swedish. At this time most of the community was still vacant land.

Between 1920 and 1930, many single-family homes were built. Some small apartments and three-flats appeared. The population more than doubled during this decade to almost 18,000. Growth continued through the Depression and World War II. After the war, construction of single-family homes picked up and Washington Heights reached residential maturity before 1950. In that year, the population was approaching 25,000. During the 1950s. blacks moved into Washington Heights, chiefly in the area east of Halsted Street. By 1960, they constituted 12 percent of the community population, which was now almost 30,000. In 1960, Irish, Germans and Swedes were most numerous among the white foreign stock.

In the decade that followed the white population dropped by almost two-thirds, but more than 25,000 blacks moved in and the total population reached an all-time high. Black families, long forced to live in the crowded areas of the city began to spread out in search of better homes and jobs. In the most recent decade blacks have continued to replace whites. They now constitute 98 percent of the population of Washington Heights. The total population remained relatively stable during the 1970s.

Today, Washington Heights is a middle-class neighborhood, near the center of many socio-economic distributions for the city, yet troubled by high unemployment (13 percent) and poverty (10 percent) rates. Median family income is $4,500 above the city median, and a third of all families live in relative affluence, reporting incomes in excess of $30,000 in 1979. The population is very young by today's standards (almost 40 percent are 20 years or younger). Two-thirds of all families with children under 18 are headed jointly by both parents, compared to slightly over one-third for the city as a whole. Washington Heights is an area of single-family homes (more than three-fourths of all housing units) and the rate of owner occupation is the same as 20 years ago, when the area was predominantly white. The value of single-family homes is average for the city. As community areas in Chicago go, the housing in Washington Heights is relatively new, much of it having been built in the decade after World War II when the residential area was finally occupied.

Annie Ruth Leslie

Community Area 73 — Washington Heights
Population and Housing Characteristics, 1930-1980

	1980	1970	1960	1950	1940	1930
Total Population......	36,453	36,540	29,793	24,488	19,370	17,865
% Male.................	46.9	47.9	48.0	48.6	49.3	50.0
% Female...............	53.1	52.1	52.0	51.4	50.7	50.0
% White................	1.4	24.8	87.3	99.7	99.7	99.6
% Black................	98.2	74.8	12.5	0.2	0.3	0.2
% Other Nonwhite Races....	0.4	0.4	0.2	0.1	0.0	0.2
% Under 5 Years Old......	6.7	8.0	9.2	9.1	6.9	10.1
% 5-19 Years Old..........	30.2	33.7	24.2	21.7	25.7	26.6
% 20-44 Years Old.........	36.0	32.9	28.5	35.9	40.6	45.1
% 45-64 Years Old.........	22.2	18.0	27.4	26.4	21.6	14.2
% 65 Years and Older.....	4.9	7.4	10.7	6.9	5.2	4.0
Median School Years....	12.5	12.1	11.7	11.9	9.1	*
Total Housing Units....	10,245	10,098	9,068	6,947	5,228	*
% In One-Unit Structures.	75.4	73.8	78.4	*	*	*
% Owner Occupied.........	75.6	74.8	74.5	70.0	54.1	*
% Renter Occupied........	22.3	21.8	23.2	29.2	43.2	*
% Vacant................	2.1	3.4	2.3	0.8	2.7	*
% 1+ Persons per Room....	8.8	10.3	7.3	7.9	*	*

Community Area 73 — Washington Heights
Selected Characteristics of Census Tracts: 1980

Tract Number	Total	7301	7302	7303	7304	7305	7306	7307
Total Population.............	36453	3144	12349	1589	5166	6351	4716	3138
% Male........................	46.9	47.4	46.2	46.4	47.0	47.1	47.2	48.1
% Black.......................	98.1	99.4	98.8	97.4	95.7	98.8	97.6	98.1
% Other Nonwhite..............	0.4	0.2	0.4	0.1	0.7	0.3	0.5	0.4
% Of Spanish Origin...........	0.5	0.8	0.3	0.0	0.7	0.6	0.4	0.6
% Foreign Born................	0.6	0.9	0.4	0.0	0.8	0.8	0.7	0.5
% Living In Group Quarters........	0.4	0.0	0.1	0.0	2.5	0.0	0.0	0.0
% 13 Years Old And Under......	22.2	17.7	23.3	23.8	21.9	20.6	23.2	23.7
% 14-20 Years Old.............	17.0	15.0	16.0	20.5	17.8	17.3	17.6	17.9
% 21-64 Years Old.............	55.9	59.6	56.7	52.3	54.9	55.8	55.1	54.1
% 65-74 Years Old.............	3.3	5.5	2.7	2.2	3.3	4.4	2.8	3.2
% 75 Years Old And Over.......	1.6	2.3	1.4	1.2	2.1	1.9	1.4	1.2
% In Different House..........	20.8	25.1	23.9	41.2	21.3	13.2	16.4	15.7
% Families With Female Head...	29.3	24.6	32.8	27.5	27.9	24.7	29.7	29.9
Median School Years Completed....	12.5	12.6	12.5	12.4	12.6	12.4	12.5	12.4
Median Family Income, 1979.....$$	23422	28033	21323	24879	24643	22113	25734	25741
% Income Below Poverty Level....	10.0	3.5	13.4	2.3	7.4	12.6	8.0	9.4
% Income Of $30,000 Or More.....	33.7	43.3	27.4	37.3	38.9	33.1	33.7	39.6
% White Collar Workers..........	52.0	52.8	50.8	60.5	54.7	51.0	51.3	50.4
% Civilian Labor Force Unemployed.	12.9	11.5	15.9	11.0	11.2	14.2	10.7	13.1
% Riding To Work By Automobile...	68.3	70.4	66.4	68.4	69.9	71.7	67.6	65.2
Mean Commuting Time - Minutes...	40.5	39.1	42.7	45.7	35.9	38.0	40.5	42.7
Population Per Household...........	3.6	3.4	3.4	3.7	3.8	3.8	3.8	3.9
Total Housing Units...........	10245	955	3680	445	1350	1692	1279	844
% Condominiums.................	0.0	0.0	0.0	0.0	0.0	0.0	0.0	0.0
% Built 1970 Or Later..............	4.5	2.2	4.5	3.1	3.4	3.6	5.3	9.7
% Owner Occupied...............	75.6	92.5	58.1	67.9	85.1	89.4	81.2	85.9
% With 1+ Persons per Room........	8.8	7.2	8.4	8.1	8.3	9.2	9.8	10.8
Median Value: Owner Units.....$$	41000	45100	39600	41000	41100	40100	40800	40400
Median Rent: Rental Units.....$$	216	194	220	225	218	192	189	189
Median Number Of Rooms: All Units.	5.6	5.6	5.3	5.6	5.6	5.6	5.6	5.6

Community Area 73 — Washington Heights
Selected Characteristics of Census Tracts: 1970

Tract Number	TOTAL	7301	7302	7303	7304	7305	7306	7307
Total Population.............	36540	3732	11477	1252	5002	7032	4905	3140
% Male........................	47.8	49.1	47.2	47.9	46.7	48.2	48.1	49.2
% Black.......................	74.7	98.5	71.6	0.0	50.4	94.3	74.9	82.2
% Other Nonwhite..............	0.4	0.6	0.3	0.0	0.5	0.4	0.2	1.0
% Of Spanish Language.........	1.6	1.1	1.3	0.0	2.2	3.1	1.1	0.0
% Foreign Born................	2.4	0.0	2.9	10.2	3.8	0.7	1.5	2.9
% Living In Group Quarters........	0.6	0.2	0.1	0.0	3.3	0.6	0.2	0.0
% 13 Years Old And Under......	29.5	27.5	28.3	19.0	27.5	31.9	32.7	33.1
% 14-20 Years Old.............	13.8	16.6	12.1	11.9	14.2	16.0	13.5	12.4
% 21-64 Years Old.............	49.3	52.4	50.1	49.0	48.5	48.2	48.3	48.3
% 65-74 Years Old.............	4.8	2.4	6.3	13.0	5.9	2.7	3.3	3.9
% 75 Years Old And Over.......	2.6	1.1	3.2	7.1	4.0	1.1	2.3	2.3
% In Different House..........	43.1	76.0	27.0	79.9	62.4	49.5	33.4	15.0
% Families With Female Head...	12.1	9.6	13.9	15.2	13.1	10.9	10.5	10.3
Median School Years Completed....	12.1	12.1	12.2	11.7	12.3	12.0	12.2	12.0
Median Family Income, 1969......$$	12086	12202	11441	12138	13246	12098	12286	12370
% Income Below Poverty Level.....	6.4	8.7	5.3	4.5	5.8	8.9	3.9	8.6
% Income of $15,000 or More.....	30.8	30.8	26.5	31.9	38.7	31.5	31.0	33.2
% White Collar Workers..........	23.1	23.0	23.3	27.4	28.3	21.0	22.6	17.9
% Civilian Labor Force Unemployed.	4.8	4.8	4.5	4.5	3.6	6.2	5.8	5.0
% Riding To Work By Automobile....	65.4	73.5	60.4	43.4	61.0	73.6	70.7	65.0
Population Per Household...........	3.7	4.1	3.4	2.9	3.7	4.2	3.9	3.9
Total Housing Units...........	10100	945	3577	443	1335	1689	1283	828
% Condominiums & Cooperatives.....	0.8	0.8	1.5	0.0	0.4	0.6	0.0	0.0
% Built 1960 Or Later..............	15.3	33.7	7.3	14.2	14.4	31.7	7.6	8.5
% Owner Occupied...............	73.9	90.4	55.6	67.9	79.9	88.5	81.1	86.5
% With 1+ Persons Per Room........	11.3	15.0	8.8	4.6	10.8	15.5	11.9	12.8
Median Value: Owner Units.....$$	20200	22700	20000	18800	19600	20800	19600	19900
Median Rent: Rental Units......$$	137	130	143	134	128	121	111	111
Median Number Of Rooms: All Units.	5.4	5.4	5.2	5.3	5.4	5.6	5.5	5.4

Mount Greenwood

In 1877 George Waite surveyed the ridge just west of 111th Street in what is today Morgan Park and found the land ideal for use as a cemetery. He obtained a state charter in 1879 for 80 acres with the option to develop 80 more. The ridge was covered with white oaks, black oaks, hickory, aspen, and many other small trees, which led Waite to call the area "Mount Greenwood."

The adjacent community of Mount Greenwood grew as a response to the cemetery traffic on Chicago's Southwest Side. Slow transportation and poor roads made funeral observances all-day affairs. A strip of restaurants and saloons grew up around 111th Street and Sacramento Avenue, provding weary travelers with a chance for refreshment and rest after the funeral and before the long trek home. The saloons also attracted the residents of neighboring Morgan Park, which was a dry community, and the race track patrons from just west of the settlement. Horse races took place at the Worth Track west of the Mount Greenwood Cemetery, and greyhound races took place at another nearby track until the Humane Society closed them down in 1905. Besides the restaurateurs and saloon-keepers, the earliest settlers were truck farmers of Dutch and German extraction.

In 1907 Mount Greenwood was incorporated as a village, primarily to stifle the repeated attempts of Morgan Park drys to close their saloons. Businessmen persuaded nearby property owners to agree to incorporation, since under Illinois law villages of 300 or more had the right to license retail liquor establishments. Bartenders were sworn in as part-time policemen as a practical measure to keep an eye on rowdy drinkers.

Years later the first real estate boom was initiated by Jake Hovland, who subdivided the land between 107th and 111th streets between Kedzie and Sacramento Avenue. An early conflict ensued between the developers and cemetery officials over a drainage ditch. The local citizenry felt it might pollute their water source and become a health hazard so an ordinance was passed against it in 1916. When that action was ignored by the Mount Greenwood Cemetery officials the local residents ended the "Battle of the Ditch" by filling it in themselves.

Between 1905 and 1919, 300 new residential structures were built east of Central Park Avenue between 107th and 113th streets. They were mostly one-story single-family frame dwellings. In the 1920s a citywide building boom resulted in the construction of 500 more new structures in the original section and extending south to 115th Street. There were still no water mains, street lights, or sewers and in 1927 Mount Greenwood was annexed to Chicago by election, with the expectation that improvements would be forthcoming. At that time the only means of transportation were the trolley cars and buses on 111th Street and most residents had to depend upon their automobiles to get anywhere. In 1936 the Federal Works Progress Administration began to install sewage systems, erect street lights and pave streets. In addition to the native American populaton of German, Dutch, and Irish descent, a mixture of Lithuanian, Norwegian, and Swedish immigrants came to live in the area in the thirties. By 1940, however, there were still many vacant lots east of Kedzie Avenue. The small section from 107th to 109th Street, between Millard and Hamlin Avenue, was annexed to Chicago by ordinance in that year.

The population almost tripled between 1940 and 1950 due to the increasing industrial activity in plants and factories in the South and Southwest city and suburbs. The population continued to grow the following decade, with leading nationalities among the foreign stock those of Dutch, German, and Polish descent. In 1960 the area between Crawford and Central Park Avenue, 107th to 109th streets was annexed to Chicago. This added 1,787 people and 357 housing units to the

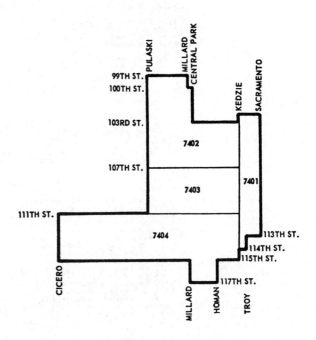

community. Today, Mount Greenwood is surrounded by suburbs on three sides. Oak Lawn is to the west, Evergreen Park is on the north, Alsip and Merrionette Park are to the south. Its eastern boundary is shared with the Chicago communities of Beverly and Morgan Park. Mount Greenwood has been called the land of the Seven Holy Tombs because of the large number of cemeteries in its vicinity. These include Mount Greenwood, Ever Rest, Oak Hill, Lincoln, Mount Hope, Mount Olivet, and Beverly. St. Casimir Church, located within the community, also has a cemetery on its property. The population is primarily white with a very small pocket of blacks living in the southern end of the community. Median family income and single-family housing values are well above the city norm and 84 percent of the homes are owner-occupied. Three- fourths of the residents have lived in their homes for at least five years.

Mount Greenwood is characterized by a variety of well-maintained brick and frame structures throughout the community. Several large apartment complexes and condominiums are located on the major thoroughfares. The housing is relatively new, most of it having been built since World War II. Mount Greenwood did not achieve residential maturity until after 1960. There is a commercial strip on 111th Street but neighboring suburban shopping malls draw much of the business. The community has a quiet, residential look about it.

Antoinette LoBosco

Community Area 74 — Mount Greenwood
Population and Housing Characteristics, 1930-1980

	1980	1970	1960	1950	1940	1930
Total Population.......	20,084	23,186	21,941	12,331	4,390	3,310
% Male...................	47.9	47.7	48.8	50.7	51.6	51.7
% Female.................	52.1	52.3	51.2	49.3	48.4	48.3
% White..................	99.0	99.8	99.9	100.0	100.0	100.0
% Black..................	0.5	0.1	0.0	0.0	–	–
% Other Nonwhite Races...	0.5	0.1	0.1	0.1	0.0	0.0
% Under 5 Years Old......	5.8	6.7	11.4	13.3	9.1	10.4
% 5-19 Years Old.........	22.6	31.5	31.0	25.9	30.5	35.8
% 20-44 Years Old........	30.4	25.3	31.3	41.1	37.7	36.6
% 45-64 Years Old........	25.7	27.3	20.6	15.9	19.1	14.0
% 65 Years and Older.....	15.5	9.2	5.7	3.8	3.6	3.8
Median School Years....	12.4	12.1	11.4	9.7	8.0	*
Total Housing Units....	6,812	6,361	5,676	3,203	1,128	*
% In One-Unit Structures.	86.1	91.7	97.8	*	*	*
% Owner Occupied........	83.8	90.1	91.6	88.5	67.2	*
% Renter Occupied........	14.6	9.1	6.8	9.8	30.5	*
% Vacant.................	1.6	0.8	1.6	1.7	2.3	*
% 1+ Persons per Room....	4.8	11.4	12.3	13.0	*	*

Community Area 74 — Mount Greenwood
Selected Characteristics of Census Tracts: 1980

Tract Number	Total	7401	7402	7403	7404
Total Population.............	20084	3493	6068	5237	5286
% Male.......................	47.9	49.0	47.0	47.0	49.0
% Black......................	0.5	0.0	0.3	0.0	1.4
% Other Nonwhite.............	0.5	0.8	0.6	0.3	0.4
% Of Spanish Origin..........	0.8	1.4	0.8	0.3	0.7
% Foreign Born...............	6.0	6.9	4.9	5.6	7.0
% Living In Group Quarters...	1.7	0.0	5.3	0.0	0.4
% 13 Years Old And Under.....	17.4	17.6	17.2	18.7	16.2
% 14-20 Years Old............	12.9	11.7	15.4	11.4	12.3
% 21-64 Years Old............	54.2	54.3	53.5	54.1	55.2
% 65-74 Years Old............	9.8	10.4	8.9	10.2	10.0
% 75 Years Old And Over......	5.7	6.0	5.0	5.6	6.3
% In Different House.........	25.2	22.7	21.4	28.3	28.2
% Families With Female Head..	9.1	10.2	8.7	7.7	10.3
Median School Years Completed	12.4	12.3	12.5	12.4	12.4
Median Family Income, 1979......$$	24794	22188	25771	25078	25229
% Income Below Poverty Level....	2.9	3.0	2.6	3.1	3.0
% Income Of $30,000 Or More....	34.8	30.7	39.7	33.1	34.0
% White Collar Workers.......	52.0	47.7	54.7	54.7	48.9
% Civilian Labor Force Unemployed.	4.6	6.8	4.8	3.5	4.0
% Riding To Work By Automobile....	76.6	73.3	75.7	77.6	79.1
Mean Commuting Time - Minutes....	31.5	30.7	29.4	32.1	34.1
Population Per Household..........	2.9	2.8	3.2	2.9	2.8
Total Housing Units..........	6812	1267	1809	1796	1940
% Condominiums...............	0.2	0.0	0.6	0.0	0.0
% Built 1970 Or Later........	6.7	2.1	4.3	2.9	15.6
% Owner Occupied.............	83.8	86.0	93.3	86.8	70.9
% With 1+ Persons Per Room....	4.8	7.4	5.6	3.5	3.8
Median Value: Owner Units.......$$	49600	45800	51500	49700	52000
Median Rent: Rental Units.......$$	271	183	273	273	283
Median Number Of Rooms: All Units.	5.2	5.1	5.4	5.3	5.1

Community Area 74 — Mount Greenwood
Selected Characteristics of Census Tracts: 1970

Tract Number	TOTAL	7401	7402	7403	7404
Total Population.............	23186	4060	7106	6256	5764
% Male.......................	47.7	47.5	45.8	48.5	49.4
% Black......................	0.1	0.0	0.1	0.0	0.3
% Other Nonwhite.............	0.1	0.1	0.1	0.1	0.1
% Of Spanish Language........	0.2	0.0	0.0	0.2	0.8
% Foreign Born...............	6.8	9.1	6.0	6.4	6.5
% Living In Group Quarters...	2.2	0.0	6.2	0.4	0.8
% 13 Years Old And Under.....	25.3	23.8	25.6	24.3	27.2
% 14-20 Years Old............	14.5	12.1	16.1	14.2	14.6
% 21-64 Years Old............	51.0	52.8	49.5	52.3	50.1
% 65-74 Years Old............	6.0	6.9	5.9	6.1	5.4
% 75 Years Old And Over......	3.2	4.4	3.0	3.1	2.7
% In Different House.........	72.2	66.3	73.8	72.9	73.6
% Families With Female Head..	7.9	9.6	7.5	7.3	7.7
Median School Years Completed.	12.1	11.7	12.3	12.3	12.1
Median Family Income, 1969......$$	13152	11750	13769	13207	13447
% Income Below Poverty Level....	4.0	6.8	1.8	4.0	4.5
% Income of $15,000 or More....	36.8	27.5	41.0	38.0	37.9
% White Collar Workers.......	27.1	20.2	31.5	28.6	25.0
% Civilian Labor Force Unemployed.	2.2	2.2	2.2	2.1	2.4
% Riding To Work By Automobile....	67.9	70.1	64.0	68.4	70.6
Population Per Household..........	3.6	3.3	3.8	3.5	3.7
Total Housing Units..........	6389	1263	1767	1802	1557
% Condominiums & Cooperatives....	0.0	0.0	0.0	0.0	0.0
% Built 1960 Or Later........	13.9	13.4	13.3	10.2	19.2
% Owner Occupied.............	89.7	85.7	92.9	87.9	91.6
% With 1+ Persons Per Room....	11.7	11.0	14.2	9.8	12.1
Median Value: Owner Units.......$$	21600	19700	22500	21600	22100
Median Rent: Rental Units.......$$	127	107	157	148	113
Median Number Of Rooms: All Units.	5.2	5.0	5.3	5.2	5.2

Morgan Park

The history of Morgan Park dates back to the time when Pottawatomie Indians inhabited the heavily-wooded Blue Island Ridge area and exchanged their furs with the few white traders that ventured into the territory. The ridge was desirable as the only elevated land in an otherwise marshy region. It is a table of land approximately six miles long, two miles wide, lying 30 to 40 feet above the Chicago plain. Residents of the Village of Blue Island, platted at the south end of the ridge, referred to the area as "North Blue Island." In 1833 the Indians signed an agreement with the United States government to vacate the land and move westward. Soon after, John Blackstone purchased 3,000 acres of land. Bears, wolves, and deer roamed the densely wooded ridge area and it is reported that criminals took advantage of the cover to hide in ravines. One such hideaway at the base of the ridge around 108th Street and Longwood Drive was known as "Horse Thief Hollow."

The community is named for Thomas Morgan, an Englishman who purchased most of Blackstone's land in 1844. It extended from 91st Street and to 115th streets around the ridge area. He built his home at 92nd Street and Pleasant Avenue and called it "Upwood" after his father's home in England. The land was fenced for farming, cattle and sheep ranching, and used for a hunting ground. The Rock Island Railroad laid tracks through the territory in 1852 but there was no resident service to Chicago. Later, other settlers purchased land near the Morgan farm. They used the Vincennes Trail along the ridge and another that paralleled the tracks at the base of the ridge to get to the city.

Morgan died in 1857. After the Civil War his children sold the land to a group of entrepreneurs who had formed the Blue Island Land and Building Company. They platted the area as a subdivision of Washington Heights (much of which today is Beverly) and selected the name "Morgan Park" for the extension south of 107th street to Lyon Avenue, and Western Avenue to about Ashland Avenue. It included both the desirable ridge and lowland areas. Beginning in 1870 it was widely advertised as a residential suburb built in the style of an old English park. Chicagoans were given free transportation and lunch to come out and visit its charming parks and winding streets. The establishment of several major religious and educational institutions in the community further enhanced its attractiveness. The Mount Vernon Military Academy, which became the Morgan Park Military Academy, was founded in 1873, and the Chicago Female College of Morgan Park began operation in 1875. The Baptist Theological Union was located in Morgan Park on five acres of land contributed by the Blue Island Land and Building Company between 1877 and 1892. In 1881, William Rainey Harper founded the American Institute of Hebrew. By the late 1880s 2,800 people lived in Morgan Park and 46 Rock Island trains stopped there daily.

The spacious ridge mansions on Chicago's only hilly area lent a further status to living in the area. Professionals and businessmen were attracted to the Beverly-Morgan Park area. In 1882 Morgan Park was incorporated as a village and in the 1890s surface lines were laid on most of the major thoroughfares, including Vincennes Avenue, Western Avenue between 111th and 119th streets and 111th Street between Ashland and California avenues. This further accelerated its growth. A small business section developed by the Rock Island junction at 110th Street and Monterey Avenue. A strip of land between Halsted and Peoria avenues from 111th to 115th streets was annexed to Chicago in 1890 as part of the village of West Roseland and later became part of Morgan Park. A long fight for annexation to Chicago ended in 1914 by election with a margin of only 15 votes. Morgan Park was larger then than it is now, the northwestern parcel between 99th and 107th streets,

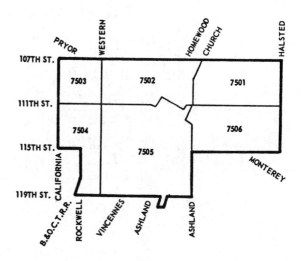

Western and California avenues having drifted to Beverly. With annexation came improvement to the whole village. Today, Morgan Park's boundaries are 107th to 115th streets between Halsted and California avenues, and 115th to 119th streets from Ashland Avenue to the vicinity of Rockwell Street.

Chicago has several integrated neighborhoods but perhaps Morgan Park is unique in that blacks have been a part of this community for most of the century. A small settlement was first recorded in 1915 east of Vincennes Avenue near the Rock Island on unimproved land that was mostly swamp. By 1920 they were 12 percent of the populaton, which was 5,804. Other residents were mostly of English, German, Swedish, and Irish descent, with only a small proportion of foreign born. In the 1920s the population more than doubled and the proportion of blacks increased to 35 percent. Residential growth was rapid as existing subdivisions were redivided and new lands opened up west of Western Avenue and south of 115th Street. Land values and rents skyrocketed. Residential structures varied from small brick buildings south of Monterey Avenue between the Rock Island and Vincennes Avenue, mansions on Longwood Drive, brick and frame dwellings between 107th and 111th streets and apartment buildings east of Longwood Drive between 108th and 110th streets. Irish workers became numerous in the area between Vincennes Road and the Rock Island. Blacks settled primarily in a triangular area east of Vincennes Road, to the Pennsylvania tracks between 107th and 119th streets. A number of blacks were employed at the Pullman car works and in the large industrial plants of the South Side. Others were service employees or did domestic work in Morgan Park. In 1950 Morgan Park reported a 25 percent increase in the number of foreign born at a time when the foreign born population of the city was declining by about that proportion. Leading nationalities included the Swedish, Germans, and Irish. By 1960 an increase in the number of Irish settlers had made them the predominant group, followed by the Germans, English, and Swedish.

A retail area developed at 111th Street (which was once Morgan Avenue) and Hale Avenue, the center of the area. Shoppers were also attracted outside the area to the South Michigan Avenue area of Roseland and to the Loop. Today, suburban Evergreen Plaza at 95th Street and Western Avenue draws many shoppers, and retail areas dot the major thoroughfares in the community.

In 1960 the Morgan Park Military Academy dropped the military aspect of its program to concentrate on scholastic achievement. Students are now bused into the restyled Morgan Park Academy from a

Community Area 75 — Morgan Park
Population and Housing Characteristics, 1930-1980

	1980	1970	1960	1950	1940	1930
Total Population.......	29,315	31,016	27,912	22,618	15,645	12,747
% Male..................	46.7	46.4	47.7	48.0	48.5	48.7
% Female................	53.3	53.6	52.3	52.0	51.5	51.3
% White.................	36.7	52.0	64.8	60.2	60.4	64.8
% Black.................	62.5	47.7	35.1	39.7	39.5	35.1
% Other Nonwhite Races..	0.8	0.3	0.1	0.1	0.1	0.1
% Under 5 Years Old.....	7.1	7.6	10.2	11.0	7.0	8.7
% 5-19 Years Old........	27.5	30.9	27.6	22.2	26.9	28.0
% 20-44 Years Old.......	33.8	27.2	27.4	36.1	36.4	39.1
% 45-64 Years Old.......	19.9	22.2	24.2	22.7	22.2	18.8
% 65 Years and Older....	11.7	12.1	10.6	8.0	7.5	5.4
Median School Years....	12.6	12.3	12.0	12.0	10.1	*
Total Housing Units....	9,121	9,050	7,858	6,053	4,036	*
% In One-Unit Structures.	75.0	71.8	70.5	*	*	*
% Owner Occupied.........	73.1	71.2	68.0	69.0	53.5	*
% Renter Occupied........	24.1	26.7	29.5	30.9	44.2	*
% Vacant.................	2.8	2.1	2.5	1.1	2.3	*
% 1+ Persons per Room....	6.4	9.3	11.4	12.7	*	*

Community Area 75 — Morgan Park
Selected Characteristics of Census Tracts: 1980

Tract Number	Total	7501	7502	7503	7504	7505	7506	8233. 1
Total Population..............	29315	6323	3967	2686	3371	7304	5664	0
% Male.........................	46.7	47.0	47.1	46.3	47.8	45.3	47.2	-
% Black........................	62.5	98.9	39.8	0.1	0.2	66.6	99.2	-
% Other Nonwhite...............	0.8	0.5	1.5	1.0	1.1	0.8	0.5	-
% Of Spanish Origin............	1.0	0.8	1.4	0.7	1.0	1.2	0.7	-
% Foreign Born.................	2.6	0.9	3.4	2.2	5.9	3.0	1.9	-
% Living In Group Quarters.....	1.1	0.0	0.3	0.0	0.2	4.1	0.1	-
% 13 Years Old And Under.......	21.8	24.8	21.2	19.8	16.6	22.9	21.5	-
% 14-20 Years Old..............	14.8	18.1	13.2	10.3	10.0	15.2	15.6	-
% 21-64 Years Old..............	51.7	51.4	54.3	49.5	55.2	49.3	52.5	-
% 65-74 Years Old..............	6.5	3.5	6.3	11.6	11.6	5.2	6.4	-
% 75 Years Old And Over........	5.2	2.2	5.1	8.8	6.5	6.8	4.0	-
% In Different House...........	25.8	16.6	49.5	18.0	24.0	32.8	15.4	-
% Families With Female Head....	27.2	30.6	21.2	15.0	8.8	32.9	33.0	-
Median School Years Completed....	12.6	12.5	13.4	13.0	12.7	12.5	12.3	-
Median Family Income, 1979......$$	23735	20684	27422	27604	26886	23614	19623	-
% Income Below Poverty Level...	9.6	15.0	7.2	1.0	4.8	11.9	11.1	-
% Income Of $30,000 Or More.....	34.1	31.1	42.2	40.9	42.2	32.7	23.4	-
% White Collar Workers.........	59.5	56.4	64.8	63.4	63.7	58.1	54.9	-
% Civilian Labor Force Unemployed.	11.6	18.0	7.1	5.7	3.1	10.6	17.9	-
% Riding To Work By Automobile....	71.1	74.2	73.5	75.9	73.0	64.6	70.7	-
Mean Commuting Time - Minutes...	37.8	41.5	35.3	30.7	33.4	40.0	40.9	-
Population Per Household...........	3.3	3.9	2.9	2.8	2.8	3.4	3.4	-
Total Housing Units...........	9121	1681	1394	988	1205	2142	1711	0
% Condominiums................	1.3	0.0	5.7	0.0	1.7	1.0	0.0	-
% Built 1970 Or Later.........	5.2	6.2	2.6	1.7	2.9	8.4	6.1	-
% Owner Occupied..............	73.1	75.3	63.2	77.2	87.3	66.3	75.3	-
% With 1+ Persons Per Room....	6.4	11.3	2.7	2.4	1.9	7.9	8.5	-
Median Value: Owner Units......$$	46900	43700	54400	54800	53800	45100	40100	-
Median Rent: Rental Units......$$	214	166	258	248	238	230	163	-
Median Number Of Rooms: All Units.	5.6	5.6	5.6	5.6	5.6	5.6	5.5	-

Community Area 75 — Morgan Park
Selected Characteristics of Census Tracts: 1970

Tract Number	TOTAL	7501	7502	7503	7504	7505	7506
Total Population.............	31016	6534	3827	3011	3958	7537	6149
% Male........................	46.4	47.7	45.2	46.1	46.9	44.2	48.5
% Black.......................	47.7	94.6	4.5	0.0	0.0	34.9	94.6
% Other Nonwhite..............	0.3	0.3	0.7	0.2	0.2	0.2	0.4
% Of Spanish Language.........	0.6	0.1	0.0	0.8	0.0	1.4	0.4
% Foreign Born................	2.9	0.7	2.5	5.7	5.0	4.4	1.0
% Living In Group Quarters....	1.4	0.2	0.9	0.0	0.6	4.2	0.9
% 13 Years Old And Under......	26.7	33.5	22.9	22.8	20.1	26.4	28.6
% 14-20 Years Old.............	13.2	14.8	10.6	9.4	14.9	13.0	14.1
% 21-64 Years Old.............	48.0	46.2	49.1	50.7	52.0	45.0	49.1
% 65-74 Years Old.............	7.3	3.6	10.2	11.4	8.8	7.8	5.7
% 75 Years Old And Over.......	4.8	1.9	7.2	5.7	4.3	7.8	2.5
% In Different House..........	56.5	35.4	51.1	64.1	74.9	53.9	69.1
% Families With Female Head......	14.3	15.7	15.8	12.3	10.1	16.1	14.0
Median School Years Completed.....	12.3	12.0	12.7	12.7	12.5	12.3	11.9
Median Family Income, 1969......$$	12620	11905	13945	14732	14472	12231	10865
% Income Below Poverty Level....	6.7	9.4	2.6	2.3	5.3	9.4	6.5
% Income of $15,000 or More....	36.5	30.3	43.2	48.5	46.7	37.6	22.8
% White Collar Workers.........	30.4	20.8	46.3	37.8	38.0	33.3	16.6
% Civilian Labor Force Unemployed.	4.4	6.2	2.1	1.9	2.1	4.3	7.1
% Riding To Work By Automobile....	64.8	64.8	63.7	70.2	63.7	60.8	68.4
Population Per Household..........	3.5	4.0	3.0	3.1	3.4	3.4	3.7
Total Housing Units...........	9052	1645	1319	988	1185	2222	1693
% Condominiums & Cooperatives.....	1.9	5.5	3.6	0.6	0.0	0.9	0.4
% Built 1960 Or Later.........	18.3	26.3	18.3	7.8	4.5	14.6	31.2
% Owner Occupied..............	69.3	71.5	59.6	77.4	86.3	58.6	72.1
% With 1+ Persons Per Room....	9.6	15.4	3.7	3.4	1.9	9.3	13.6
Median Value: Owner Units......$$	22500	22300	23200	24600	24700	21100	20200
Median Rent: Rental Units......$$	125	87	147	165	156	132	97
Median Number Of Rooms: All Units.	5.4	5.6	5.5	5.5	5.6	5.2	5.2

wide arc of city and suburban neighborhoods that extends from northwest Indiana to 55th Street in Chicago.

Between 1930 and 1960 the population of Morgan Park more than doubled with the largest growth period occurring in the forties. During that time the proportion of blacks remained fairly stable, fluctuating between 35 and 39 percent. The black population was considered an isolated satellite community. Racial change came to the Morgan Park area in the 1960s, primarily as a result of the general black growth on the South Side. Between 1960 and 1970 the community's population continued to climb to 31,043, its highest ever, due to an increase of over 50 percent in the number of blacks. By 1980, the number of blacks had increased again by 24 percent. Blacks now make up 63 percent of the community population.

Morgan Park has both integrated and racially segregated areas. The population east of Ashland Avenue is almost entirely black; the population west of Western Avenue almost entirely white; and the area between is approximately 60 percent white north of 111th Street, and 67 percent black south of 111th Street. As expected, the middle area has shown the greatest amount of residential change over the last decade. About 50 percent of the population has lived in their homes for at least 5 years in the area north of 111th Street, compared to the community average of 74 percent. The median value of homes is slightly lower than that of the city as a whole but almost three-fourths are owner-occupied.

In many ways Morgan Park and Beverly are like one community. In both can be found a diversity of architectural styles that has led to the designation of the area as a National Historic District from 87th to 115th Street, between Prospect Avenue and Hoyne and Seeley avenues. Victorian, French Provincial, Cape Cod, Swiss Chalet, Georgian, Dutch Colonial, and other styles have lent a country-like atmosphere to these communities. Both Beverly and Morgan Park have been influenced by the same cultural and educational institutions, and both have tried to maintain racial stability within their environs. The Beverly Area Planning Association (BAPA), which serves as an umbrella organization for other groups, has been instrumental in this last endeavor, though their boundaries exclude the large segment of blacks living east of Ashland Avenue in Morgan Park. Whether white flight and black resegregation will occur in Morgan Park remains to be seen.

Antoinette LoBosco

Community Area 76

O'Hare

The O'Hare community area has its origins in the development of its namesake, O'Hare International Airport. Following the Japanese attack on Pearl Harbor, the federal government began to look for sites in order to build C-54 transport planes. By June 1942, the War Department had decided upon a strip of land 18 miles northwest of downtown Chicago at Orchard Place as the location for a huge Douglas Aircraft Company plant. Orchard Place had been the name of a railroad station, so called because it was located on an orchard acreage donated by a pioneer developer. Federal officials then bought 1,000 acres of land, and contracted arrangements for water and sewer facilities with city officials. Within 18 months, the plant and the airfield were completed. The Douglas plant would become the largest aircraft manufacturing facility in the country, employing 21,000 workers at it peak. The field was Chicago Orchard Airport, and this is the origin of the unusual ORD baggage symbol so familiar to air travelers.

Although the Douglas site was shut down in the summer of 1945, after the plant had manufactured 655 transport planes during the war, there were other plans for the facility. It had become apparent that Midway Airport could not handle the postwar volume of air traffic. A 21-man committee, comprised of various representatives from airline companies, government aviation agencies, and city and county agencies, was commissioned to choose a location for a second Chicago airport. In November, 1945, the committee recommended the old Douglas site. In 1947, the city asked for the site from the war property disposal agency and got it for nothing with an additional 5,000 acres. On June 22, 1949, the name of the Orchard Airport was changed, by city council resolution, to O'Hare Field, Chicago International Airport. The field was named for a Chicagoan, World War II hero Edward H. "Butch" O'Hare.

On October 30, 1955, O'Hare Field was opened to scheduled airline traffic. Before long it became apparent that the new airport would have to be able to accommodate jet aircraft. This meant longer runways and more land. The O'Hare Field site eventually grew to 7,800 acres, some of which extends into DuPage County.

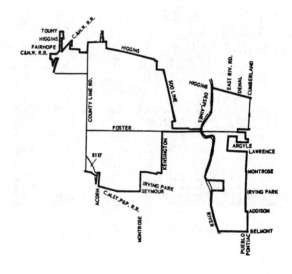

In the beginning, the remote airfield was connected to the city by the thin ribbon of Higgins Road. To secure its legal hold on O'Hare Field, city officials continually added surrounding acreage. Nine hundred acres of forest preserve, bounded approximately by Higgins Road, the Des Plaines River, East River Road, and Belmont Avenue, were annexed in March 1958. As O'Hare Field became Chicago's primary airport, the community of O'Hare began to take shape. Prior to 1960, it had consisted of a smattering of expensive homes surrounded by forest preserve. The 1960 census noted a residential population of 763. By the middle 1960s, however, the first bricks were laid for rows of tract homes, and by the end of that decade more than 6,000 lived there. By the end of the 1970s, O'Hare had become a community of attractive single-family homes, condominiums, and apartment complexes. Among these apartment structures is The Pavilion, a massive 1,130-unit high-rise complex.

Community Area 76 -- O'Hare
Population and Housing Characteristics, 1930-1980

	1980	1970	1960	1950	1940	1930
Total Population.......	11,054	6,342	763	*	*	*
% Male..................	48.1	49.2	*	*	*	*
% Female................	51.9	50.8	*	*	*	*
% White.................	95.7	98.5	*	*	*	*
% Black.................	1.5	0.2	*	*	*	*
% Other Nonwhite Races...	2.8	1.3	*	*	*	*
% Under 5 Years Old.....	4.5	10.1	*	*	*	*
% 5-19 Years Old........	11.8	17.5	*	*	*	*
% 20-44 Years Old.......	48.7	45.9	*	*	*	*
% 45-64 Years Old.......	24.2	22.4	*	*	*	*
% 65 Years and Older....	10.8	4.1	*	*	*	*
Median School Years....	12.7	12.8	*	*	*	*
Total Housing Units....	5,737	2,403	242	*	*	*
% In One-Unit Structures.	12.5	27.1	*	*	*	*
% Owner Occupied........	31.9	27.5	76.9	*	*	*
% Renter Occupied........	64.0	67.5	14.9	*	*	*
% Vacant...............	4.1	5.0	8.2	*	*	*
% 1+ Persons per Room....	1.7	4.3	11.7	*	*	*

Community Area 76 -- O Hare
Selected Characteristics of Census Tracts: 1980

Tract Number	Total	7608	7609	7705	7706	7707	7708	8117	8400	8408
Total Population.............	11068	10962	92	3	0	0	0	0	11	0
% Male.......................	48.1	48.0	-	-	-	-	-	-	-	-
% Black......................	1.5	1.4	-	-	-	-	-	-	-	-
% Other Nonwhite.............	2.8	2.7	-	-	-	-	-	-	-	-
% Of Spanish Origin..........	2.6	2.5	-	-	-	-	-	-	-	-
% Foreign Born...............	16.0	16.1	-	-	-	-	-	-	-	-
% Living In Group Quarters...	0.0	0.0	-	-	-	-	-	-	-	-
% 13 Years Old And Under.....	10.5	10.3	-	-	-	-	-	-	-	-
% 14-20 Years Old............	7.4	7.4	-	-	-	-	-	-	-	-
% 21-64 Years Old............	71.4	71.4	-	-	-	-	-	-	-	-
% 65-74 Years Old............	7.2	7.3	-	-	-	-	-	-	-	-
% 75 Years Old And Over......	3.5	3.6	-	-	-	-	-	-	-	-
% In Different House.........	61.0	60.7	-	-	-	-	-	-	-	-
% Families With Female Head..	18.3	18.5	-	-	-	-	-	-	-	-
Median School Years Completed..	12.7	12.7	-	-	-	-	-	-	-	-
Median Family Income, 1979......$$	23884	23871	-	-	-	-	-	-	-	-
% Income Below Poverty Level....	2.8	2.8	-	-	-	-	-	-	-	-
% Income Of $30,000 Or More....	33.5	33.4	-	-	-	-	-	-	-	-
% White Collar Workers........	64.1	63.9	-	-	-	-	-	-	-	-
% Civilian Labor Force Unemployed.	4.2	4.2	-	-	-	-	-	-	-	-
% Riding To Work By Automobile....	81.5	81.6	-	-	-	-	-	-	-	-
Mean Commuting Time - Minutes....	29.1	29.1	-	-	-	-	-	-	-	-
Population Per Household..........	2.0	2.0	-	-	-	-	-	-	-	-
Total Housing Units..........	5737	5694	39	1	0	0	0	0	3	0
% Condominiums...............	20.6	20.7	-	-	-	-	-	-	-	-
% Built 1970 Or Later........	62.4	62.2	-	-	-	-	-	-	-	-
% Owner Occupied.............	31.9	31.6	-	-	-	-	-	-	-	-
% With 1+ Persons Per Room....	1.7	1.6	-	-	-	-	-	-	-	-
Median Value: Owner Units......$$	100700	100500	-	-	-	-	-	-	-	-
Median Rent: Rental Units......$$	340	339	-	-	-	-	-	-	-	-
Median Number Of Rooms: All Units.	4.0	4.0	-	-	-	-	-	-	-	-

Community Area 76 -- O'Hare
Selected Characteristics of Census Tracts: 1970

Tract Number	TOTAL	7601	7603	7604	7605	7606
Total Population.............	6342	200	1364	2577	2034	167
% Male.......................	49.2	47.0	49.8	49.0	49.1	52.7
% Black......................	0.2	0.0	0.1	0.0	0.4	0.0
% Other Nonwhite.............	1.0	3.0	0.0	0.0	2.5	3.0
% Of Spanish Language........	-	-	-	-	-	-
% Foreign Born...............	9.1	0.0	11.1	7.5	11.6	7.2
% Living In Group Quarters...	0.3	0.0	1.2	0.0	0.0	1.2
% 13 Years Old And Under.....	20.3	31.5	22.9	20.5	15.8	37.1
% 14-20 Years Old............	8.7	11.0	14.1	6.2	7.6	13.8
% 21-64 Years Old............	66.9	52.5	55.1	69.2	74.9	49.0
% 65-74 Years Old............	2.9	4.0	5.2	3.2	1.1	0.0
% 75 Years Old And Over......	1.2	1.0	2.7	0.9	0.6	0.0
% In Different House.........	68.0	47.6	37.3	89.5	59.4	85.1
% Families With Female Head..	8.2	13.2	5.3	7.5	10.5	2.6
Median School Years Completed....	12.2	11.2	12.1	12.4	12.2	11.6
Median Family Income, 1969......$$	13883	7429	14882	13150	14614	9250
% Income Below Poverty Level....	2.6	17.7	0.0	4.2	0.0	0.0
% Income of $15,000 or More.....	40.8	16.1	49.4	36.5	46.9	15.2
% White Collar Workers........	59.5	20.2	57.4	62.9	58.5	30.8
% Civilian Labor Force Unemployed.	1.2	0.0	1.0	2.1	0.0	0.0
% Riding To Work By Automobile....	86.6	52.5	83.4	92.7	84.1	68.8
Population Per Household..........	2.8	3.3	3.7	2.6	2.5	4.2
Total Housing Units..........	2402	64	369	1117	811	41
% Condominiums & Cooperatives.....	3.0	0.0	0.0	6.4	0.0	-
% Built 1960 Or Later............	28.8	78.5	5.5	5.6	43.3	-
% Owner Occupied.................	27.5	50.0	87.0	18.2	9.2	-
% With 1+ Persons Per Room.......	4.3	15.0	7.7	2.6	3.1	-
Median Value: Owner Units.......$$	40500	-	40500	-	-	-
Median Rent: Rental Units......$$	179	98	182	179	178	-
Median Number Of Rooms: All Units.	4.1	4.6	5.5	4.0	3.8	-

The 11,000 residents who live today in O'Hare's variegated housing are primarily Italians, Poles, Germans, and Irish, along with a small number of blacks and Hispanics. The people of O'Hare are relatively affluent, with a median family income in 1979 of almost $24,000, among the city's top 20. The median value of single-family homes is more than $100,000, third in the city, and most of the housing has been built in the last decade. Many of these residents were attracted by O'Hare's suburban environment and the region's accessibility to downtown Chicago via the Kennedy Expressway. In addition, the area transportation accessibility was increased by the completion of the CTA surface line to the River Road station in 1983.

The residential growth of O'Hare is matched by the emergence of business establishments in the area, evident from the high-rise corporate structures which dot the Kennedy Expressway. One of the earliest headquarters in the community area was the Midwest office of the Teamsters Union, located in the International Tower, a 10-story building built in the early 1970s. Over time, more organizations began to establish offices in the community, attracted by the proximity of the airport, and the easy access to the Loop. McDonnell Douglas and International Harvester both established corporate offices in the O'Hare Towers, while Sperry Univac moved in next door to the O'Hare Towers. In May, 1983, Bally Corporation, manufacturers of pinball machines, moved into the President Plaza. As expected, this business growth has spurred real estate values; property values in the community have risen from $6 to $8 per square foot in 1978 to $10 to $12 per square foot in 1983.

While the proximity of the airport has been a major factor in attracting business to the O'Hare community, the noise generated from the airport has made life uncomfortable for many of the residents. The Chicago Aviation Department, however, has promised that the skies will be quieter in the future. A federal law which requires quieter engines on all commercial aircraft will take effect in 1985. Furthermore, attempts are being made to divert flight paths over forests and factories instead of over area homes. Thus, while noise will always be part of the O'Hare environment, there are signs that relief is in sight.

Winston McDowell

Community Area 77

Edgewater

Earlier editions of the *Fact Book* have conjoined the communities of Edgewater and Uptown as Community Area 3. However, in mid-1980, it was announced by the Chicago Department of Planning that Edgewater would be officially designated as a separate community area divided from Uptown by Foster Avenue.

One of the earliest settlers in the Edgewater area was a Luxembourger named Nicholas Krantz. In 1848, he constructed the first notable structure in the area, a frame homestead on the northeast corner of what is today Ridge and Clark streets. The homestead, called Seven Mile House in view of its distance from the Chicago City Hall, functioned as a tavern, inn, and local meeting place for the settlers of that era. Edgewater remained relatively rural and sparsely populated until the turn of the century. In the late nineteenth century, the area was known the "celery-growing capital of the Middle West."

Two railroad lines passed through Edgewater in these early years. The Chicago, Milwaukee and St. Paul Railroad ran along the route now used by the CTA elevated train, and the predecessor of the Chicago and North Western Railroad ran by Ravenswood Avenue—the western boundry of Edgewater. Until 1890, the nearest stop for Edgewater residents on the Chicago, Milwaukee and St. Paul line was to the north in Evanston. The Chicago and North Western began service between Chicago and Waukegan in 1855 and shortly after opened a station near the entrance to the Rosehill Cemetery.

The clearing of the dense woods and underbrush and the subdivision and platting of Edgewater for residential construction began in the 1880s and 1890s. The name "Edgewater" was given by the developer John Lewis Cochran to the first subdivision that he purchased in the area in 1885. This subdivision was bounded by what is today Broadway, Bryn Mawr, Lake Michigan and Foster Avenue. Cochran had grand designs for Edgewater and installed wide macadam streets, stone sidewalks, and a drainage system in an attempt to attract residents to the new area. Advertisements in the late 1880s celebrated Edgewater as "the only electric lighted suburb adjacent to Chicago." The settlers of Edgewater at this time were primarily German, Scandinavian and Irish. In 1889, Edgewater was annexed by the City of Chicago as part of the City of Lake View.

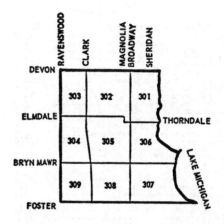

Edgewater began to grow rapidly after the turn of the century. In 1900, the North Western Elevated Railroad was opened to Wilson Avenue and in 1907 the elevated service was extended through Howard Street. Before and after World War I, as Italians began to settle on the Near North Side, a large number of Swedes moved into Edgewater from their Oak Street settlement. The southwest corner of Edgewater centering around Clark Street between Foster and Bryn Mawr avenues became a favored residential location for many Swedes. This area became known as "Andersonville" from the name of the local school district. Germans and Irish also moved from older residential areas into Edgewater.

During the period from 1900 to 1920, the area west of Broadway was the site of mostly single-family residential construction that grew slowly but steadily. The land east of Broadway soon became extremely valuable for high rise hotels and apartment complexes. Apartment flats began to be constructed alongside the elevated train route on Kenmore and Winthrop avenues replacing the earlier single-family homes that had been built there. This stretch of apartment blocks, which extends south into the Uptown community area, has become known as the "Winthrop-Kenmore Corridor." North Sheridan Road also became developed during this period as a preserve of large single-family mansions.

Building construction stopped in Edgewater during the First World War, but quickly resumed during the 1920s. In 1922, the last area of virgin land in Edgewater was subdivided. The density of population along the Winthrop-Kenmore Corridor increased with the building of several courtyard apartments and approximately 40 furnished apartment hotel buildings. Edgewater at this time was regarded as one of

Community Area 77 -- Edgewater
Population and Housing Characteristics, 1930-1980

	1980	1970	1960	1950	1940	1930
Total Population	58,561	61,598	51,579	54,606	55,503	53,938
% Male	47.3	45.5	44.7	54.4	45.1	46.6
% Female	52.7	54.5	55.3	54.6	54.9	53.4
% White	71.9	93.9	97.8	99.5	99.7	99.7
% Black	11.1	0.6	0.1	0.2	0.2	0.2
% Other Nonwhite Races	17.0	5.5	2.1	0.3	0.1	0.1
% Under 5 Years Old	5.4	5.3	6.9	6.5	4.4	4.9
% 5-19 Years Old	13.5	14.7	14.8	13.0	15.7	16.8
% 20-44 Years Old	43.4	36.9	30.5	38.4	45.0	49.8
% 45-64 Years Old	19.3	25.3	31.1	30.7	26.5	22.5
% 65 Years and Older	18.4	17.8	16.7	11.4	8.4	5.7
Median School Years	12.8	12.4	12.1	11.9	11.7	*
Total Housing Units	32,613	30,519	23,588	20,052	19,168	*
% In One Unit Structures	4.6	5.7	7.6	*	*	*
% Owner Occupied	23.2	15.4	16.6	17.0	13.2	*
% Renter Occupied	66.6	79.1	75.8	80.9	79.8	*
% Vacant	10.2	5.5	7.6	2.1	7.0	*
% 1+ Persons per Room	5.9	4.5	4.5	11.8	*	*

Community Area 77 -- Edgewater
Selected Characteristics of Census Tracts: 1980

Tract Number	Total	301	302	303	304	305	306	307	308	309
Total Population	58561	11978	6449	3062	2629	7546	9001	8718	5534	3644
% Male	47.3	46.3	48.0	44.4	46.4	48.2	45.3	49.1	49.0	48.6
% Black	11.1	21.1	2.2	1.6	1.4	3.4	21.0	17.0	2.2	0.4
% Other Nonwhite	17.0	12.5	13.4	13.2	28.6	25.9	11.0	16.3	26.2	17.3
% Of Spanish Origin	13.3	5.9	8.0	10.0	20.1	27.0	11.4	13.4	15.0	18.6
% Foreign Born	29.0	25.0	21.2	23.0	43.1	37.2	29.3	28.9	30.1	32.2
% Living In Group Quarters	3.6	9.4	0.7	0.2	6.8	1.6	1.8	3.6	2.5	0.4
% 13 Years Old And Under	12.2	8.3	15.3	15.3	12.7	18.5	8.8	9.3	15.0	15.7
% 14-20 Years Old	8.5	8.2	11.2	7.7	11.4	11.4	5.3	5.2	10.4	10.4
% 21-64 Years Old	60.8	62.2	61.6	55.0	62.5	59.0	59.5	65.5	59.1	57.4
% 65-74 Years Old	9.9	12.1	6.7	12.1	8.0	6.1	12.6	10.9	8.5	9.3
% 75 Years Old And Over	8.5	9.3	5.2	9.9	5.4	4.9	13.8	9.2	7.0	7.2
% In Different House	60.1	64.9	45.8	59.7	62.3	66.0	65.6	60.7	57.7	44.3
% Families With Female Head	26.4	33.2	21.7	18.1	15.7	27.1	37.5	33.5	20.7	18.0
Median School Years Completed	12.8	13.5	13.5	12.5	12.6	12.6	12.7	12.9	12.6	12.2
Median Family Income, 1979...$$	19860	20748	23822	19816	21719	18328	18759	18536	19868	19200
% Income Below Poverty Level	11.2	13.6	8.8	9.1	7.9	14.6	15.3	10.0	6.8	6.4
% Income Of $30,000 Or More	28.1	34.1	36.0	19.1	29.1	18.3	23.9	31.8	31.4	21.9
% White Collar Workers	64.9	73.7	66.8	63.1	56.3	51.3	69.5	65.9	61.5	56.5
% Civilian Labor Force Unemployed	7.2	6.0	5.1	4.0	5.3	9.1	8.7	9.0	6.2	9.0
% Riding To Work By Automobile	45.1	39.3	55.3	51.2	42.4	39.2	41.1	44.3	51.5	58.2
Mean Commuting Time - Minutes	31.5	33.9	28.6	34.5	25.7	32.0	31.9	33.8	28.1	28.8
Population Per Household	1.9	1.6	2.4	2.1	2.4	2.6	1.6	1.6	2.4	2.5
Total Housing Units	32613	7563	2784	1522	1111	3174	6359	6122	2441	1537
% Condominiums	21.3	37.0	1.1	5.0	3.2	5.4	28.7	32.5	1.0	0.0
% Built 1970 Or Later	12.0	15.3	0.2	17.2	3.6	0.2	7.1	31.0	0.8	3.6
% Owner Occupied	23.2	24.7	29.0	25.0	25.6	20.8	17.2	22.5	26.6	29.6
% With 1+ Persons Per Room	5.9	5.4	3.1	3.6	9.1	8.2	7.7	6.3	4.6	3.7
Median Value: Owner Units...$$	61100	-	62000	60200	53800	53900	-	-	76000	55700
Median Rent: Rental Units...$$	225	232	234	221	204	221	230	218	226	216
Median Number Of Rooms: All Units	3.5	3.1	5.0	4.1	4.2	4.6	2.7	2.9	5.0	4.9

Community Area 77 -- Edgewater
Selected Characteristics of Census Tracts: 1970

Tract Number	TOTAL	0301	0302	0303	0304	0305	0306	0307	0308	0309
Total Population	61598	11871	7253	2750	2887	8117	10051	8457	5974	4238
% Male	45.5	43.7	46.8	45.1	43.9	45.9	43.3	47.4	47.3	47.1
% Black	0.6	0.8	0.2	0.2	0.3	0.7	0.6	1.5	0.1	0.0
% Other Nonwhite	5.5	2.9	5.3	1.6	7.5	8.8	3.7	6.7	8.9	5.1
% Of Spanish Language	7.9	4.1	2.6	5.1	13.8	11.9	9.2	12.0	6.2	8.7
% Foreign Born	21.3	18.6	13.7	14.8	30.1	23.6	26.0	23.1	20.6	22.2
% Living In Group Quarters	3.1	7.5	0.6	0.0	2.0	1.5	1.3	5.5	3.1	0.6
% 13 Years Old And Under	13.6	4.8	23.4	15.9	20.1	20.8	5.9	10.0	18.3	20.2
% 14-20 Years Old	8.2	7.9	11.4	8.1	8.7	10.1	4.7	6.1	9.3	9.9
% 21-64 Years Old	60.4	68.9	51.8	59.3	57.0	55.5	66.6	63.6	54.0	52.2
% 65-74 Years Old	11.3	11.9	8.5	11.1	9.2	8.6	13.9	13.1	10.9	11.3
% 75 Years Old And Over	6.6	6.4	4.9	5.7	5.0	5.0	8.8	7.3	7.5	6.3
% In Different House	38.2	22.3	52.8	51.6	51.6	46.4	28.5	26.2	53.3	53.2
% Families With Female Head	13.2	11.8	14.1	15.3	12.5	14.8	11.6	15.0	12.8	13.0
Median School Years Completed	12.4	12.8	12.4	12.3	12.2	12.1	12.5	12.3	12.2	12.1
Median Family Income, 1969...$$	11844	14134	11802	10558	11582	11259	13008	10190	11528	11735
% Income Below Poverty Level	5.6	3.7	3.7	3.5	3.2	5.4	7.7	9.8	4.7	6.6
% Income of $15,000 or More	32.0	45.8	29.8	18.8	27.1	23.9	41.8	25.4	29.1	21.2
% White Collar Workers	40.4	54.3	35.6	35.5	33.9	27.4	47.1	37.1	35.2	23.5
% Civilian Labor Force Unemployed	2.6	2.8	3.1	0.8	2.1	3.6	2.1	3.9	1.6	1.6
% Riding To Work By Automobile	43.5	43.7	45.8	48.2	43.1	45.0	40.9	37.9	46.6	48.5
Population Per Household	2.1	1.7	2.9	2.3	2.5	2.6	1.6	1.7	2.6	2.7
Total Housing Units	30494	7096	2558	1233	1174	3147	6311	5098	2279	1598
% Condominiums & Cooperatives	5.1	9.5	0.9	1.8	0.0	0.3	7.5	6.9	0.3	0.0
% Built 1960 Or Later	30.3	52.7	1.3	19.3	5.0	0.8	56.7	29.2	1.0	2.6
% Owner Occupied	10.2	0.8	26.8	21.9	25.2	18.4	1.1	1.5	27.9	28.8
% With 1+ Persons Per Room	4.5	2.9	4.9	2.0	6.1	6.1	3.7	7.7	2.9	4.7
Median Value: Owner Units...$$	21600	-	22900	20900	20200	18400	-	-	23200	19300
Median Rent: Rental Units...$$	135	156	128	129	115	120	151	132	120	114
Median Number Of Rooms: All Units	3.4	2.9	5.0	4.3	4.2	4.6	2.7	2.6	5.0	4.9

Chicago's most prestigious communities. A prominent symbol of Edgewater's affluence was the Edgewater Beach Hotel which opened in 1916 at 5349 North Sheridan Road. The Edgewater building boom peaked in 1926 and property values reached their height in 1928.

Construction in Edgewater stopped with the onset of the Depression in the 1930s and did not resume until after the Second World War. The extension of Lake Shore Drive north to Foster in 1933, the parking problems created in Edgewater as a result of the increasing number of automobiles, and the growth of Evanston as a shopping area contributed to Edgewater's decline during the '30s and '40s.

In 1930, of the major foreign-born ethnic groups in Edgewater, the Swedes were the largest group with 39 percent, followed by the Germans with 17 percent, the Irish with 8 percent, and the Russians with 6 percent. The Germans lived north of the Andersonville Swedish community and the Irish lived primarily in the central strip of Edgewater between Clark and Broadway from Foster to Devon. The area east of Broadway had a smaller foreign-born ppulation and no single ethnic group was predominant in this area.

After the Second World War, many of the larger homes and apartments in Edgewater were broken up into smaller units to accommodate the increased demand for housing. Beginning in the mid-1950s and continuing into the 1970s, the large homes on North Sheridan Road were torn down and a strip of high-rise apartments constructed in their place. By 1974, approximately 6,150 apartment units had been built in the eight blocks from 5600 to 6400 North Sheridan Road, making this an area with one of the highest population densities in the city.

The development of the suburbs in the 1950s coincides with the decline of Edgewater's population from almost 55,000 in 1950 to less than 52,000 in 1960. The urban decay that had become apparent in the Uptown community to the south and along the Winthrop-Kenmore Corridor spawned efforts by residents to establish the Edgewater Community Council in 1960. This organization has spearheaded efforts to stop the increase of crime in the area, to prevent further urban decay along the Corridor, to control lakefront development, and to restore many of the deteriorated buildings in Edgewater.

Between 1960 and 1970, Edgewater's population increased by ten thousand to 61,598. This large increase is attributable to the replacement of single-family and two- to six-flats with high- and low-rise apartment buildings. Rehabilitation of existing structures has occurred mostly in the southern portions of the Winthrop-Kenmore Corridor and some apartment buildings have been converted into condominiums. Several "four-plus-one" apartment buildings have replaced single-family homes on the Winthrop-Kenmore Corridor, especially near the Granville and Thorndale elevated train stops. As of 1970, 57 percent of the housing in Edgewater had been built before 1939 but 30 percent had been built in the previous decade. Several hundred more units, amounting to 12 percent of the current stock, were built in the 1970s.

After the Second World War, many of the descendants of the early Scandinavian immigrants began leaving Edgewater, first to the neighboring community of Rogers Park and then to northern suburbs such as Glenview and Evanston. However, a Swedish presence still remains in Andersonville where the Swedish American Museum opened in 1976. Newer ethnic groups began moving into Edgewater during the '60s and '70s including Asian, Hispanic, and Middle-Eastern groups as well as Greeks, blacks, and American Indians.

Broadway and Clark streets are Edgewater's prime commercial streets today containing many small businesses, family-owned restaurants, retail shopping stores and banking and real estate firms. In addition, Broadway has many automobile and repair businesses. Other commercial areas in Edgewater are located in the vicinity of the elevated stops of Berwyn, Bryn Mawr, Thorndale and Granville and along the northern border street of Devon. Some light manufacturing plants are located on Ravenswood Avenue between Foster and Peterson. A few smaller industrial concerns are located along Clark Street.

In 1982, a large block of lakefront land at Granville and North Sheridan Road was purchased by the Park District for community use and the conversion of the National Guard Armory at Broadway and Thorndale Avenue into a multi-recreational facility for Edgewater is expected to begin soon. These developments will help rectify a lack of recreational space and facilities in the community.

Rodney Nelson

Other Cities of 25,000 or More Population in the Consolidated Statistical Area

Revised Census Bureau Housing and Population Totals

After compiling the total numbers of inhabitants and housing units reported in this section for suburban communities in 1980 and 1970, the U. S. Bureau of the Census reported corrections for certain of them. These changes are usually based on reassignments of certain areas, either included in or excluded from the municipality.

	Number of Inhabitants	Number of Housing Units
1980		
Addison	29,826	10,070
Downers Grove	42,691	15,715
Elgin	63,668	24,794
Elk Grove Village	28,679	9,698
Hanover Park	28,719	9,287
Lombard	36,879	13,286
Naperville	42,601	14,236
Tinley Park	26,178	8,627
Wilmette	28,221	9,980
1970		
Bolingbrook	7,643	1,843
Calumet City	33,107	10,912
Elk Grove Village	21,707	5,606
Elmhurst	48,887	14,024
Evanston	80,113	27,873
Joliet	78,887	26,186
Lombard	36,194	10,551
Maywood	29,019	8,728
Park Ridge	42,614	13,233
Skokie	68,322	21,067

Addison

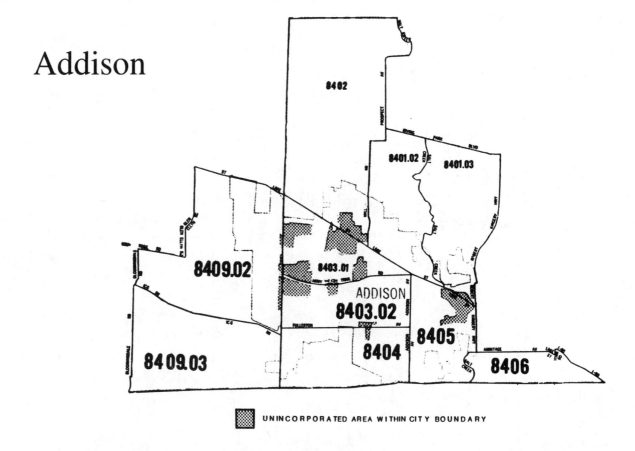

■ UNINCORPORATED AREA WITHIN CITY BOUNDARY

Addison lies in DuPage County, 20 miles west of Chicago's Loop. It consists of nine square miles of incorporated land and has a planning perimeter of 12 square miles. The city is named for Joseph Addison, the English writer. Until 1950, Addison was a quiet rural village of less than 1,000 population. Since that time its growth in all respects has been phenomenal. Today it is an ordered mixture of industrial and residential areas which are home to nearly 30,000 people.

Before the first white settlers arrived, the Pottawatomie Indians had a village along Salt Creek near the present Elmhurst Country Club. In 1833 Hezekiah Dunklee and Mason Smith staked out claims in a grove of trees on the west side of Salt Creek near what is now Lake Street (U.S. Highway 20). The area became known as Dunklee's Grove. Other early settlers included Steunkel, Krage, Fischer, Franzen, Lester, Kotermun, Kruse, Fiene, and Buchholz; the names indicate their German origins.

In 1837 there were 30 families living in Dunklee's Grove. In 1842 the name was changed to Addison and by 1849 the settlement had an English and German Lutheran church-school, the St. Paul Christian Day School. It stood near the corner of Army Trail Road and May Street. Another early meeting place for the 200-odd residents was the Salt Creek House, which was an inn and a stop on the early stagecoach line.

Army Trail Road was used by General Winfield Scott and the U.S. Army during the Black Hawk War in 1832. Lake Street, which angles through Addison and provides entry to the Tri-State Tollway, was established as a stagecoach route from Chicago to Bloomingdale in 1836. In the early 20th century the Elgin-to-Chicago road races were held along this road although it was not paved until 1922.

In the 1850s the Addison windmill was constructed to grind grain for nearby farmers. By this time Addison consisted of a blacksmith shop, cobbler's shop, a physician's office, general store (known as the Century), and a steam grist mill which later became a cheese factory. In 1864 the Missouri Synod of the Lutheran Church moved its teachers seminary to Addison. The first class consisted of 43 male students, and the seminary was an important institution in the community until it was moved to River Forest and became Concordia Teachers College in the

1920s. In 1873 the Evangelical Lutheran Home Orphanage was established, to be supplemented by the two-story Kinderheim, built in 1902.

In 1884 the Village of Addison was incorporated with Buchholz as its first President. The Illinois Central Railroad ran the first train into Addison in 1890 and by 1894 there were 450 residents in the village. The population had grown to 591 in 1900. Although several farms were sold for subdividing in the 1910s, not much construction was undertaken. The Village of Addison led a detached rural life for several decades. The population rose to a high of 916 in 1930, dropping to 813 by 1950.

In the decade that followed, developers began building in earnest to meet increased housing demands, and Addison's growth began. By 1960 the population had risen to 6,741. It increased 263 percent during the next 10 years, bringing the total to more than 24,000 in 1970. In the 1970s Addison experienced another increase of more than 20 percent to almost 30,000, as the extension to the Eisenhower Expressway (Interstate Highway 290) was built.

The largest single descent group in 1980 was Italian, followed by German, Polish, Mexican, Cuban and Irish. Residents of Spanish origin constituted 6 percent of the population. Addison has a relatively young population. Thirty-two percent of the residents are under 18 years of age and less than 5 percent are over 65. The median age in this community is 26.6 compared to nearby Downers Grove, where the median is 32. If the experience of other communities is repeated, Addison may experience a population loss in this decade as the young people leave parental homes for school and work.

The number of housing units in Addison has grown to more than 10,000, of which almost a third have been built in the most recent decade. In 1980 61 percent of the units were single-family homes and 57 percent were owner-occupied. Drops in those percentages in the most recent decade reflect increased construction of apartment houses. At the same time the percentage of overcrowded units dropped from eight in 1970 to less than five in 1980. The latter figure is still relatively high for a suburban area. In 1979 the Village sponsored a $25 million residential bond issue, participation in which was limited to Addison. It allowed purchase of residences at an interest rate of about 8.5 percent

Addison
Population and Housing Characteristics, 1930-1980

	1980	1970	1960	1950	1940	1930
Total Population.......	29,826	24,482	6,741	813	819	916
% Male..................	49.8	50.1	50.5	*	*	*
% Female................	50.2	49.9	49.5	*	*	*
% White.................	94.0	99.4	99.8	*	*	*
% Black.................	0.8	0.1	0.0	*	*	*
% Other Nonwhite Races...	5.2	0.5	0.2	*	*	*
% Under 5 Years Old......	7.6	13.0	22.2	*	*	*
% 5-19 Years Old.........	28.1	32.2	26.8	*	*	*
% 20-44 Years Old........	42.1	40.6	41.9	*	*	*
% 45-64 Years Old........	17.8	11.7	7.0	*	*	*
% 65 Years and Older.....	4.4	2.5	2.1	*	*	*
Median School Years......	12.5	12.3	12.2	*	*	*
Total Housing Units....	10,070	6,798	1,750	*	*	*
% In one-Unit Structures.	56.5	65.4	92.1	*	*	*
% Owner Occupied.........	57.4	63.6	84.1	*	*	*
% Renter Occupied........	39.5	34.3	10.2	*	*	*
% Vacant.................	3.1	2.1	5.7	*	*	*
% 1+ Persons per Room....	4.6	8.4	13.6	*	*	*

Place 15 — Addison, Illinois
Selected Characteristics of Census Tracts: 1980

Tract Number	Total	8401.02	8401.03	8402	8403.01	8403.02	8404	8405	8406	8407	8409.02	8409.03
Total Population.............	29759	5114	433	1740	5885	7164	541	5627	0	0	3228	27
% Male.......................	49.8	49.9	51.7	49.9	49.9	50.1	49.9	50.3	–	–	47.5	–
% Black......................	0.8	0.3	0.0	0.0	0.3	0.6	0.7	0.0	–	–	5.0	–
% Other Nonwhite.............	5.1	8.0	3.2	2.7	2.9	6.3	7.4	3.8	–	–	5.6	–
% Of Spanish Origin..........	5.8	11.3	6.2	2.4	3.6	6.5	10.4	3.7	–	–	4.3	–
% Foreign Born...............	12.6	19.8	8.6	16.8	11.5	10.4	13.8	8.8	–	–	12.5	–
% Living In Group Quarters...	0.1	0.1	0.0	0.0	0.6	0.0	0.0	0.0	–	–	0.0	–
% 13 Years Old And Under.....	23.4	24.9	26.1	29.3	23.1	22.5	22.9	19.8	–	–	26.5	–
% 14-20 Years Old............	14.6	13.5	14.3	12.9	17.5	15.3	15.7	14.5	–	–	10.7	–
% 21-64 Years Old............	57.6	56.9	52.9	54.4	54.9	58.5	56.4	60.2	–	–	60.2	–
% 65-74 Years Old............	3.0	3.4	5.3	2.1	3.1	2.5	3.5	3.8	–	–	1.7	–
% 75 Years Old And Over......	1.4	1.4	1.4	1.4	1.5	1.3	1.5	1.8	–	–	0.9	–
% In Different House.........	49.3	56.0	40.9	60.0	49.2	46.3	42.4	32.6	–	–	71.3	–
% Families With Female Head..	11.6	13.3	9.0	2.1	8.4	12.4	11.0	10.6	–	–	20.3	–
Median School Years Completed	12.5	12.3	12.7	12.4	12.6	12.5	12.6	12.5	–	–	12.8	–
Median Family Income, 1979.....$$	27413	23346	34812	33481	31060	24933	27800	27800	–	–	24773	–
% Income Below Poverty Level....	3.3	4.4	6.3	1.1	2.1	2.9	9.0	2.1	–	–	6.4	–
% Income Of $30,000 Or More..	42.1	29.9	73.9	62.6	54.1	35.7	34.7	42.8	–	–	37.1	–
% White Collar Workers.......	52.6	38.7	66.5	52.6	54.7	54.6	55.3	52.1	–	–	63.3	–
% Civilian Labor Force Unemployed.	3.6	3.9	0.0	4.8	3.3	4.5	7.6	2.1	–	–	3.4	–
% Riding To Work By Automobile....	91.2	90.5	95.8	89.4	93.6	91.2	84.4	90.0	–	–	91.5	–
Mean Commuting Time - Minutes...	23.1	20.0	20.1	24.7	25.9	22.8	25.5	21.0	–	–	26.7	–
Population Per Household......	3.1	3.1	3.6	3.8	3.4	3.0	3.5	3.0	–	–	2.6	–
Total Housing Units..........	10037	1702	126	489	1860	2421	167	1968	0	0	1291	13
% Condominiums...............	5.1	0.8	0.0	0.0	6.8	11.5	3.6	0.2	–	–	5.8	–
% Built 1970 Or Later........	31.5	13.4	30.8	53.6	36.3	28.4	9.5	3.9	–	–	90.4	–
% Owner Occupied.............	57.0	46.5	89.7	91.0	62.1	56.2	85.0	66.7	–	–	30.3	–
% With 1+ Persons Per Room...	4.6	8.8	0.8	1.8	3.3	5.7	5.8	2.9	–	–	2.7	–
Median Value: Owner Units.......$$	76900	69300	131000	92400	96900	70900	64500	66900	–	–	98900	–
Median Rent: Rental Units.......$$	265	257	165	363	274	270	250	234	–	–	278	–
Median Number Of Rooms: All Units.	5.1	4.6	5.6	5.6	5.6	4.9	5.4	5.2	–	–	4.5	–

Addison
Selected Characteristics of Census Tracts: 1970

Tract Number	TOTAL	8401	8402	8403	8404	8405	8406	8407	8409
Total Population.............	24482	19009	6485	12787	1007	8360	7278	6674	13931
% Male.......................	50.1	49.7	50.5	50.1	49.6	50.2	49.3	50.5	49.8
% Black......................	0.1	0.0	0.0	0.1	0.0	0.1	0.0	0.1	0.1
% Other Nonwhite.............	0.5	0.4	0.5	0.4	0.4	0.4	0.4	0.4	0.7
% Of Spanish Language........	2.7	5.0	0.4	2.3	7.7	1.1	3.8	4.1	2.7
% Foreign Born...............	5.8	8.2	5.7	6.1	0.5	4.0	7.5	6.3	5.1
% Living In Group Quarters...	0.3	0.5	0.0	0.4	0.6	0.3	0.0	0.1	0.1
% 13 Years Old And Under.....	35.8	33.2	31.7	37.1	34.5	33.0	27.3	33.2	39.6
% 14-20 Years Old............	10.6	10.7	12.5	10.4	14.7	12.5	11.5	11.8	10.1
% 21-64 Years Old............	51.1	52.1	50.7	50.2	47.3	51.0	53.8	51.7	47.9
% 65-74 Years Old............	1.7	2.5	3.3	1.6	2.6	2.5	5.9	2.3	1.6
% 75 Years Old And Over......	0.8	1.5	1.9	0.8	1.0	1.0	3.5	1.1	0.8
% In Different House.........	43.3	47.6	55.3	36.4	75.6	58.2	60.6	53.5	38.9
% Families With Female Head..	5.2	4.8	4.0	3.9	7.6	5.8	5.7	5.2	3.8
Median School Years Completed	12.4	12.2	12.4	12.5	12.1	12.3	12.4	12.2	12.3
Median Family Income, 1969.....$$	13303	13441	13857	13453	13588	12964	13653	13751	13247
% Income Below Poverty Level....	2.2	2.8	1.3	1.3	4.0	4.8	2.4	4.3	2.5
% Income of $15,000 or More.....	34.7	37.5	41.0	35.5	37.8	34.1	40.6	40.7	35.4
% White Collar Workers.......	34.0	27.7	39.0	35.6	12.7	33.2	40.3	30.2	31.5
% Civilian Labor Force Unemployed.	2.1	2.6	1.8	2.0	5.4	3.2	1.2	2.1	2.0
% Riding To Work By Automobile....	88.5	87.3	80.6	88.8	85.9	88.0	81.4	84.9	86.0
Population Per Household......	3.7	3.7	3.8	3.8	4.2	3.6	3.4	3.7	4.1
Total Housing Units..........	6798	5320	1752	3395	238	2351	2210	1823	3517
% Condominiums & Cooperatives....	0.1	0.0	0.0	0.0	0.0	0.2	0.4	0.0	0.0
% Built 1960 Or Later........	67.1	56.4	29.3	78.9	9.2	43.1	16.1	50.5	70.2
% Owner Occupied.............	63.5	72.1	87.6	68.8	85.7	68.9	86.5	76.6	83.1
% With 1+ Persons Per Room...	8.4	8.7	7.3	7.2	16.8	9.3	5.3	8.8	10.1
Median Value: Owner Units.......$$	28300	27000	28400	31200	21600	24800	26500	26000	27000
Median Rent: Rental Units.......$$	168	166	162	167	145	167	147	152	180
Median Number Of Rooms: All Units.	5.0	5.2	5.5	5.4	5.3	5.0	5.6	5.3	5.6

(nearly 2 percent lower than most other rates at the time), and the funds were totally utilized. The five large areas of single-family residences are between the Eisenhower extension and Lake Street, two areas around Driscoll High School (a Catholic school), southwest of the Addison Golf Course, and east of the Illinois Central and Gulf Railroad tracks and Addison Road.

Addison has grown to include 500 industrial facilities ranging from small factories to large warehouses such as those of Ace Hardware and United Parcel Service. While this growth has been recent and rapid, it has been well planned. There are more than 1,200 acres of land zoned for industry with 800 acres under-roof. In most cases these are in industrial parks with modern facilities and landscaped grounds. In 1979 Addison was the first metropolitan community to issue industrial revenue bonds offering financing to industry at a low rate. An Addison Chamber of Commerce was activated in 1947. In the 1950s the

Addison Industrial Association was formed with about a half dozen members to improve various road conditions and by 1983 the group had over 260 members. Its concerns have expanded to include civic responsibility in government as well as improvement of services and utilities. It works closely with the vocational programs of area schools.

There are six shopping areas in Addison including the Green Meadows plaza on Lake Street. The Oak Brook and Yorktown shopping centers are to the south of the community and the new Stratford Square Mall is just a few miles west on Army Trail Road. Although there is no train station in town, there is access to both North Western and Milwaukee Railroad commuter stations in nearby communities as well as good roads to Chicago. About three-fourths of all workers who live in Addison commute to some other place to work.

Gail Danks Welter

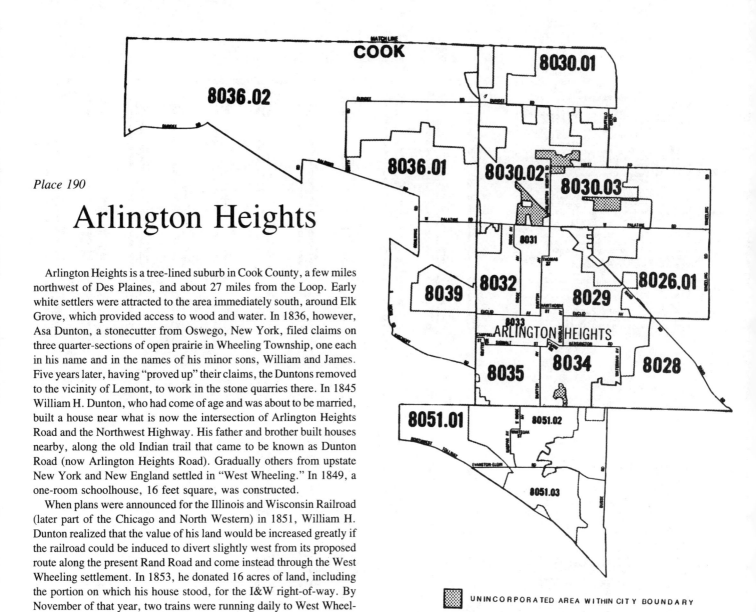

UNINCORPORATED AREA WITHIN CITY BOUNDARY

Place 190

Arlington Heights

Arlington Heights is a tree-lined suburb in Cook County, a few miles northwest of Des Plaines, and about 27 miles from the Loop. Early white settlers were attracted to the area immediately south, around Elk Grove, which provided access to wood and water. In 1836, however, Asa Dunton, a stonecutter from Oswego, New York, filed claims on three quarter-sections of open prairie in Wheeling Township, one each in his name and in the names of his minor sons, William and James. Five years later, having "proved up" their claims, the Duntons removed to the vicinity of Lemont, to work in the stone quarries there. In 1845 William H. Dunton, who had come of age and was about to be married, built a house near what is now the intersection of Arlington Heights Road and the Northwest Highway. His father and brother built houses nearby, along the old Indian trail that came to be known as Dunton Road (now Arlington Heights Road). Gradually others from upstate New York and New England settled in "West Wheeling." In 1849, a one-room schoolhouse, 16 feet square, was constructed.

When plans were announced for the Illinois and Wisconsin Railroad (later part of the Chicago and North Western) in 1851, William H. Dunton realized that the value of his land would be increased greatly if the railroad could be induced to divert slightly west from its proposed route along the present Rand Road and come instead through the West Wheeling settlement. In 1853, he donated 16 acres of land, including the portion on which his house stood, for the I&W right-of-way. By November of that year, two trains were running daily to West Wheeling. Dunton immediately laid out a town site on his land. The town was originally to be called Bradley, after a friend of his but, when another place named Bradley, Illinois was discovered, he renamed the town Dunton. In 1854 a store and the railroad station (called Elk Grove) appeared. The name of the station was changed a year later when a post office, also called Dunton, was established.

With rapid transportation to Chicago, the village of Dunton began to attract settlers. Numerous migrants from Hanover, Germany, including the Busse, Sigwalt and Klehm families, moved into the area. John Klehm acquired land near the railroad right-of-way on which he planted potatoes to sell in Chicago, and where he started the Klehm

Arlington Heights
Population and Housing Characteristics, 1930-1980

	1980	1970	1960	1950	1940	1930
Total Population.......	66,116	64,884	27,878	8,768	5,668	4,997
% Male.................	48.6	49.0	49.1	49.2	49.5	51.2
% Female...............	51.4	51.0	50.9	50.8	50.5	48.8
% White................	97.0	99.5	99.9	99.9	99.9	99.9
% Black................	0.4	0.0	0.0	0.0	0.1	0.1
% Other Nonwhite Races...	2.6	0.5	0.1	0.1	-	-
% Under 5 Years Old......	5.6	8.9	14.2	10.4	7.7	8.0
% 5-19 Years Old.........	26.7	34.2	30.6	22.1	24.2	26.5
% 20-44 Years Old........	37.2	34.1	34.0	38.0	39.7	41.0
% 45-64 Years Old........	22.8	18.1	16.2	21.8	19.8	16.8
% 65 Years and Older.....	7.7	4.7	5.0	7.7	8.6	7.7
Median School Years....	13.8	14.1	12.7	12.1	8.6	*
Total Housing Units....	23,202	18,714	7,545	2,556	1,608	*
% In One-Unit Structures.	68.7	73.3	94.9	*	*	*
% Owner Occupied.........	71.6	70.7	83.6	74.4	52.8	*
% Renter Occupied........	24.8	24.5	11.5	23.1	43.3	*
% Vacant................	3.6	4.8	4.9	2.5	3.9	*
% 1+ Persons per Room....	0.9	3.2	7.1	4.4	*	*

Place 190 — Arlington Heights, Illinois
Selected Characteristics of Census Tracts: 1980

Tract Number	Total	8026.01	8028	8029	8030.01	8030.02	8030.03	8031	8032	8033	8034
Total Population.............	66116	2811	4689	5816	111	10407	5572	3803	4858	4282	6697
% Male.................	48.6	48.3	48.4	49.2	46.8	49.0	48.7	48.3	45.6	45.4	48.9
% Black................	0.4	1.5	0.1	0.1	0.0	0.3	0.4	0.2	0.2	0.3	0.2
% Other Nonwhite.......	2.6	4.1	2.8	1.5	3.6	2.7	3.0	1.8	2.3	2.5	2.0
% Of Spanish Origin....	1.7	1.8	1.4	1.3	0.9	1.2	1.5	1.5	2.0	1.8	1.5
% Foreign Born.........	6.9	9.5	6.4	4.1	0.0	6.3	8.6	5.1	7.5	9.5	6.3
% Living In Group Quarters	1.7	0.0	0.0	0.6	0.0	0.0	0.0	0.0	9.9	0.0	0.0
% 13 Years Old And Under	20.5	17.1	16.3	21.2	38.7	26.8	25.7	20.9	19.3	14.9	21.1
% 14-20 Years Old......	13.1	12.8	14.9	15.5	5.4	13.3	14.6	14.3	9.9	10.7	11.6
% 21-64 Years Old......	58.7	64.2	60.2	57.2	55.9	55.9	56.0	57.6	55.9	55.5	59.3
% 65-74 Years Old......	4.4	3.7	4.7	3.9	0.0	2.7	2.4	4.4	5.3	10.4	5.3
% 75 Years Old And Over	3.3	2.2	3.8	2.2	0.0	1.2	1.3	2.8	9.6	8.6	2.7
% In Different House...	42.3	67.3	34.2	34.1	100.0	38.2	44.7	32.2	43.6	48.5	42.1
% Families With Female Head	7.8	12.9	6.3	6.9	0.0	6.3	5.7	9.6	7.7	13.3	8.6
Median School Years Completed...	13.8	13.6	14.2	13.3	16.1	14.2	13.6	13.7	12.9	12.8	14.7
Median Family Income, 1979...$$	33323	27472	34904	33772	24000	35783	33902	32527	31617	30887	35185
% Income Below Poverty Level....	1.9	3.9	2.0	2.4	20.8	0.7	3.6	0.6	0.9	2.5	1.3
% Income Of $30,000 Or More.....	59.7	42.3	63.5	59.8	16.7	65.2	62.5	57.7	58.2	54.5	63.4
% White Collar Workers...	77.1	76.5	77.9	71.7	100.0	79.8	76.0	73.5	76.3	75.9	82.5
% Civilian Labor Force Unemployed.	2.9	3.3	3.7	3.7	0.0	2.2	3.1	1.3	2.5	4.0	3.2
% Riding To Work By Automobile....	83.1	88.5	87.8	83.6	64.0	84.8	86.3	84.1	81.6	77.3	74.9
Mean Commuting Time - Minutes...	28.1	29.0	26.9	26.0	47.8	29.8	29.6	26.4	30.9	28.1	29.6
Population Per Household.........	2.9	2.5	2.9	3.4	3.7	3.3	3.4	3.1	2.8	2.3	3.0
Total Housing Units...........	23194	1190	1644	1750	42	3214	1736	1237	1570	1912	2314
% Condominiums...............	10.1	40.8	11.0	0.0	-	4.6	10.7	0.0	1.0	14.0	6.7
% Built 1970 Or Later........	25.1	24.0	3.0	8.2	-	49.8	46.8	9.2	3.8	16.0	10.5
% Owner Occupied.............	71.1	47.4	83.8	90.7	-	72.6	81.5	84.3	80.6	54.9	81.5
% With 1+ Persons Per Room......	0.9	0.6	1.1	1.1	-	0.3	0.4	1.1	1.2	1.1	0.9
Median Value: Owner Units.......$$	93400	114100	91100	88900	-	100400	116400	77000	70900	80300	93000
Median Rent: Rental Units....$$	333	335	286	365	-	352	325	347	278	269	335
Median Number Of Rooms: All Units.	5.6	4.6	5.6	5.6	-	5.6	5.6	5.6	5.6	4.9	5.6

Tract Number	8035	8036.02	8039	8051.01	8051.02	8051.03	8645.04
Total Population.............	5880	0	466	3199	4688	2837	0
% Male.................	47.6	-	77.0	47.1	49.3	52.7	-
% Black................	0.3	-	16.3	0.2	0.3	1.0	-
% Other Nonwhite.......	1.7	-	0.2	3.0	3.2	5.4	-
% Of Spanish Origin....	1.2	-	39.3	1.1	1.1	2.5	-
% Foreign Born.........	4.9	-	22.8	6.5	7.3	10.8	-
% Living In Group Quarters	1.1	-	89.7	4.7	0.0	0.0	-
% 13 Years Old And Under	18.2	-	8.2	19.0	21.4	9.8	-
% 14-20 Years Old......	14.8	-	18.7	11.5	15.2	7.2	-
% 21-64 Years Old......	58.6	-	71.9	58.8	58.4	77.8	-
% 65-74 Years Old......	5.0	-	1.1	5.2	3.3	3.2	-
% 75 Years Old And Over	3.4	-	0.2	5.5	1.7	1.9	-
% In Different House...	31.8	-	74.3	51.3	32.0	81.5	-
% Families With Female Head	6.6	-	-	5.6	5.7	22.0	-
Median School Years Completed...	14.0	-	14.1	13.8	13.8	13.8	-
Median Family Income, 1979...$$	35124	-	-	31353	36830	24669	-
% Income Below Poverty Level....	1.9	-	-	3.8	2.9	0.6	-
% Income Of $30,000 Or More.....	63.4	-	-	53.7	66.6	30.2	-
% White Collar Workers...	76.1	-	37.5	79.6	77.9	76.2	-
% Civilian Labor Force Unemployed.	2.3	-	0.0	2.9	4.3	1.8	-
% Riding To Work By Automobile....	77.5	-	95.7	85.0	85.2	87.1	-
Mean Commuting Time - Minutes...	28.7	-	20.2	24.6	27.2	26.8	-
Population Per Household.........	3.1	-	3.2	2.7	3.2	1.8	-
Total Housing Units...........	1961	0	18	1179	1629	1798	0
% Condominiums...............	11.0	-	-	19.3	28.8	0.0	-
% Built 1970 Or Later........	13.1	-	-	60.9	27.0	41.3	-
% Owner Occupied.............	89.7	-	-	58.4	81.7	8.2	-
% With 1+ Persons Per Room......	0.8	-	-	0.7	1.4	1.3	-
Median Value: Owner Units.......$$	91800	-	-	123100	99600	114800	-
Median Rent: Rental Units....$$	325	-	-	388	406	331	-
Median Number Of Rooms: All Units.	5.6	-	-	5.2	5.6	3.6	-

Arlington Heights
Selected Characteristics of Census Tracts: 1970

Tract Number	TOTAL	8026	8028	8029	8030	8031	8032	8033	8034	8035	8036
Total Population	65058	15506	17469	7184	22676	4514	6000	5305	7070	6845	20660
% Male	49.0	50.3	48.9	49.1	49.7	49.0	48.2	47.5	49.0	49.2	50.2
% Black	0.0	0.1	0.0	0.1	0.0	0.0	0.0	0.0	0.0	0.1	0.1
% Other Nonwhite	0.5	0.6	0.3	0.3	0.6	0.3	0.3	0.7	0.1	0.5	0.5
% Of Spanish Language	1.0	1.8	1.3	1.6	1.9	0.0	2.7	0.8	0.0	0.3	1.6
% Foreign Born	3.5	5.2	3.5	3.5	3.6	4.7	2.8	5.2	4.3	2.9	3.5
% Living In Group Quarters	0.6	0.1	0.0	0.3	0.0	0.0	3.2	0.8	0.0	0.3	0.3
% 13 Years Old And Under	31.5	31.4	29.0	34.3	39.4	32.0	31.6	24.4	29.7	32.3	37.7
% 14-20 Years Old	12.6	11.0	14.2	15.7	9.9	12.6	11.5	14.0	13.0	16.9	12.4
% 21-64 Years Old	51.2	54.5	51.4	46.1	48.5	49.3	50.4	52.0	52.0	46.5	46.8
% 65-74 Years Old	2.9	1.9	3.5	2.5	1.3	4.1	2.6	6.0	3.6	2.7	2.0
% 75 Years Old And Over	1.8	1.1	2.0	1.4	0.8	2.0	3.9	3.6	1.8	1.6	1.1
% In Different House	39.5	30.7	61.1	50.3	29.1	50.8	54.3	50.9	51.3	53.6	39.7
% Families With Female Head	4.3	4.1	5.2	4.6	2.4	4.5	4.1	6.5	4.9	4.3	2.5
Median School Years Completed	12.9	12.8	12.8	12.8	12.8	12.7	12.7	12.7	13.4	13.0	12.9
Median Family Income, 1969 $$	17034	15967	16580	16440	15171	15100	14839	15386	18408	18281	17493
% Income Below Poverty Level	1.4	2.2	2.0	1.8	1.9	2.0	1.6	1.5	0.5	2.9	1.8
% Income of $15,000 or More	59.0	54.3	57.1	55.4	50.7	50.4	48.8	51.5	62.4	64.1	60.9
% White Collar Workers	55.7	54.7	50.0	50.3	50.4	49.5	49.2	48.3	57.6	58.4	55.9
% Civilian Labor Force Unemployed	1.8	1.6	1.7	2.6	2.5	2.1	1.1	3.1	2.3	2.5	2.1
% Riding To Work By Automobile	78.3	86.3	79.6	77.1	84.3	81.2	81.6	69.0	69.3	75.3	78.1
Population Per Household	3.6	3.5	3.6	4.2	4.1	4.1	3.7	3.6	3.6	4.1	4.2
Total Housing Units	18710	5084	4870	1724	5919	1243	1616	1686	2036	1692	5086
% Condominiums & Cooperatives	0.7	0.0	2.9	0.0	0.0	0.0	0.0	0.0	0.3	0.0	0.0
% Built 1960 Or Later	58.6	76.1	29.7	40.1	80.5	39.5	20.9	31.5	25.1	39.2	66.0
% Owner Occupied	70.0	57.3	81.5	88.7	81.1	80.4	84.9	57.1	85.5	89.5	89.3
% With 1+ Persons Per Room	3.2	2.2	5.1	5.8	4.5	3.8	6.0	3.3	3.0	4.8	3.4
Median Value: Owner Units $$	35500	39300	30400	33400	36500	30000	28700	31600	37400	37000	38800
Median Rent: Rental Units $$	194	204	174	188	202	204	173	173	175	184	154
Median Number Of Rooms: All Units	6.0	5.8	5.6	6.3	6.6	5.9	5.6	5.2	6.3	6.6	7.2

Tract Number	8039	8051	8645
Total Population	7077	25709	12835
% Male	49.5	49.8	50.5
% Black	0.0	0.2	0.2
% Other Nonwhite	0.3	0.9	0.8
% Of Spanish Language	2.8	1.7	4.0
% Foreign Born	3.3	4.2	4.1
% Living In Group Quarters	0.0	0.9	1.4
% 13 Years Old And Under	33.3	30.3	34.1
% 14-20 Years Old	12.9	9.9	11.0
% 21-64 Years Old	50.5	56.6	50.8
% 65-74 Years Old	2.4	2.0	2.5
% 75 Years Old And Over	1.0	1.2	1.7
% In Different House	54.5	29.4	40.6
% Families With Female Head	4.6	4.1	3.5
Median School Years Completed	12.5	12.8	12.9
Median Family Income, 1969 $$	13298	14783	16961
% Income Below Poverty Level	1.8	1.6	2.1
% Income of $15,000 or More	34.9	48.4	56.9
% White Collar Workers	34.0	47.2	52.1
% Civilian Labor Force Unemployed	2.1	1.8	2.0
% Riding To Work By Automobile	86.1	86.1	81.2
Population Per Household	3.8	3.3	3.8
Total Housing Units	1898	8353	3736
% Condominiums & Cooperatives	0.0	0.0	0.0
% Built 1960 Or Later	18.6	88.5	54.9
% Owner Occupied	85.3	45.4	74.0
% With 1+ Persons Per Room	9.3	3.0	4.6
Median Value: Owner Units $$	23200	36200	43500
Median Rent: Rental Units $$	182	195	146
Median Number Of Rooms: All Units	5.2	5.1	6.4

Nursery, a business that is still operated in Arlington Heights by his descendants. The town began to take shape. A Presbyterian society grew out of a meeting in Dunton's barn in 1855 and, a year after that, a Presbyterian church was built. A second store was built in 1855 and this was followed in 1856 by the first hotel. The Elk Grove Methodist congregation relocated in Dunton in 1858 and built a church there in 1860, the same year that St. Peter's Lutheran Church was established. A new school, built of brick, was erected in 1870.

By 1874, there were about 150 dwellings in the village. As an impetus to development, real estate developers persuaded the voters that Arlington was a more attractive sounding name than Dunton and would draw more homeowners. Once again, a search of the records showed the pre-existence of a town called Arlington in Illinois, so the word "Heights" was added to the name, on the basis of the altitude of the village, 704 feet above sea level, thus 106 feet above the level of Chicago. The first census of Arlington Heights, taken in 1880, showed 995 residents.

Arlington Heights was finally incorporated in 1887, and the first mayor was elected in 1888. In the census of 1890, Arlington Heights reported a population of 1,424. A fire department was formed in 1894, and the first graveled street was put down in 1898. Work on the first storm sewer and a municipal water system was commenced in 1902. In 1910, the village board authorized construction of a sanitary sewer. A one-story village hall was built in 1913. Nevertheless, growth was slow, because Arlington Heights had little local industry, and places more accessible to Chicago were absorbing the suburban migration. After the First World War, the village began to grow rapidly, from 2,250 in 1920 to nearly 5,000 a decade later. A $1.5 million sewer system was built by the village, and private interests laid out two improved subdivisions, Scarsdale and Stonegate.

In 1927, the village acquired its best-known landmark when California millionaire H. D. Brown put together a package of land adjacent to the village, comprised of many of the old German pioneer farms, and built the Arlington Park race track. In the following years the Arlington Classic and the Arlington Futurity races became famous. In 1940, B. F. Lindheimer and John Allen assumed control of the track and began an elaborate program of improvements. The track was shut down for three years in 1943, because of wartime materials and transportation shortages.

The Depression had temporarily halted the plans for growth in Arlington Heights. Real estate values declined, tax collections were reduced, and business was poor. In the last half of the 1930s, Arlington Heights was able to secure an unusual amount of government and private investment in public facilities, and this led to some growth in population. In 1940 Arlington Heights had a population of 5,668. A residential suburb with little industry, the race track closed, Arlington Heights experienced little growth during the Second World War.

After the war, however, the village became part of the northward suburban movement of the Chicago area population. Arlington Heights tripled in size between 1950 and 1960, from less than 9,000 to more than 28,000. That number doubled again during the next decade, growing to 65,000 by 1970. The growth rate dropped dramatically during the 1970s, however, and the 1980 population was 66,000. The moderate growth of the 1970s was caused in part by rigorous adherence to an updated comprehensive plan designed to maintain low population density. Current growth is further limited by the fact that 57 percent of the land zoned for residential use was occupied by 1980.

Through zoning and other means, the community has retained its essential character as a residential suburb. During the 1970s, the number of homes grew faster than the number of residents. In 1980, there were more than 23,000 housing units in Arlington Heights, up almost 25 percent since 1970, and more than triple the number available 20 years ago. Despite trends toward condominium and apartment construction, the village remains a community of single-family (73 percent), owner-occupied (74 percent) homes. The median value of single-family homes in 1980 was $93,000, almost twice the median reported for Chicago. Residential units now occupy about 44 percent of the developed land in the village.

B. F. Lindheimer died in 1960 and his daughter, Marje Everett, assumed control of Arlington Park, mounting an even more aggressive and imaginative program of development. In the late 1960s she converted the property to a year-around facility by constructing a convention center, consisting of a five-story exhibit hall, a large restaurant and a 13-story hotel. A proposal for night racing at the track generated strong protest from local residents. This caused the village board to consider annexation of Arlington Park, which was negotiated at great length and finally approved late in 1969.

The Arlington Park annexation was one of a series between 1957 and 1981, which nearly tripled the village's land area from 5.9 to 15.8 square miles, thus allowing authorities to set aside new land for commercial and industrial expansion. During the 1970s, village officials sought to generate additional revenues by attracting new industry to Arlington Heights. By 1980, a total of 965 acres was zoned for commerical use, 88 percent of which was already in use. Most of the village's commercial development during the last ten years occurred northwest of the central business district, primarily along Rand Road north of Euclid Avenue. Another 564 acres were zoned for manufacturing; 77 percent of this land had been developed by 1980. The number of light manufacturing firms in Arlington Heights increased from 23 in 1963 to 86 in 1977. Light industry, for the most part, these plants produce metal products, machinery, and building products. Honeywell, Inc., a manufacturer of computers and electronic components, is the largest employer. An increasing number of research and development firms have located in the village's newly-developed industrial parks, especially in the Arlington Research Center complex.

Arlington Heights is an affluent community. In 1980, more than three-fourths of the labor force was engaged in white-collar occupations and the median family income was more than $36,000, about twice that of Chicago. Forty-four percent of all employed residents worked in Chicago in 1980, while 10 percent worked in Arlington Heights and 42 percent worked in other suburbs. In 1980, 64,124 residents were white, 288 were black, and 1,255 were of Asian descent, about equal parts Japanese, Filipino, Korean, Chinese and Asian Indians. Almost 2 percent are Hispanic.

Village authorities and residents have sought actively to protect property values and maintain the high socio-economic status of the community. A housing development featuring homes costing less than $12,000 encountered considerable local opposition in the 1950s. Nearly two decades later, a proposal to build subsidized housing in the heart of town for low-income and minority families touched off intense controversy and resulted in a prolonged legal battle. The village board rejected the housing proposal in 1972, and the developers brought suit in federal court, charging that the decision was racially discriminatory. In 1977, the U.S. Supreme Court exonerated Arlington Heights, but a later appellate court decision forced the village to permit construction of the 190-unit subsidized housing complex. This was scheduled for completion in the autumn of 1982.

M.W.H.

Place 280

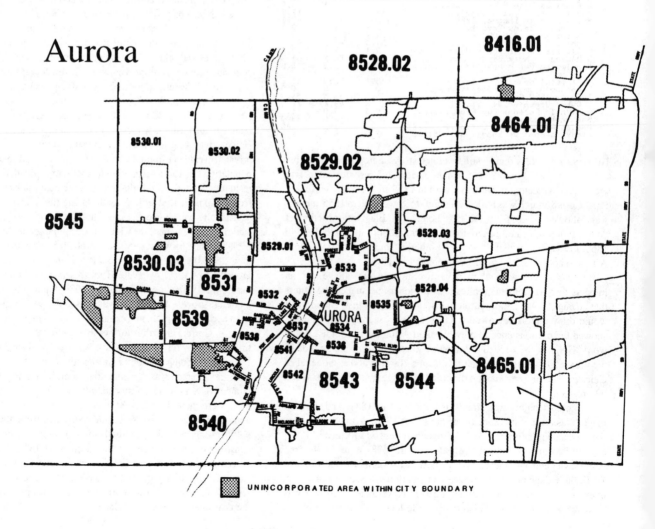

UNINCORPORATED AREA WITHIN CITY BOUNDARY

Aurora straddles the Fox River in the southeastern corner of Kane County, 38 miles west of Chicago. It is the principal city in the Fox River Valley.

When the first settler, Joseph McCarty of Elmira, New York, came to this region in 1834, he found a large Pottawatomie village by the river. There were between 300 and 500 Indians in the vicinity and trade was established bartering bread and tobacco for fish. The possibiity of water power from the swift current of the river and the hope that the island in the river would facilitate constructing a dam convinced McCarty and his brother Samuel to stake a claim of 460 acres on the east bank of the river. By the end of the year, there were perhaps 15 settlers in the area. The following year, land was surveyed and the town of McCarty's Mills was laid out on the east bank. A way mill, grist mill, and woolen mill were established once the dam was completed in 1835.

Platted in 1836, the little community had 30 families and a post office. The McCarty brothers arranged to have Aurora made a stage stop on the route between Chicago and Galena. The stage stop and the post office required a name. Some historians attest that Aruora, New York, was the origin of the city's name. Others insist that Aurora was chosen as the closest in meaning to the name of a friendly Pottawatomie chief, Waubonsie (morning light). In 1843, this settlement on the east bank was incorporated, with a voting population of more than 100. In 1842, Theodore Lake laid out the village of West Aurora on the west bank of the river, which was incorporated in 1854, inaugurating a rivalry that lasted until the two villages were merged in 1857.

In 1849, the increasing population and commerce gave rise to plans for a railway spur to connect with the Galena and Chicago Union Railroad route to Chicago at a point 12 miles northeast of Aurora. The Aurora Branch Railway was chartered in the same year and construction began in 1850. The name was changed in 1855 to the Chicago, Burlington and Quincy Railroad. The railroad located maintenance yards in Aurora in 1856, making the railroad a major industry. In 1864, the railroad built its own tracks from Aurora to Chicago. Other industries were established during the 1850s—a wagon and carriage work, machine shops, a brewery, a soap factory, and a planing mill. From a population of about 1,200 in 1850, Aurora had grown to a total of 11,162 in 1870. Growth as an industrial center continued until the depression of 1873. In 1881, Aurora became one of the first towns in the nation to light its streets with electricity. The impressive yellow glow from atop the 150 foot steel towers gave the city its current sobriquet, "City of Light."

Growth resumed in the 1880s, and continued without major interruption until the Depression of the 1930s. In 1880, the major industry was the Burlington shops, and there were few other manufacturing plants. The commercial centers on the east and on the west sides of the river had both grown. The residential area covered some 200 blocks, with the larger portion located on the east side.

During the 1880s and 1890s, special inducements were offered to attract new industries to Aurora in an attempt at diversification. The Burlington shops employed nearly 2,000 people, while all other industries in 1876 employed fewer than 300 workers. The building of the Chicago and North Western and the Elgin, Joliet and Eastern Railroads not only offered competition with the Burlington, but provided rail connections with other areas. By 1890, there were some 90 manufacturing plants employing between 4,000 and 5,000 workers.

Aurora
Population and Housing Characteristics, 1930-1980

	1980	1970	1960	1950	1940	1930
Total Population.......	81,293	74,182	63,715	50,576	47,170	46,589
% Male....................	48.4	48.5	48.6	48.3	48.6	49.3
% Female..................	51.6	51.5	51.4	51.7	51.4	50.7
% White...................	80.7	92.9	96.4	97.6	97.9	98.0
% Black...................	10.4	6.6	3.5	2.3	2.1	2.0
% Other Nonwhite Races...	8.9	0.5	0.1	0.1	0.0	0.0
% Under 5 Years Old......	10.0	9.9	11.6	9.5	6.9	7.9
% 5-19 Years Old.........	25.8	28.8	25.4	19.5	22.3	25.4
% 20-44 Years Old........	38.2	32.9	32.3	36.5	39.8	41.1
% 45-64 Years Old........	16.1	18.8	20.5	24.5	22.7	19.1
% 65 Years and Older.....	9.9	9.6	10.2	10.0	8.3	6.5
Median School Years....	12.4	12.1	11.2	10.8	8.7	*
Total Housing Units....	29,413	24,244	20,163	15,422	13,384	*
% In One-Unit Structures.	62.3	62.0	71.8	*	*	*
% Owner Occupied.........	59.3	58.2	64.0	63.8	51.3	*
% Renter Occupied........	36.4	38.0	33.0	34.5	47.0	*
% Vacant.................	4.3	3.8	3.0	1.7	1.7	*
% 1+ Persons per Room....	6.4	8.0	8.6	6.5	*	*

Place 280 — Aurora, Illinois
Selected Characteristics of Census Tracts: 1980

Tract Number	Total	8416.01	8464.01	8465.01	8528.02	8529.01	8529.02	8529.03	8529.04	8530.01	8530.02
Total Population..............	81293	26	56	1601	4	3744	4518	1635	697	948	5551
% Male........................	48.4	–	–	50.9	–	48.3	48.9	46.8	46.1	48.1	48.4
% Black.......................	10.4	–	–	1.9	–	24.7	8.3	8.4	30.7	6.3	12.3
% Other Nonwhite..............	8.9	–	–	3.6	–	3.7	5.2	3.3	13.6	1.8	7.2
% Of Spanish Origin...........	17.8	–	–	1.1	–	8.0	8.9	10.9	23.8	4.4	8.5
% Foreign Born................	8.1	–	–	4.6	–	2.8	4.8	4.6	4.6	2.0	5.2
% Living In Group Quarters....	1.6	–	–	0.0	–	2.1	0.0	11.8	0.0	0.0	0.1
% 13 Years Old And Under......	25.1	–	–	26.7	–	22.5	22.4	20.8	31.1	30.4	27.9
% 14-20 Years Old.............	12.5	–	–	4.6	–	12.6	13.2	11.4	16.1	7.2	12.4
% 21-64 Years Old.............	52.5	–	–	66.8	–	53.4	58.4	55.0	46.1	59.9	55.8
% 65-74 Years Old.............	5.4	–	–	1.4	–	7.3	3.9	3.9	3.9	1.7	2.5
% 75 Years Old And Over.......	4.5	–	–	0.4	–	4.2	2.1	9.0	2.9	0.8	1.3
% In Different House..........	52.4	–	–	99.5	–	41.9	55.5	64.9	67.3	74.1	56.7
% Families With Female Head...	17.9	–	–	2.8	–	22.2	18.8	17.2	43.1	13.7	22.3
Median School Years Completed...	12.4	–	–	14.7	–	12.5	12.5	12.5	11.8	13.9	12.5
Median Family Income, 1979...$$	23035	–	–	31160	–	22395	22647	25841	24167	25385	22680
% Income Below Poverty Level....	6.6	–	–	0.8	–	4.8	8.1	4.0	4.3	2.7	4.9
% Income Of $30,000 Or More.....	29.7	–	–	56.1	–	31.6	29.0	28.8	39.6	28.1	30.5
% White Collar Workers..........	46.5	–	–	74.8	–	48.8	53.1	61.3	31.3	78.9	50.8
% Civilian Labor Force Unemployed.	6.8	–	–	2.5	–	9.1	5.2	3.0	12.3	0.0	7.9
% Riding To Work By Automobile....	89.5	–	–	88.2	–	87.3	95.5	96.2	77.1	90.1	90.8
Mean Commuting Time - Minutes...	19.1	–	–	33.5	–	18.1	17.6	23.4	12.2	22.3	19.8
Population Per Household........	2.9	–	–	2.7	–	2.8	2.7	2.6	3.4	3.0	2.9
Total Housing Units..........	29406	8	19	830	2	1365	1888	610	209	325	1997
% Condominiums.................	3.6	–	–	31.0	–	0.0	7.7	19.7	0.0	18.8	16.7
% Built 1970 Or Later..........	18.6	–	–	98.7	–	5.5	37.3	62.0	17.6	84.7	25.6
% Owner Occupied...............	58.3	–	–	64.8	–	69.1	43.4	40.5	62.7	92.3	54.2
% With 1+ Persons Per Room.....	6.4	–	–	0.2	–	4.4	3.9	4.8	10.3	0.3	4.8
Median Value: Owner Units.......$$	49100	–	–	79900	–	52900	59000	66500	34900	64900	51900
Median Rent: Rental Units....$$	219	–	–	350	–	225	263	261	150	365	243
Median Number Of Rooms: All Units.	5.2	–	–	5.6	–	5.3	4.7	4.4	5.0	5.6	4.9

Place 280 — Aurora , Illinois
Selected Characteristics of Census Tracts: 1980

Tract Number	8530.03	8531	8532	8533	8534	8535	8536	8537	8538	8539	8540
Total Population	7134	2463	5423	3076	6670	4018	6531	360	1724	5970	3725
% Male	46.3	48.0	48.7	48.4	50.2	49.8	48.4	65.0	52.3	47.0	47.1
% Black	6.8	3.3	12.1	1.7	11.0	27.1	18.9	10.0	5.9	2.0	15.8
% Other Nonwhite	3.0	4.9	11.1	8.7	25.5	13.5	17.2	7.5	17.0	1.6	6.9
% Of Spanish Origin	3.5	7.7	15.1	19.0	55.6	33.1	42.8	17.5	31.6	3.0	10.9
% Foreign Born	3.9	5.0	7.6	10.6	26.6	11.8	12.4	9.0	14.8	3.4	4.9
% Living In Group Quarters	0.2	2.3	1.6	0.0	0.0	0.0	1.8	24.7	0.0	4.6	5.2
% 13 Years Old And Under	22.8	20.8	26.7	20.5	31.1	30.7	28.2	11.4	27.2	18.0	26.4
% 14-20 Years Old	10.3	11.6	12.7	13.1	15.0	13.4	12.7	5.8	15.4	13.9	14.0
% 21-64 Years Old	56.4	54.3	50.3	53.3	47.7	48.1	47.2	69.2	50.3	53.1	47.4
% 65-74 Years Old	5.9	7.3	4.8	8.1	3.7	5.2	5.9	6.9	3.6	8.5	5.3
% 75 Years Old And Over	4.7	6.0	5.4	4.9	2.5	2.6	6.0	6.7	3.5	6.4	6.9
% In Different House	55.0	36.6	60.2	45.3	51.6	48.7	59.0	56.6	39.5	36.1	53.3
% Families With Female Head	14.7	13.2	20.9	12.1	18.7	22.0	20.5	29.0	23.7	8.6	23.9
Median School Years Completed	12.7	12.3	12.5	12.2	9.2	11.3	10.2	12.1	11.4	13.9	12.5
Median Family Income, 1979 $$	26056	22992	22092	22372	20045	18986	18661	7452	18427	30646	27225
% Income Below Poverty Level	3.1	2.0	7.1	5.6	11.6	15.0	11.7	33.3	14.9	1.0	11.4
% Income Of $30,000 Or More	37.0	29.5	23.2	33.8	17.4	14.8	19.6	0.0	23.9	52.1	45.6
% White Collar Workers	58.1	42.8	40.1	46.2	19.2	26.0	23.4	32.0	29.9	71.1	61.8
% Civilian Labor Force Unemployed	5.2	5.5	8.1	6.9	9.5	10.3	10.8	11.4	7.2	2.4	7.2
% Riding To Work By Automobile	93.2	91.0	81.7	96.8	89.9	93.1	91.0	46.6	79.4	83.2	89.3
Mean Commuting Time - Minutes	19.8	17.1	16.3	20.5	18.2	21.1	19.6	9.6	18.0	15.6	19.6
Population Per Household	2.5	2.8	2.8	2.9	3.7	3.4	3.1	1.8	3.2	2.6	3.2
Total Housing Units	2896	887	2090	1120	1876	1230	2209	269	593	2236	1126
% Condominiums	2.3	0.0	0.0	0.0	0.0	0.0	0.0	0.0	0.0	3.1	0.0
% Built 1970 Or Later	45.8	4.6	6.1	7.1	3.1	3.1	11.0	2.5	3.2	4.1	22.8
% Owner Occupied	53.5	81.4	42.5	70.0	58.3	68.4	42.1	1.5	42.2	76.2	64.3
% With 1+ Persons Per Room	1.7	4.5	6.3	6.3	17.8	13.2	15.0	6.6	11.4	1.6	6.6
Median Value: Owner Units $$	64400	44400	44300	46300	35300	36800	36200	-	36400	67200	77300
Median Rent: Rental Units $$	239	211	214	210	210	208	185	155	207	217	187
Median Number Of Rooms: All Units	5.0	5.2	5.0	5.3	5.2	5.0	4.7	2.8	5.2	5.6	5.6

Tract Number	8541	8542	8543	8544	8545
Total Population	3678	3924	6516	955	346
% Male	47.4	49.0	48.2	47.5	52.6
% Black	6.1	1.4	3.2	37.6	2.6
% Other Nonwhite	11.0	5.2	3.8	14.9	3.5
% Of Spanish Origin	23.1	10.4	7.0	33.5	1.4
% Foreign Born	7.4	4.5	4.4	14.0	0.0
% Living In Group Quarters	3.2	0.3	0.7	0.0	0.0
% 13 Years Old And Under	25.6	23.7	21.4	41.6	30.1
% 14-20 Years Old	12.9	12.6	11.2	12.5	12.1
% 21-64 Years Old	50.3	53.3	53.1	44.4	56.1
% 65-74 Years Old	5.2	5.7	8.1	1.2	1.2
% 75 Years Old And Over	6.0	4.6	6.3	0.4	0.6
% In Different House	57.2	54.4	41.7	66.8	92.6
% Families With Female Head	18.1	12.3	12.2	43.8	1.5
Median School Years Completed	12.2	12.6	12.4	7.9	14.3
Median Family Income, 1979 $$	21767	22445	22593	11591	40239
% Income Below Poverty Level	1.7	5.8	2.7	31.4	0.0
% Income Of $30,000 Or More	21.1	26.3	22.4	12.4	69.1
% White Collar Workers	33.4	49.7	46.7	15.8	89.8
% Civilian Labor Force Unemployed	9.3	5.8	3.2	15.7	7.8
% Riding To Work By Automobile	86.9	91.1	91.0	92.3	97.5
Mean Commuting Time - Minutes	18.1	19.0	19.0	23.6	21.6
Population Per Household	3.0	2.8	2.7	3.5	3.7
Total Housing Units	1266	1452	2513	288	102
% Condominiums	0.0	0.0	0.0	4.9	0.0
% Built 1970 Or Later	2.7	0.0	7.0	36.8	94.9
% Owner Occupied	59.3	61.6	71.3	21.5	91.2
% With 1+ Persons Per Room	8.9	3.7	2.8	18.1	0.0
Median Value: Owner Units $$	41200	47600	43300	35400	119600
Median Rent: Rental Units $$	207	208	209	199	-
Median Number Of Rooms: All Units	5.1	5.6	5.2	4.2	5.6

Aurora
Selected Characteristics of Census Tracts: 1970

Tract Number	TOTAL	8416	8464	8465	8528	8529	8530	8531	8532	8533	8534
Total Population	74389	6398	4918	8110	9168	14733	12079	3554	6170	3305	6520
% Male	48.5	49.3	49.3	49.4	49.3	50.2	49.5	49.9	47.6	49.1	49.1
% Black	6.6	0.3	0.2	0.1	1.5	4.9	0.8	6.5	8.5	0.7	13.0
% Other Nonwhite	0.6	0.3	0.1	0.5	0.3	0.4	0.4	0.3	0.5	0.7	1.4
% Of Spanish Language	7.3	3.3	0.3	0.2	2.2	4.9	1.9	4.1	5.8	11.9	20.7
% Foreign Born	4.7	6.5	2.2	3.5	3.9	3.6	3.0	2.3	4.0	9.0	6.1
% Living In Group Quarters	1.9	0.7	0.2	1.4	6.0	2.3	1.8	3.8	1.2	0.9	0.6
% 13 Years Old And Under	27.9	29.9	31.6	30.9	31.1	30.8	32.7	25.2	29.2	26.0	32.1
% 14-20 Years Old	12.5	12.4	13.1	14.3	12.6	12.1	10.3	13.1	11.7	13.3	12.4
% 21-64 Years Old	50.0	51.3	50.2	48.2	49.2	50.9	53.8	51.6	47.3	49.3	46.7
% 65-74 Years Old	5.7	4.6	3.4	3.4	4.3	3.9	2.1	5.7	6.4	6.7	5.3
% 75 Years Old And Over	3.9	1.8	1.8	3.3	2.8	2.3	1.1	4.4	5.6	4.7	3.6
% In Different House	53.3	56.2	44.9	53.3	50.8	53.3	40.9	54.3	45.3	67.5	53.4
% Families With Female Head	9.2	5.9	5.2	5.8	6.2	6.1	5.4	6.4	11.7	9.3	13.7
Median School Years Completed	12.1	12.4	12.7	12.7	12.3	12.2	12.5	12.0	12.1	12.0	9.8
Median Family Income, 1969 $$	11274	12849	14822	15486	12674	12105	12272	11337	10809	11406	8947
% Income Below Poverty Level	3.9	4.0	1.4	3.5	3.0	2.7	1.4	4.3	3.6	2.4	9.1
% Income of $15,000 or More	24.7	32.8	48.8	52.1	31.3	29.8	25.7	30.6	22.9	22.0	12.2
% White Collar Workers	27.3	32.1	47.1	48.3	31.2	28.6	38.1	21.1	28.9	19.8	14.2
% Civilian Labor Force Unemployed	2.8	1.4	2.3	3.3	1.8	3.3	1.8	4.4	0.9	2.5	4.0
% Riding To Work By Automobile	84.6	84.9	83.2	75.1	86.3	86.9	90.5	80.7	86.0	89.0	83.1
Population Per Household	3.1	3.4	3.6	3.6	3.4	3.4	3.4	3.2	2.9	3.3	3.4
Total Housing Units	24237	1941	1507	2252	2621	4355	3628	1075	2221	1014	2018
% Condominiums & Cooperatives	0.1	0.0	0.0	0.0	0.0	0.1	0.0	0.0	0.0	0.0	0.4
% Built 1960 Or Later	18.4	27.7	55.4	37.5	31.1	40.8	68.3	7.9	9.9	7.9	2.3
% Owner Occupied	58.1	68.5	68.9	75.6	73.1	66.0	57.4	76.2	40.4	73.2	51.8
% With 1+ Persons Per Room	8.0	7.4	5.6	5.0	6.9	9.5	6.3	7.2	7.6	8.3	14.6
Median Value: Owner Units $$	18800	22200	28800	32900	23100	21800	22600	17400	17500	18100	14600
Median Rent: Rental Units $$	121	164	183	133	137	142	145	118	116	108	109
Median Number Of Rooms: All Units	5.0	5.1	5.3	6.3	5.5	5.0	5.0	5.0	4.8	5.2	4.9

Aurora
Selected Characteristics of Census Tracts: 1970

Tract Number	8535	8536	8537	8538	8539	8540	8541	8542	8543	8544	8545
Total Population	3799	5072	374	2468	7773	8139	4045	4318	7350	6688	5424
% Male	48.3	47.6	61.2	51.5	47.8	49.3	47.4	46.3	47.9	50.3	50.1
% Black	19.6	21.2	6.4	2.7	2.1	1.4	6.6	0.0	0.3	3.3	0.1
% Other Nonwhite	0.8	1.2	5.1	0.6	0.2	0.3	0.6	0.4	0.4	0.3	0.2
% Of Spanish Language	19.6	12.8	9.7	12.6	4.7	2.6	6.6	3.9	0.6	8.8	2.3
% Foreign Born	4.8	7.9	3.8	5.6	3.7	2.5	5.5	3.2	4.8	1.9	1.4
% Living In Group Quarters	0.0	1.0	0.0	1.0	4.8	0.0	2.9	1.5	0.8	0.0	0.0
% 13 Years Old And Under	28.4	28.7	13.4	29.3	23.3	29.8	26.8	25.9	25.1	32.5	32.3
% 14-20 Years Old	12.9	13.1	8.6	12.6	15.5	12.3	11.4	13.6	11.6	12.2	11.5
% 21-64 Years Old	49.8	47.8	58.8	50.8	49.0	51.5	49.3	48.5	49.8	50.1	49.2
% 65-74 Years Old	5.1	6.0	12.8	4.7	8.0	4.4	6.4	6.5	8.5	3.8	4.4
% 75 Years Old And Over	3.8	4.5	6.4	2.7	4.3	2.1	6.1	5.5	5.0	1.4	2.6
% In Different House	64.3	48.3	25.0	51.5	57.6	53.9	57.3	56.7	69.5	58.8	51.1
% Families With Female Head	9.7	12.2	11.1	10.2	7.9	7.5	10.4	11.3	8.1	8.0	3.4
Median School Years Completed	10.6	10.4	8.3	10.1	12.7	12.2	10.9	12.3	12.0	11.0	12.4
Median Family Income, 1969 $$	9494	9682	5727	10525	13871	13156	10743	11421	10988	11278	12532
% Income Below Poverty Level	8.0	8.5	30.0	4.1	3.5	2.3	1.6	2.4	2.7	5.0	4.2
% Income of $15,000 or More	18.2	15.2	0.0	25.3	43.6	37.1	16.2	24.0	18.9	22.1	33.4
% White Collar Workers	11.8	14.1	28.0	16.1	46.0	30.9	16.8	26.7	25.5	14.7	30.1
% Civilian Labor Force Unemployed	1.3	5.3	15.2	1.0	3.0	3.2	4.8	1.6	2.9	2.5	1.2
% Riding To Work By Automobile	87.2	83.0	32.5	82.0	77.6	88.5	83.8	83.6	83.9	91.6	80.6
Population Per Household	3.3	3.1	1.5	3.1	2.9	3.4	3.0	3.0	3.0	3.5	3.6
Total Housing Units	1196	1707	263	836	2575	2484	1369	1496	2449	1630	1566
% Condominiums & Cooperatives	0.0	0.0	0.0	0.0	0.0	0.0	0.5	0.0	0.0	0.0	0.0
% Built 1960 Or Later	16.7	2.8	2.1	0.7	6.2	37.1	6.1	3.1	4.8	30.8	36.3
% Owner Occupied	67.9	46.0	6.5	36.8	68.5	74.7	53.8	57.4	76.8	77.1	70.9
% With 1+ Persons Per Room	10.9	12.7	11.0	14.9	3.5	7.2	9.7	5.2	4.9	13.7	6.3
Median Value: Owner Units $$	15500	15300	-	14900	27500	24000	16100	18700	16900	15100	26500
Median Rent: Rental Units $$	121	108	74	101	118	121	111	111	110	125	106
Median Number Of Rooms: All Units	4.9	4.7	1.2	4.6	5.5	5.3	4.8	5.3	5.2	4.7	5.8

Residential and commercial areas increased in extent, spreading along the flood plain, up the valley slopes, and over the uplands.

During the first 30 years of the 20th century, the greatest gains in manufacturing were made in the production of steel products, and by 1920, there were eight factories manufacturing machinery, and five companies producing steel office furniture and factory equipment. Five railroads including the Burlington operated through Aurora, making it a major transportation center. There were six bridges across the Fox River within the city limits. During this period, the north end of Stolp's Island was filled in, and developed as a commercial center. Aurora College located in Aurora in 1912.

The 1920s were a decade of rapid population growth and industrial expansion. Existing factories were enlarged and additional plants built. The production of steel products shows the greatest increase — machinery, pressed steel products, hardware, and foundry products. Population increased from 36,397 in 1920 to 46,589 in 1930. In 1930, persons of German stock predominated, comprising 15 percent of the total population, followed by much smaller numbers of Romanians, Swedes, Irish, English, and Luxembourgers. A small black population comprised only 2 percent of the total in 1930.

This period of growth was halted by the Depression, during which the population of Aurora remained relatively stable. By 1940, Aurora occupied an area of eight square miles, much of it vacant. The city still had nearly 150 manufacturing establishments employing more than 8,000 persons. There was no concentrated manufacturing district — most plants located along the railroad tracks. The better residential areas were on the west side, while the older and larger residential area was on the east side of the river.

Aurora's growth resumed after the Second World War, especially during the 1950s, as a result of the city's success in attracting new industry and because of the combination of rail transport and available space along the river and adjoining the tracks. Between 1950 and 1960, population increased 26 percent from 50,576 to 63,715. After 1960, the city continued to increase in population although the rate was much slower — 14 percent in the 1960s, 9 percent in the 1970s. Much of the most recent increase was due to annexation. The irregular boundaries of the city now encompass 27 square miles. As the city grew, its ethnic composition changed. Those of German descent remain the most common European nationality, but the rapid influx of Mexicans has made them an important component of the population of Aurora. The Hispanic population has grown from less than a thousand in 1960 to almost 15,000 in 1980. The black population, which was less than 4 percent of the total in 1960, has slowly risen to more than ten percent in 1980. The majority of black residents is concentrated in the north and northeastern parts of the city. In these same areas the percentage of Hispanics is two to five times greater than the blacks. The number of housing units has increased by almost half in the last 20 years, and more than 18 percent were built in the last decade. In 1980, more than half the population had changed residence within the last five years.

In 1977 there were 157 manufacturing establishments in Aurora, employing 16,000 persons. The majority of these were in machinery manufacturing. Seventy-three service industries employed over 6,000 persons. The median family income was $4,000 higher than the Chicago median in 1979. Less than 7 percent lived in poverty, while 30 percent lived in the relative affluence of an income of $30,000 or more. About seven percent of the labor force is unemployed. More than half of those employed work in Aurora.

Aurora is witness to the dawn of a new era. Threatened by competition from suburban shopping centers, a declining image and age, the old city has seen the light. In the early 1970s initial renovation of the downtown business district was begun and century-old buildings were replaced. Not until the early 1980s, however, did major changes take place. The cornerstone of the entire downtown development is the Art-Deco Paramount building built in 1931. This rundown structure was restored in 1978 and exhibits the alternative to urban blight. Governmental and community funds of more than $25 million have financed a new fire station, a civic center complex, replacement of storefront sidewalks and several other revitalization projects. The Burlington Northern Railroad's roundhouse property is the proposed site of the modern commuter transportation center. Community groups are involved in home rehabilitation in older neighborhoods throughout the city and in preserving the local architectural heritage through renovation of old residences.

The consistent availability of employment with the city and the county validates predictions of continued growth. Aurora is on the fringes of the high technology corridor which has developed on both sides of the East-West Tollway. The National Accelerator Laboratory is only seven miles northeast and closer in are several computer centers. The population is projected to be greater than 150,000 by the year 2000. Due to the vast open areas around the city, more than half of this population will live in the extensive open areas that were brought within the city limits in the last five years.

Marlene J. Aitken

Berwyn

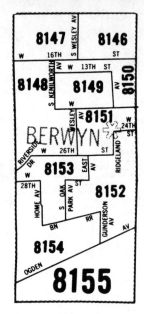

The city of Berwyn is located nine miles west of Chicago's Loop on 3.8 square miles of land in Cook County. It is bounded by Roosevelt Road on the north, Lombard Avenue on the east, Pershing Road on the south and Harlem Avenue to the west. The city is home to almost 47,000 residents, many of whom have lived there for decades. It has always been a "dormitory" suburb characterized by well-kept brick bungalows on small but well-tended lots.

Originally much of the land upon which present Berwyn is built belonged to the Illinois and Michigan Canal Company, which obtained it in 1845 from the state. By 1848 the canal connecting the Illinois River and Lake Michigan was completed and a plank road was built on the property. This road eventually became Ogden Avenue and runs diagonally through the southern portion of the city. In the 1860s settlers began moving into this area. One of the early realtors, T.F. Baldwin, developed an area he called La Vergue. Baldwin sold a right-of-way to the Chicago Burlington and Quincy Railroad which was joined by other railroads as the rail network spread west of Chicago. In the 1880s a large number of Swedes moved into the area north of the Burlington tracks between East and Oak Park avenues. This area became known as Upsala. The northern portion of the land owned by the Illinois and Michigan Canal Company was eventually obtained by the Mutual Life Insurance Company which by 1887 had it surveyed and subdivided.

Berwyn developed quickly after 1890, when realtors Charles E. Piper and Wilbur J. Andrews built a subdivision, complete with streets, sidewalks, and sewers, relying on Chicago to supply its residents. The name was chosen from a Pennsylvania Railroad timetable by Piper and Andrews. Berwyn was a part of Cicero Township until it was recognized as a separate subdivision in 1890. In 1901 Berwyn, along with Oak Park, split off from the township as independent villages. In the first decade of the 20th century Berwyn grew rapidly, becoming a residential suburb for Chicago workers. The first Czechoslovakian families arrived in northern Berwyn in 1907 and in the decades that followed Czechs became the predominant nationality. In 1908 Berwyn was chartered as a city. Berwyn was developed and settled during the first three decades of this century. It grew from a population of 5,841 in 1910 to 14,150 in 1920. During these years much of the housing was in the form of flat-roofed one-story structures built in the southern portion of the city. These were sold on the assumption that once the owner saved enough money he would construct a second story. The building would then become a two-family flat.

In the 1920s the population increased 232 percent to 47,027, and the city experienced a building boom. Construction was basically of two-story brick bungalows which often went up in three months or less. However, municipal building codes were rigidly enforced resulting in substantial and well-built structures. Homes in Berwyn were considered somewhat better than those in Stickney to the south or Cicero to the east. By the end of the 1920s all vacant land was filled up in Berwyn. As in Cicero, a large proportion of the population was of Czechoslovakian stock and in 1930, 38 percent of the total fell into that category.

Industry was not allowed within Berwyn's city limits so it was from the outset a dormitory suburb. Many of the workers from Berwyn were employed in Cicero at the Hawthorne Works of the Western Electric Company as well as by other plants there and in Chicago. A catastrophe occurred in July, 1915 when the Eastland, a lake excursion boat which had been chartered for its workers by Western Electric, suddenly capsized in the Chicago River and drowned 812 persons. Most of those on board were from Berwyn.

During the Depression Berwyn's growth slowed and the population grew by only 1,400 persons during the 1930s. That decade brought many municipal improvements supported by federal aid. The population continued to increase over the next two decades rising to a peak of 54,224 in 1960. Since then the population has declined, by 2,000 during the 1960s, and by almost 6,000 during the 1970s. By 1980 the population had dropped below its 1930 level to stand at 46,849, and this took Berwyn off the list of the 10 most populous Chicago suburbs.

The loss of population seems related to the age structure of Berwyn. In 1980, the median age was 42.3, one of the oldest in the area. The percentage of the population 65 years and above was 22.3, and one out of every three persons in Berwyn was 60 years old or more. Only 18 percent of the population was less than 19 years of age. Almost two-thirds of the 19,751 households in Berwyn consist of one or two persons. In addition, while the population decreased by more than 10 percent during the 1970s the number of households decreased by less than 1 percent. This suggests an "empty nest" situation whereby the children in a family have moved out, leaving the parents in a house which used to have five people living in it, and an aging population with many widowed survivors living alone.

The stability of the population is reflected in the fact that 41 percent of the homeowners have lived in their houses for 20 years or more. One of the factors which tends to stabilize the population is the emphasis on cultural and national heritage. The Czechoslovak Society of America is headquartered in Berwyn and the city boasts other nationality-based organizations. The community also has a variety of ethnic restaurants and stores, many located along Cermak Road, which is the major shopping area. A relatively large number (14 percent) are foreign born. While several nationalities are represented (e.g. Germans, Poles, and Italians) in Berwyn's population, the community has been and still is almost all white. Two percent of the residents are of Spanish origin.

Berwyn's residents are basically middle-class with the median family income in 1979 at $23,178. Four percent of all families lived in poverty, while more than 30 percent earned more than $30,000. Sixty percent of all workers are in white-collar occupations. Most home prices in the community ranged from $40,000-$70,000 with a few up to $125,000. The median home value in 1980 was more than $10,000 higher than the Chicago median.

In the future Berwyn will need to attract young couples and families. One attraction is its location with respect to Chicago and neighboring industrial centers. While the housing stock is old it is sound and well-kept, suggesting a pride in the community on the part of residents. There were a dozen banks and savings and loan associations in Berwyn in 1981, all of which were growing. Eight local business associations were active in the community in 1980. The Berwyn business district includes a major retail center, the Cermak Plaza at Cermak Road and Harlem Avenue. There are two other shopping areas farther south. The MacNeal Memorial Hospital (427 beds) is constructing a new building at a cost of $62 million in the city. An aging Berwyn continues to be quietly active.

Gail Danks Welter

Berwyn
Population and Housing Characteristics, 1930-1980

	1980	1970	1960	1950	1940	1930
Total Population.......	46,849	52,502	54,224	51,280	48,451	47,027
% Male.................	45.8	46.3	47.7	48.4	49.6	50.4
% Female...............	54.2	53.7	52.3	51.4	50.4	49.6
% White................	98.5	99.6	99.9	100.0	100.0	100.0
% Black................	–	0.0	0.0	0.0	0.0	0.0
% Other Nonwhite Races...	1.5	0.4	0.0	0.0	0.0	0.0
% Under 5 Years Old.....	4.4	5.5	7.4	7.8	5.7	8.0
% 5-19 Years Old.......	17.0	19.6	19.1	17.0	20.5	25.8
% 20-44 Years Old.......	31.4	27.8	30.6	38.9	45.4	47.3
% 45-64 Years Old.......	25.0	30.1	30.4	28.6	23.3	15.7
% 65 Years and Older.....	22.2	17.0	12.5	7.7	5.1	3.2
Median School Years.....	12.2	11.9	10.5	10.5	9.2	8.8	*

Total Housing Units....	20,467	30,341	19,287	16,058	14,132	*
% In One-Unit Structures.	46.3	47.1	51.5	*	*	*
% Owner Occupied........	58.7	59.5	61.4	62.5	54.8	*
% Renter Occupied........	39.4	38.6	36.4	36.6	43.6	*
% Vacant...............	1.9	1.9	2.2	0.9	1.6	*
% 1+ Persons per Room....	1.6	2.8	3.2	5.6	*	*

Place 495 — Berwyn, Illinois
Selected Characteristics of Census Tracts: 1980

Tract Number	Total	8146	8147	8148	8149	8150	8151	8152	8153	8154	8155
Total Population.............	46849	4740	4739	4912	4854	3005	3250	5532	3434	5710	6673
% Male.......................	45.8	48.2	48.0	43.8	41.3	45.0	45.4	47.1	46.4	45.4	46.5
% Black......................	0.0	0.0	0.0	0.0	0.1	0.1	0.0	0.0	0.0	0.0	0.0
% Other Nonwhite.............	1.5	2.0	2.8	1.0	1.3	1.3	0.7	1.6	1.3	1.4	1.0
% Of Spanish Origin..........	2.4	3.6	3.3	1.3	2.5	2.4	2.6	2.9	2.2	1.9	1.8
% Foreign Born...............	13.0	9.7	13.7	17.1	15.6	15.7	18.2	12.0	9.4	10.8	10.6
% Living In Group Quarters...	0.4	0.0	0.0	0.0	0.0	0.0	0.0	0.3	0.0	3.0	0.0
% 13 Years Old And Under.....	13.4	17.6	17.2	9.8	9.4	11.3	12.0	14.7	14.4	12.3	14.5
% 14-20 Years Old............	9.4	11.5	10.0	7.1	6.8	8.9	9.5	10.5	10.1	10.5	9.5
% 21-64 Years Old............	54.9	54.5	56.9	53.5	53.7	54.1	52.0	56.2	54.8	56.0	55.4
% 65-74 Years Old............	13.7	10.0	10.6	17.8	17.6	16.0	16.1	12.0	12.5	12.2	13.8
% 75 Years Old And Over......	8.6	6.4	5.3	11.8	13.3	9.7	10.4	6.6	8.2	9.0	6.7
% In Different House.........	34.5	33.9	47.0	32.6	35.9	35.4	23.6	39.3	27.5	37.3	28.6
% Families With Female Head..	15.1	16.7	18.5	10.7	21.6	13.6	15.8	17.0	13.9	12.5	11.8
Median School Years Completed..	12.2	12.1	12.1	12.1	12.2	12.1	12.1	12.2	12.3	12.5	12.2
Median Family Income, 1979.....$$	23178	22646	19789	27236	20136	22361	20518	22960	23821	25797	23495
% Income Below Poverty Level..	4.0	6.0	6.7	3.1	2.3	3.8	5.4	4.1	4.1	2.2	3.4
% Income Of $30,000 Or More...	30.5	28.0	23.9	41.9	24.0	29.6	25.6	25.9	34.0	37.1	31.8
% White Collar Workers.......	59.6	52.7	52.4	60.7	67.5	55.0	58.8	59.0	62.5	65.4	59.2
% Civilian Labor Force Unemployed.	5.3	6.7	8.3	4.2	4.2	4.6	5.2	4.1	4.8	4.7	4.0
% Riding To Work By Automobile....	73.7	79.6	78.5	73.2	70.5	72.7	70.1	75.0	68.6	65.2	80.6
Mean Commuting Time - Minutes...	26.1	24.7	24.1	29.3	28.4	26.6	27.6	25.7	28.3	24.6	24.5
Population Per Household......	2.4	2.7	2.5	2.2	1.9	2.3	2.3	2.4	2.5	2.3	2.6
Total Housing Units..........	20464	1880	1959	2310	2649	1376	1441	2331	1373	2516	2629
% Condominiums...............	0.1	0.0	0.0	0.0	0.0	0.0	0.0	0.0	0.0	1.1	0.0
% Built 1970 Or Later........	2.3	1.5	4.9	1.8	1.4	0.0	2.4	2.7	1.5	3.0	2.7
% Owner Occupied.............	58.0	64.4	54.2	61.3	27.9	54.3	62.8	62.8	74.9	48.4	78.9
% With 1+ Persons Per Room...	1.6	2.4	3.0	1.1	1.1	1.0	1.4	1.5	1.5	1.4	1.5
Median Value: Owner Units.......$$	58500	53600	54500	62500	63400	59900	54200	52700	59700	62700	59500
Median Rent: Rental Units.......$$	213	193	213	226	214	205	192	208	213	219	227
Median Number Of Rooms: All Units.	5.0	5.1	4.9	5.0	4.5	5.1	5.3	4.9	5.2	4.7	5.1

Berwyn
Selected Characteristics of Census Tracts: 1970

Tract Number	TOTAL	8146	8147	8148	8149	8150	8151	8152	8153	8154	8155
Total Population.............	52502	5572	5206	5475	5567	3322	3640	6534	3596	6547	7043
% Male.......................	46.3	48.5	47.6	44.9	42.8	46.1	45.4	47.7	45.6	45.3	47.6
% Black......................	0.0	0.0	0.0	0.0	0.0	0.0	0.0	0.0	0.0	0.0	0.0
% Other Nonwhite.............	0.3	0.2	0.1	0.0	0.1	0.2	0.5	0.5	0.4	1.1	0.2
% Of Spanish Language........	1.3	1.6	2.2	0.4	1.3	0.0	1.5	2.5	1.1	1.6	0.1
% Foreign Born...............	11.4	7.2	7.5	13.2	18.0	13.9	17.9	12.2	10.7	9.7	7.8
% Living In Group Quarters...	0.5	0.0	0.0	0.0	0.0	0.2	0.2	0.0	0.0	3.6	0.0
% 13 Years Old And Under.....	17.1	23.0	20.2	11.6	11.6	14.6	13.6	20.0	16.2	18.1	18.5
% 14-20 Years Old............	9.3	10.2	11.3	8.2	7.2	7.9	8.8	9.2	10.1	9.9	10.1
% 21-64 Years Old............	56.6	53.5	56.6	57.8	57.7	56.1	56.3	56.3	56.1	56.4	58.1
% 65-74 Years Old............	10.7	8.1	7.9	14.8	15.2	12.6	13.0	8.6	12.1	9.1	8.9
% 75 Years Old And Over......	6.3	5.3	4.1	7.6	8.3	8.8	8.3	5.9	5.5	6.5	4.3
% In Different House.........	67.0	68.3	68.3	72.1	59.3	63.1	73.5	68.1	66.6	60.6	70.9
% Families With Female Head..	10.8	10.7	10.7	11.2	14.5	10.4	13.9	10.5	10.8	8.8	8.2
Median School Years Completed..	11.5	11.0	11.0	11.5	11.1	11.0	10.5	11.1	12.1	12.3	11.6
Median Family Income, 1969....$$	11836	11357	11250	12694	11285	11447	10470	11070	12130	13703	12564
% Income Below Poverty Level...	3.5	4.0	5.4	1.9	4.0	2.2	7.1	4.9	1.5	1.7	2.6
% Income of $15,000 or More...	29.7	27.8	24.7	31.4	23.9	29.0	23.5	26.8	30.8	43.1	32.3
% White Collar Workers.......	26.9	24.3	24.1	29.6	29.5	26.6	24.7	24.4	29.7	33.8	22.3
% Civilian Labor Force Unemployed.	2.2	2.6	3.0	2.2	3.0	3.5	3.6	2.3	1.1	1.7	1.5
% Riding To Work By Automobile....	68.7	76.8	71.3	69.5	61.9	68.7	60.7	70.3	66.1	62.1	75.5
Population Per Household......	2.6	2.9	2.8	2.5	2.2	2.5	2.5	2.7	2.7	2.6	2.8
Total Housing Units..........	20335	1918	1892	2286	2623	1373	1463	2464	1363	2453	2500
% Condominiums & Cooperatives...	0.5	0.8	0.7	0.3	0.8	0.6	0.0	0.3	0.0	0.3	0.8
% Built 1960 Or Later........	8.5	4.5	9.1	12.7	4.1	3.3	11.7	7.0	13.5	10.8
% Owner Occupied.............	59.1	64.2	58.2	62.5	30.0	54.0	65.3	63.8	75.3	47.4	80.3
% With 1+ Persons Per Room...	2.8	4.7	3.8	1.6	1.4	2.0	2.2	3.9	2.2	3.2	2.8
Median Value: Owner Units.......$$	23200	21200	21700	25800	26200	23500	22600	21300	23400	25600	23600
Median Rent: Rental Units.......$$	121	106	117	136	121	122	106	115	123	129	132
Median Number Of Rooms: All Units.	4.9	5.0	4.9	5.0	4.4	5.1	5.2	4.8	5.1	4.6	5.0

Bolingbrook

The Village of Bolingbrook is a relatively new community about 30 miles southwest of Chicago, near the interchange of Interstate Highway 55 and Illinois Route 53. Most of it is situated in Will County, except for a few residential developments to the northeast, which extend into DuPage County. It was incorporated in 1965 and has a governing body that includes an elected President, Board of Trustees, and Village Manager.

Bolingbrook developed as a frontier area on the other side of what was known as the "Indian Boundary Line." The first permanent white settlers arrived around 1830. Scotch residents reportedly voted to separate from DuPage County because they thought the Germans to the north drank too much. Population growth was sluggish well into the 20th century; land that was not kept vacant became cornfields.

There are several different accounts of how the town came to be called Bolingbrook. The most credible is that the Dover Construction Company selected the name to promote an English imagery in a subdivision built in 1961. The Earl of Bolingbroke is a character in several Shakespeare plays. In any case, residents formally adopted the name at the time of incorporation.

In 1965 the population numbered 5,357. Since then, Bolingbrook has been one of the fastest growing communities in the metropolitan area. By 1970, the population had grown to 8,504, then skyrocketed by 400 percent in the next decade. More than 37,000 live in Bolingbrook today. Total land area expanded from one square mile in 1964 to almost 10 square miles. The eastern sector is the oldest part of town; the main growth area is in the western part.

Bolingbrook got off to a shaky start during this period because of overly-eager builders who built poorly-constructed, inexpensive single-family frame homes. Young couples with small children were attracted to the area. Schools were kept in session the year around to accommodate their numbers. Old Chicago Amusement Center (including a shopping mall), called the world's largest closed-in recreation center, went bankrupt. Many of the small specialty shops were too expensive and too elitist in appeal for the general public. The shopping center is now empty, a silent challenge to Bolingbrook's image as a "boom town".

During the past few years the Village has been catching up with its own growth. By 1979 it had enough schools to return to the traditional 10-month school year. Bolingbrook has its own fire and police departments, and boasts a police force that is 75 percent college educated. Through zoning regulations, economic development and planning commissions are attempting to direct the pattern of industrial and residential growth. This is not an easy task, given that Bolingbrook is a community of subdivisions. About 40 such areas exist in various stages of completion, separated by cornfields. They have recently been grouped into eight "neighborhoods" to facilitate census counts and revenue assessments.

There is no downtown area, although small commercial centers are located at Highway 53 and Boughton Road, and Schmitt and Boughton roads. Other main streets include Naperville, Briarcliffe and Rockhurst roads, Lily Cache Lane and Janes Avenue. Residents generally travel to shopping centers in Aurora (Fox Valley), Lombard (Yorktown), and Oakbrook. There is no major industry in Bolingbrook. About 40 percent of the labor force travels at least 20 miles to their jobs (most of them to Chicago). Clow International Airport is on the western outskirts of the Village and accommodates single- and twin-engine planes.

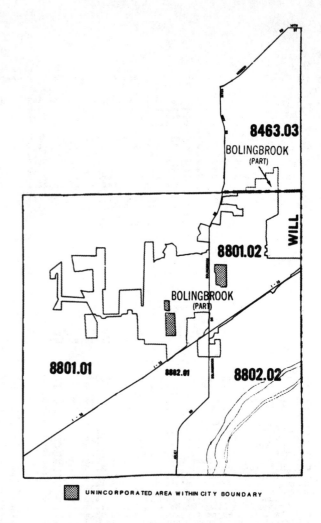

UNINCORPORATED AREA WITHIN CITY BOUNDARY

A majority of the residents are white. Blacks make up 7 percent of the population, Asians about 4 percent, and another 4.5 percent are Spanish-speaking. One recent survey showed blacks are dispersed throughout the community. This is an unusual growth pattern; in the city and other suburbs, black minorities are concentrated in certain neighborhoods.

Bolingbrook's residents are mobile. More than two-thirds have moved into their houses within the last five years. Nevertheless, this is a family-oriented community. Of the 11,773 housing units, 65 percent are single-family dwellings, and 77 percent are owner occupied. More than 80 percent of all units were built within the last 10 years. The value of single-family dwellings is, on the average, about a third higher than in the city.

The population of Bolingbrook is young and relatively affluent. Almost 40 percent are 18 or younger, less than 2 percent are 65 or older. More than 40 percent of all families reported incomes of $30,000 or more in 1979; less than 3 percent lived in poverty at that time. Almost two-thirds of the resident labor force is in white-collar occupations.

Bolingbrook is still a very new community. This suburb may experience a natural population decline in years to come, as youngsters leave home and mobile adults move on to opportunities located elsewhere. Now that growth is slowing down, community planners will be able to concentrate on developing cohesion among its many subdivisions.

Antoinette LoBosco

Bolingbrook
Population and Housing Characteristics, 1930-1980

	1980	1970	1960	1950	1940	1930
Total Population.......	37,261	7,275	*	*	*	*
% Male..................	504	50.1	*	*	*	*
% Female................	49.6	49.9	*	*	*	*
% White.................	87.2	99.6	*	*	*	*
% Black.................	6.8	0.0	*	*	*	*
% Other Nonwhite Races...	6.0	0.4	*	*	*	*
% Under 5 Years Old......	12.8	13.3	*	*	*	*
% 5-19 Years Old.........	29.7	38.9	*	*	*	*
% 20-44 Years Old........	48.1	36.7	*	*	*	*
% 45-64 Years Old.......	7.7	9.5	*	*	*	*
% 65 Years and Older.....	1.7	1.6	*	*	*	*
Median School Years....	12.9	12.2	*	*	*	*
Total Housing Units....	11,773	1,727	*	*	*	*
% In One-Unit Structures.	79.9	99.1	*	*	*	*
% Owner Occupied.........	77.6	91.9	*	*	*	*
% Renter Occupied........	16.1	4.6	*	*	*	*
% Vacant................	6.3	3.5	*	*	*	*
% 1+ Persons per Room....	2.2	6.6	*	*	*	*

Place 563 — Bolingbrook , Illinois
Selected Characteristics of Census Tracts: 1980

Tract Number	Total	8463.03	8801.01	8801.02	8802.01	8802.02
Total Population............	37261	1154	18077	18030	0	0
% Male...................	50.4	50.8	50.5	50.2	–	–
% Black..................	6.8	4.5	6.3	7.4	–	–
% Other Nonwhite.........	6.0	9.0	5.8	5.9	–	–
% Of Spanish Origin......	4.5	3.6	4.2	4.9	–	–
% Foreign Born...........	6.2	8.3	6.0	6.3	–	–
% Living In Group Quarters........	0.0	0.0	0.0	0.0	–	–
% 13 Years Old And Under..........	33.8	39.3	35.1	32.1	–	–
% 14-20 Years Old.........	9.7	5.2	8.1	11.6	–	–
% 21-64 Years Old.........	54.8	54.4	55.6	54.0	–	–
% 65-74 Years Old.........	1.3	0.8	0.9	1.6	–	–
% 75 Years Old And Over...	0.5	0.3	0.3	0.6	–	–
% In Different House......	67.7	97.2	74.8	59.1	–	–
% Families With Female Head...	7.8	2.1	7.2	8.8	–	–
Median School Years Completed....	12.9	13.3	12.9	12.9	–	–
Median Family Income, 1979......$$	27679	31450	27012	28164	–	–
% Income Below Poverty Level....	2.8	1.3	2.9	2.8	–	–
% Income Of $30,000 Or More.....	40.9	57.0	37.7	43.2	–	–
% White Collar Workers.......	63.6	71.6	61.6	65.1	–	–
% Civilian Labor Force Unemployed.	4.4	1.4	4.1	4.9	–	–
% Riding To Work By Automobile...	90.1	88.5	89.5	90.7	–	–
Mean Commuting Time - Minutes...	34.6	36.6	35.3	33.8	–	–
Population Per Household..........	3.4	3.7	3.3	3.5	–	–
Total Housing Units..........	11773	321	5813	5639	0	0
% Condominiums.................	7.3	0.0	9.8	5.1	–	–
% Built 1970 Or Later.............	80.9	100.0	92.2	68.2	–	–
% Owner Occupied..............	77.2	97.5	76.9	76.3	–	–
% With 1+ Persons Per Room......	2.2	1.6	1.9	2.5	–	–
Median Value: Owner Units....$$	65200	86700	64700	64600	–	–
Median Rent: Rental Units.......$$	273	–	248	305	–	–
Median Number Of Rooms: All Units.	5.6	5.6	5.6	5.6	–	–

Bolingbrook
Selected Characteristics of Census Tracts: 1970

Tract Number	TOTAL	8463	8801	8802
Total Population.............	7651	21351	9109	10928
% Male.....................	50.1	51.0	50.7	49.9
% Black....................	0.0	0.4	0.1	0.0
% Other Nonwhite...........	0.4	0.7	0.5	0.6
% Of Spanish Language......	6.0	1.9	6.1	4.8
% Foreign Born.............	2.0	4.3	2.2	1.4
% Living In Group Quarters........	0.1	0.4	0.1	0.1
% 13 Years Old And Under..........	43.0	36.5	43.0	40.8
% 14-20 Years Old...........	9.8	9.1	8.9	13.2
% 21-64 Years Old..........	45.6	52.1	46.6	44.6
% 65-74 Years Old..........	1.1	1.5	1.0	1.0
% 75 Years Old And Over...........	0.6	0.8	0.5	0.4
% In Different House........	55.1	30.2	44.4	58.6
% Families With Female Head.......	2.7	2.6	2.7	3.8
Median School Years Completed....	12.2	12.8	12.3	11.9
Median Family Income, 1969......$$	12070	14197	12526	12720
% Income Below Poverty Level.....	2.9	1.6	2.9	3.2
% Income of $15,000 or More.....	21.2	43.0	26.1	27.6
% White Collar Workers......	23.0	53.8	29.4	18.6
% Civilian Labor Force Unemployed.	2.5	1.4	2.0	2.9
% Riding To Work By Automobile....	92.6	82.8	88.9	93.3
Population Per Household..........	4.4	3.6	4.3	4.5
Total Housing Units..........	1726	6607	2255	2477
% Condominiums & Cooperatives.....	0.0	1.6	3.4	0.0
% Built 1960 Or Later.............	87.9	87.3	91.3	60.4
% Owner Occupied..................	91.9	64.0	84.4	91.8
% With 1+ Persons Per Room........	6.7	4.5	6.3	18.4
Median Value: Owner Units.......$$	21300	30200	22400	18900
Median Rent: Rental Units.......$$	145	195	152	146
Median Number Of Rooms: All Units.	6.2	5.7	6.1	5.3

Burbank

Burbank is a newly-incorporated city located just southwest of Chicago. It is bounded by the suburban communities of Bedford Park, Oak Lawn, and Bridgeview. The city was named after two existing community focal points, the Luther Burbank School and the Burbank Fire Department. Burbank's early history cannot be separated from that of Stickney Township, by which it is surrounded. Marshy land, which made up the entire southwest Chicago metropolitan area, kept residential growth at a minimum here as it did in the city. As late as the 1920s the district was almost entirely farmland and prairie. Roads from Chicago typically ended in mud or gravel paths as they approached Stickney Township. Early settlers sometimes constructed their homes from discarded packing cases and boxcars from nearby rail lines. Truck farming was common.

Residential growth over the years has been stimulated by the development of the industrial and commercial complex formed by the Clearing Industrial District, Midway Airport, Ford City Shopping Center, and other scattered industrial and retail establishments that line Cicero and Harlem avenues. Real estate developers first subdivided the land in the early 1930s but building construction came to a halt with the Depression. The few services that were available were provided by the township. The area that makes up Burbank was referred to as South Stickney or Burbank Manor by people who lived there. The post-World War II Southwest Side building and population boom contributed to the growth of Stickney Township. By 1959 South Stickney had installed a public water and sewer system.

The question of incorporation arose as the township population continued to grow. Burbank was the only concentration of over 10,000 people in Cook County not governed by a village or city government, though it encompassed 4 of the 6.5 square miles of the area. Residents were divided over the issue. Some were satisfied with the growing assortment of services the township provided and feared incorporation would lead to excessive taxation. Others favored annexation to a neighboring suburban village or town. In 1969 a fact-finding committee determined that revenue sources would offset the anticipated tax burden but the question of incorporation was not settled until after Chicago annexed an unincorporated part of Stickney Township west of Cicero Avenue. Bridgeview had also indicated an interest in some extensively improved area located nearby. Residents finally approved incorporation as the City of Burbank in April, 1970.

The present population is 28,462. Though the decennial census for Burbank begins with 1980, several previous counts were taken by various civic and governmental units. The 1960 population was estimated at 20,720 for this part of Stickney Township. A municipal census taken by volunteer civic groups came up with a 1970 total of 26,383. A federal census in January, 1971, set an unofficial count at 27,768, including 1,160 annexed residents. By 1976 no fewer than five government agencies had taken their own population counts. This prompted another special federal census in July of that year and the population was recorded at 29,448. According to the federal figures,

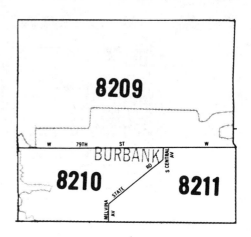

Burbank has grown in the last 10 years, though the population dropped slightly during the four years between 1976 and 1980.

A majority of residents are white, less than 1 percent is black, and another 3 percent are of Spanish orgin. In 1980 7 percent of the population was foreign born. Leading nationalities include Poles, Italians, Germans, Irish, English, and Czechs. Burbank is a primarily residential community. Eighty four percent of the homes owner-occupied and the median value is $59,100, substantially above the Chicago median. Most homes are single-family housing units and a majority of the multiple-family dwellings are concentrated along 79th and 87th Streets.

Burbank is often referred to as a "bedroom" community since most of the residents work in nearby industrial and commercial centers. About half of the employed residents work in Chicago. The Clearing Industrial District, Midway Airport, and Ford City Shopping Center are important employment centers. Public transportation is not an important factor in commuting to work; almost everyone drives an automobile. To some extent, Burbank serves as a corridor for industrial and commercial traffic, especially 79th Street, Central, Cicero, and Harlem avenues. A small industrial area is located in the northeast sector. Several community services are still provided at the township level. These include health care, a recreational park system, youth center, office of aging and public library.

Twenty-eight percent of the residential labor force was employed in manufacturing in 1980. This figure dropped from 33 percent in 1970 as the retail and service sectors grew. This trend is in keeping with the national shift of jobs into white-collar service industry occupations.

The principal shopping area is located at 79th Street and Cicero Avenue. Residents also frequent Chicago's Ford City and Scottsdale shopping centers, just across from this intersection, and several other plazas in nearby Oak Lawn and Bridgeview. Business establishments line 79th and 87th streets, Cicero and Harlem avenues. Scattered vacant land parcels dot the community with some larger undeveloped areas located along the periphery.

Antoinette LoBosco

Burbank
Population and Housing Characteristics, 1930-1980

	1980	1970	1960	1950	1940	1930
Total Population.......	28,462	–	*	*	*	*
% Male..................	49.2	–	*	*	*	*
% Female................	50.8	–	*	*	*	*
% White.................	98.2	–	*	*	*	*
% Black.................	–	–	*	*	*	*
% Other Nonwhite Races....	1.8	–	*	*	*	*
% Under 5 Years Old.....	6.3	–	*	*	*	*
% 5-19 Years Old.........	27.3	–	*	*	*	*
% 20-44 Years Old........	34.6	–	*	*	*	*
% 45-64 Years Old........	23.4	–	*	*	*	*
% 65 Years and Older.....	8.4	–	*	*	*	*
Median School Years....	12.2	–	*	*	*	*
Total Housing Units....	8,682	–	*	*	*	*
% In One-Unit Structures.	83.4	–	*	*	*	*
% Owner Occupied........	83.5	–	*	*	*	*
% Renter Occupied........	15.7	–	*	*	*	*
% Vacant................	0.8	–	*	*	*	*
% 1+ Persons per Room....	4.8	–	*	*	*	*

Place 743 — Burbank , Illinois
Selected Characteristics of Census Tracts: 1980

Tract Number	Total	8209	8210	8211
Total Population.............	28462	9428	10588	8446
% Male...........................	49.2	48.9	49.3	49.3
% Black..........................	0.0	0.0	0.0	0.1
% Other Nonwhite.................	1.8	2.5	1.4	1.5
% Of Spanish Origin..............	3.1	3.9	2.3	3.2
% Foreign Born...................	7.3	9.1	6.9	5.8
% Living In Group Quarters.......	1.1	1.3	0.7	1.6
% 13 Years Old And Under.........	20.2	21.2	20.3	18.9
% 14-20 Years Old................	15.5	15.2	16.0	15.2
% 21-64 Years Old................	55.9	55.7	56.3	55.7
% 65-74 Years Old................	5.5	5.1	4.9	6.6
% 75 Years Old And Over..........	2.9	2.8	2.5	3.5
% In Different House.............	31.2	32.5	31.9	29.0
% Families With Female Head......	9.1	9.7	8.6	8.8
Median School Years Completed....	12.2	12.2	12.3	12.2
Median Family Income, 1979......$$	26367	26158	26802	26088
% Income Below Poverty Level.....	2.8	3.6	2.5	2.4
% Income Of $30,000 Or More.....	37.3	33.4	39.7	38.6
% White Collar Workers...........	46.2	44.9	45.1	49.1
% Civilian Labor Force Unemployed.	6.1	6.3	5.7	6.4
% Riding To Work By Automobile....	89.2	88.1	91.7	87.4
Mean Commuting Time - Minutes...	26.7	27.6	26.7	25.7
Population Per Household.........	3.3	3.2	3.4	3.2
Total Housing Units..........	8682	2919	3141	2622
% Condominiums...................	1.1	3.3	0.0	0.0
% Built 1970 Or Later............	11.7	13.7	11.1	10.3
% Owner Occupied.................	83.0	78.2	86.9	83.9
% With 1+ Persons Per Room.......	4.8	5.8	4.8	3.6
Median Value: Owner Units.......$$	59100	57500	61000	58200
Median Rent: Rental Units.......$$	262	258	262	266
Median Number Of Rooms: All Units.	5.3	5.1	5.6	5.4

Burbank
Selected Characteristics of Census Tracts: 1970

Tract Number	TOTAL	8209	8210	8211
Total Population.............	29900	10804	11777	9129
% Male...........................	49.5	49.5	49.8	48.9
% Black..........................	0.0	0.0	0.0	0.0
% Other Nonwhite.................	0.2	0.6	0.1	0.3
% Of Spanish Language............	2.0	4.1	3.5	0.4
% Foreign Born...................	3.8	4.2	3.9	3.8
% Living In Group Quarters.......	0.9	1.0	0.7	1.2
% 13 Years Old And Under.........	32.7	33.9	33.1	30.7
% 14-20 Years Old................	13.2	12.1	13.3	14.3
% 21-64 Years Old................	50.0	50.3	49.8	49.8
% 65-74 Years Old................	2.6	2.5	2.3	3.2
% 75 Years Old And Over..........	1.6	1.1	1.5	2.1
% In Different House.............	67.4	57.6	69.2	72.4
% Families With Female Head......	6.0	6.6	5.3	6.5
Median School Years Completed....	11.8	11.7	12.0	11.4
Median Family Income, 1969......$$	12511	12336	12617	12609
% Income Below Poverty Level.....	3.2	3.7	4.5	1.3
% Income of $15,000 or More.....	29.2	27.8	30.0	30.0
% White Collar Workers...........	20.5	18.9	20.6	21.1
% Civilian Labor Force Unemployed.	2.9	3.1	3.5	1.7
% Riding To Work By Automobile....	87.5	86.8	89.4	87.7
Population Per Household.........	3.9	3.9	4.0	3.8
Total Housing Units..........	7671	2794	2985	2380
% Condominiums & Cooperatives.....	0.1	0.0	0.2	0.3
% Built 1960 Or Later............	36.8	45.6	40.0	23.6
% Owner Occupied.................	86.2	80.8	86.9	86.7
% With 1+ Persons Per Room.......	13.1	15.8	12.4	11.8
Median Value: Owner Units.......$$	20900	20200	22000	20000
Median Rent: Rental Units.......$$	151	143	158	156
Median Number Of Rooms: All Units.	5.2	5.0	5.3	5.3

Calumet City

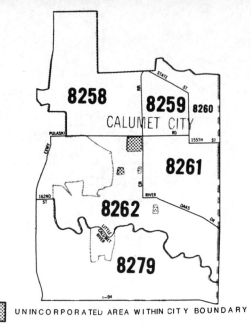

UNINCORPORATED AREA WITHIN CITY BOUNDARY

Calumet City is an old "state line" suburb located in Cook County about 23 miles south of Chicago's Loop. Its boundaries encompass 15 square miles of land within which are located some forest preserve areas and Holy Cross Cemetery. The Little Calumet River runs along the southern boundary of the city. Most of the area north of Michigan City Road is residential as is the southeastern section of the city.

Calumet City was called West Hammond when it was founded in 1893. Many of the early residents were from Hammond or worked in the nearby industrial region in northwestern Indiana. The city was incorporated in 1911 as West Hammond, but the name was changed to Calumet City in 1924 to avoid confusion with a southern Illinois town named Hammond.

Calumet City's location has played an important part in its history. It is only a few blocks west of Hammond's main business district. As the industrial area grew, Calumet City did also. On one hand it served as a dormitory suburb for the industrial cities, and at the same time as an after-hours community.

A number of saloons had opened by 1900 when the city was known for being "wide-open." Many of the customers were steel and slaughterhouse workers. In 1910 Virginia Brooks led an attempt to clean up the town. This resulted in scandalous revelations prompting the election of a reform ticket in 1912. However, when Virginia Brooks moved to Chicago in 1913 the situation reverted to its former status.

As prohibition spread, another aspect of the city's location became important. Although dependent on the Gary-Hammond region for employment, Calumet City was under the jurisdiction of another state government. In 1916 Indiana became a dry state and Calumet City's after-hours strip prospered. Eventually federal prohibition brought some new but not insurmountable difficulties. The forms and ways of doing business changed slightly for the taverns and night spots, some of which became speakeasies. Despite many raids by federal agents, the general prosperity of the 1920s kept the saloon business alive. The Depression finally did, for a time, wipe out the "recreational" industry in Calumet City.

The city continued to grow along with the surrounding industrial areas, increasing from nearly 4,000 at the turn of the century to about 6,000 in 1910 and more than 8,000 in 1920. By 1930 there were 12,298 residents in Calumet City, but population growth slowed during the Depression. Only an additional 1,000 residents were counted in 1940.

The post World War II prosperity brought a new population boom to Calumet City and by 1960 residents numbered 25,000—an increase of 58 percent over the 1950 figure. By this time the city's liquor and amusement businesses had recovered and reportedly expanded to include some illegal operations. However, the city's revenue from the licensing of these establishments helped keep real estate taxes down.

Much of the city's postwar growth was due to the expansion of nearby steel-making industries and oil refineries. Several chemical plants chose to locate in Calumet City during this period and a section of the city's northern area was zoned for industry. The Calumet Expressway (Interstate Highway 94) was built along the western boundary in the late 1950s. In 1968 Calumet City celebrated its diamond jubilee.

Between 1960 and 1970 the population again increased about 58 percent, to 32,956. Building was taking place in outlying areas. Nearly 23 percent of all current housing units were built in the 1960s and another 35 percent were constructed in the 1970s. By 1980 the population had increased to almost 40,000.

While many residents have always worked in nearby communites, Calumet City has attracted some light industries and many service businesses. Together these firms employ more than 1,400 workers.

The city has been actively trying to attract new business and industry. The city Planning Commission and Chamber of Commerce are both interested in expanding the city's commercial and industrial base. The Klarich-Calumet Expressway Industrial Plaza covers 10 acres, and the River Oaks West Business Park covers 60 acres. The former is located in the northern section of the community near the expressway, and the River Oaks Park is found in the southwestern section.

In addition to these industrial and business areas, Calumet City is the location of a major retail center, the River Oaks Shopping Center located at the intersection of 159th street and Route 83. This $35 million center houses 80 stores and with the adjacent River Oaks West Center draws many customers. In addition to these there are merchants in the downtown area and some neighborhood shops on Sibley, Torrence and Burnham avenues. Downtown Hammond is only a few blocks east.

The housing in Calumet City is varied. The median home value in 1980 was $49,000 with prices ranging from about $28,000 to $90,000. Newer homes in the outlying area averaged $70,000. Of the 15,655 occupied housing units in 1980, 62 percent were owner-occupied. Most of these were two- and three-bedroom units. Almost half the homeowners have moved in during the most recent decade. One of the newest residential areas in the city is River Oaks, on the southwest side, where several hundred condominium units have been built. Two 144-unit senior citizen complexes have also been built and occupied.

Of the total workforce in Calumet City, 50 percent were employed in white-collar occupations and the median family income was figured at $25,628 in 1980. Five percent of the nearly 11,000 families had incomes below the poverty level in 1979, while nearly 37 percent reported totals of $30,000 or more. Seven percent of the resident labor force was unemployed in 1980. About 13 percent still work in the declining steel industry.

The population of Calumet City has been overwhelmingly white. In 1960 there were only 23 blacks. By 1980 blacks comprised 6 percent and Spanish-speaking residents accounted for 4 percent of the total. The median age rose from 27.6 in 1970 to 32.8 in 1980 following the national trend of an aging population. The percentage 18 years of age or less dropped from 37 to 23. The relative number of those 65 and over doubled from 6 to 12 percent. Nearly 60 percent of the households had only one or two persons, suggesting many residual "empty nest" households maintained by couples after the children have moved away.

The future of Calumet City is problematic. As in the past, the city's fortunes are dependent on those of the Gary-Hammond industrial area. The slowdowns, shutdowns and general decline of heavy industry may have negative effects on the well being of residents, and ultimately the city itself.

Gail Danks Welter

Calumet City
Population and Housing Characteristics, 1930-1980

	1980	1970	1960	1950	1940	1930
Total Population.......	39,697	32,956	25,000	15,799	13,241	12,298
% Male..................	48.5	49.5	49.7	50.0	50.6	51.4
% Female................	51.5	50.5	50.3	50.0	49.4	48.6
% White.................	91.9	99.7	99.9	99.8	99.7	99.8
% Black.................	5.9	0.1	0.1	0.2	0.3	0.2
% Other Nonwhite Races...	2.2	0.2	0.0	0.0	0.0	0.0
% Under 5 Years Old.....	6.1	9.3	13.2	11.4	7.3	10.4
% 5-19 Years Old........	20.4	28.3	26.0	20.8	27.4	33.1
% 20-44 Years Old.......	37.1	34.2	37.1	42.3	42.8	41.7
% 45-64 Years Old.......	24.6	21.8	17.9	20.8	18.6	11.7
% 65 Years and Older....	11.8	6.4	5.8	4.7	3.9	3.1
Median School Years....	12.3	12.0	10.9	9.3	8.3	*
Total Housing Units....	16,253	10,871	7,531	4,693	3,435	*
% In One-Unit Structures.	51.2	60.5	71.1	*	*	*
% Owner Occupied........	59.9	62.4	69.3	59.9	47.8	*
% Renter Occupied........	37.2	34.3	27.0	37.6	51.1	*
% Vacant................	2.9	3.3	3.7	2.5	1.1	*
% 1+ Persons per Room....	2.8	7.7	10.5	11.8	*	*

Place 800 — Calumet City, Illinois
Selected Characteristics of Census Tracts: 1980

Tract Number	Total	8258	8259	8260	8261	8262	8279
Total Population.............	39697	15246	3566	3955	6895	10035	0
% Male..................	48.5	48.3	49.7	48.6	48.0	48.7	-
% Black.................	5.9	4.3	0.0	0.3	0.1	16.8	-
% Other Nonwhite.........	2.1	2.7	2.0	3.0	1.4	1.5	-
% Of Spanish Origin......	3.8	4.1	3.6	6.5	2.9	3.1	-
% Foreign Born..........	6.9	10.2	4.4	8.4	4.3	4.0	-
% Living In Group Quarters........	0.0	0.0	0.0	0.0	0.0	0.0	-
% 13 Years Old And Under........	16.8	16.2	16.6	17.5	16.4	17.8	-
% 14-20 Years Old.............	11.5	11.1	14.4	11.6	11.0	11.6	-
% 21-64 Years Old.............	59.9	60.9	57.3	55.8	57.9	62.1	-
% 65-74 Years Old.............	8.2	8.5	8.4	10.0	9.4	6.0	-
% 75 Years Old And Over........	3.7	3.3	3.3	5.1	5.4	2.5	-
% In Different House........	40.7	48.4	38.4	40.3	28.4	38.3	-
% Families With Female Head......	16.0	12.8	12.8	28.0	17.4	16.6	-
Median School Years Completed....	12.3	12.3	12.3	12.3	12.1	12.6	-
Median Family Income, 1979......$$	25628	25991	26849	18582	24616	27038	-
% Income Below Poverty Level....	5.0	3.3	4.3	12.9	6.4	4.0	-
% Income Of $30,000 Or More.....	36.8	37.0	40.9	25.1	34.6	40.9	-
% White Collar Workers.........	50.5	50.6	45.1	41.1	49.2	55.9	-
% Civilian Labor Force Unemployed....	7.1	7.3	6.8	8.4	7.9	6.2	-
% Riding To Work By Automobile....	87.0	88.1	83.8	78.5	86.7	89.3	-
Mean Commuting Time - Minutes...	25.3	25.4	23.3	21.2	25.0	27.4	-
Population Per Household........	2.5	2.5	2.8	2.3	2.5	2.6	-
Total Housing Units..........	16247	6320	1296	1813	2854	3964	0
% Condominiums..............	4.7	1.1	0.0	0.0	3.0	15.2	-
% Built 1970 Or Later.........	35.4	58.5	16.2	8.0	11.3	34.6	-
% Owner Occupied.............	59.4	53.5	72.6	42.4	65.8	67.8	-
% With 1+ Persons Per Room......	2.8	3.2	3.4	4.1	1.7	2.1	-
Median Value: Owner Units.......$$	49000	61000	46600	32700	44400	45800	-
Median Rent: Rental Units.......$$	239	258	218	174	185	276	-
Median Number Of Rooms: All Units.	4.8	4.7	4.9	4.5	5.0	5.0	-

Calumet City
Selected Characteristics of Census Tracts: 1970

Tract Number	TOTAL	8258	8259	8260	8261	8262	8279
Total Population.............	33107	8154	3752	4899	7547	9221	5064
% Male..................	49.5	50.4	50.2	48.2	48.8	49.5	49.9
% Black.................	0.1	0.0	0.2	0.3	0.0	0.1	0.0
% Other Nonwhite.........	0.2	0.3	0.3	0.4	0.1	0.2	0.2
% Of Spanish Language......	1.4	2.1	0.9	0.3	1.7	1.8	2.4
% Foreign Born..........	3.9	3.6	3.2	7.0	5.0	1.8	3.3
% Living In Group Quarters......	0.2	0.0	0.4	0.3	0.0	0.4	0.0
% 13 Years Old And Under........	27.3	28.2	27.2	24.1	22.1	32.5	32.0
% 14-20 Years Old.............	11.7	8.8	12.8	11.3	12.4	13.4	12.4
% 21-64 Years Old.............	54.7	59.3	54.5	54.0	55.1	50.7	51.4
% 65-74 Years Old.............	4.3	2.9	3.5	7.0	6.9	2.4	2.8
% 75 Years Old And Over........	2.0	0.9	1.9	3.5	3.6	1.0	1.4
% In Different House........	54.4	23.4	64.8	50.4	66.9	68.3	53.3
% Families With Female Head.......	7.5	4.4	6.9	13.0	10.0	5.0	4.5
Median School Years Completed.......	12.1	12.3	11.9	10.4	11.4	12.3	12.2
Median Family Income, 1969......$$	11823	12651	11570	9712	11186	12713	12763
% Income Below Poverty Level....	3.4	1.2	1.7	10.4	3.2	2.8	2.7
% Income of $15,000 or More.....	26.0	30.3	22.1	15.2	27.1	29.3	33.4
% White Collar Workers.........	24.5	29.6	19.0	16.8	22.4	27.5	27.7
% Civilian Labor Force Unemployed.	2.9	3.0	1.8	4.0	3.2	2.6	1.6
% Riding To Work By Automobile....	82.8	85.9	82.1	75.5	82.5	85.1	88.1
Population Per Household..........	3.1	2.9	3.4	3.4	3.2	3.0	3.7
Total Housing Units..........	10862	2875	1133	1905	2631	2460	1409
% Condominiums & Cooperatives.....	0.1	0.2	0.0	0.0	0.0	0.0	0.0
% Built 1960 Or Later.........	34.1	87.1	25.4	5.5	9.2	24.2	31.4
% Owner Occupied.................	62.4	52.6	72.1	42.3	65.9	81.7	83.8
% With 1+ Persons Per Room......	7.7	6.9	9.9	7.2	5.9	10.0	8.1
Median Value: Owner Units.......$$	19300	24200	19900	14000	18500	18700	19400
Median Rent: Rental Units.......$$	121	145	110	88	93	141	145
Median Number Of Rooms: All Units.	4.8	4.6	4.9	4.4	4.9	5.2	5.3

Chicago Heights

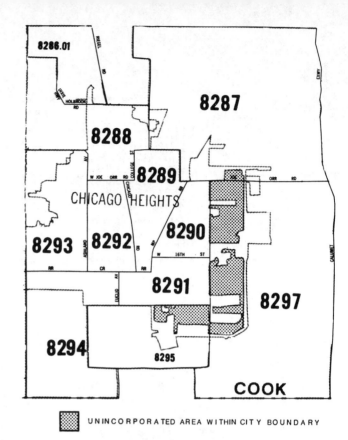

UNINCORPORATED AREA WITHIN CITY BOUNDARY

In a setting of factories and mills is Chicago Heights, a city whose population numbers approximately 37,000. It is located in the southeastern corner of Cook County, twenty-four miles south of the Loop. It is a city indebted to industry for its welfare and growth.

Migrants to what was then known as the Thorn Grove settlement began to arrive in 1832 after the resolution of the Black Hawk War. The early settlers were of Scotch and Irish descent and made their way to northern Illinois by way of the Sauk Trail. The first white settler, Absolam Wells, came in the Spring of 1833, but the first permanent settler in Thorn Grove was Adam Brown. He built the first log cabin at 13th Street and Chicago Road. Dominating the settlement were members of four families of Scottish descent who found the gently rolling prairies and magnificent forest a wonderful place to live. The families included the McCoys and the McEldowneys. Most settlers lived along two roads, the Hubbard Trail, which came from Vincennes, and the Sauk Trail which originated in Detroit. The village was inhabited by more than 100 people in 1849, with a store and a few outlying farmhouses.

Thorn Grove became Bloom in 1849 in honor of a German patriot, Robert Bluhm. By this time, settlers had come from the eastern part of the United States as well as Eastern Europe and Switzerland. In 1853, the Joliet and Northern Indiana Railroad ran a branch line into Bloom for the convenience of the farmers. The town of Bloom responded liberally to President Lincoln's call for volunteers during the Civil War. About 44 men enlisted, many of them being members of the 8th Illinois Cavalry, which fought in the Battle of Gettysburg.

The Chicago and Eastern Illinois Railroad built tracks in 1869 and with the railroads came the end of isolation and the beginning of business activity. By 1876, Bloom was a small agricultural community with 1,500 residents with large and small farms, small industrial shops, five stores and a school.

The present name and industrial character of Chicago Heights dates from 1890. The Chicago Heights Land Association, headed by Charles Wacker, a well-known Chicago businessman, and Martin Kilgallen purchased 4,000 acres at $125 per acre, then persuaded manufacturers to establish plants there. The land, which had a limestone base under the soil, was appealing because it could support the weight of heavy industry. The offer of free land, low water rates, a splendid transportation system, sufficient housing for workers and shipping rates comparable to Chicago interested, among the early business enterprises, Inland Steel, which built a plant in 1893. Inland Steel played a major role in the economic success of the community and helped attract other industries to the area.

Among the other business concerns were the Victoria Hotel, designed by Louis Sullivan, at the Northwest corner of Halsted and Illinois streets, McEldowney and Company Bank, on Calumet Street, Monarch Motor Company and the American Brake Shoe and Foundry Company.

Bloom was incorporated as the Village of Chicago Heights on September 24, 1892, by a unanimous vote of the townspeople. The name Chicago Heights came from the fact the area is located on the Valparaiso Moraine, 694 feet above sea level, one of the highest elevations in Cook County. In 1901, Chicago Heights was incorporated as a city.

With the growth of industry came increased population. Most of those coming to Chicago Heights were foreign-born citizens who were recruited by labor contractors in Eastern and Southern Europe. Economics, the need for work and labor contractors also drew black and Mexican immigrants from the southwestern United States and Mexico. Ethnic neighborhoods developed and one, called "The Hill", was comprised mostly of Italians, Poles, Czechs and other European

people. Industrial plants and millworkers' houses occupied the East side of the city and the West side consisted of more spacious residences of mill officials and Chicago commuters.

The city's Carnegie Library was erected with a $15,000 gift from Andrew Carnegie in 1902. Services were needed by the increasing population, and a transportation system was designed. St. James Hospital opened a 50-bed unit in 1911 and, in 1913, a new post office was built at the intersection of 16th and Halsted streets. About the same time, the Chicago Heights Country Club developed on 52 acres of land.

By the turn of the century, the population was more than 5,000. In 1910, it was almost 15,000 and, in 1920, nearly 20,000. As an industrial satellite city, rather than a suburb, Chicago Heights experienced phenomenal growth until the Depression of the 1930s. During that decade there was virtually no change. More than one-half of the city's population was on relief rolls or employed in one of the federal government's work-making projects. Three city banks failed — First State, Commercial, and First National — and business firms found the going harder than ever. On some days, they made no sales at all. Teachers were paid in scrip, or "promissory" money. The construction of Bloom High School was completed in 1934 and recently it became the first suburban school to be listed in the National Registry of Historic Places, for an architectural style emphasizing geometric form popular during the Depression. During Prohibition, Chicago Heights became notorious when some citizens were involved in violation of the 18th Amendment because of the illegal production and sale of liquor.

Some new industry was attracted to the city when it became accessible for shipping through the completion of the Calumet Waterway in 1935 and, with the advent of World War II, there was again prosperity in Chicago Heights. The number of residents increased by about 2,000. Expansion of businesses continued after 1950, facilitated by the work of a committee which had some success in attracting new industry. The population increased during the 1950s by 29 percent, most of which was accounted for by the annexation of an area known as Beacon Hills.

The years after the war brought changes. The black population grew from 10 percent in 1940 to 19 percent in 1980. By 1960, the number of school-aged children had increased dramatically. Children under 18 years now constituted 38 percent of the population. Kennedy School was opened in 1964, and the new Bloom Freshman-Sophomore di-

Chicago Heights
Population and Housing Characteristics, 1930-1980

	1980	1970	1960	1950	1940	1930
Total Population........	37,026	40,900	34,331	24,551	22,461	22,321
% Male..................	48.0	48.8	49.3	49.4	50.4	51.9
% Female................	52.0	51.2	50.7	50.6	49.6	48.1
% White.................	65.1	82.0	80.9	83.2	90.1	89.5
% Black.................	28.8	17.4	19.0	16.8	9.9	9.9
% Other Nonwhite Races...	6.1	0.6	0.1	0.0	0.0	0.6
% Under 5 Years Old.....	8.5	10.0	14.5	10.3	7.2	8.9
% 5-19 Years Old.........	27.5	31.9	26.1	20.7	25.4	32.3
% 20-44 Years Old.......	34.5	31.5	35.1	41.4	41.8	39.8
% 45-64 Years Old.......	19.9	19.5	17.2	20.3	20.9	16.0
% 65 Years and Older.....	9.6	7.1	7.1	7.3	4.7	3.0
Median School Years....	12.3	11.9	10.1	8.8	7.9	*
Total Housing Units....	12,730	12,340	10,036	7,054	5,867	*
% In One-Unit Structures.	58.0	57.1	60.3	*	*	*
% Owner Occupied........	59.2	57.8	57.9	47.6	42.8	*
% Renter Occupied........	37.1	38.3	37.3	50.5	55.5	*
% Vacant................	3.7	3.9	4.8	1.9	1.7	*
% 1+ Persons per Room....	7.4	11.0	12.4	12.3	*	*

Place 1055 — Chicago Heights , Illinois
Selected Characteristics of Census Tracts: 1980

Tract Number	Total	8286.01	8287	8288	8289	8290	8291	8292	8293	8294	8295
Total Population.............	37026	96	640	6525	3505	4324	5383	5776	8139	2592	46
% Male........................	48.0	–	41.6	49.5	49.6	45.1	49.5	47.9	46.8	49.1	–
% Black.......................	28.8	–	36.4	8.8	3.3	94.4	18.6	3.3	26.2	89.0	–
% Other Nonwhite..............	6.2	–	1.1	1.2	11.4	1.9	21.0	4.9	2.6	3.5	–
% Of Spanish Origin...........	11.4	–	1.4	2.3	19.8	4.5	35.7	11.1	6.9	4.5	–
% Foreign Born................	6.6	–	1.3	5.0	10.6	1.7	15.1	6.7	3.8	4.5	–
% Living In Group Quarters....	1.1	–	0.0	0.0	0.2	0.0	0.1	3.6	2.5	0.0	–
% 13 Years Old And Under......	24.1	–	29.7	21.0	20.9	30.3	24.9	16.5	25.2	36.1	–
% 14-20 Years Old.............	13.9	–	12.0	15.3	12.6	16.0	13.7	11.5	12.3	19.9	–
% 21-64 Years Old.............	52.4	–	52.0	57.7	54.0	45.6	48.7	57.3	53.5	41.9	–
% 65-74 Years Old.............	6.2	–	4.7	4.3	8.2	5.4	8.5	9.0	5.6	1.5	–
% 75 Years Old And Over.......	3.3	–	1.6	1.7	4.2	2.8	4.2	5.6	3.3	0.6	–
% In Different House..........	41.1	–	39.4	34.4	51.2	39.4	40.3	38.3	48.2	32.4	–
% Families With Female Head...	26.9	–	56.2	9.1	21.6	63.4	23.7	14.8	26.8	31.7	–
Median School Years Completed...	12.3	–	12.4	12.7	11.8	11.0	9.2	12.5	12.5	12.3	–
Median Family Income, 1979.....$$	21206	–	18750	28008	17457	9738	18670	23049	22580	17561	–
% Income Below Poverty Level...	12.9	–	20.4	3.2	14.8	34.1	15.1	6.5	13.4	11.2	–
% Income Of $30,000 Or More.....	27.4	–	18.0	44.0	16.4	8.9	21.4	30.6	31.1	15.9	–
% White Collar Workers........	46.8	–	49.8	59.8	34.7	29.4	34.9	47.5	55.5	32.1	–
% Civilian Labor Force Unemployed.	8.9	–	12.8	6.5	7.2	16.7	13.8	7.4	6.5	12.2	–
% Riding To Work By Automobile....	86.7	–	84.9	86.2	89.3	75.5	87.0	90.3	86.3	90.0	–
Mean Commuting Time - Minutes...	22.4	–	19.1	27.8	16.2	18.2	18.5	20.7	24.6	25.1	–
Population Per Household.......	3.1	–	2.6	3.3	2.7	3.3	3.0	2.6	3.0	4.7	–
Total Housing Units..........	12728	28	289	1987	1443	1438	1940	2173	2813	596	21
% Condominiums................	0.2	–	0.0	0.0	0.0	0.8	0.0	0.0	0.4	0.0	–
% Built 1970 Or Later.........	13.1	–	81.9	2.4	9.1	4.5	12.5	1.2	26.5	24.4	–
% Owner Occupied..............	57.9	–	13.1	93.3	49.1	26.2	44.3	67.5	56.3	74.5	–
% With 1+ Persons Per Room....	7.4	–	2.9	2.7	3.8	15.5	11.7	3.1	5.9	26.0	–
Median Value: Owner Units.......$$	45800	–	–	52500	39000	23200	28300	46900	52900	28700	–
Median Rent: Rental Units.....$$	186	–	311	202	205	121	157	193	246	201	–
Median Number Of Rooms: All Units.	5.2	–	4.4	5.6	4.9	4.8	5.0	5.5	5.1	5.3	–

Tract Number	8297
Total Population.............	0
% Male........................	–
% Black.......................	–
% Other Nonwhite..............	–
% Of Spanish Origin...........	–
% Foreign Born................	–
% Living In Group Quarters....	–
% 13 Years Old And Under......	–
% 14-20 Years Old.............	–
% 21-64 Years Old.............	–
% 65-74 Years Old.............	–
% 75 Years Old And Over.......	–
% In Different House..........	–
% Families With Female Head......	–
Median School Years Completed....	–
Median Family Income, 1979......$$	–
% Income Below Poverty Level...	–
% Income Of $30,000 Or More.....	–
% White Collar Workers........	–
% Civilian Labor Force Unemployed.	–
% Riding To Work By Automobile....	–
Mean Commuting Time - Minutes...	–
Population Per Household..........	–
Total Housing Units..........	0
% Condominiums................	–
% Built 1970 Or Later..............	–
% Owner Occupied...............	–
% With 1+ Persons Per Room......$$	–
Median Value: Owner Units.......$$	–
Median Rent: Rental Units.....$$	–
Median Number Of Rooms: All Units.	–

vision on Sauk Trial opened its doors to 1,050 freshmen in September, 1964. The number of inhabitants grew to more than 40,000 in 1970.

A 1971 neighborhood analysis revealed concentrated areas of blight on the east side of the city near the industrial area. At the same time, the downtown area had deteriorated. Since the later 1970s Chicago Heights has added a $3.2 million bank-office building, a new city hall, a new police station, and most recently, the Otto Mall. The Otto Mall houses the post office and has spaces for other businesses. These attempts to revitalize the downtown area have been met with competition from outlying shopping centers and a generally declining economy.

The commission form of government has been in existence since 1921, with a mayor and four commissioners elected for four-year terms. School Districts 170 and 206 levy their own taxes and have their own school boards. The Jones Community Center, first organized in 1917 to assist new immigrants, still stands on East 15th Street, supported by voluntary contributions, and provides a food pantry, services for senior citizens, a nursery and an after-school program for children. Bloom Community College was opened in 1958 and has been renamed Prairie State University.

In the early 1960s a 172-family unit public housing project was constructed on the east side. Two other public housing units, Golden Towers I and II, were built in 1971 for senior citizens. Since 1976, the city has received more than $8 million in community development block grants for the rehabilitation of the city and restoration of aged housing.

The population has decreased 9.5 percent since the historic high in 1970. Unlike other "empty nest" suburbs, Chicago Heights has re-

Chicago Heights
Selected Characteristics of Census Tracts: 1970

Tract Number	TOTAL	8286	8287	8288	8289	8290	8291	8292	8293	8294	8295
Total Population	40900	10287	7425	10215	4839	5750	6412	6326	8832	7291	4923
% Male	48.8	48.8	51.8	49.6	48.8	48.6	49.0	47.3	48.8	50.3	48.2
% Black	17.4	0.1	0.4	0.8	2.7	87.6	20.2	0.1	1.4	8.8	0.1
% Other Nonwhite	0.6	0.2	0.4	0.4	0.9	1.1	0.7	0.4	0.3	1.1	0.4
% Of Spanish Language	7.1	0.5	0.6	0.1	15.0	7.3	17.6	2.7	2.6	5.9	6.3
% Foreign Born	6.2	3.6	3.5	4.7	10.2	1.7	8.6	8.3	5.8	6.2	8.0
% Living In Group Quarters	0.6	0.0	2.9	0.1	0.7	0.8	0.2	0.3	1.1	0.2	1.7
% 13 Years Old And Under	30.7	26.6	35.3	33.8	23.2	37.2	28.9	23.1	30.2	37.1	25.4
% 14-20 Years Old	12.6	13.7	11.4	12.7	11.1	15.0	13.1	11.8	13.1	10.0	12.4
% 21-64 Years Old	49.5	52.0	49.6	49.5	54.6	42.3	49.8	52.4	51.0	50.7	52.8
% 65-74 Years Old	4.4	5.1	2.4	2.7	6.8	4.0	5.1	7.8	3.3	1.5	5.3
% 75 Years Old And Over	2.7	2.5	1.2	1.3	4.2	1.5	3.1	4.8	2.4	0.7	4.1
% In Different House	56.8	51.1	34.9	65.2	46.2	50.7	59.4	64.9	49.5	34.9	70.0
% Families With Female Head	11.3	4.4	4.0	4.1	12.6	27.7	13.8	10.1	7.3	6.2	7.3
Median School Years Completed	12.0	12.8	12.6	12.7	9.3	9.3	8.9	12.1	12.5	12.8	10.8
Median Family Income, 1969 $$	11153	16351	14193	15998	10227	7041	9145	11996	12689	11782	10970
% Income Below Poverty Level	8.4	1.8	1.3	2.5	7.7	24.0	11.4	4.2	4.7	4.1	6.2
% Income of $15,000 or More	27.3	55.5	44.1	53.8	16.7	9.0	16.8	34.9	34.6	30.0	21.2
% White Collar Workers	27.6	52.7	44.2	50.0	17.0	7.0	12.3	36.1	39.9	49.9	16.8
% Civilian Labor Force Unemployed	3.9	2.8	1.6	2.7	2.6	8.5	6.0	3.4	2.2	2.5	4.5
% Riding To Work By Automobile	80.6	69.3	81.5	79.8	79.1	69.1	79.9	81.5	84.0	74.2	83.7
Population Per Household	3.4	3.4	3.7	3.9	2.8	3.9	3.3	3.0	3.5	3.6	3.1
Total Housing Units	12339	3018	2051	2665	1866	1558	1974	2190	2595	2041	1566
% Condominiums & Cooperatives	0.0	3.5	1.3	0.0	0.0	0.0	0.0	0.0	0.0	46.7	0.4
% Built 1960 Or Later	21.7	44.3	78.9	32.9	10.6	10.2	3.9	4.1	47.2	9.5	19.2
% Owner Occupied	57.8	90.9	79.4	93.4	40.9	31.1	42.6	65.5	64.6	31.0	67.0
% With 1+ Persons Per Room	11.0	2.3	6.0	7.1	7.8	25.2	13.8	5.6	6.8	7.9	9.7
Median Value: Owner Units $$	21000	30200	27000	24600	16300	14800	12900	20800	24700	16100	17400
Median Rent: Rental Units $$	94	137	165	117	90	77	86	102	137	130	94
Median Number Of Rooms: All Units	5.1	6.1	5.8	5.9	4.5	4.6	4.8	5.3	5.3	5.3	4.8

Tract Number	8297
Total Population	6208
% Male	48.4
% Black	79.5
% Other Nonwhite	1.3
% Of Spanish Language	3.6
% Foreign Born	0.8
% Living In Group Quarters	0.6
% 13 Years Old And Under	41.7
% 14-20 Years Old	17.0
% 21-64 Years Old	37.6
% 65-74 Years Old	2.4
% 75 Years Old And Over	1.3
% In Different House	40.3
% Families With Female Head	17.7
Median School Years Completed	10.2
Median Family Income, 1969 $$	8936
% Income Below Poverty Level	23.7
% Income of $15,000 or More	16.4
% White Collar Workers	10.5
% Civilian Labor Force Unemployed	11.1
% Riding To Work By Automobile	80.6
Population Per Household	4.8
Total Housing Units	1394
% Condominiums & Cooperatives	5.2
% Built 1960 Or Later	57.7
% Owner Occupied	54.9
% With 1+ Persons Per Room	32.7
Median Value: Owner Units $$	16900
Median Rent: Rental Units $$	71
Median Number Of Rooms: All Units	5.1

mained youthful; nearly a third of the current population is less than 18 years old. The largest white ancestry group is Italian, many of whom serve in city administration. Unlike most suburbs, substantial numbers of black (29 percent) and Hispanic (11 percent) people live in Chicago Heights. About one-third of the labor force works within the city limits. The median family income is larger than that of Chicago. Unemployment, paralleling national averages, had risen to more than 10 percent in 1983. Approximately 37 percent are employed in blue-collar occupations. Thirteen percent of all residents were living below the poverty level in 1979.

Though the number of permits for new construction continues to decline, the quantity of housing units in Chicago Heights has increased by 20 percent since 1960. Percentages of single-family and owner-occupied units have edged upward during that time, and the percentage of overcrowded units has dropped. Compared to other suburbs, the cost of single-family housing in Chicago Heights is modest; the median value of owner-occupied homes is lower than in Chicago.

Today, after the proliferation of other suburbs, the virtual demise of its once-bustling downtown business district, the decline of the railroad and the shift away from heavy industry, Chicago Heights is no longer a rapid-growth community and much of the dynamism of the turn of the century community boosters is gone. Current growth is limited by the lack of large parcels of land suitable for residential development. City officials actively continue attempts at attracting new businesses and industries.

Patricia Booth Levenberg

Cicero

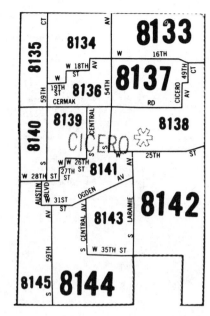

Cicero, named for the statesman and orator, is located eight miles west of Chicago's Loop on 5.8 square miles of land. It is bounded by Chicago on the north and east, Stickney on the south and Berwyn on the west. It is the largest incorporated town and the second largest industrial center in the state. Cicero's character has been influenced by the high proportion of Eastern European residents who came to the town in the early decades of this century. Over the years they have given Cicero an ethnic character which can be seen in the shops and restaurants.

In the mid-1800s there were about 10 families living on the swampy lowlands which became Cicero. The Galena and Chicago Union Railroad began operating through the area in 1849, and in 1857 a township government was formed. The town was named on the suggestion of Augustus Porter after his hometown of Cicero, New York. At the first election nine of the 14 total voters were elected to office. The same year two more railroads were built through the township: the Galena and Chicago Union Railroad through the north portion and the Chicago, Alton and St. Louis Railroad through the south. The construction of various improvements such as drainage ditches and roads connecting the township settlements drew workers to the area. William Ogden supervised the draining of a shallow fork of the Chicago River (known as "Mud Lake" or "Ogden's Ditch" into the Des Plaines River.

Cicero grew slowly until the Civil War when its farmlands increased in value and drew many homesteaders from the East. In 1863 the Chicago, Burlington and Quincy Railroad was built through the township with trains running the next year. Cicero was changed from a governmental to an incorporated town by a special charter in 1863. In 1869 Cicero received a city charter which called for local self government and interdicted high taxation. Construction of drainage systems and road building were major activities at this time. By 1869 the population was estimated at 3,000, which was substantially reduced that year with an annexation to Chicago leaving 1,545 people counted in the 1870 census. Annexations by Chicago also occurred in 1889 and 1899 as the city expanded westward. The incorporations of Oak Park and Berwyn in 1901 left Cicero within its present boundaries.

Two early land speculators were Hetty Green and Porteus Weare, who encouraged the delineation of boulevards when the area was still covered by cornfields. Weare built a 20-room frame house on the northeast corner of 52nd Avenue and 25th Street and named it Ranch 47.

The town's growth pattern was unique. Rather than spreading out from a central point, several small disparate settlements developed in widely-separated areas. Morton Park was the hub along the Burlington Railway; Hawthorne grew up to the east by limestone quarries; Grant Works was an area of company-built homes near the Grant Locomotive Works, which moved to Cicero in 1890 and went bankrupt two years later; other sections include Clyde, Drexel and Warren Park. As roads improved and railroad transportation progressed these separate enclaves converged, so that by 1900 Cicero was a settled community with a population of 16,310.

The excellent rail transportation and low tax rates drew both industry and residents to the town. The population more than tripled from 1910 to 1920. The largest employer, the Hawthorne Works of the Western Electric Company opened in 1903 and by 1922 had expanded to include all operations formerly handled in New York. By 1930 there were at least 115 factories and workshops in Cicero.

The relatively low taxes which had attracted industry to Cicero in turn enabled it to maintain low taxes and draw more residents. Thus between 1910 and 1930 Cicero's population more than quadrupled, rising to 66,602 in 1930. The Depression was felt deeply by Cicero

with its industrial concentration, and population declined slightly during the 1930s. Population increased during the 1940s and again in the 1950s to a peak of 69,130 in 1960. Since then the population has decreased, down 3 percent in the 1960s and down 9 percent in the 1970s, resulting in a population of 61,232 in 1980. It is, however, still one of the 10 most populous suburbs of Chicago.

Almost two-thirds of Cicero's housing was built before 1940 and nearly 20 percent antedates 1914. In two of the neighborhoods (Grant Works and Hawthorne) nearly 60 percent of the homes were built before 1914. A third of all housing units in Cicero are single-family dwellings and another third are in two-family structures. Many of the rental units are in three- and six-flat buildings. Forty-seven percent of all units were owner-occupied and the median home value in 1980 was more than $50,000. The more expensive homes (up to about $75,000) are mostly located along Austin Boulevard.

Population figures for Cicero have shown a consistent increase in the proportion of older residents. In 1950 only 7 percent of the population was 65 years of age or more, but that increased to 11 percent in 1960 and to 16 percent in 1980. Otherwise, population composition has changed little over the years. Although other close-in suburbs have become to some extent integrated, Cicero has continued to be overwhelmingly white. In 1980, 9 percent of the population was of Spanish origin, but there were only 74 blacks residing in the town. This situation has led to difficulties in obtaining federal funds for community development and housing rehabilitation which are needed in view of the town's aged housing stock.

Cicero is second only to Chicago on the list of Illinois manufacturing centers and has 150 industrial establishments. Of these the largest has been the Hawthorne Works of Western Electric which in the mid-1960s employed 30,000 workers. The operations cover 141 acres of land in the town. However, since the 1970s, Western Electric has been phasing out the operations here and the plant now employs about 4,200 workers. The plant is scheduled for final shutdown by 1986. This, coupled with the loss a few years ago of a large forging operation, suggests major problems for the aging community. Without the tax revenue from these industrial establishments and the ability to attract federal funds, the community deterioration, which has officials worried, may continue unchecked. The loss of jobs may also encourage more movement of young people and families out of the community. Plans are being made to improve the situation through land clearance and tougher enforcement of building codes as well as a long-range comprehensive plan to modernize the Cermak Road business area with an ethnic "Old World" approach.

Cicero
Population and Housing Characteristics, 1930-1980

	1980	1970	1960	1950	1940	1930
Total Population.......	61,232	67,058	69,130	67,544	64,712	66,602
% Male....................	48.4	48.4	49.0	49.6	50.5	51.5
% Female..................	51.6	51.6	51.0	50.4	49.5	48.5
% White...................	95.6	99.7	100.0	100.0	100.0	100.0
% Black...................	0.1	0.0	0.0	0.0	0.0	0.0
% Other Nonwhite Races...	4.3	0.3	0.0	0.0	0.0	0.0
% Under 5 Years Old......	6.3	7.2	8.8	8.8	6.1	7.5
% 5-19 Years Old.........	20.1	21.3	21.1	17.4	20.7	28.7
% 20-44 Years Old........	34.1	31.2	33.1	41.8	45.2	44.9
% 45-64 Years Old........	23.6	28.1	26.3	24.5	23.3	16.0
% 65 Years and Older.....	15.9	12.2	10.7	7.5	4.7	2.9
Median School Years....	11.9	11.1	9.7	8.8	8.3	*
Total Housing Units....	25,870	25,393	23,938	20,842	18,165	*
% In One-Unit Structures.	31.5	32.7	39.1	*	*	*
% Owner Occupied.........	48.5	49.5	53.3	52.2	46.3	*
% Renter Occupied........	47.4	47.7	43.7	46.6	52.3	*
% Vacant.................	4.1	2.8	3.0	1.2	1.4	*
% 1+ Persons per Room....	3.5	4.8	5.6	8.3	11.9	*

Place 1085 — Cicero, Illinois
Selected Characteristics of Census Tracts: 1980

Tract Number	Total	8133	8134	8135	8136	8137	8138	8139	8140	8141	8142
Total Population............	61232	5951	5509	4992	3373	5420	6166	4585	3353	2962	5609
% Male........................	48.4	49.5	47.6	47.7	46.9	47.8	50.0	48.2	46.5	48.3	50.7
% Black.......................	0.1	0.0	0.0	0.0	0.0	0.0	0.0	0.5	0.0	0.1	0.8
% Other Nonwhite.............	4.2	6.9	2.7	2.0	3.2	9.8	7.6	4.5	2.8	2.3	4.3
% Of Spanish Origin..........	8.6	22.5	7.2	3.0	5.7	15.7	12.9	7.4	4.5	5.6	8.3
% Foreign Born...............	13.3	23.4	12.9	11.7	15.9	21.8	14.4	16.3	12.5	13.3	7.6
% Living In Group Quarters...	1.2	0.0	0.0	0.0	0.0	0.0	0.3	8.9	0.0	0.0	5.6
% 13 Years Old And Under.....	17.7	24.8	19.3	15.4	15.3	17.9	19.9	16.2	13.6	17.5	18.5
% 14-20 Years Old............	10.3	11.1	11.8	10.5	11.3	9.2	10.2	9.3	8.6	10.2	10.8
% 21-64 Years Old............	56.0	52.4	54.3	55.1	55.3	56.3	55.4	52.7	55.2	57.2	58.1
% 65-74 Years Old............	10.3	7.3	9.2	11.6	11.6	10.4	9.0	12.7	14.3	9.7	8.8
% 75 Years Old And Over......	5.6	4.4	5.3	7.3	6.5	6.3	5.4	9.1	8.2	5.4	3.8
% In Different House.........	42.9	60.1	44.6	40.1	37.9	42.0	52.1	40.9	36.1	48.9	51.0
% Families With Female Head..	20.2	29.1	18.0	16.0	22.9	19.5	21.0	22.0	17.2	26.3	22.9
Median School Years Completed	11.9	10.4	12.0	12.1	11.4	11.9	11.8	11.3	12.0	11.1	11.8
Median Family Income, 1979....$$	20804	17715	22149	22491	21144	20536	18145	19536	21167	19312	18665
% Income Below Poverty Level....	6.8	13.0	3.7	5.8	6.0	7.3	9.1	7.7	3.5	7.4	9.5
% Income Of $30,000 Or More.....	23.5	15.3	28.1	27.1	26.9	19.3	15.6	23.7	27.3	14.9	20.9
% White Collar Workers........	44.7	34.3	46.1	50.0	45.6	45.6	38.0	47.0	49.3	42.0	40.9
% Civilian Labor Force Unemployed.	6.4	7.6	7.2	5.6	5.0	7.1	6.4	11.5	4.1	6.4	7.0
% Riding To Work By Automobile....	72.7	63.4	77.1	73.3	68.8	67.0	64.4	71.3	69.6	66.1	74.3
Mean Commuting Time - Minutes	24.3	23.5	23.7	24.2	25.0	27.2	25.0	25.7	22.2	27.9	23.6
Population Per Household...........	2.5	2.6	2.7	2.5	2.4	2.4	2.4	2.4	2.3	2.3	2.5
Total Housing Units...........	25861	2573	2146	2112	1488	2353	2808	1832	1493	1410	2318
% Condominiums................	0.0	0.0	0.0	0.0	0.0	0.0	0.0	0.0	0.0	0.0	0.0
% Built 1970 Or Later.........	2.7	3.3	0.0	0.4	1.4	1.6	1.1	3.0	0.7	2.1	6.8	4.2
% Owner Occupied..............	47.3	27.6	55.8	51.2	48.4	36.8	34.3	48.5	52.4	36.2	38.9
% With 1+ Persons Per Room.......$$	3.5	8.2	3.0	1.8	2.1	3.8	4.7	3.5	1.9	3.6	3.9
Median Value: Owner Units........$$	50800	36000	47500	54000	45900	47100	43800	46800	52200	38100	41500
Median Rent: Rental Units........$$	186	170	191	201	186	185	175	190	187	182	167
Median Number Of Rooms: All Units.	4.7	4.4	5.2	5.2	4.6	4.9	4.5	4.5	4.9	4.1	4.4

Tract Number	8143	8144	8145
Total Population............	3126	6155	4031
% Male........................	48.2	48.4	47.7
% Black.......................	0.0	0.0	0.0
% Other Nonwhite.............	2.5	1.4	1.5
% Of Spanish Origin..........	5.8	3.0	1.6
% Foreign Born...............	6.9	4.9	8.4
% Living In Group Quarters...	0.0	0.4	0.0
% 13 Years Old And Under.....	17.4	16.1	13.8
% 14-20 Years Old............	10.8	10.0	10.2
% 21-64 Years Old............	58.0	60.5	58.2
% 65-74 Years Old............	9.5	9.9	12.8
% 75 Years Old And Over......	4.3	3.6	5.0
% In Different House.........	37.4	33.3	23.5
% Families With Female Head..	18.1	14.7	10.6
Median School Years Completed	12.0	12.1	12.2
Median Family Income, 1979....$$	22384	23349	24395
% Income Below Poverty Level....	5.2	6.0	1.7
% Income Of $30,000 Or More.....	26.7	27.1	33.8
% White Collar Workers........	41.0	51.9	52.2
% Civilian Labor Force Unemployed.	5.6	6.2	2.1
% Riding To Work By Automobile....	81.3	85.1	81.1
Mean Commuting Time - Minutes...	22.2	23.1	22.9
Population Per Household...........	2.5	2.6	2.6
Total Housing Units...........	1287	2400	1641
% Condominiums................	0.0	0.0	0.0
% Built 1970 Or Later.........	1.6	4.8	4.2
% Owner Occupied..............	56.2	70.9	73.2
% With 1+ Persons Per Room.......	3.7	4.2	1.8
Median Value: Owner Units........$$	53100	56600	60600
Median Rent: Rental Units........$$	204	219	217
Median Number Of Rooms: All Units.	4.7	5.0	4.8

Cicero
Selected Characteristics of Census Tracts: 1970

Tract Number	TOTAL	8133	8134	8135	8136	8137	8138	8139	8140	8141	8142
Total Population	67058	6633	5959	5493	3685	6023	6778	4455	3837	3450	5716
% Male	48.4	49.9	47.4	47.8	47.5	47.6	49.5	47.4	47.1	48.4	48.7
% Black	0.0	0.0	0.0	0.0	0.0	0.0	0.0	0.0	0.0	0.0	0.0
% Other Nonwhite	0.3	0.0	0.9	0.4	0.2	0.1	0.5	0.3	0.2	0.3	0.2
% Of Spanish Language	1.3	1.1	1.4	2.0	2.2	1.6	2.6	0.4	1.7	2.0	0.5
% Foreign Born	12.4	17.5	14.3	13.2	16.8	19.2	10.8	13.6	10.5	15.0	7.0
% Living In Group Quarters	0.3	0.6	0.1	0.3	0.3	1.0	0.5	0.0	0.3	0.2	0.2
% 13 Years Old And Under	20.0	23.1	20.9	17.5	17.2	17.2	20.1	18.7	16.9	20.5	22.5
% 14-20 Years Old	10.0	9.2	11.1	9.9	9.3	9.0	9.1	10.3	9.4	8.3	10.0
% 21-64 Years Old	57.8	57.2	55.7	56.4	58.3	58.5	57.4	56.6	57.4	58.6	58.0
% 65-74 Years Old	7.8	6.1	7.8	10.6	9.2	9.4	8.8	8.8	10.7	7.6	6.2
% 75 Years Old And Over	4.4	4.4	4.6	5.7	6.1	5.8	4.6	5.7	5.6	5.0	3.3
% In Different House	68.1	62.7	65.7	66.5	73.3	63.1	58.8	69.7	61.5	58.8	78.4
% Families With Female Head	11.4	12.9	9.8	12.2	12.3	13.5	12.4	12.4	11.4	10.9	11.9
Median School Years Completed	10.7	10.0	11.1	11.2	10.3	10.7	10.4	10.2	10.9	10.6	10.5
Median Family Income, 1969....$$	11265	10612	11215	11591	11036	11357	11009	10815	10812	11093	10674
% Income Below Poverty Level	4.2	3.9	5.2	4.7	5.0	4.1	3.8	6.9	3.9	5.2	4.3
% Income of $15,000 or More	23.6	19.4	24.2	25.5	21.0	26.8	21.5	20.2	24.0	21.4	17.7
% White Collar Workers	19.5	15.0	20.3	28.8	16.6	20.5	17.8	16.0	23.0	18.2	16.4
% Civilian Labor Force Unemployed	2.8	2.9	4.6	2.2	2.2	2.6	3.0	2.4	2.1	2.0	2.3
% Riding To Work By Automobile	64.5	49.9	61.7	69.3	69.5	55.7	51.9	69.1	64.5	58.5	72.2
Population Per Household	2.7	2.7	2.9	2.7	2.6	2.6	2.5	2.6	2.6	2.5	2.7
Total Housing Units	25388	2574	2103	2077	1442	2407	2787	1737	1502	1430	2188
% Condominiums & Cooperatives	0.3	0.2	0.6	0.3	0.4	0.5	0.7	0.0	0.3	0.6	0.0
% Built 1960 Or Later	9.4	10.4	6.5	3.3	3.9	2.9	4.8	7.9	6.8	14.5	7.7
% Owner Occupied	49.2	30.6	57.8	53.4	51.2	36.4	36.2	53.7	52.9	38.6	41.5
% With 1+ Persons Per Room	4.8	7.1	4.0	2.8	3.6	3.4	4.8	4.6	3.2	5.6	6.2
Median Value: Owner Units.......$$	21000	16300	20700	22500	19800	21200	19100	19300	21000	16100	17600
Median Rent: Rental Units.......$$	107	93	111	116	106	106	104	111	114	105	88
Median Number Of Rooms: All Units	4.7	4.4	5.2	5.1	4.6	4.9	4.6	4.5	4.8	4.0	4.3

Tract Number	8143	8144	8145
Total Population	3392	7312	4325
% Male	49.6	48.8	48.6
% Black	0.0	0.0	0.0
% Other Nonwhite	0.0	0.2	0.4
% Of Spanish Language	0.4	0.8	0.4
% Foreign Born	10.5	5.5	8.6
% Living In Group Quarters	0.2	0.3	0.0
% 13 Years Old And Under	22.1	21.9	19.0
% 14-20 Years Old	9.6	12.1	11.1
% 21-64 Years Old	58.5	59.3	60.7
% 65-74 Years Old	6.3	4.9	6.3
% 75 Years Old And Over	3.5	1.9	2.9
% In Different House	85.3	72.3	76.6
% Families With Female Head	10.5	9.3	7.6
Median School Years Completed	10.9	11.3	11.4
Median Family Income, 1969.....$$	11353	12271	12465
% Income Below Poverty Level	1.4	3.1	2.9
% Income of $15,000 or More	23.6	28.6	32.2
% White Collar Workers	19.9	19.4	22.6
% Civilian Labor Force Unemployed	3.9	3.6	2.0
% Riding To Work By Automobile	72.9	81.3	72.0
Population Per Household	2.9	3.1	2.9
Total Housing Units	1214	2424	1503
% Condominiums & Cooperatives	0.0	0.0	0.0
% Built 1960 Or Later	22.1	22.8	15.0
% Owner Occupied	56.3	70.6	77.6
% With 1+ Persons Per Room	5.6	5.8	4.7
Median Value: Owner Units.......$$	21300	21800	23600
Median Rent: Rental Units.......$$	122	135	127
Median Number Of Rooms: All Units	4.7	4.9	4.9

The physical deterioration in Cicero has been affected by the age of the structures, the inability to get federal funding and the loss of tax dollars. The long political debate over the now defunct Crosstown Expressway plan was a contributing factor. Up to 600 parcels of land would have been in the path of the proposed Crosstown route along the Cicero Avenue right of way on the eastern border. Because of the anticipated demolition, these parcels were not well tended and contributed to the physical deterioration in the community.

Cicero is an old town, historically dependent on industry which has kept taxes relatively low and attracted workers for its own and other nearby plants. In the 1930s it was largely made up of foreign-born residents from Eastern Europe (primarily Czechoslovakian). Today many of their descendants are still there. One of every five home-owners has lived in his home for 40 years or more and one of every 10 renters has been in his apartment for 30 years or more.

While Cicero has problems to face in the future with an aging housing stock and the loss of major industries, it still has many attractions. Rail and bus lines criss-cross the suburb providing excellent transportation to and from Chicago and other suburbs, and the Eisenhower and Stevenson Expressways are nearby. The Cermak Road shopping area provides a wide variety of stores and there are five other scattered shopping sites as well at nearby Cermak Plaza in Berwyn.

Despite its attractions the town of Cicero, known for its tight-knit ethnic character, has many problems to face in the future. The decade of the 1980s is likely to bring many changes, and at this point few of them appear to be positive.

Gail Danks Welter

Des Plaines

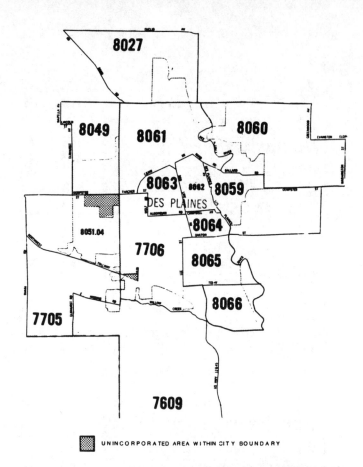

UNINCORPORATED AREA WITHIN CITY BOUNDARY

Des Plaines is in Cook County, about 21 miles northwest of the Loop, just northwest of Park Ridge, and north of O'Hare Airport. The forested site along the Des Plaines River attracted the attention of volunteer soldiers in the Black Hawk War, who marched by on their way to and from that campaign. The first white settler in the area came in 1835. The first industry came in 1841, when Luther Jefferson constructed a large windmill near what is now the southeast corner of Oaktown and Des Plaines avenues. This was soon replaced by a large grist and lumber mill, along with a general store catering to nearby farmers. The lumber mill provided timbers for the Northwestern Plank Road (Milwaukee Avenue), which was built from Chicago to Jefferson Park in the 1840s, and ties for the railroad which came a decade later. A few years later, a flour mill was built on the banks of the Des Plaines River, just north of the present Miner Street bridge and east of River Road (Des Plaines Avenue).

The first survey of the area was in 1851. In 1853, E. Chittenden opened a tavern for the Illinois and Wisconsin Land Company, which had been organized to buy up land along the Illinois and Wisconsin Railroad (later the Chicago and North Western). A small settlement began, which in 1859 received the name "Town of Rand," in honor of Socrates Rand, owner of the flour mill and one of the first settlers.

A number of German families settled in and around the town. They erected the first church, which was Lutheran, in 1876. In 1869, the name of the town was changed to Des Plaines, the name used by the railroad station since 1854. In 1873, Des Plaines was incorporated as a village, bounded approximately by Perry Street, Miner Street, Thacker Street, and Graceland Avenue. When Des Plaines first appeared in the census in 1880, its population was 818.

During the 1880s, the Northwestern Plank Road was extended to Des Plaines. Among the industries in Des Plaines during this period was a brickyard, a cheese and butter factory, and a cider mill. Blacksmithing and horse-shoeing for the nearby farmers were also important. The population increased steadily from 1880 to about 1920, with Des Plaines primarily a service center for the surrounding farmland. Des Plaines became known as the "garden spot of Cook County" and a residence for retired farmers.

Before the onset of paved roads and extensive automobile transportation, Des Plaines was about a day's travel from the Chicago markets. As the Cook County highway system developed, Des Plaines became strategically located at the intersections of Ballard Road, Rand Road, Northwest Highway, and River Road. As Des Plaines became more accessible to the Chicago markets, many of the truck farms in the immdediate area were bought up by speculators and subdividers, and the importance of agriculture in the local economy began to decline.

During the 1920s, all of the northern suburbs experienced rapid population increases. Des Plaines more than doubled in population during this decade, to a total of 8,798 in 1930, but part of this was due to annexations. The village of Riverview, which once had been a more important town than Des Plaines, but whose industrial development was halted by a series of fires, was annexed. By 1926, all streets within the Des Plaines city limits had been paved and the city had attracted several new industries. The Depression brought this period of growth to a stop while Des Plaines was still a town of fewer than 10,000 persons. By 1940, there was little indication of Des Plaines' future as a middle-class residential suburb.

After the Second World War, Des Plaines began a period of rapid growth as a residential, home-owning suburb. One factor in its growth was its favorable location with respect to automobile transportation, making it attractive for suburban tract developments. In 1951, one of Chicago's largest home builders began developing 525 home sites in

the area bounded by Dempster Street, Wolf Road, Algonquin Road, and Second Avenue. As the plans for O'Hare Airport were developed and construction began one-half mile south of Des Plaines, retail business in the city increased. The employment at O'Hare, first in construction, then permanently in its operation, along with the expectation of attracting new industries desirous of a convenient northern suburban location, led Des Plaines officials to anticipate a period of continued rapid growth.

The population of Des Plaines more than doubled between 1950 and 1960, increasing from 14,994 to 34,886. Some of this increase (6,852 persons) was the result of annexations during the decade. In 1960, Germans were still the leading nationality among the foreign stock. Des Plaines continued to grow rapidly during the following decade, increasing by more than 60 percent to 57,239. The rate of growth began to slow during the first half of the 1970s, however, and the total number began to decline in the second half of the decade. The 1980 count showed 53,568 residents, a drop of 6 percent since 1970. This loss can be attributed to several factors—the demolition of some older and dilapidated housing, children growing up and moving away, and an increase in the number of young couples wanting smaller families. In Des Plaines the number of young persons, under 18 years of age, has decreased by almost 7,200, more than a third, in the last decade. This is almost twice the decline in the total population.

The overwhelming majority of the Des Plaines population is white, more than 51,000. There are 160 blacks, compared to five in 1960, and nearly 1,500 of Asian descent, mostly Asian Indians, Filipinos, Koreans and Japanese. Four percent of the population is of Spanish origin.

There was only moderate housing growth in the housing stock in the 1970s, compared to the 70 percent growth in the previous decade. About three-fourths of all Des Plaines housing is in single-family units, and slightly more than three-fourths is owner-occupied. The median values of owner-occupied homes in Des Plaines, $75,500, is 60 percent higher than the median value of Chicago homes.

For a time after the Second World War, Des Plaines tried to control its industrial development by requiring new industrial plants to be built outside the city limits. If plant operations did not generate unacceptable

Des Plaines
Population and Housing Characteristics, 1930-1980

	1980	1970	1960	1950	1940	1930
Total Population	53,568	57,239	34,886	14,994	9,518	8,798
% Male	48.7	49.1	49.4	50.0	49.8	51.4
% Female	51.3	50.9	50.6	50.0	50.2	48.6
% White	95.5	99.3	99.9	99.9	100.0	99.9
% Black	0.3	0.1	0.0	0.0	-	0.1
% Other Nonwhite Races	4.2	0.6	0.1	0.1	0.0	0.1
% Under 5 Years Old	5.4	8.5	12.6	11.8	7.3	8.8
% 5-19 Years Old	23.5	30.5	28.2	22.1	25.0	27.9
% 20-44 Years Old	36.0	33.6	34.7	39.4	40.8	42.0
% 45-64 Years Old	24.5	21.2	18.9	20.6	20.9	16.6
% 65 Years and Older	10.6	6.2	5.6	6.1	6.0	4.7
Median School Years	12.6	12.6	12.2	11.9	8.8	*
Total Housing Units	19,287	17,140	10,151	4,437	2,655	*
% In One-Unit Structures	71.2	73.8	87.2	*	*	*
% Owner Occupied	75.5	75.0	81.1	74.9	54.9	*
% Renter Occupied	22.6	23.0	14.2	20.3	39.5	*
% Vacant	1.9	2.0	4.7	4.8	5.6	*
% 1+ Persons per Room	2.4	5.1	7.5	6.7	*	*

Place 1460 — Des Plaines, Illinois
Selected Characteristics of Census Tracts: 1980

Tract Number	Total	7609	7705	7706	8027	8049	8051.04	8059	8060	8061	8062
Total Population	53568	7	0	5898	639	5397	6511	1377	543	9483	5515
% Male	48.7	-	-	49.7	52.6	49.3	49.7	42.6	50.5	48.3	46.0
% Black	0.3	-	-	0.1	0.0	0.3	0.3	0.3	0.0	0.2	0.1
% Other Nonwhite	4.6	-	-	2.4	1.7	4.2	7.6	3.1	2.2	5.3	3.6
% Of Spanish Origin	4.0	-	-	2.9	2.8	1.2	3.3	3.3	9.0	2.8	6.8
% Foreign Born	11.0	-	-	8.7	9.5	10.3	14.9	13.9	6.2	12.0	9.3
% Living In Group Quarters	1.7	-	-	0.5	26.4	0.0	0.0	28.0	0.0	2.0	0.0
% 13 Years Old And Under	17.5	-	-	16.4	18.0	19.2	19.7	11.8	18.6	17.7	11.5
% 14-20 Years Old	13.1	-	-	14.1	27.7	17.0	13.8	9.2	13.4	13.5	8.8
% 21-64 Years Old	58.9	-	-	59.6	48.0	57.2	60.3	51.9	56.9	59.2	61.0
% 65-74 Years Old	6.4	-	-	6.9	3.9	4.2	3.9	9.7	7.7	5.9	10.5
% 75 Years Old And Over	4.1	-	-	3.0	2.3	2.4	2.2	17.4	3.3	3.6	8.2
% In Different House	41.3	-	-	32.2	27.5	33.2	53.3	59.5	74.7	33.9	58.7
% Families With Female Head	9.8	-	-	7.8	1.6	6.3	10.9	9.1	11.0	8.7	16.7
Median School Years Completed	12.6	-	-	12.5	12.8	12.7	12.7	12.7	12.8	12.7	12.6
Median Family Income, 1979 $$	28807	-	-	30081	37214	31699	27440	30000	32182	31122	25882
% Income Below Poverty Level	2.1	-	-	1.1	0.0	0.8	2.5	2.8	11.3	2.6	1.7
% Income Of $30,000 Or More	46.5	-	-	50.3	70.6	56.6	41.7	50.0	58.9	54.1	40.1
% White Collar Workers	62.6	-	-	57.0	79.9	68.1	61.5	69.2	50.0	66.6	67.6
% Civilian Labor Force Unemployed	3.4	-	-	2.9	0.0	4.6	3.8	2.3	5.6	1.5	2.9
% Riding To Work By Automobile	85.9	-	-	87.0	85.4	88.9	88.1	74.4	91.1	84.7	75.0
Mean Commuting Time - Minutes	23.9	-	-	23.6	20.3	23.9	24.9	25.1	21.3	24.2	25.6
Population Per Household	2.8	-	-	3.0	3.1	3.3	2.8	2.3	3.0	3.0	2.0
Total Housing Units	19281	1	0	2007	150	1665	2376	479	183	3181	2839
% Condominiums	6.0	-	-	0.0	0.0	2.2	7.3	34.7	0.0	0.3	25.0
% Built 1970 Or Later	14.2	-	-	9.9	0.0	8.7	9.6	47.2	21.5	12.1	38.7
% Owner Occupied	75.0	-	-	95.0	98.7	86.2	52.1	58.0	82.0	83.9	38.7
% With 1+ Persons Per Room	2.4	-	-	1.6	0.7	1.7	3.1	1.8	2.8	2.2	2.1
Median Value: Owner Units $$	73800	-	-	72600	87500	89400	84400	80700	75300	78600	66200
Median Rent: Rental Units $$	285	-	-	308	-	311	309	276	250	260	278
Median Number Of Rooms: All Units	5.6	-	-	5.6	5.6	5.6	5.5	4.9	5.6	5.6	4.3

Tract Number	8063	8064	8065	8066
Total Population	4909	2732	6998	3559
% Male	48.5	48.8	49.0	50.0
% Black	0.0	0.1	0.3	0.3
% Other Nonwhite	1.8	1.8	5.3	3.1
% Of Spanish Origin	3.4	3.7	6.5	5.9
% Foreign Born	6.7	7.7	13.6	11.9
% Living In Group Quarters	0.0	5.3	0.0	0.0
% 13 Years Old And Under	16.4	17.0	20.1	20.2
% 14-20 Years Old	11.0	10.4	13.5	12.5
% 21-64 Years Old	59.0	56.1	59.6	59.4
% 65-74 Years Old	9.2	7.9	4.8	5.7
% 75 Years Old And Over	4.3	8.6	2.0	2.2
% In Different House	32.8	43.2	45.9	31.6
% Families With Female Head	10.6	11.3	12.7	6.4
Median School Years Completed	12.7	12.6	12.6	12.4
Median Family Income, 1979 $$	27014	28806	27592	26273
% Income Below Poverty Level	1.2	4.4	1.6	4.0
% Income Of $30,000 Or More	40.1	47.1	42.5	33.5
% White Collar Workers	65.4	63.7	57.1	50.7
% Civilian Labor Force Unemployed	4.1	6.7	2.8	6.6
% Riding To Work By Automobile	84.9	91.4	88.0	92.7
Mean Commuting Time - Minutes	20.7	25.2	23.0	24.3
Population Per Household	2.7	2.8	3.0	2.9
Total Housing Units	1848	953	2332	1267
% Condominiums	0.0	0.0	2.6	0.0
% Built 1970 Or Later	1.7	1.8	6.1	15.9
% Owner Occupied	87.7	78.7	79.6	88.5
% With 1+ Persons Per Room	1.7	2.0	3.5	3.6
Median Value: Owner Units $$	67800	68900	67400	68300
Median Rent: Rental Units $$	241	266	284	179
Median Number Of Rooms: All Units	5.6	5.6	5.5	5.4

Des Plaines
Selected Characteristics of Census Tracts: 1970

Tract Number	TOTAL	7602	8027	8049	8051	8059	8060	8061	8062	8063	8064
Total Population	57239	8360	10771	16036	25709	9388	22462	9577	4981	6891	2874
% Male	49.1	49.4	49.4	49.4	49.8	47.2	48.6	49.4	47.4	49.0	49.0
% Black	0.1	0.0	0.6	0.0	0.2	0.1	0.2	0.1	0.1	0.0	0.0
% Other Nonwhite	0.6	0.4	1.0	0.6	0.9	1.0	0.6	0.6	0.7	0.5	0.0
% Of Spanish Language	2.0	2.9	1.0	0.5	1.7	1.0	1.8	1.7	5.5	0.5	2.3
% Foreign Born	5.7	5.6	5.3	4.2	4.2	6.3	7.5	3.6	8.7	4.9	6.1
% Living In Group Quarters	0.6	0.1	4.6	0.1	0.9	2.8	1.5	0.6	2.0	0.0	0.0
% 13 Years Old And Under	28.6	24.7	34.5	31.3	30.3	27.2	28.4	29.4	22.2	25.1	24.0
% 14-20 Years Old	11.8	12.9	13.3	12.6	9.9	12.8	8.5	12.2	11.0	11.7	12.2
% 21-64 Years Old	53.4	57.5	49.1	50.9	56.6	53.3	58.0	52.8	53.7	54.9	52.2
% 65-74 Years Old	4.0	3.2	1.9	3.3	2.0	3.8	3.1	3.7	7.7	5.7	7.1
% 75 Years Old And Over	2.2	1.7	1.1	1.8	1.2	2.9	2.0	1.9	5.4	2.7	4.5
% In Different House	57.0	52.7	47.0	56.4	29.4	56.1	32.3	62.5	46.2	64.8	62.9
% Families With Female Head	6.0	6.0	3.5	5.0	4.1	4.7	6.3	5.3	11.1	5.8	5.3
Median School Years Completed	12.5	12.4	12.7	12.7	12.8	12.7	12.7	12.6	12.3	12.5	12.2
Median Family Income, 1969....$$	14056	13045	17283	17230	14783	18426	13831	14921	11992	14419	13529
% Income Below Poverty Level	2.2	2.7	1.9	1.7	1.6	1.5	2.4	1.6	1.5	2.5	3.3
% Income of $15,000 or More	42.8	35.8	60.9	59.9	48.4	63.9	41.1	49.4	30.7	46.0	37.4
% White Collar Workers	36.8	29.5	47.7	51.2	47.2	53.1	51.5	41.2	30.7	39.1	31.5
% Civilian Labor Force Unemployed	2.2	1.3	1.3	1.3	1.8	1.7	1.8	1.8	1.8	1.5	2.7
% Riding To Work By Automobile	83.2	88.6	79.9	78.4	86.1	78.0	84.7	81.1	71.3	82.3	82.4
Population Per Household	3.4	3.1	4.0	3.7	3.3	3.5	3.0	3.5	2.8	3.2	3.2
Total Housing Units	17134	2774	2634	4358	8353	2748	8062	2752	1754	2171	925
% Condominiums & Cooperatives	0.2	0.0	0.0	0.8	0.2	0.0	0.2	0.2	0.5	0.4	0.0
% Built 1960 Or Later	40.1	57.8	81.2	48.1	88.5	43.7	84.4	33.9	16.4	15.3	10.9
% Owner Occupied	74.8	73.6	77.1	82.8	45.4	80.2	34.2	83.8	45.3	83.3	79.9
% With 1+ Persons Per Room	5.1	4.7	4.0	3.7	3.0	3.1	2.8	4.8	4.4	4.1	4.0
Median Value: Owner Units....$$	30000	29900	38400	35700	36200	39200	31100	32000	26200	27600	25700
Median Rent: Rental Units....$$	172	165	221	181	195	181	185	165	146	163	160
Median Number Of Rooms: All Units	5.4	4.6	6.6	6.2	5.1	6.1	4.6	5.7	4.8	5.4	5.4

Tract Number	8065	8066
Total Population	8598	4251
% Male	49.4	50.2
% Black	0.1	0.0
% Other Nonwhite	0.4	0.3
% Of Spanish Language	1.0	1.4
% Foreign Born	6.2	6.7
% Living In Group Quarters	0.5	0.4
% 13 Years Old And Under	31.1	31.8
% 14-20 Years Old	12.9	10.7
% 21-64 Years Old	51.9	52.6
% 65-74 Years Old	2.9	3.5
% 75 Years Old And Over	1.3	1.4
% In Different House	58.1	65.3
% Families With Female Head	6.2	5.3
Median School Years Completed	12.4	12.3
Median Family Income, 1969....$$	13441	13046
% Income Below Poverty Level	3.6	2.4
% Income of $15,000 or More	38.5	32.5
% White Collar Workers	34.4	31.3
% Civilian Labor Force Unemployed	3.1	3.5
% Riding To Work By Automobile	84.7	86.8
Population Per Household	3.7	3.5
Total Housing Units	2377	1225
% Condominiums & Cooperatives	0.5	0.0
% Built 1960 Or Later	29.3	26.9
% Owner Occupied	71.6	90.7
% With 1+ Persons Per Room	8.6	8.5
Median Value: Owner Units....$$	26700	26800
Median Rent: Rental Units....$$	172	116
Median Number Of Rooms: All Units	5.2	5.1

noise levels or noxious fumes, Des Plaines would then annex the site. Prominent among industries in Des Plaines is a large petroleum research and development organization, and a manufacturer of hydraulic and pneumatic cylinders. Retail business in Des Plaines draws on a large area. For many years, the old central business disrict failed to expand with the population, much of the increasing business going to outlying shopping centers. However, the Des Plaines Mall and a high rise shopping and office center were built in the downtown area in 1977. The development of shopping facilities in Des Plaines restored a balance between residential, commercial and industrial land use.

Developments through the years have enhanced Des Plaines' strategic location with respect to transportation. The Chicago and North Western Railroad runs through the heart of the old business section, and 56 daily commuter trains reach the Loop, many in 28 minutes. The junction of the Tri-State Tollway, the Northwest Tollway, and the Kennedy Expressway is at the city's southern boundary, providing rapid automobile routes to the entire metropolitan area. O'Hare Field, adjacent, is an attraction to businesses that use air freight. Access to transportation made Des Plaines a city of commuters. Today about 300 industrial firms employ almost 28,000 people. While 35 percent of the resident labor force commutes to work elsewhere in the metropolitan area, an equal or greater number commute to jobs in Des Plaines.

M.W.H.

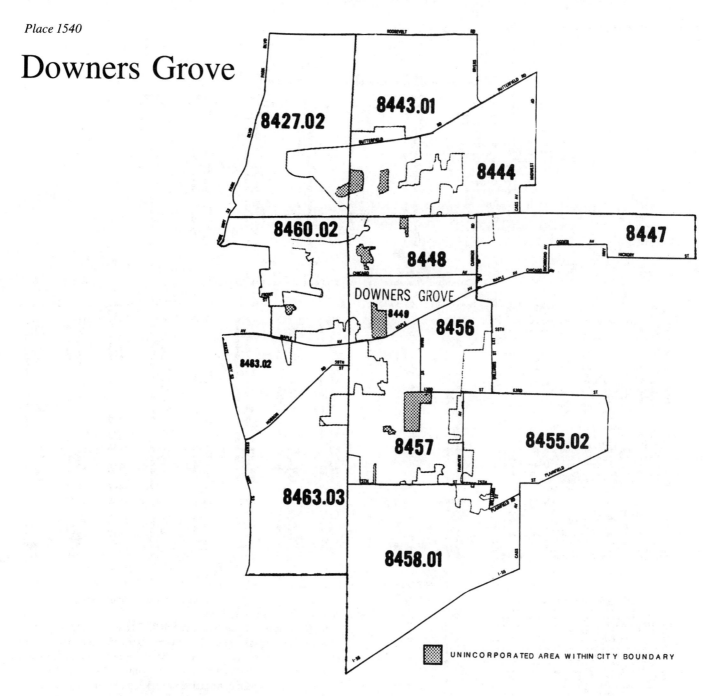

Downers Grove

UNINCORPORATED AREA WITHIN CITY BOUNDARY

Downers Grove is located on 12 square miles of land 23 miles from Chicago's Loop in DuPage County. Early settlers were farmers and later, with the coming of the railroad, commuters were drawn to the community. The outward expansion of industry and people has made Downers Grove, with its trees and areas of open land, very attractive. While it is an old comunity most of the growth in population and land area has come about in the last few decades.

The founding of Downers Grove is dated at 1832 with the arrival of Pierce Downer, who came from New York to visit his son Stephen. Downer filed a 160-acre claim on an oak grove at the intersection of two ancient Indian trails, at a favorite campsite of Chief Waubonsee. Adelaide Downer arrived in 1834 to keep house for her father and married another early settler, Gary Smith. By 1835 there were three log cabins and four people. However, that year the Dexter Stanley family, Edwin Bush, and Daniel Narramore settled in Downers Grove. Israel P. Blodgett, who would operate a station on the Underground Railroad in Downers Grove, joined them from the Naper settlement in 1836. By 1850 nearly 80 families had settled in the combined area of Downers Grove, Cass, and Lisle. The Downers Grove settlement was clustered around Maple Avenue and the center of present day Downers Grove

south of the tracks. In 1850 the first Downers Grove Township meeting was held and the population was listed at 967 people.

In 1862 there were eight merchants in the community. Although there were fewer than 350 inhabitants, 119 men joined the Union Army from Downers Grove. Despite the war, construction of the Chicago, Burlington and Quincy branch railway from Chicago to Aurora began in 1862, and the first passenger train arrived from Aurora in 1864. The coming of the railroad brought changes to the community, with the first subdivision platted by Henry Carpenter in 1863 covering the present business section.

In 1873 Downers Grove was incorporated as a village with about 350 people. A year later the village was described as having 90 homes, three general stores, a meat market, coal and lumber yard, drug store, two-story brick schoolhouse, four organized churches and one hotel. The Village prospered and in the 1880s more land was subdivided south of 55th Street and east of Main Street.

Two businesses still in operation today were started in 1883 and 1884; the Downers Grove Reporter (the oldest paper in DuPage County) and Mochel's Hardware Store. In 1890 the Village had a population of 960 and was still growing.

Downers Grove
Population and Housing Characteristics, 1930-1980

	1980	1970	1960	1950	1940	1930
Total Population.......	42,691	32,751	21,154	11,886	9,526	8,977
% Male..................	48.4	49.1	48.6	48.8	49.3	49.4
% Female................	51.6	50.9	51.4	51.2	50.7	50.6
% White.................	95.2	99.3	99.7	99.8	99.8	99.7
% Black.................	1.1	0.2	0.1	0.2	0.2	0.2
% Other Nonwhite Races...	3.7	0.5	0.2	-	0.0	0.1
% Under 5 Years Old.....	6.7	8.7	11.5	10.2	6.2	8.8
% 5-19 Years Old........	23.7	29.5	28.9	23.0	25.4	26.8
% 20-44 Years Old........	39.8	33.5	32.2	36.3	39.7	41.5
% 45-64 Years Old........	20.4	21.0	21.0	23.6	21.9	17.4
% 65 Years and Older.....	9.4	7.3	6.4	6.9	6.8	5.5
Median School Years....	13.5	12.7	12.5	12.3	10.5	*
Total Housing Units.....	15,715	10,729	6,202	3,507	2,696	*
% In One-Unit Structures.	69.9	73.4	92.4	85.9	84.4	*
% Owner Occupied.........	74.4	70.3	83.8	80.1	61.0	*
% Renter Occupied........	21.9	23.8	13.0	17.8	37.1	*
% Vacant.................	3.7	5.9	3.2	2.1	1.9	*
% 1+ Persons per Room....	1.1	4.0	6.2	6.0	5.9	*

Place 1540 — Downers Grove, Illinois
Selected Characteristics of Census Tracts: 1980

Tract Number	Total	8427.02	8443.01	8444	8447	8448	8449	8455.02	8456	8457	8458.01
Total Population.............	42572	0	2	3070	879	7378	6768	432	7501	11664	118
% Male........................	48.4	-	-	48.3	49.3	49.3	46.4	51.6	48.8	48.8	46.6
% Black.......................	1.1	-	-	5.5	1.7	0.2	0.6	0.0	0.2	1.2	5.9
% Other Nonwhite..............	3.7	-	-	8.0	10.1	1.5	1.2	2.5	2.1	6.3	1.7
% Of Spanish Origin...........	1.4	-	-	2.0	1.3	0.7	1.1	0.2	1.0	0.3	0.0
% Foreign Born................	6.5	-	-	8.7	10.0	5.2	5.1	0.0	5.5	8.8	0.0
% Living In Group Quarters....	1.0	-	-	13.7	0.0	0.0	0.1	0.0	0.0	0.0	0.0
% 13 Years Old And Under......	20.4	-	-	20.8	29.4	19.1	16.9	33.1	19.4	24.2	16.9
% 14-20 Years Old.............	11.5	-	-	18.9	15.4	10.3	10.1	12.3	11.2	11.4	5.1
% 21-64 Years Old.............	58.7	-	-	57.4	51.8	59.2	56.5	53.0	60.0	59.5	78.0
% 65-74 Years Old.............	5.9	-	-	1.8	2.0	7.5	9.1	1.6	6.1	3.4	0.0
% 75 Years Old And Over.......	3.5	-	-	1.1	1.5	4.0	7.3	0.0	3.4	1.4	0.0
% In Different House..........	46.9	-	-	61.0	27.6	33.4	40.4	36.2	44.2	56.7	100.0
% Families With Female Head...	8.4	-	-	6.1	8.3	8.4	8.9	2.4	4.8	8.8	33.3
Median School Years Completed.	13.5	-	-	15.7	15.7	12.9	13.3	13.4	13.5	14.1	12.8
Median Family Income, 1979......$$	31478	-	-	44111	36124	27908	30008	36158	31828	33314	23750
% Income Below Poverty Level...	1.9	-	-	0.0	0.0	0.0	1.5	0.0	2.0	1.7	0.0
% Income Of $30,000 Or More...	55.1	-	-	83.6	79.1	44.4	50.0	76.8	57.4	60.7	33.3
% White Collar Workers........	72.0	-	-	75.7	75.9	68.6	70.9	73.5	71.5	76.3	64.0
% Civilian Labor Force Unemployed.	3.3	-	-	3.0	0.0	4.2	3.8	0.0	3.6	2.9	0.0
% Riding To Work By Automobile...	79.1	-	-	78.8	83.9	81.3	72.4	74.8	77.9	80.9	82.9
Mean Commuting Time - Minutes...	29.1	-	-	25.4	32.4	27.8	25.9	36.0	27.4	32.8	32.1
Population Per Household.........	2.8	-	-	3.4	3.8	2.8	2.5	3.9	2.7	3.1	2.0
Total Housing Units...........	15865	0	1	803	235	2727	2835	112	2848	3892	64
% Condominiums................	13.4	-	-	17.4	0.0	11.1	4.5	0.0	5.9	19.1	0.0
% Built 1970 Or Later.........	33.3	-	-	51.6	58.5	9.7	17.3	92.2	19.0	60.1	100.0
% Owner Occupied..............	74.4	-	-	87.3	87.2	83.6	65.2	97.3	72.3	87.4	1.6
% With 1+ Persons Per Room....	1.1	-	-	0.6	3.8	1.3	0.7	0.0	1.0	0.9	0.0
Median Value: Owner Units......$$	79300	-	-	128800	97900	69200	72200	117000	75600	90400	-
Median Rent: Rental Units......$$	283	-	-	369	445	310	262	-	272	368	345
Median Number Of Rooms: All Units.	5.6	-	-	5.6	5.6	5.6	5.4	5.6	5.6	5.6	4.1

Tract Number	8460.02	8463.02	8463.03
Total Population.............	2703	58	1999
% Male........................	46.2	-	50.9
% Black.......................	0.7	-	2.6
% Other Nonwhite..............	2.4	-	3.2
% Of Spanish Origin...........	2.6	-	4.4
% Foreign Born................	4.9	-	5.9
% Living In Group Quarters....	0.0	-	0.0
% 13 Years Old And Under......	12.5	-	21.7
% 14-20 Years Old.............	8.4	-	12.8
% 21-64 Years Old.............	57.0	-	62.6
% 65-74 Years Old.............	14.1	-	2.0
% 75 Years Old And Over.......	8.0	-	1.0
% In Different House..........	35.4	-	70.1
% Families With Female Head...	13.8	-	17.3
Median School Years Completed.	12.8	-	13.0
Median Family Income, 1979......$$	24782	-	27317
% Income Below Poverty Level...	5.1	-	3.4
% Income Of $30,000 Or More...	37.7	-	43.6
% White Collar Workers........	67.5	-	64.2
% Civilian Labor Force Unemployed.	2.9	-	3.8
% Riding To Work By Automobile...	82.7	-	82.4
Mean Commuting Time - Minutes...	25.2	-	34.9
Population Per Household.........	2.1	-	2.3
Total Housing Units...........	1382	16	950
% Condominiums................	46.9	-	0.0
% Built 1970 Or Later.........	27.6	-	55.2
% Owner Occupied..............	67.9	-	25.4
% With 1+ Persons Per Room....	1.6	-	2.3
Median Value: Owner Units......$$	65100	-	81100
Median Rent: Rental Units......$$	285	-	270
Median Number Of Rooms: All Units.	4.4	-	4.0

Despite a disagreement over the path of a proposed right-of-way for Main Street, the street (then known as Rogers) was opened to the Plank Road (now Odgen Avenue), and Highland (then known as Main Street) was cut through as it is now. This facilitated the settling of a new 225 acre subdivision north of the railroad tracks. Another subdivision opened in the 1890s reflected the new immigration pattern of eastern Europeans. This was the Gostyn subdivision named after a community in Poland. In 1891 the first Catholic church in Downers Grove was founded. The 1890s also saw the opening of Downers Grove's first bank, a nine-hole golf course (the Chicago Golf Course, later moved to Wheaton), a water works, electric company, telephone service and a volunteer fire department.

By 1900 the population had grown to 2,103 and the early years of the new century brought more improvements to the community. The electric plant was modernized, a new bank was organized in 1910, and a new passenger railroad station was built in 1912. In 1912 the Kindergarten Extension Association selected Downers Grove as the site for their second building which eventually became the Avery Coonley Experimental School, which is nationally known. In 1915 the residents went to the polls to vote for a change to the commission form of municipal government, which went into effect in 1917.

After the passage of the State Forest Preserve Act, 80 acres of land were purchased in 1920 from Marshall Field III, whose estate was just west of town. The other 83 acres became the Maple Grove Forest Preserve. The passage of the 19th amendment brought women to the polls and helped elect Lottie Holman O'Neill, a Downers Grove resident, the first woman member of the illinois General Assembly in 1922. She served almost continuously from 1922 until her retirement in 1963. Another famous Downers Grove resident, Dr. James Breasted, became the first head of the Oriental Institute of the University of Chicago in 1919.

In 1920 the population of the Village was 3,543 and by 1930 it had grown to 8,977. Some of the new residents of the 1920s were attracted by the opening of new subdivisions on the south and west of the Village where the Field estate had been. The 1930s brought the closing of all the banks in the Village. Despite the trying times Downers Grove celebrated its centennial in 1932 with parades, pageants and fireworks.

Downers Grove
Selected Characteristics of Census Tracts: 1970

Tract Number	TOTAL	8427	8443	8444	8447	8448	8449	8455	8456	8457	8458
Total Population	32751	14501	11096	4202	6687	9535	8132	11370	8547	7578	12828
% Male	49.1	50.4	48.5	50.4	49.6	49.3	47.6	49.4	49.5	49.9	50.6
% Black	0.2	0.2	0.7	2.2	0.1	0.1	0.2	0.0	0.2	0.0	0.3
% Other Nonwhite	0.5	0.5	1.0	0.4	0.3	0.3	0.5	0.8	0.7	0.4	0.7
% Of Spanish Language	0.9	1.3	3.2	0.7	1.3	0.9	1.5	1.1	0.8	0.2	1.4
% Foreign Born	3.9	2.6	5.3	3.8	6.7	5.3	4.4	4.4	3.3	2.5	6.4
% Living In Group Quarters	0.3	1.1	0.2	7.8	0.4	0.0	0.2	0.1	0.0	0.1	0.5
% 13 Years Old And Under	27.9	36.3	30.1	26.8	27.2	26.5	23.9	31.4	28.3	32.9	32.6
% 14-20 Years Old	11.4	12.4	11.7	16.0	12.1	11.5	11.6	9.8	11.8	11.5	10.7
% 21-64 Years Old	53.4	48.6	54.4	51.8	53.0	54.9	53.0	55.2	53.5	51.4	53.3
% 65-74 Years Old	4.8	1.8	2.6	3.2	5.0	5.0	7.2	2.6	4.2	3.0	2.2
% 75 Years Old And Over	2.5	0.9	1.2	2.2	2.8	2.1	4.2	1.1	2.3	1.3	1.3
% In Different House	45.2	46.0	26.1	26.4	55.9	52.8	57.0	28.8	45.4	45.4	40.0
% Families With Female Head	5.6	2.8	6.8	2.9	5.4	5.6	7.7	3.7	4.8	4.3	3.8
Median School Years Completed	12.7	13.0	12.8	12.9	12.6	12.6	12.6	12.7	12.7	12.7	12.6
Median Family Income, 1969......$$	14524	17436	14767	19658	14527	14057	14839	14366	14988	14735	14247
% Income Below Poverty Level	2.2	0.7	3.0	1.6	2.2	2.0	1.4	1.3	2.5	1.5	2.7
% Income of $15,000 or More	46.9	60.8	48.3	66.2	46.8	43.7	49.1	44.6	49.9	48.1	44.6
% White Collar Workers	49.5	58.4	51.0	56.0	40.6	46.8	47.2	45.2	49.3	43.5	43.9
% Civilian Labor Force Unemployed	1.8	2.3	2.4	2.4	3.4	1.9	1.9	1.8	1.3	2.1	1.9
% Riding To Work By Automobile	76.6	80.2	85.5	86.1	76.7	75.5	73.1	80.1	78.7	79.5	87.3
Population Per Household	3.2	4.0	3.4	3.6	3.4	3.4	3.2	3.0	3.4	3.3	3.7
Total Housing Units	10727	3696	3819	1197	2024	3111	2888	3046	2666	2250	4265
% Condominiums & Cooperatives	2.0	0.0	4.8	1.3	0.0	0.0	4.5	0.2	0.0	0.0	0.0
% Built 1960 Or Later	41.1	70.7	77.0	72.9	23.9	32.3	24.8	71.0	41.9	49.7	63.5
% Owner Occupied	68.3	88.0	61.8	72.8	84.9	72.4	62.7	65.4	73.4	80.4	56.3
% With 1+ Persons Per Room	4.0	3.5	4.4	3.8	4.6	5.0	3.9	3.8	4.2	4.8	7.4
Median Value: Owner Units......$$	27200	34400	29100	50100	30800	24700	24400	33700	28000	28600	28000
Median Rent: Rental Units......$$	173	213	202	186	148	200	154	194	167	184	187
Median Number Of Rooms: All Units	5.3	7.0	5.1	6.6	5.8	5.2	5.2	5.5	5.4	5.8	5.3

Tract Number	8460	8463
Total Population	8134	21351
% Male	49.7	51.0
% Black	0.3	0.4
% Other Nonwhite	0.4	0.7
% Of Spanish Language	1.3	1.9
% Foreign Born	6.1	4.3
% Living In Group Quarters	0.0	0.4
% 13 Years Old And Under	30.0	36.5
% 14-20 Years Old	12.2	9.1
% 21-64 Years Old	52.3	52.1
% 65-74 Years Old	3.8	1.5
% 75 Years Old And Over	1.7	0.8
% In Different House	49.4	30.2
% Families With Female Head	6.2	2.6
Median School Years Completed	12.4	12.8
Median Family Income, 1969......$$	13542	14197
% Income Below Poverty Level	5.6	1.6
% Income of $15,000 or More	38.5	43.0
% White Collar Workers	37.1	53.8
% Civilian Labor Force Unemployed	1.9	1.4
% Riding To Work By Automobile	81.0	82.8
Population Per Household	3.4	3.6
Total Housing Units	2474	6607
% Condominiums & Cooperatives	4.3	1.6
% Built 1960 Or Later	35.2	87.3
% Owner Occupied	69.8	64.0
% With 1+ Persons Per Room	6.9	4.5
Median Value: Owner Units......$$	25200	30200
Median Rent: Rental Units......$$	172	195
Median Number Of Rooms: All Units	5.4	5.7

The population of Downers Grove has always been almost all white European stock. In 1980, 1 percent of the total was black and 1 percent was Hispanic. As in most suburbs the population has aged since 1960; the percentage under 18 has dropped from 39 to 27; the percentage 65 and over has grown from 6 to 9.

In 1960, Downers Grove had only 6,202 housing units, by 1970 10,729, by 1980 nearly 16,000. This reflects the large population increases during these two decades. About three-fourths of all units are single-family homes and about the same proportion is owner-occupied. Several new developments are underway in the southern portion of the suburb and over 400 senior citizen units are currently occupied. The median value for for a single-family home in 1980 was $79,400 (about $20,000 less than in nearby Naperville) although prices range from $65,000 to $200,000. More than half the families in Downers Grove reported incomes in excess of $30,000 in 1979 and almost three-fourths are white-collar workers. Three percent of the labor force is unemployed and 2 percent of all families live in poverty.

Part of the continuing growth in the last few decades was due to Downers Grove's location. The opening of the Congress Street (Eisenhower) Expressway in the 1960s brought another means of direct access to Chicago. Downers Grove is also close to the tollway system. This "tollway corridor" between Oak Brook and Naperville has drawn many firms, especially those in high technology and research. This has brought many new residents to the western suburbs including Downers Grove.

The Village has two main industrial parks — Ellsworth to the west and Oak Grove Center of Commerce of the north. There are over 90 manufacturing concerns employing over 6,000 workers; and over 150 service establishments employing more than 4,000 persons. In the last few years the northwest section of Downers Grove has been targeted by developers for new office complexes. This situation has caused Downers Grove officials to put some restrictions on building which serve to ensure quality.

Downers Grove has a major retail center, Downers Park, opened in 1979. Downtown, the Main Street area offers extensive shopping, and there are four other shopping centers.

In 1983, an off-price retail center opened on Butterfield Road just east of Finley Road containing 19 stores, all of which had committed themselves to the project before the center opened. George Williams College is located on the north side. Downers Grove is meeting its problems of growth and attempting to meld a forward-looking community.

Gail Danks Welter

One of the first WPA projects in Illinois was the paving of Highland Avenue north to Roosevelt Road. This led to the re-laying of all brick streets in the Village bringing some employment for Village residents. Federal funds were also used for construction of a new water tower and a gymnasium addition. In 1940, after nearly a decade without a local bank, the Citizen's National Bank of Downers Grove opened its doors taking in $100,000 worth of deposits in the first day.

By 1940, there were 9,527 residents in the Village, only 550 more than a decade before. World War II brought about change in the previously bleak economic picture. At the end of the war Downers Grove faced many new problems brought by rapid growth. In 1950, there were 11,865 residents and by 1960 21,154, an increase of nearly 80 percent. Industry was added to the Village in the 1950s, one of the first firms being Pepperidge Farm.

In 1962, Downers Grove changed to the village manager form of government and the next year the village annexed 262 acres around Dunham and 63rd Streets. In the 1960s, after much debate, apartment units and shopping areas were finally included in the zoning revisions. By 1970, the Village had 32,715 residents. During the 1970s the Village provided and financed its own bus service, which still operates independently of the RTA. The Village Complex was completed, the new public library was built, and a new hospital was opened. Growth continued throughout the 1970s, bringing the population to 42,691 in 1980.

Elgin

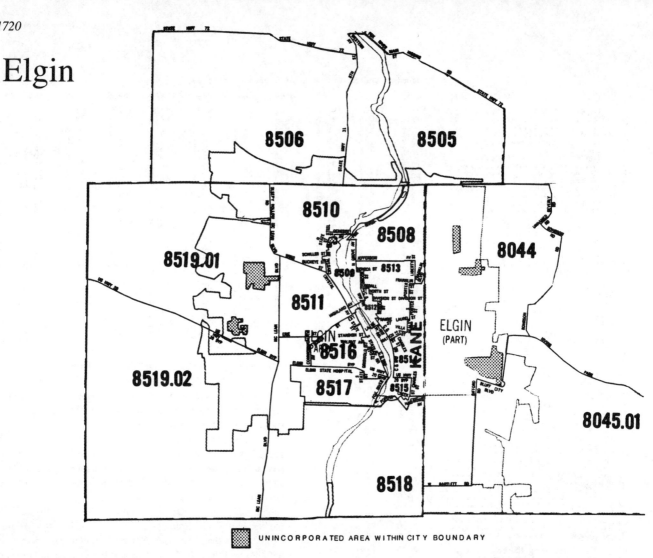

UNINCORPORATED AREA WITHIN CITY BOUNDARY

Elgin lies 36 miles west and slightly north of Chicago, on the Fox River at an altitude of about 700 feet. It is located primarily in Kane County, but portions of it cross the county line into Cook County. The name comes from the title of a Scotch song that was a favorite of the pioneer settlers. Elgin was first settled in 1835, after the Black Hawk War and the treaty which removed Indians from the area. James Gifford and his brother Hezekiah came from New York and built a home there. James Gifford wanted the proposed Frink and Walker Chicago-Galena stage coach line to run past his cabin and with the help of another settler, Samuel Kimball, he laid out a road to Belvidere, which the coaches used as a route, beginning the following year. James Gifford and Kimball dammed the Fox River, and set up a sawmill and a grist mill. In 1838, B.W. Raymond, who would become the third mayor of Chicago, began to promote industrial activities in the vicinity. Several general stores were opened, as well as a woolen factory, a hardware store, a stone mill, and a banking office.

Elgin was incorporated as a village in 1847. Two years later, after Raymond pledged some of his land as an incentive, the Galena and Chicago Union (later the Chicago and North Western) Railroad reached Elgin, and for two years Elgin was its western terminal. Construction of the Fox River Road north to Richmond at the Wisconsin border also contributed to improved transportation which in turn brought new settlers. The village grew steadily and in 1854 Elgin was incorporated as a city. The Elgin Academy opened in 1856. A financial depression in 1857 and the Civil War temporarily halted Elgin's growth.

Elgin became the center of a prosperous dairy region. Milk shipments to Chicago began in 1852, and cheese and butter manufacture commenced soon after. Beginning in the 1860s, Elgin grew rapidly into the hub of the dairy industry, manufacturing butter and cheese, condenseries, cream separators, silos, butter tubs, malted milk, and other products. As a boy, Gail Borden had observed the problems of Western travelers who got off the train at Elgin in preserving food. In 1865 he invented a process for condensing milk and, in 1866, the Borden Condensed Milk Factory opened in Elgin. It was soon followed by the Elgin Milk Condensing Company. The Elgin Board of Trade, which began operations in 1872 to guide local dairy activities, became an important force in setting national prices of butter and cheese for almost a half century. The Board stopped operations in 1917, at the request of the World War I Food Administration.

At the same time, another major industry located in Elgin — in 1864, Raymond bought the National Watch Company of Chicago and relocated it in Elgin on a 35-acre tract of land. The Elgin National Watch Company used interchangeable parts and a modified assembly line so that they could produce watches comparable to Swiss products in quality at considerably lower prices. The Elgin Packing Company followed several years later. The immediate post-Civil War period also brought the construction of an iron bridge across the river, several frame stores, a large wooden warehouse, three churches, and about 55 dwellings. Excellent water power, combined with fairly rapid rail service to Chicago, contributed to Elgin's attractiveness to industry. This was enhanced in 1873 with the completion of the first part of the Chicago and Pacific Railroad from Chicago to Elgin. The Northern Illinois State Mental Hospital opened in 1872, with facilities for 300 patients. The population nearly doubled from 1860 to 1870, and continued to increase between 1870 and 1880.

The growth of industry and population continued through the 1880s. The David C. Cook religious publishing company located in Elgin,

Elgin
Population and Housing Characteristics, 1930-1980

	1980	1970	1960	1950	1940	1930
Total Population.......	63,668	55,691	49,447	44,223	38,333	35,929
% Male...................	47.9	47.0	47.7	47.3	48.1	48.4
% Female.................	52.1	53.0	52.3	52.7	51.9	51.6
% White..................	87.4	94.7	96.7	98.2	98.8	99.1
% Black..................	6.6	4.8	3.2	1.7	1.2	0.9
% Other Nonwhite Races...	6.0	0.5	0.1	0.1	0.0	0.0
% Under 5 Years Old......	8.8	8.5	9.2	7.8	5.4	6.6
% 5-19 Years Old.........	22.5	24.5	20.5	15.8	17.9	19.6
% 20-44 Years Old........	39.5	31.6	30.3	37.1	41.5	43.8
% 45-64 Years Old........	17.2	22.1	26.5	27.5	25.2	21.7
% 65 Years and Older.....	12.0	13.3	13.5	11.8	10.0	8.3
Median School Years.....	12.5	12.1	10.5	10.3	8.7	*
Total Housing Units.....	24,794	18,434	14,801	11,944	10,189	**
% In One-Unit Structures.	56.9	57.2	65.7	*	*	**
% Owner Occupied.........	56.4	57.1	59.7	59.6	51.7	**
% Renter Occupied........	39.4	39.9	36.8	38.8	46.2	**
% Vacant.................	4.2	3.0	3.5	1.6	2.1	**
% 1+ Persons per Room....	4.2	5.6	6.4	5.9	*	**

Place 1720 — Elgin, Illinois
Selected Characteristics of Census Tracts: 1980

Tract Number	Total	8044	8045.01	8505	8506	8508	8509	8510	8511	8512	8513
Total Population............	63798	10975	45	24	520	5724	765	6051	6916	415	8586
% Male......................	47.9	48.5	–	–	53.1	47.2	49.5	46.6	47.2	57.6	48.9
% Black.....................	6.6	11.1	–	–	2.5	2.0	17.0	3.0	3.0	6.7	14.0
% Other Nonwhite............	6.0	5.8	–	–	2.5	2.2	17.0	4.4	4.1	27.2	12.8
% Of Spanish Origin.........	10.2	7.4	–	–	3.3	5.1	33.9	3.5	8.1	30.4	28.7
% Foreign Born..............	6.8	5.5	–	–	1.1	4.3	17.8	5.0	4.3	28.4	16.1
% Living In Group Quarters..	2.8	0.2	–	–	0.0	0.0	0.0	4.2	0.5	25.5	0.9
% 13 Years Old And Under....	22.0	26.8	–	–	36.2	19.7	27.5	16.3	19.2	15.2	26.0
% 14-20 Years Old...........	11.2	10.3	–	–	9.8	9.6	11.1	13.4	10.6	14.2	12.6
% 21-64 Years Old...........	54.7	56.3	–	–	53.7	55.3	52.5	55.0	54.5	59.8	52.3
% 65-74 Years Old...........	6.8	4.0	–	–	0.2	8.9	5.4	9.9	8.7	6.5	4.9
% 75 Years Old And Over.....	5.2	2.5	–	–	0.2	6.4	3.5	5.4	7.0	4.3	4.2
% In Different House........	53.5	56.9	–	–	74.6	42.4	57.5	64.5	42.9	58.8	57.0
% Families With Female Head.	17.2	16.5	–	–	2.8	11.3	21.1	17.7	14.7	34.1	24.0
Median School Years Completed	12.5	12.6	–	–	15.4	12.6	12.1	12.7	12.7	12.2	12.1
Median Family Income, 1979....$$	23193	25103	–	–	32761	23728	17396	22238	25071	13958	18050
% Income Below Poverty Level.	5.3	5.6	–	–	0.0	1.1	4.0	1.1	4.3	0.0	15.0
% Income Of $30,000 Or More..	29.6	32.7	–	–	61.6	29.3	16.7	28.7	35.0	0.0	17.4
% White Collar Workers.......	53.3	57.6	–	–	79.1	54.9	29.8	65.8	55.7	31.2	38.9
% Civilian Labor Force Unemployed.	5.8	6.0	–	–	7.1	4.8	14.9	3.5	2.4	15.0	10.0
% Riding To Work By Automobile....	88.6	92.4	–	–	94.0	85.9	89.6	86.5	86.3	61.8	87.0
Mean Commuting Time - Minutes...	20.1	21.8	–	–	17.6	19.9	15.0	21.2	18.5	21.4	19.9
Population Per Household.........	2.6	2.9	–	–	3.7	2.6	2.8	2.3	2.6	2.5	2.8
Total Housing Units..........	24892	4117	18	4	143	2281	294	2674	2794	146	3295
% Condominiums...............	1.1	1.4	–	–	0.0	0.0	0.0	3.5	0.0	0.0	0.0
% Built 1970 Or Later........	25.5	56.9	–	–	100.0	1.3	5.5	54.2	4.2	0.0	1.7
% Owner Occupied.............	55.5	60.5	–	–	97.2	74.6	43.5	53.8	69.6	4.1	32.8
% With 1+ Persons Per Room...	4.2	4.4	–	–	1.4	1.4	9.9	1.7	2.3	18.7	10.7
Median Value: Owner Units......$$	62200	66800	–	–	83500	58300	42200	73300	60000	–	47600
Median Rent: Rental Units......$$	229	252	–	–	–	224	201	273	225	170	202
Median Number Of Rooms: All Units.	4.9	5.2	–	–	5.6	5.5	4.6	4.5	5.3	3.3	4.5

Tract Number	8514	8515	8516	8517	8518	8519.01	8519.02
Total Population.............	5613	977	5453	703	2209	7813	1009
% Male.......................	49.1	45.4	45.0	56.0	46.5	47.8	48.7
% Black......................	8.5	13.6	2.3	15.1	2.5	1.7	7.1
% Other Nonwhite.............	9.6	8.3	3.1	0.3	2.0	3.5	6.2
% Of Spanish Origin..........	17.3	20.1	4.5	2.7	2.6	3.0	5.8
% Foreign Born...............	8.5	7.1	2.4	7.7	4.3	4.5	5.4
% Living In Group Quarters...	1.6	0.0	1.9	100.0	0.0	4.5	0.0
% 13 Years Old And Under.....	24.9	24.6	18.0	0.0	19.3	20.5	29.2
% 14-20 Years Old............	12.1	11.9	9.7	5.0	9.7	12.5	10.3
% 21-64 Years Old............	51.2	52.6	51.8	79.2	54.4	57.1	57.7
% 65-74 Years Old............	6.4	7.4	10.3	10.2	10.5	4.7	2.1
% 75 Years Old And Over......	5.5	3.6	10.2	5.5	6.0	5.2	0.7
% In Different House.........	48.6	47.9	48.4	34.8	54.3	57.5	81.3
% Families With Female Head..	19.1	32.3	16.9	–	19.5	12.9	17.4
Median School Years Completed	12.2	12.1	12.3	11.7	12.6	12.8	12.8
Median Family Income, 1979....$$	20897	17417	21266	–	25048	28490	24471
% Income Below Poverty Level.	8.3	18.6	3.3	–	2.5	2.4	4.6
% Income Of $30,000 Or More..	21.7	14.5	23.2	–	30.0	44.8	24.5
% White Collar Workers.......	38.6	35.3	48.5	–	59.5	62.3	56.6
% Civilian Labor Force Unemployed.	6.4	7.8	6.0	–	6.1	5.0	2.3
% Riding To Work By Automobile....	90.6	84.7	89.1	–	86.4	90.2	97.6
Mean Commuting Time - Minutes...	18.1	20.1	18.8	–	20.6	20.8	24.0
Population Per Household.........	2.9	2.3	2.3	0.0	2.4	2.8	3.0
Total Housing Units..........	2054	458	2442	0	971	2845	356
% Condominiums...............	0.0	0.0	0.0	–	0.0	3.1	7.6
% Built 1970 Or Later........	2.1	26.5	13.6	–	40.1	34.3	93.8
% Owner Occupied.............	57.6	21.2	51.8	–	56.0	55.5	59.0
% With 1+ Persons Per Room...	7.4	4.2	1.9	–	2.0	2.2	5.1
Median Value: Owner Units......$$	51700	39600	55500	–	60100	80100	64700
Median Rent: Rental Units......$$	214	173	182	–	195	264	304
Median Number Of Rooms: All Units.	5.1	3.9	4.7	–	4.7	5.1	4.9

employing 350 people. Many other industries were attracted, in part by deliberate promotional activities, including a shoe factory, a watch case factory, a shirt factory, and a silver plate factory. The Elgin National Bank was established in 1892. Another severe depression from 1893 to 1897 brought that boom to an end.

Since 1890, Elgin has not experienced any new periods of very rapid growth. There has been steady growth each decade, sufficient to accumulate into a large quantity over time. Because of Elgin's distance from Chicago, population growth has been tied very closely to developments in its own economic base. Between 1900 and 1910, a mill which developed into the largest independent manufacturer of pure and artificial silk in the nation, a butter producer, and another bank all located in Elgin. The watch company built the Elgin Observatory in 1909. Population increased moderately during the decade from 22,433 to 25,976.

The unprecedented period of prosperity of the 1920s brought many new industries to Elgin. Among the new industries were a machine shop, a street sweeper company, and a producer of asphalt products. The Elgin Watchmakers College was established. As a result of this increased economic activity, population grew from 27,454 in 1920 to almost 36,000 in 1930. In 1930, Germans were the single largest nationality among the foreign stock, constituting 22 percent of the total population. Population growth and economic activity declined during the Depression 1930s — population increased by only 2,400 in that

Elgin
Selected Characteristics of Census Tracts: 1970

Tract Number	TOTAL	8044	8045	8505	8506	8508	8509	8510	8511	8512	8513
Total Population	55691	6166	10216	3337	2505	6959	890	3252	7965	579	8887
% Male	47.0	49.5	49.2	48.1	49.9	47.2	48.9	47.6	47.1	54.2	45.7
% Black	4.8	2.2	0.4	0.0	0.1	0.7	34.4	1.0	1.8	9.5	14.2
% Other Nonwhite	0.5	0.5	0.4	0.2	0.1	0.2	0.4	0.4	0.3	0.7	1.1
% Of Spanish Language	5.3	3.2	3.4	0.0	0.0	1.7	24.3	2.9	4.5	30.8	10.9
% Foreign Born	3.8	3.2	4.0	2.7	3.1	3.8	3.1	2.5	4.3	1.8	5.3
% Living In Group Quarters	7.3	0.8	1.0	1.7	0.0	0.6	0.9	3.2	0.6	1.4	1.8
% 13 Years Old And Under	23.6	29.4	36.4	26.0	31.3	23.4	32.4	23.5	23.0	15.2	25.1
% 14-20 Years Old	10.9	11.6	10.0	12.9	13.3	11.7	12.4	11.3	12.0	9.0	11.3
% 21-64 Years Old	52.2	52.7	50.1	49.7	51.9	50.6	48.4	54.5	51.5	55.8	49.4
% 65-74 Years Old	8.2	4.7	2.4	6.4	2.2	9.4	4.7	8.2	8.5	10.9	7.7
% 75 Years Old And Over	5.2	1.7	1.1	5.0	1.4	4.9	2.1	2.6	5.0	9.2	6.5
% In Different House	50.0	56.0	41.0	58.5	36.3	61.3	40.7	20.4	57.3	40.0	50.4
% Families With Female Head	9.8	7.3	4.2	7.8	3.6	9.2	19.0	4.0	8.7	17.7	14.2
Median School Years Completed	12.1	12.2	12.3	12.4	12.9	12.2	10.6	12.4	12.4	8.9	11.3
Median Family Income, 1969 $$	11555	12668	12596	12197	18835	12025	10370	12757	12190	9313	10480
% Income Below Poverty Level	4.2	2.6	3.2	4.4	2.1	2.7	2.8	1.8	3.7	23.8	6.1
% Income of $15,000 or More	27.3	32.8	30.4	31.4	67.0	27.9	12.6	33.7		6.2	22.2
% White Collar Workers	30.2	32.4	28.5	39.3	55.7	32.8	14.9	34.9	37.1	13.7	22.3
% Civilian Labor Force Unemployed	3.3	2.3	2.3	0.7	0.6	2.7	5.1	3.1	1.9	11.2	5.7
% Riding To Work By Automobile	84.0	87.1	83.9	87.9	88.8	83.3	91.1	86.7	85.2	44.0	80.8
Population Per Household	2.9	3.2	3.7	3.2	3.6	2.9	3.3	2.9	2.9	1.8	2.7
Total Housing Units	18433	1958	2875	1105	762	2435	286	1138	2783	376	3357
% Condominiums & Cooperatives	0.0	0.0	3.0	0.0	0.0	0.2	0.0	0.0	0.0	0.0	0.0
% Built 1960 Or Later	22.7	49.9	75.5	16.6	80.9	7.1	9.2	76.0	12.7	1.7	3.9
% Owner Occupied	57.1	69.4	75.7	68.5	64.0	71.3	46.5	73.8	69.0	2.7	34.1
% With 1+ Persons Per Room	5.6	6.1	8.6	3.5	1.3	3.4	14.1	4.1	4.6	9.0	8.7
Median Value: Owner Units $$	20700	24900	24900	22100	44300	20000	14600	30400	22100	-	16800
Median Rent: Rental Units $$	124	152	169	119	204	128	105	157	129	80	109
Median Number Of Rooms: All Units	4.8	4.9	5.3	5.4	6.4	5.2	4.6	4.6	5.1	1.7	4.4

Tract Number	8514	8515	8516	8518	8519
Total Population	5835	760	5714	6098	8672
% Male	47.8	48.3	44.5	49.6	48.7
% Black	4.5	2.1	4.5	0.5	0.2
% Other Nonwhite	0.6	0.3	0.3	0.6	0.7
% Of Spanish Language	7.7	24.6	2.2	1.5	1.3
% Foreign Born	3.5	11.3	2.3	2.6	2.9
% Living In Group Quarters	2.4	0.0	38.1	6.0	1.2
% 13 Years Old And Under	24.9	25.3	14.8	32.2	30.7
% 14-20 Years Old	11.0	12.0	8.4	10.8	11.2
% 21-64 Years Old	50.0	51.1	55.1	50.6	53.3
% 65-74 Years Old	8.5	7.2	12.9	4.8	2.8
% 75 Years Old And Over	5.7	4.5	8.8	1.7	2.1
% In Different House	51.0	56.0	52.0	59.5	31.7
% Families With Female Head	11.4	14.3	11.6	5.2	4.1
Median School Years Completed	11.3	11.0	11.0	12.1	12.6
Median Family Income, 1969 $$	10617	9233	10391	12038	13595
% Income Below Poverty Level	6.2	6.6	6.0	2.6	2.5
% Income of $15,000 or More	24.2	15.3	18.9	25.2	39.8
% White Collar Workers	21.9	26.6	23.0	25.5	41.2
% Civilian Labor Force Unemployed	3.3	1.9	3.4	2.4	1.7
% Riding To Work By Automobile	84.6	58.5	85.6	89.1	87.0
Population Per Household	2.9	2.9	2.7	3.4	3.4
Total Housing Units	1985	268	2107	1825	2579
% Condominiums & Cooperatives	0.0	0.0	0.0	0.0	0.0
% Built 1960 Or Later	4.0	2.0	10.7	28.1	79.3
% Owner Occupied	56.7	50.0	60.2	79.2	60.3
% With 1+ Persons Per Room	6.7	8.1	3.5	8.7	5.1
Median Value: Owner Units $$	17900	15700	18600	21100	29500
Median Rent: Rental Units $$	114	108	121	115	170
Median Number Of Rooms: All Units	4.9	4.6	4.8	5.0	5.0

decade. Transportation changes brought an end to butter manufacture. In the World War II and postwar periods, economic expansion and population growth resumed. During the war, the Elgin National Watch Company employed 5,500, making munitions timing devices. Between 1950 and 1960, population increased from 44,000 to 49,000. Elgin was cited as an All-America city in 1956. Germans remained the dominant nationality among the foreign stock in 1960, followed by Swedes and English.

In 1960, the Elgin Watch Company, the watch case factory, and the Elgin State Hospital, now grown to 4,700 patients, were among the largest employers in the city. However, times had changed in the watch industry. The 13-story factory had become outmoded and was torn down. Eventually, the whole operation was shut down and the watch case factory, the watchmakers college and the observatory followed. Despite this, the Elgin industrial base continued to grow. A new industrial district grew on the south edge of town along a bypass for U.S. Highway 20. The building of the Northwest Tollway facilitated automobile and truck transportation. Today, eight industrial districts in Elgin occupy more than 1,600 acres.

After relatively slow housing growth between 1930 and 1960, the pace of construction in Elgin has picked up in recent decades. There are now almost 25,000 housing units, a fourth of which were built in the most recent decade. Fifty-five percent of the 1980 units were owner-occupied and 61 percent were in single-family structures. The growth of the latter figure from 1970 indicates increasing attention to single-unit construction. The median values of owner-occupied units is average for suburbs. There has been considerable housing mobility in recent years; about half the population of 1980 had lived in a different house five years before.

The population of Elgin passed 50,000 in 1970 and stands today at an all-time high, just under 64,000. Seven percent of the residents are black and 10 percent are of Spanish origin. Unlike some other suburbs, Elgin retains a relatively large number of young people. Twenty-eight percent are 18 years of age or younger. More than half of the resident labor force works in white-collar occupations, and 57 percent work in Elgin itself. Six percent are unemployed and 5 percent of all families lived in poverty during 1979. Thirty percent of the families reported an income in excess of $30,000 in that year.

Elgin remains an economically independent community located relatively far from the city of Chicago. Its labor supply is drawn not only from the city itself, but from the many surrounding communities and rural settlements from which the city is easily accessible by a network of modern highways. Downtown Elgin is a major retail center, with four large department stores and more than 500 other stores and specialty shops.

M.W.H.

Elk Grove Village

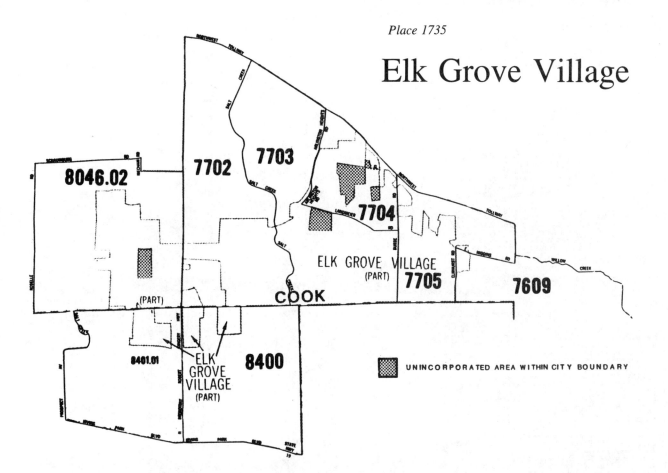

Elk Grove Village is in an area often designated as the Northwest Corridor. It is approximately 22 miles from Chicago's Loop, just northwest of O'Hare International Airport. The dense grove of trees in the area was the natural habitat of elk when the white settlers came, and they named the area for the game they found there. The first white settlers traveled west from Vermont in 1834. Among them were Aaron Miner and Eli Skinner, who had served in the Revolutionary War before traveling to the Midwest. They are two of the five soldiers from that war buried in Illinois. Their graves are in the Elk Grove Cemetery. In 1848, the arrival of the Busse family began a period of German settlement in the area.

During the years following settlement until the mid-1950s, Elk Grove was quite similar to many other rural communities. Most of the residents made their living by dairy or truck farming. There was no railroad to Elk Grove itself, but the farmers had access to two nearby lines, the North Western to the north in Arlington Heights, and the Milwaukee Road to the south, with stations in Wood Dale and Itasca. World War II brought increased activity to the entire Elk Grove region. Douglas Aircraft began to produce planes for military use on land in nearby Orchard Place, providing employment for some area residents. After the war, the plant and surrounding land became the base for the construction of the Douglas-Orchard Airport, which became O'Hare International Airport.

Elk Grove Village itself was developed as a planned community by the Central Texas Company (Centex), a Dallas land development group. Centex wanted to create an entire community, including industrial as well as residential areas, and spent several years exploring the metropolitan area for a large enough parcel of land — about 1500 acres. Elk Grove Township was the site chosen in 1954. Determining factors in the choice were the proximity of the newly-opened airport, the two railroads in the area that could provide spur lines into the village, and the network of highways which were being rapidly improved.

The incorporation of Elk Grove Village took place on July 19, 1956. Its boundaries were established at Higgins Road on the north, State Road on the west, Devon Avenue on the south and York Road on the

east. The first homes built were tract houses in the northwest corner of the new village, in the area bounded by Higgins, State, Oakton and Wildwood. A choice of four different floor plans were offered, with variations in the front window and entry treatment. Prices ranged from $15,000 to $22,000. Residential areas were laid out with "curvilinear streets," and underground cables were used for light and phone lines for the first time in the Chicago area. A shopping center, school and neighborhood parks were planned.

When Elk Grove Village had been incorporated for four years, the first federal census showed 6,600 residents, a substantial increase over the 116 counted in 1956. The Junior Women's Club was one of the first important civic groups in the new community. In 1959, the group organized the Elk Grove Village Public Library, first located in one of the Centex model homes, by collecting "a buck and a book" from the earliest homeowners. Village residents during this period faced problems with unpaved roads, a lack of nearby shopping and medical facilities, and land that needed re-landscaping. The moving vans and construction equipment in the area were constant signs of the village's growth. Throughout the 1960s, annexations added to the size of both the residential and industrial portions of Elk Grove Village. By 1966, the end of the village's first decade, there were three shopping centers, a high school, a hospital, a new building for the library, and several new elementary schools.

Firms began to occupy the Centex industrial park in 1958, and this area grew steadily, though more slowly than the residential section. The park is now occupied by more than 2,200 businesses with a work force of over 42,300 people. Buildings throughout the area are well landscaped, and almost residential in appearance. Industrial areas have been annexed over the years so that at this time the industrial park includes portions of DuPage County. It is roughly bounded by Devon Avenue on the south, Higgins Road and the Tollway on the north, Tonne Road on the west, and O'Hare Field on the east, and serves as a buffer between the airport and the residential parts of Elk Grove Village.

Most of Elk Grove Village's growth occurred during the 1960s,

Elk Grove Village
Population and Housing Characteristics, 1930–1980

	1980	1970	1960	1950	1940	1930
Total Population.......	28,679	24,516	6,608	*	*	*
% Male..................	49.4	50.0	49.6	*	*	*
% Female................	50.6	50.0	50.4	*	*	*
% White.................	93.0	99.2	100.0	*	*	*
% Black.................	0.8	0.1	-	*	*	*
% Other Nonwhite Races..	6.2	0.7	0.0	*	*	*
% Under 5 Years Old.....	7.3	12.1	28.0	*	*	*
% 5-19 Years Old........	28.1	37.0	19.1	*	*	*
% 20-44 Years Old.......	41.4	37.4	47.0	*	*	*
% 45-64 Years Old.......	18.5	11.4	4.7	*	*	*
% 65 Years and Older....	4.7	2.1	1.2	*	*	*
Median Shcool Years....	12.9	12.6	12.7	*	*	*
Total Housing Units....	9,698	6,248	1,867	*	*	*
% In One-Unit Structures.	70.5	87.2	99.7	*	*	*
% Owner Occupied........	71.0	88.7	89.6	*	*	*
% Renter Occupied.......	25.1	9.0	1.6	*	*	*
% Vacant...............	3.9	2.3	8.8	*	*	*
% 1+ Persons per Room....	1.7	5.6	6.8	*	*	*

Place 1735 -- Elk Grove Village , Illinois
Selected Characteristics of Census Tracts: 1980

Tract Number	Total	7609	7702	7703	7704	7705	8046.02	8051.02	8400	8401.01
Total Population.............	28907	57	9868	8209	4059	11	6475	228	0	0
% Male.......................	49.4	-	47.7	49.6	50.7	-	50.8	49.6	-	-
% Black......................	0.8	-	1.0	0.7	0.4	-	0.9	0.0	-	-
% Other Nonwhite.............	6.2	-	3.3	3.9	5.4	-	14.1	0.4	-	-
% Of Spanish Origin..........	2.6	-	2.2	2.0	3.6	-	2.6	2.2	-	-
% Foreign Born...............	8.4	-	7.2	6.2	7.9	-	12.7	21.8	-	-
% Living In Group Quarters...	0.4	-	1.0	0.1	0.0	-	0.0	0.0	-	-
% 13 Years Old And Under.....	23.0	-	20.2	19.6	21.2	-	32.9	18.9	-	-
% 14-20 Years Old............	14.1	-	16.2	15.4	14.5	-	8.9	15.8	-	-
% 21-64 Years Old............	58.2	-	56.1	61.0	60.3	-	56.4	59.6	-	-
% 65-74 Years Old............	3.0	-	4.7	2.6	2.8	-	1.3	3.1	-	-
% 75 Years Old And Over......	1.7	-	2.8	1.4	1.2	-	0.5	2.6	-	-
% In Different House.........	50.1	-	44.1	46.2	43.5	-	68.8	93.5	-	-
% Families With Female Head..	9.4	-	12.4	11.8	9.7	-	3.5	5.9	-	-
Median School Years Completed....	12.9	-	12.9	12.8	12.8	-	13.7	12.6	-	-
Median Family Income, 1979...$$	30578	-	32153	29127	28638	-	31525	35616	-	-
% Income Below Poverty Level....	1.2	-	1.2	1.1	2.1	-	1.1	0.0	-	-
% Income Of $30,000 Or More.....	52.3	-	57.0	47.5	46.6	-	56.1	51.4	-	-
% White Collar Workers.......	68.4	-	71.0	65.7	63.7	-	73.0	46.7	-	-
% Civilian Labor Force Unemployed..	2.7	-	2.9	2.6	2.4	-	3.0	0.0	-	-
% Riding To Work By Automobile....	92.4	-	91.8	94.6	92.4	-	90.7	80.7	-	-
Mean Commuting Time - Minutes...	24.6	-	23.6	21.1	23.6	-	32.8	13.9	-	-
Population Per Household.........	3.1	-	2.9	2.9	3.1	-	3.6	3.0	-	-
Total Housing Units...	9774	22	3475	2883	1409	4	1904	77	0	0
% Condominiums..............	9.4	-	22.5	4.3	0.0	-	0.6	0.0	-	-
% Built 1970 Or Later........	46.2	-	54.0	16.7	20.5	-	97.6	9.1	-	-
% Owner Occupied.............	70.8	-	69.7	63.6	65.1	-	86.9	87.0	-	-
% With 1+ Persons Per Room...	1.7	-	1.0	2.1	2.9	-	0.8	4.0	-	-
Median Value: Owner Units.......$$	78300	-	85000	67400	67300	-	92300	86100	-	-
Median Rent: Rental Units....$$	325	-	299	325	336	-	491	225	-	-
Median Number Of Rooms: All Units.	5.6	-	5.6	5.6	5.5	-	5.6	5.6	-	-

Elk Grove Village
Selected Characteristics of Census Tracts: 1970

Tract Number	TOTAL	7601	7701	8046	8051	8401
Total Population.............	20346	28396	2359	8686	25709	19009
% Male.......................	50.0	50.0	49.8	50.2	49.8	49.7
% Black......................	0.1	0.1	0.0	0.2	0.2	0.0
% Other Nonwhite.............	0.7	0.7	0.7	0.6	0.9	0.4
% Of Spanish Language........	1.4	1.9	5.9	2.8	1.7	5.0
% Foreign Born...............	3.1	3.4	7.9	3.0	4.2	8.2
% Living In Group Quarters...	0.1	0.1	0.0	0.0	0.9	0.5
% 13 Years Old And Under.....	39.6	38.5	31.1	34.1	30.3	33.2
% 14-20 Years Old............	10.3	10.3	11.5	11.6	9.9	10.7
% 21-64 Years Old............	48.0	49.0	52.2	52.0	56.6	52.1
% 65-74 Years Old............	1.5	1.6	3.3	1.5	2.0	2.5
% 75 Years Old And Over......	0.7	0.7	1.9	0.8	1.2	1.5
% In Different House.........	41.2	41.2	59.0	41.4	29.4	47.6
% Families With Female Head..	4.5	4.4	5.9	4.2	4.1	4.8
Median School Years Completed....	12.7	12.7	12.7	12.3	12.8	12.2
Median Family Income, 1969...$$	14155	14051	12586	13760	14783	13441
% Income Below Poverty Level....	1.8	1.8	4.5	2.2	1.6	2.8
% Income of $15,000 or More.....	42.9	42.3	30.4	40.1	48.4	37.5
% White Collar Workers.......	43.9	43.1	22.0	42.2	47.2	27.7
% Civilian Labor Force Unemployed..	1.9	2.1	2.2	2.1	1.8	2.6
% Riding To Work By Automobile....	89.0	87.1	83.3	86.8	86.1	87.3
Population Per Household.........	4.0	3.9	3.7	3.7	3.3	3.7
Total Housing Units..........	6246	7434	650	2515	8353	5320
% Condominiums & Cooperatives.....	0.1	0.1	0.0	0.0	0.0	2.3
% Built 1960 Or Later........	72.6	72.6	19.9	65.2	88.5	56.4
% Owner Occupied.............	88.6	84.8	84.0	62.8	45.4	72.1
% With 1+ Persons Per Room...$$	5.6	5.7	9.4	5.0	3.0	8.7
Median Value: Owner Units....$$	29900	30200	24500	31400	36200	27000
Median Rent: Rental Units....$$	204	202	128	182	195	166
Median Number Of Rooms: All Units.	5.8	5.7	5.3	5.8	5.1	5.2

although the population has continued to increase more slowly since. The village grew from 6,600 to 24,500 between 1960 and 1970. By 1980 the population neared 30,000. Of the current residents, 1 percent are black and 3 percent are Hispanic. As is often the case with new suburbs, the population is young; the median age is less than 30, and almost a third are 18 years of age or younger. More than two-thirds of the labor force is in white-collar work, and more than half of all families reported incomes of $30,000 or more in 1979. Three percent are unemployed and 1 percent lived in poverty in 1979. Many residents came to live in Elk Grove Village because they worked in the industrial park, and some who came to live in the village later found jobs there as well. Nevertheless, 70 percent of the workers commute to some place outside the village. Many residents are employed by the airport and airlines. Transportation needs for those who commute into Chicago are met by the two railroads and the network of roads and tollways in the area.

Housing in the village now includes not only single-family homes, but also apartments, condominiums, townhomes and quadroplex units. The number of housing units increased by more than 50 percent during the most recent 10 years. Reflective of the increased construction of multiple-unit housing, the relative number of single-family homes has declined, but still comprises three-fourths of the housing units in Elk Grove Village. Seventy-one percent of all units are currently owner-occupied, and the median value of owner-occupied units is more than 50 percent greater than the Chicago median.

Adjoining Elk Grove Village is the Busse Woods Forest Preserve area, a part of the Upper Salt Creek Watershed Plan. The area includes Busse Lake, which covers a territory of 590 acres. The preserve was formed in 1916, when 19 farmers sold their wood lots, parcels of land apart from their farms which were used for firewood, for $200 per acre. In 1924 the William Busse family purchased and donated a herd of 10 elk from Wyoming. The present herd now have their own corner at the intersection of Route 72 (Higgins Road) and Arlington Heights Road, where they were relocated to make it easier for visitors to view them at close range. Since 1963 the Forest Preserve has protected the area from changes that might be disruptive.

Elk Grove Village is governed by a village president, a board of six trustees, and a full-time village clerk. There is a professional village manager appointed jointly by the president and board. The Fire Department's pre-Fire Plan, which originated in Elk Grove Village because of its dual responsibility for both homes and industrial buildings, has brought national recognition. The library, nearing its quarter-century mark in 1984, has been expanded several times, and has nearly 100,000 books, as well as films, art prints, video cassettes, statuary, travel and community information. The closing of an elementary school that was no longer needed has provided space for a Senior Center, which serves as a meeting place for the ever growing number in this age group. The Elk Grove Historical Society, formed in 1975, is located on Biesterfield Road in a house which dates back to 1865, and has been restored as a typical Midwest farmhouse of the period 1850 to 1875. Elk Grove Village has participated in the Greater O'Hare Association of Industry and Commerce. The village's well-landscaped industrial buildings bring a pleasant balance to the residential community, and visitors from all over the world come to study, and in many cases, copy ideas used there.

Mary J. McCarthy

Place 1770

Elmhurst

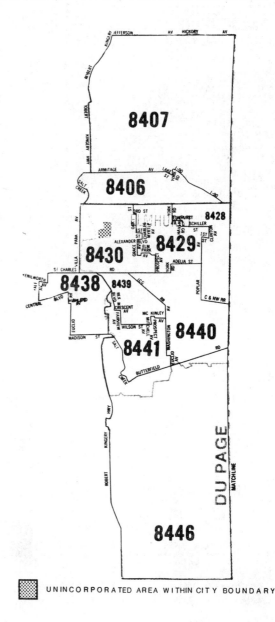

In 1834, after the departure of most of the Indians, Frederick Graue and his family settled on prairie land 17 miles west of Chicago, a portion of which would later become part of the pioneer community, Cottage Hill. In the 1840s he received 320 additional acres of land which comprise much of the north side of today's Elmhurst. Another early settler, Gerry Bates, came to Elmhurst in 1842. An inn called Hill Cottage was opened on Bates' land in 1843 by his brother-in-law, John L. Hovey. This became the first post office in the community, baptized Cottage Hill in 1845. The transposition of words was suggested by the Postmaster General since many other places were know as Hill-this or Hill-that. Bates also gave land for a right-of-way to the Galena and Chicago Union Railroad in the 1840s in return for building the station known as Cottage Hill across from his house on Park Avenue.

Cottage Hill was platted originally by Gerry Bates in 1854. Two years later Thomas Barbour Bryan bought 1,000 acres in the small village. By 1857 the population was listed as 200 and was concentrated in the area between York and Addison streets and along the railroad tracks. During the 1850s and 1860s Cottage Hill was composed mainly of farms, a few small businesses and several mansions used as summer homes by people such as the Bryans. Their mansion, known as Byrd's Nest (Bryan married a woman from the Byrd family of Virginia) was completed in 1859 and contained 21 rooms. Among other mansions of the time were Hawthorne, owned by Lucian Hagans, Clover Lawn (the former Hill Cottage moved to a new location) owned by G.P.A. Healey, and White Birch (called Lancaster Lodge by a subsequent owner and now a part of the library) owned by Seth Wadhams.

By the late 1860s Cottage Hill had been subtly changed from its original prairie land by the planting of hundreds of trees. John R. Case Sr. and his family planted an orchard consisting of 1,000 cherry trees and 600 apple trees. Others had planted many elm trees along the main streets of the village which eventually suggested its new name. The village then consisted of a post office, railway station, a few stores and saloons, as well as a Catholic and a Protestant church. The latter was Byrd's Nest Chapel built in the former bowling alley on that estate. In

▨ UNINCORPORATED AREA WITHIN CITY BOUNDARY

231

Elmhurst
Population and Housing Characteristics, 1930-1980

	1980	1970	1960	1950	1940	1930
Total Population......	44,276	50,547	36,991	21,273	15,458	14,055
% Male.................	48.4	48.6	48.7	49.3	49.2	50.0
% Female...............	51.6	51.4	51.3	50.7	50.8	50.0
% White................	96.5	99.2	99.9	99.8	99.8	99.8
% Black................	0.4	0.3	0.0	0.1	0.1	0.1
% Other Nonwhite Races...	3.1	0.5	0.1	0.1	0.1	0.1
% Under 5 Years Old......	5.8	7.5	10.6	9.6	6.5	10.0
% 5-19 Years Old........	25.0	32.2	29.1	22.1	25.6	25.7
% 20-44 Years Old........	34.2	28.5	30.6	37.1	40.1	43.3
% 45-64 Years Old........	23.8	23.7	22.9	24.5	21.9	16.6
% 65 Years and Older.....	11.2	8.1	6.8	6.7	5.9	4.4
Median School Years....	13.0	12.9	12.6	12.2	11.1	*
Total Housing Units....	14,999	14,594	10,593	6,270	4,227	*
% In One-Unit Structures..	83.8	87.4	91.7	*	*	*
% Owner Occupied........	83.0	84.1	84.7	76.1	35.2	*
% Renter Occupied.......	16.0	15.0	13.2	21.5	35.2	*
% Vacant...............	1.0	0.9	2.1	2.4	29.6	*
% 1+ Persons per Room....	1.7	4.9	5.6	5.9	*	*

Place 1770 -- Elmhurst , Illinois
Selected Characteristics of Census Tracts: 1980

Tract Number	Total	8401.03	8406	8407	8428	8429	8430	8439	8440	8441	8446
Total Population.............	44276	38	5025	6519	4651	4951	3803	4082	8514	4633	2060
% Male.......................	48.4	—	47.9	49.3	49.0	46.7	47.5	48.4	49.0	49.2	47.9
% Black......................	0.4	—	0.2	0.2	0.1	1.7	1.4	0.2	0.1	0.0	0.5
% Other Nonwhite.............	3.0	—	1.7	7.3	3.4	1.8	1.9	1.0	2.1	2.0	7.2
% Of Spanish Origin..........	2.1	—	1.2	6.3	1.5	2.2	1.2	1.3	1.3	1.3	1.2
% Foreign Born...............	7.0	—	6.2	12.4	7.9	4.8	6.1	6.7	5.1	3.9	11.6
% Living In Group Quarters...	1.9	—	0.0	3.7	0.0	12.5	0.0	0.0	0.0	0.0	0.0
% 13 Years Old And Under.....	19.0	—	18.5	23.5	18.3	15.0	18.2	19.1	20.0	17.7	16.8
% 14-20 Years Old............	13.4	—	10.5	12.7	12.3	18.4	11.3	12.4	14.6	15.0	10.5
% 21-64 Years Old............	56.4	—	57.7	55.7	57.5	52.2	53.5	56.3	56.6	60.1	59.1
% 65-74 Years Old............	6.9	—	8.3	4.0	7.4	8.3	10.5	7.3	5.7	5.2	9.6
% 75 Years Old And Over......	4.3	—	5.0	4.1	4.4	6.1	6.5	4.9	3.2	2.0	4.0
% In Different House.........	37.5	—	43.6	40.1	42.6	47.0	39.3	28.0	29.6	25.0	55.7
% Families With Female Head..	8.7	—	10.7	8.2	9.0	9.9	13.6	6.6	7.1	7.9	8.6
Median School Years Completed	13.0	—	12.8	12.5	14.3	13.5	13.6	13.0	13.0	13.7	12.9
Median Family Income, 1979.....$$	30407	—	28294	28252	34531	30294	29561	27587	32954	32312	30308
% Income Below Poverty Level....	1.3	—	0.9	1.9	0.0	0.0	3.0	2.8	1.7	0.5	1.0
% Income Of $30,000 Or More....	51.4	—	43.4	44.6	57.9	51.1	48.4	42.9	59.0	58.7	51.1
% White Collar Workers.......	68.6	—	65.7	50.1	77.9	74.7	71.2	71.8	68.7	73.5	76.5
% Civilian Labor Force Unemployed.	3.5	—	2.9	3.9	3.1	2.6	1.4	4.7	3.8	4.8	4.0
% Riding To Work By Automobile...	83.9	—	83.5	94.0	78.2	67.0	79.2	83.7	86.6	89.0	91.1
Mean Commuting Time - Minutes...	23.6	—	23.8	22.5	25.9	22.0	26.3	24.0	22.6	24.4	22.4
Population Per Household......	2.9	—	2.7	3.3	3.0	2.7	2.6	2.9	3.2	3.2	2.7
Total Housing Units..........	14995	13	1882	2007	1580	1663	1505	1446	2674	1449	776
% Condominiums...............	2.9	—	0.0	10.4	0.0	0.0	7.2	0.0	0.0	0.0	16.1
% Built 1970 Or Later........	9.9	—	8.2	31.3	0.3	2.8	8.6	0.8	3.9	1.2	47.8
% Owner Occupied.............	82.3	—	77.1	81.4	91.6	61.0	76.8	83.5	93.1	95.9	69.2
% With 1+ Persons Per Room...	1.7	—	1.0	4.3	0.9	1.8	1.4	1.5	1.3	1.3	0.8
Median Value: Owner Units......$$	74200	—	67900	68100	81800	82700	72400	67300	84800	74700	78300
Median Rent: Rental Units....$$	288	—	274	328	315	274	271	235	339	417	453
Median Number Of Rooms: All Units.	5.6	—	5.6	5.5	5.6	5.6	5.6	5.6	5.6	5.6	5.6

Elmhurst
Selected Characteristics of Census Tracts: 1970

Tract Number	TOTAL	8401	8406	8407	8428	8429	8430	8439	8440	8441	8446
Total Population.............	46392	19009	7278	6674	5364	5905	4182	6521	10789	5745	5861
% Male.......................	48.6	49.7	49.3	50.5	47.5	48.2	47.6	48.1	48.4	49.2	49.6
% Black......................	0.3	0.0	0.0	0.1	0.0	2.3	0.1	0.1	0.1	0.1	0.0
% Other Nonwhite.............	0.4	0.4	0.4	0.4	0.2	0.5	0.3	0.3	0.4	0.8	0.5
% Of Spanish Language........	1.7	5.0	3.8	4.1	0.3	1.7	0.3	2.0	1.0	0.8	1.6
% Foreign Born...............	5.1	8.2	7.5	6.3	6.1	5.5	5.1	4.0	4.0	3.8	3.9
% Living In Group Quarters...	1.7	0.5	0.6	0.1	0.1	12.8	0.0	0.3	0.2	0.2	0.0
% 13 Years Old And Under.....	27.4	33.2	27.3	33.2	24.3	21.6	22.7	27.5	29.6	31.2	25.8
% 14-20 Years Old............	13.7	10.7	11.5	11.8	13.8	19.5	11.4	12.3	13.7	14.9	13.1
% 21-64 Years Old............	50.8	52.1	51.8	51.7	52.2	48.1	53.5	51.0	50.0	50.5	54.2
% 65-74 Years Old............	5.3	2.5	5.9	2.3	6.3	6.9	8.3	6.0	4.4	2.2	5.0
% 75 Years Old And Over......	2.8	1.5	3.5	1.1	3.5	3.9	4.1	3.3	2.3	1.1	1.9
% In Different House.........	60.9	47.6	60.6	53.5	57.9	48.4	60.6	59.9	63.6	73.9	57.8
% Families With Female Head..	6.4	4.8	5.7	5.7	5.2	7.1	8.2	8.7	7.2	4.4	4.6
Median School Years Completed..	12.7	12.2	12.4	12.2	12.8	12.9	12.6	12.7	12.8	12.8	12.6
Median Family Income, 1969.....$$	14955	13441	13653	13751	17326	14754	13896	14671	17561	15566	15194
% Income Below Poverty Level.....	2.0	2.8	2.4	4.3	1.8	1.4	2.6	2.1	2.1	0.8	1.0
% Income of $15,000 or More.....	49.7	37.5	40.6	40.7	58.6	48.5	43.2	47.3	59.3	52.2	50.6
% White Collar Workers.......	46.3	27.7	40.3	30.2	58.8	43.9	40.9	44.3	54.8	49.0	48.7
% Civilian Labor Force Unemployed.	1.7	2.6	1.2	2.1	1.7	1.9	2.0	1.5	1.8	2.0	2.3
% Riding To Work By Automobile....	78.1	87.3	81.4	84.9	79.3	56.8	76.5	78.1	81.7	88.9	85.7
Population Per Household......	3.4	3.7	3.4	3.7	3.3	3.1	2.9	3.4	3.7	4.0	3.4
Total Housing Units..........	14594	5320	2210	1823	2121	1680	1475	1913	2943	1446	1762
% Condominiums & Cooperatives.....	0.4	2.3	0.4	0.0	0.0	0.0	3.7	0.0	0.0	0.0	0.0
% Built 1960 Or Later........	17.2	56.4	16.1	50.5	7.3	8.4	3.2	3.9	24.6	33.0	40.4
% Owner Occupied.............	83.8	72.1	86.5	76.6	81.9	67.4	69.0	90.8	90.2	97.7	82.7
% With 1+ Persons Per Room...	4.9	8.7	5.3	8.8	2.4	3.7	3.8	4.4	4.7	7.2	3.4
Median Value: Owner Units......$$	28600	27000	26500	26000	32500	31100	27500	25200	31900	29900	35400
Median Rent: Rental Units.....	153	166	147	152	148	138	159	158	146	167	221
Median Number Of Rooms: All Units.	5.7	5.2	5.6	5.3	5.9	5.6	5.2	5.6	6.0	5.8	5.8

1869, on Thomas B. Bryan's suggestion, the village changed its name to Elmhurst — roughly meaning elm forest.

The Chicago fire brought many new people to Elmhurst which was then perceived to be a country retreat from the noisy city. During the 1870s the northwest section of the community between Addison and Myrtle streets was subdivided into plots by a man named Emerson. While his sales campaign, which included a railway excursion, picnics, free beer and concerts, was not a great success, it did bring a few new residents to the village.

In 1871 Elmhurst College was founded by the German Evangelical Synods of the West and Northwest. Its purpose was to prepare students to enter the theological seminary and to train teachers for the German Evangelical schools. The prescribed course corresponded to four years of high school plus a small amount of college credit. Not until 1934 did Elmhurst College become accredited as a four year college. Since then it has grown to an enrollment of more than 1,000 students. While it maintains the traditional liberal arts program, it has expanded to include a Center for Business and Economics and a Center for Special Programs.

By 1880 Henry L. Glos had begun a campaign which resulted in the Village of Elmhurst being incorporated in 1882 with Glos as President of the Board of Trustees. One of the early concerns of the Board of Trustees was air pollution produced by animal and human refuse. The 1880s brought street grading, sidewalks, a city hall, street lamps and restrictions on local saloon activities. By 1885 estimates of the population ranged from 300 to 725. Elmhurst included nearly 40 businesses, one of which, the Elmhurst-Chicago Stone Company, is still operating. Most businesses were located a block north and south of the tracks, along York Street, and along First Street. The 1880s also saw the construction of a brick school, and the organization of 2 new churches. By the 1890s the census listed 1,050 persons, and Elmhurst had running water, a fire department and an electric light company.

By the turn of the century Elmhurst had a population of 1,728 after annexation of an area running west between the Chicago and North Western tracks and St. Charles Road. After a near doubling in population during the next decade the largely voluntary services of village officials were becoming inadequate. In 1909 a special election was held to decide on a petition for incorporation as a city. The vote was nearly evenly split, necessitating a canvassing of the population which resulted in approval of the petition. Thus in 1910, with a population of 2,360, Elmhurst became a city.

At the start of the 1920s the population was 4,594 but grew rapidly during the decade to 14,000 in 1930. Elmhurst was an attractive suburb with its exclusive and well-landscaped homes on the south side of town near St. Charles road, its abundance of tree-lined streets, and its ease of access to Chicago. Four railroads passed through the town with the Chicago and North Western and the Chicago, Aurora and Elgin providing commuter service. The main highways were paved in the early 1920s, stimulating further city growth as the popularity of automobiles increased. The Elmhurst Community Hospital was dedicated in 1926 and has grown over the years to its current capacity of more than 500 beds. The Elmhurst Public Library was also established in this decade in the former Wadhams mansion. One of the most famous residents of Elmhurst was Carl Sandburg who lived there from 1919 to 1930, producing much of the work for which he is known during that period.

The decade of the 1930s brought little increase in population or in economic activity. While continuing to discourage industry the city did drop its restrictions on apartment buildings, hoping to draw new residents. Despite the slow economic recovery Elmhurst celebrated its centennial in 1936 with a huge parade, plays, and concerts.

Following World War II Elmhurst once again began a period of growth. During the mid-1940s the St. Charles West apartments were opened at a cost of $3 million. Due in part to the availability of vacant land for residential expansion, Elmhurst's population went from 15,000 in 1940 to 21,000 in 1950. In 1953 the city manager form of government was instituted and city services were extensively improved and expanded. The plans for the Congress Street Expressway (now the Eisenhower) increased Elmhurst's attractiveness by cutting auto commuter time into Chicago in half, from 40 to 20 minutes. During the 1950s the population increased by 74 percent to 36,991.

In an effort to broaden the tax base in the mid-1950s, Elmhurst established the Elmhurst Industrial Park zoned for light industry. It is located in the northwestern section of the community. By 1962, with several annexations, the park covered 600 acres and within a few years 120 companies were located there. In 1980 there were 1,324 business establishments in the city employing 22,537 persons. The bulk of these businesses were in the services and wholesale and retail trade categories. Besides the original downtown shopping area of Elmhurst there are the Vallette and Spring Road districts and the Elmhurst Plaza. The Oak Brook shopping plaza is two miles southwest and the Yorktown center is also nearby.

By 1970 the population had grown to 46,000. Most of the housing units in the city had been built after World War II. The 1960s saw an increase of 4,000 housing units, approximately the same number constructed during the 1950s. The population declined to 44,000 in 1980. The city had little open land for expansion and building. Between 1970 and 1980 only about 400 additional housing units were constructed resulting in approximately 15,000 units. Of these, 86 percent were single-family homes and 84 percent were owner-occupied.

The population is almost all white. In 1980 less than .5 percent of the population was black and only 3 percent were of other non-white races. The predominant nationality among foreign stock continues to be German and only 2 percent are of Spanish origin. The population of Elmhurst has aged since 1960. Those less than 18 years old have decreased by 10 percent and those 65 and more have increased by 5 percent. The median income in 1979 was $23,530 and the median home value in 1980 was $74,200. Three percent of all workers are unemployed and 1 percent of all families live in poverty.

The settlement pattern in Elmhurst was similar to other areas in that it followed the available transportation lines. The south side of Elmhurst with its old stately mansions continues to be an exclusive section, while newer homes may be found scattered throughout the community. Since Elmhurst did not grow as early or rapidly as some of its neighbors its ability to expand was limited by previously made boundaries, such as Villa Park to the west and the Cook County line to the east. Although the city did not encourage industry until the early 1960s its efforts seem successful.

Gail Danks Welter

Evanston

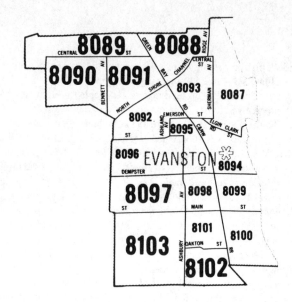

Evanston lies in Cook County and is located on Lake Michigan, 12 miles north of the Loop. It is bounded on the south by Chicago, on the west by Skokie, and on the north by Wilmette. Prior to settlement it was an area of Indian trails and swamps; the only high ground lay along two ridges, the present routes of Ridge and Chicago avenues. The earliest white settlers built cabins scattered along these ridges, and lived by farming and wood-cutting. Their community was centered around Major Edward Mulford's tavern on the west ridge, just 10 miles from the Chicago courthouse, and became known as Ridgeville. In 1842 the settlers built a schoolhouse, though the area was still only sparsely populated, and so swampy that travel was difficult.

The development of the city of Evanston proper began with the founding of Northwestern University, located in the northeastern corner of the city along the lake shore. Nine members of the Methodist Episcopal Church met in Chicago in 1850 for the purpose of founding a university. They bought 379 acres at a lake shore site which was not low, wet and swampy. By 1855, Northwestern University had a three-story building and 10 students were enrolled that fall. Two other colleges were located nearby. Northwestern Female College also opened in the fall of 1855 and Garrett Biblical Institute had been founded in 1853.

In 1854, the settlement adjoining the University was platted with a rectangular street grid, and a drainage commission began reclaiming swampy land. At the time of the first assessment in 1853, property in town was valued at $6,000. The opening of the Chicago and Milwaukee Railroad (later merged with the Chicago and North Western) along the north shore between Chicago and Waukegan in 1855 spurred residential settlement.

In 1863, Evanston was incorporated as a town, with H.B. Hurd as president. The following year property values were assessed at $125,000. Population increased steadily during the next 20 years, reaching 4,400 by the time of the 1880 census. In 1871, a free public library was opened. In 1872, the town was re-incorporated as a village. The laying of gas and water pipes began and two years later a water works was built. In that year, business property downtown was selling for $75 to $150 per foot. At that time, there were a number of Protestant churches in Evanston. They included Baptist, Methodist Episcopal, Methodist Congregational, Episcopal, Presbyterian, and a Swedish Methodist Episcopal, reflecting a growing Swedish population.

In 1873 the Evanston College for Ladies merged with Northwestern University, and educator Frances Willard became Dean of the University's Women's College. After her resignation, she became active in the temperance movement and served as president of the Women's Christian Temperance Union. Evanston, which had been dry by charter since its founding, became the organization's national headquarters.

The population of Evanston doubled in the decade from 1880 to 1890 and again from 1890 to 1900, reaching 19,259 by the turn of the century. Several annexations, including the villages of North Evanston and South Evanston, increased the territory included in the village. In 1892, Evanston was incorporated as a city with a mayor-council form of government. Enrollment and employment at Northwestern University continued to grow. According to local legend, the ice cream sundae was invented in Evanston during this period. Seltzer water was banned on the sabbath, so druggists in the town removed it and served ice cream with syrup, calling the dish a "sundae."

By the turn of the century, the Chicago, North Shore, and Milwaukee Line was operating between Wilson Avenue in Chicago and Waukegan. In 1908, the Chicago rapid transit system was extended to Central Street near the northern border of Evanston, and in 1912 to Linden Street in Wilmette. With such easy access to downtown Chicago, population continued its rapid growth, from 19,259 in 1900 to 37,234 in 1920, and 63,338 in 1930. The resulting building boom was largely uncontrolled until 1921. The City Council passed Evanston's first zoning ordinance, with the hope of preventing overcrowding of the land, arresting the encroachment of business and industry into residential areas, separating apartment houses from single-family dwellings and conserving property values. Throughout this period, Evanston, with its close-in location, its railroad and elevated connections with Chicago, its lake shore location and its outstanding educational facilities, was in the forefront of the rapidly-growing north suburban area. Germans and Swedes were the predominant nationalities among the foreign stock in 1930, followed by the English and Canadians.

As was true of the entire metropolitan area, rapid population growth in Evanston came to a halt with the Depression. Growth in Evanston could not have continued at the same level in any case, for the available land for new construction was limited.

After the Second World War and through the succeeding decade, growth resumed, but at a slower pace. Some of the increase in population recorded between 1940 and 1950 is artificial, since it results from a change in the census procedures with regard to enumeration of college students. In 1945, building restrictions were relaxed permitting some industrial development in Evanston. According to the 1958 Census of Manufacturers, there were 139 manufacturing establishments in Evanston employing 4,981 persons. However, Evanston remained primarily a residential community with a small industrial and commercial base. In 1952, Evanston adopted a council-manager form of government. The property tax is the single largest source of revenue for the city, and because of a fairly high level of public services and educational facilities, the tax rate is high.

Until the mid-1950s, Evanston was a key retail center, serving the entire North Shore and the area west to Elgin. However, in 1956, the opening of the Old Orchard shopping center in neighboring Skokie signaled the beginning of a long-term decline, gradual but steady, in Evanston's retail sales. Several of the city's major stores have closed. Beginning in the late 1960s, however, Evanston's losses in retail space have been replaced by new office space development. Large office buildings and national headquarters have begun to dominate the city's central business district. In response to the changing character of the downtown, the city has taken steps to increase parking space in the area. Smaller specialty stores have become a more important part of the retail sector, and the restaurant trade has grown, partly as a result of changes in Evanston's liquor laws, which for the first time permitted the sale of alcohol.

The population of Evanston increased gradually between 1950 and 1970. Like many surrounding communities, the city experienced a

Evanston
Population and Housing Characteristics, 1930-1980

	1980	1970	1960	1950	1940	1930
Total Population.......	73,706	79,808	79,283	73,641	65,389	63,338
% Male...................	46.6	45.4	46.0	46.5	45.7	46.7
% Female.................	53.4	54.6	54.0	53.5	54.3	53.3
% White..................	74.5	82.1	88.0	90.3	90.7	92.1
% Black..................	21.4	16.1	11.5	9.5	9.2	7.8
% Other Nonwhite Races...	4.1	1.8	0.5	0.2	0.1	0.1
% Under 5 Years Old......	4.8	7.0	8.4	7.6	5.6	7.4
% 5-19 Years Old.........	20.7	23.4	20.6	17.5	20.3	22.0
% 20-44 Years Old........	42.8	34.3	32.9	39.0	42.9	46.0
% 45-64 Years Old........	17.6	21.3	25.4	26.2	23.7	19.4
% 65 Years and Older.....	14.1	14.0	12.7	9.7	7.5	5.2
Median School Years....	15.4	14.6	12.8	12.5	12.4	*
Total Housing Units....	29,295	27,782	27,050	20,947	19,177	*
% In One-Unit Structures.	36.2	37.1	40.8	*	*	*
% Owner Occupied.........	46.9	41.2	41.4	40.6	28.3	*
% Renter Occupied........	49.8	56.6	54.0	57.9	66.3	*
% Vacant.................	3.3	2.2	4.6	1.5	5.4	*
% 1+ Persons per Room....	2.2	3.4	4.3	6.7	7.8	*

Place 1845 -- Evanston , Illinois
Selected Characteristics of Census Tracts: 1980

Tract Number	Total	8087	8088	8089	8090	8091	8092	8093	8094	8095	8096
Total Population.............	73706	6985	2333	3775	4074	3444	4799	4884	4227	3467	3427
% Male.......................	46.6	51.8	44.1	45.3	42.7	45.8	45.0	47.6	41.6	49.6	48.1
% Black......................	21.4	6.5	3.2	1.1	1.1	2.3	96.6	12.5	5.1	11.7	71.8
% Other Nonwhite.............	4.0	4.2	3.2	1.9	2.0	1.9	1.4	7.9	3.7	5.6	1.9
% Of Spanish Origin..........	2.3	1.9	2.3	0.5	1.5	1.0	1.1	2.1	1.4	1.7	3.2
% Foreign Born...............	11.4	6.7	7.8	5.4	11.4	8.4	8.4	16.4	11.0	10.1	10.2
% Living In Group Quarters...	11.1	64.6	11.8	0.4	5.8	3.2	0.0	16.6	27.8	8.2	0.0
% 13 Years Old And Under.....	14.5	5.0	15.3	17.7	19.4	19.0	19.3	12.1	5.7	8.2	19.3
% 14-20 Years Old............	14.0	51.5	14.9	7.7	8.5	8.0	14.9	7.6	15.9	7.3	14.2
% 21-64 Years Old............	57.4	37.4	57.1	55.4	48.8	56.6	50.8	65.4	44.3	67.1	55.2
% 65-74 Years Old............	7.0	3.3	7.0	10.8	7.5	7.1	9.7	7.4	9.5	8.0	6.4
% 75 Years Old And Over......	7.1	2.7	5.7	8.4	15.6	9.3	5.3	7.5	24.6	9.4	4.8
% In Different House.........	55.0	82.9	43.9	37.5	41.7	46.4	32.3	63.3	59.4	63.5	48.1
% Families With Female Head..	22.0	9.6	11.6	16.1	9.3	13.6	44.8	19.0	14.2	18.2	26.9
Median School Years Completed.	15.4	16.1	16.1	16.1	16.1	16.1	11.3	16.1	14.8	16.1	12.7
Median Family Income, 1979......$$	28264	46442	36145	34016	37287	35304	15445	25236	35751	27415	24640
% Income Below Poverty Level....	3.8	3.4	1.3	0.0	0.0	0.7	13.5	5.8	2.6	2.6	4.3
% Income Of $30,000 Or More.....	46.1	69.3	66.7	60.5	64.4	61.7	9.5	38.4	57.2	45.7	38.0
% White Collar Workers..........	77.7	76.7	84.0	89.8	86.5	88.3	49.1	81.1	77.8	85.3	52.3
% Civilian Labor Force Unemployed.	3.5	3.7	1.4	3.0	1.9	2.5	9.1	2.4	5.1	2.7	7.1
% Riding To Work By Automobile....	55.2	23.0	45.1	60.2	66.2	62.1	62.7	45.0	34.8	43.9	69.8
Mean Commuting Time - Minutes....	27.1	17.7	27.3	30.1	27.4	26.2	24.2	27.2	24.1	28.9	27.1
Population Per Household..........	2.3	2.5	2.4	2.4	2.6	2.4	3.1	2.1	1.6	1.9	3.1
Total Housing Units..........	29276	1024	967	1630	1540	1432	1647	2030	1950	1774	1140
% Condominiums...................	10.3	28.4	12.9	9.1	7.9	8.9	0.0	5.7	7.2	12.1	0.0
% Built 1970 Or Later............	3.3	4.6	6.0	3.2	3.4	3.2	2.5	11.3	5.2	3.3	2.4
% Owner Occupied.................	46.2	73.3	49.9	76.6	84.1	64.0	46.1	28.8	17.3	25.3	62.5
% With 1+ Persons Per Room.......$$	2.2	1.0	0.3	0.4	0.3	0.2	9.2	0.9	1.8	1.7	5.3
Median Value: Owner Units.......$$	88600	159300	109800	98400	108100	96900	57400	94900	186400	124600	68400
Median Rent: Rental Units.......$$	312	351	327	351	437	333	235	296	350	328	270
Median Number Of Rooms: All Units.	5.0	5.6	5.6	5.6	5.6	5.6	5.2	4.4	3.0	4.0	5.6

Tract Number	8097	8098	8099	8100	8101	8102	8103
Total Population.............	4024	3098	2670	4776	4952	5421	7350
% Male.......................	49.6	47.3	48.1	45.6	47.1	44.7	46.5
% Black......................	49.9	24.5	2.6	4.1	31.5	16.8	17.3
% Other Nonwhite.............	3.5	2.9	2.8	1.9	4.8	5.6	8.1
% Of Spanish Origin..........	7.5	2.2	1.1	1.0	4.7	1.8	3.6
% Foreign Born...............	21.9	7.5	7.3	8.2	12.2	12.9	20.6
% Living In Group Quarters...	0.3	13.3	0.0	0.0	0.8	2.1	2.4
% 13 Years Old And Under.....	19.2	14.1	17.2	10.7	20.2	14.0	16.9
% 14-20 Years Old............	13.4	10.0	9.9	5.0	10.1	6.9	9.9
% 21-64 Years Old............	58.4	65.2	66.0	74.2	62.3	66.1	57.7
% 65-74 Years Old............	5.7	5.9	4.3	5.7	4.4	7.2	8.9
% 75 Years Old And Over......	3.3	4.8	2.7	4.5	3.0	5.8	6.6
% In Different House.........	40.9	54.1	55.0	65.2	62.2	70.1	42.2
% Families With Female Head..	23.0	27.1	19.3	27.2	34.7	28.2	14.1
Median School Years Completed....	12.6	14.6	16.1	16.1	14.7	14.6	14.5
Median Family Income, 1979......$$	25294	29865	36745	29899	20440	24154	29951
% Income Below Poverty Level....	3.8	4.1	0.9	2.3	8.3	4.8	1.6
% Income Of $30,000 Or More.....	34.6	49.7	65.6	49.8	25.9	37.7	49.8
% White Collar Workers..........	58.8	79.3	88.7	91.6	76.3	81.3	74.5
% Civilian Labor Force Unemployed.	5.1	1.0	1.7	1.1	4.0	4.4	2.9
% Riding To Work By Automobile....	70.3	59.3	47.3	49.8	58.4	59.1	73.8
Mean Commuting Time - Minutes...	25.1	25.7	34.0	31.2	27.5	31.4	27.0
Population Per Household..........	2.9	2.4	2.5	1.9	2.4	2.1	2.6
Total Housing Units..........	1404	1175	1174	2713	2174	2688	2814
% Condominiums...................	1.1	4.9	21.3	23.8	8.9	18.5	2.2
% Built 1970 Or Later............	1.2	0.6	1.7	4.1	0.5	0.9	1.9
% Owner Occupied.................	60.6	35.7	41.6	28.9	31.1	32.1	67.8
% With 1+ Persons Per Room.......	6.1	1.9	0.2	0.7	3.0	1.6	2.4
Median Value: Owner Units.......$$	65400	97600	179800	126900	78200	80400	71200
Median Rent: Rental Units.......$$	272	287	351	344	293	308	299
Median Number Of Rooms: All Units.	5.3	4.9	4.6	4.6	4.6	4.5	5.4

Evanston
Selected Characteristics of Census Tracts: 1970

Tract Number	TOTAL	8087	8088	8089	8090	8091	8092	8093	8094	8095	8096
Total Population	80113	5581	2905	4069	4360	3839	5863	4778	4194	3251	4065
% Male	45.4	50.4	41.0	44.9	43.7	44.0	45.5	44.7	34.3	46.4	47.0
% Black	16.1	2.3	0.6	0.3	0.5	0.6	97.2	11.8	4.4	8.6	65.2
% Other Nonwhite	1.8	1.9	1.4	1.0	0.5	1.2	0.7	2.5	1.0	3.4	0.9
% Of Spanish Language	1.8	0.5	1.5	1.3	1.3	1.1	1.3	2.6	1.5	0.6	3.3
% Foreign Born	9.1	4.4	6.3	5.2	6.8	8.5	1.5	9.9	10.8	12.9	7.1
% Living In Group Quarters	8.0	55.2	14.3	0.7	4.8	2.3	1.3	6.5	30.0	11.3	0.6
% 13 Years Old And Under	19.8	8.3	20.7	21.9	22.1	22.4	26.9	18.7	8.7	13.4	27.2
% 14-20 Years Old	12.9	45.4	17.6	8.6	8.9	10.4	11.9	13.1	13.1	7.6	12.2
% 21-64 Years Old	53.2	36.8	48.1	51.2	46.9	49.8	51.2	56.6	44.5	57.3	51.9
% 65-74 Years Old	8.1	5.8	9.2	11.3	10.5	9.5	7.0	6.9	13.2	11.3	5.9
% 75 Years Old And Over	6.0	3.7	4.5	7.1	11.7	7.9	3.0	4.7	20.6	10.4	3.0
% In Different House	49.2	28.9	44.3	61.4	62.2	52.7	64.1	43.5	44.3	32.5	63.4
% Families With Female Head	12.7	8.3	12.1	10.5	7.5	10.7	24.9	12.6	14.4	14.2	14.7
Median School Years Completed	13.2	16.4	15.1	15.4	15.2	14.1	10.9	14.8	14.2	14.1	12.2
Median Family Income, 1969 $$	13932	21518	15754	18148	19414	15922	8714	12259	18381	14083	11269
% Income Below Poverty Level	3.9	0.6	6.0	2.1	0.7	4.0	10.5	6.9	3.1	1.0	5.7
% Income of $15,000 or More	44.4	70.4	52.2	61.2	64.6	53.1	18.3	39.4	59.9	44.3	27.8
% White Collar Workers	49.9	49.6	60.7	64.4	67.9	55.8	10.0	51.3	62.3	54.8	25.7
% Civilian Labor Force Unemployed	3.1	2.4	6.7	2.3	2.9	0.5	6.0	2.2	3.3	4.0	2.9
% Riding To Work By Automobile	56.7	31.4	39.0	65.4	68.4	66.6	64.0	49.1	39.6	48.5	66.9
Population Per Household	2.7	2.6	2.7	2.7	2.8	2.8	3.4	2.5	1.9	2.2	3.5
Total Housing Units	27768	983	933	1526	1497	1379	1736	1792	1571	1333	1152
% Condominiums & Cooperatives	3.9	21.6	2.1	5.9	0.0	3.2	0.6	1.8	6.1	6.1	0.5
% Built 1960 Or Later	12.4	15.3	5.9	5.6	18.2	11.6	11.2	7.3	24.1	20.3	9.6
% Owner Occupied	37.3	40.4	48.3	66.6	70.7	53.4	44.2	26.3	11.5	13.0	61.5
% With 1+ Persons Per Room	3.4	0.8	1.6	0.5	1.0	1.5	15.2	3.7	2.1	2.1	9.6
Median Value: Owner Units $$	33700	50100	40400	38800	41400	34800	22800	35500	50100	43000	24800
Median Rent: Rental Units $$	165	206	167	197	261	177	135	150	178	179	147
Median Number Of Rooms: All Units	5.0	5.8	5.4	5.9	6.1	5.6	5.0	4.7	3.7	4.2	5.4

Tract Number	8097	8098	8099	8100	8101	8102	8103
Total Population	4261	3572	3300	6058	5586	6480	8030
% Male	48.3	47.1	46.2	44.8	47.4	45.0	47.5
% Black	30.6	25.1	1.9	1.4	14.0	1.2	0.9
% Other Nonwhite	1.1	1.8	1.1	1.7	2.6	3.8	2.9
% Of Spanish Language	3.1	3.0	1.4	2.0	2.9	0.7	1.9
% Foreign Born	11.0	9.9	11.2	10.2	10.5	11.2	14.4
% Living In Group Quarters	0.0	1.3	1.4	1.8	0.9	2.1	1.7
% 13 Years Old And Under	25.3	24.0	23.4	19.1	21.7	16.7	20.0
% 14-20 Years Old	11.7	11.3	11.2	6.2	9.2	8.0	11.1
% 21-64 Years Old	53.6	53.6	56.0	61.7	58.0	61.6	57.2
% 65-74 Years Old	5.6	6.6	5.8	8.1	6.8	9.5	7.2
% 75 Years Old And Over	3.7	4.5	3.7	5.0	4.3	4.2	4.5
% In Different House	59.0	44.4	51.2	35.7	40.9	43.1	62.5
% Families With Female Head	12.7	15.6	12.7	11.1	15.1	12.3	8.5
Median School Years Completed	12.2	12.9	16.0	15.3	12.9	13.0	12.7
Median Family Income, 1969 $$	10986	12021	17857	14181	12525	13805	14427
% Income Below Poverty Level	5.1	8.0	2.3	2.6	4.3	2.2	2.1
% Income of $15,000 or More	26.6	41.8	56.8	44.8	35.8	42.0	45.9
% White Collar Workers	30.8	44.9	61.3	66.4	51.6	54.8	50.7
% Civilian Labor Force Unemployed	4.2	4.1	1.4	3.4	2.2	2.7	2.7
% Riding To Work By Automobile	72.2	59.2	49.5	52.9	56.4	58.7	66.7
Population Per Household	3.1	2.8	2.9	2.4	2.6	2.4	2.9
Total Housing Units	1408	1294	1151	2549	2150	2664	2745
% Condominiums & Cooperatives	0.9	1.5	1.3	3.8	3.3	8.3	1.9
% Built 1960 Or Later	14.1	4.9	4.8	11.2	14.1	14.3	12.4
% Owner Occupied	53.6	29.3	28.2	11.3	23.3	17.2	65.2
% With 1+ Persons Per Room	7.4	5.7	1.2	1.2	3.5	1.6	1.8
Median Value: Owner Units $$	23800	35200	50100	45200	28900	32000	29600
Median Rent: Rental Units $$	134	141	180	175	151	170	167
Median Number Of Rooms: All Units	5.1	4.7	5.4	4.6	4.6	4.6	5.3

population decline between 1970 and 1980, but these losses were primarily due to an overall decline in household size. The population has also become slightly younger, in contrast to surrounding communities. This difference is probably attributable to the variety of housing available in Evanston and the relatively large number of rental units. The city has been racially mixed for over a century, and the black population has increased steadily, growing from 12 percent in 1960 to 21 percent in 1980. Residentially, blacks are concentrated in the central portion of the city. There has also been an increase in the Hispanic population, although persons of Spanish origin still constituted only about 2 percent of the population in 1980.

Evanston has a substantial employment base, including office, retail and industrial jobs, and a large portion of its residents work within the city. The Chicago, North Shore and Milwaukee Line abandoned its commuter service in 1955. However, transportation to the Loop is still afforded by the elevated line and the Chicago and North Western Railroad.

Evanston has remained a suburb of relatively high socio-economic status. Since it is an older community, the housing stock is older, but in relatively good condition. The city has an active code enforcement program, and provides rehabilitation assistance for low-income residents. There is a substantial preservation program which includes several hundred landmark buildings. Some new residential construction occurred during the 1950s, especially in the southwestern corner of the city, but at present there is virtually no vacant land for new building. Compared to other North Shore suburbs, there are a relatively large number of multi-unit housing structures.

During the 1970s, substantial work was done to maintain public facilities, including street and sidewalk repair, a street tree planting program, and parks renovation. Future plans include two sites for new mixed-use development on the edges of the central business district, and a transportation center which would connect the Chicago and North Western and CTA elevated lines.

Marjorie DeVault

Glenview

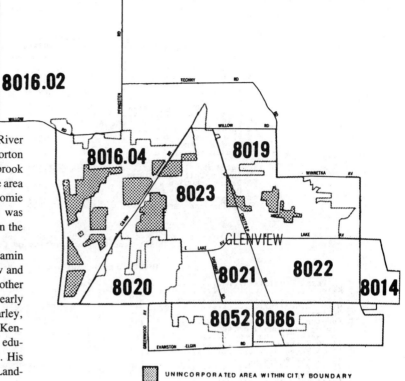

UNINCORPORATED AREA WITHIN CITY BOUNDARY

Glenview is located in Cook County, between the Des Plaines River and the North Branch of the Chicago River. It is bordered by Morton Grove on the south, Skokie and Wilmette on the east, and Northbrook and Northfield on the north. The first white settlers moved into the area (then called Northfield Township) in 1833, when the Pottawatomie Indians were moved beyond the Mississippi River. The land was mainly prairie and settlement began along old Indian trails and in the occasional grove of oak trees.

The first Glenview settlers were Dardenus Bishop and Benjamin Troops, who built houses in the vicinity of the present Glenview and Waukegan roads, an area referred to as South Northfield. Several other families arrived in the area during the next three years. These early residents were mostly English farmers, who grew oats, corn, barley, wheat, potatoes, horse radish, onions and vegetables. Dr. John Kennicott, the area's first physician and also a horticulturalist and educational leader, settled in the western part of Northfield in 1836. His home was the "The Grove," which is now a National Historic Landmark and part of the Glenview Park District.

Mail service to the area began in 1836, on stagecoaches which traveled along the Milwaukee Road (now Milwaukee Avenue). The first school was built in 1843, and post offices were established in the Grove in 1848, and in South Northfield (the center of the present day village) in 1853. The 1850 census showed that Northfield was the most densely populated township in the area outside of Chicago, with 1,013 residents. During the 1850s there was a second wave of immigration, and several German families came to the area.

However, the township continued to be a farming community and the population grew slowly, to 1,534 in 1860 and 1,705 in 1870. In 1872, the Chicago and Milwaukee Railroad built a track through the Glenview area in order to handle the large shipments of building supplies that were needed for rebuilding after the Chicago fire. A rail stop in the village of South Northfield provided better access to the city and opened up opportunities for tile manufacturing and dairy and truck farming. A large nursery business was also established in the town. A second railroad track was laid in 1892 in anticipation of the Columbian Exposition to be held in Chicago.

The name of "South Northfield" was awkward and confusing. Over the years the village was also referred to as "North Branch" and "Oak Glen", and the railroad named its stop in Glenview "Barr," after a company administrator. The villagers decided on the present name at a special meeting in 1895.

In the early 1890s members of the Swedenborg Society of Chicago (followers of Emanuel Swedenborg) decided to relocate in the Glenview area in order to build a community focused around the doctrines of their church. They bought 40 acres of land near the present intersection of Glenview and Shermer roads. Their members began to build homes, and by 1894 there were eight families living in "The Park" and 20 pupils in their school. These new settlers were mostly professional people who commuted to Chicago, and the character of Glenview began to change. the concentration of people in the area created a need for more services, and the village incorporated in 1899 with a population of 351 and a land area of 1.5 square miles. The first village mayor was Hugh Burnham, a Swedenborgian and nephew of the Chicago architect and planner, Daniel Burnham.

Following incorporation, sidewalks and street lights were installed and a bridge was built on Waukegan Road. Gas and electric utilities were established in 1910, a volunteer fire department was organized in

1912, and water distribution started in 1916. The ease of commuting to Chicago and the presence of the Swedenborg Society attracted more white-collar residents to Gleview. During the 1920s, several roads were paved, a zoning ordinance was adopoted, and a chamber of commerce and park district were formed. Several golf clubs were established in the area. In 1931, the village voted to adopt a council-manager form of government and in 1932 the first manager was appointed. In spite of these improvements, Glenview remained a small town up to the time of the Depression, with a population of only 1,886 in 1930. Despite the Depression, the population grew to 2,500 in 1940.

During the late 1930s, the U.S. Navy began to use to Curtiss-Reynolds Airfield in Glenview for high-speed aircraft. Eventually, a 319-acre tract became the Glenview Naval Air Station, where Navy and Marine Corps aviators received primary flight training. In 1942, construction began on the $12,500,000 Naval Reserve Aviation Base. During World War II, 9000 cadets received their training at the base. In 1946, primary training at the base was discontinued, but the Naval Air Station has continued to grow, now serving as a reserve training base. It is national headquarters for the Naval and Marine Air Reserve Training Commands.

The Construction of the Edens Expressway in 1952 began a period of much more rapid growth for Glenview which has continued through the late 1970s. Between 1950 and 1960 the village population tripled in size from 6,142 to 18,132. Further growth brought the number to residents to almost 25,000 in 1970. In 1971, the Naval Air Station (by then covering almost 13,000 acres) was annexed to the village. This was Glenview's largest annexation, and increased its popoulation to more than 32,000 today. Like many suburbs, modern Glenview is almost entirely white. There are fewer than 300 blacks, compared to more than 30,000 whites. A handful of American Indians and about a thousand of Asiatic descent — Koreans, Filipinos, Japanese, Chinese and Asian Indians — completed the population.

The number of housing units has doubled since 1960, growing faster in the most recent decade because of annexation of the Naval Air Station. Although new residential construction has consisted largely of apartments and condominiums, Glenview remains overwhelmingly a place of single-family (83 percent), owner-occupied (79 percent) units. Twenty years ago, more than 5 percent of all homes in Glenview were

Glenview
Population and Housing Characteristics, 1930-1980

	1980	1970	1960	1940	1940	1930
Total Population.......	32,060	24,880	18,132	6,142	2,500	1,886
% Male..................	49.1	48.7	49.3	49.2	49.2	52.2
% Female................	50.9	51.3	50.7	50.8	50.8	47.8
% White.................	95.4	99.4	99.9	99.7	99.5	100.0
% Black.................	0.9	0.1	0.1	0.2	0.5	–
% Other Nonwhite Races...	3.7	0.6	0.0	0.1	0.0	–
% Under 5 Years Old......	6.0	6.9	12.9	12.3	7.7	9.4
% 5-19 Years Old........	25.5	32.5	30.3	24.1	24.8	*
% 20-44 Years Old.......	35.3	27.9	32.4	39.1	41.5	*
% 45-64 Years Old.......	24.7	25.6	19.9	19.7	19.4	17.1
% 65 Years and Older.....	8.6	7.0	4.4	4.8	6.6	5.4
Median School Years......	14.6	13.5	12.9	12.6	9.7	*
Total Housing Units....	10,994	7,194	5,056	1,710	711	*
% In One-Unit Structures.	80.0	89.1	95.7	86.8	79.2	**
% Owner Occupied........	79.3	86.8	89.1	80.1	62.4	**
% Renter Occupied........	17.7	12.0	6.7	15.3	32.9	***
% Vacant.................	2.9	1.2	4.2	4.6	4.6	**
% 1+ Persons per Room....	0.8	2.5	5.2	6.6	7.3	**

Place 2225 — Glenview , Illinois
Selected Characteristics of Census Tracts: 1980

Tract Number	Total	8014	8016.02	8016.04	8019	8020	8021	8022	8023	8052	8086
Total Population............	32060	3100	0	4253	5201	4416	3298	4412	1834	3991	1555
% Male......................	49.1	48.5	–	50.0	47.1	49.1	49.1	47.7	56.3	49.0	49.5
% Black.....................	0.9	0.2	–	0.4	0.1	1.4	0.3	0.1	8.7	0.2	0.3
% Other Nonwhite............	3.7	3.5	–	7.8	2.7	4.5	1.6	1.5	6.4	3.8	1.6
% Of Spanish Origin.........	1.4	1.5	–	1.3	1.6	1.6	0.4	1.5	3.8	1.0	0.8
% Foreign Born..............	7.4	3.8	–	11.1	8.7	9.1	5.5	5.4	4.2	9.9	5.5
% Living In Group Quarters..	1.3	0.0	–	0.0	2.8	0.0	0.0	0.3	14.9	0.0	0.0
% 13 Years Old And Under....	20.3	19.3	–	31.0	15.4	18.3	20.4	16.0	30.2	19.8	16.9
% 14-20 Years Old...........	12.5	12.0	–	14.3	12.7	13.1	11.2	11.9	9.2	13.8	11.5
% 21-64 Years Old...........	58.6	60.3	–	52.9	59.3	61.9	57.1	58.5	60.0	58.8	60.6
% 65-74 Years Old...........	5.6	5.7	–	1.4	7.1	4.5	7.8	8.7	0.2	5.5	8.0
% 75 Years Old And Over.....	3.0	2.7	–	0.4	5.5	2.2	3.5	4.9	0.4	2.2	3.0
% In Different House........	38.7	28.1	–	37.8	39.9	46.9	33.7	34.8	93.5	29.2	22.8
% Families With Female Head.	8.3	5.8	–	4.1	12.4	14.6	8.7	8.3	6.7	7.0	5.8
Median School Years Completed....	14.7	15.9	–	15.8	14.7	14.1	15.3	15.7	12.7	12.9	14.7
Median Family Income, 1979......$$	36344	37066	–	43140	41067	33503	36669	51827	14446	30817	34274
% Income Below Poverty Level.	1.6	0.5	–	2.1	2.4	1.2	0.8	1.1	1.4	2.5	1.3
% Income Of $30,000 Or More.	62.9	66.9	–	74.0	69.4	56.7	65.7	77.0	7.6	54.1	62.6
% White Collar Workers......	79.8	85.9	–	84.5	81.9	70.3	83.6	87.8	62.0	75.3	73.1
% Civilian Labor Force Unemployed.	2.5	1.2	–	2.4	3.4	1.8	1.8	3.8	1.4	2.0	4.6
% Riding To Work By Automobile...	82.3	86.4	–	90.1	85.5	84.9	79.7	76.9	56.0	86.6	81.0
Mean Commuting Time - Minutes...	25.7	31.1	–	29.3	25.7	23.4	24.7	27.4	14.8	25.6	24.8
Population Per Household.........	3.0	3.0	–	4.0	2.6	2.7	2.9	2.8	3.1	3.2	2.8
Total Housing Units..........	10994	1064	0	1098	2000	1719	1146	1621	509	1281	556
% Condominiums..............	10.7	0.0	–	0.0	27.3	24.2	2.2	10.3	4.3	0.0	0.0
% Built 1970 Or Later.......	22.2	1.6	–	51.6	30.6	48.6	4.0	13.5	15.2	4.2	1.2
% Owner Occupied............	79.3	95.8	–	96.1	81.4	57.2	87.9	74.1	18.3	94.1	95.0
% With 1+ Persons Per Room..	0.8	0.2	–	0.5	0.5	1.5	0.5	0.3	3.2	.1	0.9
Median Value: Owner Units.......$$	111900	99200	–	140400	131900	105600	100500	143300	–	86100	94800
Median Rent: Rental Units....$$	322	475	–	501	323	317	348	420	171	445	408
Median Number Of Rooms: All Units.	5.6	5.6	–	5.6	5.6	5.3	5.6	5.6	4.6	5.6	5.6

Glenview
Selected Characteristics of Census Tracts: 1970

Tract Number	TOTAL	8014	8016	8019	8020	8021	8022	8023	8052	8086
Total Population.............	24880	3584	16274	6687	8695	3883	4733	2076	9207	2407
% Male.......................	48.7	50.0	49.4	47.7	49.2	49.4	48.5	58.4	49.4	49.0
% Black......................	0.1	0.0	0.1	0.0	0.2	0.0	0.1	4.8	0.1	0.0
% Other Nonwhite.............	0.6	0.9	0.6	0.7	0.3	0.4	0.1	3.7	0.8	0.5
% Of Spanish Language........	1.4	2.6	1.6	1.0	0.3	0.0	2.1	2.7	1.8	0.9
% Foreign Born...............	5.7	6.8	4.6	7.0	5.2	2.4	4.2	4.6	7.8	6.7
% Living In Group Quarters...	0.9	0.0	1.2	2.5	1.1	0.0	0.0	15.2	2.1	0.1
% 13 Years Old And Under.....	27.3	30.7	35.8	24.2	32.4	25.7	24.7	35.4	33.3	23.1
% 14-20 Years Old............	13.0	11.4	12.4	12.3	14.5	13.6	12.2	11.9	12.6	13.6
% 21-64 Years Old............	52.6	53.0	47.8	53.1	48.6	54.4	53.4	52.4	49.0	54.7
% 65-74 Years Old............	4.3	3.7	2.2	5.9	2.4	4.2	6.5	0.1	2.3	6.1
% 75 Years Old And Over......	2.7	1.2	1.8	4.5	2.1	2.0	3.2	0.1	2.8	2.5
% In Different House.........	56.3	50.0	31.3	49.6	62.6	64.4	50.1	4.6	58.1	69.6
% Families With Female Head..	6.0	4.3	3.4	7.4	7.2	5.1	6.7	0.9	4.6	5.3
Median School Years Completed...$$	13.5	14.8	13.0	13.0	12.8	14.0	13.9	12.5	12.8	12.8
Median Family Income, 1969.....$$	19137	18627	18923	17857	15729	17104	24822	7076	16818	19561
% Income Below Poverty Level.....	2.2	1.9	3.4	2.8	2.8	5.2	1.7	5.1	1.4	2.1
% Income of $15,000 or More.....	64.4	65.1	65.3	57.1	52.8	57.0	76.0	3.5	57.9	65.0
% White Collar Workers.......	59.1	69.6	55.3	56.8	47.1	60.6	64.0	19.4	50.7	48.4
% Civilian Labor Force Unemployed.	2.0	2.0	1.6	1.5	2.9	1.9	2.9	5.3	1.3	1.7
% Riding To Work By Automobile....	77.6	79.3	84.7	80.9	82.0	77.3	72.9	74.4	86.0	73.3
Population Per Household.........	3.5	3.6	4.1	3.0	3.9	3.4	3.2	3.7	3.9	3.4
Total Housing Units..........	7194	1000	4076	2153	2230	1134	1513	474	2312	715
% Condominiums & Cooperatives.....	1.8	0.0	0.0	0.0	0.0	0.0	0.0	0.0	0.0	0.0
% Built 1960 Or Later.......	26.1	28.2	63.6	47.5	31.1	10.6	33.9	18.9	35.0	15.2
% Owner Occupied............	85.1	97.6	89.7	80.7	86.4	86.7	70.1	12.4	90.3	91.2
% With 1+ Persons Per Room..	2.5	1.4	3.6	2.5	4.0	2.0	2.0	17.6	4.2	2.8
Median Value: Owner Units.......$$	41900	41400	50100	49600	34400	39400	50100	–	35400	42300
Median Rent: Rental Units....$$	213	267	183	167	181	196	243	91	219	175
Median Number Of Rooms: All Units.	6.2	6.4	7.3	5.7	6.4	6.2	6.4	4.1	6.3	6.3

overcrowded (with more than one person per room), but today that figure is less than 1 percent. At $110,600 the median value of owner-occupied homes in Glenview is one of the highest in the metropolitan area, and well over the median value of homes in Chicago.

Since 1970 the overall growth of the village has slowed somewhat, since there has been less land available for development. However, industrial development has continued. During the late 1960s and 1970s Glenview became the site of several major corporate headquarters, including Scott Foresman, Kraft and Zenith. The village has en-couraged this type of development. Because of it, Glenview has become what one source described as "a happy combination of luxury housing and tax-paying, non-polluting industries." The village itself has built a new village hall, a commuter plaza at the Milwaukee Railroad depot, and new police and fire department buildings, and plans a new public works yard and garage. In 1977 the village purchased two independent water distribution companies and in 1980 extended the provision of Lake Michigan water to residents on the far west side of the village.

The trend since 1960 has been toward more planning by the village. Zoning ordinances were modernized in 1964. Because of the early establishment of zoning in Glenview and a history of consistency in enforcement, residential and industrial areas have been kept intact, and very few mixed areas have developed. During the early 1970's, an Appearance Commission was formed to monitor the construction of businesses and multi-family dwellings. In 1973, Glenview joined with

Northbrook and Northfield, along with area school and park districts, to form the Techny Area Joint Planning Commission. The establishment of this group marked the first time in Illinois that municipalities and special districts had shared powers in a new unit of government. The group adopted common land use and boundary agreements in 1975. As a part of this plan, Glenview has participated in the construction of three water retention basins in the Techny area.

Marjorie DeVault

Place 2445

Hanover Park

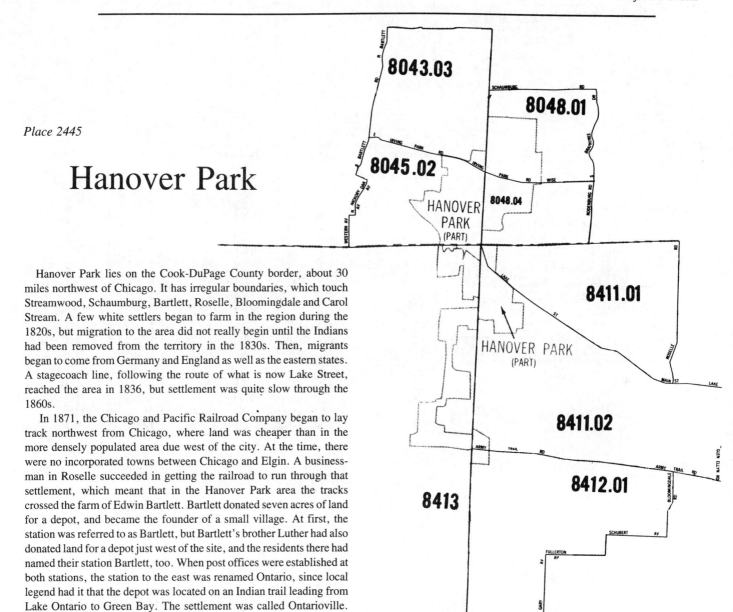

Hanover Park lies on the Cook-DuPage County border, about 30 miles northwest of Chicago. It has irregular boundaries, which touch Streamwood, Schaumburg, Bartlett, Roselle, Bloomingdale and Carol Stream. A few white settlers began to farm in the region during the 1820s, but migration to the area did not really begin until the Indians had been removed from the territory in the 1830s. Then, migrants began to come from Germany and England as well as the eastern states. A stagecoach line, following the route of what is now Lake Street, reached the area in 1836, but settlement was quite slow through the 1860s.

In 1871, the Chicago and Pacific Railroad Company began to lay track northwest from Chicago, where land was cheaper than in the more densely populated area due west of the city. At the time, there were no incorporated towns between Chicago and Elgin. A businessman in Roselle succeeded in getting the railroad to run through that settlement, which meant that in the Hanover Park area the tracks crossed the farm of Edwin Bartlett. Bartlett donated seven acres of land for a depot, and became the founder of a small village. At first, the station was referred to as Bartlett, but Bartlett's brother Luther had also donated land for a depot just west of the site, and the residents there had named their station Bartlett, too. When post offices were established at both stations, the station to the east was renamed Ontario, since local legend had it that the depot was located on an Indian trail leading from Lake Ontario to Green Bay. The settlement was called Ontarioville. Bartlett was appointed the first postmaster and laid out the village. Within a few years, there was a grain elevator, a church and a store which also served as a hotel. During the 1880s, a few more homes were built on Bartlett's land near the railroad tracks. The residents organized an elementary school district in 1910, with classes held in a garage. However, growth was very slow. By 1920, the population of Ontarioville was only 250. The neighboring town of Bartlett incorporated in 1891, but it grew slowly also. As the automobile became more important, Lake Street, which ran through the village of Ontarioville, became a major thoroughfare. However, a by-pass was built north of the village. The result was that development shifted toward the Cook County part of Ontarioville and away from the older DuPage County section.

During the 1920s, communities closer to Chicago began to grow as a suburban real estate boom developed. In Ontarioville, a single farm was subdivided and put up for sale as the Grant's Highway subdivision (so called because it was on Lake Street, then known as Grant's Highway). Only a few homes were built. However, the community grew slowly through the decade and by 1929 had a population of about 350. The village constructed a school building in anticipation of future growth. During the Depression few people moved to Ontarioville. However, after World War II a new building boom began in the suburbs. Again, a few families moved to Ontarioville, but commuting to the city was still relatively difficult, and the community remained basically rural.

Hanover Park
Population and Housing Characteristics, 1930-1980

	1980	1970	1960	1950	1940	1930
Total Population.......	28,719	11,916	*	*	*	*
% Male.................	50.7	49.8	*	*	*	*
% Female...............	49.3	50.2	*	*	*	*
% White................	92.0	99.4	*	*	*	*
% Black................	1.4	0.0	*	*	*	*
% Other Nonwhite Races...	6.6	0.6	*	*	*	*
% Under 5 Years Old......	11.5	15.4	*	*	*	*
% 5-19 Years Old.........	28.8	36.5	*	*	*	*
% 20-44 Years Old........	49.1	39.3	*	*	*	*
% 45-64 Years Old........	8.8	7.4	*	*	*	*
% 65 Years and Older.....	1.8	1.4	*	*	*	*
Median School Years....	12.8	12.3	*	*	*	*
Total Housing Units....	9,287	2,879	*	*	*	*
% In One-Unit Structures.	75.8	89.2	*	*	*	*
% Owner Occupied.........	76.0	84.4	*	*	*	*
% Renter Occupied........	19.0	10.7	*	*	*	*
% Vacant.................	5.0	4.9	*	*	*	*
% 1+ Persons per Room....	3.3	7.7	*	*	*	*

Place 2445 — Hanover Park , Illinois
Selected Characteristics of Census Tracts: 1980

Tract Number	Total	8043.03	8045.02	8048.01	8048.04	8411.01	8411.02	8412.01	8413
Total Population.............	28850	68	7991	6883	3216	1063	3893	316	5420
% Male........................	50.7	–	50.3	50.5	50.1	49.9	51.8	52.2	51.1
% Black.......................	1.4	–	0.7	1.7	0.2	1.8	3.0	0.9	1.3
% Other Nonwhite..............	6.7	–	8.3	6.5	2.8	4.3	5.7	12.7	7.7
% Of Spanish Origin...........	6.1	–	10.6	4.4	3.2	6.2	5.5	2.5	3.6
% Foreign Born................	9.4	–	12.8	7.6	6.0	7.6	8.1	22.5	9.1
% Living In Group Quarters....	0.0	–	0.0	0.0	0.0	0.0	0.0	0.0	0.0
% 13 Years Old And Under......	30.1	–	28.6	33.3	26.5	21.5	32.9	25.9	30.7
% 14-20 Years Old.............	11.7	–	14.9	12.2	19.1	6.7	8.1	3.5	5.8
% 21-64 Years Old.............	56.4	–	54.0	52.9	52.3	69.1	57.9	70.3	62.5
% 65-74 Years Old.............	1.2	–	1.8	1.0	1.3	2.3	0.7	0.3	0.8
% 75 Years Old And Over.......	0.5	–	0.7	0.6	0.8	0.4	0.4	0.0	0.1
% In Different House..........	62.3	–	54.7	52.1	36.3	82.5	76.5	100.0	89.1
% Families With Female Head...	9.3	–	13.3	9.7	7.3	13.5	6.4	3.6	5.8
Median School Years Completed....	12.8	–	12.4	12.9	12.6	13.0	13.6	14.5	13.5
Median Family Income, 1979..... $$	27036	–	25033	26830	29703	24957	29476	25069	27129
% Income Below Poverty Level.....	2.9	–	6.2	1.3	2.2	0.0	2.0	5.4	2.2
% Income Of $30,000 Or More.....	38.1	–	33.3	35.6	48.7	26.0	48.2	17.2	39.5
% White Collar Workers...........	59.3	–	46.2	64.5	54.7	68.8	66.4	66.8	65.7
% Civilian Labor Force Unemployed.	5.7	–	7.7	4.5	5.7	4.5	3.6	0.0	6.3
% Riding To Work By Automobile....	88.6	–	88.7	88.0	89.7	88.8	86.3	92.9	90.0
Mean Commuting Time - Minutes...	33.8	–	29.5	33.7	33.2	32.4	37.9	44.1	37.2
Population Per Household..........	3.3	–	3.4	3.6	4.0	2.3	3.3	2.7	2.9
Total Housing Units..........	9352	37	2539	1985	816	504	1314	129	2028
% Condominiums................	11.1	–	0.4	19.8	0.0	58.7	26.0	0.0	0.0
% Built 1970 Or Later.........	67.0	–	42.4	66.6	1.5	94.1	99.1	100.0	95.0
% Owner Occupied..............	74.6	–	55.1	86.6	93.4	73.4	81.3	87.6	76.2
% With 1+ Persons Per Room....	3.3	–	7.8	2.6	1.2	0.7	1.3	1.7	1.3
Median Value: Owner Units....... $$	67000	–	65300	67300	66000	59000	70300	64900	68100
Median Rent: Rental Units....... $$	276	–	263	372	392	346	408	–	244
Median Number Of Rooms: All Units.	5.6	–	5.2	5.6	5.6	4.9	5.6	5.6	5.6

Hanover Park
Selected Characteristics of Census Tracts: 1970

Tract Number	TOTAL	8043	8045	8048	8411	8412	8413
Total Population............	11735	17768	10216	22268	7222	8610	5492
% Male........................	49.8	50.5	49.2	50.3	49.5	50.7	50.4
% Black.......................	0.0	0.0	0.4	0.1	0.1	0.4	0.1
% Other Nonwhite..............	0.6	0.5	0.4	0.6	0.1	0.2	0.4
% Of Spanish Language.........	4.9	4.7	3.4	2.9	1.2	3.1	3.6
% Foreign Born................	4.5	2.4	4.0	5.0	4.3	3.8	3.1
% Living In Group Quarters........	0.0	0.0	1.0	0.1	1.2	0.0	2.0
% 13 Years Old And Under........	44.1	44.4	36.4	42.7	32.1	44.1	34.1
% 14-20 Years Old.............	8.5	8.9	10.0	7.2	12.6	9.8	12.0
% 21-64 Years Old.............	45.9	45.4	50.1	48.8	49.9	44.5	49.7
% 65-74 Years Old.............	1.0	0.7	2.4	0.9	3.4	1.1	2.9
% 75 Years Old And Over.......	0.5	0.5	1.1	0.4	2.0	0.5	1.3
% In Different House..........	37.3	39.3	41.0	25.8	57.9	51.1	40.3
% Families With Female Head.......	2.6	3.0	4.2	2.4	5.2	3.2	4.0
Median School Years Completed....	12.4	12.3	12.3	12.6	12.4	12.5	12.4
Median Family Income, 1969..... $$	12902	12531	12596	13465	12938	13334	14398
% Income Below Poverty Level.....	2.2	2.2	3.2	2.5	5.5	1.9	2.5
% Income of $15,000 or More.....	28.2	27.7	30.4	35.6	32.8	34.5	45.9
% White Collar Workers...........	31.2	25.2	28.5	40.5	30.6	32.7	40.3
% Civilian Labor Force Unemployed.	4.0	3.1	3.2	1.6	1.9	1.5	3.1
% Riding To Work By Automobile....	87.3	89.8	83.9	88.1	82.4	85.4	84.7
Population Per Household..........	4.4	4.4	3.7	4.1	3.7	4.5	3.8
Total Housing Units..........	2879	4289	2875	5606	2057	1988	1480
% Condominiums & Cooperatives.....	0.2	0.1	3.0	0.1	0.0	0.0	0.0
% Built 1960 Or Later.............	92.6	74.4	75.5	94.8	31.2	83.0	44.1
% Owner Occupied..............	84.2	86.6	75.7	89.3	75.3	88.9	79.0
% With 1+ Persons Per Room......	7.7	12.8	8.6	3.6	8.6	11.3	6.3
Median Value: Owner Units....... $$	28200	23000	24900	30000	27500	23500	31900
Median Rent: Rental Units....... $$	176	206	169	199	163	190	159
Median Number Of Rooms: All Units.	6.3	5.4	5.3	6.5	5.3	5.9	6.0

During the mid-1950s developers began to move into the rural territory northwest of Chicago, where they could subdivide the open farmland and build many houses in a small area. The construction of O'Hare Airport speeded this development. In 1957, a developer bought a group of farms northwest of Ontarioville and incorporated the area as the village of Streamwood. Hoffman Estates was being developed to the northeast, and the residents of Ontarioville began to worry about losing control of their area to these new communities.

Two village residents, Emil Rinne and Arthur Schlueter, began to promote the the idea of incorporation. Many residents initially opposed incorporation, wanting to maintain the rural character of their community, but they could see the inevitability of the rapid development occurring in Streamwood, and voted for incorporation in 1958. Only the Cook County part of Ontarioville was incorporated, since governing the village would be easier if it were in a single county, and since the DuPage County part of the village was in no danger of being surrounded by new development. The new village was to be called Hanover, the name of its township, but since there was already a Hanover in Illinois, it was named Hanover Park instead. The new village had a population of 305.

When they incorporated, the residents of Hanover Park planned to zone all of the land in the village into five-acre lots in order to preserve the area's rural character. However, village leaders saw that if they followed this plan Hanover Park would develop more slowly than the surrounding communities and would not be able to annex much of the surrounding land. Thus in 1959 village officials began to make plans with a newly-established real estate company, Hanover Builders. The next year, the company began construction of the Hanover Park First Addition. This subdivision, which contained almost 400 homes, had been sold by early summer of 1961, and brought an influx of new people to the community. In a single year, the population grew from 450 to 1,845. Hanover Builders constructed several shell-houses to serve as temporary classrooms for the children, and donated land for the construction of a new school building. Work was begun on a municipal water system.

Hanover Park continued to grow during the 1960s, primarily through development by two companies, Hanover Builders and Three-H (Hanover Highlands Incorporated). Several more subdivisions were built, all consisting of single-family detached homes, and in 1962, the first two-apartment buildings were constructed. Homes in the area sold quickly, since they were medium-priced, and since two arterial streets, Lake Street and Irving Park Road, provided relatively good routes to the city. In 1963, a shopping center developed by Hanover Builders opened at Barrington Road and Walnut Avenue, and in 1967 construction began on the Tradewinds shopping mall at Irving Park and Barrington roads. By 1970, the Cook County part of Hanover Park was almost completely developed, and the village's population was 11,735.

The growth of Streamwood and Hoffman Estates to the north prevented further expansion in that direction. However, the area to the south, in DuPage County, was still virtually undeveloped. In the early 1970s, the village began to annex southern sections of land purchased by Larwin, a California developer. This company began to build not only detached, single-family homes, but also townhouses, which were to become the predominant type of new housing built in the 1970s.

By the early 1970s, Hanover Park was being referred to as a "builder's town," with few restrictions on new development, and the village was beginning to feel the impact of its explosive growth. A special census indicated that Hanover Park had 19,609 residents in 1972, an increase of more than two-thirds in the first two years of the decade. There were problems with the municipal water system, and many of the village's roads needed work. In 1971, the residents adopted a mayor-manager form of government in an attempt to deal with such problems. Additional taxes were raised through several referenda. Development was slower because of worsening financial conditions, but the population continued to increase.

Today, the population of Hanover Park approaches 29,000, 6 percent of whom are Hispanic. Racially, the residents are 92 percent white, 1 percent black and 4 percent Asian. Of the latter, the most numerous are Asian Indians and Filipinos. Unlike other suburbs, which have lost population in recent years as family nests empty, Hanover Park remains extremely youthful, 37 percent being younger than 18 years. The village is populated primarily by middle-income white families. Most residents work in Chicago, though there is more and more suburban employment as more industries move to the surrounding area. The number of housing units more than tripled in the 1970s, and today there are more than 9,000. Eighty percent of all units are single-family homes, and 80 percent are owner-occupied. The corresponding percentages a decade ago were almost 90, and this change reflects the redirection of housing construction in the village. The median value of owner-occupied homes is more than 45 percent higher than the Chicago median.

During the last 10 years, the water system and the roads have been improved, and flood control is being developed. Hanover Park has developed a "fair share" policy, under which developers are required to make donations to the various taxing bodies in the area. The village is beginning to promote office and light and industrial development as a way of increasing its tax base. Although this is more prevalent in surrounding communities, Hanover Park has made plans to develop a new industrial park in conjunction with the neighboring village of Roselle. Retail development in the village has been more extensive, and draws shoppers from a large surrounding area. Most retail establishments are concentrated along Irving Park Road, though new retail development is occurring farther south at Lake Street. A Cook County Community development grant is being used for rehabilitation work on low- and moderate-income apartment buildings. In addition, Hanover Park is part of a joint action water committee which is working to obtain Lake Michigan water for a group of northwestern suburbs. In 1982, the village changed from an all-volunteer to a paid fire department.

Growth has been slower in the late 1970s and early 1980s, although small annexations have continued. The village annexed old Ontarioville, which had never incorporated, in 1982. According to a tentative boundary agreement with Carol Stream, Hanover Park will not expand any farther south than Army Trail Road. A comprehensive plan for the village was developed in 1976 and revised in 1981. Following this plan, the village is doing major work on the town center, at Lake Street and Barrington Road. This central core development will have three parts: a downtown area, with high-rise office and residential contruction; an historic district, which will preserve building facades in the old Ontarioville section; and a retail center just north of the downtown area on Lake Street.

Marjorie DeVault

Harvey

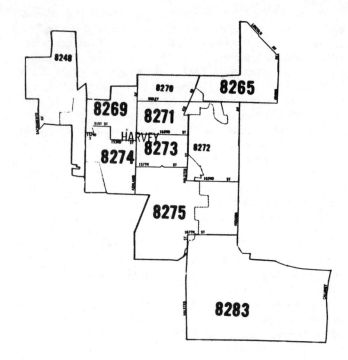

The City of Harvey, in Cook County, lies a few miles south of Chicago, and about 20 miles from the Loop. Southwest of Lake Calumet, which provides a shipping gateway to the Great Lakes, Harvey is crossed by major routes for transportation by water, railway, and expressway. The mix of transportation facilities and open land for industrial expansion prompted developers to promote the town as an ideal industrial and residential site with easy access to Chicago via the Illinois Central Railroad commuter line, which offered service as early as 1871.

Originally known as South Lawn, the area was part of a land grant from the state to the Illinois Central Railroad in the 1850s. In 1871 a syndicate comprised of six men took the first formal action to create the community that would later become known as Harvey. They divided a plot of 1,700 acres into blocks and recorded the entire area. To attract settlers, the syndicate offered lots at $100 each with free transportation to and from Chicago for one year. John Gay was the first settler, receiving a deed for two lots in 1874. Gay had few neighbors until the area began its growth, about the time Harvey L. Hopkins built the Hopkins mower works in 1880. In 1891, the Harvey Land Association, another syndicate, purchased land from Albert G. Spalding. Spalding, founder of the sporting-goods firm, had intended to create a community named after himself, but failed. The syndicate also purchased land from Turlington W. Harvey, lumber merchant and philanthropist. The town name, "Harvey," was a compromise. Turlington Harvey preferred "Turlington," but William H. Pease, who succeeded John Gay as postmaster, suggested "Harvey" as a combination honoring both Turlington Harvey and Harvey Hopkins. Turlington Harvey was reluctant but Pease settled the issue by registering the name with the U.S. Post Office. Harvey was incorporated as a village in 1891, later as a city in 1895.

One of Harvey's most colorful and best-known residents was Lucy Page Gaston, who achieved national recognition as a reformer opposed to the use of whiskey and cigarettes. The Harvey Land Association had included in the original property deeds a clause which provided the forfeiture of any property used as a saloon. Although the stipulations were unenforceable, the clause was used by the Association in its attempt to establish a temperance town. In the late '90s, the legality of the temperance clause was challenged by the opening of a saloon. Gaston and a band of Harvey residents initiated a series of test cases in the Cook County Courts which attracted nationwide attention.

Historically, Harvey had had problems with flooding because the low-lying land offered poor drainage. The area has a base of rock which results in inadequate absorption of water. Five major floods struck Harvey — in 1892, 1902, 1947, 1954 and 1957. The first two floods led to the establishment of the Calumet Union Drainage District, which provided for the construction of two major drainage ditches leading to the Calumet River. The 1954 flood was the worst disaster in the city's history and caused more than $1 million in damages. In 1955, voters approved a $1.5 million sewer rehabilitation program. Damage from the 1957 flood was not as severe as from previous floods.

From the start Harvey made rapid progress in industrial development. By 1892 Harvey had 10 industrial plants, 850 residences, 73 miles of streets, and five railroads with 70 passenger trains daily. The Harvey Land Association planned a town with 100 factories and 25,000 residents. Two belt lines — the Chicago Central and the Chicago and Calumet Terminal Railroads — plenty of open space, and proximity to Chicago without paying Chicago taxes were benefits Harvey could offer to prospective industrial occupants. Two manufacturing districts were separated by natural barriers from residential and commercial areas. One was southeast and the other northwest, bounded by the Chicago and Grand Trunk Railroad.

Industrial development and population growth went hand in hand. In 1900, the population was 5,395. Residents were attracted by Illinois Central commuter service to Chicago, the city's temperance policy, and the local availability of jobs that required some skill, as contrasted with the demand for common labor in nearby areas. Early immigrants were of Scotch, Swedish, German, and Polish descent. The population increased from 9,216, in 1920, to 16,374 in 1930. In 1930, Poles and Germans were the predominant foreign stock. Blacks comprised 2 percent of the population.

In the early 1920s, the Illinois Central Railroad electrified its system. The central power station was just north of Harvey on the Little Calumet River, and the main switchyards and repair shops just south of Harvey. Harvey's position as a rail center was enhanced and for much of this period residential development was unable to keep up with the demand for housing. Harvey workers were forced to find housing in Chicago, Blue Island, and Kensington. The city annexed land and residential development increased.

Expansion came to a halt with the onset of the Depression, but World War II and the ensuing prosperity stimulated a fresh growth of population and industry. Between 1950 and 1960, the population rose from 20,683 to 29,071 — an increase of 41 percent. In 1960, Poles were the single largest group among the foreign stock, followed by Germans and English. In the 1950s the black population began a steady and dramatic growth. In 1940, there had been 560 blacks in Harvey. By 1960 the black population had grown to 7 percent of the total. In 1970, the total population reached 34,636 and the black proportion increased to 31 percent. In 1980, the total population increased slightly, to 35,810. The black population is now 23,491 — almost two-thirds.

The postwar expansion of Harvey is reflected in housing growth. Since 1960, more than 2,000 units have been added, yet today 10.8 percent are overcrowded, a slight increase in the last 20 years. In 1980, 59 percent of the units were owner-occupied; 60 percent were in single-family structures. The median value of owner-occupied single-family homes is about two-thirds that of the city median.

Stephanie A. Rusnak

Harvey
Population and Housing Characteristics, 1930-1980

	1980	1970	1960	1950	1940	1930
Total Populaiton.......	35,810	34,636	29,071	20,683	17,878	16,374
% Male..................	48.0	49.0	50.0	50.0	50.5	51.8
% Female................	52.0	51.0	50.0	50.0	49.5	48.2
% White.................	31.6	68.5	93.1	95.1	96.9	97.5
% Black.................	65.6	30.9	6.8	4.9	3.1	2.5
% Other Nonwhite Races...	2.8	0.6	0.1	0.0	0.0	0.0
% Under 5 Years Old......	9.8	10.0	12.4	10.6	8.5	10.3
% 5-19 Years Old.........	30.8	29.9	26.1	22.2	26.1	29.0
% 20-44 Years Old........	34.9	32.7	34.8	40.5	42.3	43.1
% 45-64 Years Old........	16.8	20.0	20.0	20.8	18.8	14.3
% 65 Years and Older.....	7.7	7.4	6.7	5.9	4.3	3.3
Median School Years....	12.2	11.7	10.4	9.6	8.5	*
Total Housing Units....	11,452	11,207	9,334	6,066	4,870	*
% In One-Unit Structures.	60.3	57.7	63.3	*	*	*
% Owner Occupied.........	59.5	57.1	60.0	57.9	42.9	*
% Renter Occupied........	38.0	38.8	34.5	40.3	55.2	*
% Vacant.................	2.5	4.1	5.5	1.8	1.9	*
% 1+ Persons per Room....	10.8	10.7	12.3	*	*	*

Place 2490 — Harvey , Illinois
Selected Characteristics of Census Tracts: 1980

Tract Number	Total	8248	8265	8269	8270	8271	8272	8273	8274	8275	8283
Total Population.............	35810	1687	0	7253	4564	3835	1121	4904	6293	6147	6
% Male....................	48.0	49.9	-	46.4	49.1	46.2	50.1	50.3	46.6	48.6	-
% Black....................	65.6	46.5	-	95.4	56.0	53.0	0.6	63.7	92.2	36.8	-
% Other Nonwhite...........	2.8	3.9	-	0.9	1.7	3.8	1.1	6.9	0.8	4.2	-
% Of Spanish Origin........	4.6	5.7	-	0.9	1.6	3.7	4.5	10.2	1.5	10.1	-
% Foreign Born.............	4.3	2.5	-	0.7	4.3	3.7	6.1	10.9	1.5	6.8	-
% Living In Group Quarters.	1.7	0.0	-	0.3	0.0	8.0	0.0	0.0	3.7	0.7	-
% 13 Years Old And Under...	27.7	27.4	-	31.1	25.1	25.9	14.6	29.0	31.6	24.5	-
% 14-20 Years Old..........	14.7	15.8	-	16.1	13.8	11.4	11.8	14.3	16.4	14.8	-
% 21-64 Years Old..........	49.8	49.4	-	47.1	53.5	47.9	59.2	49.1	46.9	53.5	-
% 65-74 Years Old..........	4.8	5.4	-	3.9	5.0	7.4	8.2	4.5	3.2	5.1	-
% 75 Years Old And Over....	2.9	2.1	-	1.7	2.6	7.4	6.2	3.1	2.0	2.0	-
% In Different House.......	40.7	26.9	-	37.9	40.8	56.5	27.4	51.0	34.1	38.0	-
% Families With Female Head.	32.3	24.5	-	46.3	20.9	23.7	14.4	33.4	37.1	26.1	-
Median School Years Completed.	12.2	12.2	-	12.1	12.4	12.1	12.1	12.0	12.2	12.2	-
Median Family Income, 1979......$$	20441	20651	-	17671	24186	20906	23333	18438	18686	21040	-
% Income Below Poverty Level....	16.7	15.3	-	25.2	10.5	14.1	9.4	18.9	19.3	12.2	-
% Income Of $30,000 Or More.	23.9	31.5	-	25.3	25.8	29.0	30.1	16.8	19.8	22.6	-
% White Collar Workers........	40.1	45.7	-	38.0	43.9	41.2	40.7	40.5	36.7	39.5	-
% Civilian Labor Force Unemployed.	14.5	8.8	-	21.2	9.0	13.1	9.9	21.5	13.7	10.1	-
% Riding To Work By Automobile....	83.2	96.1	-	81.2	86.0	82.4	75.4	79.0	82.2	84.6	-
Mean Commuting Time - Minutes...	26.9	30.9	-	29.7	28.8	27.3	17.0	27.3	27.2	23.4	-
Population Per Household.....	3.2	3.1	-	3.5	3.1	3.1	2.6	3.0	3.4	3.2	-
Total Housing Units..........	11449	561	0	2140	1496	1186	460	1769	1839	1996	2
% Condominiums..............	0.0	0.2	-	0.0	0.0	0.0	0.0	0.0	0.0	0.0	-
% Built 1970 Or Later.............	5.4	26.0	-	4.9	3.3	0.0	6.7	0.0	13.4	2.6	-
% Owner Occupied.................	58.5	78.4	-	51.8	73.9	62.8	64.8	36.9	55.6	66.5	-
% With 1+ Persons Per Room........	10.8	7.1	-	16.7	6.4	9.3	3.2	12.1	13.3	8.3	-
Median Value: Owner Units......$$	33800	32200	-	30400	37200	31900	38800	30400	31700	37000	-
Median Rent: Rental Units.....$$	178	189	-	183	195	190	150	156	189	173	-
Median Number Of Rooms: All Units.	4.9	4.7	-	4.8	5.2	5.0	4.7	4.6	4.9	5.1	-

Harvey
Selected Characteristics of Census Tracts: 1970

Tract Number	TOTAL	8248	8265	8269	8270	8271	8272	8273	8274	8275	8283
Total Population.............	34636	6474	7416	8314	4693	1922	6128	4670	6746	6890	4236
% Male....................	49.0	50.1	48.9	48.8	49.1	46.8	50.0	50.0	47.9	49.3	49.4
% Black....................	30.9	3.0	0.1	71.1	0.3	6.8	51.5	2.1	59.3	17.0	0.9
% Other Nonwhite...........	0.5	0.4	0.2	0.6	0.4	0.6	0.7	0.5	0.6	0.6	0.1
% Of Spanish Language......	1.3	1.2	0.8	1.1	3.0	0.0	1.2	0.9	4.3	1.8	2.1
% Foreign Born.............	3.3	2.9	3.0	1.1	6.9	2.8	1.3	6.0	2.7	1.9	2.8
% Living In Group Quarters.	0.7	0.4	0.0	0.5	0.0	0.0	0.9	0.6	1.5	1.5	0.8
% 13 Years Old And Under...	28.9	31.7	26.7	32.8	25.6	25.9	29.9	21.1	34.0	30.2	33.1
% 14-20 Years Old..........	12.6	13.2	14.8	13.5	12.4	12.7	14.4	10.5	13.5	12.5	13.2
% 21-64 Years Old..........	51.1	50.8	51.8	48.2	54.6	51.7	51.7	47.9	53.4	51.7	47.9
% 65-74 Years Old..........	4.9	3.0	4.2	3.9	4.9	6.2	5.2	9.6	3.5	3.4	3.6
% 75 Years Old And Over....	2.5	1.3	2.4	1.6	2.6	3.4	2.5	5.3	2.3	2.2	2.3
% In Different House.......	52.9	63.8	65.9	45.6	69.6	59.7	64.4	49.4	42.5	56.3	69.7
% Families With Female Head.	10.8	6.8	7.3	15.3	7.3	9.0	12.7	11.2	12.4	8.9	5.0
Median School Years Completed.	11.7	10.5	12.2	11.8	12.0	12.1	10.6	11.7	11.2	12.0	12.3
Median Family Income, 1969......$$	11035	12074	12659	9910	12252	11123	10467	10387	10703	11612	12000
% Income Below Poverty Level....	7.7	3.1	5.4	13.7	2.4	6.6	11.8	5.7	11.4	5.0	3.2
% Income of $15,000 or More....	23.5	21.7	32.1	18.4	29.9	26.0	20.5	18.0	23.2	24.6	30.9
% White Collar Workers........	19.7	18.0	29.9	15.5	24.8	24.3	18.1	18.6	20.0	18.3	29.0
% Civilian Labor Force Unemployed.	3.8	3.4	2.7	5.4	2.4	4.5	4.1	4.7	3.0	3.0	3.6
% Riding To Work By Automobile....	76.7	82.3	71.5	78.9	78.1	77.3	77.7	65.6	77.1	80.6	82.3
Population Per Household..........	3.6	3.6	3.5	3.5	3.4	3.1	3.5	2.4	3.7	3.4	3.7
Total Housing Units..........	11207	1827	2125	2534	1487	645	1799	2020	1889	2038	1137
% Condominiums & Cooperatives.....	0.0	0.0	0.0	0.0	0.0	0.0	0.4	0.0	0.3	0.0	0.0
% Built 1960 Or Later..........	23.8	27.3	15.9	31.3	22.5	8.8	11.1	9.1	27.6	28.6	32.6
% Owner Occupied..............	57.1	76.1	83.7	51.8	71.8	60.6	62.0	35.8	60.6	65.9	85.0
% With 1+ Persons Per Room.....	10.7	13.6	8.5	15.3	7.4	5.8	14.8	4.4	16.8	11.6	10.8
Median Value: Owner Units......$$	17400	16200	19200	18100	18000	17100	16200	16100	16800	17500	20800
Median Rent: Rental Units.....$$	103	111	125	112	116	108	87	84	117	102	109
Median Number Of Rooms: All Units.	4.8	4.9	5.3	4.7	5.0	5.0	5.0	4.4	4.9	5.0	5.2

Highland Park

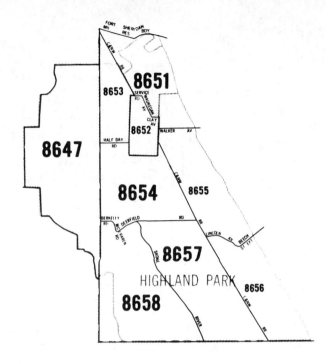

Highland Park is on the western shore of Lake Michigan, 25 miles north of Chicago. It is in the southeast corner of Lake County, bordered by Glencoe on the south, Lake Forest and Highwood on the north, and Bannockburn and Deerfield on the west. Unique to the eastern part of the city are the many ravines which wind through the wooded area, high bluffs and public beaches on Lake Michigan.

Originally the wilderness home of Pottawatomie tribes, the area's first white settlement consisted of a few cabins in swamps near the Skokie River. In 1847, the village of St. Johns (now part of Fort Sheridan) was founded as a shipping town, with a warehouse and a sawmill. Another village, Port Clinton, founded in 1850, grew up a little to the south of St. Johns, under the stimulus of Jacob A. Bloom. Bloom had contracted to supply lumber for the Chicago plank roads, and he was ambitious in the development of a lake port. In 1851, the first ship docked at Port Clinton, which by then had some 100 inhabitants, a steam sawmill, a turning lathe, and two dry goods stores. In the early 1850s, Port Clinton rivaled Waukegan as a port, and great hopes were held for its success in competition with Chicago and Milwaukee. In 1854, a severe cholera epidemic put an end to this first developmental phase.

Walter Gurnee then bought up the stock of the Port Clinton Land Company and formed the Highland Park Building Company. His plans were for residential rather than commercial development, taking advantage of what is now the Chicago and North Western Railroad between Chicago and Waukegan, opened in 1855.

The original plat was a strip of land 3/4 of a mile wide between the lake and the railroad, and 2.5 miles long, about 1,200 acres altogether. Growth during the 1850s was moderate, but was interrupted by the Civil War. After the war, many settlers were attracted to the area, including many Irish and Germans. In 1869, Highland Park was incorporated, primarily to eliminate saloons. A non-denominational religious organization was formed and in the next few years a Baptist church and a Catholic church were built.

The extension of Sheridan Road to Highland Park in the 1870s was another spur to residential growth. In 1872, two landscape artists laid out a rustic suburban development in a wooded area north of the main settlement. When Highland Park first appeared in the census, in 1880, its population was 1,154. From then until 1930 the pattern was one of fairly steady growth along with increasing accessibility to Chicago.

In 1898, the Bluff City Electric Railroad (later the Chicago, North Shore, and Milwaukee) came through Highland Park. In 1899, Highland Park annexed Ravinia, now the site of the Ravinia Festival, which was started as a "traffic builder" for the Chicago, North Shore and Milwaukee Railroad. The city became an attractive residential area for wealthy Chicagoans. The establishment of Fort Sheridan, a U.S. Army post on 700 acres of the former site of the town of St. Johns, in 1887, led to an increase in business and residential settlement in the city.

In about 1910, the Chicago Rapid Transit Company extended its lines as far as Highland Park. Though growth slowed during the war years, it resumed during the 1920s. Additional territory on the north and west was annexed to the city, and a Zoning Commission was formed which actively boosted Highland Park as a high status residential area. The development of the north shore suburbs during this period was assisted by the construction of the Skokie Valley route of the Chicago, North Shore, and Milwaukee Railroad. With commuting time reduced to 34 minutes, there were many new subdivisions and sharply increasing land values.

By the end of the 1920s, Highland Park consisted of an older core on the wooded ridge between the lake and Skokie Valley, and of newer areas in the valley and on the ridges to the west of the river. Although Highland Park was noted for its numerous private golf clubs, it was becoming too large to remain an exclusive residential area. Its business center by 1925 was the third largest on the north shore, following Evanston and Waukegan. In 1930, Germans, Italians, Swedes, and English were the leading nationalities among the foreign stock.

During the Depression, and until the end of the Second World War, residential growth in Highland Park virtually ceased. Growth resumed in the postwar years. A city plan of 1947 envisioned a population of 26,000 by 1970. Increases in business, public improvements and services, and construction accompanied the postwar growth in population.

The planner's visions were more than realized, for by 1970, Highland Park's population totalled 32,263. In 1980 the population declined to 30,611, but in the 30 years between 1950 and 1980, the city witnessed a population increase of 82 percent. The relatively high socio-economic status of Highland Park is reflected in the fact that in 1980 the median family income was estimated at almost $34,000, one of the higher per capita incomes in the nation for cities over 25,000 in population. Highland Park is occupied largely by executives, business people, and professionals, a large number of whom commute daily into the Chicago Loop. As a suburban bedroom community, Highland Park contains homes ranging from a low of $60,000 to over $1 million. The median value for owner-occupied single-family homes was $124,800 in 1980, which ranks twenty-fourth in the Chicago Metropolitan area. The continuing growth and improvement of Highland Park is reflected by the fact that during the 12 months ending May 1, 1981, the city issued 1,864 permits for $21,851,260 in new construction and remodeling. Of the 10,550 housing units in the city in 1980, 68 percent were single-family homes and 80 percent were owner-occupied units. More than 13 percent of all housing units in Highland Park have been built in the last 10 years.

Continuing growth has not spoiled Highland Park, for it remains a mature, upper-middle class community with a wide range of excellent services, public facilities, and cultural activities. Included among the City's many assets are the 332-bed Highland Park Hospital, a high school with a national reputation for academic excellence, numerous architectural landmarks, and the world-renowned Ravinia Music Festival, summer home of the Chicago Symphony Orchestra. In national competition, the National Municipal League named Highland Park an All-America City in 1959 and gave it an honorable mention in 1979.

In 1976, Highland Park published an updated Comprehensive Master Plan for the City. A revised Zoning Ordinance adopted in 1978

Highland Park
Population and Housing Characteristics, 1930–1980

	1980	1970	1960	1950	1940	1930
Total Population.......	30,611	32,263	25,532	16,808	14,476	12,203
% Male.................	48.7	48.3	47.6	47.2	47.3	47.5
% Female...............	51.3	51.7	52.4	52.8	52.7	52.5
% White................	95.5	97.6	97.8	97.6	98.4	98.4
% Black................	1.8	1.8	2.0	2.3	1.6	1.5
% Other Nonwhite Races...	2.7	0.6	0.2	0.1	0.0	0.1
% Under 5 Years Old......	6.0	7.9	10.4	9.2	6.7	8.1
% 5–19 Years Old........	25.8	32.4	28.0	21.3	23.3	25.2
% 20–44 Years Old.......	35.0	31.0	32.2	37.5	42.6	43.3
% 45–64 Years Old.......	24.1	21.7	24.7	24.7	21.5	18.7
% 65 Years and Older....	9.1	7.0	7.1	7.3	5.9	4.7
Median School Years....	15.9	13.4	13.0	12.5	12.1	*
Total Housing Units....	10,550	9,391	7,384	4,814	3,847	*
% In One-Unit Structures.	82.7	81.5	87.2	*	*	*
% Owner Occupied.........	79.7	76.0	77.8	71.3	55.4	*
% Renter Occupied........	18.3	21.9	18.5	25.8	40.2	*
% Vacant.................	2.0	2.1	3.7	2.9	4.4	*
% 1+ Persons per Room....	1.2	2.5	2.9	4.6	*	*

Place 2595 — Highland Park, Illinois
Selected Characteristics of Census Tracts: 1980

Tract Number	Total	8647	8651	8653	8654	8655	8656	8657	8658
Total Population.............	30611	3827	959	2388	4290	3834	3931	6115	5267
% Male.......................	48.7	49.4	49.8	48.9	48.7	47.2	48.4	48.6	49.5
% Black......................	1.8	0.9	22.8	2.0	1.7	1.3	0.9	0.8	0.8
% Other Nonwhite.............	2.7	2.2	7.5	1.9	7.1	1.9	1.1	1.5	2.0
% Of Spanish Origin..........	2.7	1.3	3.4	1.6	9.7	2.7	0.7	2.0	0.9
% Foreign Born...............	9.3	9.2	10.3	11.5	19.5	8.7	4.3	6.8	6.9
% Living In Group Quarters...	1.0	0.0	0.0	0.0	2.9	2.5	2.1	0.2	0.0
% 13 Years Old And Under.....	20.8	24.4	39.2	22.0	16.0	16.7	18.0	21.0	23.0
% 14–20 Years Old............	12.0	13.7	7.5	12.5	10.9	13.1	11.3	11.8	12.2
% 21–64 Years Old............	58.1	57.0	51.9	61.9	59.3	55.5	56.9	58.1	60.0
% 65–74 Years Old............	5.6	3.3	0.4	2.2	8.1	8.4	8.0	6.2	3.3
% 75 Years Old And Over......	3.5	1.6	0.9	1.3	5.7	6.3	5.7	2.9	1.5
% In Different House.........	36.9	36.6	98.0	34.0	43.8	34.9	26.2	31.3	38.5
% Families With Female Head..	7.8	4.8	6.7	7.3	13.3	8.5	7.1	8.1	7.1
Median School Years Completed..	15.9	16.1	12.8	16.0	12.9	16.1	16.1	16.1	16.1
Median Family Income, 1979...$$	42903	48814	18018	40763	30845	45580	61513	48196	41730
% Income Below Poverty Level.	1.5	2.4	0.0	0.0	2.6	1.7	0.0	1.6	1.8
% Income Of $30,000 Or More...	69.5	76.3	2.5	73.4	53.2	71.7	81.7	74.4	71.0
% White Collar Workers.......	81.2	82.9	53.4	82.7	68.0	81.1	88.7	84.9	83.7
% Civilian Labor Force Unemployed.	2.4	3.2	0.0	1.0	3.3	2.9	1.3	2.5	2.5
% Riding To Work By Automobile....	74.8	80.2	81.5	79.1	72.2	63.6	61.9	76.6	84.6
Mean Commuting Time – Minutes...	28.2	28.8	6.6	32.7	19.1	31.2	35.0	30.7	28.0
Population Per Household.....	3.0	3.4	3.6	3.2	2.5	2.8	2.9	3.0	3.2
Total Housing Units..........	10540	1168	270	755	1762	1408	1360	2114	1703
% Condominiums...............	3.8	0.0	0.0	0.0	7.5	6.0	0.0	0.6	10.0
% Built 1970 Or Later........	13.4	26.1	12.5	7.1	14.8	12.4	0.9	8.0	23.5
% Owner Occupied.............	78.9	92.7	3.0	93.9	51.9	68.2	88.4	87.4	93.4
% With 1+ Persons Per Room...	1.2	0.4	5.6	0.9	3.6	0.4	0.2	0.5	0.9
Median Value: Owner Units.......$$	124800	133600	—	117700	85200	170500	164300	124500	101100
Median Rent: Rental Units...$$	286	400	235	297	277	320	291	341	493
Median Number Of Rooms: All Units.	5.6	5.6	5.1	5.6	5.2	5.6	5.6	5.6	5.6

Highland Park
Selected Characteristics of Census Tracts: 1970

Tract Number	TOTAL	8647	8651	8653	8654	8655	8656	8657	8658
Total Population.............	32263	3260	3060	2780	4293	4179	4366	6700	6185
% Male.......................	48.3	49.2	50.9	49.4	46.7	46.1	47.2	48.9	49.4
% Black......................	1.8	0.6	8.7	0.8	0.9	1.6	2.2	1.0	1.1
% Other Nonwhite.............	0.6	0.1	3.0	0.0	1.5	0.2	0.1	0.6	0.3
% Of Spanish Language........	1.6	0.4	3.8	3.4	1.7	1.1	1.2	1.6	2.1
% Foreign Born...............	8.2	5.7	5.4	8.8	15.0	8.4	5.1	8.4	5.9
% Living In Group Quarters...	0.9	0.2	0.0	0.0	1.8	2.2	2.1	0.6	0.0
% 13 Years Old And Under.....	28.6	32.2	38.8	32.2	22.9	24.4	23.4	29.1	34.1
% 14–20 Years Old............	12.6	13.0	11.8	13.7	10.2	13.4	13.1	12.7	12.4
% 21–64 Years Old............	51.8	50.4	48.7	51.0	55.2	52.0	53.5	51.3	50.1
% 65–74 Years Old............	4.4	3.0	0.2	1.9	6.2	6.2	5.9	4.7	2.2
% 75 Years Old And Over......	2.6	1.4	0.4	1.2	4.6	4.0	4.0	2.3	1.2
% In Different House.........	57.9	61.6	0.0	62.6	53.7	54.5	65.7	64.1	59.4
% Families With Female Head..	5.1	3.3	0.8	4.1	9.8	6.1	4.5	4.9	3.7
Median School Years Completed...	14.1	14.5	12.9	14.4	12.4	15.3	15.8	14.7	14.5
Median Family Income, 1969...$$	20749	21774	10897	22206	13431	26113	33152	21525	21148
% Income Below Poverty Level..	2.3	2.3	1.4	2.1	3.7	3.9	2.6	0.8	2.2
% Income of $15,000 or More....	67.3	75.4	20.9	79.4	41.6	75.2	82.0	69.2	72.6
% White Collar Workers.......	61.6	68.5	33.5	67.4	39.4	69.6	70.9	64.8	64.1
% Civilian Labor Force Unemployed.	2.1	1.4	4.7	1.8	2.3	1.6	1.0	1.6	1.9
% Riding To Work By Automobile....	68.6	81.2	55.5	77.4	65.4	57.8	58.6	65.6	81.3
Population Per Household......	3.5	3.8	4.1	3.9	2.8	3.3	3.4	3.5	3.9
Total Housing Units..........	9387	869	758	728	1542	1292	1295	1927	1606
% Condominiums & Cooperatives.....	0.1	0.0	0.0	0.0	0.0	0.0	0.0	0.3	0.0
% Built 1960 Or Later........	22.3	31.5	49.9	29.6	15.4	11.4	7.2	25.1	44.9
% Owner Occupied.............	76.0	94.1	0.3	92.3	50.6	67.4	87.5	85.6	95.3
% With 1+ Persons Per Room.......	2.5	2.0	6.8	2.2	3.5	1.2	0.7	2.1	2.3
Median Value: Owner Units.......$$	46100	48200	—	44100	31400	50100	50100	45600	43900
Median Rent: Rental Units...$$	161	167	120	181	141	219	177	190	215
Median Number Of Rooms: All Units.	6.6	7.0	5.8	6.9	5.0	7.1	7.7	6.8	7.0

reflected the specifications of the Master Plan by providing for increased densities and mixed uses. The City of Highland Park is encouraging the office and commercial revitalization of the central business district on a partnership basis. To that end the City purchased a square block of property in its downtown central business district. A private developer will construct a mixed-use retail-office complex on the site. The 40-acre central business district is more than 100 years old and the streets and utilities are being replaced and a landscaping plan put in place. A tax increment financing program has been implemented to finance this work from new property taxes generated as a result of the public improvements — at no cost to existing residential taxpayers. The street and utility replacement will improve the aesthetic quality of the city's streets and as an end result will generate additional sales and property tax income. The dynamic "target block" and streets programs demonstrate that Highland Park is committed to the redevelopment of its commercial areas to preserve the unique character of the community and to continue to provide high quality amenities.

Esther Benjamin

Hoffman Estates

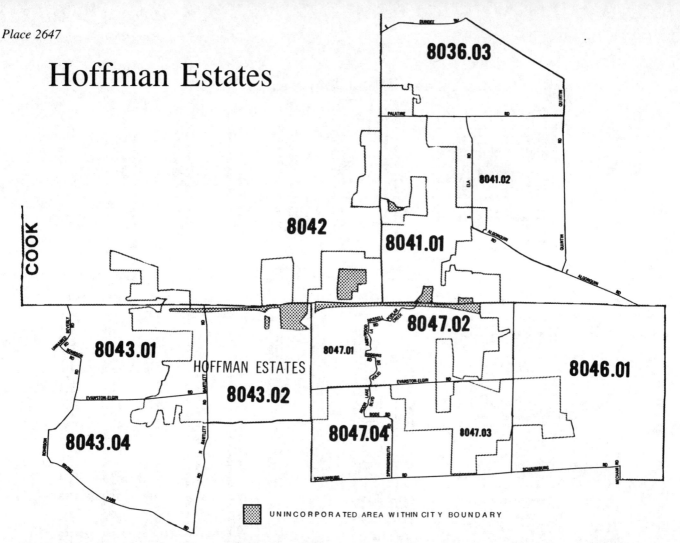

UNINCORPORATED AREA WITHIN CITY BOUNDARY

The village of Hoffman Estates is located 29 miles northwest of the Chicago Loop along the Northwest Tollway. The major portion of the village lies within Cook County and recent annexations into Kane County give a total land area of 17.25 square miles. Included in the village limits are 300 acres of land which make up the Poplar Creek and the Paul Douglas Forest preserves. The area is dotted by several artificial lakes.

The Hoffman Estates community began in 1955 as a subdivision in Schaumburg Township built by Sam and Jack Hoffman (Father and Son Construction Company). Township history dates back to the 1830s when a few New England families first cleared some land and erected cabins. Then, in the early 1840s, Johann Sunderlage from Hanover, Germany, came to the township with three other families and settled along what is now Higgins Road. This was the start of a German predominance in the township that lasted for more than a century.

After World War I and during the Depression, many of the descendants of the German farmers began to sell their land to businessmen from Chicago, who often retained the farmers as farm managers. Arthur Hammerstein, a theatrical entrepreneur, and his film star wife, Dorothy Dalton, purchased such a farm, the buildings of which eventually became the first village hall. The Marshall Field family owned a large livestock operation called Fieldale which is now the Hilldale Townhouse and Golf Complex.

The Hoffmans purchased a 160-acre farm for subdivision in 1954 and Cook County approved the development in February, 1955. At this time, Schaumburg Township did not have an incorporated village within its boundaries. Some residents, fearing that they would lose control of the township, decided to incorporate land surrounding the new subdivision in order to control it and other possible local development. The surrounding area became the village of Schaumburg, incorporated in December, 1955. The first residents of the new subdivision

were mostly young families who shopped and worked elsewhere. The increase in school children flooded the newly-constructed Schaumburg School and high school students were bussed into Palatine High School. By 1959, the F. and S. Construction Company had built four schools. A Lutheran Church and a Catholic Church were organized and constructed. Community services began with the organization of a volunteer fire department and the Hammerstein Library (later incorporated in the township government).

At this point, members of the Hoffman Estates Homeowners Association realized that some form of government was needed. Schaumburg was approached, but Hoffman Estates was denied both annexation and incorporation. Some community residents opposed incorporation because they feared increased taxation and industrial and commercial development. Nevertheless, incorporation was approved and, on November 7, 1959, the first village president, six trustees, a clerk, and a police magistrate were elected. Public services included a municipal police department and a volunteer fire department which was later reorganized as a county fire protection district. In 1962, the Interstate Commerce Commission ruled for the village in its condemnation proceedings against Citizens Utilities. The village then acquired its own water facility. In May, 1964, voters approved the formation of the Hoffman Estates Park District as a separate taxing and governing body.

The population at the time of incorporation was less than 8,000 and the incorporated area around the intersection of Roselle and Higgins roads was approximately three square miles. Nearly half of the population was Roman Catholic and there were neither blacks nor recognizable nationality groups among the whites. Later, it was discovered that Schaumburg did not completely surround Hoffman Estates and more land was annexed to the north and west. Growth was rapid in the following decade. The population increased by 160 percent, to more than 22,000 in 1970. By that time, an area which had been open

Hoffman Estates
Population and Housing Characteristics, 1930-1980

	1980	1970	1960	1950	1940	1930
Total Population	37,272	22,238	8,296	*	*	*
% Male	50.6	50.4	50.9	*	*	*
% Female	49.4	49.6	49.1	*	*	*
% White	93.3	99.4	99.8	*	*	*
% Black	1.3	0.1	-	*	*	*
% Other Nonwhite Races	5.4	0.5	0.2	*	*	*
% Under 5 Years Old	9.3	12.0	26.1	*	*	*
% 5-19 Years Old	26.8	38.8	27.3	*	*	*
% 20-44 Years Old	48.6	38.3	42.7	*	*	*
% 45-64 Years Old	13.1	9.4	3.2	*	*	*
% 65 Years and Older	2.2	1.5	0.7	*	*	*
Median School Years	13.4	12.4	12.7	*	*	*
Total Housing Units	13,214	5,809	1,995	*	*	*
% In One-Unit Structures	72.3	82.1	99.7	*	*	*
% Owner Occupied	69.5	75.6	89.9	*	*	*
% Renter Occupied	24.7	16.3	4.1	*	*	*
% Vacant	5.8	8.1	6.0	*	*	*
% 1+ Persons per Room	1.5	5.9	13.1	*	*	*

Place 2647 — Hoffman Estates, Illinois
Selected Characteristics of Census Tracts: 1980

Tract Number	Total	8036.03	8041.01	8041.02	8042	8043.01	8043.02	8046.01	8047.01	8047.02	8047.03
Total Population	37272	748	6372	337	1609	9	19	2727	5172	10728	9549
% Male	50.6	50.0	50.0	51.0	51.6	-	-	50.5	52.0	49.9	50.8
% Black	1.3	1.7	0.5	0.0	1.2	-	-	0.8	2.4	1.0	1.9
% Other Nonwhite	5.3	7.0	7.0	8.9	11.5	-	-	3.2	3.6	3.0	7.1
% Of Spanish Origin	3.2	1.6	1.9	0.0	3.3	-	-	4.5	3.1	2.2	5.2
% Foreign Born	7.8	7.7	7.9	7.0	15.4	-	-	8.5	10.0	4.7	8.7
% Living In Group Quarters	0.5	0.0	0.0	0.0	0.0	-	-	0.0	3.5	0.0	0.0
% 13 Years Old And Under	25.5	31.3	33.4	34.4	31.8	-	-	22.7	19.7	25.4	22.6
% 14-20 Years Old	12.2	5.7	8.6	10.4	6.4	-	-	15.0	7.3	15.9	13.9
% 21-64 Years Old	60.0	62.8	56.4	53.1	61.0	-	-	59.1	68.8	56.8	61.4
% 65-74 Years Old	1.3	0.1	1.1	1.2	0.7	-	-	2.1	1.5	1.1	1.4
% 75 Years Old And Over	1.0	0.0	0.5	0.9	0.2	-	-	1.0	2.7	0.8	0.8
% In Different House	60.5	100.0	75.4	96.6	100.0	-	-	34.6	86.7	42.9	54.5
% Families With Female Head	9.1	3.5	2.8	.5	2.0	-	-	7.2	16.8	10.1	12.6
Median School Years Completed	13.4	16.1	14.0	15.5	15.9	-	-	12.7	14.5	13.1	12.9
Median Family Income, 1979...$$	29865	29417	34203	40425	34967	-	-	29063	26810	31049	26224
% Income Below Poverty Level	2.6	0.0	1.8	0.0	1.1	-	-	2.5	3.2	1.3	5.1
% Income Of $30,000 Or More	49.5	46.7	65.1	65.5	70.8	-	-	45.5	36.3	53.9	37.1
% White Collar Workers	69.0	68.6	72.6	100.0	85.6	-	-	60.4	74.4	72.1	59.2
% Civilian Labor Force Unemployed	3.9	1.8	2.9	0.0	2.3	-	-	6.6	3.0	3.0	5.5
% Riding To Work By Automobile	91.7	89.3	87.6	88.5	90.0	-	-	92.2	93.1	93.0	92.1
Mean Commuting Time - Minutes	29.2	35.2	33.6	35.8	33.6	-	-	26.7	30.0	26.8	28.4
Population Per Household	3.0	3.1	3.6	3.9	3.3	-	-	3.4	2.2	3.4	2.8
Total Housing Units	13214	310	1853	96	508	2	5	819	2382	3358	3880
% Condominiums	15.4	0.0	0.0	0.0	0.0	-	-	0.0	31.9	18.8	16.5
% Built 1970 Or Later	56.4	100.0	91.2	100.0	98.2	-	-	0.0	90.8	32.2	41.6
% Owner Occupied	68.2	67.4	93.8	89.6	89.8	-	-	91.3	49.0	78.7	50.6
% With 1+ Persons Per Room	1.5	0.4	0.4	0.0	0.8	-	-	1.4	0.9	0.8	3.5
Median Value: Owner Units...$$	76900	86500	91100	164100	94900	-	-	66300	66800	76700	67400
Median Rent: Rental Units...$$	324	458	501	0	501	-	-	375	358	359	274
Median Number Of Rooms: All Units	5.6	5.6	5.6	5.6	5.6	-	-	5.6	4.9	5.6	5.2

Hoffman Estates
Selected Characteristics of Census Tracts: 1970

Tract Number	TOTAL	8036	8041	8042	8043	8046	8047
Total Population	22238	20660	8468	7607	17768	8686	19587
% Male	50.4	50.2	50.1	48.4	50.5	50.2	50.4
% Black	0.1	0.1	0.1	0.1	0.0	0.2	0.1
% Other Nonwhite	0.5	0.5	0.5	0.3	0.5	0.6	0.4
% Of Spanish Language	2.5	1.6	2.3	1.9	4.7	2.8	2.2
% Foreign Born	3.1	3.5	4.5	4.0	2.4	3.0	3.4
% Living In Group Quarters	0.1	0.3	1.6	1.4	0.0	0.1	0.1
% 13 Years Old And Under	39.7	37.7	30.4	26.1	44.4	34.1	40.5
% 14-20 Years Old	12.1	12.4	11.8	13.2	8.9	11.6	11.3
% 21-64 Years Old	46.7	46.8	53.0	51.5	45.4	52.0	46.7
% 65-74 Years Old	1.0	2.0	3.0	5.7	1.5	1.5	1.0
% 75 Years Old And Over	0.6	1.1	1.8	3.6	0.5	0.8	0.5
% In Different House	45.7	39.7	39.3	51.7	39.3	41.4	41.3
% Families With Female Head	3.8	2.5	2.9	6.1	3.0	4.2	3.5
Median School Years Completed	12.7	12.9	12.9	12.7	12.3	12.5	12.7
Median Family Income, 1969...$$	14549	17493	19412	15194	12531	13760	14658
% Income Below Poverty Level	1.7	1.8	1.2	3.9	2.8	2.2	2.0
% Income of $15,000 or More	46.5	60.9	69.5	50.5	27.7	40.1	47.3
% White Collar Workers	44.7	55.9	57.9	46.9	25.2	42.2	46.8
% Civilian Labor Force Unemployed	2.2	2.1	2.3	1.9	3.1	2.1	2.1
% Riding To Work By Automobile	89.2	78.1	81.6	70.7	89.8	86.8	90.4
Population Per Household	4.2	4.2	3.5	3.5	4.4	3.7	4.2
Total Housing Units	5808	5086	2683	2948	4289	2515	4958
% Condominiums & Cooperatives	0.0	0.0	2.5	0.0	0.1	0.0	0.0
% Built 1960 Or Later	70.2	66.0	73.5	25.9	74.4	65.2	76.0
% Owner Occupied	75.6	89.3	69.1	68.7	86.6	62.8	79.4
% With 1+ Persons Per Room	5.9	3.4	2.8	4.2	12.8	5.4	5.4
Median Value: Owner Units...$$	28600	38800	45600	32200	23000	31400	29700
Median Rent: Rental Units...$$	185	154	177	142	206	182	178
Median Number Of Rooms: All Units	6.2	7.2	6.7	5.9	5.4	5.8	6.4

farmland scarcely more than a decade before was covered by almost 6,000 housing units, more than 80 percent single-family and owner-occupied.

The village election of 1969 was the most highly contested in the village's history. Until this election, the municipal government was controlled by a group of independents who used various names for their party. Several members of the village board began to suspect that other members were involved in illegal actions. This prompted the local Republican and Democratic organizations to run full slates against the independents. The Republicans won the election and have dominated

village government ever since. Then, in 1970, the federal courts found two former presidents and three former village trustees guilty of taking bribes from a developer and they were sentenced to prison.

The village was not out of trouble yet, because it soon found itself embroiled in a scandal surrounding the failure of the City Savings Association. When the court made its final decision, Hoffman Estates was ordered to rezone 440 acres of land along Palatine Road so that investors of the defunct savings association could get some of their money back. This rezoning created an area of higher density than originally planned.

In 1970, the village voted to hire a village manager. The new municipal building on Gannon Drive and Golf Road, the first in the state of Illinois to be fully accessible to the handicapped, was completed and dedicated in 1972. In 1975, the fire department was changed from a county to a municipal department. In 1982, the Supreme Court ruled for the Village of Hoffman Estates and upheld its 1978 Drug Ordinance. The ordinance, which restricts the sale of drug-related materials to adults and requires the seller to keep a record of all customers, has become a model for other communities throughout the United States.

Growth continued in the 1970s, when the number of residents increased by another 15,000, and Hoffman Estates grew to more than 37,000 total. All but 2,500 of these are white, the largest racial minority being 1,500 Asiatics, about a third of whom are Asian Indians. The black populaton is a little over 1 percent of the total. About 3 percent are of Spanish origin. Hoffman Estates continues to be a child-rearing suburb, almost a third are less than 18 years old, while the proporation of 65 or more years is very small, just over 2 percent.

The number of housing units is more than twice the number in 1970, and the proportion of single-famly homes continues to exceed 80 percent. More than two-thirds of all homes are owner-occupied and the median value of these is more than $30,000 higher than in Chicago, although not quite as high as the median in neighboring Schaumburg. Commercial and industrial development has been slow, but now includes the Suburban Medical Center, a 356-bed acute care hospital, Popular Creek Music Theater, a 20,000 capacity open-air entertainment complex and Pfizer, Inc., midwest distribution center. The Hoffman Estates business district consists of six shopping centers. The village has created a business development committee and local businessmen have formed the Hoffman Estates Businessmen's Association in order to promote the expansion of the business community.

Today, prices of homes go as high as $150,000, though some developers have begun to build smaller houses at lower prices. The recession of the early 1980s has caused a reduction in home sales and has also resulted in reduced village revenues. Population, housing and business development have slowed down, temporarily at least, but the village has 2,000 incorporated acres for future development.

Marilyn Hepburn Lind

Place 2865

Joliet

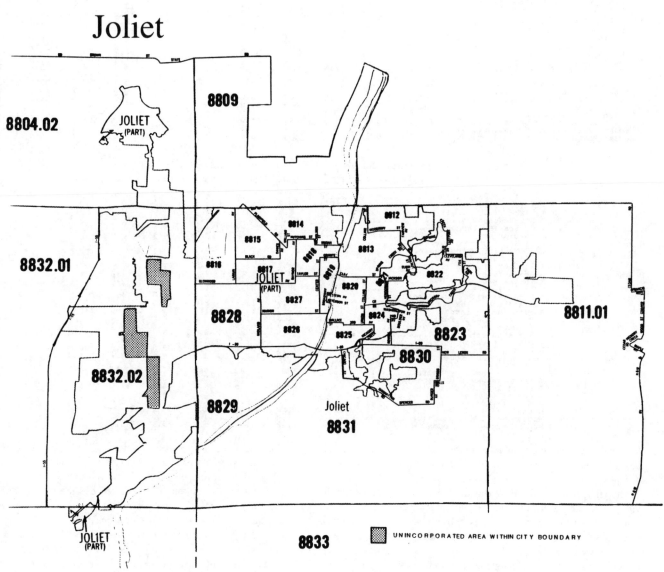

Joliet lies on the Des Plaines River, 40 miles southwest of Chicago, and is the only large city in Will County. The city was renamed in honor of Canadian-born surveyor and frontiersman Louis Jolliet who, along with Father Jacques Marquette, explored the area in 1673. Early pioneers could ford the Des Plaines River where Joliet now stands, making it a logical settling point. However, it was not settled until 1833, when the Charles Reed family crossed the river to build a small log cabin on the western shore. Soon others followed, attracted by the fertile prairie soil, soft coal, ample timber, and the transportation afforded by the river. They also found extensive limestone deposits that could be quarried for use as a building material.

One of those attracted to this area was James B. Campbell, a commissioner for the newly proposed Illinois and Michigan Canal. Late in 1833 he bought 80 acres and the next year filed a plat for the town of "Juliet" (named for his daughter). Farther north was the village of Romeo, which became Romeoville. The plain was dominated by a 60-foot limestone hill, Mount Juliet, later Joliet Mound. The now extinct mound was made of glacial deposits which were quarried to build the city.

When the town was chartered by the state in 1852 it adopted the name Joliet.

In 1848, the Illinois Waterway Canal was opened. This event influenced the development of the state by linking Chicago with the Mississippi River. Joliet is bisected by the canalized stream which flows through the nothern part of town at street level. With its new barge transportation, Joliet entered into an era of industrialization. Quarried limestone was often shipped as far as New York, and provided the construction material for the Indiana State Prison, the Illinois State House, and the Lincoln Monument at Springfield.

The Rock Island Railroad came to Joliet in 1852 and was quickly followed by other lines. Although the railroad eventually caused the decline of the canal, it did foster the manufacturing of steel which was further aided by the local availability of soft coal. Soon Bessemer plants, rail and rod mills and blast furnaces were followed by plants manufacturing products such as galvanized and barbed wire, and nails needed for the growing agricultural West. The American Steel and Wire Division of United States Steel remains one of Joliet's largest industries.

In 1888, the Elgin, Joliet and Eastern Railway companies incorporated, contributing to the development of Joliet's iron and steel industry by providing a new route for the shipping of heavy raw materials, iron ore and limestone. The line linked Joliet with the southern end of Lake Michigan, the Calumet industrial region, Waukegan and Aurora.

The residential development of Joliet was closely related to the industrial development. Attracted by employment opportunities, people of many nationalities came to settle in Joliet bringing their various heritages and cultures. Growth was especially rapid from 1870 through the early 20th century as the population increased from 7,263 in 1870 to 42,993 in 1930. The growing labor force was a heterogeneous mixture of Germans, Italians and Yugoslavians among the largest groups followed by the Irish, Poles, English, Swedes and Czechoslovakians. Joliet's population experienced a slight decline during the Depression years, but with wartime preparation and government constructuion of nearby ordinance plants, industrial activity again grew. Blacks made up only 3 percent of the population in 1930. During World War II, however, black immigration speeded up. Cities such as Joliet and Rockford, which encountered difficulty in filling jobs, recruited black migrants.

Following the war, Joliet began improving its water and sewer system, and other municipal services, attracting additional population and industry. Population increased 22 percent in the 1940s to 51,601 in 1950, due mainly to annexation. By 1960, the population had grown to nearly 67,000 and Italians and Germans were still the leading nationality groups. The black population had increased during the postwar years, constituting 7 percent of the 1960 population. However, 17 percent of the black population were inmates of the old State Prison.

The population increased by a sixth in the next two decades to the 1980 total of 77,956. The last two decades have seen an increase in black and Spanish-speaking populations. The 1980 census showed blacks made up 20 percent of Joliet's population and 8 percent of the total was of Spanish origin.

Although included in the Chicago Standard Metropolitan Statiscial Area, Joliet is large enough to be a metropolitan center with suburbs of its own. There are 325 area manufacturing firms, 33 of which are among Fortune 500 companies. Local industries produce over 2,800 different items. The Mobil Oil plant at Joliet is one of the state's largest. Founded in Joliet in 1972, International Games Inc., maker of "Uno" (the card game) keeps its international headquarters here. Among other industries are firms such as Dow Chemical, Caterpillar, Olin Corporation and Uniroyal. Joliet industry also includes numerous smaller firms with more than three-fourths of the companies employing 50 or fewer persons.

Railroad and truck lines have gradually increased their use of Joliet as a transfer point for freight. In addition, the Illinois Deep Waterway (Chicago Ship Canal), carries shipments of coal, fuel oil, chemicals, grain and many other manufactured goods. Joliet is also situated at the crossroads of two major interstate highways, I-80 and I-55, making it less than one hour away from Chicago and O'Hare Airport.

This city at the crossroads is a "home-rule" community operating under a council-manager form of government. Joliet has an area of 23 square miles presided over by a mayor and eight councilmen. Administrative duties are carried out by a city manager. Recently, Joliet initiated a process of developing public-private relationships to encourage further development of the city. Various local groups have cooperated to assist in expansion by utilizing industrial revenue bonds, tax increment financing, urban development action grants and SBA programs for small business loans .

Joliet is a mixture of the old and new. its architectural landscape offers a host of modern business structures such as the new Louis Joliet Mall, a major retail center consisting of more than 100 stores, theaters,

Joliet
Population and Housing Characteristics, 1930-1980

	1980	1970	1960	1950	1940	1930
Total Population.......	77,956	80,378	66,780	51,601	42,365	42,993
% Male.................	48.2	48.1	49.4	48.2	49.0	50.4
% Female...............	51.8	51.9	50.6	51.8	51.0	49.6
% White................	74.0	87.7	93.0	96.2	96.9	96.9
% Black................	20.1	11.8	6.9	3.8	3.1	3.0
% Other Nonwhite Races...	5.9	0.5	0.1	0.0	0.0	0.1
% Under 5 Years Old......	8.3	8.6	11.0	8.8	6.1	7.3
% 5-19 Years Old........	24.4	28.9	24.6	19.4	22.6	26.5
% 20-44 Years Old........	35.7	30.0	32.6	37.8	40.5	41.3
% 45-64 Years Old........	18.5	21.5	21.7	24.6	23.2	19.1
% 65 Years and Older.....	13.1	11.0	10.1	9.4	7.6	5.8
Median School Years....	12.3	12.0	10.9	9.8	8.5	*
Total Housing Units....	29,816	26,521	20,968	15,510	11,718	*
% In One-Unit Structures.	59.7	62.0	67.5	*	*	*
% Owner Occupied.........	58.1	59.3	60.2	57.0	43.9	*
% Renter Occupied........	37.8	36.3	34.9	41.0	54.6	*
% Vacant................	4.1	4.4	4.9	2.0	1.5	*
% 1+ Persons per Room....	4.8	8.3	9.6	8.5	*	*

Place 2865 — Joliet, Illinois
Selected Characteristics of Census Tracts: 1980

Tract Number	Total	8804.02	8809	8811.01	8812	8813	8814	8815	8816	8817	8818
Total Population	77956	300	0	9	4340	6496	5390	3457	5775	4079	3736
% Male	48.2	47.7	–	–	49.2	59.4	47.4	44.8	50.2	46.6	45.7
% Black	20.1	0.0	–	–	83.0	25.7	0.1	0.3	14.6	0.3	1.1
% Other Nonwhite	5.9	0.0	–	–	1.5	21.9	0.7	0.5	2.8	1.0	1.1
% Of Spanish Origin	8.4	2.3	–	–	2.3	39.1	1.7	1.0	2.8	1.0	2.3
% Foreign Born	6.5	8.1	–	–	0.8	19.1	4.5	3.4	3.4	3.4	3.4
% Living In Group Quarters	4.8	0.0	–	–	2.5	0.0	7.1	0.0	0.0	0.0	9.7
% 13 Years Old And Under	22.1	27.3	–	–	34.1	24.1	15.2	15.3	21.0	16.7	15.7
% 14-20 Years Old	12.7	5.7	–	–	16.6	16.8	11.2	10.2	13.6	10.4	15.1
% 21-64 Years Old	52.2	63.0	–	–	46.1	51.2	57.1	56.4	61.3	53.3	53.9
% 65-74 Years Old	7.4	3.3	–	–	2.3	5.1	11.0	9.8	3.0	11.8	10.7
% 75 Years Old And Over	5.7	0.7	–	–	0.9	2.8	8.5	8.2	11.8	11.8	10.7
% In Different House	47.3	69.4	–	–	50.1	51.7	28.1	31.6	58.7	31.8	49.4
% Families With Female Head	22.3	2.0	–	–	45.0	24.5	12.3	10.6	18.3	8.7	16.4
Median School Years Completed	12.3	12.7	–	–	12.1	10.7	12.1	12.6	12.7	12.9	12.4
Median Family Income, 1979 $$	22694	24306	–	–	16528	18472	22292	26339	26526	28370	21358
% Income Below Poverty Level	9.1	6.3	–	–	30.1	14.7	2.0	1.9	7.3	1.0	4.7
% Income Of $30,000 Or More	30.7	32.3	–	–	23.4	16.8	27.0	43.9	45.7		29.2
% White Collar Workers	48.7	54.2	–	–	31.9	24.9	48.0	56.6	57.4	74.0	54.9
% Civilian Labor Force Unemployed	9.3	9.0	–	–	13.7	18.1	6.8	7.0	5.9	4.7	7.4
% Riding To Work By Automobile	91.8	100.0	–	–	95.0	87.3	90.9	91.2	94.7	96.5	83.0
Mean Commuting Time - Minutes	18.7	16.8	–	–	26.2	18.2	17.9	15.8	17.4	19.2	18.9
Population Per Household	2.7	2.9	–	–	3.6	3.4	2.5	2.7	2.6	2.6	2.3
Total Housing Units	29803	106	0	4	1284	1787	2204	1218	2442	1642	1536
% Condominiums	1.8	0.9	–	–	1.8	0.0	0.0	0.0	1.3	1.3	0.0
% Built 1970 Or Later	14.0	64.7	–	–	22.7	1.0	0.8	3.6	24.3	1.9	0.6
% Owner Occupied	55.5	91.5	–	–	41.7	51.2	76.0	93.5	48.2	83.6	59.9
% With 1+ Persons Per Room	4.8	1.0	–	–	15.4	13.5	1.2	2.4	0.9	1.5	
Median Value: Owner Units $$	45700	64400	–	–	32500	24500	42800	50800	63400	63100	41700
Median Rent: Rental Units $$	184	325	–	–	180	146	189	248	206	250	203
Median Number Of Rooms: All Units	5.0	5.6	–	–	4.9	5.0	4.9	5.2	4.7	5.6	5.0

Tract Number	8819	8820	8821	8822	8823	8824	8825	8826	8827	8828	8829
Total Population	2824	4113	2568	938	844	3762	3598	5682	5314	5604	450
% Male	45.6	48.4	48.8	49.9	47.3	48.2	46.3	49.1	46.8	43.0	50.4
% Black	14.3	57.3	15.0	12.7	8.3	52.9	80.7	1.2	0.4	5.1	0.0
% Other Nonwhite	3.7	13.7	27.3	11.5	4.9	12.5	6.2	1.6	2.1	2.4	1.6
% Of Spanish Origin	5.9	16.2	37.2	21.5	9.2	13.5	6.7	3.0	2.5	2.9	6.7
% Foreign Born	5.2	14.3	18.8	13.3	9.1	4.1	3.8	3.3	4.0	5.2	9.9
% Living In Group Quarters	0.8	8.4	0.0	0.7	0.0	0.0	0.0	0.0	0.5	12.2	0.0
% 13 Years Old And Under	18.4	28.5	29.3	26.7	25.7	33.4	31.4	18.8	19.1	16.2	21.3
% 14-20 Years Old	11.4	11.8	14.0	15.6	8.8	14.6	14.7	12.0	11.5	9.7	11.1
% 21-64 Years Old	51.2	47.4	47.2	50.3	53.6	45.9	44.9	55.4	54.5	50.0	54.9
% 65-74 Years Old	10.8	5.3	5.3	4.5	6.8	3.7	4.9	9.0	9.2	12.7	8.0
% 75 Years Old And Over	8.2	7.0	4.2	3.0	5.2	2.3	4.0	4.8	5.8	11.3	4.7
% In Different House	48.5	56.1	45.5	65.5	38.7	47.9	41.3	40.4	44.5	54.1	12.3
% Families With Female Head	29.0	48.6	20.8	17.9	16.5	33.0	48.7	11.3	13.9	18.0	16.4
Median School Years Completed	12.2	11.8	11.8	11.9	12.0	11.8	11.9	12.4	12.7	12.3	11.0
Median Family Income, 1979 $$	15579	12602	19512	20000	21098	17459	15301	24883	24109	25143	21875
% Income Below Poverty Level	14.6	34.3	16.9	16.2	5.7	20.7	19.1	3.3	1.3	5.3	0.0
% Income Of $30,000 Or More	19.9	16.1	20.6	19.0	21.7	17.0	25.7	31.0	31.6	34.7	26.0
% White Collar Workers	45.0	36.9	29.4	20.4	36.5	24.4	32.8	48.5	55.1	55.3	37.0
% Civilian Labor Force Unemployed	13.0	19.1	17.5	5.2	2.6	12.8	13.8	10.3	7.8	6.3	24.7
% Riding To Work By Automobile	85.3	80.3	90.6	81.6	95.6	91.8	92.9	94.4	94.9	90.7	92.4
Mean Commuting Time - Minutes	17.0	16.8	18.7	24.5	19.4	24.7	18.4	17.9	18.2	18.2	18.7
Population Per Household	2.1	2.5	3.3	3.2	2.7	3.4	3.1	2.7	2.6	2.4	2.8
Total Housing Units	1693	1965	918	315	344	1230	1325	2185	2186	2223	166
% Condominiums	0.0	0.0	0.0	0.0	0.0	0.0	0.0	0.0	0.0	14.3	0.0
% Built 1970 Or Later	12.2	1.3	1.3	2.9	2.9	1.6	1.9	2.3	3.6	39.6	0.0
% Owner Occupied	21.2	14.4	50.7	63.2	60.2	54.4	35.0	75.7	58.9	53.8	81.9
% With 1+ Persons Per Room	3.7	11.5	11.5	5.6	3.2	10.6	8.7	2.2	1.6	3.0	4.4
Median Value: Owner Units $$	32600	26100	27600	31400	34200	29800	27200	44000	49200	43300	37200
Median Rent: Rental Units $$	167	155	166	182	182	173	148	206	210	211	230
Median Number Of Rooms: All Units	4.1	3.7	5.2	5.2	5.1	5.2	5.0	5.2	5.2	4.5	5.0

Tract Number	8830	8831	8832.01	8832.02	8833
Total Population	1409	426	0	6824	18
% Male	31.4	49.8	–	49.9	–
% Black	19.8	86.2	–	3.5	–
% Other Nonwhite	1.5	1.6	–	2.4	–
% Of Spanish Origin	2.2	1.4	–	2.2	–
% Foreign Born	11.1	0.0	–	5.4	–
% Living In Group Quarters	41.8	0.0	–	1.7	–
% 13 Years Old And Under	7.5	27.2	–	24.2	–
% 14-20 Years Old	5.7	14.6	–	13.4	–
% 21-64 Years Old	25.0	51.4	–	56.3	–
% 65-74 Years Old	17.9	5.2	–	4.1	–
% 75 Years Old And Over	43.9	1.6	–	2.1	–
% In Different House	63.4	30.1	–	61.9	–
% Families With Female Head	23.3	21.9	–	9.2	–
Median School Years Completed	10.2	12.1	–	12.9	–
Median Family Income, 1979 $$	25833	24000	–	28252	–
% Income Below Poverty Level	5.4	11.3	–	1.3	–
% Income Of $30,000 Or More	34.4	46.8	–	44.0	–
% White Collar Workers	34.4	43.4	–	62.7	–
% Civilian Labor Force Unemployed	10.6	2.5	–	3.8	–
% Riding To Work By Automobile	90.3	95.4	–	95.2	–
Mean Commuting Time - Minutes	17.1	21.6	–	18.7	–
Population Per Household	1.9	3.3	–	2.9	–
Total Housing Units	447	138	0	2433	12
% Condominiums	0.0	0.0	–	4.9	–
% Built 1970 Or Later	61.1	0.0	–	61.2	–
% Owner Occupied	28.9	67.4	–	63.8	–
% With 1+ Persons Per Room	2.6	10.8	–	1.3	–
Median Value: Owner Units $$	34800	27500	–	71500	–
Median Rent: Rental Units $$	162	156	–	254	–
Median Number Of Rooms: All Units	3.2	5.5	–	5.6	–

Joliet
Selected Characteristics of Census Tracts: 1970

Tract Number	TOTAL	8804	8809	8811	8812	8813	8814	8815	8816	8817	8818
Total Population	78827	11028	7684	10049	4358	5865	6731	4453	5644	4980	4304
% Male	48.1	49.7	49.6	50.2	48.2	50.1	48.4	45.3	49.8	47.3	42.4
% Black	11.8	0.0	0.1	0.0	73.0	19.4	0.6	0.7	2.9	0.9	0.1
% Other Nonwhite	0.5	0.3	0.4	0.2	0.4	1.3	0.2	0.3	0.3	0.2	0.3
% Of Spanish Language	4.1	1.6	1.7	0.9	3.9	22.2	0.2	1.3	1.1	1.0	2.9
% Foreign Born	4.3	1.5	3.3	2.6	2.1	10.7	5.8	2.1	3.0	4.7	4.1
% Living In Group Quarters	2.7	0.1	0.0	0.3	0.5	1.1	0.0	6.0	0.0	0.0	10.6
% 13 Years Old And Under	26.1	32.6	28.0	32.5	41.5	28.6	22.4	22.8	29.2	20.9	17.2
% 14-20 Years Old	13.1	12.7	13.1	12.0	14.5	12.9	12.0	14.2	13.0	12.8	16.6
% 21-64 Years Old	49.8	49.5	54.0	50.4	40.5	48.5	54.8	52.2	55.4	51.7	50.4
% 65-74 Years Old	6.6	3.2	3.5	3.5	2.2	6.2	7.1	5.7	1.4	9.9	10.0
% 75 Years Old And Over	4.4	1.9	1.3	1.7	1.3	3.8	3.8	5.1	0.9	4.7	5.1
% In Different House	57.9	54.8	58.5	54.5	49.8	62.5	70.1	72.6	48.3	65.7	63.7
% Families With Female Head	10.9	4.8	6.3	4.3	22.6	16.2	8.4	6.8	5.8	8.7	10.9
Median School Years Completed	12.0	12.3	11.3	12.3	10.3	8.8	11.1	12.4	12.7	12.7	11.3
Median Family Income, 1969 $$	11233	12520	11570	13051	9203	8632	11686	13773	13788	14778	10462
% Income Below Poverty Level	6.1	3.2	2.1	3.2	18.9	13.6	3.9	1.6	2.3	2.4	4.4
% Income of $15,000 or More	27.7	30.9	24.2	34.4	16.4	11.2	25.9	41.1	40.2	49.0	22.7
% White Collar Workers	27.8	27.6	22.3	32.9	13.3	7.9	19.0	35.2	47.8	51.6	23.5
% Civilian Labor Force Unemployed	3.7	2.2	3.6	3.1	3.4	5.1	4.9	1.0	1.7	1.6	2.2
% Riding To Work By Automobile	89.0	90.0	92.1	86.0	92.1	84.4	93.6	88.9	93.7	91.1	81.8
Population Per Household	3.1	3.7	3.3	3.6	4.3	3.0	3.3	3.0	3.3	3.2	2.7
Total Housing Units	26514	3067	2507	2805	1041	1903	2309	1304	1920	1712	1493
% Condominiums & Cooperatives	0.1	0.0	0.2	0.0	0.0	0.0	0.3	0.6	0.0	0.0	0.0
% Built 1960 Or Later	17.0	40.8	36.8	41.7	53.2	2.8	9.2	14.1	76.6	15.3	3.3
% Owner Occupied	59.2	80.7	63.0	84.0	53.4	49.9	76.4	86.6	51.2	77.6	61.6
% With 1+ Persons Per Room	8.3	8.1	10.3	7.3	25.8	12.9	6.8	7.3	6.3	3.2	4.3
Median Value: Owner Units $$	17700	22100	16300	22700	13200	10900	16400	20500	25600	26100	15600
Median Rent: Rental Units $$	98	120	135	123	84	74	97	133	141	152	102
Median Number Of Rooms: All Units	4.9	5.4	4.5	5.5	4.9	4.8	4.8	5.0	4.7	5.3	5.0

Tract Number	8819	8820	8821	8822	8823	8824	8825	8826	8827	8828	8829
Total Population	2956	4597	2768	6247	5224	3859	3949	6748	6088	4437	2740
% Male	47.4	47.7	48.1	49.1	48.4	47.9	47.9	48.4	47.1	48.6	49.5
% Black	1.5	32.5	3.3	1.5	0.2	5.0	59.9	0.5	0.1	0.5	0.3
% Other Nonwhite	0.2	0.6	0.7	0.4	0.4	0.7	0.5	0.2	0.7	0.3	0.1
% Of Spanish Language	2.5	4.5	7.5	3.0	5.0	5.7	1.5	1.9	2.9	2.5	10.8
% Foreign Born	6.8	4.7	8.5	2.3	2.6	3.4	1.2	2.3	4.3	3.8	7.5
% Living In Group Quarters	1.8	7.5	3.4	0.4	0.1	0.2	0.9	0.5	0.5	5.0	0.3
% 13 Years Old And Under	19.0	20.2	24.2	30.9	24.7	27.4	31.6	24.9	23.0	29.6	26.2
% 14-20 Years Old	9.1	10.8	12.2	12.6	11.9	11.7	14.9	12.2	12.8	14.1	11.9
% 21-64 Years Old	52.6	49.0	48.4	48.7	52.8	49.1	45.2	51.6	50.9	48.2	52.7
% 65-74 Years Old	12.3	10.2	8.5	5.4	7.3	6.7	5.1	6.8	8.6	4.0	5.6
% 75 Years Old And Over	7.1	9.8	6.6	2.4	3.3	5.2	3.2	4.4	4.7	4.1	3.6
% In Different House	48.0	40.6	61.0	61.3	69.3	54.6	40.3	65.7	60.4	60.5	63.2
% Families With Female Head	14.9	20.6	12.9	8.1	7.7	11.0	17.9	9.0	8.9	8.8	9.8
Median School Years Completed	10.8	10.1	9.7	10.6	11.0	10.5	9.6	12.1	12.4	12.1	10.1
Median Family Income, 1969 $$	10171	8451	9196	9714	11009	10061	8348	11538	12710	11963	9846
% Income Below Poverty Level	7.5	12.6	6.0	4.3	6.7	9.4	13.1	3.6	1.7	1.8	5.8
% Income of $15,000 or More	15.4	15.6	12.6	17.7	19.5	19.4	16.6	28.8	36.3	29.7	20.6
% White Collar Workers	29.6	18.8	17.1	16.8	17.4	18.4	9.7	30.7	36.6	27.9	14.0
% Civilian Labor Force Unemployed	6.0	5.8	5.7	4.6	4.1	6.9	3.6	3.9	2.5	3.1	3.0
% Riding To Work By Automobile	88.3	79.8	83.8	90.8	91.0	91.4	87.6	94.9	88.6	87.9	79.8
Population Per Household	2.3	2.3	2.9	3.4	3.1	3.0	3.3	3.1	3.0	3.6	3.1
Total Housing Units	1332	2074	988	1907	1754	1354	1264	2195	2121	1195	926
% Condominiums & Cooperatives	0.8	0.0	0.0	0.0	0.0	0.0	0.0	0.0	0.3	0.0	0.0
% Built 1960 Or Later	15.6	9.2	0.0	8.8	5.9	0.9	3.0	4.3	5.9	23.3	6.3
% Owner Occupied	29.7	16.8	47.3	75.1	77.4	56.0	42.7	74.7	59.0	72.8	65.1
% With 1+ Persons Per Room	4.6	8.0	7.2	12.8	8.4	8.2	13.6	6.4	5.7	12.7	8.8
Median Value: Owner Units $$	13100	12800	12500	12500	13600	13800	12500	17500	19100	18000	13500
Median Rent: Rental Units $$	84	81	88	90	95	97	94	102	114	148	83
Median Number Of Rooms: All Units	4.1	3.3	4.9	4.8	4.7	5.0	4.8	5.0	5.1	5.0	4.6

Tract Number	8830	8831	8832	8833
Total Population	2910	7143	9895	8221
% Male	48.0	49.3	51.6	50.8
% Black	23.7	33.0	1.8	0.2
% Other Nonwhite	0.9	0.5	0.2	0.7
% Of Spanish Language	2.5	1.0	2.0	1.7
% Foreign Born	5.2	1.5	1.9	1.6
% Living In Group Quarters	5.9	0.0	2.9	0.4
% 13 Years Old And Under	27.1	34.6	36.3	30.7
% 14-20 Years Old	12.1	13.8	13.6	11.8
% 21-64 Years Old	46.9	47.1	48.2	50.0
% 65-74 Years Old	6.7	2.8	1.2	4.7
% 75 Years Old And Over	7.2	1.7	0.8	2.9
% In Different House	64.5	62.3	49.0	53.6
% Families With Female Head	11.4	10.6	3.4	4.7
Median School Years Completed	10.9	11.6	12.5	12.0
Median Family Income, 1969 $$	10679	12211	13505	11282
% Income Below Poverty Level	8.0	6.5	2.7	4.4
% Income of $15,000 or More	24.6	29.1	40.0	26.8
% White Collar Workers	14.9	19.3	38.1	19.8
% Civilian Labor Force Unemployed	4.4	4.8	2.2	3.9
% Riding To Work By Automobile	90.1	91.5	93.6	82.3
Population Per Household	3.3	3.8	3.9	3.4
Total Housing Units	862	1913	2956	2479
% Condominiums & Cooperatives	0.0	0.0	0.0	0.0
% Built 1960 Or Later	8.6	36.3	79.3	28.1
% Owner Occupied	69.3	73.4	81.4	66.7
% With 1+ Persons Per Room	10.2	16.6	8.0	8.3
Median Value: Owner Units $$	14800	17400	25000	19400
Median Rent: Rental Units $$	89	103	152	103
Median Number Of Rooms: All Units	4.9	5.1	5.4	5.4

restaurants, and services. In constrast to this is the revitalized downtown business center. The Ruebens Rialto Square Theater, opened in 1926, was modeled after the great Baroque palace at Versailles and has been listed on the National Register of Historical Places. It was refurbished at a cost of $6.5 million and now combines a spectacular theater with offices and shops.

More than 60 percent of Joliet's housing is single-family and 55 percent is owner-occupied. Home prices range from $25,000 to $70,000. Many rental properties are also situated on the west side along with new condominium developments, schools, churches and the growing commercial areas. The trend here, as in many suburban areas is toward multi-family structures.

Gail Danks Welter

Lansing

Lansing is a south suburban community of 29,039 residents and is located 26 miles southeast of Chicago's Loop along the Indiana state line. Among the early settlers was the John Lansing family who came to this part of the country in 1846. Lansing laid out the original town plot in 1865 and his brother, Henry, was named the first postmaster. The Village took its name from this pioneer family.

Many Dutch and German immigrants in search of rich farmland were also among the early settlers. Until the year 1862, however, there were no outlets for water to drain away when the creeks and rivers overflowed their banks. The farmers who lived along the trail from Thornton to Ridge Road banded together to dig a ditch from Dyer to Highland, Indiana to help the drainage problems. They were finally solved when Cook County connected the Grand Calumet River with the Illinois and Michigan Canal.

In 1856, the Pennsylvania Railroad established a station in the Lansing area. Later, the Grand Trunk Railroad also established a route through Lansing. The GTR shipped the area's crops of corn, oats, and rye to markets in Chicago. In addition to farming, an important step in economic development was the growth of the brick industry. In 1877, the Harlan Brickyard opened, followed in 1892 by the Illinois Brick Company which, at peak periods, operated four yards producing quality brick for all purposes. The Pennsylvania Railroad built a depot and switch tracks to haul bricks to Chicago where construction was booming in anticipation of the Columbian Exposition.

Lansing was incorporated on April 18, 1893, with a population of 200. Fifty-three votes were cast to elect J.B. McDonald the first President. Six trustees, a village clerk and police magistrate were also elected. A treasurer was then appointed and construction of the Village Hall, on a site at what is now Lake and Henry streets, was completed in 1894. At the turn of the century, 830 people lived in Lansing.

The rise of the nearby Calumet industrial area was a significant factor in the growth of Lansing. Industrial development was encouraged by the natural harbor site along the southern shores of Lake Michigan, which in turn provided a transportation network conducive to steel production. Inland Steel came to the area in 1901. Soon after, the acceleration of automobile production made an important contribution to expansion of heavy industry in the Calumet Region. Attracted by the availability of jobs, the population grew to 1,060 in 1910. The first subdivision of homes was begun north of Ridge Road between Lake and Henry streets. The state chartered the first bank in Lansing the previous year. Road contracting began and the first concrete street, Ridge Road, was completed in 1916. By 1920, the population was 1,409.

Lansing's airport, one of the earliest in the country and second chartered in the state, was built by Henry Ford in 1924. It has recently been purchased by the Village but in the early period had been used by such notable flight pioneers as Amelia Earhardt and Wiley Post.

Considerable upgrading of municipal services took place. The fire department was organized in 1922. A new position of Chief of Police was introduced in 1927.

A great deal of business expansion occurred in the decade between 1920 and 1930. Building material firms developed out of the need for home, school, and church construction. The first Ford agency appeared in 1926. The Chamber of Commerce and the Board of Realtors were organized at this time. By the end of the decade the population was nearly 3,400.

During the early Depression years the first Lansing State Bank failed, as well as many small businesses. In the years previous, the steel mills of the Calumet area had provided 40,000 jobs but by 1932 none was operating at more than 15 percent capacity. School teachers were

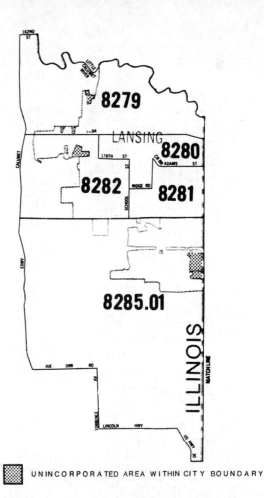

UNINCORPORATED AREA WITHIN CITY BOUNDARY

paid with scrip or anticipatory warrants during the worst years. Barracks were built at the Thornton Forest Preserve to house young men hired by the Civilian Conservation Corps for $1 per day. They were employed by the CCC to build bridges, lay trails, and erect pavillions in the forest preserves. Despite the bad times, Lansing grew by a third during the 1930s.

During World War II the Calumet steel mills and factories operated at capacity with defense tools the priority products. During the war years the barracks built in the Depression housed young German war prisoners who worked the area's sugar beet fields by day and, despite a language barrier, shared lunches with school children. By 1950, the number of residents had almost doubled again, to nearly 8,700.

The postwar economic recovery made home ownership available to millions of Americans who were provided governmental mortgage assistance. The Gold Coast subdivision of Lansing north of the Tri-State Expressway developed in the early 1950s. The population grew rapidly. Lansing experienced its largest increase in the 1950s, when it grew to more than 18,000.

The exodus from southside Chicago neighborhoods to southern suburban communities reflected a national trend of movement from central cities to outlying areas in the 1960s. During this period, the construction industry had mastered techniques for large-scale home building and land was plentiful in the outlying metropolitan area. Additionally, mortgage loans were more readily available for new homes, compared to financing renovation of older housing in the central cities. Tax advantages were an added incentive toward the purchase of a home. Future residents were attracted by the advantages of newer and better suburban homes. Personal incomes had risen and larger homes were desired by many. Many others relocated to avoid dealing with the difficulties of living in a large multi-ethnic environment. In Lansing, the last large tract of farmland (southeast section) was subdivided for housing in 1964. Nearly 26,000 people lived in Lansing in 1970. The number of housing units had increased by 57 percent during the decade.

Lansing
Population and Housing Characteristics, 1930-1980

	1980	1970	1960	1950	1940	1930
Total Population.......	29,039	25,805	18,098	8,682	4,462	3,378
% Male...................	48.5	49.3	49.5	49.6	50.4	52.1
% Female.................	51.5	50.7	50.5	50.4	49.6	47.9
% White..................	97.9	99.7	100.0	100.0	100.0	99.6
% Black..................	1.1	0.1	0.0	0.0	–	–
% Other Nonwhite Races...	1.0	0.2	0.0	–	–	0.4
% Under 5 Years Old......	6.2	8.6	12.5	14.0	9.4	14.2
% 5-19 Years Old.........	23.6	31.3	32.1	25.2	30.2	31.2
% 20-44 Years Old........	36.6	32.3	35.1	41.1	42.6	39.2
% 45-64 Years Old........	23.6	21.9	16.4	16.0	13.4	12.1
% 65 Years and Older.....	9.9	5.9	4.0	3.7	4.4	3.3
Median School Years....	12.5	12.3	12.1	10.9	8.5	*
Total Housing Units....	10,673	7,689	4,856	2,410	1,175	*
% In One-Unit Structures.	68.4	78.9	94.7	85.5	82.3	**
% Owner Occupied.........	69.0	77.0	88.9	81.2	63.5	**
% Renter Occupied........	28.2	21.4	9.2	15.9	34.0	**
% Vacant.................	2.8	1.5	1.9	2.9	2.6	**
% 1+ Persons per Room....	1.9	6.6	11.4	11.4	15.8	*

Place 3130 — Lansing, Illinois
Selected Characteristics of Census Tracts: 1980

Tract Number	Total	8279	8280	8281	8282	8285.01
Total Population.............	29039	5152	5720	5212	7489	5466
% Male........................	48.5	49.8	48.6	46.7	48.0	49.7
% Black.......................	1.1	4.9	0.6	0.0	0.4	0.0
% Other Nonwhite..............	1.0	2.0	0.7	0.7	0.7	0.8
% Of Spanish Origin...........	2.1	3.9	1.8	1.7	1.7	1.5
% Foreign Born................	4.1	6.5	2.6	3.9	3.8	4.1
% Living In Group Quarters....	0.2	0.0	0.8	0.0	0.0	0.0
% 13 Years Old And Under......	18.7	20.0	18.8	16.9	16.4	22.2
% 14-20 Years Old.............	12.8	12.4	13.4	12.8	11.9	14.0
% 21-64 Years Old.............	58.5	60.3	58.5	55.5	59.7	58.1
% 65-74 Years Old.............	6.6	4.9	5.9	9.7	7.8	4.1
% 75 Years Old And Over.......	3.4	2.4	3.4	5.0	4.2	1.6
% In Different House..........	32.6	38.9	30.4	25.1	39.0	27.4
% Families With Female Head...	9.4	11.4	11.7	7.7	9.2	6.8
Median School Years Completed..	12.5	12.5	12.5	12.4	12.5	12.7
Median Family Income, 1979......$$	26707	26651	25166	26045	26321	30451
% Income Below Poverty Level...	2.0	1.7	2.2	3.0	1.6	1.6
% Income Of $30,000 Or More.....	40.4	38.0	35.7	34.5	41.4	52.2
% White Collar Workers.........	54.9	49.4	53.3	51.5	57.2	61.7
% Civilian Labor Force Unemployed.	5.2	6.2	6.4	6.1	3.6	4.3
% Riding To Work By Automobile...	90.9	90.9	92.8	88.5	90.6	91.1
Mean Commuting Time - Minutes...	22.8	26.5	20.4	20.1	22.3	24.3
Population Per Household..........	2.8	2.8	2.9	2.7	2.5	3.2
Total Housing Units..........	10672	1912	1960	1972	3081	1747
% Condominiums.................	3.9	2.2	0.6	0.8	7.5	6.5
% Built 1970 Or Later..........	26.5	34.7	23.5	8.5	24.8	44.0
% Owner Occupied...............	69.0	63.8	76.5	75.5	55.5	82.8
% With 1+ Persons Per Room.....	1.9	1.9	3.2	2.0	1.4	1.3
Median Value: Owner Units.......$$	57800	52000	52700	54000	60300	65800
Median Rent: Rental Units.......$$	271	298	282	223	264	278
Median Number Of Rooms: All Units.	5.2	5.1	5.3	5.3	4.7	5.6

Lansing
Selected Characteristics of Census Tracts: 1970

Tract Number	TOTAL	8279	8280	8281	8282	8285
Total Population.............	25805	5064	5404	5737	8169	13189
% Male........................	49.3	49.9	49.0	48.7	49.4	49.7
% Black.......................	0.1	0.0	0.0	0.0	0.2	0.1
% Other Nonwhite..............	0.2	0.2	0.0	0.1	0.3	0.9
% Of Spanish Language.........	1.0	2.4	2.0	0.6	0.7	4.9
% Foreign Born................	3.8	3.3	2.9	5.1	3.7	3.7
% Living In Group Quarters....	0.2	0.0	1.0	0.0	0.0	0.4
% 13 Years Old And Under......	28.0	32.0	28.8	23.5	26.3	38.4
% 14-20 Years Old.............	13.2	12.4	15.2	13.9	12.4	12.2
% 21-64 Years Old.............	52.9	51.4	50.2	53.0	55.5	46.9
% 65-74 Years Old.............	3.8	2.8	3.3	6.3	3.8	1.8
% 75 Years Old And Over.......	2.1	1.4	2.5	3.3	1.9	0.7
% In Different House..........	53.4	53.3	66.1	60.2	50.5	51.7
% Families With Female Head...	4.9	4.5	5.9	5.1	4.5	3.5
Median School Years Completed..	12.3	12.2	12.3	12.0	12.3	12.1
Median Family Income, 1969......$$	13069	12763	13117	12551	13114	12499
% Income Below Poverty Level....	3.2	2.7	3.7	4.1	3.7	2.6
% Income of $15,000 or More.....	34.9	33.4	35.0	33.0	35.2	29.4
% White Collar Workers.........	32.6	27.7	27.7	28.3	36.8	22.3
% Civilian Labor Force Unemployed.	2.2	1.6	1.5	3.5	2.5	2.0
% Riding To Work By Automobile....	88.4	88.1	90.8	85.0	88.0	91.2
Population Per Household..........	3.4	3.7	3.7	3.2	3.2	4.2
Total Housing Units..........	7685	1409	1431	1846	2646	3247
% Condominiums & Cooperatives.....	1.2	0.0	0.0	0.7	3.0	0.0
% Built 1960 Or Later..........	38.3	31.4	15.1	15.2	54.1	49.3
% Owner Occupied...............	75.8	83.8	94.0	76.1	58.3	88.1
% With 1+ Persons Per Room.....	6.6	8.1	9.1	5.7	5.7	17.0
Median Value: Owner Units.......$$	21100	19400	19800	19800	22200	19100
Median Rent: Rental Units.......$$	149	145	131	124	161	133
Median Number Of Rooms: All Units.	5.2	5.3	5.4	5.1	4.7	5.2

Development of a metropolitan expressway system (Dan Ryan, Calumet Expressway, Calumet Skyway and Tri-State Tollway) in the last two decades has allowed industry to move from the city. Seven new industries located in Lansing during this period. The decentralization of industry influenced employees to move closer to their places of employment and the completion of the expressway system facilitated the trip for workers who commute. Today the Kingery Expressway traverses the Village and connects one mile west of Lansing with the Calumet Expressway and the beginning of the Tri-State Tollway System.

Home building decelerated in the late 1970s because of the scarcity of mortgage money. The general downward trend in the economy also affected the business community. Some small businesses closed while other major proposed developments, such as an office complex and a 150-store shopping center, never materialized. Nevertheless, Lansing today is the location of more than 200 businesses. Among these, a significant contributor to the Village's tax base is the 400,000 sq. ft. Scot Lad food distribution plant. This firm recently purchased more than 100 Chicago area food stores from the A & P chain. Food processors and distributors are the largest employers in Lansing.

The current population of Lansing is 29,000, up more than 3,000 in the most recent decade. While German, Irish, Polish, and English constitute a greater proportion in Lansing than in Chicago, blacks compose a significantly smaller proportion. While a Dutch population was once somewhat concentrated in Lansing, it no longer constitutes a

substantial proportion. The median income in 1979 was $26,707 per family. Two percent of all families lived in poverty, while more than 40 percent reported incomes greater than $30,000.

The number of housing units in Lansing has grown to more than 10,000, of which more than a fourth were built during the 1970s. Only 9 percent were built prior to 1940. This reflects postwar expansion. Sixty-nine percent of all housing units are owner-occupied while 71 percent are single-family homes.

The median value of all owner-occupied single-family units is presently $57,800. There has been a slow but gradual trend toward the construction of multiple-unit structures. Approximately one-fourth of all housing now contains five or more units.

Taking note of the increasing numbers of older people, Lansing has been granted a loan from the Department of Housing and Urban Development for construction of a 60-unit senior apartment complex. This complex will provide housing for handicapped or persons 62 years of age and older. This age cohort constitutes 13 percent of the population and there is a waiting list of 235 seniors for the soon-to-be completed housing facility.

Looking at the future, a seven-member industrial commission has been appointed to encourage more high technology firms to locate in Lansing. They are presently engaged in a data gathering project to provide interested industries with complete and vital information necessary for establishing business in the area.

Jane Cronin

Place 3315

Lombard

As in most of northern Illinois the Pottawatomie Indians were the first inhabitants of the Lombard area. Following the Black Hawk War, the brothers Ralph and Morgan Babcock settled along the DuPage River in 1833. The early settlement was called Babcock's Grove. The brothers were joined in 1834 by Deacon Winslow Churchill, his wife and 11 children. The Churchill family settled on land which eventually became part of neighboring Glen Ellyn. Other early settlers included Moses Stacy who built a hostelry west of the DuPage River at the convergence of five roads (the area known locally as Five Corners) 1837. Stacy's Tavern served as a stop on the stagecoach line between Chicago and points west, and in the early 1840s became a delivery point for U.S. mail addressed to Babcock's Grove.

Sheldon Peck was an artist who specialized in drawings of medical operations. He hired and personally paid the salary for the first teacher in the community. In 1850 Peck's home, as well as that of another early settler, Thomas Filer, became a stop on the Underground Railroad. Peck's son, Charles, helped found the Academy of Design in Chicago, which later became the Art Institute, and he served a term as its vice president. In 1849, the Galena and Chicago Union Railroad was operating through Babcock's Grove to Turner Junction (now West Chicago). By 1851 the community consisted of five frame houses, one store, a depot, and a small building owned by the railroad and used as a hotel. That same year the Congregational Church of Babcock's Grove was formed. In 1856 a second track was laid to handle the railway traffic. Some of the residents commuted to work in Chicago even at this early date. By the mid-1860s a one-room frame schoolhouse, three-story hotel, and a German school had been built.

Babcock's Grove, which had grown up on both sides of the DuPage River, was developing into two separate towns. After six other names had been tried the town west of the river would eventually become Glen

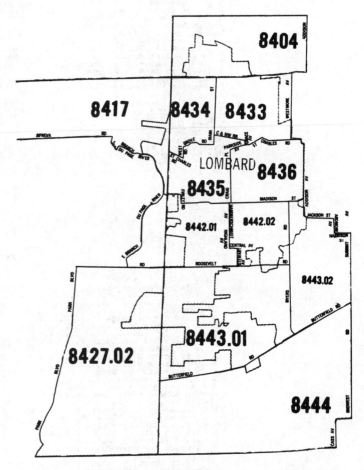

Ellyn. In 1869 the settlement of Babcock's Grove east of the river, concentrated along the railroad tracks on what is now St. Charles Road and Park Avenue, was incorporated as Lombard. It was named after Josiah Lombard, a financier and real estate broker who bought more

Lombard
Population and Housing Characteristics, 1930-1980

	1980	1970	1960	1950	1940	1930
Total Population.......	36,879	35,977	22,561	9,817	7,075	6,197
% Male...................	49.1	49.0	49.1	49.0	48.8	50.2
% Female.................	50.9	51.0	50.9	51.0	51.2	49.8
% White..................	96.4	99.6	99.9	99.9	99.9	100.0
% Black..................	0.6	0.0	0.0	0.0	0.1	0.0
% Other Nonwhite Races....	3.0	0.4	0.1	0.1	0.0	0.0
% Under 5 Years Old......	6.6	9.0	13.7	11.5	7.9	10.3
% 5-19 Years Old.........	23.9	34.1	30.1	23.1	25.8	29.0
% 20-44 Years Old........	40.1	32.7	33.8	37.4	38.1	40.8
% 45-64 Years Old........	21.7	19.1	17.1	22.2	22.3	15.2
% 65 Years and Older.....	7.7	5.1	5.3	5.3	5.9	4.7
Median School Years....	12.9	12.6	12.4	12.3	8.2	*
Total Housing Units....	13,286	10,500	6,251	2,835	1,980	*
% In One-Unit Structures.	69.8	81.2	93.5	90.6	89.6	*
% Owner Occupied.........	73.3	77.9	85.2	85.6	65.7	*
% Renter Occupied........	23.3	16.0	10.7	11.9	32.0	*
% Vacant.................	3.4	6.2	4.1	2.5	2.3	*
% 1+ Persons per Room....	1.5	6.4	9.8	8.2	8.7	*

Place 3315 — Lombard , Illinois
Selected Characteristics of Census Tracts: 1980

Tract Number	Total	8404	8417	8421	8427.02	8432	8433	8434	8435	8436	8442.01
Total Population.............	37295	531	168	18	422	0	6076	3871	4829	7292	4428
% Male.......................	49.1	52.7	44.6	–	46.9	–	49.6	50.6	47.7	48.0	51.4
% Black......................	0.6	0.0	0.0	–	1.2	–	0.1	0.3	0.0	0.1	0.0
% Other Nonwhite.............	3.0	2.8	4.8	–	37.4	–	4.8	0.8	0.9	1.2	1.8
% Of Spanish Origin..........	1.5	4.7	5.4	–	0.7	–	1.7	1.5	0.8	1.3	1.3
% Foreign Born...............	5.7	8.5	0.0	–	15.1	–	6.4	3.7	3.1	4.2	6.1
% Living In Group Quarters...	0.6	0.0	0.0	–	0.0	–	0.0	0.0	0.0	0.1	3.0
% 13 Years Old And Under.....	19.7	23.0	20.8	–	27.3	–	25.9	22.2	16.8	21.2	19.1
% 14-20 Years Old............	12.4	12.4	8.9	–	6.2	–	11.4	14.6	12.3	12.4	13.5
% 21-64 Years Old............	60.2	58.9	61.3	–	62.8	–	57.7	56.8	57.1	56.8	61.3
% 65-74 Years Old............	5.1	4.0	4.2	–	3.3	–	3.7	4.5	8.4	6.0	4.2
% 75 Years Old And Over......	2.7	1.7	4.8	–	0.5	–	1.3	2.0	5.4	3.6	1.9
% In Different House.........	43.0	20.6	40.5	–	100.0	–	33.3	43.3	40.8	35.8	38.0
% Families With Female Head...	9.6	5.3	4.5	–	2.6	–	6.7	9.3	9.1	10.3	7.1
Median School Years Completed.	12.8	12.4	12.7	–	14.6	–	12.7	12.7	12.9	12.7	12.8
Median Family Income, 1979...$$	28404	26932	19038	–	30485	–	27636	29494	29343	27126	27413
% Income Below Poverty Level..	1.5	0.0	0.0	–	0.0	–	1.8	3.5	0.5	0.7	1.9
% Income Of $30,000 Or More...	45.2	36.5	17.2	–	59.2	–	41.3	48.4	48.8	40.7	41.7
% White Collar Workers.......	67.8	57.0	65.0	–	74.7	–	61.9	61.9	71.4	64.1	61.7
% Civilian Labor Force Unemployed.	4.0	2.3	0.0	–	0.0	–	4.8	7.2	2.7	4.1	6.5
% Riding To Work By Automobile....	85.5	94.8	64.8	–	97.8	–	85.2	85.8	77.5	90.7	86.2
Mean Commuting Time - Minutes...	26.6	29.3	13.3	–	25.8	–	29.7	27.7	24.5	25.8	26.8
Population Per Household......	2.9	3.1	3.0	–	3.4	–	3.3	3.2	2.6	3.0	3.1
Total Housing Units..........	13439	182	62	8	158	0	1854	1222	1893	2510	1395
% Condominiums...............	12.0	17.6	0.0	–	0.0	–	0.0	0.0	8.7	0.0	3.7
% Built 1970 Or Later........	24.6	25.3	8.1	–	96.9	–	27.4	9.1	7.7	5.5	8.9
% Owner Occupied.............	73.3	79.1	58.1	–	72.8	–	93.4	87.0	70.3	79.0	84.0
% With 1+ Persons Per Room....	1.5	1.8	3.6	–	1.6	–	1.8	2.2	1.0	1.5	1.6
Median Value: Owner Units....$$	69300	68000	–	–	88400	–	68000	66300	69100	67400	66200
Median Rent: Rental Units....$$	332	317	229	–	501	–	298	327	274	263	281
Median Number Of Rooms: All Units.	5.6	5.4	5.6	–	5.6	–	5.6	5.6	5.6	5.6	5.6

Tract Number	8442.02	8443.01	8443.02	8444
Total Population.............	3568	5231	858	3
% Male.......................	48.5	49.5	45.9	–
% Black......................	0.1	3.4	1.0	–
% Other Nonwhite.............	2.6	5.2	3.4	–
% Of Spanish Origin..........	1.5	2.2	1.3	–
% Foreign Born...............	4.8	9.3	6.5	–
% Living In Group Quarters...	0.0	1.3	0.0	–
% 13 Years Old And Under.....	20.9	10.8	15.0	–
% 14-20 Years Old............	17.2	7.9	14.8	–
% 21-64 Years Old............	56.7	73.9	62.5	–
% 65-74 Years Old............	3.2	5.1	4.7	–
% 75 Years Old And Over......	2.0	2.2	3.0	–
% In Different House.........	24.6	76.2	64.3	–
% Families With Female Head...	5.7	21.1	30.4	–
Median School Years Completed.	12.9	14.4	12.7	–
Median Family Income, 1979.....$$	30270	30658	26553	–
% Income Below Poverty Level....	0.0	1.8	0.0	–
% Income Of $30,000 Or More....	51.0	52.4	37.2	–
% White Collar Workers.......	71.0	78.5	73.2	–
% Civilian Labor Force Unemployed.	2.2	1.9	6.5	–
% Riding To Work By Automobile....	88.1	84.2	82.6	–
Mean Commuting Time - Minutes...	24.1	27.0	25.1	–
Population Per Household......	3.5	2.0	2.4	–
Total Housing Units..........	1028	2761	365	1
% Condominiums...............	0.0	47.0	17.0	–
% Built 1970 Or Later........	3.9	70.9	25.1	–
% Owner Occupied.............	96.0	42.0	32.3	–
% With 1+ Persons Per Room....	0.9	1.0	2.5	–
Median Value: Owner Units....$$	77900	89400	94400	–
Median Rent: Rental Units....$$	356	379	306	–
Median Number Of Rooms: All Units.	5.6	4.3	4.1	–

than 200 acres of land, built several homes and assisted in the town's incorporation.

The 1870 census of York Township (including Villa Park, Elmhurst and Lombard) showed 1,799 persons and 569 horses. Among those persons living in Lombard at the time were Allen B. Wrisley, owner of the Soap company of the same name which manufctured OlivilO, "the only soap that could be spelled from either end," Josiah T. Reade, who founded the largest private library in Illinois and was instrumental in starting Lombard's library, and Col. William R. Plum, whose hobby of gardening eventually led to the establishment of Lilacia Park. The 1870s also saw the establishment of Lombard's oldest current business, the Hammerschmidt Brick and Tile Company. It expanded into a grain and fuel business and celebrated its centennial in 1978.

During the 1880s the town council was unable to provide needed services, especially street paving and sidewalks. Historically, one of Lombard's biggest problems has been drainage. Mud impeded the early settlers and continued to plague the population until after World War I. These problems resulted in a lack of growth in the town which exacerbated the financial situation. Businesses in Lombard of the 1880s included a cheese factory, tannery, well drilling, grocery and hotel, as well as the brickyards and a lucrative house moving business.

In 1891 Ellen Martin, a resident and a lawyer, led a 15-woman delegation which demanded to be allowed to vote in the local elections. Under the special charter of the incorporated town the word "male" had not been used; the only voting stipulation being "citizens . . . above the age of 21." Thus the women voted in the election and were among the first in the country to do so, although for a time their suffrage was limited to education issues. The 1890s also brought the addition of several subdivisions, and by the turn of the century the new telephone exchange served 600 users.

By 1900 Lombard had grown from about 100 or 150 to 590 residents. Growth had come without building codes or zoning laws. In 1902 passenger service started on the electric "third rail." The Aurora, Wheaton and Chicago Railway (later the Chicago, Aurora and Elgin Railroad, whose abandoned track bed is now the Prairie Path) went through the south end of town. In the following year Lombard was incorporated as a village.

By 1910, 883 Lombard residents had electricity, a bank, a water tower, and by 1912 its first newspaper begun by two local women. With a population of 1,331 in 1920 the community had added indoor plumbing, a post office building, an active volunteer fire department, a

Lombard
Selected Characteristics of Census Tracts: 1970

Tract Number	TOTAL	8404	8417	8421	8427	8432	8433	8434	8435	8436	8442
Total Population	34043	1007	6080	6376	14501	7431	6722	4426	5224	7965	11873
% Male	49.0	49.6	49.3	48.1	50.4	48.9	49.3	49.8	47.8	48.8	49.2
% Black	0.0	0.0	1.1	0.3	0.2	0.1	0.0	0.1	0.1	0.0	0.0
% Other Nonwhite	0.4	0.4	0.2	0.5	0.5	0.6	0.3	0.1	0.1	0.2	0.6
% Of Spanish Language	1.2	7.7	2.9	0.6	1.3	0.5	1.8	0.2	1.1	0.4	0.9
% Foreign Born	3.9	0.5	4.9	2.3	2.6	4.4	4.6	3.9	4.2	4.6	3.2
% Living In Group Quarters	0.3	0.6	0.9	0.8	1.1	0.0	0.0	0.1	0.3	0.0	0.5
% 13 Years Old And Under	31.1	34.5	31.6	28.7	36.3	32.0	34.1	31.5	27.9	29.3	32.7
% 14-20 Years Old	13.0	14.7	12.6	12.8	12.4	12.2	13.6	12.1	13.4	12.5	14.0
% 21-64 Years Old	50.7	47.3	51.3	52.6	48.6	50.1	48.8	51.2	49.8	52.1	49.6
% 65-74 Years Old	3.3	2.6	3.0	4.0	1.8	3.8	2.3	3.5	5.9	4.0	2.4
% 75 Years Old And Over	1.8	1.0	1.5	1.9	0.9	1.9	1.2	1.7	3.0	2.2	1.4
% In Different House	54.9	75.6	50.4	51.9	46.0	64.1	62.8	66.2	57.2	55.9	54.6
% Families With Female Head	5.3	7.6	4.2	6.4	2.8	7.2	5.5	4.7	6.7	5.4	5.0
Median School Years Completed	12.6	12.1	12.5	14.0	13.0	12.2	12.4	12.4	12.6	12.5	12.6
Median Family Income, 1969 $$	14087	13588	13233	16877	17436	12759	13436	13221	13971	13789	14308
% Income Below Poverty Level	1.9	4.0	2.7	2.5	0.7	4.3	0.9	2.0	1.5	1.5	3.0
% Income of $15,000 or More	43.2	37.8	37.2	57.7	60.8	32.7	38.1	35.6	44.3	41.5	44.7
% White Collar Workers	43.3	12.7	37.6	60.4	58.4	31.5	35.3	36.4	47.1	41.5	44.3
% Civilian Labor Force Unemployed	2.3	5.4	1.7	1.4	2.3	3.7	2.5	2.7	2.7	3.0	2.0
% Riding To Work By Automobile	81.7	85.9	84.2	73.7	80.2	83.9	87.6	81.2	70.4	84.3	81.3
Population Per Household	3.6	4.2	3.5	3.4	4.0	3.6	4.0	3.7	3.4	3.5	3.8
Total Housing Units	10500	238	1905	1916	3696	2101	1730	1214	1630	2300	3206
% Condominiums & Cooperatives	0.3	0.0	0.0	0.0	0.0	0.3	0.0	0.0	0.0	0.0	0.0
% Built 1960 Or Later	38.6	9.2	48.0	29.5	70.7	26.5	24.9	23.6	14.5	27.8	44.0
% Owner Occupied	77.6	85.7	60.1	77.9	88.0	76.5	81.3	88.6	75.0	77.7	81.3
% With 1+ Persons Per Room	6.4	16.8	6.3	3.3	3.5	10.0	9.9	7.5	5.7	6.6	7.1
Median Value: Owner Units $$	26200	21600	24700	33100	34400	22300	23400	23700	25900	25300	26900
Median Rent: Rental Units $$	172	145	189	173	213	147	179	208	145	166	185
Median Number Of Rooms: All Units	5.4	5.3	5.2	5.9	7.0	5.1	5.4	5.5	5.5	5.3	5.6

Tract Number	8443	8444
Total Population	11096	4202
% Male	48.5	50.4
% Black	0.7	2.2
% Other Nonwhite	1.0	0.4
% Of Spanish Language	3.2	0.7
% Foreign Born	5.3	3.8
% Living In Group Quarters	0.2	7.8
% 13 Years Old And Under	30.1	26.8
% 14-20 Years Old	11.7	16.0
% 21-64 Years Old	54.4	51.8
% 65-74 Years Old	2.6	3.2
% 75 Years Old And Over	1.2	2.2
% In Different House	26.1	26.4
% Families With Female Head	6.8	12.9
Median School Years Completed	12.8	12.9
Median Family Income, 1969 $$	14767	19658
% Income Below Poverty Level	3.0	1.6
% Income of $15,000 or More	48.3	66.2
% White Collar Workers	51.0	56.0
% Civilian Labor Force Unemployed	2.4	2.4
% Riding To Work By Automobile	85.5	86.1
Population Per Household	3.4	3.6
Total Housing Units	3819	1197
% Condominiums & Cooperatives	4.8	1.3
% Built 1960 Or Later	77.0	72.9
% Owner Occupied	61.8	72.8
% With 1+ Persons Per Room	4.4	3.8
Median Value: Owner Units $$	29100	50100
Median Rent: Rental Units $$	202	186
Median Number Of Rooms: All Units	5.1	6.6

The 1950s were a time of building, expansion of services, and organizational growth. A new shopping center was built, the Park District acquired over 90 additional acres of land and a new Chamber of Commerce was formed. A 1954 census showed the population at 14,043, an increase of over 4,000 persons in four years. A year later the population had increased to 16,284. Water, sewer and paving needs as well as a burgeoning school population kept officials busy throughout the 1950s. At the end of that decade Lombard had a population of 22,500.

Two hundred acres of land north of North Avenue were annexed in 1960 and zoned for manufacturing and light industry. In 1963 the National College of Chiropractic was dedicated and a new library building was opened. From 1960 to 1967 the population rose from 21,000 to 31,314 as a result of annexation and building on open lands.

In the fall of 1968 the Yorktown shopping center opened its doors. It was then considered the largest enclosed mall, covering approximately 130 acres and housing 100 stores. The area around Yorktown was zoned for high density residential development and several apartment complexes were built. Yorktown and its surrounding apartments formed an expanding base of revenue for Lombard. Yorktown has become a major retail center. In addition to downtown shopping there are two other major shopping centers.

Lombard gained 11,500 residents during the 1960s bringing the population to 34,000 in 1970.

The 1970s brought further building of apartments and condominiums as well as a new civic center. Continuing recognition of Lombard as "The Lilac Village" resulted in a crowd of nearly 50,000 attending the Lilac Festival parade in May, 1974 and nearly 75,000 in 1975.

By 1980 Lombard had grown to a village with nearly 37,000 residents. The population is nearly all white with less than 1 percent black and only 1.5 percent Hispanic residents. Its consistently residential character is reflected in the high proportion of single-family housing units which, while having dropped from over 93 percent in 1960, is still high at 73 percent. Home ownership is correspondingly high with more than 73 percent of the units owner-occupied. The income per household is $27,137 and the homes are in the $50,000 to $130,000 range. The Lilac Village continues to grow as a residential community and to expand by offering new opportunities for light industry interested in relocating.

Gail Danks Welter

Catholic church and school, and a women's club. Despite the lack of paved streets and continued problems with mud in which many travelers got stuck, the community experienced a post-war building boom. Finally in 1923 about a third of the streets were paved, resulting in an immediate rise in building permits. The next year a zoning commission was created and an ordinance drafted to help coordinate the village's growth. The population nearly quadrupled in the next 10 years.

In 1927 Colonel Plum died, leaving a bequest to the village of 2.5 acres for a park and his house for a library. By the time of his death the lilac collection he had amassed contained over 200 varieties and was known nationwide. The next year the Helen Plum Memorial Library was opened containing the collection of 3,000 books originally owned by Josiah Reade. The newly formed park district board bought five additional acreas of land adjoining the former Plum estate and hired Jens Jensen of the Chicago Park District to lay out and supervise Lilacia Park.

The first Lilac Fete was held in 1930 at which point there were more than 6,000 residents. In 1939 15,000 visitors attended the festival. The Great Depression affected Lombard as it did most communities with bank closings, as well as the closing of a local school. Nevertheless the population grew by 800 during the 1930s. The economy picked up with the war demands, but Lombard changed little since it discouraged any incoming industry. A post-war building boom began in 1946 and homes were built in several subdivisions. In 1950 alone 400 new homes were built and the population went from 7,000 in 1940 to 9,800 in 1950.

Maywood

Maywood is located 11 miles west of Chicago's Loop in Cook County. It is bounded by the Des Plaines River on the east, Roosevelt Road and Harvard streets on the south, 25th and the Indian Harbor Belt Railway on the west, and the Chicago and North Western Railway on the north. Maywood has historically been composed of industrial and residential areas, but recent movements of industry out of the Chicago area have reduced its economic base.

Maywood was a planned community from the outset. In 1868, Colonel W. T. Nichols came from Vermont and contracted for a purchase of land 1.75 miles long and a half mile wide through which the Chicago and North Western Railway now passes. He organized the Maywood Company, named after his daughter, May, chartered in 1869, and began laying out streets and planting trees. A 15-acre plot was reserved for a park in the center of what would become the village. On the northwest corner of this was erected the Maywood Hotel, the first building in the village. In 1870, several other buildings were erected including a general store, railroad depot, a brick school and a meeting house, a post office and about 30 homes. Four blocks were set aside by the Maywood Company for church purposes and one block was to be donated to any religious society that would build a church on it, the first being the Presbyterian Society in 1873.

The stock of the Maywood Company continued to rise in value and the firm branched out from real estate to industry. The Chicago Fire in 1871 brought new residents to Maywood and 100 homes were built that year. In 1884, the Company built a plant for the manufacture of farm implements and a three-story brick building, the third floor of which was a public hall capable of seating 800 persons. The financial panic of 1873 stopped nearly all growth for some 15 years. However, in 1881 Maywood was incorporated as a village. By 1884, it was estimated the village included almost 1,000 people.

In 1885, the Norton Can Works moved to Maywood from Chicago. The Norton factory was joined with others across the nation to form the American Can Company in 1901. The Maywood plant grew until in 1930 it included three factories and a laboratory unit extending from 6th to 14th avenues. It became the major employment source for the village, employing from 1,500 to 4,500 workers, even during the Depression.

Growth resumed after that and, at the turn of the century, 4,532 people lived in the village. One attraction to Maywood was the excellent transportation, with the Chicago and North Western Railroad, Chicago and Great Western Railroad, and the Aurora, Elgin and Chicago electric line, which connected to Chicago's elevated system, all servicing the community. In 1903 alone, 100 new homes were built and the next year 125. Village services expanded with a new fire station and 10 miles of bricked streets laid in 1904. Growth was steady in the early decades of the century with the population nearly doubling by 1910 to 8,033. By 1920, the total stood at 12,072.

The 1920s brought accelerated population growth in Maywood. By 1930, the population had grown to almost 26,000. Maywood devised a zoning ordinance in 1922. An attempt was made to preserve the single-family home character of the community while planning for business and industry as well as apartments. In comparison to nearby communities, Maywood was considered a well-to-do residential district. The village had well-planned, beautiful tree-lined streets and was bordered on the east by the Des Plaines River and forest preserves. It offered a range of single-family homes in a nice atmosphere. However, the direction of growth was toward smaller flats and apartment buildings to house employees of the industrial centers to the west.

The Depression brought a slowing of growth in Maywood as it did in most places. The population increased by only 800 during the 1930s. In 1930, a small black population made up 3 percent of the total and by 1940 it had grown to 4 percent.

The population size of Maywood has not changed much since 1940. The Village is surrounded by incorporated areas which have made growth through annexation nearly impossible. Annexations during the 1950s brought 71 persons into Maywood's territory. While the population increased nominally between 1940 and 1950, the 1950s brought a small decrease, partially due to the construction of Interstate Highway 290 through the southern part of Maywood, which necessitated the relocation of some homes.

Maywood's total population reached 29,000, its high to this time, in 1960 and then dropped by a thousand during the most recent decade. This decline was contrary to predictions that the population would be 35,000 by 1975. However, the change in economic conditions and the transfer of many industries and businesses out of the metropolitan region have made growth more problematic.

As growth in Maywood slowed down after 1940, blacks began to move in. The relative number of blacks doubled to 9 percent in 1950, again to 19 percent in 1960 and again to 40 percent in 1970. In the most recent decade, this group continued to increase until in 1980 the black population constituted three-fourths of the total.

The housing situation in Maywood has been fairly stable since 1950. Only 750 housing units have been added to the 1950 total of 8,027, indicating the built-up nature of the village. Most of the housing was built before 1950, and 5 percent has been built during the last 10 years. Owner-occupied units made up 60 percent of the total in 1980. Rental units range from single-family homes to apartment houses with five or more units, the latter making up 44 percent of the total occupied rental units.

As of 1980, 5 percent of the total housing units were vacant. The age distribution of Maywood's residents in 1980 suggests a relatively young population. Of the total population, a third were under 18 years of age and only one in twelve was over 65. The median age was 29.1. The median family income in 1979 was $21,668. Eleven percent of all families lived below the poverty level.

Village statistics collected in 1983 showed 83 industries and 466 commercial enterprises in Maywood. These figures indicated a slight rise in the number of establishments since 1980. However, these are small employers and they have not been able to offset the loss in the 1970s of the American Can Company and, earlier, of the Canada Dry Company, which had employed 4,000 people. Those moves left a large number of people out of work.

Maywood is attempting to attract new industry. The old site of the American Can Company is now the Maywood Industrial Center, although developing it has presented problems since originally it had its own utilities. Maywood's symbol, "Phoenix Rising" suggests village officials are cognizant of the problems and are attempting to deal with them in a positive manner.

Gail Danks Welter

Maywood
Population and Housing Characteristics, 1930-1980

	1980	1970	1960	1950	1940	1930
Total Population.......	27,998	38,036	27,330	27,473	26,648	25,829
% Male.................	47.7	48.2	481.1	48.3	49.4	50.4
% Female...............	52.3	51.8	51.9	51.7	50.6	49.6
% White................	21.6	57.6	80.6	90.8	95.5	97.1
% Black................	75.1	41.3	19.1	9.1	4.5	2.8
% Other Nonwhite Races.	3.3	1.1	0.3	0.1	0.0	0.1
% Under 5 Years Old....	8.2	9.3	11.1	9.1	6.5	8.8
% 5-19 Years Old.......	29.5	30.6	23.9	19.5	24.5	26.7
% 20-44 Years Old......	36.6	32.7	31.6	37.6	41.3	44.0
% 45-64 Years Old......	17.5	19.0	23.5	25.4	21.7	16.3
% 65 Years and Older...	8.2	8.4	9.9	8.4	6.0	4.2
Median School Years....	12.2	12.2	11.1	10.8	9.0	*
Total Housing Units....	8,777	9,023	8,364	8,027	7,338	*
% In One-Unit Structures.	57.6	57.4	60.4	*	*	*
% Owner Occupied........	60.7	60.6	61.1	59.2	46.0	*
% Renter Occupied.......	36.3	36.6	35.8	39.5	52.2	*
% Vacant...............	3.0	2.8	3.1	1.3	1.8	*
% 1+ Persons per Room....	8.7	9.8	8.9	9.8	*	*

Place 3635 — Maywood , Illinois
Selected Characteristics of Census Tracts: 1980

Tract Number	Total	8172	8173	8174	8175	8176	8177	8179
Total Population.............	27998	5775	3179	3796	4476	4516	6256	0
% Male.......................	47.7	46.7	46.2	49.1	46.5	49.7	48.0	—
% Black......................	75.1	96.9	96.9	18.9	71.3	69.8	84.4	—
% Other Nonwhite.............	3.4	0.6	1.0	12.6	3.9	3.9	0.8	—
% Of Spanish Origin..........	6.8	0.9	2.0	29.9	7.8	4.2	1.7	—
% Foreign Born...............	5.5	1.5	1.5	21.3	4.6	3.3	3.8	—
% Living In Group Quarters...	1.3	0.0	0.0	0.7	7.4	0.0	0.0	—
% 13 Years Old And Under.....	24.9	26.3	23.2	22.1	22.0	26.0	27.6	—
% 14-20 Years Old............	14.7	14.3	15.1	12.3	14.3	14.9	16.4	—
% 21-64 Years Old............	52.1	53.7	51.1	55.3	50.5	51.9	50.5	—
% 65-74 Years Old............	4.8	4.1	7.4	5.9	6.3	4.0	3.1	—
% 75 Years Old And Over......	3.4	1.5	3.3	4.4	6.9	3.1	2.4	—
% In Different House.........	36.0	36.5	20.4	44.1	43.8	41.9	28.9	—
% Families With Female Head..	29.0	37.5	43.7	16.8	36.2	28.1	17.5	—
Median School Years Completed...	12.2	12.3	10.6	12.2	12.3	12.5	12.4	—
Median Family Income, 1979...$$	21668	20456	15639	23968	20200	20904	25980	—
% Income Below Poverty Level....	11.0	11.0	27.0	7.2	15.1	6.9	5.4	—
% Income Of $30,000 Or More.....	29.0	27.1	18.6	33.3	22.7	25.7	39.5	—
% White Collar Workers.......	46.9	44.5	32.6	50.5	49.7	49.2	48.9	—
% Civilian Labor Force Unemployed.	9.7	11.5	12.9	5.2	13.3	8.8	7.8	—
% Riding To Work By Automobile....	86.4	85.8	92.6	86.1	85.1	84.9	86.7	—
Mean Commuting Time - Minutes...	23.8	24.1	20.1	19.3	25.6	22.5	28.0	—
Population Per Household..........	3.3	3.4	3.2	3.1	2.9	3.3	3.8	—
Total Housing Units..........	8777	1789	1053	1266	1539	1461	1669	0
% Condominiums...............	0.0	0.0	0.0	0.0	0.0	0.0	0.0	—
% Built 1970 Or Later........	4.8	2.9	1.8	2.1	14.9	4.2	1.9	—
% Owner Occupied.............	59.6	50.5	49.2	61.8	40.5	60.6	91.1	—
% With 1+ Persons Per Room...	8.7	8.7	10.8	7.8	10.0	7.8	7.7	—
Median Value: Owner Units.......$$	44800	44600	38500	51300	42400	43200	45000	—
Median Rent: Rental Units....$$	213	225	184	206	198	233	240	—
Median Number Of Rooms: All Units.	5.3	5.2	5.2	5.5	4.6	5.4	5.6	—

Maywood
Selected Characteristics of Census Tracts: 1970

Tract Number	TOTAL	8172	8173	8174	8175	8176	8177	8179
Total Population.............	29019	6657	4057	3642	5320	4480	5880	6670
% Male.......................	48.2	47.2	47.9	46.3	49.2	50.3	48.2	49.3
% Black......................	41.3	89.3	90.1	0.1	26.0	1.8	22.9	5.9
% Other Nonwhite.............	1.1	0.8	0.5	0.5	1.6	1.5	1.6	1.5
% Of Spanish Language........	3.6	0.9	0.7	6.3	3.8	7.6	3.8	1.8
% Foreign Born...............	4.6	2.5	2.2	6.4	5.6	5.2	6.2	7.8
% Living In Group Quarters...	0.9	0.4	1.7	1.1	1.1	1.4	0.0	0.1
% 13 Years Old And Under.....	28.9	31.2	31.2	24.7	28.3	25.9	29.9	23.0
% 14-20 Years Old............	12.4	14.0	13.7	11.4	11.7	12.4	10.9	9.8
% 21-64 Years Old............	50.3	50.2	48.7	50.8	50.6	52.4	49.3	59.4
% 65-74 Years Old............	5.4	3.0	4.6	7.8	5.8	6.2	6.3	5.3
% 75 Years Old And Over......	3.0	1.7	1.8	5.3	3.5	3.1	3.5	2.5
% In Different House.........	56.4	60.7	62.8	59.2	45.7	57.4	54.3	54.9
% Families With Female Head..	12.5	13.2	20.1	11.6	12.9	11.5	7.7	6.9
Median School Years Completed...	12.1	12.0	11.1	12.2	12.1	12.4	12.2	12.4
Median Family Income, 1969...$$	11573	10266	9592	12419	12205	12140	12848	12438
% Income Below Poverty Level....	6.4	10.0	8.5	2.7	7.0	4.2	4.1	2.5
% Income of $15,000 or More.....	27.3	21.5	16.7	30.5	32.4	27.7	33.7	33.9
% White Collar Workers.......	22.7	14.2	8.0	26.2	27.1	36.3	24.5	37.3
% Civilian Labor Force Unemployed.	4.3	6.0	5.5	3.5	3.3	1.3	5.2	3.0
% Riding To Work By Automobile....	78.8	80.3	79.3	83.2	74.4	76.3	80.0	83.4
Population Per Household..........	3.4	3.7	3.6	3.1	3.1	3.2	3.5	2.9
Total Housing Units..........	9021	1812	1131	1201	1783	1411	1683	2347
% Condominiums & Cooperatives.....	0.6	0.5	1.2	0.0	1.0	0.0	0.7	1.7
% Built 1960 Or Later........	9.1	21.8	12.6	4.1	8.6	3.0	2.3	24.2
% Owner Occupied.............	60.1	54.1	46.2	60.3	45.7	62.6	88.8	61.4
% With 1+ Persons Per Room......	9.8	13.1	17.5	5.8	9.0	5.8	8.1	4.5
Median Value: Owner Units......$$	19500	19400	17000	21000	20100	18700	19700	23100
Median Rent: Rental Units....$$	126	134	117	122	123	127	140	144
Median Number Of Rooms: All Units.	5.2	5.1	5.0	5.5	4.9	5.2	5.5	4.7

Mount Prospect

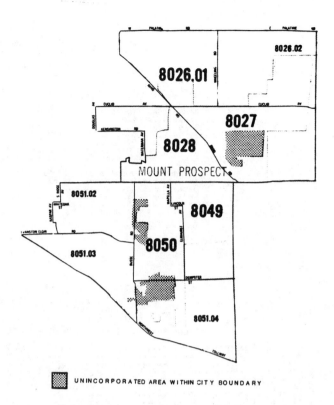

UNINCORPORATED AREA WITHIN CITY BOUNDARY

Mount Prospect is in Cook County, about 24 miles northwest of the Loop, just northwest of Des Plaines and north of O'Hare Airport. Its growth, in the span of a lifetime, has been phenomenal. At the outset of World War I, it was an unincorporated community of less than 300, and by the beginning of World War II still had fewer than 2,000 residents. Today more than 50,000 live there. The first white settlers, Yankee farmers Edward Burke and Owen Rooney, established homesteads in the heart of today's downtown Mount Prospect after the signing of an Indian treaty in 1831. Other New Englanders followed from 1833 to 1843, clearing and farming the land. By 1845, however, most of these early settlers had recommenced their migration westward, spurred on by an influx of German immigrants in the early 1840s.

The settlement's first place of worship, St. John's Lutheran Church, was founded in 1848 with the Rev. Francis Hoffman as its pastor. In 1854, the newly-formed Illinois and Wisconsin Railroad (now the Chicago and North Western) began service to the northwest villages, but did not open a depot in the settlement until 1886. Encouraged by the opportunities offered by railroad expansion, many of the remaining Yankee families moved to the nearby railroad towns of Arlington Heights and Des Plaines. Eager for land, several German and Irish families bought up their homesteads.

In 1871, Chicago real estate entrepreneur Ezra C. Eggleston bought the Burke and Rooney farms, on which he planned to build a four-block residential subdivision. Eggleston named the proposed development Mount Prospect — "Mount" because the altitude is 667 feet above sea level and approximately 70 feet above the elevation of Lake Michigan, and "Prospect" because he anticipated significant returns on his investment. Eggleston suffered heavy losses in the Chicago Fire and the Depression of 1873, however, and his planned community was never constructed. The subdivision was sold for taxes in 1882 after several lengthy court battles with his creditors, and the remainder of the land was returned to the original owners.

A small group of German farmer-businessmen began to move to the site of Eggleston's subdivision in the early 1880s. They decided to keep the name Mount Prospect. Among these were William Wille, who built a cheese factory in 1880, John Meyne, who opened a blacksmith shop in 1887, and John Conrad Moehling, who opened the village's first general store in 1882 on the corner of Northwest Highway and Main Street. Moehling was appointed the first village postmaster in 1885 and also served as the first depot agent for the Mount Prospect station which the railroad opened in 1886 at Moehling's request. The most important newcomer was William Busse, who moved to Mount Prospect in 1898. Busse built the village's first hardware store as well as its second general store, became a deputy sheriff, and served as a County Commissioner from the early 1900s to 1954. He opened the area's first Buick agency and in 1911 organized the Mount Prospect State Bank with his son William Busse, Jr. serving as its first president.

The community grew slowly during its first half century. In 1893 its population was only 35 people. Twenty years later the village still fell short of 300 residents needed for official incorporation. The villagers felt a need for local government, however, and in 1911 several leading businessmen established the Mount Prospect Improvement Association which, acting as an unofficial government, brought about the installation of electric lights and the creation of a volunteer fire department. A newborn infant became Mount Prospect's 300th resident in May, 1917 and the village immediately incorporated. William Busse served as the first Village President from 1917 to 1929.

Mount Prospect experienced a spurt of population growth and civic expansion during the 1920s. The number of residents increased to

1,225 in 1930. The community built its first village hall in 1923 on Northwest Highway east of Main Street. Two years later Central School, the village's first all-brick elementary school, opened at the corner of Central Road and Main Street. A bond issue enabled the village to open its first paved streets to traffic in 1927, and the installation of sewers and sidewalks soon followed.

Mount Prospect's rapid growth was halted by the onset of the Depression. Declines in real estate values and business activities disrupted the local economy and resulted in a major drop in tax revenues. Many families lost their homes and residential construction ceased almost entirely by 1932. Despite the economic hardships of the times, community residents pitched in to help their less fortunate neighbors and few families were forced to leave the village. The Benjamin Electric Company in neighboring Des Plaines was a major employer of Mount Prospect residents during the Depression. Most of the other villagers who had jobs commuted to Chicago.

The village's prospects for the future rebounded during the early years of World War II. The J.P. Crofoot Company, a manufacturer of staples, moved to downtown Mount Prospect in 1944 and became a leading employer. The end of the Second World War spurred new growth as more than 2,500 new residents established homes in the village in a five-year span. The community population increased to just over 4,000 in 1950. Encouraged by this new growth, village officials constructed a new and larger village hall in 1949.

The movement of white, middle-class Chicagoans contributed to Mount Prospect's accelerating growth rate during the next three decades. The population reached a total of 18,906 in 1960. Faced with the complexities of a growing populace, village officials adopted a council-manager form of government in 1955.

The village population nearly doubled between 1960 and 1970, from 18,906 to 34,995. This rapid growth stimulated the local economy and in 1962 the Randhurst Corporation opened the Randhurst Shopping Center at the intersection of Rand Road, Main Street and Kensington Road. Randhurst, with its 95 small shops and three major department stores, was the first (and for many years the largest) totally enclosed, air-conditioned shopping mall in the nation.

The population boom continued unabated for the first half of the 1970s, passing the 50,000 mark in 1976. The rate of growth slowed in

Mount Prospect
Population and Housing Characteristics, 1930-1980

	1980	1970	1960	1950	1940	1930
Total Population.......	52,634	34,995	18,906	4,009	1,720	1,225
% Male.................	49.4	49.2	49.7	49.8	50.5	52.0
% Female...............	50.6	50.8	50.3	50.2	49.5	48.0
% White................	95.6	99.6	99.8	100.0	100.0	99.4
% Black................	0.6	0.0	0.0	–	–	0.6
% Other Nonwhite Races...	3.8	0.4	0.2	–	–	
% Under 5 Years Old......	5.4	8.6	13.7	12.5	9.4	10.4
% 5-19 Years Old.........	24.8	34.5	31.6	23.5	*	*
% 20-44 Years Old........	38.4	31.6	35.4	40.1	*	*
% 45-64 Years Old........	24.2	20.5	15.5	19.7	18.1	13.5
% 65 Years and Older.....	7.1	4.8	3.9	4.2	4.7	4.7
Median School Years....	12.9	12.7	12.7	12.4	*	*
Total Housing Units....	19,513	9,699	5,108	1,171	*	*
% In One-Unit Structures.	62.9	84.5	95.5	91.3	*	*
% Owner Occupied.........	65.1	80.7	87.5	84.8	*	*
% Renter Occupied........	31.1	16.3	7.2	12.8	*	*
% Vacant.................	3.8	2.9	5.2	2.3	*	*
% 1+ Persons per Room....	1.5	4.7	5.9	5.0	*	*

Place 3930 — Mount Prospect, Illinois
Selected Characteristics of Census Tracts: 1980

Tract Number	Total	8026.01	8026.02	8027	8028	8049	8050	8051.02	8051.03	8051.04	8061
Total Population.............	52634	641	4920	9293	7512	7628	11554	3102	6229	1755	0
% Male.......................	49.4	47.9	49.9	48.6	49.3	48.6	48.3	50.7	50.2	58.3	–
% Black......................	0.6	0.0	0.0	0.5	0.3	0.1	0.8	0.0	1.8	3.2	–
% Other Nonwhite.............	3.8	0.3	3.1	3.4	3.5	2.4	3.9	2.0	1.8	2.4	–
% Of Spanish Origin..........	2.3	1.2	1.5	2.9	1.3	0.8	2.4	0.5	5.2	5.5	–
% Foreign Born...............	10.8	4.1	11.1	11.3	10.2	8.7	10.9	12.0	13.7	9.9	–
% Living In Group Quarters...	0.0	0.0	0.0	0.2	0.0	0.0	0.0	0.0	0.0	0.0	–
% 13 Years Old And Under.....	18.4	5.3	22.3	21.7	18.5	17.6	18.2	19.0	15.6	8.7	–
% 14-20 Years Old............	13.5	7.6	17.8	16.0	11.4	13.7	13.0	17.2	11.2	4.8	–
% 21-64 Years Old............	60.9	73.0	55.7	56.5	60.9	59.0	59.7	58.3	69.7	84.7	–
% 65-74 Years Old............	4.7	11.7	2.8	3.5	6.1	6.2	6.0	3.9	2.6	1.2	–
% 75 Years Old And Over......	2.4	2.3	1.4	2.3	3.2	3.4	3.1	1.6	0.9	0.6	–
% In Different House.........	44.4	70.5	28.2	39.1	35.5	36.1	44.6	33.0	74.3	95.0	–
% Families With Female Head...	10.2	23.5	4.9	9.6	7.1	9.1	14.0	4.5	15.7	21.4	–
Median School Years Completed....	12.9	14.4	13.0	12.8	12.9	13.5	12.8	12.8	13.0	15.4	–
Median Family Income, 1979...$$	30617	42327	35026	31169	29804	33139	29903	33180	26836	20990	–
% Income Below Poverty Level.....	2.2	0.0	0.5	1.7	1.8	1.8	3.0	1.8	3.6	4.4	–
% Income Of $30,000 Or More.....	51.9	87.4	64.5	53.8	49.3	58.3	49.8	61.5	35.4	5.0	–
% White Collar Workers...........	68.5	83.6	68.5	68.0	68.3	71.5	68.4	61.1	67.4	70.5	–
% Civilian Labor Force Unemployed.	3.1	4.9	3.6	5.0	3.0	2.7	2.7	1.8	2.5	2.4	–
% Riding To Work By Automobile...	86.3	84.7	91.2	87.8	80.6	76.1	88.9	91.7	88.8	93.4	–
Mean Commuting Time – Minutes...	26.2	34.5	27.1	24.9	26.4	27.5	25.1	25.4	28.6	22.7	–
Population Per Household..........	2.8	2.0	3.6	3.3	2.9	3.0	3.0	2.6	3.4	2.2	1.7
Total Housing Units..........	19508	405	1426	2966	2594	2603	4508	924	2972	1110	0
% Condominiums...............	8.7	93.6	0.0	4.1	1.7	3.6	16.4	0.0	10.7	0.0	–
% Built 1970 Or Later........	31.9	98.7	12.2	21.9	3.2	3.3	46.6	12.1	55.4	86.7	–
% Owner Occupied.............	65.1	69.6	93.6	67.5	89.8	86.2	61.8	96.8	27.6	1.4	–
% With 1+ Persons Per Room...	1.5	0.0	0.9	1.8	0.9	0.9	1.5	1.1	2.1	2.0	–
Median Value: Owner Units...$$	88500	–	98700	95200	71400	87000	90900	89100	96500	–	–
Median Rent: Rental Units...$$	319	385	501	319	319	303	288	390	330	338	–
Median Number Of Rooms: All Units.	5.6	5.2	5.6	5.6	5.6	5.6	5.2	5.6	4.1	3.8	–

Mount Prospect
Selected Characteristics of Census Tracts: 1970

Tract Number	TOTAL	8026	8027	8028	8049	8050	8051	8061
Total Population.............	34995	15506	10771	17469	16036	9701	25709	9577
% Male.......................	49.2	50.3	49.4	48.9	49.4	49.1	49.8	49.4
% Black......................	0.0	0.1	0.6	0.0	0.0	0.0	0.2	0.1
% Other Nonwhite.............	0.3	0.6	0.5	0.3	0.6	0.2	0.9	0.6
% Of Spanish Language........	1.0	1.8	1.0	1.3	0.5	0.7	1.7	1.7
% Foreign Born...............	3.9	5.2	5.3	3.5	4.2	4.1	4.2	3.6
% Living In Group Quarters...	0.4	0.1	4.6	0.0	0.1	0.1	0.9	0.6
% 13 Years Old And Under.....	31.3	31.4	34.5	29.0	31.3	31.1	30.3	29.4
% 14-20 Years Old............	12.9	11.0	13.3	14.2	12.6	12.7	9.9	12.2
% 21-64 Years Old............	51.1	54.5	49.1	51.4	50.9	52.7	56.6	52.8
% 65-74 Years Old............	3.0	1.9	1.9	3.5	3.3	2.4	2.0	3.7
% 75 Years Old And Over......	1.7	1.1	1.1	1.9	1.8	1.0	1.2	1.9
% In Different House.........	57.1	30.7	47.0	61.1	56.4	49.2	29.4	62.5
% Families With Female Head...	4.5	4.1	3.5	5.2	5.0	4.5	4.1	5.3
Median School Years Completed...	12.7	12.8	12.7	12.8	12.7	12.9	12.8	12.6
Median Family Income, 1969......$$	16503	15967	17283	16580	17230	16845	14783	14921
% Income Below Poverty Level....	1.8	2.2	1.9	2.0	1.7	2.2	1.6	1.6
% Income of $15,000 or More.....	56.4	54.3	60.9	57.1	59.9	57.4	48.4	49.4
% White Collar Workers..........	50.0	54.7	47.7	50.0	51.2	54.6	47.2	41.2
% Civilian Labor Force Unemployed.	2.3	1.6	1.3	1.7	2.5	2.3	1.8	1.8
% Riding To Work By Automobile....	77.3	86.3	79.9	79.6	78.4	77.6	86.1	81.1
Population Per Household..........	3.7	3.5	4.0	3.6	3.7	3.6	3.3	3.5
Total Housing Units..........	9699	5084	2634	4870	4358	2849	8353	2752
% Condominiums & Cooperatives.....	0.5	0.0	0.0	2.9	0.8	0.0	0.0	0.2
% Built 1960 or Later..........	41.7	76.1	81.2	29.7	48.1	60.0	88.5	33.9
% Owner Occupied..............	80.2	57.3	77.1	81.5	82.8	72.3	45.4	83.8
% With 1+ Persons Per Room....	4.7	2.2	4.0	4.0	5.1	3.7	3.0	4.8
Median Value: Owner Units.......$$	32900	39300	38400	30400	35700	36800	36200	32000
Median Rent: Rental Units.....$$	182	204	221	174	181	185	195	165
Median Number Of Rooms: All Units.	5.9	5.8	6.6	5.6	6.2	5.8	5.1	5.7

the second half of the decade and the 1980 figure stands at 52,634. A small percentage of the increase during the 1960s and 1970s is accounted for by a series of annexations of residential subdivisions in adjacent sections of unincorported Cook County. Mount Prospect's total land area in 1982 was 9.92 square miles.

Increased pressures to provide expanded municipal services to a growing population prompted village officials to seek new sources of revenue. Major revisions to the village's Comprehensive Plan in the late 1970s succeeded in attracting new industry and light manufacturing to the community. A notable addition is the Kensington Center for Business, a 300-acre industrial park.

Despite recent industrial growth, Mount Prospect remains primarily a residential community. Of its 19,500 housing units, more than two-thirds are single-family dwellings, and almost two-thirds are owner-occupied. Nine percent of all units have been built in the last 10 years and there are nearly four times as many units as there were in 1950, just after the war. In the 30 years since that time, there has been increased construction of multiple-unit housing.

Mount Prospect remains a predominantly white community, although increasing numbers of several minority groups established homes there during the late 1970s. Less than 1 percent of the total population is black, and slightly less than 3 percent is of Asian descent. Two percent of the total is Hispanic.

The birth rate dropped significantly in the latter half of the 1970s. In 1980, less than 6 percent of the population were children under five years of age while 16 percent were 55 years old or older. Declining enrollments forced several school closings between 1978 and 1982. An increasing percentage of the population is comprised of "empty-nesters" whose children have matured and left home. Confronted with an aging population, village authorities initiated several innovative programs to provide more services to the elderly, including a subsidized cab fare program, a modern senior activity center, a day care center for the very elderly, three subsidized senior citizen housing complexes, and Central Village, a condominum complex for "mature adults."

Mount Prospect remains an affluent community. In 1979, 68 percent of its work force was employed in white-collar occupations and the median family income was $30,000. Civic leaders generated a series of local economic programs during the late 1970s to enhance the village's position as an attractive residential and commercial center. A 10-year community beautification and revitalization program adopted in 1976 focuses on fostering retail and professional growth in the central business district. This program has successfully attracted a nmber of small businesses which offer specialized goods and services not available at neighboring shopping centers. Village officials project significant economic growth throughout the 1980s.

Richard Fritz

Place 3990

Naperville

Naperville has grown from a small farming settlement of 41 families in the 1830s into one of the fastest growing cities in Illinois. It is located in the southwestern corner of DuPage County and is spread over 22 square miles of land.

The Pottawatomie Indians occupied much of northeastern Illinois. They had four villages within what is now DuPage County and were generally friendly to the white settlers. Many of the major area roads in use today were originally Indian paths. It is widely believed that the Indian tradition of burning off small shrubs and trees helped to account for the fertile soil found by the pioneers. The town was named after the first white settlers, Joseph and John Naper, both Great Lakes sailing captains. They arrived in the winter of 1831 and started a trading post. Joseph also built a saw mill, completed the first land survey and laid out the town's streets.

The Black Hawk War broke out in 1831. The few families in the Naper settlement at that time were warned by friendly Pottawatomies that the Sauk were on the warpath. The settlers fled to the rebuilt Fort Dearborn in Chicago and upon their return found many of their homes damaged. The only death attributed to the hostilities came shortly after the end of the war, during the construction of Fort Payne in Naperville. Indian relations were settled in 1833 by a treaty with the Pottawatomie tribes which ceded five million acres of land to the United States.

UNINCORPORATED AREA WITHIN CITY BOUNDARY

261

Naperville
Population and Housing Characteristics, 1930-1980

	1980	1970	1960	1950	1940	1930
Total Population	42,601	23,885	12,933	7,013	5,272	5,118
% Male	49.2	49.1	49.3	49.4	48.8	48.9
% Female	50.8	50.9	50.7	50.6	51.2	51.1
% White	96.6	99.3	99.8	99.8	100.0	99.6
% Black	0.7	0.2	0.1	0.1	0.0	-
% Other Nonwhite Races	2.7	0.5	0.1	0.1	0.0	0.4
% Under 5 Years Old	7.3	7.8	12.5	10.2	7.1	8.4
% 5-19 Years Old	30.2	36.8	28.8	21.3	22.5	24.1
% 20-44 Years Old	39.5	31.9	34.5	39.9	39.9	40.5
% 45-64 Years Old	17.6	18.0	17.3	19.7	20.6	18.5
% 65 Years and Older	5.5	5.6	6.9	8.9	9.9	8.4
Median School Years	15.5	13.1	12.7	12.2	10.0	*
Total Housing Units	14,236	6,602	3,672	1,976	1,499	*
% In One-Unit Structures	79.5	79.9	82.3	69.7	74.2	*
% Owner Occupied	76.3	75.1	74.4	65.1	60.7	*
% Renter Occupied	16.4	21.6	22.3	33.4	37.8	*
% Vacant	7.2	3.3	3.3	1.5	1.5	*
% 1+ Persons per Room	0.6	3.8	6.4	8.1	6.2	*

Place 3990 — Naperville, Illinois
Selected Characteristics of Census Tracts: 1980

Tract Number	Total	8426.02	8461.01	8461.03	8462.01	8462.02	8462.03	8463.04	8464.01	8464.02	8465.02
Total Population	42330	18	3506	2380	8372	7514	4439	10	244	6684	8262
% Male	49.2	-	50.7	50.2	49.8	49.1	50.0	-	52.0	48.1	48.3
% Black	0.7	-	0.4	1.2	0.6	0.6	1.5	-	0.0	0.8	0.5
% Other Nonwhite	2.7	-	2.7	2.7	2.6	2.8	3.0	-	3.3	2.6	2.2
% Of Spanish Origin	1.0	-	0.7	2.7	0.5	0.6	1.6	-	1.6	0.9	1.1
% Foreign Born	4.5	-	4.0	2.4	4.1	3.9	4.5	-	11.6	6.1	3.8
% Living In Group Quarters	2.0	-	0.0	21.6	0.0	0.0	2.2	-	0.0	2.1	1.0
% 13 Years Old And Under	25.5	-	25.5	14.3	26.9	27.9	30.8	-	26.6	23.1	23.7
% 14-20 Years Old	13.2	-	12.5	23.1	12.6	13.6	13.1	-	6.6	11.7	12.7
% 21-64 Years Old	55.8	-	57.0	52.1	56.1	56.1	52.9	-	66.0	57.9	55.2
% 65-74 Years Old	2.9	-	3.1	5.9	2.9	1.5	1.2	-	0.8	3.2	3.8
% 75 Years Old And Over	2.6	-	1.9	4.7	1.5	1.0	2.0	-	0.0	4.0	4.5
% In Different House	61.8	-	46.2	60.2	66.5	51.9	79.4	-	100.0	67.2	56.8
% Families With Female Head	5.4	-	4.8	10.7	3.9	4.4	4.6	-	8.1	8.7	5.6
Median School Years Completed	15.5	-	15.8	15.7	15.9	15.7	16.1	-	13.9	15.0	14.9
Median Family Income, 1979 $$	36685	-	36494	28906	39464	36623	37872	-	38356	36384	35774
% Income Below Poverty Level	1.5	-	2.5	2.7	1.0	0.5	1.2	-	0.0	1.1	2.5
% Income Of $30,000 More	69.2	-	69.1	46.6	74.5	74.1	73.7	-	64.4	66.9	65.1
% White Collar Workers	79.4	-	79.6	61.0	78.6	82.3	86.5	-	81.5	83.0	77.0
% Civilian Labor Force Unemployed	1.9	-	4.2	0.9	1.8	0.9	1.0	-	0.0	2.1	2.7
% Riding To Work By Automobile	79.1	-	77.6	63.3	82.6	80.4	79.1	-	95.2	79.2	79.5
Mean Commuting Time - Minutes	29.2	-	27.5	23.9	30.7	31.3	35.1	-	26.9	27.9	25.5
Population Per Household	3.2	-	3.2	2.5	3.3	3.5	3.6	-	2.8	3.0	3.0
Total Housing Units	14057	9	1140	798	2668	2229	1444	3	91	2394	2890
% Condominiums	7.8	-	0.0	0.0	1.8	0.7	21.9	-	42.9	27.3	0.8
% Built 1970 Or Later	54.6	-	40.9	14.6	52.1	57.2	98.5	-	90.4	61.5	39.2
% Owner Occupied	76.3	-	80.5	51.4	82.0	86.0	67.0	-	87.9	79.2	72.5
% With 1+ Persons Per Room	0.6	-	0.8	1.3	0.3	0.3	0.8	-	1.1	0.7	0.9
Median Value: Owner Units $$	98400	-	103700	75500	110400	92500	120700	-	-	115400	86900
Median Rent: Rental Units $$	315	-	304	261	343	334	354	-	500	345	235
Median Number Of Rooms: All Units	5.6	-	5.6	5.6	5.6	5.6	5.6	-	5.6	5.6	5.6

Tract Number	8801.01	8803
Total Population	815	86
% Male	48.8	-
% Black	0.9	-
% Other Nonwhite	6.9	-
% Of Spanish Origin	0.7	-
% Foreign Born	10.4	-
% Living In Group Quarters	0.0	-
% 13 Years Old And Under	31.7	-
% 14-20 Years Old	10.6	-
% 21-64 Years Old	55.3	-
% 65-74 Years Old	1.7	-
% 75 Years Old And Over	0.7	-
% In Different House	76.4	-
% Families With Female Head	3.8	-
Median School Years Completed	16.1	-
Median Family Income, 1979 $$	34642	-
% Income Below Poverty Level	2.6	-
% Income Of $30,000 Or More	68.3	-
% White Collar Workers	82.8	-
% Civilian Labor Force Unemployed	1.5	-
% Riding To Work By Automobile	83.3	-
Mean Commuting Time - Minutes	34.0	-
Population Per Household	3.5	-
Total Housing Units	274	117
% Condominiums	0.0	-
% Built 1970 Or Later	85.2	-
% Owner Occupied	82.5	-
% With 1+ Persons Per Room	0.4	-
Median Value: Owner Units $$	110100	-
Median Rent: Rental Units $$	501	-
Median Number Of Rooms: All Units	5.6	-

Naperville was historically the first town chartered in Cook County. It was platted with 80 acres in 1835. Despite the opposition of Cook County officials, DuPage County was formed from a corner of Cook in 1839. The success of this effort was attributed to the influence of Joseph Naper on the Illinois General Assembly, where he was a delegate in 1836 and 1837. Naperville became the first county seat, due in part to its being the oldest town in the county. By 1850, it had a population of 1,628, which grew to 2,055 by 1855. The Plank Road connected Naperville and Chicago at that time and because of this a railroad was not constructed between the two towns at an early date. Instead, the first railroad line into DuPage County connected Wheaton and Chicago and influenced the later removal of the county seat to Wheaton. Interest in Naperville increased with the completion of the Chicago, Burlington and Quincy Railroad through the community in 1863-1864. Although the local economy was still based heavily on farming, several industries began operating after that. These included the manufacture of buggies and plows, two breweries and other concerns.

In 1857, an attempt was made to move the county seat to Wheaton. The rationale for this was that a county seat should be centrally located, approximately one day's ride from any part of the county. Naperville, located in the southwestern corner of the county, was less accessible than the more centrally-placed Wheaton. The proposal was turned down by the General Assembly, but finally passed in 1867. Naperville officials resisted the removal of county records and attempted to challenge the relocation of the county seat. Most of the records were taken to Wheaton in 1868. Those few records not taken to Wheaton (Books 15 to 20) were transferred to Cook County pending a court appeal, and were destroyed by the Chicago Fire in 1871.

Naperville
Selected Characteristics of Census Tracts: 1970

Tract Number	TOTAL	8416	8426	8461	8462	8463	8464	8465	8801	8803
Total Population	27924	6398	11322	8186	10122	21351	4918	8110	9109	1794
% Male	49.1	49.3	47.9	49.5	51.3	51.0	49.3	49.4	50.7	50.6
% Black	0.2	0.3	0.1	1.0	0.1	0.4	0.2	0.1	0.1	0.0
% Other Nonwhite	0.6	0.3	0.2	0.4	0.6	0.7	0.1	0.5	0.5	0.3
% Of Spanish Language	0.6	3.3	1.3	0.7	0.6	1.9	0.3	0.2	6.1	0.0
% Foreign Born	3.5	6.5	3.2	2.9	3.4	4.3	2.2	3.5	2.2	1.1
% Living In Group Quarters	2.7	0.7	6.8	7.5	4.9	0.4	0.2	1.4	0.1	0.0
% 13 Years Old And Under	30.7	29.9	30.8	28.5	31.8	36.5	31.6	30.9	43.0	30.9
% 14-20 Years Old	15.2	12.4	14.1	16.9	16.5	9.1	13.1	14.3	8.9	13.3
% 21-64 Years Old	48.5	51.3	46.5	48.0	48.2	52.1	50.2	48.2	46.6	50.3
% 65-74 Years Old	3.3	4.6	3.9	4.2	2.3	1.5	3.4	3.4	1.0	3.6
% 75 Years Old And Over	2.2	1.8	4.7	2.5	2.5	0.8	1.8	3.3	0.5	1.9
% In Different House	42.7	56.2	39.4	41.9	37.8	30.2	44.9	53.3	44.4	51.4
% Families With Female Head	4.5	5.9	4.4	5.7	2.8	2.6	5.2	5.8	2.7	3.2
Median School Years Completed	13.1	12.4	13.0	12.8	13.9	12.8	12.7	12.7	12.3	12.4
Median Family Income, 1969 $$	16818	12849	18177	14873	18702	14197	14822	15486	12526	12146
% Income Below Poverty Level	2.9	4.0	4.1	2.9	2.4	1.6	1.4	3.5	2.9	8.1
% Income of $15,000 or More	57.9	32.8	63.1	49.3	67.2	43.0	48.8	52.1	26.1	24.6
% White Collar Workers	56.3	32.1	54.6	45.7	63.1	53.8	47.1	48.3	29.4	26.9
% Civilian Labor Force Unemployed	1.9	1.4	1.4	2.9	1.0	1.4	2.3	3.3	2.0	2.7
% Riding To Work By Automobile	72.0	84.9	76.3	69.3	72.9	82.8	83.2	75.1	88.9	72.4
Population Per Household	3.6	3.4	3.9	3.3	3.9	3.6	3.6	3.7	4.3	3.7
Total Housing Units	6602	1941	2781	2418	3038	6607	1507	2252	2255	485
% Condominiums & Cooperatives	0.0	0.0	0.0	0.0	0.0	1.6	0.0	0.0	3.4	0.0
% Built 1960 Or Later	46.2	27.7	44.3	30.4	65.1	87.3	55.4	37.5	91.3	41.0
% Owner Occupied	75.1	68.5	86.9	65.3	75.6	64.0	68.9	75.6	84.4	72.2
% With 1+ Persons Per Room	3.8	7.4	4.3	5.2	2.7	4.5	5.6	5.0	6.3	6.4
Median Value: Owner Units $$	35700	22200	33900	31400	39200	30200	28800	32900	22400	34500
Median Rent: Rental Units $$	157	164	163	138	198	195	183	133	152	107
Median Number Of Rooms: All Units	6.4	5.1	6.5	5.6	6.6	5.7	5.6	6.3	6.1	6.5

In 1870, North Western College (now North Central College), was moved from Plainfield to Naperville. The relocation was prompted by the lack of railroad access in Plainfield and facilitated by an offer of funds and a building to house the college made by residents of Napervillle. The college had begun in 1861 under the sponsorship of the Evangelical Association of North America. It was a co-educational institution based on ardent abolitionist views and a non-sectarian policy. Today it is a private, four-year coeducational liberal arts college with an enrollment of 1,000, affiliated with the United Methodist Church.

Naperville grew slowly in the 1800s and by 1900 housed 2,629 residents. Its population had grown by 1930 to 5,000, and to 13,000 by 1960. The community has grown much more rapidly since 1960, nearly doubling by 1970 (22,617) and again in the most recent decade to bring the current population to 42,330. Despite these large increases Naperville continues to be overwhelmingly white — an attribute it has in common with much of DuPage County.

Much of this growth has been part of the process of suburbanization which began after World War II. Naperville is located 30 miles from Chicago and is only 30 minutes away by train or 45-60 minutes driving by expressway. However, most recently, industries have been relocating in Naperville, employing area residents. Included among these large corporations are: Bell's Indian Hill Laboratories employing 4,500; the Amoco Research Center employing 1,500; Northern Illinois Gas employing 3,000; and two additions, Nalco Chemical and the Midwest facility of the Wall Street Journal. These developments have changed the character of Naperville, which is fast becoming a center of scientific research, technology and communication.

Housing in Naperville has increased with the community's rapid population growth since 1960. At that time, there were 3,700 housing units. During the 1960s, this number increased to 6,600, and grew by 121 percent during the next decade, to more than 14,000 units in 1980. This increase came predominantly in the form of single-family dwellings and townhouses, and occurred despite a nationwide home building slump in the late 1970s. Many of the recently-constructed homes fall in the $100,000 to $300,000 range, reflecting the influx of professional and technical workers recruited by the industrial research facilities. This can also be seen in the 1980 median family income ($36,685) and the median home value ($98,400).

A part of the community's attractiveness to both industry and families is its extensive area, which provides opportunity for expansion. Naperville is still surrounded by open farmland, with scenic horse farms and forest preserves nearby. Area shopping facilities include several large plazas which contain well-known branch stores. In the late 1970s, a new enclosed shopping mall was opened on Naperville's western border providing further retail facilities.

In town are more specialized shops and retail businesses. Some of the latter are located in restored old homes. The architecture of many of these restored homes is Greek Revival, popular in the mid-1800s. In the center of town is a 12-acre pioneer village known as Naper Settlement. It is composed of a collection of older homes and other buildings of historic importance which were carefully moved to their present location under the sponsorship of the Naperville Heritage Society.

Naperville, while growing rapidly, is trying to preserve its identity. The emphasis on community history and the restoration of older buildings is compatible with its expanding 20th century research facilities. The rural character of its outlying areas combines with its suburban amenities to provide an atmosphere attractive to many, and this is the basis of the dramatic population expansion of the 1970s.

Gail Danks Welter

Niles

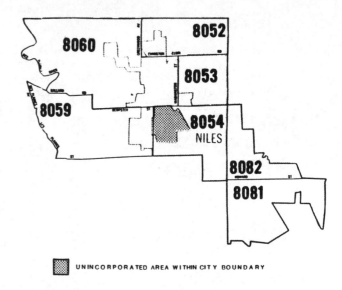

UNINCORPORATED AREA WITHIN CITY BOUNDARY

Niles is just northwest of Chicago, bounded by the city on the south and southwest, Park Ridge and Des Plaines on the west, Glenview on the north, Morton Grove and Skokie on the east. It is located in two different townships; the part of the village east of Harlem Avenue is in Niles Township, while the area west of Harlem is in Maine Township. It was at the junction of the wagon road to Milwaukee and the North Branch Road (now Milwaukee Avenue and Waukegan Road), so many travelers passed through the area. John Schadiger and Julius Perren are credited with building the first rough house in the area, in 1832 or 1833. In 1834, several other families appeared. According to local legend, John Ebinger and his son Christian, who were among these early residents, were traveling along Milwaukee Road in search of good farmland when their horse was bitten by a rattlesnake and they had to stop at Niles. They were joined there by two older Ebinger brothers.

The small settlement that developed was referred to as Dutchman's Point, because it was located on a point of land in the Chicago River and because the settlers were Germans. There were also early settlers of Polish and Bohemian stock in the southern part of present-day Niles. By 1836, Dutchman's Point had a store and a postmaster named Phillips. In 1837, John Marshall and Benjamin Hall opened the first hotel, called the North Branch. The first school was established in 1838, with four pupils taught by a Scotchman named Ballantine, although there was no schoolhouse until 1849.

Niles Township was organized in 1850. By that time, there was a steam sawmill in the area. Many of the residents were engaged in supplying the timber to Chicago, where it was needed both for fuel and for railroad buildings. Truck farming was another industry in the area, and it became increasingly important as the woodlands were cleared. The 1870s brought increasing trade with the city. There were several sawmills in the area and a brickyard, established in 1871. By 1884, the village had two stores, two hotels, a harness shop, two blacksmith shops and eight saloons, as well as two schools, two churches and one physician. The village of Niles was incorporated in 1899, with a population of 200. There is no record of the origin of the name Niles for either township or village, but residents speculate that, like Niles, Michigan, both were named for William Ogden Niles, publisher of the Niles Register, a national newspaper of the time.

Following incorporation, the village grew slowly but steadily, and gradually began to provide more services. A volunteer fire department was organized in 1910. St. Hedwig's Industrial School, a Catholic orphanage for Polish Children which opened in 1911, added 200 nuns and priests to the population. In 1917, with financial assistance from the City of Chicago, the North Branch Road, a major thoroughfare, was improved and renamed Waukegan Road. By 1920, Niles had 1,258 residents. The first bank opened in 1921, and the village was connected to the City of Chicago water distribution system in 1924. During Prohibition, bootlegging was common at restaurants and taverns in the unincorporated parts of Niles Township, and the Roger Touhy and Al Capone gangs were active in the area. There was some real estate speculation in Niles during the late 1920s and the 1930s, but it was less extensive than that in surrounding communities and growth was relatively slow.

The Depression virtually halted the growth of Niles, with the population barely increasing from 2,135 in 1930 to 2,168 in 1940. However, several WPA and CCC projects contributed to the development of village services during this period. Cinder streets were maintained, sidewalks were built, the North Branch of the Chicago River was cleaned, and sewers and water mains were installed. During the early 1930s, inventor Robert Ilg, a Niles resident, constructed a half-size replica of the Leaning Tower of Pisa, designed to conceal a large water tank at Ilg Park. Later, he donated the tower and a 4.5-acre parcel of land to the YMCA, which built a $4-million facility on the site in 1966. The Tam O'Shanter Golf Course, another landmark in the area, was the site of many major golf tournaments during the 1940s and 1950s. It was sold in 1965, but half of the course was converted into a nine-hole municipal course by the Niles Park District in 1971.

During the 1950s, Niles experienced its most significant residential, industrial and commercial growth. Population increased from less than 3,600 in 1950 to more than 20,000 in 1960. The number of residential units, primarily single-family homes increased to nearly 6,000. An industrial area began to develop in the southeastern section of the village. The A.B. Dick Company moved to Niles and opened a complete industrial plant in 1949. It has become a 13-acre facility under a single roof. Teletype Corporation purchased a small building in Niles for a manufacturing plant in 1950, and by 1962 had established several other plants, an office building, and a research and development center in Niles and neighboring Skokie. Two important retail centers developed by the early 1960s. The Golf Mill Shopping Center opened in 1959, on an 88-acre tract of land bounded by Golf Road, Milwaukee Avenue and Greenwood Avenue. In 1961, the Golf Mill Theater, with 1,800 seats, was added to the complex. The smaller Lawrencewood Shopping Center was built in 1962 at the intersection of Waukegan Road and Oakton Street.

The village responded to this growth with additional services. In the late 1950s, park and library districts were organized. The village built a new police department facility in 1964, and in 1967-68, the first public housing for senior citizens in the metropolitan area. During the early 1960s, the village eliminated a gambling strip along Milwaukee Avenue, and reorganized and modernized the police and fire departments. In recognition of these achievements, Niles received an "All-American City" award in 1964.

Since 1970, the population of Niles has remained relatively stable. After reaching a historical high of 31,432 in that year, the number of residents dropped by about a thousand in the most recent decade. The village has retained a balance between residential, commercial and industrial development. Housing is still predominantly (71 percent) single-family, though multi-family dwellings have been built, mainly in the northern portions of the village. Three-fourths of all units are owner-occupied, less than 2 percent are overcrowded, and the median value of single-family homes there is higher than that of the adjacent Edison Park area in Chicago. Niles has no real "downtown," but Milwaukee Avenue is a central commercial area which bisects the village. Commercial concentrations also exist along Harlem Avenue south of Howard Street, and at several major intersections, including Golf and Washington, Dempster and Greenwood, Dempster and Harlem, and Oakton and Waukegan. The Tam O'Shanter Golf Course

Niles
Population and Housing Characteristics, 1930-1980

	1980	1970	1960	1950	1940	1930
Total Population.......	30,363	31,432	20,393	3,587	2,168	2,135
% Male...................	47.7	48.8	49.4	50.2	52.1	53.7
% Female................	52.3	51.2	50.6	49.8	47.9	46.3
% White.................	96.0	99.6	99.9	99.9	99.9	100.0
% Black.................	0.2	0.1	0.0	0.0	0.1	–
% Other Nonwhite Races...	3.8	0.3	0.1	0.1	0.0	–
% Under 5 Years Old......	3.8	7.8	13.5	13.4	5.9	7.4
% 5-19 Years Old........	21.3	30.1	26.8	27.7	*	*
% 20-44 Years Old........	31.0	32.1	37.2	38.9	*	*
% 45-64 Years Old........	28.7	23.1	17.3	16.6	15.7	10.1
% 65 Years and Older.....	15.3	7.0	5.1	5.1	3.4	2.7
Median School Years....	12.5	12.3	12.1	10.9	*	*
Total Housing Units....	10,731	9,064	5,908	906	*	*
% In One-Unit Structures.	69.5	76.7	89.5	79.1	*	*
% Owner Occupied........	71.0	76.6	86.3	79.0	*	*
% Renter Occupied........	24.4	22.2	7.3	16.2	*	*
% Vacant................	4.6	1.1	6.4	4.7	*	*
% 1+ Persons per Room....	1.8	5.0	6.6	12.4	*	*

Place 4135 — Niles, Illinois
Selected Characteristics of Census Tracts: 1980

Tract Number	Total	8052	8053	8054	8059	8060	8081	8082
Total Population.............	30363	1129	1190	10610	3194	5618	3244	5378
% Male...................	47.7	46.1	48.2	48.6	46.7	46.7	46.4	48.6
% Black..................	0.2	1.1	0.0	0.0	0.0	0.6	0.4	0.1
% Other Nonwhite........	3.8	4.5	6.6	2.1	3.2	7.6	1.9	3.8
% Of Spanish Origin.......	1.6	0.5	1.1	0.5	1.1	4.5	1.1	1.7
% Foreign Born...........	16.8	23.4	13.4	14.8	14.3	22.5	21.0	12.8
% Living In Group Quarters.	5.9	23.5	0.0	0.3	10.0	5.1	27.6	0.3
% 13 Years Old And Under..	13.7	17.2	15.3	12.8	15.0	15.5	8.6	15.0
% 14-20 Years Old........	13.2	14.3	16.1	13.7	16.7	10.6	10.4	13.8
% 21-64 Years Old........	57.7	50.1	60.5	61.0	51.7	59.7	47.2	60.1
% 65-74 Years Old........	8.5	6.1	5.5	8.9	6.4	8.6	11.8	8.2
% 75 Years Old And Over...	6.8	12.3	2.6	3.6	10.3	5.6	22.0	2.9
% In Different House.......	34.5	44.1	27.2	22.3	30.1	62.5	44.6	25.6
% Families With Female Head.	10.4	7.2	8.4	9.0	6.7	12.2	14.0	13.6
Median School Years Completed..	12.5	12.6	12.8	12.5	12.6	12.6	12.2	12.6
Median Family Income, 1979......$$	28447	35527	30123	29597	34717	25250	24130	27912
% Income Below Poverty Level....	2.2	0.0	0.0	0.0	1.7	3.9	0.0	2.7
% Income Of $30,000 Or More.....	45.9	64.6	50.5	49.0	58.7	35.6	31.4	45.3
% White Collar Workers.........	62.9	63.5	70.9	60.1	71.3	66.3	56.8	62.0
% Civilian Labor Force Unemployed.	3.0	1.4	3.5	2.4	4.8	3.8	3.4	2.5
% Riding To Work By Automobile....	85.3	97.3	77.3	84.6	87.2	85.5	81.0	88.0
Mean Commuting Time - Minutes...	25.4	25.4	27.8	24.9	28.9	27.2	22.5	23.8
Population Per Household......	2.8	3.8	2.9	2.8	3.4	2.5	2.3	2.9
Total Housing Units..........	10727	238	414	3763	870	2489	1087	1866
% Condominiums...............	5.7	0.0	0.0	0.0	0.0	21.2	4.4	1.8
% Built 1970 Or Later.........	9.9	10.8	3.6	1.6	9.9	30.3	5.5	3.2
% Owner Occupied.............	71.0	89.9	66.2	85.9	87.7	39.5	56.7	82.3
% With 1+ Persons Per Room...	1.8	2.6	0.5	1.5	1.2	2.1	2.2	2.4
Median Value: Owner Units.......$$	79700	118100	82400	79800	91000	76000	77200	73400
Median Rent: Rental Units.......$$	282	267	280	254	284	297	269	307
Median Number Of Rooms: All Units.	5.3	5.6	5.6	5.3	5.6	4.5	4.7	5.6

Niles
Selected Characteristics of Census Tracts: 1970

Tract Number	TOTAL	8052	8053	8054	8059	8060	8081	8082
Total Population.............	31432	9207	9292	14213	9388	22462	2884	6363
% Male...................	48.8	49.4	49.2	49.4	47.2	48.6	45.6	49.8
% Black..................	0.1	0.1	0.0	0.0	0.1	0.2	0.1	0.0
% Other Nonwhite........	0.4	0.8	0.5	0.3	1.0	0.6	0.1	0.6
% Of Spanish Language.....	1.5	1.8	1.1	0.8	1.0	1.8	1.8	2.6
% Foreign Born...........	9.0	7.8	5.6	8.2	6.3	7.5	11.1	7.9
% Living In Group Quarters.	1.9	2.1	0.0	0.0	2.8	1.5	18.9	0.6
% 13 Years Old And Under..	27.0	33.3	32.5	26.2	27.2	28.4	18.5	27.3
% 14-20 Years Old........	12.0	12.6	14.2	13.7	12.8	8.5	9.4	12.5
% 21-64 Years Old........	54.0	49.0	50.4	54.4	53.3	58.0	50.4	54.7
% 65-74 Years Old........	3.9	2.3	1.7	3.6	3.8	3.1	7.5	3.7
% 75 Years Old And Over...	3.1	2.8	1.2	2.1	2.9	2.0	14.1	1.7
% In Different House.......	59.2	58.1	66.0	68.0	56.1	32.3	62.9	66.0
% Families With Female Head.	5.6	4.6	4.3	5.5	4.7	6.3	8.8	5.1
Median School Years Completed..	12.3	12.8	12.7	12.3	12.7	12.7	11.1	12.4
Median Family Income, 1969......$$	14159	16818	16879	14091	18426	13831	13476	15070
% Income Below Poverty Level....	1.4	1.4	0.9	0.9	1.5	2.4	1.2	2.7
% Income of $15,000 or More.....	44.2	57.9	57.9	43.2	63.9	41.1	40.5	50.3
% White Collar Workers.........	39.6	50.7	49.6	36.8	53.1	51.5	39.9	39.7
% Civilian Labor Force Unemployed.	1.8	1.3	2.0	1.1	1.1	1.8	1.6	3.7
% Riding To Work By Automobile....	85.8	86.0	86.3	88.2	78.0	84.7	81.3	81.4
Population Per Household..........	3.4	3.9	4.0	3.5	3.5	3.0	3.1	3.5
Total Housing Units..........	9064	2312	2369	4088	2748	8062	763	1829
% Condominiums & Cooperatives.....	0.2	0.0	0.0	0.4	0.2	0.2	0.0	0.0
% Built 1960 Or Later...........	40.8	35.0	47.4	21.7	43.7	84.4	28.1	37.6
% Owner Occupied.............	76.4	90.3	92.4	86.1	80.2	34.2	70.4	81.5
% With 1+ Persons Per Room......	5.0	4.2	3.8	5.5	3.1	2.8	5.0	5.9
Median Value: Owner Units.......$$	31800	35400	37200	31200	39200	31100	31800	31100
Median Rent: Rental Units.......$$	170	219	162	164	181	185	151	212
Median Number Of Rooms: All Units.	5.4	6.3	6.2	5.3	6.1	4.6	5.1	5.5

serves as a buffer between primarily residential areas and the village's industrial section in the southeast, which occupies about 18 percent of its total land area. The A.B. Dick Company is still the village's largest employer. However, Niles supports a variety of light industries and small businesses. In 1981, the village contained more than 230 service and industrial establishments employing more than 23,000 persons. Two major highways, the Edens Expressway and the Tri-State Toll-way, pass just east and west of the village, respectively. In addition, Niles is served by three public bus services: Nortran, the Chicago Transportation Authority (in the southern portion), and a unique no-fare intra-community courtesy bus system. The village is a part of the Oakton Community College system, and is also the site of Niles College (formerly St. Hedwig's Orphanage), a seminary and branch of Loyola University.

Marjorie DeVault

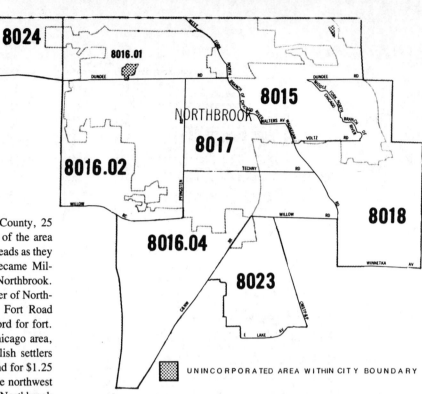

8024

8016.01

8015

NORTHBROOK

8017

8016.02

8016.04

8018

8023

▨ UNINCORPORATED AREA WITHIN CITY BOUNDARY

Northbrook

Northbrook is located on the northern edge of Cook County, 25 miles north of downtown Chicago. The first inhabitants of the area were the Pottawatomie Indians who left arrows and spearheads as they camped along the streams and prairies. Indian trails became Milwaukee Avenue and Waukegan Road, major highways to Northbrook. The presence of the Pottawatomie is evidenced in a number of Northbrook streets. Waukegan Road was once called Little Fort Road because the word "Waukegan" was the Pottawatomie word for fort. When the Treaty of 1833 forced Indians to leave the Chicago area, more white men moved into Northfield Township. English settlers came through the Erie Canal and reportedly purchased land for $1.25 per acre. One English family, the Shermans, settled on the northwest quarter of Section 10 (site of the present downtown Northbrook business district).

German settlers arrived in search of suitable farmlands, having left their homeland because of economic depression, political oppression, and religious persecution. Among these German farmers was Frederick Schermer whose name was memorialized in 1901 when the town was incorporated as Shermerville. In 1872, the Chicago Milwaukee, St. Paul and Pacific Railroad Company laid a single track through the area. The depot was named "Shermer" as a concession to the family whose farm was traversed by the tracks.

The Chicago Fire of 1871 created a great demand for bricks for the reconstruction of the city. Two brickyards were developed on the northern edge of Shermer, the National Brick Company and the Illinois Brick Company. The clay pit at the Illinois Brick Company covered approximately 35 acres and was about 40 feet deep. In its peak years between 1915 and 1920, the Illinois Brick Company employed 125 men. It closed in the 1940s, while the National Brick Company operated until the 1950s.

As the population grew from a few hundred settlers so did the need for civic improvements. Incorporation appeared to be the only solution for installation of safe and serviceable sidewalks. A population of 300 was necessary to hold elections, so residents of Bach Town where many of the brickmakers were housed had to be included. Opposition to incorporation was substantial because of the threat of higher taxation. The referendum for incorporation passed by one vote.

The village was incorporated as Shermerville in 1901. One of the earliest ordinances passed was to order the repair and scraping of streets. A 1902 ordinance called for cutting down thistles on the roads and for painting a bridge across the creek. Contracts were awarded to the North Shore Electric Company in 1910 to install street lights. At that time, the population was 441. In 1916, water mains wre installed and a pumping station was built for a 1,500 foot well. By 1920, the population had grown to 554. During the early 1920s, a complete system of sanitary and storm drainage was installed and a modern disposal station was erected on a three-acre site donated by the Illinois Brick Company.

At this time, the townspeople began to consider a change in the name of Shermerville, thinking a change in name might create a more desirable, less European image. A petition wtih 126 signatures asking for a change of name was filed with the Village Board in 1922. The name "North Brook", submitted by E. D. Landwehr because the

Middle Forks of the North Branch of the Chicago River ran through town, received the majority of votes cast. The name was officially changed to Northbrook in 1923.

By 1925, Northbrook had achieved the distinciton of having the most concrete road mileage of any comparable community in the state. The Village sponsored a "Good Roads Celebration" which was attended by 2,000 visitors. The population was then 525 residents. In 1927, the Village Board authorized the purchase of water from the neighboring town of Glencoe and mains were built to bring the water to town.

Gas mains were installed in 1930 and a new Village Hall was constructed with the proceeds of the first two "Northbrook Days." This village-wide celebration was sponsored by the Northbrook Civic Association and has continued for 52 years. By 1930, the population exceeded 1,100.

During the Depression years, the Northbrook Civic Association provided lunch to the children whose families were unemployed. The population remained stable during the 1930s.

When World War II ended, the sleepy community began to expand, far beyond the modest dreams of its earlier inhabitants. The first postwar census, in 1950, showed 3,300 residents in Northbrook. To safeguard the future development of Northbrook, a Plan Commission was created. The Park District acquired a prime piece of property in the downtown area, a fire station was built, and a post office was opened with city mail delivery. The need for a township high school was realized in 1947 with the formation of District 225. After much litigation and Illinois Supreme Court decisions, plans for Glenbrook North High School were approved and the school opened in fall of 1953. Within five years of its opening, Glenbrook North High School was one of three Illinois high schools among the top ten schools nationally ranked on the basis of academic excellence.

The population growth of Northbrook continued to accelerate during the 1950s, and more than 11,000 lived there by the end of the decade. Edens Highway was completed and the village was no longer an isolated community. Annexations and demands for rezoning and additional services kept the Village Board active. A master plan was developed and a comprehensive zoning ordinance adopted. The caucus system was initiated and a council-manager form of government was adopted in 1953.

Northbrook
Population and Housing Characteristics, 1930-1980

	1980	1970	1960	1950	1940	1930
Total Population.......	30,778	27,297	11,635	3,348	1,265	1,193
% Male...................	49.5	49.5	50.1	50.7	52.1	51.1
% Female.................	50.5	50.5	49.9	49.3	47.9	48.9
% White..................	96.3	99.4	99.7	100.0	100.0	100.0
% Black..................	0.2	0.1	0.2	0.0	-	-
% Other Nonwhite Races...	3.5	0.5	0.1	-	-	-
% Under 5 Years Old......	5.7	10.6	16.5	15.9	8.5	9.5
% 5-19 Years Old.........	27.6	35.1	29.4	21.5	*	*
% 20-44 Years Old........	33.2	32.5	37.0	42.7	*	*
% 45-64 Years Old........	25.5	17.0	14.0	16.0	21.3	16.6
% 65 Years and Older.....	7.9	4.8	3.1	3.9	5.3	6.5
Median School Years......	15.4	14.3	13.7	12.7	*	*
Total Housing Units....	9,934	7,034	3,099	957	*	*
% In One-Unit Structures.	87.8	95.4	97.4	89.9	*	*
% Owner Occupied.........	88.1	90.0	90.3	84.6	*	*
% Renter Occupied........	8.0	7.7	6.0	14.8	*	*
% Vacant.................	3.8	2.2	3.7	0.5	*	*
% 1+ Persons per Room....	0.7	2.5	4.2	5.6	*	*

Place 4190 -- Northbrook , Illinois
Selected Characteristics of Census Tracts: 1980

Tract Number	Total	8015	8016.01	8016.02	8016.04	8017	8018	8023	8024
Total Population.............	30778	4926	2925	8664	3494	8517	2218	0	34
% Male.......................	49.5	50.5	49.5	49.6	47.5	49.4	50.1		
% Black......................	0.2	0.8	0.1	0.1	0.2	0.1	0.3	-	-
% Other Nonwhite.............	3.5	2.5	3.5	3.5	7.3	2.4	4.1	-	-
% Of Spanish Origin..........	1.7	1.4	5.2	1.1	2.0	1.3	1.4	-	-
% Foreign Born...............	8.2	8.5	10.6	8.1	12.6	6.1	6.5	-	-
% Living In Group Quarters...	2.3	8.2	0.0	0.0	8.4	0.1	0.0	-	-
% 13 Years Old And Under.....	21.7	18.2	21.3	23.8	21.8	22.0	21.3	-	-
% 14-20 Years Old............	12.5	11.4	13.1	13.6	9.9	13.1	12.0	-	-
% 21-64 Years Old............	57.8	57.9	59.3	58.2	53.3	58.2	59.8	-	-
% 65-74 Years Old............	4.6	7.2	4.9	2.9	5.0	4.4	5.1	-	-
% 75 Years Old And Over......	3.3	5.3	1.5	1.5	10.0	2.3	1.8	-	-
% In Different House.........	40.7	37.3	40.0	43.5	57.3	34.9	32.4	-	-
% Families With Female Head..	7.2	7.2	7.3	6.8	7.0	7.4	7.7	-	-
Median School Years Completed	15.4	15.3	14.5	16.1	15.2	15.4	15.5	-	-
Median Family Income, 1979...$$	42297	43371	43855	47459	45812	38820	32462	-	-
% Income Below Poverty Level.	1.5	0.4	0.0	0.6	1.4	2.4	6.1	-	-
% Income Of $30,000 Or More..	72.3	71.7	75.3	80.2	72.2	68.3	54.8	-	-
% White Collar Workers.......	81.5	84.7	72.9	84.6	83.5	79.2	80.2	-	-
% Civilian Labor Force Unemployed.	2.4	3.3	3.0	2.8	0.7	1.5	3.7	-	-
% Riding To Work By Automobile....	83.5	79.7	86.5	84.8	87.9	80.8	86.2	-	-
Mean Commuting Time - Minutes....	27.2	26.8	24.7	29.9	30.5	25.2	25.2	-	-
Population Per Household..........	3.1	3.0	3.1	3.1	3.1	3.1	3.1	-	-
Total Housing Units..........	9930	1592	965	2749	1074	2770	746	0	34
% Condominiums...............	16.1	9.9	21.2	20.4	41.8	5.6	6.3	-	-
% Built 1970 Or Later........	33.8	12.5	47.9	54.6	73.7	10.1	10.3	-	-
% Owner Occupied.............	88.1	82.9	90.5	91.6	83.2	88.3	92.1	-	-
% With 1+ Persons Per Room...	0.7	0.9	1.0	1.4	0.6	0.5	1.1	-	-
Median Value: Owner Units.......$$	128400	121200	140600	156000	163400	104600	87700	-	-
Median Rent: Rental Units.......$$	436	413	373	501	460	429	493	-	-
Median Number Of Rooms: All Units.	5.6	5.6	5.6	5.6	5.6	5.6	5.6	-	-

Northbrook
Selected Characteristics of Census Tracts: 1970

Tract Number	TOTAL	8015	8016	8017	8018	8023	8024
Total Population.............	25422	6955	16274	9266	6988	2076	4525
% Male.......................	49.5	50.1	49.4	49.6	47.4	58.4	48.2
% Black......................	0.1	0.3	0.1	0.0	0.3	4.8	0.0
% Other Nonwhite.............	0.5	0.3	0.6	0.3	0.4	3.7	0.3
% Of Spanish Language........	1.1	1.5	1.6	0.7	0.5	2.7	4.7
% Foreign Born...............	4.4	5.5	4.6	3.3	7.3	4.6	4.8
% Living In Group Quarters...	1.7	4.4	1.2	0.2	7.5	15.2	2.8
% 13 Years Old And Under.....	34.7	30.2	35.8	34.0	28.7	35.4	33.2
% 14-20 Years Old............	11.8	12.3	12.4	12.3	11.8	11.9	10.5
% 21-64 Years Old............	48.8	49.3	47.8	49.6	50.9	52.4	47.7
% 65-74 Years Old............	2.6	4.0	2.2	2.5	4.3	0.1	4.9
% 75 Years Old And Over......	2.2	4.2	1.8	1.6	4.2	0.1	3.7
% In Different House.........	34.6	47.7	31.3	46.9	51.1	4.6	46.6
% Families With Female Head..	3.7	4.1	3.4	3.9	5.5	0.9	6.4
Median School Years Completed	14.3	13.9	13.0	14.6	14.3	12.5	12.3
Median Family Income, 1969...$$	19994	20542	18923	18962	20708	7076	13147
% Income Below Poverty Level.	2.0	1.4	3.4	1.2	2.8	5.1	3.5
% Income of $15,000 or More..	69.5	70.6	65.5	66.5	67.6	35.5	39.3
% White Collar Workers.......	62.5	61.0	55.3	59.0	65.7	19.4	33.6
% Civilian Labor Force Unemployed.	1.4	1.0	1.6	1.3	1.1	5.3	0.7
% Riding To Work By Automobile....	78.9	79.2	84.7	75.5	70.6	74.4	84.0
Population Per Household..........	3.9	3.7	4.1	3.8	3.6	3.7	3.5
Total Housing Units..........	7033	1829	4076	2447	1816	474	1310
% Condominiums & Cooperatives.....	0.4	0.7	0.0	0.0	1.0	0.0	13.4
% Built 1960 Or Later........	50.8	28.1	63.6	37.4	24.3	18.9	69.7
% Owner Occupied.............	89.6	86.9	89.7	89.4	89.1	12.4	52.1
% With 1+ Persons Per Room...	2.5	3.4	3.6	2.1	2.4	17.6	6.9
Median Value: Owner Units.......$$	48500	44600	50100	41000	47500	-	28500
Median Rent: Rental Units.......$$	212	197	183	222	245	91	171
Median Number Of Rooms: All Units.	7.1	6.5	7.3	6.5	6.6	4.1	5.1

The downtown shopping area, once a dozen stores and taverns scattered along Shermer Road, was expanded as new streets were laid in former pastures. Light manufacturing areas sprung up as Culligan, General Fireguard, and Hanson Scale moved their plants into the blossoming town. Northbrook was assuming a new image as an industrial community with the arrival of more businesses. The "new look" of the fifties was evident when new factories and new labor forces entered the community. Further expansion of village services, annexations, and zoning occupied the Village Board. By 1964, North-brook could cease to rely upon neighboring Glencoe for water and became the first off-shore community in the Chicago metropolitan area with direct access to Lake Michigan through its own water pumping station and filtration services. A Human Relations Board was formed as the population increased. Through the ownership of its water supply, the Village was able to regulate and control the expansion of the area by establishing policies relating to the lot sizes of single-family dwellings.

During the 1970s, Northbrook achieved national prominence a-mong retail developers with the opening of Northbrook Court, a

130-acre shopping center which attracted more than 100 specialty shops and restaurants surrounding the magnet stores of Lord and Taylor, Neiman Marcus, Sears Roebuck and Company, and I. Magnin. This major retail center provides the village with sales tax receipts amounting to 25 percent of its operating revenues, and draws more than 750,000 visitors monthly.

To plan and protect the development of the Techny lands contiguous to Northbrook and its neighbors, Northfield and Glenview, the Techny Area Joint Planning Commission was formed in 1973. The 1,100 acres of fertile land on Waukegan and Willow roads has been owned by the Society of the Divine Word since the early 1900s.

For the last 20 years, Northbrook speed skaters have participated in the Winter Olympics. In 1972, five of the skaters represented the United States in Sapporo, Japan, and returned with two gold medals. Top-ranked bicycle track racers compete for national honors in the 700-foot BMX Bicycle Track in Meadowhill Park. As the 1980s approached, the Village Board continued to explore methods of maintaining orderly growth. Northbrook has almost tripled in size since 1960, to nearly 31,000. The population is 96 percent white and affluent in the extreme. THe median family income is well over twice that of Chicago. Almost three-fourths of all Northbrook families reported incomes of $30,000 or more in 1979. More than 80 percent of the resident labor force are white-collar workers. The median of the resident education distribution indicates three years of college. Ninety

percent of all housing units are single-family dwellings, and this is down from 97 percent 20 years ago. Eighty-eight percent of all units are occupied by people who own them. Property values of the single-family homes and condominiums remain high because of the stringent building codes, zoning, and the quality of the educational, cultural and commercial environment. The median value of owner-occupied single-family units exceeds that of any community area in Chicago except the Near North Side. Although some have grown up and moved away since 1960, Northbrook remains an area of many young people; almost a third of the total population is less than 18 years old, down from a high of 45 percent 20 years ago.

Northbrook has become first in commercial development in the six-county area surrounding Chicago. More than 51 percent of taxes are paid by commerce and industry, among which are the corporate headquarters of Allstate Insurance, Household International, Culligan International, A.C. Nielsen, Combined Insurance Company of America, General Binding Corporation, Underwriters Laboratories, Inc., and International Minerals and Chemical Corporation. Northbrook's proximity to Interstate Highways I-294 and I-94, to O'Hare International Airport 16 miles to the southwest, and to the Milwaukee Road railway, adds to its desirability as a commuter suburb for white-collar workers and professionals.

Helen Reif Nordland

Place 4195

North Chicago

The City of North Chicago is a shoreline community, 32 miles north of Chicago, with Waukegan to its north and Lake Bluff to its south in Lake County, Illinois.

After the Pottawatomie Indians ceded the last of their land to the United States in 1833, the area which eventually became North Chicago was utilized as farmland settlement was clustered along Green Bay Road, the former Indian trail. Five Points was the first east and west crossroad, enabling a lumberman named Swain to get his logs out to Green Bay Road. The road extended west to Libertyville and north to Waukegan.

On January 10, 1881, farmers on both sides of Waukegan Township and Shields Township were visited by real estate agents offering extravagant prices for their farms. Land that had previously sold for $80 an acre was suddenly $500 an acre and later $1,000 an acre. The town was laid out in 15,000 lots, each 25 by 125 feet, some of which sold for $40 per front foot. Carl E. Saylor was given the contract to sell the lots and to advertise the town. The selling points were that the town was ideal for manufacturing and was "dry." This town was called South Waukegan and its motto was "No Saloons."

Development was rapid. In 1892, the Chicago and North Western Railway erected a depot. A post office was established, and the first hotel was built. That same year a deed passed from the Wadsworth family to the Washburn-Moen Manufacturing Company for the land upon which its mill would be erected. Two more factories followed: The Lanyon Zinc Oxide Company (later called the Vulcan Louisville Zinc Works) and the Morrow Brothers Harness Factory, manufacturers of pads for horse collars.

Other manufacturers followed. The Chicago Hardware Company erected its plant in 1896. The Chicago Hardware Foundry Company began operating in 1900 and the National Envelope Company in 1905. By 1912, 14 manufacturers had located here, making this a town of opportunity for workingmen.

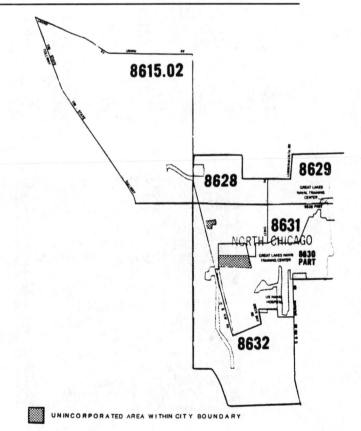

UNINCORPORATED AREA WITHIN CITY BOUNDARY

Incorporated as a village in 1895, South Waukegan changed its name to North Chicago in 1901. The city was incorporated in 1909. Many residents of the city were of Croatian, Slovenian, and Polish origin, attracted here by the availability of jobs. The population increased from 1,150 in 1900 to 3,306 in 1910. Some of the early churches were Methodist, Presbyterian and Catholic. Foss Park, established in 1907. was located on 33 wooded acres on the shore of Lake Michigan and provided one of the best recreational beaches on the North Shore.

North Chicago
Population and Housing Characteristics, 1930-1980

	1980	1970	1960	1950	1940	1930
Total Population.......	38,774	47,275	22,938	8,628	8,465	8,466
% Male..................	68.8	74.8	49.9	50.6	51.5	52.0
% Female................	31.2	25.2	50.1	49.4	48.5	48.0
% White.................	67.1	81.7	76.6	90.3	92.5	93.3
% Black.................	27.1	16.7	22.3	9.6	7.5	6.2
% Other Nonwhite Races...	5.8	1.6	1.1	0.1	-	0.5
% Under 5 Years Old......	6.8	5.9	16.4	9.6	8.6	9.0
% 5-19 Years Old.........	38.5	44.8	26.8	20.9	24.2	34.4
% 20-44 Years Old........	41.7	37.8	38.9	43.8	43.8	40.6
% 45-64 Years Old........	9.0	8.4	13.3	19.1	19.9	13.7
% 65 Years and Older.....	4.0	3.1	4.6	6.6	3.5	2.2
Median School Years....	12.5	12.1	10.6	8.9	8.0	*
Total Housing Units......	7,463	6,425	5,846	2,465	2,173	**
% In One-Unit Structures.	39.6	33.0	41.7	37.1	39.6	**
% Owner Occupied.........	37.1	35.7	37.9	49.8	45.7	**
% Renter Occupied........	56.7	61.1	58.4	49.6	53.2	**
% Vacant.................	6.2	3.2	3.7	0.6	1.1	**
% 1+ Persons per Room....	7.3	13.1	21.0	15.2	19.2	**

Place 4195 — North Chicago , Illinois
Selected Characteristics of Census Tracts: 1980

Tract Number	Total	8615.02	8628	8629	8630	8631	8632
Total Population.............	38774	0	2032	6159	24596	2664	3323
% Male.......................	68.8	-	42.8	47.1	81.1	49.5	49.1
% Black......................	27.1	-	83.0	45.7	9.5	61.6	60.5
% Other Nonwhite.............	5.8	-	4.3	7.8	6.0	4.9	2.3
% Of Spanish Origin..........	5.1	-	3.6	13.1	3.5	5.4	2.3
% Foreign Born...............	5.0	-	4.4	6.8	4.9	4.2	3.6
% Living In Group Quarters...	43.3	-	0.0	0.0	68.2	0.0	0.0
% 13 Years Old And Under.....	17.4	-	37.4	21.9	13.0	24.5	23.6
% 14-20 Years Old............	34.1	-	16.6	12.9	45.4	15.0	15.4
% 21-64 Years Old............	44.5	-	43.2	51.1	40.5	53.0	55.9
% 65-74 Years Old............	2.7	-	1.9	9.5	0.7	4.8	3.5
% 75 Years Old And Over......	1.4	-	4.5	4.4	0.4	2.7	1.6
% In Different House.........	76.1	-	51.9	37.4	95.8	37.0	42.6
% Families With Female Head.......	20.9	-	63.3	31.7	1.7	30.8	22.3
Median School Years Completed...	12.5	-	12.5	12.0	12.6	12.5	12.5
Median Family Income, 1979....$$	16850	-	12400	20104	15057	19971	22463
% Income Below Poverty Level.....	7.5	-	25.0	8.5	2.0	4.8	9.1
% Income Of $30,000 Or More.....	15.3	-	4.8	21.1	6.6	18.1	30.8
% White Collar Workers...........	44.9	-	35.5	42.0	54.5	40.5	46.7
% Civilian Labor Force Unemployed.	5.3	-	11.8	5.8	3.5	3.6	4.4
% Riding To Work By Automobile....	38.9	-	92.3	85.3	22.7	89.2	95.1
Mean Commuting Time - Minutes....	12.0	-	18.9	21.7	8.9	19.1	23.2
Population Per Household..........	3.1	-	3.2	2.7	3.7	3.0	3.0
Total Housing Units..........	7462	0	652	2463	2280	934	1133
% Condominiums...............	4.0	-	0.0	0.4	2.5	0.0	20.7
% Built 1970 Or Later........	23.4	-	45.5	6.5	34.2	5.8	37.9
% Owner Occupied.............	37.1	-	13.2	47.2	6.8	55.1	74.8
% With 1+ Persons Per Room........	7.3	-	13.1	7.6	4.9	8.8	6.9
Median Value: Owner Units.......$$	45200	-	46100	42800	-	45000	48200
Median Rent: Rental Units.......$$	219	-	211	178	234	214	248
Median Number Of Rooms: All Units.	4.9	-	4.3	4.6	5.4	4.9	4.9

North Chicago
Selected Characteristics of Census Tracts: 1970

Tract Number	TOTAL	8615	8628	8629	8630	8631	8632
Total Population.............	47275	6783	1003	6597	34276	3005	5650
% Male.......................	74.8	49.4	45.9	47.5	84.9	48.7	49.5
% Black......................	16.6	0.1	83.6	33.8	6.7	34.1	26.0
% Other Nonwhite.............	1.7	0.5	1.3	0.8	1.8	2.5	1.2
% Of Spanish Language........	2.4	2.4	6.6	3.1	1.9	5.8	1.0
% Foreign Born...............	3.0	2.3	0.6	9.5	1.6	5.6	3.5
% Living In Group Quarters...	53.2	0.2	0.0	0.2	73.3	0.3	0.5
% 13 Years Old And Under.....	16.9	29.9	47.6	22.6	12.9	27.1	31.3
% 14-20 Years Old............	44.2	12.5	16.1	13.3	55.5	15.8	12.9
% 21-64 Years Old............	35.9	52.7	33.7	53.8	30.3	50.3	51.0
% 65-74 Years Old............	1.8	3.5	1.5	6.0	0.7	4.1	3.5
% 75 Years Old And Over......	1.3	1.4	1.2	4.3	0.6	2.6	1.4
% In Different House.........	18.9	53.5	35.6	65.8	3.5	57.1	57.1
% Families With Female Head.......	9.2	6.7	35.0	14.7	0.9	11.2	7.0
Median School Years Completed....	12.1	12.2	10.9	10.9	12.3	11.7	12.5
Median Family Income, 1969....$$	8899	12057	6434	10338	7735	10359	13744
% Income Below Poverty Level.....	7.2	5.2	21.1	9.0	5.8	5.8	4.0
% Income of $15,000 or More.....	15.2	27.7	3.7	22.7	7.1	21.7	40.9
% White Collar Workers...........	19.2	25.1	11.1	17.1	28.8	24.9	34.0
% Civilian Labor Force Unemployed.	4.3	1.9	15.1	3.4	6.5	3.0	1.6
% Riding To Work By Automobile....	33.0	91.7	85.7	70.5	23.3	81.4	89.7
Population Per Household..........	3.6	3.4	4.4	2.9	4.3	3.2	3.6
Total Housing Units..........	6424	2078	227	2427	2164	979	1609
% Condominiums & Cooperatives.....	0.0	0.0	0.0	0.0	0.0	0.0	0.0
% Built 1960 Or Later.............	24.5	44.2	74.7	8.4	38.7	13.1	45.7
% Owner Occupied.................	35.7	80.0	35.7	46.6	7.8	47.9	75.8
% With 1+ Persons Per Room........	13.1	7.2	31.3	9.2	14.3	11.3	10.1
Median Value: Owner Units.......$$	18700	23500	19300	18200	-	19700	27000
Median Rent: Rental Units.......$$	109	135	74	104	112	114	139
Median Number Of Rooms: All Units.	4.7	4.8	4.6	4.4	4.9	4.6	5.2

After the turn of the century, there was evident need for a Midwestern naval training facility. Through the efforts of Congressman George Foss, a site consisting of 182 acres just south of North Chicago was approved. Members of the Merchants Club and the Commercial Club of Chicago raised more than $100,000 for the purchase of this land, which they presented free to the government. Admiral Albert A. Ross oversaw the construction of the $3.5 million facility which was dedicated October 28, 1911. This base, known as the Great Lakes Naval Training Station, has provided basic training for more than three million men and women since 1911. By 1920, the population of North Chicago had grown to 5,839.

The North Chicago Veteran's Administration Hospital was opened in 1926, upon the site of the former one-room schoolhouse on the southern side of Five Points. This large neuropsychiatric hospital was renamed Downey's Veteran's Administration Hospital in 1939. In 1976, its operation was broadened to include general medicine and surgery, and its name was changed back to North Chicago Veteran's Administration Hospital. It is now affiliated with the University of

Health Sciences, The Chicago Medical School, which opened in North Chicago in October, 1980, on a 93-acre site. This is a $100 million campus for training physicians and professionals in allied health fields and for providing graduate-level education for biomedical researchers and teachers.

During the Depression years, North Chicago's population leveled at 8,465 residents. During World War II the citizens of North Chicago, through a special bond drive, purchased a fighter plane named the "Spirit of Chicago" which was sent across the seas to aid the war effort. Not many people moved into North Chicago during the war and the population was 8,625 in 1950.

The greatest expansion of the city occurred during the 1950s. North Chicago established its own high school district. The western boundary was pushed past Lewis Avenue. By 1960, 23,000 residents called North Chicago home. With the annexation of Great Lakes Naval Training Center and the Veterans Administration Hospital, the population swelled to more than 47,000 in the 1970 census. Several black families settled in North Chicago around the turn of the century, and their number has progressively increased. By 1960, blacks constituted a fifth of the population. The annexations of the 1960s changed the percentage bases, and the black population dropped to 17 percent, despite an increase in their number. Much of the numerical increase can be accounted for by sailors at Great Lakes Naval Training Center.

During the most recent decade, the population of North Chicago dropped to less than 39,000. Activity at the Great Lakes Center declined with the end of the Vietnam hostilities. There has been some industrial shrinkage, and considerable migration of young people, who made up 41 percent of the 1960 population, but whose numbers have dropped off to 25 percent today. Blacks now constitute 27 percent of the total, and 5 percent are Hispanic. North Chicago is a lower-middle class community, 15 percent of whose families earned incomes greater than 30,000 in 1979, while 7.5 percent reported an income below the poverty level. Forty-five percent of all workers are in white-collar occupations, and many work in North Chicago itself.

The number of housing units has been increasing steadily in the last two decades. In the 1970s, construction emphasis turned more to single-family housing, which has grown to 46 percent of all units. About a fourth of all housing in North Chicago has been built in the last 10 years. Today, 37 percent of all units are owner-occupied, and the median value of a single-family dwelling is $2,000 less than the median in Chicago.

North Chicago's urban renewal site, northwest of Lewis Avenue and Argonne Drive, is an open, aesthetically pleasing, 173-acre tract of of land. Two multiple-family developments are situated at the center. A supermarket is on the northeast parcel. A church, school and park have been developed. The North Chicago City Hall was constructed in 1966 on the southeast pacrel. A community center was constructed too. Recently, a new city garage facility was located behind the supermarket. Approximately 65 acres remain undeveloped and of these approximately 20 acres are heavily wooded.

Industry and business still play a vital role in North Chicago. Abbott Laboratories, a pharmaceutical company, employs more than 6,700 persons. Their plant facility is located on Sheridan Road. As older industrial buildings were vacated, they were rehabilitated by entrepreneurs who then leased out space to other businesses and industries. The Coleman Industries is an example of this succession.

North Chicago remains an attracive location for heavy industry. With its supply of Lake Michigan water, the port of Waukegan nearby for shipping, two freight lines, its industrial zoning, access to two major highways (U.S. 41 and Interstate 294), and local labor market, it should continue as a manufacturing city with a small town atmosphere.

Mary L. Robinson

Place 4270

Oak Forest

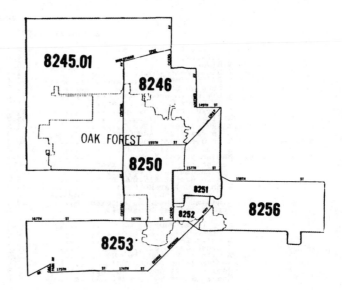

Oak Forest is located in southwest Cook County on 4.5 square miles of land. Before 1893 the settlement was known as New Bremen, or more popularly Bremen, the township name taken from that of the German city where many early residents embarked on their voyage to America. The history of Oak Forest by that name began with its inclusion in the Rock Island Railroad's timetable in 1893. The name Oak Forest was chosen for the large stand of oaks near the boxcar used as the first depot. The settlement was a farming community for the most part before 1900. The inclusion of Oak Forest as a stop on the Rock Island line was basically for the delivery of farm goods to the Chicago market. Very few persons lived in what is now Oak Forest at that time.

The Cook County Board decided to establish a County Poor Farm in Bremen Township in 1907. The institution was situated on some 254 acres in what would become Oak Forest. Nineteen infirmary buildings were built between 1909 and 1910, and a spur line of the railroad was constructed into the grounds, the latter becoming known as Oak Forest. in 1910 the first Superintendent of the Infirmary was named and in December of that year, 1,731 inmates were transferred from the overcrowded Dunning facility. The poor farm was known as the Oak Forest Infirmary or the Oak Forest Institution. It housed indigent poor, alcoholics, mentally ill, and persons with advanced cases of tuberculosis. The Infirmary instituted a new concept in care of the destitute poor by assigning almost all of the maintenance and food provision activities to the aging patients.

After 1910 two developers began purchasing land near the Infirmary. The Kaiser subdivision was located at 159th and Cicero near the focus of business at that time. However, with the advent of World War I, Kaiser allowed the name to be changed to Arbor Park Estates. The second developer, a man named McIntosh, was buying land along 155th Street. Businesses began to open, one of the most successful being the mortuary. The Infirmary and the surrounding settlement of fewer than 100 people supported two of these. Streets were lengthened and a post office was opened at the depot in 1912.

Oak Forest
Population and Housing Characteristics, 1930–1980

	1980	1970	1960	1950	1940	1930
Total Population.......	26,096	17,870	3,724	*	*	*
% Male...................	49.6	50.1	49.9	*	*	*
% Female.................	50.4	49.9	50.1	*	*	*
% White..................	96.2	99.8	100.0	*	*	*
% Black..................	2.0	0.0	–	*	*	*
% Other Nonwhite Races...	1.8	0.2	–	*	*	*
% Under 5 Years Old......	8.1	14.9	14.7	*	*	*
% 5–19 Years Old.........	28.9	31.6	29.6	*	*	*
% 20–44 Years Old........	40.2	39.3	33.7	*	*	*
% 45–64 Years Old........	15.9	11.4	15.7	*	*	*
% 65 Years and Older.....	6.9	2.8	6.3	*	*	*
Median School Years....	12.6	12.4	11.0	*	*	*
Total Housing Units....	8,039	4,873	1,078	*	*	*
% In One-Unit Structures.	72.4	83.3	91.6	*	*	*
% Owner Occupied.........	77.0	79.3	74.2	*	*	*
% Renter Occupied........	20.2	17.7	14.5	*	*	*
% Vacant.................	2.8	3.0	11.3	*	*	*
% 1+ Persons per Room....	2.3	7.0	13.2	*	*	*

Place 4270 — Oak Forest , Illinois
Selected Characteristics of Census Tracts: 1980

Tract Number	Total	8245.01	8246	8250	8251	8252	8253	8256
Total Population.............	26096	11784	4527	4618	1056	2212	1834	65
% Male.......................	49.6	49.2	49.4	49.8	51.0	50.8	50.1	–
% Black......................	2.0	0.3	0.0	0.1	45.4	0.0	0.2	–
% Other Nonwhite.............	1.8	2.0	1.3	2.1	0.9	1.4	1.4	–
% Of Spanish Origin..........	1.7	1.5	1.2	2.4	2.0	2.2	2.1	–
% Foreign Born...............	3.3	4.0	2.2	2.3	10.7	2.2	1.3	–
% Living In Group Quarters...	4.1	0.1	0.0	0.0	100.0	6.6	0.0	–
% 13 Years And Under.........	25.0	26.3	21.5	23.4	0.0	33.1	34.1	–
% 14–20 Years Old............	13.5	14.3	15.2	13.6	1.1	13.4	11.6	–
% 21–64 Years Old............	54.6	54.9	58.0	56.5	40.4	51.3	52.1	–
% 65–74 Years Old............	4.0	3.0	3.6	4.3	22.9	1.8	1.8	–
% 75 Years Old And Over......	2.9	1.5	1.7	2.3	35.5	0.4	0.4	–
% In Different House.........	42.3	43.0	38.4	41.7	63.8	27.1	52.8	–
% Families With Female Head..	9.1	8.3	10.0	11.0	–	8.7	7.3	–
Median School Years Completed..	12.6	12.8	12.7	12.4	7.9	12.6	12.7	–
Median Family Income, 1979.....$$	28027	29526	28435	24070	–	25000	29207	–
% Income Below Poverty Level....	2.2	1.8	0.0	4.3	–	7.4	6.1	–
% Income Of $30,000 Or More....	42.8	48.4	44.2	29.3	–	37.0	44.5	–
% White Collar Workers.......	57.3	62.7	58.0	45.6	–	57.2	52.0	–
% Civilian Labor Force Unemployed.	4.7	5.0	5.1	4.8	–	2.1	5.3	–
% Riding To Work By Automobile....	85.5	87.0	84.9	83.9	–	88.1	82.6	–
Mean Commuting Time – Minutes...	29.8	29.9	27.9	30.1	–	34.7	27.8	–
Population Per Household.....	3.2	3.4	3.1	2.8	0.0	3.8	3.7	–
Total Housing Units..........	8036	3576	1581	1759	10	588	502	20
% Condominiums...............	6.2	4.5	21.6	0.0	–	0.0	0.0	–
% Built 1970 Or Later........	34.9	45.4	33.6	23.8	–	7.6	36.4	–
% Owner Occupied.............	76.0	76.6	81.0	58.4	–	97.1	94.6	–
% With 1+ Persons Per Room...	2.3	1.8	2.3	3.1	–	3.1	2.2	–
Median Value: Owner Units.......$$	65600	70200	61600	59200	–	62200	66000	–
Median Rent: Rental Units.......$$	270	322	210	223	–	238	342	–
Median Number Of Rooms: All Units.	5.6	5.6	5.6	5.0	–	5.6	5.6	–

Oak Forest
Selected Characteristics of Census Tracts: 1970

Tract Number	TOTAL	8245	8246	8250	8251	8252	8253	8256
Total Population.............	19271	13094	8289	4086	2253	2358	7453	7420
% Male.......................	50.1	49.8	49.7	50.0	46.4	49.4	50.2	49.9
% Black......................	0.0	0.0	2.1	0.0	15.6	0.0	0.0	29.0
% Other Nonwhite.............	0.2	0.2	0.3	0.3	0.8	0.3	0.2	0.3
% Of Spanish Language........	1.9	1.0	0.7	3.6	0.6	2.7	0.0	4.8
% Foreign Born...............	3.0	2.8	3.1	4.3	20.3	1.1	2.2	2.2
% Living In Group Quarters...	0.1	0.6	1.2	0.0	99.3	0.0	0.1	0.1
% 13 Years Old And Under.....	38.8	39.1	34.2	32.3	0.3	46.4	32.1	36.2
% 14–20 Years Old............	8.7	8.1	13.0	11.9	0.5	5.3	13.8	14.5
% 21–64 Years Old............	49.7	49.5	47.4	50.7	28.5	47.4	49.2	46.1
% 65–74 Years Old............	1.8	2.0	3.1	3.4	22.0	0.3	3.2	2.1
% 75 Years Old And Over......	1.0	1.2	2.3	1.7	48.8	0.5	1.7	1.1
% In Different House.........	32.8	27.3	60.5	52.0	29.8	22.4	48.6	55.6
% Families With Female Head..	3.6	2.7	6.2	6.8	0.0	1.5	4.9	7.4
Median School Years Completed..	12.5	12.5	12.1	12.2	8.6	12.4	12.3	12.1
Median Family Income, 1969.....$$	12949	13635	12744	11763	37500	11683	12707	12156
% Income Below Poverty Level.....	1.9	1.6	3.9	3.1	0.0	0.0	4.1	4.0
% Income of $15,000 or More.....	33.4	38.1	30.7	27.2	100.0	27.4	32.7	30.6
% White Collar Workers.......	34.9	40.6	25.1	24.1	48.4	30.2	26.5	22.6
% Civilian Labor Force Unemployed.	2.0	1.1	3.3	2.5	0.0	3.5	2.9	3.0
% Riding To Work By Automobile....	81.1	80.8	82.6	81.3	10.3	79.9	75.8	85.1
Population Per Household.....	3.8	4.0	3.9	3.2	5.3	4.3	3.7	4.2
Total Housing Units..........	4873	3349	2203	1331	0	559	2067	1784
% Condominiums & Cooperatives.....	0.0	0.3	0.0	0.0	–	0.0	0.0	0.0
% Built 1960 Or Later........	79.8	86.6	30.8	54.0	–	96.0	33.9	9.7
% Owner Occupied.............	79.3	90.1	85.6	54.7	–	97.1	80.6	86.7
% With 1+ Persons Per Room...	7.0	5.2	11.5	10.0	–	8.1	8.1	16.5
Median Value: Owner Units.......$$	25900	28000	19500	19700	–	23200	21100	16900
Median Rent: Rental Units.......$$	135	176	126	123	–	183	138	137
Median Number Of Rooms: All Units.	5.9	6.2	5.5	4.7	–	6.0	5.6	5.4

The 1920s brought a 10-acre peony farm and nursery, a firecracker factory and, before the passage of the 18th Amendment, a number of speakeasies. The center of the town was 159th Street and Cicero Avenue. Electricity did not reach Oak Forest until 1927. During this decade a movement developed among some of the approximately 400 residents to adopt the name Arbor Park rather than Oak Forest. They felt it would reduce the stigma attached to the town from the Oak Forest Poor Farm. However, this effort was not successful.

The 1930s was a time of poverty for many Oak Forest residents. Many moved farther from the center of town, constructing two-car Harris garages to live in and growing their own food. Tramps who lived on Chicago's skid-row in summer came to Oak Forest in the winter. Living in the forests nearby, bodies of these men were frequently found in local ditches. By 1932, the Oak Forest Infirmary had become overcrowded, with a total of 4,292 inmates. More than 500 tuberculosis patients were housed in open-sided tents thought to be therapeutic. The Institute supplied water to some households, customers for businesses, and employment. Residents attended movies that were shown there.

In 1940, the population had grown to 611 and the Oak Forest

Taxpayers Association was formed. This group governed the community until its incorporation and dissolved shortly after that. Until its incorporation Oak Forest was considered a wide-open town with many taverns open 24 hours a day and no police protection. At that time the community needed many improvements such as street paving and lights and a more adequate supply of water.

In May, 1947, the Village of Oak Forest was incorporated with a population of 1,618. The first mayor was William Barr. During the 1940s the village was able to organize a volunteer fire department, pave 159th Street, and organize School District 145.

The population in 1950 was 1,856 and doubled during the following decade. The increases were attributable to the general exodus to suburbia and the attractions of Oak Forest itself. The village had good transportation to the city and a great deal of open land for building. The first subdivision, Friendly Oaks, was built in the northern section of the village. Two other subdivisions were developed west of Central Avenue and south of 151st Street.

The Oak Forest Institute discontinued its poor farm operations in 1954. In 1956 the Institute was licensed to operate as two hospitals, one for the chronically ill and the other for tuberculosis patients. In 1957 it was renamed the Oak Forest Hospital. Many improvements and additions were made during the 1950s. In 1959 the tuberculosis hospital was closed and became instead a geriatric center.

Oak Forest experienced its greatest growth in the 1960s when the population went from 3,724 to almost 18,000. During this decade an average of two families per day moved into the suburb. Its growth was accelerated by annexations and the offering of reasonably-priced homes for young middle-class families. Road improvements were a major concern as new areas opened up. Many of the subdivisions were rather isolated due to the odd boundaries of the suburb and several homeowners associations worked for local community improvement. Despite some construction of smaller shopping plazas such as Oak Plaza and the Friendly Oaks Shopping Plaza, the suburb suffered from a general lack of shopping and industry until the 1970s.

In the 1970s, with the population well over its projected 10,400 mark, the Village of Oak Forest changed its form of government to that of a city, and the first election of aldermen was held in 1973. During this decade also the city began buying Lake Michigan water from Oak Lawn and continued making municipal improvements. The Oak Forest Hospital became the world's largest long-term general disease hospital and gained international recognition for its operations.

The population in Oak Forest increased 46 percent during the last 10 years to more than 26,000 in 1980. Two percent were black and 2 percent of Spanish origin. Many of the residents came from the Southwest Side of Chicago. The "newness" of the suburb was reflected in the fact that a third of its population was 18 years of age or less, and only 7 percent were 65 or more. Two percent of all families lived in poverty during 1979, while more than 42 percent reported incomes of $30,000 or more.

The housing in Oak Forest also reflected its recent growth. Only 17 percent of the housing units were built before 1960, 48 percent were built during the 1960s and 35 percent during the 1970s. Three-fourths of the housing units were owner-occupied and three-fourths were in single-family homes. Median value of single-family homes was $65,600. Oak Forest's growth pattern differed from that of some other suburbs because it allowed only 10 housing units per acre compared to other suburbs where 20 to 40 housing units were common. Besides, some of the land originally zoned for multi-family apartments has been rezoned back to single-family homes. There were some six-flat apartment buildings, most of which were successfully rented before completion, and more were planned. Oak Forest recently opened its $1 million municipal building. Shopping is available at four plazas and centers as well as at a number of businesses along Cicero Avenue and U.S. 6. Three larger shopping centers are located in nearby suburbs.

One of the problems Oak Forest has had is its lack of a tax base. It never had a real downtown area, and while sales revenues provided over half a million dollars a year there has been little industry until recently. Oak Forest had only seven manufacturing concerns employing some 120 people. There are 25 service firms doing business in Oak Forest and employing over 860 workers in addition to the 2,200 employed at Oak Forest Hospital. The Oak Forest Industrial Park at 167th Street opened a few years ago and by 1980 nearly 55 acres of the total 75 were under developmemt.

Gail Danks Welter

Place 4290

Oak Lawn

Oak Lawn is situated on 8.34 square miles of land in Cook County about 14 miles southwest of Chicago's Loop. Before becoming known as Oak Lawn the community was called Black Oaks Grove, and then Agnes. Like most Chicago suburbs Oak Lawn developed and grew from a farming community. Unlike some other communities it did not flourish immediately with the arrival of the railroad, but continued as a sleepy town until after the turn of the century.

While 1,273 acres of land in what is now Oak Lawn was purchased as early as 1835 by a land broker named Julian Hatch, the first settler seems to have been a John Simpson who arrived in 1842. He purchased a heavily-wooded half section of land along what is now 95th Street near Central Avenue. He established his farm in 1858 and the same

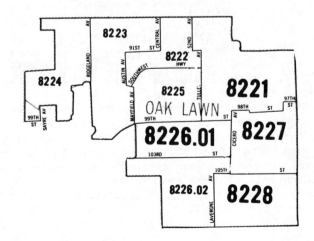

Oak Lawn
Population and Housing Characteristics, 1930-1980

	1980	1970	1960	1950	1940	1930
Total Population	60,590	60,305	27,471	8,751	3,483	2,045
% Male	47.2	48.5	49.7	50.8	51.3	51.4
% Female	52.8	51.5	50.3	49.2	48.7	48.6
% White	98.3	99.7	99.9	100.0	100.0	99.9
% Black	0.1	0.0	0.0	—	—	0.1
% Other Nonwhite Races	1.6	0.3	0.1	0.0	—	—
% Under 5 Years Old	5.0	8.1	14.9	15.9	8.8	11.5
% 5-19 Years Old	24.0	33.4	29.4	20.9	29.3	*
% 20-44 Years Old	30.2	29.2	35.6	43.7	41.8	*
% 45-64 Years Old	26.5	21.8	16.0	16.2	16.2	13.1
% 65 Years and Older	14.3	7.5	4.1	3.3	3.9	4.4
Median School Years	12.5	12.3	12.1	11.6	8.6	*
Total Housing Units	21,191	16,771	7,475	2,534	980	*
% In One-Unit Structures	66.9	78.7	97.7	*	*	*
% Owner Occupied	76.9	80.2	89.6	87.7	70.8	*
% Renter Occupied	21.4	18.3	5.3	8.4	24.9	*
% Vacant	1.7	1.5	5.1	3.9	4.3	*
% 1+ Persons per Room	2.8	8.5	10.4	13.0	*	*

Place 4290 -- Oak Lawn, Illinois
Selected Characteristics of Census Tracts: 1980

Tract Number	Total	8221	8222	8223	8224	8225	8226.01	8226.02	8227	8228
Total Population	60590	9316	4358	8505	4830	5134	5222	6102	8994	8129
% Male	47.2	45.7	49.5	48.8	49.6	47.7	48.8	48.1	43.9	46.2
% Black	0.1	0.1	0.0	0.1	0.0	0.2	0.0	0.0	0.0	0.0
% Other Nonwhite	1.6	2.5	1.0	1.7	1.8	0.9	0.8	1.9	1.9	0.0
% Of Spanish Origin	1.2	1.6	1.0	1.7	1.4	1.4	0.7	1.4	1.1	0.7
% Foreign Born	6.8	9.6	2.3	6.2	8.1	3.9	3.9	5.9	9.2	6.6
% Living In Group Quarters	1.1	3.1	0.0	2.9	0.0	2.3	0.0	0.2	0.0	0.0
% 13 Years Old And Under	16.7	15.1	20.1	20.2	22.3	18.1	18.5	16.1	11.7	13.6
% 14-20 Years Old	14.1	13.4	14.1	13.7	14.4	14.5	14.2	17.1	11.9	15.2
% 21-64 Years Old	54.8	54.1	57.2	54.5	55.3	52.4	58.0	57.1	52.5	55.0
% 65-74 Years Old	8.7	10.6	6.1	6.8	5.6	8.7	6.1	6.4	13.6	9.9
% 75 Years Old And Over	5.6	6.8	2.6	4.8	2.4	6.4	3.1	3.3	10.4	6.3
% In Different House	32.0	35.7	25.1	35.8	30.8	30.3	29.7	38.8	26.4	31.6
% Families With Female Head	9.3	11.4	10.2	10.4	7.7	8.1	6.0	10.5	8.6	9.3
Median School Years Completed	12.5	12.5	12.5	12.3	12.2	12.4	12.7	12.8	12.5	12.6
Median Family Income, 1979 $$	27813	26027	29234	25814	26792	27832	29030	29304	28115	30991
% Income Below Poverty Level	2.6	3.5	2.3	3.8	3.2	1.7	2.9	2.6	1.8	1.3
% Income Of $30,000 Or More	44.7	37.0	47.1	38.1	41.7	45.8	47.9	48.6	46.2	53.5
% White Collar Workers	58.0	59.8	52.0	45.4	44.6	56.9	63.8	65.7	63.9	64.2
% Civilian Labor Force Unemployed	5.9	6.1	6.9	6.2	5.8	4.3	7.4	4.4	5.4	6.7
% Riding To Work By Automobile	86.0	82.2	90.7	89.8	89.1	85.1	89.8	87.3	79.7	86.1
Mean Commuting Time - Minutes	30.0	29.3	29.5	28.4	26.3	28.0	30.0	29.4	34.4	31.5
Population Per Household	2.9	2.7	3.3	3.1	3.2	3.0	3.2	2.9	2.4	2.9
Total Housing Units	21189	3446	1338	2777	1523	1682	1655	2120	3763	2885
% Condominiums	10.9	7.5	0.0	10.2	4.3	0.0	0.7	14.4	29.6	9.4
% Built 1970 Or Later	23.8	21.8	4.0	27.3	31.5	5.1	13.2	51.4	20.9	28.8
% Owner Occupied	76.5	76.3	94.0	79.5	81.0	85.1	91.4	64.9	68.6	68.9
% With 1+ Persons Per Room	2.8	1.5	3.2	4.4	4.6	3.3	2.5	2.1	1.6	2.5
Median Value: Owner Units $$	66200	67900	61500	58900	61400	64600	67000	80200	70000	68900
Median Rent: Rental Units $$	276	253	277	253	268	231	389	295	273	288
Median Number Of Rooms: All Units	5.4	5.2	5.6	5.2	5.4	5.6	5.6	5.4	4.9	5.4

Oak Lawn
Selected Characteristics of Census Tracts: 1970

Tract Number	TOTAL	8221	8222	8223	8224	8225	8226	8227	8228
Total Population	60305	9181	4887	8097	4401	5535	10346	9752	8207
% Male	48.5	47.2	49.2	49.7	50.6	48.0	49.3	47.0	48.4
% Black	0.0	0.0	0.0	0.0	0.0	0.0	0.0	0.0	0.0
% Other Nonwhite	0.3	0.6	0.3	0.2	0.9	0.2	0.0	0.2	0.2
% Of Spanish Language	1.1	1.7	0.0	2.0	2.0	0.7	0.8	0.5	0.4
% Foreign Born	5.1	6.5	3.5	5.0	2.8	4.2	4.0	7.1	5.4
% Living In Group Quarters	0.8	1.0	0.0	2.8	0.0	1.8	0.3	0.1	0.1
% 13 Years Old And Under	29.9	24.7	28.3	31.2	32.4	28.1	36.4	23.7	34.2
% 14-20 Years Old	12.8	12.7	14.9	12.0	12.9	12.9	13.4	11.3	13.8
% 21-64 Years Old	49.8	54.0	51.7	48.7	50.2	48.7	45.9	52.9	46.7
% 65-74 Years Old	4.8	5.8	3.5	4.3	2.9	5.9	2.6	8.3	3.6
% 75 Years Old And Over	2.7	2.8	1.7	3.9	1.5	4.4	1.5	3.9	1.8
% In Different House	57.0	53.9	64.8	62.9	64.3	56.8	62.6	44.4	54.9
% Families With Female Head	7.2	8.1	5.5	7.7	6.6	8.2	4.0	9.9	6.5
Median School Years Completed	12.2	12.3	12.3	11.1	12.0	12.2	12.2	12.4	12.4
Median Family Income, 1969 $$	13824	13343	14174	11889	11892	13259	15156	14785	14676
% Income Below Poverty Level	2.5	2.8	1.2	3.9	4.4	2.1	1.8	1.5	3.4
% Income of $15,000 or More	41.5	38.0	43.4	27.8	29.0	37.5	50.6	48.4	47.5
% White Collar Workers	35.7	38.3	28.5	20.7	20.8	30.9	45.1	44.2	41.0
% Civilian Labor Force Unemployed	2.6	2.6	1.6	3.2	3.2	2.8	2.2	2.2	3.1
% Riding To Work By Automobile	82.3	78.5	86.4	85.4	86.6	78.4	85.6	81.2	79.6
Population Per Household	3.6	3.2	3.9	3.7	3.8	3.6	4.3	3.1	4.1
Total Housing Units	16771	2878	1271	2178	1169	1538	2441	3279	2047
% Condominiums & Cooperatives	1.6	0.3	0.0	0.2	0.0	0.0	0.0	7.9	0.0
% Built 1960 Or Later	45.4	43.0	19.3	30.0	29.3	30.4	42.0	75.8	56.6
% Owner Occupied	78.6	77.7	95.2	83.0	83.1	84.9	93.0	50.3	85.7
% With 1+ Persons Per Room	8.5	6.4	9.9	11.5	13.3	8.3	9.8	4.3	9.9
Median Value: Owner Units $$	26500	25900	22900	19500	19800	24500	31000	31100	31100
Median Rent: Rental Units $$	171	158	143	127	164	148	217	184	180
Median Number Of Rooms: All Units	5.4	5.1	5.5	5.1	5.1	5.4	6.0	4.9	5.9

year Worth Township built a major road known as the Black Oaks Grove Road. By 1860 the new settlement of Black Oaks Grove had its first school. After the Civil War a number of German immigrants came to the area and Trinity Lutheran Church was organized in 1874. A post office was functioning in the community for a brief period from 1874-1875 but was discontinued, probably from lack of use.

In 1879 a Colonel Ralph Plumb, railroad builder, signed an agreement with John and Charles Simpson, John Simpson Jr., and Franklin Chamberlain. Plumb agreed to route the proposed railroad through Black Oaks Grove with a station for freight and passengers and a telegraph office. Local residents agreed to accept this, offering $650 and 15 acres of land. In addition, they would subdivide and establish a town wherein Colonel Plumb would own half the lots. By 1881 the line was ready for service. The station master, Henry Crouch, applied for a post office and named the community Agnes after his wife. In 1882 the area from Simpson Road to 95th Street and Cook to Tulley avenues was subdivided and recorded as the Village of Oak Lawn. The same year the post office name was also changed.

In the late 1800s the Campbell's Oak Lawn Subdivision, and after that the Minnick Subdivision were built. Erasmus Minnick built a house at the corner of 54th and (now) East Shore Drive which is still standing. He also contracted to have the Oak Lawn Lake dug. By 1902 a telephone service was located in Oak Lawn, but shortly thereafter was returned to Evergreen Park due to a lack of subscribers. In 1905 a larger school was built near the depot and during the first few years of this century two more churches were organized.

During the early 1900s residents were beginning to consider incorporation for several reasons. First, Chicago had been annexing nearby unincorporated areas and, while there were some advantages to this, it meant a loss of self-determination. Second, a gas pipeline was to be laid through Evergreen Park and was offered to Oak Lawn if it were to be incorporated by 1909. The inability of the township to provide adequate police and fire protection was another consideration. So in 1909 Oak Lawn Village, encompassing the area between 87th and 99th streets and Central to Cicero avenues was incorporated.

By 1911 the gas line which had figured prominently in the community's incorporation was considered obsolete and electric street lights were installed on 95th Street. In doing so many of the black oaks were cut down. Roads were soon graded and oiled and a city hall was built for the 289 residents. During this decade the village had a pickle making business, a hardware store, and little else. By 1920 the population had grown to 489.

The 1920s brought more subdivision along 95th, 87th, and 79th streets, and west of Western Avenue from 70th to 111th streets. Consideration for the site of a race track enhanced the village's attractiveness and a zoning committee was formed in 1927. This committee came up with a plan which is used today and termed "superblocks." These were areas of commercial zoning providing an outer layer, then a layer of apartments which in turn surrounded single family homes. Although the plan was scrapped a decade later, the shopping strips along 95th, Cicero Avenue, and 87th Street were developed on this basis. While population was increasing, transportation to workplaces was still inadequate, but apparently offset by the attractiveness of this area.

By 1930 Oak Lawn had 2,045 residents and, unlike many places, continued to grow during the Depression. WPA and CWA projects such as the library in 1936 and Covington School in 1937 brought some improvements to the community. The 1940 census showed 3,483 residents in Oak Lawn. In 1944 the Park District was organized and in 1945 it bought the lake for a park. Shortly thereafter it built a field

house and made other improvements on the property. By the end of the 1940s (largely due to a water emergency in 1944) Oak Lawn approved a permanent water connection to Chicago. Today Oak Lawn supplies water to several neighborhing communities.

Oak Lawn grew to 8,751 by 1950. The following decade brought a rush of population growth. In 1953 the city adopted the city manager form of government. Territory was annexed and by the mid-1950s Oak Lawn covered 6 square miles, much of it undeveloped. The area south of 95th Street required a great deal of investment in streets and other improvements before subdivisions began to appear. The 1960 census showed that the population of Oak Lawn had tripled during the decade, and now stood at more than 27,000. The 1960s brought more annexations which helped increase the population from 27,471 in 1960 to more than 49,000 by 1966. In 1970 60,305 people resided in Oak Lawn. The peak population was reached from 1973 to 1976 with 63,500 residents. In 1971 under a new state constitution, Oak Lawn became a home rule unit.

By 1980 the population had seemingly stabilized at 60,590, close to its 1970 figure. The population of Oak Lawn has remained white. Only five blacks lived there in 1960, and only 38 in 1980. Spanish-origin residents comprised 1 percent of the total in 1980, a approximately the same proportion as in 1970. The population has aged appreciably in the last 20 years. Twenty-five percent of the population is 18 years or under in age, down from 43 percent in 1960. Fourteen percent are 65 or older, up from 4 percent. The median age of residents in Oak Lawn in 1980 was 36.3, having risen from 28.5 in 1970.

Of the 21,000 housing units in Oak Lawn more than 76 percent were owner-occupied in 1980. Some 13,500 units were single-family detached homes whose prices ranged from $40,000-$125,000. Rental units comprised only 22 percent and rents ranged from $235 to $400. The bulk of housing (61.5 percent) in the community was built between 1950 and 1970.

Most workers in Oak Lawn commute to jobs in Chicago and to other southside communities and 58 percent are in white-collar occupations. The median family income for 1980 was $27,813. These figures suggest that Oak Lawn was a solidly middle-class community in 1980.

While industry has played a small part in Oak Lawn's history, recent zoning has included an industrial park. The Oak Lawn Industrial Park covers 200 acres and is served by two rail lines. There are 41 manufacturing concerns in Oak Lawn employing over 750 workers. Including Christ Hospital 110 service firms employed nearly 6,000 people.

Gail Danks Welter

Place 4295

Oak Park

Oak Park is located about nine miles west of Chicago's Loop in Cook County. It is bordered on the north and east by Chicago, on the south by Roosevelt Road, with Berwyn and Cicero beyond, and on the west by Harlem Avenue, which separates it from Forest Park and River Forest. It is rectangular in shape and covers 4.6 square miles. Slow to grow in early years, Oak Park reached its population peak in 1940 and, although declining steadily since, was still one of the 10 most populous Chicago suburbs in 1980.

The history of Oak Park began in 1833 with the settlement by Joseph Kettlestrings, who had come with his wife from Baltimore, of a quarter section of land bounded by Harlem, Oak Park and North avenues. For a time the settlement was known as Kettlestrings' Grove, but soon became Oak Ridge. The first school was opened in the 1850s on land

Oak Park
Population and Housing Characteristics, 1930-1980

	1980	1970	1960	1950	1940	1930
Total Population.......	54,887	62,511	61,093	63,529	66,015	63,982
% Male..................	46.1	45.1	45.2	45.5	45.9	47.0
% Female................	53.9	54.9	54.8	54.5	54.1	53.0
% White.................	85.2	98.8	99.6	99.8	99.8	99.7
% Black.................	10.8	0.2	0.1	0.1	0.1	0.2
% Other Nonwhite Races..	4.0	1.0	0.3	0.1	0.1	0.1
% Under 5 Years Old.....	6.2	6.5	7.8	7.5	4.6	6.1
% 5-19 Years Old........	20.9	23.9	21.0	16.6	19.4	21.8
% 20-44 Years Old.......	41.7	29.2	27.6	33.8	40.5	43.4
% 45-64 Years Old.......	17.1	24.1	28.7	30.4	26.8	22.5
% 65 Years and Older....	14.1	16.3	14.9	11.7	8.7	6.2
Median School Years....	14.5	13.2	12.5	12.3	12.1	6.2
Total Housing Units....	23,442	23,206	21,555	20,374	19,719	*
% In One-Unit Structures.	41.6	42.5	49.8	*	*	*
% Owner Occupied........	48.9	45.5	49.1	50.0	42.5	*
% Renter Occupied.......	48.2	52.0	47.8	48.4	54.4	*
% Vacant...............	2.9	2.5	3.1	1.6	3.1	*
1+ Persons per Room....	1.3	3.0	3.0	5.3	6.4	*

Place 4295 -- Oak Park , Illinois
Selected Characteristics of Census Tracts: 1980

Tract Number	Total	8121	8122	8123	8124	8125	8126	8127	8128	8129	8130
Total Population.............	54887	5001	4209	5573	3765	4022	3825	3432	5559	5347	4680
% Male.......................	46.1	48.1	47.8	41.7	46.1	43.3	49.4	44.6	42.8	46.3	48.0
% Black......................	10.8	13.5	1.6	3.1	2.0	22.5	29.5	9.4	7.9	4.2	22.3
% Other Nonwhite.............	4.0	4.0	3.7	2.3	2.0	3.0	4.5	2.5	4.9	4.6	4.7
% Of Spanish Origin..........	2.5	2.0	2.5	2.0	1.3	2.8	2.8	1.7	2.7	2.7	3.5
% Foreign Born...............	7.6	9.2	7.4	7.7	4.6	5.7	4.7	5.6	11.8	8.8	5.6
% Living In Group Quarters...	1.2	0.0	2.0	5.0	0.6	2.3	0.2	0.2	0.0	2.7	0.0
% 13 Years Old And Under.....	17.9	21.9	19.5	10.7	20.0	19.4	17.7	13.5	8.3	19.4	24.9
% 14-20 Years Old............	10.6	10.6	12.2	7.8	14.6	10.8	8.8	10.0	5.8	13.5	12.5
% 21-64 Years Old............	57.3	56.8	52.9	56.2	53.8	56.8	65.6	58.8	62.5	55.5	55.8
% 65-74 Years Old............	7.4	6.2	8.5	11.8	6.5	7.4	4.1	7.2	11.2	6.4	4.2
% 75 Years Old And Over......	6.8	4.4	6.9	13.5	5.2	5.6	3.7	10.5	12.1	5.1	2.7
% In Different House.........	47.1	44.6	38.3	49.5	30.8	59.7	65.1	52.1	64.2	36.4	44.1
% Families With Female Head..	19.5	14.8	9.2	21.6	10.0	26.4	30.4	24.4	35.8	14.2	19.4
Median School Years Completed.	14.5	14.4	15.8	14.3	16.1	14.5	15.3	15.0	14.0	14.3	14.3
Median Family Income, 1979.....$$	27413	28194	38827	27885	37757	24589	23179	25714	23676	27557	26405
% Income Below Poverty Level..	2.8	2.7	0.4	2.3	0.5	5.5	3.2	1.6	2.5	2.5	5.8
% Income Of $30,000 Or More..	42.8	44.6	69.2	42.0	67.8	36.2	34.2	41.4	34.0	39.9	41.2
% White Collar Workers.......	76.9	76.4	86.0	82.8	88.4	71.3	77.5	80.5	79.6	77.5	68.7
% Civilian Labor Force Unemployed.	4.4	3.2	2.3	4.3	3.0	4.4	6.7	7.8	3.8	3.0	6.4
% Riding To Work By Automobile....	62.2	70.6	72.4	57.8	60.6	56.8	61.6	60.8	50.0	63.1	62.1
Mean Commuting Time - Minutes.	27.2	29.7	23.0	26.3	30.3	27.9	28.6	29.5	27.8	25.8	28.2
Population Per Household.........	2.4	2.9	3.0	1.9	3.0	2.3	2.2	2.1	1.6	2.8	3.1
Total Housing Units..........	23438	1760	1398	2896	1256	1802	1850	1763	3587	1901	1558
% Condominiums...............	6.2	0.0	1.5	19.0	2.9	1.8	5.7	13.4	12.4	1.8	0.0
% Built 1970 Or Later........	4.6	1.0	1.1	8.4	2.5	11.6	2.2	6.6	9.9	1.6	1.1
% Owner Occupied.............	48.3	76.1	87.1	40.6	79.9	32.0	24.9	29.3	17.4	64.9	65.0
% With 1+ Persons Per Room...	1.3	1.4	1.0	0.5	0.6	1.2	1.7	0.9	1.0	1.2	2.7
Median Value: Owner Units.......$$	68000	62600	103900	74200	96400	72100	67600	81800	71600	63100	61600
Median Rent: Rental Units.......$$	258	263	253	283	286	232	257	288	254	244	244
Median Number Of Rooms: All Units.	5.1	5.6	5.6	4.7	5.6	4.4	4.4	4.2	3.8	5.6	5.6

Tract Number	8131	8132
Total Population.............	4999	4475
% Male.......................	48.4	47.5
% Black......................	14.5	3.2
% Other Nonwhite.............	6.6	4.8
% Of Spanish Origin..........	3.7	1.7
% Foreign Born...............	8.2	9.0
% Living In Group Quarters...	0.0	0.0
% 13 Years Old And Under.....	21.9	19.9
% 14-20 Years Old............	10.9	11.3
% 21-64 Years Old............	57.4	56.2
% 65-74 Years Old............	5.9	7.1
% 75 Years Old And Over......	3.9	5.6
% In Different House.........	44.1	36.0
% Families With Female Head..	23.7	15.4
Median School Years Completed.	12.8	12.9
Median Family Income, 1979.....$$	22991	25377
% Income Below Poverty Level..	4.9	1.2
% Income Of $30,000 Or More..	30.1	36.7
% White Collar Workers.......	66.0	71.3
% Civilian Labor Force Unemployed.	5.3	2.5
% Riding To Work By Automobile....	69.9	65.2
Mean Commuting Time - Minutes.	25.8	24.4
Population Per Household.........	2.7	2.7
Total Housing Units..........	1974	1693
% Condominiums...............	0.0	0.0
% Built 1970 Or Later........	0.0	0.0
% Owner Occupied.............	55.6	62.8
% With 1+ Persons Per Room...	2.8	1.4
Median Value: Owner Units.......$$	53200	60800
Median Rent: Rental Units.......$$	231	245
Median Number Of Rooms: All Units.	5.3	5.6

donated by Kettlestrings. It soon became a meeting place and was also used for Sunday School and church services. The settlement grew very slowly and by 1870 there were less than 500 residents. The Chicago Fire of the next year led to an increase in population and a small land boom. In 1872 Oak Park gained its own railroad depot (having deprived nearby Harlem of theirs) and the community grew. It was in this year the name Oak Park appeared on the depot and the post office.

Two early settlers of Oak Park were James Scoville and H. W. Austin. In addition to subdividing part of Oak Park, Scoville undertook the installation of a water system in 1878. He also built and endowed the Scoville Institute, completed in 1888. This was a library and civic

center for the community which still stands. Austin was known for his opposition to intoxicating beverages and helped Oak Park resist the establishment of bars and saloons. At one point he bought a saloon from the owner on the spot and dumped the liquor in the street. Austin was not the only prohibitionist among the leaders of Oak Park. Clauses interdicting use for saloons were common features of land deeds in Oak Park and an enactment of the legislature in 1907 conferring local option to enable Oak Park to bar saloons legally was almost superfluous.

By 1877 the Chicago and North Western was running 39 trains daily from Oak Park to Chicago. A decade later there were two more railroads serving Oak Park, giving residents a choice of over 120 daily trains to and from Chicago. Despite the relatively high cost of land in Oak Park the population continued to grow. In 1887 38 percent of the 1,136 residents listed in the community directory had a business there.

Other improvements in the years before incorporation included a police and fire department, drainage and sewers, streets and sidewalks, telephone service, house numbering and gas. In 1885 the township newspaper, the Cicero Vindicator, moved there. By 1902 there were two weekly newspapers serving the community, The Oak Leaves, and the Oak Park Reporter. Oak Park is well-known for 25 residences designed by Frank Lloyd Wright during the years he lived there, including his own home at Forest and Chicago avenues.

Oak Park was not incorporated as a separate entity until 1902. Since 1867 it had been under the jurisdiction of Cicero Township along with Cicero, Austin, Berwyn, and a few smaller settlements. The township law was such that no one unit could vote itself out unilaterally; the entire electorate had to vote on the question. A dispute arose between Austin, Cicero and the other towns, which came to head in an 1898 election on whether Austin should be taken into Chicago. The majority

Oak Park
Selected Characteristics of Census Tracts: 1970

Tract Number	TOTAL	8121	8122	8123	8124	8125	8126	8127	8128	8129	8130
Total Population	62511	5293	4578	6014	4495	4439	4566	4096	6266	6531	5477
% Male	45.1	47.3	46.9	41.7	46.8	42.6	42.8	44.8	41.5	45.4	47.7
% Black	0.2	0.1	0.1	0.1	0.6	0.3	0.1	0.5	0.1	0.1	0.3
% Other Nonwhite	1.0	0.6	0.2	0.8	0.4	1.2	1.1	1.5	1.5	1.3	1.2
% Of Spanish Language	1.9	0.3	2.1	2.8	2.6	4.1	3.5	0.1	2.0	0.7	0.6
% Foreign Born	7.8	10.5	8.2	11.0	6.5	8.0	10.9	7.0	8.0	5.5	4.2
% Living In Group Quarters	1.2	0.0	1.7	4.1	0.6	3.1	0.8	0.5	0.1	2.9	0.0
% 13 Years Old And Under	21.1	21.8	22.0	15.0	26.0	17.4	17.0	18.7	10.8	26.5	28.2
% 14-20 Years Old	10.7	10.9	12.4	8.7	13.5	11.9	9.1	9.8	7.1	13.6	12.4
% 21-64 Years Old	52.0	50.6	50.6	53.5	47.6	54.7	53.3	53.8	59.7	47.7	47.3
% 65-74 Years Old	9.9	10.5	8.9	13.3	7.4	9.1	12.2	10.9	14.3	7.3	7.5
% 75 Years Old And Over	6.4	6.2	6.1	9.4	5.5	6.9	8.3	6.7	8.1	4.9	4.6
% In Different House	54.4	59.3	67.0	39.7	49.9	52.0	57.8	47.9	39.8	56.7	61.0
% Families With Female Head	13.5	10.5	8.8	14.6	10.8	15.4	19.1	15.8	17.1	12.8	12.7
Median School Years Completed	12.8	12.5	13.9	12.9	14.9	12.7	12.7	13.3	12.8	12.7	12.7
Median Family Income, 1969 $$	13823	12902	21321	14399	19805	13199	12538	14918	13957	13420	13517
% Income Below Poverty Level	3.2	3.4	3.3	3.3	1.9	3.5	5.7	1.7	2.7	4.8	1.4
% Income of $15,000 or More	43.0	35.6	70.6	46.7	68.9	38.7	35.0	49.6	43.8	40.8	40.4
% White Collar Workers	49.4	40.6	71.3	53.4	70.5	44.2	53.0	57.5	46.7	44.6	45.8
% Civilian Labor Force Unemployed	2.3	1.9	2.7	1.9	0.8	2.1	2.9	2.1	1.5	3.3	1.3
% Riding To Work By Automobile	57.4	61.1	73.7	54.5	67.7	55.1	45.5	50.9	47.2	57.8	62.9
Population Per Household	2.7	3.0	3.3	2.3	3.4	2.5	2.3	2.5	1.9	3.3	3.4
Total Housing Units	23198	1770	1405	2669	1334	1721	1993	1683	3354	1958	1626
% Condominiums & Cooperatives	1.5	0.3	0.0	6.0	0.0	0.0	1.1	1.7	3.7	0.0	0.0
% Built 1960 Or Later	11.1	4.9	3.4	23.9	3.2	10.4	7.1	27.4	23.4	3.7	3.0
% Owner Occupied	44.1	75.6	86.1	24.1	71.7	34.3	19.7	21.1	8.5	63.0	63.4
% With 1+ Persons Per Room	3.0	2.6	1.6	1.6	3.7	1.9	2.9	2.6	4.6	4.6	4.9
Median Value: Owner Units $$	26200	25300	43100	28200	37300	28200	27500	30900	28000	23900	22900
Median Rent: Rental Units $$	145	140	170	167	152	137	141	177	149	135	140
Median Number Of Rooms: All Units	5.1	5.8	6.8	6.9	4.8	4.2	4.2	3.8	5.9	5.9	

Tract Number	8131	8132
Total Population	5481	5275
% Male	46.6	47.2
% Black	0.3	0.0
% Other Nonwhite	0.9	0.8
% Of Spanish Language	2.5	1.8
% Foreign Born	7.0	6.9
% Living In Group Quarters	0.0	0.0
% 13 Years Old And Under	23.4	26.6
% 14-20 Years Old	9.1	10.0
% 21-64 Years Old	54.0	50.5
% 65-74 Years Old	8.6	8.0
% 75 Years Old And Over	4.9	4.9
% In Different House	59.8	66.1
% Families With Female Head	11.0	12.9
Median School Years Completed	12.3	12.4
Median Family Income, 1969 $$	11668	12514
% Income Below Poverty Level	2.3	1.7
% Income of $15,000 or More	25.2	30.1
% White Collar Workers	35.4	40.5
% Civilian Labor Force Unemployed	3.6	3.3
% Riding To Work By Automobile	62.0	60.5
Population Per Household	2.8	3.1
Total Housing Units	1989	1696
% Condominiums & Cooperatives	0.0	0.0
% Built 1960 Or Later	2.6	1.8
% Owner Occupied	55.6	63.9
% With 1+ Persons Per Room	4.4	4.4
Median Value: Owner Units $$	20800	22800
Median Rent: Rental Units $$	126	131
Median Number Of Rooms: All Units	5.1	5.7

voted for this, but the Superior Court of Illinois declared that annexation unconstitutional. However, in 1899 the Supreme Court of Illinois upheld the incorporation of Austin into Chicago. In 1901 a petition for separation of Oak Park from Cicero was filed; the first board was elected at the end of that year and took office January 1, 1902.

The village prospered, growing in population to 19,444 in 1910 and to 39,858 in 1920. Village officials were concerned about preserving the single-family residential character of the community. To that end Oak Park was the first large suburban community to exercise its prerogatives under state zoning laws. Most of the village was permanently zoned against business, industrial, apartment, and hotel land uses. These zoning restrictions prevented Oak Park from being overrun by industry but left it in a difficult tax position, since large revenues were needed to provide services to the growing number of residents. Industrial land use was only one-third of one percent as late as 1940. Commercial activity grew to accommodate the larger population and the most important shopping area in the 1920s was the Marion, Wisconsin, and Lake Street district. A 1927 announcement that The Hub (a large Chicago department Store) was going to open an outlet in Oak Park heralded the solution to the tax problem. Within the next decade 10 other large retailers followed The Hub into Oak Park. By 1940 Oak Park was the shopping center for Chicago's western suburbs, serving some 500,000 customers.

The 1920s were a time of growth and by 1924 it was estimated there were 6,300 single-family homes, 952 two-flats, 16 three-flats and 76 larger apartment buildings. By 1925 Oak Park was calling itself the "world's largest village." At the end of the 1920s Oak Park had 64,000 residents and was solidly built up. Because of the shortage of vacant land small apartment houses began to appear in several areas.

Unlike many suburbs, Oak Park grew during the 1930s and reached its historic population peak in 1940 with more than 66,000 residents. However, Oak Park did not grow in the years following World War II. There was no industrial base. Housing was in short supply and expensive. All the land around Oak Park was incorporated so that there was none available for expansion, and the available land was already built up. The population dropped to 63,000 in 1950 and to 61,000 in 1960. The new shopping centers in other western suburbs were beginning to take sales from the downtown business district. The existing housing stock was aging and real estate values were in decline. The construction of small apartment structures facilitated a population increase of 1,400 in the 1960s, but Oak Park surrendered its title of largest village to Skokie in 1970.

Oak Park began to change in the 1970s. Exercising another municipal option made available by the latest Illinois Constitution, the village created a special tax district to pay for the reshaping of the downtown area into a shopping mall. The Village Mall, completed in 1974 at a cost of $2.5 million, is a major retail center. A permit was issued for the construction of a 30-story apartment building nearby, and three senior citizen housing complexes were built, culminating in a 19-story center south of the Mall. A new civic center was built on Madison Street, near the eastern city limits. An era came to an end in Oak Park when the serving of liquor in restaurants was legalized.

Beginning in the mid-1950s, whites began moving out of West Side community areas of Chicago, which were nearby, and similar to Oak Park, to be succeeded by blacks. The turnover was rapid and bewildering, accelerated by a now familiar array of panic tactics employed by illegitimate real estate operators. Oak Park had passed a fair housing ordinance in 1968 but, when whites began to move out of blocks adjacent to Chicago and the panic threatened to spread into Oak Park, a concerted effort was commenced by community groups to integrate the village peacefully. The black population had grown from less than 100 individuals to almost 3 percent of the total in 1970. A housing referral service was organized to make it possible for blacks to move in a pattern different from the block-by-block change which had so quickly resegregated the West Side of Chicago. Building maintenance was monitored and code violations were reported in an effort to prevent deterioration and the exploitation of tenants. These measures have not stopped white flight; the total population dropped by almost 8,000 in the 1970s despite an influx of blacks that has made them 11 percent of the current total. However, no census tract in Oak Park has more than 30 percent blacks and there are no visible deteriorating areas that might become centers of poverty in the near future.

Because land availability is always a problem, more rental and condominium apartment buildings are projected. The number of housing units has increased by less than 10 percent in the last 20 years. Almost four-fifths of the current units are in structures built before 1950. The drop in single-family dwellings from 50 to 45 percent of the total units reflects the emphasis on multiple-unit structures in recent construction. Half of the non-vacant units are owner-occupied, and this is about the same as in 1960. Oak Park is a substantial middle-class community, though not a rich one. The median value of single-family homes is $66,300 and the median family income in 1979 was somewhat more than $27,000. Three percent of all families lived in poverty at that time.

While the population of Oak Park declined 12 percent during the last decade the number of households decreased by less than .5 percent. The households are smaller than they were. Almost two-thirds of the total households consist of one or two persons, much as it is in aging suburbs such as Berwyn or Cicero. However, the median age in Oak Park has dropped from 36 to 31 in the last 10 years. The relative number at the extremes of the age distribution, those under 18 or more than 65, is about the same as it was 20 years ago. The growth has been recorded by young adults, ages 25-39, who were 16 percent of the 1970 population, but who are 28 percent of the current total. Many of these are single or married without children. As potential spouses and parents, they could enlarge the households and revive population growth in Oak Park in the 1980s.

Gail Danks Welter
M.W.H.

Place 4465

Palatine

Palatine is located in the northwestern part of Cook County, approximately 30 miles from the Loop. It is bounded by Arlington Heights on the east, Rolling Meadows and Schaumburg on the south, Inverness on the west, and forest preserves and unincorporated land on the north. Before permanent settlement began, the Pottawatomie Indians traveled through the area. Although there is no evidence of permanent Indian villages, well-established trails existed along the routes of what are now Rand and Algonquin roads. The Indians were removed from the area after the Black Hawk War, but they continued to return occasionally to visit their burial grounds through the 1840s.

As the Indians left, white settlers from New England began to arrive. They were attracted by the relatively open land, with good soil for farming, interspersed with woodland groves which provided fuel and building material. The early residents built in the four groves which existed in the area: Deer Grove in the north, Plum Grove in the southeast, Highland Grove in the southwest, and Englishman's Grove (now the village of Inverness) in the western part of the township. George Ela, who came from Lebanon, New Hampshire, and settled in Deer Grove in 1835, was the first white man to build in the area. By the 1840s, there were small settlements in all of the groves. The residents organized schools and worship services. In Plum Grove there was a tavern, Wickliffe House, which was used by many travelers on Algonquin Road. Most of the grove settlers were from the eastern United States, though some of these had come from England, Scotland and Ireland. Plum Grove was settled almost entirely by people from the area around Stockbridge, Vermont. However, later settlers were predominantly German.

Palatine township was organized in 1850 in accord with Illinois state law. Its name was suggested by a man who had moved to the area from Palatine, New York. The village of Palatine came into being when the Chicago and North Western Railroad (then called the Illinois and Wisconsin) began to extend its line past Arlington Heights in 1853. At first the train stopped in Deer Grove, but the grade was so steep that the trains which stopped there couldn't regain enough power to go on to Barrington. Three alternate sites were considered. Two area residents, Joel Wood and Mason Sutherland, brought the railroad to the site of present-day Palatine by raising $10,000 to buy stock in the company. Many of the buildings in Deer Grove, including the post office, were moved to the new location. A depot was built in 1855. In the same year, Wood platted the village and donated land for a school, cemetery and churches, and Elisha Pratt moved his store to the right-of-way south of

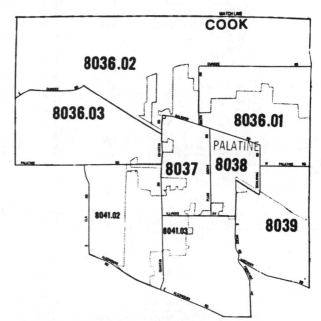

the track and became the first merchant in Palatine. A grist mill was established, but it operated for only a short time.

After the arrival of the railroad, the village of Palatine began to develop. The first church was organized in 1857 and a schoolhouse was built in 1860. A high school was organized in 1876 by Charles Cutting, principal of the grade school. Students came from the entire area between Woodstock and Jefferson Park.

Palatine incorporated as a village in 1866 and was chartered in 1869. The villagers adopted a trustee form of government, which has continued to the present. Until the 1920s, the town served primarily as the business center for the surrounding farming community. It contained flax and flour mills, a planing mill and lumber yard, grain elevators and a freight depot, and numerous small businesses such as wagon and blacksmith shops and hardware and drug stores. In 1871, the Chicago Fire destroyed Henry Godkneckt's cigar-making business and he moved the enterprise to Palatine. By 1884 the village had a population of 1,000.

Around the turn of the century, Palatine began to urbanize, with the introduction of gas, telephone and oiled gravel streets. Also in the early 1900s, Palatine citizens began to promote the idea of an interurban railroad that would connect Palatine with the Lake County resort area. The Palatine, Lake Zurich and Wauconda Railroad began operation in 1911. For the next few years the steam engine, nicknamed "Maud," carried thousands of Chicago area people from Palatine to Deer Grove,

Palatine
Population and Housing Characteristics, 1930-1980

	1980	1970	1960	1950	1940	1930
Total Population	32,166	25,904	11,504	4,079	2,222	2,118
% Male	49.1	49.3	48.6	49.0	49.5	50.0
% Female	50.9	50.7	51.4	51.0	50.5	50.0
% White	97.1	99.4	99.8	100.0	100.0	100.0
% Black	0.3	0.1	0.0	0.0	0.0	0.0
% Other Nonwhite Races	2.6	0.5	0.2	0.0	0.0	0.0
% Under 5 Years Old	5.7	10.2	14.0	14.5	6.7	8.2
% 5-19 Years Old	28.3	36.5	29.7	20.0	*	*
% 20-44 Years Old	38.9	33.4	36.2	39.3	*	*
% 45-64 Years Old	20.6	15.5	14.7	19.0	21.0	21.6
% 65 Years and Older	6.5	4.4	5.3	7.2	9.7	7.1
Median School Years	13.7	12.8	12.4	12.2	*	*
Total Housing Units	11,092	6,902	3,215	1,175	*	*
% In One-Unit Structures	68.3	84.8	84.8	80.0	*	*
% Owner Occupied	71.3	79.6	79.8	78.1	*	*
% Renter Occupied	24.5	17.3	15.9	21.9	*	*
% Vacant	4.2	3.1	4.3	-	*	*
% 1+ Persons per Room	1.0	3.8	7.0	5.9	*	*

Place 4465 -- Palatine, Illinois
Selected Characteristics of Census Tracts: 1980

Tract Number	Total	8036.01	8036.02	8036.03	8037	8038	8039	8041.02	8041.03
Total Population	32166	12816	1684	7	6548	4569	2338	3724	480
% Male	49.1	49.6	48.0	—	48.7	48.9	47.7	49.5	50.2
% Black	0.3	0.4	1.1	—	0.2	0.1	0.1	0.5	0.0
% Other Nonwhite	2.6	1.9	2.8	—	3.6	2.8	2.1	3.0	6.0
% Of Spanish Origin	1.9	0.8	2.6	—	3.8	3.1	1.5	1.1	0.2
% Foreign Born	6.7	4.6	12.4	—	7.8	8.0	10.4	5.6	9.6
% Living In Group Quarters	0.8	1.4	0.0	—	0.9	0.2	0.0	0.0	0.0
% 13 Years Old And Under	21.2	23.6	8.6	—	18.4	18.5	14.8	29.0	34.2
% 14-20 Years Old	14.3	17.7	3.9	—	11.9	11.8	10.2	18.0	9.0
% 21-64 Years Old	58.0	54.9	80.6	—	60.0	59.4	63.2	50.5	55.8
% 65-74 Years Old	3.6	1.8	5.0	—	4.9	6.8	7.5	1.0	0.6
% 75 Years Old And Over	2.9	2.0	1.9	—	4.7	3.5	4.3	1.4	0.4
% In Different House	49.0	40.6	90.9	—	53.3	41.7	49.0	54.6	100.0
% Families With Female Head	8.1	6.5	24.4	—	10.5	11.7	13.2	2.6	1.0
Median School Years Completed	13.7	14.3	14.9	—	13.0	12.9	12.8	15.9	14.6
Median Family Income, 1979 $$	33443	36870	28601	—	27752	28877	30560	49956	50254
% Income Below Poverty Level	1.6	0.6	0.0	—	2.1	4.1	2.3	1.1	0.0
% Income Of $30,000 Or More	60.8	71.7	44.8	—	43.7	46.2	51.9	86.1	100.0
% White Collar Workers	73.2	76.7	79.7	—	64.4	65.4	71.6	88.2	70.7
% Civilian Labor Force Unemployed	3.8	3.2	2.7	—	4.0	4.1	7.0	3.7	0.0
% Riding To Work By Automobile	84.0	84.8	83.4	—	82.2	84.1	81.4	89.2	73.2
Mean Commuting Time - Minutes	27.8	28.2	31.6	—	24.2	26.5	28.8	30.0	38.1
Population Per Household	3.0	3.6	1.8	—	2.6	2.8	2.3	4.2	3.8
Total Housing Units	11091	3769	1013	2	2528	1659	1077	909	134
% Condominiums	9.7	2.0	19.8	—	1.8	0.8	68.5	0.0	0.0
% Built 1970 Or Later	36.2	27.1	82.3	—	19.9	4.5	67.2	81.7	100.0
% Owner Occupied	71.3	80.6	21.6	—	58.0	79.9	78.6	97.4	94.0
% With 1+ Persons Per Room	1.0	0.6	0.6	—	1.8	1.2	1.1	0.3	0.0
Median Value: Owner Units $$	88900	93300	84000	—	76200	68700	83000	134100	165800
Median Rent: Rental Units $$	327	345	366	—	277	275	340	501	—
Median Number Of Rooms: All Units	5.6	5.6	3.7	—	5.3	5.6	4.8	5.6	5.6

Palatine
Selected Characteristics of Census Tracts: 1970

Tract Number	TOTAL	8036	8037	8038	8039	8041
Total Population	26050	20660	7517	5123	7077	8468
% Male	49.3	50.2	48.7	49.1	49.5	50.1
% Black	0.1	0.1	0.0	0.0	0.0	0.1
% Other Nonwhite	0.6	0.5	0.4	0.5	0.3	0.5
% Of Spanish Language	0.9	1.6	1.2	2.7	2.8	2.3
% Foreign Born	3.8	3.5	4.0	7.0	3.3	4.5
% Living In Group Quarters	0.3	0.3	0.8	0.3	0.0	1.6
% 13 Years Old And Under	34.8	37.7	28.9	27.8	33.3	30.4
% 14-20 Years Old	12.9	12.4	13.9	13.1	12.9	11.8
% 21-64 Years Old	47.9	46.8	50.2	52.2	50.5	53.0
% 65-74 Years Old	2.8	2.0	4.0	4.6	2.4	3.0
% 75 Years Old And Over	1.7	1.1	3.0	2.3	1.0	1.8
% In Different House	44.7	39.7	50.0	63.7	54.5	39.3
% Families With Female Head	4.4	2.5	6.9	6.0	4.6	2.9
Median School Years Completed	12.8	12.9	12.5	12.6	12.5	12.9
Median Family Income, 1969 $$	16072	17493	14687	14114	13298	19412
% Income Below Poverty Level	2.2	1.8	3.8	2.1	1.8	1.2
% Income of $15,000 or More	54.6	60.9	48.1	43.4	34.9	69.5
% White Collar Workers	50.5	55.9	43.5	40.3	34.0	57.9
% Civilian Labor Force Unemployed	2.2	2.1	1.4	3.3	2.1	2.3
% Riding To Work By Automobile	78.0	78.1	79.8	73.3	86.1	81.6
Population Per Household	3.9	4.2	3.4	3.4	3.8	3.5
Total Housing Units	6901	5086	2265	1538	1898	2683
% Condominiums & Cooperatives	0.0	0.0	0.0	0.0	0.0	2.5
% Built 1960 Or Later	54.8	66.0	42.4	14.0	18.6	73.5
% Owner Occupied	79.6	89.3	62.8	80.7	85.3	69.1
% With 1+ Persons Per Room	3.8	3.4	5.2	5.4	9.3	2.8
Median Value: Owner Units $$	32900	38800	28900	25600	23200	45600
Median Rent: Rental Units $$	169	154	167	164	182	177
Median Number Of Rooms: All Units	6.6	7.2	5.4	5.5	5.2	6.7

Lake Zurich and Wauconda for weekend outings. However, as automobiles and paved roads became more common, the railroad faced increasing financial difficulties, and it was dissolved in 1920. The Cook County Fairgrounds were located in Palatine from 1913 until the early 1930s, and the fair drew many visitors from the surrounding area.

The increasingly easy transportation to Chicago led to a period of rapid real estate development in the 1920s. The population of Palatine increased from 1,210 in 1920 to 2,213 in 1930. Sewers and concrete streets and sidewalks were built. However, the Depression ended the building boom, leaving many of the developing areas deserted. During the 1930s, the area became a truck farming center. Mexican laborers came to work on the farms, and some of them stayed to live in Palatine.

Following World War II, suburban development started again, and Palatine began to develop as a commuter suburb. Delinquent subdivisions were rebuilt and new development continued. The decades since the 1950s have been a period of tremendous increase in population, as the village has grown from 4,000 in 1950 to more than 30,000 in 1980. Palatine has matured as an upper-middle income community. The median family income was more than $33,000 in 1979, and more than three-fifths of all families earned incomes in excess of $30,000.

Two percent of the families reported incomes below the poverty line. Almost three-fourths of all workers are white-collar, and 4 percent of the labor force was unemployed in 1980. The current population is 97 percent white. Two percent are Hispanic and 4 percent were born abroad. Since 1960, the number of housing units has increased at a faster rate than the number of residents. More than a third of all housing has been built in the most recent decade. Overcrowding, a minor problem in the 1950s, has dropped to 1 percent from 7. Housing in Palatine contains a three-to-one mixture of single- and multi-family homes, more than 70 percent owner-occupied.

Many residents work in Chicago, though some light industry provides employment opportunities in the village. Sellstrom's was one of the first manufacturers to move to the area in the early 1960s. Palatine's present industrial area is located mainly west of Hicks Road. The world headquarters of Square D Company, which manufactures electrical equipment, employs more than 20,000 people. The village is encouraging further development of office-research complexes and light

industry, but taking care to preserve its mainly residential character. Currently, about 250 acres are zoned for industrial development.

Palatine has a downtown retail area and three outlying shopping malls. A federally-financed program has been utilized for some rehabilitation of the downtown area. In recent years, because of diminishing water well supplies, the village has been working to obtain Lake Michigan water via a pipeline consortium with neighboring municipalities. This project should be completed by 1984. Palatine is the site of Harper College, a two-year community college. The North Western Railroad provides transportation to the city. The village has built a commuter center at the center of town with station, shops and parking. It has also developed a community center, in a vacated high school campus, which houses the village administration and police department, park district offices, some recreational facilities and a theater. The Palatine Historical Society is housed nearby in a restored home, built in 1873, which has been listed in the National Register of Historic Places.

Marjorie DeVault

Park Forest

Park Forest is built on 3,000 acres of land, mostly in Cook County, approximately 27 miles south and slightly west of the Loop. Park Forest was a completely planned community, developed to meet the immediate post World War II needs of veterans by building reasonably priced rental apartments. In 1947 a group of four entrepreneurs headed by Philip Klutznick formed a corporation called American Community Builders. Their aim was to erect a complete community for middle income familes with all housing elements, a shopping center and an industrial park. It was served by a commuter railroad, the Illinois Central, which could reach the Loop in 38 minutes. This made Park Forest an attractive place to the first wave of colonists, who were academics, professional people and young, mobile corporate executives, 60 percent of whom worked in the Loop.

When the first houses were opened in 1948, the multi-family rental units were clustered in courts on winding streets with large open space. They were islands in a sea of mud but large numbers of young migrants kept coming from Chicago. The townhouse area contained 3,010 dwelling units or 11 dwellings per acre. The turnover of residents in the rental areas in those early days was nearly 35 percent yearly. The typical residents were 31 years old, with a college education, the parents of two children.

Soon after the first housing, Park Forest Plaza was constructed, the first mall-type regional shopping center in the midwest, strategically planned in the center of Park Forest. At one time there were 60 shops in the plaza.

The first census in 1950 showed a population of 8,000. Within two years there were 16,000 residents, 40 percent of whom were younger than 14 years, and the median age was 26 years. Twelve hundred single-family residences were completed in one year. Population increased 270 percent from 1950 to 1960, at which time it stood at almost 30,000, almost half of which was less than 18 years old. Park Forest was incorporated as a village in 1949. Since 1951, the village has had a council-manager form of government. During the 1950s three key bond issues provided for the construction of Village Hall, building of the public garage works, Westwood Recreation Building and construction of a library. Building and capital development became less of an issue in the 1960s and by 1961 the pace of building had decelerated.

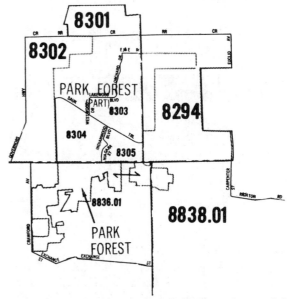

Land to the south of the village, acquired in 1955, was later made into a green belt area. Of the original 3,010 townhouses, 1,998 sold as cooperative units in the early 1960s. The remainder are rental and condominium units. A group representing 22 Protestant denominations organized the United Protestant Church.

The 1970 population was 30,638, the historic high, but the baby boom in Park Forest had passed. The elementary schools in the village had enrolled 1,100 kindergarten pupils in 1960 and added no more than 600 pupils in any year between 1969-1972. The decade that followed 1970 brought problems of racial change, aging of housing, the press of urbanization, and the lack of adequate transportation. The village budget totalled $6 million in 1970 including $1 million spent for a new commuter parking lot. In 1976, Freedom Hall, a bicentennial building, was formally dedicated as a cultural and community center.

In 1951, the Commission on Human Relations was founded to consider steps necessary to integrate the village racially; however, the desire for integration was by no means unanimous. The first black family did not move in until 1959. The 1960 census counted eight black residents in Park Forest, and there were nearly 700 10 years later. In three years between 1970 and 1973, Park Forest's black population increased from two to 7 percent. Most of the increase occurred in the townhouses. Park Forest School District 163 implemented mandatory

Park Forest
Population and Housing Characteristics, 1930-1980

	1980	1970	1960	1950	1940	1930
Total Population.......	26,222	30,638	29,993	8,138	*	*
% Male...................	48.4	49.4	49.8	50.7	*	*
% Female.................	51.6	50.6	50.2	49.3	*	*
% White..................	84.7	96.6	99.4	99.8	*	*
% Black..................	12.1	2.3	0.0	0.1	*	*
% Other Nonwhite Races...	3.2	1.1	0.6	0.1	*	*
% Under 5 Years Old......	8.3	11.5	18.8	25.3	*	*
% 5-19 Years Old.........	26.4	33.4	30.2	16.2	*	*
% 20-44 Years Old........	39.8	35.6	41.2	53.7	*	*
% 45-64 Years Old........	19.7	16.3	8.2	4.0	*	*
% 65 Years and Older.....	5.8	3.2	1.6	0.8	*	*
Median School Years....	13.4	12.8	13.5	14.7	*	*
Total Housing Units....	9,247	8,542	7,841	2,705	*	*
% In One-Unit Structures.	81.0	89.5	98.9	*	*	*
% Owner Occupied.........	61.9	76.7	56.3	0.4	*	*
% Renter Occupied........	35.9	22.1	39.6	84.7	*	*
% Vacant.................	2.2	1.2	4.1	14.7	*	*
% 1+ Persons per Room....	1.6	4.2	7.2	2.4	*	*

Place 4535 — Park Forest , Illinois
Selected Characteristics of Census Tracts: 1980

Tract Number	Total	8294	8301	8302	8303	8304	8305	8836.01	8838.01
Total Population.............	26222	4744	3892	3415	5583	3711	1566	2370	941
% Male.........................	48.4	47.8	49.6	49.1	47.4	49.1	48.0	49.5	43.6
% Black........................	12.1	17.0	10.9	10.4	14.2	5.6	5.1	8.2	33.7
% Other Nonwhite..............	3.1	2.7	3.4	2.3	2.6	1.9	2.8	2.1	18.7
% Of Spanish Origin...........	2.4	2.9	1.6	2.0	2.6	2.2	2.7	2.7	3.7
% Foreign Born................	4.4	3.7	4.4	4.6	4.4	3.5	6.7	2.4	13.3
% Living In Group Quarters....	1.8	0.0	0.0	13.6	0.0	0.0	0.0	0.0	0.0
% 13 Years Old And Under......	23.3	27.7	22.3	21.7	22.0	21.3	18.7	24.4	32.8
% 14-20 Years Old.............	12.9	10.9	16.5	21.7	10.4	10.3	10.1	10.8	11.3
% 21-64 Years Old.............	58.0	57.2	58.1	53.8	58.9	61.3	61.0	60.8	45.9
% 65-74 Years Old.............	3.8	2.9	1.9	2.2	5.0	5.0	6.8	2.6	6.3
% 75 Years Old And Over.......	2.0	1.2	1.2	0.6	3.8	2.1	3.4	1.4	3.7
% In Different House..........	46.1	46.8	39.2	39.3	57.5	36.0	32.1	53.1	78.1
% Families With Female Head...	18.2	24.3	8.8	11.7	25.1	12.9	8.8	12.5	49.1
Median School Years Completed....	13.4	13.0	14.9	14.3	13.1	12.9	13.3	13.0	12.5
Median Family Income, 1979.....$$	25156	22986	33949	28538	21753	24739	27235	25771	10203
% Income Below Poverty Level..	3.4	3.2	0.8	2.5	3.5	3.5	2.2	2.8	22.9
% Income Of $30,000 Or More....	36.1	28.2	64.1	46.3	25.2	31.4	40.2	35.8	3.1
% White Collar Workers........	68.9	64.7	79.0	73.4	67.0	61.2	67.2	72.3	71.0
% Civilian Labor Force Unemployed.	5.0	5.0	3.0	5.8	6.7	3.3	3.1	6.7	7.5
% Riding To Work By Automobile....	78.6	78.9	74.7	76.0	75.1	85.9	84.5	80.5	75.2
Mean Commuting Time - Minutes.	30.1	31.7	33.1	28.4	30.4	27.7	28.7	28.4	30.9
Population Per Household.........	2.9	2.9	3.4	3.3	2.5	2.8	2.7	2.9	2.6
Total Housing Units..........	9247	1679	1153	899	2333	1356	579	876	372
% Condominiums................	6.6	11.9	0.0	0.0	12.6	0.0	0.0	11.4	4.0
% Built 1970 Or Later.........	6.7	0.0	0.5	2.1	5.4	0.5	0.0	19.5	84.7
% Owner Occupied..............	61.5	41.8	96.6	93.3	35.1	82.3	87.7	67.4	0.0
% With 1+ Persons Per Room.....	1.6	2.5	0.8	1.7	0.9	1.3	1.2	1.8	6.1
Median Value: Owner Units.....$$	49500	34900	64400	57200	44900	44700	47700	47700	-
Median Rent: Rental Units......$$	223	193	446	364	213	331	324	320	275
Median Number Of Rooms: All Units.	5.6	5.5	5.6	5.6	5.2	5.3	5.6	5.4	4.0

Park Forest
Selected Characteristics of Census Tracts: 1970

Tract Number	TOTAL	8294	8301	8302	8303	8304	8305	8836	8838
Total Population.............	30638	7291	4872	6183	6948	5419	1101	7240	11517
% Male.........................	49.4	50.3	50.8	49.2	48.4	48.0	49.3	50.2	50.3
% Black........................	2.3	8.8	1.0	1.0	3.6	1.9	0.3	1.3	0.0
% Other Nonwhite..............	1.2	1.1	3.0	0.5	0.9	0.4	2.1	0.8	0.2
% Of Spanish Language.........	1.6	5.9	1.5	1.2	1.7	0.3	0.0	1.7	2.1
% Foreign Born................	4.7	6.2	4.0	3.4	5.1	3.3	5.5	3.3	2.6
% Living In Group Quarters........	0.0	0.2	0.0	0.0	0.0	0.0	0.0	0.0	0.0
% 13 Years Old And Under......	33.5	37.1	36.3	30.4	32.0	30.4	25.4	34.7	32.1
% 14-20 Years Old.............	12.4	10.0	16.1	16.2	10.0	12.3	14.1	11.8	12.5
% 21-64 Years Old.............	50.9	50.7	46.0	49.7	53.5	53.0	55.1	49.4	49.9
% 65-74 Years Old.............	2.0	1.5	0.9	2.1	3.0	2.6	3.3	2.5	3.5
% 75 Years Old And Over.......	1.2	0.7	0.7	1.6	1.5	1.6	2.1	1.6	2.0
% In Different House..........	43.4	34.9	51.4	52.0	35.0	51.2	57.5	53.5	55.9
% Families With Female Head......	5.7	6.2	2.5	6.4	8.2	5.5	5.8	4.2	4.6
Median School Years Completed......	13.1	12.8	14.6	12.9	12.9	12.8	15.1	12.5	12.1
Median Family Income, 1969......$$	13951	11782	19283	15569	12381	12889	14250	13089	12356
% Income Below Poverty Level....	2.8	4.1	0.8	1.0	2.5	4.4	5.6	4.0	3.2
% Income of $15,000 or More....	43.3	30.0	74.1	52.3	31.3	35.4	46.6	37.7	31.4
% White Collar Workers........	59.4	49.9	71.7	53.3	58.7	49.4	59.5	45.8	27.5
% Civilian Labor Force Unemployed.	2.7	2.5	2.2	4.7	2.4	2.8	1.1	2.8	2.4
% Riding To Work By Automobile....	69.5	74.2	66.5	72.9	69.2	66.7	68.2	80.5	89.0
Population Per Household.........	3.6	3.6	4.4	3.8	3.2	3.4	3.3	3.7	3.7
Total Housing Units..........	8541	2041	1125	1690	2187	1594	343	1993	3204
% Condominiums & Cooperatives.....	18.1	46.7	0.0	3.3	24.6	3.5	0.0	0.0	0.0
% Built 1960 Or Later.........	10.1	9.5	66.1	13.8	1.2	1.2	0.0	28.1	33.4
% Owner Occupied..............	58.6	31.0	97.2	80.0	23.0	81.4	89.8	79.9	83.0
% With 1+ Persons Per Room......	4.2	3.7	2.0	5.6	3.0	6.0	2.1	6.3	7.8
Median Value: Owner Units.......$$	21100	16100	30000	22600	21500	17500	19300	20000	20000
Median Rent: Rental Units.......$$	143	130	255	139	141	152	150	134	103
Median Number Of Rooms: All Units.	5.6	5.3	7.3	6.0	5.2	5.1	5.4	5.7	5.6

busing in 1973 after part of adjacent Chicago Heights resegregated rapidly. In 1974, the village board passed ordinances which set up a fair housing review board. Today, 12 percent of the residents are black. They live in every area of Park Forest and there is no concentration.

In the most recent decade, the population of Park Forest dropped by 14 percent to 26,000. Some of this is attributable to the outmigration of children who have come of age, although almost a third of the total are less than 18 years old. The largest group of residents today is between 25-34 years of age. In 1950, Park Forest had only 68 residents who were 65 years or older. By 1980, they had 2,922.

Except for the forest preserve property on the southern boundaries of the village, most open space around the village has been developed. The changing age structure and limited expansion potential have curbed population growth. Upward mobility has become a factor in moving out of Park Forest to suburbs where higher priced homes are available.

Park Forest is a middle-class community. The median family income is more than $25,000, a third of all families earned incomes of $30,000 or more in 1979, while three percent were unable to exceed the poverty level. Sixty-nine percent of the labor force works in white-collar occupations, 44 percent is female, 24 percent works in Chicago, and five percent is unemployed. The median value of owner-occupied single-family homes is $2,000 greater than the Chicago median.

Today, Park Forest is still a very visually attractive community with shaded, ground-hugging homes on curved, landscaped streets. There are nineteen parks totalling more than 275 acres. Of the 9,200 housing units in the village, 90 percent are in single-family dwellings and 61 percent are owner-occupied. The construction pace has slowed; only 7 percent of all units were built in the last 10 years.

In June 1983, the Park Forest Plaza was purchased for rehabilitation and expansion. Although it is a major retail center, the plaza has been in difficulty for a decade with the opening of Lincoln Mall and other suburban shopping centers. It is particularly important to the village because of the revenue it provides. The industrial site planned for the north edge of town has never developed as hoped. Some small firms are still located there. Twice recognized as an All American City (1953 and

1977) by the National Muncipal League, Park Forest is one of the most written about communities in the United States. There are hundreds of volunteers active on 20 or more village advisory boards; a unique spirit of volunteerism still exists. Aunt Martha's Youth Service Center, Inc., now located in the plaza, is a not-for-profit volunteer counseling agency serving teens and their families which began in 1972 and now has a $1.5 million annual budget. In 1978, a grass roots campaign raised $144,000 to landscape Freedom Hall. Most recently, School District 163 passed a $30,000 per year bond issue, unusual today. Park Forest continues to be noted for its physical resources, community facilities and excellent schools. It is experiencing problems that affect many urban communities, increasing costs and declining revenue base. The racial integration of Park Forest will continue to be a dynamic force in its development.

Patricia Booth Levenberg

Place 4540

Park Ridge

Park Ridge is in Cook County, adjacent to the northwest corner of Chicago, adjoining O'Hare Field, Des Plaines, and Niles, 18 miles from the Loop. The ridge on which it is located is one of the highest points in the county.

The first inhabitants of the area were Indians. They were forced out by the terms of the treaty that closed the Black Hawk War. The opening of the Erie Canal, which connected the Atlantic Ocean with the Great Lakes, and the end of the War of 1812, which removed the threat of harrassment by British troops, stimulated migration from the densely populated East. New settlers began to farm in the areas surrounding the growing city of Chicago.

Park Ridge, which was first called Smith's Ridge, was settled by New England and upstate New York farmers. One of the first to arrive in the area was Captain Mancel Talcott and his son, Mancel Junior. Talcott's farm was located in what is now the uptown section of Park Ridge. Responding to the call of the gold fields of California the younger Talcott went and returned a wealthy man. He started a stone business, became involved in banking in Chicago, and eventually became a member of the Chicago City Council.

During the 1840s more settlers came to the ridge to establish farms. Generally, the settlers who came were New Englanders. others were from the German city states. However, the New England influence on the area was so strong that when townships were established, this township was called Maine after the New England state.

George Penny came in 1853, looking for clay suitable for brickmaking. He found both the clay and a business partner, Robert Meacham, a fellow New Englander, who lived on Smith's ridge. They developed the clay pits and a brickyard, which were located near the present center of town The salmon-colored bricks were shipped to Chicago. In its peak period the brickyard and its 125 employees produced five million bricks a year.

Penny and Meacham needed a fast, cheap way to get their bricks to market in Chicago. Their answer seemed to be in the extension of the Illinois and Wisconsin Railroad (Chicago and North Western). There was no station planned for the brickmaking community, which was called Pennyville. However, Penny convinced the railroad officials to have two daily train stops. In return, he had to build the station and maintain it for ten years. Penny, a modest man, decided that the name

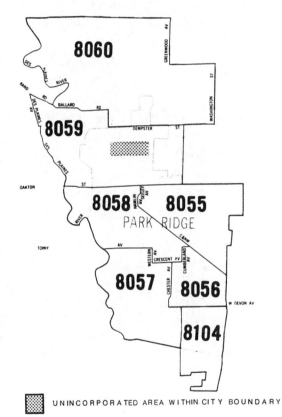

UNINCORPORATED AREA WITHIN CITY BOUNDARY

of the community should be changed. In 1858, the little settlement was renamed Brickton.

Some churches that still serve the community were founded in the early period. An Episcopal congregation (now St. Mary's) and a Methodist (First United Methodist) were founded during the 1850s. The Methodists built a church whose steeple could be seen for miles around because of the elevation of the ridge. Growth in the tiny community seemed to have slowed during the Civil War. As the War ended in 1865 so did the Penny and Meacham Brick Company. The clay pits were nearly exhausted and within a few years the business petered out. Residents raised vegetables and poultry, and a few commuters worked in Chicago. Following the War, several members of Chicago's affluent class built summer homes in Brickton. One of these was George B. Carpenter.

The three-day Fire that nearly destroyed the entire North Side of Chicago brought large numbers of people into the northwest area.

Park Ridge
Population and Housing Characteristics, 1930-1980

	1980	1970	1960	1950	1940	1930
Total Population.......	38,704	42,466	32,659	16,602	12,062	10,417
% Male..................	47.6	47.6	48.3	47.9	47.8	48.6
% Female................	52.4	52.4	51.7	52.1	52.2	51.4
% White.................	98.1	99.4	99.9	99.9	99.9	99.9
% Black.................	0.2	0.1	0.0	0.1	0.1	0.1
% Other Nonwhite Races...	1.7	0.5	0.0	0.0	0.0	—
% Under 5 Years Old......	4.2	6.1	9.8	8.6	5.7	8.9
% 5-19 Years Old.........	23.7	30.5	29.0	23.9	26.6	26.7
% 20-44 Years Old........	30.3	27.1	29.1	33.4	38.5	42.3
% 45-64 Years Old........	28.4	26.8	24.8	27.1	23.3	17.4
% 65 Years and Older.....	13.4	9.5	7.3	7.0	5.9	4.7
Median School Years....	13.3	12.6	12.6	12.4	12.2	*
Total Housing Units....	13,538	13,191	9,670	4,888	3,280	*
% In One-Unit Structures.	80.1	78.7	91.0	*	*	*
% Owner Occupied........	85.0	80.1	86.8	85.3	66.5	*
% Renter Occupied........	14.1	17.7	9.3	12.7	32.1	*
% Vacant................	0.9	2.2	3.9	2.0	1.4	*
% 1+ Persons per Room....	1.1	2.9	3.4	2.7	*	*

Place 4540 — Park Ridge, Illinois
Selected Characteristics of Census Tracts: 1980

Tract Number	Total	8055	8056	8057	8058	8059	8060	8104
Total Population.............	38704	7557	5071	7574	7726	5827	599	4350
% Male......................	47.6	47.4	48.4	48.1	47.4	46.8	44.7	48.3
% Black.....................	0.2	0.0	0.0	0.1	0.0	0.5	0.2	0.5
% Other Nonwhite............	1.8	1.6	1.3	1.5	1.8	2.3	4.3	2.1
% Of Spanish Origin.........	0.9	1.1	0.8	0.7	0.5	0.9	2.5	1.2
% Foreign Born..............	8.1	7.5	5.1	5.4	9.9	12.6	17.5	6.3
% Living In Group Quarters..	1.4	0.8	0.0	0.0	0.0	0.3	0.0	0.9
% 13 Years Old And Under....	16.2	16.7	20.1	14.8	13.9	15.5	13.0	18.4
% 14-20 Years Old...........	13.2	13.2	14.5	13.1	12.4	13.5	9.0	13.6
% 21-64 Years Old...........	57.2	55.7	54.9	58.4	60.1	57.0	62.8	54.8
% 65-74 Years Old...........	8.3	8.5	6.0	9.2	8.4	7.3	8.8	8.5
% 75 Years Old And Over.....	5.3	6.0	4.5	4.4	5.1	6.6	6.3	4.7
% In Different House........	31.5	32.4	22.6	29.8	32.3	38.5	28.9	32.4
% Families With Female Head.	8.7	8.7	8.7	8.8	9.2	9.0	15.0	6.9
Median School Years Completed.	13.3	13.6	14.0	13.9	13.0	13.6	12.8	13.4
Median Family Income, 1979.....$$	34131	34748	31496	35716	32830	34477	26667	36371
% Income Below Poverty Level....	1.3	1.8	1.9	0.8	1.1	1.3	3.9	0.9
% Income Of $30,000 Or More.....	61.3	64.6	54.7	65.1	57.7	60.9	34.3	67.3
% White Collar Workers........	77.2	77.9	75.1	82.5	77.5	72.6	75.3	74.5
% Civilian Labor Force Unemployed.	2.7	1.8	3.6	2.6	3.0	3.0	0.0	2.9
% Riding To Work By Automobile...	79.0	75.6	75.5	82.1	80.6	77.5	67.8	83.5
Mean Commuting Time - Minutes...	27.2	29.6	27.2	24.2	27.3	28.8	26.9	26.6
Population Per Household.........	2.9	2.8	3.2	2.7	2.7	3.0	2.3	3.0
Total Housing Units...........	13535	2706	1600	2821	2871	1813	288	1436
% Condominiums...............	7.9	1.2	1.1	22.7	11.2	3.5	0.0	0.0
% Built 1970 Or Later........	7.6	4.7	1.1	8.7	10.3	14.7	8.0	3.5
% Owner Occupied.............	84.2	78.5	90.2	89.1	85.0	80.6	33.3	91.5
% With 1+ Persons Per Room......	1.1	1.4	1.1	0.6	0.9	1.5	2.6	1.2
Median Value: Owner Units.......$$	92900	99400	89900	95600	88200	100800	111900	85500
Median Rent: Rental Units......$$	298	277	285	425	291	324	296	262
Median Number Of Rooms: All Units.	5.6	5.6	5.6	5.6	5.6	5.6	4.3	5.6

Park Ridge
Selected Characteristics of Census Tracts: 1970

Tract Number	TOTAL	8055	8056	8057	8058	8059	8060	8104
Total Population.............	42614	8344	6268	5868	9194	9388	22462	5054
% Male......................	47.6	47.2	48.1	48.9	48.2	47.2	48.6	47.5
% Black.....................	0.1	0.2	0.0	0.0	0.0	0.1	0.2	0.0
% Other Nonwhite............	0.6	0.5	0.5	0.4	0.3	1.0	0.6	0.3
% Of Spanish Language.......	1.0	0.5	0.9	0.2	1.7	1.0	1.8	1.6
% Foreign Born..............	5.8	4.8	5.9	3.6	6.6	6.3	7.5	5.6
% Living In Group Quarters..	1.0	1.9	0.1	0.0	0.6	2.3	1.5	0.4
% 13 Years Old And Under....	24.8	23.6	28.9	22.7	24.0	27.2	28.4	25.8
% 14-20 Years Old...........	13.0	13.0	13.0	12.5	13.2	12.8	8.5	12.8
% 21-64 Years Old...........	52.7	52.0	47.7	55.9	54.5	53.3	58.0	52.7
% 65-74 Years Old...........	6.1	7.1	6.8	6.3	5.6	3.8	3.1	6.1
% 75 Years Old And Over.....	3.4	4.3	3.6	2.5	2.8	2.9	2.0	2.6
% In Different House........	62.4	61.9	69.7	51.9	68.2	56.1	32.3	65.2
% Families With Female Head.	6.2	6.1	5.4	5.9	6.1	4.7	6.3	7.3
Median School Years Completed.	12.8	12.9	13.0	13.1	12.7	12.7	12.7	12.6
Median Family Income, 1969.....$$	17472	17825	16946	19770	17079	18426	13831	15081
% Income Below Poverty Level....	1.8	1.2	1.5	0.9	2.5	1.5	2.4	3.5
% Income of $15,000 or More.....	59.7	59.4	57.3	70.9	58.3	63.9	41.1	50.3
% White Collar Workers........	54.1	57.9	58.5	65.9	49.0	53.1	51.5	45.3
% Civilian Labor Force Unemployed.	1.9	2.0	1.2	1.4	2.6	1.7	1.8	2.7
% Riding To Work By Automobile....	76.1	74.0	74.8	83.1	80.1	78.0	84.7	76.8
Population Per Household..........	3.3	3.2	3.6	3.1	3.2	3.5	3.0	3.4
Total Housing Units...........	13188	2609	1762	1980	2939	2748	8062	1519
% Condominiums & Cooperatives.....	1.2	0.0	0.0	3.5	2.1	0.2	0.2	0.8
% Built 1960 Or Later............	23.7	19.3	7.0	39.1	24.6	43.7	84.4	12.2
% Owner Occupied.................	78.9	81.0	90.6	67.5	81.6	80.2	34.2	88.3
% With 1+ Persons Per Room........	2.9	2.3	3.9	2.3	2.9	3.1	2.8	3.3
Median Value: Owner Units.......$$	37000	40700	34200	37700	34900	39200	31100	33800
Median Rent: Rental Units......$$	175	169	156	301	168	181	185	168
Median Number Of Rooms: All Units.	5.9	6.1	6.3	5.7	5.6	6.1	4.6	6.0

Many urban dwellers were afraid to rebuild in the city. Others, the growing middle-class of industrial and business managers, salesmen, and small factory owners, wanted to establish their homes in the green areas of the country and yet be near the city and their jobs. Brickton's park-like setting and the availability of cheap, quick transportation to the city made it a desirable place to live.

In the years following the Chicago fire, Brickton began to grow. Houses began to dot the landscape. The community was in need of a governing body, safe water supply, better roads and sanitary conditions and most of all, protection from fires. Leading residents got together and applied to the state for incorporation as a village. Residents were asked to submit new names for the chartered village. From more than 100 entries, the name Park Ridge was chosen since the community was built on a ridge and its homes were in park-like settings. The name changing ceremonies took place on July 4, 1873. Residents gathered at the highest point on the ridge and at exactly noon a hot air balloon with the name Brickton was sent aloft. The balloon barely cleared the steeple of the Methodist Church and headed straight for Lake Michigan. A note was affixed to the balloon but was never returned to the village.

In the next decades things began happening on the ridge. At the 1890 census, there were 987 persons living in Park Ridge. An electric light system was started, a new school was built, and the police department got its start with the hiring of a full-time officer. A volunteer fire department was organized. By 1902, Park Ridge had telephones, a high school district had been formed for Maine Township, and a Vincentian priest had begun commuting to Park Ridge on Sundays to say mass and minister to the Catholic population. In 1900, Park Ridge had 1,340 residents. After the demise of the brick industry, no major new industries were established in the village, and Park Ridge continued to grow as a residential community. By 1910, the community had grown again, to a population of 2,009. Village officials applied for city incorporation and the City of Park Ridge came into being in that year.

After World War I, there was a serious housing shortage and the City of Park Ridge began to boom. Its population in the decade following grew almost 200 percent. The population in 1920 was 3,383 and by 1930 there were 10,417 people living in Park Ridge. The homes that were built during this era were large substantial houses on large-sized lots. A zoning ordinance and building code adopted in 1922 helped safeguard the city from land speculation and over-building. Apartments and duplex dwellings were banned, and minimum standards of 80 front feet, or 1/6 acre were set for building lots. The uptown-area commercial district also grew during this period. Two movie houses, a new bank building, and several commercial structures were built during the 1920s.

The Depression of the 1930s brought difficult times to Park Ridge. Great numbers of people were unemployed and some were forced to go on relief. The community rallied to help its own needy. Vacant farm land surrounding the city went under the plow again and food was grown to help the hungry of the community. Nevertheless, the population grew to more than 12,000 in 1940.

During World War II, the Douglas Aircraft Company built a large plant at what is now O'Hare Airport. Hundreds of people worked at the plant and they needed housing. To provide that housing, the federal government participated in a building program that resulted in the hundreds of two-story Georgian homes that now cover the blocks of southwest Park Ridge.

After the war the City of Park Ridge grew at a rapid rate especially in the southwest, west and northwest sectors. By 1950, the population was more than 16,000 and it doubled in the period between 1950 and 1960. The city began to seek more businesses, and decided to permit some new apartment house construction. Additional retail stores and office buildings were sought, in part to increase the tax base in face of rapidly increasing educational expenditures. Aetna Insurance Group moved to Park Ridge from Chicago, being one of some 150 new businesses entering Park Ridge in the decade from 1950 to 1960. The land area of the community increased through annexation and the city adopted a city manager-council form of government.

Many of the families buying homes in the city were headed by World War II veterans. The ample availability of money for housing mortgages stimulated new subdivision development in Park Ridge, and these new homes sold quickly. During the early 1950s and 1960s the chief concerns of community officials were the building and maintenance of good schools and park facilities to keep the community attractive to families with children. The city government provided its citizens with excellent roads, sewer and water systems and public protection. Resurrection Hospital opened in 1954 and Lutheran General Hospital in 1960. Maine Township High School district added three new schools. In 1970, the population of Park Ridge reached its largest size to date, more than 47,000.

Since 1960, Park Ridge has experienced relative stability. The city is fully developed, with no vacant land remaining. Population dropped by 3,900 during the most recent decade, mainly because of declining family size in the community. The residents of Park Ridge tend to be white and affluent. Three percent are non-white, 1 percent reports a Spanish origin and 8 percent are foreign born. More than 60 percent of all families earned income in excess of $30,000 in 1979, 84 percent of all housing units are owner-occupied and the median value of such units is nearly twice the median in Chicago.

The city is primarily a bedroom community, and has maintained the character of a New England town transplanted to the Midwest. Single-family housing units still predominate, though rising land values have stimulated some condominium development. There is virtually no industry in the community and only scattered commercial development, with most major shopping outside the city. Some office development has occurred along the North Western Railroad tracks and along Higgins Road, though this kind of development has been extensive, and less actively encouraged, than in surrounding communities.

Lorraine Murray

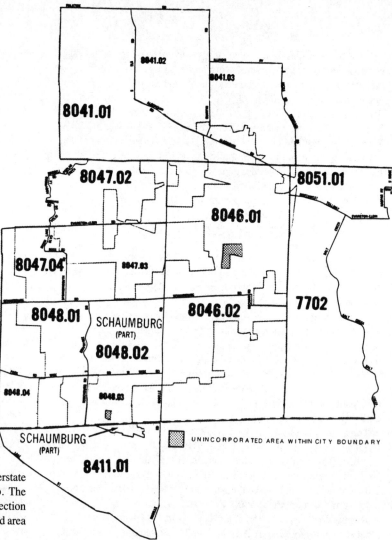

UNINCORPORATED AREA WITHIN CITY BOUNDARY

Place 5215

Schaumburg

Schaumburg is located along the Northwest Tollway (Interstate Highway 290), about 27 miles northwest of the Chicago Loop. The majority of the village lies within Cook County with one small section in DuPage County. By the end of 1982, the total incorporated land area was 18.3 square miles.

The name Schaumburg was taken from the name of the township and the little unincorporated crossroads community called Schaumburg Center, located at the intersection of Schaumburg and Roselle roads. Township history dates back to the 1830s when several New England families settled in the area and gave the name "Sarah's Grove" to a stand of oak trees near the center of the township. German immigrants began to enter the area in the early 1840s and when the township was formally organized in 1850, the name was chosen because the majority of those living near the center of the township came from the principality of Schaumburg-Lippe, Germany. German dominance of the township was established further in 1864 when the majority of members of St. Peter Evangelical Lutheran Church voted to join the Missouri Synod.

By the turn of the century, Schaumburg Center had a general store, several taverns, a creamery, a blacksmith and several houses. The church provided education for its membership and four or five public schools were in use periodically. A small bank was eventually established, but the little community did not develop during the first half of the 20th century because there were no main highways or railroads in the area. The township residents went into Roselle or Elgin for important business and shopping. After 1940, some farmers began to sell their land because they had no one to carry on in their stead. More land was sold after World War II, some of it for the proposed subdivision of Hoffman Estates, which was seen as a threat to the quiet rural life of the township. In order to contain the subdivision, a movement for incorporation began with the first referendum resulting in failure. Then, a second vote was taken in December, 1955, with different proposed boundaries, and incorporation was approved by a vote of 56 to 7.

Politics in Schaumburg has been dominated by a group of people formally organized as the Schaumburg United Party (SUP). They are basically an independent group and although challenged occasionally by other independents, have never lost an election. Beyond the village level, the residents tend to support the Republican party.

Schaumburg's population in 1956, after incorporation, was 130 and its incorporated area was two square miles. At this time, village services were almost nonexistent because life continued much the same as before. Another reason for the slow development of services was Schaumburg's policy of not levying a municipal real estate tax. The development of the Weathersfield subdivision in 1959 resulted in an increased population of 986 in 1960. The cost of necessary village services was covered by the tax revenues from new businesses. Pure Oil (later Union Oil) was Schaumburg's first major office facility and it provided the necessary revenues.

Business and industry began to boom in 1960 when Interstate Highway 90 was developed. For several years, the location of the expressway was debated by the state of Illinois. When the plan was approved to accommodate Arlington Park race track, it also served as the impetus for the development of the Woodfield Mall shopping center. Woodfield, a major retail center finished in 1971, provided enough sales tax to make up one third of the total village budget in 1980. Industrial growth began in 1967 when Motorola, Inc., located its communication division north of the tollway at Meacham and Algonquin roads. Since then, continued growth along the tollway has given the area the name of the Golden Corridor.

New job opportunities and transportation access to Chicago provided by the Tollway encouraged the phenomenal growth of the 1960s, during which the population grew from less than a thousand to nearly

Shaumburg
Population and Housing Characteristics, 1930-1980

	1980	1970	1960	1950	1940	1930
Total Population	53,305	18,730	*	*	*	*
% Male	49.9	50.3	*	*	*	*
% Female	50.1	49.7	*	*	*	*
% White	95.0	99.5	*	*	*	*
% Black	1.2	0.1	*	*	*	*
% Other Nonwhite Races	3.8	0.4	*	*	*	*
% Under % Years Old	8.1	15.9	*	*	*	*
% 5-19 Years Old	25.4	31.0	*	*	*	*
% 20-44 Years Old	49.7	41.8	*	*	*	*
% 45-64 Years Old	12.1	9.6	*	*	*	*
% 65 Years and Older	4.7	1.7	*	*	*	*
Median School Years	13.0	12.5	*	*	*	*
Total Housing Units	20,931	5,014	*	*	*	*
% In One-Unit Structures	56.0	91.5	*	*	*	*
% Owner Occupied	61.9	86.5	*	*	*	*
% Renter Occupied	32.7	9.3	*	*	*	*
% Vacant	5.4	4.2	*	*	*	*
% 1+ Persons per Room	1.0	3.2	*	*	*	*

Place 5215 — Schaumberg , Illinois
Selected Characteristics of Census Tracts: 1980

Tract Number	Total	7702	8041.01	8041.02	8041.03	8046.01	8046.02	8047.02	8047.03	8047.04	8048.01
Total Population	53305	0	4	88	1070	3398	8993	2757	6524	6917	8869
% Male	49.9	-	-	-	66.8	51.5	48.9	51.7	46.6	49.9	50.1
% Black	1.2	-	-	-	2.6	2.4	0.5	2.3	1.1	2.4	0.5
% Other Nonwhite	3.8	-	-	-	4.6	6.5	3.5	4.5	4.2	4.2	2.2
% Of Spanish Origin	1.8	-	-	-	1.0	2.8	1.2	1.4	1.6	2.8	1.3
% Foreign Born	7.4	-	-	-	10.4	11.0	8.6	6.6	6.2	5.6	5.7
% Living In Group Quarters	0.3	-	-	-	0.0	0.0	0.0	0.0	2.1	0.0	0.0
% 13 Years Old And Under	24.9	-	-	-	2.1	10.6	23.3	15.5	25.2	31.4	25.5
% 14-20 Years Old	9.8	-	-	-	3.3	5.4	8.1	9.6	7.4	8.7	14.6
% 21-64 Years Old	60.5	-	-	-	94.6	80.1	64.2	69.9	52.3	58.9	55.8
% 65-74 Years Old	2.7	-	-	-	0.0	2.6	3.6	3.5	5.0	0.8	3.0
% 75 Years Old And Over	2.0	-	-	-	0.1	1.3	0.9	1.5	10.1	0.3	1.1
% In Different House	65.5	-	-	-	97.4	80.4	68.4	78.1	70.0	88.9	38.8
% Families With Female Head	9.3	-	-	-	3.6	14.3	8.6	10.0	10.7	11.3	7.8
Median School Years Completed	13.0	-	-	-	15.8	15.0	13.0	14.9	12.9	14.0	12.7
Median Family Income, 1979 $$	29257	-	-	-	24667	27984	31127	26793	28265	28086	28627
% Income Below Poverty Level	1.9	-	-	-	0.0	0.0	0.8	2.0	2.1	2.7	2.3
% Income Of $30,000 Or More	47.4	-	-	-	30.6	46.7	55.2	39.6	45.9	44.7	45.1
% White Collar Workers	70.5	-	-	-	87.0	71.8	72.4	75.3	73.8	77.3	61.3
% Civilian Labor Force Unemployed	3.3	-	-	-	2.2	2.3	2.6	3.2	5.4	2.8	4.0
% Riding To Work By Automobile	91.3	-	-	-	92.5	85.3	92.0	94.5	91.0	91.3	91.5
Mean Commuting Time - Minutes	30.0	-	-	-	30.9	26.7	30.8	26.3	33.2	31.1	30.3
Population Per Household	2.7	-	-	-	1.5	1.8	2.7	2.0	2.5	3.0	3.3
Total Housing Units	20929	0	2	42	857	2119	3579	1475	2609	2418	2758
% Condominiums	21.3	-	-	-	0.0	27.6	48.3	0.0	19.6	18.1	8.9
% Built 1970 Or Later	76.2	-	-	-	52.9	88.5	88.3	83.1	97.0	94.0	24.0
% Owner Occupied	60.9	-	-	-	0.9	29.7	81.0	16.7	63.3	65.7	81.7
% With 1+ Persons Per Room	1.0	-	-	-	0.4	1.6	0.7	0.7	1.1	1.1	1.4
Median Value: Owner Units $$	83300	-	-	-	-	112100	99700	110100	74700	87400	70000
Median Rent: Rental Units $$	354	-	-	-	387	372	346	325	396	348	349
Median Number Of Rooms: All Units	5.4	-	-	-	4.3	4.1	5.4	3.9	5.3	5.6	5.6

Tract Number	8048.02	8048.03	8048.04	8051.01	8411.01
Total Population	13399	770	499	0	17
% Male	50.0	49.0	48.9	-	-
% Black	0.7	3.2	4.2	-	-
% Other Nonwhite	4.0	5.2	3.6	-	-
% Of Spanish Origin	2.1	3.5	1.2	-	-
% Foreign Born	7.6	11.4	10.0	-	-
% Living In Group Quarters	0.0	0.0	0.0	-	-
% 13 Years Old And Under	30.1	18.1	20.4	-	-
% 14-20 Years Old	11.3	10.0	10.4	-	-
% 21-64 Years Old	56.0	65.2	65.1	-	-
% 65-74 Years Old	1.8	5.1	3.2	-	-
% 75 Years Old And Over	0.8	1.7	0.8	-	-
% In Different House	56.8	69.1	85.6	-	-
% Families With Female Head	7.2	30.3	24.6	-	-
Median School Years Completed	12.8	12.5	12.7	-	-
Median Family Income, 1979 $$	29677	24306	27885	-	-
% Income Below Poverty Level	2.2	0.0	4.9	-	-
% Income Of $30,000 Or More	48.6	33.1	42.3	-	-
% White Collar Workers	66.8	65.2	59.2	-	-
% Civilian Labor Force Unemployed	3.3	3.6	1.7	-	-
% Riding To Work By Automobile	92.1	90.3	90.0	-	-
Mean Commuting Time - Minutes	29.1	34.1	32.1	-	-
Population Per Household	3.3	2.1	2.2	-	-
Total Housing Units	4293	423	346	0	8
% Condominiums	14.7	2.8	81.5	-	-
% Built 1970 Or Later	69.8	84.7	92.0	-	-
% Owner Occupied	75.7	12.8	43.4	-	-
% With 1+ Persons Per Room	1.0	.9	0.0	-	-
Median Value: Owner Units $$	85200	103800	77300	-	-
Median Rent: Rental Units $$	349	286	304	-	-
Median Number Of Rooms: All Units	5.6	4.1	4.6	-	-

19,000. A construction boom raised the number of housing units to more than 5,000, more than 90 percent of which was in single-family units, owner-occupied.

As revenues and population increased, village services also increased. The original village hall had been located in the remodeled Jennings barn in 1963. The new facility on Schaumburg Road was completed in 1975. Park District facilities, organized in 1963 by voter referendum, also grew to include the 200-acre Spring Valley Nature Center, numerous parks, three swimming pools, and a new recreation complex that houses a gymnasium, racquetball courts, meeting rooms and offices. Park District property totals over 637 acres of land.

Schaumburg has easy access to the Northwest Tollway, Interstate Highway 290 and Routes 72 and 58, yet traffic is its major problem. Most major roads, not already widened into four lanes, will be widened. The village has also tried to increase commuter facilities by opening a new commuter station on the Milwaukee Road line. Several years ago they annexed Roselle Field and renamed it Schaumburg Airport but, because of its closeness to O'Hare Field, service will be limited.

In 1982, Schaumburg found itself almost at its geographical limits. However, on land already incorprated, plans exist for the development of commercial land including the Woodfield 76 Metro Center. This

285

Schaumburg
Selected Characteristics of Census Tracts: 1970

Tract Number	TOTAL	8041	8046	8047	8048	8051	8411
Total Population.............	18730	8468	8686	19587	22268	25709	7222
% Male.......................	50.3	50.1	50.2	50.4	50.3	49.8	49.5
% Black......................	0.1	0.1	0.2	0.1	0.1	0.2	0.1
% Other Nonwhite.............	0.5	0.5	0.6	0.4	0.6	0.9	0.1
% Of Spanish Language........	2.1	2.3	2.8	2.2	2.9	1.7	1.2
% Foreign Born...............	4.9	4.5	3.0	3.4	5.0	4.2	4.3
% Living In Group Quarters...	0.1	1.6	0.1	0.1	0.1	0.9	1.2
% 13 Years Old And Under.....	40.0	30.4	34.1	40.5	42.7	30.3	32.1
% 14-20 Years Old............	7.5	11.8	11.6	11.3	7.2	9.9	12.6
% 21-64 Years Old............	50.8	53.0	52.0	46.7	48.8	56.6	49.9
% 65-74 Years Old............	1.1	3.0	1.5	1.0	0.9	2.0	3.4
% 75 Years Old And Over......	0.6	1.8	0.8	0.5	0.4	1.2	2.0
% In Different House.........	22.5	39.3	41.4	41.3	25.8	29.4	57.9
% Families With Female Head..	2.4	2.9	4.2	3.5	2.4	4.1	5.2
Median School Years Completed	12.6	12.9	12.5	12.7	12.6	12.8	12.4
Median Family Income, 1969...$$	13888	19412	13760	14658	13465	14783	12938
% Income Below Poverty Level..	3.1	1.2	2.2	2.0	2.5	1.6	5.5
% Income of $15,000 or More...	39.8	69.5	40.1	47.3	35.6	48.4	32.8
% White Collar Workers.......	43.4	57.9	42.2	46.8	40.5	47.2	30.6
% Civilian Labor Force Unemployed.	1.4	2.3	2.1	2.1	1.6	1.8	1.9
% Riding To Work By Automobile....	86.3	81.6	86.8	90.4	88.1	86.1	82.4
Population Per Household......	3.9	3.5	3.7	4.2	4.1	3.3	3.7
Total Housing Units.........	5013	2683	2515	4958	5606	8353	2057
% Condominiums & Cooperatives....	0.0	2.5	0.0	0.0	0.1	0.0	0.0
% Built 1960 Or Later........	92.2	73.5	65.2	76.0	94.8	88.5	31.2
% Owner Occupied.............	86.6	69.1	62.8	79.4	89.3	45.4	75.3
% With 1+ Persons Per Room...	3.2	2.8	5.4	5.4	3.6	3.0	8.6
Median Value: Owner Units....$$	31400	45600	31400	29700	30000	36200	27500
Median Rent: Rental Units....$$	191	177	182	178	199	195	163
Median Number Of Rooms: All Units.	6.5	6.7	5.8	6.4	6.5	5.1	5.3

project will provide housing for 9,000 people, offices, stores, hotels, and service businesses. The village of Schaumburg is also working on plans for a cultural center which will be called The Prairie Center for the Arts.

Not all of Schaumburg's planned projects have been successful. The spectacular "Outer Planets" project would have included a 126-story structure and other buildings, housing for 30,000 people and a monorail. Another failed project was to have been a major professional sports stadium. Lack of financial backing caused these failures.

Schaumburg's population continued to grow rapidly in the most recent decade, recorded at more than 53,000 in 1980 and estimated at more than 55,000 today. Projections of 100,000 by the year 2000 have been made, but economic conditions in the 1980s have slowed down the housing market. Although Schaumburg Township's population was, at one time, predominantly German, the ethnic character of the population of the Village of Schaumburg disappeared after the development of Weathersfield. Today there are no discernible European ethnic groups in the village, although 7 percent are foreign born and 2 percent are Hispanic. Five percent, mostly Asiatics, are non-white. The residents are comfortably middle-class. More than 70 percent of the labor force is white-collar, nearly half of the families, reported incomes of $30,000 or more in 1979. Two percent of all families lived in poverty in 1979, and 3 percent of all workers were unemployed in 1980.

Although more people live in multiple-family residences, single-family homes, which can cost as much as $150,000, account for two-thirds of all housing units, the number of which grew at a faster rate than the number of residents during the 1970s. If planned projects, such as Woodfield 76, are developed in the next few years, Schaumburg's population will increase mostly through multiple-family units. This increase in population will also cause a proportionate increase in traffic problems.

Marilyn Hepburn Lind

Place 5365

Skokie

Skokie is located on flat land in Cook County, with Evanston on the east, Morton Grove and Niles on the west, Wilmette on the north, and Lincolnwood on the south separating Skokie from Chicago. In the early days Pottawatomie Indians and French fur traders traveled through the wooded and swampy area. Permanent settlement began along the North Branch of the Chicago River, and at Dutchman's Point, now Niles. The first house in present-day Skokie was erected by Henry Harms in 1854 on the site of the present village hall. Gradually others settled in the area. In 1858, Harms started a general store, and a schoolhouse was established just south of the village. In 1867, a German Evangelical Lutheran church was organized, with a membership of about 35. The next year a Catholic church was established, and in 1873 a schoolhouse was constructed by the church.

These early settlers were largely German immigrants. By the time the village was incorporated in 1888 as Niles Center, there was an additional settlement of immigrants from Luxembourg. Until the 1920s the village grew very gradually. It remained a community of German farmers whose main cash crop was vegetables for the growing Chicago market. Greenhousing, begun in 1874, was another important source

of income. There was virtually no industrial development in the area, and no new influx of settlers. The village did not participate in the rapid population growth of other North Shore communities in the early years of the century. It had neither the transportation lines to Chicago nor the lakefront facilities enjoyed by places such as Evanston.

Skokie
Population and Housing Characteristics, 1930-1980

	1980	1970	1960	1950	1940	1930
Total Population.......	60,278	68,627	59,364	14,832	7,172	5,007
% Male..................	47.4	48.8	49.0	49.6	*	*
% Female................	52.6	51.2	51.0	50.4	*	*
% White.................	90.8	99.0	99.6	99.9	99.9	*
% Black.................	1.0	0.2	0.2	0.1	0.1	0.0
% Other Nonwhite Races...	8.2	0.8	0.2	0.0	-	*
% Under 5 Years Old.....	4.5	6.2	12.3	12.6	8.7	13.4
% 5-19 Years Old........	19.0	29.1	27.9	20.9	24.9	24.6
% 20-44 Years Old.......	30.9	29.8	34.9	40.7	45.2	44.9
% 45-64 Years Old.......	31.0	27.3	20.2	21.1	17.3	13.8
% 65 Years and Older....	14.6	7.6	4.7	4.7	3.9	3.3
Median School Years....	13.2	13.2	12.6	12.3	*	*
Total Housing Units....	22,809	21,158	17,165	4,470	2,023	*
% In One-Unit Structures.	63.1	67.9	75.1	*	*	*
% Owner Occupied........	74.5	74.6	80.7	72.9	38.9	*
% Renter Occupied........	24.2	24.3	15.6	23.0	56.5	*
% Vacant................	1.3	1.1	3.7	4.1	4.6	*
% 1+ Persons per Room....	1.4	2.0	3.5	5.0	*	*

Place 5365 -- Skokie , Illinois
Selected Characteristics of Census Tracts: 1980

Tract Number	Total	8067	8068	8069	8070	8071	8072	8073	8074	8075	8076
Total Population..............	60278	4480	7586	4063	4935	4007	5869	6730	5641	3185	6116
% Male.......................	47.4	49.2	47.1	45.4	46.4	49.6	48.4	45.2	46.9	47.2	47.9
% Black......................	1.0	4.0	0.6	0.2	0.4	5.2	1.4	0.0	0.3	0.3	0.3
% Other Nonwhite.............	8.2	5.5	6.6	7.8	8.2	9.6	10.0	6.6	7.3	12.5	12.4
% Of Spanish Origin..........	2.7	1.2	2.1	2.9	2.7	1.9	3.2	2.8	2.2	3.4	3.3
% Foreign Born...............	19.8	12.2	20.8	21.7	19.7	16.6	17.8	19.6	20.8	21.7	21.2
% Living In Group Quarters...	1.0	0.0	3.8	0.0	2.6	0.3	0.0	0.0	0.0	0.1	0.0
% 13 Years Old And Under.....	14.2	17.5	12.2	11.5	13.5	19.1	16.2	11.8	13.9	14.8	14.7
% 14-20 Years Old............	10.7	11.6	11.6	11.6	9.1	12.1	9.7	9.4	9.2	11.0	10.9
% 21-64 Years Old............	60.6	60.7	62.2	57.7	59.1	61.2	64.0	60.4	59.4	60.3	61.7
% 65-74 Years Old............	9.9	7.0	9.1	13.1	11.2	5.4	7.2	12.8	11.4	9.4	9.8
% 75 Years Old And Over......	4.6	3.3	4.8	6.0	7.1	2.2	2.8	5.7	6.2	4.6	3.0
% In Different House.........	36.0	38.6	41.8	35.8	44.5	41.6	30.9	37.4	36.6	19.6	32.4
% Families With Female Head...	10.6	9.6	10.5	9.7	15.9	8.3	8.5	12.3	14.2	6.5	9.2
Median School Years Completed	13.2	15.5	13.6	12.8	12.9	14.9	13.6	12.8	12.8	13.1	12.9
Median Family Income, 1979......$$	30858	40441	33764	29535	24306	39622	32653	28996	26811	30822	30665
% Income Below Poverty Level....	1.9	2.1	2.3	0.5	3.1	1.5	2.1	1.1	1.9	2.3	2.1
% Income Of $30,000 Or More.....	52.3	68.4	59.0	48.1	33.3	68.5	55.3	47.6	42.6	52.6	52.1
% White Collar Workers..........	79.0	84.9	85.9	79.6	76.3	88.6	80.8	75.9	74.8	79.4	76.5
% Civilian Labor Force Unemployed.	2.7	1.6	3.4	2.5	2.5	2.9	3.3	1.9	2.6	1.2	3.6
% Riding To Work By Automobile....	80.4	76.5	86.6	78.1	74.5	87.1	80.4	78.8	78.1	82.4	81.6
Mean Commuting Time - Minutes...	26.6	29.2	27.9	23.7	26.1	29.5	29.0	24.5	24.5	26.2	26.5
Population Per Household.......	2.7	3.0	2.7	2.5	2.4	3.1	2.9	2.3	2.5	2.9	2.9
Total Housing Units..........	22805	1527	2788	1613	2024	1290	2030	2989	2310	1114	2161
% Condominiums...............	8.7	5.2	15.1	31.9	6.8	0.1	0.0	13.8	3.2	0.0	3.0
% Built 1970 Or Later...........	8.9	6.5	9.5	46.2	4.3	3.6	2.1	10.8	1.1	1.3	1.2
% Owner Occupied...............	73.8	93.3	72.6	83.5	48.5	90.9	88.6	55.8	57.9	90.1	89.0
% With 1+ Persons Per Room.....	1.4	0.9	1.4	1.1	1.8	0.7	1.5	1.1	1.2	1.8	1.7
Median Value: Owner Units.......$$	84400	98900	94700	81500	72600	99800	82800	77600	81100	77800	74500
Median Rent: Rental Units.......$$	311	393	351	120	297	357	352	327	291	279	324
Median Number Of Rooms: All Units.	5.6	5.6	5.6	5.4	4.6	5.6	5.6	5.0	5.2	5.6	5.6

Tract Number	8077	8078
Total Population..............	4924	2742
% Male.......................	46.8	51.8
% Black......................	0.5	0.1
% Other Nonwhite.............	6.6	6.0
% Of Spanish Origin..........	3.6	2.9
% Foreign Born...............	24.3	20.5
% Living In Group Quarters...	0.0	5.4
% 13 Years Old And Under.....	13.2	14.7
% 14-20 Years Old............	9.7	14.6
% 21-64 Years Old............	57.9	59.8
% 65-74 Years Old............	13.5	7.4
% 75 Years Old And Over......	5.7	3.6
% In Different House.........	32.7	31.6
% Families With Female Head...	13.4	10.6
Median School Years Completed	12.8	13.9
Median Family Income, 1979......$$	28125	37889
% Income Below Poverty Level....	3.3	0.9
% Income Of $30,000 Or More.....	45.3	62.5
% White Collar Workers..........	68.5	78.1
% Civilian Labor Force Unemployed.	2.9	2.5
% Riding To Work By Automobile....	79.9	80.4
Mean Commuting Time - Minutes...	26.1	27.0
Population Per Household.......	2.5	3.0
Total Housing Units..........	2091	868
% Condominiums...............	13.3	0.0
% Built 1970 Or Later...........	15.6	4.3
% Owner Occupied...............	63.4	95.5
% With 1+ Persons Per Room.....	2.1	1.5
Median Value: Owner Units.......$$	80300	90100
Median Rent: Rental Units.......$$	272	383
Median Number Of Rooms: All Units.	5.0	5.6

The first major land boom and the development of the village as a residential suburb of Chicago was stimulated by the development of rapid transit to the city. The elevated line to Evanston was extended to Dempster Street in Niles Center in 1925, and in 1926 the Skokie Valley Route of the Chicago, North Shore, and Milwaukee Railway was completed. Land speculators foresaw the possibility of developing Skokie as a densely-populated apartment house area with rapid commuting to Chicago, and large-scale subdivision followed. Between 1925 and 1927, many public improvements were introduced. A street system was laid out paralleling section lines, with 24- and 30-foot lots.

Water, gas, and electricity lines were laid out, as well as sidewalks. Many houses and small flats were constructed, and the population, which had been 763 in 1920, reached 5,007 by 1930.

The real estate boom in Skokie was short-lived. With the Depression, new construction in the area virtually halted. Thousands of 30-foot lots which had been laid out in the hopes of selling them became worthless. Taxes and assessments were unpaid and mounted, and many lots were abandoned. Much of Skokie took on the aspect of a ghost town; there were hundreds of acres of land with streets, sidewalks, telephone lines, water and sewer lines, but with no buildings. As late as 1948, it was estimated that there were 30,000 vacant lots in Skokie, many of which were being farmed. Recovery began slowly in the 1940s. After the Second World War, Skokie took major steps fostering a new period of rapid expansion. The thousands of vacant lots presented a difficult problem, for many were abandoned or in arrears. In 1946, many lot titles were cleared, and a new zoning plan was completed. Much of the property zoned as commercial was reclassified as residential, and lots were revised to provide for single-family homes with 40- to 55-foot frontages. Light industrial zones lined the railroad tracks, and heavy industry was zoned for the southeastern corner of the village, near Chicago. In 1940, the village adopted its present name, Skokie, an Indian word for a swamp north of the village which had given the larger region the name "Skokie Valley."

In contrast to the growth in the late 1920s, the growth in the late 1940s did not depend on the rapid transit systems. In 1948, service was abandoned on the elevated line between Evanston and Skokie. After the Second World War, the automobile and the single-family home were the dominant factors in Skokie's growth. The opening of the Edens Expressway provided a major route to the city. Because Skokie

Skokie
Selected Characteristics of Census Tracts: 1970

Tract Number	TOTAL	8067	8068	8069	8070	8071	8072	8073	8074	8075	8076
Total Population	68322	5107	8646	3336	5979	4405	7018	7749	6751	3685	7118
% Male	48.8	49.8	49.0	50.2	48.5	49.4	49.3	48.0	47.7	47.8	49.0
% Black	0.2	0.4	0.3	0.1	0.1	0.3	0.1	0.2	0.0	0.1	0.1
% Other Nonwhite	0.9	1.4	0.4	1.2	0.8	0.3	0.9	1.3	1.1	0.8	1.3
% Of Spanish Language	1.4	2.1	1.2	0.2	2.2	1.3	1.3	0.4	2.6	2.0	1.8
% Foreign Born	10.0	6.3	8.1	5.6	12.6	9.6	9.7	9.3	12.8	15.7	11.3
% Living In Group Quarters	0.7	0.0	0.0	1.8	0.0	2.0	0.1	0.2	0.0	0.2	0.0
% 13 Years Old And Under	22.9	27.1	22.7	30.7	22.8	24.9	23.1	20.5	21.3	20.2	21.9
% 14-20 Years Old	13.7	14.8	15.6	14.7	9.6	14.9	16.3	10.5	11.3	15.2	14.6
% 21-64 Years Old	55.9	51.5	55.6	51.2	57.3	55.1	54.5	59.2	57.1	55.9	57.2
% 65-74 Years Old	5.2	4.7	3.5	2.3	6.4	3.4	4.1	7.0	7.2	6.0	4.4
% 75 Years Old And Over	2.4	1.9	2.6	1.0	3.8	1.6	1.9	2.7	3.0	2.8	1.9
% In Different House	63.9	65.6	61.0	69.4	50.5	70.4	73.7	56.8	58.3	69.7	74.9
% Families With Female Head	6.5	4.0	7.2	4.6	8.4	4.7	5.4	7.6	8.5	5.9	5.3
Median School Years Completed	12.8	14.3	12.9	12.9	12.5	14.0	12.8	12.7	12.6	12.7	12.7
Median Family Income, 1969 $$	16423	22925	17817	16069	13303	21513	17863	14699	14094	16253	15382
% Income Below Poverty Level	2.3	2.2	3.1	2.3	2.3	2.1	2.3	2.0	1.7	1.3	2.3
% Income of $15,000 or More	55.1	76.6	59.8	54.6	37.9	73.5	60.6	48.1	44.3	54.5	51.5
% White Collar Workers	55.9	69.6	62.3	58.2	49.9	71.9	61.3	50.4	54.1	46.9	47.9
% Civilian Labor Force Unemployed	2.3	3.4	2.9	3.0	1.6	1.7	1.9	1.8	2.9	1.8	2.6
% Riding To Work By Automobile	79.5	76.5	84.0	80.2	73.9	83.8	78.6	77.6	75.9	79.2	83.3
Population Per Household	3.3	3.7	3.3	3.9	3.0	3.5	3.6	2.8	3.0	3.4	3.4
Total Housing Units	21153	1421	2563	870	1971	1259	1981	2773	2289	1102	2126
% Condominiums & Cooperatives	4.6	0.4	8.0	0.0	13.1	0.8	0.9	4.2	6.9	0.0	3.1
% Built 1960 Or Later	23.6	12.9	32.3	37.7	21.0	25.9	8.8	42.4	22.0	17.2	13.8
% Owner Occupied	69.9	94.3	63.2	92.6	38.8	91.6	90.8	46.2	53.0	91.5	88.3
% With 1+ Persons Per Room	2.0	1.6	1.3	2.9	3.6	0.4	1.4	2.5	2.3	2.2	1.9
Median Value: Owner Units $$	36700	45300	43900	33500	30400	46900	36500	32800	34700	32800	32100
Median Rent: Rental Units $$	181	216	196	206	175	213	192	185	174	149	175
Median Number Of Rooms: All Units	5.7	6.8	5.8	5.9	4.6	6.8	6.1	5.0	5.2	5.8	5.8

Tract Number	8077	8078
Total Population	5462	2987
% Male	47.7	51.4
% Black	0.1	0.2
% Other Nonwhite	0.6	0.0
% Of Spanish Language	1.3	0.0
% Foreign Born	10.7	7.0
% Living In Group Quarters	0.0	5.8
% 13 Years Old And Under	20.6	23.2
% 14-20 Years Old	11.6	17.9
% 21-64 Years Old	58.3	52.1
% 65-74 Years Old	6.7	4.9
% 75 Years Old And Over	2.7	1.8
% In Different House	59.3	63.3
% Families With Female Head	7.6	4.4
Median School Years Completed	12.5	12.9
Median Family Income, 1969 $$	15035	18862
% Income Below Poverty Level	4.1	0.7
% Income of $15,000 or More	50.1	67.0
% White Collar Workers	47.6	61.8
% Civilian Labor Force Unemployed	2.2	0.8
% Riding To Work By Automobile	81.7	80.1
Population Per Household	3.0	3.4
Total Housing Units	1869	834
% Condominiums & Cooperatives	7.7	0.0
% Built 1960 Or Later	20.5	21.8
% Owner Occupied	56.3	95.1
% With 1+ Persons Per Room	2.5	1.2
Median Value: Owner Units $$	33300	39300
Median Rent: Rental Units $$	170	200
Median Number Of Rooms: All Units	5.1	6.2

was close to the city and was already subdivided, it became one of the most rapidly growing municipalities in the Chicago area.

Along with the rapid growth of resident population there was an an increase in light industry. Between 1945 and 1952, 93 industrial establishments began operations in the Skokie area. Most of these plants were relocating from Chicago into newer single-story buildings.

During the 1950s these trends continued. There was a high volume of construction throughout the decade, both residential and commercial. Real estate values rose, reflecting in part an emphasis by the city on commercial development with high land values. By 1958, Skokie was an industrial as well as a residential suburb. In 1958 Skokie had 174 establishments employing 12,524 persons as compared with 6,253 employees in 1954. Many of the establishments were involved in the manufacture of professional and scientific instruments. In 1957, Skokie adopted a village manager form of government and in 1959 voted down a proposal to become a city.

A major local political issue has concerned the relative emphasis Skokie should give to commercial and residential land use. Between 1950 and 1960, the population of Skokie quadrupled. Annexations

account for virtually none of this population growth — only 68 persons resided in territory annexed during the decade. Leading nationalities among the foreign stock in 1960 were Russians, Poles, and Germans. Of 147 black residents in 1960, 143 were females, primarily domestic servants. Although the village had considerable industrial development, its proximity to Chicago led to its development as a dormitory suburb as well. In 1960, 56 percent of all workers in Skokie worked in the city of Chicago.

Skokie contains a major retail center, built in 1956, which includes the Old Orchard Shopping Plaza bounded by Harrison Street, Skokie Road, Simpson Street, and the Edens Expressway. It was one of the first shopping malls in the nation, and has continued to grow through the 1970s.

Skokie's population continued to grow until 1970, when it began to decline slightly. During the 1970s the population has matured. Household size has decreased and the percentage of the population over 60 years old has increased from 12 percent in 1970 to 22 percent in 1980. Schools have been closed and are being used for other purposes, and new housing for senior citizens has been built. An increasing number of people of Asian descent have moved into the village. The community is solidly middle-class. Four-fifths of the labor force is in white-collar work, and more than half the families reported 1979 incomes greater than $30,000. Three-fourths of all housing units are owner-occupied, and the average value of a single-family owner-occupied home is more than $84,000.

Approximately 30,000 square feet of new office space was constructed during the 1970s, and this kind of building is expected to continue. The opening of an additional complete interchange on the Edens Expressway, at Old Orchard Road, has stimulated development in the northwest corner of the village. In addition, the village has provided for the issuance of industrial development bonds.

In 1969, Skokie residents voted, along with others in Niles and Maine Townships, to establish a two-year junior college, and Oakton Community College began operation the next year. It is presently located in Des Plaines, with a branch in Skokie. The village has doubled the size of its municipal building, and a major addition to the public library made it the second largest in the state.

Marjorie DeVault

Tinley Park

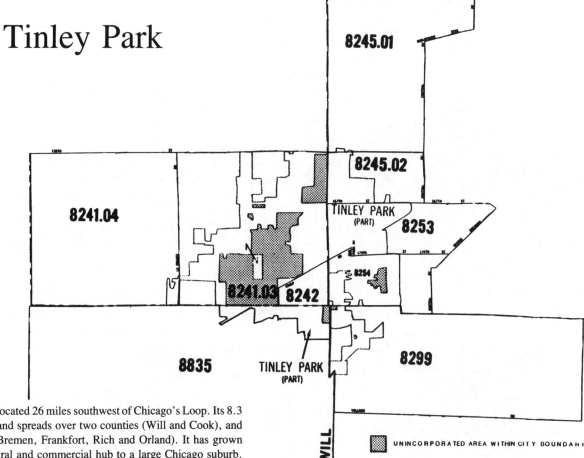

8245.01

8245.02

8241.04

TINLEY PARK (PART)

8253

8254

8241.03 8242

8835

TINLEY PARK (PART)

8299

WILL

UNINCORPORATED AREA WITHIN CITY BOUNDARY

Tinley Park is located 26 miles southwest of Chicago's Loop. Its 8.3 square miles of land spreads over two counties (Will and Cook), and four townships (Bremen, Frankfort, Rich and Orland). It has grown from an agricultural and commercial hub to a large Chicago suburb. Despite its growth, the village has continued to have a small town atmosphere, and decendants of many of the original families still live there. It enjoys the benefits of careful planning and nearness to Chicago's cultural and economic opportunities.

The community which became Tinley Park began in 1835 with the arrival of the John Fulton family. These first white settlers were dairy farmers who had come by covered wagon from New York State. They established a 160-acre homestead, and by the early 1840s were buying up additional land. In the late 1840s, after the failure of the liberal-nationalist revolution in Germany, many German immigrants began settling in the area. A large number of these immigrants were from Bremen, and named their new home "New Bremen".

The Chicago and Rock Island Railroad began construction of its main line between Joliet and Chicago in 1851, and the New Bremen settlement was located on this line. This was the most important economic factor in the community's growth. Nearly every man in the settlement was employed by the railroad in some capacity during its construction. The earlier settlers were joined by more immigrants, drawn to the area by employment opportunities offered by the railroad. Many of these stayed to farm, start businesses or just make their homes in the settlement.

New Bremen began to grow as an agricultural and commercial center after the railroad's arrival. A wheat grinding mill was built in 1872 by George Bortels and was powered by a huge windmill. Artists were attracted to the area by the picturesque sight of the windmill towering over the land. When it was finally torn down some years later, stones from it were used in building several turn-of-the-century homes.

By 1890, many residents felt it was time to incorporate since the village had become a fairly important commercial center. The name Tinley Park was chosen to honor the Tinley brothers, Sam, Charles and Edward, all of whom helped build the Rock Island Railroad. In 1892, the Village of Tinley Park was incorporated. The census of 1900 counted 300 residents. In 1912, the first bank was opened and is still serving the community.

Tinley Park grew very slowly during the first half of the 20th century. The total population was 309 in 1910, 493 in 1920, and did not exceed 1,000 until 1940. In 1950, the total was still short of 2,500. It wasn't until the 1950s that the village began to experience a population boom which has not slowed. During that decade, the total grew to nearly 6,400, and by 1970 the population exceeded 12,000. By the late 1970s, Tinley Park was the fastest growing community in Cook County. Between 1970 and 1980, the population increased more than 100 percent to 26,000.

Tinley Park's population is quite young. The median age is 27.6 years. Almost a third are 18 years of age or less, and only 7 percent 65 or above. These are familiar characteristics of a rapidly growing suburb.

The median family income in the village for 1979 was $26,901. This was lower than in some other southwestern suburbs such as Oak Lawn and Oak Forest. However, the slightly younger population of Tinley Park may account for part of this. Only 3 percent of the families in the village had incomes below the poverty level. Of the 12,000 employed persons, more than half were working in white-collar occupations in 1980. This suggests that Tinley Park is a solid young middle-class community.

Many of the older homes in Tinley Park, found along Oak Park Avenue, have undergone restoration while newer housing develop-ments have opened. Most of the housing units are very new. Sixty-one percent of the dwelling units in the village have been built in the last decade; 80 percent since 1960. The median home value in 1980 was $65,300 with prices ranging from $54,000 to $150,000. More than 70 percent of the units are single-family dwellings and more than 70 percent are owner-occupied. Three complexes have been designed especially for senior citizens. Despite the industry-wide slowdown in the late 1970s and early 1980s, home construction has continued in Tinley Park.

Tinley Park
Population and Housing Characteristics, 1930-1980

	1980	1970	1960	1950	1940	1930
Total Popualation.......	26,178	12,382	6,392	2,326	1,136	823
% Male.....................	48.9	49.5	50.2	50.8	50.8	*
% Female...................	51.1	50.5	49.8	49.2	49.2	*
% White....................	96.7	97.6	99.9	100.0	100.0	*
% Black....................	1.8	2.1	0.0	0.0	0.0	*
% Other Nonwhite Races...	1.5	0.3	0.1	0.0	0.0	*
% Under 5 Years Old.......	9.6	10.7	15.3	16.9	7.0	*
% 5-19 Years Old.........	25.2	33.2	32.2	*	*	*
% 20-44 Years Old........	43.5	35.5	35.0	*	*	*
% 45-64 Years Old........	15.3	15.9	12.5	15.7	21.3	*
% 65 Years and Older.....	6.4	4.7	5.0	6.0	8.4	*
Median School Years....	12.5	12.2	12.1	*	*	*
Total Housing Units....	8,627	3,266	1,647	727	*	*
% In One-Unit Structures.	66.0	86.0	99.1	*	*	*
% Owner Occupied.........	70.8	79.4	86.2	77.3	*	*
% Renter Occupied........	26.2	16.0	10.7	14.9	*	*
% Vacant.............	3.0	4.6	3.1	7.8	*	*
% 1+ Persons per Room....	1.7	8.2	13.1	*	*	*

Place 5745 -- Tinley Park , Illinois
Selected Characteristics of Census Tracts: 1980

Tract Number	Total	8241.03	8242	8245.01	8245.02	8253	8254	8299	8835
Total Population.............	26171	11552	927	4	3004	6265	4390	9	20
% Male..................	48.9	49.6	61.8	–	47.7	47.9	46.6	–	–
% Black....................	1.8	0.3	39.9	–	0.6	0.0	1.0	–	–
% Other Nonwhite.........	1.5	2.4	2.2	–	0.7	0.6	0.9	–	–
% Of Spanish Origin.......	1.5	2.2	1.5	–	1.1	0.9	1.1	–	–
% Foreign Born...........	4.3	4.5	2.1	–	6.0	3.5	4.4	–	–
% Living In Group Quarters........	4.1	0.0	100.0	–	4.7	0.0	0.0	–	–
% 13 Years Old And Under.........	25.0	30.6	0.6	–	21.1	20.9	24.0	–	–
% 14-20 Years Old........	11.4	10.9	9.4	–	14.7	11.6	10.6	–	–
% 21-64 Years Old........	57.1	55.5	88.2	–	54.6	59.3	53.4	–	–
% 65-74 Years Old........	3.9	2.0	1.3	–	4.5	5.3	7.0	–	–
% 75 Years Old And Over..	2.6	0.9	0.4	–	5.1	2.9	5.0	–	–
% In Different House......	50.0	52.4	73.2	–	58.8	39.4	47.7	–	–
% Families With Female Head...	9.3	7.3	–	–	12.2	10.9	10.9	–	–
Median School Years Completed....	12.5	12.6	7.9	–	12.5	12.5	12.5	–	–
Median Family Income, 1979....$$	26901	26908	–	–	30016	26244	26488	–	–
% Income Below Poverty Level.....	2.7	2.7	–	–	3.3	2.9	2.1	–	–
% Income Of $30,000 Or More.....	39.5	38.7	–	–	50.1	35.6	40.4	–	–
% White Collar Workers....	55.8	53.1	–	–	55.7	58.5	58.7	–	–
% Civilian Labor Force Unemployed.	4.9	5.2	–	–	4.1	5.8	3.2	–	–
% Riding To Work By Automobile....	84.5	89.0	–	–	87.4	79.7	78.3	–	–
Mean Commuting Time - Minutes...	32.6	34.3	–	–	29.5	31.3	33.0	–	–
Population Per Household......	3.0	3.3	0.0	–	3.0	2.7	2.8	–	–
Total Housing Units..........	8623	3633	0	1	1003	2345	1631	2	8
% Condominiums...................	8.6	13.3	–	–	14.1	0.0	7.2	–	–
% Built 1970 Or Later.....	60.8	80.6	–	–	54.9	32.3	61.4	–	–
% Owner Occupied...............	70.3	82.2	–	–	69.3	58.5	61.9	–	–
% With 1+ Persons Per Room.....	1.7	1.8	–	–	1.9	1.8	1.5	–	–
Median Value: Owner Units......$$	65300	68400	–	–	64000	59500	64300	–	–
Median Rent: Rental Units.....$$	273	286	–	–	278	274	245	–	–
Median Number Of Rooms: All Units.	5.6	5.6	–	–	5.6	5.2	5.2	–	–

Tinley Park
Selected Characteristics of Census Tracts: 1970

Tract Number	TOTAL	8241	8242	8245	8253	8254	8299	8835
Total Population.............	12572	14423	605	13094	7453	3038	4924	10424
% Male...................	49.5	49.4	54.2	49.8	50.2	49.2	49.5	50.0
% Black...................	2.1	0.0	43.3	0.0	0.0	0.0	0.0	0.0
% Other Nonwhite.........	0.3	0.4	0.3	0.2	0.2	0.3	0.1	0.4
% Of Spanish Language.....	0.7	1.1	0.0	1.0	0.0	1.2	2.9	0.6
% Foreign Born...........	2.1	1.7	0.0	2.8	2.2	2.2	2.6	2.8
% Living In Group Quarters........	4.9	0.0	100.0	0.6	0.1	0.3	0.2	0.8
% 13 Years Old And Under.........	32.8	37.8	5.3	39.1	32.1	32.8	35.5	33.7
% 14-20 Years Old........	12.4	11.4	9.8	8.1	13.8	13.2	14.1	11.9
% 21-64 Years Old........	50.2	47.8	75.0	49.5	49.2	47.5	46.7	48.1
% 65-74 Years Old........	2.9	2.0	4.8	2.0	3.2	4.3	2.6	3.9
% 75 Years Old And Over.........	1.8	1.0	5.1	1.2	1.7	2.2	1.1	2.4
% In Different House........	44.4	48.3	18.8	27.3	48.6	55.0	62.8	56.5
% Families With Female Head.......	4.7	4.2	–	2.7	4.9	4.8	4.1	4.5
Median School Years Completed.......	12.3	12.3	9.0	12.3	12.5	12.3	12.6	12.2
Median Family Income, 1969......$$	12798	13301	–	13635	12707	13214	14587	13022
% Income Below Poverty Level....	3.5	1.6	–	1.6	4.1	1.8	1.9	3.4
% Income of $15,000 or More.....	31.7	37.1	–	38.1	32.7	34.5	47.4	36.5
% White Collar Workers....	29.9	29.5	–	40.6	26.5	32.7	40.2	28.0
% Civilian Labor Force Unemployed.	1.4	2.2	–	1.1	2.9	1.8	3.1	3.0
% Riding To Work By Automobile....	75.6	87.8	–	80.8	75.8	72.8	78.8	81.0
Population Per Household.........	3.8	4.1	–	4.0	3.7	3.8	4.1	3.7
Total Housing Units.........	3265	3706	0	3349	2067	824	1299	2840
% Condominiums & Cooperatives.....	0.3	0.0	–	0.3	0.0	0.0	0.0	0.0
% Built 1960 Or Later.....	47.7	57.1	–	86.6	33.9	38.1	40.7	38.0
% Owner Occupied........	79.1	81.7	–	90.1	80.6	78.6	84.9	80.7
% With 1+ Persons Per Room......	8.2	9.7	–	5.2	8.1	10.9	9.1	8.3
Median Value: Owner Units......$$	22400	23100	–	28000	21100	22200	22500	21500
Median Rent: Rental Units.....$$	152	162	–	176	138	150	138	123
Median Number Of Rooms: All Units.	5.6	5.8	–	6.2	5.6	5.3	6.0	5.6

The Tinley Park State Mental Health Center and the William A. Howe Center cover a combined 627-acre site. They are both owned and operated by the State of Illinois, which is probably the community's largest employer. The Mental Health Center provides 4,000 patients annually with short-term psychiatric care. The Howe Developmental Disability Center houses retarded patients on a long-term basis.

Nineteen manufacturing firms are currently located in Tinley Park and employ some 550 people. There are also 41 service firms which have nearly 1,200 employees. The village is attempting to build a strong base of clean, light industry, technological research and corporate offices. To this end, it offers financial and tax incentives to new industry.

The growing retail establishment in Tinley Park includes two major retail centers, the 125-acre Brementowne Mall and the Tinley Park Shopping Center on 167th Street, which is connected to downtown Tinley Park by scattered businesses along Oak Park Avenue. Shopping is also available at Orland Square, in nearby Orland Park.

Planning has been an important part of community government since incorporation when various committees were appointed to review the community's needs. Ten major commissions have operated for a number of years and have provided residents with another means of input into community government. One of these, the Long Range Planning Commission, has monitored village growth and planned

utilities and services in anticipation of an eventual population of 40,000. They have also decided to limit the ultimate size of the village to 16 square miles.

According to transportation experts, Tinley Park has the greatest potential for industrial growth of all Chicagoland communities. Its location near the Interstate-80 and Interstate-57 expressways and service by the Rock Island and the Pennsylvania Railroads give it access to many markets. The village has 2,500 acres zoned for industry along the I-80 corridor, 500 acres of which are already occupied. The 77-acre Sandalwood Industrial Park is nearly built up completely, and the 70-acre New Gateway Industrial Park is about to begin development. In addition, there are the Tinley Park Industrial Parks covering 151 combined acres and the Thornton Industrial Park of 65 acres also located in the village.

Tinley Park gives the imrpession of a well-planned and burgeoning community. While population has continued to expand, it has not strained the village's resources since the expansion was planned. New residents have been absorbed readily into the fabric of the community since they have much in common with those already there. With its careful plan for the future, Tinley Park is likely to continue as a popular family community which will increasingly be supported by a solid industrial base.

Gail Danks Welter

Place 6075

Waukegan

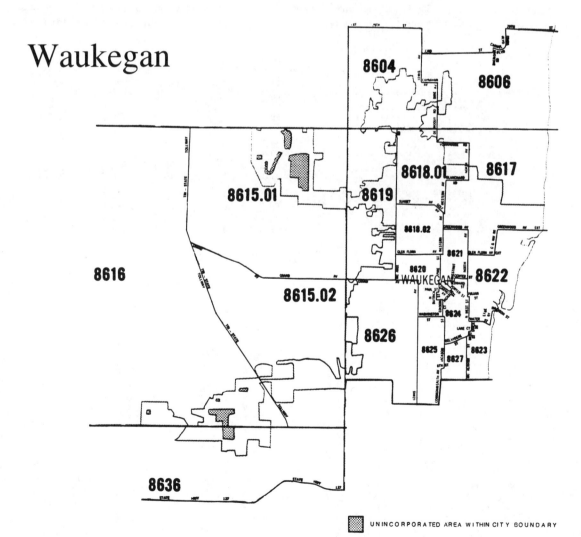

▨ UNINCORPORATED AREA WITHIN CITY BOUNDARY

Waukegan is in Lake County, Illinois, about 39 miles north of the Loop and a few miles south of the Wisconsin border. It is built on a bluff about 50 feet above Lake Michigan, and on the plain between the bluff and the lake shore.

Title to the land in the vicinity was ceded to the U.S. by Indians in 1829. In 1835, Thomas Jenkins of Chicago erected a two-story frame structure under the bluff, north of the ravine and east of the present Chicago and North Western Railroad tracks. In 1836, farmers began settling the prairie west of the lake. Surveying of the area by the government began and, in 1839, Lake County was established. In 1841, the town of Little Fort was incorporated, and two months later it was made the county seat. It possessed an excellent harbor, providing a means for shipping furs, hides, timber, and agricultural produce to markets. The settlement prospered, and by 1847 there was a population of more than 1,200, occupying some 300 dwellings and business establishments. In 1849, the name of the town was changed from Little Fort to its Indian equivalent, Waukegan. The first train of the Illinois and Wisconsin Railroad (not the Chicago and North Western) made a trip from Chicago to Waukegan in three hours in 1855, providing another transportation link between Waukegan and the rapidly growing city of Chicago.

Although Glen Flora Springs was popular and Waukegan hoped to develop as a major tourist attraction, the depression of 1878 dashed these hopes. Between 1870 and 1880, Waukegan lost population, and in the next decade it increased only a little beyond its population of 1870. The westward movement following the Civil War slowed the agricultural development of the area, as local papers advertised land in Kansas and Nebraska. Shipping on the Great Lakes was becoming concentrated in Chicago, Milwaukee, and other ports, leaving Waukegan behind.

In 1889, the Waukegan and Southern Railroad (later the Elgin, Joliet, and Eastern) opened a terminal in Waukegan, providing the city with good connections with all railroads passing in or out of Chicago. In 1895, the Bluff City Electric Street Railway (later the Chicago, North Shore, and Milwaukee) orginated in Waukegan and, by the turn of the century, was operating between Chicago and Waukegan. Two years later the first manufacturing industry located in Waukegan. Within a few years there was a wire mill, a starch factory, and a sugar refinery, and Waukegan entered a new period of growth. At the turn of the century, the population of Waukegan was 9,426. Ten years later it had grown to 16,069. Additional stimulus to commerce came during World War I, when Waukegan acquired the name "Camp Town" because of its proximity to the Great Lakes Naval Training Center a few miles to the south. The 1920 census showed a growth in population to 19,226. The general prosperity continued through the 1920s, with additional industries and a rapid expansion of public services.

By 1930, Waukegan had a population of 33,499. About 1,000 were black, representing a large increase in a community whose origins date back to free black settlement in Lake County as early as 1835. The earliest settlers of Little Fort had been largely native Americans, many of them from New England, along with some English, Scotch, and Irish. Persons of German origin formed the next major group of settlers. Around the turn of the century, many of the new inhabitants were Scandinavians, Germans, and Irish. The last of the immigrant groups to settle came around the time of the first World War, and included significant numbers of persons from Lithuania, Latvia, Yu-

Waukegan
Population and Housing Characteristics, 1930-1980

	1980	1970	1960	1950	1940	1930
Total Population.......	67,653	65,269	55,719	38,946	34,241	33,499
% Male....................	48.5	48.2	48.9	49.9	50.4	52.6
% Female..................	51.5	51.8	51.1	50.1	49.6	47.4
% White...................	72.5	86.2	91.6	94.0	96.5	96.9
% Black...................	18.5	12.9	8.0	5.9	3.4	3.0
% Other Nonwhite Races...	9.0	0.9	0.4	0.1	0.1	0.1
% Under 5 Years Old......	8.6	9.3	12.8	9.5	7.4	8.8
% 5-19 Years Old.........	24.4	28.8	25.1	19.6	23.2	25.8
% 20-44 Years Old........	38.1	33.4	35.0	41.2	43.8	45.9
% 45-64 Years Old........	19.0	20.6	20.0	22.8	20.6	16.0
% 65 Years and Older.....	9.9	7.9	7.1	6.9	5.0	3.5
Median School Years.....	12.4	12.2	11.7	10.9	8.7	*
Total Housing Units....	25,679	21,787	17,253	11,481	9,676	*
% In One-Unit Structures.	52.2	55.8	63.2	*	*	*
% Owner Occupied.........	52.2	55.7	54.9	53.7	40.6	*
% Renter Occupied........	42.8	40.5	40.9	44.7	57.6	*
% Vacant.................	5.0	3.8	4.2	1.6	1.8	*
% 1+ Persons per Room....	6.8	9.5	11.4	10.9	*	*

Place 6075 — Waukegan , Illinois
Selected Characteristics of Census Tracts: 1980

Tract Number	Total	8604	8606	8615.01	8615.02	8616	8617	8618.01	8618.02	8619	8620
Total Population.............	67653	970	20	717	575	19	4628	4981	5024	5470	6126
% Male..........................	48.5	50.9	–	48.3	44.5	–	47.8	49.0	47.2	49.9	47.6
% Black.........................	18.5	17.4	–	4.5	18.8	–	1.2	4.1	23.0	6.1	29.4
% Other Nonwhite................	9.1	6.2	–	8.6	5.6	–	4.1	5.0	7.0	4.6	5.4
% Of Spanish Origin.............	13.7	6.9	–	6.6	3.0	–	3.1	6.8	6.4	8.2	8.4
% Foreign Born..................	10.6	4.3	–	8.9	4.9	–	6.1	5.1	6.0	6.1	6.4
% Living In Group Quarters......	2.6	0.0	–	0.0	0.0	–	0.4	0.0	1.9	0.3	0.0
% 13 Years Old And Under........	22.0	25.9	–	27.1	18.3	–	19.6	23.0	23.6	20.2	20.6
% 14-20 Years Old...............	13.0	17.8	–	9.2	7.3	–	11.9	14.0	14.3	14.0	12.8
% 21-64 Years Old...............	55.0	53.6	–	61.8	68.9	–	57.8	57.6	56.3	60.2	53.9
% 65-74 Years Old...............	6.2	1.9	–	1.7	3.1	–	6.8	4.0	2.9	3.9	8.6
% 75 Years Old And Over.........	3.7	0.8	–	0.3	2.4	–	3.9	1.4	2.8	1.6	4.2
% In Different House............	49.0	60.7	–	93.1	100.0	–	34.3	39.6	50.7	47.8	37.1
% Families With Female Head.....	21.4	8.2	–	19.9	40.7	–	10.6	14.3	23.7	15.3	19.9
Median School Years Completed...	12.4	12.8	–	13.0	13.7	–	12.9	12.6	12.5	12.7	12.4
Median Family Income, 1979......$$	22692	28911	–	24712	18190	–	32002	27581	20904	26936	22315
% Income Below Poverty Level...	7.2	4.6	–	5.0	14.1	–	1.8	2.4	6.6	2.1	4.1
% Income Of $30,000 Or More.....	29.2	44.9	–	32.2	20.1	–	55.7	40.9	22.4	41.1	27.6
% White Collar Workers.........	50.6	58.9	–	78.2	64.4	–	69.7	54.9	49.2	57.6	51.4
% Civilian Labor Force Unemployed.	7.9	3.9	–	2.8	0.0	–	4.2	8.1	5.7	7.3	8.3
% Riding To Work By Automobile..	90.4	94.0	–	98.6	92.5	–	90.1	95.4	92.8	92.4	88.7
Mean Commuting Time - Minutes...	19.1	19.9	–	22.2	15.7	–	15.5	18.2	19.0	19.9	21.5
Population Per Household.........	2.7	3.4	–	2.8	1.9	–	2.8	2.9	2.8	2.7	2.7
Total Housing Units........	25671	292	7	283	385	8	1694	1806	1811	2179	2320
% Condominiums................	1.2	0.0	–	63.6	0.0	–	0.0	0.0	0.7	0.0	0.0
% Built 1970 Or Later.........	16.0	12.3	–	97.3	97.5	–	8.3	10.3	13.0	33.6	3.6
% Owner Occupied..............	51.7	91.1	–	79.2	0.8	–	79.6	66.8	43.4	52.8	70.3
% With 1+ Persons Per Room....	6.8	3.5	–	0.8	3.3	–	2.3	4.3	6.7	3.8	5.1
Median Value: Owner Units......$$	50400	62200	–	51700	–	–	67400	49800	47500	52600	48400
Median Rent: Rental Units...$$	226	294	–	409	288	–	245	258	237	297	216
Median Number Of Rooms: All Units.	4.7	5.6	–	5.6	3.6	–	5.6	4.9	4.4	4.5	5.0

Place 6075 -- Waukegan , Illinois
Selected Characteristics of Census Tracts: 1980

Tract Number	8621	8622	8623	8624	8625	8626	8627	8636
Total Population.............	4512	4070	4490	6094	5343	10346	4234	34
% Male.........................	47.0	52.2	48.6	47.9	49.0	47.3	50.6	-
% Black........................	5.6	9.4	66.8	12.8	22.5	11.8	42.4	-
% Other Nonwhite...............	5.9	11.3	12.5	20.1	10.2	8.2	16.8	-
% Of Spanish Origin............	8.4	18.7	20.8	32.8	14.4	8.7	43.5	-
% Foreign Born.................	6.4	14.4	12.3	19.4	10.7	10.4	26.4	-
% Living In Group Quarters.....	0.0	8.3	1.4	0.7	11.9	5.3	0.0	-
% 13 Years Old And Under.......	21.1	18.8	26.6	24.9	20.8	18.2	30.1	-
% 14-20 Years Old..............	10.4	13.8	14.9	13.8	14.6	10.1	15.7	-
% 21-64 Years Old..............	54.5	57.0	45.9	50.7	53.8	58.1	48.4	-
% 65-74 Years Old..............	8.4	5.7	6.5	6.2	6.7	9.0	4.3	-
% 75 Years Old And Over........	5.6	4.7	6.1	4.4	4.2	4.6	1.5	-
% In Different House...........	50.3	61.9	49.2	55.1	43.6	52.2	51.8	-
% Families With Female Head....	17.0	22.7	45.9	22.5	25.6	21.0	25.2	-
Median School Years Completed..	12.6	12.7	10.4	12.3	11.7	12.4	10.0	-
Median Family Income, 1979...$$	22381	21761	14830	17254	20269	23381	14013	-
% Income Below Poverty Level...	2.4	11.4	16.9	14.6	11.2	3.3	23.7	-
% Income Of $30,000 Or More....	26.0	28.2	13.0	17.6	18.4	30.3	14.0	-
% White Collar Workers.........	55.5	57.1	23.1	39.3	39.0	53.7	25.6	-
% Civilian Labor Force Unemployed.	5.4	9.0	11.7	11.7	8.6	7.0	13.0	-
% Riding To Work By Automobile...	90.6	84.7	83.8	89.5	91.4	89.0	91.9	-
Mean Commuting Time - Minutes...	19.2	20.6	21.8	20.3	19.1	17.5	20.1	-
Population Per Household........	2.5	2.4	3.0	2.7	2.9	2.5	3.5	-
Total Housing Units..........	1883	1842	1620	2403	1683	4147	1293	15
% Condominiums.................	2.2	0.7	0.0	0.4	1.8	0.4	0.0	-
% Built 1970 Or Later..........	2.5	15.2	10.6	12.6	10.2	25.3	0.0	-
% Owner Occupied...............	56.6	27.5	25.8	37.2	65.2	50.6	42.5	-
% With 1+ Persons Per Room.....	2.8	7.0	18.5	10.2	7.7	4.1	20.4	-
Median Value: Owner Units...$$	48300	59500	34200	39400	43200	56200	37300	-
Median Rent: Rental Units......	236	209	145	201	218	244	191	-
Median Number Of Rooms: All Units.	5.2	3.8	3.9	4.3	4.9	4.5	4.6	-

Waukegan
Selected Characteristics of Census Tracts: 1970

Tract Number	TOTAL	8604	8606	8615	8616	8617	8618	8619	8620	8621	8622
Total Population.............	65134	2545	4188	6783	9508	6389	10086	6497	7300	4775	4291
% Male.........................	48.2	51.2	50.2	49.4	50.7	48.9	48.3	49.5	47.5	47.0	48.0
% Black........................	12.9	0.4	0.2	0.1	0.1	0.3	3.6	0.5	26.0	0.6	7.5
% Other Nonwhite...............	0.9	0.7	0.4	0.5	0.6	0.7	1.3	0.6	0.9	0.6	1.2
% Of Spanish Language..........	7.2	4.0	1.3	2.4	2.2	0.4	4.4	3.7	1.4	2.1	8.3
% Foreign Born.................	6.6	3.4	1.5	2.3	3.4	2.3	4.6	3.3	3.7	4.8	8.8
% Living In Group Quarters.....	1.0	0.3	0.0	0.2	0.0	0.0	1.0	0.7	0.2	0.0	2.9
% 13 Years Old And Under.......	27.7	33.0	28.0	29.9	36.1	28.1	32.9	34.1	25.0	25.4	24.7
% 14-20 Years Old..............	12.0	12.1	11.1	12.5	12.0	12.4	11.9	10.9	12.6	10.4	12.7
% 21-64 Years Old..............	52.4	50.1	55.1	52.7	48.3	52.9	52.0	51.5	52.9	52.7	49.3
% 65-74 Years Old..............	5.0	2.9	4.5	3.5	2.4	4.4	1.8	2.6	6.2	7.8	7.8
% 75 Years Old And Over........	3.0	1.8	1.3	1.4	1.2	2.2	1.5	0.9	3.2	3.7	5.5
% In Different House...........	53.8	52.1	44.7	53.5	44.5	62.3	50.6	54.1	64.8	53.4	44.5
% Families With Female Head....	10.3	4.4	5.6	6.7	4.6	6.8	8.0	5.6	8.9	9.5	14.7
Median School Years Completed..	12.2	12.0	12.1	12.2	12.2	12.2	12.6	12.4	12.3	12.4	12.3
Median Family Income, 1969...$$	11478	11850	11580	12057	12847	14761	11738	12564	11790	12043	9519
% Income Below Poverty Level...	6.4	0.8	3.5	5.2	2.0	3.3	4.2	4.6	4.0	3.2	12.0
% Income of $15,000 or More....	28.0	30.1	24.9	27.7	34.4	48.6	26.6	26.9	29.7	30.0	25.1
% White Collar Workers.........	28.3	21.1	24.2	25.1	27.8	41.9	33.4	29.0	23.8	39.8	28.3
% Civilian Labor Force Unemployed.	3.3	4.2	3.5	1.9	3.1	2.3	3.0	2.3	2.6	3.6	2.4
% Riding To Work By Automobile...	85.2	96.6	92.5	91.7	91.8	90.9	90.7	91.0	86.9	88.5	73.8
Population Per Household........	3.1	3.7	3.0	3.4	3.9	3.3	3.4	3.6	3.0	2.9	2.6
Total Housing Units..........	21784	701	1393	2078	2553	1959	3086	1832	2454	1737	1686
% Condominiums & Cooperatives.....	0.3	0.0	0.4	0.0	0.0	0.0	0.0	0.0	0.2	3.1	0.0
% Built 1960 Or Later..........	23.0	31.5	53.0	44.2	46.5	24.0	48.9	42.4	9.1	15.7	11.8
% Owner Occupied...............	55.4	84.5	79.8	80.0	82.2	77.2	58.4	78.8	67.6	54.0	29.8
% With 1+ Persons Per Room.....	9.5	10.1	7.9	7.2	11.0	7.0	13.0	11.4	7.8	3.9	8.5
Median Value: Owner Units...$$	19800	22000	18800	23500	22100	25000	18600	19400	19100	19400	22800
Median Rent: Rental Units...$$	123	116	129	135	136	141	156	166	121	134	108
Median Number Of Rooms: All Units.	4.7	5.3	4.4	4.8	5.4	5.1	4.5	4.8	4.8	5.1	3.9

Tract Number	8623	8624	8625	8626	8627	8636
Total Population.............	4793	6533	4316	9888	4212	4128
% Male.........................	48.5	48.1	48.5	49.2	48.4	50.4
% Black........................	75.3	7.0	9.9	1.4	26.9	0.2
% Other Nonwhite...............	0.5	0.9	0.6	1.0	1.2	0.4
% Of Spanish Language..........	11.7	19.1	8.8	3.5	26.8	0.3
% Foreign Born.................	5.2	11.5	8.1	6.7	16.0	5.3
% Living In Group Quarters.....	2.9	0.4	0.2	2.0	0.0	4.7
% 13 Years Old And Under.......	32.7	24.8	24.1	21.7	29.7	27.8
% 14-20 Years Old..............	12.5	12.9	12.6	11.9	12.3	13.9
% 21-64 Years Old..............	47.1	51.2	54.4	59.1	50.5	48.2
% 65-74 Years Old..............	5.3	7.0	5.6	4.6	4.0	4.4
% 75 Years Old And Over........	2.4	4.2	3.4	2.8	3.6	5.8
% In Different House...........	48.6	48.2	62.7	51.7	45.5	55.3
% Families With Female Head....	26.1	12.2	9.0	6.8	16.3	5.5
Median School Years Completed..	9.6	11.4	12.0	12.2	9.8	12.6
Median Family Income, 1969...$$	6743	9275	11203	11814	9588	15375
% Income Below Poverty Level...	23.8	8.9	2.4	3.6	10.9	5.7
% Income of $15,000 or More....	12.2	20.1	25.4	28.4	12.2	51.4
% White Collar Workers.........	7.7	24.9	23.5	31.1	9.7	42.5
% Civilian Labor Force Unemployed.	6.7	5.9	2.8	2.1	5.0	2.9
% Riding To Work By Automobile...	69.0	81.7	81.7	89.1	84.6	79.2
Population Per Household........	3.4	2.8	3.0	2.8	3.1	3.5
Total Housing Units..........	1466	2432	1463	3588	1465	1141
% Condominiums & Cooperatives.....	0.0	0.0	0.0	0.0	0.0	0.0
% Built 1960 Or Later..........	8.9	12.2	11.4	44.6	0.9	27.4
% Owner Occupied...............	28.4	36.3	66.6	60.0	41.4	75.9
% With 1+ Persons Per Room.....	20.7	10.3	7.5	6.1	14.6	4.8
Median Value: Owner Units...$$	15100	16200	17900	21500	15900	30700
Median Rent: Rental Units...$$	102	112	117	141	106	145
Median Number Of Rooms: All Units.	4.3	4.3	4.7	4.3	4.5	5.9

goslavia, and Italy. In 1930, Germans, Swedes, Finns, Lithuanians, and Yugoslavians were the leading nationalities among the foreign stock.

Unemployment was high in Waukegan during the Depression, and the population remained stable. Extensive civil works programs were undertaken on a municipal golf course, parks, highways, schools, library, and a new city hall. During 1936-38, there were a number of bitter labor disputes.

In the early 1940s, the manufacturing sector of the town was converted to war production. The rapid enlargement of the Great Lakes Naval Training Center again stimulated business in Waukegan. After the war, industrial expansion continued, and population again began to increase. Between 1950 and 1960, the population of Waukegan increased 43 percent from 38,946 to 55,719. A considerable share of this increase in population was the result of annexation—6,274 persons resided in territory annexed during the decade. by 1960, the Naval Training Center contained 16,289 persons in the armed forces. As a result of its distance from Chicago and the existence of local industrial employment, only a small percentage of all workers residing in Waukegan work in the city of Chicago. The Chicago, North Shore, and Milwaukee Railroad abandoned its commuter service in 1955.

Since 1960, Waukegan has continued to grow, though more slowly. The population went up about 16 percent between 1960 and 1970, and 3 percent to 67,653, between 1970 and 1980. The black population has been increasing since about 1940, constituting about 8 percent of the total in 1960, and just over 18 percent in 1980. As in other industrial areas, the Hispanic population has also begun to increase, reaching almost 14 percent by 1980. Non-whites are now 28 percent of the population of Waukegan. The city has also added new territory through annexations to the northwest and southwest. This new area includes the Lakehurst Shopping Center, a major retail center, and some light industry in the northwestern section, near the airport.

Waukegan has continued to provide industrial employment for many of its residents, and has kept unemployment relatively low. The Waukegan Flats, the lake plain below the bluff, has served as the industrial and rail center for the city, with residential and commerical areas on the bluff. The American Steel and Wire Mill, part of U.S. Steel and successor to Waukegan's first manufacturing plant, closed in 1981; however, other major companies remain in the area, including Johnson Motors and Johns-Manville. Recently, Cherry Electric opened a large new plant in Waukegan. Abbott Laboratories, in neighboring North Chicago, is one of Waukegan's largest employers, and American Hospital has built a new multi-plant operation near the western boundary of the city.

Although the Waukegan plaza was a major retail center in the past, and Waukegan still is the location of almost 700 retail outlets, the city's shopping district has faced competition from newer outlying shopping malls since the mid-1960s. Several of the major downtown stores have closed; however, the city has had considerable success in transforming these buildings to other uses. A community college is housed in one former department store. The city has also capitalized on the fact that it is the county seat and administrative center for Lake County. Much of the downtown area now houses law and professional offices and financial institutions that provide for the demands of county courthouse business. The city has done substantial street and sidewalk work and plans new mixed-use development as part of the downtown revitalization.

Waukegan's hinterland to the west was once valuable primarily as an agricultural area but, with its many lakes, it is becoming increasingly valuable for recreational and residential uses. The city has developed a 750-slip marina in the harbor area, and is a noted salmon fishing center.

Waukegan tends to be similar in socio-economic status to the city of Chicago. Eight percent of workers are unemployed and 7 percent of families live in poverty. The majority of the city's housing is single-family and owner-occupied, though there has been some large apartment construction in recent years. New construction has been primarily in the northern and western sections. The city's poorest minority residents tend to be concentrated on the south side, but the rest of the city is residentially mixed. The near-north section, close to the downtown area, has been designated an Historic Distrct, and substantial rehabilitation work is underway.

Marjorie DeVault

Place 6190

Wheaton

UNINCORPORATED AREA WITHIN CITY BOUNDARY

Wheaton is located 25 miles west of Chicago, the seat of DuPage County for more than 100 years. It covers approximately 8.4 square miles with a population of 43,043 in 1980. It is bounded roughly by the towns of Glen Ellyn on the east, Winfield on the west, Carol Stream on the north and Naperville to the south. Wheaton, as much of DuPage County, was originally a farming settlement. The Pottawatomie tribes were the principal inhabitants of the area when white settlers arrived in the 1830s. One of the first settlers was Erastus Gary. He and his brother built a mill and dam in the early 1830s in what is now Winfield. Warren Wheaton laid claim in 1838 to some 600-700 acres of prairie near what are now Naperville and Roosevelt roads. He was joined by his brother, Jesse, who staked out 300 acres of adjoining land. These claims stretched for three miles over what is now Wheaton. Most early settlers came from New England, and Connecticut in particular. Many of them traced their origins to England and Wales. They brought with them Puritan backgrounds and respect for hard work and education. The Wheaton settlement was described as a transformation of New England to the Illinois prairie.

In 1848, the Wheaton brothers persuaded William B. Ogden, then president of the Chicago and Galena Railroad, to build the line through their land, which they planned to subdivide for residents. The inducement of a free five-mile right-of-way through the Wheaton and Gary farms was readily accepted by the railroad since owners along the proposed route to the north were demanding exorbitant fees for right-of-ways through their lands. In return, the railroad built a station, calling it Wheaton. The town site was platted and recorded in 1853 by the Wheaton brothers. In that same year, the Illinois Institute, a college, was opened under the sponsorship of the Wesleyans. It was intended to stand against evils such as slavery, liquor and secret societies. The college was taken over by the Congregationalists in 1859 and renamed Wheaton College. For many years, the four-year co-educational institution was better known than the town itself, sending missionaries to the far corners of the world. The farming community prospered as a result of the railroad which carried the local goods to a Chicago market, and in 1859 the Village of Wheaton was incorporated.

After several years of attempting to move the county seat from Naperville, located in the southwest corner of the county, the change was approved by the Illinois General Assembly in 1867. Shortly thereafter, a courthouse was built. After some commotion due to the refusal of Naperville officials to allow the county records to be moved, and a night raid, the records were finally transferred to Wheaton in 1868.

The 1870s brought construction of the first graded school in the community, the establishment of a branch of the National Bank of Chicago which later became the Gary-Wheaton Bank, and other village improvements. Real estate sales increased after the Chicago Fire, since the village offered commuter service to the city, schools, a college, churches and a business district. However, as in other areas, the Panic of 1873 ultimately slowed construction and growth. From the late 1880s on (except for a brief period after the repeal of national Prohibition), Wheaton has prohibited the sale of alcoholic beverages of any sort. In 1880, the village changed to a municipal form of government and began improvement and construction of streets, sidewalks, sanitary sewers and a central water system. A new courthouse was built

Wheaton
Population and Housing Characteristics, 1930-1980

	1980	1970	1960	1950	1940	1930
Total Population.......	43,043	31,138	24,312	11,638	7,389	7,258
% Male..................	48.2	48.4	48.4	47.1	47.7	48.8
% Female................	51.8	51.6	51.6	52.9	52.3	51.2
% White.................	94.8	97.6	98.4	97.8	98.8	98.1
% Black.................	2.5	1.9	1.4	2.0	1.1	1.8
% Other Nonwhite Races...	2.7	0.5	0.2	0.2	0.1	0.1
% Under 5 Years Old......	6.8	8.2	11.9	9.8	6.4	7.6
% 5-19 Years Old.........	24.7	33.4	31.2	23.2	24.2	26.0
% 20-44 Years Old........	41.6	32.0	34.5	39.0	38.8	40.5
% 45-64 Years Old........	18.9	19.4	16.6	20.4	22.7	19.5
% 65 Years and Older.....	7.9	6.9	5.8	5.6	7.7	6.4
Median School Years....	14.7	13.1	12.9	12.7	12.2	*
Total Housing Units....	15,238	8,757	6,464	3,052	2,088	*
% In One-Unit Structures.	69.7	80.4	88.6	79.4	81.4	*
% Owner Occupied.........	68.2	74.4	81.1	75.2	57.7	*
% Renter Occupied........	26.2	23.4	15.0	21.9	39.4	*
% Vacant.................	5.6	2.2	3.9	2.9	2.9	*
% 1+ Persons per Room....	1.1	4.2	7.2	7.5	5.1	*

Place 6190 — Wheaton, Illinois
Selected Characteristics of Census Tracts: 1980

Tract Number	Total	8416.02	8417	8418	8419	8424	8425	8426.01	8426.02	8427.01
Total Population.............	43043	0	10	4367	6337	4848	2968	10981	1961	11571
% Male.....................	48.2	–	–	49.4	48.3	49.1	50.2	46.7	49.3	48.1
% Black....................	2.5	–	–	0.3	2.1	7.4	0.8	2.0	0.4	2.7
% Other Nonwhite...........	2.7	–	+	2.4	2.6	3.2	1.0	2.1	2.5	3.6
% Of Spanish Origin........	1.4	–	–	1.4	1.0	1.2	1.9	1.9	1.3	1.2
% Foreign Born.............	5.9	–	–	6.0	4.8	7.8	4.8	5.2	7.2	6.3
% Living In Group Quarters.	6.7	–	–	0.8	26.4	3.3	4.1	8.0	0.0	0.0
% 13 Years Old And Under...	20.2	–	–	21.5	15.3	21.0	17.0	18.5	22.5	24.2
% 14-20 Years Old..........	13.5	–	–	11.7	28.6	10.8	14.2	11.0	14.3	9.1
% 21-64 Years Old..........	58.3	–	–	58.7	51.0	59.4	57.2	57.4	57.6	63.0
% 65-74 Years Old..........	4.4	–	–	5.4	3.2	5.1	7.3	5.6	3.8	2.7
% 75 Years Old And Over....	3.5	–	–	2.7	2.0	3.7	4.4	7.4	1.8	0.9
% In Different House.......	58.4	–	–	46.9	66.4	52.6	39.2	52.8	54.7	72.1
% Families With Female Head..	9.9	–	–	7.6	5.3	11.8	9.4	11.7	3.1	11.6
Median School Years Completed..	14.7	–	–	15.9	15.3	13.9	14.9	14.0	16.1	14.6
Median Family Income, 1979......$$	31185	–	–	32629	31281	26362	32170	30894	51881	30877
% Income Below Poverty Level....	1.9	–	–	2.3	1.1	0.4	3.8	3.1	1.3	1.3
% Income Of $30,000 Or More.....	53.5	–	–	56.7	52.7	38.6	56.0	52.3	88.4	53.3
% White Collar Workers.........	76.5	–	–	79.0	68.0	67.9	80.0	77.5	87.1	80.2
% Civilian Labor Force Unemployed.	2.8	–	–	2.7	3.8	3.4	3.0	2.7	2.2	3.5
% Riding To Work By Automobile....	76.6	–	–	78.5	61.4	79.1	69.5	75.3	77.2	85.0
Mean Commuting Time - Minutes...	27.2	–	–	24.0	23.1	24.3	24.0	29.3	31.0	30.3
Population Per Household.......	2.8	–	–	3.0	3.0	2.7	2.8	2.7	3.5	2.7
Total Housing Units..........	15232	0	2	1472	1598	1790	1066	4101	632	4571
% Condominiums...............	11.6	–	–	5.2	0.0	1.4	1.4	16.5	0.0	21.5
% Built 1970 Or Later........	42.9	–	–	7.7	17.1	4.5	3.2	49.5	46.6	81.2
% Owner Occupied.............	66.2	–	–	84.6	69.3	65.7	69.2	62.5	88.1	65.5
% With 1+ Persons Per Room......	1.1	–	–	1.2	1.4	3.0	1.1	1.0	0.0	0.6
Median Value: Owner Units.......$$	81100	–	–	80000	83400	67600	86600	78300	142700	83500
Median Rent: Rental Units.......$	292	–	–	289	262	236	236	351	501	300
Median Number Of Rooms: All Units.	5.6	–	–	5.6	5.6	5.6	5.6	5.5	5.6	5.6

Wheaton
Selected Characteristics of Census Tracts: 1970

Tract Number	TOTAL	8416	8417	8418	8419	8424	8425	8426	8427
Total Population	31138	6398	6080	8763	5320	6262	4225	11322	14501
% Male	48.4	49.3	49.3	49.3	52.2	48.2	42.4	47.9	50.4
% Black	1.9	0.3	1.1	0.2	2.3	6.0	1.3	0.1	0.2
% Other Nonwhite	0.5	0.3	0.2	0.4	1.0	0.3	0.9	0.2	0.5
% Of Spanish Language	1.7	3.3	2.9	2.1	1.9	2.4	1.3	1.3	1.3
% Foreign Born	3.8	6.5	4.9	3.0	2.8	4.5	5.6	3.2	2.6
% Living In Group Quarters	5.8	0.7	0.9	1.5	18.4	0.1	11.9	6.8	1.1
% 13 Years Old And Under	27.5	29.9	31.6	31.8	22.1	27.2	22.5	30.8	36.3
% 14-20 Years Old	16.3	12.4	12.6	14.2	23.6	12.1	21.5	14.1	12.4
% 21-64 Years Old	49.3	51.3	51.3	48.3	48.0	52.9	46.0	46.5	48.6
% 65-74 Years Old	4.1	4.6	3.0	3.2	4.0	5.0	6.0	3.9	1.8
% 75 Years Old And Over	2.8	1.8	1.5	2.5	2.2	2.8	4.0	4.7	0.9
% In Different House	44.8	56.2	50.4	46.2	35.8	54.0	46.1	39.4	46.0
% Families With Female Head	5.7	5.9	4.2	4.1	5.1	5.1	8.8	4.4	2.8
Median School Years Completed	13.1	12.4	12.5	13.0	13.9	12.7	13.2	13.0	13.0
Median Family Income, 1969......$$	15055	12849	13233	15533	14000	13178	14227	18177	17436
% Income Below Poverty Level	3.5	4.0	2.7	1.4	4.7	2.7	3.6	4.1	0.7
% Income of $15,000 or More	50.2	32.8	37.2	52.2	45.9	38.6	46.3	63.1	60.8
% White Collar Workers	50.2	32.1	37.6	49.7	45.7	46.8	46.5	54.6	58.4
% Civilian Labor Force Unemployed	1.6	1.4	1.7	2.2	1.2	2.7	1.1	1.4	2.3
% Riding To Work By Automobile	72.8	84.9	84.2	79.9	61.7	84.2	57.8	76.3	80.2
Population Per Household	3.4	3.4	3.5	3.8	3.2	3.2	3.0	3.9	4.0
Total Housing Units	8754	1941	1905	2295	1408	2023	1252	2781	3696
% Condominiums & Cooperatives	0.0	0.0	0.0	0.0	0.0	0.0	0.0	0.0	0.0
% Built 1960 Or Later	28.9	27.7	48.0	34.6	38.9	30.6	7.9	44.3	70.7
% Owner Occupied	74.4	68.5	60.1	89.4	61.2	64.4	62.6	86.9	88.0
% With 1+ Persons Per Room	4.2	7.4	6.3	3.9	4.1	5.8	3.0	4.3	3.5
Median Value: Owner Units......$$	29000	22200	24700	30000	29100	24800	31000	33900	34400
Median Rent: Rental Units......$$	155	164	189	171	156	160	129	163	213
Median Number Of Rooms: All Units	5.8	5.1	5.2	6.1	5.4	5.1	5.8	6.5	7.0

around the turn of the century and the Chicago, Aurora and Elgin electric line was laid to Wheaton providing yet another railroad connection with Chicago.

In 1900, 2,345 people lived in Wheaton, and this had increased to 4,137 in 1920. Between 1920 and 1930, some 3,000 persons came to Wheaton and building activity increased. The Depression era brought a slowdown of business, population and housing growth but, after World War II, construction and all forms of economic activity increased. By 1950, almost 12,000 people lived in Wheaton.

In the 1950s, as post-war suburbanization went into full swing, the population rose to over 24,000. During the 1960s, the population increased 28 percent more to 31,000. The latest figures show a population increase of 38 percent in the 1970s bringing the total number of residents to the present 43,000. While Wheaton, like most of Chicago's western suburbs, has always been and continues to be predominantly white, it has a black community dating back to the turn of the century. Several black families moved to the town during the construction of the Chicago, Aurora and Elgin Railroad. Today, there are more than a thousand black residents.

For most of Wheaton's history, farming was a major industry. However, after World War II, the number of farms throughout the county declined dramatically, mainly because of the expense of mechanization and increased taxes. Wheaton was attractive to many families who left Chicago and it became a bedroom community through most of the 1960s. This was due in a large part to the commuter service of the Chicago and North Western and, until its demise, the Aurora and Elgin railroad lines. Later, Wheaton residents who wished to commute by automobile had access to expressways into the city.

The character of Wheaton has been greatly influenced by the success of Wheaton College. Over the years, the strong Christian orientation of the college and the community (which has over 35 churches) has attracted religious activities to the area. Today the city has approximately 34 Christian mission boards, publishing houses and service organizations, many of them located in the northeastern section bordering Carol Stream.

In the 1970s, new employment opportunities opened in DuPage County. While Wheaton itself has never had any heavy industry or office parks, it is close to those in Naperville and Carol Stream. Downtown Wheaton is composed mainly of small retail and service establishments, much as it has been throughout its history. There is no major shopping center within the boundaries of Wheaton, although a few plazas have developed along major thoroughfares such as Main Street, Geneva Road and Butterfield Road to the south.

Settlement began near what has always been the downtown section along Main and Front streets. New housing construction then proceeded to the north and slightly east. Even today many of the early homes can be found in these areas, some still owned by the same families. More recent construction, especially during the 1970s, has taken place in the south of Wheaton, where a number of farms have been broken up into housing developments.

Between 1970 and 1980, the number of housing units increased by 74 percent, bringing the total number to 15,238. Most units are owner-ccupied (68 percent in 1980) and single-family homes. There are some small apartment houses found throughout the city, especially near Wheaton College and along Roosevelt Road. In the 1970s Wheaton Towers, a twin tower complex of 20 stories was constructed in downtown Wheaton on the site of the old Aurora and Elgin Railroad yards. Twelve percent of all current housing units are condominums.

In the early 1970s, reflecting the growth in DuPage County, new county facilities were opened on the southwest side of Wheaton along County Farm Road. Further construction and expansion of Wheaton College was also accomplished during the last decade including the completion of the Billy Graham Center, named for one of the College's most famous alumni.

Other Wheaton residents have gone on to metropolitan, national and world prominence. From the pioneer community came Elbert Gary, son of Erastus Gary, who became the President of United States Steel and for whom the Indiana suburb is named. Wheaton was home to John Gates, founder of the Texaco Corporation, and to Red Grange, the legendary athlete. It became home to Robert R. McCormick, later publisher of the Chicago Tribune, whose house and grounds are preserved with the Cantigny Gardens and Museum.

The current population of Wheaton is affluent and well educated, the latter in part a result of the presence of Wheaton College. The education median suggests an average of two to three years of college. More than half of all families earned incomes greater than $30,000 in 1979, while 2 percent lived in poverty. More than three-fourths of the resident labor force are white-collar workers, while 3 percent are unemployed. The median value of single-family homes is three-fourths higher than in Chicago.

The college and the courthouse are the stable centers of the town, whose function has changed through the years from farm service center to dormitory suburb. The movement of industry and technics to the suburbs may foreshadow another adjustment, as the relation between the city and the metropolitan area continues to evolve. Continued growth could bring new problems to Wheaton, but the town appears to be built around a solid and diversifying base.

Gail Danks Welter

Wilmette

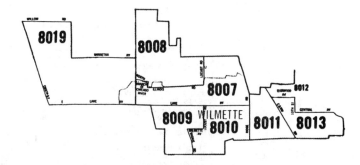

Wilmette lies in Cook County and is located on Lake Michigan, just north of Evanston and Skokie, about 15 miles north of the Loop. The village is named for Antoine Ouilmette, a French-Canadian fur trader who first came to Chicago in 1790. In 1796 or 1797, he married Archange Chevallier, a one-quarter Pottawatomie Indian. They lived on the north bank of the Chicago River (on the site of the present Wrigley Building) until about 1826 when they moved to a cabin on the lake shore near present-day Lake Street in Wilmette. In 1829, the Treaty of Prairie du Chien gave the United States title to much land in northern Illinois. In recognition of the help of Antoine Ouilmette in persuading the Indians to sign the treaty, a grant was made "to Archange Ouilmette, a Pottawatomie woman, wife of Antoine, two sections for herself and her children on Lake Michigan . . ." The Ouilmette Reservation, comprising about 1,280 acres, including the area from the lake shore to present-day 15th Street, and from Elmwood Avenue to Central Street in Evanston. The Ouilmette family lived on the Reservation until 1838. All the land was sold by 1846.

The early settlement of Wilmette came as a northward movement from Evanston by persons in search of farmland. They settled along the Green Bay Trail, a high path along a cliff that ran from Fort Dearborn to Fort Howard in Green Bay, Wisconsin. The trail was subsequently almost entirely swallowed up by the lake. Here the first industry, log banking, was set up. As forests were cleared, timber was rolled down the cliff and floated on the lake to saw mills.

Later, in 1857, John Westerfield acquired farmland on the Ouilmette reservation, and built a pickle factory in the vicinity of what is now Lake Avenue and Sheridan Road, as well as a vinegar factory near the present waterworks.

Transportation during the earliest days of settlement was by horse or by boat. In 1854, the first accommodation train made the 36-mile run from Chicago to Waukegan over the nearly-completed Chicago and North Western tracks in three hours, making the entire North Shore area more accessible. Wilmette is first listed as a regular stop in the May, 1870, edition of *The Official Railway Guide,* with six trains per day.

The Village of Wilmette was laid out in 1869. The first plat included about 525 acres surrounding the intersection of Wilmette Avenue and Central Street. When the village was formally incorporated in 1872, with Westerfield as its first president, the population was slightly more than 300, the minimum for incorporation under Illinois statutes. The boundaries of the village were, roughly, Chestnut Street on the north, Lake Michigan on the east, Isabella on the south and Ridge Avenue on the west. In 1880, when Wilmette first appeared in the census, its population was 419.

During the 1840s, immigrants from near Trier, Germany had begun to farm the area west of Ridge Avenue. In 1874, they incorporated the separate village of Gross Point; however, it was dissolved, mainly because of bankruptcy, in 1919. Despite the slow growth of population during the 1870s this was a period of extensive development of the town. There are said to have been some 60 homes in the village, many of them owned by Chicago businessmen. Wilmette had a grocery, meat market, furniture store, two shoe stores, a tin shop, and a broom factory. There were some 12 miles of graded streets. In 1873, a new brick depot was built. A one-room school was erected at the corner of Tenth Street and Central Avenue in 1871. During the 1880s, Population increased by 1,000, reaching 1,458 at the 1890 census.

In 1894, partly as a result of increasing problems of local services for the steadily increasing population, a referendum was held on the question of annexation to Evanston. The vote was 165 for annexation, 168 against, and the two towns have remained separate ever since.

Wilmette was one of the north shore residential suburbs which attracted population continually from before 1900 until the Depression of the 1930s. During each decade from 1890 to 1930, the population increased more than 50 percent. Transportation to Chicago improved during this period. The elevated line to Evanston was extended to Linden Street in Wilmette in 1912. The Chicago and North Western Railroad continued to provide commuter service, and the Chicago, North Shore, and Milwaukee Electric Line provided additional services until it was abandoned in 1955.

The first annexation to Wilmette occurred in 1912, when a small triangle at the northern edge and just west of the C.& N.W. tracks was added. A rectangular section west and south of the irregular boundary line was added in 1914 and 1915. In addition, 22 acres were added to the land area of the village between 1908 and 1910, when the land excavated in the digging of the North Shore Channel of the Sanitary District Canal was dumped into the lake between the inlet, near Greenleaf Avenue, and Washington Avenue. The Wilmette Park District was formed in 1908 to claim this land under the law which stated that man-made land unoccupied and within the boundaries of an organized park district could be taken for park purposes.

Early in the 1920s, a Plan Commission was organized in recognition of the need to protect Wilmette's character as a high-quality residential suburb. In 1922, a zoning ordinance was passed, allowing business development in a fairly large area centering around the Chicago and North Western station, a smaller area at the terminal of the North-western elevated, and a small area at the intersection of Ridge and Wilmette avenues. Industrial areas were limited to a few places along the railroad tracks, while the rest of the city was zoned for residences. Provision was made for the elevation of the tracks of the Chicago and North Western Railroad and the Chicago, North Shore, and Milwaukee Line, but these plans were never carried out.

Annexations to the village continued. Most of Gross Point Village was annexed to Wilmette in two stages, the first in 1924 and the second in 1926. The 1926 annexation also included previously unincorporated land as far west as the C.& N.W. tracks and the east fork of the North Branch of the Chicago River. "Connecticut Village" was annexed in 1939, and in 1942, an unclaimed "No Man's Land" between Wilmette and Kenilworth on the north, which was part residential, part commercial, and part "honky-tonk," was annexed. From an area of 2.9 square miles in the early 1920s, Wilmette reached its present size of 5.3 square miles.

Wilmette was dependent for its growth on new home construction, as it had little industrial or institutional employment to attract residents. In 1926, the National College of Education, the oldest private elementary teachers' college in the U.S., founded in Chicago in 1886, moved to Wilmette. In 1920, construction of the Bahai Temple was begun, but was not to be completed for more than 30 years. By 1930, the population of Wilmette had reached 15,233. Germans were the predominant group among the foreign stock in 1930, followed by Swedes, Canadians, and English.

Just as the entire metropolitan area experienced slow growth during the 1930s, so did Wilmette's period of rapid growth end for a while.

Place 6255 — Wilmette

Wilmette
Population and Housing Characteristics, 1930-1980

	1980	1970	1960	1950	1940	1930
Total Population.......	28,221	32,134	28,268	18,162	17,226	15,233
% Male.................	47.6	48.1	47.9	47.1	46.3	47.3
% Female...............	52.4	51.9	52.1	52.9	53.7	52.7
% White................	96.4	99.2	99.2	99.1	98.6	98.6
% Black................	0.3	0.3	0.6	0.7	1.3	1.3
% Other Nonwhite Races.	3.3	0.5	0.2	0.2	0.1	0.1
% Under 5 Years Old....	4.9	6.2	10.7	8.2	5.9	6.8
% 5-19 Years Old.......	24.9	33.7	29.1	23.3	24.3	27.3
% 20-44 Years Old......	30.2	27.2	28.7	31.9	38.5	38.0
% 45-64 Years Old......	27.3	23.3	22.7	26.8	24.0	22.6
% 65 Years and Older...	12.7	9.6	8.8	9.8	7.3	5.3
Median School Years....	16.1	14.0	13.8	12.8	12.5	*
Total Housing Units....	9,980	9,583	7,974	5,004	4,387	*
% In One-Unit Structures.	82.8	82.9	89.8	*	*	*
% Owner Occupied.......	84.0	81.0	83.3	80.2	61.0	*
% Renter Occupied......	14.5	15.8	12.9	18.2	34.8	*
% Vacant...............	1.5	3.2	3.8	1.6	4.2	*
% 1+ Persons per Room..	2.4	1.5	2.2	3.4	*	*

Place 6255 — Wilmette, Illinois
Selected Characteristics of Census Tracts: 1980

Tract Number	Total	8007	8008	8009	8010	8011	8012	8013	8019
Total Population.............	28229	4940	189	4852	5145	4613	4033	4321	136
% Male.......................	47.6	47.1	52.4	49.1	47.9	48.3	46.9	46.1	46.3
% Black......................	0.3	0.3	0.0	0.4	0.3	0.3	0.3	0.5	0.0
% Other Nonwhite.............	3.3	3.2	9.0	5.2	4.4	2.7	1.0	2.3	5.1
% Of Spanish Origin..........	1.2	0.7	0.5	1.6	1.3	1.5	1.3	0.7	2.2
% Foreign Born...............	8.1	7.7	0.0	12.1	10.4	7.0	4.9	6.4	0.0
% Living In Group Quarters...	1.1	3.5	0.0	0.6	0.2	0.1	0.3	2.1	0.0
% 13 Years Old And Under.....	18.5	19.5	14.8	18.0	16.2	21.2	18.0	18.6	14.0
% 14-20 Years Old............	12.4	12.0	23.3	13.2	12.0	11.2	13.4	12.1	10.3
% 21-64 Years Old............	56.4	55.9	58.7	62.1	60.7	55.3	49.5	53.3	55.1
% 65-74 Years Old............	7.3	8.1	2.6	4.8	6.9	6.7	10.6	7.6	14.7
% 75 Years Old And Over......	5.4	4.5	0.0	1.9	4.3	5.6	8.6	8.4	5.9
% In Different House.........	35.9	40.9	0.0	25.2	35.2	38.0	35.8	44.3	0.0
% Families With Female Head..	8.7	7.1	2.9	9.4	10.1	8.5	6.6	10.4	0.0
Median School Years Completed.	16.1	16.1	16.1	15.1	15.7	16.1	16.1	16.1	16.1
Median Family Income, 1979....$$	41304	50320	44671	38096	39520	35026	54739	39894	66893
% Income Below Poverty Level....	2.0	1.3	0.0	2.8	2.8	0.9	1.5	2.0	12.3
% Income Of $30,000 Or More....	71.6	80.4	61.1	69.4	68.1	59.7	84.5	69.5	63.2
% White Collar Workers.......	85.4	90.9	100.0	83.2	83.1	80.4	89.5	86.7	100.0
% Civilian Labor Force Unemployed.	2.6	0.3	26.7	2.3	3.2	2.8	2.0	3.6	7.5
% Riding To Work By Automobile...	67.8	67.0	84.4	79.2	79.0	64.2	49.6	55.0	100.0
Mean Commuting Time - Minutes...	29.8	31.7	30.0	26.3	27.2	27.6	34.9	34.3	23.3
Population Per Household.........	2.9	3.0	3.6	3.1	2.7	2.8	2.8	2.7	2.8
Total Housing Units.........	9982	1585	54	1591	1931	1686	1494	1592	49
% Condominiums...............	7.1	0.0	0.0	0.0	10.6	0.0	30.6	2.8	—
% Built 1970 Or Later........	5.3	4.4	23.3	2.5	8.5	1.0	9.6	4.9	—
% Owner Occupied.............	83.1	92.7	92.6	90.8	81.9	78.1	88.4	66.8	—
% With 1+ Persons Per Room...	0.5	0.5	0.0	0.4	0.5	0.9	0.2	0.2	—
Median Value: Owner Units....$$	121800	148400	—	103700	110200	101900	169400	123900	—
Median Rent: Rental Units....$$	374	501	—	457	366	341	442	343	—
Median Number Of Rooms: All Units.	5.6	5.6	5.6	5.6	5.6	5.6	5.6	5.6	—

Wilmette
Selected Characteristics of Census Tracts: 1970

Tract Number	TOTAL	8007	8008	8009	8010	8011	8012	8013	8019
Total Population.............	32134	5554	2218	6093	5755	5292	4308	4908	6687
% Male.......................	48.1	47.6	47.1	49.4	49.0	47.6	48.0	46.8	47.7
% Black......................	0.3	0.2	0.8	0.3	0.1	0.3	0.4	0.2	0.0
% Other Nonwhite.............	0.6	0.3	0.2	0.6	1.1	0.9	0.2	0.4	0.7
% Of Spanish Language........	1.5	0.9	0.4	3.3	1.3	0.0	2.2	1.3	1.0
% Foreign Born...............	5.2	2.8	11.3	5.5	5.9	7.9	3.8	4.9	7.0
% Living In Group Quarters...	1.4	5.8	0.0	0.8	0.1	0.5	0.2	1.1	2.5
% 13 Years Old And Under.....	27.2	25.0	21.4	30.7	27.8	27.7	24.4	26.8	24.2
% 14-20 Years Old............	13.6	12.2	14.2	15.3	14.1	11.1	15.9	13.1	12.3
% 21-64 Years Old............	49.6	51.3	54.4	50.7	51.0	48.8	47.1	47.2	53.1
% 65-74 Years Old............	6.0	6.6	6.9	2.4	4.6	7.6	8.6	7.3	5.9
% 75 Years Old And Over......	3.7	4.8	3.2	0.9	2.6	4.8	4.1	5.7	4.5
% In Different House.........	62.4	61.8	60.7	66.1	60.5	65.8	56.1	61.1	49.6
% Families With Female Head..	6.5	4.5	6.3	3.7	7.4	8.8	6.1	9.4	7.4
Median School Years Completed....	15.2	16.0	13.4	14.1	14.3	14.8	16.1	15.5	13.0
Median Family Income, 1969....$$	21809	27035	21277	22308	19836	17445	32932	19849	17857
% Income Below Poverty Level.....	2.5	1.1	2.8	1.5	1.6	4.8	4.6	1.8	2.8
% Income of $15,000 or More.....	71.8	82.4	64.6	74.4	66.3	58.7	83.7	69.0	57.1
% White Collar Workers.......	68.2	73.4	53.7	67.4	62.5	60.4	78.8	72.2	56.8
% Civilian Labor Force Unemployed.	2.7	2.1	3.0	2.8	3.6	1.8	2.7	2.5	1.5
% Riding To Work By Automobile....	69.4	60.4	77.4	86.4	79.6	68.8	59.9	50.5	80.9
Population Per Household.........	3.4	3.4	3.1	3.9	3.5	3.2	3.3	3.2	3.0
Total Housing Units.........	9582	1563	755	1578	1690	1671	1465	1542	2153
% Condominiums & Cooperatives.....	3.0	0.0	0.0	0.6	2.8	0.0	13.2	2.4	6.0
% Built 1960 Or Later........	21.1	10.5	25.3	36.1	29.2	6.0	34.4	8.6	47.5
% Owner Occupied.............	78.0	92.3	78.3	90.7	76.3	77.0	62.0	67.4	80.7
% With 1+ Persons Per Room...	1.5	0.8	1.1	1.1	2.2	2.3	0.7	1.6	2.5
Median Value: Owner Units....$$	46500	50100	48300	45800	45100	35900	50100	42900	49600
Median Rent: Rental Units....	220	258	193	275	226	180	301	197	167
Median Number Of Rooms: All Units.	6.7	7.1	6.3	6.9	6.4	6.3	7.4	6.8	5.7

Few civic improvements were made during the Depression, though in 1930 an ordinance created the administrative office of village manager. For most of the time since then, Wilmette has retained the village manager form of government.

Wilmette did not particpate at first in the postwar resurgence of suburban growth. In the late 1940s, a "Study of Wilmette" delineated the civic needs that had accumulated during the war years and the Depression. A Planning Board was formed in 1947, and presented a set of propositions to the voters in 1948. Bond issues were approved for a new library, police station, and extensions of sewers and water lines.

New schools were approved then and in subsequent years, along with a municipal garage and the purchase of land for park purposes.

Between 1950 and 1960, particularly the latter half of the decade, Wilmette had another period of rapid growth of population and housing. The area annexed in the 1920s, then still mainly farmland, was completely developed, mostly with single-family homes, by 1970. Three large tracts were retained for parks. A 1958 change in the zoning ordinance allowed for the construction of townhouses as a buffer between commercial areas and those of single-family homes. It also allowed for highrise construction along the lakeshore at the northern

298

end of the village. Six such apartment buildings, now condominiums, were erected in the late 1960s. Population increased from 18,162 in 1950 to 28,268 in 1960. Germans, Russians, and English were the leading nationalities among the foreign stock in 1960. Of the 156 black residents in 1960, 136 were females, primarily domestic servants.

The Wilmette Plan Commission, established in the late '60s, hired a professional planning firm to do a comprehensive study of Wilmette in terms of future needs and services. Using this study as the basis, a Comprehensive Plan was developed and formally adopted in 1974.

Two planned shopping centers are located in Wilmette. Edens Plaza, a major retail center bounded by Skokie Road, Lake Avenue and the Edens Expressway, opened in 1956. Plaza del Lago, opened in 1968, included the row of shops known as Spanish Court, which was built in the 1920s in what was then "No Man's Land." During the early 1970s Wilmette's business districts faced increasing competition from these centers, plus others in the northern suburbs. In 1974, the council for Commercial Renewal was formed to address this problem.

The population reached a historic high of 32,134 in the 1970 census. Wilmette celebrated its Centennial in 1972. In 1974, the Wilbus system

was begun to link the western section of the village with the east-side transportation centers, as well as other bus lines outside the village limits. A new village Administration Center, a C.& N.W. Railway station, and Centennial Park, with indoor ice and tennis facilities and an outdoor swimming pool, were all opened in the 1970s.

Wilmette continues to be a residential suburb of high socio-economic status. The median education indicates an average of four years of college. The median family income was more than $40,000 in 1979. The median value of a home in Wilmette is more than $120,000, and 83 percent of all housing units are owner-occupied. A survey of village residents showed that 20 percent of those employed work in the Loop and another 20 percent work in other parts of Chicago, while 28 percent work in Wilmette or Evanston and 29 percent work elsewhere in the suburbs. Wilmette has maintained its character as a village of single-family homes. There are few local businesses other than retail trade establishments. The 1980 census showed a drop in population to 28,221. Some of the decrease is due to declining fertility rates and out-migration of young people growing up and leaving home.

Eileen S. Ramm

Place 680

East Chicago, Indiana

East Chicago, a port city in Lake County, northwestern Indiana, adjoins Gary on the east, Hammond on the southwest, Whiting on the northwest and Lake Michigan on the north. The city is an industrial suburb whose growth was the result of the Indiana Harbor and the Indiana Harbor Canal, and excellent rail transportation. Industrially, East Chicago has few peers for a city its size. In addition to basic steel manufacturing and oil refineries, the industrial diversification includes refractories, chemical plants, aluminum smelting, tools and machinery, forgings and fabrication, and products of wood, paper, concrete, iron, steel, petroleum and textiles. Seventy percent of its land area of 12.3 square miles is occupied by industry, the highest concentration of such land use for any city in the country. Only 10.7 percent of the land is in residential use. Since East Chicago is completely hemmed in by other municipalities and has nowhere to expand, this has imposed a ceiling on population growth.

Originally perceived as a wasteland with no commercial advantage, the area remained an uninhabitable marsh and swamp until the end of the 19th century. The expansion of the steel industry in the Chicago area was largely responsible for the origin and development of East Chicago. As the land for industrial expansion became scarce and expensive in the Chicago area, industrialists and speculators began to seek sites across the state line in Indiana. Such elements as railroad and transportation facilities, the availability of an inexpensive water supply, level land, and an unlimited market from which to obtain labor were contributing factors in the location and growth of the city.

Early in November, 1881, Jacob and Caroline Forsythe sold 8,000 acres of land for $1 million to William W. Green. On the same day, Green transferred this tract, upon which the greater part of East Chicago now stands, to the East Chicago Improvement Company. The Company's financiers, impressed by the industrial expansion in Chicago saw possibilities of profitable investment in adjacent Indiana. In 1887 the East Chicago Improvement Company was sold to the Calumet Canal and Improvement Company, controlled by Joseph Thatcher Torrence. With two others, Marcus M. Towle and James N. Young, he organized the Chicago and Calumet Terminal Belt Line Railroad, to

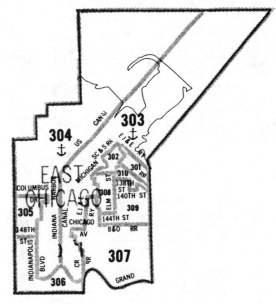

construct rail connections for industries locating in the area. Later that year, the Towle-Torrence interests, operating as the Standard Steel and Iron Company, plotted the first subdivision, extending from Railroad Avenue on the east to Indianapolis Boulevard on the west and from the Baltimore and Ohio Chicago Terminal to 151st Street. In 1889, a petition was filed for the incorporation of the town of East Chicago. In 1893, East Chicago was incorporated as a city. There were 1,255 inhabitants in 1890, and 3,411 in 1900.

Among early industries located in East Chicago were the William Graver Tank Works (1888) which manufactured storage tanks for the oil refinery at Whiting; the Famous Manufacturing Company, which made farm machinery and later high-wheeled roadsters; and the Grasselli Chemical Company (now Dupont), which came in 1892, producing chemicals used in the making of petroleum products.

In 1901 the Block interests purchased 50 acres from the Lake Michigan Land Company for the development of Inland Steel. With the coming of Inland, the city was advertised as a "Twentieth Century Wonder" and the East Chicago Land Company undertook a campaign to attract workers and residents. This began the influx of workers from Europe which lasted until 1914.

Place 680 — East Chicago, Indiana

East Chicago, Indiana
Population and Housing Characteristics, 1930–1980

	1980	1970	1960	1950	1940	1930
Total Population.......	39,786	46,982	57,669	54,263	54,637	54,784
% Male.................	48.8	49.3	51.7	52.7	52.1	55.9
% Female...............	51.2	50.7	48.3	47.3	46.9	44.1
% White................	47.8	71.6	76.0	81.4	88.7	90.6
% Black................	29.7	27.4	23.9	18.5	11.2	9.3
% Other Nonwhite Races..	22.5	1.0	0.1	0.1	0.1	0.1
% Under 5 Years Old.....	9.3	8.9	13.5	10.2	8.2	10.2
% 5-19 Years Old.......	26.2	30.2	25.5	21.0	26.6	30.4
% 20-44 Years Old.......	32.3	30.0	34.8	42.7	43.1	45.6
% 45-64 Years Old.......	21.7	22.1	18.9	21.0	19.3	12.4
% 65 Years and Older....	10.5	8.8	7.3	5.1	2.8	1.4
Median School Years....	11.3	9.8	8.8	8.8	7.6	*
Total Housing Units....	14,934	15,664	17,475	14,677	13,259	*
% In One-Unit Structures.	34.1	31.7	33.2	*	*	*
% Owner Occupied........	39.3	37.7	34.4	37.1	33.3	*
% Renter Occupied.......	52.4	55.8	61.9	61.5	66.0	*
% Vacant...............	8.3	6.5	3.7	1.4	0.7	*
% 1+ Persons per Room...	9.3	14.9	20.6	19.9	*	*

Place 680 — East Chicago, Indiana
Selected Characteristics of Census Tracts: 1980

Tract Number	Total	301	302	303	303.99	304	304.99	305	306	307	308
Total Population.............	39786	1271	2373	5355	93	4066	17	4317	5225	3214	5630
% Male.......................	48.8	42.3	51.5	47.8	-	49.2	-	48.6	48.5	48.7	49.5
% Black......................	29.7	92.2	23.6	87.6	-	4.8	-	1.6	0.2	41.2	10.6
% Other Nonwhite.............	22.5	4.7	38.3	5.6	-	25.9	-	26.4	15.1	18.7	32.6
% Of Spanish Origin..........	42.3	9.5	71.0	10.4	-	55.7	-	46.3	32.6	37.0	60.1
% Foreign Born...............	15.7	4.5	20.7	1.7	-	15.4	-	10.6	14.3	13.5	28.7
% Living In Group Quarters...	0.7	0.0	0.0	2.2	-	0.0	-	0.0	0.0	1.5	0.2
% 13 Years Old And Under.....	24.2	31.6	29.3	29.4	-	25.4	-	22.7	20.0	22.5	22.1
% 14-20 Years Old...........	13.4	12.8	17.2	15.2	-	11.0	-	13.6	11.0	13.9	13.0
% 21-64 Years Old...........	51.9	52.6	47.2	45.6	-	50.3	-	51.6	58.0	53.5	53.5
% 65-74 Years Old...........	6.9	2.1	3.8	6.6	-	8.6	-	8.0	7.7	6.9	7.3
% 75 Years Old And Over.....	3.6	0.8	2.5	3.2	-	4.8	-	4.1	3.3	3.2	4.1
% In Different House........	36.0	62.1	31.4	26.4	-	33.4	-	53.4	29.0	34.6	35.9
% Families With Female Head..	31.4	59.4	38.2	58.4	-	21.9	-	18.1	21.9	26.9	22.2
Median School Years Completed..	11.3	12.1	9.7	11.0	-	10.8	-	12.2	12.1	11.9	10.3
Median Family Income, 1979.....$$	20945	14273	13478	11548	-	21329	-	23762	25068	19275	22668
% Income Below Poverty Level...	15.9	21.7	39.6	36.0	-	13.2	-	9.1	9.2	10.8	9.9
% Income Of $30,000 Or More....	25.8	12.3	24.6	11.9	-	22.2	-	27.1	34.1	28.4	27.5
% White Collar Workers.........	32.0	32.6	30.7	22.8	-	33.4	-	40.6	39.6	25.4	31.9
% Civilian Labor Force Unemployed.	11.1	12.1	18.7	21.7	-	13.2	-	6.5	6.5	10.6	9.3
% Riding To Work By Automobile....	82.9	76.0	67.0	78.0	-	82.9	-	84.3	85.5	90.3	86.3
Mean Commuting Time - Minutes....	17.8	16.3	19.6	19.0	-	16.2	-	19.2	16.4	19.6	18.1
Population Per Household..........	2.9	2.7	3.3	3.1	-	2.6	-	2.7	2.6	3.1	2.9
Total Housing Units...........	14925	498	864	1844	0	1712	0	1703	2123	1097	2041
% Condominiums................	0.5	2.0	0.0	1.7	-	0.8	-	0.0	0.0	0.0	0.0
% Built 1970 Or Later.........	8.5	61.0	6.5	19.5	-	11.3	-	2.3	1.7	2.7	1.7
% Owner Occupied..............	39.3	4.2	17.5	25.9	-	35.2	-	46.0	48.2	57.0	46.8
% With 1+ Persons Per Room....	9.3	8.7	16.5	13.2	-	8.2	-	7.1	6.1	8.2	8.6
Median Value: Owner Units......$$	35600	-	30000	24000	-	26300	-	37900	37600	36700	37600
Median Rent: Rental Units......$$	131	187	124	97	-	130	-	156	135	120	147
Median Number Of Rooms: All Units.	4.5	4.0	4.0	4.4	-	4.2	-	4.8	4.5	4.9	4.9

Tract Number	309	310
Total Population.............	5563	2662
% Male.......................	49.2	47.7
% Black......................	26.4	63.9
% Other Nonwhite.............	30.4	21.4
% Of Spanish Origin..........	55.5	30.9
% Foreign Born...............	22.8	16.6
% Living In Group Quarters...	0.0	0.0
% 13 Years Old And Under.....	22.9	24.4
% 14-20 Years Old...........	14.8	12.3
% 21-64 Years Old...........	53.9	49.6
% 65-74 Years Old...........	5.6	7.8
% 75 Years Old And Over.....	2.8	4.0
% In Different House........	34.3	41.0
% Families With Female Head..	20.6	46.8
Median School Years Completed...$$	11.1	9.3
Median Family Income, 1979.....$$	23680	19813
% Income Below Poverty Level...	10.7	15.9
% Income Of $30,000 Or More....	35.4	17.1
% White Collar Workers.........	32.5	18.6
% Civilian Labor Force Unemployed.	8.7	10.2
% Riding To Work By Automobile....	80.2	87.8
Mean Commuting Time - Minutes....	17.1	17.6
Population Per Household..........	3.3	2.5
Total Housing Units...........	1859	1184
% Condominiums................	0.0	1.2
% Built 1970 Or Later.........	8.5	5.6
% Owner Occupied..............	52.6	20.9
% With 1+ Persons Per Room....	10.8	9.1
Median Value: Owner Units......$$	39800	29600
Median Rent: Rental Units......$$	130	103
Median Number Of Rooms: All Units.	4.9	3.9

East Chicago grew rapidly. By 1910 the population had soared to 19,098, an increase of over 400 percent in 10 years. In 1920 it had 34,967 inhabitants, having almost doubled since 1910, and in 1930 54,784, or 5,000 persons per square mile. By then East Chicago had reached residential maturity if not saturation. Since so much of the city's area was occupied by industries and railroads, little space was left for additional residents.

Four major waves of newcomers to East Chicago increased the city's population. First were Scotch, Irish, Welsh, English and Germans before 1914. Since World War I required increased production of steel and war material, more workers were needed and the second wave came from the American South, Canada, and from Mexico. The third wave followed in the 1940s when World War II created another increased demand for steel production and other manufacturing, recruits coming mainly from the Southern states. These were followed by a fourth group from Puerto Rico. After falling slightly during the Depression and World War II eras, the number of inhabitants reached an all time high in 1960, at 57,669. At that time, about 24 percent of the population was black, and more than 16 percent was Latin American.

East Chicago consists of six community areas. The basis of the major division is the Indiana Harbor Ship Canal and the switching yards of the Indiana Harbor Belt Line Railroad which divide the city into two almost equal parts. The west side of the barrier is known as East Chicago and is the area of original settlement. The east side, adjacent to Lake Michigan and the Inland Steel Company complex, is known as Indiana Harbor. This bifurcation has led to a nickname, the "Twin City" for East Chicago.

There are four other distinct communities. Located between East Chicago and Indiana Harbor are New Addition and Calumet. New Addition is a small community north of Columbus Drive, between Kennedy Avenue and the Pennsylvania Railroad. It is cut off from Indiana Harbor by the New York Central Railroad yards and the O.F. Jordan Company. Calumet is a somewhat larger community, bounded by Chicago Avenue on the north, the Indiana Harbor Belt Line Railroad on the west, U.S. Lead Refining Company and E.I. Dupont De Ne Mours on the south, and the Cities Service Oil Refineries on the east. In the northern part of town, west of Indiana Harbor and in the middle of the Youngstown Sheet and Tube Company complex is Marktown.

Marktown, a 200-home island community surrounded by industry on the city's north side, is a designated historical landmark. It was chosen as a landmark because the neighborhood has remained virtually the same since its founding. Marktown was established by Chicago

300

East Chicago
Selected Characteristics of Census Tracts: 1970

Tract Number	TOTAL	0301	0302	0303	030399	0304	030499	0305	0306	0307	0308
Total Population	46982	1229	4190	6108	53	4265	54	4529	6257	3868	6062
% Male	49.3	46.9	52.1	47.6	-	50.0	-	48.7	49.4	48.1	49.5
% Black	27.4	85.9	20.3	86.5	-	0.5	-	0.2	0.0	34.6	7.1
% Other Nonwhite	1.0	0.7	1.1	0.4	-	1.1	-	0.5	0.4	0.9	2.0
% Of Spanish Language	26.8	15.1	62.8	7.8	-	31.7	-	14.3	6.9	14.6	37.3
% Foreign Born	13.2	1.2	18.6	1.7	-	12.9	-	9.9	9.7	13.5	29.0
% Living In Group Quarters	0.9	0.2	2.9	0.2	-	0.7	-	0.2	0.1	2.1	0.3
% 13 Years Old And Under	27.4	36.7	32.0	32.7	-	26.9	-	21.4	23.7	27.0	23.5
% 14-20 Years Old	13.4	16.1	15.3	14.9	-	11.9	-	10.8	13.4	13.4	11.5
% 21-64 Years Old	50.4	42.7	46.2	45.1	-	52.4	-	55.1	54.8	51.3	53.7
% 65-74 Years Old	5.6	3.3	4.8	5.4	-	5.2	-	7.7	4.6	5.2	7.0
% 75 Years Old And Over	3.1	1.2	1.7	1.9	-	3.6	-	5.0	3.5	3.1	4.3
% In Different House	54.9	42.9	34.0	58.0	-	52.0	-	60.7	71.5	68.1	58.9
% Families With Female Head	16.1	30.1	18.5	26.5	-	13.3	-	12.3	11.5	15.8	10.6
Median School Years Completed	9.8	9.9	7.4	9.2	-	9.9	-	12.0	10.7	9.9	10.0
Median Family Income, 1969 $$	9208	8000	8091	7701	-	9622	-	10060	10286	8881	10544
% Income Below Poverty Level	11.5	29.6	14.0	21.3	-	9.9	-	6.0	7.7	8.8	4.7
% Income of $15,000 or More	16.5	9.3	11.6	10.2	-	17.1	-	20.7	21.5	13.1	21.6
% White Collar Workers	13.9	9.0	6.4	8.6	-	11.8	-	26.7	16.7	14.3	15.9
% Civilian Labor Force Unemployed	4.2	7.2	5.1	6.9	-	3.5	-	3.3	2.6	3.3	2.2
% Riding To Work By Automobile	67.1	63.1	43.7	70.1	-	69.8	-	73.2	74.3	74.8	62.1
Population Per Household	3.2	3.7	3.4	3.6	-	2.9	-	2.7	3.0	3.3	3.1
Total Housing Units	15659	366	1340	1912	0	1569	0	1758	2189	1201	2024
% Condominiums & Cooperatives	0.3	0.0	0.0	0.4	-	0.0	-	0.0	0.0	0.8	0.5
% Built 1960 Or Later	7.9	47.3	12.4	4.7	-	1.7	-	2.6	3.2	5.1	1.4
% Owner Occupied	37.4	15.3	15.1	29.8	-	36.6	-	46.8	49.2	50.8	48.0
% With 1+ Persons Per Room	14.9	25.9	23.1	22.8	-	12.8	-	6.3	9.9	16.0	11.0
Median Value: Owner Units $$	16700	-	16600	12300	-	12600	-	17300	17500	16400	17400
Median Rent: Rental Units $$	72	83	66	65	-	73	-	86	68	72	79
Median Number Of Rooms: All Units	4.4	4.1	3.8	4.2	-	4.3	-	4.6	4.4	4.5	4.8

Tract Number	0309	0310
Total Population	6074	4293
% Male	50.0	48.2
% Black	20.9	60.8
% Other Nonwhite	2.0	0.7
% Of Spanish Language	43.5	30.4
% Foreign Born	16.9	8.5
% Living In Group Quarters	0.4	0.2
% 13 Years Old And Under	29.4	29.1
% 14-20 Years Old	14.3	13.8
% 21-64 Years Old	49.0	46.8
% 65-74 Years Old	4.6	7.2
% 75 Years Old And Over	2.6	3.1
% In Different House	42.8	46.0
% Families With Female Head	12.7	24.7
Median School Years Completed	9.5	8.9
Median Family Income, 1969 $$	9414	7780
% Income Below Poverty Level	10.1	20.0
% Income of $15,000 or More	18.1	9.7
% White Collar Workers	13.4	6.0
% Civilian Labor Force Unemployed	4.7	7.3
% Riding To Work By Automobile	67.4	61.3
Population Per Household	3.6	3.0
Total Housing Units	1763	1537
% Condominiums & Cooperatives	0.0	0.8
% Built 1960 Or Later	13.9	22.3
% Owner Occupied	39.9	17.7
% With 1+ Persons Per Room	17.2	16.8
Median Value: Owner Units $$	22200	14800
Median Rent: Rental Units $$	79	64
Median Number Of Rooms: All Units	4.7	3.9

Industrialist Clayton Marks in 1917 to house workers of the Mark Manufacturing Company, now known as Youngstown Sheet and Tube Company. The Youngstown complex surrounds the neighborhood on three sides, and the Standard Oil Refinery seals the circle on the north. In Marktown as in many European villages, people park on the sidewalks and walk in the streets. The streets are so narrow that if automobiles were parked the normal way no one could get through.

Finally, in the southwest corner of the city, south of the Grand Calumet River and cut off by the Indiana East-West Toll Road and the Chicago, South Shore and South Bend Railroad, is Roxanna.

East Chicago has two major shopping districts. Indiana Harbor's main retail area is centered around Main Street and Broadway. The central business district of East Chicago proper is located along Chicago Avenue and Indianapolis Boulevard.

The years since the population peak of 1960 have witnessed a precipitous decline. The 1980 population was 39,786, down 15 percent since 1970, 31 percent since 1960. This out-migration is not the product of racial turnover; both whites and blacks are leaving East Chicago. The white population is now 19,036, having dropped by 57 percent since its crest in 1950. The 1980 count of blacks showed 11,802 living in East Chicago, 14 percent less than the number in 1960. The population of East Chicago has been sustained by an influx of Latin

Americans. The number of residents of Spanish origin in 1980 was 16,818, and they now comprise more than 42 percent of the city population. Blacks are 30 percent of the total.

Sixteen percent of all East Chicago residents are foreign born and 45 percent do not speak English at home. Among the residue of white European stock, Polish are the most numerous of the descent groups. The population is young, almost a third are 18 years or younger. There are contrasts in socio-economic status. Although the median family income was higher than Chicago's in 1979, and 39 percent of all families reported incomes over $25,000, one-sixth of the families lived in poverty, and 11 percent of the workers were unemployed in 1980.

The population loss may be attributed in part to the desire to resettle in the growing suburban area farther south in Lake County, and in part to discontinuities in the industrial economy of the late 1970s. However, the major problem seems to be the dwindling and deteriorating housing stock. In 1960, there were 17,475 housing units in East Chicago; this dropped by more than 10 percent in the following decade. By 1980, the number had declined to 14,934, another 4 percent loss. Perhaps because of the lack of vacant land for new subdivisions, housing construction languished even during the growing years. In 1980, only 19 percent of all housing units were in structures built in the previous 30 years. Thirty-nine percent of all units are owner-occupied, and this percentage has not changed since 1960. The median value of single-family homes is about three-fourths that of Chicago.

In the early 1960s, many residents of East Chicago were compelled to move out of the city because government housing programs eliminated so many low-rent (and substandard) housing units. The effect of the demolition programs resulted in the decline of units in multiple-dwelling structures from 67 to 62 percent in the last 20 years. The percentage in overcrowded units has dropped from 21 to nine. New residential building programs were initiated to help stem the outward flight and plans were made for revival of commercial areas. In the following decade new housing and rehabilitation developments accounted for about 1,600 new low-income dwelling units.

The future of East Chicago may turn less on industrial development than on the provision of adequate housing and a desirable environment for those who work there. Given the recent increase of housing opportunities in nearby suburbs, and the scarcity of living space in the city, it seems unlikely that the number of residents will again reach the size of 20 years ago. However much smaller, housing rehabilitation and new construction should lead to an optimum and stable population.

Janice K. Bella

Gary

Gary, the third largest city in Indiana, is located in the northwest corner of the state at the southern end of Lake Michigan. It is a 20th century city, built on an area that was covered by sand dunes and scrub oaks in 1906. Gary originated as a result of a dilemma that faced the United States Steel Corporation, which was losing income in 1905 because of its inability to meet steel demands in the developing Midwest market. The corporation dispatched its attorney, Armanis F. Knotts, to secure a site for the development of a large new complex of steel plants in the Midwest.

In 1905, Knotts and the U. S. Steel Corporation Board Chairman, Elbert H. Gary, for whom the city was to be named, selected an uninhabited area of swamps and sand dunes along the southern shore of Lake Michigan as the location for a midwest steel center. Judge Gary originally favored a site near Waukegan, but Knotts convinced him that the Indiana location was best suited for the company's needs. Decisive factors in the selection included proximity to the expanding centers of population and industry, particularly St. Louis, Detroit, and Chicago; accessibility by water and rail to Minnesota iron ore, Michigan Limestone, and Appalachian coal; a seemingly inexhaustible water supply for industrial use from both Lake Michigan and the nearby Grand Calumet River; the possibility of an adequate harbor for ore freighters given the depth of Lake Michigan at Gary; availability of plentiful and inexpensive land for future expansion; favorable state and local laws (no state or municipal government in Indiana can build highways or construct in front of the lakeside steel proerty); and an accessible labor supply.

In 1906, U.S. Steel purchased 1,500 acres of lowland near the lake for the major mill site. Later that year the company purchased the higher land to the south and east to build a town. In all, the corporation acquired 9,000 acres of land, including seven miles of shoreline, for aproximately $7.2 million, or $800 an acre. On April 18, 1906, the first stake was driven into the sand at 5th Avenue and Broadway. At the time the city was incorporated in July, more than 300 people lived there. The steel furnaces went into operation in February, 1907 and by the end of that year there were some 10,000 residents.

By 1910, there were 4,204 employees at U.S. Steel. Construction had begun on two subsidiaries, the American Bridge Company and the American Sheet and Tin Plate Plant. In 1912, the Gary Screw and Bolt company was founded, the first major industry in the area that was not a U.S. Steel Subsidiary. A second nonsubsidiary, U.S. Drawn Steel Company, was organized in 1918.

The building of the massive $85 million dollar plant facilities took priority over the needs of the adjacent $15 million dollar town. Nevertheless, Knotts convinced the U.S. Steel Corporation to invest in the development of a city. To accomplish this another subsidiary of U.S. Steel, the Gary Land Company, was created. The company's primary purpose was the construction of living quarters on the north side of Gary. The Gary Land Company developed U.S. Steel's 800-acre First Subdivision in 1906, which extended south to the Wabash Railroad tracks near 9th Avenue.

The planning responsibilities of the Gary Land Coompany did not extend beyond the north side of Gary; the south side was allowed to develop in an ad hoc fashion. The differences were striking. The north side of Gary housed the professional, managerial, and skilled people, who were mostly American-born citizens or people from England, Ireland, Germany, and northern Europe. The south side housed the steel workers, from southern and eastern Europe.

The city annexed Glen Park in 1909, Tolleston in 1910, Miller in 1918 and Aetna in 1924, expanding Gary's residential area. It continued to grow throughout the 1920s. In 1930, less than 25 years after its founding, Gary had a population of 100,426. Foreign white stock comprised 45 percent of the city's population, and the predominant nationalities were the Poles, Czechoslovakians, Yugoslavians, and Germans.

Although industrial output, employment and housing construction dropped during the Depression, the population continued to grow, reaching almost 112,000 by 1940. With the onset of the Second World War, Gary's industrial facilitites were utilized to full capacity. With continued prosperity after the war, the city continued to experience rapid population growth. Between 1940 and 1950, Gary's population increased from 111,719 to 133,911. In 1950, the population of Gary included 11 percent foregn-born, 29 percent black, and 59 percent native whites.

Over the next 10 years, Gary's population increased by a third, to its historic peak of 178,320 in 1960. By 1960, blacks comprised 39 percent of the population. Most resided in the south central portion of the city, between the Wabash Railroad tracks on the north and the Little Calumet River on the south. Poles, Yugoslavians, and Czechoslovakians were the dominant nationalities among the foreign stock in 1960; followed by two newer immigrant groups, Mexicans and Puerto Ricans. The latter two groups resided near the predominantly black area in the western portion of the city. A building boom more than doubled the number of housing units.

Between 1960 and 1970 the number of residents dropped to 175,415, signalling the beginning of suburbanization. In 1970, 53 percent of the city's population was black. The number of housing units grew, but by only 3.8 percent, proportionately the smallest housing unit increase since the creation of Gary in 1906. The percentage of housing units owner-occupied increased from 55 to 60.

Today, the city spans an area of 45 square miles and consists of approximately 2,880 blocks. Gary is divided into four major areas: Downtown, the erstwhile central business district, centers on Broadway and runs to 9th Avenue on the south. Westside is divided from the east by Broadway. The Westside includes all or part of five community areas: Burnswick, Tolleston, Black Oak, Glen Park and Midtown. Glen Park and Midtown have been subdivided in such a fashion that half of each community is located in Westside and the other half in Eastside. Eastside is bordered on the east by Interstate Highway 65 and on the West by Broadway. The Eastside is comprised of five community areas: Pulaski, Emerson, Marshalltown, Aetna and Miller, as well as the eastern halves of Glen Park and Midtown. The fourth area, still the dominant feature of the Gary skyline, is the United States Steel Corporation property, which fronts on Lake Michigan to the north, is divided from the city proper by Interstate Highway 90, and extends to the western city limits at Cline Avenue.

The 1980 population of Gary was 151,953, a drop of 13 percent for the decade, almost 15 percent since the numerical crest of 1960. The black population, which has almost tripled in the last 30 years, reached more than 100,000, 71 percent of the total. More than half of the white

Gary, Indiana
Population and Housing Characteristics, 1930-1980

	1980	1970	1960	1950	1940	1930
Total Population.......	151,953	175,415	178,320	133,911	111,719	100,426
% Male.................	47.2	48.3	49.8	51.1	52.0	54.4
% Female...............	52.8	51.7	50.2	48.9	48.0	45.6
% White................	25.2	46.7	61.1	70.6	81.6	82.2
% Black................	70.8	52.8	38.8	29.3	18.3	17.8
% Other Nonwhite Races..	4.0	0.5	0.1	0.1	0.1	0.0
% Under 5 Years Old....	10.0	9.2	13.3	10.9	7.6	9.5
% 5-19 Years Old.......	28.8	33.2	28.3	21.5	24.8	28.0
% 20-44 Years Old......	33.9	30.1	33.5	41.7	44.5	47.5
% 45-64 Years Old......	19.1	19.9	18.5	20.9	20.0	13.3
% 65 Years and Older...	8.2	7.6	6.4	5.0	3.1	1.7
Median School Years....	12.1	10.9	10.1	9.7	8.4	*
Total Housing Units....	54,446	54,252	52,289	38,283	30,520	*
% In One-Unit Structures.	63.5	59.2	60.1	*	*	*
% Owner Occupied........	54.9	55.7	54.7	51.4	34.8	*
% Renter Occupied.......	36.0	39.4	41.4	46.1	63.5	*
% Vacant...............	9.1	4.9	3.9	2.5	1.7	*
% 1+ Persons per Room....	8.7	15.8	19.0	17.2	*	*

Place 905 — Gary, Indiana
Selected Characteristics of Census Tracts: 1980

Tract Number	Total	101	102	102.99	103	104	105	106	107	108	109
Total Population.............	151953	6049	8241	0	12966	4487	3835	4742	2525	1471	4165
% Male.....................	47.2	48.9	47.4	–	47.4	43.9	45.8	46.9	46.7	53.2	46.7
% Black....................	70.8	52.2	53.8	–	84.5	93.9	92.5	94.0	64.7	72.3	87.5
% Other Nonwhite...........	4.0	2.7	4.6	–	6.2	1.8	2.5	1.6	15.6	9.2	6.5
% Of Spanish Origin........	7.1	4.7	7.3	–	12.4	2.6	5.3	2.3	23.0	12.8	9.2
% Foreign Born.............	3.6	4.0	4.4	–	3.2	1.4	1.6	1.1	7.6	4.9	1.3
% Living In Group Quarters..	0.5	0.0	0.0	–	1.4	0.0	0.0	0.6	8.4	0.2	0.0
% 13 Years Old And Under....	26.7	24.3	28.3	–	29.6	27.4	30.8	28.6	29.7	25.3	33.3
% 14-20 Years Old..........	13.9	11.6	10.8	–	18.8	17.1	12.6	14.1	12.8	12.6	16.2
% 21-64 Years Old..........	51.1	57.5	53.2	–	47.6	50.0	54.3	53.4	47.2	53.6	47.1
% 65-74 Years Old..........	5.3	4.0	5.1	–	2.4	4.1	1.7	2.7	5.6	5.6	2.5
% 75 Years Old And Over....	2.9	2.5	2.6	–	1.6	1.4	0.5	1.2	4.8	2.9	0.9
% In Different House.......	38.0	44.1	52.7	–	24.5	28.8	37.4	37.3	44.6	50.6	44.2
% Families With Female Head..	36.8	17.8	34.9	–	37.5	45.2	45.1	33.5	43.8	58.0	44.7
Median School Years Completed..	12.1	13.4	12.3	–	12.0	12.1	12.5	12.5	10.8	12.1	12.0
Median Family Income, 1979...$$	19477	28605	21250	–	19242	18854	18333	23080	17712	14833	19355
% Income Below Poverty Level.	18.0	5.7	14.6	–	19.6	25.7	13.7	9.1	30.3	36.1	25.1
% Income Of $30,000 Or More..	23.7	47.0	21.0	–	24.8	24.5	16.2	32.9	8.1	11.8	20.0
% White Collar Workers.....	36.4	62.0	38.7	–	28.6	38.4	37.4	43.6	22.5	19.0	31.6
% Civilian Labor Force Unemployed.	14.5	9.5	11.6	–	17.6	15.2	11.2	9.8	16.2	29.8	21.7
% Riding To Work By Automobile....	88.9	94.0	90.3	–	91.1	90.5	92.1	90.9	80.4	69.7	80.7
Mean Commuting Time - Minutes...	23.0	22.3	22.2	–	21.9	23.1	23.0	17.9	23.8	21.6	22.7
Population Per Household.........	3.1	2.9	2.9	–	3.8	3.2	2.9	3.2	3.3	2.3	3.7
Total Housing Units..........	54381	2189	3347	0	3635	1472	1429	1602	916	729	1311
% Condominiums...............	0.4	0.0	0.9	0	0.8	0.8	1.2	0.0	0.0	0.0	0.0
% Built 1970 Or Later.......	7.8	11.2	21.7	–	13.1	17.1	1.5	0.4	0.9	1.7	1.3
% Owner Occupied............	54.9	75.9	39.9	–	61.4	53.1	36.4	62.8	41.7	14.4	56.0
% With 1+ Persons Per Room..	8.7	2.3	5.3	–	17.3	11.2	7.4	7.6	9.8	9.5	13.2
Median Value: Owner Units.......$$	25200	45200	28100	–	23500	27300	24100	28800	17600	19000	18800
Median Rent: Rental Units......$$	142	187	200	–	161	128	129	162	138	140	145
Median Number Of Rooms: All Units.	4.8	5.6	4.5	–	4.9	4.8	4.4	5.2	4.9	3.5	5.1

Tract Number	110	111	112	113	114	115	116	117	118	119	120
Total Population.............	1486	1219	2999	3135	2753	7143	5712	2683	435	802	3696
% Male.....................	46.9	54.6	46.0	47.3	46.9	47.1	47.6	47.4	36.3	45.1	45.2
% Black....................	79.3	63.3	70.2	88.2	94.0	98.9	97.8	96.2	97.9	93.5	99.3
% Other Nonwhite...........	6.1	9.4	10.3	4.7	1.1	0.5	0.5	0.2	0.0	0.7	0.4
% Of Spanish Origin........	12.9	16.0	18.7	8.7	3.9	0.5	0.8	1.0	0.0	0.5	0.9
% Foreign Born.............	2.4	8.7	7.5	2.4	1.7	0.2	0.8	1.7	0.0	2.5	0.6
% Living In Group Quarters..	0.1	0.0	1.5	0.0	0.0	0.0	0.1	2.1	0.0	0.0	0.0
% 13 Years Old And Under....	31.6	27.3	29.8	31.1	23.8	25.9	19.9	22.1	22.5	15.8	33.3
% 14-20 Years Old..........	15.3	11.6	13.7	13.6	18.6	15.2	13.5	12.9	12.9	7.9	17.7
% 21-64 Years Old..........	47.2	50.5	45.4	48.5	52.8	51.4	55.0	54.1	21.6	60.5	44.0
% 65-74 Years Old..........	3.8	6.6	5.4	1.9	5.4	3.0	7.6	7.5	26.0	10.7	3.5
% 75 Years Old And Over....	2.2	4.0	5.7	1.6	2.0	1.0	2.4	2.9	17.0	5.1	1.4
% In Different House.......	46.1	63.0	48.6	37.2	22.0	24.1	17.6	40.0	31.1	47.4	29.5
% Families With Female Head..	53.7	58.1	46.7	43.4	46.9	33.6	34.0	54.2	71.1	41.9	61.4
Median School Years Completed..	11.0	11.4	11.4	12.3	11.7	12.3	12.2	11.6	7.9	12.1	11.1
Median Family Income, 1979...$$	12235	8676	15000	20000	17750	24623	23048	12162	8333	20208	10521
% Income Below Poverty Level.	37.0	44.4	30.2	20.9	16.2	14.5	13.0	28.9	40.6	14.3	36.0
% Income Of $30,000 Or More..	11.7	7.5	14.7	25.2	23.4	39.4	32.4	18.7	0.0	21.3	14.4
% White Collar Workers.....	18.8	14.5	30.4	36.3	32.4	40.7	42.9	28.6	27.8	32.6	26.4
% Civilian Labor Force Unemployed.	30.4	42.9	19.1	17.1	21.9	12.2	12.6	18.3	39.1	11.4	25.7
% Riding To Work By Automobile....	87.1	52.9	83.2	84.4	89.2	92.3	90.8	78.6	27.8	78.9	85.0
Mean Commuting Time - Minutes...	24.4	26.6	23.4	22.0	24.7	24.9	21.2	27.5	17.4	23.7	34.1
Population Per Household.........	3.2	2.4	2.9	3.7	3.3	3.7	3.1	2.7	1.9	2.2	3.8
Total Housing Units..........	624	697	1290	1043	1029	1961	1955	1124	233	385	996
% Condominiums...............	0.0	0.0	0.0	0.0	0.0	0.7	0.0	0.0	0.0	0.0	2.7
% Built 1970 Or Later.......	0.0	0.0	8.8	0.0	0.0	18.4	3.4	1.3	92.8	2.4	6.0
% Owner Occupied............	28.4	14.6	26.1	50.2	49.4	75.6	71.2	39.3	1.3	38.7	44.1
% With 1+ Persons Per Room..	9.9	7.9	7.9	8.9	10.4	11.8	8.6	5.3	7.0	3.3	19.3
Median Value: Owner Units.......$$	16000	15000	18300	25300	21500	28500	26200	21100	–	23600	19900
Median Rent: Rental Units......$$	141	123	138	158	142	153	141	132	85	135	87
Median Number Of Rooms: All Units.	4.7	3.1	4.5	5.3	5.0	5.6	5.2	4.6	3.1	4.4	4.8

population left in the 1970s; whites are now about one-fourth of the population of Gary. Among the remaining whites the largest descent group is Polish. Seven percent of the current total population is Hispanic.

The Gary population retains a sizeable number of young people, as more than a third are less than 19 years of age. More than a third of the households with children 18 or under are female-headed. The median family income in 1979 was less than $20,000 and 18 percent of the families lived in poverty. Fourteen percent of the resident labor force was unemployed.

Housing in Gary is aging. Three-quarters of all units were built before 1960, half before 1950, and a quarter before 1940. Areas of the city are dotted with substandard housing units and corrective measures have been adopted. Gary was one of the first cities in the country designated for federal funds under the Model Cities program. By the early 1970s, over $86 million in federal money had been allocated to revitalize the socio-economic life of the run-down areas. Private foundation funds were also used. Since 1960, the percentage of units in multiple-family structures has dropped from 40 to 33, and the percentage of overcrowded units from 19 to 9.

Today, Gary is a city in some distress. The city is virtually a one-industry town with almost half of the more than 61,000 employees working in the steel mills. Much of its industry is absentee-owned. Businesses, as well as people, are moving out. The Downtown area,

Place 905 — Gary , Indiana
Selected Characteristics of Census Tracts: 1980

Tract Number	121	122	123	124	125	126	127	128	129	130	131
Total Population............	5475	4927	2209	2679	5049	652	3037	2722	2261	6383	7177
% Male..................	49.1	45.3	48.8	48.3	44.0	47.9	45.2	44.4	43.5	48.4	46.9
% Black.................	29.6	98.8	97.9	99.0	98.8	99.4	98.4	98.9	99.5	60.4	57.7
% Other Nonwhite........	6.6	0.3	0.6	0.5	0.5	0.6	0.2	0.7	0.4	6.1	4.1
% Of Spanish Origin.....	15.5	0.7	0.7	0.4	1.2	2.0	0.5	0.4	0.5	10.0	8.8
% Foreign Born..........	4.8	0.3	0.3	0.3	0.4	2.9	0.2	1.7	0.0	5.8	6.1
% Living In Group Quarters	0.0	1.5	0.0	0.0	1.4	0.0	0.0	0.0	0.0	0.0	0.0
% 13 Years Old And Under.	31.1	23.6	19.7	19.1	28.0	21.5	22.9	19.5	27.9	30.1	25.4
% 14-20 Years Old........	13.1	13.1	10.1	13.7	15.0	17.5	11.7	12.2	12.4	14.0	10.1
% 21-64 Years Old........	52.2	52.8	50.4	53.9	44.1	50.9	49.5	48.8	49.4	49.3	51.9
% 65-74 Years Old........	2.3	6.3	13.9	9.1	8.0	6.7	9.5	11.4	7.2	4.3	7.2
% 75 Years Old And Over..	1.3	4.1	5.8	4.1	5.0	3.4	6.5	8.1	3.1	2.4	5.4
% In Different House.....	45.5	32.1	30.8	19.7	33.8	15.6	19.9	36.1	33.9	45.8	42.3
% Families With Female Head	19.9	49.4	64.3	41.2	68.6	37.1	51.3	58.2	54.2	30.7	25.1
Median School Years Completed	12.2	11.9	10.2	12.2	11.5	12.0	11.4	11.0	11.5	12.0	12.1
Median Family Income, 1979..$$	21839	15769	9430	17444	8627	21136	11828	11176	11500	20009	22272
% Income Below Poverty Level..	9.9	27.6	35.3	16.1	39.4	25.8	21.8	27.2	29.4	16.1	10.3
% Income Of $30,000 Or More...	24.1	25.9	5.1	24.6	13.3	26.5	13.5	16.2	8.7	19.4	29.9
% White Collar Workers..	32.4	33.5	18.8	42.4	29.6	44.7	35.8	34.0	38.5	35.6	43.0
% Civilian Labor Force Unemployed.	9.3	15.8	16.6	17.2	17.9	23.3	18.3	23.0	13.3	13.4	12.5
% Riding To Work By Automobile....	93.7	88.1	69.8	87.9	75.1	89.0	82.5	83.2	79.7	88.6	90.0
Mean Commuting Time - Minutes...	20.9	23.1	19.0	24.2	25.2	17.1	24.5	24.1	24.3	25.0	21.0
Population Per Household...	3.5	2.9	2.1	3.0	2.9	3.6	2.8	2.6	3.0	3.3	2.7
Total Housing Units.........	1646	1787	1285	979	1942	428	1302	1225	778	2054	2761
% Condominiums..........	0.0	0.0	0.0	0.0	1.3	0.0	0.0	0.0	3.9	0.0	0.5
% Built 1970 Or Later...	1.8	3.3	1.8	1.2	3.2	30.5	1.9	1.4	3.7	1.8	6.4
% Owner Occupied........	79.8	41.5	19.1	63.0	34.0	38.1	47.5	45.2	44.7	65.4	62.2
% With 1+ Persons Per Room.....	10.2	8.8	6.7	6.4	10.6	16.7	7.8	6.6	9.1	11.7	5.3
Median Value: Owner Units.....$$	23200	25000	19000	29900	20900	30300	21900	18400	20500	22300	26600
Median Rent: Rental Units.....$$	185	134	94	110	87	150	105	103	132	166	163
Median Number Of Rooms: All Units.	5.1	4.6	4.0	5.0	4.6	4.2	4.7	4.6	4.2	4.9	4.8

Tract Number	132	133	134	411	412	413.01
Total Population............	6001	3623	9215	5227	2073	2699
% Male..................	48.6	48.2	47.3	50.4	49.4	49.3
% Black.................	40.7	50.2	32.0	0.3	44.6	1.3
% Other Nonwhite........	7.4	5.2	7.7	5.0	4.1	2.2
% Of Spanish Origin.....	10.9	9.4	11.1	12.5	7.6	4.1
% Foreign Born..........	8.8	6.9	10.9	1.6	2.7	4.9
% Living In Group Quarters	0.0	0.0	0.3	0.0	0.0	0.1
% 13 Years Old And Under.	25.4	29.0	25.8	26.4	23.5	20.8
% 14-20 Years Old........	11.1	12.3	10.2	15.1	16.0	12.4
% 21-64 Years Old........	52.7	51.5	54.2	52.4	50.3	57.6
% 65-74 Years Old........	7.2	4.9	6.7	4.2	6.7	6.4
% 75 Years Old And Over..	3.6	2.3	3.0	1.8	3.5	2.8
% In Different House.....	51.7	56.5	49.5	35.8	38.1	61.0
% Families With Female Head	20.6	25.8	21.8	14.2	29.7	22.0
Median School Years Completed	12.3	12.2	12.3	10.3	9.9	11.8
Median Family Income, 1979..$$	23385	21569	22965	18723	15347	17645
% Income Below Poverty Level..	7.1	11.7	9.0	13.5	24.2	8.6
% Income Of $30,000 Or More...	26.7	21.1	30.5	15.9	12.2	16.8
% White Collar Workers..	38.9	31.3	39.4	18.4	29.0	33.5
% Civilian Labor Force Unemployed.	10.6	15.5	9.7	10.0	13.3	11.8
% Riding To Work By Automobile....	92.9	91.5	92.8	95.1	89.1	90.7
Mean Commuting Time - Minutes...	24.0	26.6	22.8	23.0	23.3	24.3
Population Per Household...	3.0	3.2	3.0	3.2	3.0	2.4
Total Housing Units.........	2117	1214	3184	1749	791	1172
% Condominiums..........	0.0	0.0	0.0	0.0	0.0	0.0
% Built 1970 Or Later...	1.7	1.6	13.5	7.2	7.0	32.2
% Owner Occupied........	75.6	76.9	68.5	67.4	60.4	73.1
% With 1+ Persons Per Room.....	5.4	7.9	6.3	10.3	10.0	3.9
Median Value: Owner Units.....$$	27000	23800	30000	20300	18500	30300
Median Rent: Rental Units.....$$	163	174	220	155	128	149
Median Number Of Rooms: All Units.	5.2	5.1	4.9	4.7	4.8	4.2

Gary
Selected Characteristics of Census Tracts: 1970

Tract Number	TOTAL	0101	0102	010299	0103	0104	0105	0106	0107	0108	0109
Total Population............	175415	6114	7779	33	13831	4836	4401	4477	3762	2774	5170
% Male..................	48.3	49.4	48.3	—	48.8	47.7	47.9	47.0	48.8	53.0	47.2
% Black.................	52.8	1.2	6.0	—	61.1	85.4	58.4	28.4	20.2	19.6	44.9
% Other Nonwhite........	0.5	0.5	0.7	—	0.8	0.1	0.2	0.9	1.5	0.4	1.2
% Of Spanish Language...	8.1	2.7	5.8	—	25.5	2.6	7.7	6.7	44.6	23.2	23.6
% Foreign Born..........	5.8	6.0	5.5	—	3.4	2.6	4.1	8.0	11.7	13.8	9.0
% Living In Group Quarters	0.6	0.0	0.2	—	1.6	0.0	0.0	0.3	4.1	0.0	0.0
% 13 Years Old And Under.	29.6	27.1	28.9	—	40.0	37.4	31.3	21.4	28.1	20.8	31.2
% 14-20 Years Old........	14.4	14.2	11.4	—	14.8	13.7	9.5	11.1	13.7	8.5	14.9
% 21-64 Years Old........	48.5	52.5	53.3	—	41.5	44.6	53.9	55.4	46.7	56.6	46.5
% 65-74 Years Old........	4.9	4.2	4.4	—	2.2	3.1	3.7	7.9	7.0	8.5	4.4
% 75 Years Old And Over..	2.7	2.0	2.0	—	1.5	1.2	1.6	4.2	4.5	5.7	2.9
% In Different House.....	54.6	63.5	43.1	—	36.6	51.9	37.5	48.2	42.8	39.3	35.3
% Families With Female Head	16.2	6.5	13.4	—	10.6	17.4	12.9	11.1	13.0	16.1	16.8
Median School Years Completed	11.1	12.8	12.3	—	10.7	11.4	12.3	12.2	8.8	9.5	10.4
Median Family Income, 1969...$$	9819	15752	11242	—	10116	10099	10574	12366	8533	8023	9218
% Income Below Poverty Level..	13.5	3.1	10.0	—	10.2	16.3	8.2	3.6	10.7	16.8	16.3
% Income of $15,000 or More...	19.2	52.8	27.2	—	13.8	20.9	19.7	32.6	8.6	10.2	14.8
% White Collar Workers..	18.0	53.2	26.9	—	12.5	16.2	29.1	31.8	11.6	15.3	8.3
% Civilian Labor Force Unemployed.	5.5	1.4	3.0	—	4.5	5.4	4.3	4.8	4.8	7.2	6.7
% Riding To Work By Automobile....	76.4	90.5	87.8	—	86.4	85.4	83.3	81.2	61.2	50.8	69.8
Population Per Household...	3.4	3.4	3.0	—	4.5	3.9	3.1	2.8	3.2	2.1	3.5
Total Housing Units.........	54244	1873	2643	0	3135	1260	1464	1663	1182	1447	1574
% Condominiums & Cooperatives.....	0.4	0.3	0.5	—	0.6	0.6	0.5	0.5	0.0	0.0	0.0
% Built 1960 Or Later...	10.6	20.9	40.4	—	25.9	15.1	8.7	4.1	0.5	1.4	0.7
% Owner Occupied........	55.3	83.7	53.2	—	75.8	69.9	44.1	62.3	47.8	12.9	57.9
% With 1+ Persons Per Room.....	15.8	4.7	8.8	—	31.3	22.6	10.9	4.4	18.9	9.9	17.1
Median Value: Owner Units.....$$	15000	23400	16100	—	14200	16000	15100	17400	12400	13400	13200
Median Rent: Rental Units.....$$	80	122	129	—	82	62	90	101	80	86	87
Median Number Of Rooms: All Units.	4.6	5.5	4.6	—	4.8	4.7	4.3	4.9	4.3	2.8	4.5

which centers at the historic 5th and Broadway location, has lost more than half its businesses, and empty buildings and boarded-up store-fronts are widespread. Like the people, the businesses have moved to the suburbs. A local government campaign to increase and upgrade housing units has had mixed results. Some new housing complexes have been built, other areas marked for rehabilitation, but construction has barely kept pace with demolitions. The economy of Gary is largely dependent on the steel, automobile and construction industries, all of which are currently in recession. If they revive, Gary will begin to grow again.

Gary
Selected Characteristics of Census Tracts: 1970

Tract Number	0110	0111	0112	0113	0114	0115	0116	0117	0118	0119	0120
Total Population	2319	2775	3974	3840	4374	7227	8188	4147	1381	1013	4769
% Male	49.2	54.7	49.5	48.2	48.0	49.8	47.9	48.7	50.6	49.7	46.2
% Black	26.1	17.9	25.3	26.8	87.2	98.3	95.8	91.9	91.2	85.1	98.3
% Other Nonwhite	3.0	1.3	0.9	1.0	0.5	0.1	0.4	0.2	0.1	0.7	0.1
% Of Spanish Language	12.8	25.8	24.5	16.8	4.1	0.5	0.6	1.1	1.9	13.6	0.6
% Foreign Born	22.4	22.1	10.5	9.9	1.6	0.3	1.1	2.6	0.0	6.4	0.0
% Living In Group Quarters	0.0	0.9	0.3	0.7	0.2	0.3	0.2	0.6	7.5	5.1	0.0
% 13 Years Old And Under	25.9	22.9	26.3	25.8	35.6	36.3	29.1	28.9	31.5	21.6	38.3
% 14-20 Years Old	12.8	11.3	14.5	14.5	15.6	18.5	17.0	13.5	11.2	13.3	22.3
% 21-64 Years Old	51.0	50.8	48.1	48.0	44.2	43.1	48.7	51.9	49.9	58.1	36.9
% 65-74 Years Old	5.8	9.4	6.5	6.9	2.5	1.6	3.5	3.8	5.4	4.4	1.8
% 75 Years Old And Over	4.5	5.7	4.6	4.8	2.1	0.5	1.7	1.9	2.0	2.5	0.7
% In Different House	37.1	29.5	38.8	44.2	57.4	63.2	69.1	50.7	25.6	60.2	73.1
% Families With Female Head	15.9	16.4	14.6	15.0	21.8	9.5	15.2	21.7	46.0	18.1	29.0
Median School Years Completed	9.0	8.9	10.2	12.1	11.4	11.7	11.1	11.3	9.7	11.2	10.1
Median Family Income, 1969 $$	8149	7568	8657	10518	8911	10834	10347	8946	3547	10195	8348
% Income Below Poverty Level	11.7	26.8	13.3	8.0	18.4	9.9	12.0	14.7	59.6	11.9	30.3
% Income of $15,000 or More	10.5	10.8	9.7	22.2	14.8	25.8	25.6	10.9	0.0	17.8	13.8
% White Collar Workers	10.4	8.2	9.8	23.1	15.0	15.1	16.7	12.4	9.2	13.4	6.9
% Civilian Labor Force Unemployed	7.2	7.8	8.9	5.2	6.8	5.6	4.6	4.4	22.9	4.4	9.4
% Riding To Work By Automobile	60.6	39.1	58.0	66.0	77.6	81.9	77.8	68.4	41.0	77.8	77.6
Population Per Household	2.9	2.2	3.0	3.1	3.9	4.7	3.8	3.2	2.8	2.7	4.8
Total Housing Units	857	1529	1442	1338	1188	1568	2213	1348	586	373	1022
% Condominiums & Cooperatives	0.0	0.0	0.0	0.6	1.0	0.8	1.1	0.4	0.0	0.0	0.9
% Built 1960 Or Later	0.6	0.0	0.0	0.0	4.5	42.5	9.8	0.0	0.0	0.0	7.6
% Owner Occupied	32.0	11.8	33.1	48.1	53.5	89.0	69.0	37.3	6.5	39.9	48.1
% With 1+ Persons Per Room	11.7	11.8	12.5	10.6	22.8	26.5	18.8	15.6	20.9	7.3	37.4
Median Value: Owner Units $$	13200	13600	13900	15700	13200	15500	15100	14200	–	16100	12000
Median Rent: Rental Units $$	81	71	87	86	85	94	82	86	61	88	75
Median Number Of Rooms; All Units	4.2	2.4	4.2	4.7	4.6	5.4	4.9	4.3	3.6	4.3	4.8

Tract Number	0121	0122	0123	0124	0125	0126	0127	0128	0129	0130	0131
Total Population	6227	7022	5186	4450	8539	1806	4593	4763	3053	6631	6909
% Male	49.7	47.4	46.5	47.6	45.4	47.8	47.4	47.1	46.7	49.4	47.1
% Black	0.4	98.5	99.1	98.8	99.5	99.8	99.6	99.3	98.7	6.7	0.4
% Other Nonwhite	0.4	0.1	0.1	0.1	0.2	0.1	0.2	0.3	0.3	0.7	0.3
% Of Spanish Language	8.5	0.0	0.6	1.0	1.6	3.3	0.5	0.2	1.0	13.0	4.6
% Foreign Born	3.9	0.3	0.1	0.0	0.2	0.0	0.2	0.7	0.0	13.0	15.0
% Living In Group Quarters	0.0	1.4	0.8	0.8	1.2	0.1	0.6	0.2	0.1	0.1	0.2
% 13 Years Old And Under	33.1	30.3	27.6	29.0	32.3	31.9	29.4	25.7	32.8	26.6	18.9
% 14-20 Years Old	14.4	15.9	12.7	16.4	16.1	17.8	14.4	13.8	18.1	13.6	12.4
% 21-64 Years Old	49.5	46.7	48.7	48.0	42.3	42.0	46.4	49.2	44.0	50.6	55.2
% 65-74 Years Old	2.1	4.6	8.1	4.7	6.1	6.0	7.1	7.8	4.0	5.6	8.8
% 75 Years Old And Over	0.9	2.5	2.9	1.9	3.2	2.3	2.8	3.6	1.1	3.6	4.7
% In Different House	58.4	53.9	51.0	72.1	58.7	66.3	59.6	71.0	61.5	56.9	64.6
% Families With Female Head	7.1	21.5	34.7	22.3	39.2	23.0	27.7	25.3	25.1	11.2	9.4
Median School Years Completed	12.1	10.1	9.3	10.8	10.0	9.3	10.4	10.0	9.8	10.2	11.1
Median Family Income, 1969 $$	10766	8285	5387	8419	5441	8328	8078	7857	7891	9699	10885
% Income Below Poverty Level	5.2	17.3	37.5	16.1	37.5	27.8	20.2	24.8	16.6	6.4	5.0
% Income of $15,000 or More	19.8	14.2	3.5	16.8	7.2	11.4	13.2	9.1	9.2	17.1	26.1
% White Collar Workers	18.0	11.9	8.9	16.4	10.5	12.4	13.4	9.1	8.9	15.7	22.7
% Civilian Labor Force Unemployed	1.7	9.0	8.9	5.0	10.4	9.6	7.7	7.1	12.9	4.3	3.0
% Riding To Work By Automobile	87.5	67.5	68.0	72.8	68.8	71.1	65.4	65.4	76.1	83.5	79.8
Population Per Household	3.9	3.5	2.7	3.6	3.4	4.2	3.4	3.1	4.1	3.2	2.8
Total Housing Units	1636	2062	2172	1275	2600	455	1448	1629	784	2099	2466
% Condominiums & Cooperatives	0.6	1.3	0.0	0.4	0.5	0.0	0.0	0.3	0.0	0.0	5.2
% Built 1960 Or Later	14.0	23.8	0.8	4.7	2.0	13.8	2.7	2.6	2.7	11.7	5.2
% Owner Occupied	85.1	40.5	14.9	57.3	32.3	69.0	46.6	45.9	48.7	69.6	70.3
% With 1+ Persons Per Room	17.1	20.1	15.5	18.4	20.9	24.9	18.0	14.8	30.4	12.8	7.8
Median Value: Owner Units $$	14200	15100	12100	16300	12900	12700	12500	11500	12200	13600	15400
Median Rent: Rental Units $$	116	75	65	69	65	67	72	71	80	84	101
Median Number Of Rooms; All Units	5.0	4.4	3.8	4.8	4.3	4.9	4.5	4.4	4.2	4.7	4.6

Tract Number	0132	0133	0134	0411	0412	0413
Total Population	6304	4176	8572	6930	2694	7707
% Male	48.2	49.7	48.5	51.4	48.9	50.0
% Black	0.0	0.3	0.0	0.4	52.6	0.0
% Other Nonwhite	0.0	0.3	0.4	0.6	0.3	0.4
% Of Spanish Language	7.6	5.1	3.7	8.9	11.2	4.5
% Foreign Born	13.2	13.3	12.5	2.2	3.2	3.1
% Living In Group Quarters	0.0	0.2	0.3	0.1	0.5	0.0
% 13 Years Old And Under	20.6	28.4	24.7	34.9	35.1	28.4
% 14-20 Years Old	13.3	14.6	13.8	14.6	16.3	13.5
% 21-64 Years Old	54.2	50.4	54.4	47.1	42.3	52.7
% 65-74 Years Old	7.3	4.0	4.1	2.7	5.0	3.8
% 75 Years Old And Over	4.7	2.5	3.0	0.8	1.3	1.6
% In Different House	66.5	63.9	65.2	54.2	60.5	57.1
% Families With Female Head	8.6	8.7	7.3	6.5	14.4	6.1
Median School Years Completed	12.1	11.1	11.8	9.2	9.2	11.4
Median Family Income, 1969 $$	11649	11322	11843	9546	7263	11215
% Income Below Poverty Level	2.7	3.8	3.1	7.0	24.9	6.9
% Income of $15,000 or More	25.4	20.6	26.4	15.1	10.4	25.4
% White Collar Workers	27.2	14.3	19.2	11.5	9.6	14.7
% Civilian Labor Force Unemployed	3.9	2.5	2.0	4.6	10.6	4.7
% Riding To Work By Automobile	79.5	82.6	84.5	90.9	87.0	92.4
Population Per Household	3.0	3.5	3.4	3.8	3.9	3.3
Total Housing Units	2120	1217	2576	1844	737	2339
% Condominiums & Cooperatives	0.2	0.0	0.3	0.0	0.0	0.3
% Built 1960 Or Later	2.7	2.7	21.5	22.1	18.9	31.7
% Owner Occupied	78.3	82.3	79.0	68.5	66.6	81.8
% With 1+ Persons Per Room	6.8	13.1	10.2	23.5	24.8	10.6
Median Value: Owner Units $$	15800	14400	16900	10600	9800	15400
Median Rent: Rental Units $$	94	94	115	84	69	93
Median Number Of Rooms; All Units	5.0	4.8	4.9	4.5	4.5	4.6

United States Steel is currently constructing a new furnace at Gary, utilizing the highly-efficient continuous casting technology, which will produce as much as one-third of the entire U.S. Steel output.

As the industrial base of the country moves west, transportation conditions will tend to make the Chicago-Northwest Indiana district even more important in the geography of the steel industry. However, the new production techniques will require fewer workers, and many steel workers who are currently laid off will never be recalled.

The 1960 *Fact Book* envisioned a Gary of 250,000 inhabitants. However, if the basic industries do not revive and begin to diversify, Gary must adjust to a new industrial geography, in which the city may play a greater role while providing fewer opportunities.

Janice K. Bella

Hammond, Indiana

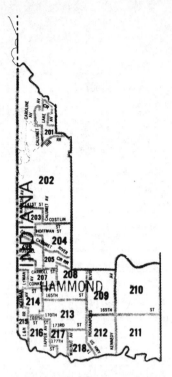

Hammond is an L-shaped city on the Indiana-Illinois border about 20 miles southeast of the Loop. Its L-shaped square mile area consists of a large rectangle south of East Chicago between the Grand Calumet and Little Calumet Rivers and a narrow strip bordering the state line extending roughly five miles north to Lake Michigan. The city has common boundaries with Chicago, Calumet City, Lansing, East Chicago and Gary. It is part of the Calumet industrial region and many workers make their living in the steel and oil plants nearby.

During the early 19th century, the area now occupied by Hammond was covered by sand and swamp. In 1850 a cholera epidemic in Chicago led Ernest Hohman, a German immigrant tailor, to live for a time with friends in Merrillville. While commuting between there and his shop in Chicago he became familiar with the Calumet area. Hammond had its beginnings the following year, when Hohman bought 39 acres on the north bank of the river and built the Hohman Inn, a six-room log structure which soon began to attract travelers. Hohman built a bridge across the river and a road which led in the direction of Crown Point, A small settlement developed around the inn, and he began to buy up the surrounding land.

In 1869 George H. Hammond, a Detroit butcher and entrepreneur who had developed a refrigerated railroad car, built a slaughterhouse across the river from the Hohman Inn, in partnership with Marcus M. Towle. An ice house and a boarding house for the workers were soon added. The beef was shipped on the Michigan Central Railroad, which was accessible at the Gibson Station, two miles away. The plant was known at the State Line Slaughter House and by the autumn it was shipping dressed beef to Chicago and Boston. Within 10 years, shipments were being made to Liverpool. Hammond died at the age of 48, in 1886, but the slaughterhouse continued to operate. By 1891 the Hammond plant employed more than a thousand workers and, with Armour, Swift and Morris, was rated one of the "Big Four" of meatpacking. Hammond had retained his Detroit plant and later built a large slaughterhouse in Omaha.

A Chicago land speculator had filed the plat of a "Town of Hohman" in 1870, but this never materialized. Hammond was not interested in the development of the land around his plant, preferring to live in Detroit. However his partner Marcus Towle built an imposing home near the slaughterhouse, established the first store and became the first postmaster. The post office was called State Line, but mail routing was often confused with another State Line located in Illinois. At Towle's urging the name of the post office was changed to Hammond in 1873. In 1875, with land he had purchased from Hohman's widow, Towle platted a town of Hammond. Five years later the first federal census counted 699 residents. During the 1880s Hammond became important as a rail center with the construction of the Erie, Nickel Plate and Monon system tracks. The community became a city in 1884, and Towle served as the first mayor. He severed his connection with the slaughterhouse and began selling homes to the workers. To support his construction activities he built a lumber yard, a sawmill, planing mill, sash and door factory and a dock on the Calumet River to receive the lumber. Caroline Hohman proved an able administrator of her husband's estate. Beginning in the 1880s she built the Hohman Opera House Block, Hammond's first business district. Thomas Hammond, younger brother of the packing magnate, left the business in 1886 to participate in local finance and politics. He succeeded Towle as mayor, organized the Commercial Bank of Hammond in 1892 and headed the Hammond Land and Improvement Company, which brought the Conkey Printing Company and other industries to Hammond.

In 1892 the first electric street railway began operation on Hohman Avenue. This brought shoppers from East Chicago and Whiting to Hammond, and the retail district of Hammond developed faster. The construction of the Chicago, Lake Shore and South Bend Railroad (later the Chicago, South Shore and South Bend) in 1908 made downtown Chicago accessible to Hammond residents. Commuting developed as they found work in Chicago, and Chicago workers established homes in Hammond. The 1890 population was 5,428 and this grew to 12,376 at the turn of the century. Hammond attracted numerous German immigrants, many of whom were butchers and sausage makers who worked at the meatpacking plant.

The slaughterhouse remained the major industry until it was destroyed by fire in 1901. By that time, the meatpacking operation covered four acres and employed 1,800 men. The management made no effort to rebuild the plant. This led to massive unemployment, which was exacerbated by a strike at the printing company. Led by Mayor Armanis F. Knotts, who would later choose the Gary site for the United States Steel Corporation, the city undertook an aggressive campaign to attract new and more diversified industry. A distilling company was established in 1902, a potato machinery factory in 1903, a piano manufacturer and a surgical instrument company came in 1904. The Standard Steel Car Company started construction of a large plant in 1906. Despite the out-migration of hundreds of workers after the destruction of the slaughterhouse, the 1910 population reached 20,928, 30 percent of whom were German foreign stock. In 1911 Hammond annexed all the remaining unincorporated territory in North Township north of the Little Calumet River, including the village of Hessville and the Gibson Railroad Yards.

During the next 20 years, industry grew rapidly as the result of the extensive rail network and the availability of vacant land. The development of Gary as a major steel center during this period stimulated the growth of Hammond as a center of lighter industry. World War I brought near-capacity production and employment in the Calumet Region. An attempt in 1919 by the American Federation of Labor to organize the employees of the Standard Steel Car Company, which was now the largest employer, led to a strike and later a riot in which four were killed and 60 wounded. An attempt in the mid-1920s to annex suburban Highland and Munster was met with hostility and dropped. By 1930 the Conkey Printing Company employed 600 persons in a 14-acre plant, Lever Brothers had located a soap factory in in Hammond which employed 500, and a large corn products company had set up a 100-acre plant. From a population of 36,000 in 1920 the population of Hammond, fed by migration from depressed farm areas in

Hammond, Indiana
Population and Housing Characteristics, 1930-1980

	1980	1970	1960	1950	1940	1930
Total Population	93,714	107,790	111,698	87,594	70,184	64,560
% Male	49.0	49.1	50.0	50.6	51.3	52.1
% Female	51.0	50.9	50.0	49.4	48.7	47.9
% White	89.5	95.4	97.7	98.7	99.1	99.0
% Black	6.4	4.3	2.2	1.3	0.9	1.0
% Other Nonwhite Races	4.1	0.3	0.1	0.0	0.0	0.0
% Under 5 Years Old	8.2	8.6	12.3	11.3	8.4	10.3
% 5-19 Years Old	23.8	29.6	26.8	21.6	25.6	20.5
% 20-44 Years Old	35.2	31.0	34.7	41.7	43.3	43.9
% 45-64 Years Old	22.1	23.0	19.7	20.0	18.9	13.7
% 65 Years and Older	10.7	7.8	6.5	5.4	3.8	2.6

Place 1040 — Hammond, Indiana
Selected Characteristics of Census Tracts: 1980

Tract Number	Total	201	202	203	204	205	206	207	208	209	210
Total Population	93714	5615	7440	4385	4638	5506	3646	5279	3393	3877	10314
% Male	49.0	48.1	49.6	48.7	48.8	49.5	50.4	47.5	48.3	48.5	49.3
% Black	6.4	0.0	0.1	1.8	0.1	4.1	7.7	43.5	66.5	0.5	0.1
% Other Nonwhite	4.1	1.6	2.9	6.5	7.3	10.7	8.7	5.7	3.3	2.5	2.8
% Of Spanish Origin	8.3	2.6	7.6	13.2	18.2	22.1	13.9	10.8	6.3	5.1	6.6
% Foreign Born	5.1	8.4	6.9	8.5	5.4	5.3	5.5	3.7	1.9	3.5	4.8
% Living In Group Quarters	0.4	1.4	0.8	0.0	0.3	0.0	0.7	0.7	3.5	0.0	0.0
% 13 Years Old And Under	21.7	15.7	18.3	21.7	24.5	29.3	28.5	27.2	25.7	17.3	21.7
% 14-20 Years Old	12.3	10.7	11.3	13.3	12.1	12.6	10.3	15.5	13.9	9.2	14.6
% 21-64 Years Old	55.4	56.0	57.7	53.1	53.0	50.7	47.9	49.8	50.1	61.9	57.0
% 65-74 Years Old	7.1	10.9	9.2	8.0	7.2	4.7	8.2	4.7	7.0	7.7	4.7
% 75 Years Old And Over	3.6	6.6	3.5	3.9	3.2	2.7	5.1	2.9	3.3	3.8	2.0
% In Different House	39.9	31.9	33.0	32.5	43.5	55.7	57.8	55.0	37.4	49.5	35.1
% Families With Female Head	17.6	10.6	16.6	23.4	18.8	20.3	29.2	24.8	36.4	14.4	11.1
Median School Years Completed	12.2	12.3	12.2	11.8	11.1	11.3	11.8	11.8	10.9	12.4	12.3
Median Family Income, 1979 $$	22978	25441	22748	19656	18563	19915	16346	18173	15238	24952	26396
% Income Below Poverty Level	6.9	1.5	5.9	9.3	13.0	10.0	24.5	16.2	25.6	2.2	1.7
% Income Of $30,000 Or More	27.8	37.1	28.6	19.0	16.6	15.4	11.4	14.5	18.3	31.1	37.7
% White Collar Workers	40.2	48.2	42.1	36.3	29.0	28.6	28.8	32.7	27.7	46.9	36.7
% Civilian Labor Force Unemployed	8.8	6.2	7.8	11.5	15.6	13.2	12.8	14.2	13.7	6.0	7.2
% Riding To Work By Automobile	89.2	80.0	89.2	83.8	79.0	92.6	73.3	85.9	84.3	88.0	93.8
Mean Commuting Time - Minutes	20.0	20.8	19.0	17.1	18.2	17.2	20.3	20.4	20.3	20.7	19.6
Population Per Household	2.7	2.5	2.6	2.7	2.8	3.1	2.4	3.2	3.0	2.3	3.1
Total Housing Units	36075	2288	3016	1721	1801	1991	1789	1790	1166	1688	3407
% Condominiums	0.3	0.0	0.0	0.0	0.0	0.6	0.0	0.0	0.0	0.0	0.3
% Built 1970 Or Later	5.9	1.4	5.6	5.3	3.2	9.2	16.1	2.1	1.8	19.0	3.8
% Owner Occupied	61.7	67.4	70.1	54.4	57.4	49.3	17.8	53.5	52.6	52.5	81.7
% With 1+ Persons Per Room	4.5	2.0	3.8	5.8	5.1	9.6	9.3	8.4	8.1	2.8	4.2
Median Value: Owner Units $$	38100	44200	36100	32000	30800	26400	21500	29500	25400	36600	40900
Median Rent: Rental Units $$	178	176	161	155	163	169	134	163	137	240	220
Median Number Of Rooms: All Units	4.9	5.1	4.6	4.8	4.7	4.6	3.3	5.2	4.9	4.4	5.2

Tract Number	211	212	213	214	215	216	217	218	401
Total Population	8738	3390	6387	4411	4600	4659	4055	3259	122
% Male	50.8	49.5	48.6	48.0	50.3	48.1	46.8	49.1	48.4
% Black	5.9	0.0	0.3	0.8	0.7	0.0	4.9	0.2	0.0
% Other Nonwhite	3.1	2.0	2.6	5.1	3.8	1.4	4.7	2.1	5.7
% Of Spanish Origin	6.3	5.1	3.9	8.5	5.0	3.4	8.7	4.4	25.4
% Foreign Born	4.0	5.0	4.4	4.4	7.1	4.0	3.3	4.7	6.7
% Living In Group Quarters	0.1	0.0	0.0	0.0	0.2	0.0	1.2	0.0	0.0
% 13 Years Old And Under	21.2	16.9	17.2	21.7	18.0	19.5	27.4	22.8	21.3
% 14-20 Years Old	14.4	11.2	11.1	10.8	10.9	12.5	13.3	13.3	11.5
% 21-64 Years Old	59.2	58.8	59.9	53.0	57.6	53.9	52.1	57.4	56.6
% 65-74 Years Old	3.9	9.8	8.1	8.7	7.4	11.6	4.6	4.8	5.7
% 75 Years Old And Over	1.4	3.4	3.6	5.7	6.2	5.9	3.5	1.7	4.9
% In Different House	45.8	35.5	36.0	45.1	40.8	28.1	33.6	26.3	57.4
% Families With Female Head	14.4	12.5	13.7	16.6	15.9	8.8	33.5	8.9	5.9
Median School Years Completed	12.3	12.5	12.4	12.3	12.5	12.3	12.1	12.2	10.8
Median Family Income, 1979 $$	24698	24762	25477	21409	24844	23162	22254	24978	25938
% Income Below Poverty Level	2.0	2.3	2.4	6.0	3.4	3.4	16.9	2.8	14.3
% Income Of $30,000 Or More	32.2	33.5	32.9	23.1	36.7	27.6	28.5	29.0	14.3
% White Collar Workers	40.1	50.2	43.6	37.2	54.8	44.3	42.9	40.2	39.3
% Civilian Labor Force Unemployed	7.9	3.7	7.4	6.6	6.7	7.8	10.8	8.7	0.0
% Riding To Work By Automobile	91.0	92.6	93.2	92.4	90.0	92.7	93.3	94.5	89.3
Mean Commuting Time - Minutes	20.6	21.5	19.5	20.5	20.1	20.7	21.5	24.1	18.6
Population Per Household	2.7	2.7	2.6	2.5	2.3	2.6	3.0	3.1	2.7
Total Housing Units	3441	1257	2471	1832	2135	1796	1377	1060	49
% Condominiums	1.9	0.0	0.0	0.0	0.0	0.0	0.9	0.0	–
% Built 1970 Or Later	14.0	1.0	4.3	4.2	3.3	1.4	1.5	0.8	–
% Owner Occupied	50.8	85.5	69.1	61.4	48.0	85.9	61.4	92.8	–
% With 1+ Persons Per Room	4.7	2.0	2.7	2.8	2.7	1.5	5.3	3.9	–
Median Value: Owner Units $$	43000	45100	42600	34500	52600	40500	35900	37300	–
Median Rent: Rental Units $$	220	209	218	180	174	189	56	256	–
Median Number Of Rooms: All Units	4.7	5.2	4.9	5.0	4.8	5.3	4.8	5.3	–

Lake County and further downstate, grew to more than 64,000 in 1930. The leading nationality groups among the white foreign stock were the Germans, Poles and Czechoslovakians. Blacks comprised 1 percent of the total population.

The Depression brought this period of sustained growth to an end as manufacturing employment dropped off sharply. In 1932 every bank in Hammond was closed for almost the entire year, and the municipal employees were paid with checks dated 90 days ahead. State and federal relief measures began to alleviate the worst conditions by 1933. In 1938, reclamation of the Lake George swamplands was begun. Industry revived in the late 1930s and 4,500 persons were employed in more than 90 manufacturing establishments by the end of the decade, by which time the population had grown to more than 70,000. During World War II Hammond industries were again called on to produce at capacity.

Hammond continued to grow during the postwar years. The population grew to more than 87,000 in 1950. Between 1950 and 1960, it increased 28 percent to 111,698. Leading nationalities among the foreign stock were the Poles, Germans, Czechoslovakians, and Hungarians. During this period, Hammond had a diversified manufacturing base, but depended heavily on steel, oil and agricultural products for employment. There was additional growth as a trucking center, with carload freight for Chicago being transferred to trucks in Hammond. Correspondingly, Hammond became a distributing center for a number of major companies. In 1958 there were 123 manufacturing establishments in Hammond employing 10,583 persons. In 1960, 44 percent of the workers residing in Hammond worked there, and another 25 percent worked in East Chicago.

Despite the decreasing supply of vacant land, particularly land desirable for residential development away from railroads and indus-

Hammond
Selected Characteristics of Census Tracts: 1970

Tract Number	TOTAL	0201	0202	0203	0204	0205	0206	0207	0208	0209	0210
Total Population	107790	6497	9077	5046	5489	5734	3441	6159	5194	3777	12276
% Male	49.1	48.5	49.9	49.0	48.8	49.4	51.7	49.0	48.2	50.0	49.3
% Black	4.3	0.0	0.1	0.1	0.1	0.1	1.2	13.8	68.0	0.1	0.0
% Other Nonwhite	0.3	0.1	0.1	0.5	0.5	0.4	1.4	0.2	0.1	0.6	0.2
% Of Spanish Language	3.1	1.9	1.9	5.4	7.6	8.6	3.3	5.2	3.7	0.9	3.7
% Foreign Born	4.8	8.3	6.0	8.0	6.2	5.0	3.9	6.1	3.5	5.3	3.4
% Living In Group Quarters	0.3	0.1	1.0	0.3	0.6	0.0	1.7	1.4	0.3	0.0	0.2
% 13 Years Old And Under	26.7	20.3	25.2	25.0	25.6	28.5	25.2	27.8	34.1	23.6	31.4
% 14-20 Years Old	13.1	12.1	12.2	13.3	12.5	14.3	12.4	13.4	13.6	11.4	14.3
% 21-64 Years Old	52.4	55.7	55.2	52.8	53.7	49.5	51.7	47.8	45.9	56.7	50.6
% 65-74 Years Old	5.1	7.9	4.7	5.6	5.2	5.3	6.9	6.3	4.3	5.9	2.5
% 75 Years Old And Over	2.7	4.0	2.7	3.3	2.9	2.3	3.8	4.7	2.1	2.4	1.1
% In Different House	61.2	67.1	68.3	65.3	64.4	51.1	38.9	40.6	56.1	67.5	65.7
% Families With Female Head	9.4	9.9	9.0	10.6	9.2	9.3	15.3	12.4	17.2	8.3	6.0
Median School Years Completed	11.7	12.2	11.3	10.4	10.2	9.8	9.8	10.5	9.8	11.6	12.1
Median Family Income, 1969 $$	10899	11569	10829	10567	9449	9561	7892	9197	8733	11186	11549
% Income Below Poverty Level	5.4	4.0	4.8	1.9	5.1	10.0	10.0	7.8	17.6	5.6	2.3
% Income of $15,000 or More	22.4	26.8	24.0	16.1	16.0	16.1	10.0	15.2	11.8	20.2	24.2
% White Collar Workers	20.9	29.3	17.3	13.6	13.5	12.6	15.3	14.7	8.0	21.7	19.4
% Civilian Labor Force Unemployed	3.9	3.8	2.8	2.9	3.1	5.2	6.7	6.2	8.1	2.3	3.7
% Riding To Work By Automobile	82.7	72.3	79.3	75.6	70.9	82.9	67.5	75.1	81.4	86.4	92.1
Population Per Household	3.1	2.9	3.1	3.1	3.0	3.0	3.3	2.5	3.1	3.0	3.7
Total Housing Units	35613	2304	2971	1722	1920	1869	1576	2056	1562	1300	3319
% Condominiums & Cooperatives	0.4	0.3	0.2	0.2	0.0	0.3	0.0	0.4	0.7	0.0	0.7
% Built 1960 Or Later	10.9	4.2	15.2	3.6	6.4	0.9	0.9	1.4	0.9	3.5	24.7
% Owner Occupied	62.2	66.3	71.6	55.6	56.8	52.4	21.1	48.7	45.8	66.5	82.4
% With 1+ Persons Per Room	9.9	5.6	9.5	9.9	9.9	11.1	10.6	12.0	19.8	8.4	12.5
Median Value: Owner Units $$	16400	19400	15600	13900	13500	12300	11200	14600	12200	15600	17000
Median Rent: Rental Units $$	97	94	89	86	88	87	82	94	76	109	121
Median Number Of Rooms: All Units	4.7	5.0	4.5	4.7	4.5	4.5	3.2	4.8	4.4	4.5	5.0

Tract Number	0211	0212	0213	0214	0215	0216	0217	0218	0401
Total Population	9352	4149	7681	4863	5036	5280	4823	3916	2429
% Male	51.6	48.8	48.2	48.0	48.4	48.1	47.3	49.2	50.5
% Black	0.3	0.0	0.0	0.4	0.1	0.0	3.4	0.0	0.5
% Other Nonwhite	0.3	0.1	0.2	0.2	0.3	0.3	0.0	0.1	0.5
% Of Spanish Language	1.7	2.2	1.5	0.5	3.1	0.0	3.7	0.0	4.7
% Foreign Born	3.8	2.8	5.8	2.9	3.8	4.6	3.3	2.2	8.9
% Living In Group Quarters	0.2	0.0	0.2	0.0	0.3	0.3	0.0	0.0	0.3
% 13 Years Old And Under	30.0	22.7	23.9	23.8	20.3	20.6	34.3	32.5	27.4
% 14-20 Years Old	13.5	13.9	14.5	9.5	11.0	11.9	14.8	14.9	12.8
% 21-64 Years Old	53.4	56.4	55.4	53.2	54.4	55.6	44.8	49.0	52.2
% 65-74 Years Old	2.0	5.0	3.9	9.0	8.7	8.3	3.8	2.6	4.6
% 75 Years Old And Over	1.1	2.0	2.2	4.5	5.5	3.5	2.4	1.0	3.0
% In Different House	59.9	71.3	66.7	60.6	49.7	72.2	58.2	63.4	52.4
% Families With Female Head	5.5	6.5	7.9	9.7	9.6	7.6	19.1	6.9	12.7
Median School Years Completed	12.1	12.3	12.2	11.6	12.5	12.1	11.1	12.1	10.5
Median Family Income, 1969 $$	11370	13413	11859	9991	12750	11341	9862	11743	9610
% Income Below Poverty Level	4.5	2.0	2.4	3.3	2.1	3.3	15.3	3.4	5.2
% Income of $15,000 or More	24.9	39.1	26.4	17.0	34.3	24.7	16.0	28.0	11.7
% White Collar Workers	23.1	33.7	27.7	18.7	37.3	25.2	17.2	21.4	17.3
% Civilian Labor Force Unemployed	3.0	2.4	3.7	3.9	4.0	2.0	5.7	2.4	3.9
% Riding To Work By Automobile	91.0	88.6	84.1	81.8	82.6	84.2	90.6	90.5	69.8
Population Per Household	3.2	3.2	3.2	2.8	2.5	3.0	3.6	3.8	3.2
Total Housing Units	3126	1346	2434	1824	2111	1785	1353	1035	783
% Condominiums & Cooperatives	2.2	0.0	0.2	0.0	0.2	0.0	0.4	0.0	0.0
% Built 1960 Or Later	47.6	9.7	12.8	2.7	5.0	1.7	4.2	4.8	5.7
% Owner Occupied	52.0	75.4	71.4	62.0	47.8	84.5	62.5	91.2	44.3
% With 1+ Persons Per Room	12.0	6.4	8.1	5.7	3.4	5.0	14.9	12.0	13.2
Median Value: Owner Units $$	17300	19200	18100	15000	22800	17400	15900	15700	12800
Median Rent: Rental Units $$	126	115	129	93	97	112	51	127	76
Median Number Of Rooms: All Units	4.6	4.9	4.7	4.8	4.7	5.1	4.7	5.1	4.5

try, and the lack of prospects for annexing land, Hammond anticipated a population maximum of 125,000 by 1980, but that was not to be. The number of residents dropped by 4,000 in the 1960s as the suburban fringe to the south developed, and by 14,000 in the 1970s as job opportunities in Calumet region industries began to shrink. The baby boom fertility rates dropped while teenagers matured and moved away. The many railroads and the patchwork zoning of residential and industrial areas made planning for expansion difficult.

The number of housing units in Hammond has increased while the population dropped. Eighteen percent of all current units have been built in the last 20 years. The fact that the percentage of units in single-family homes has dropped by 5 percent to 68 percent suggests greater concentration on structures with multiple-units. In 1980, 62 percent of all units were owner-occupied, and the value of a single owner-occupied unit was greater than in Gary or East Chicago. The percentage in overcrowded housing has declined by two-thirds since 1960. The commercial center is at State Street and Hohman Avenue.

Hammond continues to be a city of whites, although the black population has grown from 2 to 6 percent in the last 20 years. Among the whites, the most numerous descent groups are Polish, English and German. Eight percent are of Spanish origin, 5 percent are foreign born and 13 percent speak a language other than English at home. The median income of Hammond residents is higher than that of Gary or East Chicago, and fewer families lived in poverty in 1979. Of the resident labor force, 42 percent work in manufacturing, 57 percent work outside of Hammond and 9 percent were unemployed in 1980. Though dependent on Gary and Whiting, Hammond has its own diversified industrial base. Although the population maximum has probably been reached, prospects in Hammond are modestly optimistic as industry recovers in the 1980s.

M.W.H.

Highland, Indiana

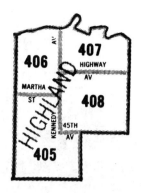

Highland lies 28 miles southeast of Chicago and is located in the extreme northwest corner of the State of Indiana. It is bounded by Hammond on the north and by Schererville on the south. The east and west sides are contiguous with the neighboring communities of Munster and Griffith.

As the prehistoric Lake Chicago drained, it left a great sand ridge and marshes known as the "Northern Swamps." The early inhabitants were Pottawatomie and Miami Indians. French missionaries later explored and mapped this section, labeling it Calumet. The first settlers in Highland were the Johnston family who arrived in 1847. They were attracted by the abundance of wildlife as well as the rich farmlands. Judith Johnston set up the first school, teaching pupils in her home for the first 11 years. An elementary school has been named in her honor. Although the original log cabin no longer stands, a plaque commemorating these first homesteaders has been placed on the site at the intersection of Grace Street and Ridge Road.

The Johnstons were soon followed by German immigrants who harvested crops of corn and wheat. Gradually, Dutch settlers moved in to work as tenant farmers. They grew most of the cabbage for Highland's first industry, a sauerkraut factory that was later purchased by Libby, McNeill and Libby. By the turn of the century a second sauerkraut factory had been founded. Other early industry included a cement block company and a brick factory.

In 1882, the town then known as Clough Postal Station was plotted by John H. Clough, Charles G. Wicker and John Condit Smith. The following year surveyors from the Erie Railroad stood atop the dunes, which were once the shoreline of Lake Michican, and marked the spot on the map as "Highlands." In 1905 the Chicago-Southern Indiana Railroad was built through Highland. This line was later absorbed by the New York Central. Highland became an agricultural center in the Calumet Region. Early shipments were made to the southern states and sometime later to Chicago.

It wasn't until 1910 that Highland incorporated as a town with a population of 304. Charles Wirth was elected as the first Town Board President and remained on the board until 1931. The decade from 1920 (population 542) to 1930 (population 1,583) brought the largest 10-year percentage increase in number of residents. An effort to preserve the last stand of timber in Highland led to the creation of Wicker Park. A major portion of this land was donated by the Wicker estate and the 200-acre park named for that family is located at the corner of Ridge Road and U. S. Highway 41.

In the late 1920s, the City of Hammond took legal steps to annex the Town of Highland as well as neighboring Munster. A great majority of Highland residents were opposed, unwilling to trade an ample water supply and fire and police protection for higher taxes and "remote" government. This issue was not resolved until 1948 when a bill was introduced into the General Assembly which prohibited annexation of either ridge town. In 1945, a referendum to become a city was defeated and never seriously considered again.

Population growth continued in the 1930s, despite the Depression. The Farmers and Merchants Bank, the first in Highland, closed in 1932, involving thousands of dollars in town funds. Nearly every bank in northwest Indiana closed as well during the Depression years.

World War II ended the Depression and sent the Calumet industries into production at full capacity. Highland continued to grow in the postwar era. The population more than doubled from 1940 (2,723) to 1950 (5,878), reflecting the general trend of the Calumet Region. The industrial cities to the north, where the giant steel and oil industries as well as hundreds of smaller enterprises are located, had increased in population and many who preferred suburban living had moved to the towns immediately south to establish homes and raise families. The majority of workers living in Highland were employed in the steel and oil industries, general manufacturing and transportation. A small percentage owned and operated retail stores and service enterprises in town. Industrial workers continued to move into Highland in the 1950s and by the end of that decade the population had nearly tripled again to more than 16,000.

By 1970, the population had increased to nearly 25,000. The current (1980) population is 25,935. One percent are black and 2.5 percent of Spanish origin. Among the European descended, the largest number is Polish, followed by Germans, English and Dutch. The median family income in 1979 was more than $29,000, and 62 percent of the families reported incomes in excess of $25,000. Only 2 percent of the families lived in poverty.

Almost three-fourths of the housing in Highland was built in a 30-year period between 1940 and 1970. Only 6 percent of all housing units were constructed before then. Twenty-two percent was built in the most recent decade. Thirteen percent of all housing is now in structures containing five or more units. The percentage in single-family units has dropped in the last 20 years, but is still high at 84. Seventy-nine percent of all units are owner-occupied and the median value of single-family owner-occupied housing units is $58,500.

Highland's residential growth has been facilitated by the town's proximity to a vast industrial complex, with its numerous oil refineries and steel companies. A third of the resident labor force works in manufacturing. A network of roads link Highland to the industrial region. Principal north-south routes are U. S. 41 (Indianapolis Boulevard) and State 912 (Cline Avenue), which tie in with Interstate Highways 80, 90, and 94. Interstate Highway 65 is a short distance west and provides a quick route to Indianapolis. Ninety-five percent of all workers drive to work. The average travel time is 20 minutes.

Retail sections are centered in the older business district along Highway Avenue, the newer area of 45th Avenue and Ridge Road, as well as along Route 41. There are more than 200 retail establishments in the Highland community. Gas stations comprise the largest number, followed by food stores, automotive dealers and apparel shops. There are 26 wholesale outlets with more than 200 employees.

In an effort to maintain its neighborhood image, zoning is limited to light industry, of which the three largest employers are a dairy and two manufacturers; one of which makes tools and the other refrigeration equipment. Indiana Bell Telephone Company has a district headquarters in Highland and is currently the largest local employer. The Town of Highland is administered by five trustees and a clerk-treasurer. Each is elected to a four-year term. Water is supplied by Lake Michigan via Hammond. There is a 34-member regular police force and an eight-member special unit. The fire Department is a volunteer 55-member unit. A new communications system was completed in the Spring of 1980 and is used jointly by the police department, fire department, public works and civil defense.

Recently, the sewer system has been elaborated as part of a multi-million dollar federally-funded project. In addition, 45th Avenue has been broadened into a four-lane highway in the hope of attracting new

Highland, Indiana
Population and Housing Characteristics, 1930-1980

	1980	1970	1960	1950	1940	1930
Total Population.......	25,935	24,947	16,284	5,878	2,723	1,553
% Male.................	49.4	49.2	50.7	51.2	52.3	52.1
% Female...............	50.6	50.8	49.3	48.8	47.7	47.9
% White................	98.5	99.6	100.0	100.0	100.0	99.1
% Black................	0.1	0.0	0.0	–	0.0	0.1
% Other Nonwhite Races...	1.4	0.4	0.0	–	–	0.0
% Under 5 Years Old......	6.8	9.5	15.7	14.7	11.6	14.2
% 5-19 Years Old.........	26.8	35.2	29.8	25.6	27.9	*
% 20-44 Years Old........	36.5	33.8	37.5	42.5	44.9	*
% 45-64 Years Old........	23.1	18.0	14.1	14.2	13.2	10.9
% 65 Years and Older.....	6.8	3.5	2.9	3.0	2.4	2.8
Median School Years......	12.6	12.4	12.2	11.2	8.8	*
Total Housing Units....	8,638	6,690	4,389	1,677	716	*
% In One Unit Structures.	82.0	91.0	98.1	88.7	84.2	*
% Owner Occupied.........	79.3	87.0	87.1	81.4	73.9	*
% Renter Occupied........	19.3	11.9	8.9	14.4	25.6	*
% Vacant.................	1.4	1.1	4.0	4.2	0.6	*
% 1+ Persons per Room....	2.9	11.6	14.0	15.9	24.6	*

Place 1080 — Highland , Indiana
Selected Characteristics of Census Tracts: 1980

Tract Number	Total	405	406	407	408
Total Population.............	25935	6240	4569	5943	9183
% Male..................	49.4	50.5	48.9	48.6	49.3
% Black................	0.1	0.4	0.0	0.0	0.0
% Other Nonwhite.........	1.4	1.6	1.4	1.2	1.3
% Of Spanish Origin........	2.5	2.5	2.9	2.2	2.6
% Foreign Born............	4.1	5.1	3.7	4.0	3.7
% Living In Group Quarters...	0.2	0.0	0.0	0.0	0.4
% 13 Years Old And Under....	21.1	24.2	18.8	20.8	20.4
% 14-20 Years Old..........	14.1	11.6	11.5	14.4	16.9
% 21-64 Years Old..........	58.0	59.3	59.1	57.9	56.8
% 65-74 Years Old..........	4.7	3.5	7.6	4.9	3.9
% 75 Years Old And Over......	2.1	1.5	3.1	1.9	2.1
% In Different House........	37.5	52.0	43.9	25.8	32.6
% Families With Female Head......	8.9	8.0	10.6	7.7	9.6
Median School Years Completed....	12.6	12.7	12.6	12.5	12.6
Median Family Income, 1979......$$	29039	29339	26166	29089	30288
% Income Below Poverty Level.....	2.3	1.8	3.8	3.1	1.4
% Income Of $30,000 Or More.....	47.0	47.5	38.1	47.4	51.0
% White Collar Workers..........	51.5	50.9	52.8	50.4	52.0
% Civilian Labor Force Unemployed..	4.5	4.5	4.1	5.1	4.4
% Riding To Work By Automobile....	94.7	94.2	92.7	95.4	95.6
Mean Commuting Time - Minutes...	21.8	22.2	21.1	21.0	22.3
Population Per Household........	3.0	2.9	2.7	3.2	3.2
Total Housing Units..........	8637	2186	1708	1881	2862
% Condominiums.............	1.0	0.0	3.2	0.0	1.1
% Built 1970 Or Later...........	22.2	61.3	6.4	4.8	13.0
% Owner Occupied..........	79.3	58.8	79.3	93.5	85.7
% With 1+ Persons Per Room....	2.9	2.1	2.1	3.8	3.3
Median Value: Owner Units.......$$	58500	66100	46700	55800	60700
Median Rent: Rental Units.......$$	259	274	220	249	245
Median Number Of Rooms: All Units.	5.3	5.1	5.1	5.3	5.4

Highland
Selected Characteristics of Census Tracts: 1970

Tract Number	TOTAL	0405	0406	0407	0408
Total Population.............	24947	2865	5177	7121	9784
% Male..................	49.2	48.9	48.8	49.3	49.4
% Black................	0.0	0.0	0.0	0.0	0.0
% Other Nonwhite.........	0.4	0.5	0.5	0.3	0.3
% Of Spanish Language........	2.1	0.0	4.2	1.7	1.9
% Foreign Born............	3.4	4.1	4.6	2.6	3.1
% Living In Group Quarters.....	0.1	0.4	0.2	0.1	0.0
% 13 Years Old And Under.....	32.9	31.1	28.7	33.7	35.1
% 14-20 Years Old..........	12.9	11.6	12.8	13.8	12.8
% 21-64 Years Old..........	50.6	53.6	53.3	49.4	49.2
% 65-74 Years Old..........	2.4	2.4	3.6	2.1	2.0
% 75 Years Old And Over..........	1.1	1.2	1.5	1.0	1.0
% In Different House........	65.0	34.9	65.1	74.7	66.5
% Families With Female Head.......	4.8	5.6	5.5	5.0	4.0
Median School Years Completed.......	12.4	12.4	12.3	12.4	12.4
Median Family Income, 1969......$$	12773	11680	12418	12829	13161
% Income Below Poverty Level....	2.6	2.5	3.3	2.8	2.2
% Income of $15,000 or More.....	32.8	28.0	34.9	32.9	33.1
% White Collar Workers.........	29.8	26.5	31.9	28.4	30.6
% Civilian Labor Force Unemployed.	2.8	3.7	4.3	2.6	1.6
% Riding To Work By Automobile....	90.8	93.2	89.0	89.8	91.9
Population Per Household..........	3.8	3.5	3.5	3.9	3.9
Total Housing Units..........	6685	831	1517	1814	2523
% Condominiums & Cooperatives.....	0.0	0.0	0.0	0.0	0.0
% Built 1960 Or Later.............	39.9	64.8	18.6	23.0	56.6
% Owner Occupied..........	87.0	77.0	82.5	93.4	88.4
% With 1+ Persons Per Room....	11.6	9.0	10.0	13.5	11.9
Median Value: Owner Units.......$$	21500	23600	18000	21000	22300
Median Rent: Rental Units.......$$	136	149	129	138	135
Median Number Of Rooms: All Units.	5.1	5.0	5.0	5.1	5.2

businesses west of Indianapolis Boulevard, the last area available for commercial development. Looking to the future, an active Economic Development Commission predicts the land most likely to be developed into an industrial park will be the farm land at the south end of town.

The southeast corner of Highland joins with neighboring Griffith and Schererville to form the location of Hoosier Prairie, an acreage preserving natural vegetation in the heart of the heavily-industrialized region. A more distinctive landmark is The Monument of Flags. In 1971, at the urging of the National Council for the Encouragement of Patriotism, the governors of eight states spanning the length of U. S. Highway 41 issued proclamations officially dedicating the highway as "The Highway of Flags" in tribute to American men and women serving in the armed forces. Each home and place of business along the highway was asked to display the flag every day. The monument, located at the southeast corner of Ridge Road and Indianapolis Boulevard, was dedicated on Memorial Day, 1975. It stands in North Township Memorial Park, which was dedicated to the memory of those who died in World War I by ex-president Coolidge in 1929.

Jane Cronin

Merrillville, Indiana

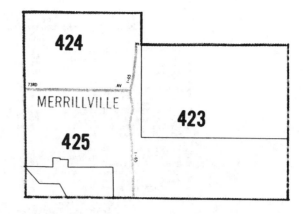

Merrillville is located 33 miles southeast of Chicago. It borders Gary to the north and is bounded by Hobart and Crown Point to the east and south. Schererville and Griffith are the neighboring towns that border the western edge.

An early Indian trading post was located east of Broadway between County Route 330 and Deerpath Road. A man named McGwinn, one of the earliest settlers, arriving in 1834, established residence in a small clearing in the heavily wooded area. Thus, the first of the area's many names, McGwinn's Village, was derived. The following year, the flamboyant Jeremiah Wiggins stopped and laid claim to considerable farmland. Noted for his "gift of gab" and intriguing trinkets, he soon earned the trust of the Pottawatomies. He was even permitted to plow their sacred burial grounds to clear the way for additional corn fields. Soon after, the Indians moved to western reservations and white settlers cleared dense woods and plowed virgin prairie to plant crops. At this time the area was renamed Wiggins Point.

Wiggins Point became a popular stop for wagon trains bound for Chicago, Joliet, and Kankakee. As westward expansion accelerated, routes emanating from Wiggins Point proliferated in all directions. A number of businesses, stores and hotels emerged to support the growing stagecoach trade. Among them was the California Exchange Hotel, built in 1842 by the Pierce family, by the old Sauk Trail (73rd Avenue) to Chicago's Fort Dearborn. Some confusion surrounds the name change from Wiggins Point to Centerville. It is said that when Jeremiah Wiggins died in 1838, residents thought the name Centerville was more dignified for a thriving community.

Somewhat later the name was changed to Merrillville in honor of William and Dudley Merrill, successful brothers who had a great impact on the town's early growth. Recognizing the value of owning property along the Sauk Trail, they purchased land there. They owned and operated a cheese factory, started in 1835; a general merchandise store, founded in 1840; and a Blacksmith shop begun in 1850. All of these enterprises thrived, particularly during the 1849 Gold Rush. From their land, the Merriills created the first subdivision.

The first public school in Ross Township was operational as early as 1838. The school building was replaced in 1870, remodeled in 1917, and subsequently converted for use as the present-day Town Hall. Merrillville remained the community's name until the town and its neighboring settlements, Deep River, Ross, Turkey Creek, Ainsworth, Lottaville and Rexville, organized collectively under the central government of Ross Township in 1848.

The John Wood grist mill was originally built in 1851 as a distillery and, later in 1854, it was converted to use as a steam mill for grinding wheat and flour. Millers were much in demand in early America because each neighborhood wanted the time and labor-saving services of a grist mill. After the mill was built, farmers came considerable distances and often waited several hours, sometimes days, to have their grain ground. It attracted shopkeepers and artisans such as coopers and blacksmiths. The mill served the area well and was in use until 1930.

The decades that followed settlement brought changing agricultural needs and milling techniques, but no urban growth in Ross Township. It wasn't until the 1940s that the first genuine subdivision, Forest Hills, was developed. The developer planned irregular lots and curved streets, leaving the surrounding woods as undisturbed as possible. These homes were built along County Route 330 and Broadway. Through the end of World War II the the majority of Ross Township residents remained rural farmers.

After the war, widespread opportunities developed in the industrial cities to the north of Merrillville. The Gary steel mills, in particular, attracted large numbers of workers to the area. In the 1950s newer tract subdivisions were first built near the Gary city limits. These new housing developments used the Gary sanitary sewage system. The 1940s and 1950s brought an increase in school construction that paralleled residential expansion.

While the Town Hall had its roots in the early history of Ross Township, the desire for self-government did not materialize until 1950. With a population of approximately 5,000, some residents expressed a need for government to control growth. Others failed to see any advantages to self-government, thinking the area would become a large city which could lead to higher taxes. There was considerable opposition from surrounding cities (Gary, Hobart, and Crown Point) to a proposed separate political entity for the area. All hope for independence died in 1969, when a bill, passed by both Indiana legislative houses to allow Merrillville to become a town, was "lost" on its way to the governor for signature.

Although the formal incorporation of Merrillville was not realized at this time, the problems associated with growth continued. The 1970 census for the communities of Merrillville, Lottaville and Rexville listed a population of 15,918. Much of this growth can be attributed to a mass migration by persons who had suffered property losses caused by panic selling as residential neighborhoods changed in Gary. The influx of new residents necessitated additional services. Among the problems of the late 1960s and early 1970s were planning, zoning, and flood and traffic control. In attempting to solve one of these problems, the Merrillville Conservancy District was created in 1962 to provide sanitary sewage facilities.

Location was a pivotal factor in the rapid development. Perhaps of more significance to overall expansion was the completion of Interstate Highway 65 in 1968. It linked Merrillville to the entire national highway system. I-65 offers access to Interstate Highways 80, 94 and 90 as well as U.S. Route 6 directly to the north. Lincoln Highway (U. S. 30) bisects important north-south U. S. 41 and in-town state roads 53 (Broadway) and 55 (Taft).

Merrillville was finally incorporated in 1971. Merrillville's first decade as a town was a time of unprecedented commercial expansion. Most of the development has occurred in and around the intersection of Interstate Highway 65 and U. S. Route 30. The cornerstone is a multi-million dollar shopping mall completed in September, 1974. Since that time, there has been a series of groundbreakings and dedications of numerous operations centers. Among these are a $13 million corporate complex of a major insurance firm, the area's largest financial institution, several office parks, a 400-bed medical facility, a mental health center, a residence center for seniors, a multi-million dollar hotel-theatre, a convention complex, the county's largest bowling alley, and a tennis and health center.

Growth of this magnitude and rapidity precipitated problems within the community as well as outside. The latter involved a four-year lawsuit with Hobart over annexation of 15 square miles, including the lucrative tax- producing mall. Having won the court battle, Merrillville

Merriville, Indiana
Population and Housing Characteristics, 1930-1980

	1980	1970	1960	1950	1940	1930
Total Population.......	27,677	15,918	*	*	*	*
% Male.................	48.4	49.0	*	*	*	*
% Female...............	51.6	51.0	*	*	*	*
% White................	97.9	99.9	*	*	*	*
% Black................	0.1	-	*	*	*	*
% Other Nonwhite Races...	2.0	0.1	*	*	*	*
% Under 5 Years Old......	6.1	7.3	*	*	*	*
% 5-19 Years Old.........	25.8	34.6	*	*	*	*
% 20-44 Years Old........	34.5	30.6	*	*	*	*
% 45-64 Years Old........	24.2	22.6	*	*	*	*
% 65 Years and Older.....	9.4	4.9	*	*	*	*
Median School Years....	12.5	12.3	*	*	*	*
Total Housing Units....	9,292	4,337	*	*	*	*
% In One-Unit Structures.	80.5	91.9	*	*	*	*
% Owner Occupied.........	78.8	88.0	*	*	*	*
% Renter Occupied........	19.6	10.7	*	*	*	*
% Vacant................	1.6	1.3	*	*	*	*
% 1+ Persons per Room....	2.4	7.5	*	*	*	*

Place 1536 -- Merrillville, Indiana
Selected Characteristics of Census Tracts: 1980

Tract Number	Total	423	424	425
Total Population.............	27677	673	18149	8855
% Male...................	48.4	52.3	47.9	48.9
% Black..................	0.1	0.1	0.2	0.0
% Other Nonwhite.........	2.0	2.7	1.8	2.4
% Of Spanish Origin......	4.9	4.5	4.8	5.1
% Foreign Born...........	8.7	10.7	9.5	7.0
% Living In Group Quarters..	0.7	0.0	1.0	0.1
% 13 Years Old And Under...	19.8	24.1	17.3	24.4
% 14-20 Years Old........	13.7	13.1	13.5	14.4
% 21-64 Years Old........	57.1	57.1	58.0	55.2
% 65-74 Years Old........	6.4	4.0	7.4	4.4
% 75 Years Old And Over...	3.0	1.8	3.7	1.7
% In Different House......	37.8	52.4	34.5	43.6
% Families With Female Head.....	9.8	1.8	11.8	6.9
Median School Years Completed..	12.5	12.1	12.5	12.5
Median Family Income, 1979.....$$	27653	24489	27973	27543
% Income Below Poverty Level....	2.5	0.0	2.5	2.9
% Income Of $30,000 Or More.....	41.5	23.2	43.4	39.0
% White Collar Workers.......	53.5	45.6	55.8	49.4
% Civilian Labor Force Unemployed.	5.9	7.3	5.8	6.0
% Riding To Work By Automobile...	96.0	91.6	95.8	97.0
Mean Commuting Time - Minutes...	21.9	30.9	21.5	22.0
Population Per Household.........	3.0	3.3	2.9	3.3
Total Housing Units..........	9282	214	6329	2739
% Condominiums...........	1.9	0.0	2.7	0.0
% Built 1970 Or Later...........	29.9	38.2	27.3	35.4
% Owner Occupied.............	78.8	77.6	75.6	86.2
% With 1+ Persons Per Room.......	2.4	1.5	2.1	3.3
Median Value: Owner Units.......$$	55100	75100	56700	50800
Median Rent: Rental Units.......$$	259	195	259	268
Median Number Of Rooms: All Units.	5.6	5.6	5.4	5.6

Merrillville
Selected Characteristics of Census Tracts: 1970

Tract Number	TOTAL	0423	0424	0425
Total Population.............	15918	4455	17297	7093
% Male...................	49.0	50.4	49.1	50.3
% Black..................	0.0	0.2	0.0	0.2
% Other Nonwhite.........	0.1	0.1	0.1	0.2
% Of Spanish Language....	3.6	3.5	3.9	1.7
% Foreign Born...........	5.8	2.5	5.7	4.4
% Living In Group Quarters..	0.2	0.0	0.2	4.0
% 13 Years Old And Under...	28.8	33.2	29.5	32.7
% 14-20 Years Old........	14.4	13.0	13.9	11.3
% 21-64 Years Old........	52.0	49.2	51.9	49.2
% 65-74 Years Old........	3.2	3.2	2.9	3.1
% 75 Years Old And Over...	1.7	1.4	1.7	3.7
% In Different House......	66.4	59.9	61.9	49.5
% Families With Female Head......	4.8	4.2	4.7	4.4
Median School Years Completed..	12.4	12.2	12.4	12.2
Median Family Income, 1969.....$$	13965	12316	13793	12667
% Income Below Poverty Level....	2.7	4.2	2.3	5.0
% Income of $15,000 or More.....	42.5	26.0	41.8	30.0
% White Collar Workers.......	29.1	22.6	29.3	23.3
% Civilian Labor Force Unemployed.	2.4	3.3	2.6	2.7
% Riding To Work By Automobile....	89.9	91.4	91.0	89.3
Population Per Household.........	3.7	3.9	3.7	3.8
Total Housing Units..........	4335	1163	4686	1812
% Condominiums & Cooperatives.....	0.0	0.0	0.0	0.0
% Built 1960 Or Later.............	49.6	36.3	52.7	55.9
% Owner Occupied.............	88.0	87.1	88.0	88.7
% With 1+ Persons Per Room.......	7.5	11.0	7.9	8.3
Median Value: Owner Units.......$$	24300	20300	24400	19900
Median Rent: Rental Units.......$$	144	115	148	127
Median Number Of Rooms: All Units.	5.4	5.3	5.4	5.4

was then required to revise the town's master plan. There were several lawsuits within the town as well, when disagreement arose between the Planning Department and the Town Board. The Board found discrepancies with what its voting constituency desired and what the Planning Department would allow.

During the early 1970s many permits were issued for retail, office, industrial and residential construction. New construction demanded an upgrading of streets and sanitation facilities. Problems were compounded each time new pavement cut down on soil absorbency. The Merrillville Conservancy District expanded lines to the south for service to the new hospital and and shopping complex. Recently, ground was broken for a $10 million federally-funded sewer project. Traffic congestion was somewhat eased in 1975, when 61st street was reconstructed to form a four-lane road between Broadway and I-65. In December, 1981, an eight-year effort to widen Indiana Highway 53 (Broadway) to five lanes was completed.

In 1980, the population of Merrillville was 27,677, Five percent are of Spanish origin. Of the whites claiming a single ancestry, the largest group is German, followed by Polish. Nine percent of Merrillville's residents are foreign born and 16 percent speak a language other than

English at home. Of the current labor force, one third works in manufacturing and two-thirds work outside Merrillville. In 1979, 59 percent of all families earned incomes of $25,000 or more, while 2.5 percent lived in poverty.

Despite the town's rapid change to a major regional center of commerce, its spacious residential suburban look has been maintained. There are currently 9,135 housing units, of which 85 percent are single-family dwellings and 77 percent are owner-ocupied. The me-

dian value of owner-occupied housing units is $52,500. The housing is very new; almost a third of the units were built in the last 10 years and more than 85 percent have been built since the end of World War II.

According to the Economic Development Commission, projected development in the 1980s will center on industrial growth rather than the past focus on retail and office center construction.

Jane Cronin

Place 2080

Portage, Indiana

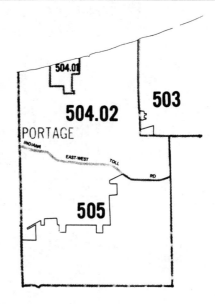

Portage occupies an area of 22 square miles in Portage Township which is located in the northwest corner of Porter County, Indiana. Located just south of the rolling sand dunes at the southern tip of Lake Michigan, Portage lies 35 miles east of Chicago. In 1822 Joseph Bailly became the first known white settler in this area. A French fur trader, Bailly established a post and built his home on the bank of the nearby Calumet River, near the Pottawatomie Trail, which was the main pathway connecting Chicago and Michigan. As traffic along this road flourished, so did Bailly's business. He became the first innkeeper in the Dunes area. Other settlers began to trickle into the Portage Township area, many from Ohio and Michigan. It is believed that Portage got its name from Portage County, Ohio, from which some of the settlers came.

In 1833 Samuel Putnam Robbins came to the area from Hocking County, Ohio. He settled on what is now known as Robbins Road and purchased 160 acres of land. Robbins was joined by other pioneers, including Jacob Wolf, whose homestead established there in the spring of 1834 grew to be the largest farm, encompassing 4,500 acres for stock raising and dairy farming.

In the spring of 1836, Porter County was created and divided into 10 townships. The first Portage Township election was held three weeks later in Jacob Wolf's home. The first school was begun in 1840. The township grew rather slowly. Its only store was owned by Isaac Crisman, for whom a town in Portage Township was named. The town of Crisman was established in 1853 when Benjamin Crisman gave an acre of land for the location of a Michigan Central Railroad depot.

In 1852 the Michigan Central Railroad (now part of the New York Central system) was built, connecting Chicago and New York. Two others began construction through Portage, the Peninsular, later called the Grand Trunk; and the Baltimore, Pittsburgh and Chicago, later known as the Baltimore and Ohio. The railroad junction began to attract businesses. By the 1860s Portage was the site of 18 houses and shipped 100 to 200 cans of milk daily from its depot to Chicago on the Baltimore and Ohio trains.

The population of Portage Township rose to 1,014 in 1900. In the decades that followed it became a highly-productive agricultural region. Between 1930 and 1970, Portage Township changed from a rural farm area that encompassed the three small settlements of Crisman, McCool, and Garyton, into one of the fastest growing communities in Indiana. On June 29, 1959, these communities were incorporated into the Town of Portage and in 1968 became the City of Portage.

This development can be attributed primarily to the construction of two large steel mills in the area. The location here of the Midwest Division of National Steel in 1959 was followed by the construction of the Bethlehem Steel plant in 1963. The population of 8,000 at that time soared to 22,000 in 1975, at which time it was predicted the growth

would continue and reach at least 27,000 in 1980. The Port of Indiana, the outlet to deep water trade, was finally opened in 1969, as Bethlehem Steel unloaded the first shipment of ore. The 269-acre Port of Indiana is located between the property of Midwest Steel and Bethlehem Steel, owned and operated by the State of Indiana. An estimated six million tons of foreign and domestic commerce is handled by the Port each year, carried by the ships of 14 nations.

The railroads and steel plants increased the need for housing and schools in the Portage area. The township population in the 1950 census was 5,500 and as many as 10,000 were projected by 1956. The newly-industrialized area began to attract business. The first shopping center was constructed on 10 acres near the entrance to Midwest Steel. Farmland was being sold for homesites, bringing nearly $7,000 per acre in 1959. The imminence of a seaport within the county serving Lake Michigan opened up the prospect of commerce on the St. Lawrence Seaway. There was a railroad switch yard to handle water-to-rail and rail-to-water shipments and freight trains to link Portage to Chicago and other industrial areas.

Incorporation of the town of Portage was proposed. Industrialization of the area had, however, met with two disapproving factions. Property owners in Ogden Dunes, a small portion of Portage County at the tip of Lake Michigan, were against heavy industry there, fearing it would interfere with the public's use of the beaches. A "Save the Dunes" campaign was started, led by Senator Paul Douglas of Illinois. Also against the increasing industrialization of the area was a Portage Township farm group which argued that it would destroy highly productive agricultural land.

The discussion of incorporation went on for years until April, 1959, when area residents learned of a recently enacted state law which prohibited the incorporation of a town within three miles of the corporate limits of a second-class city (such as Gary, which abuts the township line). This meant there could be no town of Portage unless the residents acted before the new law became effective in July.

Portage, Indiana
Population and Housing Characteristics, 1930-1980

	1980	1970	1960	1950	1940	1930
Total Population.......	27,409	19,127	11,822	*	*	*
% Male.................	49.6	50.3	50.8	*	*	*
% Female...............	50.4	49.7	49.2	*	*	*
% White................	97.5	99.7	99.9	*	*	*
% Black................	0.1	0.1	0.1	*	*	*
% Other Nonwhite Races...	2.4	0.2	0.0	*	*	*
% Under 5 Years Old......	8.9	10.7	16.2	*	*	*
% 5-19 Years Old........	27.4	35.5	30.7	*	*	*
% 20-44 Years Old........	40.6	35.6	36.6	*	*	*
% 45-64 Years Old........	17.7	15.2	13.4	*	*	*
% 65 Years and Older.....	5.4	3.0	3.1	*	*	*
Median School Years......	12.4	12.1	10.8	*	*	*
Total Housing Units....	9,591	5,181	3,259	*	*	*
% In One-Unit Structures.	67.3	82.7	99.2	*	*	*
% Owner Occupied........	72.1	82.7	81.0	*	*	*
% Renter Occupied........	23.3	15.2	13.7	*	*	*
% Vacant...............	4.6	2.1	5.2	*	*	*
% 1+ Persons per Room....	3.2	6.0	21.6	*	*	*

Place 2080 — Portage , Indiana
Selected Characteristics of Census Tracts: 1980

Tract Number	Total	503	504.02	505
Total Population.............	27409	366	10237	16806
% Male......................	49.6	44.0	50.4	49.3
% Black.....................	0.1	0.0	0.1	0.1
% Other Nonwhite.............	2.4	0.5	2.8	2.2
% Of Spanish Origin..........	5.0	0.8	5.3	4.8
% Foreign Born...............	3.2	4.7	3.0	3.3
% Living In Group Quarters......	0.5	0.0	0.0	0.7
% 13 Years Old And Under........	25.0	4.4	26.2	24.7
% 14-20 Years Old...........	13.0	3.8	13.5	12.9
% 21-64 Years Old...........	56.6	69.7	57.0	56.0
% 65-74 Years Old...........	3.8	15.0	2.4	4.4
% 75 Years Old And Over........	1.7	7.1	0.9	2.0
% In Different House..........	51.4	30.2	52.0	51.5
% Families With Female Head.....	12.2	21.4	11.9	12.3
Median School Years Completed....	12.4	12.3	12.4	12.3
Median Family Income, 1979.....$$	26225	22262	26460	26122
% Income Below Poverty Level....	4.6	0.0	5.3	4.3
% Income Of $30,000 Or More.....	35.7	39.2	36.0	35.4
% White Collar Workers.........	39.7	56.1	38.7	40.0
% Civilian Labor Force Unemployed.	8.9	8.8	8.9	8.9
% Riding To Work By Automobile....	95.9	95.7	94.2	97.1
Mean Commuting Time - Minutes...	23.6	33.2	20.6	25.3
Population Per Household..........	3.0	1.6	3.0	3.0
Total Housing Units..........	9591	247	3548	5796
% Condominiums...............	0.2	0.0	0.0	0.3
% Built 1970 Or Later..........	46.8	64.2	43.8	48.0
% Owner Occupied..............	72.2	77.3	70.9	72.7
% With 1+ Persons Per Room......	3.2	0.0	3.7	3.1
Median Value: Owner Units......$$	52200	—	54500	50800
Median Rent: Rental Units.......$$	236	269	236	236
Median Number Of Rooms: All Units.	5.1	4.1	5.1	5.2

Portage
Selected Characteristics of Census Tracts: 1970

Tract Number	TOTAL	0503	0504	0505
Total Population.............	19127	4649	9146	19225
% Male......................	50.3	50.9	50.6	50.5
% Black.....................	0.1	0.3	0.2	0.2
% Other Nonwhite.............	0.2	0.2	0.3	0.2
% Of Spanish Language.........	1.7	2.0	2.0	1.3
% Foreign Born...............	2.7	3.4	1.9	2.4
% Living In Group Quarters........	0.1	1.5	0.1	0.4
% 13 Years Old And Under........	34.6	29.7	33.3	37.3
% 14-20 Years Old...........	12.8	12.9	11.8	12.1
% 21-64 Years Old...........	49.6	51.8	51.5	48.1
% 65-74 Years Old...........	1.8	3.5	2.0	1.7
% 75 Years Old And Over........	1.1	2.2	1.4	0.9
% In Different House..........	49.0	54.3	50.0	43.1
% Families With Female Head......	4.7	6.6	4.2	4.2
Median School Years Completed....	12.1	12.2	12.4	12.1
Median Family Income, 1969......$$	11910	11744	12864	11655
% Income Below Poverty Level....	3.5	7.3	4.1	3.0
% Income of $15,000 or More.....	26.3	26.2	35.3	22.5
% White Collar Workers.........	16.6	22.5	28.4	14.1
% Civilian Labor Force Unemployed.	3.8	4.4	4.3	2.6
% Riding To Work By Automobile....	93.3	86.1	92.1	92.0
Population Per Household..........	3.8	3.3	3.6	3.9
Total Housing Units..........	5181	1496	2608	5000
% Condominiums & Cooperatives.....	0.2	0.0	0.0	0.2
% Built 1960 Or Later..........	51.6	28.3	54.8	61.7
% Owner Occupied..............	82.5	71.3	84.5	82.4
% With 1+ Persons Per Room......	12.8	8.4	10.4	12.0
Median Value: Owner Units......$$	18000	17400	20300	16900
Median Rent: Rental Units.......$$	126	109	135	117
Median Number Of Rooms: All Units.	5.1	5.0	5.1	5.2

The proposed town was surveyed and a census was taken showing a population of 9,824 (2,541 heads of households and 1,879 residential land owners, making it a fifth-class city) and petitions were signed. On June 13 the vote was overwhelmingly in favor of incorporation (2,140 to 213). Twelve days later the new town, consisting of seven wards, held its first election. As one of its first official acts, the new town of Portage approved the disannexation of a group of farmers in south Portage who wanted to remain in the unincorporated township.

A plan was developed which set up a central business area, using U.S. Highway 20 as the main street. The steel and railroad industries which had provided the impetus for the growth of Portage granted the town $30,000 for incorporation. In October of that first year, a special census revealed an increased population of 10,737. This conferred upon Portage fourth-class city status, meaning added funds in state gasoline and alcohol tax rebates.

A seven-member board Port Authority was created, awaiting approval of the Port, for buying and selling of docks and real estate, and channel control. Eight and one-half square miles was set aside for proposed industry, and a plan for a future Portage of 120,000 residents was formulated. Some envisioned a plan for as many as 250,000 people. In the 1960s much tract housing was built in Portage, consisting mainly of two-story dwellings. Two shopping centers were erected along major highways.

The population of Portage increased from 11,822 in 1960 to 19,127 in 1970. The number of housing units increased to more than 5,000 in 1970 from the 1960 figure of 3,000. In the light of extravagant earlier projections the 40 percent growth, to more than 27,000 population, of the most recent decade has been almost disappointing. The current population of Portage is 98 percent white, including 5 percent of Spanish origin. The largest white European descent groups are German and English. As in many suburbs the relative number of young people has dropped considerably in the last 20 years, although those 18 years or younger are still a third of the population. Thirty-nine percent of the resident labor force work in manufacturing and 49 percent are white-collar workers. The median family income in 1979 was more than $26,000, and 5 percent of Portage families reported incomes below the poverty line at that time.

A construction boom in Portage in the 1970s produced new housing at a rate twice that of the growth in population. There are now 9,600 units of which two-thirds are single-family structures. Almost three-fourths of all units are owner-occupied. The median value of Portage homes in 1980 was $51,300. The housing is very new, half of it having been built in the last ten years, and three-fourths since 1960.

The presence of Bethlehem and Midwest Steel, and other industries related to steel production, has provided a solid basis for Portage's growth. Air Products and Chemicals, Enamel Products and Plating Co., ITT Henze Service, and Levy Company are some of the other industries located in the Portage area. Portage is ideally situated for industrial activity. It is served by the Port of Indiana, multiple railroads, and the Indiana Toll Road, Interstates 80, 90 and 94, U.S. Routes 6, 12 and 20, and State Routes 149 and 249.

Despite industrial and residential attractions, Portage has problems. Dependent upon the steel industry for employment and revenue, it has been hurt by several mill cutbacks Bethlehem and Midwest Steel felt necessary in recent years. Much of the Portage work force at all levels has been affected by the mill cutbacks. Nine percent of the workers were unemployed in 1980. The generous projections for a thriving, expanding Portage are not as realistic as they were when originally formulated. This city's future, like its past, seems to rest with the steel industry. It appears doubtful in today's economic climate that the predicted future growth for Portage will be realized, although it will be one of the vital parts of the northwest Indiana industrial urban complex.

Gail Danks Welter

Place 1280

Kenosha, Wisconsin

Kenosha is located on the Lake Michigan shore in the southeastern corner of Wisconsin, about 60 miles north of Chicago and 30 miles south of Milwaukee. There is evidence that three Pottawatomie Indian villages existed in or near what is now Kenosha. The land was wooded, with many streams and low marshy areas near the lake. The Indians called the area Kenosha (or Kenozia), their word for "pike," because these fish were so plentiful in the lake and streams. The Pottawatomie were moved out of southern Wisconsin as a result of the Black Hawk War.

As the Indians left the area, settlers from the eastern states began to arrive. The first settlers in Kenosha were members of the "Western Emigration Company," a land company formed in Hannibal, New York, under the leadership of John Bullen and Reverend Jason Lothrop. Four representatives of the company (Warters Towslee, Sydney Roberts and Charles Turner, later joined by John Bullen, Jr.) were sent to find a site for settlement that had both a natural harbor and good surrounding farmland. On June 5, 1835 they decided to settle at Kenosha, which they referred to as "Pike." More members of the company arrived by wagon with their families, and by the end of the year the village had a population of 32. Other settlers, who were not part of the land company, claimed parts of the farmland surrounding the village. A store was built during the first year and Reverend Lothrop taught school, with 27 pupils, in his log cabin.

The residents of Pike foresaw that the future of their town would be linked with its development as a lake port. They built their main street close to the harbor, and in 1837 they changed the name of the village to Southport, to indicate that it was the southernmost harbor in Wisconsin. The site was surveyed by United States Engineers in 1837 to determine the cost of the developing the harbor. Development slowed because of a nationwide depression, but there was a continuing need for a lake port in the area. In 1840 work began on the Kenosha site.

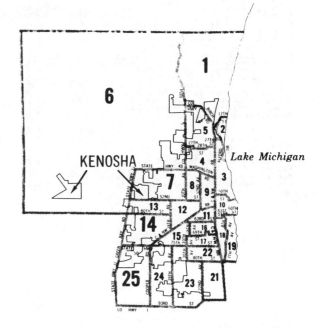

By 1840 Southport had a population of 337, and incorporated as a village, with Michael Frank as its first president. By this time the town had several sawmills as well as shops and a tavern. During the 1840s it added numerous small industries, such as bakeries and breweries, a warehouse for storing wheat, and a flour mill. It became a trading center for the surrounding country as far west as the Rock River, and shipped lead from the mines in the Galena area. Improvements on the harbor, including a lighthouse, continued during this period. In 1845 a free public school was established in Southport, a result of the work of village president Michael Frank and Reuben Deming, a minister who had come from Vermont. Irish and German settlers joined those from England, Scotland and the eastern United States. Among those who came in the 1840s were the Simmons family whose son, Zalmon Simmons, was to found the Simmons Company and play an important part in Kenosha's development.

Kenosha, Wisconsin
Population and Housing Characteristics, 1930-1980

	1980	1970	1960	1950	1940	1930
Total Population	77,685	78,805	67,899	54,368	48,765	50,262
% Male	48.4	48.4	50.0	49.9	50.5	51.2
% Female	51.6	51.6	50.0	50.1	49.5	48.8
% White	93.9	97.2	98.5	99.5	99.6	99.6
% Black	3.6	2.4	1.4	0.5	0.4	0.4
% Other Nonwhite Races	2.5	0.4	0.1	0.0	0.0	0.0
% Under 5 Years Old	7.3	9.0	11.6	10.3	6.5	9.1
% 5-19 Years Old	25.3	30.6	26.5	20.2	25.3	29.3
% 20-44 Years Old	36.5	30.3	32.2	37.6	39.6	42.3
% 45-64 Years	19.3	20.1	20.1	23.7	22.8	15.5
% 65 Years and Older	11.6	10.0	9.6	8.2	5.8	3.8
Median School Years	12.3	11.7	10.3	9.5	8.4	*
Total Housing Units	29,411	24,872	21,072	16,351	13,350	*
% In One-Unit Structures	61.2	63.2	61.7	*	*	*
% Owner Occupied	61.8	64.7	64.2	58.2	42.8	*
% Renter Occupied	33.4	32.9	33.5	40.3	54.4	*
% Vacant	4.8	2.4	2.3	1.5	2.8	*
% 1+ Persons per Room	3.0	8.7	11.2	9.6	10.9	*

Place 1280 — Kenosha, Wisconsin
Selected Characteristics of Census Tracts: 1980

Tract Number	Total	1	2	3	4	5	6	7	8	9	10
Total Population	77685	1236	934	3557	3983	5168	1501	4131	2486	4191	1608
% Male	48.4	48.1	49.0	47.3	47.6	46.6	49.9	47.7	48.1	47.9	54.5
% Black	3.6	3.7	5.0	0.7	0.1	1.5	3.2	18.3	12.8	2.4	9.3
% Other Nonwhite	2.5	2.6	0.3	2.0	0.8	1.9	1.9	4.0	3.5	5.2	7.5
% Of Spanish Origin	4.0	1.5	0.7	3.5	1.1	2.0	2.0	7.1	5.8	8.9	13.3
% Foreign Born	5.8	1.7	1.8	5.6	7.2	8.4	5.2	4.2	7.5	9.0	8.8
% Living In Group Quarters	3.1	0.0	98.6	5.8	0.0	0.0	16.8	2.4	0.0	0.0	24.3
% 13 Years Old And Under	21.0	21.2	0.7	18.5	15.4	21.7	11.3	26.9	22.0	24.3	15.3
% 14-20 Years Old	13.9	7.4	66.7	12.3	14.8	15.6	12.3	14.4	13.9	11.8	11.3
% 21-64 Years Old	53.5	62.3	32.5	52.3	56.4	51.0	61.7	51.1	52.1	52.4	57.2
% 65-74 Years Old	6.6	6.6	0.0	8.6	9.2	7.2	4.9	3.7	7.3	6.7	8.1
% 75 Years Old And Over	5.0	2.4	0.0	8.3	4.2	4.5	9.8	3.9	4.7	4.8	8.1
% In Different House	44.4	78.5	90.7	49.6	27.1	28.7	75.1	52.6	33.2	54.3	64.5
% Families With Female Head	19.4	25.7	0.0	24.8	11.8	13.2	32.6	30.1	31.4	31.4	34.3
Median School Years Completed	12.3	12.6	16.0	12.3	12.3	12.3	12.4	12.2	12.0	12.2	12.1
Median Family Income, 1979 $$	22313	21594	-	18511	22967	25901	21821	20945	18918	16354	16214
% Income Below Poverty Level	6.4	7.4	-	2.7	2.7	3.6	12.2	9.8	10.6	14.2	11.8
% Income Of $30,000 Or More	27.5	24.1	-	17.0	29.9	35.4	13.7	21.3	18.2	13.7	16.0
% White Collar Workers	44.3	49.6	56.6	44.9	42.3	42.3	45.7	32.3	29.8	36.2	37.7
% Civilian Labor Force Unemployed	7.6	8.5	2.4	11.3	2.7	5.6	10.0	9.4	6.9	12.7	15.3
% Riding To Work By Automobile	88.6	91.2	46.0	86.8	89.8	92.5	95.2	89.4	84.9	81.4	80.0
Mean Commuting Time - Minutes	16.2	18.1	18.2	14.9	13.8	14.1	19.5	17.5	16.7	18.2	18.1
Population Per Household	2.7	2.2	2.2	2.5	2.8	2.9	1.7	2.9	2.6	2.6	2.1
Total Housing Units	29384	579	6	1442	1451	1767	808	1416	989	1781	874
% Condominiums	0.5	15.7	-	0.0	0.0	0.7	3.2	0.0	0.0	0.0	0.0
% Built 1970 Or Later	18.1	90.1	-	2.1	3.9	27.7	82.9	31.2	6.1	0.7	25.7
% Owner Occupied	61.8	33.0	-	53.9	86.2	73.2	6.7	46.8	57.8	44.2	15.2
% With 1+ Persons Per Room	3.0	1.1	-	2.4	3.0	4.5	1.5	6.1	5.0	3.6	3.9
Median Value: Owner Units $$	45700	61700	-	37100	46800	52800	-	42600	35100	36000	31900
Median Rent: Rental Units $$	188	268	-	166	181	92	226	199	189	167	160
Median Number Of Rooms: All Units	4.9	4.3	-	4.9	5.0	5.0	3.2	4.7	4.8	4.8	3.4

Tract Number	11	12	13	14	15	16	17	18	19	20	21
Total Population	3406	4229	3783	5885	3991	3512	2874	2492	2704	8	4206
% Male	52.2	49.2	49.3	48.9	48.3	48.5	47.3	48.4	47.1	-	48.9
% Black	4.0	1.7	1.1	0.4	0.3	19.8	2.8	3.0	0.2	-	1.5
% Other Nonwhite	8.9	2.9	1.2	1.0	0.9	4.2	2.5	2.8	0.7	-	1.7
% Of Spanish Origin	15.0	4.4	2.9	1.1	1.3	8.2	3.9	4.4	1.7	-	2.6
% Foreign Born	9.3	11.1	5.1	4.2	4.8	6.2	3.0	5.4	3.6	-	5.2
% Living In Group Quarters	7.1	0.6	0.0	0.0	0.3	0.4	0.5	1.2	0.9	-	2.4
% 13 Years Old And Under	21.5	18.6	24.7	23.8	20.9	25.1	23.8	22.2	18.2	-	21.0
% 14-20 Years Old	12.5	12.3	13.0	14.4	11.7	15.0	12.9	11.8	11.1	-	14.3
% 21-64 Years Old	51.6	55.7	54.9	54.7	53.1	51.0	49.5	55.1	53.3	-	55.9
% 65-74 Years Old	7.3	8.0	4.7	4.7	8.4	4.9	4.9	6.7	8.8	-	5.1
% 75 Years Old And Over	7.1	5.4	2.6	2.4	6.0	3.9	6.7	4.3	8.7	-	3.7
% In Different House	59.6	42.6	38.6	34.1	37.4	68.5	40.6	41.2	31.3	-	49.6
% Families With Female Head	33.0	24.4	18.0	7.9	18.6	35.2	15.5	21.0	11.0	-	17.2
Median School Years Completed	11.9	12.1	12.4	12.6	12.3	12.1	12.3	12.5	14.3	-	12.3
Median Family Income, 1979 $$	14727	21643	21691	28457	22500	13927	19705	23832	29770	-	22386
% Income Below Poverty Level	19.6	7.3	6.9	1.3	2.8	19.5	6.8	9.9	3.4	-	6.0
% Income Of $30,000 Or More	8.6	27.0	24.1	44.8	23.8	9.5	20.7	32.3	49.4	-	28.4
% White Collar Workers	32.0	36.9	44.7	53.6	42.5	31.2	39.1	46.8	72.6	-	40.3
% Civilian Labor Force Unemployed	20.6	6.9	8.1	4.1	5.3	14.5	5.0	12.7	5.2	-	7.2
% Riding To Work By Automobile	74.6	80.5	93.7	92.2	89.2	84.1	90.9	87.6	89.2	-	94.6
Mean Commuting Time - Minutes	17.3	13.7	16.0	15.7	18.7	16.9	16.3	18.2	14.7	-	17.2
Population Per Household	2.4	2.5	2.9	3.2	2.7	2.7	2.7	2.8	2.6	-	2.8
Total Housing Units	1475	1790	1331	1859	1522	1439	1044	982	1103	8	1517
% Condominiums	0.0	0.0	0.0	0.0	0.0	0.0	0.0	0.0	0.0	-	1.1
% Built 1970 Or Later	1.2	0.8	16.9	25.4	0.5	2.1	0.0	5.9	5.9	-	41.6
% Owner Occupied	28.8	60.3	62.4	92.6	78.7	41.8	78.4	61.4	67.7	-	67.2
% With 1+ Persons Per Room	4.1	2.5	3.5	2.4	2.0	4.8	2.8	2.9	0.6	-	3.4
Median Value: Owner Units $$	30000	38200	46500	55800	39100	32300	38500	38600	66700	-	46500
Median Rent: Rental Units $$	165	178	223	254	184	164	176	171	209	-	259
Median Number Of Rooms: All Units	4.3	4.7	4.8	5.3	5.1	4.9	5.6	5.1	5.6	-	4.8

Place 1280 -- Kenosha , Wisconsin
Selected Characteristics of Census Tracts: 1980

Tract Number	22	23	24	25
Total Population.............	3925	4805	2894	176
% Male........................	47.8	46.4	48.3	51.1
% Black.......................	0.0	0.2	0.7	0.0
% Other Nonwhite..............	0.6	1.6	1.2	0.0
% Of Spanish Origin...........	1.0	1.8	1.3	2.3
% Foreign Born................	1.9	5.2	2.4	0.0
% Living In Group Quarters....	0.0	2.0	0.0	0.0
% 13 Years Old And Under......	17.1	19.0	25.1	29.0
% 14-20 Years Old.............	11.5	14.2	14.4	11.9
% 21-64 Years Old.............	55.9	53.5	53.7	54.5
% 65-74 Years Old.............	8.9	7.4	4.5	4.0
% 75 Years Old And Over.......	6.5	6.0	2.3	0.6
% In Different House..........	32.4	32.7	57.1	57.8
% Families With Female Head...	11.3	9.2	6.1	10.0
Median School Years Completed.	12.5	12.4	12.6	12.4
Median Family Income, 1979.....$$	22500	26546	26645	35773
% Income Below Poverty Level...	1.2	2.7	1.4	0.0
% Income Of $30,000 Or More...	27.8	36.8	39.8	64.2
% White Collar Workers........	54.8	50.5	58.7	30.2
% Civilian Labor Force Unemployed.	3.8	4.1	3.0	0.0
% Riding To Work By Automobile...	91.8	90.3	93.8	89.8
Mean Commuting Time - Minutes...	16.1	15.0	17.3	15.9
Population Per Household.......	2.6	2.8	3.1	3.3
Total Housing Units..........	1506	1699	938	58
% Condominiums................	0.0	0.0	0.0	0.0
% Built 1970 Or Later.........	1.6	37.8	59.4	50.9
% Owner Occupied..............	89.3	74.9	78.7	86.2
% With 1+ Persons Per Room....	1.4	2.3	2.0	0.0
Median Value: Owner Units.......$$	46700	56700	62100	-
Median Rent: Rental Units.....$$	192	164	227	-
Median Number Of Rooms: All Units.	5.2	5.1	5.6	5.6

Kenosha
Selected Characteristics of Census Tracts: 1970

Tract Number	TOTAL	0001	0002	0003	0004	0005	0006	0007	0008	0009
Total Population.............	78805	236	983	4307	4745	4577	411	3263	3054	5153
% Male........................	48.4	55.1	54.1	47.3	48.6	48.7	40.4	49.4	49.6	48.2
% Black.......................	2.4	0.0	3.1	1.8	0.1	0.3	0.7	14.0	6.1	1.8
% Other Nonwhite..............	0.3	4.7	0.2	0.2	0.1	0.2	0.0	0.4	0.8	0.3
% Of Spanish Language.........	2.8	0.0	0.0	2.7	0.0	0.8	0.0	0.1	6.3	4.5
% Foreign Born................	6.2	0.0	0.7	5.7	6.2	3.7	30.7	4.7	13.4	14.4
% Living In Group Quarters....	2.5	0.0	93.7	0.8	0.0	0.0	78.8	0.1	0.2	0.5
% 13 Years Old And Under......	28.1	41.9	1.5	26.9	26.1	36.2	6.8	32.5	26.6	29.0
% 14-20 Years Old.............	13.2	5.5	68.9	11.7	14.5	12.4	3.4	12.3	14.2	12.0
% 21-64 Years Old.............	48.7	52.1	29.7	49.1	51.5	48.2	18.4	51.2	48.9	48.3
% 65-74 Years Old.............	5.8	0.4	0.3	7.2	4.7	2.1	12.4	2.5	6.3	5.8
% 75 Years Old And Over.......	4.2	0.0	0.0	5.1	3.1	1.0	59.1	1.4	4.0	5.0
% In Different House..........	39.1	75.9	80.4	37.2	22.3	34.0	64.0	52.5	47.2	44.6
% Families With Female Head...	10.0	-	-	13.5	5.7	4.1	-	10.9	13.5	17.3
Median School Years Completed...$$	11.9	12.1	13.8	10.9	12.1	12.2	7.3	11.6	10.4	10.1
Median Family Income, 1969.....$$	10191	10867	-	9302	11110	11152	-	10356	8830	8681
% Income Below Poverty Level...	6.1	-	-	12.7	1.5	3.2	-	3.5	6.9	9.4
% Income of $15,000 or More....	17.9	-	50.3	28.6	23.5	19.4	--	16.1	10.5	9.7
% White Collar Workers........	41.6	-	50.3	40.9	38.8	43.1	-	37.8	33.3	33.9
% Civilian Labor Force Unemployed.	4.7	5.9	13.4	6.0	2.8	1.7	-	3.5	5.8	3.6
% Riding To Work By Automobile...	84.0	96.5	23.2	81.2	83.3	90.4	-	89.1	78.0	79.9
Population Per Household.......	3.2	3.5	2.8	2.9	3.4	4.0	3.6	3.3	3.1	3.0
Total Housing Units..........	24848	84	22	1506	1411	1151	25	999	990	1795
% Condominiums & Cooperatives.....	0.1	-	-	0.5	0.0	0.0	-	0.0	0.0	0.7
% Built 1960 Or Later.........	17.6	-	-	4.6	14.5	60.5	-	56.9	13.1	0.7
% Owner Occupied..............	64.7	-	-	51.6	86.7	90.4	-	43.4	58.3	45.1
% With 1+ Persons Per Room....	8.5	-	-	6.5	9.6	13.9	-	12.6	8.4	7.1
Median Value: Owner Units.......$$	16400	-	-	13200	17700	18700	-	16100	13300	12800
Median Rent: Rental Units.....$$	91	-	-	82	89	167	-	118	97	84
Median Number Of Rooms: All Units.	4.9	-	-	4.9	5.1	5.1	-	4.5	4.7	4.8

Tract Number	0010	0011	0012	0013	0014	0015	0016	0017	0018
Total Population.............	1623	4410	5084	3641	4763	4792	3499	3258	3018
% Male........................	52.1	49.5	49.4	49.5	48.1	47.7	47.3	48.0	47.2
% Black.......................	12.9	1.5	0.8	0.2	0.0	0.4	14.6	0.0	1.7
% Other Nonwhite..............	0.6	0.4	0.5	0.2	0.2	0.4	0.3	0.4	0.8
% Of Spanish Language.........	10.2	8.2	2.1	2.2	0.5	1.1	4.6	1.5	9.4
% Foreign Born................	6.3	8.2	10.7	3.2	3.6	4.5	5.8	6.2	5.0
% Living In Group Quarters....	7.4	4.4	0.5	0.0	0.0	0.3	0.7	1.1	1.0
% 13 Years Old And Under......	20.0	25.6	25.2	33.6	30.6	27.4	30.9	27.0	28.0
% 14-20 Years Old.............	11.3	11.8	11.8	10.5	13.0	12.5	12.4	12.6	12.4
% 21-64 Years Old.............	52.3	49.0	50.9	50.8	51.0	48.0	45.3	44.9	46.7
% 65-74 Years Old.............	8.3	6.6	7.3	3.7	4.0	7.8	7.0	9.0	7.0
% 75 Years Old And Over.......	8.0	7.1	4.8	1.4	1.4	4.3	4.4	6.4	6.0
% In Different House..........	55.5	53.0	39.3	34.9	37.6	26.6	43.1	27.5	45.7
% Families With Female Head...	21.0	18.7	12.6	7.0	4.6	11.1	18.1	10.0	14.7
Median School Years Completed...$$	7.0	10.1	10.5	12.2	12.2	11.8	10.6	12.1	11.9
Median Family Income, 1969.....$$	8342	7936	9240	10596	11818	9354	8317	10203	9567
% Income Below Poverty Level...	14.7	17.0	6.8	4.6	4.9	5.7	9.6	1.8	12.0
% Income of $15,000 or More....	3.8	8.4	11.6	12.5	28.5	17.1	8.3	16.7	15.6
% White Collar Workers........	37.5	26.1	30.0	40.9	48.6	41.6	29.1	46.4	38.7
% Civilian Labor Force Unemployed.	8.6	5.6	5.3	3.7	4.3	5.8	5.2	2.5	7.1
% Riding To Work By Automobile...	64.1	66.2	74.6	90.4	95.4	86.7	84.4	85.4	79.7
Population Per Household.......	2.1	2.7	2.9	3.5	3.6	3.1	3.0	3.1	3.0
Total Housing Units..........	792	1641	1825	1045	1336	1548	1523	1057	1000
% Condominiums & Cooperatives.....	0.0	0.0	0.0	0.0	0.0	0.0	0.0	0.0	0.0
% Built 1960 Or Later.........	2.5	4.4	2.2	52.5	38.5	4.9	0.7	9.4	7.4
% Owner Occupied..............	14.0	30.7	59.0	71.8	93.0	74.5	44.2	79.0	60.0
% With 1+ Persons Per Room....	7.6	7.9	6.8	12.0	8.5	7.3	9.3	6.1	8.9
Median Value: Owner Units.......$$	11500	11900	14000	16900	19400	14200	12600	14300	14000
Median Rent: Rental Units.....$$	84	83	86	133	126	94	83	93	86
Median Number Of Rooms: All Units.	3.0	4.4	4.6	4.8	5.1	4.9	4.8	5.4	5.1

Kenosha
Selected Characteristics of Census Tracts: 1970

Tract Number	0019	0021	0022	0023	0024	0025
Total Population.............	3164	3824	4702	3951	1442	5
% Male.........................	45.2	48.5	47.1	48.7	50.9	–
% Black........................	0.0	0.4	0.0	0.2	0.0	–
% Other Nonwhite..............	0.2	0.3	0.2	0.4	0.0	–
% Of Spanish Language..........	0.0	2.6	0.7	2.3	2.7	–
% Foreign Born.................	4.5	3.2	4.4	3.3	3.6	–
% Living In Group Quarters.....	1.5	2.9	0.1	0.0	1.0	–
% 13 Years Old And Under.......	21.7	33.3	24.4	31.3	30.9	–
% 14-20 Years Old..............	13.3	13.1	12.6	13.8	14.6	–
% 21-64 Years Old..............	49.0	47.7	50.3	49.5	47.6	–
% 65-74 Years Old..............	10.0	2.5	9.0	3.4	4.2	–
% 75 Years Old And Over........	5.9	3.4	3.8	1.9	2.8	–
% In Different House...........	40.0	51.2	26.8	29.6	39.1	–
% Families With Female Head....	6.5	6.1	5.3	4.4	8.9	–
Median School Years Completed..	13.0	12.2	12.2	12.3	12.3	–
Median Family Income, 1969.....$$	14750	10826	11417	12091	11219	–
% Income Below Poverty Level....	4.2	3.6	2.2	1.9	1.3	–
% Income of $15,000 or More.....	48.9	17.0	27.2	25.2	21.0	–
% White Collar Workers..........	71.4	42.8	55.2	51.5	40.1	–
% Civilian Labor Force Unemployed.	5.0	4.1	3.0	2.0	6.2	–
% Riding To Work By Automobile....	83.1	92.9	88.9	93.7	90.7	–
Population Per Household..........	2.9	3.7	3.1	3.7	3.6	–
Total Housing Units..........	1103	1010	1509	1080	394	2
% Condominiums & Cooperatives.....	0.0	0.0	0.0	0.0	0.0	–
% Built 1960 Or Later.............	4.9	61.7	4.7	39.4	39.6	–
% Owner Occupied..................	68.4	79.0	87.8	89.2	87.3	–
% With 1+ Persons Per Room........	3.1	15.3	5.7	10.0	8.4	–
Median Value: Owner Units.......$$	24200	17100	17300	19200	19000	–
Median Rent: Rental Units.......$$	105	138	100	130	105	–
Median Number Of Rooms: All Units.	5.7	4.9	5.0	5.1	5.1	–

In 1850 Kenosha reincorporated as a city and adopted its present name. Michael Frank became the city's first mayor. At the same time, Kenosha County separated from Racine County. A new county court house and jail were built by subscription, since the legislature ruled that the residents should not be re-taxed to support the erection of a second county building.

The harbor was still seen as the key to the city's development, and the citizens consistently supported taxation for its continued improvement. By 1859 they had completed a channel 11 feet deep, which was enough to admit the largest ships then traveling on the lakes. The city's industrial base also began to develop during the 1850s. The Bain Wagon Works, founded in 1852, was to become the world's largest manufacturer of wagons. The N.R. Allen tannery, established in 1856, and the Kenosha Malt House (1857), which later became the Pettit Malting Company, were also founded during this period.

During the 1850s, railroads began to reach the area around Kenosha. The citizens were concerned about the effect of the railroads on harbor traffic, and wanted a railroad in Kenosha. Both the city and county bonded themselves heavily and work was begun on a line which ran from Kenosha to Harvard, Illinois. It was completed in 1861, after long delays, but it was never successful and was sold to the Chicago and North Western Railroad in 1864. However, the heavy railroad debts which remained were a problem for the city through the 1880s. In 1884 Zalmon Simmons was elected mayor, and by the end of that year, through his personal leadership and some material assistance, he had made an arrangement to settle the city's debts through a $200,000 bond issue. Kenosha's population grew slowly during this period, but the city's industries continued to develop. Bain wagons were in great demand because of their strength and endurance. Simmons went into manufacturing, and many small industries such as foundries and tanneries were established.

Once the railroad debt was settled, the city began to progress again. Significant gifts from Simmons and Bain aided in the construction of a new police station and courthouse. By the late 1880s, Kenosha was a lively town with many active civic organizations and a growing cultural life. Its population had grown from 5,093 in 1880 to 6,532 in 1890, its biggest 10-year increase since incorporation.

During the 1890s there was a tremendous growth in manufacturing in Kenosha, and an increasing demand for workers. In the early 1900s agents were sent to Chicago to recruit workers, and Italian and Polish immigrants began to come to the city. The rapid growth of industry also created a demand for improved city services. In 1895 a private water company was purchased by the city, and in 1905 two paid fire-fighters were hired. A library, run by a public corporation, opened in 1896. Simmons donated a library building, designed by Chicago planner Daniel Burnham and surrounded by parkland, which became an important landmark in the city. By the turn of the century the population had grown to 11,606. It grew to 21,371 by 1910.

Production increased in Kenosha with the start of World War I. By January, 1916, industries in Kenosha were employing more than 10,000 workers. Even more workers were needed, and immigration from Europe, mostly Italy, continued through the 1920s. The city continued to develop. A park commission was established in 1912. The heirs of Zalmon Simmons donated their property on what was then Washington Island to be renamed Simmons Island and improved as a park site in memory of Simmons. A zoning ordinance was adopted in 1923.

By 1920 Kenosha's population was 40,472, the third largest in Wisconsin. The city had 84 industries, 13 of which had an annual production of $500,000 or more. New industries continued to be attracted to the city. Jeffrey Motors, the Badger Ice Cream Company and an artificial ice plant were all established in Kenosha during the 1920s, and the Snap-On Wrench Company moved to the city in 1929. In 1925 a master plan for the city was developed by Harlan Barthemew. Additional park land was acquired along the lakeshore for future public use. The population topped 50,000 in 1930.

During the Depression, unemployment was high in Kenosha. Some jobs were provided through the WPA and other federal projects to improve water and sewage systems, park facilities and the post office building. By the late 1930s conditions began to improve. Several large corporations were established: Nash Motors (later AMC), Cooper (later Jockey International) and American Brass (later Anaconda). Kenosha's wage scale was the highest in the state, but work was still scarce. The 1940 census showed the population at 48,765, a 3 percent loss and the first time in the city's history that the population had declined. However, World War II and the ensuing peacetime prosperity again stimulated the growth of Kenosha's industry, and led to a new period of development. The population was already back over 50,000 by 1950.

The two decades following 1950 were a period of expansion and annexation, as Kenosha gained from growth in the Milwaukee and Chicago areas. The population was approaching 70,000 by 1960 and

318

80,000 by 1970. Throughout the city's history, its central location, with good transportation, and its skilled labor force have been attractive to various industries. Today Kenosha's diversified industrial base includes corporations such as American Motors-Renault, Anaconda Brass, Snap-On Tools, Eaton Corporation, Ocean Spray and Jockey International. The harbor has been developing steadily. At present, it can accommodate five ocean-going vessels at a time, and handles 80,000 tons of freight per year.

The current population is 94 percent white, 4 percent black. Four percent are of Spanish origin. Among the whites, the predominant descent group is German, followed at some remove by Italian, English and Polish. Eleven percent speak a language other than English at home. The city has remained a blue-collar town, where 42 percent work in manufacturing. Almost one-fourth commute outside Kenosha to work. The median family income in 1979 was $4,000 higher than the Chicago median, and 6 percent of the families lived in poverty.

The number of housing units in Kenosha increased by 18 percent, despite the population loss. More than 60 percent of all units are in single-family homes, and more than 60 percent are owner-occupied. More than half of Kenosha's housing has been built since World War II. The median value of single-family units is lower than Chicago's. A policy of controlled annexation has kept the city compact, so that Kenosha has neither urban "sprawl" nor a suburban ring. Much of the lakefront is held for park land.

The most recent decade has been a period of stability. The city's population has declined slightly, but the total in Kenosha County has grown. Retail sales volume is being lost, north to Racine and Milwaukee and south to Waukegan and Chicago. Kenosha's retail development has never been particularly strong, and the city has faced increasing competition from surrounding areas with the development of large shopping malls near the interstate highway system in the mid-1960s. However, Kenosha is planning for continued development. A downtown revitalization project will include a condominium development, shops and public use areas, and a 400-slip marina. The merger of American Motors and Renault in 1980 and the re-tooling of one of the company's plants have provided new jobs in the city. In addition, a new industrial park is being developed on the west side of the city near its airport and major airport expansion is planned over the next several years.

Marjorie DeVault

Part II
Non-Census Statistics

In this section, data pertaining to several characteristics not reported in the U.S. Census are presented for the Community Areas of Chicago. The sources of these data and the contents of the tables are as follows:

Components of Population Change

The change in the size of the population residing in a specified area between two points in time is conventionally subdivided into two major components: (1) natural increase, or the excess of births over deaths, and (2) net migration, or the difference between the number of in-migrants to the area and the number of out-migrants from the area. These components usually are computed in the following steps: (1) natural increase equals births minus deaths, and (2) net migration equals "difference between population at the beginning and at the end of the time interval" minus "natural increase." That is, the components can be computed if the following information is available: (1) a count of the population of the area at the beginning and end of the time interval, and (2) a count of the number of births and deaths occurring in the area during the time interval.

The procedure outlined above was used to obtain components of population change for community areas (CAs) in Chicago during the decade 1970-1980. The results are presented in Table II-1. Several implications of this method of computation should be noted. First, net migration is computed as a residual, that is, it is the difference between the change in population size (as enumerated in the 1970 and 1980 Censuses) and the excess of births over deaths (as reported to the Illinois Department of Public Health). Consequently, small percentage errors in the census enumerations of population may yield much larger percentage errors in the estimates of net migration, particularly when the ratio of net migration to enumerated population is low. This error will not occur, of course, if the two censuses have the same rate of under-enumeration (or over-enumeration). Second, if the two censuses do not have equivalent rates of under- or over-enumeration the measure of the change in population size itself is subject to error, and all of this error is allocated to the "net migration" component. This principle applies to subgroups of the population as well. For example, the under-enumeration of blacks is often greater than that of non-blacks and consequently black components of change may be subject to greater error than non-black components. Finally, errors in the reporting of births and deaths and in their allocation to CAs not only affect the measurement of the natural increase component, but also affect the estimated size of net migration. While the reporting of births and deaths is known to be virtually complete in Illinois, much less is known about possible differences between the allocation of births and deaths to CAs on the basis of residence addresses reported on the birth and death certificates, and the allocation of the census population to CAs on the basis of residence as enumerated in the 1970 and 1980 censuses. If there are sizeable differences in residence allocation on vital statistics records and residence allocation in the census, the components of population change could be significantly affected, particularly in CAs with large institutions for the aged or homes for unwed mothers. With these limitations in mind, the estimated number of "net migrants" should be used with caution when it represents a small proportion of the total population, that is, when the ratio of net migration per 100 population in 1970 (shown in Table II-1 as "% change") is small.

In interpreting the components of population change expressed as ratios to the 1970 population, it should be noted that the ratio for the natural increase component shown in the seventh column of Table II-1 relates (1) the difference between all births and deaths occurring to residents of an area during the decade, to (2) the 1970 population of the area. This component, therefore, cannot be used as a measure of the natural increase occurring to the 1970 population itself, since it includes births and deaths occurring to in-migrants to the area after they arrive, and it excludes births and deaths occurring to out-migrants after they leave. The natural increase component, expressed as a ratio to the 1970 population, is properly interpreted as a measure of the proportionate increase in the population of the area resulting from the excess of births over deaths occurring to residents of the area during the decade 1970-1980. Similarly, the net migration component, in the ninth column, expressed as a ratio to the 1970 population, measures the proportionate increase (or decrease, if negative) in population resulting from migration into and out of the area during the decade. The sum of these two components equals the proportionate change in total population during the decade.

Computation of the components of population change requires, for each community area, population figures for the beginning and end points of the interval, and a count of the total number of births and deaths occurring during the interval. The population figures are those of the 1970 and 1980 censuses, and pertain to April 1 of each year. For community areas and the City of Chicago, counts of births and deaths from 1970 to 1980 were provided by the Illinois Department of Public Health. The categorization of race into "black" and "non-black" minimizes errors resulting from ambiguities in the reporting of race for the 1980 census.

Building Permits

Table II-2 displays the number of dwelling units in buildings obtaining permits for new construction, demolition, repairs (court ordered and general) and alterations. The information presented in this table was drawn from Housing Chicago and Region, Appendices B-D, 1981, published by the Metropolitan Housing and Planning Council. The Council compiled this information from building permit data made available by the City of Chicago, Department of Inspectional Services.

Some comments about the utilization of these data are in order. If one wishes to know the net change in the housing stock between 1970 and 1980, the most reliable source of data is the 1970 and 1980 censuses. Building permit data should not be used for this purpose because there is an undercount in demolitions and possibly new constructions as well. However, despite this drawback, the building permit data provide valuable rough estimates of the nature and extent of change in the housing stock from 1970 to 1980 since, unlike the census data, they provide information on the actual components of change, that is, demolitions and new constructions. For example, the census data may indicate very little activity or change between 1970 and 1980 in the net housing stock for a given community area, even though there may have been a large number of demolitions and new constructions during this period.

Subsidized Housing

There are several different programs of federally subsidized housing in Chicago that reflect the shifting housing policies of the federal government over the past fifty years. As new housing programs were initiated earlier programs were often modified or dropped entirely. Therefore, the existing distribution of various types of subsidized housing represents a physical residue of historically changing social needs coupled with the political and economic factors that influenced the evolution of housing policies at both the federal and local levels.

The different types of subsidized housing are generally known or labeled by the specific Congressional legislative acts that brought them into existence. In Table II-3 the specific types of subsidized housing are identified as follows:

(1) Public Housing. Public Housing was created by Congress with the Housing Act of 1937, that provided Federal funds to local housing authorities to construct and own housing, choose tenants and operate public housing projects for low income tenants within specified federal guidelines. Specific public housing projects have been designated for the elderly, other projects for low income families.

(2) Section 221(d)(3). Housing Congressional amendment to the Housing Act in 1961 provided federal loans for below-market interest rates to not-for-profit organizations to build or rehabilitate housing for moderate income families. A similar amendment, Section 202 housing, was specifically geared to elderly housing.

(3) Section 235 and 236 Housing. A congressional amendment to the Housing Act in 1968 provided federal funds to subsidize the interest rates paid by either for-profit or not-for-profit developers on their mortgage loans for either rental units (Section 236) or single-family-owned units (Section 235) to moderate income families. The units were not publically owned but owned by either the developers or the individual occupants of the units.

(4) Section 8. In 1974 a comprehensive amendment of the Housing Act, Section 8, provided for three distinct programs each of which could be provided either to income families or to the elderly. Section 8 federal funds would be provided for rental assistance for; (a) new construction where a minimum of 20 percent of the tenants of a development are federally subsidized; (b) rehabilitation of sound housing to be rented to qualified tenants; or (c) existing housing occupied by qualified tenants who are eligible for subsidized rental assistance.

The data in Table II-3 are provided by permission from two sources: *Subsidized Housing in Chicago: A Spatial Survey and Analysis,* by Elizabeth Warren (1980); and *Subsidized Housing in the Chicago Suburbs,* by Elizabeth Warren (1981), both published by the Center for Urban Policy, Loyola University of Chicago.

Public Assistance Recipients

Persons may receive financial assistance under one of five programs: (1) "State Supplemental Payments to the Aged, Blind or Disabled" provides cash grants to individuals in need who are 65 years or older, or who are any age, but are blind or severely disabled and are in need and meet other eligibility requirements; (2) "Aid to Families with Dependent Children" provides cash grants to children under 16 years of age, or up to 18 if still registered for the WIN Demonstration Program, and to responsible relatives, on the basis of need due to absence, incapacity, or unemployment of one or both parents and provided other eligibility requirements are met; (3) "General Assistance" provides cash grants to those persons who are in need but who are ineligible for other cash grants; (4) "Medical Assistance" provides medical care to persons receiving one of the cash grants mentioned above or to other persons who do not need assistance to meet their general living costs but who do require help in meeting the cost of medical bills; and (5) "Food Stamp Program" provides food coupons to persons who do not need assistance to meet general living costs, but who do require help in meeting food costs or to most persons eligible for one of the cash grants mentioned above.

Table II-4 classifies recipients by race and type of public aid received in Chicago Community areas. While the three categories of cash grants (Aid to the Aged, Blind and Disabled, Aid to Families with Dependent Children, and General Assistance) are mutually exclusive, recipients of these grants generally receive food stamps and medical assistance as well. Persons classified as receiving "Food Stamps, No Grant" of "Medical Assistance, No Grant" are not receiving any cash grants. They may be receiving only food stamps or only medical assistance, or both.

Data for this table were drawn from a computer print-out produced by the Chicago Health Systems Agency, 205 Randolph Street, Chicago. A copy of the computer print-out is available at the Chicago Municipal Library.

Parks

The data on parks are based on information supplied by the Records and Estimates Division Planning Group of the Chicago Park District. The Chicago Park District is the principal park and recreation authority in the City, although some facilities are jointly operated wtih the Board of Education or the Chicago Housing Authority.

The Chicago Park District is responsible for horticultural and zoological gardens, 16 major beaches, 15 minor beaches, 8 harbors, 88 swimming pools, 19 bicycle paths, and 250 indoor field houses. Over 85 million visitations are made annually to the district's facilities.

To permit some assessment of the park and recreation facilities available to each community area, the various parks were divided into several classes, following Park District usage. The six city-wide parks are omitted from the acreage statistics allocated to community areas in Table II-5, although they are included in the totals reported for the City of Chicago. Each of these parks exceeds 300 acres in size, and tends to attract persons from many community areas. The area and location of each city-wide park is shown below:

Park	Acreage	Community Areas
Burnham	598.0	33, 35, 36, 39, 41
Grant	308.6	32, 33
Jackson	542.9	41, 42
Lincoln	1185.0	3, 6. 7, 77
Marquette	320.9	66
Washington	366.8	40

Close to half of the total park acreage in Chicago was in these parks. Their combined acreage was 3,322.6, as compared to 3,905.1 acres in all other parks.

The remaining parks — sectional parks, community parks, neighborhood parks, playgrounds, playlots, and passive recreation areas, may more meaningfully be regarded as serving nearby communities. Each of these parks was assigned to the community in which it is located and their data on acreage are summarized by community.

The first four columns of Table II-5 report the number of parks of each type located in each community area. The fifth column reports the total acreage of all parks itemized in the first four columns. These statistics were reported as of December 1980.

The omission of city-wide parks from the figures shown for community areas understates the park acreage located in certain areas.

Column totals do not exactly match City of Chicago totals. Certain community and minor parks are located within the bounds of more than one community area. In such a case that park was counted as one park within each community area it is a part of, while total acreage was evenly divided among the community areas involved. These community areas are shown with an asterisk. Total acreage by community area contains slight errors due to rounding inaccuracies. Again, the total for the City of Chicago is accurate.

Juvenile Delinquency

Table II-6 reports 1980 data on police and court contacts with juveniles separately for each community area in Chicago. These data are extracted from a larger compilation of statistics on juvenile delinquency reported in the volume Youth Problems in the City: A Data Inventory (1980), published by the Illinois Institute for Juvenile Research. Persons interested in obtaining delinquency estimates at the census tract level should consult that volume.

Geographic Cross-Referencing

Finally, Table II-8 provides a geographical cross-reference guide for the various administrative districts within the City of Chicago. Organized by community area and census tract, the table shows the 1982 Congressional District, 1982 Legislative District, 1981 City Ward, Police District, School district and Zip Code in which each census tract is located. Many tracts are located within more than one district. In those instances, all of the districts in which a tract is situated are reported.

The maps used to cross-reference most of these data were published by the Citizens Information Bureau of Illinois. Due to a slight non-correspondence of scales when overlaying the maps, there were several instances when the placement of the tracts became a matter of judgment. This situation occurred most frequently in the assignment of tracts to City Wards. When possible, enlarged maps were used as aids.

Maps were insufficient to designate Zip Codes, however, and especially at border streets since Zip Codes often include both sides of a street. Instead, data were taken from an annual publication of the Donnelley Marketing Information Services known as the Marketing Profile Analysis, 1982 edition.

According to the Bureau of the Census, a suffix .99 on a tract number indicates a tract populated entirely by persons aboard merchant or military ships. Such crews do not generally appear on maps: "the tracts relate to the water area and/or piers and docks associated with the on-shore tract(s) having the same 4-digit basic code."

In Table II-7 two of five ".99" tracts are excluded because no population figures appear in the Census tables. They are tracts 4601.99 and 4211.99.

Table II-1. Components of Population Change, Chicago Community Areas, 1970-1980

| Community Area | Total Population | | | Components of Population Change | | | | | |
| | | | | | | Natural Increase | | Net Migration | |
	1970	1980	Change	Births	Deaths	Number	% Change	Number	% Change
Chicago Total									
Total......	3,369,359	3,005,072	-364,287	577,622	358,714	218,908	6.5	-583,195	-17.3
Black......	1,102,620	1,197,000	94,380	277,106	104,803	172,303	15.6	-77,923	-7.1
Non-black..	2,266,739	1,808,072	-458,667	300,516	253,911	46,605	2.1	-505,272	-22.3
1. Rogers Park									
Total......	60,787	55,525	-5,262	8,504	7,752	752	1.2	-6,014	-9.9
Black......	760	5,225	4,465	1,029	189	840	110.5	3,625	477.0
Non-black..	60,027	50,300	-9,727	7,475	7,563	-88	-0.1	-9,639	-16.1
2. West Ridge									
Total......	65,432	61,129	-4,303	6,385	8,534	-2,149	-3.3	-2,154	-3.3
Black......	91	442	351	70	60	10	11.0	341	374.7
Non-black..	65,341	60,687	-4,654	6,315	8,474	-2,159	-3.3	-2,495	-3.8
3. Uptown (Includes Edgewater)									
Total......	136,436	122,975	-13,461	23,993	21,486	2,507	1.8	-15,968	-11.7
Black......	3,417	16,217	12,800	1,506	816	690	20.2	12,110	354.4
Non-black..	133,019	106,758	-26,261	22,487	20,670	1,817	1.4	-28,078	-21.1
4. Lincoln Square									
Total......	47,751	43,954	-3,797	6,188	6,127	61	0.1	-3,858	-8.1
Black......	55	236	181	60	24	36	65.5	145	263.6
Non-black..	47,696	43,718	-3,978	6,128	6,103	25	0.1	-4,003	-8.4
5. North Center									
Total......	39,410	35,161	-4,249	5,577	4,723	854	2.2	-5,103	-12.9
Black......	140	412	272	116	38	78	55.7	194	138.6
Non-black..	39,270	34,749	-4,521	5,461	4,685	776	2.0	-5,297	-13.5
6. Lake View									
Total......	114,943	97,519	-17,424	16,559	13,062	3,497	3.0	-20,921	-18.2
Black......	892	6,757	5,865	1,020	176	844	94.6	5,021	562.9
Non-black..	114,051	90,762	-23,289	15,539	12,886	2,653	2.3	-25,942	-22.7
7. Lincoln Park									
Total......	67,804	57,146	-10,658	9,547	6,698	2,849	4.2	-13,507	-19.9
Black......	4,904	4,909	5	1,595	461	1,134	23.1	-1,129	-23.0
Non-black..	62,900	52,237	-10,663	7,952	6,237	1,715	2.7	-12,378	-19.7
8. Near North Side									
Total......	70,269	67,167	-3,102	9,641	7,777	1,864	2.7	-4,966	-7.1
Black......	26,076	22,000	-4,076	6,872	1,852	5,020	19.3	-9,096	-34.9
Non-black..	44,193	45,167	974	2,769	5,925	-3,156	-7.1	4,130	9.3
9. Edison Park									
Total......	13,241	12,457	-784	987	1,463	-476	-3.6	-308	-2.3
Black......	--	--	--	6	3	3	--	-3	--
Non-black..	13,241	12,457	-784	981	1,460	-479	-3.6	-305	-2.3
10. Norwood Park									
Total......	41,827	40,585	-1,242	3,265	5,262	-1,997	-4.8	755	1.8
Black......	1	7	6	5	1	4	--	2	--
Non-black..	41,826	40,578	-1,248	3,260	5,261	-2,001	-4.8	753	1.8
11. Jefferson Park									
Total......	27,553	24,583	-2,970	2,514	3,405	-891	-3.2	-2,079	-7.5
Black......	2	5	3	13	3	10	--	-7	--
Non-black..	27,551	24,578	-2,973	2,501	3,402	-901	-3.3	-2,072	-7.5
12. Forest Glen									
Total......	20,531	18,991	-1,540	1,577	2,217	-640	-3.1	-900	-4.4
Black......	4	11	7	10	10	0	--	7	--
Non-black..	20,527	18,980	-1,547	1,567	2,207	-640	-3.1	-907	-4.4

Table II-1. Components of Population Change, Chicago Community Areas, 1970-1980

| | Total Population | | | | | Components of Population Change | | | |
| | | | | | | Natural Increase | | Net Migration | |
Community Area	1970	1980	Change	Births	Deaths	Number	% Change	Number	% Change
13. North Park									
Total......	16,732	15,273	-1,459	1,481	1,896	-415	-2.5	-1,044	-6.2
Black......	432	143	-289	22	13	9	2.1	-298	-69.0
Non-black..	16,300	15,130	-1,170	1,459	1,883	-424	-2.6	-746	-4.6
14. Albany Park									
Total......	47,092	46,075	-1,017	7,651	5,033	2,618	5.6	-3,635	-7.7
Black......	30	279	249	56	14	42	--	207	--
Non-black..	47,062	45,796	-1,266	7,595	5,019	2,576	5.5	-3,842	-8.2
15. Portage Park									
Total......	63,608	57,349	-6,259	6,265	8,045	-1,780	-2.8	-4,479	-7.0
Black......	21	51	30	51	14	37	--	-7	--
Non-black..	63,587	57,298	-6,289	6,214	8,031	-1,817	-2.9	-4,472	-7.0
16. Irving Park									
Total......	54,900	49,489	-5,411	6,971	6,451	520	0.9	-5,931	-10.8
Black......	27	63	36	27	20	7	--	29	--
Non-black..	54,873	49,426	-5,447	6,944	6,431	513	0.9	-5,960	-10.9
17. Dunning									
Total......	43,856	37,860	-5,996	3,631	4,626	-995	2.3	-5,001	-11.4
Black......	311	183	-128	19	7	12	3.9	-140	-45.0
Non-black..	43,545	37,677	-5,868	3,612	4,619	-1,007	2.3	-4,861	-11.2
18. Montclare									
Total......	11,675	10,793	-882	1,051	1,513	-462	-4.0	-420	-3.6
Black......	1	0	-1	3	2	1	--	-2	--
Non-black..	11,674	10,793	-881	1,048	1,511	-463	-4.0	-418	-3.6
19. Belmont Cragin									
Total......	57,399	53,371	-4,028	6,121	7,414	-1,293	-2.3	-2,735	-4.8
Black......	10	43	33	37	11	26	--	7	--
Non-black..	57,389	53,328	-4,061	6,084	7,403	-1,319	-2.3	-2,742	-4.8
20. Hermosa									
Total......	19,838	19,547	-291	2,901	2,355	546	2.8	-837	-4.2
Black......	8	74	66	36	13	23	--	43	--
Non-black..	19,830	19,473	-357	2,865	2,342	523	2.6	-880	-4.4
21. Avondale									
Total......	35,806	33,527	-2,279	5,250	4,114	1,136	3.2	-3,415	-9.5
Black......	11	60	49	32	6	26	--	23	--
Non-black..	35,795	33,467	-2,328	5,218	4,108	1,110	3.1	-3,438	-9.6
22. Logan Square									
Total......	88,555	84,768	-3,787	18,067	9,158	8,909	10.1	-12,696	-14.3
Black......	629	2,236	1,607	577	99	478	76.0	1,129	179.5
Non-black..	87,926	82,532	-5,394	17,490	9,059	8,431	9.6	-13,825	-15.7
23. Humboldt Park									
Total......	71,726	70,879	-847	17,043	6,066	10,977	15.3	-11,824	-16.5
Black......	13,921	25,215	11,294	6,155	1,247	4,908	35.3	6,386	45.9
Non-black..	57,805	45,664	-12,141	10,888	4,819	6,069	10.5	-18,210	-31.5
24. West Town									
Total......	124,800	96,428	-28,372	28,766	11,477	17,289	13.9	-45,661	-36.6
Black......	5,518	8,671	3,152	2,762	730	2,032	36.8	1,120	20.3
Non-black..	119,282	87,787	-31,524	26,004	10,747	15,257	12.8	-46,781	-39.2
25. Austin									
Total......	127,981	138,026	10,045	28,872	12,028	16,844	13.2	-6,799	-5.3
Black......	41,583	101,831	60,248	21,185	4,004	17,181	41.3	43,067	103.6
Non-black..	86,398	36,195	-50,203	7,687	8,024	-337	-0.4	-49,866	-57.7

Table II-1. Components of Population Change, Chicago Community Areas, 1970-1980

| | Total Population | | | Components of Population Change | | | | | |
| | | | | | | Natural Increase | | Net Migration | |
Community Area	1970	1980	Change	Births	Deaths	Number	% Change	Number	% Change
26. West Garfield Park									
Total......	48,464	33,865	-14,599	11,237	3,217	8,020	16,5	-22,619	-46.7
Black......	46,929	33,475	-13,454	11,154	2,828	8,326	17.7	-21,780	-46.4
Non-black..	1,535	390	-1,145	83	389	-306	-19.9	-839	-54.7
27. East Garfield Park									
Total......	52,185	31,580	-20,605	11,688	4,205	7,483	14.3	-28,088	-53.8
Black......	51,121	31,263	-19,858	11,523	3,819	7,704	15.1	-27,562	-53.9
Non-black..	1,064	317	-747	165	386	-221	-20.8	-526	-49.4
28. Near West Side									
Total......	78,703	57,305	-21,398	17,539	9,121	8,418	10.7	-29,816	-37.9
Black......	56,822	42,810	-14,012	13,775	5,189	8,586	15.1	-22,598	-39.8
Non-black..	21,881	14,495	-7,386	3,764	3,932	-168	-0.8	-7,218	-33.0
29. North Lawndale									
Total......	94,772	61,534	-33,238	21,048	6,840	14,208	15.0	-47,446	-50.1
Black......	91,274	59,370	-31,904	20,244	6,043	14,201	15.5	-46,105	-50.5
Non-black..	3,498	2,164	-1,334	804	797	7	0.2	-1,341	-38.3
30. South Lawndale									
Total......	62,895	75,204	12,309	17,029	5,882	11,147	17.7	1,162	1.8
Black......	6,447	6,476	29	865	392	473	7.3	-444	6.9
Non-black..	56,448	68,728	12,280	16,164	5,490	10,674	18.9	1,606	2.8
31. Lower West Side									
Total	44,498	44,951	453	12,582	3,966	8,616	19.4	-8,163	-18.3
Black......	1,068	477	-591	249	76	173	16.2	-764	-71.5
Non-black..	43,430	44,474	1,044	12,333	3,890	8,443	19.4	-7,399	-17.0
32. Loop									
Total......	4,936	6,462	1,526	331	1,479	-1,148	-23.3	2,674	54.2
Black......	587	1,231	644	108	210	-102	-17.4	746	127.1
Non-black..	4,349	5,231	882	223	1,269	-1,046	-24.1	1,928	44.3
33. Near South Side									
Total......	8,767	7,243	-1,524	1,977	1,050	927	10.6	-2,451	-28.0
Black......	7,487	6,819	-668	1,829	773	1,056	14.1	-1,724	-23.0
Non-black..	1,280	424	-856	148	277	-129	-10.1	-727	-56.8
34. Armour Square									
Total......	13,058	12,475	-583	2,004	1,536	468	3.6	-1,051	-8.0
Black......	4,131	3,162	-969	747	632	115	2.8	-1,084	-26.2
Non-black..	8,927	9,313	386	1,257	904	353	4.0	33	0.4
35. Douglas									
Total......	47,734	35,700	-12,034	8,459	4,722	3,737	7.8	-15,771	33.0
Black......	41,783	30,905	-10,878	7,406	4,420	2,986	7.1	-13,864	33.2
Non-black..	5,951	4,795	-1,156	1,053	302	751	12.6	-1,907	-32.0
36. Oakland									
Total......	18,291	16,748	-1,543	4,920	1,777	3,143	17.2	-4,686	-25.6
Black......	18,085	16,647	-1,438	4,908	1,725	3,183	17.6	-4,621	-25.6
Non-black..	206	101	-105	12	52	-40	-19.4	-65	-31.6
37. Fuller Park									
Total......	7,372	5,832	-1,540	1,472	974	498	6.8	-2,038	-27.6
Black......	7,142	5,757	-1,385	1,459	947	512	13.3	-1,897	-26.6
Non-black..	230	75	-155	13	27	-14	-6.1	-141	-61.3
38. Grand Boulevard									
Total......	80,150	53,741	-26,409	14,416	10,672	3,744	4.7	-30,153	-37.6
Black......	79,595	53,428	-26,167	14,358	10,445	3,913	4.9	-30,080	-37.8
Non-black...	555	313	-242	58	227	-169	-30.4	-73	-13.2

Table II-1. Components of Population Change, Chicago Community Areas, 1970-1980

| | Total Population | | | | | Components of Population Change | | | |
| | | | | | | Natural Increase | | Net Migration | |
Community Area	1970	1980	Change	Births	Deaths	Number	% Change	Number	% Change
39. Kenwood									
Total......	26,908	21,974	-4,934	4,155	3,635	520	1.9	-5,454	-20.3
Black......	21,222	17,024	-4,198	3,687	2,822	865	4.1	-5,063	-23.9
Non-black..	5,686	4,950	-736	468	813	-345	-6.1	-391	-6.9
40. Washington Park									
Total......	46,024	31,935	-14,089	8,067	5,731	2,336	5.1	-16,425	-35.7
Black......	45,636	31,726	-13,910	8,034	5,653	2,381	5.2	-16,291	-35.7
Non-black..	388	209	-179	33	78	-45	-11.6	-134	-34.5
41. Hyde Park									
Total......	33,559	31,198	-2,361	4,193	3,003	1,190	3.5	-3,551	-10.6
Black......	10,424	11,610	1,186	2,060	960	1,100	10.6	86	0.8
Non-black..	23,135	19,588	-3,547	2,133	2,043	90	0.4	-3,637	-15.7
42. Woodlawn									
Total......	53,814	36,323	-17,491	9,112	6,531	2,581	4.8	-20,072	-37.3
Black......	51,556	34,759	-16,797	8,935	6,003	2,932	5.7	-19,729	-38.3
Non-black..	2,258	1,564	-694	177	528	-351	-15.5	-343	-15.2
43. South Shore									
Total......	80,660	77,743	-2,917	16,386	7,581	8,805	10.9	-11,722	-14.5
Black......	55,638	73,929	18,291	15,623	4,688	10,935	19.7	7,356	13.2
Non-black..	25,022	3,814	-21,208	763	2,893	-2,130	-8.5	-19,078	-76.2
44. Chatham									
Total......	47,287	40,725	-6,562	6,871	4,284	2,587	5.5	-9,149	-19.3
Black......	46,114	40,113	-6,001	6,829	4,028	2,801	6.1	-8,802	-19.1
Non-black..	1,173	612	-561	42	256	-214	-18.2	-347	-29.6
45. Avalon Park									
Total	14,412	13,792	-620	2,194	1,059	1,135	7.9	-1,755	-12.2
Black......	11,912	13,258	1,346	2,163	778	1,385	11.6	-39	-0.3
Non-black..	2,500	534	-1,966	31	281	-250	-10.0	-1,716	-68.6
46. South Chicago									
Total......	45,655	46,422	767	10,053	4,345	5,708	12.5	-4,941	-10.8
Black......	10,230	22,186	11,956	3,904	1,098	2,806	27.4	9,150	89.4
Non-black..	35,425	24,236	-11,189	6,149	3,247	2,902	8.2	-14,091	-39.8
47. Burnside									
Total......	3,181	3,942	761	723	337	386	12.1	375	11.8
Black......	91	3,491	3,400	542	89	453	497.8	2,947	3238.5
Non-black..	3,090	451	-2,639	181	248	-67	-2.2	-2,572	-83.2
48. Calumet Heights									
Total......	20,123	20,505	382	3,086	1,462	1,624	8.1	-1,242	-6.2
Black......	9,038	17,795	8,757	2,416	791	1,625	18.0	7,132	78.9
Non-black..	11,085	2,710	-8,375	670	671	-1	0.0	-8,374	-75.5
49. Roseland									
Total......	62,512	64,372	1,860	12,116	5,542	6,574	10.6	-4,714	-7.5
Black......	34,445	62,749	28,304	11,354	3,860	7,494	21.8	20,810	60.4
Non-black..	28,067	1,623	-26,444	762	1,682	-920	-3.3	-25,524	-90.9
50. Pullman									
Total......	10,893	10,341	-552	1,798	915	883	8.1	-1,435	-13.2
Black......	5,236	7,896	2,660	1,307	371	936	17.9	1,724	32.9
Non-black..	5,657	2,445	-3,212	491	544	-53	-0.9	-3,159	-55.8
51. South Deering									
Total......	19,271	19,400	129	3,330	1,503	1,827	9.5	-1,698	-8.8
Black......	3,067	10,631	7,564	1,775	418	1,357	44.2	6,207	202.4
Non-black..	16,204	8,769	-7,435	1,555	1,085	470	2.9	-7,905	-48.8

Table II-1. Components of Population Change, Chicago Community Areas, 1970-1980

| | Total Population | | | Components of Population Change | | | | | |
| | | | | Births | Deaths | Natural Increase | | Net Migration | |
Community Area	1970	1980	Change			Number	% Change	Number	% Change
52. East Side				2,612	2,577	35	0.1	-3,353	-13.6
Total......	24,649	21,331	-3,318	12	3	9	--	-7	--
Black......	23	25	2	2,600	2,574	26	0.1	-3,346	-13.6
Non-black..	24,626	21,306	3,320						
53. West Pullman				10,904	3,296	7,608	18.9	-3,022	-7.5
Total......	40,318	44,904	4,586	5,923	1,087	4,836	72.5	29,195	437.7
Black......	6,670	40,701	34,031	4,981	2,209	2,772	8.2	-32,217	-95.7
Non-black..	33,648	4,203	-29,445						
54. Riverdale				3,647	772	2,875	19.1	-4,354	-30.0
Total......	15,016	13,539	-1,479	3,533	698	2,835	19.9	-3,975	-27.9
Black......	14,229	13,089	-1,140	114	74	40	5.1	-379	-48.0
Non-black..	789	450	-339						
55. Hegewisch				1,454	1,077	377	3.3	-151	-1.3
Total......	11,346	11,572	226	15	7	8	--	-1	--
Black......	22	29	7	1,439	1,070	369	3.3	-150	-1.3
Non-black..	11,324	11,543	219						
56. Garfield Ridge				4,237	3,428	809	1.9	-5,862	-13.6
Total......	42,988	37,935	-5,053	1,053	152	901	25.7	780	22.2
Black......	3,505	5,186	1,681	3,184	3,276	-92	-0.2	-6,642	-16.8
Non-black..	39,483	32,749	-6,734						
57. Archer Heights				1,184	1,291	-107	-1.0	-1,319	-11.8
Total......	11,134	9,708	-1,426	11	8	3	--	4	--
Black......	1	8	7	1,173	1,283	-110	-1.0	-1,323	-11.9
Non-black..	11,133	9,700	-1,433						
58. Brighton Park				5,012	4,253	759	2.1	-5,607	-15.7
Total......	35,618	30,770	-4,848	34	17	17	--	-17	--
Black......	34	34	0	4,978	4,236	742	2.1	-5,590	-15.7
Non-black..	35,584	30,736	-4,848						
59. McKinley Park				2,353	1,863	490	3.1	-2,874	-18.4
Total......	15,632	13,248	-2,384	18	3	15	--	-14	--
Black......	4	5	1	2,335	1,860	475	3.0	-2,860	-18.3
Non-black..	15,628	13,243	-2,385						
60. Bridgeport				5,885	4,027	1,858	5.3	-6,102	-17.4
Total......	35,167	30,923	-4,244	81	23	58	--	-63	--
Black......	45	40	-5	5,804	4,004	1,800	5.1	-6,039	-17.2
Non-black..	35,122	30,883	-4,239						
61. New City				13,057	6,329	6,728	11.1	-11,685	-19.2
Total......	60,817	55,860	-4,957	2,918	594	2,324	108.0	7,763	360.7
Black......	2,152	12,239	10,087	10,139	5,735	4,404	7.5	-19,448	-33.2
Non-black..	58,665	43,621	-15,044						
62. West Elsdon				1,158	1,607	-449	-3.2	-813	-5.8
Total......	14,059	12,797	-1,262	12	4	8	--	-6	--
Black......	5	7	2	1,146	1,603	-457	-3.2	-807	-5.7
Non-black..	14,054	12,790	-1,264						
63. Gage Park				3,102	3,776	-674	-2.5	-1,579	-5.9
Total......	26,698	24,445	-2,253	24	11	13	--	149	--
Black......	1	163	162	3,078	3,765	-687	-2.6	-1,728	-6.5
Non-black..	26,697	24,282	-2,415						
64. Clearing				3,055	2,115	940	3.8	-2,844	-11.6
Total......	24,488	22,584	-1,904	7	7	0	--	4	--
Black......	1	5	4	3,048	2,108	940	3.8	-2,848	-11.6
Non-black..	24,487	22,579	-1,908						

Community Area	Total Population			Components of Population Change					
						Natural Increase		Net Migration	
	1970	1980	Change	Births	Deaths	Number	% Change	Number	% Change
65. West Lawn									
Total......	18,597	24,748	6,151	2,382	3,006	-624	-3.4	6,775	36.4
Black......	10	52	42	23	10	13	--	29	--
Non-black..	18,587	24,696	6,109	2,359	2,996	-637	-3.4	6,746	36.3
66. Chicago Lawn									
Total......	48,435	46,568	-1,867	5,792	7,190	-1,398	-2.9	-469	-1.0
Black......	10	4,782	4,772	357	46	311	--	4,461	--
Non-black..	48,425	41,786	-6,639	5,435	7,144	-1,709	-3.5	-4,930	-10.2
67. West Englewood									
Total......	61,910	62,069	159	14,944	5,263	9,681	15.6	-9,522	-15.4
Black......	29,914	60,882	30,968	13,008	3,280	9,728	32.5	21,240	71.0
Non-black..	31,996	1,187	-30,809	1,936	1,983	-47	-0.1	-30,762	-96.1
68. Englewood									
Total......	89,713	59,075	-30,638	18,058	7,260	10,798	12.0	-41,436	-46.2
Black......	86,485	58,395	-28,090	17,918	6,799	11,119	12.9	-39,209	-45.3
Non-black..	3,228	680	-2,548	140	461	-321	-9.9	-2,227	-69.0
69. Greater Grand Crossing									
Total......	54,414	45,218	-9,196	8,659	5,988	2,671	4.9	-11,867	-21.8
Black......	53,353	44,660	-8,693	8,598	5,739	2,859	5.4	-11,552	-21.7
Non-black..	1,061	558	-503	61	249	-188	-17.7	-315	-29.7
70. Ashburn									
Total......	47,161	40,477	-6,684	3,804	4,501	-697	-1.5	-5,987	12.7
Black......	503	1,084	581	133	325	-192	-38.2	773	153.7
Non-black..	46,658	39,363	-7,265	3,671	4,176	-505	-1.1	-6,760	-14.5
71. Auburn Gresham									
Total......	68,854	65,132	-3,722	13,718	5,376	8,342	12.1	-12,064	-17.5
Black......	47,308	64,093	16,785	12,999	3,689	9,310	19.7	7,475	15.8
Non-black..	21,546	1,039	-20,507	719	1,687	-968	-4.5	-19,539	-90.7
72. Beverly									
Total......	26,771	23,360	-3,411	2,845	3,032	-187	-0.7	-3,224	-12.0
Black......	30	3,178	3,148	329	65	264	--	2,884	--
Non-black..	26,741	20,182	-6,559	2,516	2,967	-451	-1.7	-6,108	-22.8
73. Washington Heights									
Total......	36,540	36,453	-87	6,413	2,625	3,788	10.4	-3,875	-10.6
Black......	27,307	35,778	8,471	6,199	1,951	4,248	15.6	4,223	15.5
Non-black..	9,233	675	-8,558	214	674	-460	-5.0	-8,098	-87.7
74. Mount Greenwood									
Total......	23,186	20,084	-3,102	2,105	2,382	-277	-1.2	-2,825	-12.2
Black......	22	93	71	14	8	6	--	65	--
Non-black..	23,164	19,991	-3,173	2,091	2,374	-283	-1.2	-2,890	-12.5
75. Morgan Park									
Total......	31,016	29,315	-1,701	4,920	3,394	1,526	4.9	-3,227	-10.4
Black......	14,794	18,320	3,526	3,353	1,403	1,950	13.2	1,576	10.7
Non-black..	16,222	10,995	-5,227	1,567	1,991	-424	-2.6	-4,803	-29.6
76. O'Hare									
Total......	6,342	11,068	4,726	1,305	525	780	12.3	3,946	62.2
Black......	11	165	154	17	3	14	--	140	--
Non-black..	6,331	10,903	4,572	1,288	522	766	12.1	3,808	60.1

Table II-2. Type of Building Permits of Dwelling Units

for Chicago Community Areas 1970-1980

COMMUNITY AREA	New Construction Number Dwelling Units In Building						Demolition Number Dwelling Units in Building					
	Total	1	2-4	5-7	8+	Other	Total	1	2-4	5-7	8+	Other
1 Rogers Park	503	59	11	39	337	57	695	49	35	11	464	136
2 West Ridge	899	233	63	112	409	82	70	32	24	0	0	14
3 Uptown*	3,346	25	28	42	2,954	297	2,686	48	285	535	1,500	318
4 Lincoln Square	197	32	25	7	119	14	225	37	77	12	66	33
5 North Center	21	15	6	0	0	0	175	23	64	12	20	56
6 Lake View	2,722	145	130	46	2,125	276	860	47	345	66	280	122
7 Lincoln Park	4,567	675	77	82	3,227	506	1,792	107	979	106	316	284
8 Near North	6,897	63	13	0	4,855	1,966	2,168	68	861	221	367	651
9 Edison Park	373	65	16	28	209	55	39	27	9	0	0	3
10 Norwood Park	1,896	364	98	301	881	252	50	37	6	0	0	7
11 Jefferson Park	409	90	157	25	120	17	75	50	14	0	0	11
12 Forest Glen	207	180	18	0	9	0	18	16	2	0	0	0
13 North Park	404	15	7	18	104	260	15	9	4	0	0	2
14 Albany Park	53	35	16	0	0	2	167	26	45	0	76	20
15 Portage Park	513	79	145	44	203	42	168	67	60	6	9	26
16 Irving Park	237	66	40	0	107	24	175	45	61	0	24	45
17 Dunning	868	274	81	71	234	208	105	74	25	0	0	6
18 Montclare	65	44	19	0	0	2	25	6	7	0	12	0
19 Belmont Cragin	255	46	91	20	71	27	92	33	29	0	0	30
20 Hermosa	8	4	2	0	0	2	74	11	26	12	18	7
21 Avondale	39	23	9	6	0	1	139	22	64	7	0	46
22 Logan Square	37	21	16	0	0	0	986	110	495	54	180	147
23 Humboldt Park	99	53	3	0	36	7	1,626	141	619	135	458	273
24 West Town	241	62	5	0	159	15	4,056	252	2,074	465	582	683
25 Austin	572	45	8	0	306	213	2,417	197	545	76	871	728
26 W Garfield Pk	29	7	8	6	8	0	2,100	84	752	165	965	134
27 E Garfield Pk	205	8	16	12	168	1	3,345	96	1,319	321	1,241	368
28 Near West Side	2,468	454	9	5	1,897	103	4,414	137	2,225	410	753	898
29 North Lawndale	104	12	61	24	0	7	5,461	147	1,597	631	2,294	792
30 South Lawndale	351	9	4	0	0	338	492	93	226	0	72	101
31 Lower West Side	146	19	4	0	0	123	582	46	347	47	20	122
32 Loop	4,232	1	12	0	2,008	2,211	82	4	16	6	35	21
33 Near South Side	784	0	0	0	399	385	202	2	31	18	47	104
34 Armour Square	494	133	42	0	310	9	155	14	76	12	8	45
35 Douglas	1,049	41	0	0	749	259	848	15	378	87	218	150
36 Oakland	771	0	0	5	667	99	831	4	210	74	428	115
37 Fuller Park	87	87	0	0	0	0	429	85	221	6	77	40
38 Grand Boulevard	757	11	0	0	648	98	3,516	73	1,129	587	1,417	30

*Includes Edgewater

330

COMMUNITY AREA	New Construction Number Dwelling Units In Building						Demolition Number Dwelling Units in Building					
	Total	1	2-4	5-7	8+	Other	Total	1	2-4	5-7	8+	Other
39 Kenwood	2,309	266	0	218	1,825	0	1,736	15	386	172	1,008	155
40 Washington Park	386	8	0	0	300	78	1,718	40	326	363	802	187
41 Hyde Park	138	18	0	0	112	8	231	3	17	12	184	15
42 Woodlawn	554	40	0	0	313	201	4,540	39	409	721	2,956	415
43 South Shore	281	36	0	0	79	166	1,010	76	208	118	338	270
44 Chatham	193	158	2	5	0	28	167	36	63	0	45	23
45 Avalon	70	50	3	0	0	17	72	19	22	0	0	31
46 South Chicago	500	69	2	0	429	0	488	91	256	24	20	97
47 Burnside	92	92	0	0	0	0	19	7	8	0	0	4
48 Calumet Heights	89	87	2	0	0	0	75	29	35	0	0	11
49 Roseland	362	322	0	0	0	40	440	187	162	0	30	61
50 Pullman	44	44	0	0	0	0	44	5	23	0	15	1
51 South Deering	84	44	0	0	0	40	52	5	13	0	32	2
52 East Side	285	245	4	0	0	36	44	21	22	0	0	1
53 West Pullman	398	201	0	0	180	17	211	65	98	0	0	48
54 Riverdale	8	8	0	0	0	0	29	15	12	0	0	2
55 Hegewisch	51	29	8	0	0	14	11	2	5	0	0	4
56 Garfield Ridge	676	212	90	29	267	78	58	41	10	6	0	1
57 Archer Heights	152	15	59	0	31	47	50	34	14	0	0	2
58 Brighton Park	130	62	10	0	0	58	100	25	59	12	0	4
59 McKinley Park	50	22	0	0	15	13	142	21	25	6	24	66
60 Bridgeport	346	190	36	5	0	115	359	57	171	6	34	91
61 New City	282	182	2	10	0	88	1,467	253	819	84	133	178
62 West Elsdon	219	46	50	21	78	24	20	11	6	0	0	3
63 Gage Park	77	29	8	2	0	38	64	11	45	0	0	8
64 Clearing	714	109	96	216	193	100	53	18	7	6	22	0
65 West Lawn	248	65	83	18	0	82	41	27	12	0	0	2
66 Chicago Lawn	131	35	20	5	17	54	82	25	35	0	0	22
67 West Englewood	303	242	9	0	12	40	1,268	364	589	41	96	178
68 Englewood	514	243	2	0	243	26	3,803	338	1,392	331	1,141	601
69 Greater Grand Cr	247	101	2	12	99	33	811	89	321	35	304	62
70 Ashburn	409	192	21	6	136	54	8	4	4	0	0	0
71 Auburn Gresham	194	165	5	0	0	24	288	78	104	0	75	31
72 Beverly	34	34	0	0	0	0	29	7	20	0	0	2
73 Washington Hts	377	207	2	0	0	168	106	64	36	0	0	6
74 Mount Greenwood	534	90	0	0	402	42	19	15	0	0	0	4
75 Morgan Park	516	353	5	0	28	130	258	122	81	6	0	49
76 O'Hare	1,441	73	29	60	1,065	214	6	3	0	0	0	3
Total	50,343	7,879	1,790	1,500	29,143	10,031	61,274	4,596	21,097	6,016	20,077	9,488

Table II-2. Type of Building Permits of Dwelling Units

for Chicago Community Areas 1970-1980

| | Repairs | | Alterations |
| | Court Ordered | General | |
Community Area	Total Dwel. Units	Total Dwel. Units	Total Dwel. Units
1 Rogers Park	2,737	642	995
2 West Ridge	786	745	866
3 Uptown*	13,879	4,035	16,458
4 Lincoln Square	1,179	169	328
5 North Center	730	112	219
6 Lake View	9,464	3,345	6,460
7 Lincoln Park	6,083	4,109	5,121
8 Near North	8,093	6,123	15,269
9 Edison Park	75	185	78
10 Norwood Park	368	1,336	2,253
11 Jefferson Park	135	310	94
12 Forest Glen	71	175	81
13 North Park	217	151	81
14 Albany Park	1,515	53	398
15 Portage Park	352	447	413
16 Irving Park	1,068	225	297
17 Dunning	175	563	135
18 Montclare	64	38	48
19 Belmont Cragin	458	296	220
20 Hermosa	306	21	98
21 Avondale	851	49	391
22 Logan Square	3,208	111	568
23 Homboldt Park	1,816	133	492
24 West Town	4,939	427	908
25 Austin	3,525	615	790
26 W Garfield Pk	1,034	64	203
27 E Garfield Pk	1,907	280	433
28 Near West Side	1,816	949	1,017
29 North Lawndale	3,121	737	6,112
30 South Lawndale	1,185	307	378
31 Lower West Side	2,567	491	10,365
32 Loop	994	957	
33 Near South Side	315	352	326
34 Armour Square	449	192	233
35 Douglas	478	905	554
36 Oakland	583	773	788
37 Fuller Park	129	96	34
38 Grand Boulevard	3,055	565	354

Table II-2. Type of Building Permits of Dwelling Units
for Chicago Community Areas 1970-1980

| | Repairs | | Alterations |
| | Court Ordered | General | |
COMMUNITY AREA	Total Dwel. Units	Total Dwel. Units	Total Dwel. Units
39 Kenwood	2,826	1,862	659
40 Washington Park	1,935	351	356
41 Hyde Park	2,359	198	2,508
42 Woodlawn	2,321	427	500
43 South Shore	3,875	738	1,495
44 Chatham	950	294	344
45 Avalon	274	52	83
46 South Chicago	922	535	500
47 Burnside	91	78	30
48 Calumet Heights	121	66	107
49 Roseland	808	388	469
50 Pullman	122	47	47
51 South Deering	134	92	118
52 East Side	127	181	126
53 West Pullman	902	381	192
54 Riverdale	68	13	52
55 Hegewisch	36	33	42
56 Garfield Ridge	96	492	579
57 Archer Heights	160	121	35
58 Brighton Park	391	140	124
59 McKinley Park	327	28	126
60 Bridgeport	1,603	288	448
61 New City	1,872	318	524
62 West Elsdon	79	372	43
63 Gage Park	206	113	47
64 Clearing	148	593	68
65 West Lawn	119	186	81
66 Chicago Lawn	664	86	208
67 West Englewood	1,775	403	456
68 Englewood	2,478	990	451
69 Greater Grand Cr	1,296	283	1,087
70 Ashburn	44	333	56
71 Auburn Gresham	1,269	323	382
72 Beverly	54	37	64
73 Washington Hts	381	337	142
74 Mount Greenwood	39	446	47
75 Morgan Park	213	506	193
76 O'Hare	938	1,347	75
Total	110,712	44,437	77,959

*Includes Edgewater

Table II-3. Total Number of Subsidized Housing Units Under Four Government
Programs in Chicago's Community Areas, January 1980

Community Area	Public Housing Units			"Section 8" Units							Section 221 (d)(3)	Section 236
					Existing		Rehabilitation		New Construction			
	Total	Elder	Family	Total	Elder	Family	Elder	Family	Elder	Family		
1. Rogers Park.....	450	0	450	338	287	27	0	18	0	6	25	85
2. West Ridge......	0	0	0	157	49	8	0	0	100	0	0	0
*3. Uptown..........	1282	78	1204	2468	744	297	0	457	703	267	2411	671
4. Lincoln Square..	0	0	0	98	82	16	0	0	0	0	0	0
5. North Center....	396	396	0	19	18	0	0	1	0	0	0	0
6. Lake View.......	708	27	681	834	185	61	108	312	79	89	646	400
7. Lincoln Park....	1329	519	810	448	20	7	181	36	104	100	45	591
8. Near North Side.	4094	3573	521	921	16	116	0	0	576	213	640	206
9. Edison Park.....	0	0	0	0	0	0	0	0	0	0	0	0
10. Norwood Park....	0	0	0	6	6	0	6	6	0	0	0	132
11. Jefferson Park..	0	0	0	4	4	0	0	0	0	0	0	0
12. Forest Glen.....	0	0	0	0	0	0	0	0	0	0	0	0
13. North Park......	0	0	0	15	15	0	0	0	0	0	0	0
14. Albany Park.....	0	0	0	116	100	16	0	0	0	0	61	0
15. Portage Park....	0	0	0	22	19	3	0	0	0	0	0	0
16. Irving Park.....	0	0	0	30	27	3	0	0	0	0	0	0
17. Dunning........	0	0	0	6	6	0	0	0	0	0	0	0
18. Montclare.......	0	0	0	5	4	1	0	0	0	0	0	0
19. Belmont Cragin..	0	0	0	17	17	0	0	0	0	0	0	0
20. Hermosa........	0	0	0	6	6	0	0	0	0	0	0	0
21. Avondale........	1	1	0	16	10	6	0	0	0	0	0	0
22. Logan Square....	0	0	0	467	26	19	0	233	0	189	0	37
23. Humboldt Park...	193	36	157	27	4	23	0	0	0	0	38	0
24. West Town.......	651	15	636	39	2	11	0	26	0	0	479	253
25. Austin..........	169	0	169	113	28	67	0	18	0	0	0	0
26. W. Garfield Park	814	0	814	63	1	23	0	39	0	0	0	23
27. E. Garfield Park	161	161	0	207	3	73	0	35	0	96	189	150
28. Near West Side..	6859	6614	245	582	3	9	0	26	394	150	108	272
29. North Lawndale..	626	626	0	654	18	255	0	183	120	78	624	526
30. South Lawndale..	475	125	350	3	1	2	0	0	0	0	0	0
31. Lower West Side.	212	0	212	1	0	1	0	0	0	0	0	0
32. Loop............	0	0	0	249	0	0	0	59	190	0	0	0
33. Near South Side.	1504	1140	364	120	1	2	117	0	0	0	448	250
34. Armour Square...	1077	569	508	139	1	0	0	0	138	0	0	0
35. Douglas........	4941	4674	267	329	49	26	0	4	150	100	1075	384
36. Oakland........	2924	2646	278	44	16	28	0	0	0	0	0	732
37. Fuller Park.....	436	97	339	1	0	1	0	0	0	0	0	0
38. Grand Blvd......	4530	3949	581	571	76	51	0	67	190	187	12	831
39. Kenwood.........	92	0	92	115	62	53	0	0	0	0	923	631
40. Washington Pk...	1746	1746	0	117	62	55	0	0	0	0	195	229

* includes Edgewater

334

Table II-3. Total Number of Subsidized Housing Units Under Four Government
Programs in Chicago's Community Areas, January 1980

Community Area	Public Housing Units			"Section 8" Units							Section 221 (d)(3)	Section 236
					Existing		Rehabilitation		New Construction			
	Total	Elder	Family	Total	Elder	Family	Elder	Family	Elder	Family		
41. Hyde Park.......	34	12	22	394	84	44	73	101	92	0	159	0
42. Woodlawn........	300	10	290	858	121	140	0	95	354	148	785	584
43. South Shore.....	0	0	0	1301	116	182	187	816	0	0	50	206
44. Chatham........	0	0	0	93	53	40	0	0	0	0	49	0
45. Avalon Park.....	0	0	0	4	1	3	0	0	0	0	0	0
46. South Chicago...	298	0	298	32	5	27	0	0	0	0	0	357
47. Burnside........	0	0	0	144	0	0	0	0	72	72	56	0
48. Calumet Heights.	0	0	0	5	1	4	0	0	0	0	0	0
49. Roseland........	128	128	0	45	15	30	0	0	0	0	0	0
50. Pullman.........	0	0	0	140	0	1	0	139	0	0	803	0
51. South Deering...	475	447	28	3	0	3	0	0	0	0	0	0
52. East Side.......	0	0	0	3	2	1	0	0	0	0	0	0
53. West Pullman....	0	0	0	24	1	23	0	0	0	0	0	180
54. Riverdale.......	1963	1963	0	19	1	18	0	0	0	0	766	0
55. Hegewisch.......	0	0	0	1	0	1	0	0	0	0	0	0
56. Garfield Ridge..	615	615	0	4	1	3	0	0	0	0	46	0
57. Archer Heights..	0	0	0	2	2	0	0	0	0	0	0	0
58. Brighton Park...	0	0	0	9	6	3	0	0	0	0	0	0
59. McKinley Park...	0	0	0	2	2	0	0	0	0	0	0	0
60. Bridgeport......	152	138	14	2	1	1	0	0	0	0	0	0
61. New City........	0	0	0	72	14	10	0	0	0	48	0	0
62. Elston..........	0	0	0	1	0	1	0	0	0	0	0	0
63. Gage Park.......	0	0	0	8	8	0	0	0	0	0	0	0
64. Clearing........	0	0	0	0	0	0	0	0	0	0	0	0
65. West Lawn.......	0	0	0	3	2	1	0	0	0	0	0	0
66. Chicago Lawn....	0	0	0	39	13	5	0	0	0	21	0	0
67. West Englewood..	0	0	0	28	7	21	0	0	0	0	6	60
68. Englewood.......	635	93	542	189	61	88	0	40	0	0	375	394
69. Gr Grand Cr.....	0	0	0	110	26	84	0	0	0	0	268	799
70. Ashburn.........	0	0	0	5	5	0	0	0	0	0	0	0
71. Auburn Gresham..	0	0	0	52	11	41	0	0	0	0	156	0
72. Beverly.........	0	0	0	4	2	2	0	0	0	0	0	0
73. Washington Hts..	0	0	0	11	1	10	0	0	0	0	0	0
74. Mt. Greenwood...	0	0	0	9	7	2	0	0	0	0	0	0
75. Morgan Park.....	0	0	0	20	7	13	0	0	0	0	0	0
76. O'Hare..........	0	0	0	0	0	0	0	0	0	0	0	0
Total	40270	30398	9872	13003	2544	2062	666	2705	3262	1764	11438	8983

The statistics presented above are drawn from Elizabeth Warren,
Subsidized Housing in Chicago. These statistics have been updated through May, 1980,
by the Leadership Council for Metropolitan Open Communities (See
Housing Chicago and Region, 1981, Appendix F, page 48, Metropolitan
Housing and Planning Council). According to the Council, the total number
of Section 8 housing units was 13,936 by May of 1980.

Table II-4. Recipients of Public Assistance, by Race and by Type of Assistance

Community Areas in City of Chicago, December, 1980

Community Area	Total	Aid to Aged, Blind and Disabled					Aid to Families with Dependent Children				
		Total	White	Black	Spanish	Other	Total	White	Black	Spanish	Other
Chicago	651,222	24,835	7,301	15,089	2,126	319	436,454	45,689	338,647	49,689	2,429
1 Rogers Park	5,144	419	368	35	9	7	1,891	685	916	207	83
2 West Ridge	2,550	223	204	2	7	10	424	346	12	47	19
3 Uptown	21,194	1,959	1,485	272	134	68	9,663	3,350	3,512	1,898	903
4 Lincoln Square	2,768	214	176	1	22	15	1,300	877	15	348	60
5 North Center	3,513	152	107	3	32	10	2,129	1,366	121	615	25
6 Lake View	8,639	697	513	39	129	16	4,523	1,963	732	1,718	110
7 Lincoln Park	4,975	356	266	61	23	6	2,367	871	913	560	23
8 Near North	15,289	510	270	214	22	4	10,806	136	10,578	75	17
9 Edison Park	64	2	2	0	0	0	20	20	0	0	0
10 Norwood Park	291	27	25	0	0	2	86	86	0	0	0
11 Jefferson Park	273	29	25	0	2	2	120	117	0	0	3
12 Forest Glen	79	3	3	0	0	0	21	21	0	0	0
13 North Park	550	55	50	1	2	2	109	81	0	24	4
14 Albany Park	5,235	237	83	0	41	13	3,313	1,860	66	1,216	171
15 Portage Park	1,123	115	99	0	10	6	430	374	27	17	12
16 Irving Park	2,505	207	175	1	24	7	1,282	1,013	19	223	27
17 Dunning	537	31	31	0	0	0	165	162	0	3	0
18 Montclare	275	43	38	0	5	0	82	79	0	3	0
19 Belmont Cragin	1,910	121	97	0	23	1	941	793	10	127	11
20 Hermosa	2,195	116	71	1	41	3	1,443	632	24	782	5
21 Avondale	2,785	182	112	2	62	6	1,722	877	27	801	17
22 Logan Square	17,128	741	351	32	350	8	12,185	3,083	1,016	8,018	68
23 Humboldt Park	21,246	583	134	231	205	13	15,970	1,584	8,707	5,627	52
24 West Town	29,758	1,179	440	183	545	11	20,300	3,599	3,612	12,958	131
25 Austin	40,688	1,141	124	961	37	19	30,083	808	28,604	622	49
26 W Garfield Park	15,601	419	4	415	0	0	1,838	61	11,749	14	14
27 E Garfield Park	16,267	755	11	741	2	1	11,144	52	11,069	4	19
28 Near West Side	31,225	911	165	718	23	5	22,293	377	21,472	415	29
29 North Lawndale	29,239	882	21	847	9	5	21,840	175	21,453	201	11
30 South Lawndale	8,351	270	108	63	95	4	5,705	1,233	994	3,465	13
31 Lower West Side	6,031	181	91	12	76	2	4,077	958	154	2,947	18
32 Loop	634	81	39	39	1	2	232	13	218	1	0
33 Near South Side	6,084	80	8	72	0	0	4,931	174	4,625	124	8
34 Armour Square	2,569	83	18	45	1	19	1,451	128	1,245	40	38
35 Douglas	16,912	370	7	360	1	2	11,594	44	11,523	9	18
36 Oakland	11,917	165	0	164	1	0	9,172	29	9,126	2	15
37 Fuller Park	2,744	113	3	110	0	0	1,637	5	1,631	1	0
38 Grand Boulevard	33,014	1,356	16	1,339	0	1	22,178	102	22,015	38	3
39 Kenwood	6,686	465	4	461	0	0	3,737	23	3,703	9	2

Table II-4. Recipients of Public Assistance, by Race and by Type of Assistance

Community Areas in City of Chicago, December, 1980

COMMUNITY AREA	Total	Aid to Aged, Blind and Disabled					Aid to Families with Dependent Children			
		Total	White	Black	Spanish	Other	Total	White	Black	Spanish	Other
40 Washington Park	18,558	719	5	714	0	0	13,036	58	12,956	22	0
41 Hyde Park	2,523	197	42	152	0	3	1,302	76	1,212	10	4
42 Woodlawn	16,008	10,411	46	994	0	1	9,143	49	9,074	7	13
43 South Shore	21,579	741	12	726	2	1	14,782	77	14,671	28	6
44 Chatham	7,665	456	12	444	0	0	4,652	23	4,624	0	5
45 Avalon Park	1,984	90	4	86	0	0	1,254	9	1,242	3	0
46 South Chicago	8,386	258	30	174	53	1	5,801	468	3,922	1,392	19
47 Burnside	937	24	3	21	0	0	701	10	678	13	0
48 Calumet Heights	2,194	98	4	92	2	0	1,390	21	1,306	63	0
49 Roseland	16,074	373	11	362	0	0	11,073	87	10,970	14	2
50 Pullman	1,737	35	8	25	2	0	1,236	45	1,117	14	0
51 South Deering	3,212	68	13	52	3	0	2,229	329	1,534	360	6
52 East Side	942	38	35	1	2	0	575	399	28	148	0
53 West Pullman	10,661	137	5	132	0	0	7,975	93	7,796	82	4
54 Riverdale	6,969	19	2	17	0	0	5,810	30	5,769	11	0
55 Hegewisch	405	20	16	2	2	0	197	175	17	5	0
56 Garfield Ridge	2,596	43	18	20	3	2	1,869	297	1,558	10	4
57 Archer Heights	286	13	11	0	2	0	136	119	3	14	0
58 Brighton Park	2,189	67	59	1	7	0	1,228	1,006	16	206	0
59 McKinley Park	1,229	36	33	1	2	0	782	649	14	115	4
60 Bridgeport	3,474	129	112	5	12	0	2,254	1,725	29	500	0
61 New City	12,697	372	190	146	32	4	9,316	2,464	4,961	1,840	51
62 West Elsdon	240	45	12	3	0	0	103	92	2	9	0
63 Gage Park	1,318	71	50	2	8	1	735	561	73	87	14
64 Clearing	604	26	23	3	0	0	324	283	7	34	0
65 West Lawn	396	16	15	1	0	0	153	149	3	1	0
66 Chicago Lawn	4,039	168	124	29	14	1	2,610	1,222	1,021	307	60
67 West Englewood	25,268	586	17	568	0	1	19,126	187	18,888	30	21
68 Englewood	28,931	1,062	10	1,051	0	1	21,194	68	21,085	25	16
69 Greater Grand Cr	13,811	713	9	702	0	2	8,949	47	8,893	7	2
70 Ashburn	823	38	28	10	0	0	202	109	85	8	0
71 Auburn Gresham	16,345	565	5	556	1	3	11,021	37	10,963	14	7
72 Beverly	635	21	8	13	0	0	414	56	349	6	3
73 Washington Hts	6,843	170	1	169	0	0	4,685	19	4,659	3	4
74 Mount Greenwood	333	14	170	12	2	0	155	137	18	0	0
75 Morgan Park	4,300	113	17	95	1	0	2,978	55	2,902	11	10
76 O'Hare Area	494	13	12	0	0	1	171	150	13	6	2
Uncategorized	26,549	797	433	293	44	27	13,689	6,149	6,241	1,125	174

Table II-4. Recipients of Public Assistance, by Race and by Type of Assistance:

Community Areas in City of Chicago, December, 1980

| | General Assistance | | | | | Medical Assistance No Grant | | | | |
Community Area	Total	White	Black	Spanish	Other	Total	White	Black	Spanish	Other
Chicago	72,758	9,580	56,349	6,195	334	78,976	28,782	41,904	6,904	1,345
1 Rogers Park	597	351	196	44	6	1,863	1,505	226	97	35
2 West Ridge	267	249	5	10	3	1,395	1,230	68	52	45
3 Uptown	3,091	1,536	966	379	110	5,062	3,683	744	340	295
4 Lincoln Square	265	218	13	36	6	800	685	17	51	47
5 North Center	334	231	10	90	3	610	448	30	103	29
6 Lake View	1,341	684	309	323	25	1,298	824	83	334	57
7 Lincoln Park	505	218	197	86	4	1,233	840	238	123	22
8 Near North	1,705	325	1,334	43	3	1,404	396	1,058	32	8
9 Edison Park	3	3	0	0	0	33	31	1	0	1
10 Norwood Park	16	15	0	1	0	138	132	0	2	4
11 Jefferson Park	20	19	1	0	0	68	59	0	6	3
12 Forest Glen	8	8	0	0	0	39	33	1	2	3
13 North Park	47	42	0	4	1	313	251	30	19	13
14 Albany Park	599	448	11	107	33	796	552	18	154	72
15 Portage Park	82	79	1	2	0	357	325	9	15	8
16 Irving Park	242	194	2	33	458	551	458	8	57	28
17 Dunning	50	50	0	0	191	222	191	9	16	6
18 Montclare	19	14	1	4	96	101	96	0	4	1
19 Belmont Cragin	117	94	2	20	478	554	478	13	50	13
20 Hermosa	223	98	5	119	153	285	153	7	114	11
21 Avondale	232	147	4	78	302	453	302	13	112	26
22 Logan Square	1,334	398	95	830	1,006	2,063	1,006	98	905	54
23 Humboldt Park	2,097	210	1,104	773	289	1,662	289	694	625	54
24 West Town	3,332	642	751	1,931	1,391	3,553	1,391	447	1,612	103
25 Austin	4,619	178	4,365	70	629	3,154	629	2,370	128	27
26 W Garfield Pk	1,846	8	1,833	2	14	898	14	881	0	3
27 E Garfield Pk	2,328	18	2,305	2	10	1,187	10	1,169	3	5
28 Near West Side	3,145	327	2,722	79	278	2,849	278	2,479	79	13
29 North Lawndale	3,166	30	3,114	20	92	2,014	92	1,929	18	2
30 South Lawndale	564	132	152	279	394	1,241	394	430	404	13
31 Lower West Side	500	136	21	342	260	707	260	63	372	12
32 Loop	239	83	148	8	0	49	22	25	1	1
33 Near South Side	344	8	332	4	0	406	4	398	0	4
34 Armour Square	186	27	147	5	7	518	83	322	12	101
35 Douglas	1,485	11	1,471	3	0	2,309	92	2,207	0	10
36 Oakland	961	5	956	0	0	1,014	5	1,007	0	2
37 Fuller Park	369	4	365	0	0	3,289	5	383	0	1
38 Grand Boulevard	4,202	27	4,168	6	1	3,213	56	3,150	5	2
39 Kenwood	1,103	4	1,097	2	0	953	106	840	4	3

Table II-4. Recipients of Public Assistance, by Race and by Type of Assistance:

Community Areas in City of Chicago, December, 1980

COMMUNITY AREA	General Assistance					Medical Assistance No Grant				
	Total	White	Black	Spanish	Other	Total	White	Black	Spanish	Other
40 Washington Park	2,350	18	2,331	1	0	1,456	9	1,443	1	3
41 Hyde Park	461	14	442	2	3	325	26	294	3	2
42 Woodlawn	2,758	9	2,745	3	1	1,803	172	1,626	0	5
43 South Shore	2,988	38	2,924	25	1	1,799	122	1,666	9	2
44 Chatham	1,182	3	1,179	0	0	775	10	762	3	0
45 Avalon Park	313	2	313	0	0	193	5	188	0	0
46 South Chicago	918	74	688	153	3	816	119	534	155	8
47 Burnside	111	1	110	0	0	67	2	65	0	0
48 Calumet Heights	294	3	285	6	0	233	14	207	11	1
49 Roseland	2,025	24	1,999	0	2	1,825	87	1,732	6	0
50 Pullman	231	27	196	2	6	141	23	117	1	0
51 South Deering	315	37	234	43	1	358	115	154	88	1
52 East Side	62	50	4	8	0	168	138	5	25	0
53 West Pullman	1,187	31	1,142	14	0	875	32	832	10	1
54 Riverdale	486	5	481	0	0	405	10	395	0	0
55 Hegewisch	54	48	2	4	0	82	71	6	5	0
56 Garfield Ridge	207	61	138	8	0	321	149	162	8	2
57 Archer Heights	37	33	4	0	0	65	62	0	3	0
58 Brighton Park	227	185	9	31	2	458	378	22	38	20
59 McKinley Prk	137	104	2	31	0	176	141	8	27	0
60 Bridgeport	322	242	9	70	1	493	380	18	84	11
61 New City	1,293	402	724	159	8	1,117	534	386	196	1
62 West Elsdon	28	26	1	0	1	55	53	0	0	2
63 Gage Park	136	94	15	25	2	249	205	14	25	5
64 Clearing	74	62	3	8	1	113	104	6	1	2
65 West Lawn	32	32	0	0	0	140	138	1	0	1
66 Chicago Lawn	459	225	165	64	5	509	351	114	34	10
67 West Englewood	2,914	44	2,860	5	5	1,737	35	1,697	2	3
68 Englewood	3,277	28	3,245	2	2	2,032	24	2,002	3	3
69 Greater Grand Cr	1,856	13	1,841	1	1	1,298	8	1,290	0	0
70 Ashburn	63	41	22	0	0	470	249	215	5	1
71 Auburn Gresham	2,128	14	2,114	0	0	1,700	53	1,643	3	1
72 Beverly	58	7	51	0	0	87	50	36	0	1
73 Washington Hts	855	5	848	1	1	727	37	686	1	3
74 Mount Greenwood	22	22	0	0	0	87	87	0	0	0
75 Morgan Park	475	12	463	0	0	436	58	376	1	1
76 O'Hare Area	2	2	0	0	0	268	261	0	5	2
Uncategorized	838	179	559	94	6	9,256	7,062	1,737	341	116

Table II-4. Recipients of Public Assistance, by Race and by Type of Assistance:

Community Areas in City of Chicago, December, 1980

Food Stamps, No Grant

Community Area	Total	White	Black	Spanish	Other
Chicago	38,199	8,295	25,856	3,698	350
1 Rogers Park	374	268	49	51	6
2 West Ridge	241	214	1	24	2
3 Uptown	1,419	793	252	285	89
4 Lincoln Square	189	132	3	48	6
5 North Center	288	206	8	71	3
6 Lake View	780	504	83	178	15
7 Lincoln Park	524	327	117	76	4
8 Near North	774	127	623	22	2
9 Edison Park	6	6	0	0	0
10 Norwood Park	24	24	0	0	0
11 Jefferson Park	36	32	0	3	1
12 Forest Glen	8	8	0	0	0
13 North Park	26	16	0	8	2
14 Albany Park	290	140	10	124	16
15 Portage Park	139	132	0	6	1
16 Irving Park	223	198	0	22	3
17 Dunning	69	66	0	3	0
18 Montclare	30	29	0	1	0
19 Belmont Cragin	177	155	1	20	1
20 Hermosa	128	80	0	48	0
21 Avondale	196	137	1	57	1
22 Logan Square	805	326	43	426	10
23 Humboldt Park	934	149	488	289	8
24 West Town	1,394	505	205	668	16
25 Austin	1,691	146	1,486	50	9
26 W Garfield Pk	600	2	596	0	2
27 E Garfield Pk	853	8	843	90	2
28 Near West Side	2,027	108	1,854	60	5
29 North Lawndale	1,310	10	1,274	16	10
30 South Lawndale	571	108	214	245	4
31 Lower West Side	566	152	85	382	1
32 Loop	33	14	19	0	0
33 Near South Side	323	11	310	0	2
34 Armour Square	331	59	219	10	43
35 Douglas	1,154	20	1,131	0	3
36 Oakland	605	0	604	0	1
37 Fuller Park	236	13	223	0	0
38 Grand Boulevard	2,065	24	2,035	2	4
39 Kenwood	428	4	423	1	0

Table II-4. Recipients of Public Assistance, by Race and by Type of Assistance:

Community Areas in City of Chicago, December, 1980

Food Stamps, No Grant

Community Area	Total	White	Black	Spanish	Other
40 Washington Park	997	12	982	0	3
41 Hyde Park	238	21	212	0	5
42 Woodlawn	1,263	5	1,255	0	3
43 South Shore	1,269	27	1,236	4	2
44 Chatham	600	2	595	3	0
45 Avalon Park	134	2	132	0	0
46 South Chicago	593	57	423	100	13
47 Burnside	34	0	34	0	0
48 Calumet Heights	179	9	160	9	1
49 Roseland	778	8	768	2	0
50 Pullman	94	9	85	0	0
51 South Deering	242	60	134	44	4
52 East Side	99	73	13	10	3
53 West Pullman	487	14	461	11	1
54 Riverdale	249	5	244	0	0
55 Hegewisch	52	39	8	5	0
56 Garfield Ridge	156	82	69	4	1
57 Archer Heights	35	33	1	1	0
58 Brighton Park	209	174	10	24	1
59 McKinley Park	98	84	4	10	0
60 Bridgeport	276	205	13	52	6
61 New City	599	280	209	108	2
62 West Elsdon	39	35	1	3	0
63 Gage Park	127	106	12	9	0
64 Clearing	67	59	6	2	0
65 West Lawn	55	49	4	1	1
67 West Englewood	905	52	847	4	2
68 Englewood	1,366	17	1,348	0	1
69 Greater Grand Cr	995	5	988	0	2
70 Ahsburn	50	18	32	0	0
71 Auburn Gresham	931	6	923	0	2
72 Beverly	55	20	35	0	0
73 Washington Hts	406	4	402	0	0
74 Mount Greenwood	55	45	10	0	0
75 Morgan Park	298	18	278	0	2
76 O'Hare	40	37	1	1	1
Uncategorized	1,969	1,162	651	135	21

Table II-5. Number of Parks and Acreage in Parks: Community Areas in the City of Chicago, 1980

Number of Parks

Community Area	Total	Sectional	Community	Minor	Acreage in Parks
1. Rogers Park.....	30	-	3	27	58.6
2. West Ridge......	12*	1	5*	6	184.2
3. Uptown..........	12	-	1	11	15.6
4. Lincoln Square..	8*	-	2*	6	55.9
5. North Center....	8	-	2	6	22.0
6. Lake View.......	12#	-	2	10	5.8
7. Lincoln Park....	16#	-	3	13	36.7
8. Near North Side.	11	-	3	8	28.3
9. Edison Park.....	4	-	2	2	20.6
10. Norwood Park....	11	-	3	8	51.4
11. Jefferson Park..	4	-	1	3	16.4
12. Forest Glen....	7	-	3	4	26.7
13. North Park......	7*	-	4*	3	93.4
14. Albany Park.....	8*	-	2*	6	25.0
15. Portage Park....	7	-	4	3	70.6
16. Irving Park.....	8	1	4	3	95.4
17. Dunning........	3	-	3	-	39.7
18. Montclare.......	3	-	1	2	11.1
19. Belmont Cragin..	4	1	1	2	66.2
20. Hermosa.........	2	-	2	-	12.8
21. Avondale........	9	-	2	7	11.3
22. Logan Square....	13	-	2	11	20.3
23. Humboldt Park...	16	-	2	14	16.7
24. West Town.......	17	1	5	11	249.2
25. Austin.........	22	1	3	18	199.3
26. W. Garfield Pk..	2	-	-	2	1.3
27. E. Garfield Pk..	11	1	1	9	194.8
28. Near West Side..	19	-	4	15	60.6
29. North Lawndale..	15	1	1	13	185.0
30. South Lawndale..	7	-	2	5	25.7
31. Lower West Side.	8	-	2	6	26.8
32. The Loop........	1#	-	-	1	.9
33. Near South Side.	2#	-	-	2	91.6
34. Armour Square...	4	-	1	3	13.3
35. Douglas.........	8#	-	6	2	65.6
36. Oakland.........	5#	-	-	5	14.4
37. Fuller Park.....	4	-	1	3	14.2
38. Grand Boulevard.	12	-	1	11	16.1
39. Kenwood.........	7#	-	1	6	16.7
40. Washington Pk...	3#	-	-	3	2.7

Table II-5. Number of Parks and Acreage in Parks:
Community Areas in the City of Chicago, 1980

Number of Parks

Community Area	Total	Sectional	Community	Minor	Acreage in Parks
41. Hyde Park........	10#	-	-	10	93.7
42. Woodlawn.........	11#	-	-	11	3.6
43. South Shore......	9	2	-	7	147.6
44. Chatham.........	6	-	2	4	49.3
45. Avalon Park.....	2	-	1	1	28.4
46. South Chicago...	4	-	2	2	38.3
47. Burnside........	1	-	-	1	5.5
48. Calumet Heights.	2	-	1	1	20.0
49. Roseland........	7	-	4	3	103.8
50. Pullman.........	4	-	1	3	27.4
51. South Deering...	6	-	1	5	31.3
52. East Side.......	6	1	1	4	225.1
53. West Pullman....	7	-	4	3	44.1
54. Riverdale.......	3	-	2	1	39.8
55. Hegewisch.......	2	-	1	1	20.3
56. Garfield Ridge..	6*	-	3	3	51.3
57. Archer Heights..	4	-	2	2	27.4
58. Brighton Park...	2	-	1	1	13.9
59. McKinley Park...	5	1	-	4	73.3
60. Bridgeport......	9	-	2	7	17.8
61. New City........	12	1	2	9	86.2
62. West Elsdon.....	2	-	1	1	21.0
63. Gage Park.......	3	-	1	2	34.6
64. Clearing........	4*	-	1	3	36.9
65. West Lawn.......	1	-	1	-	16.7
66. Chicago Lawn....	2#	-	-	2	.6
67. West Englewood..	8	1	1	6	85.9
68. Englewood.......	11	-	2	9	44.6
69. Gr Grand Cr.....	13	-	2	11	38.6
70. Ashburn.........	8	-	5	3	73.8
71. Auburn Gresham..	8	-	3	5	53.9
72. Beverly.........	9	-	3	6	39.6
73. Washington Hts..	5	-	2	3	40.3
74. Mount Greenwood.	2	-	1	1	26.2
75. Morgan Park.....	13	-	2	11	49.8
76. O'Hare..........	-	-	-	-	-
77. Edgewater.......	15	-	1	14	24.8
Chicago Total.......	580	13	138	429	7227.6

* This community shares a community or sectional park with another community.
# This community also contains all or a portion of a citywide park.
Note: Figures for Chicago Total include six citywide parks covering
3,322.6 acres which are not allocated to Community Areas.

343

Table II-6. Police Contacts with Juveniles and Juvenile Court Referrals, 1980, Chicage Community Areas

Community Area	Population Aged 10-17 (1980)	Police Contacts Total	Police Contacts Rate per 1000 Youth	Court Referrals Total	Court Referrals Rate per 1000 Youth
1. Rogers Park.....	3818	448	117.3	146	38.2
2. West Ridge......	5452	253	46.4	82	15.0
3. Uptown.........	4941	1268	256.6	447	90.5
4. Lincoln Square..	4223	420	99.5	121	28.6
5. North Center....	3866	723	187.0	257	66.5
6. Lake View.......	6627	955	144.1	308	46.5
7. Lincoln Park....	3266	371	113.6	145	44.4
8. Near North Side.	5041	1203	238.6	422	83.7
9. Edison Park.....	1547	45	29.1	11	7.1
10. Norwood Park....	4485	135	30.1	29	6.5
11. Jefferson Park..	2422	124	51.3	27	11.1
12. Forest Glen.....	2411	60	24.9	22	9.1
13. North Park......	1512	104	68.8	29	19.2
14. Albany Park.....	5300	740	139.6	231	43.6
15. Portage Park....	5981	410	68.6	122	20.4
16. Irving Park.....	5227	687	131.4	170	32.5
17. Dunning........	4220	206	48.8	56	13.3
18. Montclare.......	1131	31	27.4	10	8.8
19. Belmont Cragin..	5295	320	60.4	91	17.2
20. Hermosa........	2324	277	119.2	80	34.4
21. Avondale........	3474	403	116.0	125	36.0
22. Logan Square....	11070	1505	136.0	564	50.9
23. Humboldt Park...	11857	1420	119.8	547	46.1
24. West Town.......	14021	2115	150.9	632	45.1
25. Austin.........	22365	2655	118.7	912	40.8
26. W. Garfield Pk..	6473	674	104.1	214	33.1
27. E. Garfield Pk..	5515	863	156.5	287	52.0
28. Near West Side..	9731	2007	206.2	659	67.7
29. North Lawndale..	11937	1728	144.8	555	46.5
30. South Lawndale..	10065	1120	111.3	417	41.4
31. Lower West Side.	6221	478	76.8	126	20.3
32. The Loop........	98	31	316.3	10	102.0
33. Near South Side.	1188	292	245.8	64	53.9
34. Armour Square...	1657	113	68.2	46	27.8
35. Douglas.........	4374	1017	232.5	348	79.6
36. Oakland.........	3806	945	248.3	272	71.5
37. Fuller Park.....	963	196	203.5	54	56.1
38. Grand Boulevard.	9262	2867	309.5	1012	109.3
39. Kenwood.........	2244	339	151.1	94	41.9
40. Washington Pk...	5373	1651	307.3	614	114.3

Table II-6. Police Contacts with Juveniles and Juvenile Court Referrals, 1980, Chicage Community Areas

Community Area	Population Aged 10-17 (1980)	Police Contacts Total	Police Contacts Rate per 1000 Youth	Court Referrals Total	Court Referrals Rate per 1000 Youth
41. Hyde Park.......	2149	162	75.4	72	33.5
42. Woodlawn........	4894	743	151.8	304	62.1
43. South Shore.....	9811	1554	158.4	590	60.1
44. Chatham........	4185	513	122.6	161	38.5
45. Avalon Park.....	2180	242	111.0	100	45.9
46. South Chicago...	7038	1086	154.3	314	44.6
47. Burnside.......	754	83	110.1	18	23.9
48. Calumet Heights.	3438	329	95.7	65	18.9
49. Roseland.......	11514	1356	117.8	389	33.8
50. Pullman........	1752	108	61.6	27	15.4
51. South Deering...	3407	435	127.7	105	30.8
52. East Side.......	2696	246	91.3	53	19.7
53. West Pullman....	8566	957	111.7	285	33.3
54. Riverdale.......	3139	516	164.4	218	69.4
55. Hegewisch.......	1624	81	49.9	23	14.2
56. Garfield Ridge..	5074	359	70.8	97	19.1
57. Archer Heights..	932	35	37.6	11	11.8
58. Brighton Park...	3243	343	105.8	94	29.0
59. McKinley Park...	1619	206	127.2	65	40.1
60. Bridgeport......	3907	518	132.6	183	46.8
61. New City........	8414	1323	157.2	462	54.9
62. East Elsdon.....	1249	77	61.6	22	17.6
63. Gage Park.......	2650	285	107.6	106	40.0
64. Clearing........	2891	142	49.1	28	9.7
65. West Lawn.......	2916	143	49.0	32	11.0
66. Chicago Lawn....	5302	633	119.4	170	32.1
67. West Englewood..	12414	2021	162.8	675	54.4
68. Englewood.......	10214	1416	138.6	472	46.2
69. Gr Grand Cr.....	5493	744	135.4	221	40.2
70. Ashburn........	5589	239	42.8	71	12.7
71. Auburn Gresham..	10520	1048	99.6	303	28.8
72. Beverly........	3326	132	39.7	25	7.5
73. Washington Hts..	6371	610	95.8	186	29.2
74. Mount Greenwood.	2610	89	34.1	24	9.2
75. Morgan Park.....	4661	337	72.3	81	17.4
76. O'Hare..........	*	*	*	*	*
77. Edgewater.......	3842	490	127.5	147	38.3

* Not reported because of unreliable data

Source: Illinois Institute for Juvenile Research, Youth Problems in the City: A Data Inventory, 1980.

345

Table II-7. Geographical Area Cross-Reference

Tract Number	Congressional District 1982	Legislative District 1982	Wards, 1981	Police District	Public School District	Zipcode 606
CA01--Rogers Park						
0101	09	02	49	6-24	02	26
0102	09	02	49	6-24	02	26,45
0103	09	02	49	6-24	02	26
0104	09	02	49	6-24	02	26,60
0105	09	02	49	6-24	02	26,60
0106	09	02	49	6-24	02	26,60
0107	09	02	49,50	6-24	02	26,45
0108	09	02	49,50	6-24	02	26,60
0109	09	02	49	6-24	02	26,60
CA02--West Ridge						
0201	11	02	50	6-24	02	45
0202	11	02	50	6-24	02	45
0203	11	01,02	50	6-24	02	45
0204	11	02	50	6-24	02	45
0205	11	01,02	50	6-24	02	26,45,59,60
0206	11	01	50	6-24	02	45,59
0207	11	01,03	40,50	6-20,24	02	59
0208	11	01,03	40,50	6-20,24	02	59
0209	11	01	50	6-24	02	59,60
CA03--Uptown						
0310	11	03	47	6-19	02	40
0311	09	03	48	6-20	02	40
0312	09	03	48	6-20	02	40
0313	09	03	48	6-20	02	40
0314	09	03	46	6-20,23	02	13,40
0315	09	03	46,48	6-20	02	13,40
0316	09	03	46,48	6-20	02	13,40
C317	09	03	46	6-20	02	13,40
0318	11	03	47	6-19	02,03	40
0319	11	03	46,47	6-19,20	02,03	13,40
0320	09	03	46	6-23	02,03	13
C321	09	03	46	6-23	02	13
CA04--Lincoln Square						
0401	11	03	40	6-20	02	25,40
0402	11	03	40	6-19,20	01,02	25,59
0403	11	03	40	6-19,20	01,02	25,59
0404	11	03	40,47	6-19	02	25,40
0405	11	03	47	6-19	02,03	25,40
0406	11	03	47	6-19	02,03	25
0407	11	06	40	6-19	01	25
0408	11	03	47	6-19	01	18,25
0409	08	03	47	6-19	03	18,25
0410	11	03	47	6-19	03	13,25,40
CA05--North Center						
0501	08	03	47	6-19	03	13,,8
0502	08	03	47	6-19	03	18
0503	08	03	47	6-19	01	18
0504	08	03	47	6-19	03	18
0505	08	03	47	6-19	03	18
0506	08	03	47	6-19	03	13,18
0507	08	04	47	6-19	03	13,18,57
0508	08	04	47	6-19	03	18
0509	08	04	47	6-19	03	18
0510	08	04	32,47	6-19	03,05	18
0511	08	04	32,47	6-19	03,05	18
0512	08	04	32,47	6-19	03,05	18,57
0513	08,09	04	32	6-19	05	14,18,57
0514	08	04	32	6-19	05	18,47
0515	08	04	32	6-19	05	18

Table II-7. Geographical Area Cross-Reference

Tract Number	Congres-sional District 1982	Legisla-tive District 1982	Wards, 1981	Police District	Public School District	Zipcode 606
0601--LAKEVIEW						
0601	09	04	46	6-19,23	03	13,40
0602	08	03	47	6-19	03	13
0603	08	03,04	47	6-19	03	13
0604	08	04	46	6-19	03	13
0605	09	03	46	6-23	02,03	13
0606	09	03	46	6-23	02,03	13
0607	09	03	46	6-23	02	13
0608	09	03	46	6-23	02	13
0609	09	03	46	6-23	02,03	13,57
0610	09	03	46	6-23	03	13
0611	09	04	44	6-23	03	13
0612	09	04	44	6-19,23	03	13
0613	09	04	47	6-19	03	13,57
0614	09	04	44	6-19	03	13,57
0615	09	04	44	6-19	03	13,57
0616	09	04	44	6-23	03	13,57
0617	09	04	44	6-23	03	13,57
0618	09	03	46	6-23	02	13,57
0619	09	03	44	6-23	03	57
0620	09	04	44	6-23	03	57
0621	09	04	44	6-23	03	57
0622	09	04	44	6-19,23	03	57
0623	09	04	44	6-19	03	57
0624	09	04	44	6-19	03	57
0625	09	04	32	6-19	03,05	57
0626	09	04	32	6-19	03,05	14,57
0627	09	04	44	6-19	03,05	14,57
0628	09	04	44	6-19	03	14,57
0629	09	04	44	6-19,23	03	14,57
0630	09	04	44	6-19,23	03	14,57
0631	09	04	44	6-23	03	57
0632	09	03	44	6-23	03	57
0633	09	03,04	43,44	6-23	03	14,57
0634	09	04	44	6-23	03	14,57
CA07--Lincoln Park						
0701	09	04	43	6-23	03	14
0702	09	04	43	6-19,23	03	14
0703	09	04	43	6-19,23	03	14
0704	09	04	43	6-19	03	14
0705	08	04	43	6-19	03	14
0706	08	04	32,43	6-19	03	14
0707	08	04	32	6-19	05	14,47
0708	08	04	32	6-18	03,05	14
0709	09	04	43	6-18	03	14
0710	09	04	43	6-18	03	14
0711	09	04	43	6-18	03	14
0712	09	04	43	6-18	03	14
0713	09	04	43	6-18	03	14
0714	09	04	43	6-18	03	14
0715	09	04	43	6-18	03	14,22
0716	09	04	43	6-18	03	14
0717	09	04	43	6-18	03	10,14
0718	09	04	42,43	6-18	03	10,14
0719	09	04	42	6-18	03	14,22
0720	09	04	42	6-18	03	14,22

Table II-7. Geographical Area Cross-Reference

Tract Number	Congressional District 1982	Legislative District 1982	Wards, 1981	Police District	Public School District	Zipcode 606
CA08--Near North Side						
0801	09	04	43	6-18	03	10
0802	09	04	42,43	6-18	03	10
0803	09	04	42	6-18	03	10
0804	07	04	42	6-18	03	10
0805	07	04	43	6-18	03	10
0806	07	04	42	6-18	03	22
0807	07	04	42	6-18	03	10,22
0808	07	04	42	6-18	03	10
0809	07	04	42	6-18	03	10
0810	07	04	42	6-18	03	10
0811	07	04	42	6-18	03	10
0812	07	04	42,43	6-18	03	10,11
0813	07	04	42,43	6-18	03	11
0814	07	04	42	6-18	03	11
0815	07	04	42	6-18	03	10,11
0816	07	04	42	6-18	03	10
0817	07	04	42	6-18	03	10
0818	07	04	42	6-18	03	10
0819	07	04	42	6-18	03	10
CA09--Edison Park						
0901	11	07	41	5-16	01	48
0902	11	07	41	5-16	01	31,48
0903	11	07	41	5-16	01	31
CA10--Norwood Park						
1001	11	07	41,45	5-16	01	46
1002	11	07	41	5-16	01	31,46
1003	11	07	41	5-16	01	31,46
1004	11	07	41	5-16	01	31
1005	11	07	41	5-16	01	31,56
1006	11	07	41,45	5-16	01	30,56
1007	11	07	45	5-16	01	30,56
CA11--Jefferson Park						
1101	11	07	41,45	5-16	01	30,46
1102	11	07	45	5-16	01	30,46
1103	11	07	45	5-16	01	30,31,56
1104	11	07	45	5-16	01	30
1105	11	07	45	5-16	01	30
CA12--Forest Glen						
1201	11	07	41	5-16	01	46,48
1202	11	01	39	5-16	01	46
1203	11	01	39	5-17	01	46,59
1204	11	01,07	45	5-16	01	30,46
CA13--North Park						
1301	11	01	39,40	5-17	01	46,59
1302	11	01	39	5-17	01	30,46
1303	11	01	39,40	5-17	01	59
1304	11	03	40	5-17	01	25
1305	11	01	39	5-17	01	25,30,59
CA14--Albany Park						
1401	11	03	40	5-17	01	25
1402	11	01	39	5-17	01	25
1403	11	01	39	5-17	01	25,30
1404	11	01	39	5-17	01	30
1405	11	01	39	5-17	01	30,41
1406	11	01	39	5-17	01	18,25,30
1407	11	01	39,40	5-17	01	18,25
1408	11	06	40	5-17	01	18,25

Table II-7. Geographical Area Cross-Reference

Tract Number	Congres- sional District 1982	Legisla- tive District 1982	Wards, 1981	Police District	Public School District	Zipcode 606
CA15--Portage Park						
1501	11	01	45	5-17	01	41
1502	11	01,07	45	5-16	01	30,41
1503	11	07	38,45	5-16	01	30,34,41
1504	11	07	38,45	5-16	01	30,34
1505	11	07	38	5-16	01	30,34
1506	11	07	38	5-16	01	34
1507	11	07	38	5-16	04	34,41
1508	11	07	38,45	5-16	04	41
1509	11	01	38,45	5-17	04	41
1510	08	06	30,38	5-16,17	04	41
1511	11	06	38	5-16	04	34,41
1512	11	06	38	5-16	04	34
CA16--Irving Park						
1601	11	01	45	5-17	01	30,41
1602	11	01	45	5-17	01	30,41
1603	08	01	33	5-17	01	41
1604	08	01	33	5-17	01	18,41
1605	08	01	33	5-17	01	18
1606	08	06	33,40	5-17	01	18
1607	08	06	33	5-17	01	18
1608	08	06	33,35	5-17	01	18
1609	08	01	35	5-17	01	18,41
1610	08	01	35	5-17	04	41
1611	08	01	35	5-17	04	41
1612	08	06	30	5-17	04	41
1613	08	06	30	5-17	04	41
CA17--Dunning						
1701	11	07	38	5-16	01	34,56
1702	11	07	38	5-16	01	34
1703	11	07	38	5-16	01	34
1704	11	08	38	5-16	01	34
1705	11	08	38	5-16	01	34
1706	11	08	36	5-16	01	34
1707	11	08	36	5-16	04	34
1708	11	08	36	5-16	04	34
1709	08	08	36	5-25	04	34,35
1710	11	07,08	36,38	5-16	04	34
1711	11	07	38	5-16	04	34
CA18--Montclare						
1801	08	08	36	5-25	04	34,35
1802	08	08	36	5-25	04	35
1803	08	08	36	5-25	04	35
CA19--Belmont Cragin						
1901	08	06	30	5-25	04	41
1902	08	06	30	5-25	04	39,41
1903	08	06	36,37	5-25	04	34,39,41
1904	08	06,08	36	5-25	04	34,39
1905	08	08	36	5-25	04	34,35
1906	08	06,08	36	5-25	04	39
1907	08	06	37	5-25	04	39
1908	08	06	30	5-25	04	39
1909	08	06	30	5-25	04,05	39
1910	08	06	30	5-25	05	39
1911	08	06	30,37	5-25	04	39
1912	08	06	37	5-25	04	39
1913	08	06,08	36,37	5-25	04	39
1914	08	08	36	5-25	04	35,39
CA20--Hermosa						
2001	08	06	30	5-25	04	39,41
2002	08	06	30	5-25	04,05	39
2003	08	06	30	5-25	05	39
2004	08	06	35,30	5-25	05	39,47
2005	08	06	30	5-25	05	39
2006	08	05	35	5-25	05	39,47

Table II-7. Geographical Area Cross-Reference

Tract Number	Congressional District 1982	Legislative District 1982	Wards, 1981	Police District	Public School District	Zipcode 606
CA21--Avondale						
2101	08	06	33	5-17	01,05	18
2102	08	06	35	5-17	01,05	18
2103	08	01,06	35	5-17	01,05	18,41
2104	08	06	30	5-25	04	41
2105	08	06	35	5-25	05	18,41,47
2106	08	06	05	5-14	05	18,47
2107	08	06	33	5-14	05	18,47
2108	08	06	33	5-14	05	18,47
2109	08	04	33	5-14	05	18,47
CA22--Logan Square						
2201	08	06	32	5-14	05	14,47
2202	08	06	32	5-14	05	47
2203	08	06	32	5-14	05	47
2204	08	06	33	5-14	05	47
2205	08	06	33	5-14	05	47
2206	08	06	35	5-14	05	47
2207	08	06	30,35	5-25	05	39,47
2208	08	06	30	5-25	04,05	39
2209	08	06	35	5-25	05	39,47
2210	08	05	35	5-14	05	47
2211	08	05,06	35	5-14	05	47
2212	08	05,06	33	5-14	05,06	47
2213	08	05,06	33	5-14	05,06	47
2214	08	05,06	33	5-14	05,06	47
2215	08	05,06	32	5-14	05,06	47
2216	08	05,06	32	5-14	05,06	47
2217	08	05	32	5-14	05	47
2218	08	05	32	5-14	05	14,22,47
2219	08	05	32	5-14	06	22
2220	08	05	32	5-14	06	22,47
2221	08	05	32	5-14	06	47
2222	08	05	32	5-14	06	47
2223	08	05	32	5-14	06	47
2224	08	05	33	5-14	06	47
2225	08	05	33	5-14	06	47
2226	08	05	33	5-14	06	47
2227	08	05	31	5-14	05	47
2228	08	05	31,35	5-14	05	47
2229	08	05	35	5-25	05	47
CA23--Humboldt Park						
2301	08	05	31	5-14	06	47
2302	08	05	31	5-14	05	47
2303	08	05	31	5-14	05	47
2304	08	05	30,31	5-25	05	39,47
2305	08	05,06	30	5-25	05	39
2306	08	05,06	30,37	5-25	05	39,51
2307	08	05	31	5-25	05	47,51
2308	08	05	31	5-14	05	47,51
2309	08	05	31	5-14	05	47,51
2310	08	05	31	4-11	05	51
2311	08	05	31	4-11	05	51
2312	08	05,09	31	4-11	05	51
2313	08	05	30,37,31	4-11	05	51
2314	07	09	38	4-11	05	24
2315	07	09	27,28	4-11	05,07	24,51
2316	07	10	27	4-11	05,07	12,24,51
2317	07	10	26,27	4-13	05	12,22
2318	08	05	31	4-13	06	22,51
CA24--West Town						
2401	08	05	32	5-14	06	22
2402	08	05	32	5-14	06	22
2403	08	05	32	5-14	06	22,47
2404	08	05	32	5-14	06	47

Table II-7. Geographical Area Cross-Reference

Tract Number	Congressional District 1982	Legislative District 1982	Wards, 1981	Police District	Public School District	Zipcode 606
CA24--WEST TOWN						
2405	08	05	32	5-14	06	47
2406	08	05	31	5-14	06	47
2407	08	05	31	5-14	06	47
2408	08	05	31	5-14	06	47
2409	08	05	31	4-13,5-14	06	22,47,51
2410	08	05	31	5-14	06	22,47
2411	08	05	26	5-14	06	22,47
2412	08	05	32	5-14	06	22,47
2413	08	05	32	5-14	06	22,47
2414	08	05	26	5-14	06	22,47
2415	08	05	26,32	5-14	06	22
2416	08	05	32	5-14	06	22
2417	08	05	32	5-14	06	22
2418	08	05	26	4-13	06	10,22
2419	08	05	26	4-13	06	22
2420	08	05	26	4-13	06	22
2421	08	05	26	4-13	06	22
2422	08	05	26	4-13	06	22
2423	08	05	26	4-13	06	22
2424	08	05	26	4-13	06	22
2425	08	05	26	4-13	06	22
2426	08	05	26,31	4-13,5-14	06	22
2427	08	05	31	4-13	06	22
2428	08	05	26	4-13	05,06	12,22
2429	08	05	26	4-13	06	12,22
2430	08	05	26	4-13	06	12,22
2431	08	05	26	4-13	06	22
2432	08	05	26	4-13	06	22
2433	08	05	26	4-13	06	22
2434	08	05	26	4-13	06	22
2435	08	05	26	4-13	06	22
2436	08	05	26	4-13	06	10
CA25--Austin						
2501	08	06	30,37	5-25	05	39
2502	08	06	37	5-25	04	39
2503	08	06	37	5-25	04	39
2504	08	06,08	36,37	5-25	04	39
2505	08	08	36	5-25	04	35,39
2506	07	08	37	5-25	04	39,51
2507	07	08	37	5-25	04	39,51
2508	07	06,08	37	5-25	04	39,51
2509	07	06	37	5-25	04,05	39,51
2510	07	06	37	4-11,5-25	04,05	51
2511	07	08	28,37	5-15	04	51
2512	07	08	37	5-15	04	51
2513	07	08	37	5-15	04	51
2514	07	08	39	5-15	07	44,51
2515	07	08	29	5-15	04,07	44,51
2516	07	08	28	5-15	07	44,51
2517	07	09	28	4-11,5-15	05,07	44,51
2518	07	09	28,29	4-11,5-15	07	44
2519	07	08	29	5-15	07	44
2520	07	08	29	5-15	07	44
2521	07	09	39	5-15	07	44
2522	07	09	28,29	4-11,5-15	07	44
2523	07	09	24,28,29	4-11,5-15	07,10	44
2524	07	09	29	5-15	07	44,50
CA26--West Garfield Park						
2601	07	09	28	4-11	07	24
2602	07	09	28	4-11	07	24
2603	07	09	28	4-11	07	24
2604	07	09	28	4-11	07	24
2605	07	09	28	4-11	07,10	24,44
2606	07	09	28	4-11	07	24
2607	07	09	28	4-11	07	24
2608	07	09	28	4-11	07	24
2609	07	09	24	4-11	10	24
2610	07	09	24	4-11	07,10	24

Table II-7. Geographical Area Cross-Reference

Tract Number	Congres- sional District 1982	Legisla- tive District 1982	Wards, 1981	Police District	Public School District	Zipcode 606
CA27--East Garfield Park						
2701	07	10	27	4-13	09	12
2702	07	10	27	4-13	07,09	12
2703	07	10	27,28	4-11	07	12,24
2704	07	09	27,28	4-11	07	24
2705	07	09	27,28	4-11	07,10	24
2706	07	10	27	4-11	07	12,24
2707	07	10	27	4-13	09	12
2708	07	10	27	4-13	09	12
2709	07	10	27	4-13	09	12
2710	07	10	27	4-11	09	12
2711	07	10	27	4-11	09	12
2712	07	10	27	4-11	09	12
2713	07	10	27	4-11	07	12,24
2714	07	09,10	27	4-11	07	24
2715	07	09	24	4-11	10	24
2716	07	10	24,27	4-11	10,09	12,24
2717	07	10	27	4-11	09,08	12
2718	07	10	25	4-11	09,08	12
2719	07	10	25	4-11	09	12
CA28--Near West Side						
2801	07	10	27	4-12	09	06
2802	07	10	27	4-12	09	06,22
2803	07	10	27	4-12,13	09	06
2804	07	10	27	4-13	09	12
2805	07	10	27	4-13	09	12
2806	07	10	27	4-13	09	12
2807	07	10	27	4-13	09	12
2808	07	10	37	4-11	09	12
2809	07	10	27	4-12	09	12
2810	07	10	27	4-13	09	12
2811	07	10	27	4-13	09	12
2812	07	10	27	4-12	09	12
2813	07	10	27	4-12	09	12
2814	07	10	27	4-13	09	12
2815	07	10	27	4-12,13	09	12
2816	07	10	27	4-12,13	09	07,12
2817	07	10	27	4-12	09	06
2818	07	10	27	4-12	09	06,07
2819	07	10	27	4-12,1-01	09	06,07
2820	07	10	27	4-12,1-01	09	07
2821	07	10	01	4-12	09	07
2822	07	10	01	4-12	09	07
2823	07	10	01	4-12	09	07
2824	07	10	27	4-12	09	07
2825	07	10	27	4-12	09	12
2826	07	10	27	4-12	09	12
2827	07	10	25	4-11	08,09	08,12
2828	07	10	25	4-12	09	08,12
2829	07	10	25	4-12	09	07,12
2830	07	10	25	4-12	09	07,12
2831	07	10	01	4-12	09	07
2832	07	10	01	4-12	09	07,08
2833	07	10	01	4-12	09	07
2834	07	10	01	4-12	09	07
2835	07	10	01	4-12,1-01	09	07
2836	07	10	01	4-12,1-01	09	07,16
2837	07	10	01	4-12	09	07,08
2838	07	10	01	4-12	09	08
2839	07	10	01	4-12	08,09	08
2840	07	10	25	4-12	08,09	08
2841	07	10	25	4-12	09	08
2842	07	10	25	4-12	09	08
2843	07	10	25	4-10	08	08
CA29--North Lawndale						
2901	07	10	25	4-11	08,09	08,12
2902	07	10	25	4-11	08	12
2903	07	09	24	4-11	08	12
2904	07	09	24	4-11	10	24

Table II-7. Geographical Area Cross-Reference

Tract Number	Congres- sional District 1982	Legisla- tive District 1982	Wards, 1981	Police District	Public School District	Zipcode 606
CA29--North Lawndale						
2905	07	09	24	4-11	10	24
2906	07	09	24	4-11	10	24
2907	07	09	24	4-11	10	24
2908	07	09	24	4-11	10	24
2909	07	09	24	4-10	10	23,24
2910	07	09	24	4-10	10	23
2911	07	09	24	4-10	10	23,24
2912	07	09	24	4-10	10	23,24
2913	07	09	24	4-10	08,10	23
2414	07	09	24,25	4-10	08	12,23
2915	07	10	25	4-10	08	08
2916	07	10	25	4-10	08	08
2917	07	09	24,25	4-10	08	23
2918	07	09	24	4-10	08,10	23
2919	07	09	22,24	4-10	08,10	23
2920	07	09	22	4-10	08,10	23
2921	07	09	24	4-10	10	23
2922	07	09	24	4-10	10	23
2923	07	09	24	4-10	10	23
2424	07	09	24	4-10	10	23
2925	07	09	24	4-10	10	23
2926	07	11	22	4-10	10	23
2927	07	11	27	4-10	10	23
CA30--South Lawndale						
3001	05	10	25	4-10	08	08
3002	05	10	25	4-10	08	08,23
3003	07	10	22	4-10	08	23
3004	07	09	22	4-10	08,10	23
3005	05	11	22	4-10	10	23
3006	05	10	22	4-10	10	23
3007	05	10	22	4-10	10	23
3008	05	10	22	4-10	10	23
3009	05	10	22	4-10	08	23
3010	05	10	25	4-10	08	08,23
3011	05	10	22	4-10	08	08,23
3012	05	10	25	4-10	08	08
3013	05	11	25,12	4-10,3-09	08	08,23
3014	05	11	12	4-10	08	23
3015	05	10	12	4-10	10	23
3016	05	11	12	4-10	10	23
3017	05	11	22	4-10	10	23
3018	05	11	22	4-10	10	23
3019	05	11	22	4-10,3-08	10,12	23
3020	05	11	12	4-10,3-08	10,12	23,32
CA31--Lower West Side						
3101	07	10	01	4-12	08	16
3102	07	10	01	4-12	08	08,16
3103	05	10	01	4-12	08	08
3104	05	10	01	4-12	08	08
3105	05	10	01	4-12	08	08
2106	05	10	01	4-12	08	08
3107	05	10	25,01	4-12	08	08
3108	05	10	25	4-12	08	08
3109	05	10	25	4-12	08	08
3110	05	10	25	4-12	08	08
3111	05	10	25	4-10	08	08
3112	05	10	25	4-10	08	08
3113	05	10,11	25,11,12	4-10,3-09	08	08
3114	05	10,11	25,11,12	4-10,3-09	08	08
3115	05	10	01	4-12	08	08
CA32--Loop						
3201	07	10	01	1-01	11	01,11
3201.99	07	10	01	1-01	11	01,11
3202	07	10	01	1-01	11	01,06
3203	07	10	01	1-01	11	06
3204	07	10	01	1-01	11	04,05
3205	07	10	01	1-01	11	04,05,06,07
3206	07	10	01	1-01	11	05

Table II-7. Geographical Area Cross-Reference

Tract Number	Congressional District 1982	Legislative District 1982	Wards, 1981	Police District	Public School District	Zipcode 606
CA33--Near South Side						
3301	07	10	01	1-01,21	11	05,16
3302	07	10	01	1-01,21	11	05,16
3303	01	10	01	1-21	11	16
3304	01	12	01	1-21	11	16
3305	01	12	01	1-21	11	16
CA34--Armour Square						
3401	07	10	01	1-21,3-09	11	16
3402	01,05	10	01	1-21,3-09	11	16
3403	05	10	01	1-21	11	16
3404	01,05	10	01	1-21	11	16
3405	01,05	11	11	3-09	11	16
3406	01	12	02,11	3-09	11	09,16
CA35--Douglas						
3501	01	12	02	1-21	11	16
3502	01	12	02	1-21	11	16
3503	01	12	02	1-21	11	16
3504	01	12	01	1-21	11	16
3505	01	12	11	1-21	11	16
3506	01	12	02	1-21	11	16
3507	01	12	02	1-21	11	16
3508	01	12	02	1-21	11	16
3509	01	12	02	1-21	11	16
3510	01	12	02	1-21	11	16
3511	01	12	02	1-02	11	16,53
3512	01	12	02	1-02	11	16,53
3513	01	12	02	1-02	11	16,53
3514	01	12	02	1-02	11	09,16,53
3515	01	12	02	1-02	11	09
CA36--Oakland						
3601	01	12	02	1-21	11	16,53
3602	01	12	02	1-21,02	11	53
3603	01	12	02	1-21	11	53
3604	01	12	04	1-21	11,14	53
3605	01	12	04	1-21	11,14	53
CA37--Fuller Park						
3701	01	12	11	3-09	13	09
3702	01	12	03,11	3-09	13	09
3706	01	12	03	1-02,3-09	13	09
3704	01	12	03	1-02,3-09	13	09
CA38--Grand Boulevard						
3801	01	12	04	1-02	11,14	53
3802	01	12	02	1-02	11,14	53
3803	01	12	02	1-02	11,14	53
3804	01	12	02	1-02	11,13	09,53
3805	01	12	02	1-02	13	09
3806	01	12	02	1-02	13	09
3807	01	12	03	1-02	13	09,53
3808	01	12	03	1-02	14	53
3809	01	12	03,04	1-02	14	53
3810	01	12	03,04	1-02	14	53
3811	01	12	03,04	1-02	14	53
3812	01	12	03,04	1-02	13,14	15,53
3813	01	12	03	1-02	13,14	15,53
3814	01	12	03	1-02	13,14	09,15,53
3815	01	12	03	1-02	13	09,53
3816	01	12	03	1-02	13	09
3817	01	12	03	1-02	13	09
3818	01	12	03	1-02	13	15
3819	01	12	04	1-02	13	15
3820	01	12	04	1-02	13	15,53
CA39--Kenwood						
3901	01	12	04	1-21	14	53
3902	01	12	04	1-21	14	53
3903	01	12	04	1-21	14	53
3904	01	12	04	1-21	13,14	15,53
3905	01	13	04	1-21	14	15,53
3906	01	13	04	1-21	14	15
3907	01	13	04	1-21	14	15

Table II-7. Geographical Area Cross-Reference

Tract Number	Congres- sional District 1982	Legisla- tive District 1982	Wards, 1981	Police District	Public School District	Zipcode 606
CA40--Washington Park						
4001	01	12	03	1-02	13	09,15
4002	01	12	03	1-02	13	09
4003	01	12	04,20	1-02,03	13,14	09,15,37
4004	01	12	03,20	1-02	13	37
4005	01	12	03,20	1-02	13	37,21
4006	01	12	03	1-02,03	13,16	21
4007	01	12	20	1-03	13,16	21,37
4008	01	16	20	1-03	13,16	21,37
CA41--Hyde Park						
4101	01	13	04	1-21	14	15
4102	01	13	04	1-21	14	15
4103	01	12	04	1-21	14	15
4104	01	12	04	1-21	13,14	15
4105	01	12,13	04	1-21	13,14	15
4106	01	13	04	1-21	14	15
4107	01	13	04	1-21	14	15
4108	01	13	04	1-21	14	15,37
4109	01	13	04,05	1-21	14	15,37
4110	01	13	05	1-21,03	14	15,37
4111	01	13	04,05	1-21	14	37
4112	01	13	05	1-21	14	15,37
4113	01	13	05	1-21	14	15,37
4114	01	13	05	1-21	14	15,37
CA42--Woodlawn						
4201	01	13	05	1-21,03	14	37
4202	01	13	05,20	1-21,03	14	37
4203	01	13	20	1-21,03	14	37
4204	01	13	20	1-21,03	14	37
4205	01	16	20	1-03	14	37
4206	01	16	20	1-03	13,14	37
4207	01	16	20	1-03	14	37,49
4208	01	13	20	1-03	14	37,49
4209	01	13	20	1-03	14	37,49
4210	01	13	20	1-03	14	37,49
4211	01	13	05,20	1-03	14	37,49
4212	01	16	05,20	1-03	14,17	37
CA43--South Shore						
4301	01	13	05	1-03	17	49
4302	01	13	05	1-03	14,17	49
4303	01	13	20	1-03	14	37,19,49
4304	01	13	06	1-03	17	19,49
4305	01	13	05	1-03	17	49
4306	01	13	05	1-03	17	49
4307	01	13	05	1-03	17	49
4308	01	13	05	1-03	17	49
4309	01	13	05	1-03	17	49
4310	01	13	06	2-04	17	19
4311	01	13	08	2-04	17	49
4312	01	13	05,08	2-04	17	49
4313	02	13	07	1-03,2-04	17	49
4314	02	13	05,07	1-03,2-04	17	49
CA44--Chatham						
4401	01	13	08	2-04,06	17	19
4402	01	18	06	2-06	17	19
4403	01	16	06	2-06	17	19
4404	01	16	17	2-06	16,18	20
4405	01	18	21	2-06	18	20
4406	01	18	06	2-06	17,19	19
4407	01	18	06	2-06	17	19
4408	01	18	08	2-04,06	17,19	19
4409	01	18	06	2-06	19	19
CA45--Avalon Park						
4501	01	13	06	2-04	17	19
4502	01	13	08	2-04	17	17,19
4503	01	13	08	2-04	17,19	17

Table II-7. Geographical Area Cross-Reference

Tract Number	Congressional District 1982	Legislative District 1982	Wards, 1981	Police District	Public School District	Zipcode 606
CA46--South Chicago						
4601	02	18	07,10	2-04	17,19	17,49
4602	02	18	07	2-04	17,19	17
4603	02	13	07	2-04	17,19	17,49
4604	02	13	07	2-04	17,19	17,49
4605	01	13	08	2-04	17,19	17,49
4606	02	18	07	2-04	19	17
4607	02	18	07	2-04	19	17
4608	02	18	10	2-04	19	17
4609	02	18	07	2-04	19	17
4610	02	18	10	2-04	19	17
CA47--Burnside						
4701	01	18	08	2-04	17,19	19
CA48--Calumet Heights						
4801	01	18	08	2-04	17,19	17
4802	01	18	08	2-04	17	17,19
4803	01	18	08	2-04	19	17,19
4804	01	18	07,08,10	2-04	19	17
4805	02	18	07	2-04	19	17
CA49--Roseland						
4901	01	18	21	2-06	18	20
4902	01	18	21	2-06	18	20,28
4903	01	18	06	2-06	18,19	19
4904	01	18	06	2-06	19	19
4905	01	17	06	2-05	18,19	19,28
4906	01	17	21	2-05	18	28
4907	01	17	21	2-05	18	28
4908	01	17	06,08,21	2-05	18,19	28
4909	02	17	09	2-05	20	28
4910	02	17	34	2-05	20	28
4911	02	17	34	2-22	18,20	28
4912	02	17	34	2-22	18,20	28
4913	02	17	34	2-05	20	28
4914	02	17	09	2-05	20	28
CA50--Pullman						
5001	01	18	08	2-05	19	19,28
5002	02	17	09	2-05	20	28
5003	02	17	09	2-05	20	28
CA51--South Deering						
5101	02	18	10	2-04	19	17
5102	02	18	10	2-04	19	17
5103	01	18	10	2-04	19	17
5104	02	18	09,10	2-04	19,20	17,28,33
5104.99	02	18	09,10	2-04	19,20	17,28,33
5105	02	18	10	2-04	19	17
CA52--East Side						
5201	02	18	10	2-04	19	17
5202	02	18	10	2-04	19	17
5202.99	02	18	10	2-04	19	17
5203	02	18	10	2-04	19	17
5204	02	18	10	2-04	19	17
5205	02	18	10	2-04	19,20	17
5206	02	18	10	2-04	19,20	17
CA53--West Pullman						
5301	02	17	09	2-05	20	28
5302	02	17	34	2-05	18,20	28
5303	02	17	34	2-05	18	28,43
5304	02	17	34	2-05	18	28,43
5305	02	17	09,34	2-05	18,20	28,43
5306	02	17	09	2-05	20	28
CA54--Riverdale						
5401	02	17	09	2-05	20	27,28

Table II-7. Geographical Area Cross-Reference

Tract Number	Congres- sional District 1982	Legisla- tive District 1982	Wards, 1981	Police District	Public School District	Zipcode 606
CA55--Hegewisch						
5501	02	18	10	2-04	20	17,33
5502	02	18	10	2-04	20	28,33
CA56--Garfield Ridge						
5601	05	24	22	3-08,4-10	10,12	32
5602	05	24	22	3-08	12	38
5603	05	24	23	3-08	12	38
5604	05	24	23	3-08	12	32
5605	05	24	23	3-08	12	32
5606	05	24	23	3-08	12	38
5607	05	24	23	3-08	12	38
5608	05	24	23	3-08	12	38
5609	05	24	23	3-08	12	38
5610	05	24	23	3-08	12	38
5611	05	24	23	3-08	12	38
5612	05	24	23	3-08	12	38
5613	03	24	23	3-08	12	32,38
CA57--Archer Heights						
5701	05	11,24	12	3-08	12	32
5702	05	11,24	22,23	3-08	12	32
5703	05	24	23	3-08	12	32
5704	05	24	23	3-08	12	32
5705	05	24	23	3-08	12	32
CA58--Brighton Park						
5801	05	11	12	3-09	08	32
5802	05	11	12	3-09	08	32
5803	05	11	12	3-08	12	32
5804	05	11	12	3-08	12	32
5805	05	11	12	3-09	08	32
5806	05	11	12	3-09	08	32
5807	05	11	12	3-09	08	09,32
5808	05	11	12	3-09	08	09,32
5809	05	11	12	3-09	08	32
5810	05	24	12	3-08	12	32
5811	05	11	14	3-09	08	09,32
CA59--McKinley Park						
5901	05	11	11	3-09	11	08,09
5902	05	11	11	3-09	11	08,09
5903	05	11	12	3-09	08,11	08,09
5904	05	11	12	3-09	08	08,09,32
5905	05	11	12	3-09	08,11	09
5906	05	11	12	3-09	11	09
5907	05	11	11	3-09	11	09
CA60--Bridgeport						
6001	05	11	11	3-09	11	16
6002	05	11	11	3-09	11	16
6003	05	11	11	3-09	11	16
6004	05	11	11	3-09	11	08,16
6005	05	11	11	3-09	11	16
6006	05	11	11	3-09	11	08
6007	05	11	11	3-09	11	08
6008	05	11	11	3-09	11	08,09,16
6009	05	11	11	3-09	11	08
6010	05	11	11	3-09	11	16,08
6011	05	11	11	3-09	11	16
6012	05	11	11	3-09	11	16
6013	05	11	11	3-09	11	08,16
6014	05	11	11	3-09	11	09
6015	05	11	11	3-09	11	09,16
6016	05	11	11	3-09	11	09

Table II-7. Geographical Area Cross-Reference

Tract Number	Congres- sional District 1982	Legisla- tive District 1982	Wards, 1981	Police District	Public School District	Zipcode 606
CA61--New City						
6101	05	11	11	3-09	11,13	09
6102	05	11	11	3-09	13	09
6103	05	11	12	3-09	08,13	09
6104	05	11	11,12	3-09	13	09
6105	05	11	11	3-09	13	09
6106	05	11	11	3-09	13	09
6107	05	11	11	3-09	13	09
6108	05	11	11	3-09	13	09
6109	01	11	11	3-09	12,13	09
6110	01	11	11	3-09	12,13	09
6111	05	11	14	3-09	12,13	09
6112	05	11	14	3-09	12,13	09
6113	05	11	14	3-09	12,13	09
6114	05	11	14	3-09	08,12	09
6115	05	11	12,14	3-09	08,12	09
6116	05	11	14	3-09	12	09
6117	05	11	14	3-09	12	09
6118	05	11	14	3-09	12	09
6119	05	11	14	3-09	12	09
6120	01	12	11	3-09	12	09
6121	01	12	03,11	3-09	12	09
6122	01	12	03,11	3-09	13	09
CA62--West Elsdon						
6201	05	24	23	3-08	12	32
6202	05	24	23	3-08	12	32
6203	03	15	13	3-08	12	29,32
6204	03	24	23	3-08	12	29,32
CA63--Gage Park						
6301	05	11	14	3-09	12	09
6302	05	11	14	3-09	12	09,32
6303	05	24	12,13	3-08	12	32
6304	05	11	12,13	3-09	12	32
6305	05	11	13	3-09	12	09,32
6306	03	15	14	3-08	12	36
6307	03	11	14	3-08	12	29,32,36
6308	03	11	14	3-08	12	29,32
6309	03	24	13	3-08	12	29,32
CA64--Clearing						
6401	03	15	13	3-08	12,15	29,38
6402	03	15	13	3-08	12	38
6403	03	15,24	13,23	3-08	12	38
6404	03	24	23	3-08	12	38
6405	03	24	23	3-08	12	38
6406	03	15,24	13,23	3-08	12	38
6407	03	15	13	3-08	12	38
6408	03	15	13	3-08	15	29,38
CA65--West Lawn						
6501	03	15	13	3-08	12,15	29
6502	03	15	13	3-08	12,15	29
6503	03	15	13	3-08	15	29
6504	03	15	13	3-08	15	29
6505	03	15	13	3-08	15	29,52
CA66--Chicago Lawn						
6601	03	15	15	3-08	12,15	36
6602	03	15	15	3-08	15	29,36
6603	03	15	15	3-08	15	29
6604	03	15	13	3-08	12,15	29
6605	03	15	13,15	3-08	15	29
6606	03	15	15	3-08	15	29,36
6607	02	15	15	3-08	15	36
6608	03	15	15	3-08	15	29,36
6609	03	15	13,15	3-08	15	29,36
6610	03	15	15	3-08	15	29,36
6611	03	15	13,15	3-08	15	29

Table II-7. Geographical Area Cross-Reference

Tract Number	Congressional District 1982	Legislative District 1982	Wards, 1981	Police District	Public School District	Zipcode 606
CA67--West Englewood						
6701	02	16	14,16	3-07	12	36
6702	02	16	14	3-07	12	36
6703	02	16	14	3-07	12	36
6704	02	16	14	3-07	12	36
6705	02	15	14,15	3-07	12,15	36
6706	02	16	15	3-07	12,15	36
6707	02	16	16	3-07	12,15	09,36
6708	02	16	16	3-07	12,15	36
6709	02	16	16	3-07	12,15	36
6710	02	16	16	3-07	15	36
6711	02	16	16	3-07	15	36
6712	02	16	16	3-07	15	36
6713	02	16	15	3-07	15	36
6714	02	15	15	3-07	15	36
6715	02	16	15,16	3-07	15	36
6716	02	16	16	3-07	15	36
6717	02	16	16	3-07	15	36
6718	02	16	17	3-07	15,16	36
6719	02	16	17	3-07	15	36
6720	02	16	15	3-07	15	36
CA68--Englewood						
6801	01	12	03	1-02,03	13,16	21
6802	01	12	03	3-07	13,16	21
6803	01	12	03,16	3-07	12,13	21
6804	01,02	12	16	3-07	12,13	21
6805	02	16	16	3-07	12,13	21,36
6806	02	16	16	3-07	13,16	21,36
6807	02	12	16	3-07	13,16	21
6808	01	12	03,16	3-07	13,16	21
6809	01	12	16	3-07	16	21
6810	02	12	16	3-07	16	21,36
6811	02	16	16	3-07	16	21,36
6812	01	16	16	3-07	16	21
6813	01	16	17	3-07,2-06	16	20,21
6814	02	16	17	3-07	16	20,21,36
CA69--Greater Grand Crossing						
6901	01	16	20	1-03	16,17	37
6902	01	12	03	1-03,3-07	16	21,37
6903	01	16	17	3-07	16	21
6904	01	16	20	1-03	16,17	19,37
6905	01	16	20	1-03	14,17	19,37
6906	01	13	20	1-03	14,17	19,37
6907	01	13	06	1-03	17	19
6908	01	13	06	1-03	17	19
6909	01	16	06	1-03	17	19
6910	01	16	06	1-03	16,17	19
6911	01	16	17	3-07	16	19,21
6912	01	16	17	2-06	16	20
6913	01	16	06	2-06	16,17	19
6914	01	16	06	2-06	17	19
6915	01	13	06	2-06	17	19
CA70--Ashburn						
7001	03	15	18	3-08	15	20,52
7002	03	15	13	3-08	15	52
7003	03	15	18	3-08	15	52
7004	03	15	18	3-08	15	52
7005	03	15	18	3-08,2-06	15	20,52

Table II-7. Geographical Area Cross-Reference

Tract Number	Congressional District 1982	Legislative District 1982	Wards, 1981	Police District	Public School District	Zipcode 606
CA71--Auburn Gresham						
7101	01	16	17	2-06	16	20
7102	02	16	17	2-06	15.16	20
7103	02	16	17	2-06	15	20
7104	02	16	17,18	2-06	15	20
7105	02	16	18	2-06	15	20
7106	02	18	18	2-06	16	20
7107	02	18	18	2-06	15,16	20
7108	02	16	17	2-06	16	20
7109	01	16	21	2-06	16,18	20
7110	02	16	17,21	2-06	18	20
7111	02	18	18	2-06	16,18	20
7112	02	18	18	2-06	15	20
7113	02	18	21	2-22	18	20
7114	02	18	21	2-22	18	20
7115	01	18	21	2-22	18	20
CA72--Beverly						
7201	03	14	19	2-22	18	20,43
7202	03	14	19	2-22	18	43
7203	03	14	19	2-22	18	43
7204	03	14	19	2-22	18	42,43,55
7205	03	14	19	2-22	18	42,43,55
7206	03	14	19	2-22	18	43
7207	03	14	19	2-22	18	43
CA73--Washington Heights						
7301	01	18	21	2-22	18	20,28
7302	02	18	21	2-22	18	20,43
7303	02	18	21	2-22	18	20
7304	02	18	21	2-22	18	28,43
7305	01	17,18	21	2-22	18	28
7306	02	18	21	2-22	18	28,43
7307	02	17	34	2-22	18	28,43
CA74--Mount Greenwood						
7401	03	14	19	2-22	18	42,55
7402	03	14	19	2-22	18	42,55
7403	03	14	16	2-22	18	55
7404	03	14	19	2-22	18	55
CA75--Morgan Park						
7501	02	17	34	2-22	18	28,43
7502	03	14	19	2-22	18	43
7503	03	14	19	2-22	18	43,55
7504	03	14	19	2-22	18	43,55
7505	02,03	14,17	19,34	2-22,05	18	43
7506	02	17	34	2-22	18	28,43
CA76--O'Hare						
7608	11	07,08	41	5-16	01	31,34,56;60171
7609	11	26	41	5-16	01	66
CA77--Edgewater						
0301	09	02	48,49	6-24	02	60
0302	09	02	48,49	6-24	02	60
0303	09	01	50	6-24	02	60
0304	09	03	40	6-20	02	60
0305	09	02,03	40,48,49	6-20	02	60
0306	09	02	48	6-20	02	60
0307	09	02,03	48	6-20	02	40,60
0308	09	02,03	48	6-20	02	40,60
0309	11	03	40	6-20	02	40,60

Part III
Detailed Census Statistics for Chicago Community Areas

TABLE III-1 GENERAL CHARACTERISTICS OF THE POPULATION,
BY COMMUNITY AREA: CITY OF CHICAGO, 1980

	01	02	03	04	05	06	07	08	09
TOTAL POPULATION	55,525	61,129	64,414	43,954	35,161	97,519	57,146	67,167	12,457
SEX									
TOTAL PERSONS	55,525	61,129	64,414	43,954	35,161	97,519	57,146	67,158	12,457
MALE	26,516	27,992	32,891	20,465	16,651	46,975	27,827	31,420	5,711
FEMALE	29,009	33,137	31,523	23,489	18,510	50,544	29,319	35,738	6,746
AGE									
TOTAL PERSONS	55,525	61,129	64,414	43,954	35,161	97,519	57,146	67,158	12,45?
UNDER 1 YEAR	783	679	1,178	637	534	1,225	644	817	88
1 AND 2 YEARS	1,178	1,133	1,970	1,022	1,012	2,006	952	1,451	188
3 AND 4 YEARS	1,042	1,137	1,892	959	877	1,688	891	1,543	185
5 YEARS	527	555	856	470	490	844	401	617	94
6 YEARS	477	529	851	439	414	796	437	699	94
7 TO 9 YEARS	1,489	1,746	2,409	1,425	1,507	2,450	1,326	2,433	370
10 TO 13 YEARS	1,844	2,529	2,974	1,899	1,785	3,104	1,671	2,517	644
14 YEARS	435	677	721	551	487	836	357	567	207
15 YEARS	487	750	743	558	492	848	372	581	237
16 YEARS	485	716	738	610	563	875	419	706	226
17 YEARS	567	780	821	605	539	964	447	670	233
18 YEARS	909	695	810	594	528	945	531	774	221
19 YEARS	1,221	772	992	672	608	1,112	627	873	218
20 YEARS	1,271	722	1,029	721	629	1,373	707	1,027	200
21 YEARS	1,373	825	1,166	751	639	1,511	726	1,094	207
22 TO 24 YEARS	5,005	2,885	4,315	2,382	2,090	7,871	4,777	4,830	546
25 TO 29 YEARS	8,907	5,113	7,446	4,137	3,352	15,339	11,290	8,720	749
30 TO 34 YEARS	5,673	4,516	6,148	3,453	2,743	11,765	8,674	7,051	650
35 TO 44 YEARS	5,367	6,124	7,425	4,770	3,806	11,653	7,790	8,114	1,273
45 TO 54 YEARS	4,112	6,267	5,815	4,579	3,637	7,995	4,501	6,781	1,576
55 TO 59 YEARS	2,088	3,923	2,768	2,444	1,962	4,124	2,033	3,582	990
60 AND 61 YEARS	800	1,660	1,029	968	658	1,508	788	1,309	403
62 TO 64 YEARS	1,178	2,534	1,378	1,405	1,023	2,285	1,102	1,664	536
65 TO 74 YEARS	4,136	8,641	4,642	4,495	2,919	7,729	3,057	5,094	1,424
75 TO 84 YEARS	3,213	4,280	3,179	2,690	1,487	5,421	2,037	2,990	747
85 YEARS AND OVER	958	941	1,119	718	380	1,252	589	654	151
FEMALE	29,009	33,137	31,523	23,489	18,510	50,544	29,319	35,738	6,746
UNDER 1 YEAR	420	300	553	318	269	611	330	447	48
1 AND 2 YEARS	586	521	919	502	520	977	495	809	103
3 AND 4 YEARS	503	586	896	485	414	869	447	747	95
5 YEARS	265	267	391	260	241	406	188	298	43
6 YEARS	241	256	402	197	196	403	231	337	53
7 TO 9 YEARS	753	841	1,133	701	727	1,202	652	1,254	185
10 TO 13 YEARS	892	1,259	1,474	985	831	1,497	818	1,228	321
14 YEARS	205	317	334	252	254	401	170	262	95
15 YEARS	228	367	382	290	236	423	204	273	107
16 YEARS	260	342	344	292	284	430	197	372	105
17 YEARS	288	387	389	285	266	489	223	269	126
18 YEARS	395	348	394	326	244	500	239	389	108
19 YEARS	616	404	478	341	304	569	305	450	106
20 YEARS	668	372	485	381	310	685	368	555	111
21 YEARS	700	401	559	401	314	795	400	663	90
22 TO 24 YEARS	2,529	1,584	2,037	1,249	1,079	4,051	2,719	2,720	266
25 TO 29 YEARS	4,382	2,653	3,528	2,028	1,699	7,382	6,040	5,069	372
30 TO 34 YEARS	2,571	2,263	2,732	1,687	1,422	5,642	4,301	3,931	341
35 TO 44 YEARS	2,494	3,210	3,354	2,385	1,978	5,432	3,373	3,874	703
45 TO 54 YEARS	2,078	3,324	2,584	2,379	1,908	3,870	2,047	3,266	827
55 TO 59 YEARS	1,147	2,290	1,325	1,362	1,079	2,201	981	1,719	540
60 AND 61 YEARS	472	963	518	557	363	901	412	701	229
62 TO 64 YEARS	689	1,463	728	836	592	1,348	593	901	303
65 TO 74 YEARS	2,665	5,134	2,682	2,765	1,784	4,980	1,826	2,925	846
75 TO 84 YEARS	2,256	2,656	2,066	1,723	937	3,653	1,376	1,873	515
85 YEARS AND OVER	706	600	836	502	259	827	384	406	108
RACE									
TOTAL PERSONS	55,525	61,129	64,414	43,954	35,161	97,519	57,146	67,167	12,457
WHITE	42,653	54,593	36,869	37,048	29,745	75,176	47,616	43,163	12,326
BLACK	5,225	442	9,703	236	412	6,757	4,909	22,000	0
AMERICAN INDIAN	166	68	957	179	219	456	127	59	10
ESKIMO	4	0	14	1	0	1	6	0	0
ALEUT	2	3	6	1	0	4	2	4	0
JAPANESE	496	493	870	394	179	1,227	549	283	14
CHINESE	889	739	986	284	87	442	187	183	7
FILIPINO	758	980	2,097	1,218	830	1,751	673	248	23
KOREAN	465	1,192	670	1,163	211	603	87	58	21
ASIAN INDIAN	1,016	1,079	1,014	523	137	1,034	156	187	6
VIETNAMESE	152	3	1,216	88	20	44	12	4	0
HAWAIIAN	10	3	18	3	1	23	24	21	0
GUAMANIAN	4	1	18	10	3	30	14	2	0
SAMOAN	7	2	1	2	0	9	0	2	0
OTHER	3,678	1,531	9,975	2,804	3,317	9,962	2,784	953	50
SPANISH ORIGIN									
TOTAL PERSONS	55,525	61,129	64,414	43,954	35,161	97,519	57,146	67,167	12,457
NOT OF SPANISH ORIGIN	48,904	58,863	49,430	38,981	28,477	79,186	51,155	65,223	12,337
MEXICAN	4,071	484	7,842	1,654	2,588	8,079	2,963	1,089	69
PUERTO RICAN	418	253	2,888	736	2,312	6,166	2,117	339	8
CUBAN	561	549	847	685	376	859	147	90	7
OTHER SPANISH	1,571	980	3,407	1,898	1,408	3,229	764	426	36
RACE: PERSONS OF SPANISH ORIGIN									
TOTAL	6,621	2,266	14,984	4,973	6,684	18,333	5,991	1,944	120
WHITE	3,954	1,644	6,308	3,057	3,560	9,139	3,358	1,073	90
BLACK	130	6	287	8	22	199	109	188	0
AMERICAN INDIAN, ESKIMO, ALEUT, AND ASIAN AND PACIFIC ISLANDER	98	52	330	132	93	270	116	27	9
OTHER	2,439	564	8,059	1,776	3,009	8,725	2,408	656	21

TABLE III-1 GENERAL CHARACTERISTICS OF THE POPULATION, BY COMMUNITY AREA: CITY OF CHICAGO, 1980

	10	11	12	13	14	15	16	17	18
TOTAL POPULATION	40,585	24,583	18,991	15,273	46,075	57,349	49,489	37,860	10,793
SEX									
TOTAL PERSONS	40,585	24,583	18,991	15,273	46,075	57,349	49,489	37,860	10,793
MALE	18,980	11,306	8,911	7,085	22,544	26,512	23,351	18,060	4,944
FEMALE	21,605	13,277	10,080	8,188	23,531	30,837	26,138	19,800	5,849
AGE									
TOTAL PERSONS	40,585	24,583	18,991	15,273	46,075	57,349	49,489	37,860	10,793
UNDER 1 YEAR	311	208	166	167	914	581	696	311	91
1 AND 2 YEARS	610	393	298	323	1,540	1,041	1,192	618	177
3 AND 4 YEARS	631	369	277	280	1,462	1,009	1,110	655	164
5 YEARS	323	172	177	158	686	505	510	319	104
6 YEARS	289	171	170	149	655	525	491	358	91
7 TO 9 YEARS	1,143	666	681	483	2,079	1,733	1,711	1,142	312
10 TO 13 YEARS	1,928	1,068	1,071	665	2,521	2,606	2,437	1,864	500
14 YEARS	550	325	303	196	639	762	643	517	160
15 YEARS	631	354	335	198	699	830	698	589	139
16 YEARS	658	330	329	227	662	860	722	625	179
17 YEARS	731	345	373	226	779	923	727	625	153
18 YEARS	639	377	293	316	728	850	695	575	181
19 YEARS	661	337	282	409	795	948	782	610	163
20 YEARS	671	371	229	340	884	933	901	680	179
21 YEARS	629	369	239	322	931	1,006	826	626	188
22 TO 24 YEARS	1,733	1,182	730	805	2,852	3,046	2,902	1,726	484
25 TO 29 YEARS	2,390	1,743	923	1,179	4,640	4,376	4,684	2,510	752
30 TO 34 YEARS	2,316	1,500	996	1,053	3,910	3,610	3,796	2,108	606
35 TO 44 YEARS	3,896	2,303	2,229	1,590	5,196	5,528	5,458	3,755	960
45 TO 54 YEARS	5,235	2,889	2,501	1,562	4,412	6,528	5,130	4,701	1,270
55 TO 59 YEARS	3,469	1,944	1,425	959	2,127	4,143	2,868	3,142	853
60 AND 61 YEARS	1,342	837	514	369	775	1,581	1,082	1,159	343
62 TO 64 YEARS	1,932	1,311	836	556	1,056	2,494	1,712	1,721	535
65 TO 74 YEARS	5,043	3,197	2,299	1,684	3,014	6,703	4,665	4,499	1,327
75 TO 84 YEARS	2,162	1,468	1,108	846	1,651	3,362	2,404	1,958	670
85 YEARS AND OVER	662	354	207	211	468	866	647	467	212
FEMALE	21,605	13,277	10,080	8,188	23,531	30,837	26,138	19,800	5,849
UNDER 1 YEAR	144	105	93	87	448	274	370	155	46
1 AND 2 YEARS	290	202	162	164	726	503	567	280	89
3 AND 4 YEARS	322	187	149	141	704	499	522	317	79
5 YEARS	165	77	82	74	319	231	276	158	58
6 YEARS	143	75	84	70	344	249	251	180	48
7 TO 9 YEARS	560	325	340	238	985	867	852	549	146
10 TO 13 YEARS	973	494	491	314	1,215	1,300	1,171	873	259
14 YEARS	265	157	155	102	303	366	324	255	77
15 YEARS	293	184	158	104	363	390	351	289	73
16 YEARS	333	176	158	105	336	455	370	301	89
17 YEARS	361	175	197	112	373	458	370	273	93
18 YEARS	342	177	137	159	351	460	349	264	84
19 YEARS	325	147	131	243	422	483	422	288	96
20 YEARS	312	189	121	176	434	478	478	342	103
21 YEARS	284	197	99	168	478	537	436	292	105
22 TO 24 YEARS	839	584	342	445	1,382	1,499	1,483	822	225
25 TO 29 YEARS	1,163	853	466	595	2,283	2,177	2,307	1,235	379
30 TO 34 YEARS	1,170	772	519	553	1,837	1,765	1,848	1,017	294
35 TO 44 YEARS	2,086	1,205	1,209	819	2,625	2,883	2,747	1,942	515
45 TO 54 YEARS	2,809	1,545	1,287	839	2,264	3,414	2,595	2,529	669
55 TO 59 YEARS	1,854	1,086	785	521	1,161	2,326	1,603	1,714	466
60 AND 61 YEARS	718	486	284	211	420	907	611	604	169
62 TO 64 YEARS	1,069	755	471	304	589	1,454	998	956	303
65 TO 74 YEARS	2,901	1,951	1,304	958	1,779	4,032	2,826	2,630	786
75 TO 84 YEARS	1,407	921	710	528	1,063	2,260	1,541	1,223	443
85 YEARS AND OVER	477	252	146	158	327	570	470	312	155
RACE									
TOTAL PERSONS	40,585	24,583	18,991	15,273	46,075	57,349	49,489	37,860	10,793
WHITE	39,988	24,123	18,384	13,244	34,070	55,907	44,832	37,202	10,655
BLACK	7	5	11	143	279	51	63	183	0
AMERICAN INDIAN	21	13	6	19	248	47	83	12	5
ESKIMO	2	0	0	0	9	2	2	0	0
ALEUT	1	1	0	0	0	0	1	0	0
JAPANESE	44	46	64	177	383	56	150	24	7
CHINESE	50	39	84	178	434	116	187	20	5
FILIPINO	104	99	130	444	1,506	250	1,000	96	11
KOREAN	115	79	158	467	2,230	210	643	81	1
ASIAN INDIAN	51	38	39	245	1,594	123	512	20	12
VIETNAMESE	0	1	0	21	331	2	26	2	1
HAWAIIAN	4	0	0	1	10	0	5	4	0
GUAMANIAN	0	0	0	0	9	0	2	0	0
SAMOAN	1	0	0	0	5	1	0	1	0
OTHER	197	139	115	334	4,967	584	1,983	215	96
SPANISH ORIGIN									
TOTAL PERSONS	40,585	24,583	18,991	15,273	46,075	57,349	49,489	37,860	10,793
NOT OF SPANISH ORIGIN	40,195	24,188	18,696	14,427	37,001	55,863	45,222	37,247	10,614
MEXICAN	156	169	95	203	3,250	720	1,746	275	78
PUERTO RICAN	67	54	38	141	2,357	253	1,152	125	32
CUBAN	34	39	67	205	947	148	301	42	21
OTHER SPANISH	133	133	95	297	2,520	365	1,068	171	48
RACE: PERSONS OF SPANISH ORIGIN									
TOTAL	390	395	295	846	9,074	1,486	4,267	613	179
WHITE	298	320	240	617	5,056	1,095	2,659	498	139
BLACK	0	0	0	7	18	4	4	1	0
AMERICAN INDIAN, ESKIMO, ALEUT, AND ASIAN AND PACIFIC ISLANDER	6	12	17	30	190	21	66	7	1
OTHER	86	63	38	192	3,810	366	1,538	107	39

TABLE III-1 GENERAL CHARACTERISTICS OF THE POPULATION,
BY COMMUNITY AREA: CITY OF CHICAGO, 1980

	19	20	21	22	23	24	25	26	27
TOTAL POPULATION	53,371	19,547	33,527	84,768	70,875	96,428	138,026	33,865	31,580
SEX									
TOTAL PERSONS	53,371	19,547	33,527	84,768	70,866	96,428	138,026	33,865	31,580
MALE	25,077	9,489	16,225	42,203	34,266	48,337	64,431	15,610	14,585
FEMALE	28,294	10,058	17,302	42,565	36,600	48,091	73,595	18,255	16,995
AGE									
TOTAL PERSONS	53,371	19,547	33,527	84,768	70,866	96,428	138,026	33,865	31,580
UNDER 1 YEAR	597	327	572	1,973	1,725	2,207	3,224	837	786
1 AND 2 YEARS	1,143	604	901	3,219	2,948	4,026	5,382	1,400	1,238
3 AND 4 YEARS	1,038	582	879	3,140	3,088	3,878	5,351	1,416	1,206
5 YEARS	530	299	399	1,503	1,539	1,869	2,584	694	562
6 YEARS	506	262	390	1,432	1,472	1,785	2,679	688	590
7 TO 9 YEARS	1,616	871	1,228	4,428	4,658	5,635	8,769	2,295	1,926
10 TO 13 YEARS	2,429	1,087	1,581	5,405	5,708	6,767	11,050	3,011	2,635
14 YEARS	661	312	416	1,372	1,501	1,745	2,741	817	682
15 YEARS	669	303	451	1,385	1,590	1,770	2,822	888	705
16 YEARS	752	290	512	1,456	1,556	1,875	2,866	835	762
17 YEARS	784	332	514	1,452	1,502	1,864	2,886	922	731
18 YEARS	751	307	505	1,476	1,449	1,929	2,827	853	726
19 YEARS	815	381	514	1,552	1,447	2,026	2,859	833	761
20 YEARS	814	383	547	1,758	1,447	1,974	2,899	815	697
21 YEARS	808	376	610	1,706	1,387	1,811	2,776	741	654
22 TO 24 YEARS	2,671	1,116	1,895	5,281	4,151	5,792	8,226	1,973	1,804
25 TO 29 YEARS	4,116	1,697	3,004	7,867	5,954	8,523	12,483	2,570	2,359
30 TO 34 YEARS	3,529	1,475	2,633	6,641	5,112	6,981	10,790	1,953	1,708
35 TO 44 YEARS	4,978	2,014	3,756	8,857	7,493	9,678	15,603	3,263	2,868
45 TO 54 YEARS	6,011	1,949	3,555	7,478	5,786	7,768	11,741	3,190	2,990
55 TO 59 YEARS	4,012	1,049	2,053	3,975	2,542	4,396	5,003	1,236	1,530
60 AND 61 YEARS	1,658	424	873	1,421	941	1,718	1,809	462	554
62 TO 64 YEARS	2,441	593	1,177	2,031	1,296	2,156	2,240	495	640
65 TO 74 YEARS	6,319	1,513	2,932	5,060	2,982	5,388	5,420	1,133	1,671
75 TO 84 YEARS	2,876	800	1,291	2,248	1,269	2,184	2,396	454	637
85 YEARS AND OVER	847	201	330	652	321	683	600	91	158
FEMALE	28,294	10,058	17,302	42,565	36,600	48,091	73,595	18,255	16,995
UNDER 1 YEAR	301	149	267	961	833	1,071	1,619	397	392
1 AND 2 YEARS	543	304	447	1,623	1,446	1,921	2,708	685	619
3 AND 4 YEARS	511	276	444	1,561	1,527	1,833	2,673	675	606
5 YEARS	269	144	186	751	743	909	1,257	349	278
6 YEARS	245	114	185	703	680	888	1,241	333	300
7 TO 9 YEARS	779	409	585	2,223	2,334	2,832	4,419	1,135	949
10 TO 13 YEARS	1,171	540	773	2,651	2,805	3,380	5,628	1,512	1,393
14 YEARS	317	138	191	653	740	848	1,422	402	339
15 YEARS	338	144	219	697	784	904	1,391	438	371
16 YEARS	367	149	245	713	775	913	1,437	427	374
17 YEARS	369	161	274	716	793	914	1,478	466	361
18 YEARS	398	175	264	784	687	920	1,477	445	356
19 YEARS	401	201	261	798	738	971	1,506	459	396
20 YEARS	391	200	263	876	752	989	1,574	434	368
21 YEARS	402	206	337	805	731	886	1,521	407	351
22 TO 24 YEARS	1,356	546	942	2,616	2,178	2,846	4,526	1,126	1,007
25 TO 29 YEARS	2,019	830	1,428	3,775	3,171	4,203	6,944	1,492	1,316
30 TO 34 YEARS	1,665	717	1,223	3,227	2,719	3,414	5,993	1,144	990
35 TO 44 YEARS	2,586	987	1,854	4,253	4,057	4,675	8,387	1,962	1,648
45 TO 54 YEARS	3,216	1,000	1,861	3,692	3,020	3,898	6,355	1,803	1,709
55 TO 59 YEARS	2,168	560	1,136	2,030	1,312	2,228	2,766	653	808
60 AND 61 YEARS	937	234	472	753	470	878	994	263	285
62 TO 64 YEARS	1,376	343	634	1,043	676	1,108	1,242	274	342
65 TO 74 YEARS	3,725	890	1,705	2,798	1,656	2,847	3,130	635	955
75 TO 84 YEARS	1,872	503	870	1,406	776	1,353	1,499	276	388
85 YEARS AND OVER	572	138	236	457	197	462	408	63	94
RACE									
TOTAL PERSONS	53,371	19,547	33,527	84,768	70,879	96,428	138,026	33,865	31,580
WHITE	51,379	15,803	29,120	60,382	24,820	53,123	28,649	246	223
BLACK	43	74	60	2,236	25,215	8,671	101,831	33,475	31,263
AMERICAN INDIAN	35	44	106	322	124	373	86	20	17
ESKIMO	0	1	0	3	1	9	2	0	0
ALEUT	0	1	0	4	4	6	1	1	0
JAPANESE	31	29	63	90	42	52	44	18	7
CHINESE	85	42	64	185	50	111	97	3	0
FILIPINO	377	331	590	599	1,080	767	2,065	22	3
KOREAN	73	35	83	49	18	59	54	0	0
ASIAN INDIAN	62	58	132	178	72	100	118	1	0
VIETNAMESE	40	2	33	60	0	107	95	0	4
HAWAIIAN	3	0	5	3	3	8	15	2	0
GUAMANIAN	0	8	12	56	76	8	18	0	0
SAMOAN	3	4	0	4	0	0	3	0	0
OTHER	1,240	3,115	3,259	20,597	19,374	33,034	4,948	77	63
SPANISH ORIGIN									
TOTAL PERSONS	53,371	19,547	33,527	84,768	70,879	96,428	138,026	33,865	31,580
NOT OF SPANISH ORIGIN	50,299	13,446	26,664	40,939	42,007	41,735	129,878	33,587	31,317
MEXICAN	1,321	2,011	2,521	14,961	8,876	23,477	3,824	178	225
PUERTO RICAN	963	3,374	3,087	23,792	17,769	28,469	2,805	18	13
CUBAN	203	172	386	1,590	318	376	209	10	6
OTHER SPANISH	585	544	869	3,486	1,909	2,371	1,310	72	19
RACE: PERSONS OF SPANISH ORIGIN									
TOTAL	3,072	6,101	6,863	43,829	28,872	54,693	8,148	278	263
WHITE	2,167	3,099	3,831	23,534	9,759	22,891	3,264	42	28
BLACK	0	21	10	232	258	372	490	194	205
AMERICAN INDIAN, ESKIMO, ALEUT, AND ASIAN AND PACIFIC ISLANDER	65	43	93	251	184	194	156	1	1
OTHER	840	2,938	2,929	19,812	18,671	31,236	4,238	41	29

TABLE III-1 GENERAL CHARACTERISTICS OF THE POPULATION,
BY COMMUNITY AREA: CITY OF CHICAGO, 1980

	28	29	30	31	32	33	34	35	36
TOTAL POPULATION	57,305	61,534	75,204	44,951	6,462	7,243	12,475	35,700	16,748
SEX									
TOTAL PERSONS	57,296	61,523	75,204	44,951	6,462	7,243	12,475	35,700	16,748
MALE	27,004	28,250	40,118	23,453	3,618	2,980	5,914	15,150	7,135
FEMALE	30,292	33,273	35,086	21,498	2,844	4,263	6,561	20,550	9,613
AGE									
TOTAL PERSONS	57,296	61,523	75,204	44,951	6,462	7,243	12,475	35,700	16,748
UNDER 1 YEAR	1,314	1,462	2,045	1,162	47	196	177	684	457
1 AND 2 YEARS	2,368	2,429	3,454	2,066	33	346	310	1,223	774
3 AND 4 YEARS	2,406	2,447	3,577	2,199	16	367	306	1,324	790
5 YEARS	1,251	1,217	1,626	1,029	17	184	151	700	403
6 YEARS	1,270	1,246	1,554	915	7	176	136	611	390
7 TO 9 YEARS	3,795	4,216	4,614	2,615	27	564	516	2,028	1,368
10 TO 13 YEARS	4,695	5,689	5,028	3,049	43	605	784	2,153	1,853
14 YEARS	1,216	1,517	1,186	776	15	140	192	531	483
15 YEARS	1,286	1,544	1,192	705	11	143	206	556	470
16 YEARS	1,270	1,625	1,192	813	12	151	239	535	495
17 YEARS	1,264	1,562	1,467	878	17	149	236	599	505
18 YEARS	1,196	1,450	1,609	970	47	146	223	772	472
19 YEARS	1,257	1,419	1,879	975	64	159	245	870	414
20 YEARS	1,206	1,345	1,864	1,018	77	147	230	755	393
21 YEARS	1,208	1,264	1,920	991	83	158	249	859	373
22 TO 24 YEARS	3,800	3,463	5,470	3,049	278	498	777	2,414	963
25 TO 29 YEARS	5,263	4,543	8,006	4,390	662	711	1,065	3,426	1,182
30 TO 34 YEARS	3,412	3,476	5,920	3,142	652	481	763	2,412	786
35 TO 44 YEARS	4,543	5,625	7,201	4,282	871	522	1,170	3,124	1,145
45 TO 54 YEARS	4,498	5,432	5,134	3,471	974	367	1,421	2,899	1,089
55 TO 59 YEARS	2,280	2,462	2,357	1,736	573	196	651	1,589	477
60 AND 61 YEARS	750	923	866	660	218	66	253	614	179
62 TO 64 YEARS	1,085	1,140	1,182	908	344	87	332	771	239
65 TO 74 YEARS	2,998	2,818	3,058	2,116	893	340	1,075	2,469	580
75 TO 84 YEARS	1,311	993	1,401	808	419	278	613	1,373	366
85 YEARS AND OVER	354	216	402	228	62	66	155	409	102
FEMALE	30,292	33,273	35,086	21,498	2,844	4,263	6,561	20,550	9,613
UNDER 1 YEAR	653	700	1,017	572	24	91	83	336	240
1 AND 2 YEARS	1,183	1,221	1,703	1,033	15	174	147	568	386
3 AND 4 YEARS	1,182	1,215	1,759	1,074	5	180	143	599	377
5 YEARS	617	574	781	475	9	94	76	338	195
6 YEARS	647	634	749	469	4	94	71	284	192
7 TO 9 YEARS	1,857	2,148	2,274	1,218	16	288	271	1,068	691
10 TO 13 YEARS	2,279	2,898	2,461	1,499	17	312	405	1,098	891
14 YEARS	609	730	575	392	7	54	86	281	264
15 YEARS	588	785	591	351	5	75	100	292	249
16 YEARS	620	830	570	400	6	84	103	291	238
17 YEARS	637	772	654	400	7	67	113	303	247
18 YEARS	628	715	659	482	18	75	117	373	257
19 YEARS	598	745	783	441	30	83	112	420	205
20 YEARS	663	743	715	423	31	81	120	399	210
21 YEARS	705	672	787	418	31	105	123	453	236
22 TO 24 YEARS	2,107	1,927	2,242	1,377	104	319	386	1,393	571
25 TO 29 YEARS	2,868	2,549	3,328	1,966	260	476	509	2,059	794
30 TO 34 YEARS	1,951	2,129	2,554	1,442	250	304	396	1,508	555
35 TO 44 YEARS	2,635	3,352	3,269	1,992	332	345	628	1,999	810
45 TO 54 YEARS	2,516	3,130	2,458	1,649	379	249	749	1,789	739
55 TO 59 YEARS	1,173	1,395	1,129	809	229	123	315	1,004	330
60 AND 61 YEARS	367	497	454	333	91	42	149	378	120
62 TO 64 YEARS	578	617	606	495	188	50	198	513	133
65 TO 74 YEARS	1,654	1,603	1,781	1,140	508	262	675	1,629	365
75 TO 84 YEARS	769	553	917	507	251	188	387	882	250
85 YEARS AND OVER	208	139	270	141	27	48	99	293	68
RACE									
TOTAL PERSONS	57,305	61,534	75,204	44,951	6,462	7,243	12,475	35,700	16,748
WHITE	9,350	1,038	33,513	20,746	4,724	248	4,030	3,546	56
BLACK	42,810	59,370	6,476	477	1,231	6,819	3,162	30,905	16,647
AMERICAN INDIAN	47	29	169	201	14	7	6	23	2
ESKIMO	0	0	1	0	0	0	0	2	0
ALEUT	2	0	0	4	0	0	0	0	0
JAPANESE	33	16	7	7	35	2	7	62	6
CHINESE	254	1	60	23	57	14	4,945	272	0
FILIPINO	535	45	131	60	62	4	9	255	1
KOREAN	82	6	11	2	19	4	0	59	0
ASIAN INDIAN	393	15	31	27	58	59	7	256	0
VIETNAMESE	8	0	2	1	1	2	15	20	1
HAWAIIAN	18	9	1	2	0	2	1	4	0
GUAMANIAN	3	0	15	7	0	0	0	0	0
SAMOAN	0	0	0	0	0	0	0	0	0
OTHER	3.770	1,005	34,787	23,394	261	82	287	296	35
SPANISH ORIGIN									
TOTAL PERSONS	57,305	61,534	75,204	44,951	6,462	7,243	12,475	35,700	16,748
NOT OF SPANISH ORIGIN	51,600	59,881	19,504	10,084	6,240	7,135	11,872	35,387	16,651
MEXICAN	4,794	1,411	51,208	32,178	121	48	549	148	48
PUERTO RICAN	494	123	2,428	1,557	28	31	10	24	16
CUBAN	46	28	126	44	11	5	9	20	0
OTHER SPANISH	371	91	1,938	1,088	62	24	35	121	33
RACE: PERSONS OF SPANISH ORIGIN									
TOTAL	5,705	1,653	55,700	34,867	222	108	603	313	97
WHITE	2,039	383	21,069	11,523	57	8	347	77	2
BLACK	358	336	147	74	8	31	4	136	90
AMERICAN INDIAN, ESKIMO, ALEUT, AND ASIAN AND PACIFIC ISLANDER	65	3	170	133	6	4	12	16	0
OTHER	3,243	931	34,314	23,137	151	65	240	84	5

TABLE III-1 GENERAL CHARACTERISTICS OF THE POPULATION,
BY COMMUNITY AREA: CITY OF CHICAGO, 1980

	37	38	39	40	41	42	43	44	45
TOTAL POPULATION	5,832	53,741	21,974	31,935	31,198	36,323	77,743	40,725	13,792
SEX									
TOTAL PERSONS	5,832	53,741	21,974	31,935	31,198	36,323	77,743	40,725	13,792
MALE	2,630	24,493	10,079	14,454	15,831	16,630	35,626	18,302	6,410
FEMALE	3,202	29,248	11,895	17,481	15,367	19,693	42,117	22,423	7,382
AGE									
TOTAL PERSONS	5,832	53,741	21,974	31,935	31,198	36,323	77,743	40,725	13,792
UNDER 1 YEAR	108	1,145	355	713	363	698	1,553	603	187
1 AND 2 YEARS	168	1,979	619	1,239	581	1,189	2,603	1,033	313
3 AND 4 YEARS	178	1,994	571	1,227	500	1,084	2,549	958	334
5 YEARS	90	976	259	573	256	533	1,199	449	178
6 YEARS	100	1,032	229	596	253	529	1,290	413	164
7 TO 9 YEARS	331	3,418	916	2,015	842	1,808	4,001	1,568	657
10 TO 13 YEARS	467	4,331	1,071	2,523	1,037	2,335	4,886	1,942	965
14 YEARS	114	1,202	304	693	238	631	1,150	536	300
15 YEARS	140	1,220	296	680	297	678	1,306	526	290
16 YEARS	114	1,270	283	756	271	630	1,249	575	308
17 YEARS	128	1,239	290	721	306	620	1,220	606	317
18 YEARS	121	1,077	233	656	642	648	1,156	575	328
19 YEARS	141	1,147	296	609	768	639	1,210	593	279
20 YEARS	123	1,081	310	611	751	675	1,336	703	274
21 YEARS	97	1,019	318	539	780	648	1,448	679	304
22 TO 24 YEARS	286	2,546	1,361	1,568	3,171	1,950	5,057	2,220	719
25 TO 29 YEARS	386	3,314	2,395	2,117	4,782	2,692	9,064	3,598	1,010
30 TO 34 YEARS	272	2,535	1,983	1,552	3,226	2,290	7,139	2,799	875
35 TO 44 YEARS	462	4,491	2,520	2,702	3,627	3,408	9,590	4,219	1,920
45 TO 54 YEARS	475	4,585	2,210	2,924	2,860	3,643	7,660	5,411	1,936
55 TO 59 YEARS	301	2,520	1,196	1,616	1,338	1,970	3,228	3,259	788
60 AND 61 YEARS	89	995	419	643	461	749	1,189	1,139	239
62 TO 64 YEARS	157	1,287	614	817	646	1,041	1,491	1,454	263
65 TO 74 YEARS	580	4,323	1,765	2,347	1,787	3,073	3,365	3,332	588
75 TO 84 YEARS	341	2,428	942	1,189	1,053	1,691	1,438	1,259	201
85 YEARS AND OVER	63	587	219	309	362	471	366	276	55
FEMALE	3,202	29,248	11,895	17,481	15,367	19,693	42,117	22,423	7,382
UNDER 1 YEAR	57	559	176	358	168	335	760	302	86
1 AND 2 YEARS	79	982	351	631	274	579	1,296	491	169
3 AND 4 YEARS	87	994	287	629	250	518	1,250	509	156
5 YEARS	51	448	136	268	125	255	613	227	94
6 YEARS	47	538	117	289	122	248	641	225	74
7 TO 9 YEARS	182	1,719	452	1,007	412	880	1,935	800	346
10 TO 13 YEARS	239	2,150	547	1,266	505	1,161	2,465	945	503
14 YEARS	60	606	172	337	107	325	612	270	132
15 YEARS	71	605	137	334	124	336	613	268	153
16 YEARS	58	649	135	374	138	320	635	312	144
17 YEARS	51	652	146	369	155	319	684	312	167
18 YEARS	59	578	132	350	265	323	619	294	149
19 YEARS	85	610	168	338	314	328	672	321	145
20 YEARS	58	559	189	339	309	350	777	378	143
21 YEARS	47	556	181	338	344	374	859	369	148
22 TO 24 YEARS	135	1,452	697	887	1,415	1,003	2,995	1,236	360
25 TO 29 YEARS	214	1,942	1,273	1,215	2,281	1,542	5,015	2,059	581
30 TO 34 YEARS	145	1,513	1,094	946	1,585	1,288	3,921	1,588	484
35 TO 44 YEARS	290	2,671	1,331	1,630	1,816	1,866	5,157	2,349	1,153
45 TO 54 YEARS	261	2,498	1,205	1,643	1,448	2,001	4,162	3,185	1,035
55 TO 59 YEARS	168	1,355	632	877	679	1,119	1,815	1,787	408
60 AND 61 YEARS	52	511	224	352	248	420	653	622	123
62 TO 64 YEARS	85	737	365	455	347	595	830	815	136
65 TO 74 YEARS	344	2,482	1,019	1,344	985	1,837	1,972	1,875	323
75 TO 84 YEARS	236	1,490	588	712	701	1,036	906	727	132
85 YEARS AND OVER	41	392	141	193	250	335	260	157	38
RACE									
TOTAL PERSONS	5,832	53,741	21,974	31,935	31,198	36,323	77,743	40,725	13,792
WHITE	47	175	4,352	93	17,354	1,261	2,825	343	378
BLACK	5,757	53,428	17,024	31,726	11,610	34,759	73,929	40,113	13,258
AMERICAN INDIAN	5	29	28	18	78	23	83	58	21
ESKIMO	0	0	0	0	0	0	2	0	0
ALEUT	0	0	0	0	2	0	4	1	0
JAPANESE	0	19	78	6	405	26	64	8	20
CHINESE	0	2	70	1	508	19	23	14	1
FILIPINO	0	11	69	0	174	17	76	6	15
KOREAN	0	0	34	1	143	12	10	3	0
ASIAN INDIAN	0	1	69	3	239	24	23	5	9
VIETNAMESE	0	2	5	0	29	0	3	0	0
HAWAIIAN	2	11	5	10	7	17	16	14	0
GUAMANIAN	0	0	1	0	2	8	2	0	0
SAMOAN	0	0	0	0	3	0	0	0	0
OTHER	21	63	239	77	644	157	683	160	90
SPANISH ORIGIN									
TOTAL PERSONS	5,832	53,741	21,974	31,935	31,198	36,323	77,743	40,725	13,792
NOT OF SPANISH ORIGIN	5,761	53,391	21,733	31,730	30,477	36,038	76,826	40,454	13,683
MEXICAN	53	275	105	127	225	150	305	98	50
PUERTO RICAN	0	9	36	16	91	32	99	40	11
CUBAN	0	10	8	5	40	13	33	25	8
OTHER SPANISH	18	56	92	57	365	90	480	108	40
RACE: PERSONS OF SPANISH ORIGIN									
TOTAL	71	350	241	205	721	285	917	271	109
WHITE	10	5	67	10	402	29	95	7	9
BLACK	50	332	116	176	122	199	617	203	73
AMERICAN INDIAN, ESKIMO, ALEUT, AND ASIAN AND PACIFIC ISLANDER	0	0	8	2	29	10	10	7	6
OTHER	11	13	50	17	168	47	195	54	21

	46	47	48	49	50	51	52	53	54
TOTAL POPULATION	46,422	3,942	20,505	64,372	10,341	19,400	21,331	44,904	13,539
SEX									
TOTAL PERSONS	46,422	3,942	20,505	64,372	10,341	19,400	21,331	44,904	13,539
MALE	22,365	1,843	9,659	30,230	4,847	9,158	10,438	21,366	5,847
FEMALE	24,057	2,099	10,846	34,142	5,494	10,242	10,893	23,538	7,692
AGE									
TOTAL PERSONS	46,422	3,942	20,505	64,372	10,341	19,400	21,331	44,904	13,539
UNDER 1 YEAR	972	75	244	1,090	166	318	285	945	323
1 AND 2 YEARS	1,701	147	482	1,866	289	557	463	1,692	644
3 AND 4 YEARS	1,742	138	506	1,871	305	594	492	1,821	621
5 YEARS	883	79	264	967	138	321	211	986	327
6 YEARS	871	82	303	967	155	303	199	933	361
7 TO 9 YEARS	2,692	283	1,071	3,657	543	1,199	816	3,297	1,215
10 TO 13 YEARS	3,445	350	1,575	5,201	832	1,647	1,175	4,213	1,560
14 YEARS	876	91	449	1,513	219	446	341	1,023	352
15 YEARS	878	112	514	1,543	232	417	379	1,093	405
16 YEARS	886	114	442	1,595	242	451	401	1,107	414
17 YEARS	953	87	458	1,662	227	446	400	1,130	408
18 YEARS	907	95	404	1,548	211	432	416	998	348
19 YEARS	1,032	91	411	1,449	201	419	410	909	340
20 YEARS	925	85	377	1,400	180	398	452	853	288
21 YEARS	859	76	355	1,344	191	345	388	759	270
22 TO 24 YEARS	2,762	194	865	3,354	555	978	1,230	2,158	729
25 TO 29 YEARS	4,152	291	1,231	4,444	705	1,424	1,435	3,490	1,102
30 TO 34 YEARS	3,368	303	1,352	4,061	757	1,386	1,205	3,862	848
35 TO 44 YEARS	5,035	506	3,621	8,296	1,437	2,621	2,166	6,028	1,168
45 TO 54 YEARS	4,411	331	2,818	7,208	1,117	1,988	2,612	3,740	891
55 TO 59 YEARS	1,965	116	1,022	3,077	431	843	1,530	1,366	348
60 AND 61 YEARS	680	36	317	989	155	284	612	434	100
62 TO 64 YEARS	946	61	355	1,124	208	354	872	515	118
65 TO 74 YEARS	2,281	129	666	2,747	578	821	1,909	1,068	265
75 TO 84 YEARS	958	59	316	1,070	214	325	776	370	78
85 YEARS AND OVER	242	11	87	329	53	83	156	114	16
FEMALE	24,057	2,099	10,846	34,142	5,494	10,242	10,893	23,538	7,692
UNDER 1 YEAR	483	38	127	521	79	153	152	462	166
1 AND 2 YEARS	857	71	238	895	141	284	251	829	308
3 AND 4 YEARS	848	71	256	888	140	279	233	893	325
5 YEARS	454	36	115	469	65	143	87	473	192
6 YEARS	424	36	148	504	82	156	98	457	194
7 TO 9 YEARS	1,302	145	532	1,804	287	590	407	1,649	617
10 TO 13 YEARS	1,692	181	764	2,590	391	800	576	2,140	801
14 YEARS	423	52	208	791	112	215	163	514	199
15 YEARS	465	59	265	741	111	214	175	554	210
16 YEARS	447	64	216	765	113	238	182	525	194
17 YEARS	458	48	232	832	125	229	213	602	206
18 YEARS	469	43	203	780	89	210	213	498	169
19 YEARS	502	42	220	710	109	221	218	459	187
20 YEARS	460	50	200	750	102	209	218	457	147
21 YEARS	425	48	186	692	104	168	188	386	144
22 TO 24 YEARS	1,387	94	445	1,758	279	495	571	1,164	421
25 TO 29 YEARS	2,195	158	695	2,391	381	752	693	1,998	695
30 TO 34 YEARS	1,756	172	800	2,300	425	816	611	2,218	566
35 TO 44 YEARS	2,732	284	2,059	4,876	845	1,490	1,110	3,282	779
45 TO 54 YEARS	2,298	178	1,437	3,897	580	1,095	1,322	1,948	589
55 TO 59 YEARS	1,009	61	528	1,616	244	412	827	682	217
60 AND 61 YEARS	368	21	155	520	84	149	333	228	59
62 TO 64 YEARS	541	38	187	627	116	196	468	262	74
65 TO 74 YEARS	1,323	66	378	1,555	333	472	1,024	581	171
75 TO 84 YEARS	589	36	198	659	125	205	466	205	51
85 YEARS AND OVER	150	7	54	211	32	51	94	72	11
RACE									
TOTAL PERSONS	46,422	3,942	20,505	64,372	10,341	19,400	21,331	44,904	13,539
WHITE	12,759	364	1,582	1,212	1,982	6,043	20,081	2,587	357
BLACK	22,186	3,491	17,795	62,749	7,896	10,631	25	40,701	13,089
AMERICAN INDIAN	63	6	19	33	14	37	38	18	10
ESKIMO	0	0	0	0	1	0	0	0	0
ALEUT	3	0	0	0	0	1	0	2	0
JAPANESE	10	2	15	40	7	12	8	9	1
CHINESE	2	0	1	9	6	2	3	1	0
FILIPINO	10	0	73	61	1	2	7	3	0
KOREAN	4	0	3	2	1	0	9	7	0
ASIAN INDIAN	7	0	15	8	4	5	9	5	0
VIETNAMESE	2	0	2	8	0	0	0	5	3
HAWAIIAN	5	2	9	2	3	4	0	14	0
GUAMANIAN	0	0	0	0	0	0	0	1	0
SAMOAN	0								
OTHER	11,371	77	991	248	426	2,657	1,157	1,546	79
SPANISH ORIGIN									
TOTAL PERSONS	46,422	3,942	20,505	64,372	10,341	19,400	21,331	44,904	13,539
NOT OF SPANISH ORIGIN	28,193	3,842	19,024	63,822	9,699	14,637	18,653	42,595	13,363
MEXICAN	15,960	91	1,258	356	552	4,445	2,384	2,006	147
PUERTO RICAN	1,486	1	122	46	12	173	134	89	2
CUBAN	34	3	14	18	3	7	1	16	0
OTHER SPANISH	749	5	87	130	75	138	159	198	27
RACE: PERSONS OF SPANISH ORIGIN									
TOTAL	18,229	100	1,481	550	642	4,763	2,678	2,309	176
WHITE	6,792	37	519	108	244	2,121	1,635	606	21
BLACK	413	21	128	325	24	122	0	260	105
AMERICAN INDIAN, ESKIMO, ALEUT, AND ASIAN AND PACIFIC ISLANDER	40	0	14	7	4	14	17	13	0
OTHER	10,984	42	820	110	370	2,506	1,026	1,430	50

TABLE III-1 GENERAL CHARACTERISTICS OF THE POPULATION,
BY COMMUNITY AREA: CITY OF CHICAGO, 1980

	55	56	57	58	59	60	61	62	63
TOTAL POPULATION	11,572	37,935	9,708	30,770	13,248	30,923	55,860	12,797	24,445
SEX									
TOTAL PERSONS	11,572	37,929	9,708	30,770	13,248	30,923	55,860	12,797	24,445
MALE	5,773	18,180	4,648	14,749	6,391	15,000	27,771	5,969	11,552
FEMALE	5,799	19,749	5,060	16,021	6,857	15,923	28,089	6,828	12,893
AGE									
TOTAL PERSONS	11,572	37,929	9,708	30,770	13,248	30,923	55,860	12,797	24,445
UNDER 1 YEAR	116	407	115	455	225	523	1,417	121	343
1 AND 2 YEARS	227	727	187	756	364	874	2,392	225	591
3 AND 4 YEARS	215	758	168	692	378	825	2,408	215	623
5 YEARS	131	382	82	332	187	451	1,116	94	273
6 YEARS	133	392	75	322	179	404	1,064	103	251
7 TO 9 YEARS	418	1,407	255	1,119	562	1,287	3,288	351	851
10 TO 13 YEARS	739	2,225	395	1,519	771	1,866	4,049	498	1,227
14 YEARS	222	658	129	410	196	508	1,054	178	328
15 YEARS	236	763	144	444	208	514	1,035	182	362
16 YEARS	210	706	137	435	227	476	1,154	193	356
17 YEARS	217	722	127	435	217	543	1,122	198	377
18 YEARS	211	736	155	482	214	597	1,090	188	372
19 YEARS	234	758	151	531	238	580	1,211	172	393
20 YEARS	237	689	176	533	250	599	1,209	206	404
21 YEARS	227	696	189	578	261	600	1,174	204	436
22 TO 24 YEARS	613	1,914	601	1,867	783	1,944	3,563	678	1,274
25 TO 29 YEARS	747	2,408	772	2,588	1,167	2,655	4,775	901	1,976
30 TO 34 YEARS	666	2,278	539	1,860	847	2,130	3,718	758	1,541
35 TO 44 YEARS	1,371	3,854	818	2,788	1,281	3,059	5,182	1,031	2,126
45 TO 54 YEARS	1,386	4,710	1,129	3,222	1,289	2,971	4,804	1,553	2,531
55 TO 59 YEARS	889	3,184	965	2,333	908	1,920	2,548	1,192	1,656
60 AND 61 YEARS	384	1,218	381	987	389	820	992	497	719
62 TO 64 YEARS	451	1,871	544	1,397	466	1,142	1,305	756	1,054
65 TO 74 YEARS	937	3,336	1,033	3,239	1,110	2,543	2,874	1,631	2,784
75 TO 84 YEARS	272	890	309	1,100	407	839	1,025	534	1,260
85 YEARS AND OVER	83	240	132	346	124	253	291	138	337
FEMALE	5,799	19,749	5,060	16,021	6,857	15,923	28,089	6,828	12,893
UNDER 1 YEAR	70	192	55	218	116	251	707	68	165
1 AND 2 YEARS	115	356	90	356	181	426	1,112	116	294
3 AND 4 YEARS	112	356	69	342	165	388	1,168	103	311
5 YEARS	59	176	37	163	81	194	547	34	135
6 YEARS	61	183	35	152	85	208	497	44	117
7 TO 9 YEARS	207	728	125	563	279	625	1,600	181	397
10 TO 13 YEARS	356	1,086	199	756	371	934	2,019	250	608
14 YEARS	101	347	62	186	88	241	504	85	151
15 YEARS	119	366	65	225	102	264	495	103	168
16 YEARS	117	342	80	213	109	236	562	89	174
17 YEARS	97	349	62	210	117	268	528	104	193
18 YEARS	101	358	76	232	115	311	524	96	208
19 YEARS	98	381	78	284	119	294	593	80	223
20 YEARS	111	356	89	276	141	303	622	97	193
21 YEARS	111	353	92	296	134	307	587	105	221
22 TO 24 YEARS	273	882	292	938	382	956	1,717	328	626
25 TO 29 YEARS	355	1,197	355	1,265	567	1,273	2,302	430	956
30 TO 34 YEARS	332	1,144	273	888	412	1,066	1,821	365	720
35 TO 44 YEARS	718	2,127	412	1,388	636	1,552	2,626	547	1,058
45 TO 54 YEARS	694	2,603	600	1,709	687	1,564	2,473	856	1,332
55 TO 59 YEARS	444	1,702	568	1,198	495	1,044	1,326	665	917
60 AND 61 YEARS	191	635	185	539	211	438	529	278	394
62 TO 64 YEARS	240	984	278	776	261	609	732	439	599
65 TO 74 YEARS	508	1,806	578	1,856	657	1,471	1,646	921	1,697
75 TO 84 YEARS	158	578	210	764	261	537	669	353	820
85 YEARS AND OVER	51	162	95	228	85	163	183	91	216
RACE									
TOTAL PERSONS	11,572	37,935	9,708	30,770	13,248	30,923	55,860	12,797	24,445
WHITE	11,236	31,945	9,464	28,219	12,242	27,410	32,102	12,586	22,737
BLACK	29	5,116	8	34	5	40	12,239	7	163
AMERICAN INDIAN	17	15	18	75	10	91	81	10	29
ESKIMO	0	1	0	0	0	0	0	1	0
ALEUT	0	0	0	0	0	0	1	0	0
JAPANESE	7	11	0	12	3	8	13	1	11
CHINESE	0	17	6	18	2	437	40	8	20
FILIPINO	1	241	12	228	39	75	59	16	60
KOREAN	29	22	0	57	3	6	8	6	0
ASIAN INDIAN	3	46	3	11	13	16	33	1	45
VIETNAMESE	1	1	0	3	0	3	7	0	0
HAWAIIAN	1	7	0	2	9	1	12	0	0
GUAMANIAN	0	1	0	2	1	0	2	0	2
SAMOAN	0	1	0	0	0	0	0	0	1
OTHER	248	511	197	2,109	920	2,836	11,263	161	1,377
SPANISH ORIGIN									
TOTAL PERSONS	11,572	37,935	9,708	30,770	13,248	30,923	55,860	12,797	24,445
NOT OF SPANISH ORIGIN	10,854	36,369	9,354	26,231	11,119	24,339	35,915	12,500	21,744
MEXICAN	582	1,205	278	3,947	1,952	5,952	17,234	218	2,134
PUERTO RICAN	42	102	26	216	66	323	1,812	37	339
CUBAN	0	14	19	35	5	2	33	3	8
OTHER SPANISH	94	245	31	341	106	307	866	39	220
RACE: PERSONS OF SPANISH ORIGIN									
TOTAL	718	1,566	354	4,539	2,129	6,584	19,945	297	2,701
WHITE	528	1,124	239	2,674	1,235	3,870	9,012	197	1,525
BLACK	0	32	0	1	0	6	122	0	0
AMERICAN INDIAN, ESKIMO, ALEUT, AND ASIAN AND PACIFIC ISLANDER	2	30	3	55	9	56	59	7	8
OTHER	188	380	112	1,809	885	2,652	10,752	93	1,168

367

TABLE III-1 GENERAL CHARACTERISTICS OF THE POPULATION, BY COMMUNITY AREA: CITY OF CHICAGO, 1980

	64	65	66	67	68	69	70	71	72
TOTAL POPULATION	22,584	24,748	46,568	62,069	59,075	45,218	40,477	65,132	23,360
SEX									
TOTAL PERSONS	22,584	24,748	46,568	62,069	59,075	45,218	40,477	65,132	23,360
MALE	11,152	11,772	22,052	28,939	26,857	20,331	19,621	30,388	11,133
FEMALE	11,432	12,976	24,516	33,130	32,218	24,887	20,856	34,744	12,227
AGE									
TOTAL PERSONS	22,584	24,748	46,568	62,069	59,075	45,218	40,477	65,132	23,360
UNDER 1 YEAR	290	239	749	1,353	1,371	720	435	1,183	322
1 AND 2 YEARS	460	444	1,376	2,460	2,218	1,251	781	2,026	660
3 AND 4 YEARS	467	459	1,268	2,482	2,251	1,270	840	2,104	723
5 YEARS	237	233	597	1,151	1,104	564	452	1,026	301
6 YEARS	238	194	562	1,287	1,139	663	411	1,001	318
7 TO 9 YEARS	798	743	1,947	4,184	3,756	2,085	1,447	3,750	1,065
10 TO 13 YEARS	1,269	1,224	2,516	5,873	4,794	2,594	2,202	4,863	1,566
14 YEARS	348	396	653	1,558	1,299	691	735	1,363	403
15 YEARS	428	397	710	1,590	1,334	727	846	1,372	442
16 YEARS	419	437	704	1,652	1,357	712	891	1,428	468
17 YEARS	427	462	719	1,741	1,430	769	915	1,494	447
18 YEARS	427	437	741	1,626	1,393	679	844	1,362	378
19 YEARS	424	446	740	1,586	1,272	735	833	1,340	330
20 YEARS	456	463	800	1,486	1,322	774	861	1,361	328
21 YEARS	470	396	810	1,285	1,182	758	749	1,377	347
22 TO 24 YEARS	1,343	1,246	2,476	3,595	3,409	2,470	2,071	3,715	1,054
25 TO 29 YEARS	1,825	1,714	3,955	4,832	4,467	3,613	2,635	5,315	1,759
30 TO 34 YEARS	1,499	1,270	3,087	4,016	3,238	2,807	2,244	4,871	1,924
35 TO 44 YEARS	2,313	2,238	4,139	6,560	5,277	4,192	3,706	8,391	2,306
45 TO 54 YEARS	2,898	2,971	4,231	5,510	5,590	4,872	5,462	7,499	2,224
55 TO 59 YEARS	1,680	2,149	2,700	2,210	2,630	3,121	3,472	2,924	1,238
60 AND 61 YEARS	633	861	1,114	680	907	1,144	1,227	966	419
62 TO 64 YEARS	885	1,259	1,731	810	1,228	1,528	1,617	1,065	731
65 TO 74 YEARS	1,618	2,765	4,952	1,762	3,338	4,310	3,163	2,283	2,097
75 TO 84 YEARS	605	1,036	2,607	630	1,478	1,779	1,268	845	1,209
85 YEARS AND OVER	127	269	684	150	291	390	370	208	301
FEMALE	11,432	12,976	24,516	33,130	32,218	24,887	20,856	34,744	12,227
UNDER 1 YEAR	131	108	408	635	696	373	200	608	151
1 AND 2 YEARS	218	217	699	1,227	1,106	638	390	965	304
3 AND 4 YEARS	226	230	617	1,222	1,137	643	415	1,036	338
5 YEARS	117	96	295	567	545	270	211	515	143
6 YEARS	111	92	281	620	562	325	195	550	154
7 TO 9 YEARS	368	362	949	2,070	1,848	1,066	703	1,844	525
10 TO 13 YEARS	606	601	1,207	2,927	2,408	1,324	1,077	2,413	754
14 YEARS	182	173	309	769	624	345	373	687	195
15 YEARS	196	192	350	786	643	356	401	695	209
16 YEARS	209	200	335	824	712	365	443	696	235
17 YEARS	199	225	360	880	765	387	440	743	217
18 YEARS	208	230	386	831	737	347	440	683	177
19 YEARS	212	230	381	800	675	387	388	691	142
20 YEARS	231	224	397	790	717	433	416	734	162
21 YEARS	231	188	450	705	647	419	351	745	176
22 TO 24 YEARS	645	640	1,234	1,952	1,822	1,371	1,023	2,024	535
25 TO 29 YEARS	867	840	1,983	2,809	2,540	1,987	1,275	3,019	905
30 TO 34 YEARS	729	602	1,473	2,316	1,912	1,574	1,082	2,783	972
35 TO 44 YEARS	1,181	1,184	2,092	3,799	3,162	2,368	1,958	4,736	1,198
45 TO 54 YEARS	1,512	1,619	2,127	3,133	3,204	2,856	2,973	4,021	1,150
55 TO 59 YEARS	849	1,137	1,463	1,220	1,447	1,767	1,821	1,547	690
60 AND 61 YEARS	343	464	607	348	531	642	603	503	228
62 TO 64 YEARS	489	678	977	442	676	877	839	552	429
65 TO 74 YEARS	922	1,586	2,963	964	1,966	2,473	1,764	1,278	1,240
75 TO 84 YEARS	369	669	1,717	391	941	1,035	796	528	788
85 YEARS AND OVER	81	189	456	103	195	259	279	148	210
RACE									
TOTAL PERSONS	22,584	24,748	46,568	62,069	59,075	45,218	40,477	65,132	23,360
WHITE	22,227	24,344	38,660	818	377	281	38,651	754	19,947
BLACK	5	52	4,782	60,882	58,395	44,660	1,084	64,093	3,178
AMERICAN INDIAN	15	9	59	29	40	49	32	39	16
ESKIMO	0	0	0	0	0	0	0	0	0
ALEUT	0	0	0	1	0	0	0	0	1
JAPANESE	7	4	22	20	13	7	22	16	5
CHINESE	8	20	61	3	3	4	52	7	9
FILIPINO	6	25	338	7	22	12	74	9	31
KOREAN	5	10	46	6	2	1	8	4	4
ASIAN INDIAN	2	5	33	6	2	4	58	8	34
VIETNAMESE	2	5	9	0	1	1	1	0	11
HAWAIIAN	0	0	1	11	11	19	3	10	0
GUAMANIAN	0	0	0	0	0	3	0	0	0
SAMOAN	0	0	0	1	1	0	0	1	0
OTHER	300	279	2,557	284	207	177	491	189	124
SPANISH ORIGIN									
TOTAL PERSONS	22,584	24,748	46,568	62,069	59,075	45,218	40,477	65,132	23,360
NOT OF SPANISH ORIGIN	21,668	24,149	41,628	61,383	58,578	44,952	39,572	64,669	23,052
MEXICAN	715	469	3,797	392	257	135	654	225	206
PUERTO RICAN	52	23	663	184	116	30	73	35	15
CUBAN	33	22	37	19	13	11	19	26	9
OTHER SPANISH	116	85	443	91	111	90	159	177	78
RACE: PERSONS OF SPANISH ORIGIN									
TOTAL	916	599	4,940	686	497	266	905	463	308
WHITE	677	427	2,962	102	41	10	625	16	198
BLACK	0	0	20	336	358	194	2	385	27
AMERICAN INDIAN, ESKIMO, ALEUT, AND ASIAN AND PACIFIC ISLANDER	1	2	51	11	7	7	16	3	10
OTHER	238	170	1,907	237	91	55	262	59	73

	73	74	75	76	77
TOTAL POPULATION	36,453	20,084	29,315	11,068	58,561
SEX					
TOTAL PERSONS	36,453	20,084	29,315	11,054	58,561
MALE	17,088	9,616	13,679	5,319	27,690
FEMALE	19,365	10,468	15,636	5,735	30,871
AGE					
TOTAL PERSONS	36,453	20,084	29,315	11,054	58,561
UNDER 1 YEAR	563	250	495	152	809
1 AND 2 YEARS	942	450	794	174	1,271
3 AND 4 YEARS	931	456	790	173	1,054
5 YEARS	475	203	373	64	507
6 YEARS	479	224	383	64	469
7 TO 9 YEARS	1,904	757	1,462	220	1,368
10 TO 13 YEARS	2,791	1,152	2,093	309	1,694
14 YEARS	829	336	577	86	460
15 YEARS	878	368	658	107	530
16 YEARS	898	363	674	100	551
17 YEARS	975	391	659	114	607
18 YEARS	922	362	612	97	751
19 YEARS	858	393	582	142	962
20 YEARS	825	374	566	170	1,125
21 YEARS	745	349	542	203	1,206
22 TO 24 YEARS	2,056	1,057	1,490	990	4,328
25 TO 29 YEARS	2,362	1,412	2,092	1,669	7,179
30 TO 34 YEARS	2,120	1,109	1,799	1,122	5,414
35 TO 44 YEARS	4,998	1,799	3,424	1,229	6,168
45 TO 54 YEARS	4,938	2,246	3,066	1,319	5,636
55 TO 59 YEARS	1,934	1,457	1,465	717	2,937
60 AND 61 YEARS	576	605	552	281	1,106
62 TO 64 YEARS	656	860	736	361	1,653
65 TO 74 YEARS	1,210	1,970	1,916	801	5,821
75 TO 84 YEARS	469	922	1,171	335	4,004
85 YEARS AND OVER	119	219	344	55	951
FEMALE	19,365	10,468	15,636	5,735	30,871
UNDER 1 YEAR	303	119	239	80	383
1 AND 2 YEARS	478	233	393	81	614
3 AND 4 YEARS	487	234	383	82	501
5 YEARS	243	98	194	35	250
6 YEARS	257	105	188	33	220
7 TO 9 YEARS	937	382	709	115	670
10 TO 13 YEARS	1,378	515	1,046	151	822
14 YEARS	404	151	299	49	219
15 YEARS	441	191	326	65	263
16 YEARS	475	180	342	40	273
17 YEARS	477	201	326	54	295
18 YEARS	493	183	292	55	409
19 YEARS	451	188	293	67	519
20 YEARS	412	175	298	107	584
21 YEARS	375	178	260	122	620
22 TO 24 YEARS	1,054	515	770	557	2,070
25 TO 29 YEARS	1,278	687	1,084	835	3,385
30 TO 34 YEARS	1,230	540	962	495	2,461
35 TO 44 YEARS	2,955	906	1,923	591	2,921
45 TO 54 YEARS	2,632	1,217	1,618	658	2,791
55 TO 59 YEARS	951	765	812	369	1,626
60 AND 61 YEARS	279	324	315	164	636
62 TO 64 YEARS	326	483	394	194	1,009
65 TO 74 YEARS	656	1,153	1,129	493	3,878
75 TO 84 YEARS	316	596	779	212	2,781
85 YEARS AND OVER	77	149	262	31	671
RACE					
TOTAL PERSONS	36,453	20,084	29,315	11,068	58,561
WHITE	523	19,883	10,758	10,592	42,075
BLACK	35,778	93	18,320	165	6,514
AMERICAN INDIAN	25	13	21	8	336
ESKIMO	0	0	0	0	5
ALEUT	0	0	0	0	0
JAPANESE	10	4	19	60	1,295
CHINESE	16	14	6	14	1,033
FILIPINO	0	8	20	40	1,301
KOREAN	4	5	5	24	665
ASIAN INDIAN	0	5	10	51	1,033
VIETNAMESE	0	0	8	1	311
HAWAIIAN	3	0	2	0	12
GUAMANIAN	1	0	2	0	15
SAMOAN	0	0	0	6	0
OTHER	93	59	144	107	3,966
SPANISH ORIGIN					
TOTAL PERSONS	36,453	20,084	29,315	11,068	58,561
NOT OF SPANISH ORIGIN	36,276	19,930	29,035	10,780	50,756
MEXICAN	88	104	188	109	2,944
PUERTO RICAN	30	16	18	46	954
CUBAN	10	1	5	26	1,441
OTHER SPANISH	49	33	69	107	2,466
RACE: PERSONS OF SPANISH ORIGIN					
TOTAL	177	154	280	288	7,805
WHITE	5	116	97	218	4,819
BLACK	134	1	94	2	146
AMERICAN INDIAN, ESKIMO, ALEUT, AND					
ASIAN AND PACIFIC ISLANDER	0	1	13	5	199
OTHER	38	36	76	63	2,641

TABLE III-2 FAMILY AND DISABILITY CHARACTERISTICS
OF THE POPULATION, BY COMMUNITY AREA: CITY OF CHICAGO, 1980

	01	02	03	04	05	06	07	08	09
MARITAL STATUS									
MALE, 15 YRS. AND OVER	22,606	23,354	26,142	16,763	12,997	40,392	24,479	26,158	4,784
SINGLE	10,620	6,592	11,772	5,715	4,430	18,826	12,440	12,403	1,458
NOW MARRIED, EXCEPT SEPARATED	9,047	14,761	9,624	8,981	6,911	15,318	8,101	8,651	3,009
SEPARATED	538	225	1,200	307	231	1,226	697	1,058	18
WIDOWED	716	884	1,159	646	508	1,174	610	867	161
DIVORCED	1,685	892	2,387	1,114	917	3,848	2,631	3,179	138
FEMALE, 15 YRS. AND OVER	25,144	28,790	25,421	19,789	15,058	44,178	25,988	30,356	5,803
SINGLE	9,282	6,457	7,922	5,116	3,798	16,533	11,724	13,266	1,446
NOW MARRIED, EXCEPT SEPARATED	8,782	14,798	9,127	8,869	6,841	14,906	7,935	8,205	3,012
SEPARATED	702	286	1,484	486	442	1,287	770	1,614	40
WIDOWED	3,974	5,434	4,176	3,531	2,463	6,448	2,579	3,763	1,043
DIVORCED	2,404	1,815	2,712	1,787	1,514	5,004	2,980	3,508	262
PERSONS IN HOUSEHOLD									
NUMBER OF HOUSEHOLDS	26,245	24,962	28,259	18,753	14,067	52,167	31,781	36,488	4,715
1 PERSON	12,237	7,022	13,543	6,756	4,260	27,093	18,008	21,845	1,122
2 PERSONS	7,747	9,286	6,618	5,711	4,168	14,808	8,464	8,608	1,656
3 PERSONS	2,849	3,870	3,049	2,628	2,303	4,738	2,620	2,474	708
4 PERSONS	1,761	2,599	2,324	2,007	1,731	2,879	1,499	1,812	570
5 PERSONS	1,001	1,346	1,235	956	892	1,337	702	923	372
6 OR MORE PERSONS	650	839	1,490	695	713	1,312	488	826	287
HOUSEHOLD TYPE AND RELATIONSHIP									
PERSONS IN HOUSEHOLDS	52,668	59,950	60,246	43,160	35,076	96,523	55,193	63,814	12,457
IN FAMILY HOUSEHOLD:									
HOUSEHOLDER	11,288	17,150	12,515	11,038	9,070	19,698	10,285	12,424	3,505
SPOUSE	8,161	14,197	8,201	8,376	6,571	14,131	7,552	7,720	2,959
OTHER RELATIVES	14,096	19,445	20,209	14,755	13,274	23,501	11,398	16,474	4,700
NONRELATIVES	793	331	1,155	370	398	1,207	585	699	26
IN NONFAMILY HOUSEHOLD:									
MALE HOUSEHOLDER	7,016	2,459	8,704	3,018	2,016	14,986	10,528	11,419	295
FEMALE HOUSEHOLDER	7,995	5,395	6,992	4,607	2,944	17,293	10,841	12,528	898
NONRELATIVES	3,319	973	2,470	996	803	5,707	4,004	2,550	74
IN GROUP QUARTERS:									
INMATE OF INSTITUTION	1,458	1,085	1,648	693	60	83	846	834	0
OTHER	1,399	94	2,520	101	25	913	1,107	2,510	0
FAMILY TYPE BY PRESENCE OF OWN CHILDREN UNDER 18 YEARS									
HOUSEHOLDS	26,245	24,962	28,259	18,753	14,067	52,167	31,781	36,488	4,715
MARRIED-COUPLE FAMILY:									
WITH OWN CHILDREN	3,582	5,154	4,703	3,774	3,246	5,842	2,851	1,954	1,140
WITHOUT OWN CHILDREN	4,806	9,145	4,041	4,755	3,523	8,829	4,774	5,816	1,838
FAMILY WITH MALE HOUSEHOLDER, NO WIFE PRESENT:									
WITH OWN CHILDREN	135	132	280	170	153	374	179	229	6
WITHOUT OWN CHILDREN	576	606	722	521	430	1,099	481	265	79
FAMILY WITH FEMALE HOUSEHOLDER, NO HUSBAND PRESENT:									
WITH OWN CHILDREN	1,191	689	2,226	778	1,076	2,093	1,371	3,163	107
WITHOUT OWN CHILDREN	1,115	1,408	941	1,174	817	1,894	736	987	379
NONFAMILY HOUSEHOLD	14,840	7,828	15,346	7,581	4,822	32,036	21,389	24,074	1,166
LANGUAGE SPOKEN AT HOME AND ABILITY TO SPEAK ENGLISH									
PERSONS 5 TO 17 YEARS	6,290	8,309	10,126	6,490	6,303	10,539	5,500	8,858	2,101
SPEAK ONLY ENGLISH AT HOME	3,914	5,185	5,414	3,341	4,541	5,967	3,893	8,506	1,895
SPEAK A LANGUAGE OTHER THAN ENGLISH AT HOME:	777	297	2,167	736	1,162	3,151	1,029	67	11
SPANISH LANGUAGE SPOKEN AT HOME:									
SPEAK ENGLISH VERY WELL OR WELL	138	35	791	175	110	614	270	83	0
SPEAK ENGLISH NOT WELL OR NOT AT ALL	1,046	2,463	1,181	2,024	420	724	293	202	195
OTHER LANGUAGE SPOKEN AT HOME	415	329	573	214	70	83	15	0	0
PERSONS 18 YEARS AND OVER	46,176	49,874	49,264	34,845	26,408	82,113	49,122	54,561	9,895
SPEAK ONLY ENGLISH AT HOME	32,315	32,854	29,895	20,577	18,362	59,318	40,420	49,312	8,193
SPEAK A LANGUAGE OTHER THAN ENGLISH AT HOME:	2,700	1,052	5,288	2,092	2,522	8,178	2,893	1,197	39
SPANISH LANGUAGE SPOKEN AT HOME:									
SPEAK ENGLISH VERY WELL OR WELL	1,774	301	4,273	992	1,142	3,639	1,108	397	24
SPEAK ENGLISH NOT WELL OR NOT AT ALL	6,967	12,938	7,458	8,855	3,792	9,730	4,398	3,364	1,477
OTHER LANGUAGE SPOKEN AT HOME	2,420	2,729	2,350	2,329	590	1,248	303	291	162
TYPE OF GROUP QUARTERS									
PERSONS IN GROUP QUARTERS	2,875	1,166	4,197	804	67	1,017	2,010	3,339	0
INMATE OF MENTAL HOSPITAL	0	227	189	52	0	46	0	26	0
INMATE OF HOME FOR THE AGED	1,464	740	1,365	575	47	23	641	121	0
INMATE OF OTHER INSTITUTION	27	118	16	68	13	41	6	416	0
IN MILITARY BARRACKS	0	0	0	0	0	0	0	0	0
IN COLLEGE DORMITORY	1,157	0	0	0	0	170	719	2,020	0
OTHER IN GROUP QUARTERS	227	81	2,627	109	7	737	644	756	0
WORK DISABILITY STATUS									
NONINSTITUTIONAL PERSONS 16 TO 64 YEARS	38,659	37,517	41,408	28,187	22,764	69,586	44,132	46,874	8,019
WITH A WORK DISABILITY									
IN LABOR FORCE	1,165	993	1,454	799	561	2,187	773	1,081	210
NOT IN LABOR FORCE:									
PREVENTED FROM WORKING	971	872	3,438	986	1,190	2,011	1,045	1,249	230
NOT PREVENTED FROM WORKING	266	145	429	197	220	485	130	427	30
NO WORK DISABILITY	36,257	35,507	36,087	26,205	20,793	64,903	42,184	44,117	7,549
PUBLIC TRANSPORTATION DISABILITY STATUS									
NONINSTITUTIONAL PERSONS 16 TO 64 YEARS									
WITH A PUBLIC TRANSPORTATION DISABILITY	605	668	1,756	510	575	1,205	499	675	161
NO PUBLIC TRANSPORTATION DISABILITY	38,054	36,849	39,652	27,677	22,189	68,381	43,633	46,199	7,858
NONINSTITUTIONAL PERSONS 65 YEARS AND OVER									
WITH A PUBLIC TRANSPORTATION DISABILITY	1,036	1,528	1,808	995	871	2,074	932	1,020	265
NO PUBLIC TRANSPORTATION DISABILITY	6,083	11,399	6,021	6,344	3,870	12,162	4,253	7,431	2,057

	10	11	12	13	14	15	16	17	18
MARITAL STATUS									
MALE, 15 YRS. AND OVER	16,057	9,556	7,324	5,854	17,092	22,039	18,894	15,043	4,147
SINGLE	4,736	2,802	2,096	1,909	5,786	6,854	6,152	4,629	1,195
NOW MARRIED, EXCEPT SEPARATED	10,209	5,927	4,811	3,540	9,609	13,078	10,337	9,196	2,563
SEPARATED	78	75	35	47	300	263	312	109	37
WIDOWED	580	356	204	153	476	859	699	537	188
DIVORCED	454	396	178	205	921	985	1,394	572	164
FEMALE, 15 YRS. AND OVER	18,743	11,655	8,524	6,998	18,487	26,548	21,805	17,033	5,047
SINGLE	4,430	2,659	1,986	2,094	4,474	6,424	5,399	3,794	1,164
NOW MARRIED, EXCEPT SEPARATED	10,198	5,905	4,804	3,522	9,355	13,001	10,260	9,173	2,572
SEPARATED	114	98	53	74	536	324	457	152	58
WIDOWED	3,250	2,336	1,363	966	2,595	5,149	3,615	3,047	1,006
DIVORCED	751	657	318	342	1,527	1,650	2,074	867	247
PERSONS IN HOUSEHOLD									
NUMBER OF HOUSEHOLDS	14,995	9,914	6,803	5,399	16,272	22,760	20,489	13,879	4,103
1 PERSON	3,120	2,661	1,238	1,210	4,003	6,537	6,959	2,921	1,043
2 PERSONS	5,373	3,620	2,536	1,936	4,451	7,470	6,195	4,877	1,345
3 PERSONS	2,575	1,535	1,154	921	2,916	3,647	3,076	2,401	691
4 PERSONS	2,075	1,120	938	742	2,414	2,665	2,190	1,947	500
5 PERSONS	1,069	632	562	370	1,393	1,432	1,215	1,026	382
6 OR MORE PERSONS	783	346	375	220	1,095	1,009	854	707	142
HOUSEHOLD TYPE AND RELATIONSHIP									
PERSONS IN HOUSEHOLDS	40,155	24,582	18,991	14,109	45,684	57,032	49,006	37,350	10,677
IN FAMILY HOUSEHOLD:									
HOUSEHOLDER	11,601	7,078	5,526	3,953	11,555	15,756	12,739	10,745	3,013
SPOUSE	9,905	5,732	4,696	3,399	8,742	12,515	9,791	8,876	2,436
OTHER RELATIVES	14,946	8,519	7,336	4,914	19,136	20,758	17,124	14,177	4,027
NONRELATIVES	138	125	52	84	600	308	468	166	34
IN NONFAMILY HOUSEHOLD:									
MALE HOUSEHOLDER	932	815	358	506	2,161	2,268	3,295	954	362
FEMALE HOUSEHOLDER	2,384	2,067	929	949	2,569	4,784	4,559	2,190	751
NONRELATIVES	249	246	94	304	921	643	1,030	242	54
IN GROUP QUARTERS:									
INMATE OF INSTITUTION	254	0	0	251	345	92	360	509	94
OTHER	176	1	0	913	46	225	123	1	22
FAMILY TYPE BY PRESENCE OF OWN CHILDREN UNDER 18 YEARS									
HOUSEHOLDS	14,995	9,914	6,803	5,399	16,272	22,760	20,489	13,879	4,103
MARRIED-COUPLE FAMILY:									
WITH OWN CHILDREN	3,540	2,038	1,798	1,315	5,026	5,006	4,404	3,375	950
WITHOUT OWN CHILDREN	6,419	3,805	2,923	2,078	4,116	7,569	5,516	5,579	1,549
FAMILY WITH MALE HOUSEHOLDER, NO WIFE PRESENT:									
WITH OWN CHILDREN	77	47	53	21	136	100	101	96	15
WITHOUT OWN CHILDREN	402	280	129	128	445	641	495	399	129
FAMILY WITH FEMALE HOUSEHOLDER, NO HUSBAND PRESENT:									
WITH OWN CHILDREN	300	218	125	168	991	665	1,000	295	142
WITHOUT OWN CHILDREN	965	658	453	249	868	1,782	1,190	1,026	231
NONFAMILY HOUSEHOLD	3,292	2,868	1,322	1,440	4,690	6,997	7,783	3,109	1,087
LANGUAGE SPOKEN AT HOME AND ABILITY TO SPEAK ENGLISH									
PERSONS 5 TO 17 YEARS	6,327	3,468	3,474	2,291	8,837	8,770	7,785	6,088	1,697
SPEAK ONLY ENGLISH AT HOME	5,666	2,950	2,968	1,457	4,695	7,309	6,113	5,038	1,248
SPEAK A LANGUAGE OTHER THAN ENGLISH AT HOME:	76	45	46	130	1,496	151	565	45	66
SPANISH LANGUAGE SPOKEN AT HOME:									
SPEAK ENGLISH VERY WELL OR WELL	19	6	25	0	378	0	89	9	0
SPEAK ENGLISH NOT WELL OR NOT AT ALL	548	451	435	669	1,837	1,250	960	967	383
OTHER LANGUAGE SPOKEN AT HOME	18	16	0	35	431	60	58	29	0
PERSONS 18 YEARS AND OVER	32,708	20,144	14,780	12,226	33,348	45,925	38,735	30,188	8,664
SPEAK ONLY ENGLISH AT HOME	25,448	15,406	11,581	7,742	17,446	33,917	27,856	22,367	6,245
SPEAK A LANGUAGE OTHER THAN ENGLISH AT HOME:	146	224	178	471	3,341	766	1,869	383	148
SPANISH LANGUAGE SPOKEN AT HOME:									
SPEAK ENGLISH VERY WELL OR WELL	12	5	28	93	1,926	168	461	55	21
SPEAK ENGLISH NOT WELL OR NOT AT ALL	6,249	3,814	2,663	3,370	7,934	9,304	7,066	5,955	1,794
OTHER LANGUAGE SPOKEN AT HOME	853	695	330	550	2,701	1,770	1,483	1,428	456
TYPE OF GROUP QUARTERS									
PERSONS IN GROUP QUARTERS	432	0	0	1,130	372	323	479	518	114
INMATE OF MENTAL HOSPITAL	0	0	0	0	0	0	0	358	0
INMATE OF HOME FOR THE AGED	255	0	0	214	337	0	271	0	89
INMATE OF OTHER INSTITUTION	0	0	0	34	0	90	91	159	0
IN MILITARY BARRACKS	0	0	0	0	0	0	0	0	0
IN COLLEGE DORMITORY	0	0	0	741	0	12	0	0	0
OTHER IN GROUP QUARTERS	177	0	0	141	35	221	117	1	25
WORK DISABILITY STATUS									
NONINSTITUTIONAL PERSONS 16 TO 64 YEARS	26,279	15,831	11,879	9,921	29,670	36,664	32,441	24,208	6,898
WITH A WORK DISABILITY									
IN LABOR FORCE	694	359	235	268	829	990	907	673	175
NOT IN LABOR FORCE:									
PREVENTED FROM WORKING	842	607	201	243	998	1,238	1,312	803	286
NOT PREVENTED FROM WORKING	266	154	78	72	191	257	211	224	69
NO WORK DISABILITY	24,477	14,711	11,365	9,338	27,652	34,179	30,011	22,508	6,368
PUBLIC TRANSPORTATION DISABILITY STATUS									
NONINSTITUTIONAL PERSONS 16 TO 64 YEARS									
WITH A PUBLIC TRANSPORTATION DISABILITY	505	298	112	172	614	723	778	473	88
NO PUBLIC TRANSPORTATION DISABILITY	25,774	15,533	11,767	9,749	29,056	35,941	31,663	23,735	6,810
NONINSTITUTIONAL PERSONS 65 YEARS AND OVER									
WITH A PUBLIC TRANSPORTATION DISABILITY	1,032	727	399	230	791	1,690	1,174	1,013	439
NO PUBLIC TRANSPORTATION DISABILITY	6,583	4,289	3,223	2,298	3,994	9,224	6,203	5,901	1,681

TABLE III-2 FAMILY AND DISABILITY CHARACTERISTICS
OF THE POPULATION, BY COMMUNITY AREA: CITY OF CHICAGO, 1980

	19	20	21	22	23	24	25	26	27
MARITAL STATUS									
MALE, 15 YRS. AND OVER	20,693	7,219	12,937	30,857	22,735	34,107	43,618	9,940	9,836
SINGLE	6,208	2,261	4,095	11,272	8,950	13,488	18,056	4,821	4,615
NOW MARRIED, EXCEPT SEPARATED	12,392	4,100	7,260	15,482	10,915	16,075	19,409	3,259	2,946
SEPARATED	229	143	270	996	1,005	1,441	2,447	870	1,002
WIDOWED	858	257	465	1,134	736	1,189	1,258	371	551
DIVORCED	1,006	458	847	1,973	1,129	1,914	2,448	619	722
FEMALE, 15 YRS. AND OVER	24,158	7,984	14,224	31,439	25,492	34,409	52,628	12,767	12,119
SINGLE	5,369	1,857	3,243	8,257	8,103	9,904	18,937	5,355	4,850
NOW MARRIED, EXCEPT SEPARATED	12,167	3,992	6,855	14,675	10,694	15,056	19,327	3,251	2,917
SEPARATED	345	258	459	1,757	2,183	2,384	4,649	1,591	1,538
WIDOWED	4,724	1,254	2,430	4,080	2,649	4,328	5,491	1,432	1,720
DIVORCED	1,553	623	1,237	2,670	1,863	2,737	4,224	1,138	1,094
PERSONS IN HOUSEHOLD									
NUMBER OF HOUSEHOLDS	21,194	7,089	13,160	29,317	21,230	32,233	41,350	9,257	9,895
1 PERSON	5,741	1,784	3,831	8,125	4,554	8,717	8,417	1,729	2,638
2 PERSONS	6,840	2,007	3,982	6,992	4,206	7,048	9,166	1,713	1,976
3 PERSONS	3,646	1,209	2,225	4,781	3,608	5,244	7,558	1,467	1,493
4 PERSONS	2,680	1,048	1,636	3,987	3,362	4,363	6,439	1,390	1,253
5 PERSONS	1,394	545	730	2,432	2,337	3,043	4,093	1,018	875
6 OR MORE PERSONS	893	496	756	3,000	3,163	3,818	5,677	1,940	1,660
HOUSEHOLD TYPE AND RELATIONSHIP									
PERSONS IN HOUSEHOLDS	53,071	19,471	33,464	83,823	70,374	95,529	136,578	33,412	31,473
IN FAMILY HOUSEHOLD:									
HOUSEHOLDER	14,743	5,038	8,657	19,864	16,078	22,000	31,819	7,088	6,674
SPOUSE	11,559	3,767	6,239	13,531	9,874	13,737	17,906	2,904	2,601
OTHER RELATIVES	19,423	8,169	12,533	37,617	37,220	46,209	73,068	20,135	17,714
NONRELATIVES	354	210	473	1,489	1,185	1,604	2,382	815	828
IN NONFAMILY HOUSEHOLD:									
MALE HOUSEHOLDER	2,172	855	2,003	5,091	2,706	5,516	4,986	973	1,616
FEMALE HOUSEHOLDER	4,168	1,160	2,562	4,522	2,612	4,606	4,812	1,079	1,481
NONRELATIVES	652	272	997	1,709	699	1,857	1,605	418	559
IN GROUP QUARTERS:									
INMATE OF INSTITUTION	242	51	0	434	157	314	618	45	32
OTHER	58	25	63	511	335	585	830	408	75
FAMILY TYPE BY PRESENCE OF OWN CHILDREN UNDER 18 YEARS									
HOUSEHOLDS	21,194	7,089	13,160	29,317	21,230	32,233	41,350	9,257	9,895
MARRIED-COUPLE FAMILY:									
WITH OWN CHILDREN	4,872	1,987	3,085	8,073	6,522	8,833	11,282	1,879	1,305
WITHOUT OWN CHILDREN	7,041	1,886	3,495	6,075	3,743	5,725	7,500	1,305	1,283
FAMILY WITH MALE HOUSEHOLDER, NO WIFE PRESENT:									
WITH OWN CHILDREN	145	43	114	445	477	499	752	224	165
WITHOUT OWN CHILDREN	580	277	427	946	540	1,258	1,063	259	333
FAMILY WITH FEMALE HOUSEHOLDER, NO HUSBAND PRESENT:									
WITH OWN CHILDREN	711	488	792	3,170	3,738	4,431	8,071	2,664	2,635
WITHOUT OWN CHILDREN	1,665	414	863	1,464	1,183	1,782	3,137	896	1,113
NONFAMILY HOUSEHOLD	6,180	1,994	4,384	9,144	5,027	9,705	9,545	2,030	3,061
LANGUAGE SPOKEN AT HOME AND ABILITY TO SPEAK ENGLISH									
PERSONS 5 TO 17 YEARS	8,005	3,749	5,583	18,316	19,636	23,674	36,515	10,119	8,530
SPEAK ONLY ENGLISH AT HOME	6,019	2,139	3,190	6,673	10,879	7,318	33,041	9,959	8,397
SPEAK A LANGUAGE OTHER THAN ENGLISH AT HOME:	500	1,138	1,399	9,211	6,879	12,172	2,161	88	76
SPANISH LANGUAGE SPOKEN AT HOME:									
SPEAK ENGLISH VERY WELL OR WELL	28	270	151	1,752	1,364	3,078	237	12	16
SPEAK ENGLISH NOT WELL OR NOT AT ALL	1,381	198	686	574	470	1,011	1,025	60	41
OTHER LANGUAGE SPOKEN AT HOME	77	4	157	106	44	95	51	0	0
PERSONS 18 YEARS AND OVER	42,579	14,343	25,625	58,164	43,582	62,760	87,642	20,093	19,820
SPEAK ONLY ENGLISH AT HOME	26,693	7,895	13,644	24,620	23,211	20,332	76,165	19,593	19,348
SPEAK A LANGUAGE OTHER THAN ENGLISH AT HOME:	1,407	2,496	2,639	15,659	9,943	17,422	3,516	244	259
SPANISH LANGUAGE SPOKEN AT HOME:									
SPEAK ENGLISH VERY WELL OR WELL	335	1,146	1,236	9,395	5,708	12,104	1,404	36	29
SPEAK ENGLISH NOT WELL OR NOT AT ALL	10,978	2,282	5,462	6,875	3,819	9,938	5,658	207	184
OTHER LANGUAGE SPOKEN AT HOME	3,166	524	2,644	1,615	901	2,964	899	13	0
TYPE OF GROUP QUARTERS									
PERSONS IN GROUP QUARTERS	305	61	20	858	550	817	1,493	455	117
INMATE OF MENTAL HOSPITAL	0	0	0	0	157	31	118	41	37
INMATE OF HOME FOR THE AGED	246	55	0	347	0	178	454	0	0
INMATE OF OTHER INSTITUTION	0	0	0	32	0	12	17	0	0
IN MILITARY BARRACKS	0	0	0	0	0	0	0	0	0
IN COLLEGE DORMITORY	0	0	0	0	2	0	24	0	0
OTHER IN GROUP QUARTERS	59	6	20	479	391	596	880	414	80
WORK DISABILITY STATUS									
NONINSTITUTIONAL PERSONS 16 TO 64 YEARS	34,163	12,403	22,117	53,098	42,043	58,300	84,766	20,033	18,808
WITH A WORK DISABILITY									
IN LABOR FORCE	1,010	353	679	1,755	1,209	1,745	2,867	592	574
NOT IN LABOR FORCE:									
PREVENTED FROM WORKING	1,494	590	1,033	3,166	2,822	3,873	4,986	1,549	1,967
NOT PREVENTED FROM WORKING	204	58	140	522	433	690	970	370	434
NO WORK DISABILITY	31,455	11,402	20,265	47,655	37,579	51,992	75,943	17,522	15,833
PUBLIC TRANSPORTATION DISABILITY STATUS									
NONINSTITUTIONAL PERSONS 16 TO 64 YEARS									
WITH A PUBLIC TRANSPORTATION DISABILITY	772	221	421	1,491	1,312	1,603	2,364	723	849
NO PUBLIC TRANSPORTATION DISABILITY	33,391	12,182	21,696	51,607	40,731	56,697	82,402	19,310	17,959
NONINSTITUTIONAL PERSONS 65 YEARS AND OVER									
WITH A PUBLIC TRANSPORTATION DISABILITY	1,403	513	778	1,252	740	1,370	1,686	487	701
NO PUBLIC TRANSPORTATION DISABILITY	8,387	1,951	3,760	6,255	3,780	6,794	6,449	1,191	1,765

TABLE III-2 FAMILY AND DISABILITY CHARACTERISTICS
OF THE POPULATION, BY COMMUNITY AREA: CITY OF CHICAGO, 1980

	28	29	30	31	32	33	34	35	36
MARITAL STATUS									
MALE, 15 YRS. AND OVER	17,716	18,147	28,353	16,374	3,510	1,689	4,624	10,468	3,853
SINGLE	9,343	8,581	11,812	6,506	1,522	862	1,860	5,130	2,327
NOW MARRIED, EXCEPT SEPARATED	5,080	5,981	14,216	8,416	1,223	491	2,258	3,141	864
SEPARATED	1,281	1,613	702	336	187	119	100	776	256
WIDOWED	853	789	609	458	138	106	246	538	215
DIVORCED	1,159	1,183	1,014	658	440	111	160	883	191
FEMALE, 15 YRS. AND OVER	21,265	23,153	23,767	14,766	2,747	2,976	5,279	15,978	6,377
SINGLE	9,204	9,343	6,568	4,190	922	1,241	1,548	6,663	3,036
NOW MARRIED, EXCEPT SEPARATED	4,874	5,986	12,255	7,427	913	478	2,199	3,160	908
SEPARATED	2,549	3,010	995	674	84	414	222	1,589	933
WIDOWED	2,864	2,831	2,720	1,632	524	481	1,017	2,648	878
DIVORCED	1,774	1,983	1,229	843	304	362	293	1,918	622
PERSONS IN HOUSEHOLD									
NUMBER OF HOUSEHOLDS	18,630	17,266	19,197	13,034	3,853	2,419	4,505	14,319	4,894
1 PERSON	5,867	3,088	3,294	2,635	2,689	835	1,379	6,362	1,340
2 PERSONS	3,712	3,440	3,411	2,543	943	422	1,018	3,053	868
3 PERSONS	2,632	3,073	3,080	2,025	149	399	667	2,067	709
4 PERSONS	2,142	2,616	3,258	1,961	47	318	639	1,288	564
5 PERSONS	1,626	1,995	2,480	1,437	23	212	400	627	448
6 OR MORE PERSONS	2,651	3,054	3,674	2,433	2	233	402	922	965
HOUSEHOLD TYPE AND RELATIONSHIP									
PERSONS IN HOUSEHOLDS	55,382	60,937	70,461	44,760	5,342	6,963	12,446	33,190	16,662
IN FAMILY HOUSEHOLD:									
HOUSEHOLDER	11,581	13,463	15,339	9,695	1,028	1,558	2,940	7,575	3,425
SPOUSE	4,257	5,353	11,193	6,813	850	396	2,031	2,814	778
OTHER RELATIVES	30,581	36,005	37,230	23,141	458	3,987	5,718	15,055	10,696
NONRELATIVES	896	1,487	1,519	906	21	94	86	455	199
IN NONFAMILY HOUSEHOLD:									
MALE HOUSEHOLDER	3,525	1,815	1,875	1,766	1,523	318	603	2,367	523
FEMALE HOUSEHOLDER	3,232	1,904	2,120	1,503	1,311	545	910	4,411	926
NONRELATIVES	1,310	910	1,185	936	151	65	158	513	115
IN GROUP QUARTERS:									
INMATE OF INSTITUTION	902	268	4,610	81	266	19	3	747	23
OTHER	1,012	318	133	110	854	261	26	1,763	63
FAMILY TYPE BY PRESENCE OF OWN CHILDREN UNDER 18 YEARS									
HOUSEHOLDS	18,630	17,266	19,197	13,034	3,853	2,419	4,505	14,319	4,894
MARRIED-COUPLE FAMILY:									
WITH OWN CHILDREN	2,614	3,209	8,206	4,871	125	278	1,097	1,179	445
WITHOUT OWN CHILDREN	1,971	2,444	3,253	2,183	776	156	1,004	1,743	326
FAMILY WITH MALE HOUSEHOLDER, NO WIFE PRESENT:									
WITH OWN CHILDREN	178	276	358	296	16	8	54	135	62
WITHOUT OWN CHILDREN	431	639	940	692	22	12	149	199	70
FAMILY WITH FEMALE HOUSEHOLDER, NO HUSBAND PRESENT:									
WITH OWN CHILDREN	5,195	5,120	1,691	1,165	24	912	369	3,270	2,160
WITHOUT OWN CHILDREN	1,513	1,881	1,003	759	76	176	343	1,090	410
NONFAMILY HOUSEHOLD	6,728	3,697	3,746	3,068	2,814	877	1,489	6,703	1,421
LANGUAGE SPOKEN AT HOME AND ABILITY TO SPEAK ENGLISH									
PERSONS 5 TO 17 YEARS	16,290	18,830	17,778	10,843	126	2,166	2,463	7,749	5,972
SPEAK ONLY ENGLISH AT HOME	14,940	18,147	3,418	2,148	113	2,119	1,396	7,508	5,856
SPEAK A LANGUAGE OTHER THAN ENGLISH AT HOME:	896	463	10,920	5,747	0	35	67	96	84
SPANISH LANGUAGE SPOKEN AT HOME:									
SPEAK ENGLISH VERY WELL OR WELL	262	65	3,243	2,868	0	0	11	0	0
SPEAK ENGLISH NOT WELL OR NOT AT ALL	150	145	169	80	13	12	770	140	32
OTHER LANGUAGE SPOKEN AT HOME	42	10	28	0	0	0	219	5	0
PERSONS 18 YEARS AND OVER	35,008	36,379	48,187	28,647	6,223	4,176	9,252	24,719	8,755
SPEAK ONLY ENGLISH AT HOME	29,175	34,794	14,357	6,889	5,409	3,996	4,770	22,854	8,547
SPEAK A LANGUAGE OTHER THAN ENGLISH AT HOME:	2,160	870	15,925	8,820	198	24	223	297	54
SPANISH LANGUAGE SPOKEN AT HOME:									
SPEAK ENGLISH VERY WELL OR WELL	1,569	316	14,416	10,386	64	30	112	33	7
SPEAK ENGLISH NOT WELL OR NOT AT ALL	1,935	361	2,964	2,182	520	126	2,194	1,443	117
OTHER LANGUAGE SPOKEN AT HOME	169	38	525	370	32	0	1,953	92	30
TYPE OF GROUP QUARTERS									
PERSONS IN GROUP QUARTERS	1,978	598	4,839	185	1,102	288	30	2,532	75
INMATE OF MENTAL HOSPITAL	289	36	81	0	0	8	0	52	0
INMATE OF HOME FOR THE AGED	189	205	273	0	0	0	0	456	0
INMATE OF OTHER INSTITUTION	169	42	4,378	80	214	9	0	229	0
IN MILITARY BARRACKS	0	0	0	0	0	0	0	0	0
IN COLLEGE DORMITORY	119	25	12	0	338	0	0	1,776	0
OTHER IN GROUP QUARTERS	1,212	290	95	105	550	271	30	19	75
WORK DISABILITY STATUS									
NONINSTITUTIONAL PERSONS 16 TO 64 YEARS	32,330	35,526	41,638	27,280	4,657	3,824	7,816	21,407	8,714
WITH A WORK DISABILITY									
IN LABOR FORCE	933	1,199	946	340	179	60	227	707	266
NOT IN LABOR FORCE:									
PREVENTED FROM WORKING	3,348	3,524	1,423	996	317	198	397	1,752	873
NOT PREVENTED FROM WORKING	556	840	293	110	17	77	61	415	166
NO WORK DISABILITY	27,493	29,963	38,976	25,834	4,144	3,489	7,131	18,533	7,409
PUBLIC TRANSPORTATION DISABILITY STATUS									
NONINSTITUTIONAL PERSONS 16 TO 64 YEARS									
WITH A PUBLIC TRANSPORTATION DISABILITY	1,950	1,968	769	652	170	49	212	898	353
NO PUBLIC TRANSPORTATION DISABILITY	30,380	33,558	40,869	26,628	4,487	3,775	7,604	20,509	8,361
NONINSTITUTIONAL PERSONS 65 YEARS AND OVER									
WITH A PUBLIC TRANSPORTATION DISABILITY	1,189	997	836	390	92	130	341	710	311
NO PUBLIC TRANSPORTATION DISABILITY	3,476	2,933	3,791	2,684	1,304	519	1,524	3,006	737

TABLE III-2 FAMILY AND DISABILITY CHARACTERISTICS
OF THE POPULATION, BY COMMUNITY AREA: CITY OF CHICAGO, 1980

	37	38	39	40	41	42	43	44	45
MARITAL STATUS									
MALE, 15 YRS. AND OVER	1,876	16,412	7,993	9,660	13,724	12,124	25,967	14,569	4,872
SINGLE	788	7,663	3,067	4,334	6,840	5,078	9,955	4,523	1,805
NOW MARRIED, EXCEPT SEPARATED	638	3,975	3,019	2,526	4,942	3,654	10,401	6,896	2,395
SEPARATED	160	1,947	739	1,134	590	1,277	2,135	1,032	248
WIDOWED	147	1,470	434	762	308	876	903	655	120
DIVORCED	143	1,357	734	904	1,044	1,239	2,573	1,463	304
FEMALE, 15 YRS. AND OVER	2,400	21,252	9,657	12,696	13,404	15,392	32,545	18,654	5,822
SINGLE	742	8,029	3,131	4,628	5,069	5,037	11,124	5,028	1,817
NOW MARRIED, EXCEPT SEPARATED	643	3,961	3,005	2,522	4,856	3,649	10,287	6,905	2,385
SEPARATED	235	2,938	891	1,835	660	1,835	3,394	1,555	373
WIDOWED	557	4,316	1,502	2,360	1,431	3,036	3,566	2,537	593
DIVORCED	223	2,008	1,128	1,351	1,388	1,835	4,174	2,629	654
PERSONS IN HOUSEHOLD									
NUMBER OF HOUSEHOLDS	1,930	18,601	10,006	11,028	14,545	14,138	31,393	16,361	4,276
1 PERSON	638	7,193	4,327	3,750	6,556	5,513	10,950	4,803	694
2 PERSONS	426	3,622	2,833	2,438	4,401	3,331	8,043	5,241	957
3 PERSONS	219	2,193	1,318	1,500	1,861	1,985	5,201	2,973	914
4 PERSONS	228	1,737	791	1,124	1,140	1,410	3,646	1,717	725
5 PERSONS	132	1,431	388	753	345	850	1,820	863	481
6 OR MORE PERSONS	287	2,425	349	1,463	242	1,049	1,733	764	505
HOUSEHOLD TYPE AND RELATIONSHIP									
PERSONS IN HOUSEHOLDS	5,784	52,910	21,509	31,657	28,480	35,143	77,459	40,684	13,768
IN FAMILY HOUSEHOLD:									
HOUSEHOLDER	1,221	10,509	5,048	6,559	6,398	7,862	18,659	10,880	3,424
SPOUSE	569	3,483	2,824	2,233	4,570	3,292	9,579	6,502	2,255
OTHER RELATIVES	3,022	28,215	7,396	16,638	6,849	15,802	32,839	16,143	6,885
NONRELATIVES	144	1,185	454	847	444	927	1,618	727	286
IN NONFAMILY HOUSEHOLD:									
MALE HOUSEHOLDER	241	4,003	2,391	2,083	4,190	2,910	6,556	2,299	346
FEMALE HOUSEHOLDER	450	4,182	2,595	2,344	3,870	3,303	6,152	3,239	453
NONRELATIVES	137	1,333	801	953	2,159	1,047	2,056	894	119
IN GROUP QUARTERS:									
INMATE OF INSTITUTION	12	372	333	65	2	631	208	0	0
OTHER	36	459	132	213	2,716	549	76	41	24
FAMILY TYPE BY PRESENCE OF OWN CHILDREN UNDER 18 YEARS									
HOUSEHOLDS	1,930	18,601	10,006	11,028	14,545	14,138	31,393	16,361	4,276
MARRIED-COUPLE FAMILY:									
WITH OWN CHILDREN	221	1,488	1,139	950	1,945	1,504	5,128	2,285	1,338
WITHOUT OWN CHILDREN	372	1,941	1,795	1,436	2,762	2,147	4,611	4,238	897
FAMILY WITH MALE HOUSEHOLDER, NO WIFE PRESENT:									
WITH OWN CHILDREN	42	189	186	138	95	172	600	170	42
WITHOUT OWN CHILDREN	83	565	245	290	238	332	759	440	147
FAMILY WITH FEMALE HOUSEHOLDER, NO HUSBAND PRESENT:									
WITH OWN CHILDREN	347	4,649	1,262	2,703	961	2,597	5,478	2,018	549
WITHOUT OWN CHILDREN	138	1,757	490	1,034	519	1,256	2,297	1,702	537
NONFAMILY HOUSEHOLD	727	8,012	4,889	4,477	8,025	6,130	12,520	5,508	766
LANGUAGE SPOKEN AT HOME AND ABILITY TO SPEAK ENGLISH									
PERSONS 5 TO 17 YEARS	1,510	14,847	3,601	8,593	3,527	7,781	16,328	6,635	3,162
SPEAK ONLY ENGLISH AT HOME	1,479	14,645	3,377	8,455	3,076	7,530	15,749	6,382	3,080
SPEAK A LANGUAGE OTHER THAN ENGLISH AT HOME:	9	78	114	56	54	69	200	116	41
SPANISH LANGUAGE SPOKEN AT HOME:									
SPEAK ENGLISH VERY WELL OR WELL	0	7	11	6	6	13	7	7	0
SPEAK ENGLISH NOT WELL OR NOT AT ALL	22	117	99	66	352	161	320	91	34
OTHER LANGUAGE SPOKEN AT HOME	0	0	0	10	39	8	52	39	7
PERSONS 18 YEARS AND OVER	3,868	33,776	16,834	20,163	26,201	25,579	54,703	31,496	9,805
SPEAK ONLY ENGLISH AT HOME	3,758	33,111	15,824	19,721	22,584	24,542	52,045	30,365	9,437
SPEAK A LANGUAGE OTHER THAN ENGLISH AT HOME:	19	336	266	175	675	418	894	516	177
SPANISH LANGUAGE SPOKEN AT HOME:									
SPEAK ENGLISH VERY WELL OR WELL	0	27	13	13	24	30	106	62	0
SPEAK ENGLISH NOT WELL OR NOT AT ALL	91	287	681	236	2,684	516	1,488	510	177
OTHER LANGUAGE SPOKEN AT HOME	0	15	50	18	234	73	170	43	14
TYPE OF GROUP QUARTERS									
PERSONS IN GROUP QUARTERS	20	753	429	246	2,724	1,148	273	22	14
INMATE OF MENTAL HOSPITAL	0	0	0	0	0	175	34	0	0
INMATE OF HOME FOR THE AGED	0	392	322	37	0	161	172	0	0
INMATE OF OTHER INSTITUTION	0	0	13	0	0	296	0	0	0
IN MILITARY BARRACKS	0	0	0	0	0	0	0	0	0
IN COLLEGE DORMITORY	0	74	0	7	2,428	357	22	0	0
OTHER IN GROUP QUARTERS	20	287	94	202	296	159	45	22	14
WORK DISABILITY STATUS									
NONINSTITUTIONAL PERSONS 16 TO 64 YEARS	3,134	28,904	14,266	17,750	23,501	21,313	51,867	27,827	9,607
WITH A WORK DISABILITY									
IN LABOR FORCE	129	964	422	759	576	705	1,636	1,130	311
NOT IN LABOR FORCE:									
PREVENTED FROM WORKING	294	3,405	937	2,341	547	2,102	2,715	1,349	381
NOT PREVENTED FROM WORKING	72	657	124	376	180	382	501	324	85
NO WORK DISABILITY	2,639	23,878	12,783	14,274	22,198	18,124	47,015	25,024	8,830
PUBLIC TRANSPORTATION DISABILITY STATUS									
NONINSTITUTIONAL PERSONS 16 TO 64 YEARS									
WITH A PUBLIC TRANSPORTATION DISABILITY	142	1,595	480	1,253	314	930	1,574	899	179
NO PUBLIC TRANSPORTATION DISABILITY	2,992	27,309	13,786	16,497	23,187	20,383	50,293	26,928	9,428
NONINSTITUTIONAL PERSONS 65 YEARS AND OVER									
WITH A PUBLIC TRANSPORTATION DISABILITY	282	1,750	482	1,046	517	986	892	909	175
NO PUBLIC TRANSPORTATION DISABILITY	702	5,305	2,269	2,782	2,754	3,875	4,121	3,958	669

	46	47	48	49	50	51	52	53	54
MARITAL STATUS									
MALE, 15 YRS. AND OVER	15,666	1,228	7,153	21,560	3,497	6,393	8,423	13,873	3,246
SINGLE	5,884	526	2,348	8,567	1,349	2,437	2,728	5,148	1,778
NOW MARRIED, EXCEPT SEPARATED	7,821	545	4,046	9,948	1,650	3,229	4,821	7,077	1,130
SEPARATED	598	44	231	1,105	148	195	96	599	132
WIDOWED	497	32	144	616	106	177	354	308	77
DIVORCED	866	81	384	1,324	244	355	424	741	129
FEMALE, 15 YRS. AND OVER	17,574	1,469	8,458	25,680	4,197	7,622	8,926	16,121	4,890
SINGLE	5,261	511	2,416	8,303	1,249	2,295	2,119	5,101	2,015
NOW MARRIED, EXCEPT SEPARATED	7,623	541	4,068	9,978	1,635	3,190	4,768	7,044	1,162
SEPARATED	1,036	130	427	1,883	259	404	131	1,175	672
WIDOWED	2,047	127	721	2,750	490	831	1,380	1,168	430
DIVORCED	1,607	160	826	2,766	564	902	528	1,633	611
PERSONS IN HOUSEHOLD									
NUMBER OF HOUSEHOLDS	14,379	1,015	6,167	18,058	3,384	5,669	7,436	11,732	3,393
1 PERSON	3,158	144	757	2,765	788	830	1,561	1,363	332
2 PERSONS	3,270	178	1,530	4,029	779	1,204	2,162	2,046	501
3 PERSONS	2,519	191	1,409	3,344	582	1,127	1,415	2,234	694
4 PERSONS	2,129	193	1,170	3,046	561	998	1,159	2,419	637
5 PERSONS	1,511	77	689	2,072	338	715	708	1,471	392
6 OR MORE PERSONS	1,792	232	612	2,802	336	795	431	2,199	837
HOUSEHOLD TYPE AND RELATIONSHIP									
PERSONS IN HOUSEHOLDS	46,293	3,931	20,467	63,909	10,304	19,331	21,222	44,852	13,496
IN FAMILY HOUSEHOLD:									
HOUSEHOLDER	10,850	866	5,284	14,926	2,512	4,654	5,757	10,145	3,036
SPOUSE	7,134	505	3,871	9,284	1,537	3,006	4,612	6,654	1,033
OTHER RELATIVES	23,317	2,261	9,951	34,603	5,106	10,117	8,830	25,184	8,829
NONRELATIVES	774	76	255	1,276	174	351	145	840	180
IN NONFAMILY HOUSEHOLD:									
MALE HOUSEHOLDER	1,738	93	377	1,495	394	392	689	859	139
FEMALE HOUSEHOLDER	1,883	80	533	1,692	461	58:	1,012	741	220
NONRELATIVES	597	50	196	633	120	230	177	429	59
IN GROUP QUARTERS:									
INMATE OF INSTITUTION	12	0	0	370	0	0	1	0	0
OTHER	117	11	38	93	37	69	108	52	43
FAMILY TYPE BY PRESENCE OF OWN CHILDREN UNDER 18 YEARS									
HOUSEHOLDS	14,379	1,015	6,167	18,058	3,384	5,669	7,436	11,732	3,393
MARRIED-COUPLE FAMILY:									
WITH OWN CHILDREN	4,386	349	2,234	5,317	883	2,093	2,017	4,878	855
WITHOUT OWN CHILDREN	2,891	151	1,682	4,097	723	1,242	2,511	2,029	214
FAMILY WITH MALE HOUSEHOLDER, NO WIFE PRESENT:									
WITH OWN CHILDREN	233	14	46	300	52	66	58	289	98
WITHOUT OWN CHILDREN	458	34	188	445	96	103	280	307	104
FAMILY WITH FEMALE HOUSEHOLDER, NO HUSBAND PRESENT:									
WITH OWN CHILDREN	1,865	208	701	2,943	521	713	402	1,934	1,371
WITHOUT OWN CHILDREN	1,005	87	454	1,777	229	498	492	718	396
NONFAMILY HOUSEHOLD	3,541	172	862	3,179	880	954	1,676	1,577	355
LANGUAGE SPOKEN AT HOME AND ABILITY TO SPEAK ENGLISH									
PERSONS 5 TO 17 YEARS	11,662	1,206	4,911	17,137	2,570	5,295	4,023	13,744	5,071
SPEAK ONLY ENGLISH AT HOME	7,157	1,104	4,496	16,649	2,292	4,290	3,188	12,907	4,969
SPEAK A LANGUAGE OTHER THAN ENGLISH AT HOME:	3,561	45	216	250	218	681	335	436	27
SPANISH LANGUAGE SPOKEN AT HOME:									
SPEAK ENGLISH VERY WELL OR WELL	678	0	36	31	21	107	44	145	23
SPEAK ENGLISH NOT WELL OR NOT AT ALL	260	49	145	203	39	204	441	256	52
OTHER LANGUAGE SPOKEN AT HOME	6	8	18	4	0	13	15	0	0
PERSONS 18 YEARS AND OVER	30,405	2,371	14,399	42,416	6,990	12,661	16,089	26,720	6,857
SPEAK ONLY ENGLISH AT HOME	18,911	2,134	12,934	41,047	6,223	9,172	11,810	24,496	6,667
SPEAK A LANGUAGE OTHER THAN ENGLISH AT HOME:	6,461	34	625	536	215	1,609	1,068	876	43
SPANISH LANGUAGE SPOKEN AT HOME:									
SPEAK ENGLISH VERY WELL OR WELL	2,965	0	139	87	125	686	284	579	29
SPEAK ENGLISH NOT WELL OR NOT AT ALL	1,898	190	689	709	351	1,009	2,408	706	118
OTHER LANGUAGE SPOKEN AT HOME	170	13	12	37	76	185	519	63	0
TYPE OF GROUP QUARTERS									
PERSONS IN GROUP QUARTERS	89	0	44	413	3	46	104	5	33
INMATE OF MENTAL HOSPITAL	0	0	0	0	0	0	0	0	0
INMATE OF HOME FOR THE AGED	0	0	0	285	0	0	0	0	0
INMATE OF OTHER INSTITUTION	14	0	0	60	0	0	0	0	0
IN MILITARY BARRACKS	0	0	0	0	0	0	0	0	0
IN COLLEGE DORMITORY	6	0	0	0	0	0	48	0	0
OTHER IN GROUP QUARTERS	69	0	44	68	3	46	56	5	33
WORK DISABILITY STATUS									
NONINSTITUTIONAL PERSONS 16 TO 64 YEARS	28,783	2,381	14,172	41,425	6,697	12,288	14,173	27,368	7,365
WITH A WORK DISABILITY									
IN LABOR FORCE	689	45	316	1,334	204	275	355	786	148
NOT IN LABOR FORCE:									
PREVENTED FROM WORKING	1,185	65	589	2,171	327	408	510	1,347	504
NOT PREVENTED FROM WORKING	185	19	86	566	28	138	160	198	131
NO WORK DISABILITY	26,724	2,252	13,181	37,354	6,138	11,467	13,148	25,037	6,582
PUBLIC TRANSPORTATION DISABILITY STATUS									
NONINSTITUTIONAL PERSONS 16 TO 64 YEARS									
WITH A PUBLIC TRANSPORTATION DISABILITY	610	47	409	1,296	196	294	234	830	274
NO PUBLIC TRANSPORTATION DISABILITY	28,173	2,334	13,763	40,129	6,501	11,994	13,939	26,538	7,091
NONINSTITUTIONAL PERSONS 65 YEARS AND OVER									
WITH A PUBLIC TRANSPORTATION DISABILITY	652	8	241	857	108	264	399	393	60
NO PUBLIC TRANSPORTATION DISABILITY	2,793	191	827	3,100	676	1,000	2,413	1,141	299

	55	56	57	58	59	60	61	62	63
MARITAL STATUS									
MALE, 15 YRS. AND OVER	4,653	14,648	3,914	11,880	4,895	11,529	19,137	5,065	9,243
SINGLE	1,517	4,874	1,248	4,019	1,751	4,155	7,590	1,487	2,997
NOW MARRIED, EXCEPT SEPARATED	2,707	8,754	2,311	6,435	2,591	5,960	9,375	3,214	5,246
SEPARATED	46	113	36	169	82	231	588	37	134
WIDOWED	145	424	146	496	188	454	650	159	402
DIVORCED	238	483	173	761	283	729	934	168	464
FEMALE, 15 YRS. AND OVER	4,718	16,325	4,388	13,285	5,491	12,656	19,935	5,947	10,715
SINGLE	1,048	4,148	1,027	3,146	1,391	3,398	5,860	1,319	2,529
NOW MARRIED, EXCEPT SEPARATED	2,694	8,756	2,298	6,360	2,574	5,813	8,825	3,196	5,191
SEPARATED	45	314	46	246	142	354	1,138	50	179
WIDOWED	660	2,311	800	2,538	941	2,043	2,690	1,093	2,190
DIVORCED	271	796	217	995	443	1,048	1,422	289	626
PERSONS IN HOUSEHOLD									
NUMBER OF HOUSEHOLDS	4,157	12,624	3,689	12,214	4,810	11,377	17,100	4,833	9,340
1 PERSON	902	1,954	877	3,611	1,292	3,161	3,755	997	2,542
2 PERSONS	1,283	4,103	1,201	3,812	1,376	3,078	3,790	1,789	2,895
3 PERSONS	716	2,458	688	2,010	834	1,852	2,800	918	1,561
4 PERSONS	629	1,955	493	1,360	633	1,518	2,436	628	1,120
5 PERSONS	315	1,174	253	777	320	929	1,829	271	648
6 OR MORE PERSONS	312	980	177	644	355	839	2,490	230	574
HOUSEHOLD TYPE AND RELATIONSHIP									
PERSONS IN HOUSEHOLDS	11,568	37,879	9,700	30,602	13,236	30,855	55,619	12,763	24,417
IN FAMILY HOUSEHOLD:									
HOUSEHOLDER	3,167	10,516	2,761	8,184	3,461	7,788	12,627	3,785	6,530
SPOUSE	2,611	8,406	2,194	6,077	2,470	5,560	8,189	3,080	5,003
OTHER RELATIVES	4,677	16,440	3,603	11,587	5,619	13,111	28,603	4,681	9,641
NONRELATIVES	61	263	85	297	129	351	885	51	206
IN NONFAMILY HOUSEHOLD:									
MALE HOUSEHOLDER	444	697	323	1,636	546	1,497	2,082	312	957
FEMALE HOUSEHOLDER	516	1,400	626	2,373	360	2,051	2,301	766	1,816
NONRELATIVES	92	157	108	448	151	497	932	88	264
IN GROUP QUARTERS:									
INMATE OF INSTITUTION	0	4	0	110	0	0	0	0	0
OTHER	4	46	8	58	12	68	241	34	28
FAMILY TYPE BY PRESENCE OF OWN CHILDREN UNDER 18 YEARS									
HOUSEHOLDS	4,157	12,624	3,689	12,214	4,810	11,377	17,100	4,833	9,340
MARRIED-COUPLE FAMILY:									
WITH OWN CHILDREN	1,250	3,399	857	2,711	1,206	2,873	5,255	1,079	2,267
WITHOUT OWN CHILDREN	1,413	5,172	1,386	3,641	1,209	2,711	3,180	2,059	2,938
FAMILY WITH MALE HOUSEHOLDER, NO WIFE PRESENT:									
WITH OWN CHILDREN	22	104	22	85	68	83	312	14	44
WITHOUT OWN CHILDREN	139	364	113	346	163	458	754	100	282
FAMILY WITH FEMALE HOUSEHOLDER, NO HUSBAND PRESENT:									
WITH OWN CHILDREN	156	658	134	588	364	955	2,094	130	314
WITHOUT OWN CHILDREN	198	902	245	931	396	865	1,272	405	770
NONFAMILY HOUSEHOLD	979	2,025	932	3,912	1,404	3,432	4,233	1,046	2,725
LANGUAGE SPOKEN AT HOME AND ABILITY TO SPEAK ENGLISH									
PERSONS 5 TO 17 YEARS	2,238	7,256	1,313	5,054	2,604	6,272	13,855	1,834	3,955
SPEAK ONLY ENGLISH AT HOME	2,029	6,624	950	3,666	2,222	4,711	8,640	1,535	3,050
SPEAK A LANGUAGE OTHER THAN ENGLISH AT HOME:	50	226	51	705	287	901	3,592	45	358
SPANISH LANGUAGE SPOKEN AT HOME:									
SPEAK ENGLISH VERY WELL OR WELL	0	19	12	105	46	217	1,015	0	61
SPEAK ENGLISH NOT WELL OR NOT AT ALL	140	365	300	529	43	421	496	249	473
OTHER LANGUAGE SPOKEN AT HOME	19	22	0	49	6	22	112	5	13
PERSONS 18 YEARS AND OVER	8,743	28,778	7,936	23,801	9,677	22,489	35,928	10,402	18,938
SPEAK ONLY ENGLISH AT HOME	6,803	22,604	5,100	14,068	7,322	15,915	19,787	7,771	13,532
SPEAK A LANGUAGE OTHER THAN ENGLISH AT HOME:	250	839	163	1,724	767	1,962	5,335	137	1,150
SPANISH LANGUAGE SPOKEN AT HOME:									
SPEAK ENGLISH VERY WELL OR WELL	68	159	34	682	218	1,203	5,147	0	245
SPEAK ENGLISH NOT WELL OR NOT AT ALL	1,468	4,603	2,139	5,776	1,230	2,775	3,978	2,133	3,240
OTHER LANGUAGE SPOKEN AT HOME	154	573	500	1,551	140	634	1,681	361	771
TYPE OF GROUP QUARTERS									
PERSONS IN GROUP QUARTERS	0	57	2	164	11	43	211	34	29
INMATE OF MENTAL HOSPITAL	0	0	0	0	0	0	0	0	0
INMATE OF HOME FOR THE AGED	0	0	0	109	0	0	0	0	0
INMATE OF OTHER INSTITUTION	0	18	0	0	0	0	0	0	0
IN MILITARY BARRACKS	0	0	0	0	0	0	0	0	0
IN COLLEGE DORMITORY	0	0	0	0	0	0	2	0	0
OTHER IN GROUP QUARTERS	0	39	2	55	11	43	209	34	29
WORK DISABILITY STATUS									
NONINSTITUTIONAL PERSONS 16 TO 64 YEARS	7,846	25,710	6,698	20,020	8,521	19,979	33,740	8,515	15,260
WITH A WORK DISABILITY									
IN LABOR FORCE	165	658	176	774	317	585	977	254	397
NOT IN LABOR FORCE:									
PREVENTED FROM WORKING	467	1,160	358	938	452	1,131	1,796	360	741
NOT PREVENTED FROM WORKING	40	179	18	174	86	171	256	67	142
NO WORK DISABILITY	7,174	23,713	6,146	18,134	7,666	18,092	30,711	7,834	13,980
PUBLIC TRANSPORTATION DISABILITY STATUS									
NONINSTITUTIONAL PERSONS 16 TO 64 YEARS									
WITH A PUBLIC TRANSPORTATION DISABILITY	233	800	214	445	227	617	950	258	460
NO PUBLIC TRANSPORTATION DISABILITY	7,613	24,910	6,484	19,575	8,294	19,362	32,790	8,257	14,800
NONINSTITUTIONAL PERSONS 65 YEARS AND OVER									
WITH A PUBLIC TRANSPORTATION DISABILITY	244	708	204	1,030	229	566	843	319	777
NO PUBLIC TRANSPORTATION DISABILITY	1,032	3,767	1,262	3,632	1,411	3,073	3,390	1,984	3,598

	64	65	66	67	68	69	70	71	72
MARITAL STATUS									
MALE, 15 YRS. AND OVER	9,004	9,719	17,149	18,628	17,851	15,477	15,882	21,690	8,339
SINGLE	2,878	3,043	5,810	8,454	7,959	5,358	5,337	8,193	2,781
NOW MARRIED, EXCEPT SEPARATED	5,287	5,903	9,186	7,518	6,177	6,403	9,616	10,022	5,009
SEPARATED	108	68	332	1,171	1,550	1,282	87	1,332	61
WIDOWED	270	373	793	536	884	916	466	578	254
DIVORCED	461	332	1,028	949	1,281	1,518	376	1,565	234
FEMALE, 15 YRS. AND OVER	9,473	11,097	19,751	23,093	23,292	19,903	17,292	26,126	9,663
SINGLE	2,261	2,660	5,133	8,767	8,586	5,549	4,578	8,691	2,633
NOW MARRIED, EXCEPT SEPARATED	5,251	5,902	9,120	7,521	6,187	6,370	9,617	10,019	4,998
SEPARATED	108	104	445	2,462	2,848	2,060	144	2,127	128
WIDOWED	1,295	1,945	3,766	2,154	3,359	3,441	2,374	2,501	1,429
DIVORCED	558	486	1,287	2,189	2,312	2,483	579	2,788	475
PERSONS IN HOUSEHOLD									
NUMBER OF HOUSEHOLDS	8,067	8,989	17,600	16,086	17,787	16,968	12,817	19,260	7,602
1 PERSON	1,671	1,917	5,283	2,029	3,949	4,764	1,565	3,452	1,594
2 PERSONS	2,514	2,985	5,035	2,919	3,820	5,002	3,787	4,208	2,213
3 PERSONS	1,485	1,578	2,640	2,733	2,937	2,980	2,826	3,806	1,247
4 PERSONS	1,193	1,206	2,111	2,664	2,559	1,839	2,204	3,164	1,078
5 PERSONS	782	718	1,250	2,081	1,706	1,136	1,361	2,059	677
6 OR MORE PERSONS	422	585	1,281	3,660	2,816	1,247	1,074	2,571	793
HOUSEHOLD TYPE AND RELATIONSHIP									
PERSONS IN HOUSEHOLDS	22,545	24,722	46,386	62,034	58,777	45,111	40,144	65,029	23,348
IN FAMILY HOUSEHOLD:									
HOUSEHOLDER	6,180	6,936	11,664	13,304	12,960	11,349	11,071	15,268	5,972
SPOUSE	5,129	5,747	8,764	6,921	5,606	5,924	9,412	9,364	4,889
OTHER RELATIVES	9,026	9,777	18,744	37,230	32,746	20,012	17,707	33,886	10,329
NONRELATIVES	121	60	511	1,416	1,543	1,140	119	1,510	147
IN NONFAMILY HOUSEHOLD:									
MALE HOUSEHOLDER	785	648	2,321	1,257	2,048	2,358	506	1,938	551
FEMALE HOUSEHOLDER	1,078	1,408	3,615	1,296	2,731	3,225	1,177	2,144	1,227
NONRELATIVES	226	146	767	610	1,143	1,103	152	919	233
IN GROUP QUARTERS:									
INMATE OF INSTITUTION	0	0	0	7	0	22	303	71	0
OTHER	39	26	182	28	298	85	30	32	12
FAMILY TYPE BY PRESENCE OF OWN CHILDREN UNDER 18 YEARS									
HOUSEHOLDS	8,067	8,989	17,600	16,086	17,787	16,968	12,817	19,260	7,602
MARRIED-COUPLE FAMILY:									
WITH OWN CHILDREN	2,338	2,244	4,213	4,699	2,858	2,346	4,443	5,545	2,467
WITHOUT OWN CHILDREN	2,946	3,533	4,723	2,504	2,831	3,868	5,027	3,877	2,284
FAMILY WITH MALE HOUSEHOLDER, NO WIFE PRESENT:									
WITH OWN CHILDREN	40	22	139	435	327	258	58	320	80
WITHOUT OWN CHILDREN	186	283	611	452	631	581	381	587	171
FAMILY WITH FEMALE HOUSEHOLDER, NO HUSBAND PRESENT:									
WITH OWN CHILDREN	331	283	836	4,065	4,565	2,430	428	2,957	291
WITHOUT OWN CHILDREN	395	628	1,251	1,534	1,910	1,987	807	1,891	542
NONFAMILY HOUSEHOLD	1,831	1,996	5,827	2,397	4,665	5,498	1,673	4,083	1,767
LANGUAGE SPOKEN AT HOME AND ABILITY TO SPEAK ENGLISH									
PERSONS 5 TO 17 YEARS	4,121	3,941	8,373	19,089	16,348	8,866	7,777	16,470	5,041
SPEAK ONLY ENGLISH AT HOME	3,729	3,504	6,357	18,549	16,006	8,665	7,379	16,058	4,880
SPEAK A LANGUAGE OTHER THAN ENGLISH AT HOME:	139	72	896	353	182	97	171	158	43
SPANISH LANGUAGE SPOKEN AT HOME:									
SPEAK ENGLISH VERY WELL OR WELL	4	10	140	16	30	9	9	42	7
SPEAK ENGLISH NOT WELL OR NOT AT ALL	238	350	923	151	130	88	196	208	111
OTHER LANGUAGE SPOKEN AT HOME	11	5	57	20	0	7	22	4	0
PERSONS 18 YEARS AND OVER	17,267	19,650	34,779	36,669	36,887	33,114	30,648	43,353	16,625
SPEAK ONLY ENGLISH AT HOME	14,357	15,671	23,984	35,698	35,850	32,211	26,862	42,119	15,632
SPEAK A LANGUAGE OTHER THAN ENGLISH AT HOME:	377	260	2,033	521	589	358	345	600	151
SPANISH LANGUAGE SPOKEN AT HOME:									
SPEAK ENGLISH VERY WELL OR WELL	108	72	595	75	6	52	25	29	12
SPEAK ENGLISH NOT WELL OR NOT AT ALL	2,019	3,077	6,347	360	427	484	2,971	524	795
OTHER LANGUAGE SPOKEN AT HOME	406	570	1,820	15	15	9	445	81	35
TYPE OF GROUP QUARTERS									
PERSONS IN GROUP QUARTERS	46	25	201	8	339	65	322	100	12
INMATE OF MENTAL HOSPITAL	0	0	0	0	0	0	0	0	0
INMATE OF HOME FOR THE AGED	0	0	0	0	0	0	303	70	0
INMATE OF OTHER INSTITUTION	0	0	0	8	0	28	0	0	0
IN MILITARY BARRACKS	0	0	0	0	0	0	0	0	0
IN COLLEGE DORMITORY	0	0	0	0	23	0	0	2	0
OTHER IN GROUP QUARTERS	46	25	201	0	316	37	19	28	12
WORK DISABILITY STATUS									
NONINSTITUTIONAL PERSONS 16 TO 64 YEARS	15,740	16,450	27,980	37,645	34,668	27,975	27,609	43,098	13,982
WITH A WORK DISABILITY									
IN LABOR FORCE	440	400	699	1,115	1,084	836	529	1,254	310
NOT IN LABOR FORCE:									
PREVENTED FROM WORKING	636	558	1,195	2,445	3,360	2,355	793	1,995	285
NOT PREVENTED FROM WORKING	50	121	238	586	671	385	165	468	91
NO WORK DISABILITY	14,614	15,371	25,848	33,499	29,553	24,399	26,122	39,381	13,296
PUBLIC TRANSPORTATION DISABILITY STATUS									
NONINSTITUTIONAL PERSONS 16 TO 64 YEARS									
WITH A PUBLIC TRANSPORTATION DISABILITY	380	330	741	1,107	1,701	1,218	507	1,044	263
NO PUBLIC TRANSPORTATION DISABILITY	15,360	16,120	27,239	36,538	32,967	26,757	27,102	42,054	13,719
NONINSTITUTIONAL PERSONS 65 YEARS AND OVER									
WITH A PUBLIC TRANSPORTATION DISABILITY	356	590	1,418	568	1,266	1,343	723	712	542
NO PUBLIC TRANSPORTATION DISABILITY	1,993	3,470	6,793	1,921	3,841	5,159	3,866	2,575	3,067

TABLE III-2 FAMILY AND DISABILITY CHARACTERISTICS
OF THE POPULATION, BY COMMUNITY AREA: CITY OF CHICAGO, 1980

	73	74	75	76	77
MARITAL STATUS					
MALE, 15 YRS. AND OVER	12,661	7,625	10,163	4,703	23,737
SINGLE	4,826	2,461	3,755	1,507	10,315
NOW MARRIED, EXCEPT SEPARATED	6,289	4,593	5,236	2,454	9,888
SEPARATED	550	63	311	100	705
WIDOWED	291	287	369	100	855
DIVORCED	705	221	492	542	1,974
FEMALE, 15 YRS. AND OVER	14,878	8,631	12,185	5,109	27,192
SINGLE	4,945	2,259	3,610	1,446	9,091
NOW MARRIED, EXCEPT SEPARATED	6,267	4,600	5,248	2,419	9,601
SEPARATED	931	60	519	85	847
WIDOWED	1,265	1,347	1,801	586	4,923
DIVORCED	1,470	365	1,007	573	2,730
PERSONS IN HOUSEHOLD					
NUMBER OF HOUSEHOLDS	10,114	6,684	8,792	5,467	29,249
1 PERSON	1,332	1,240	1,594	2,166	14,694
2 PERSONS	2,102	2,092	2,330	1,990	8,270
3 PERSONS	2,011	1,158	1,505	701	2,967
4 PERSONS	1,766	987	1,375	403	1,728
5 PERSONS	1,343	651	910	143	900
6 OR MORE PERSONS	1,560	556	1,078	64	690
HOUSEHOLD TYPE AND RELATIONSHIP					
PERSONS IN HOUSEHOLDS	36,314	19,737	28,990	11,054	56,456
IN FAMILY HOUSEHOLD:					
HOUSEHOLDER	8,503	5,345	7,038	2,920	12,524
SPOUSE	5,894	4,500	4,990	2,358	9,021
OTHER RELATIVES	19,438	8,355	14,411	2,710	14,889
NONRELATIVES	643	62	374	43	720
IN NONFAMILY HOUSEHOLD:					
MALE HOUSEHOLDER	739	462	707	1,329	7,665
FEMALE HOUSEHOLDER	792	898	1,121	1,250	9,113
NONRELATIVES	305	115	349	444	2,524
IN GROUP QUARTERS:					
INMATE OF INSTITUTION	58	0	269	0	719
OTHER	81	347	56	0	1,386
FAMILY TYPE BY PRESENCE OF OWN CHILDREN UNDER 18 YEARS					
HOUSEHOLDS	10,114	6,684	8,792	5,467	29,249
MARRIED-COUPLE FAMILY:					
WITH OWN CHILDREN	3,162	2,117	2,508	732	3,350
WITHOUT OWN CHILDREN	2,740	2,509	2,425	1,602	5,730
FAMILY WITH MALE HOUSEHOLDER, NO WIFE PRESENT:					
WITH OWN CHILDREN	206	29	116	17	193
WITHOUT OWN CHILDREN	271	118	286	129	712
FAMILY WITH FEMALE HOUSEHOLDER, NO HUSBAND PRESENT:					
WITH OWN CHILDREN	1,386	167	892	170	1,363
WITHOUT OWN CHILDREN	808	395	746	264	1,157
NONFAMILY HOUSEHOLD	1,541	1,349	1,819	2,553	16,744
LANGUAGE SPOKEN AT HOME AND ABILITY TO SPEAK ENGLISH					
PERSONS 5 TO 17 YEARS	9,360	3,845	6,907	1,078	6,253
SPEAK ONLY ENGLISH AT HOME	9,119	3,732	6,649	840	3,793
SPEAK A LANGUAGE OTHER THAN ENGLISH AT HOME:	109	8	87	6	1,110
SPANISH LANGUAGE SPOKEN AT HOME:					
SPEAK ENGLISH VERY WELL OR WELL	0	0	0	7	231
SPEAK ENGLISH NOT WELL OR NOT AT ALL	132	100	133	214	928
OTHER LANGUAGE SPOKEN AT HOME	0	5	38	11	191
PERSONS 18 YEARS AND OVER	24,649	15,083	20,329	9,467	49,302
SPEAK ONLY ENGLISH AT HOME	24,134	13,828	19,419	7,275	33,441
SPEAK A LANGUAGE OTHER THAN ENGLISH AT HOME:	183	112	265	177	3,300
SPANISH LANGUAGE SPOKEN AT HOME:					
SPEAK ENGLISH VERY WELL OR WELL	14	0	11	20	2,183
SPEAK ENGLISH NOT WELL OR NOT AT ALL	300	997	598	1,643	8,844
OTHER LANGUAGE SPOKEN AT HOME	18	146	36	352	1,534
TYPE OF GROUP QUARTERS					
PERSONS IN GROUP QUARTERS	137	346	290	0	2,080
INMATE OF MENTAL HOSPITAL	0	0	0	0	11
INMATE OF HOME FOR THE AGED	68	0	267	0	621
INMATE OF OTHER INSTITUTION	0	0	0	0	15
IN MILITARY BARRACKS	0	0	0	0	0
IN COLLEGE DORMITORY	0	162	0	0	700
OTHER IN GROUP QUARTERS	69	184	23	0	733
WORK DISABILITY STATUS					
NONINSTITUTIONAL PERSONS 16 TO 64 YEARS	24,820	12,796	18,248	8,522	39,629
WITH A WORK DISABILITY					
IN LABOR FORCE	646	301	523	240	1,179
NOT IN LABOR FORCE:					
PREVENTED FROM WORKING	1,143	484	793	164	1,626
NOT PREVENTED FROM WORKING	148	67	183	25	345
NO WORK DISABILITY	22,883	11,944	16,749	8,093	36,479
PUBLIC TRANSPORTATION DISABILITY STATUS					
NONINSTITUTIONAL PERSONS 16 TO 64 YEARS					
WITH A PUBLIC TRANSPORTATION DISABILITY	642	271	520	106	791
NO PUBLIC TRANSPORTATION DISABILITY	24,178	12,525	17,728	8,416	38,838
NONINSTITUTIONAL PERSONS 65 YEARS AND OVER					
WITH A PUBLIC TRANSPORTATION DISABILITY	418	534	607	167	1,584
NO PUBLIC TRANSPORTATION DISABILITY	1,312	2,577	2,556	1,024	8,579

	01	02	03	04	05	06	07	08	09
NATIVITY AND PLACE OF BIRTH									
TOTAL PERSONS	55,525	61,129	64,414	43,954	35,161	97,519	57,146	67,157	12,457
NATIVE:									
BORN IN STATE OF RESIDENCE	27,229	33,313	24,963	21,325	21,537	47,018	29,587	36,045	10,056
BORN IN DIFFERENT STATE	11,762	7,777	17,064	6,502	5,672	26,946	19,373	25,168	1,042
BORN ABROAD, AT SEA, ETC.	470	322	1,956	552	1,351	3,769	1,137	444	20
FOREIGN BORN	16,064	19,717	20,431	15,575	6,601	19,786	7,049	5,500	1,339
ANCESTRY									
TOTAL PERSONS	55,525	61,129	64,414	43,954	35,161	97,519	57,146	67,157	12,457
SINGLE ANCESTRY GROUP:									
DUTCH	134	41	127	79	118	297	259	279	88
ENGLISH	1,703	1,123	2,968	1,193	837	3,762	3,040	3,406	155
FRENCH	321	144	368	103	175	614	392	378	27
GERMAN	3,231	4,317	2,883	4,865	5,570	7,809	4,059	3,413	1,422
GREEK	582	2,416	349	4,443	221	684	256	504	172
HUNGARIAN	489	814	277	349	344	1,100	260	453	45
IRISH	3,686	2,693	2,762	1,972	2,483	4,792	3,108	2,873	1,516
ITALIAN	925	1,239	871	1,050	1,118	2,012	1,693	1,150	932
NORWEGIAN	195	87	186	124	102	321	251	233	124
POLISH	1,916	3,640	1,389	1,437	1,236	3,098	1,961	1,459	2,033
PORTUGUESE	62	0	19	12	0	20	36	8	0
RUSSIAN	3,475	6,917	1,018	866	86	3,474	1,493	2,356	31
SCOTTISH	131	126	153	124	104	381	340	417	25
SWEDISH	477	602	642	773	235	911	478	516	276
UKRAINIAN	361	519	118	86	69	307	130	115	107
OTHER	17,150	12,537	31,009	11,940	8,980	30,772	11,333	20,455	622
MULTIPLE ANCESTRY GROUP	14,516	13,265	9,614	10,154	10,349	23,994	14,862	13,718	4,323
ANCESTRY NOT SPECIFIED:									
OTHER	2,995	7,809	3,735	1,831	1,332	5,061	2,626	2,696	212
NOT REPORTED	3,176	2,840	5,926	2,553	1,802	8,110	10,569	12,728	347
PERSONS IN SELECTED MULTIPLE ANCESTRY GROUPS	19,875	17,087	12,235	13,946	15,406	32,990	20,632	18,877	6,956
ENGLISH AND OTHER GROUP(S)	3,792	2,680	2,601	2,278	1,955	6,570	4,359	4,678	625
FRENCH AND OTHER GROUP(S)	1,283	1,195	897	1,036	856	2,661	1,691	1,289	315
GERMAN AND OTHER GROUP(S)	6,152	5,120	3,651	4,932	5,769	10,239	6,440	5,934	2,396
IRISH AND OTHER GROUP(S)	5,845	4,492	3,613	3,653	4,041	8,397	5,161	4,832	1,837
ITALIAN AND OTHER GROUP(S)	944	838	612	734	1,271	1,890	1,241	851	615
POLISH AND OTHER GROUP(S)	1,859	2,762	861	1,313	1,514	3,233	1,740	1,293	1,168
RESIDENCE IN 1975									
PERSONS 5 YEARS AND OVER	52,468	58,282	58,924	41,641	32,861	92,664	54,926	63,392	11,998
SAME HOUSE	17,655	31,806	19,554	20,703	17,983	35,950	20,253	28,256	8,521
DIFFERENT HOUSE IN UNITED STATES:									
SAME COUNTY	22,183	19,246	25,790	15,079	12,126	36,608	22,694	22,699	3,123
DIFFERENT COUNTY:									
SAME STATE	2,039	476	918	453	246	3,466	2,676	2,251	134
DIFFERENT STATE:									
NORTHEAST	1,148	304	734	420	161	2,558	1,742	2,107	0
NORTH CENTRAL	1,881	769	1,405	437	366	4,765	3,555	3,232	75
SOUTH	713	543	1,700	385	264	2,116	1,449	1,599	0
WEST	757	496	693	337	131	1,640	1,304	1,802	39
ABROAD	6,092	4,642	8,130	3,827	1,584	5,561	1,253	1,446	106
YEARS OF SCHOOL COMPLETED									
PERSONS 25 YEARS AND OVER	36,402	43,986	41,080	29,706	21,975	69,242	41,848	45,993	8,499
ELEMENTARY (0 TO 8 YEARS)	5,516	7,252	10,991	6,677	6,040	10,948	4,814	4,850	1,345
HIGH SCHOOL:									
1 TO 3 YEARS	4,010	4,833	6,067	4,565	4,626	7,677	3,034	4,023	1,333
4 YEARS	9,258	12,874	10,084	8,972	6,523	15,225	7,244	8,190	3,124
COLLEGE:									
1 TO 3 YEARS	6,457	8,187	6,047	4,614	2,391	12,506	6,410	8,410	1,578
4 OR MORE YEARS	11,161	10,840	7,891	4,878	2,395	22,886	20,346	20,520	1,119
SCHOOL ENROLLMENT									
PERSONS 3 YEARS AND OLDER ENROLLED IN SCHOOL	13,274	13,322	14,760	9,100	7,892	18,110	10,738	15,625	3,031
NURSERY SCHOOL	387	614	671	171	187	561	350	664	99
KINDERGARTEN AND ELEMENTARY (1 TO 8 YEARS)	4,464	5,380	7,337	4,250	4,153	7,513	3,794	6,518	1,237
HIGH SCHOOL (1 TO 4 YEARS)	1,987	3,015	2,674	2,288	2,023	2,857	1,502	2,456	887
COLLEGE	6,436	4,313	4,078	2,391	1,529	7,179	5,092	5,987	808
PRIVATE SCHOOL ENROLLMENT									
PERSONS 3 YEARS AND OLDER ENROLLED IN PRIVATE SCHOOL	5,973	5,186	3,280	2,972	2,380	6,524	4,178	5,893	1,800
NURSERY SCHOOL	235	464	271	109	116	379	244	102	74
KINDERGARTEN AND ELEMENTARY (1 TO 8 YEARS)	1,391	2,038	1,218	1,370	1,155	2,114	1,035	963	960
HIGH SCHOOL (1 TO 4 YEARS)	630	1,061	509	685	630	780	384	658	505
COLLEGE	3,717	1,623	1,282	808	479	3,251	2,515	4,170	261
VETERAN STATUS									
CIVILIAN MALES 16 AND OVER	22,351	22,916	25,703	16,567	12,718	39,972	24,261	25,828	4,629
VETERAN	4,691	6,306	5,697	4,136	3,555	9,540	6,042	7,790	1,756
NON-VETERAN	17,660	16,610	20,006	12,431	9,163	30,432	18,219	18,038	2,873
CIVILIAN FEMALES 16 AND OVER	24,887	28,502	25,017	19,548	14,842	43,915	25,659	30,060	5,712
VETERAN	283	238	351	220	175	564	210	294	57
NON-VETERAN	24,604	28,264	24,666	19,328	14,667	43,351	25,449	29,766	5,655

	10	11	12	13	14	15	16	17	18
NATIVITY AND PLACE OF BIRTH									
TOTAL PERSONS	40,586	24,583	18,991	15,273	46,075	57,349	49,489	37,860	10,793
NATIVE:									
BORN IN STATE OF RESIDENCE	31,501	18,377	13,777	8,083	22,504	41,364	32,545	27,894	7,461
BORN IN DIFFERENT STATE	3,737	2,391	2,177	2,420	5,426	5,271	6,614	3,255	884
BORN ABROAD, AT SEA, ETC.	126	64	112	141	1,428	272	750	144	32
FOREIGN BORN	5,222	3,751	2,925	4,629	16,717	10,442	9,580	6,567	2,416
ANCESTRY									
TOTAL PERSONS	40,586	24,583	18,991	15,273	46,075	57,349	49,489	37,860	10,793
SINGLE ANCESTRY GROUP:									
DUTCH	66	17	23	38	86	83	32	33	21
ENGLISH	502	407	433	254	873	711	1,080	456	122
FRENCH	90	92	47	71	222	171	218	153	38
GERMAN	4,251	2,844	2,338	904	3,688	6,252	6,160	3,824	578
GREEK	416	504	548	919	821	1,332	431	969	484
HUNGARIAN	101	89	130	279	308	358	250	250	30
IRISH	3,141	1,788	2,009	347	1,731	3,769	3,087	2,627	561
ITALIAN	4,515	2,111	1,428	346	1,255	6,011	2,060	6,938	2,796
NORWEGIAN	562	100	177	51	126	480	426	256	122
POLISH	8,160	5,947	1,876	1,272	2,246	11,262	5,631	6,535	1,334
PORTUGUESE	14	0	0	0	17	15	10	12	6
RUSSIAN	92	45	82	1,305	523	161	210	84	39
SCOTTISH	83	24	74	30	56	95	117	47	13
SWEDISH	770	308	544	811	574	663	705	415	117
UKRAINIAN	473	114	77	71	91	446	184	250	57
OTHER	2,353	1,673	1,561	3,422	18,936	4,336	9,000	2,371	526
MULTIPLE ANCESTRY GROUP	12,999	7,468	6,558	3,198	10,807	17,949	16,735	10,673	2,407
ANCESTRY NOT SPECIFIED:									
OTHER	750	368	566	1,468	1,716	1,400	1,298	766	153
NOT REPORTED	1,248	684	520	487	1,999	1,855	1,855	1,201	1,399
PERSONS IN SELECTED MULTIPLE									
ANCESTRY GROUPS	20,740	11,688	10,245	3,591	15,083	28,019	25,661	17,024	3,932
ENGLISH AND OTHER GROUP(S)	2,040	1,201	1,168	523	2,091	2,943	3,020	1,437	405
FRENCH AND OTHER GROUP(S)	940	585	550	178	1,071	1,328	1,320	724	270
GERMAN AND OTHER GROUP(S)	6,977	4,077	3,519	1,129	4,710	9,366	8,815	5,042	1,049
IRISH AND OTHER GROUP(S)	4,975	2,506	2,735	792	4,183	6,244	6,793	4,204	894
ITALIAN AND OTHER GROUP(S)	2,019	986	1,063	280	1,273	2,873	2,045	2,450	637
POLISH AND OTHER GROUP(S)	3,789	2,333	1,210	689	1,755	5,265	3,668	3,167	677
RESIDENCE IN 1975									
PERSONS 5 YEARS AND OVER	39,200	23,487	18,190	14,501	42,022	54,538	46,663	36,274	10,403
SAME HOUSE	28,145	16,197	13,472	7,374	16,993	34,415	26,387	25,705	6,957
DIFFERENT HOUSE IN UNITED STATES:									
SAME COUNTY	9,974	6,250	3,435	4,885	17,063	17,910	16,389	9,752	3,285
DIFFERENT COUNTY:									
SAME STATE	309	284	627	379	438	657	533	319	17
DIFFERENT STATE:									
NORTHEAST	73	49	19	262	356	75	218	39	0
NORTH CENTRAL	214	112	157	428	431	344	453	84	35
SOUTH	169	158	171	119	549	113	432	126	17
WEST	183	178	76	166	329	126	120	103	17
ABROAD	133	259	233	888	5,863	898	2,131	146	75
YEARS OF SCHOOL COMPLETED									
PERSONS 25 YEARS AND OVER	28,458	17,566	13,039	10,010	27,262	39,231	32,527	26,020	7,528
ELEMENTARY (0 TO 8 YEARS)	5,316	4,273	1,563	1,693	7,275	9,757	7,043	6,677	2,306
HIGH SCHOOL:									
1 TO 3 YEARS	4,770	3,014	1,358	1,013	4,379	7,149	6,393	5,163	1,301
4 YEARS	10,615	6,176	4,171	2,837	8,274	13,629	10,513	9,298	2,425
COLLEGE:									
1 TO 3 YEARS	4,313	2,331	2,572	1,672	3,398	5,148	4,534	3,127	1,033
4 OR MORE YEARS	3,444	1,772	3,375	2,795	3,936	3,548	4,044	1,755	463
SCHOOL ENROLLMENT									
PERSONS 3 YEARS AND OLDER									
ENROLLED IN SCHOOL	8,709	4,557	4,834	4,292	11,238	11,620	10,487	7,935	2,216
NURSERY SCHOOL	224	35	125	133	362	179	372	238	69
KINDERGARTEN AND ELEMENTARY (1 TO 8 YEARS)	3,725	2,149	2,202	1,556	6,138	5,542	5,136	3,828	1,033
HIGH SCHOOL (1 TO 4 YEARS)	2,712	1,412	1,329	759	2,551	3,352	2,575	2,213	669
COLLEGE	2,048	961	1,178	1,844	2,187	2,547	2,404	1,656	445
PRIVATE SCHOOL ENROLLMENT									
PERSONS 3 YEARS AND OLDER									
ENROLLED IN PRIVATE SCHOOL	4,377	2,133	2,791	2,209	2,581	6,189	3,976	3,993	1,091
NURSERY SCHOOL	181	35	112	119	194	138	259	125	54
KINDERGARTEN AND ELEMENTARY (1 TO 8 YEARS)	2,246	1,108	1,320	527	1,179	3,331	1,872	2,142	603
HIGH SCHOOL (1 TO 4 YEARS)	1,253	638	854	372	660	1,848	965	1,236	289
COLLEGE	697	352	505	1,191	548	872	880	490	145
VETERAN STATUS									
CIVILIAN MALES 16 AND OVER	15,726	9,362	7,171	5,743	16,602	21,532	18,493	14,811	4,104
VETERAN	6,086	3,383	2,537	1,421	3,801	7,573	5,767	5,184	1,292
NON-VETERAN	9,640	5,979	4,634	4,322	12,801	13,959	12,726	9,627	2,812
CIVILIAN FEMALES 16 AND OVER	18.410	11,472	8,330	6,954	18,155	26,091	21,596	16,719	5.003
VETERAN	184	105	76	42	210	240	241	162	46
NON-VETERAN	18,226	11,367	8,254	6,912	17,945	25,851	21,355	16,557	4,957

	19	20	21	22	23	24	25	26	27
NATIVITY AND PLACE OF BIRTH									
TOTAL PERSONS	53,371	19,547	33,527	84,768	70,879	96,428	138,026	33,865	31,580
NATIVE:									
BORN IN STATE OF RESIDENCE	36,077	10,934	18,971	42,476	37,278	44,263	83,614	19,450	18,200
BORN IN DIFFERENT STATE	4,845	2,569	3,741	10,011	13,534	11,996	43,580	14,125	13,146
BORN ABROAD, AT SEA, ETC.	784	2,120	1,696	12,500	9,717	13,650	1,670	24	55
FOREIGN BORN	11,665	3,924	9,119	19,781	10,350	26,519	9,162	266	179
ANCESTRY									
TOTAL PERSONS	53,371	19,547	33,527	84,768	70,879	96,428	138,026	33,865	31,580
SINGLE ANCESTRY GROUP:									
DUTCH	59	40	28	103	22	19	39	0	0
ENGLISH	698	299	451	1,298	1,060	861	1,782	382	423
FRENCH	85	60	89	300	100	246	138	53	0
GERMAN	3,594	1,270	2,114	2,855	639	1,111	2,008	123	38
GREEK	1,379	94	179	327	49	29	916	0	0
HUNGARIAN	178	111	88	188	87	129	80	0	0
IRISH	2,322	649	801	1,699	987	800	2,150	9	51
ITALIAN	6,802	712	916	1,058	1,775	2,890	5,383	19	51
NORWEGIAN	428	325	117	384	67	87	239	0	0
POLISH	15,027	2,852	9,926	10,655	3,871	10,605	2,644	8	8
PORTUGUESE	0	11	20	36	63	24	7	0	0
RUSSIAN	190	36	101	191	112	197	163	0	0
SCOTTISH	119	15	47	94	43	41	34	3	5
SWEDISH	477	132	138	176	90	108	251	0	0
UKRAINIAN	585	255	71	374	546	3,296	258	0	0
OTHER	5,033	6,195	7,858	41,241	48,990	54,738	94,937	27,952	26,472
MULTIPLE ANCESTRY GROUP	13,669	4,592	7,925	13,696	5,539	8,252	8,566	304	280
ANCESTRY NOT SPECIFIED:									
OTHER	1,162	757	731	2,578	1,904	2,595	4,157	1,122	640
NOT REPORTED	1,564	1,142	1,927	7,515	4,935	10,400	14,274	3,890	3,612
PERSONS IN SELECTED MULTIPLE ANCESTRY GROUPS	21,750	6,514	11,673	18,896	6,739	9,840	12,174	224	333
ENGLISH AND OTHER GROUP(S)	2,069	682	1,346	2,330	871	1,120	1,338	35	78
FRENCH AND OTHER GROUP(S)	1,163	250	550	1,278	393	511	889	62	22
GERMAN AND OTHER GROUP(S)	6,390	2,090	3,903	5,791	1,692	2,458	3,622	15	191
IRISH AND OTHER GROUP(S)	4,916	1,730	2,761	4,955	1,894	2,610	3,222	44	42
ITALIAN AND OTHER GROUP(S)	2,817	731	825	1,175	636	876	1,542	23	0
POLISH AND OTHER GROUP(S)	4,395	1,031	2,288	3,367	1,253	2,265	1,561	45	0
RESIDENCE IN 1975									
PERSONS 5 YEARS AND OVER	50,644	18,026	31,208	76,623	63,105	86,519	124,200	30,557	28,507
SAME HOUSE	31,795	9,613	16,847	36,415	32,243	45,087	68,158	18,108	17,727
DIFFERENT HOUSE IN UNITED STATES:									
SAME COUNTY	16,420	6,906	11,412	31,154	26,403	31,649	51,237	11,599	9,895
DIFFERENT COUNTY:									
SAME STATE	275	11	157	345	260	360	401	119	121
DIFFERENT STATE:									
NORTHEAST	180	46	98	750	104	753	143	56	0
NORTH CENTRAL	97	183	70	640	224	593	837	239	140
SOUTH	276	116	131	814	470	919	1,967	394	530
WEST	34	127	155	344	118	427	272	11	56
ABROAD	1,567	1,024	2,338	6,161	3,283	6,731	1,185	31	38
YEARS OF SCHOOL COMPLETED									
PERSONS 25 YEARS AND OVER	36,827	11,748	21,629	46,278	33,760	49,479	68,141	14,847	15,115
ELEMENTARY (0 TO 8 YEARS)	11,473	3,897	6,779	18,350	13,358	24,085	15,979	4,623	5,306
HIGH SCHOOL:									
1 TO 3 YEARS	7,257	2,470	4,671	9,602	7,888	9,998	16,152	4,521	3,863
4 YEARS	11,671	3,390	6,488	10,904	8,245	8,670	22,268	4,085	3,879
COLLEGE:									
1 TO 3 YEARS	3,752	1,087	2,019	4,178	2,635	3,447	9,348	1,332	1,687
4 OR MORE YEARS	2,674	904	1,672	3,244	1,634	3,279	4,394	286	380
SCHOOL ENROLLMENT									
PERSONS 3 YEARS AND OLDER ENROLLED IN SCHOOL	10,586	4,574	6,830	21,160	21,832	26,728	43,838	12,065	10,274
NURSERY SCHOOL	279	103	188	694	674	918	1,673	621	464
KINDERGARTEN AND ELEMENTARY (1 TO 8 YEARS)	5,276	2,612	3,672	13,250	13,777	16,937	25,588	6,990	5,902
HIGH SCHOOL (1 TO 4 YEARS)	2,912	1,005	1,863	4,528	5,390	6,251	11,093	3,448	2,870
COLLEGE	2,119	854	1,107	2,688	1,991	2,622	5,484	1,006	1,038
PRIVATE SCHOOL ENROLLMENT									
PERSONS 3 YEARS AND OLDER ENROLLED IN PRIVATE SCHOOL	4,887	1,193	2,229	4,182	2,912	4,398	6,829	863	772
NURSERY SCHOOL	190	47	54	295	182	256	739	90	81
KINDERGARTEN AND ELEMENTARY (1 TO 8 YEARS)	2,596	596	1,337	2,207	1,757	2,418	3,461	398	346
HIGH SCHOOL (1 TO 4 YEARS)	1,334	265	585	951	589	1,032	1,329	252	236
COLLEGE	767	285	253	729	384	692	1,300	123	109
VETERAN STATUS									
CIVILIAN MALES 16 AND OVER	20,313	7,093	12,640	30,002	22,084	33,219	42,077	9,409	9,580
VETERAN	6,422	1,779	3,211	6,462	4,225	5,343	10,069	1,926	1,937
NON-VETERAN	13,891	5,314	9,429	23,540	17,859	27,876	32,008	7,483	7,643
CIVILIAN FEMALES 16 AND OVER	23,886	7,829	14,009	30,961	24,587	33,437	51,323	12,338	11,716
VETERAN	202	58	172	258	189	299	428	174	62
NON-VETERAN	23,684	7,771	13,837	30,703	24,398	33,138	50,895	12,164	11,654

	28	29	30	31	32	33	34	35	36
NATIVITY AND PLACE OF BIRTH									
TOTAL PERSONS	57,305	61,534	75,204	44,951	6,420	7,243	12,475	35,700	16,748
NATIVE:									
BORN IN STATE OF RESIDENCE	35,006	35,959	32,814	18,736	2,942	4,903	6,446	21,039	11,249
BORN IN DIFFERENT STATE	16,561	24,213	8,988	4,877	2,667	2,004	1,685	12,909	5,375
BORN ABROAD, AT SEA, ETC.	574	107	1,659	1,232	76	0	57	87	9
FOREIGN BORN	5,164	1,255	31,743	20,106	735	336	4,287	1,665	115
ANCESTRY									
TOTAL PERSONS	57,305	61,534	75,204	44,951	6,420	7,243	12,475	35,700	16,748
SINGLE ANCESTRY GROUP:									
DUTCH	44	0	5	0	0	0	0	20	0
ENGLISH	907	593	430	180	199	26	84	552	244
FRENCH	84	11	78	17	23	0	19	149	0
GERMAN	286	43	546	358	249	18	131	343	0
GREEK	55	5	74	51	26	10	9	17	0
HUNGARIAN	42	0	18	26	44	0	7	10	0
IRISH	576	44	317	422	208	33	187	198	0
ITALIAN	1,220	34	387	1,042	72	0	1,516	69	0
NORWEGIAN	7	0	29	4	16	0	10	5	0
POLISH	343	84	3,502	2,460	201	0	62	189	0
PORTUGUESE	10	0	13	19	0	0	6	8	0
RUSSIAN	62	46	16	17	80	0	0	54	0
SCOTTISH	5	0	0	7	0	0	0	20	0
SWEDISH	24	0	65	7	36	8	9	87	0
UKRAINIAN	0	15	37	40	11	0	0	39	0
OTHER	37,531	51,075	58,290	31,748	1,285	6,137	7,481	26,630	13,800
MULTIPLE ANCESTRY GROUP	1,731	670	3,686	3,004	638	61	920	1,696	194
ANCESTRY NOT SPECIFIED:									
OTHER	1,110	1,762	1,186	711	119	160	322	849	241
NOT REPORTED	13,268	7,152	6,525	4,838	3,213	790	1,712	4,765	2,269
PERSONS IN SELECTED MULTIPLE ANCESTRY GROUPS	2,289	352	3,785	3,239	840	38	1,283	2,067	91
ENGLISH AND OTHER GROUP(S)	488	86	290	263	223	12	58	456	26
FRENCH AND OTHER GROUP(S)	135	54	237	137	46	0	55	147	5
GERMAN AND OTHER GROUP(S)	489	67	1,156	712	311	4	233	652	17
IRISH AND OTHER GROUP(S)	624	83	750	868	170	22	429	407	43
ITALIAN AND OTHER GROUP(S)	318	24	267	335	60	0	366	189	0
POLISH AND OTHER GROUP(S)	235	38	1,085	924	30	0	142	216	0
RESIDENCE IN 1975									
PERSONS 5 YEARS AND OVER	51,223	55,307	65,608	39,523	6,368	6,344	11,779	32,516	14,814
SAME HOUSE	30,605	36,429	30,432	20,523	2,999	4,214	7,560	19,590	9,294
DIFFERENT HOUSE IN UNITED STATES:									
SAME COUNTY	17,298	17,422	26,783	12,307	2,288	1,976	2,935	9,975	5,066
DIFFERENT COUNTY:									
SAME STATE	755	223	163	117	197	25	106	403	24
DIFFERENT STATE:									
NORTHEAST	268	40	70	104	189	14	78	349	23
NORTH CENTRAL	289	106	99	151	184	10	48	582	53
SOUTH	530	767	690	444	140	59	8	469	294
WEST	377	181	833	316	164	0	71	193	49
ABROAD	1,101	139	6,538	5,561	207	46	973	955	11
YEARS OF SCHOOL COMPLETED									
PERSONS 25 YEARS AND OVER	26,578	27,657	35,520	21,769	5,670	3,113	7,502	19,082	6,145
ELEMENTARY (0 TO 8 YEARS)	9,514	9,252	18,956	13,002	735	716	2,932	4,394	1,860
HIGH SCHOOL:									
1 TO 3 YEARS	6,421	7,596	6,844	3,331	972	918	1,538	3,386	1,756
4 YEARS	4,718	7,091	6,575	3,398	1,718	744	1,943	4,078	1,502
COLLEGE:									
1 TO 3 YEARS	2,487	2,890	2,153	1,152	961	448	541	3,276	818
4 OR MORE YEARS	3,438	828	992	886	1,284	287	548	3,948	209
SCHOOL ENROLLMENT									
PERSONS 3 YEARS AND OLDER ENROLLED IN SCHOOL	20,801	21,763	19,376	11,902	702	2,712	3,442	12,717	7,022
NURSERY SCHOOL	1,024	994	385	311	6	173	92	713	440
KINDERGARTEN AND ELEMENTARY (1 TO 8 YEARS)	11,482	12,870	12,866	7,813	33	1,591	1,674	5,668	4,133
HIGH SCHOOL (1 TO 4 YEARS)	5,241	5,978	4,237	2,717	84	594	901	2,204	1,804
COLLEGE	3,054	1,921	1,888	1,061	579	354	775	4,132	645
PRIVATE SCHOOL ENROLLMENT									
PERSONS 3 YEARS AND OLDER ENROLLED IN PRIVATE SCHOOL	2,378	1,714	4,243	2,280	403	252	1,248	3,315	394
NURSERY SCHOOL	203	287	82	54	6	39	48	195	41
KINDERGARTEN AND ELEMENTARY (1 TO 8 YEARS)	1,047	798	2,580	1,423	16	130	617	624	208
HIGH SCHOOL (1 TO 4 YEARS)	439	358	1,079	510	18	21	293	197	57
COLLEGE	689	271	502	293	363	62	290	2,299	88
VETERAN STATUS									
CIVILIAN MALES 16 AND OVER	16,965	17,190	27,738	15,957	3,577	1,596	4,525	10,096	3,619
VETERAN	2,949	3,254	3,325	2,016	1,190	330	855	2,408	643
NON-VETERAN	14,016	13,936	24,413	13,941	2,387	1,266	3,670	7,688	2,976
CIVILIAN FEMALES 16 AND OVER	20,537	22,526	23,217	14,477	2,690	2,888	5,156	15,749	6,143
VETERAN	183	207	161	105	23	43	13	207	21
NON-VETERAN	20,354	22,319	23,056	14,372	2,667	2,845	5,143	15,542	6,122

	37	38	39	40	41	42	43	44	45
NATIVITY AND PLACE OF BIRTH									
TOTAL PERSONS	5,832	53,741	21,974	31,935	31,198	36,323	77,743	40,725	13,792
NATIVE:									
BORN IN STATE OF RESIDENCE	3,103	31,665	11,563	19,023	12,017	19,044	46,303	20,910	8,104
BORN IN DIFFERENT STATE	2,638	21,613	9,190	12,622	15,066	16,379	29,366	19,000	5,464
BORN ABROAD, AT SEA, ETC.	43	35	62	10	307	54	210	94	27
FOREIGN BORN	48	428	1,159	280	3,808	846	1,864	721	197
ANCESTRY									
TOTAL PERSONS	5,832	53,741	21,974	31,935	31,198	36,323	77,743	40,725	13,792
SINGLE ANCESTRY GROUP:									
DUTCH	0	0	24	0	166	0	20	0	0
ENGLISH	31	976	413	255	1,933	396	715	457	32
FRENCH	0	18	52	8	142	42	103	80	38
GERMAN	8	8	385	22	1,642	147	217	14	20
GREEK	0	0	26	0	33	6	111	0	0
HUNGARIAN	0	0	26	0	188	6	5	20	20
IRISH	0	17	222	34	801	88	302	68	36
ITALIAN	0	0	49	0	398	51	43	9	22
NORWEGIAN	0	0	35	0	93	0	29	8	0
POLISH	0	14	70	0	466	6	86	0	49
PORTUGUESE	0	0	0	0	12	0	0	15	0
RUSSIAN	0	0	347	0	862	85	61	0	0
SCOTTISH	0	0	50	0	156	9	20	0	0
SWEDISH	0	0	72	0	281	12	84	6	0
UKRAINIAN	0	0	0	0	86	0	4	0	7
OTHER	5,220	45,438	15,632	28,268	13,248	30,761	63,233	34,795	11,349
MULTIPLE ANCESTRY GROUP	50	670	1,879	398	7,672	723	2,092	642	302
ANCESTRY NOT SPECIFIED:									
OTHER	64	1,124	820	464	1,086	823	1,981	1,080	273
NOT REPORTED	459	5,476	1,872	2,486	1,933	3,168	8,637	3,531	1,644
PERSONS IN SELECTED MULTIPLE ANCESTRY GROUPS									
ENGLISH AND OTHER GROUP(S)	35	348	2,132	229	9,639	747	1,732	340	245
FRENCH AND OTHER GROUP(S)	0	121	596	34	2,682	208	431	19	25
GERMAN AND OTHER GROUP(S)	24	121	197	33	695	108	254	154	37
IRISH AND OTHER GROUP(S)	11	24	667	17	2,858	147	487	82	56
ITALIAN AND OTHER GROUP(S)	0	64	416	89	2,156	221	490	79	105
POLISH AND OTHER GROUP(S)	0	0	65	56	391	19	35	6	5
	0	18	191	0	857	44	35	0	17
RESIDENCE IN 1975									
PERSONS 5 YEARS AND OVER	5,307	48,554	20,296	28,848	30,040	33,366	71,032	37,937	13,050
SAME HOUSE	3,782	31,946	9,829	17,429	12,199	18,597	36,725	25,485	9,987
DIFFERENT HOUSE IN UNITED STATES:									
SAME COUNTY	1,398	15,460	7,804	10,818	9,507	12,866	31,138	10,986	2,615
DIFFERENT COUNTY:									
SAME STATE	30	177	199	102	533	176	198	285	81
DIFFERENT STATE:									
NORTHEAST	15	80	557	108	2,264	374	178	113	19
NORTH CENTRAL	0	193	653	86	1,777	272	887	221	85
SOUTH	56	625	612	207	1,181	678	1,172	609	200
WEST	10	36	319	62	1,028	180	206	128	38
ABROAD	16	37	323	36	1,551	223	528	110	25
YEARS OF SCHOOL COMPLETED									
PERSONS 25 YEARS AND OVER	3,126	27,065	14,288	16,216	20,167	21,028	44,553	26,746	7,883
ELEMENTARY (0 TO 8 YEARS)	1,227	9,514	2,347	4,963	1,473	5,672	5,979	4,251	1,024
HIGH SCHOOL:									
1 TO 3 YEARS	870	8,208	2,054	4,786	1,451	5,247	8,240	4,867	1,357
4 YEARS	713	5,969	3,026	4,257	2,774	5,785	13,421	8,203	2,421
COLLEGE:									
1 TO 3 YEARS	284	2,602	2,516	1,785	3,141	2,695	10,225	6,032	1,778
4 OR MORE YEARS	32	772	4,345	425	11,328	1,629	6,688	3,393	1,303
SCHOOL ENROLLMENT									
PERSONS 3 YEARS AND OLDER									
ENROLLED IN SCHOOL	1,761	17,396	6,070	9,992	11,779	10,349	23,175	9,471	4,579
NURSERY SCHOOL	75	800	308	503	459	477	1,129	435	161
KINDERGARTEN AND ELEMENTARY (1 TO 8 YEARS)	1,002	10,369	2,592	5,984	2,413	5,462	11,331	4,530	2,015
HIGH SCHOOL (1 TO 4 YEARS)	542	4,609	1,128	2,478	1,195	2,551	5,373	2,120	1,283
COLLEGE	142	1,618	2,042	1,027	7,712	1,859	5,342	2,386	1,120
PRIVATE SCHOOL ENROLLMENT									
PERSONS 3 YEARS AND OLDER									
ENROLLED IN PRIVATE SCHOOL	109	1,098	1,963	954	8,024	1,583	4,998	2,263	1,097
NURSERY SCHOOL	12	117	150	153	310	162	595	222	100
KINDERGARTEN AND ELEMENTARY (1 TO 8 YEARS)	77	627	561	410	1,029	544	2,130	967	505
HIGH SCHOOL (1 TO 4 YEARS)	7	136	159	213	434	210	1,065	484	254
COLLEGE	13	218	1,093	178	6,251	667	1,208	590	238
VETERAN STATUS									
CIVILIAN MALES 16 AND OVER	1,792	15,718	7,894	9,218	13,521	11,729	25,159	14,330	4,768
VETERAN	362	3,632	2,265	2,308	2,833	3,430	8,981	5,115	1,623
NON-VETERAN	1,430	12,086	5,629	6,910	10,688	8,299	16,178	9,215	3,145
CIVILIAN FEMALES 16 AND OVER	2,321	20,606	9,451	12,386	13,225	15,044	31,863	18,364	5,676
VETERAN	47	172	205	134	160	182	420	185	97
NON-VETERAN	2,274	20,434	9,246	12,252	13,065	14,862	31,443	18,179	5,579

	46	47	48	49	50	51	52	53	54
NATIVITY AND PLACE OF BIRTH									
TOTAL PERSONS	46,422	3,942	20,505	64,372	10,341	19,400	21,331	44,904	13,539
NATIVE:									
BORN IN STATE OF RESIDENCE	26,918	2,591	11,533	39,121	6,355	12,520	15,575	28,965	10,008
BORN IN DIFFERENT STATE	10,570	1,112	7,840	23,960	3,249	4,564	2,643	14,307	3,338
BORN ABROAD, AT SEA, ETC.	1,090	0	133	66	27	114	103	73	31
FOREIGN BORN	7,844	239	999	1,225	710	2,202	3,010	1,559	162
ANCESTRY									
TOTAL PERSONS	46,422	3,942	20,505	64,372	10,341	19,400	21,331	44,904	13,539
SINGLE ANCESTRY GROUP:									
DUTCH	0	0	0	55	12	7	45	77	24
ENGLISH	360	160	136	714	62	107	462	474	163
FRENCH	36	0	63	55	18	47	48	6	0
GERMAN	222	23	96	88	117	224	1,371	155	54
GREEK	60	0	47	15	14	4	215	0	0
HUNGARIAN	73	54	30	42	17	17	145	35	0
IRISH	177	7	50	59	102	208	812	62	20
ITALIAN	71	14	39	83	430	230	1,436	333	11
NORWEGIAN	37	0	0	7	0	6	23	4	0
POLISH	3,228	43	216	101	93	592	2,432	492	10
PORTUGUESE	21	0	0	0	6	0	15	6	0
RUSSIAN	0	11	5	46	7	17	30	14	0
SCOTTISH	12	0	18	5	26	10	26	7	0
SWEDISH	30	0	11	34	74	0	225	37	0
UKRAINIAN	0	92	8	20	5	19	34	5	0
OTHER	34,361	2,720	16,419	56,216	7,413	13,833	5,192	37,428	10,649
MULTIPLE ANCESTRY GROUP	2,074	88	516	1,087	714	1,498	6,874	917	186
ANCESTRY NOT SPECIFIED:									
OTHER	932	69	534	1,449	180	425	690	1,301	366
NOT REPORTED	4,728	661	2,317	4,296	1,051	2,156	1,256	3,551	2,056
PERSONS IN SELECTED MULTIPLE									
ANCESTRY GROUPS	2,042	125	571	706	1,152	1,858	9,967	620	151
ENGLISH AND OTHER GROUP(S)	241	11	88	139	150	173	1,221	97	26
FRENCH AND OTHER GROUP(S)	204	0	62	115	89	138	488	48	43
GERMAN AND OTHER GROUP(S)	491	40	129	185	344	397	2,836	213	23
IRISH AND OTHER GROUP(S)	389	42	175	220	252	526	2,489	143	46
ITALIAN AND OTHER GROUP(S)	80	0	26	36	212	308	1,066	72	13
POLISH AND OTHER GROUP(S)	637	32	91	11	105	316	1,867	47	0
RESIDENCE IN 1975									
PERSONS 5 YEARS AND OVER	41,974	3,482	19,372	59,912	9,611	18,107	20,032	40,414	11,891
SAME HOUSE	26,759	1,808	15,111	44,315	6,724	12,868	13,831	28,126	7,848
DIFFERENT HOUSE IN UNITED STATES:									
SAME COUNTY	12,970	1,401	3,881	13,881	2,404	4,410	5,296	10,689	3,733
DIFFERENT COUNTY:									
SAME STATE	82	98	0	237	98	106	212	138	0
DIFFERENT STATE:									
NORTHEAST	72	0	36	132	0	156	8	27	15
NORTH CENTRAL	321	0	88	239	58	141	300	282	61
SOUTH	426	75	54	779	87	39	89	860	155
WEST	193	100	91	155	13	101	50	34	14
ABROAD	1,151	0	111	174	227	286	246	258	65
YEARS OF SCHOOL COMPLETED									
PERSONS 25 YEARS AND OVER	24,078	1,843	11,862	33,352	5,647	10,153	13,291	21,065	4,934
ELEMENTARY (0 TO 8 YEARS)	7,653	315	1,537	5,568	955	2,267	3,625	3,619	832
HIGH SCHOOL:									
1 TO 3 YEARS	4,758	486	1,708	6,757	1,164	2,127	3,091	4,350	1,419
4 YEARS	6,486	607	3,677	10,598	1,912	3,400	4,678	7,696	1,716
COLLEGE:									
1 TO 3 YEARS	3,220	308	2,800	6,996	1,202	1,623	1,240	4,046	778
4 OR MORE YEARS	1,961	127	2,140	3,433	414	736	657	1,354	189
SCHOOL ENROLLMENT									
PERSONS 3 YEARS AND OLDER									
ENROLLED IN SCHOOL	14,648	1,362	6,759	22,426	3,387	6,501	4,901	16,533	5,145
NURSERY SCHOOL	566	56	320	783	166	215	71	665	326
KINDERGARTEN AND ELEMENTARY (1 TO 8 YEARS)	8,319	749	3,341	11,314	1,688	3,658	2,512	9,595	3,581
HIGH SCHOOL (1 TO 4 YEARS)	3,661	406	1,661	6,254	915	1,852	1,566	4,196	1,560
COLLEGE	2,102	151	1,437	4,075	618	776	752	2,077	678
PRIVATE SCHOOL ENROLLMENT									
PERSONS 3 YEARS AND OLDER									
ENROLLED IN PRIVATE SCHOOL	2,983	188	2,066	3,889	691	1,618	1,655	3,169	530
NURSERY SCHOOL	234	24	241	380	94	103	12	380	63
KINDERGARTEN AND ELEMENTARY (1 TO 8 YEARS)	1,747	97	1,094	2,030	308	962	823	1,991	316
HIGH SCHOOL (1 TO 4 YEARS)	534	61	411	776	193	498	533	502	111
COLLEGE	468	6	320	703	96	55	287	296	40
VETERAN STATUS									
CIVILIAN MALES 16 AND OVER	15,113	1,155	7,015	20,751	3,373	6,194	8,199	13,315	3,063
VETERAN	3,818	366	2,423	6,271	1,045	2,016	3,064	3,992	754
NON-VETERAN	11,295	789	4,592	14,480	2,328	4,178	5,135	9,323	2,309
CIVILIAN FEMALES 16 AND OVER	17,129	1,425	8,212	24,934	4,108	7,358	8,786	15,574	4,661
VETERAN	214	31	76	347	45	116	132	143	47
NON-VETERAN	16,915	1,394	8,136	24,587	4,063	7,242	8,654	15,431	4,614

	55	56	57	58	59	60	61	62	63
NATIVITY AND PLACE OF BIRTH									
TOTAL PERSONS	11,572	37,928	9,708	30,770	13,248	30,923	55,860	12,797	24,445
NATIVE:									
BORN IN STATE OF RESIDENCE	8,331	30,548	7,284	21,712	10,581	23,147	33,256	10,139	18,270
BORN IN DIFFERENT STATE	2,231	4,181	639	2,528	1,322	2,933	8,369	1,094	2,058
BORN ABROAD, AT SEA, ETC.	49	115	54	203	63	368	877	38	326
FOREIGN BORN	961	3,084	1,731	6,327	1,282	4,475	13,358	1,526	3,791
ANCESTRY									
TOTAL PERSONS	11,572	37,928	9,708	30,770	13,248	30,923	55,860	12,797	24,445
SINGLE ANCESTRY GROUP:									
DUTCH	27	68	7	49	7	19	44	57	19
ENGLISH	238	407	75	258	224	404	930	197	290
FRENCH	59	157	20	89	30	88	92	17	37
GERMAN	400	1,855	295	1,289	895	1,146	990	515	1,368
GREEK	288	184	49	118	23	127	63	37	150
HUNGARIAN	67	93	0	43	42	42	42	13	71
IRISH	454	1,785	312	1,283	712	1,981	2,701	558	2,244
ITALIAN	320	1,855	478	666	434	3,154	298	630	821
NORWEGIAN	8	43	5	32	8	0	13	0	26
POLISH	3,501	9,792	4,828	8,823	3,036	3,533	7,195	5,031	4,343
PORTUGUESE	0	43	0	0	18	0	3	7	0
RUSSIAN	56	82	55	110	27	40	92	74	101
SCOTTISH	6	49	8	27	7	21	25	6	75
SWEDISH	86	49	19	97	28	41	74	51	104
UKRAINIAN	21	227	77	144	44	70	118	99	169
OTHER	1,459	9,275	868	7,817	2,167	8,750	31,153	1,480	6,191
MULTIPLE ANCESTRY GROUP	3,912	9,616	2,115	7,569	4,191	8,546	7,645	3,381	7,097
ANCESTRY NOT SPECIFIED:									
OTHER	178	803	262	748	339	641	1,274	165	524
NOT REPORTED	492	1,545	235	1,608	1,016	2,320	3,108	479	815
PERSONS IN SELECTED MULTIPLE ANCESTRY GROUPS	5,905	14,652	3,022	11,451	6,735	13,943	11,165	4,953	10,442
ENGLISH AND OTHER GROUP(S)	726	1,028	197	982	501	1,172	1,207	430	778
FRENCH AND OTHER GROUP(S)	341	720	120	706	315	701	621	132	547
GERMAN AND OTHER GROUP(S)	1,440	4,079	904	3,068	1,770	3,768	2,947	1,399	3,002
IRISH AND OTHER GROUP(S)	1,362	3,084	637	3,224	1,940	4,484	3,672	1,373	3,216
ITALIAN AND OTHER GROUP(S)	558	1,645	273	879	644	1,804	539	381	867
POLISH AND OTHER GROUP(S)	1,478	4,096	891	2,592	1,565	2,014	2,179	1,238	2,032
RESIDENCE IN 1975									
PERSONS 5 YEARS AND OVER	11,035	35,974	9,289	28,930	12,294	28,720	49,998	12,347	22,872
SAME HOUSE	8,457	27,882	6,790	18,150	8,064	18,144	25,408	8,590	15,173
DIFFERENT HOUSE IN UNITED STATES:									
SAME COUNTY	2,164	7,311	2,307	9,333	3,919	9,153	19,426	3,528	6,729
DIFFERENT COUNTY:									
SAME STATE	41	356	13	113	68	208	173	72	65
DIFFERENT STATE:									
NORTHEAST	15	0	0	29	31	5	139	0	107
NORTH CENTRAL	227	132	0	177	93	120	238	40	108
SOUTH	118	178	27	143	22	174	502	52	156
WEST	13	25	13	92	20	139	402	0	23
ABROAD	0	90	139	893	77	777	3,710	65	511
YEARS OF SCHOOL COMPLETED									
PERSONS 25 YEARS AND OVER	7,207	24,053	6,643	19,833	7,988	18,363	27,591	8,991	15,968
ELEMENTARY (0 TO 8 YEARS)	1,711	5,891	2,160	6,228	2,315	6,052	11,715	2,532	4,405
HIGH SCHOOL:									
1 TO 3 YEARS	1,596	5,115	1,387	4,127	1,967	4,704	6,593	1,798	3,613
4 YEARS	2,895	9,298	2,042	6,544	2,723	5,405	6,288	3,091	5,370
COLLEGE:									
1 TO 3 YEARS	812	2,457	657	1,803	613	1,305	2,014	936	1,535
4 OR MORE YEARS	193	1,292	397	1,131	370	897	981	634	1,045
SCHOOL ENROLLMENT									
PERSONS 3 YEARS AND OLDER									
ENROLLED IN SCHOOL	2,708	9,414	1,813	6,264	3,070	7,549	15,555	2,494	5,121
NURSERY SCHOOL	53	290	60	259	50	279	523	73	210
KINDERGARTEN AND ELEMENTARY (1 TO 8 YEARS)	1,422	4,492	886	3,423	1,762	4,093	9,940	1,063	2,659
HIGH SCHOOL (1 TO 4 YEARS)	817	2,865	481	1,610	809	2,059	3,705	735	1,353
COLLEGE	416	1,767	386	972	449	1,118	1,387	623	899
PRIVATE SCHOOL ENROLLMENT									
PERSONS 3 YEARS AND OLDER									
ENROLLED IN PRIVATE SCHOOL	947	3,338	823	2,463	1,292	3,438	3,590	1,241	1,856
NURSERY SCHOOL	28	144	16	158	27	160	172	31	120
KINDERGARTEN AND ELEMENTARY (1 TO 8 YEARS)	597	1,945	539	1,542	815	1,648	2,124	676	952
HIGH SCHOOL (1 TO 4 YEARS)	227	738	136	416	347	1,193	956	349	484
COLLEGE	95	511	132	347	103	437	338	185	300
VETERAN STATUS									
CIVILIAN MALES 16 AND OVER	4,521	14,117	3,815	11,695	4,741	11,217	18,571	4,992	9,115
VETERAN	1,727	5,467	1,357	3,932	1,700	3,333	4,224	1,943	3,133
NON-VETERAN	2,794	8,650	2,458	7,763	3,041	7,884	14,347	3,049	5,982
CIVILIAN FEMALES 16 AND OVER	4,601	16,040	4,343	12,987	5,420	12,395	19,391	5,826	10,520
VETERAN	89	92	7	135	44	116	232	58	58
NON-VETERAN	4,512	15,948	4,336	12,852	5,376	12,279	19,159	5,768	10,462

	64	65	66	67	68	69	70	71	72
NATIVITY AND PLACE OF BIRTH									
TOTAL PERSONS	22,584	24,748	46,568	62,069	59,075	45,218	40,477	65,132	23,360
NATIVE:									
BORN IN STATE OF RESIDENCE	18,092	20,013	31,834	39,655	34,774	23,909	33,870	39,137	19,161
BORN IN DIFFERENT STATE	2,376	1,928	5,471	21,560	23,811	20,736	3,368	25,158	3,405
BORN ABROAD, AT SEA, ETC.	44	72	485	148	102	49	161	147	42
FOREIGN BORN	2,072	2,735	8,778	706	388	524	3,078	690	752
ANCESTRY									
TOTAL PERSONS	22,584	24,748	46,568	62,069	59,075	45,218	40,477	65,132	23,360
SINGLE ANCESTRY GROUP:									
DUTCH	72	61	93	0	0	8	125	0	92
ENGLISH	334	241	727	853	649	283	567	774	507
FRENCH	72	70	106	18	51	143	80	13	70
GERMAN	1,258	1,304	2,343	70	41	33	2,728	165	1,519
GREEK	211	223	361	22	19	0	457	0	141
HUNGARIAN	74	74	136	6	5	0	116	9	27
IRISH	2,279	2,967	4,362	45	23	51	6,959	139	5,624
ITALIAN	2,059	1,459	1,549	18	0	19	2,228	14	500
NORWEGIAN	26	22	49	10	0	0	46	0	58
POLISH	4,339	5,468	3,578	63	10	0	4,326	52	523
PORTUGUESE	0	0	9	0	0	0	16	0	0
RUSSIAN	92	91	115	10	0	0	77	0	38
SCOTTISH	40	30	113	0	0	0	97	0	92
SWEDISH	147	116	161	12	7	8	352	15	316
UKRAINIAN	60	165	205	0	0	0	169	20	22
OTHER	2,413	3,285	17,307	52,497	50,262	39,015	4,829	55,816	4,011
MULTIPLE ANCESTRY GROUP	7,330	7,889	12,275	461	660	512	14,729	742	8,182
ANCESTRY NOT SPECIFIED:									
OTHER	502	409	869	1,211	1,161	897	1,091	1,891	586
NOT REPORTED	1,276	874	2,210	6,773	6,187	4,249	1,485	5,482	1,052
PERSONS IN SELECTED MULTIPLE									
ANCESTRY GROUPS	11,376	12,175	18,069	224	286	217	23,207	630	13,357
ENGLISH AND OTHER GROUP(S)	863	1,024	1,610	50	58	80	2,279	101	1,901
FRENCH AND OTHER GROUP(S)	546	633	1,162	65	41	14	1,010	88	674
GERMAN AND OTHER GROUP(S)	3,155	3,422	5,112	37	68	56	7,111	103	4,165
IRISH AND OTHER GROUP(S)	3,295	3,624	5,739	37	119	54	7,854	233	5,208
ITALIAN AND OTHER GROUP(S)	1,270	974	1,409	10	0	13	1,835	23	667
POLISH AND OTHER GROUP(S)	2,247	2,498	3,037	25	0	0	3,118	82	742
RESIDENCE IN 1975									
PERSONS 5 YEARS AND OVER	21,248	23,690	42,939	55,490	53,220	42,072	38,642	59,890	21,848
SAME HOUSE	13,907	17,462	24,419	39,668	33,636	28,865	29,534	43,611	14,278
DIFFERENT HOUSE IN UNITED STATES:									
SAME COUNTY	6,755	5,879	16,434	14,668	17,732	12,213	8,498	14,529	6,870
DIFFERENT COUNTY:									
SAME STATE	135	117	385	166	201	64	209	142	79
DIFFERENT STATE:									
NORTHEAST	0	0	66	43	44	111	24	149	101
NORTH CENTRAL	201	54	298	168	468	224	80	323	257
SOUTH	69	0	221	557	818	406	60	825	186
WEST	30	47	47	142	276	103	48	202	58
ABROAD	151	131	1,069	78	45	86	189	109	19
YEARS OF SCHOOL COMPLETED									
PERSONS 25 YEARS AND OVER	14,133	16,539	29,225	27,165	28,444	27,751	25,193	34,365	14,214
ELEMENTARY (0 TO 8 YEARS)	2,921	3,650	7,264	6,439	8,426	6,501	3,942	5,913	1,057
HIGH SCHOOL:									
1 TO 3 YEARS	3,159	3,181	5,608	7,776	8,051	6,202	3,937	7,422	1,253
4 YEARS	5,763	6,422	9,990	8,152	7,760	8,532	11,477	11,680	4,099
COLLEGE:									
1 TO 3 YEARS	1,558	2,120	3,591	3,838	3,280	4,634	3,659	6,748	3,097
4 OR MORE YEARS	732	1,166	2,772	960	927	1,882	2,178	2,602	4,708
SCHOOL ENROLLMENT									
PERSONS 3 YEARS AND OLDER									
ENROLLED IN SCHOOL	5,207	5,460	10,488	22,650	19,243	11,760	10,527	21,772	6,994
NURSERY SCHOOL	81	154	325	783	702	590	296	895	388
KINDERGARTEN AND ELEMENTARY (1 TO 8 YEARS)	2,672	2,422	5,687	12,816	10,902	6,143	4,569	11,169	3,371
HIGH SCHOOL (1 TO 4 YEARS)	1,481	1,696	2,694	6,402	5,531	2,753	3,375	5,875	1,776
COLLEGE	973	1,188	1,782	2,649	2,108	2,274	2,287	3,833	1,459
PRIVATE SCHOOL ENROLLMENT									
PERSONS 3 YEARS AND OLDER									
ENROLLED IN PRIVATE SCHOOL	1,920	2,785	4,026	2,439	1,565	1,797	4,591	4,373	3,936
NURSERY SCHOOL	57	118	215	356	248	266	149	556	338
KINDERGARTEN AND ELEMENTARY (1 TO 8 YEARS)	1,019	1,358	2,108	1,301	723	888	2,367	2,395	1,905
HIGH SCHOOL (1 TO 4 YEARS)	558	928	1,154	463	333	281	1,324	886	1,146
COLLEGE	286	381	549	319	261	362	751	536	547
VETERAN STATUS									
CIVILIAN MALES 16 AND OVER	8,793	9,525	16,822	17,825	17,113	14,983	15,538	21,013	8,155
VETERAN	3,464	3,761	5,376	4,077	3,701	4,855	6,506	6,073	2,902
NON-VETERAN	5,329	5,764	11,446	13,748	13,412	10,128	9,032	14,940	5,253
CIVILIAN FEMALES 16 AND OVER	9,296	10,974	19,369	22,288	22,614	19,469	16,951	25,370	9,436
VETERAN	80	74	217	247	241	288	194	279	88
NON-VETERAN	9,216	10,900	19,152	22,041	22,373	19,181	16,757	25,091	9,348

	73	74	75	76	77
NATIVITY AND PLACE OF BIRTH					
TOTAL PERSONS	36,453	20,084	29,315	11,056	58,561
NATIVE:					
BORN IN STATE OF RESIDENCE	21,931	17,106	20,983	7,650	26,995
BORN IN DIFFERENT STATE	14,269	1,722	7,507	1,584	13,629
BORN ABROAD, AT SEA, ETC.	34	51	52	48	935
FOREIGN BORN	219	1,205	773	1,774	17,002
ANCESTRY					
TOTAL PERSONS	36,453	20,084	29,315	11,056	58,561
SINGLE ANCESTRY GROUP:					
DUTCH	0	245	97	29	156
ENGLISH	214	301	499	151	1,841
FRENCH	0	133	49	5	423
GERMAN	144	1,218	659	817	3,950
GREEK	0	136	47	260	677
HUNGARIAN	8	86	39	19	495
IRISH	44	4,443	2,585	775	3,641
ITALIAN	5	821	301	2,148	1,029
NORWEGIAN	5	34	39	87	195
POLISH	12	1,278	431	1,491	1,788
PORTUGUESE	0	7	5	0	14
RUSSIAN	0	22	32	102	1,831
SCOTTISH	8	76	52	20	194
SWEDISH	28	312	305	89	932
UKRAINIAN	0	63	43	173	181
OTHER	31,134	1,308	16,743	1,016	21,617
MULTIPLE ANCESTRY GROUP	655	8,279	4,829	3,148	13,564
ANCESTRY NOT SPECIFIED:					
OTHER	1,270	540	831	134	2,975
NOT REPORTED	2,926	782	1,729	592	3,058
PERSONS IN SELECTED MULTIPLE					
ANCESTRY GROUPS	496	13,796	7,473	4,820	18,866
ENGLISH AND OTHER GROUP(S)	87	1,602	1,222	469	3,481
FRENCH AND OTHER GROUP(S)	75	751	588	265	1,383
GERMAN AND OTHER GROUP(S)	181	4,092	2,225	1,354	6,172
IRISH AND OTHER GROUP(S)	132	5,144	2,612	1,234	5,331
ITALIAN AND OTHER GROUP(S)	15	889	356	735	993
POLISH AND OTHER GROUP(S)	6	1,318	470	763	1,506
RESIDENCE IN 1975					
PERSONS 5 YEARS AND OVER	33,994	19,191	27,202	10,570	55,890
SAME HOUSE	26,910	14,358	20,195	4,127	22,318
DIFFERENT HOUSE IN UNITED STATES:					
SAME COUNTY	6,366	4,329	6,191	4,945	22,706
DIFFERENT COUNTY:					
SAME STATE	129	161	262	349	1,184
DIFFERENT STATE:					
NORTHEAST	17	0	29	181	754
NORTH CENTRAL	188	160	217	274	1,611
SOUTH	327	107	158	192	1,093
WEST	41	35	44	155	757
ABROAD	16	41	106	347	5,467
YEARS OF SCHOOL COMPLETED					
PERSONS 25 YEARS AND OVER	19,389	12,599	16,565	7,893	40,878
ELEMENTARY (0 TO 8 YEARS)	2,693	1,908	2,321	1,142	6,876
HIGH SCHOOL:					
1 TO 3 YEARS	3,978	2,133	2,750	1,025	4,832
4 YEARS	6,306	5,593	5,316	2,651	10,847
COLLEGE:					
1 TO 3 YEARS	4,320	1,635	3,456	1,625	7,719
4 OR MORE YEARS	2,092	1,330	2,722	1,450	10,604
SCHOOL ENROLLMENT					
PERSONS 3 YEARS AND OLDER					
ENROLLED IN SCHOOL	12,637	5,121	9,348	1,755	12,200
NURSERY SCHOOL	407	162	425	65	420
KINDERGARTEN AND ELEMENTARY (1 TO 8 YEARS)	5,835	2,334	4,426	718	4,010
HIGH SCHOOL (1 TO 4 YEARS)	3,793	1,632	2,737	359	2,207
COLLEGE	2,602	993	1,760	613	5,563
PRIVATE SCHOOL ENROLLMENT					
PERSONS 3 YEARS AND OLDER					
ENROLLED IN PRIVATE SCHOOL	2,390	3,381	3,001	696	5,072
NURSERY SCHOOL	298	110	276	65	271
KINDERGARTEN AND ELEMENTARY (1 TO 8 YEARS)	1,188	1,558	1,401	196	1,285
HIGH SCHOOL (1 TO 4 YEARS)	476	1,240	768	191	869
COLLEGE	428	473	556	244	2,647
VETERAN STATUS					
CIVILIAN MALES 16 AND OVER	12,190	7,466	9,789	4,655	23,428
VETERAN	3,994	2,919	3,304	1,567	5,842
NON-VETERAN	8,196	4,547	6,485	3,088	17,586
CIVILIAN FEMALES 16 AND OVER	14,415	8,428	11,871	5,033	26,954
VETERAN	134	67	113	62	383
NON-VETERAN	14,281	8,361	11,758	4,971	26,571

	01	02	03	04	05	06	07	08	09
LABOR FORCE STATUS									
MALES 16 AND OVER	22,366	22,928	25,734	16,589	12,723	40,017	24,297	25,828	4,629
LABOR FORCE:									
ARMED FORCES	15	12	31	22	5	45	36	0	0
CIVILIAN LABOR FORCE:									
EMPLOYED	16,091	16,555	15,852	11,722	8,851	30,947	19,278	18,533	3,457
UNEMPLOYED	1,204	787	1,985	845	812	1,953	983	1,103	175
NOT IN LABOR FORCE	5,056	5,574	7,866	4,000	3,055	7,072	4,000	6,192	997
FEMALES 16 AND OVER	24,898	28,502	25,017	19,548	14,842	43,915	25,659	30,060	5,712
LABOR FORCE:									
ARMED FORCES	11	0	0	0	0	0	0	0	0
CIVILIAN LABOR FORCE:									
EMPLOYED	14,006	14,728	11,051	10,022	7,237	25,884	17,204	16,950	2,924
UNEMPLOYED	834	532	1,102	637	449	1,325	574	964	66
NOT IN LABOR FORCE	10,047	13,242	12,864	8,889	7,156	16,706	7,881	12,146	2,722
PLACE OF WORK									
WORKERS 16 YEARS AND OVER	29,393	30,526	24,848	21,331	15,325	55,794	35,907	34,996	6,325
WORKED IN CHICAGO SMSA:									
IN CHICAGO	19,343	21,457	17,675	15,867	11,847	44,152	25,594	25,458	3,449
OUTSIDE CHICAGO	7,230	6,598	3,572	3,813	2,245	5,425	3,438	2,223	2,582
WORKED OUTSIDE CHICAGO SMSA	143	111	153	51	30	257	182	274	43
NOT REPORTED	2,677	2,360	3,448	1,600	1,203	5,960	6,693	7,041	251
CLASS OF WORKER									
EMPLOYED PERSONS 16 YEARS AND OVER	30,097	31,283	26,903	21,744	16,088	56,831	36,482	35,483	6,381
PRIVATE WAGE AND SALARY WORKER	25,719	24,934	22,855	18,569	13,855	47,086	30,016	28,738	5,014
FEDERAL GOVERNMENT WORKER	726	482	681	370	335	1,435	812	993	40
STATE GOVERNMENT WORKER	750	713	682	322	256	1,457	1,195	904	92
LOCAL GOVERNMENT WORKER	1,621	2,731	1,568	1,392	1,094	3,674	2,157	1,776	980
SELF-EMPLOYED WORKER	1,252	2,250	948	1,045	536	3,086	2,240	2,978	241
UNPAID FAMILY WORKER	29	173	169	46	12	93	62	94	14
OCCUPATION									
EMPLOYED PERSONS 16 YEARS AND OVER	30,097	31,283	26,903	21,744	16,088	56,831	36,482	35,483	6,381
EXECUTIVE, ADMINISTRATIVE, AND MANAGERIAL	3,242	4,170	2,342	1,788	1,254	8,599	7,241	8,734	618
PROFESSIONAL SPECIALTY	5,559	5,573	3,800	2,419	1,343	11,810	10,200	8,653	771
TECHNICIANS AND RELATED SUPPORT	1,268	1,106	865	497	473	1,801	1,305	834	192
SALES	2,922	4,273	2,029	2,142	1,024	5,990	4,213	4,993	631
ADMINISTRATIVE SUPPORT (INCL. CLERICAL)	7,058	7,271	4,943	5,221	3,759	11,444	5,664	5,323	1,732
PRIVATE HOUSEHOLD	125	50	157	46	74	149	33	256	11
PROTECTIVE SERVICE	424	539	406	282	469	472	328	315	490
OTHER SERVICE	3,629	2,509	3,908	2,697	1,769	6,166	2,823	3,841	373
FARMING, FORESTRY, AND FISHING	137	22	74	69	65	186	60	85	10
PRECISION PRODUCTION, CRAFT, AND REPAIR	2,118	2,635	2,309	2,414	2,131	3,681	1,710	852	677
MACHINE OPERATORS, ASSEMBLERS, AND INSPECTORS	2,307	1,779	3,991	2,684	2,172	3,918	1,520	859	481
TRANSPORTATION AND MATERIAL MOVING	631	550	821	706	563	1,188	659	337	180
HANDLERS, EQUIPMENT CLEANERS, HELPERS, AND LABORERS	677	806	1,258	779	992	1,427	726	401	215
INDUSTRY									
EMPLOYED PERSONS 16 YEARS AND OVER	30,097	31,283	26,903	21,744	16,088	56,831	36,482	35,483	6,381
AGRICULTURAL, FORESTRY, FISHERIES, AND MINING	155	83	99	95	42	205	74	140	10
CONSTRUCTION	851	924	877	808	735	1,252	630	422	253
MANUFACTURING:									
NONDURABLE GOODS	2,338	2,050	2,327	1,886	1,525	4,772	2,756	2,524	609
DURABLE GOODS	3,316	3,877	4,483	3,833	3,424	5,780	2,861	1,558	923
TRANSPORTATION	1,042	896	1,075	827	683	2,367	1,323	1,759	268
COMMUNICATIONS AND OTHER PUBLIC UTILITIES	502	489	427	447	432	1,319	817	706	283
WHOLESALE TRADE	1,304	1,890	969	984	801	2,486	1,363	1,669	305
RETAIL TRADE	5,038	5,521	3,792	3,902	2,472	8,223	4,333	4,745	905
FINANCE, INSURANCE, AND REAL ESTATE	3,447	3,256	2,526	2,006	1,237	6,135	4,650	5,286	554
BUSINESS AND REPAIR SERVICES	1,735	1,793	1,749	1,089	740	4,242	3,608	3,258	291
PERSONAL, ENTERTAINMENT, AND RECREATION SERVICES	1,369	1,166	1,392	851	654	2,531	1,301	1,759	193
PROFESSIONAL AND RELATED SERVICES:									
HEALTH SERVICES	2,886	3,130	3,007	2,259	1,251	5,876	3,907	3,794	451
EDUCATIONAL SERVICES	2,575	2,518	1,457	977	680	3,909	2,874	2,193	308
OTHER PROFESSIONAL AND RELATED SERVICES	2,344	2,235	1,819	957	627	5,172	4,269	4,245	308
PUBLIC ADMINISTRATION	1,195	1,455	904	823	785	2,562	1,716	1,425	720
MEANS OF TRANSPORTATION TO WORK									
WORKERS 16 YEARS AND OVER	29,350	30,389	25,961	21,091	15,609	55,360	35,763	34,330	6,213
CAR, TRUCK, OR VAN:									
DRIVE ALONE	8,964	14,548	7,594	8,566	6,169	15,521	10,566	6,501	3,642
CARPOOL	3,579	5,922	4,284	3,368	2,683	6,453	4,197	2,047	900
PUBLIC TRANSPORTATION	13,299	7,647	10,767	6,712	4,692	27,324	15,876	13,863	1,226
WALKED ONLY	2,809	1,610	2,450	2,079	1,814	4,505	3,733	10,577	388
OTHER MEANS	227	277	331	204	175	589	608	456	10
WORKED AT HOME	472	385	535	162	76	968	783	886	47
TRAVEL TIME TO WORK									
WORKERS 16 YEARS AND OVER WHO DID NOT WORK AT HOME	28,925	30,186	24,244	21,070	15,293	54,941	35,102	34,028	6,270
LESS THAN 5 MINUTES	528	393	457	405	306	977	1,018	1,160	76
5 TO 9 MINUTES	1,590	1,805	1,186	1,383	1,157	2,506	2,245	3,711	376
10 TO 14 MINUTES	2,397	3,163	1,576	2,493	1,531	3,800	3,218	5,363	698
15 TO 19 MINUTES	2,480	3,552	2,411	2,567	2,107	5,962	4,663	6,431	957
20 TO 29 MINUTES	4,209	5,274	4,534	4,032	3,056	11,845	9,626	8,412	1,166
30 TO 44 MINUTES	9,000	7,230	7,974	5,732	4,299	20,075	10,349	10,349	1,553
45 TO 59 MINUTES	5,392	4,664	3,537	2,716	1,790	6,195	2,732	1,595	646
60 OR MORE MINUTES	3,329	4,105	2,569	1,742	1,047	3,581	1,251	873	798

	10	11	12	13	14	15	16	17	18
LABOR FORCE STATUS									
MALES 16 AND OVER	15,732	9,375	7,171	5,743	16,637	21,549	18,499	14,811	4,104
LABOR FORCE:									
ARMED FORCES	6	13	0	0	35	17	6	0	0
CIVILIAN LABOR FORCE:									
EMPLOYED	11,474	6,504	5,271	4,272	12,148	15,440	13,288	10,300	2,936
UNEMPLOYED	498	289	241	204	912	808	897	490	108
NOT IN LABOR FORCE	3,754	2,569	1,659	1,267	3,542	5,284	4,308	4,021	1,060
FEMALES 16 AND OVER	18,417	11,472	8,330	6,954	18,155	26,091	21,596	16,719	5,003
LABOR FORCE:									
ARMED FORCES	7	0	0	0	0	0	0	0	0
CIVILIAN LABOR FORCE:									
EMPLOYED	9,031	5,684	3,918	3,645	9,191	12,729	10,743	7,590	2,188
UNEMPLOYED	349	219	104	169	681	619	685	350	104
NOT IN LABOR FORCE	9,030	5,569	4,308	3,140	8,283	12,743	10,168	8,779	2,711
PLACE OF WORK									
WORKERS 16 YEARS AND OVER	19,936	11,875	8,942	7,780	20,489	27,467	23,324	16,921	4,977
WORKED IN CHICAGO SMSA:									
IN CHICAGO	12,585	7,974	6,187	5,751	14,846	19,520	17,892	10,453	2,778
OUTSIDE CHICAGO	6,159	3,092	2,368	1,272	4,383	6,459	4,287	5,645	1,347
WORKED OUTSIDE CHICAGO SMSA	65	49	40	81	38	53	66	113	0
NOT REPORTED	1,127	760	347	676	1,222	1,435	1,079	710	852
CLASS OF WORKER									
EMPLOYED PERSONS 16 YEARS AND OVER	20,505	12,188	9,189	7,917	21,339	28,169	24,031	17,890	5,124
PRIVATE WAGE AND SALARY WORKER	16,249	10,274	6,868	6,163	18,617	24,154	20,666	15,104	4,248
FEDERAL GOVERNMENT WORKER	425	229	175	93	356	554	443	338	102
STATE GOVERNMENT WORKER	323	133	185	341	380	450	322	208	41
LOCAL GOVERNMENT WORKER	2,778	1,135	1,291	708	1,128	2,057	1,679	1,678	588
SELF-EMPLOYED WORKER	686	370	639	543	784	900	865	537	145
UNPAID FAMILY WORKER	44	47	31	69	74	54	56	25	0
OCCUPATION									
EMPLOYED PERSONS 16 YEARS AND OVER	20,505	12,188	9,189	7,917	21,339	28,169	24,031	17,890	5,124
EXECUTIVE, ADMINISTRATIVE, AND MANAGERIAL	2,207	1,182	1,304	1,051	1,727	2,594	2,006	1,611	346
PROFESSIONAL SPECIALTY	2,062	1,108	1,593	1,564	1,697	2,143	2,409	1,249	356
TECHNICIANS AND RELATED SUPPORT	559	278	228	244	823	769	620	395	42
SALES	1,865	1,173	1,207	875	1,722	2,392	1,920	1,667	540
ADMINISTRATIVE SUPPORT (INCL. CLERICAL)	4,968	3,366	1,996	1,660	4,672	7,517	6,100	4,183	1,274
PRIVATE HOUSEHOLD	26	5	4	32	53	65	60	10	33
PROTECTIVE SERVICE	1,229	402	369	154	313	808	666	769	135
OTHER SERVICE	1,691	888	676	668	2,175	2,756	2,153	1,659	440
FARMING, FORESTRY, AND FISHING	86	72	9	18	37	74	82	60	14
PRECISION PRODUCTION, CRAFT, AND REPAIR	2,786	1,751	963	717	2,967	4,010	3,177	2,521	773
MACHINE OPERATORS, ASSEMBLERS, AND INSPECTORS	1,585	1,049	339	550	3,370	2,949	2,859	2,063	691
TRANSPORTATION AND MATERIAL MOVING	662	466	187	173	625	958	947	688	222
HANDLERS, EQUIPMENT CLEANERS, HELPERS, AND LABORERS	779	448	314	211	1,158	1,134	1,032	1,015	258
INDUSTRY									
EMPLOYED PERSONS 16 YEARS AND OVER	20,505	12,188	9,189	7,917	21,339	28,169	24,031	17,890	5,124
AGRICULTURAL, FORESTRY, FISHERIES, AND MINING	138	72	35	15	30	86	68	76	6
CONSTRUCTION	1,057	597	385	292	978	1,454	1,151	980	361
MANUFACTURING:									
NONDURABLE GOODS	1,449	1,064	766	575	2,135	2,600	2,418	1,571	577
DURABLE GOODS	3,597	2,431	1,095	941	4,840	5,706	4,836	3,853	958
TRANSPORTATION	1,147	751	361	258	1,012	1,457	1,016	972	329
COMMUNICATIONS AND OTHER PUBLIC UTILITIES	715	408	242	96	449	854	572	536	116
WHOLESALE TRADE	868	530	452	347	985	1,295	1,286	840	173
RETAIL TRADE	3,147	1,796	1,471	1,252	3,227	4,487	3,682	3,053	924
FINANCE, INSURANCE, AND REAL ESTATE	1,790	1,280	863	611	1,976	2,855	2,156	1,514	397
BUSINESS AND REPAIR SERVICES	749	498	515	407	1,027	1,332	1,349	880	187
PERSONAL, ENTERTAINMENT, AND RECREATION SERVICES	478	324	225	290	773	795	741	439	210
PROFESSIONAL AND RELATED SERVICES:									
HEALTH SERVICES	1,451	745	556	724	1,643	1,591	1,602	865	204
EDUCATIONAL SERVICES	1,271	542	708	1,213	747	1,213	1,122	773	202
OTHER PROFESSIONAL AND RELATED SERVICES	782	497	780	610	811	1,101	995	471	123
PUBLIC ADMINISTRATION	1,866	653	735	286	706	1,343	1,037	1,067	357
MEANS OF TRANSPORTATION TO WORK									
WORKERS 16 YEARS AND OVER	20,038	11,843	8,921	7,709	20,754	27,434	23,196	17,526	5,003
CAR, TRUCK, OR VAN:									
DRIVE ALONE	11,552	6,107	5,137	3,565	8,712	13,737	10,530	10,136	2,797
CARPOOL	3,074	1,900	1,418	1,223	3,968	4,486	3,929	2,967	747
PUBLIC TRANSPORTATION	3,975	3,107	1,743	1,706	6,177	7,008	6,509	3,546	1,034
WALKED ONLY	1,125	658	476	1,032	1,541	1,877	1,811	658	368
OTHER MEANS	115	12	43	37	138	133	156	72	24
WORKED AT HOME	197	59	104	146	218	193	261	147	33
TRAVEL TIME TO WORK									
WORKERS 16 YEARS AND OVER WHO DID NOT WORK AT HOME	19,736	11,813	8,828	7,581	20,274	27,247	23,053	16,735	4,962
LESS THAN 5 MINUTES	267	105	83	353	158	385	357	160	96
5 TO 9 MINUTES	1,335	525	780	773	1,118	1,479	1,458	823	430
10 TO 14 MINUTES	1,853	1,084	903	742	1,364	2,232	2,065	1,347	423
15 TO 19 MINUTES	2,555	1,569	1,228	882	2,459	3,116	3,335	1,897	447
20 TO 29 MINUTES	3,905	2,851	1,576	1,280	4,000	5,992	4,686	3,556	929
30 TO 44 MINUTES	5,388	3,302	2,496	1,861	6,341	7,878	6,510	4,923	1,616
45 TO 59 MINUTES	2,489	1,539	1,083	827	2,861	3,644	2,771	1,784	415
60 OR MORE MINUTES	1,944	838	679	863	1,973	2,521	1,871	2,245	606

TABLE III-4 LABOR FORCE CHARACTERISTICS OF THE POPULATION, BY COMMUNITY AREA: CITY OF CHICAGO, 1980

	19	20	21	22	23	24	25	26	27
LABOR FORCE STATUS									
MALES 16 AND OVER	20,313	7,093	12,640	30,023	22,089	33,236	42,122	9,409	9,580
LABOR FORCE:									
ARMED FORCES	0	0	0	21	5	17	45	0	0
CIVILIAN LABOR FORCE:									
EMPLOYED	14,144	5,131	8,949	20,533	13,719	20,824	26,268	4,527	3,787
UNEMPLOYED	902	471	820	2,129	1,951	2,443	4,364	1,342	1,202
NOT IN LABOR FORCE	5,267	1,491	2,871	7,340	6,414	9,952	11,445	3,540	4,591
FEMALES 16 AND OVER	23,886	7,829	14,015	30,961	24,596	33,437	51,355	12,343	11,731
LABOR FORCE:									
ARMED FORCES	0	0	6	0	9	0	32	5	15
CIVILIAN LABOR FORCE:									
EMPLOYED	11,506	3,649	6,747	13,850	9,893	12,416	23,647	4,518	3,714
UNEMPLOYED	723	270	598	1,452	1,535	1,632	3,718	1,026	744
NOT IN LABOR FORCE	11,657	3,910	6,664	15,659	13,159	19,389	23,958	6,794	7,258
PLACE OF WORK									
WORKERS 16 YEARS AND OVER	24,586	8,594	14,703	33,378	22,049	31,731	47,479	8,681	6,986
WORKED IN CHICAGO SMSA:									
IN CHICAGO	18,083	6,125	10,660	22,710	15,335	21,925	29,491	5,474	4,670
OUTSIDE CHICAGO	4,756	1,540	2,523	5,500	3,774	4,724	10,906	1,716	1,071
WORKED OUTSIDE CHICAGO SMSA	33	25	61	123	18	23	144	28	72
NOT REPORTED	1,714	904	1,459	5,045	2,922	5,059	6,938	1,463	1,173
CLASS OF WORKER									
EMPLOYED PERSONS 16 YEARS AND OVER	25,650	8,780	15,696	34,383	23,612	33,240	49,915	9,045	7,501
PRIVATE WAGE AND SALARY WORKER	22,356	7,706	14,038	30,081	20,110	28,894	39,907	7,096	5,444
FEDERAL GOVERNMENT WORKER	476	225	260	819	729	730	2,676	540	585
STATE GOVERNMENT WORKER	262	118	185	601	572	589	1,651	338	416
LOCAL GOVERNMENT WORKER	1,661	493	812	1,965	1,739	2,075	4,569	904	895
SELF-EMPLOYED WORKER	789	225	360	838	449	948	1,029	149	129
UNPAID FAMILY WORKER	106	13	41	79	13	4	83	18	32
OCCUPATION									
EMPLOYED PERSONS 16 YEARS AND OVER	25,650	8,780	15,696	34,383	23,612	33,240	49,915	9,045	7,501
EXECUTIVE, ADMINISTRATIVE, AND MANAGERIAL	2,177	449	864	1,846	849	1,520	2,321	286	296
PROFESSIONAL SPECIALTY	1,639	476	784	2,353	1,178	2,106	3,096	359	342
TECHNICIANS AND RELATED SUPPORT	626	185	357	477	396	513	1,103	187	242
SALES	2,296	729	1,014	2,149	1,420	1,997	3,402	482	383
ADMINISTRATIVE SUPPORT (INCL. CLERICAL)	5,667	1,927	3,330	6,355	3,952	5,412	11,583	1,842	1,549
PRIVATE HOUSEHOLD	16	0	54	46	58	62	207	69	54
PROTECTIVE SERVICE	586	198	341	568	354	518	1,232	181	168
OTHER SERVICE	2,402	705	1,752	3,797	3,075	4,724	6,033	1,648	1,311
FARMING, FORESTRY, AND FISHING	42	6	15	120	52	208	79	0	31
PRECISION PRODUCTION, CRAFT, AND REPAIR	3,767	1,330	2,320	3,996	2,801	3,481	4,980	698	661
MACHINE OPERATORS, ASSEMBLERS, AND INSPECTORS	4,068	1,833	3,121	8,868	6,032	8,321	8,949	1,849	1,343
TRANSPORTATION AND MATERIAL MOVING	955	288	748	1,379	1,341	1,630	3,182	539	365
HANDLERS, EQUIPMENT CLEANERS, HELPERS, AND LABORERS	1,409	654	996	2,429	2,104	2,748	3,748	905	756
INDUSTRY									
EMPLOYED PERSONS 16 YEARS AND OVER	25,650	8,780	15,696	34,383	23,612	33,240	49,915	9,045	7,501
AGRICULTURAL, FORESTRY, FISHERIES, AND MINING	36	14	36	77	44	191	83	18	26
CONSTRUCTION	1,073	436	577	1,011	673	797	1,313	223	203
MANUFACTURING:									
NONDURABLE GOODS	2,846	1,112	1,784	4,615	3,119	4,485	5,761	899	574
DURABLE GOODS	6,677	2,451	4,555	10,051	7,267	9,576	10,786	2,200	1,382
TRANSPORTATION	1,164	372	790	1,735	1,075	1,475	3,847	663	565
COMMUNICATIONS AND OTHER PUBLIC UTILITIES	607	211	235	647	346	515	1,543	179	204
WHOLESALE TRADE	1,150	436	861	1,652	907	1,249	1,960	317	196
RETAIL TRADE	4,272	1,387	2,300	4,863	3,323	4,684	6,966	1,364	970
FINANCE, INSURANCE, AND REAL ESTATE	1,943	510	1,094	1,597	1,079	1,927	2,925	376	392
BUSINESS AND REPAIR SERVICES	1,248	313	776	1,561	849	1,560	1,715	281	290
PERSONAL, ENTERTAINMENT, AND RECREATION SERVICES	651	203	452	1,068	796	1,369	1,763	406	423
PROFESSIONAL AND RELATED SERVICES:									
HEALTH SERVICES	1,284	426	782	1,621	1,710	2,072	4,623	974	903
EDUCATIONAL SERVICES	767	316	444	1,499	959	1,316	2,551	466	524
OTHER PROFESSIONAL AND RELATED SERVICES	825	252	488	1,381	634	934	1,354	255	326
PUBLIC ADMINISTRATION	1,107	341	522	1,005	831	1,090	2,725	424	523
MEANS OF TRANSPORTATION TO WORK									
WORKERS 16 YEARS AND OVER	24,739	8,367	15,138	32,976	22,628	31,560	47,720	8,487	7,206
CAR, TRUCK, OR VAN:									
DRIVE ALONE	11,967	3,831	5,747	12,503	9,954	10,966	22,128	3,462	2,512
CARPOOL	4,224	1,711	2,556	6,694	4,172	6,051	8,523	1,644	1,209
PUBLIC TRANSPORTATION	6,131	1,953	5,035	11,001	6,672	10,829	14,841	2,924	2,992
WALKED ONLY	2,053	744	1,550	2,348	1,593	3,135	1,872	396	374
OTHER MEANS	117	60	99	155	109	332	246	39	29
WORKED AT HOME	247	68	151	275	128	247	110	22	90
TRAVEL TIME TO WORK									
WORKERS 16 YEARS AND OVER WHO DID NOT WORK AT HOME	24,248	8,504	14,588	33,117	22,004	31,392	47,390	8,656	6,892
LESS THAN 5 MINUTES	349	146	157	499	398	677	458	145	58
5 TO 9 MINUTES	1,375	316	750	1,659	1,034	1,987	1,254	356	275
10 TO 14 MINUTES	2,409	818	1,228	2,800	1,666	2,969	2,971	481	518
15 TO 19 MINUTES	2,439	873	1,744	4,192	2,662	3,826	4,778	1,015	979
20 TO 29 MINUTES	4,503	2,099	2,928	6,684	4,017	6,128	9,040	1,488	1,292
30 TO 44 MINUTES	7,056	2,684	4,702	10,415	6,717	9,391	15,311	2,695	1,858
45 TO 59 MINUTES	3,340	834	1,852	3,983	3,297	3,638	7,132	991	1,076
60 OR MORE MINUTES	2,777	734	1,227	2,885	2,213	2,776	6,446	1,485	836

390

TABLE III-4 LABOR FORCE CHARACTERISTICS OF THE POPULATION,
BY COMMUNITY AREA: CITY OF CHICAGO, 1980

	28	29	30	31	32	33	34	35	36
LABOR FORCE STATUS									
MALES 16 AND OVER	16,996	17,208	27,774	15,957	3,577	1,602	4,525	10,105	3,619
LABOR FORCE:									
ARMED FORCES	31	18	36	0	0	6	0	9	0
CIVILIAN LABOR FORCE:									
EMPLOYED	7,349	7,915	16,531	10,664	2,022	757	2,841	4,823	1,159
UNEMPLOYED	1,443	2,290	2,332	1,574	182	178	266	754	444
NOT IN LABOR FORCE	8,173	6,985	8,875	3,719	1,373	661	1,418	4,519	2,016
FEMALES 16 AND OVER	20,537	22,526	23,217	14,477	2,690	2,888	5,156	15,749	6,143
LABOR FORCE:									
ARMED FORCES	0	0	0	0	0	0	0	0	0
CIVILIAN LABOR FORCE:									
EMPLOYED	5,867	7,735	8,796	5,370	1,190	931	2,093	6,311	1,185
UNEMPLOYED	1,038	1,728	1,686	1,537	60	252	145	665	538
NOT IN LABOR FORCE	13,632	13,063	12,735	7,570	1,440	1,705	2,918	8,773	4,420
PLACE OF WORK									
WORKERS 16 YEARS AND OVER	12,676	15,000	23,892	15,429	3,104	1,633	4,756	10,839	2,065
WORKED IN CHICAGO SMSA:									
IN CHICAGO	8,480	9,590	14,628	9,976	1,495	1,263	3,351	8,386	1,588
OUTSIDE CHICAGO	1,197	2,461	5,622	2,800	133	189	554	696	219
WORKED OUTSIDE CHICAGO SMSA	69	32	71	101	29	17	67	95	0
NOT REPORTED	2,930	2,917	3,571	2,552	1,447	164	784	1,662	258
CLASS OF WORKER									
EMPLOYED PERSONS 16 YEARS AND OVER	13,216	15,650	25,327	16,034	3,212	1,688	4,934	11,134	2,344
PRIVATE WAGE AND SALARY WORKER	9,271	11,966	23,008	14,211	2,326	1,242	3,894	7,166	1,525
FEDERAL GOVERNMENT WORKER	474	882	358	271	64	108	133	940	208
STATE GOVERNMENT WORKER	1,234	732	371	315	268	95	116	898	167
LOCAL GOVERNMENT WORKER	1,874	1,804	1,018	842	251	222	476	1,965	431
SELF-EMPLOYED WORKER	337	232	471	342	285	0	297	161	13
UNPAID FAMILY WORKER	26	34	101	53	18	21	18	4	0
OCCUPATION									
EMPLOYED PERSONS 16 YEARS AND OVER	13,216	15,650	25,327	16,034	3,212	1,688	4,934	11,134	2,344
EXECUTIVE, ADMINISTRATIVE, AND MANAGERIAL	410	485	934	464	641	65	337	935	98
PROFESSIONAL SPECIALTY	2,372	924	617	828	720	210	357	2,561	149
TECHNICIANS AND RELATED SUPPORT	542	313	224	216	63	48	116	705	66
SALES	443	987	1,244	754	331	80	268	691	93
ADMINISTRATIVE SUPPORT (INCL. CLERICAL)	2,431	3,204	3,482	2,116	505	497	961	2,936	568
PRIVATE HOUSEHOLD	73	85	57	38	11	11	6	62	4
PROTECTIVE SERVICE	296	347	209	103	73	52	76	400	50
OTHER SERVICE	2,290	2,506	2,613	1,741	288	296	1,396	1,398	584
FARMING, FORESTRY, AND FISHING	60	28	233	233	26	0	0	24	39
PRECISION PRODUCTION, CRAFT, AND REPAIR	760	1,253	2,747	1,861	124	97	357	328	141
MACHINE OPERATORS, ASSEMBLERS, AND INSPECTORS	1,960	3,039	7,888	4,221	253	122	555	530	229
TRANSPORTATION AND MATERIAL MOVING	561	1,044	1,170	693	87	102	179	307	94
HANDLERS, EQUIPMENT CLEANERS, HELPERS, AND LABORERS	1,018	1,435	3,909	2,766	90	108	326	257	229
INDUSTRY									
EMPLOYED PERSONS 16 YEARS AND OVER	13,216	15,650	25,327	16,034	3,212	1,688	4,934	11,134	2,344
AGRICULTURAL, FORESTRY, FISHERIES, AND MINING	58	41	199	278	16	0	0	34	21
CONSTRUCTION	182	399	808	582	113	18	140	120	19
MANUFACTURING:									
NONDURABLE GOODS	1,192	1,648	4,197	2,622	240	114	655	559	126
DURABLE GOODS	1,945	3,346	9,157	4,867	302	222	434	644	286
TRANSPORTATION	733	1,192	1,222	954	110	88	162	718	131
COMMUNICATIONS AND OTHER PUBLIC UTILITIES	262	224	345	257	76	47	139	293	44
WHOLESALE TRADE	378	586	1,163	974	118	52	200	309	38
RETAIL TRADE	1,170	2,182	3,363	1,716	428	222	1,469	919	341
FINANCE, INSURANCE, AND REAL ESTATE	791	703	1,200	650	315	169	458	851	169
BUSINESS AND REPAIR SERVICES	521	567	1,062	682	133	120	109	452	120
PERSONAL, ENTERTAINMENT, AND RECREATION SERVICES	555	735	451	573	212	56	173	388	116
PROFESSIONAL AND RELATED SERVICES:									
HEALTH SERVICES	2,741	1,756	748	478	248	322	301	1,966	318
EDUCATIONAL SERVICES	1,125	1,003	491	495	343	64	230	2,030	268
OTHER PROFESSIONAL AND RELATED SERVICES	781	478	450	445	338	47	210	551	109
PUBLIC ADMINISTRATION	782	790	471	461	220	147	254	1,300	238
MEANS OF TRANSPORTATION TO WORK									
WORKERS 16 YEARS AND OVER	12,576	14,882	24,157	15,511	3,091	1,648	4,799	10,776	2,175
CAR, TRUCK, OR VAN:									
DRIVE ALONE	3,771	6,224	8,726	5,304	525	486	1,357	3,362	563
CARPOOL	1,414	2,407	6,827	3,545	380	57	1,424	1,137	328
PUBLIC TRANSPORTATION	4,265	5,206	6,389	4,813	1,018	867	1,221	4,371	1,066
WALKED ONLY	2,738	848	1,706	1,586	1,121	200	766	1,734	177
OTHER MEANS	215	97	382	187	30	38	28	101	0
WORKED AT HOME	173	100	127	76	17	0	3	71	41
TRAVEL TIME TO WORK									
WORKERS 16 YEARS AND OVER WHO DID NOT WORK AT HOME	12,483	14,890	23,727	15,350	3,085	1,633	4,753	10,795	2,024
LESS THAN 5 MINUTES	346	218	263	225	29	83	225	475	29
5 TO 9 MINUTES	1,488	688	711	1,075	367	70	622	959	47
10 TO 14 MINUTES	1,447	963	1,812	1,253	487	119	612	1,001	183
15 TO 19 MINUTES	2,067	1,595	3,236	1,710	617	133	521	1,355	192
20 TO 29 MINUTES	1,830	2,638	4,595	3,102	707	349	931	2,061	354
30 TO 44 MINUTES	2,710	4,553	6,877	4,845	566	382	988	3,052	590
45 TO 59 MINUTES	983	1,851	3,320	1,552	138	324	500	1,084	328
60 OR MORE MINUTES	1,612	2,384	2,913	1,588	174	173	354	808	301

TABLE III-4 LABOR FORCE CHARACTERISTICS OF THE POPULATION, BY COMMUNITY AREA: CITY OF CHICAGO, 1980

	37	38	39	40	41	42	43	44	45
LABOR FORCE STATUS									
MALES 16 AND OVER	1,797	15,745	7,894	9,223	13,547	11,729	25,210	14,330	4,775
LABOR FORCE:									
ARMED FORCES	5	27	0	5	26	0	51	0	7
CIVILIAN LABOR FORCE:									
EMPLOYED	673	4,912	4,559	3,567	8,754	5,193	16,295	9,084	3,181
UNEMPLOYED	240	1,757	588	1,040	651	1,388	2,842	1,450	360
NOT IN LABOR FORCE	879	9,049	2,747	4,611	4,116	5,148	6,022	3,796	1,227
FEMALES 16 AND OVER	2,321	20,606	9,451	12,392	13,225	15,051	31,876	18,364	5,676
LABOR FORCE:									
ARMED FORCES	0	0	0	6	0	7	13	0	0
CIVILIAN LABOR FORCE:									
EMPLOYED	693	4,693	4,663	3,377	8,005	5,072	16,812	10,244	3,335
UNEMPLOYED	150	1,303	435	804	319	1,064	2,162	980	308
NOT IN LABOR FORCE	1,478	14,610	4,353	8,205	4,901	8,908	12,889	7,140	2,033
PLACE OF WORK									
WORKERS 16 YEARS AND OVER	1,194	8,483	8,520	6,415	16,374	9,727	31,724	18,394	6,264
WORKED IN CHICAGO SMSA:									
IN CHICAGO	858	6,106	6,903	4,674	13,607	7,166	24,722	13,938	4,679
OUTSIDE CHICAGO	161	742	774	549	1,135	1,298	2,513	1,831	582
WORKED OUTSIDE CHICAGO SMSA	22	34	22	88	138	42	311	131	68
NOT REPORTED	153	1,601	821	1,104	1,494	1,221	4,178	2,494	935
CLASS OF WORKER									
EMPLOYED PERSONS 16 YEARS AND OVER	1,366	9,605	9,222	6,944	16,759	10,265	33,107	19,328	6,516
PRIVATE WAGE AND SALARY WORKER	1,002	6,829	6,468	5,144	12,766	7,356	22,662	12,443	4,367
FEDERAL GOVERNMENT WORKER	90	829	572	572	747	823	2,809	1,881	562
STATE GOVERNMENT WORKER	52	530	523	303	825	489	1,642	952	336
LOCAL GOVERNMENT WORKER	179	1,179	1,254	683	1,574	1,388	5,170	3,429	1,133
SELF-EMPLOYED WORKER	43	223	384	236	819	201	782	608	118
UNPAID FAMILY WORKER	0	15	21	6	28	8	42	15	0
OCCUPATION									
EMPLOYED PERSONS 16 YEARS AND OVER	1,366	9,605	9,222	6,944	16,759	10,265	33,107	19,328	6,516
EXECUTIVE, ADMINISTRATIVE, AND MANAGERIAL	41	304	1,132	283	1,930	560	2,871	1,404	534
PROFESSIONAL SPECIALTY	46	597	2,568	362	5,951	1,163	4,543	2,337	987
TECHNICIANS AND RELATED SUPPORT	44	193	425	173	1,426	429	1,085	627	200
SALES	43	378	604	345	1,018	568	2,234	1,321	323
ADMINISTRATIVE SUPPORT (INCL. CLERICAL)	317	2,177	1,850	1,603	3,089	2,593	8,799	5,164	1,802
PRIVATE HOUSEHOLD	26	135	53	137	97	149	188	148	5
PROTECTIVE SERVICE	83	225	194	215	244	317	1,127	624	211
OTHER SERVICE	239	2,373	929	1,480	1,461	1,805	3,999	2,455	762
FARMING, FORESTRY, AND FISHING	0	4	0	0	50	14	91	58	9
PRECISION PRODUCTION, CRAFT, AND REPAIR	148	757	438	440	524	652	2,206	1,346	467
MACHINE OPERATORS, ASSEMBLERS, AND INSPECTORS	227	1,308	557	951	372	932	2,634	1,849	613
TRANSPORTATION AND MATERIAL MOVING	68	545	222	342	342	525	1,812	1,073	333
HANDLERS, EQUIPMENT CLEANERS, HELPERS, AND LABORERS	84	609	250	613	255	558	1,518	922	270
INDUSTRY									
EMPLOYED PERSONS 16 YEARS AND OVER	1,366	9,605	9,222	6,944	16,759	10,265	33,107	19,328	6,516
AGRICULTURAL, FORESTRY, FISHERIES, AND MINING	0	17	48	0	53	37	84	39	6
CONSTRUCTION	30	198	116	162	116	223	659	337	91
MANUFACTURING:									
NONDURABLE GOODS	179	839	522	644	792	787	1,994	1,407	419
DURABLE GOODS	272	1,398	647	790	553	1,051	3,500	2,143	828
TRANSPORTATION	133	892	556	544	548	880	3,374	2,077	828
COMMUNICATIONS AND OTHER PUBLIC UTILITIES	28	180	221	184	178	208	1,083	605	266
WHOLESALE TRADE	29	263	265	220	265	311	917	516	115
RETAIL TRADE	149	1,174	991	982	1,557	1,439	4,041	2,564	671
FINANCE, INSURANCE, AND REAL ESTATE	58	660	729	377	1,195	588	2,951	1,364	461
BUSINESS AND REPAIR SERVICES	69	472	447	438	852	463	1,480	696	235
PERSONAL, ENTERTAINMENT, AND RECREATION SERVICES	68	722	321	652	540	580	1,383	800	224
PROFESSIONAL AND RELATED SERVICES:									
HEALTH SERVICES	103	971	1,319	636	2,355	1,196	3,373	1,794	600
EDUCATIONAL SERVICES	94	843	1,690	560	5,310	1,207	3,928	2,469	865
OTHER PROFESSIONAL AND RELATED SERVICES	39	366	690	265	1,622	572	1,414	679	289
PUBLIC ADMINISTRATION	115	610	660	490	823	723	2,926	1,838	618
MEANS OF TRANSPORTATION TO WORK									
WORKERS 16 YEARS AND OVER	1,308	9,009	8,868	6,457	16,047	9,769	31,937	18,448	6,338
CAR, TRUCK, OR VAN:									
DRIVE ALONE	452	2,227	3,412	1,752	4,364	3,272	13,151	7,977	3,089
CARPOOL	249	1,090	1,294	828	1,772	1,184	4,959	2,843	1,134
PUBLIC TRANSPORTATION	584	4,930	3,419	3,439	4,709	4,299	12,372	7,111	1,960
WALKED ONLY	14	654	474	324	4,567	906	1,027	303	89
OTHER MEANS	9	56	165	35	315	70	233	105	39
WORKED AT HOME	0	52	104	79	320	38	195	109	27
TRAVEL TIME TO WORK									
WORKERS 16 YEARS AND OVER WHO DID NOT WORK AT HOME	1,194	8,455	8,433	6,356	16,054	9,656	31,483	18,249	6,233
LESS THAN 5 MINUTES	6	131	78	104	402	228	343	129	56
5 TO 9 MINUTES	34	379	436	228	1,633	370	690	343	142
10 TO 14 MINUTES	12	325	680	289	2,502	635	1,471	843	294
15 TO 19 MINUTES	149	611	1,063	518	2,174	914	2,337	1,293	481
20 TO 29 MINUTES	179	1,413	1,549	790	3,186	1,426	4,529	2,584	831
30 TO 44 MINUTES	419	2,688	2,365	1,583	3,551	2,613	8,445	4,584	1,511
45 TO 59 MINUTES	167	1,472	1,020	1,227	1,319	1,439	5,387	3,980	969
60 OR MORE MINUTES	228	1,436	1,242	1,617	1,287	2,031	8,281	4,493	1,949

392

TABLE III-4 LABOR FORCE CHARACTERISTICS OF THE POPULATION,
BY COMMUNITY AREA: CITY OF CHICAGO, 1980

	46	47	48	49	50	51	52	53	54
LABOR FORCE STATUS									
MALES 16 AND OVER	15,113	1,155	7,024	20,786	3,373	6,194	8,199	13,322	3,063
LABOR FORCE:									
ARMED FORCES	0	0	9	35	0	0	0	7	0
CIVILIAN LABOR FORCE:									
EMPLOYED	9,999	701	5,001	12,229	2,172	4,046	5,651	8,620	1,358
UNEMPLOYED	1,379	92	434	2,311	316	678	414	1,409	462
NOT IN LABOR FORCE	3,735	362	1,580	6,211	885	1,470	2,134	3,286	1,243
FEMALES 16 AND OVER	17,129	1,425	8,216	24,941	4,108	7,358	8,786	15,580	4,661
LABOR FORCE:									
ARMED FORCES	0	0	4	7	0	0	0	6	0
CIVILIAN LABOR FORCE:									
EMPLOYED	7,608	606	4,829	12,217	2,081	3,728	3,557	7,482	1,334
UNEMPLOYED	880	143	397	1,527	314	454	312	1,095	452
NOT IN LABOR FORCE	8,641	676	2,986	11,190	1,713	3,176	4,917	6,997	2,875
PLACE OF WORK									
WORKERS 16 YEARS AND OVER	16,775	1,268	9,824	24,263	3,884	7,704	8,807	15,068	2,380
WORKED IN CHICAGO SMSA:									
IN CHICAGO	12,784	907	7,839	18,290	3,001	5,956	6,741	10,610	1,549
OUTSIDE CHICAGO	1,414	120	882	2,911	383	630	568	2,198	307
WORKED OUTSIDE CHICAGO SMSA	242	20	92	192	33	178	712	150	0
NOT REPORTED	2,335	221	1,011	2,870	467	940	786	2,110	524
CLASS OF WORKER									
EMPLOYED PERSONS 16 YEARS AND OVER	17,607	1,307	9,830	24,446	4,253	7,774	9,208	16,102	2,692
PRIVATE WAGE AND SALARY WORKER	13,943	992	6,401	16,803	3,093	5,861	7,996	11,856	1,861
FEDERAL GOVERNMENT WORKER	1,074	64	880	2,209	317	564	115	1,301	224
STATE GOVERNMENT WORKER	525	47	392	1,020	199	250	124	540	151
LOCAL GOVERNMENT WORKER	1,674	169	1,959	3,821	548	880	776	2,055	379
SELF-EMPLOYED WORKER	345	26	198	552	89	206	197	327	68
UNPAID FAMILY WORKER	46	9	0	41	7	13	0	23	9
OCCUPATION									
EMPLOYED PERSONS 16 YEARS AND OVER	17,607	1,307	9,830	24,446	4,253	7,774	9,208	16,102	2,692
EXECUTIVE, ADMINISTRATIVE, AND MANAGERIAL	911	76	913	1,801	318	437	503	957	156
PROFESSIONAL SPECIALTY	1,431	57	1,744	2,819	303	582	574	1,061	194
TECHNICIANS AND RELATED SUPPORT	371	32	333	534	132	247	155	354	40
SALES	846	80	565	1,595	310	517	662	926	129
ADMINISTRATIVE SUPPORT (INCL. CLERICAL)	4,096	295	2,479	5,987	1,132	2,156	1,764	4,087	645
PRIVATE HOUSEHOLD	81	8	18	106	18	27	4	57	15
PROTECTIVE SERVICE	360	13	229	902	166	165	382	505	87
OTHER SERVICE	1,925	188	907	3,047	436	744	984	1,902	497
FARMING, FORESTRY, AND FISHING	63	7	20	30	21	40	25	56	17
PRECISION PRODUCTION, CRAFT, AND REPAIR	2,242	83	762	1,923	388	977	1,700	1,754	224
MACHINE OPERATORS, ASSEMBLERS, AND INSPECTORS	2,962	216	812	2,703	466	991	1,168	2,086	343
TRANSPORTATION AND MATERIAL MOVING	945	114	589	1,608	315	398	613	1,101	182
HANDLERS, EQUIPMENT CLEANERS, HELPERS, AND LABORERS	1,374	138	459	1,391	248	493	674	1,256	163
INDUSTRY									
EMPLOYED PERSONS 16 YEARS AND OVER	17,607	1,307	9,830	24,446	4,253	7,774	9,208	16,102	2,692
AGRICULTURAL, FORESTRY, FISHERIES, AND MINING	70	7	13	24	12	40	32	46	0
CONSTRUCTION	479	67	134	443	130	214	380	406	75
MANUFACTURING:									
NONDURABLE GOODS	1,846	163	669	1,974	476	726	660	1,442	227
DURABLE GOODS	4,276	269	1,409	3,221	621	1,561	3,011	2,809	404
TRANSPORTATION	1,294	121	1,026	2,705	477	641	441	1,978	203
COMMUNICATIONS AND OTHER PUBLIC UTILITIES	556	75	377	717	178	282	302	670	43
WHOLESALE TRADE	536	49	326	796	131	302	309	656	54
RETAIL TRADE	1,576	107	1,007	2,968	501	978	1,322	1,967	423
FINANCE, INSURANCE, AND REAL ESTATE	1,283	108	681	1,889	317	495	561	1,103	170
BUSINESS AND REPAIR SERVICES	699	38	287	1,042	109	276	327	546	103
PERSONAL, ENTERTAINMENT, AND RECREATION SERVICES	563	48	311	966	100	204	176	535	63
PROFESSIONAL AND RELATED SERVICES:									
HEALTH SERVICES	1,527	77	913	2,156	335	707	572	1,308	262
EDUCATIONAL SERVICES	1,226	85	1,386	2,688	392	597	323	1,183	266
OTHER PROFESSIONAL AND RELATED SERVICES	760	68	360	837	97	232	306	469	128
PUBLIC ADMINISTRATION	916	25	931	2,020	377	519	486	984	271
MEANS OF TRANSPORTATION TO WORK									
WORKERS 16 YEARS AND OVER	16,865	1,266	9,488	23,484	4,117	7,464	8,856	15,329	2,501
CAR, TRUCK, OR VAN:									
DRIVE ALONE	7,249	557	5,115	11,184	2,032	3,592	4,921	7,614	1,190
CARPOOL	3,084	218	1,793	3,873	635	1,260	1,736	2,906	389
PUBLIC TRANSPORTATION	5,242	460	2,232	7,609	1,209	2,177	1,538	4,393	751
WALKED ONLY	1,124	31	310	623	194	360	567	299	149
OTHER MEANS	59	0	13	76	9	29	62	42	22
WORKED AT HOME	107	0	25	119	38	46	32	75	0
TRAVEL TIME TO WORK									
WORKERS 16 YEARS AND OVER WHO DID NOT WORK AT HOME	16,609	1,268	9,809	24,120	3,850	7,660	8,765	14,983	2,380
LESS THAN 5 MINUTES	123	7	138	222	36	86	146	239	66
5 TO 9 MINUTES	754	24	338	633	228	504	960	357	42
10 TO 14 MINUTES	1,165	71	487	1,100	134	646	1,433	769	220
15 TO 19 MINUTES	1,892	118	805	1,758	340	749	1,586	837	105
20 TO 29 MINUTES	3,062	124	1,359	3,398	486	933	1,799	1,591	262
30 TO 44 MINUTES	3,981	278	2,568	6,175	902	1,700	1,377	3,964	576
45 TO 59 MINUTES	2,307	319	1,952	4,388	697	1,143	441	2,683	265
60 OR MORE MINUTES	3,325	327	2,162	6,446	1,027	1,899	1,023	4,543	844

	55	56	57	58	59	60	61	62	63
LABOR FORCE STATUS									
MALES 16 AND OVER	4,521	14,163	3,821	11,695	4,741	11,223	18,582	4,992	9,115
LABOR FORCE:									
ARMED FORCES	0	46	6	0	0	6	11	0	0
CIVILIAN LABOR FORCE:									
EMPLOYED	3,192	10,002	2,657	8,006	3,342	7,509	11,955	3,379	6,116
UNEMPLOYED	292	800	182	672	269	767	1,769	210	529
NOT IN LABOR FORCE	1,037	3,315	976	3,017	1,130	2,941	4,847	1,403	2,470
FEMALES 16 AND OVER	4,601	16,040	4,343	12,987	5,420	12,395	19,391	5,826	10,520
LABOR FORCE:									
ARMED FORCES	0	0	0	0	0	0	0	0	0
CIVILIAN LABOR FORCE:									
EMPLOYED	1,963	7,523	2,115	6,062	2,415	5,397	7,962	2,842	4,564
UNEMPLOYED	93	684	122	498	230	488	1,040	125	380
NOT IN LABOR FORCE	2,545	7,833	2,106	6,427	2,775	6,510	10,389	2,859	5,576
PLACE OF WORK									
WORKERS 16 YEARS AND OVER	5,046	17,266	4,832	13,746	5,659	12,480	19,045	5,880	10,175
WORKED IN CHICAGO SMSA:									
IN CHICAGO	3,401	11,378	3,669	10,699	4,535	9,657	14,030	4,533	7,735
OUTSIDE CHICAGO	775	4,202	690	1,841	647	1,203	2,444	881	1,340
WORKED OUTSIDE CHICAGO SMSA	442	138	46	25	19	28	87	28	33
NOT REPORTED	428	1,548	427	1,181	458	1,592	2,484	438	1,067
CLASS OF WORKER									
EMPLOYED PERSONS 16 YEARS AND OVER	5,155	17,525	4,772	14,068	5,757	12,906	19,917	6,221	10,680
PRIVATE WAGE AND SALARY WORKER	4,214	14,773	4,181	12,141	4,894	10,579	17,432	5,139	8,793
FEDERAL GOVERNMENT WORKER	85	403	113	257	147	237	426	117	215
STATE GOVERNMENT WORKER	26	330	45	150	85	242	311	88	187
LOCAL GOVERNMENT WORKER	682	1,581	300	1,036	486	1,389	1,322	752	1,148
SELF-EMPLOYED WORKER	138	414	115	444	145	413	335	125	317
UNPAID FAMILY WORKER	10	24	18	40	0	46	91	0	20
OCCUPATION									
EMPLOYED PERSONS 16 YEARS AND OVER	5,155	17,525	4,772	14,068	5,757	12,906	19,917	6,221	10,680
EXECUTIVE, ADMINISTRATIVE, AND MANAGERIAL	327	911	341	872	309	885	784	470	732
PROFESSIONAL SPECIALTY	290	1,060	207	622	263	715	741	448	676
TECHNICIANS AND RELATED SUPPORT	81	464	46	318	179	312	322	157	182
SALES	509	1,475	377	1,070	441	1,042	1,193	386	805
ADMINISTRATIVE SUPPORT (INCL. CLERICAL)	1,043	4,831	1,252	3,473	1,742	3,148	3,820	1,609	2,858
PRIVATE HOUSEHOLD	7	13	7	52	7	0	30	0	0
PROTECTIVE SERVICE	379	785	107	358	195	539	518	332	447
OTHER SERVICE	517	1,310	499	1,510	468	1,313	2,404	595	1,027
FARMING, FORESTRY, AND FISHING	8	26	8	46	20	13	113	15	16
PRECISION PRODUCTION, CRAFT, AND REPAIR	892	2,611	652	1,762	687	1,357	2,490	852	1,431
MACHINE OPERATORS, ASSEMBLERS, AND INSPECTORS	538	1,906	635	1,887	664	1,402	3,767	615	1,108
TRANSPORTATION AND MATERIAL MOVING	222	1,029	232	878	366	971	1,037	292	576
HANDLERS, EQUIPMENT CLEANERS, HELPERS, AND LABORERS	342	1,104	409	1,220	416	1,209	2,698	450	822
INDUSTRY									
EMPLOYED PERSONS 16 YEARS AND OVER	5,155	17,525	4,772	14,068	5,757	12,906	19,917	6,221	10,680
AGRICULTURAL, FORESTRY, FISHERIES, AND MINING	35	43	0	52	36	6	103	0	11
CONSTRUCTION	219	657	112	418	242	483	670	142	476
MANUFACTURING:									
NONDURABLE GOODS	366	2,116	656	1,854	697	1,656	3,204	740	1,155
DURABLE GOODS	1,432	3,371	1,007	2,551	786	1,671	4,249	913	1,741
TRANSPORTATION	294	1,478	445	1,327	562	1,146	1,184	514	749
COMMUNICATIONS AND OTHER PUBLIC UTILITIES	142	456	105	269	115	362	389	207	418
WHOLESALE TRADE	150	1,092	278	868	378	963	1,681	384	886
RETAIL TRADE	916	2,719	733	2,429	978	2,243	3,105	1,017	1,602
FINANCE, INSURANCE, AND REAL ESTATE	351	1,373	442	1,228	619	1,017	1,009	593	819
BUSINESS AND REPAIR SERVICES	156	662	274	707	245	570	881	233	434
PERSONAL, ENTERTAINMENT, AND RECREATION SERVICES	100	384	99	312	131	313	468	55	234
PROFESSIONAL AND RELATED SERVICES:									
HEALTH SERVICES	234	763	133	576	194	573	882	380	562
EDUCATIONAL SERVICES	146	582	119	438	278	586	695	285	486
OTHER PROFESSIONAL AND RELATED SERVICES	115	691	161	305	183	405	560	232	343
PUBLIC ADMINISTRATION	499	1,138	208	734	313	912	837	526	764
MEANS OF TRANSPORTATION TO WORK									
WORKERS 16 YEARS AND OVER	4,901	17,052	4,627	13,602	5,580	12,553	18,658	5,868	10,265
CAR, TRUCK, OR VAN:									
DRIVE ALONE	2,912	9,189	2,115	5,862	2,363	4,912	7,705	3,024	4,998
CARPOOL	781	2,799	838	2,457	923	2,213	3,742	1,230	1,999
PUBLIC TRANSPORTATION	928	4,135	1,212	3,944	1,798	3,929	5,292	1,265	2,286
WALKED ONLY	211	791	436	1,151	422	1,306	1,628	288	805
OTHER MEANS	38	54	0	52	13	133	141	30	43
WORKED AT HOME	31	84	26	136	61	60	150	31	134
TRAVEL TIME TO WORK									
WORKERS 16 YEARS AND OVER WHO DID NOT WORK AT HOME	5,024	17,172	4,820	13,619	5,598	12,419	18,860	5,847	10,065
LESS THAN 5 MINUTES	72	194	77	283	52	120	437	29	176
5 TO 9 MINUTES	268	848	402	753	362	1,048	1,326	315	640
10 TO 14 MINUTES	595	1,381	444	1,575	676	1,661	1,532	592	987
15 TO 19 MINUTES	721	1,984	551	1,905	920	1,654	1,790	664	1,540
20 TO 29 MINUTES	1,022	3,409	750	2,379	940	2,484	3,411	1,194	1,628
30 TO 44 MINUTES	1,253	4,293	1,246	3,569	1,576	3,498	5,214	1,670	2,499
45 TO 59 MINUTES	540	2,638	798	1,884	754	1,158	2,334	647	1,164
60 OR MORE MINUTES	553	2,425	552	1,271	318	796	2,816	736	1,431

	64	65	66	67	68	69	70	71	72
LABOR FORCE STATUS									
MALES 16 AND OVER	8,793	9,536	16,822	17,849	17,161	15,028	15,550	21,041	8,155
LABOR FORCE:									
ARMED FORCES	0	11	0	24	48	45	12	28	0
CIVILIAN LABOR FORCE:									
EMPLOYED	6,738	6,855	11,284	8,878	7,593	8,143	11,710	13,487	6,051
UNEMPLOYED	429	423	955	2,622	1,951	1,570	609	2,305	295
NOT IN LABOR FORCE	1,626	2,247	4,583	6,325	7,569	5,270	3,219	5,221	1,809
FEMALES 16 AND OVER	9,296	10,974	19,369	22,293	22,614	19,477	16,951	25,414	9,436
LABOR FORCE:									
ARMED FORCES	0	0	0	5	0	8	0	44	0
CIVILIAN LABOR FORCE:									
EMPLOYED	4,830	5,100	8,610	8,750	7,581	8,269	8,266	13,198	4,528
UNEMPLOYED	343	254	486	1,945	1,417	1,140	485	1,743	154
NOT IN LABOR FORCE	4,123	5,620	10,273	11,593	13,616	10,060	8,200	10,429	4,754
PLACE OF WORK									
WORKERS 16 YEARS AND OVER	11,292	11,311	18,498	16,931	15,220	16,264	19,724	25,586	10,646
WORKED IN CHICAGO SMSA:									
IN CHICAGO	7,724	8,260	13,976	11,822	11,189	11,871	13,955	18,872	7,409
OUTSIDE CHICAGO	2,748	2,024	2,987	1,998	1,620	1,704	4,212	3,274	1,997
WORKED OUTSIDE CHICAGO SMSA	56	60	81	172	63	83	130	182	117
NOT REPORTED	764	967	1,454	2,939	2,348	2,606	1,427	3,258	1,123
CLASS OF WORKER									
EMPLOYED PERSONS 16 YEARS AND OVER	11,568	11,955	19,894	17,628	15,174	16,412	19,976	26,685	10,579
PRIVATE WAGE AND SALARY WORKER	9,696	9,728	16,540	13,053	11,775	11,242	15,303	19,106	7,331
FEDERAL GOVERNMENT WORKER	190	324	472	1,521	1,187	1,397	361	2,360	212
STATE GOVERNMENT WORKER	135	198	343	769	519	859	226	1,178	269
LOCAL GOVERNMENT WORKER	1,244	1,427	1,879	2,014	1,486	2,453	3,648	3,528	2,103
SELF-EMPLOYED WORKER	236	257	553	229	207	461	408	491	648
UNPAID FAMILY WORKER	67	21	107	42	0	0	30	22	16
OCCUPATION									
EMPLOYED PERSONS 16 YEARS AND OVER	11,568	11,955	19,894	17,628	15,174	16,412	19,976	26,685	10,579
EXECUTIVE, ADMINISTRATIVE, AND MANAGERIAL	895	962	1,204	712	571	920	1,721	1,403	1,325
PROFESSIONAL SPECIALTY	472	919	1,779	970	743	1,573	1,648	2,342	2,415
TECHNICIANS AND RELATED SUPPORT	270	372	637	463	324	411	482	607	276
SALES	959	855	1,557	965	877	1,090	2,140	1,680	1,224
ADMINISTRATIVE SUPPORT (INCL. CLERICAL)	2,883	3,054	4,747	4,242	3,502	4,136	4,637	6,868	2,277
PRIVATE HOUSEHOLD	0	26	29	79	215	121	19	71	43
PROTECTIVE SERVICE	676	645	676	489	458	466	1,769	862	527
OTHER SERVICE	832	903	2,044	2,418	2,515	2,628	1,700	3,377	618
FARMING, FORESTRY, AND FISHING	22	54	73	71	22	47	35	66	30
PRECISION PRODUCTION, CRAFT, AND REPAIR	1,682	1,786	2,583	1,600	1,252	1,351	2,469	2,407	962
MACHINE OPERATORS, ASSEMBLERS, AND INSPECTORS	1,325	1,067	2,127	2,775	2,365	1,781	1,302	3,523	307
TRANSPORTATION AND MATERIAL MOVING	764	581	1,063	1,376	875	843	894	1,636	286
HANDLERS, EQUIPMENT CLEANERS, HELPERS, AND LABORERS	788	731	1,375	1,468	1,455	1,045	1,160	1,843	289
INDUSTRY									
EMPLOYED PERSONS 16 YEARS AND OVER	11,568	11,955	19,894	17,628	15,174	16,412	19,976	26,685	10,579
AGRICULTURAL, FORESTRY, FISHERIES, AND MINING	44	48	76	57	15	14	92	49	46
CONSTRUCTION	417	444	702	499	410	363	892	622	459
MANUFACTURING:									
NONDURABLE GOODS	1,533	1,306	2,495	1,908	1,776	1,420	1,803	2,737	558
DURABLE GOODS	1,937	1,715	2,776	2,597	2,451	2,067	1,996	3,808	622
TRANSPORTATION	1,095	938	1,566	1,808	1,335	1,642	1,247	3,246	487
COMMUNICATIONS AND OTHER PUBLIC UTILITIES	339	430	628	524	362	553	876	920	395
WHOLESALE TRADE	738	618	1,200	636	561	462	1,126	717	353
RETAIL TRADE	1,898	2,073	3,239	2,245	2,133	2,126	3,822	3,537	1,206
FINANCE, INSURANCE, AND REAL ESTATE	824	1,018	1,600	1,031	885	1,104	1,346	1,803	1,334
BUSINESS AND REPAIR SERVICES	417	432	631	760	671	636	713	910	454
PERSONAL, ENTERTAINMENT, AND RECREATION SERVICES	289	217	438	731	875	872	540	810	329
PROFESSIONAL AND RELATED SERVICES:									
HEALTH SERVICES	459	595	1,525	1,910	1,374	1,529	1,277	2,657	778
EDUCATIONAL SERVICES	385	471	1,020	1,276	792	1,717	1,234	2,364	1,542
OTHER PROFESSIONAL AND RELATED SERVICES	183	456	827	491	669	561	542	844	941
PUBLIC ADMINISTRATION	1,010	1,194	1,171	1,155	865	1,346	2,470	1,661	1,075
MEANS OF TRANSPORTATION TO WORK									
WORKERS 16 YEARS AND OVER	11,145	11,705	19,103	16,900	14,512	15,729	19,470	25,652	10,254
CAR, TRUCK, OR VAN:									
DRIVE ALONE	6,623	6,307	9,482	7,068	5,233	6,548	11,423	11,871	5,514
CARPOOL	1,994	2,224	3,553	2,873	2,116	2,392	3,839	4,230	1,610
PUBLIC TRANSPORTATION	1,897	2,260	4,519	6,544	6,561	6,208	3,092	8,915	2,430
WALKED ONLY	557	829	1,335	350	467	442	939	454	526
OTHER MEANS	52	33	80	28	60	52	78	94	65
WORKED AT HOME	22	52	134	37	75	87	99	88	109
TRAVEL TIME TO WORK									
WORKERS 16 YEARS AND OVER WHO DID NOT WORK AT HOME	11,270	11,257	18,381	16,845	15,155	16,181	19,589	25,501	10,550
LESS THAN 5 MINUTES	145	194	277	68	144	103	198	175	172
5 TO 9 MINUTES	772	741	1,259	425	187	493	1,072	452	730
10 TO 14 MINUTES	960	1,215	1,512	571	442	739	2,050	794	901
15 TO 19 MINUTES	1,435	1,353	1,829	892	862	1,400	2,317	1,678	839
20 TO 29 MINUTES	2,095	1,875	2,867	1,966	1,951	2,327	3,411	3,469	1,677
30 TO 44 MINUTES	2,935	3,038	4,880	4,764	4,149	4,250	5,158	6,552	3,015
45 TO 59 MINUTES	1,094	1,332	2,393	3,364	3,291	2,761	2,539	5,272	1,533
60 OR MORE MINUTES	1,834	1,509	3,364	4,795	4,129	4,108	2,844	7,109	1,683

TABLE III-4 LABOR FORCE CHARACTERISTICS OF THE POPULATION,
BY COMMUNITY AREA: CITY OF CHICAGO, 1980

	73	74	75	76	77
LABOR FORCE STATUS					
MALES 16 AND OVER	12,197	7,479	9,801	4,674	23,472
LABOR FORCE:					
ARMED FORCES	7	13	12	19	44
CIVILIAN LABOR FORCE:					
EMPLOYED	7,933	5,342	6,231	3,840	16,488
UNEMPLOYED	1,220	301	940	209	1,389
NOT IN LABOR FORCE	3,037	1,823	2,618	606	5,551
FEMALES 16 AND OVER	14,421	8,428	11,877	5,039	26,960
LABOR FORCE:					
ARMED FORCES	6	0	6	6	6
CIVILIAN LABOR FORCE:					
EMPLOYED	7,376	3,654	5,456	3,026	14,291
UNEMPLOYED	1,054	137	596	94	993
NOT IN LABOR FORCE	5,985	4,637	5,819	1,913	11,670
PLACE OF WORK					
WORKERS 16 YEARS AND OVER	14,522	8,775	11,208	6,711	29,342
WORKED IN CHICAGO SMSA:					
IN CHICAGO	10,433	5,285	7,796	3,608	21,976
OUTSIDE CHICAGO	1,976	2,651	2,213	2,749	4,521
WORKED OUTSIDE CHICAGO SMSA	149	62	138	72	78
NOT REPORTED	1,964	777	1,061	282	2,767
CLASS OF WORKER					
EMPLOYED PERSONS 16 YEARS AND OVER	15,309	8,996	11,687	6,866	30,779
PRIVATE WAGE AND SALARY WORKER	10,235	6,493	7,851	5,194	25,971
FEDERAL GOVERNMENT WORKER	1,556	128	646	188	701
STATE GOVERNMENT WORKER	757	89	432	99	778
LOCAL GOVERNMENT WORKER	2,466	1,982	2,303	1,047	1,985
SELF-EMPLOYED WORKER	238	277	429	317	1,309
UNPAID FAMILY WORKER	57	27	26	21	35
OCCUPATION					
EMPLOYED PERSONS 16 YEARS AND OVER	15,309	8,996	11,687	6,866	30,779
EXECUTIVE, ADMINISTRATIVE, AND MANAGERIAL	935	782	1,059	932	3,901
PROFESSIONAL SPECIALTY	1,551	894	1,726	880	5,177
TECHNICIANS AND RELATED SUPPORT	548	223	319	228	1,074
SALES	1,025	976	980	714	2,965
ADMINISTRATIVE SUPPORT (INCL. CLERICAL)	3,906	1,801	2,872	1,644	6,867
PRIVATE HOUSEHOLD	39	0	50	0	192
PROTECTIVE SERVICE	422	912	559	369	543
OTHER SERVICE	1,645	894	1,092	535	3,585
FARMING, FORESTRY, AND FISHING	12	54	20	16	70
PRECISION PRODUCTION, CRAFT, AND REPAIR	1,351	1,316	941	734	2,392
MACHINE OPERATORS, ASSEMBLERS, AND INSPECTORS	1,818	365	819	331	2,389
TRANSPORTATION AND MATERIAL MOVING	1,136	419	547	232	764
HANDLERS, EQUIPMENT CLEANERS, HELPERS, AND LABORERS	921	360	703	251	860
INDUSTRY					
EMPLOYED PERSONS 16 YEARS AND OVER	15,309	8,996	11,687	6,866	30,779
AGRICULTURAL, FORESTRY, FISHERIES, AND MINING	23	26	25	34	113
CONSTRUCTION	326	520	437	295	933
MANUFACTURING:					
NONDURABLE GOODS	1,478	535	693	394	2,531
DURABLE GOODS	2,051	702	1,186	957	3,272
TRANSPORTATION	1,963	552	899	435	1,242
COMMUNICATIONS AND OTHER PUBLIC UTILITIES	516	415	367	200	551
WHOLESALE TRADE	461	319	420	382	1,331
RETAIL TRADE	1,866	1,601	1,570	920	4,623
FINANCE, INSURANCE, AND REAL ESTATE	1,043	761	1,113	677	3,380
BUSINESS AND REPAIR SERVICES	486	258	464	416	1,912
PERSONAL, ENTERTAINMENT, AND RECREATION SERVICES	384	278	284	302	1,444
PROFESSIONAL AND RELATED SERVICES:					
HEALTH SERVICES	1,349	536	1,069	492	3,459
EDUCATIONAL SERVICES	1,682	929	1,459	277	2,374
OTHER PROFESSIONAL AND RELATED SERVICES	370	276	454	322	2,312
PUBLIC ADMINISTRATION	1,311	1,288	1,247	763	1,302
MEANS OF TRANSPORTATION TO WORK					
WORKERS 16 YEARS AND OVER	14,732	8,670	11,351	6,727	29,784
CAR, TRUCK, OR VAN:					
DRIVE ALONE	7,434	5,075	6,090	4,440	9,448
CARPOOL	2,631	1,568	1,980	1,045	3,982
PUBLIC TRANSPORTATION	4,248	1,373	2,793	941	12,976
WALKED ONLY	284	541	364	232	2,765
OTHER MEANS	86	35	48	34	214
WORKED AT HOME	49	78	76	35	399
TRAVEL TIME TO WORK					
WORKERS 16 YEARS AND OVER WHO DID NOT WORK AT HOME	14,441	8,689	11,152	6,669	28,923
LESS THAN 5 MINUTES	65	118	204	55	587
5 TO 9 MINUTES	324	757	394	454	1,637
10 TO 14 MINUTES	674	951	753	737	1,904
15 TO 19 MINUTES	925	1,048	1,075	673	2,848
20 TO 29 MINUTES	2,023	1,275	1,719	1,628	5,289
30 TO 44 MINUTES	3,891	2,207	2,435	1,667	8,343
45 TO 59 MINUTES	2,631	853	1,783	665	5,071
60 OR MORE MINUTES	3,908	1,480	2,789	790	3,244

TABLE III-5 INCOME AND POVERTY STATUS OF THE POPULATION, BY COMMUNITY AREA: CITY OF CHICAGO, 1980

	01	02	03	04	05	06	07	08	09
INCOME TYPE IN 1979									
HOUSEHOLDS WITH INCOME									
EARNINGS	21,553	20,354	19,905	14,909	10,745	42,630	27,523	28,843	3,728
WAGE OR SALARY INCOME	21,006	19,379	19,434	14,481	10,480	41,157	26,457	27,203	3,625
NONFARM SELF-EMPLOYMENT INCOME	1,884	3,038	1,349	1,395	717	4,539	3,235	4,088	305
FARM SELF-EMPLOYMENT INCOME	157	195	91	94	41	284	241	391	30
INTEREST, DIVIDEND, OR NET RENTAL INCOME	11,215	15,266	7,594	8,816	5,797	22,707	13,364	15,968	3,252
SOCIAL SECURITY INCOME	5,545	8,503	6,074	5,796	3,869	11,067	4,247	6,057	1,833
PUBLIC ASSISTANCE INCOME	1,821	856	4,564	1,048	1,266	3,093	1,319	4,111	115
ALL OTHER INCOME	3,904	4,397	4,069	3,444	2,677	7,404	3,615	4,033	1,242
HOUSEHOLD INCOME IN 1979									
HOUSEHOLDS	26,245	24,962	28,259	18,753	14,067	52,167	31,781	36,488	4,715
LESS THAN $2,500	1,454	727	3,058	732	697	2,775	1,659	2,163	72
$2,500 TO $4,999	2,851	1,409	4,756	1,528	1,408	4,666	2,405	4,047	173
$5,000 TO $7,499	2,272	1,588	2,916	1,606	1,353	4,176	1,903	2,336	214
$7,500 TO $9,999	2,344	1,731	2,552	1,649	1,096	3,912	1,838	2,004	303
$10,000 TO $12,499	2,910	1,852	2,737	1,894	1,281	4,915	2,581	2,384	288
$12,500 TO $14,999	2,300	1,590	1,822	1,508	902	4,113	2,300	1,974	287
$15,000 TO $17,499	2,452	1,783	2,017	1,499	1,086	4,286	2,738	2,636	251
$17,500 TO $19,999	1,754	1,429	1,567	1,407	1,068	3,598	1,874	1,589	294
$20,000 TO $22,499	1,697	1,925	1,388	1,278	1,030	3,857	2,399	2,278	347
$22,500 TO $24,999	1,102	1,387	988	1,091	831	2,269	1,478	1,252	357
$25,000 TO $27,499	1,165	1,435	998	852	697	2,245	1,496	1,524	296
$27,500 TO $29,999	684	1,193	652	756	495	1,522	1,072	997	244
$30,000 TO $34,999	1,255	2,075	782	1,073	841	2,618	2,170	1,790	521
$35,000 TO $39,999	777	1,542	568	651	432	1,866	1,294	1,325	359
$40,000 TO $49,999	597	1,617	714	666	535	2,275	1,636	2,166	362
$50,000 TO $74,999	506	1,224	521	448	284	1,984	1,852	2,579	256
$75,000 OR MORE	125	455	223	115	31	1,090	1,086	3,444	91
FAMILY INCOME IN 1979									
FAMILIES	11,405	17,134	12,913	11,172	9,245	20,131	10,392	12,414	3,549
LESS THAN $2,500	528	330	831	304	301	726	429	697	25
$2,500 TO $4,999	614	338	1,452	359	457	975	661	1,909	17
$5,000 TO $7,499	700	572	1,089	529	637	1,046	426	844	72
$7,500 TO $9,999	731	803	1,045	845	540	1,263	472	589	150
$10,000 TO $12,499	962	896	1,216	846	731	1,488	682	449	163
$12,500 TO $14,999	774	877	1,053	875	634	1,212	455	477	157
$15,000 TO $17,499	1,000	1,145	1,041	870	756	1,539	525	497	170
$17,500 TO $19,999	766	1,006	849	898	761	1,377	430	196	235
$20,000 TO $22,499	1,051	1,469	687	881	768	1,534	752	444	231
$22,500 TO $24,999	594	1,079	589	849	707	1,074	453	289	309
$25,000 TO $27,499	688	1,198	658	718	572	1,080	472	249	264
$27,500 TO $29,999	454	1,022	509	585	458	769	349	232	206
$30,000 TO $34,999	936	1,879	547	915	699	1,419	935	597	500
$35,000 TO $39,999	617	1,417	335	595	400	1,178	561	496	346
$40,000 TO $49,999	459	1,512	535	609	523	1,437	860	891	357
$50,000 TO $74,999	435	1,154	332	407	270	1,282	1,095	1,415	263
$75,000 OR MORE	96	437	145	87	31	732	835	2,143	84
POVERTY STATUS IN 1979									
PERSONS FOR WHOM POVERTY STATUS IS DETERMINED									
INCOME IN 1979 ABOVE POVERTY LEVEL									
TOTAL	44,418	56,531	44,909	38,988	30,775	84,424	48,259	48,361	12,194
WHITE	35,876	50,893	26,710	33,511	26,952	66,052	41,234	37,878	8,172
BLACK	3,578	308	6,585	91	133	5,736	3,331	7,998	0
AMERICAN INDIAN, ESKIMO AND ALEUT	78	28	580	30	134	351	8	0	0
ASIAN AND PACIFIC ISLANDER	3,105	4,384	6,232	3,768	1,293	4,803	1,622	631	0
INCOME IN 1979 BELOW POVERTY LEVEL									
TOTAL	8,363	3,463	17,614	4,225	4,266	12,637	7,452	16,152	248
WHITE	5,391	3,059	10,129	3,658	3,270	8,993	5,216	2,751	201
BLACK	1,387	54	2,839	0	194	849	1,363	11,529	0
AMERICAN INDIAN, ESKIMO AND ALEUT	46	25	608	0	45	21	60	0	0
ASIAN AND PACIFIC ISLANDER	879	302	1,594	320	100	569	65	126	0
PERSONS FOR WHOM POVERTY STATUS IS DETERMINED	52,781	59,994	62,523	43,213	35,041	97,061	55,711	64,513	12,442
INCOME IN 1979 ABOVE POVERTY LEVEL	44,418	56,531	44,909	38,988	30,775	84,424	48,259	48,361	12,194
UNDER 55 YEARS	34,458	36,714	35,947	27,991	23,327	65,350	40,879	35,125	8,160
55 TO 59 YEARS	1,864	3,815	1,886	2,167	1,789	3,490	1,722	3,188	951
60 TO 64 YEARS	1,892	3,886	1,617	2,213	1,518	3,300	1,623	2,666	853
65 YEARS AND OVER	6,204	12,116	5,459	6,617	4,141	12,284	4,035	7,382	2,230
INCOME IN 1979 BELOW POVERTY LEVEL	8,363	3,463	17,614	4,225	4,266	12,637	7,452	16,152	248
UNDER 55 YEARS	7,137	2,323	13,628	3,286	3,315	9,851	5,940	14,318	156
55 TO 59 YEARS	173	148	872	114	159	427	182	399	0
60 TO 64 YEARS	138	181	744	103	192	407	197	366	0
65 YEARS AND OVER	915	811	2,370	722	600	1,952	1,133	1,069	92
FAMILIES WITH ONE OR MORE RELATED CHILDREN	5,173	6,200	7,752	4,984	4,667	8,770	4,616	5,724	1,289
INCOME IN 1979 ABOVE POVERTY LEVEL WITH RELATED CHILDREN:	4,196	5,786	5,458	4,443	3,963	7,264	3,664	2,845	1,262
UNDER 5 YEARS AND 5 TO 17 YEARS	602	914	998	710	629	1,283	558	532	164
UNDER 5 YEARS ONLY	1,224	1,217	1,742	1,084	829	1,923	969	503	154
5 TO 17 YEARS ONLY	2,370	3,655	2,718	2,649	2,505	4,058	2,137	1,810	944
INCOME IN 1979 BELOW POVERTY LEVEL WITH RELATED CHILDREN:	977	414	2,294	541	704	1,506	952	2,879	27
UNDER 5 YEARS AND 5 TO 17 YEARS	250	78	629	132	241	317	283	1,245	5
UNDER 5 YEARS ONLY	368	109	620	120	141	428	201	450	4
5 TO 17 YEARS ONLY	359	227	1,045	289	322	761	468	1,184	18

TABLE III-5 INCOME AND POVERTY STATUS OF THE POPULATION,
BY COMMUNITY AREA: CITY OF CHICAGO, 1980

	10	11	12	13	14	15	16	17	18
INCOME TYPE IN 1979									
HOUSEHOLDS WITH INCOME									
EARNINGS	11,975	7,493	5,545	4,528	13,285	17,817	16,139	10,900	3,115
WAGE OR SALARY INCOME	11,701	7,318	5,221	4,332	13,035	17,416	15,722	10,594	3,029
NONFARM SELF-EMPLOYMENT INCOME	952	569	935	704	1,012	1,269	1,237	794	161
FARM SELF-EMPLOYMENT INCOME	105	63	59	37	46	102	109	50	14
INTEREST, DIVIDEND, OR NET RENTAL INCOME	10,104	6,498	5,010	3,224	6,491	12,888	10,301	8,572	2,327
SOCIAL SECURITY INCOME	5,871	3,925	2,404	1,671	3,681	8,510	6,165	5,562	1,593
PUBLIC ASSISTANCE INCOME	410	259	164	163	1,195	946	952	464	197
ALL OTHER INCOME	3,495	2,398	1,501	1,003	2,752	5,406	4,114	3,386	987
HOUSEHOLD INCOME IN 1979									
HOUSEHOLDS	14,995	9,914	6,803	5,399	16,272	22,760	20,489	13,879	4,103
LESS THAN $2,500	225	196	121	120	792	490	839	244	153
$2,500 TO $4,999	722	551	243	192	1,279	1,645	1,772	817	249
$5,000 TO $7,499	756	684	213	307	1,356	1,487	1,539	985	299
$7,500 TO $9,999	815	669	263	316	1,230	1,683	1,665	870	214
$10,000 TO $12,499	1,017	687	331	434	1,420	1,934	1,714	862	340
$12,500 TO $14,999	675	682	205	342	1,215	1,693	1,587	944	285
$15,000 TO $17,499	1,020	688	341	413	1,387	1,714	1,742	893	285
$17,500 TO $19,999	695	532	362	302	1,057	1,488	1,467	889	256
$20,000 TO $22,499	1,077	785	415	375	1,174	1,671	1,491	1,110	264
$22,500 TO $24,999	987	632	351	350	881	1,302	1,120	829	281
$25,000 TO $27,499	958	669	446	286	779	1,442	1,139	814	253
$27,500 TO $29,999	965	541	391	294	664	1,154	831	714	251
$30,000 TO $34,999	1,499	787	677	455	1,035	1,687	1,387	1,380	362
$35,000 TO $39,999	1,143	587	570	320	720	1,204	908	969	225
$40,000 TO $49,999	1,476	746	712	457	776	1,355	750	889	274
$50,000 TO $74,999	817	417	782	285	401	701	431	600	68
$75,000 OR MORE	148	61	380	151	106	110	107	70	44
FAMILY INCOME IN 1979									
FAMILIES	11,703	7,046	5,481	3,959	11,582	15,763	12,706	10,770	3,016
LESS THAN $2,500	67	54	58	44	381	181	232	99	53
$2,500 TO $4,999	177	53	50	43	551	311	464	159	58
$5,000 TO $7,499	254	323	63	136	693	508	627	412	155
$7,500 TO $9,999	427	250	97	187	638	842	735	430	109
$10,000 TO $12,499	570	407	209	189	957	992	791	481	223
$12,500 TO $14,999	418	390	110	206	837	1,101	971	748	164
$15,000 TO $17,499	693	444	188	274	949	1,135	1,066	727	196
$17,500 TO $19,999	576	407	317	214	856	1,072	997	736	181
$20,000 TO $22,499	909	626	368	308	889	1,306	1,079	1,003	216
$22,500 TO $24,999	849	550	287	281	744	1,201	911	758	254
$25,000 TO $27,499	875	574	406	250	701	1,335	932	791	236
$27,500 TO $29,999	955	509	355	270	630	1,057	756	683	233
$30,000 TO $34,999	1,442	723	621	423	943	1,588	1,191	1,298	357
$35,000 TO $39,999	1,130	562	549	292	639	1,073	811	952	211
$40,000 TO $49,999	1,441	712	677	419	722	1,298	670	846	266
$50,000 TO $74,999	777	411	752	272	353	660	379	577	60
$75,000 OR MORE	143	51	374	151	99	103	94	70	44
POVERTY STATUS IN 1979									
PERSONS FOR WHOM POVERTY STATUS IS DETERMINED									
INCOME IN 1979 ABOVE POVERTY LEVEL									
TOTAL	38,936	23,660	18,530	13,415	39,767	54,442	44,706	35,837	10,111
WHITE	35,298	20,772	18,087	11,680	30,894	53,034	40,786	27,506	9,933
BLACK	0	0	0	65	233	0	0	0	0
AMERICAN INDIAN, ESKIMO AND ALEUT	0	0	0	0	165	0	0	0	0
ASIAN AND PACIFIC ISLANDER	101	84	181	970	5,815	771	2,460	32	34
INCOME IN 1979 BELOW POVERTY LEVEL									
TOTAL	1,387	900	440	869	5,830	2,785	4,352	1,480	593
WHITE	1,223	809	440	786	4,136	2,720	3,951	1,093	593
BLACK	0	0	0	10	49	0	0	0	0
AMERICAN INDIAN, ESKIMO AND ALEUT	0	0	0	0	87	0	0	0	0
ASIAN AND PACIFIC ISLANDER	42	0	0	60	804	12	169	0	0
PERSONS FOR WHOM POVERTY STATUS IS DETERMINED	40,323	24,560	18,970	14,284	45,597	57,227	49,058	37,317	10,704
INCOME IN 1979 ABOVE POVERTY LEVEL	38,936	23,660	18,530	13,415	39,767	54,442	44,706	35,837	10,111
UNDER 55 YEARS	25,095	14,919	12,350	9,223	32,024	36,040	32,863	23,490	6,495
55 TO 59 YEARS	3,409	1,967	1,389	977	1,916	4,034	2,417	2,995	794
60 TO 64 YEARS	3,295	1,985	1,364	833	1,634	4,168	2,682	2,868	823
65 YEARS AND OVER	7,137	4,789	3,427	2,382	4,193	10,200	6,744	6,484	1,999
INCOME IN 1979 BELOW POVERTY LEVEL	1,387	900	440	869	5,830	2,785	4,352	1,480	593
UNDER 55 YEARS	667	563	195	675	4,862	1,795	3,240	909	367
55 TO 59 YEARS	139	17	27	14	218	125	173	46	40
60 TO 64 YEARS	103	93	23	34	158	151	306	95	65
65 YEARS AND OVER	478	227	195	146	592	714	633	430	121
FAMILIES WITH ONE OR MORE RELATED CHILDREN	4,141	2,412	2,052	1,546	6,474	6,126	5,725	3,989	1,168
INCOME IN 1979 ABOVE POVERTY LEVEL WITH RELATED CHILDREN:	4,009	2,324	2,015	1,449	5,501	5,793	5,117	3,802	1,082
UNDER 5 YEARS AND 5 TO 17 YEARS	608	320	270	219	1,090	899	860	671	126
UNDER 5 YEARS ONLY	536	412	255	279	1,340	1,135	1,100	602	237
5 TO 17 YEARS ONLY	2,865	1,592	1,490	951	3,071	3,759	3,157	2,529	719
INCOME IN 1979 BELOW POVERTY LEVEL WITH RELATED CHILDREN:	132	88	37	97	973	333	608	187	86
UNDER 5 YEARS AND 5 TO 17 YEARS	17	7	6	31	282	74	142	32	0
UNDER 5 YEARS ONLY	10	19	0	7	227	53	138	48	11
5 TO 17 YEARS ONLY	105	62	31	59	464	206	328	107	75

398

TABLE III-5 INCOME AND POVERTY STATUS OF THE POPULATION,
BY COMMUNITY AREA: CITY OF CHICAGO, 1980

	19	20	21	22	23	24	25	26	27
INCOME TYPE IN 1979									
HOUSEHOLDS WITH INCOME									
EARNINGS	16,238	5,558	10,320	22,260	15,676	22,404	32,125	6,166	5,697
WAGE OR SALARY INCOME	15,892	5,446	10,117	21,916	15,520	21,955	31,769	6,101	5,634
NONFARM SELF-EMPLOYMENT INCOME	1,081	292	535	1,118	584	1,051	1,259	198	173
FARM SELF-EMPLOYMENT INCOME	82	0	83	90	69	84	66	29	0
INTEREST, DIVIDEND, OR NET RENTAL INCOME	11,363	2,886	5,932	8,904	4,513	7,419	8,890	864	999
SOCIAL SECURITY INCOME	7,847	2,102	3,821	7,024	4,057	7,525	7,338	1,649	2,268
PUBLIC ASSISTANCE INCOME	945	639	906	4,484	5,053	6,656	9,616	3,430	4,298
ALL OTHER INCOME	4,866	1,521	2,357	5,332	3,679	5,002	7,954	1,953	1,790
HOUSEHOLD INCOME IN 1979									
HOUSEHOLDS	21,194	7,089	13,160	29,317	21,230	32,233	41,350	9,257	9,895
LESS THAN $2,500	605	297	630	1,906	2,000	3,646	3,975	1,267	1,544
$2,500 TO $4,999	1,713	773	1,274	3,842	3,112	5,085	4,446	1,604	2,034
$5,000 TO $7,499	1,743	492	1,052	2,767	1,817	3,091	3,195	982	1,193
$7,500 TO $9,999	1,478	566	1,300	2,679	1,838	3,128	3,212	900	922
$10,000 TO $12,499	1,702	554	1,217	3,012	2,078	3,005	3,624	667	857
$12,500 TO $14,999	1,386	492	994	2,087	1,344	2,364	2,784	550	573
$15,000 TO $17,499	1,501	656	924	1,972	1,663	2,406	2,838	587	590
$17,500 TO $19,999	1,549	614	972	1,985	1,296	1,938	2,512	405	474
$20,000 TO $22,499	1,604	443	941	1,905	1,212	1,951	2,593	528	326
$22,500 TO $24,999	1,280	373	767	1,432	995	1,080	1,979	322	269
$25,000 TO $27,499	1,410	390	857	1,290	847	1,069	2,042	318	282
$27,500 TO $29,999	880	314	382	1,040	633	715	1,418	258	226
$30,000 TO $34,999	1,668	385	722	1,386	1,037	1,122	2,543	336	237
$35,000 TO $39,999	941	342	520	859	552	584	1,656	177	164
$40,000 TO $49,999	1,127	253	397	710	467	644	1,557	209	127
$50,000 TO $74,999	535	112	194	317	301	288	785	91	55
$75,000 OR MORE	72	33	17	128	38	117	191	56	22
FAMILY INCOME IN 1979									
FAMILIES	15,014	5,095	8,776	20,173	16,203	22,528	31,805	7,227	6,834
LESS THAN $2,500	159	163	275	954	1,102	1,953	2,420	742	657
$2,500 TO $4,999	360	231	353	1,749	1,979	2,554	2,834	1,188	1,370
$5,000 TO $7,499	669	249	474	1,582	1,254	2,092	2,223	791	780
$7,500 TO $9,999	830	367	695	1,602	1,379	2,088	2,232	701	699
$10,000 TO $12,499	962	369	746	1,860	1,555	2,241	2,659	519	591
$12,500 TO $14,999	933	340	602	1,578	1,061	1,774	2,095	454	489
$15,000 TO $17,499	1,112	501	749	1,555	1,373	1,929	2,298	494	423
$17,500 TO $19,999	1,289	506	751	1,521	1,135	1,527	2,005	349	367
$20,000 TO $22,499	1,328	354	789	1,528	1,023	1,647	2,160	450	264
$22,500 TO $24,999	1,167	324	635	1,289	891	925	1,728	257	215
$25,000 TO $27,499	1,285	351	689	1,090	759	899	1,733	269	233
$27,500 TO $29,999	848	307	346	920	519	597	1,392	235	207
$30,000 TO $34,999	1,583	348	675	1,208	909	921	2,212	299	221
$35,000 TO $39,999	844	327	476	783	546	481	1,526	158	159
$40,000 TO $49,999	1,057	250	364	607	440	576	1,393	196	94
$50,000 TO $74,999	523	87	140	252	249	236	720	82	50
$75,000 OR MORE	65	21	17	95	29	88	175	43	15
POVERTY STATUS IN 1979									
PERSONS FOR WHOM POVERTY STATUS IS DETERMINED									
INCOME IN 1979 ABOVE POVERTY LEVEL									
TOTAL	49,876	17,164	29,567	66,695	50,522	66,140	103,976	20,392	17,887
WHITE	43,675	14,724	25,954	48,719	21,573	39,032	26,031	188	34
BLACK	0	0	19	1,308	16,315	5,189	71,739	14,599	11,512
AMERICAN INDIAN, ESKIMO AND ALEUT	34	0	0	262	0	186	52	0	0
ASIAN AND PACIFIC ISLANDER	444	582	964	1,381	1,023	1,138	2,315	0	0
INCOME IN 1979 BELOW POVERTY LEVEL									
TOTAL	3,175	2,280	3,919	17,531	19,919	29,866	32,736	13,256	13,523
WHITE	2,740	1,671	3,318	10,739	5,880	13,974	2,710	66	18
BLACK	0	0	31	763	8,696	3,396	29,133	9,254	9,434
AMERICAN INDIAN, ESKIMO AND ALEUT	0	0	0	111	0	116	21	0	0
ASIAN AND PACIFIC ISLANDER	83	0	19	62	42	100	55	0	0
PERSONS FOR WHOM POVERTY STATUS IS DETERMINED	53,051	19,444	33,486	84,226	70,441	96,006	136,712	33,648	31,410
INCOME IN 1979 ABOVE POVERTY LEVEL	49,876	17,164	29,567	66,695	50,522	66,140	103,976	20,392	17,887
UNDER 55 YEARS	33,110	13,000	21,714	53,983	42,686	53,014	89,461	17,688	14,616
55 TO 59 YEARS	3,763	925	1,962	3,393	2,173	3,631	4,051	822	1,013
60 TO 64 YEARS	3,974	1,047	1,795	2,979	1,989	3,278	3,573	696	710
65 YEARS AND OVER	9,029	2,192	4,096	6,340	3,674	6,217	6,891	1,186	1,548
INCOME IN 1979 BELOW POVERTY LEVEL	3,175	2,280	3,919	17,531	19,919	29,866	32,736	13,256	13,523
UNDER 55 YEARS	1,958	1,823	3,191	15,292	18,289	26,385	30,049	12,032	11,681
55 TO 59 YEARS	188	72	165	554	433	784	688	450	452
60 TO 64 YEARS	268	113	121	518	351	750	755	282	472
65 YEARS AND OVER	761	272	442	1,167	846	1,947	1,244	492	918
FAMILIES WITH ONE OR MORE RELATED CHILDREN	5,951	2,651	4,179	12,292	11,516	14,641	22,002	5,472	4,762
INCOME IN 1979 ABOVE POVERTY LEVEL WITH RELATED CHILDREN:	5,539	2,256	3,650	9,080	7,842	9,394	15,841	3,115	2,414
UNDER 5 YEARS AND 5 TO 17 YEARS	974	498	663	2,278	1,883	2,505	4,040	843	660
UNDER 5 YEARS ONLY	1,153	414	873	2,228	1,536	2,225	2,696	426	383
5 TO 17 YEARS ONLY	3,412	1,344	2,114	4,574	4,423	4,664	9,105	1,846	1,371
INCOME IN 1979 BELOW POVERTY LEVEL WITH RELATED CHILDREN:	412	395	529	3,212	3,674	5,247	6,161	2,357	2,348
UNDER 5 YEARS AND 5 TO 17 YEARS	96	148	215	1,017	1,249	1,790	2,178	944	991
UNDER 5 YEARS ONLY	102	80	92	803	767	1,173	1,127	371	299
5 TO 17 YEARS ONLY	214	167	222	1,392	1,658	2,284	2,856	1,042	1,058

399

TABLE III-5 INCOME AND POVERTY STATUS OF THE POPULATION,
BY COMMUNITY AREA: CITY OF CHICAGO, 1980

	28	29	30	31	32	33	34	35	36
INCOME TYPE IN 1979									
HOUSEHOLDS WITH INCOME									
EARNINGS	9,942	11,007	15,296	10,237	2,547	1,322	3,092	8,518	2,016
WAGE OR SALARY INCOME	9,799	10,899	15,083	10,108	2,321	1,307	3,036	8,460	2,000
NONFARM SELF-EMPLOYMENT INCOME	414	356	571	455	408	22	263	319	30
FARM SELF-EMPLOYMENT INCOME	60	91	65	5	64	0	0	21	0
INTEREST, DIVIDEND, OR NET RENTAL INCOME	2,430	1,729	4,526	2,987	1,583	168	1,531	2,911	174
SOCIAL SECURITY INCOME	4,256	3,490	3,796	2,718	1,200	605	1,566	3,304	948
PUBLIC ASSISTANCE INCOME	7,585	6,640	2,380	1,526	303	937	825	4,370	3,023
ALL OTHER INCOME	3,025	3,264	3,621	2,339	711	477	772	2,478	765
HOUSEHOLD INCOME IN 1979									
HOUSEHOLDS	18,630	17,266	19,197	13,034	3,853	2,419	4,505	14,319	4,894
LESS THAN $2,500	3,190	2,115	1,392	1,370	346	241	484	1,935	971
$2,500 TO $4,999	5,189	3,492	1,951	1,454	584	822	977	3,230	1,685
$5,000 TO $7,499	2,169	1,975	1,693	1,277	533	338	424	1,389	575
$7,500 TO $9,999	1,499	1,647	1,624	1,138	299	185	327	1,291	450
$10,000 TO $12,499	1,230	1,494	1,691	1,313	243	154	370	968	456
$12,500 TO $14,999	924	1,118	1,324	992	201	195	189	810	172
$15,000 TO $17,499	850	1,161	1,878	1,170	109	134	273	763	110
$17,500 TO $19,999	682	720	1,346	799	181	51	217	894	101
$20,000 TO $22,499	567	693	1,358	745	173	63	241	704	79
$22,500 TO $24,999	404	658	996	461	147	80	239	425	43
$25,000 TO $27,499	382	472	1,051	521	143	31	134	389	76
$27,500 TO $29,999	313	384	549	398	98	35	150	312	9
$30,000 TO $34,999	355	546	893	560	174	59	188	403	64
$35,000 TO $39,999	342	307	609	285	130	20	106	206	25
$40,000 TO $49,999	255	287	501	265	133	11	86	275	46
$50,000 TO $74,999	196	197	253	253	270	0	80	237	19
$75,000 OR MORE	83	0	88	33	89	0	20	88	13
FAMILY INCOME IN 1979									
FAMILIES	11,902	13,569	15,451	9,966	1,039	1,542	3,016	7,616	3,473
LESS THAN $2,500	1,227	1,327	891	856	0	146	163	837	445
$2,500 TO $4,999	2,942	2,580	1,102	690	49	411	375	1,788	1,183
$5,000 TO $7,499	1,766	1,687	1,248	928	101	230	282	863	489
$7,500 TO $9,999	1,157	1,239	1,258	795	62	115	234	742	401
$10,000 TO $12,499	887	1,173	1,261	1,091	51	88	286	502	320
$12,500 TO $14,999	660	923	1,069	784	54	134	151	368	139
$15,000 TO $17,499	564	923	1,590	928	6	121	201	345	90
$17,500 TO $19,999	523	669	1,294	757	40	44	203	391	96
$20,000 TO $22,499	413	564	1,226	653	80	33	191	225	75
$22,500 TO $24,999	268	562	883	402	45	73	216	222	28
$25,000 TO $27,499	279	460	960	507	44	22	121	263	69
$27,500 TO $29,999	237	333	511	331	51	35	140	208	9
$30,000 TO $34,999	238	479	853	487	83	59	179	206	61
$35,000 TO $39,999	339	258	531	266	72	20	97	176	5
$40,000 TO $49,999	174	232	468	253	57	11	86	193	39
$50,000 TO $74,999	181	160	231	205	207	0	72	214	11
$75,000 OR MORE	47	0	75	33	37	0	19	73	13
POVERTY STATUS IN 1979									
PERSONS FOR WHOM POVERTY STATUS IS DETERMINED									
INCOME IN 1979 ABOVE POVERTY LEVEL									
TOTAL	27,132	34,690	55,117	32,849	4,650	4,082	9,056	18,489	5,735
WHITE	6,368	433	29,269	15,628	3,795	164	3,436	1,778	35
BLACK	13,839	30,387	1,293	109	674	3,746	1,664	13,997	5,685
AMERICAN INDIAN, ESKIMO AND ALEUT	0	30	260	63	0	0	0	0	0
ASIAN AND PACIFIC ISLANDER	1,190	53	71	56	0	49	3,746	181	0
INCOME IN 1979 BELOW POVERTY LEVEL									
TOTAL	29,299	26,165	15,212	11,814	1,198	3,135	3,404	14,618	10,933
WHITE	2,189	228	6,129	4,353	664	100	637	216	14
BLACK	20,772	23,164	1,227	149	424	3,013	1,399	12,656	10,914
AMERICAN INDIAN, ESKIMO AND ALEUT	0	0	97	23	0	0	0	0	0
ASIAN AND PACIFIC ISLANDER	181	9	0	77	76	0	1,166	92	0
PERSONS FOR WHOM POVERTY STATUS IS DETERMINED	56,431	60,855	70,329	44,663	5,848	7,217	12,460	33,107	16,668
INCOME IN 1979 ABOVE POVERTY LEVEL	27,132	34,690	55,117	32,849	4,650	4,082	9,056	18,489	5,735
UNDER 55 YEARS	22,197	28,570	47,657	27,903	2,579	3,526	6,845	13,886	4,869
55 TO 59 YEARS	1,360	1,764	1,968	1,328	464	130	516	1,131	232
60 TO 64 YEARS	860	1,513	1,807	1,307	429	107	446	1,030	156
65 YEARS AND OVER	2,715	2,843	3,685	2,311	1,178	319	1,249	2,442	478
INCOME IN 1979 BELOW POVERTY LEVEL	29,299	26,165	15,212	11,814	1,198	3,135	3,404	14,618	10,933
UNDER 55 YEARS	25,515	23,761	13,828	10,511	689	2,741	2,590	12,472	9,833
55 TO 59 YEARS	1,073	676	242	280	140	42	82	460	229
60 TO 64 YEARS	761	641	200	260	151	22	116	412	301
65 YEARS AND OVER	1,950	1,087	942	763	218	330	616	1,274	570
FAMILIES WITH ONE OR MORE RELATED CHILDREN	8,812	9,778	11,010	6,799	167	1,321	1,590	5,014	2,905
INCOME IN 1979 ABOVE POVERTY LEVEL	3,589	5,017	8,367	4,804	134	666	1,109	2,156	959
WITH RELATED CHILDREN:									
UNDER 5 YEARS AND 5 TO 17 YEARS	1,077	1,214	2,523	1,403	16	140	119	380	217
UNDER 5 YEARS ONLY	608	670	2,356	1,255	23	98	219	424	131
5 TO 17 YEARS ONLY	1,904	3,133	3,488	2,146	95	428	771	1,352	611
INCOME IN 1979 BELOW POVERTY LEVEL	5,223	4,761	2,643	1,995	33	655	481	2,858	1,946
WITH RELATED CHILDREN:									
UNDER 5 YEARS AND 5 TO 17 YEARS	2,082	1,765	865	830	8	163	93	869	771
UNDER 5 YEARS ONLY	821	829	762	403	25	120	117	551	264
5 TO 17 YEARS ONLY	2,320	2,167	1,016	762	0	372	271	1,438	911

	37	38	39	40	41	42	43	44	45
INCOME TYPE IN 1979									
HOUSEHOLDS WITH INCOME									
EARNINGS	994	8,011	7,171	5,535	12,044	7,860	25,089	13,380	3,802
WAGE OR SALARY INCOME	973	7,858	6,978	5,439	11,644	7,763	24,738	13,171	3,747
NONFARM SELF-EMPLOYMENT INCOME	44	256	597	262	1,401	225	1,095	747	189
FARM SELF-EMPLOYMENT INCOME	0	20	65	36	99	16	104	21	7
INTEREST, DIVIDEND, OR NET RENTAL INCOME	213	987	2,661	792	6,646	1,570	4,734	3,161	877
SOCIAL SECURITY INCOME	793	5,977	2,198	3,157	2,449	3,943	4,919	4,027	941
PUBLIC ASSISTANCE INCOME	685	8,653	2,035	4,824	1,040	4,785	5,957	2,069	565
ALL OTHER INCOME	318	3,341	1,649	2,239	2,578	2,751	5,668	3,407	928
HOUSEHOLD INCOME IN 1979									
HOUSEHOLDS	1,930	18,601	10,006	11,028	14,545	14,138	31,393	16,361	4,276
LESS THAN $2,500	246	3,534	1,159	1,906	926	2,313	2,562	1,023	201
$2,500 TO $4,999	424	5,337	1,314	2,511	1,469	3,257	3,804	1,486	229
$5,000 TO $7,499	268	2,527	1,060	1,724	1,254	1,485	2,505	1,178	199
$7,500 TO $9,999	258	1,827	702	1,074	1,259	1,341	2,567	1,390	271
$10,000 TO $12,499	146	1,364	867	930	1,257	1,180	3,297	1,594	276
$12,500 TO $14,999	88	903	571	569	1,043	870	2,098	1,220	189
$15,000 TO $17,499	109	692	640	428	1,084	825	2,404	1,185	362
$17,500 TO $19,999	86	609	605	357	851	530	2,232	1,095	276
$20,000 TO $22,499	56	499	598	352	946	550	1,924	1,092	265
$22,500 TO $24,999	34	297	371	291	584	411	1,603	954	235
$25,000 TO $27,499	49	190	359	194	541	374	1,161	701	226
$27,500 TO $29,999	54	126	245	176	337	196	967	590	166
$30,000 TO $34,999	48	286	391	214	659	318	1,461	998	432
$35,000 TO $39,999	13	173	306	119	481	195	1,009	651	259
$40,000 TO $49,999	32	146	261	120	745	167	1,006	682	447
$50,000 TO $74,999	19	69	301	44	790	75	623	441	204
$75,000 OR MORE	0	22	256	19	319	51	170	81	39
FAMILY INCOME IN 1979									
FAMILIES	1,203	10,589	5,117	6,551	6,520	8,008	18,873	10,853	3,510
LESS THAN $2,500	81	1,238	373	721	211	708	1,184	469	118
$2,500 TO $4,999	170	2,666	454	1,256	323	1,439	2,046	704	148
$5,000 TO $7,499	177	1,787	562	1,108	323	930	1,279	740	140
$7,500 TO $9,999	131	1,159	289	724	411	767	1,609	829	173
$10,000 TO $12,499	133	824	464	663	511	733	1,713	875	209
$12,500 TO $14,999	73	680	308	417	358	622	1,096	734	128
$15,000 TO $17,499	72	472	238	233	440	544	1,314	731	276
$17,500 TO $19,999	86	373	356	245	315	373	1,145	664	212
$20,000 TO $22,499	42	379	273	268	435	438	1,198	784	215
$22,500 TO $24,999	34	250	189	209	309	325	1,110	724	199
$25,000 TO $27,499	44	137	249	138	298	266	837	573	203
$27,500 TO $29,999	62	107	173	142	237	202	744	486	171
$30,000 TO $34,999	42	249	267	178	470	287	1,199	888	418
$35,000 TO $39,999	13	133	211	95	323	143	846	597	247
$40,000 TO $49,999	30	91	210	100	574	133	869	605	410
$50,000 TO $74,999	13	44	270	35	708	58	546	388	204
$75,000 OR MORE	0	0	231	19	274	40	138	62	39
POVERTY STATUS IN 1979									
PERSONS FOR WHOM POVERTY STATUS IS DETERMINED									
INCOME IN 1979 ABOVE POVERTY LEVEL									
TOTAL	3,341	23,170	15,941	16,125	24,012	21,457	59,184	34,778	12,236
WHITE	0	0	3,926	26	13,229	242	2,459	187	258
BLACK	2,286	12,587	11,677	10,477	9,279	19,313	56,052	34,251	11,744
AMERICAN INDIAN, ESKIMO AND ALEUT	0	0	0	47	0	0	69	0	0
ASIAN AND PACIFIC ISLANDER	0	0	210	0	891	47	93	106	31
INCOME IN 1979 BELOW POVERTY LEVEL									
TOTAL	2,475	29,880	5,646	15,670	4,700	13,743	17,981	5,787	1,494
WHITE	0	0	510	18	2,170	138	295	39	8
BLACK	1,741	14,449	5,041	11,914	2,169	12,859	17,499	5,713	1,452
AMERICAN INDIAN, ESKIMO AND ALEUT	0	0	0	16	0	0	31	0	0
ASIAN AND PACIFIC ISLANDER	0	0	12	0	206	57	17	7	14
PERSONS FOR WHOM POVERTY STATUS IS DETERMINED	5,816	53,050	21,587	31,795	28,712	35,200	77,165	40,565	13,730
INCOME IN 1979 ABOVE POVERTY LEVEL	3,341	23,170	15,941	16,125	24,012	21,457	59,184	34,778	12,236
UNDER 55 YEARS	2,375	16,236	12,143	11,493	18,856	15,323	50,286	25,293	10,325
55 TO 59 YEARS	163	1,280	921	1,084	1,128	1,371	2,868	2,936	706
60 TO 64 YEARS	143	1,381	745	943	1,192	1,424	2,064	2,306	444
65 YEARS AND OVER	660	4,273	2,132	2,605	2,836	3,339	3,966	4,243	761
INCOME IN 1979 BELOW POVERTY LEVEL	2,475	29,880	5,646	15,670	4,700	13,743	17,981	5,787	1,494
UNDER 55 YEARS	2,044	25,114	4,579	13,288	4,005	11,018	15,817	4,604	1,346
55 TO 59 YEARS	55	1,057	234	618	94	583	489	318	28
60 TO 64 YEARS	52	927	214	541	166	620	628	241	37
65 YEARS AND OVER	324	2,782	619	1,223	435	1,522	1,047	624	83
FAMILIES WITH ONE OR MORE RELATED CHILDREN	719	7,087	2,799	4,375	3,126	4,861	12,325	5,209	2,271
INCOME IN 1979 ABOVE POVERTY LEVEL WITH RELATED CHILDREN:	383	2,521	1,989	1,933	2,683	2,693	8,971	4,215	1,967
UNDER 5 YEARS AND 5 TO 17 YEARS	80	625	287	431	383	680	1,654	706	362
UNDER 5 YEARS ONLY	21	347	519	398	689	499	1,974	821	217
5 TO 17 YEARS ONLY	282	1,549	1,183	1,104	1,611	1,514	5,343	2,688	1,388
INCOME IN 1979 BELOW POVERTY LEVEL WITH RELATED CHILDREN:	336	4,566	810	2,442	443	2,168	3,354	994	304
UNDER 5 YEARS AND 5 TO 17 YEARS	143	1,804	315	985	124	719	1,041	238	89
UNDER 5 YEARS ONLY	32	596	156	278	127	414	803	184	43
5 TO 17 YEARS ONLY	161	2,166	339	1,179	192	1,035	1,510	572	172

	46	47	48	49	50	51	52	53	54
INCOME TYPE IN 1979									
HOUSEHOLDS WITH INCOME									
EARNINGS	11,566	916	5,612	15,300	2,816	4,806	5,898	10,216	2,101
WAGE OR SALARY INCOME	11,492	908	5,558	15,132	2,780	4,719	5,833	10,141	2,066
NONFARM SELF-EMPLOYMENT INCOME	492	21	263	648	114	230	287	448	86
FARM SELF-EMPLOYMENT INCOME	35	12	15	43	0	19	31	45	7
INTEREST, DIVIDEND, OR NET RENTAL INCOME	3,530	191	1,696	2,963	786	1,280	3,739	1,602	202
SOCIAL SECURITY INCOME	3,264	226	1,114	3,777	734	1,128	2,475	1,842	618
PUBLIC ASSISTANCE INCOME	2,027	191	584	3,250	459	648	384	1,843	1,717
ALL OTHER INCOME	3,259	249	1,289	4,178	794	1,443	2,265	2,490	716
HOUSEHOLD INCOME IN 1979									
HOUSEHOLDS	14,379	1,015	6,167	18,058	3,384	5,669	7,436	11,732	3,393
LESS THAN $2,500	905	12	208	999	158	297	207	591	384
$2,500 TO $4,999	1,508	94	208	1,362	306	472	495	780	693
$5,000 TO $7,499	899	35	232	1,219	185	308	447	650	413
$7,500 TO $9,999	809	92	288	1,140	259	242	552	616	307
$10,000 TO $12,499	1,048	64	289	1,392	244	459	439	842	260
$12,500 TO $14,999	911	88	353	1,151	142	285	351	733	224
$15,000 TO $17,499	1,135	70	384	1,239	225	407	345	817	189
$17,500 TO $19,999	941	54	336	1,267	300	416	420	803	149
$20,000 TO $22,499	1,217	114	397	1,188	233	448	702	969	181
$22,500 TO $24,999	891	44	424	1,031	215	407	511	747	139
$25,000 TO $27,499	689	58	406	1,002	150	317	418	778	85
$27,500 TO $29,999	693	108	342	714	189	239	377	629	137
$30,000 TO $34,999	1,000	82	600	1,331	302	502	790	1,142	99
$35,000 TO $39,999	661	46	576	1,108	237	327	445	701	42
$40,000 TO $49,999	642	48	584	1,155	105	288	503	556	55
$50,000 TO $74,999	331	0	449	657	107	216	398	302	31
$75,000 OR MORE	99	6	91	103	27	39	36	76	5
FAMILY INCOME IN 1979									
FAMILIES	10,838	843	5,305	14,879	2,504	4,715	5,760	10,155	3,038
LESS THAN $2,500	463	12	125	663	87	139	95	413	310
$2,500 TO $4,999	770	41	99	887	183	250	142	536	644
$5,000 TO $7,499	599	35	200	828	86	243	201	523	367
$7,500 TO $9,999	541	68	188	863	129	201	264	466	256
$10,000 TO $12,499	680	57	248	1,085	172	397	324	673	218
$12,500 TO $14,999	750	59	310	901	109	218	286	582	219
$15,000 TO $17,499	890	84	325	1,094	188	317	255	728	182
$17,500 TO $19,999	720	42	256	1,042	182	376	328	713	149
$20,000 TO $22,499	990	94	347	1,013	209	368	587	889	154
$22,500 TO $24,999	752	46	330	926	206	356	478	693	123
$25,000 TO $27,499	598	58	362	877	128	310	362	691	85
$27,500 TO $29,999	598	87	345	658	165	233	349	621	109
$30,000 TO $34,999	888	74	555	1,205	248	460	748	1,093	106
$35,000 TO $39,999	588	37	589	1,047	200	304	443	649	42
$40,000 TO $49,999	619	43	530	1,093	88	296	478	519	38
$50,000 TO $74,999	305	0	418	616	102	208	384	300	31
$75,000 OR MORE	87	6	78	81	22	39	36	66	5
POVERTY STATUS IN 1979									
PERSONS FOR WHOM POVERTY STATUS IS DETERMINED									
INCOME IN 1979 ABOVE POVERTY LEVEL									
TOTAL	38,423	3,213	19,064	52,389	8,795	16,736	19,924	37,954	7,125
WHITE	12,105	353	1,306	803	1,921	5,269	15,295	2,234	232
BLACK	18,200	2,792	15,010	49,882	6,588	9,351	0	28,921	6,765
AMERICAN INDIAN, ESKIMO AND ALEUT	59	0	0	0	0	0	0	0	0
ASIAN AND PACIFIC ISLANDER	0	0	70	27	0	46	32	0	0
INCOME IN 1979 BELOW POVERTY LEVEL									
TOTAL	7,886	725	1,383	11,329	1,484	2,591	1,353	6,794	6,388
WHITE	1,781	30	40	114	169	929	1,107	351	85
BLACK	3,981	695	1,063	11,081	1,243	1,191	0	5,193	6,298
AMERICAN INDIAN, ESKIMO AND ALEUT	60	0	0	0	0	0	0	0	0
ASIAN AND PACIFIC ISLANDER	0	0	30	12	0	0	0	0	0
PERSONS FOR WHOM POVERTY STATUS IS DETERMINED	46,309	3,938	20,447	63,718	10,279	19,327	21,277	44,748	13,513
INCOME IN 1979 ABOVE POVERTY LEVEL	38,423	3,213	19,064	52,389	8,795	16,736	19,924	37,954	7,125
UNDER 55 YEARS	32,647	2,851	16,355	44,375	7,359	14,339	14,394	34,491	6,468
55 TO 59 YEARS	1,650	118	985	2,687	449	715	1,604	1,321	225
60 TO 64 YEARS	1,407	66	717	2,041	322	577	1,358	890	185
65 YEARS AND OVER	2,719	178	1,007	3,286	665	1,105	2,568	1,252	247
INCOME IN 1979 BELOW POVERTY LEVEL	7,886	725	1,383	11,329	1,484	2,591	1,353	6,794	6,388
UNDER 55 YEARS	6,714	690	1,191	10,044	1,266	2,327	940	6,249	6,075
55 TO 59 YEARS	241	14	66	314	63	59	104	116	116
60 TO 64 YEARS	205	0	65	300	36	46	65	147	85
65 YEARS AND OVER	726	21	61	671	119	159	244	282	112
FAMILIES WITH ONE OR MORE RELATED CHILDREN	7,073	641	3,259	9,859	1,608	3,162	2,606	7,693	2,574
INCOME IN 1979 ABOVE POVERTY LEVEL	5,735	514	3,026	7,909	1,339	2,708	2,417	6,497	1,314
WITH RELATED CHILDREN:									
UNDER 5 YEARS AND 5 TO 17 YEARS	1,462	147	571	1,755	310	556	365	1,915	324
UNDER 5 YEARS ONLY	1,117	92	384	905	146	352	441	805	154
5 TO 17 YEARS ONLY	3,156	275	2,071	5,249	883	1,800	1,611	3,777	836
INCOME IN 1979 BELOW POVERTY LEVEL	1,338	127	233	1,950	269	454	189	1,196	1,260
WITH RELATED CHILDREN:									
UNDER 5 YEARS AND 5 TO 17 YEARS	329	43	43	638	78	177	13	475	517
UNDER 5 YEARS ONLY	305	10	31	185	35	66	46	163	124
5 TO 17 YEARS ONLY	704	74	159	1,127	156	211	130	558	619

	55	56	57	58	59	60	61	62	63
INCOME TYPE IN 1979									
HOUSEHOLDS WITH INCOME									
EARNINGS	3,371	10,269	2,983	9,166	3,638	8,718	12,691	3,673	6,908
WAGE OR SALARY INCOME	3,292	10,158	2,922	8,991	3,569	8,546	12,509	3,618	6,739
NONFARM SELF-EMPLOYMENT INCOME	156	502	203	482	185	532	378	156	405
FARM SELF-EMPLOYMENT INCOME	12	72	7	33	31	39	83	37	34
INTEREST, DIVIDEND, OR NET RENTAL INCOME	1,983	6,853	2,088	5,984	1,979	4,112	4,452	2,802	4,947
SOCIAL SECURITY INCOME	1,247	4,084	1,206	4,210	1,510	3,323	4,068	1,946	3,561
PUBLIC ASSISTANCE INCOME	200	934	126	724	418	1,203	3,043	197	540
ALL OTHER INCOME	1,180	3,302	973	2,564	1,123	2,452	3,202	1,324	2,309
HOUSEHOLD INCOME IN 1979									
HOUSEHOLDS	4,157	12,624	3,689	12,214	4,810	11,377	17,100	4,833	9,340
LESS THAN $2,500	181	324	100	562	224	730	1,403	126	332
$2,500 TO $4,999	252	717	223	1,181	496	1,248	2,223	304	871
$5,000 TO $7,499	248	674	199	1,060	456	879	1,628	283	734
$7,500 TO $9,999	271	753	245	1,023	399	1,097	1,627	319	681
$10,000 TO $12,499	262	738	340	1,158	373	1,116	1,524	358	708
$12,500 TO $14,999	174	654	225	851	310	725	1,155	315	572
$15,000 TO $17,499	214	772	238	828	328	782	1,237	334	603
$17,500 TO $19,999	211	793	313	792	283	660	1,140	324	675
$20,000 TO $22,499	358	1,008	228	920	328	789	1,051	386	696
$22,500 TO $24,999	272	843	213	653	239	529	760	227	621
$25,000 TO $27,499	311	904	235	711	286	582	715	390	598
$27,500 TO $29,999	264	663	154	398	249	435	508	215	420
$30,000 TO $34,999	434	1,210	322	705	292	666	893	422	763
$35,000 TO $39,999	241	950	185	509	155	351	451	351	365
$40,000 TO $49,999	302	916	288	468	210	476	499	274	431
$50,000 TO $74,999	136	639	163	349	157	261	253	191	240
$75,000 OR MORE	26	66	18	46	25	51	33	14	30
FAMILY INCOME IN 1979									
FAMILIES	3,178	10,599	2,757	8,302	3,406	7,945	12,867	3,787	6,615
LESS THAN $2,500	67	229	40	246	98	273	724	42	155
$2,500 TO $4,999	51	310	81	250	161	505	1,222	81	113
$5,000 TO $7,499	117	342	62	449	249	493	1,135	158	361
$7,500 TO $9,999	172	476	153	527	269	630	1,092	196	342
$10,000 TO $12,499	170	460	183	647	235	653	1,158	202	438
$12,500 TO $14,999	125	461	151	585	214	515	932	264	418
$15,000 TO $17,499	143	680	173	634	254	536	998	269	461
$17,500 TO $19,999	176	725	256	657	224	613	881	292	577
$20,000 TO $22,499	271	926	222	768	226	692	928	300	593
$22,500 TO $24,999	218	793	197	550	213	447	679	211	518
$25,000 TO $27,499	290	849	212	649	254	531	688	358	523
$27,500 TO $29,999	253	655	146	365	226	425	434	199	392
$30,000 TO $34,999	443	1,196	281	673	254	589	873	409	705
$35,000 TO $39,999	227	924	171	466	155	311	440	341	335
$40,000 TO $49,999	302	879	254	468	210	431	446	260	421
$50,000 TO $74,999	136	628	157	329	144	254	221	191	233
$75,000 OR MORE	17	66	18	39	20	47	16	14	30
POVERTY STATUS IN 1979									
PERSONS FOR WHOM POVERTY STATUS IS DETERMINED									
INCOME IN 1979 ABOVE POVERTY LEVEL									
TOTAL	10,946	35,147	9,207	27,478	11,703	26,008	41,791	12,192	22,589
WHITE	10,621	27,751	7,568	25,438	11,084	22,639	26,831	10,396	21,483
BLACK	30	3,456	0	0	0	0	6,960	0	0
AMERICAN INDIAN, ESKIMO AND ALEUT	31	0	0	69	0	0	0	0	0
ASIAN AND PACIFIC ISLANDER	0	250	0	347	34	446	103	0	109
INCOME IN 1979 BELOW POVERTY LEVEL									
TOTAL	600	2,707	501	3,148	1,536	4,856	13,867	605	1,841
WHITE	600	1,022	420	2,943	1,441	4,108	6,306	567	1,612
BLACK	0	1,596	0	0	0	0	4,915	0	0
AMERICAN INDIAN, ESKIMO AND ALEUT	0	0	0	6	0	44	0	0	0
ASIAN AND PACIFIC ISLANDER	0	0	0	0	0	30	30	0	35
PERSONS FOR WHOM POVERTY STATUS IS DETERMINED	11,546	37,854	9,708	30,626	13,239	30,864	55,658	12,797	24,430
INCOME IN 1979 ABOVE POVERTY LEVEL	10,946	35,147	9,207	27,478	11,703	26,008	41,791	12,192	22,589
UNDER 55 YEARS	8,130	24,609	6,029	19,175	8,508	19,575	34,230	7,720	15,556
55 TO 59 YEARS	834	3,317	898	2,149	862	1,663	2,115	1,213	1,327
60 TO 64 YEARS	808	2,992	932	2,164	869	1,671	1,983	1,167	1,729
65 YEARS AND OVER	1,174	4,229	1,348	3,990	1,464	3,099	3,463	2,092	3,977
INCOME IN 1979 BELOW POVERTY LEVEL	600	2,707	501	3,148	1,536	4,856	13,867	605	1,841
UNDER 55 YEARS	376	2,154	297	2,096	1,225	3,876	12,201	302	1,269
55 TO 59 YEARS	53	140	57	172	78	157	447	51	87
60 TO 64 YEARS	69	167	29	208	57	283	449	41	87
65 YEARS AND OVER	102	246	118	672	176	540	770	211	398
FAMILIES WITH ONE OR MORE RELATED CHILDREN	1,495	4,470	1,070	3,523	1,700	4,122	8,158	1,270	2,731
INCOME IN 1979 ABOVE POVERTY LEVEL WITH RELATED CHILDREN:	1,419	4,022	1,010	3,120	1,419	3,317	5,774	1,206	2,504
UNDER 5 YEARS AND 5 TO 17 YEARS	264	755	159	475	226	581	1,582	171	523
UNDER 5 YEARS ONLY	209	582	251	737	337	661	1,396	247	585
5 TO 17 YEARS ONLY	946	2,685	600	1,908	856	2,075	2,796	788	1,396
INCOME IN 1979 BELOW POVERTY LEVEL WITH RELATED CHILDREN:	76	448	60	403	281	805	2,384	64	227
UNDER 5 YEARS AND 5 TO 17 YEARS	7	190	6	135	111	256	925	5	84
UNDER 5 YEARS ONLY	20	25	7	75	78	192	499	23	38
5 TO 17 YEARS ONLY	49	233	47	193	92	357	960	36	105

TABLE III-5 INCOME AND POVERTY STATUS OF THE POPULATION,
BY COMMUNITY AREA: CITY OF CHICAGO, 1980

	64	65	66	67	68	69	70	71	72
INCOME TYPE IN 1979									
HOUSEHOLDS WITH INCOME									
EARNINGS	6,914	7,083	12,964	12,098	11,041	11,854	10,986	16,710	6,185
WAGE OR SALARY INCOME	6,841	6,938	12,747	12,020	10,949	11,641	10,872	16,526	5,902
NONFARM SELF-EMPLOYMENT INCOME	343	400	775	348	234	563	658	569	928
FARM SELF-EMPLOYMENT INCOME	101	36	86	30	33	46	28	19	103
INTEREST, DIVIDEND, OR NET RENTAL INCOME	4,193	5,430	8,450	1,726	1,829	2,872	7,907	2,854	4,829
SOCIAL SECURITY INCOME	2,170	3,263	6,512	2,609	4,761	5,084	3,816	3,266	2,550
PUBLIC ASSISTANCE INCOME	309	267	1,201	5,048	7,009	4,073	341	3,292	213
ALL OTHER INCOME	1,795	2,398	4,229	3,297	3,442	3,863	3,246	3,734	1,879
HOUSEHOLD INCOME IN 1979									
HOUSEHOLDS	8,067	8,989	17,600	16,086	17,787	16,968	12,817	19,260	7,602
LESS THAN $2,500	218	232	783	1,466	2,301	1,628	199	1,024	120
$2,500 TO $4,999	373	512	1,528	2,071	3,641	2,537	464	1,328	288
$5,000 TO $7,499	388	462	1,656	1,443	1,885	1,640	354	1,173	311
$7,500 TO $9,999	394	555	1,295	1,391	1,602	1,437	523	1,260	397
$10,000 TO $12,499	432	582	1,256	1,317	1,615	1,624	609	1,608	326
$12,500 TO $14,999	500	473	1,223	1,187	1,345	996	472	1,382	397
$15,000 TO $17,499	574	662	1,264	1,134	928	1,227	723	1,231	442
$17,500 TO $19,999	564	505	1,259	1,133	793	1,070	704	1,426	383
$20,000 TO $22,499	736	590	1,503	1,101	893	1,017	1,113	1,331	610
$22,500 TO $24,999	585	535	924	772	746	774	1,008	1,106	368
$25,000 TO $27,499	607	705	956	645	497	784	1,013	953	479
$27,500 TO $29,999	459	587	781	469	359	369	759	981	344
$30,000 TO $34,999	911	751	1,038	777	465	714	1,496	1,490	842
$35,000 TO $39,999	484	572	792	531	274	429	1,115	1,083	570
$40,000 TO $49,999	455	720	786	381	270	361	1,227	1,090	657
$50,000 TO $74,999	329	491	420	218	143	310	893	710	776
$75,000 OR MORE	58	55	136	50	30	51	145	84	292
FAMILY INCOME IN 1979									
FAMILIES	6,236	6,993	11,773	13,689	13,122	11,470	11,144	15,177	5,835
LESS THAN $2,500	116	56	310	1,060	1,336	803	100	668	72
$2,500 TO $4,999	126	132	406	1,698	2,249	1,284	154	862	60
$5,000 TO $7,499	176	180	562	1,179	1,359	963	151	826	81
$7,500 TO $9,999	204	296	639	1,149	1,311	1,018	349	880	155
$10,000 TO $12,499	221	391	723	1,164	1,281	1,169	377	1,277	171
$12,500 TO $14,999	285	346	798	1,055	981	785	366	967	258
$15,000 TO $17,499	417	467	863	993	818	814	614	882	320
$17,500 TO $19,999	425	425	1,040	942	733	691	610	997	293
$20,000 TO $22,499	635	536	1,289	929	710	770	1,009	1,081	466
$22,500 TO $24,999	474	471	714	691	605	624	956	927	311
$25,000 TO $27,499	555	670	839	601	418	599	967	809	448
$27,500 TO $29,999	439	539	686	434	307	335	733	886	313
$30,000 TO $34,999	882	721	940	721	408	597	1,457	1,348	732
$35,000 TO $39,999	487	549	731	459	212	368	1,087	1,045	504
$40,000 TO $49,999	426	697	724	353	233	342	1,203	1,010	632
$50,000 TO $74,999	327	462	407	218	131	266	871	667	727
$75,000 OR MORE	41	55	102	43	30	42	140	45	292
POVERTY STATUS IN 1979									
PERSONS FOR WHOM POVERTY STATUS IS DETERMINED									
INCOME IN 1979 ABOVE POVERTY LEVEL									
TOTAL	21,524	23,786	41,669	42,053	35,317	33,286	39,167	55,711	22,488
WHITE	19,827	23,481	35,596	526	124	32	37,861	774	14,996
BLACK	0	0	3,976	36,937	31,774	26,935	820	54,576	2,638
AMERICAN INDIAN, ESKIMO AND ALEUT	0	0	0	0	0	0	34	36	0
ASIAN AND PACIFIC ISLANDER	0	0	476	0	0	0	87	30	36
INCOME IN 1979 BELOW POVERTY LEVEL									
TOTAL	1,031	953	4,869	19,671	23,268	11,670	985	8,992	781
WHITE	963	930	3,764	143	81	38	934	44	418
BLACK	0	0	829	18,202	20,649	8,588	47	8,919	234
AMERICAN INDIAN, ESKIMO AND ALEUT	0	0	0	0	0	0	0	0	0
ASIAN AND PACIFIC ISLANDER	0	0	103	0	0	0	0	0	0
PERSONS FOR WHOM POVERTY STATUS IS DETERMINED	22,555	24,739	46,538	61,724	58,585	44,956	40,152	64,703	23,269
INCOME IN 1979 ABOVE POVERTY LEVEL	21,524	23,786	41,669	42,053	35,317	33,286	39,167	55,711	22,488
UNDER 55 YEARS	16,320	15,822	29,198	37,156	28,080	23,227	28,529	48,531	16,433
55 TO 59 YEARS	1,726	2,110	2,557	1,893	2,000	2,609	3,336	2,543	1,297
60 TO 64 YEARS	1,285	2,013	2,540	1,171	1,691	2,239	2,907	1,859	1,282
65 YEARS AND OVER	2,193	3,841	7,374	1,833	3,546	5,211	4,395	2,778	3,476
INCOME IN 1979 BELOW POVERTY LEVEL	1,031	953	4,869	19,671	23,268	11,670	985	8,992	781
UNDER 55 YEARS	678	591	3,652	18,311	20,362	9,236	655	7,983	597
55 TO 59 YEARS	86	54	166	366	769	526	59	280	29
60 TO 64 YEARS	111	89	214	338	576	617	77	220	22
65 YEARS AND OVER	156	219	837	656	1,561	1,291	194	509	133
FAMILIES WITH ONE OR MORE RELATED CHILDREN	2,807	2,687	5,481	10,364	9,029	6,068	5,107	10,186	2,940
INCOME IN 1979 ABOVE POVERTY LEVEL WITH RELATED CHILDREN:	2,650	2,566	4,815	6,733	4,974	4,149	4,960	8,479	2,834
UNDER 5 YEARS AND 5 TO 17 YEARS	392	465	1,115	2,002	1,293	761	845	1,959	629
UNDER 5 YEARS ONLY	473	448	853	802	633	640	720	1,246	468
5 TO 17 YEARS ONLY	1,785	1,653	2,847	3,929	3,048	2,748	3,395	5,274	1,737
INCOME IN 1979 BELOW POVERTY LEVEL WITH RELATED CHILDREN:	157	121	666	3,631	4,055	1,919	147	1,707	106
UNDER 5 YEARS AND 5 TO 17 YEARS	5	30	253	1,538	1,610	571	29	523	36
UNDER 5 YEARS ONLY	16	13	193	450	544	470	5	324	19
5 TO 17 YEARS ONLY	136	78	220	1,643	1,901	878	113	860	51

TABLE III-5 INCOME AND POVERTY STATUS OF THE POPULATION,
BY COMMUNITY AREA: CITY OF CHICAGO, 1980

	73	74	75	76	77
INCOME TYPE IN 1979					
HOUSEHOLDS WITH INCOME					
EARNINGS	8,997	5,206	7,161	4,934	22,518
WAGE OR SALARY INCOME	8,967	5,053	6,997	4,767	21,866
NONFARM SELF-EMPLOYMENT INCOME	289	406	539	469	1,966
FARM SELF-EMPLOYMENT INCOME	18	56	29	69	109
INTEREST, DIVIDEND, OR NET RENTAL INCOME	1,743	3,929	3,246	2,953	12,719
SOCIAL SECURITY INCOME	1,666	2,447	2,517	1,022	7,868
PUBLIC ASSISTANCE INCOME	1,523	243	1,198	88	2,039
ALL OTHER INCOME	2,180	1,820	2,240	836	4,827
HOUSEHOLD INCOME IN 1979					
HOUSEHOLDS	10,114	6,684	8,792	5,467	29,249
LESS THAN $2,500	399	123	366	121	1,935
$2,500 TO $4,999	492	296	581	148	3,320
$5,000 TO $7,499	476	404	451	176	2,657
$7,500 TO $9,999	424	393	465	300	2,773
$10,000 TO $12,499	602	421	583	369	2,826
$12,500 TO $14,999	746	415	548	383	2,106
$15,000 TO $17,499	762	448	610	506	2,040
$17,500 TO $19,999	668	394	469	436	1,750
$20,000 TO $22,499	712	561	657	643	1,712
$22,500 TO $24,999	496	462	479	385	1,208
$25,000 TO $27,499	680	453	575	303	1,142
$27,500 TO $29,999	564	367	436	298	764
$30,000 TO $34,999	980	599	782	562	1,404
$35,000 TO $39,999	734	466	557	306	1,144
$40,000 TO $49,999	842	526	669	320	1,058
$50,000 TO $74,999	504	301	431	163	1,004
$75,000 OR MORE	33	55	133	48	406
FAMILY INCOME IN 1979					
FAMILIES	8,573	5,335	6,973	2,914	12,505
LESS THAN $2,500	255	42	187	24	431
$2,500 TO $4,999	374	79	313	52	717
$5,000 TO $7,499	367	182	277	54	838
$7,500 TO $9,999	336	247	336	121	778
$10,000 TO $12,499	463	273	449	156	999
$12,500 TO $14,999	563	298	404	208	836
$15,000 TO $17,499	613	319	410	179	904
$17,500 TO $19,999	480	342	349	200	794
$20,000 TO $22,499	668	491	561	303	837
$22,500 TO $24,999	454	430	406	289	723
$25,000 TO $27,499	576	436	480	182	653
$27,500 TO $29,999	535	337	423	169	476
$30,000 TO $34,999	959	554	691	360	929
$35,000 TO $39,999	670	466	528	233	861
$40,000 TO $49,999	783	502	635	227	689
$50,000 TO $74,999	450	282	397	125	754
$75,000 OR MORE	27	55	127	32	286
POVERTY STATUS IN 1979					
PERSONS FOR WHOM POVERTY STATUS IS DETERMINED					
INCOME IN 1979 ABOVE POVERTY LEVEL					
TOTAL	32,000	19,168	25,726	10,640	48,449
WHITE	547	19,003	10,106	10,169	36,108
BLACK	31,349	0	15,408	133	4,948
AMERICAN INDIAN, ESKIMO AND ALEUT	0	0	0	0	86
ASIAN AND PACIFIC ISLANDER	0	0	0	202	5,334
INCOME IN 1979 BELOW POVERTY LEVEL					
TOTAL	4,169	751	3,193	411	8,642
WHITE	100	751	397	364	5,741
BLACK	4,058	0	2,772	13	1,619
AMERICAN INDIAN, ESKIMO AND ALEUT	0	0	0	0	111
ASIAN AND PACIFIC ISLANDER	0	0	0	19	658
PERSONS FOR WHOM POVERTY STATUS IS DETERMINED	36,169	19,919	28,919	11,051	57,091
INCOME IN 1979 ABOVE POVERTY LEVEL	32,000	19,168	25,726	10,640	48,449
UNDER 55 YEARS	27,723	13,482	20,383	8,125	34,636
55 TO 59 YEARS	1,661	1,468	1,238	687	2,620
60 TO 64 YEARS	1,078	1,389	1,273	691	2,403
65 YEARS AND OVER	1,538	2,829	2,832	1,137	8,790
INCOME IN 1979 BELOW POVERTY LEVEL	4,169	751	3,193	411	8,642
UNDER 55 YEARS	3,658	322	2,544	314	6,557
55 TO 59 YEARS	179	80	166	14	404
60 TO 64 YEARS	140	67	152	29	353
65 YEARS AND OVER	192	282	331	54	1,328
FAMILIES WITH ONE OR MORE RELATED CHILDREN	5,545	2,406	3,891	960	5,257
INCOME IN 1979 ABOVE POVERTY LEVEL	4,857	2,341	3,407	931	4,262
WITH RELATED CHILDREN:					
UNDER 5 YEARS AND 5 TO 17 YEARS	1,135	376	687	138	746
UNDER 5 YEARS ONLY	543	367	494	283	1,263
5 TO 17 YEARS ONLY	3,179	1,598	2,226	510	2,253
INCOME IN 1979 BELOW POVERTY LEVEL	688	65	484	29	995
WITH RELATED CHILDREN:					
UNDER 5 YEARS AND 5 TO 17 YEARS	215	17	145	0	259
UNDER 5 YEARS ONLY	101	8	51	6	289
5 TO 17 YEARS ONLY	372	40	288	23	447

	01	02	03	04	05	06	07	08	09
TOTAL HOUSING UNITS	28,401	26,081	33,727	19,459	14,977	56,836	35,336	41,403	4,778
VACANT SEASONAL AND MIGRATORY	1	17	13	5	8	42	21	114	1
YEAR-ROUND HOUSING UNITS	28,400	26,064	33,714	19,454	14,969	56,794	35,315	41,289	4,777
TENURE AND VACANCY STATUS									
OWNER-OCCUPIED HOUSING UNITS	3,607	11,999	3,731	5,176	5,280	11,599	8,128	9,256	3,743
RENTER-OCCUPIED HOUSING UNITS	22,692	13,005	24,480	13,487	8,750	40,378	23,526	27,121	955
VACANT HOUSING UNITS	2,101	1,060	5,503	791	939	4,817	3,661	4,912	79
FOR SALE ONLY	313	317	489	45	27	721	501	718	28
FOR RENT	1,518	499	3,640	519	478	2,924	2,224	2,905	19
HELD FOR OCCASIONAL USE	29	91	53	23	52	85	112	568	5
OTHER VACANTS	241	153	1,321	204	382	1,087	824	721	27
CONDOMINIUM HOUSING UNITS									
TOTAL	1,827	3,660	3,817	624	0	9,362	5,624	12,182	473
RENTER OCCUPIED	351	289	1,038	93	0	2,580	1,369	2,932	39
VACANT FOR SALE ONLY	273	257	384	2	0	530	368	636	16
OTHER VACANTS	64	84	277	8	0	264	211	639	9
YEAR HOUSEHOLDER MOVED INTO UNIT									
OWNER-OCCUPIED HOUSING UNITS	3,607	11,999	3,731	5,176	5,280	11,599	8,128	9,256	3,743
1979 TO MARCH 1980	597	1,137	790	450	482	1,818	1,980	2,124	220
1975 TO 1978	1,122	2,677	1,486	1,031	1,044	3,526	3,136	3,880	644
1970 TO 1974	485	2,136	492	695	731	1,719	1,127	2,292	620
1960 TO 1969	845	2,942	469	1,076	1,120	2,341	754	1,576	992
1950 TO 1959	266	2,286	284	1,134	824	1,082	465	272	918
1949 OR EARLIER	292	821	210	790	1,079	1,113	666	161	349
RENTER-OCCUPIED HOUSING UNITS	22,692	13,005	24,480	13,487	8,750	40,378	23,526	27,121	955
1979 TO MARCH 1980	8,588	3,622	9,594	3,932	2,469	15,360	9,231	8,985	277
1975 TO 1978	8,107	4,463	8,371	4,569	3,022	14,121	8,840	8,754	295
1970 TO 1974	2,573	2,063	3,319	2,018	1,340	4,992	2,667	4,241	185
1960 TO 1969	2,281	1,915	2,299	1,725	1,129	3,938	1,798	2,826	110
1950 TO 1959	729	633	503	752	409	1,360	487	970	66
1949 OR EARLIER	414	309	394	491	381	607	503	287	22
BATHROOMS									
YEAR-ROUND HOUSING UNITS	28,400	26,064	33,714	19,454	14,969	56,794	35,315	41,289	4,777
NO BATHROOM OR ONLY A HALF BATH	686	404	2,853	576	445	1,692	979	1,940	43
1 COMPLETE BATHROOM	23,760	17,168	27,813	16,673	13,092	47,593	28,364	30,012	2,794
1 COMPLETE BATHROOM PLUS HALF BATH(S)	2,001	4,604	1,019	1,338	712	1,649	1,628	1,156	1,178
2 OR MORE COMPLETE BATHROOMS	1,954	3,881	2,034	872	728	5,847	4,342	8,205	763
OCCUPIED HOUSING UNITS	26,299	25,004	28,211	18,663	14,030	51,977	31,654	36,377	4,698
NO BATHROOM OR ONLY A HALF BATH	605	404	2,198	543	377	1,523	801	1,538	43
1 COMPLETE BATHROOM	21,957	16,307	23,334	15,968	12,259	43,426	25,295	26,204	2,732
1 COMPLETE BATHROOM PLUS HALF BATH(S)	1,871	4,513	892	1,289	695	1,566	1,521	1,053	1,160
2 OR MORE COMPLETE BATHROOMS	1,866	3,780	1,787	863	699	5,462	4,037	7,573	763
NUMBER OF ROOMS									
1 ROOM	2,540	186	5,908	690	165	5,930	3,570	8,019	17
2 ROOMS	3,331	607	6,144	1,521	382	7,164	4,260	6,686	43
3 ROOMS	6,037	2,946	8,364	2,955	1,362	12,226	7,084	10,118	309
4 ROOMS	7,782	5,729	5,835	4,941	4,093	12,349	7,839	7,289	810
5 ROOMS	4,877	7,188	3,955	4,823	4,487	9,484	5,911	5,045	1,665
6 OR MORE ROOMS	3,833	9,408	3,508	4,524	4,480	9,641	6,651	4,132	1,933
KITCHEN FACILITIES									
COMPLETE KITCHEN FACILITIES	27,902	25,879	31,698	19,136	14,733	55,428	34,494	38,005	4,751
NO COMPLETE KITCHEN FACILITIES	499	178	2,021	323	244	1,353	819	3,308	27
SEWAGE DISPOSAL									
PUBLIC SEWER	28,351	25,991	33,460	19,395	14,938	56,533	35,208	41,218	4,773
SEPTIC TANK OR CESSPOOL	8	28	25	37	20	38	7	24	5
OTHER MEANS	42	38	234	27	19	210	98	71	0
AIR CONDITIONING									
NONE	15,348	5,824	23,780	8,264	7,514	24,456	14,352	13,282	833
CENTRAL SYSTEM	1,279	6,887	2,597	1,530	578	7,999	9,233	15,338	1,571
1 INDIVIDUAL ROOM UNITS	7,784	6,596	4,966	6,493	4,648	14,651	8,165	6,029	1,455
2 OR MORE INDIVIDUAL ROOM UNITS	3,990	6,750	2,376	3,172	2,237	9,675	3,563	6,664	919
HEATING EQUIPMENT									
STEAM OR HOT WATER SYSTEM	23,518	16,866	25,557	13,959	6,820	35,525	16,243	18,406	1,684
CENTRAL WARM-AIR FURNACE	3,066	7,796	4,394	4,042	3,677	10,816	10,424	12,148	2,905
ELECTRIC HEAT PUMP	199	222	287	61	42	743	776	1,370	19
OTHER BUILT-IN ELECTRIC UNITS	894	552	1,624	219	132	2,695	2,373	6,298	39
FLOOR, WALL, OR PIPELESS FURNACE	336	197	912	203	344	1,097	633	1,575	131
ROOM HEATERS WITH FLUE	264	284	582	858	3,461	4,767	3,870	1,058	0
ROOM HEATERS WITHOUT FLUE	87	116	277	111	386	809	730	244	0
FIREPLACES, STOVES, OR PORTABLE ROOM HEATERS	24	8	33	6	115	232	225	147	0
NONE	13	16	53	0	0	97	39	67	0
OCCUPIED HOUSING UNITS	26,299	25,004	28,211	18,663	14,030	51,977	31,654	36,377	4,698
TELEPHONE IN HOUSING UNIT									
WITH TELEPHONE	24,532	24,835	21,483	17,758	13,045	48,226	29,824	34,441	4,659
NO TELEPHONE	1,767	169	6,728	905	985	3,751	1,830	1,927	39
OCCUPIED HOUSING UNITS WITH VEHICLE AVAILABLE									
1	12,337	13,211	10,398	9,034	6,593	21,738	15,049	12,729	2,231
2	2,615	5,561	1,867	2,712	2,096	4,312	3,176	1,556	1,243
3 OR MORE	356	1,136	361	667	605	964	556	127	594

TABLE III-6 GENERAL HOUSING CHARACTERISTICS,
BY COMMUNITY AREA: CITY OF CHICAGO, 1980

	10	11	12	13	14	15	16	17	18
TOTAL HOUSING UNITS	15,182	10,179	6,911	5,586	17,123	23,427	21,358	14,162	4,328
VACANT SEASONAL AND MIGRATORY	2	4	4	4	4	5	8	1	0
YEAR-ROUND HOUSING UNITS	15,180	10,175	6,907	5,582	17,119	23,422	21,350	14,161	4,328
TENURE AND VACANCY STATUS									
OWNER-OCCUPIED HOUSING UNITS	11,925	6,631	6,022	3,082	5,449	13,081	8,133	10,781	2,630
RENTER-OCCUPIED HOUSING UNITS	2,992	3,329	791	2,326	10,836	9,727	12,460	3,108	1,496
VACANT HOUSING UNITS	263	215	94	174	834	614	757	272	202
FOR SALE ONLY	86	31	45	9	29	74	34	54	15
FOR RENT	74	77	20	103	586	275	453	69	127
HELD FOR OCCASIONAL USE	14	14	4	8	33	54	45	21	14
OTHER VACANTS	89	93	25	54	186	211	225	128	46
CONDOMINIUM HOUSING UNITS									
TOTAL	515	278	0	124	23	337	467	118	0
RENTER OCCUPIED	66	22	0	12	3	22	28	6	0
VACANT FOR SALE ONLY	30	0	0	1	0	13	6	14	0
OTHER VACANTS	9	4	0	2	0	8	2	0	0
YEAR HOUSEHOLDER MOVED INTO UNIT									
OWNER-OCCUPIED HOUSING UNITS	11,925	6,631	6,022	3,082	5,449	13,081	8,133	10,781	2,630
1979 TO MARCH 1980	640	394	252	270	479	778	650	576	120
1975 TO 1978	2,086	1,057	1,092	690	1,373	2,490	1,610	1,940	525
1970 TO 1974	1,764	871	1,153	530	777	1,825	1,288	1,561	306
1960 TO 1969	3,207	1,604	1,557	657	1,279	2,988	1,778	2,749	655
1950 TO 1959	3,182	1,595	1,475	611	732	2,304	1,267	2,346	605
1949 OR EARLIER	1,051	1,110	493	324	809	2,696	1,540	1,609	419
RENTER-OCCUPIED HOUSING UNITS	2,992	3,329	791	2,326	10,836	9,727	12,460	3,108	1,496
1979 TO MARCH 1980	698	786	217	709	4,108	2,393	3,723	756	311
1975 TO 1978	1,100	1,211	277	734	3,898	3,227	4,218	1,090	565
1970 TO 1974	564	579	97	402	1,150	1,638	1,788	615	277
1960 TO 1969	392	513	133	304	1,040	1,530	1,461	463	202
1950 TO 1959	136	180	55	128	392	498	722	135	93
1949 OR EARLIER	97	60	12	49	248	441	548	49	48
BATHROOMS									
YEAR-ROUND HOUSING UNITS	15,180	10,175	6,907	5,582	17,119	23,422	21,350	14,161	4,328
NO BATHROOM OR ONLY A HALF BATH	152	161	13	159	613	439	773	169	78
1 COMPLETE BATHROOM	8,719	7,463	2,412	3,300	14,245	18,315	17,774	9,352	3,160
1 COMPLETE BATHROOM PLUS HALF BATH(S)	3,922	1,520	2,629	1,409	1,376	2,573	1,626	2,788	641
2 OR MORE COMPLETE BATHROOMS	2,376	1,028	1,850	718	889	2,094	1,185	1,853	449
OCCUPIED HOUSING UNITS	14,917	9,960	6,813	5,408	16,285	22,808	20,593	13,889	4,126
NO BATHROOM OR ONLY A HALF BATH	145	161	13	159	603	410	725	164	70
1 COMPLETE BATHROOM	8,516	7,272	2,359	3,140	13,486	17,769	17,101	9,160	3,020
1 COMPLETE BATHROOM PLUS HALF BATH(S)	3,894	1,506	2,620	1,402	1,344	2,561	1,611	2,749	630
2 OR MORE COMPLETE BATHROOMS	2,362	1,021	1,821	707	852	2,068	1,156	1,816	406
NUMBER OF ROOMS									
1 ROOM	73	37	15	66	412	261	515	22	28
2 ROOMS	188	99	40	110	873	547	839	121	79
3 ROOMS	930	820	225	457	2,139	2,135	2,478	1,067	524
4 ROOMS	2,362	2,274	621	938	4,189	4,694	5,541	2,838	918
5 ROOMS	5,333	3,889	1,636	1,360	4,661	8,029	6,222	5,022	1,437
6 OR MORE ROOMS	6,294	3,056	4,370	2,651	4,845	7,756	5,755	5,091	1,342
KITCHEN FACILITIES									
COMPLETE KITCHEN FACILITIES	15,073	10,047	6,890	5,526	16,880	23,156	20,868	14,080	4,309
NO COMPLETE KITCHEN FACILITIES	96	125	14	60	243	265	490	82	19
SEWAGE DISPOSAL									
PUBLIC SEWER	15,159	10,161	6,904	5,567	17,053	23,361	21,200	14,140	4,328
SEPTIC TANK OR CESSPOOL	6	6	0	12	7	33	25	6	0
OTHER MEANS	4	5	0	7	63	27	133	16	0
AIR CONDITIONING									
NONE	2,979	2,622	983	1,249	8,847	7,564	9,551	3,313	1,365
CENTRAL SYSTEM	5,974	2,075	3,937	1,822	816	2,961	1,102	3,727	723
1 INDIVIDUAL ROOM UNITS	3,704	3,492	1,072	1,336	4,855	8,035	7,037	4,385	1,364
2 OR MORE INDIVIDUAL ROOM UNITS	2,512	1,983	912	1,179	2,605	4,861	3,668	2,737	876
HEATING EQUIPMENT									
STEAM OR HOT WATER SYSTEM	4,502	3,960	1,366	2,946	13,401	13,377	13,548	4,606	2,017
CENTRAL WARM-AIR FURNACE	10,082	5,577	5,348	2,317	2,779	8,541	5,379	8,652	2,112
ELECTRIC HEAT PUMP	73	37	33	12	70	62	52	35	0
OTHER BUILT-IN ELECTRIC UNITS	200	83	38	129	124	141	271	125	32
FLOOR, WALL, OR PIPELESS FURNACE	113	188	46	50	106	258	297	279	32
ROOM HEATERS WITH FLUE	179	276	61	88	441	910	1,496	374	135
ROOM HEATERS WITHOUT FLUE	7	32	12	39	154	105	247	55	0
FIREPLACES, STOVES, OR PORTABLE ROOM HEATERS	13	12	0	0	48	22	62	31	0
NONE	0	7	0	5	0	5	6	5	0
OCCUPIED HOUSING UNITS	14,917	9,960	6,813	5,408	16,285	22,808	20,593	13,889	4,126
TELEPHONE IN HOUSING UNIT									
WITH TELEPHONE	14,838	9,767	6,780	5,325	15,043	22,334	19,130	13,658	4,035
NO TELEPHONE	79	193	33	83	1,242	474	1,463	231	91
OCCUPIED HOUSING UNITS WITH VEHICLE AVAILABLE									
1	6,717	4,881	2,880	2,729	7,763	10,518	10,052	6,433	2,060
2	4,586	2,257	2,563	1,395	3,044	5,203	3,736	4,007	973
3 OR MORE	1,599	666	820	302	720	1,361	932	1,181	242

	19	20	21	22	23	24	25	26	27
TOTAL HOUSING UNITS	22,202	7,373	13,994	32,538	23,771	36,825	44,771	9,583	10,945
VACANT SEASONAL AND MIGRATORY	19	1	8	24	25	35	89	1	12
YEAR-ROUND HOUSING UNITS	22,183	7,372	13,986	32,514	23,746	36,790	44,682	9,582	10,933
TENURE AND VACANCY STATUS									
OWNER-OCCUPIED HOUSING UNITS	11,756	3,267	4,952	8,315	7,614	6,876	16,360	2,148	1,946
RENTER-OCCUPIED HOUSING UNITS	9,327	3,786	8,270	21,162	13,782	25,246	25,257	6,992	7,825
VACANT HOUSING UNITS	1,100	319	764	3,037	2,350	4,668	3,065	442	1,162
FOR SALE ONLY	81	8	14	79	58	130	181	8	15
FOR RENT	537	164	421	1,904	1,433	2,970	1,706	276	765
HELD FOR OCCASIONAL USE	98	17	89	163	141	241	123	15	20
OTHER VACANTS	384	130	240	891	718	1,327	1,055	143	362
CONDOMINIUM HOUSING UNITS									
TOTAL	41	0	0	0	0	66	562	0	0
RENTER OCCUPIED	2	0	0	0	0	41	73	0	0
VACANT FOR SALE ONLY	12	0	0	0	0	0	49	0	0
OTHER VACANTS	0	0	0	0	0	0	22	0	0
YEAR HOUSEHOLDER MOVED INTO UNIT									
OWNER-OCCUPIED HOUSING UNITS	11,756	3,267	4,952	8,315	7,614	6,876	16,360	2,148	1,946
1979 TO MARCH 1980	765	467	490	745	803	598	1,634	34	68
1975 TO 1978	2,525	717	1,033	1,690	1,766	1,224	4,381	147	141
1970 TO 1974	1,502	483	591	1,381	1,800	910	4,498	409	207
1960 TO 1969	2,311	634	874	1,490	1,658	1,337	3,363	1,259	636
1950 TO 1959	2,128	412	731	1,288	701	1,068	1,320	223	572
1949 OR EARLIER	2,525	554	1,233	1,748	886	1,739	1,164	76	322
RENTER-OCCUPIED HOUSING UNITS	9,327	3,786	8,270	21,162	13,782	25,246	25,257	6,992	7,825
1979 TO MARCH 1980	2,068	1,203	2,309	7,416	4,566	7,087	8,088	1,964	1,780
1975 TO 1978	3,431	1,332	2,682	7,188	4,953	9,124	9,763	2,225	2,597
1970 TO 1974	1,743	501	1,201	2,914	2,077	4,159	4,812	1,459	1,572
1960 TO 1969	1,152	396	1,007	1,853	1,361	2,586	1,811	1,127	1,275
1950 TO 1959	486	161	591	873	431	1,006	406	180	422
1949 OR EARLIER	447	193	480	891	394	1,284	377	37	179
BATHROOMS									
YEAR-ROUND HOUSING UNITS	22,183	7,372	13,986	32,514	23,746	36,790	44,682	9,582	10,933
NO BATHROOM OR ONLY A HALF BATH	600	165	447	1,416	1,293	2,959	2,005	488	907
1 COMPLETE BATHROOM	18,019	6,331	12,340	28,616	20,090	31,577	34,878	8,010	8,901
1 COMPLETE BATHROOM PLUS HALF BATH(S)	2,023	385	688	1,079	1,120	973	4,328	458	493
2 OR MORE COMPLETE BATHROOMS	1,555	481	512	1,420	1,257	1,306	3,509	622	636
OCCUPIED HOUSING UNITS	21,083	7,053	13,222	29,477	21,396	32,122	41,617	9,140	9,771
NO BATHROOM OR ONLY A HALF BATH	562	162	411	1,291	1,158	2,548	1,823	470	835
1 COMPLETE BATHROOM	17,037	6,054	11,711	25,889	18,040	27,535	32,343	7,635	7,923
1 COMPLETE BATHROOM PLUS HALF BATH(S)	1,975	381	609	981	1,032	866	4,104	448	404
2 OR MORE COMPLETE BATHROOMS	1,509	456	491	1,316	1,166	1,173	3,347	587	609
NUMBER OF ROOMS									
1 ROOM	139	29	149	870	391	990	959	273	500
2 ROOMS	460	143	333	1,804	497	1,396	2,099	373	699
3 ROOMS	2,329	635	1,331	2,744	1,989	2,964	4,263	879	1,473
4 ROOMS	5,099	1,660	4,617	9,460	5,596	12,354	8,177	1,599	2,056
5 ROOMS	8,178	2,494	4,135	7,926	7,215	8,980	13,243	2,421	2,496
6 OR MORE ROOMS	5,978	2,411	3,421	9,710	8,058	10,106	15,941	4,037	3,709
KITCHEN FACILITIES									
COMPLETE KITCHEN FACILITIES	22,060	7,256	13,779	31,661	22,867	34,896	43,409	9,266	10,458
NO COMPLETE KITCHEN FACILITIES	137	106	208	870	893	1,919	1,311	312	479
SEWAGE DISPOSAL									
PUBLIC SEWER	22,163	7,315	13,924	32,254	23,415	36,240	44,280	9,494	10,740
SEPTIC TANK OR CESSPOOL	14	14	29	100	144	111	181	29	35
OTHER MEANS	20	33	34	177	201	464	259	55	162
AIR CONDITIONING									
NONE	8,163	3,400	7,150	20,834	16,241	27,658	26,833	7,873	9,331
CENTRAL SYSTEM	2,015	446	509	832	790	864	3,396	178	145
1 INDIVIDUAL ROOM UNITS	7,818	2,319	4,553	8,009	5,072	6,724	9,956	1,211	1,212
2 OR MORE INDIVIDUAL ROOM UNITS	4,201	1,197	1,775	2,856	1,657	1,569	4,535	316	249
HEATING EQUIPMENT									
STEAM OR HOT WATER SYSTEM	13,623	4,006	7,131	17,139	13,184	13,444	27,792	6,263	6,892
CENTRAL WARM-AIR FURNACE	6,196	2,000	2,715	4,715	4,661	2,747	11,482	1,362	1,564
ELECTRIC HEAT PUMP	48	21	34	131	180	159	315	73	56
OTHER BUILT-IN ELECTRIC UNITS	214	84	181	367	358	706	800	275	119
FLOOR, WALL, OR PIPELESS FURNACE	334	107	262	660	564	818	719	341	357
ROOM HEATERS WITH FLUE	1,374	994	3,019	7,612	3,603	14,711	2,448	807	1,458
ROOM HEATERS WITHOUT FLUE	350	128	487	1,412	943	3,172	874	400	380
FIREPLACES, STOVES, OR PORTABLE ROOM HEATERS	58	17	154	453	244	1,002	208	50	58
NONE	0	5	4	42	23	56	82	7	53
OCCUPIED HOUSING UNITS	21,083	7,053	13,222	29,477	21,396	32,122	41,617	9,140	9,771
TELEPHONE IN HOUSING UNIT									
WITH TELEPHONE	20,558	6,453	12,257	24,423	17,837	23,794	37,283	7,563	8,064
NO TELEPHONE	525	600	965	5,054	3,559	8,328	4,334	1,577	1,707
OCCUPIED HOUSING UNITS WITH VEHICLE AVAILABLE									
1	9,715	3,424	6,419	12,554	8,967	13,063	17,577	3,269	3,065
2	4,538	1,484	1,889	3,895	3,165	2,800	7,586	983	834
3 OR MORE	1,192	335	309	871	678	773	1,911	307	131

	28	29	30	31	32	33	34	35	36
TOTAL HOUSING UNITS	20,074	18,595	20,941	14,701	4,334	2,488	4,684	15,173	5,210
VACANT SEASONAL AND MIGRATORY	10	3	42	28	152	1	5	5	1
YEAR-ROUND HOUSING UNITS	20,064	18,592	20,899	14,673	4,182	2,487	4,679	15,168	5,209
TENURE AND VACANCY STATUS									
OWNER-OCCUPIED HOUSING UNITS	2,047	3,698	7,142	3,231	1,628	12	952	717	201
RENTER-OCCUPIED HOUSING UNITS	16,293	13,487	12,192	9,733	2,234	2,409	3,501	13,636	4,673
VACANT HOUSING UNITS	1,724	1,407	1,565	1,709	320	66	226	815	335
FOR SALE ONLY	31	17	54	32	13	1	1	86	0
FOR RENT	1,048	836	770	742	183	44	144	561	191
HELD FOR OCCASIONAL USE	64	48	82	67	2	2	10	14	19
OTHER VACANTS	581	506	659	868	122	19	71	154	125
CONDOMINIUM HOUSING UNITS									
TOTAL	215	0	50	13	1,964	0	29	133	0
RENTER OCCUPIED	106	0	40	13	288	0	6	41	0
VACANT FOR SALE ONLY	0	0	0	0	10	0	0	56	0
OTHER VACANTS	3	0	5	0	96	0	0	2	0
YEAR HOUSEHOLDER MOVED INTO UNIT									
OWNER-OCCUPIED HOUSING UNITS	2,047	3,698	7,142	3,231	1,628	12	952	717	201
1979 TO MARCH 1980	217	147	705	220	275	135	51	695	8
1975 TO 1978	324	356	1,889	613	835	306	181	1,039	12
1970 TO 1974	343	357	1,199	520	283	296	134	431	21
1960 TO 1969	472	985	1,279	695	186	127	287	578	24
1950 TO 1959	397	1,551	874	430	15	14	77	131	53
1949 OR EARLIER	457	299	1,196	752	34	6	255	219	94
RENTER-OCCUPIED HOUSING UNITS	16,293	13,487	12,192	9,733	2,234	2,409	3,501	13,636	4,673
1979 TO MARCH 1980	3,738	2,697	4,455	2,954	776	239	883	1,589	758
1975 TO 1978	5,265	4,539	4,497	3,510	743	487	766	3,459	1,474
1970 TO 1974	2,926	3,007	1,647	1,475	253	348	775	3,035	1,333
1960 TO 1969	2,908	2,204	821	964	382	389	616	1,952	844
1950 TO 1959	870	788	292	424	70	74	219	1,029	125
1949 OR EARLIER	423	255	480	407	10	0	209	196	128
BATHROOMS									
YEAR-ROUND HOUSING UNITS	20,064	18,592	20,899	14,673	4,182	2,487	4,679	15,168	5,209
NO BATHROOM OR ONLY A HALF BATH	1,926	1,182	1,467	1,309	525	158	284	921	339
1 COMPLETE BATHROOM	16,272	15,869	17,729	12,216	2,802	2,215	4,005	13,086	4,520
1 COMPLETE BATHROOM PLUS HALF BATH(S)	1,090	748	991	536	252	107	218	318	119
2 OR MORE COMPLETE BATHROOMS	777	781	716	615	684	8	177	848	223
OCCUPIED HOUSING UNITS	18,340	17,185	19,334	12,964	3,862	2,421	4,453	14,353	4,874
NO BATHROOM OR ONLY A HALF BATH	1,558	1,109	1,332	1,055	449	140	272	737	229
1 COMPLETE BATHROOM	15,013	14,629	16,388	10,862	2,560	2,166	3,800	12,561	4,306
1 COMPLETE BATHROOM PLUS HALF BATH(S)	1,011	727	927	499	240	107	204	297	119
2 OR MORE COMPLETE BATHROOMS	758	720	687	548	613	8	177	758	220
NUMBER OF ROOMS									
1 ROOM	1,764	269	199	229	1,108	94	114	1,577	113
2 ROOMS	1,634	389	901	766	473	166	398	1,607	597
3 ROOMS	3,576	1,261	1,855	1,979	1,453	766	971	3,986	1,036
4 ROOMS	5,490	4,992	9,388	5,317	586	816	1,123	4,605	1,516
5 ROOMS	4,094	4,865	4,552	2,869	353	498	990	2,116	1,115
6 OR MORE ROOMS	3,506	6,813	4,004	3,510	209	147	1,083	1,276	832
KITCHEN FACILITIES									
COMPLETE KITCHEN FACILITIES	18,398	17,961	20,183	14,078	3,209	2,414	4,518	14,636	5,083
NO COMPLETE KITCHEN FACILITIES	1,667	619	720	598	1,054	74	166	537	118
SEWAGE DISPOSAL									
PUBLIC SEWER	19,791	18,315	20,709	14,505	4,243	2,472	4,629	15,117	5,161
SEPTIC TANK OR CESSPOOL	44	93	46	52	0	0	0	0	0
OTHER MEANS	230	172	148	119	20	16	55	56	40
AIR CONDITIONING									
NONE	15,988	15,338	13,928	10,526	925	2,239	2,348	10,921	4,856
CENTRAL SYSTEM	1,271	348	784	433	2,097	42	453	536	19
1 INDIVIDUAL ROOM UNITS	2,171	2,193	4,669	2,921	566	192	1,255	2,773	265
2 OR MORE INDIVIDUAL ROOM UNITS	635	701	1,522	796	675	15	628	943	61
HEATING EQUIPMENT									
STEAM OR HOT WATER SYSTEM	10,018	11,601	4,929	3,549	2,321	863	1,616	8,433	3,009
CENTRAL WARM-AIR FURNACE	3,298	2,391	3,360	1,375	605	313	790	2,811	383
ELECTRIC HEAT PUMP	202	139	248	173	498	8	28	236	31
OTHER BUILT-IN ELECTRIC UNITS	1,788	438	744	541	434	724	290	1,313	487
FLOOR, WALL, OR PIPELESS FURNACE	1,292	500	1,107	406	282	465	247	1,459	1,040
ROOM HEATERS WITH FLUE	2,460	2,522	7,872	6,275	79	19	1,464	643	125
ROOM HEATERS WITHOUT FLUE	801	765	2,059	1,854	27	51	143	165	91
FIREPLACES, STOVES, OR PORTABLE ROOM HEATERS	152	186	558	479	17	45	71	54	30
NONE	54	38	26	24	0	0	35	59	5
OCCUPIED HOUSING UNITS	18,340	17,185	19,334	12,964	3,862	2,421	4,453	14,353	4,874
TELEPHONE IN HOUSING UNIT									
WITH TELEPHONE	15,083	14,599	15,880	10,279	3,488	2,096	4,185	13,160	4,147
NO TELEPHONE	3,257	2,586	3,454	2,685	374	325	268	1,193	727
OCCUPIED HOUSING UNITS WITH VEHICLE AVAILABLE									
1	5,140	6,136	9,143	5,978	1,502	612	1,837	5,139	1,027
2	1,233	1,968	2,673	1,426	288	95	500	846	110
3 OR MORE	245	575	722	329	63	14	78	64	22

	37	38	39	40	41	42	43	44	45
TOTAL HOUSING UNITS	2,028	20,868	11,270	12,091	15,510	15,824	34,166	17,141	4,302
VACANT SEASONAL AND MIGRATORY	5	16	14	6	17	77	4	3	0
YEAR-ROUND HOUSING UNITS	2,023	20,852	11,256	12,085	15,493	15,747	34,162	17,138	4,302

TENURE AND VACANCY STATUS

	37	38	39	40	41	42	43	44	45
OWNER-OCCUPIED HOUSING UNITS	558	1,324	2,263	631	3,688	1,985	6,064	6,474	3,065
RENTER-OCCUPIED HOUSING UNITS	1,354	17,370	7,771	10,355	10,770	12,090	25,303	9,944	1,158
VACANT HOUSING UNITS	111	2,158	1,222	1,099	1,035	1,672	2,795	720	79
FOR SALE ONLY	2	54	55	17	89	58	157	57	8
FOR RENT	57	1,223	835	710	595	1,210	1,795	507	36
HELD FOR OCCASIONAL USE	19	127	20	46	30	22	22	4	3
OTHER VACANTS	33	754	312	326	321	382	821	152	32

CONDOMINIUM HOUSING UNITS

	37	38	39	40	41	42	43	44	45
TOTAL	0	43	1,509	68	2,742	76	1,129	189	15
RENTER OCCUPIED	0	22	257	40	469	19	174	45	1
VACANT FOR SALE ONLY	0	0	24	0	63	9	94	15	0
OTHER VACANTS	0	2	38	9	72	7	103	9	0

YEAR HOUSEHOLDER MOVED INTO UNIT

	37	38	39	40	41	42	43	44	45
OWNER-OCCUPIED HOUSING UNITS	558	1,324	2,263	631	3,688	1,985	6,064	6,474	3,065
1979 TO MARCH 1980	14	327	244	57	477	118	586	219	79
1975 TO 1978	23	608	497	75	1,044	197	1,105	544	375
1970 TO 1974	89	502	557	85	741	200	1,629	765	802
1960 TO 1969	92	599	560	110	942	320	2,384	2,732	1,645
1950 TO 1959	217	402	314	71	322	588	221	2,068	108
1949 OR EARLIER	123	626	91	243	162	562	139	146	56
RENTER-OCCUPIED HOUSING UNITS	1,354	17,370	7,771	10,355	10,770	12,090	25,303	9,944	1,158
1979 TO MARCH 1980	181	2,752	2,137	1,920	4,026	2,732	6,887	2,284	304
1975 TO 1978	425	5,238	2,860	3,185	3,770	4,192	10,529	3,294	404
1970 TO 1974	405	3,192	1,506	3,322	1,412	2,242	4,755	2,163	227
1960 TO 1969	203	2,775	925	1,772	1,037	1,857	2,664	1,831	200
1950 TO 1959	110	872	289	617	390	730	304	293	0
1949 OR EARLIER	30	801	54	529	135	337	164	79	23

BATHROOMS

	37	38	39	40	41	42	43	44	45
YEAR-ROUND HOUSING UNITS	2,023	20,852	11,256	12,085	15,493	15,747	34,162	17,138	4,302
NO BATHROOM OR ONLY A HALF BATH	73	2,311	363	1,059	410	944	1,024	338	86
1 COMPLETE BATHROOM	1,760	16,888	8,278	10,400	10,946	13,404	27,265	13,078	2,441
1 COMPLETE BATHROOM PLUS HALF BATH(S)	120	466	345	150	924	695	2,204	2,184	1,023
2 OR MORE COMPLETE BATHROOMS	66	1,198	2,284	470	3,226	726	3,673	1,541	752
OCCUPIED HOUSING UNITS	1,912	18,694	10,034	10,986	14,458	14,075	31,367	16,418	4,223
NO BATHROOM OR ONLY A HALF BATH	65	2,043	268	854	361	737	944	319	76
1 COMPLETE BATHROOM	1,671	15,208	7,268	9,571	10,155	12,043	24,901	12,433	2,402
1 COMPLETE BATHROOM PLUS HALF BATH(S)	117	427	310	136	865	629	2,080	2,148	1,003
2 OR MORE COMPLETE BATHROOMS	59	1,016	2,188	425	3,077	666	3,442	1,518	742

NUMBER OF ROOMS

	37	38	39	40	41	42	43	44	45
1 ROOM	10	1,718	680	779	1,735	1,309	1,209	200	22
2 ROOMS	154	2,189	1,774	921	2,432	1,843	2,914	565	51
3 ROOMS	284	3,204	2,777	1,658	2,922	2,600	6,515	2,716	246
4 ROOMS	392	4,138	2,715	2,835	2,801	3,070	8,554	4,091	514
5 ROOMS	442	5,001	1,645	3,078	2,133	3,501	7,379	4,708	1,206
6 OR MORE ROOMS	741	4,602	1,665	2,814	3,470	3,424	7,591	4,858	2,263

KITCHEN FACILITIES

	37	38	39	40	41	42	43	44	45
COMPLETE KITCHEN FACILITIES	2,005	19,796	10,979	11,586	14,977	14,999	33,566	16,939	4,213
NO COMPLETE KITCHEN FACILITIES	14	1,067	291	493	529	770	600	202	89

SEWAGE DISPOSAL

	37	38	39	40	41	42	43	44	45
PUBLIC SEWER	1,985	20,701	11,229	11,986	15,379	15,662	33,997	17,100	4,268
SEPTIC TANK OR CESSPOOL	13	25	10	9	7	28	66	21	27
OTHER MEANS	21	137	31	84	120	79	103	20	7

AIR CONDITIONING

	37	38	39	40	41	42	43	44	45
NONE	1,667	18,909	6,702	10,938	9,080	12,895	21,892	9,332	1,812
CENTRAL SYSTEM	103	595	2,211	177	1,586	513	1,846	1,779	700
1 INDIVIDUAL ROOM UNITS	215	1,091	1,260	806	2,951	1,882	7,324	4,419	1,126
2 OR MORE INDIVIDUAL ROOM UNITS	34	268	1,097	158	1,889	479	3,104	1,611	664

HEATING EQUIPMENT

	37	38	39	40	41	42	43	44	45
STEAM OR HOT WATER SYSTEM	645	14,203	7,224	8,671	12,470	12,229	26,796	10,376	2,056
CENTRAL WARM-AIR FURNACE	613	1,416	2,234	938	1,931	1,595	4,406	5,050	1,986
ELECTRIC HEAT PUMP	17	492	263	143	252	118	265	213	5
OTHER BUILT-IN ELECTRIC UNITS	41	1,567	728	688	379	476	1,010	367	48
FLOOR, WALL, OR PIPELESS FURNACE	176	2,127	459	1,037	170	581	630	329	51
ROOM HEATERS WITH FLUE	347	669	168	442	185	524	692	601	122
ROOM HEATERS WITHOUT FLUE	97	282	117	126	104	193	263	166	34
FIREPLACES, STOVES, OR PORTABLE ROOM HEATERS	83	54	37	28	15	28	77	32	0
NONE	0	53	40	6	0	25	27	7	0
OCCUPIED HOUSING UNITS	1,912	18,694	10,034	10,986	14,458	14,075	31,367	16,418	4,223

TELEPHONE IN HOUSING UNIT

	37	38	39	40	41	42	43	44	45
WITH TELEPHONE	1,687	14,770	8,998	9,020	13,487	11,616	29,033	15,638	4,078
NO TELEPHONE	225	3,924	1,036	1,966	971	2,459	2,334	780	145

OCCUPIED HOUSING UNITS
WITH VEHICLE AVAILABLE

	37	38	39	40	41	42	43	44	45
1	644	4,065	4,129	2,904	6,742	4,593	13,585	7,734	1,994
2	148	600	1,045	423	1,352	959	4,026	2,788	1,240
3 OR MORE	14	102	139	54	215	130	652	594	293

	46	47	48	49	50	51	52	53	54
TOTAL HOUSING UNITS	15,628	1,114	6,322	18,777	3,527	5,804	7,756	12,286	3,505
VACANT SEASONAL AND MIGRATORY	12	0	1	6	2	0	2	5	0
YEAR-ROUND HOUSING UNITS	15,616	1,114	6,321	18,771	3,525	5,804	7,754	12,281	3,505
TENURE AND VACANCY STATUS									
OWNER-OCCUPIED HOUSING UNITS	6,093	722	4,754	11,678	1,886	3,969	5,243	8,399	579
RENTER-OCCUPIED HOUSING UNITS	8,378	317	1,440	6,435	1,481	1,658	2,215	3,346	2,816
VACANT HOUSING UNITS	1,145	75	127	658	158	177	296	536	110
FOR SALE ONLY	55	8	20	162	21	34	25	94	15
FOR RENT	528	18	54	240	96	58	149	175	65
HELD FOR OCCASIONAL USE	25	0	6	16	4	4	21	14	0
OTHER VACANTS	537	49	47	240	37	81	101	253	30
CONDOMINIUM HOUSING UNITS									
TOTAL	80	0	0	0	52	0	0	0	18
RENTER OCCUPIED	3	0	0	0	18	0	0	0	11
VACANT FOR SALE ONLY	1	0	0	0	0	0	0	0	0
OTHER VACANTS	0	0	0	0	0	0	0	0	0
YEAR HOUSEHOLDER MOVED INTO UNIT									
OWNER-OCCUPIED HOUSING UNITS	6,093	722	4,754	11,678	1,886	3,969	5,243	8,399	579
1979 TO MARCH 1980	385	78	187	468	79	251	273	611	20
1975 TO 1978	1,261	190	637	1,470	293	761	872	2,129	84
1970 TO 1974	1,758	290	1,847	4,261	605	1,613	832	3,765	115
1960 TO 1969	1,382	64	1,721	3,777	675	817	1,256	1,419	305
1950 TO 1959	439	31	236	1,094	84	207	987	242	24
1949 OR EARLIER	868	69	126	608	150	324	1,023	233	31
RENTER-OCCUPIED HOUSING UNITS	8,378	317	1,440	6,435	1,481	1,658	2,215	3,346	2,816
1979 TO MARCH 1980	2,150	104	321	1,576	280	319	695	948	390
1975 TO 1978	3,358	137	600	2,416	443	626	674	1,508	744
1970 TO 1974	1,646	76	354	1,543	326	362	343	676	699
1960 TO 1969	798	0	138	418	388	184	289	92	576
1950 TO 1959	229	0	0	210	18	117	105	64	317
1949 OR EARLIER	197	0	27	272	26	46	109	58	90
BATHROOMS									
YEAR-ROUND HOUSING UNITS	15,616	1,114	6,321	18,771	3,525	5,804	7,754	12,281	3,505
NO BATHROOM OR ONLY A HALF BATH	848	36	114	548	124	115	186	297	91
1 COMPLETE BATHROOM	12,108	797	3,499	12,511	2,129	4,343	5,831	8,133	2,913
1 COMPLETE BATHROOM PLUS HALF BATH(S)	1,584	171	1,736	3,297	1,059	925	947	2,538	461
2 OR MORE COMPLETE BATHROOMS	1,082	110	973	2,408	215	421	792	1,318	40
OCCUPIED HOUSING UNITS	14,471	1,039	6,194	18,113	3,367	5,627	7,458	11,745	3,395
NO BATHROOM OR ONLY A HALF BATH	708	36	102	522	119	115	179	297	89
1 COMPLETE BATHROOM	11,171	732	3,421	12,024	1,985	4,208	5,574	7,698	2,813
1 COMPLETE BATHROOM PLUS HALF BATH(S)	1,541	161	1,726	3,250	1,048	907	922	2,490	461
2 OR MORE COMPLETE BATHROOMS	1,051	110	945	2,317	215	397	783	1,260	32
NUMBER OF ROOMS									
1 ROOM	391	1	14	241	68	26	38	33	44
2 ROOMS	514	6	63	232	33	80	79	151	85
3 ROOMS	1,428	53	239	659	281	350	433	569	330
4 ROOMS	4,153	174	601	2,193	768	842	1,441	1,643	1,147
5 ROOMS	3,780	426	2,062	6,140	1,222	2,252	2,865	4,232	1,225
6 OR MORE ROOMS	5,350	454	3,342	9,106	1,153	2,254	2,898	5,653	674
KITCHEN FACILITIES									
COMPLETE KITCHEN FACILITIES	15,198	1,084	6,252	18,384	3,418	5,740	7,663	12,043	3,440
NO COMPLETE KITCHEN FACILITIES	424	30	70	380	109	64	93	243	65
SEWAGE DISPOSAL									
PUBLIC SEWER	15,354	1,067	6,270	18,542	3,462	5,750	7,741	12,142	3,381
SEPTIC TANK OR CESSPOOL	85	28	42	97	17	44	4	91	32
OTHER MEANS	183	19	10	125	48	10	11	53	92
AIR CONDITIONING									
NONE	8,733	699	2,112	9,679	1,849	2,403	2,359	6,393	2,868
CENTRAL SYSTEM	966	127	2,230	3,031	385	1,063	2,188	2,219	71
1 INDIVIDUAL ROOM UNITS	4,520	212	1,288	4,327	941	1,669	2,260	2,790	495
2 OR MORE INDIVIDUAL ROOM UNITS	1,403	76	692	1,727	352	669	949	884	71
HEATING EQUIPMENT									
STEAM OR HOT WATER SYSTEM	7,789	308	1,303	5,643	624	1,451	2,125	2,978	1,481
CENTRAL WARM-AIR FURNACE	3,890	609	4,474	10,906	2,342	3,674	4,704	7,710	1,424
ELECTRIC HEAT PUMP	108	0	33	71	28	8	36	100	27
OTHER BUILT-IN ELECTRIC UNITS	398	25	76	211	66	39	66	242	266
FLOOR, WALL, OR PIPELESS FURNACE	409	36	109	423	112	119	58	286	90
ROOM HEATERS WITH FLUE	2,145	110	255	1,136	301	390	566	811	87
ROOM HEATERS WITHOUT FLUE	684	18	72	301	37	91	147	134	89
FIREPLACES, STOVES, OR PORTABLE ROOM HEATERS	178	8	0	65	17	25	54	18	12
NONE	21	0	0	8	0	7	0	7	29
OCCUPIED HOUSING UNITS	14,471	1,039	6,194	18,113	3,367	5,627	7,458	11,745	3,395
TELEPHONE IN HOUSING UNIT									
WITH TELEPHONE	13,251	944	5,985	17,169	3,203	5,296	7,180	10,922	3,023
NO TELEPHONE	1,220	95	209	944	164	331	278	823	372
OCCUPIED HOUSING UNITS WITH VEHICLE AVAILABLE									
1	6,718	474	2,818	7,739	1,656	2,559	3,401	5,099	1,099
2	2,483	238	2,079	4,947	730	1,359	1,986	3,455	312
3 OR MORE	621	45	428	1,353	182	412	550	742	109

TABLE III-6 GENERAL HOUSING CHARACTERISTICS,
BY COMMUNITY AREA: CITY OF CHICAGO, 1980

	55	56	57	58	59	60	61	62	63
TOTAL HOUSING UNITS	4,365	12,749	3,787	12,767	5,234	12,288	18,609	4,910	9,603
VACANT SEASONAL AND MIGRATORY	1	1	1	1	2	7	6	0	0
YEAR-ROUND HOUSING UNITS	4,364	12,748	3,786	12,766	5,232	12,281	18,603	4,910	9,603

TENURE AND VACANCY STATUS

	55	56	57	58	59	60	61	62	63
OWNER-OCCUPIED HOUSING UNITS	3,192	10,119	2,395	5,937	2,376	4,447	6,546	3,913	5,791
RENTER-OCCUPIED HOUSING UNITS	935	2,500	1,315	6,256	2,491	6,889	10,464	950	3,512
VACANT HOUSING UNITS	237	129	76	573	365	945	1,593	47	300
FOR SALE ONLY	49	20	12	29	14	29	62	8	28
FOR RENT	103	56	40	182	170	375	764	18	125
HELD FOR OCCASIONAL USE	9	8	3	85	33	101	90	3	23
OTHER VACANTS	76	45	21	277	148	440	677	18	124

CONDOMINIUM HOUSING UNITS

	55	56	57	58	59	60	61	62	63
TOTAL	0	0	0	0	0	0	0	125	0
RENTER OCCUPIED	0	0	0	0	0	0	0	11	0
VACANT FOR SALE ONLY	0	0	0	0	0	0	0	0	0
OTHER VACANTS	0	0	0	0	0	0	0	0	0

YEAR HOUSEHOLDER MOVED INTO UNIT

	55	56	57	58	59	60	61	62	63
OWNER-OCCUPIED HOUSING UNITS	3,192	10,119	2,395	5,937	2,376	4,447	6,546	3,913	5,791
1979 TO MARCH 1980	279	333	90	318	145	225	623	217	403
1975 TO 1978	488	1,284	260	1,032	349	559	1,456	704	1,102
1970 TO 1974	471	1,573	303	665	273	660	1,275	421	795
1960 TO 1969	1,002	2,477	595	1,177	442	863	929	831	1,067
1950 TO 1959	497	3,620	763	1,144	378	799	692	1,278	1,104
1949 OR EARLIER	455	835	384	1,601	789	1,341	1,571	462	1,320
RENTER-OCCUPIED HOUSING UNITS	935	2,500	1,315	6,256	2,491	6,889	10,464	950	3,512
1979 TO MARCH 1980	270	565	362	1,693	650	1,877	3,458	256	1,043
1975 TO 1978	276	815	472	2,028	826	2,064	3,515	293	1,135
1970 TO 1974	83	516	151	962	313	940	1,540	173	566
1960 TO 1969	160	380	168	707	343	792	824	154	375
1950 TO 1959	78	186	86	332	170	500	551	60	202
1949 OR EARLIER	68	27	76	534	189	716	576	14	191

BATHROOMS

	55	56	57	58	59	60	61	62	63
YEAR-ROUND HOUSING UNITS	4,364	12,748	3,786	12,766	5,232	12,281	18,603	4,910	9,603
NO BATHROOM OR ONLY A HALF BATH	171	91	129	593	226	681	973	85	293
1 COMPLETE BATHROOM	3,329	9,399	2,904	11,051	4,428	10,368	15,748	3,588	7,864
1 COMPLETE BATHROOM PLUS HALF BATH(S)	578	2,014	353	588	351	601	933	746	795
2 OR MORE COMPLETE BATHROOMS	287	1,237	401	535	229	638	948	491	651
OCCUPIED HOUSING UNITS	4,127	12,619	3,710	12,193	4,867	11,336	17,010	4,863	9,303
NO BATHROOM OR ONLY A HALF BATH	108	88	129	529	172	628	828	85	281
1 COMPLETE BATHROOM	3,165	9,289	2,827	10,559	4,140	9,510	14,381	3,546	7,590
1 COMPLETE BATHROOM PLUS HALF BATH(S)	578	2,003	353	577	334	594	901	741	789
2 OR MORE COMPLETE BATHROOMS	276	1,231	401	528	221	604	900	491	643

NUMBER OF ROOMS

	55	56	57	58	59	60	61	62	63
1 ROOM	124	56	2	105	51	45	178	7	31
2 ROOMS	49	137	45	289	83	179	481	31	148
3 ROOMS	229	524	234	810	302	822	1,097	208	807
4 ROOMS	1,116	2,375	1,126	5,105	1,622	4,258	7,046	1,325	2,530
5 ROOMS	1,727	6,405	1,558	3,527	1,427	2,944	4,175	2,215	3,149
6 OR MORE ROOMS	1,119	3,251	821	2,930	1,747	4,033	5,626	1,124	2,938

KITCHEN FACILITIES

	55	56	57	58	59	60	61	62	63
COMPLETE KITCHEN FACILITIES	4,308	12,690	3,730	12,519	5,119	12,143	18,115	4,871	9,510
NO COMPLETE KITCHEN FACILITIES	57	51	57	248	115	145	487	39	93

SEWAGE DISPOSAL

	55	56	57	58	59	60	61	62	63
PUBLIC SEWER	4,328	12,727	3,747	12,729	5,223	12,214	18,348	4,910	9,575
SEPTIC TANK OR CESSPOOL	20	7	18	14	0	37	92	0	6
OTHER MEANS	17	7	22	24	11	37	162	0	22

AIR CONDITIONING

	55	56	57	58	59	60	61	62	63
NONE	1,220	2,895	1,051	5,798	2,502	5,936	12,278	1,046	4,206
CENTRAL SYSTEM	1,465	5,743	694	744	274	720	678	1,639	697
1 INDIVIDUAL ROOM UNITS	1,096	2,726	1,399	4,472	1,687	3,886	4,230	1,439	3,082
2 OR MORE INDIVIDUAL ROOM UNITS	584	1,377	643	1,753	771	1,746	1,416	786	1,618

HEATING EQUIPMENT

	55	56	57	58	59	60	61	62	63
STEAM OR HOT WATER SYSTEM	1,152	1,548	1,751	4,732	1,854	3,119	4,705	1,125	5,013
CENTRAL WARM-AIR FURNACE	2,597	10,344	1,545	2,668	1,136	2,175	3,394	3,361	3,012
ELECTRIC HEAT PUMP	101	56	19	15	6	25	146	21	22
OTHER BUILT-IN ELECTRIC UNITS	121	222	66	253	92	193	338	195	110
FLOOR, WALL, OR PIPELESS FURNACE	18	217	61	349	216	474	824	73	163
ROOM HEATERS WITH FLUE	309	281	289	4,139	1,614	5,307	7,008	135	1,057
ROOM HEATERS WITHOUT FLUE	43	49	49	401	229	816	1,643	0	189
FIREPLACES, STOVES, OR PORTABLE ROOM HEATERS	14	24	7	198	87	163	466	0	37
NONE	10	0	0	12	0	16	78	0	0
OCCUPIED HOUSING UNITS	4,127	12,619	3,710	12,193	4,867	11,336	17,010	4,863	9,303

TELEPHONE IN HOUSING UNIT

	55	56	57	58	59	60	61	62	63
WITH TELEPHONE	4,017	12,308	3,611	11,338	4,500	10,252	14,296	4,774	9,001
NO TELEPHONE	110	303	99	855	367	1,084	2,714	89	302

OCCUPIED HOUSING UNITS
WITH VEHICLE AVAILABLE

	55	56	57	58	59	60	61	62	63
1	1,912	5,472	1,929	5,631	2,151	5,431	7,445	2,623	4,277
2	1,281	3,951	795	2,110	857	1,670	2,321	1,152	1,976
3 OR MORE	328	1,217	276	553	260	354	643	293	587

TABLE III-6 GENERAL HOUSING CHARACTERISTICS,
BY COMMUNITY AREA: CITY OF CHICAGO, 1980

	64	65	66	67	68	69	70	71	72
TOTAL HOUSING UNITS	8,300	9,153	18,168	16,986	19,309	17,672	12,875	20,126	7,885
VACANT SEASONAL AND MIGRATORY	3	1	4	6	8	1	0	4	0
YEAR-ROUND HOUSING UNITS	8,297	9,152	18,164	16,980	19,301	17,671	12,875	20,122	7,885
TENURE AND VACANCY STATUS									
OWNER-OCCUPIED HOUSING UNITS	5,622	7,126	9,488	8,206	5,225	5,556	11,662	10,008	6,235
RENTER-OCCUPIED HOUSING UNITS	2,421	1,866	8,112	7,651	12,514	11,376	1,092	9,342	1,515
VACANT HOUSING UNITS	254	160	564	1,123	1,562	739	121	772	135
FOR SALE ONLY	35	34	24	115	67	34	51	58	46
FOR RENT	150	29	321	375	759	355	20	413	34
HELD FOR OCCASIONAL USE	8	14	31	14	43	16	2	35	9
OTHER VACANTS	61	83	188	619	693	334	48	266	46
CONDOMINIUM HOUSING UNITS									
TOTAL	158	309	0	0	0	0	46	90	95
RENTER OCCUPIED	9	109	0	0	0	0	4	23	20
VACANT FOR SALE ONLY	14	0	0	0	0	0	0	16	14
OTHER VACANTS	4	14	0	0	0	0	0	25	0
YEAR HOUSEHOLDER MOVED INTO UNIT									
OWNER-OCCUPIED HOUSING UNITS	5,622	7,126	9,488	8,206	5,225	5,556	11,662	10,008	6,235
1979 TO MARCH 1980	366	451	621	558	192	205	527	330	485
1975 TO 1978	1,033	1,125	2,640	1,753	366	505	2,218	1,325	1,579
1970 TO 1974	851	1,038	1,373	3,314	721	626	2,108	3,621	1,263
1960 TO 1969	1,586	1,464	1,719	2,013	2,128	1,497	2,964	4,335	1,301
1950 TO 1959	1,424	2,291	1,523	367	1,520	2,466	3,617	213	1,006
1949 OR EARLIER	362	757	1,612	201	298	257	228	184	601
RENTER-OCCUPIED HOUSING UNITS	2,421	1,866	8,112	7,651	12,514	11,376	1,092	9,342	1,515
1979 TO MARCH 1980	947	420	2,343	1,728	2,846	2,176	240	2,138	381
1975 TO 1978	814	709	2,760	2,936	4,139	3,536	316	3,649	493
1970 TO 1974	334	269	1,202	1,927	2,892	2,394	238	2,205	256
1960 TO 1969	214	295	1,175	830	1,970	1,896	207	1,242	206
1950 TO 1959	82	143	362	152	513	1,175	83	76	113
1949 OR EARLIER	30	30	270	78	154	199	8	32	66
BATHROOMS									
YEAR-ROUND HOUSING UNITS	8,297	9,152	18,164	16,980	19,301	17,671	12,875	20,122	7,885
NO BATHROOM OR ONLY A HALF BATH	135	115	403	490	978	618	46	632	14
1 COMPLETE BATHROOM	6,259	6,291	14,856	13,080	15,984	14,589	7,897	15,075	3,280
1 COMPLETE BATHROOM PLUS HALF BATH(S)	1,214	1,514	1,688	1,581	1,079	1,278	3,187	2,770	2,605
2 OR MORE COMPLETE BATHROOMS	692	1,233	1,216	1,829	1,248	1,187	1,745	1,627	1,986
OCCUPIED HOUSING UNITS	8,043	8,992	17,600	15,857	17,739	16,932	12,754	19,350	7,750
NO BATHROOM OR ONLY A HALF BATH	102	108	393	396	862	588	26	615	14
1 COMPLETE BATHROOM	6,077	6,148	14,324	12,173	14,698	13,957	7,810	14,400	3,196
1 COMPLETE BATHROOM PLUS HALF BATH(S)	1,196	1,514	1,679	1,525	1,012	1,263	3,173	2,732	2,574
2 OR MORE COMPLETE BATHROOMS	668	1,222	1,204	1,763	1,167	1,124	1,745	1,603	1,966
NUMBER OF ROOMS									
1 ROOM	109	20	180	103	307	215	13	87	32
2 ROOMS	134	93	677	212	976	600	58	490	59
3 ROOMS	837	547	2,152	858	2,070	2,112	237	1,823	401
4 ROOMS	1,573	2,048	3,526	2,419	3,635	4,177	1,590	3,551	715
5 ROOMS	3,953	3,427	5,252	5,299	4,914	5,129	5,595	5,451	1,432
6 OR MORE ROOMS	1,691	3,017	6,377	8,089	7,399	5,438	5,382	8,720	5,246
KITCHEN FACILITIES									
COMPLETE KITCHEN FACILITIES	8,159	9,074	17,996	16,569	18,654	17,381	12,815	19,807	7,835
NO COMPLETE KITCHEN FACILITIES	141	79	167	411	635	291	60	297	50
SEWAGE DISPOSAL									
PUBLIC SEWER	8,259	9,133	18,103	16,778	19,034	17,613	12,834	19,953	7,879
SEPTIC TANK OR CESSPOOL	14	14	32	103	92	27	41	65	6
OTHER MEANS	27	6	28	99	163	32	0	86	0
AIR CONDITIONING									
NONE	1,638	1,970	7,984	12,615	15,845	12,035	2,039	11,747	2,381
CENTRAL SYSTEM	3,065	2,962	1,646	803	606	779	6,851	1,581	1,849
1 INDIVIDUAL ROOM UNITS	2,498	2,362	5,768	2,808	2,285	3,668	2,237	5,134	1,736
2 OR MORE INDIVIDUAL ROOM UNITS	1,099	1,859	2,765	754	553	1,190	1,748	1,642	1,919
HEATING EQUIPMENT									
STEAM OR HOT WATER SYSTEM	1,962	2,488	11,518	7,387	10,237	12,167	1,198	12,551	3,712
CENTRAL WARM-AIR FURNACE	5,476	5,943	5,776	6,080	4,763	3,340	11,044	5,658	3,888
ELECTRIC HEAT PUMP	71	54	12	65	198	82	77	76	50
OTHER BUILT-IN ELECTRIC UNITS	547	372	142	226	515	233	304	314	141
FLOOR, WALL, OR PIPELESS FURNACE	122	112	206	633	807	655	132	366	51
ROOM HEATERS WITH FLUE	106	178	373	1,821	2,015	861	84	751	36
ROOM HEATERS WITHOUT FLUE	16	0	115	690	513	294	33	294	7
FIREPLACES, STOVES, OR PORTABLE ROOM HEATERS	0	6	21	47	204	28	3	46	0
NONE	0	0	0	31	37	12	0	48	0
OCCUPIED HOUSING UNITS	8,043	8,992	17,600	15,857	17,739	16,932	12,754	19,350	7,750
TELEPHONE IN HOUSING UNIT									
WITH TELEPHONE	7,814	8,856	16,721	13,994	15,449	15,490	12,689	18,169	7,701
NO TELEPHONE	229	136	879	1,863	2,290	1,442	65	1,181	49
OCCUPIED HOUSING UNITS WITH VEHICLE AVAILABLE									
1	3,711	4,155	7,869	6,826	6,312	7,315	5,318	8,403	3,328
2	2,516	2,482	3,632	2,501	1,975	2,272	4,901	4,622	2,691
3 OR MORE	766	879	1,019	534	425	431	1,563	1,202	868

413

	73	74	75	76	77
TOTAL HOUSING UNITS	10,245	6,813	9,121	5,740	32,626
VACANT SEASONAL AND MIGRATORY	0	1	0	3	13
YEAR-ROUND HOUSING UNITS	10,245	6,812	9,121	5,737	32,613
TENURE AND VACANCY STATUS					
OWNER-OCCUPIED HOUSING UNITS	7,749	5,711	6,671	1,830	7,579
RENTER-OCCUPIED HOUSING UNITS	2,285	994	2,195	3,672	21,723
VACANT HOUSING UNITS	211	107	255	235	3,311
FOR SALE ONLY	22	26	51	35	674
FOR RENT	103	56	102	146	1,753
HELD FOR OCCASIONAL USE	5	3	7	16	68
OTHER VACANTS	81	22	95	38	816
CONDOMINIUM HOUSING UNITS					
TOTAL	0	11	121	1,179	6,950
RENTER OCCUPIED	0	1	12	289	1,890
VACANT FOR SALE ONLY	0	0	0	35	632
OTHER VACANTS	0	0	3	54	240
YEAR HOUSEHOLDER MOVED INTO UNIT					
OWNER-OCCUPIED HOUSING UNITS	7,749	5,711	6,671	1,830	7,579
1979 TO MARCH 1980	279	298	240	243	1,306
1975 TO 1978	894	902	1,282	719	2,189
1970 TO 1974	2,251	1,014	1,539	409	1,435
1960 TO 1969	3,613	1,357	2,311	401	1,509
1950 TO 1959	609	1,523	694	59	685
1949 OR EARLIER	103	617	605	0	455
RENTER-OCCUPIED HOUSING UNITS	2,285	994	2,195	3,672	21,723
1979 TO MARCH 1980	570	279	537	1,528	8,071
1975 TO 1978	897	352	800	1,496	7,446
1970 TO 1974	586	239	486	567	2,901
1960 TO 1969	178	95	229	78	2,363
1950 TO 1959	31	18	76	0	574
1949 OR EARLIER	23	11	67	0	368
BATHROOMS					
YEAR-ROUND HOUSING UNITS	10,245	6,812	9,121	5,737	32,613
NO BATHROOM OR ONLY A HALF BATH	191	35	67	80	954
1 COMPLETE BATHROOM	5,968	4,355	4,577	3,869	26,866
1 COMPLETE BATHROOM PLUS HALF BATH(S)	2,661	1,389	2,910	1,164	1,543
2 OR MORE COMPLETE BATHROOMS	1,425	1,034	1,567	625	3,263
OCCUPIED HOUSING UNITS	10,034	6,705	8,866	5,502	29,302
NO BATHROOM OR ONLY A HALF BATH	180	35	63	80	852
1 COMPLETE BATHROOM	5,823	4,269	4,372	3,680	24,003
1 COMPLETE BATHROOM PLUS HALF BATH(S)	2,638	1,376	2,887	1,132	1,365
2 OR MORE COMPLETE BATHROOMS	1,393	1,025	1,544	608	3,082
NUMBER OF ROOMS					
1 ROOM	24	35	20	250	4,116
2 ROOMS	102	88	61	202	4,589
3 ROOMS	450	305	473	1,224	7,801
4 ROOMS	1,048	1,099	1,076	2,222	6,286
5 ROOMS	3,361	2,675	2,515	1,109	5,370
6 OR MORE ROOMS	5,260	2,610	4,976	726	4,451
KITCHEN FACILITIES					
COMPLETE KITCHEN FACILITIES	10,087	6,784	9,003	5,715	31,997
NO COMPLETE KITCHEN FACILITIES	158	29	118	23	629
SEWAGE DISPOSAL					
PUBLIC SEWER	10,171	6,796	9,085	5,738	32,576
SEPTIC TANK OR CESSPOOL	42	12	26	0	14
OTHER MEANS	32	5	10	0	36
AIR CONDITIONING					
NONE	4,721	1,349	3,480	100	12,797
CENTRAL SYSTEM	2,023	2,635	2,279	2,290	6,284
1 INDIVIDUAL ROOM UNITS	2,306	1,680	2,240	2,089	9,156
2 OR MORE INDIVIDUAL ROOM UNITS	1,195	1,149	1,122	1,259	4,389
HEATING EQUIPMENT					
STEAM OR HOT WATER SYSTEM	3,485	1,186	2,523	2,240	21,907
CENTRAL WARM-AIR FURNACE	5,860	5,335	5,679	2,944	6,515
ELECTRIC HEAT PUMP	120	33	87	109	806
OTHER BUILT-IN ELECTRIC UNITS	181	132	158	263	2,260
FLOOR, WALL, OR PIPELESS FURNACE	126	48	129	159	443
ROOM HEATERS WITH FLUE	383	76	370	23	503
ROOM HEATERS WITHOUT FLUE	77	3	137	0	142
FIREPLACES, STOVES, OR PORTABLE ROOM HEATERS	6	0	38	0	36
NONE	7	0	0	0	14
OCCUPIED HOUSING UNITS	10,034	6,705	8,866	5,502	29,302
TELEPHONE IN HOUSING UNIT					
WITH TELEPHONE	9,606	6,642	8,608	5,471	26,884
NO TELEPHONE	428	63	258	29	2,418
OCCUPIED HOUSING UNITS WITH VEHICLE AVAILABLE					
1	4,355	2,943	3,997	3,284	12,138
2	3,206	2,213	2,635	1,543	2,842
3 OR MORE	930	768	891	309	565

	01	02	03	04	05	06	07	08	09
UNITS IN STRUCTURE									
YEAR-ROUND HOUSING UNITS	28,401	26,057	33,719	19,459	14,977	56,781	35,313	41,313	4,778
1, DETACHED	1,022	5,026	663	2,027	2,177	1,654	1,385	311	3,195
1, ATTACHED	299	789	150	181	148	412	1,005	602	23
2	1,223	3,487	1,006	3,470	5,763	5,560	3,814	416	206
3 AND 4	2,178	4,113	1,870	3,799	3,797	8,850	7,047	803	219
5 OR MORE	23,672	12,618	29,968	9,976	3,092	40,267	22,021	39,147	1,135
MOBILE HOME OR TRAILER, ETC.	7	24	62	6	0	38	41	34	0
OWNER-OCCUPIED HOUSING UNITS	3,607	11,999	3,731	5,176	5,280	11,599	8,128	10,305	3,743
1, DETACHED	868	4,861	479	1,903	1,876	1,260	951	105	3,071
1, ATTACHED	273	761	62	126	78	280	667	218	20
2	525	1,853	353	1,456	2,404	1,952	1,182	70	119
3 AND 4	369	1,477	274	1,267	765	1,751	1,207	66	36
5 OR MORE	1,572	3,037	2,563	424	157	6,343	4,110	9,846	497
MOBILE HOME OR TRAILER, ETC.	0	10	0	0	0	13	11	0	0
RENTER-OCCUPIED HOUSING UNITS	22,692	13,005	24,480	13,487	8,750	40,378	23,526	26,063	955
1, DETACHED	114	95	129	92	234	318	262	181	105
1, ATTACHED	26	28	82	55	67	115	309	317	0
2	627	1,551	614	1,879	3,037	3,146	2,263	261	87
3 AND 4	1,611	2,475	1,355	2,390	2,718	6,263	4,870	612	180
5 OR MORE	20,307	8,842	22,238	9,065	2,694	30,523	15,799	24,658	583
MOBILE HOME OR TRAILER, ETC.	7	14	62	6	0	13	23	34	0
YEAR STRUCTURE BUILT									
YEAR-ROUND HOUSING UNITS	28,401	26,057	33,719	19,459	14,977	56,781	35,313	41,313	4,778
1979 TO MARCH 1980	61	61	241	43	22	272	335	510	52
1975 TO 1978	99	197	562	86	14	1,213	999	2,951	91
1970 TO 1974	1,236	777	1,919	203	31	3,636	4,972	4,551	233
1960 TO 1969	4,141	3,955	4,340	1,059	311	8,527	3,721	11,818	753
1950 TO 1959	2,521	7,076	3,035	2,846	785	5,618	1,777	5,544	1,586
1940 TO 1949	3,580	3,826	4,022	3,011	1,971	5,719	3,042	2,501	621
1939 OR EARLIER	16,763	10,165	19,600	12,211	11,843	31,796	20,467	13,438	1,442
OWNER-OCCUPIED HOUSING UNITS	3,607	11,999	3,731	5,176	5,280	11,599	8,128	10,305	3,743
1979 TO MARCH 1980	21	18	0	13	6	25	120	256	31
1975 TO 1978	37	128	112	40	3	242	362	762	59
1970 TO 1974	155	477	329	30	5	532	2,125	1,487	176
1960 TO 1969	756	1,819	859	190	108	2,137	1,009	4,568	442
1950 TO 1959	293	4,137	259	1,209	142	1,715	117	1,239	1,335
1940 TO 1949	146	1,383	184	465	358	436	213	166	518
1939 OR EARLIER	2,199	4,037	1,988	3,229	4,658	6,512	4,182	1,827	1,182
RENTER-OCCUPIED HOUSING UNITS	22,692	13,005	24,480	13,487	8,750	40,378	23,526	26,063	955
1979 TO MARCH 1980	21	15	112	30	16	201	110	156	15
1975 TO 1978	62	69	303	46	11	846	524	1,876	32
1970 TO 1974	1,033	266	1,343	164	26	2,858	2,563	2,647	54
1960 TO 1969	3,144	1,901	3,272	847	148	5,867	2,434	6,131	299
1950 TO 1959	2,041	2,657	2,445	1,579	576	3,561	1,330	3,869	223
1940 TO 1949	3,253	2,291	2,980	2,387	1,424	4,674	2,356	1,917	91
1939 OR EARLIER	13,138	5,806	14,025	8,434	6,549	22,371	14,209	9,467	241
BEDROOMS									
YEAR-ROUND HOUSING UNITS	28,401	26,057	33,719	19,459	14,977	56,781	35,313	41,313	4,778
NONE	4,291	430	8,309	1,514	311	8,654	5,387	10,605	19
1	13,717	7,186	15,432	6,927	3,192	23,428	13,114	15,907	478
2	6,786	9,005	6,177	6,385	6,723	15,607	11,143	9,383	1,872
3	2,723	8,345	3,056	3,986	3,905	7,700	4,708	4,285	1,880
4	628	843	523	499	644	1,116	716	795	456
5 OR MORE	256	248	222	148	202	276	245	338	73
OWNER-OCCUPIED HOUSING UNITS	3,607	11,999	3,731	5,176	5,280	11,599	8,128	10,305	3,743
NONE	34	12	217	20	8	362	414	1,000	0
1	560	1,058	1,122	327	268	2,862	2,339	3,720	110
2	1,036	3,931	1,208	2,032	2,201	4,203	2,514	3,233	1,336
3	1,320	6,041	758	2,197	2,087	3,347	2,217	1,744	1,772
4	437	736	242	452	536	642	430	407	452
5 OR MORE	220	221	184	148	180	183	214	201	73
RENTER-OCCUPIED HOUSING UNITS	22,692	13,005	24,480	13,487	8,750	40,378	23,526	26,063	955
NONE	3,801	364	6,311	1,400	264	7,539	4,514	7,759	19
1	12,143	5,734	11,812	6,311	2,591	18,568	9,483	10,388	356
2	5,251	4,658	4,082	4,070	4,148	10,052	7,166	5,250	480
3	1,309	2,144	2,029	1,659	1,658	3,706	2,103	2,205	96
4	167	78	228	47	90	423	235	335	4
5 OR MORE	21	27	18	0	19	90	25	126	0
YEAR-ROUND HOUSING UNITS	28,401	26,057	33,719	19,459	14,977	56,781	35,313	41,313	4,778
STORIES IN STRUCTURE									
1 TO 3	18,722	21,566	16,590	17,020	14,503	29,746	20,240	4,313	4,711
4 TO 6	7,753	3,261	6,178	2,412	461	9,496	5,495	4,181	60
7 TO 12	1,225	188	3,458	4	4	3,724	2,542	3,231	7
13 OR MORE	701	1,042	7,493	23	9	13,815	7,036	29,588	0
PASSENGER ELEVATOR									
STRUCTURES WITH 4 OR MORE STORIES	9,679	4,491	17,129	2,439	474	27,035	15,073	37,000	67
WITH ELEVATOR	6,408	2,868	14,515	976	13	23,841	12,338	34,772	27
NO ELEVATOR	3,271	1,623	2,614	1,463	461	3,194	2,735	2,228	40

TABLE III-7 STRUCTURAL CHARACTERISTICS OF HOUSING UNITS, BY COMMUNITY AREA: CITY OF CHICAGO, 1980

	10	11	12	13	14	15	16	17	18
UNITS IN STRUCTURE									
YEAR-ROUND HOUSING UNITS	15,169	10,172	6,904	5,586	17,123	23,421	21,358	14,162	4,328
1, DETACHED	10,644	4,805	5,816	2,181	3,167	8,788	4,106	9,776	2,126
1, ATTACHED	243	64	113	71	100	97	84	190	28
2	1,447	2,922	441	1,143	3,696	6,725	6,450	1,825	847
3 AND 4	609	992	196	741	2,775	3,219	3,192	796	579
5 OR MORE	2,215	1,383	338	1,443	7,380	4,592	7,520	1,575	748
MOBILE HOME OR TRAILER, ETC.	11	6	0	0	7	5	0	0	0
OWNER-OCCUPIED HOUSING UNITS	11,930	6,631	6,022	3,082	5,449	13,081	8,133	10,781	2,630
1, DETACHED	10,233	4,526	5,613	2,086	2,844	8,332	3,742	9,226	1,977
1, ATTACHED	207	48	102	53	56	58	50	170	28
2	804	1,385	201	571	1,784	3,346	2,893	932	378
3 AND 4	117	344	56	221	506	787	690	217	175
5 OR MORE	565	328	50	151	259	558	758	236	72
MOBILE HOME OR TRAILER, ETC.	4	0	0	0	0	0	0	0	0
RENTER-OCCUPIED HOUSING UNITS	2,987	3,329	791	2,326	10,836	9,727	12,460	3,108	1,496
1, DETACHED	312	227	154	76	240	335	331	432	72
1, ATTACHED	36	16	11	18	44	35	34	15	0
2	607	1,449	206	535	1,783	3,128	3,259	858	437
3 AND 4	422	601	140	504	2,096	2,312	2,325	540	382
5 OR MORE	1,603	1,030	280	1,186	6,673	3,917	6,505	1,263	605
MOBILE HOME OR TRAILER, ETC.	7	6	0	0	7	0	0	0	0
YEAR STRUCTURE BUILT									
YEAR-ROUND HOUSING UNITS	15,169	10,172	6,904	5,586	17,123	23,421	21,358	14,162	4,328
1979 TO MARCH 1980	101	50	7	63	75	105	44	19	13
1975 TO 1978	411	139	109	41	60	247	74	204	16
1970 TO 1974	555	321	222	80	67	496	284	427	66
1960 TO 1969	2,461	1,279	703	442	597	1,389	1,171	1,802	466
1950 TO 1959	4,678	2,105	2,574	1,520	1,280	2,537	1,406	3,429	805
1940 TO 1949	3,341	1,353	1,868	1,056	3,130	2,744	2,289	3,023	743
1939 OR EARLIER	3,622	4,925	1,421	2,384	11,914	15,903	16,090	5,234	2,219
OWNER-OCCUPIED HOUSING UNITS	11,930	6,631	6,022	3,082	5,449	13,081	8,133	10,781	2,630
1979 TO MARCH 1980	37	20	7	4	0	40	11	19	5
1975 TO 1978	186	57	90	23	22	163	53	131	16
1970 TO 1974	388	141	185	26	25	242	152	234	11
1960 TO 1969	1,554	624	562	176	149	586	618	890	174
1950 TO 1959	4,064	1,581	2,203	1,182	328	1,498	280	2,641	524
1940 TO 1949	2,848	944	1,705	579	600	1,096	386	2,603	501
1939 OR EARLIER	2,853	3,264	1,270	1,092	4,325	9,456	6,633	4,263	1,399
RENTER-OCCUPIED HOUSING UNITS	2,987	3,329	791	2,326	10,836	9,727	12,460	3,108	1,496
1979 TO MARCH 1980	57	19	0	14	68	45	30	17	8
1975 TO 1978	214	71	19	18	38	71	17	62	0
1970 TO 1974	162	178	34	54	42	240	113	187	55
1960 TO 1969	878	630	139	246	414	795	532	829	272
1950 TO 1959	515	518	343	320	852	963	1,020	717	256
1940 TO 1949	456	375	124	459	2,355	1,546	1,797	372	212
1939 OR EARLIER	705	1,538	132	1,215	7,067	6,067	8,951	924	693
BEDROOMS									
YEAR-ROUND HOUSING UNITS	15,169	10,172	6,904	5,586	17,123	23,421	21,358	14,162	4,328
NONE	163	143	30	126	743	623	1,098	71	79
1	1,436	1,269	382	1,233	5,492	4,510	6,161	1,804	785
2	5,966	4,864	2,312	1,715	5,744	10,116	8,017	6,024	1,915
3	6,125	2,997	3,319	2,146	4,285	6,149	4,678	5,016	1,330
4	1,224	751	685	311	703	1,700	1,113	1,073	169
5 OR MORE	255	148	176	55	156	323	291	174	50
OWNER-OCCUPIED HOUSING UNITS	11,930	6,631	6,022	3,082	5,449	13,081	8,133	10,781	2,630
NONE	20	20	13	0	12	22	5	6	6
1	318	264	37	125	185	532	415	480	117
2	4,414	2,958	1,989	900	1,936	5,812	3,264	4,552	1,218
3	5,730	2,508	3,149	1,735	2,589	4,843	3,181	4,554	1,083
4	1,193	745	663	274	584	1,592	973	1,027	160
5 OR MORE	255	136	171	48	143	297	278	162	46
RENTER-OCCUPIED HOUSING UNITS	2,987	3,329	791	2,326	10,836	9,727	12,460	3,108	1,496
NONE	141	123	17	104	682	565	1,058	60	58
1	1,070	973	323	1,041	4,978	3,850	5,421	1,255	586
2	1,405	1,800	287	742	3,517	3,973	4,413	1,366	634
3	343	415	140	402	1,553	1,229	1,432	380	209
4	28	6	19	30	97	84	123	35	9
5 OR MORE	0	12	5	7	9	26	13	12	0
YEAR-ROUND HOUSING UNITS	15,169	10,172	6,904	5,586	17,123	23,421	21,358	14,162	4,328
STORIES IN STRUCTURE									
1 TO 3	14,546	10,001	6,896	5,431	16,228	22,727	20,057	14,110	4,321
4 TO 6	597	171	8	155	857	682	1,284	52	7
7 TO 12	26	0	0	0	38	6	0	0	0
13 OR MORE	0	0	0	0	0	6	17	0	0
PASSENGER ELEVATOR									
STRUCTURES WITH 4 OR MORE STORIES	623	171	8	155	895	694	1,301	52	7
WITH ELEVATOR	605	142	8	0	46	175	185	0	0
NO ELEVATOR	18	29	0	155	849	519	1,116	52	7

TABLE III-7 STRUCTURAL CHARACTERISTICS OF HOUSING UNITS,
BY COMMUNITY AREA: CITY OF CHICAGO, 1980

	19	20	21	22	23	24	25	26	27
UNITS IN STRUCTURE									
YEAR-ROUND HOUSING UNITS	22,197	7,362	13,987	32,531	23,760	36,815	44,720	9,578	10,937
1, DETACHED	7,554	1,828	1,855	3,017	3,662	1,644	9,648	654	424
1, ATTACHED	149	26	37	200	236	303	724	65	235
2	7,783	2,963	5,826	10,218	8,957	9,259	13,154	3,803	3,362
3 AND 4	3,518	1,387	3,731	9,098	6,328	12,055	5,877	1,867	2,857
5 OR MORE	3,193	1,158	2,538	9,985	4,571	13,534	15,294	3,189	4,051
MOBILE HOME OR TRAILER, ETC.	0	0	0	0	13	6	20	23	8
OWNER-OCCUPIED HOUSING UNITS	11,756	3,267	4,952	8,342	7,614	6,876	16,360	2,148	1,946
1, DETACHED	6,955	1,598	1,556	2,283	2,849	1,059	8,259	468	277
1, ATTACHED	89	20	14	56	116	36	418	55	114
2	3,683	1,264	2,430	3,834	3,345	2,798	5,377	1,213	988
3 AND 4	745	299	795	1,737	1,067	1,963	1,100	339	470
5 OR MORE	284	86	157	432	231	1,020	1,197	73	97
MOBILE HOME OR TRAILER, ETC.	0	0	0	0	6	0	9	0	0
RENTER-OCCUPIED HOUSING UNITS	9,327	3,786	8,270	21,135	13,782	25,246	25,257	6,992	7,825
1, DETACHED	380	164	210	452	565	490	896	162	135
1, ATTACHED	55	6	23	119	102	214	241	8	115
2	3,670	1,568	3,069	5,584	4,971	5,527	7,062	2,427	2,118
3 AND 4	2,514	1,020	2,691	6,382	4,437	8,500	4,411	1,450	1,990
5 OR MORE	2,708	1,028	2,277	8,585	3,707	10,495	12,633	2,945	3,459
MOBILE HOME OR TRAILER, ETC.	0	0	0	0	13	20	14	0	8
YEAR STRUCTURE BUILT									
YEAR-ROUND HOUSING UNITS	22,197	7,362	13,987	32,531	23,760	36,815	44,720	9,578	10,937
1979 TO MARCH 1980	21	0	9	129	66	134	215	19	23
1975 TO 1978	51	15	17	177	106	172	732	41	55
1970 TO 1974	273	70	36	109	215	629	661	117	178
1960 TO 1969	1,293	253	414	681	937	1,386	2,264	433	450
1950 TO 1959	2,492	506	1,036	2,661	2,652	2,366	6,803	912	1,221
1940 TO 1949	3,294	1,248	1,893	5,058	5,274	5,147	10,250	2,228	2,370
1939 OR EARLIER	14,773	5,270	10,582	23,716	14,510	26,981	23,795	5,828	6,640
OWNER-OCCUPIED HOUSING UNITS	11,756	3,267	4,952	8,342	7,614	6,876	16,360	2,148	1,946
1979 TO MARCH 1980	6	0	0	0	9	0	17	0	0
1975 TO 1978	33	0	9	0	4	0	257	0	0
1970 TO 1974	84	13	15	16	70	50	300	28	0
1960 TO 1969	482	100	212	168	375	124	579	62	8
1950 TO 1959	1,360	217	258	314	647	149	2,448	131	85
1940 TO 1949	1,479	345	390	752	1,130	570	3,407	382	231
1939 OR EARLIER	8,318	2,592	4,068	7,092	5,379	5,983	9,352	1,545	1,622
RENTER-OCCUPIED HOUSING UNITS	9,327	3,786	8,270	21,135	13,782	25,246	25,257	6,992	7,825
1979 TO MARCH 1980	18	0	9	129	45	117	141	19	23
1975 TO 1978	14	15	8	155	92	144	427	30	48
1970 TO 1974	184	43	15	78	140	557	336	89	173
1960 TO 1969	724	136	180	454	444	1,070	1,524	346	384
1950 TO 1959	1,024	246	709	2,083	1,786	1,899	3,893	763	974
1940 TO 1949	1,583	828	1,440	3,820	3,488	3,887	6,127	1,713	1,831
1939 OR EARLIER	5,780	2,518	5,909	14,416	7,787	17,572	12,809	4,032	4,392
BEDROOMS									
YEAR-ROUND HOUSING UNITS	22,197	7,362	13,987	32,531	23,760	36,815	44,720	9,578	10,937
NONE	242	59	204	1,339	540	965	1,847	310	538
1	3,977	1,544	2,852	7,592	4,300	5,443	10,865	2,026	2,520
2	10,811	3,100	7,010	13,207	9,811	19,104	15,684	3,108	3,596
3	5,897	2,102	3,357	9,601	7,551	9,553	11,993	3,115	3,099
4	1,016	455	410	984	1,185	1,357	3,041	856	970
5 OR MORE	254	102	154	408	373	393	1,290	163	214
OWNER-OCCUPIED HOUSING UNITS	11,756	3,267	4,952	8,342	7,614	6,876	16,360	2,148	1,946
NONE	6	0	15	14	42	0	32	25	6
1	346	116	193	496	310	380	636	96	110
2	5,915	1,399	2,570	3,235	2,878	2,996	5,536	661	621
3	4,348	1,303	1,778	3,674	3,256	2,685	6,719	930	751
4	898	347	282	620	843	647	2,375	331	316
5 OR MORE	243	102	114	303	285	168	1,062	105	142
RENTER-OCCUPIED HOUSING UNITS	9,327	3,786	8,270	21,135	13,782	25,246	25,257	6,992	7,825
NONE	198	53	175	1,219	408	743	1,580	255	463
1	3,253	1,328	2,421	6,243	3,584	4,491	9,403	1,811	2,239
2	4,446	1,580	4,109	8,539	5,972	13,478	8,956	2,326	2,435
3	1,333	731	1,432	4,791	3,554	5,806	4,659	2,058	2,008
4	92	94	103	271	216	552	475	486	618
5 OR MORE	5	0	30	72	48	176	184	56	62
YEAR-ROUND HOUSING UNITS	22,197	7,362	13,987	32,531	23,760	36,815	44,720	9,578	10,937
STORIES IN STRUCTURE									
1 TO 3	22,080	7,333	13,540	30,430	23,001	33,387	41,364	8,766	9,970
4 TO 6	117	29	441	2,044	541	2,246	2,756	549	546
7 TO 12	0	0	6	47	14	201	487	61	227
13 OR MORE	0	0	0	10	204	981	113	202	194
PASSENGER ELEVATOR									
STRUCTURES WITH 4 OR MORE STORIES	117	29	447	2,101	759	3,428	3,356	812	967
WITH ELEVATOR	8	0	13	464	316	1,417	2,035	466	477
NO ELEVATOR	109	29	434	1,637	443	2,011	1,321	346	490

	28	29	30	31	32	33	34	35	36
UNITS IN STRUCTURE									
YEAR-ROUND HOUSING UNITS	20,065	18,580	20,903	14,676	4,263	2,488	4,684	15,173	5,201
1, DETACHED	899	1,024	2,358	910	82	0	305	171	79
1, ATTACHED	1,373	148	218	114	178	0	291	496	367
2	2,091	5,174	8,424	3,190	0	20	906	542	130
3 AND 4	2,749	5,810	6,625	5,373	44	0	1,225	753	404
5 OR MORE	12,907	6,406	3,278	5,082	3,959	2,459	1,957	13,165	4,221
MOBILE HOME OR TRAILER, ETC.	46	18	0	7	0	0	0	46	0
OWNER-OCCUPIED HOUSING UNITS	2,210	3,695	7,142	3,230	1,628	884	985	3,093	212
1, DETACHED	417	664	1,944	563	78	0	177	119	38
1, ATTACHED	286	89	96	9	56	0	92	238	44
2	556	1,587	3,427	1,236	0	12	341	112	24
3 AND 4	430	932	1,391	938	44	0	215	182	31
5 OR MORE	501	423	284	484	1,450	872	160	2,442	75
MOBILE HOME OR TRAILER, ETC.	20	0	0	0	0	0	0	0	0
RENTER-OCCUPIED HOUSING UNITS	16,130	13,490	12,192	9,734	2,234	1,537	3,468	11,260	4,662
1, DETACHED	401	279	269	233	4	0	116	30	41
1, ATTACHED	1,030	44	102	82	91	0	193	228	315
2	1,312	3,296	4,518	1,623	0	0	526	318	99
3 AND 4	1,916	4,382	4,663	3,854	0	0	914	477	350
5 OR MORE	11,445	5,471	2,640	3,935	2,139	1,528	1,719	10,161	3,857
MOBILE HOME OR TRAILER, ETC.	26	18	0	7	0	9	0	46	0
YEAR STRUCTURE BUILT									
YEAR-ROUND HOUSING UNITS	20,065	18,580	20,903	14,676	4,263	2,488	4,684	15,173	5,201
1979 TO MARCH 1980	648	58	150	98	555	25	33	107	19
1975 TO 1978	924	117	252	181	472	53	240	77	157
1970 TO 1974	859	353	269	214	399	293	328	1,149	844
1960 TO 1969	2,700	1,082	692	506	1,177	1,062	489	3,614	1,613
1950 TO 1959	4,262	1,558	1,969	975	168	693	443	5,236	594
1940 TO 1949	3,105	3,052	3,791	1,686	297	115	451	2,090	773
1939 OR EARLIER	7,567	12,360	13,780	11,016	1,195	247	2,700	2,900	1,201
OWNER-OCCUPIED HOUSING UNITS	2,210	3,695	7,142	3,230	1,628	884	985	3,093	212
1979 TO MARCH 1980	78	5	22	9	141	17	14	11	0
1975 TO 1978	110	20	14	0	253	35	54	10	0
1970 TO 1974	89	46	47	36	283	269	88	94	0
1960 TO 1969	156	83	159	152	684	393	65	1,168	11
1950 TO 1959	186	125	505	106	103	0	24	954	7
1940 TO 1949	163	393	976	213	0	13	9	170	6
1939 OR EARLIER	1,428	3,023	5,419	2,714	164	157	731	686	188
RENTER-OCCUPIED HOUSING UNITS	16,130	13,490	12,192	9,734	2,234	1,537	3,468	11,260	4,662
1979 TO MARCH 1980	556	48	125	61	292	8	19	32	19
1975 TO 1978	793	76	233	181	165	18	181	56	157
1970 TO 1974	737	264	209	162	106	24	205	1,016	834
1960 TO 1969	2,441	911	467	316	482	666	420	2,380	1,517
1950 TO 1959	3,835	1,329	1,305	677	65	681	414	4,150	540
1940 TO 1949	2,521	2,469	2,496	1,223	268	92	436	1,830	697
1939 OR EARLIER	5,247	8,393	7,357	7,114	856	48	1,793	1,796	898
BEDROOMS									
YEAR-ROUND HOUSING UNITS	20,065	18,580	20,903	14,676	4,263	2,488	4,684	15,173	5,201
NONE	1,894	331	165	235	1,158	130	161	2,086	175
1	5,244	2,483	2,479	2,715	2,253	852	1,413	5,188	1,712
2	7,116	7,609	11,901	7,213	660	853	1,761	5,237	1,575
3	4,466	6,384	5,174	3,622	118	549	1,099	1,992	989
4	1,151	1,370	946	692	52	88	222	477	638
5 OR MORE	194	403	238	199	22	16	28	193	112
OWNER-OCCUPIED HOUSING UNITS	2,210	3,695	7,142	3,230	1,628	884	985	3,093	212
NONE	13	12	0	5	149	101	21	930	0
1	268	141	212	140	818	324	48	1,056	31
2	584	1,086	3,555	1,358	500	313	383	546	40
3	836	1,771	2,457	1,294	92	139	420	253	51
4	432	482	691	329	52	7	88	200	52
5 OR MORE	77	203	227	104	17	0	25	108	38
RENTER-OCCUPIED HOUSING UNITS	16,130	13,490	12,192	9,734	2,234	1,537	3,468	11,260	4,662
NONE	1,635	297	120	169	878	21	131	902	143
1	4,614	2,097	2,076	2,228	1,226	506	1,299	3,978	1,547
2	5,755	5,882	7,441	4,977	109	537	1,295	4,431	1,441
3	3,388	4,229	2,327	1,955	21	382	618	1,635	902
4	624	810	220	323	0	75	122	262	555
5 OR MORE	114	175	8	82	0	16	3	52	74
YEAR-ROUND HOUSING UNITS	20,065	18,580	20,903	14,676	4,263	2,488	4,684	15,173	5,201
STORIES IN STRUCTURE									
1 TO 3	11,653	17,600	20,190	13,802	503	149	3,707	3,494	2,349
4 TO 6	1,518	719	373	624	324	68	129	1,710	123
7 TO 12	2,176	261	10	231	937	863	572	3,220	1,109
13 OR MORE	4,718	0	330	19	2,499	1,408	276	6,749	1,620
PASSENGER ELEVATOR									
STRUCTURES WITH 4 OR MORE STORIES	8,412	980	713	874	3,760	2,339	977	11,679	2,852
WITH ELEVATOR	7,721	261	340	262	3,746	2,294	876	10,892	2,762
NO ELEVATOR	691	719	373	612	14	45	101	787	90

TABLE III-7 STRUCTURAL CHARACTERISTICS OF HOUSING UNITS,
BY COMMUNITY AREA: CITY OF CHICAGO, 1980

UNITS IN STRUCTURE	37	38	39	40	41	42	43	44	45
YEAR-ROUND HOUSING UNITS	2,019	20,863	11,270	12,079	15,506	15,769	34,166	17,141	4,302
1, DETACHED	358	368	398	213	394	552	3,069	4,866	2,696
1, ATTACHED	89	449	304	162	824	263	402	504	191
2	726	1,068	167	633	195	2,151	2,634	1,606	273
3 AND 4	311	2,974	678	1,420	679	2,811	3,911	2,439	467
5 OR MORE	535	15,963	9,700	9,615	13,408	9,971	24,130	7,722	675
MOBILE HOME OR TRAILER, ETC.	0	41	23	36	6	21	20	4	0
OWNER-OCCUPIED HOUSING UNITS	558	3,064	2,263	641	3,688	1,985	6,064	6,474	3,065
1, DETACHED	211	173	290	98	341	404	2,735	4,448	2,493
1, ATTACHED	49	199	223	26	698	126	284	374	176
2	222	276	53	144	64	717	1,056	642	151
3 AND 4	55	414	139	141	202	425	722	428	95
5 OR MORE	21	2,002	1,550	232	2,383	313	1,267	582	150
MOBILE HOME OR TRAILER, ETC.	0	0	0	8	0	0	0	0	0
RENTER-OCCUPIED HOUSING UNITS	1,354	15,630	7,771	10,345	10,770	12,090	25,303	9,944	1,158
1, DETACHED	128	127	71	99	50	115	291	354	142
1, ATTACHED	40	242	70	126	115	115	92	127	15
2	460	670	95	457	124	1,274	1,475	939	122
3 AND 4	232	2,147	410	1,151	446	2,072	2,798	1,858	365
5 OR MORE	494	12,403	7,110	8,476	10,029	8,493	20,627	6,666	514
MOBILE HOME OR TRAILER, ETC.	0	41	15	36	6	21	20	0	0
YEAR STRUCTURE BUILT									
YEAR-ROUND HOUSING UNITS	2,019	20,863	11,270	12,079	15,506	15,769	34,166	17,141	4,302
1979 TO MARCH 1980	18	182	37	41	104	74	249	15	0
1975 TO 1978	25	511	136	107	54	147	204	55	11
1970 TO 1974	346	843	1,636	347	363	716	474	202	60
1960 TO 1969	275	3,688	1,894	1,887	1,774	1,301	3,597	2,574	357
1950 TO 1959	140	1,778	1,256	1,194	884	1,532	5,181	2,797	1,088
1940 TO 1949	292	3,113	1,125	2,057	2,235	2,739	8,266	3,968	974
1939 OR EARLIER	923	10,748	5,186	6,446	10,092	9,260	16,195	7,530	1,812
OWNER-OCCUPIED HOUSING UNITS	558	3,064	2,263	641	3,688	1,985	6,064	6,474	3,065
1979 TO MARCH 1980	0	18	0	0	0	0	6	0	0
1975 TO 1978	7	14	3	0	41	14	14	23	5
1970 TO 1974	64	11	205	3	26	51	57	49	56
1960 TO 1969	54	532	643	17	113	66	410	1,217	273
1950 TO 1959	42	252	111	21	826	65	839	1,278	845
1940 TO 1949	35	249	76	103	214	244	1,179	1,336	609
1939 OR EARLIER	356	1,988	1,225	497	2,266	1,545	3,559	2,571	1,277
RENTER-OCCUPIED HOUSING UNITS	1,354	15,630	7,771	10,345	10,770	12,090	25,303	9,944	1,158
1979 TO MARCH 1980	18	164	21	30	44	62	37	15	0
1975 TO 1978	18	488	121	85	26	126	157	32	6
1970 TO 1974	282	816	1,342	312	238	612	398	146	0
1960 TO 1969	207	2,868	1,136	1,715	894	1,127	2,951	1,218	84
1950 TO 1959	92	1,375	1,053	1,061	619	1,279	3,961	1,411	223
1940 TO 1949	247	2,429	865	1,784	1,829	2,142	6,244	2,427	352
1939 OR EARLIER	490	7,490	3,233	5,358	7,120	6,742	11,555	4,695	493
BEDROOMS									
YEAR-ROUND HOUSING UNITS	2,019	20,863	11,270	12,079	15,506	15,769	34,166	17,141	4,302
NONE	13	1,757	1,409	994	2,450	1,730	2,629	422	54
1	528	6,368	4,860	3,451	6,423	5,250	14,571	5,229	604
2	637	5,183	3,293	3,703	3,294	4,789	9,760	6,163	1,360
3	680	5,076	1,019	2,998	2,008	3,070	5,419	4,154	1,430
4	150	1,918	400	835	946	670	1,269	926	699
5 OR MORE	11	561	289	98	385	260	518	247	155
OWNER-OCCUPIED HOUSING UNITS	558	3,064	2,263	641	3,688	1,985	6,064	6,474	3,065
NONE	0	128	111	11	49	13	32	21	19
1	33	588	522	63	547	186	313	242	42
2	165	758	689	205	1,049	555	1,841	2,181	982
3	268	893	397	258	1,018	807	2,391	2,967	1,273
4	81	431	288	87	685	300	1,015	842	623
5 OR MORE	11	266	256	17	340	124	472	221	126
RENTER-OCCUPIED HOUSING UNITS	1,354	15,630	7,771	10,345	10,770	12,090	25,303	9,944	1,158
NONE	13	1,528	1,116	845	2,198	1,469	2,303	393	35
1	473	5,103	3,695	3,005	5,395	4,378	12,872	4,654	553
2	410	3,796	2,309	3,216	2,022	3,768	7,186	3,696	351
3	405	3,657	552	2,541	876	2,047	2,687	1,107	139
4	53	1,313	90	660	237	313	209	68	57
5 OR MORE	0	233	9	78	42	115	46	26	23
YEAR-ROUND HOUSING UNITS	2,019	20,863	11,270	12,079	15,506	15,769	34,166	17,141	4,302
STORIES IN STRUCTURE									
1 TO 3	1,649	13,079	5,740	8,734	8,005	12,316	25,382	16,332	4,271
4 TO 6	6	2,253	985	1,126	3,152	1,619	4,114	765	31
7 TO 12	6	538	669	160	2,503	967	1,976	28	0
13 OR MORE	358	4,993	3,876	2,059	1,846	867	2,694	16	0
PASSENGER ELEVATOR									
STRUCTURES WITH 4 OR MORE STORIES	370	7,784	5,530	3,345	7,501	3,453	8,784	809	31
WITH ELEVATOR	364	5,894	5,042	2,501	6,293	2,754	6,808	221	0
NO ELEVATOR	6	1,890	488	844	1,208	699	1,976	588	31

419

TABLE III-7 STRUCTURAL CHARACTERISTICS OF HOUSING UNITS,
BY COMMUNITY AREA: CITY OF CHICAGO, 1980

	46	47	48	49	50	51	52	53	54
UNITS IN STRUCTURE									
YEAR-ROUND HOUSING UNITS	15,622	1,114	6,322	18,764	3,527	5,804	7,756	12,286	3,505
1, DETACHED	3,989	624	4,358	10,824	1,029	2,428	4,424	7,842	492
1, ATTACHED	204	51	144	1,339	1,420	1,766	185	364	1,519
2	4,025	293	615	3,108	461	774	1,673	2,125	73
3 AND 4	3,644	62	684	1,541	432	412	1,124	1,062	97
5 OR MORE	3,751	76	521	1,925	181	391	345	878	1,317
MOBILE HOME OR TRAILER, ETC.	9	8	0	27	4	33	5	15	7
OWNER-OCCUPIED HOUSING UNITS	6,093	722	4,754	11,678	1,886	3,973	5,243	8,399	579
1, DETACHED	3,306	512	4,083	9,645	972	2,198	4,129	7,039	347
1, ATTACHED	101	37	129	353	666	1,311	155	260	166
2	1,656	123	288	1,184	139	328	668	797	8
3 AND 4	722	31	156	349	68	96	232	192	11
5 OR MORE	299	19	98	144	37	11	54	111	47
MOBILE HOME OR TRAILER, ETC.	9	0	0	3	4	29	5	0	0
RENTER-OCCUPIED HOUSING UNITS	8,378	317	1,440	6,435	1,481	1,654	2,215	3,346	2,816
1, DETACHED	453	67	215	949	48	181	200	583	124
1, ATTACHED	92	14	15	933	719	406	30	93	1,343
2	2,070	140	287	1,751	260	418	923	1,227	43
3 AND 4	2,618	31	525	1,087	317	285	775	710	75
5 OR MORE	3,145	57	398	1,691	137	360	287	718	1,224
MOBILE HOME OR TRAILER, ETC.	0	8	0	24	0	4	0	15	7
YEAR STRUCTURE BUILT									
YEAR-ROUND HOUSING UNITS	15,622	1,114	6,322	18,764	3,527	5,804	7,756	12,286	3,505
1979 TO MARCH 1980	45	0	16	43	0	8	26	83	8
1975 TO 1978	180	10	6	41	0	31	104	141	37
1970 TO 1974	720	41	78	452	29	123	147	302	157
1960 TO 1969	1,062	169	1,124	2,245	998	683	730	3,122	1,056
1950 TO 1959	2,168	269	2,662	4,176	493	1,334	1,126	2,988	332
1940 TO 1949	3,115	196	1,214	5,571	523	1,625	1,634	2,389	1,364
1939 OR EARLIER	8,332	429	1,222	6,236	1,484	2,000	3,989	3,261	551
OWNER-OCCUPIED HOUSING UNITS	6,093	722	4,754	11,678	1,886	3,973	5,243	8,399	579
1979 TO MARCH 1980	7	0	5	14	0	8	14	35	0
1975 TO 1978	6	10	6	26	0	20	100	66	8
1970 TO 1974	20	41	43	267	22	84	139	175	37
1960 TO 1969	386	115	883	1,725	317	543	650	2,492	402
1950 TO 1959	854	193	2,274	2,877	398	1,068	960	2,328	27
1940 TO 1949	1,232	112	876	2,931	425	1,162	1,235	1,432	32
1939 OR EARLIER	3,588	251	667	3,838	724	1,088	2,145	1,871	73
RENTER-OCCUPIED HOUSING UNITS	8,378	317	1,440	6,435	1,481	1,654	2,215	3,346	2,816
1979 TO MARCH 1980	34	0	11	29	0	0	12	41	8
1975 TO 1978	161	0	0	15	0	11	4	56	29
1970 TO 1974	658	0	35	129	7	39	8	126	109
1960 TO 1969	604	54	221	470	664	124	61	516	606
1950 TO 1959	1,169	61	354	1,145	79	222	160	576	305
1940 TO 1949	1,675	63	309	2,426	83	415	375	848	1,315
1939 OR EARLIER	4,077	139	510	2,221	648	843	1,595	1,183	444
BEDROOMS									
YEAR-ROUND HOUSING UNITS	15,622	1,114	6,322	18,764	3,527	5,804	7,756	12,286	3,505
NONE	406	0	7	309	76	33	45	43	48
1	2,648	88	435	1,880	391	398	723	1,073	350
2	6,121	367	1,938	6,617	1,483	2,335	2,822	3,770	1,305
3	5,200	528	3,256	7,076	1,296	2,650	3,425	5,483	1,474
4	898	92	555	2,028	227	321	620	1,506	313
5 OR MORE	349	39	131	854	54	67	121	411	15
OWNER-OCCUPIED HOUSING UNITS	6,093	722	4,754	11,678	1,886	3,973	5,243	8,399	579
NONE	11	0	7	8	7	13	0	10	0
1	135	12	79	255	63	104	129	210	17
2	2,072	191	1,199	3,488	705	1,418	1,635	1,929	84
3	2,932	388	2,831	5,414	905	2,142	2,780	4,604	417
4	655	92	510	1,765	155	251	582	1,289	61
5 OR MORE	288	39	128	748	51	45	110	357	0
RENTER-OCCUPIED HOUSING UNITS	8,378	317	1,440	6,435	1,481	1,654	2,215	3,346	2,816
NONE	292	0	0	298	51	12	31	33	42
1	2,332	57	346	1,551	298	277	533	714	322
2	3,565	164	655	2,828	711	848	1,036	1,684	1,173
3	1,921	96	403	1,471	349	436	577	716	1,027
4	223	0	36	219	72	59	34	149	245
5 OR MORE	45	0	0	68	0	22	4	50	7
YEAR-ROUND HOUSING UNITS	15,622	1,114	6,322	18,764	3,527	5,804	7,756	12,286	3,505
STORIES IN STRUCTURE									
1 TO 3	14,863	1,114	6,302	18,539	3,518	5,694	7,740	12,087	3,505
4 TO 6	408	0	20	218	9	110	16	186	0
7 TO 12	343	0	0	7	0	0	0	0	0
13 OR MORE	8	0	0	0	0	0	0	13	0
PASSENGER ELEVATOR									
STRUCTURES WITH 4 OR MORE STORIES	759	0	20	225	9	110	16	199	0
WITH ELEVATOR	486	0	0	32	0	12	0	158	0
NO ELEVATOR	273	0	20	193	9	98	16	41	0

TABLE III-7 STRUCTURAL CHARACTERISTICS OF HOUSING UNITS,
BY COMMUNITY AREA: CITY OF CHICAGO, 1980

	55	56	57	58	59	60	61	62	63
UNITS IN STRUCTURE									
YEAR-ROUND HOUSING UNITS	4,365	12,741	3,787	12,767	5,234	12,288	18,602	4,910	9,603
1, DETACHED	2,437	9,972	1,766	2,645	1,354	2,213	3,163	3,420	4,449
1, ATTACHED	43	654	32	89	33	226	197	123	40
2	749	855	1,329	6,870	2,042	4,071	7,574	640	2,974
3 AND 4	287	370	353	2,451	1,093	3,763	5,555	271	1,091
5 OR MORE	213	884	307	712	712	2,015	2,113	447	1,049
MOBILE HOME OR TRAILER, ETC.	636	6	0	0	0	0	0	9	0
OWNER-OCCUPIED HOUSING UNITS	3,192	10,122	2,395	5,937	2,376	4,447	6,546	3,913	5,791
1, DETACHED	2,199	9,504	1,646	2,353	1,120	1,896	2,510	3,272	4,092
1, ATTACHED	38	104	13	57	25	23	95	114	33
2	323	384	628	2,921	854	1,658	2,716	323	1,312
3 AND 4	28	67	82	552	283	666	1,019	70	284
5 OR MORE	26	57	26	54	94	204	206	134	70
MOBILE HOME OR TRAILER, ETC.	578	6	0	0	0	0	0	0	0
RENTER-OCCUPIED HOUSING UNITS	935	2,489	1,315	6,256	2,491	6,889	10,464	950	3,512
1, DETACHED	183	389	95	234	179	281	527	125	294
1, ATTACHED	5	545	19	32	8	181	83	9	7
2	394	460	681	3,634	1,046	2,045	4,238	308	1,558
3 AND 4	215	295	271	1,753	725	2,771	3,983	197	724
5 OR MORE	98	800	249	603	533	1,611	1,633	302	929
MOBILE HOME OR TRAILER, ETC.	40	0	0	0	0	0	0	9	0
YEAR STRUCTURE BUILT									
YEAR-ROUND HOUSING UNITS	4,365	12,741	3,787	12,767	5,234	12,288	18,602	4,910	9,603
1979 TO MARCH 1980	89	28	0	34	8	54	50	28	12
1975 TO 1978	122	216	24	28	15	97	119	131	45
1970 TO 1974	363	344	190	66	22	204	456	230	49
1960 TO 1969	1,233	2,019	513	579	339	300	914	616	597
1950 TO 1959	672	6,866	970	719	248	479	1,369	2,142	752
1940 TO 1949	220	1,878	446	1,367	475	1,007	2,664	1,108	1,056
1939 OR EARLIER	1,666	1,390	1,644	9,974	4,127	10,147	13,030	655	7,092
OWNER-OCCUPIED HOUSING UNITS	3,192	10,122	2,395	5,937	2,376	4,447	6,546	3,913	5,791
1979 TO MARCH 1980	83	5	0	16	8	14	7	11	12
1975 TO 1978	106	76	13	28	8	62	23	78	11
1970 TO 1974	326	133	46	42	11	137	270	117	19
1960 TO 1969	1,148	1,451	253	439	185	158	466	375	300
1950 TO 1959	573	5,991	764	435	96	90	460	1,875	433
1940 TO 1949	92	1,485	317	443	101	150	725	970	569
1939 OR EARLIER	864	981	1,002	4,534	1,967	3,836	4,595	487	4,447
RENTER-OCCUPIED HOUSING UNITS	935	2,489	1,315	6,256	2,491	6,889	10,464	950	3,512
1979 TO MARCH 1980	6	23	0	13	0	28	43	17	0
1975 TO 1978	16	138	11	0	7	21	96	48	30
1970 TO 1974	28	195	128	10	11	61	168	102	30
1960 TO 1969	69	550	239	130	133	142	392	239	285
1950 TO 1959	87	817	200	259	146	341	767	260	306
1940 TO 1949	111	376	129	853	339	739	1,683	123	456
1939 OR EARLIER	618	390	608	4,991	1,855	5,557	7,315	161	2,405
BEDROOMS									
YEAR-ROUND HOUSING UNITS	4,365	12,741	3,787	12,767	5,234	12,288	18,602	4,910	9,603
NONE	102	11	5	99	63	73	178	8	73
1	299	668	333	1,182	544	1,158	1,802	328	1,336
2	1,649	4,134	1,488	6,997	2,490	5,765	9,018	2,289	4,354
3	2,092	6,856	1,768	3,962	1,780	4,562	5,999	1,905	3,108
4	184	971	167	358	305	629	1,277	323	564
5 OR MORE	39	101	26	169	52	101	328	57	168
OWNER-OCCUPIED HOUSING UNITS	3,192	10,122	2,395	5,937	2,376	4,447	6,546	3,913	5,791
NONE	0	0	0	12	0	0	26	0	0
1	96	152	35	140	69	168	207	79	156
2	1,056	2,871	803	2,851	955	1,545	2,361	1,715	2,550
3	1,843	6,189	1,381	2,479	1,108	2,219	2,854	1,742	2,448
4	158	824	150	327	198	423	834	320	496
5 OR MORE	39	86	26	128	46	92	264	57	141
RENTER-OCCUPIED HOUSING UNITS	935	2,489	1,315	6,256	2,491	6,889	10,464	950	3,512
NONE	39	11	5	80	31	73	113	8	63
1	173	507	298	957	412	838	1,371	236	1,126
2	502	1,193	641	3,769	1,396	3,688	5,758	552	1,677
3	200	625	354	1,382	557	2,091	2,795	151	565
4	21	138	17	29	89	199	371	3	54
5 OR MORE	0	15	0	39	6	0	56	0	27
YEAR-ROUND HOUSING UNITS	4,365	12,741	3,787	12,767	5,234	12,288	18,602	4,910	9,603
STORIES IN STRUCTURE									
1 TO 3	4,357	12,741	3,769	12,731	5,222	12,191	18,428	4,901	9,603
4 TO 6	8	0	18	36	12	97	169	9	0
7 TO 12	0	0	0	0	0	0	0	0	0
13 OR MORE	0	0	0	0	0	0	5	0	0
PASSENGER ELEVATOR									
STRUCTURES WITH 4 OR MORE STORIES	8	0	18	36	12	97	174	9	0
WITH ELEVATOR	0	0	0	0	0	0	16	0	0
NO ELEVATOR	8	0	18	36	12	97	158	9	0

TABLE III-7 STRUCTURAL CHARACTERISTICS OF HOUSING UNITS, BY COMMUNITY AREA: CITY OF CHICAGO, 1980

	64	65	66	67	68	69	70	71	72
UNITS IN STRUCTURE									
YEAR-ROUND HOUSING UNITS	8,300	9,153	18,163	16,980	19,289	17,672	12,875	20,104	7,885
1, DETACHED	4,808	6,326	7,288	6,825	3,128	3,728	11,651	7,946	6,185
1, ATTACHED	423	11	125	193	282	274	41	223	51
2	765	1,464	4,186	6,467	7,086	4,665	205	4,465	296
3 AND 4	597	505	2,408	2,025	3,248	2,565	263	2,686	230
5 OR MORE	1,707	847	4,156	1,440	5,522	6,434	709	4,750	1,123
MOBILE HOME OR TRAILER, ETC.	0	0	0	30	23	6	6	34	0
OWNER-OCCUPIED HOUSING UNITS	5,622	7,126	9,488	8,206	5,225	5,556	11,662	10,008	6,235
1, DETACHED	4,582	5,978	6,800	5,563	2,214	3,071	11,378	7,395	5,892
1, ATTACHED	382	11	78	92	116	146	27	138	44
2	346	767	1,909	2,056	2,114	1,652	112	1,825	178
3 AND 4	108	146	453	304	480	395	58	377	83
5 OR MORE	204	224	248	161	292	292	87	248	38
MOBILE HOME OR TRAILER, ETC.	0	0	0	30	9	0	0	25	0
RENTER-OCCUPIED HOUSING UNITS	2,421	1,866	8,112	7,651	12,514	11,376	1,092	9,342	1,515
1, DETACHED	203	282	384	980	795	547	178	406	218
1, ATTACHED	25	0	43	82	141	128	14	82	7
2	379	653	2,129	3,941	4,503	2,885	82	2,503	118
3 AND 4	426	342	1,819	1,483	2,485	2,034	205	2,171	126
5 OR MORE	1,388	589	3,737	1,165	4,576	5,776	607	4,171	1,046
MOBILE HOME OR TRAILER, ETC.	0	0	0	0	14	6	6	9	0
YEAR STRUCTURE BUILT									
YEAR-ROUND HOUSING UNITS	8,300	9,153	18,163	16,980	19,289	17,672	12,875	20,104	7,885
1979 TO MARCH 1980	65	14	20	88	88	27	26	30	0
1975 TO 1978	245	92	20	63	142	82	141	29	5
1970 TO 1974	592	288	159	416	641	352	233	349	34
1960 TO 1969	2,306	1,144	1,176	1,314	1,395	909	3,083	1,882	495
1950 TO 1959	2,393	3,939	2,644	2,687	1,990	2,260	7,837	3,937	1,766
1940 TO 1949	1,190	1,281	3,377	4,710	4,464	3,955	1,331	5,762	1,800
1939 OR EARLIER	1,509	2,395	10,767	7,729	10,569	10,087	224	8,115	3,785
OWNER-OCCUPIED HOUSING UNITS	5,622	7,126	9,488	8,206	5,225	5,556	11,662	10,008	6,235
1979 TO MARCH 1980	6	7	13	42	19	0	4	0	0
1975 TO 1978	68	55	5	46	2	14	137	23	5
1970 TO 1974	202	130	53	306	153	107	156	135	7
1960 TO 1969	1,400	567	635	831	279	236	2,518	1,031	221
1950 TO 1959	2,115	3,469	1,788	1,186	313	345	7,476	2,039	1,324
1940 TO 1949	1,006	1,077	1,705	1,925	908	817	1,230	2,657	1,527
1939 OR EARLIER	825	1,821	5,289	3,870	3,551	4,037	141	4,123	3,151
RENTER-OCCUPIED HOUSING UNITS	2,421	1,866	8,112	7,651	12,514	11,376	1,092	9,342	1,515
1979 TO MARCH 1980	44	7	7	18	66	27	2	26	0
1975 TO 1978	163	37	15	12	125	48	4	6	0
1970 TO 1974	370	152	103	87	460	234	77	183	27
1960 TO 1969	855	556	513	393	987	622	550	781	269
1950 TO 1959	252	415	814	1,293	1,473	1,794	275	1,708	432
1940 TO 1949	168	176	1,510	2,410	3,125	2,972	101	2,910	234
1939 OR EARLIER	569	523	5,150	3,438	6,278	5,679	83	3,728	553
BEDROOMS									
YEAR-ROUND HOUSING UNITS	8,300	9,153	18,163	16,980	19,289	17,672	12,875	20,104	7,885
NONE	125	50	366	131	369	262	25	269	93
1	1,212	777	4,230	1,686	4,174	4,570	359	4,197	593
2	2,503	3,451	6,394	6,214	6,597	6,906	3,184	6,341	2,021
3	3,956	3,842	5,611	5,982	5,786	4,423	7,776	6,862	3,155
4	389	913	1,204	2,054	1,762	1,139	1,271	1,807	1,505
5 OR MORE	115	120	358	913	601	372	260	628	518
OWNER-OCCUPIED HOUSING UNITS	5,622	7,126	9,488	8,206	5,225	5,556	11,662	10,008	6,235
NONE	14	6	14	6	6	6	6	6	
1	102	165	251	256	333	226	81	307	79
2	1,521	2,463	3,405	2,026	1,412	2,054	2,607	2,739	1,248
3	3,514	3,513	4,409	3,547	2,067	2,200	7,479	4,787	2,960
4	370	866	1,107	1,612	942	799	1,247	1,600	1,454
5 OR MORE	115	105	310	751	465	271	248	569	494
RENTER-OCCUPIED HOUSING UNITS	2,421	1,866	8,112	7,651	12,514	11,376	1,092	9,342	1,515
NONE	87	36	341	110	280	256	22	235	93
1	1,015	583	3,729	1,278	3,389	4,054	255	3,656	510
2	918	902	2,789	3,728	4,684	4,573	544	3,309	687
3	388	283	1,126	2,040	3,344	2,112	235	1,900	170
4	13	47	82	370	701	296	24	185	38
5 OR MORE	0	15	45	125	116	85	12	57	17
YEAR-ROUND HOUSING UNITS	8,300	9,153	18,163	16,980	19,289	17,672	12,875	20,104	7,885
STORIES IN STRUCTURE									
1 TO 3	8,278	8,838	17,804	16,914	17,774	16,687	12,831	19,634	7,716
4 TO 6	22	151	348	58	664	393	39	447	169
7 TO 12	0	0	11	8	93	384	0	8	0
13 OR MORE	0	164	0	0	758	208	5	15	0
PASSENGER ELEVATOR									
STRUCTURES WITH 4 OR MORE STORIES	22	315	359	66	1,515	985	44	470	169
WITH ELEVATOR	0	315	57	8	1,114	621	15	163	70
NO ELEVATOR	22	0	302	58	401	364	29	307	99

TABLE III-7 STRUCTURAL CHARACTERISTICS OF HOUSING UNITS,
BY COMMUNITY AREA: CITY OF CHICAGO, 1980

	73	74	75	76	77
UNITS IN STRUCTURE					
YEAR-ROUND HOUSING UNITS	10,245	6,813	9,121	5,738	32,626
1, DETACHED	7,629	5,831	6,491	682	1,249
1, ATTACHED	99	37	353	0	245
2	662	170	633	283	2,511
3 AND 4	863	50	453	206	2,491
5 OR MORE	980	718	1,184	4,550	26,098
MOBILE HOME OR TRAILER, ETC.	12	7	7	17	32
OWNER-OCCUPIED HOUSING UNITS	7,749	5,711	6,671	1,831	7,579
1, DETACHED	7,080	5,581	5,962	669	1,152
1, ATTACHED	77	25	194	0	152
2	300	65	221	156	1,050
3 AND 4	210	14	96	42	532
5 OR MORE	70	26	191	947	4,693
MOBILE HOME OR TRAILER, ETC.	12	0	7	17	0
RENTER-OCCUPIED HOUSING UNITS	2,285	994	2,195	3,669	21,723
1, DETACHED	436	188	410	13	88
1, ATTACHED	7	12	144	0	80
2	357	100	393	106	1,319
3 AND 4	601	36	296	143	1,746
5 OR MORE	884	651	952	3,407	18,473
MOBILE HOME OR TRAILER, ETC.	0	7	0	0	17
YEAR STRUCTURE BUILT					
YEAR-ROUND HOUSING UNITS	10,245	6,813	9,121	5,738	32,626
1979 TO MARCH 1980	22	0	0	98	147
1975 TO 1978	63	64	30	1,065	683
1970 TO 1974	372	394	446	2,418	3,075
1960 TO 1969	1,981	1,016	1,877	1,932	7,151
1950 TO 1959	3,002	2,409	2,201	219	2,942
1940 TO 1949	2,338	2,022	1,715	6	3,467
1939 OR EARLIER	2,467	908	2,852	0	15,161
OWNER-OCCUPIED HOUSING UNITS	7,749	5,711	6,671	1,831	7,579
1979 TO MARCH 1980	14	0	0	44	6
1975 TO 1978	13	30	30	507	105
1970 TO 1974	295	85	338	533	1,179
1960 TO 1969	1,457	630	1,290	606	2,252
1950 TO 1959	2,398	2,317	1,671	135	440
1940 TO 1949	1,631	1,919	1,407	6	175
1939 OR EARLIER	1,941	730	1,935	0	3,422
RENTER-OCCUPIED HOUSING UNITS	2,285	994	2,195	3,669	21,723
1979 TO MARCH 1980	8	0	0	42	78
1975 TO 1978	50	34	0	531	534
1970 TO 1974	51	309	86	1,735	1,604
1960 TO 1969	451	327	512	1,277	4,115
1950 TO 1959	565	79	527	84	2,208
1940 TO 1949	675	91	262	0	2,946
1939 OR EARLIER	485	154	808	0	10,238
BEDROOMS					
YEAR-ROUND HOUSING UNITS	10,245	6,813	9,121	5,738	32,626
NONE	83	58	57	290	6,027
1	907	598	722	1,885	14,765
2	2,756	2,225	2,712	2,546	7,686
3	4,529	3,163	4,046	1,010	3,302
4	1,581	672	1,286	0	604
5 OR MORE	389	97	298	7	242
OWNER-OCCUPIED HOUSING UNITS	7,749	5,711	6,671	1,831	7,579
NONE	8	4	30	19	320
1	112	99	108	209	2,062
2	1,783	1,829	1,635	839	2,870
3	4,080	3,045	3,471	757	1,615
4	1,438	646	1,155	0	482
5 OR MORE	328	88	272	7	230
RENTER-OCCUPIED HOUSING UNITS	2,285	994	2,195	3,669	21,723
NONE	48	54	27	263	5,006
1	780	441	582	1,578	11,012
2	893	368	984	1,596	4,102
3	424	105	479	232	1,485
4	87	17	97	0	113
5 OR MORE	53	9	26	0	5
YEAR-ROUND HOUSING UNITS	10,245	6,813	9,121	5,738	32,626
STORIES IN STRUCTURE					
1 TO 3	10,154	6,368	8,968	3,539	14,123
4 TO 6	91	445	153	793	6,970
7 TO 12	0	0	0	240	3,479
13 OR MORE	0	0	0	1,166	8,054
PASSENGER ELEVATOR					
STRUCTURES WITH 4 OR MORE STORIES	91	445	153	2,199	18,503
WITH ELEVATOR	45	430	75	2,113	17,007
NO ELEVATOR	46	15	78	86	1,496

TABLE III-8 FUELS AND FINANCIAL CHARACTERISTICS OF HOUSING UNITS, BY COMMUNITY AREA: CITY OF CHICAGO, 1980

	01	02	03	04	05	06	07	08	09
OCCUPIED HOUSING UNITS	26,299	25,004	28,211	18,663	14,030	51,977	31,654	36,368	4,698
HOUSE HEATING FUEL									
UTILITY GAS	21,837	21,600	22,454	16,489	12,692	40,394	25,046	20,810	4,427
BOTTLED, TANK, OR LP GAS	413	418	493	334	110	795	285	349	24
ELECTRICITY	1,193	1,095	2,270	391	195	4,434	3,994	9,618	74
FUEL OIL, KEROSENE, ETC.	2,285	1,637	2,344	1,308	951	5,570	1,975	4,965	148
COAL OR COKE	290	88	349	90	56	369	145	254	0
WOOD	0	0	0	0	0	0	9	0	0
OTHER FUEL	275	150	260	51	26	327	171	305	25
NO FUEL USED	6	16	41	0	0	88	29	67	0
WATER HEATING FUEL									
UTILITY GAS	22,791	22,672	23,361	17,191	13,332	42,706	26,538	22,156	4,572
BOTTLED, TANK, OR LP GAS	522	427	642	416	225	1,075	523	1,095	39
ELECTRICITY	1,226	1,075	2,002	496	198	4,031	3,253	8,959	80
FUEL OIL, KEROSENE, ETC.	1,436	694	1,662	456	212	3,569	1,103	3,560	7
OTHER	310	126	440	80	56	515	190	546	0
NO FUEL USED	14	10	104	24	7	81	47	52	0
COOKING FUEL									
UTILITY GAS	23,497	19,652	23,464	16,677	13,373	40,610	24,061	16,992	3,908
BOTTLED, TANK, OR LP GAS	243	179	489	165	60	566	214	513	29
ELECTRICITY	2,407	5,149	3,848	1,763	545	10,391	7,079	18,029	761
OTHER	28	13	73	5	22	94	34	87	0
NO FUEL USED	124	11	337	53	30	316	266	747	0
SPECIFIED OWNER-OCCUPIED NON-CONDOMINIUM HOUSING UNITS	1,114	5,168	523	1,877	1,793	1,361	1,396	277	3,004
VALUE									
LESS THAN $10,000	0	3	1	3	11	4	15	4	2
$10,000 TO $14,999	4	1	0	10	23	10	17	3	0
$15,000 TO $19,999	7	8	8	15	58	39	18	1	4
$20,000 TO $24,999	9	20	12	47	126	83	26	3	6
$25,000 TO $29,999	13	34	17	64	158	83	29	8	10
$30,000 TO $34,999	31	57	29	86	169	99	28	1	14
$35,000 TO $39,999	39	67	25	116	218	102	22	0	34
$40,000 TO $49,999	113	290	89	305	454	230	86	9	162
$50,000 TO $79,999	635	2,834	212	873	525	401	202	24	1,694
$80,000 TO $99,999	177	1,342	38	220	39	87	126	5	905
$100,000 TO $149,000	69	470	29	113	9	114	272	24	166
$150,000 TO $199,999	15	35	28	20	2	56	192	12	5
$200,000 OR MORE	2	7	35	5	1	53	363	183	2
SELECTED MONTHLY OWNER COSTS									
SPECIFIED OWNER-OCCUPIED HOUSING UNITS	1,071	5,179	523	1,833	1,775	1,338	1,276	254	2,969
WITH A MORTGAGE	729	3,219	383	961	830	792	823	215	1,414
LESS THAN $100	0	14	0	0	0	0	0	0	0
$100 TO $149	0	0	6	0	21	0	0	0	7
$150 TO $199	0	31	11	18	8	9	0	0	3
$200 TO $249	13	79	8	42	20	34	0	6	21
$250 TO $299	61	235	35	105	116	109	45	0	141
$300 TO $349	94	408	17	146	178	102	40	0	245
$350 TO $399	106	421	10	95	127	99	79	0	256
$400 TO $449	123	338	28	148	139	36	23	0	234
$450 TO $499	78	379	66	63	92	79	0	0	163
$500 TO $599	132	556	24	181	87	116	48	32	179
$600 TO $749	87	435	70	83	25	111	253	12	92
$750 OR MORE	35	323	108	80	17	97	335	159	73
NOT MORTGAGED	342	1,960	140	872	945	546	453	39	1,555
LESS THAN $50	0	0	0	0	15	0	7	0	0
$50 TO $74	0	7	5	0	7	0	0	0	0
$75 TO $99	0	14	6	16	85	28	60	0	7
$100 TO $124	24	45	16	55	164	77	43	6	200
$125 TO $149	33	129	23	143	244	90	97	0	856
$150 TO $199	173	731	59	373	343	202	80	11	394
$200 TO $249	74	650	19	135	87	47	37	0	98
$250 OR MORE	38	384	12	150	0	102	129	22	
GROSS RENT									
SPECIFIED RENTER-OCCUPIED HOUSING UNITS	22,688	13,001	24,459	13,487	8,729	40,317	23,469	26,220	955
LESS THAN $60	435	9	554	7	188	476	500	1,283	0
$60 TO $79	137	0	520	29	157	537	518	1,174	0
$80 TO $99	64	15	381	31	70	190	117	772	0
$100 TO $119	95	28	627	55	184	310	329	585	0
$120 TO $149	559	149	2,508	428	387	1,030	613	1,280	4
$150 TO $169	799	171	2,202	755	462	1,636	676	1,023	11
$170 TO $199	2,693	444	3,711	1,888	1,354	4,112	1,598	1,209	19
$200 TO $249	5,915	2,213	6,327	4,418	2,966	9,408	3,685	2,034	124
$250 TO $299	6,047	4,087	3,828	3,050	1,668	7,471	3,742	2,367	266
$300 TO $349	3,193	2,759	1,710	1,515	712	5,652	3,488	2,567	332
$350 TO $399	1,400	1,658	854	768	295	3,431	2,664	2,539	77
$400 TO $499	946	1,099	796	319	111	3,762	3,130	4,051	59
$500 OR MORE	166	190	181	27	23	1,900	2,212	5,004	27
NO CASH RENT	239	179	260	197	152	402	197	332	36
CONTRACT RENT									
SPECIFIED RENTER-OCCUPIED HOUSING UNITS	22,587	12,968	24,323	13,446	8,711	40,210	23,404	26,779	951
LESS THAN $50	352	13	530	23	100	352	361	1,170	2
$50 TO $99	310	51	956	125	607	1,153	1,122	2,559	3
$100 TO $119	161	72	690	212	459	778	563	448	6
$120 TO $139	355	81	1,632	413	639	1,142	739	670	6
$140 TO $149	342	50	1,369	328	362	766	402	610	1
$150 TO $159	575	124	1,466	619	708	1,583	668	447	15
$160 TO $169	859	134	1,560	702	583	1,603	565	600	16
$170 TO $199	3,369	771	4,440	2,643	1,870	5,562	1,965	1,153	48
$200 TO $249	6,954	3,587	6,215	4,597	2,220	8,893	3,736	2,018	196
$250 TO $299	5,167	3,903	2,837	2,384	732	6,616	3,755	2,376	326
$300 TO $399	3,460	3,587	1,739	1,136	215	7,089	5,292	5,316	257
$400 TO $499	426	347	479	56	16	2,710	2,434	3,945	27
$500 OR MORE	64	37	178	15	4	1,487	1,552	5,145	5
NO CASH RENT	193	211	232	193	196	476	250	322	43

TABLE III-8 FUELS AND FINANCIAL CHARACTERISTICS OF HOUSING UNITS,
BY COMMUNITY AREA: CITY OF CHICAGO, 1980

	10	11	12	13	14	15	16	17	18
OCCUPIED HOUSING UNITS	14,917	9,960	6,813	5,408	16,285	22,808	20,593	13,889	4,126
HOUSE HEATING FUEL									
UTILITY GAS	14,147	9,362	6,605	4,858	14,650	21,325	18,657	13,281	3,972
BOTTLED, TANK, OR LP GAS	30	34	7	80	272	106	176	74	7
ELECTRICITY	391	149	82	130	228	289	400	157	32
FUEL OIL, KEROSENE, ETC.	349	388	114	335	1,015	950	1,228	370	115
COAL OR COKE	0	8	0	0	78	91	63	0	0
WOOD	0	0	0	0	0	0	0	0	0
OTHER FUEL	0	12	5	0	42	42	63	7	0
NO FUEL USED	0	7	0	5	0	5	6	0	0
WATER HEATING FUEL									
UTILITY GAS	14,510	9,773	6,640	5,072	15,388	22,125	19,373	13,454	4,022
BOTTLED, TANK, OR LP GAS	85	42	38	94	322	188	267	124	22
ELECTRICITY	300	89	130	171	217	303	442	268	49
FUEL OIL, KEROSENE, ETC.	18	48	0	64	284	125	342	43	25
OTHER	0	8	5	0	37	67	57	0	8
NO FUEL USED	4	0	0	7	37	0	112	0	0
COOKING FUEL									
UTILITY GAS	12,628	8,958	5,218	4,407	15,373	21,213	19,216	12,595	3,831
BOTTLED, TANK, OR LP GAS	31	18	31	36	131	50	66	22	12
ELECTRICITY	2,246	984	1,557	957	760	1,504	1,188	1,263	283
OTHER	12	0	0	8	10	17	6	3	0
NO FUEL USED	0	0	7	0	11	24	117	6	0
SPECIFIED OWNER-OCCUPIED NON-CONDOMINIUM HOUSING UNITS	9,996	4,291	5,414	2,031	2,770	7,990	3,572	8,927	1,915
VALUE									
LESS THAN $10,000	6	1	0	0	3	4	6	10	3
$10,000 TO $14,999	6	6	4	2	4	9	7	14	6
$15,000 TO $19,999	17	13	3	4	17	35	33	27	10
$20,000 TO $24,999	51	28	19	2	50	82	110	73	31
$25,000 TO $29,999	76	61	27	5	75	163	142	118	32
$30,000 TO $34,999	106	91	37	18	100	227	228	218	56
$35,000 TO $39,999	171	108	39	20	162	349	243	322	72
$40,000 TO $49,999	669	433	202	110	451	1,186	779	1,085	278
$50,000 TO $79,999	5,725	2,853	1,845	1,026	1,670	5,242	1,865	5,790	1,193
$80,000 TO $99,999	2,371	613	1,498	569	187	616	128	1,094	206
$100,000 TO $149,000	723	77	1,380	248	46	64	25	169	23
$150,000 TO $199,999	65	4	290	24	3	8	4	5	4
$200,000 OR MORE	10	3	70	3	2	5	2	2	1
SELECTED MONTHLY OWNER COSTS									
SPECIFIED OWNER-OCCUPIED HOUSING UNITS	9,943	4,307	5,414	2,031	2,710	7,987	3,600	8,933	1,915
WITH A MORTGAGE	4,674	1,747	2,660	1,217	1,543	3,635	1,858	4,229	807
LESS THAN $100	0	14	0	0	0	5	0	0	0
$100 TO $149	26	6	11	0	14	14	5	24	10
$150 TO $199	58	38	19	9	12	75	14	69	13
$200 TO $249	137	49	36	0	27	120	67	202	26
$250 TO $299	609	188	83	43	119	509	203	705	97
$300 TO $349	724	274	188	101	303	678	356	712	113
$350 TO $399	635	277	346	155	177	474	343	657	93
$400 TO $449	629	248	342	182	253	378	228	602	92
$450 TO $499	392	169	308	171	180	450	149	386	97
$500 TO $599	681	320	460	250	242	538	274	519	144
$600 TO $749	534	124	514	201	164	316	192	283	116
$750 OR MORE	249	40	353	105	52	78	27	70	6
NOT MORTGAGED	5,269	2,560	2,754	814	1,167	4,352	1,742	4,704	1,108
LESS THAN $50	0	0	0	0	6	0	0	0	0
$50 TO $74	6	7	0	0	0	6	0	14	0
$75 TO $99	34	6	7	0	16	74	28	112	18
$100 TO $124	229	134	37	11	94	375	219	453	42
$125 TO $149	738	480	163	30	330	943	431	1,191	173
$150 TO $199	2,553	1,466	981	313	513	2,240	789	2,175	629
$200 TO $249	1,224	422	886	293	138	581	192	601	178
$250 OR MORE	485	45	680	167	70	133	83	158	68
GROSS RENT									
SPECIFIED RENTER-OCCUPIED HOUSING UNITS	2,981	3,322	788	2,326	10,824	9,727	12,436	3,075	1,496
LESS THAN $60	0	6	0	8	48	4	21	6	0
$60 TO $79	0	6	0	7	17	8	15	4	19
$80 TO $99	15	13	0	12	13	30	43	17	11
$100 TO $119	12	6	0	20	66	62	182	54	9
$120 TO $149	23	87	12	32	271	270	680	102	67
$150 TO $169	41	114	24	62	610	474	695	116	75
$170 TO $199	93	356	39	96	1,575	1,264	1,786	275	172
$200 TO $249	559	628	129	463	3,913	2,945	4,357	490	278
$250 TO $299	654	783	153	813	2,557	2,364	2,823	824	316
$300 TO $349	763	673	143	375	958	1,213	1,043	614	267
$350 TO $399	287	266	76	242	436	480	367	192	146
$400 TO $499	292	210	81	104	188	254	159	111	56
$500 OR MORE	77	21	50	31	34	45	35	85	13
NO CASH RENT	165	153	81	61	138	314	230	185	67
CONTRACT RENT									
SPECIFIED RENTER-OCCUPIED HOUSING UNITS	2,970	3,315	780	2,320	10,806	9,701	12,435	3,079	1,496
LESS THAN $50	8	13	1	5	26	24	30	4	7
$50 TO $99	30	68	12	14	121	189	287	55	29
$100 TO $119	51	123	16	29	157	271	424	91	55
$120 TO $139	45	142	16	40	318	347	680	96	66
$140 TO $149	22	62	10	25	194	229	363	56	52
$150 TO $159	87	148	24	54	553	535	720	141	74
$160 TO $169	44	88	11	33	603	450	705	82	60
$170 TO $199	202	401	50	174	2,409	1,571	2,796	327	191
$200 TO $249	630	815	157	719	3,822	3,307	4,259	727	359
$250 TO $299	744	712	186	680	1,833	1,677	1,410	773	309
$300 TO $399	825	536	181	434	583	719	430	460	207
$400 TO $499	90	50	25	35	25	38	22	50	11
$500 OR MORE	34	5	15	16	9	8	6	9	4
NO CASH RENT	158	152	76	62	153	336	303	208	72

TABLE III-8 FUELS AND FINANCIAL CHARACTERISTICS OF HOUSING UNITS, BY COMMUNITY AREA: CITY OF CHICAGO, 1980

	19	20	21	22	23	24	25	26	27
OCCUPIED HOUSING UNITS	21,083	7,053	13,222	29,477	21,396	32,122	41,617	9,140	9,771
HOUSE HEATING FUEL									
UTILITY GAS	19,699	6,453	12,106	26,783	18,937	29,791	36,145	7,549	8,299
BOTTLED, TANK, OR LP GAS	135	68	139	398	383	550	850	281	327
ELECTRICITY	287	104	214	481	609	779	1,213	392	205
FUEL OIL, KEROSENE, ETC.	928	385	726	1,618	1,235	770	2,832	802	731
COAL OR COKE	29	13	9	43	88	95	229	57	21
WOOD	0	0	8	7	2	7	10	0	0
OTHER FUEL	5	25	16	105	122	96	275	52	135
NO FUEL USED	0	5	4	42	20	34	63	7	53
WATER HEATING FUEL									
UTILITY GAS	20,537	6,801	12,559	27,643	19,769	30,337	37,484	8,031	8,552
BOTTLED, TANK, OR LP GAS	173	109	259	656	694	1,036	1,754	513	459
ELECTRICITY	251	46	203	379	389	262	1,085	201	208
FUEL OIL, KEROSENE, ETC.	97	78	177	632	249	220	775	235	274
OTHER	25	9	24	112	188	93	388	144	206
NO FUEL USED	0	10	0	55	107	174	131	16	72
COOKING FUEL									
UTILITY GAS	19,859	6,713	12,740	28,557	20,541	31,120	38,152	8,746	9,314
BOTTLED, TANK, OR LP GAS	54	48	75	192	213	320	471	168	196
ELECTRICITY	1,152	268	399	644	521	398	2,802	135	186
OTHER	6	9	0	72	91	50	78	46	42
NO FUEL USED	12	15	8	12	30	234	114	45	33
SPECIFIED OWNER-OCCUPIED NON-CONDOMINIUM HOUSING UNITS	6,655	1,555	1,419	2,266	2,748	1,257	8,087	501	425
VALUE									
LESS THAN $10,000	6	1	5	36	51	90	35	23	34
$10,000 TO $14,999	11	12	29	132	158	175	80	38	55
$15,000 TO $19,999	63	44	83	221	428	215	316	87	83
$20,000 TO $24,999	151	123	123	378	500	211	666	98	72
$25,000 TO $29,999	215	154	130	336	493	165	831	55	47
$30,000 TO $34,999	359	171	191	326	377	96	870	39	53
$35,000 TO $39,999	420	167	165	257	277	81	978	41	16
$40,000 TO $49,999	1,364	349	331	343	322	98	1,719	60	32
$50,000 TO $79,999	3,828	528	344	215	138	97	2,054	57	27
$80,000 TO $99,999	210	5	10	12	2	13	419	2	5
$100,000 TO $149,000	24	0	6	8	2	8	100	1	0
$150,000 TO $199,999	4	0	0	1	0	3	9	0	1
$200,000 OR MORE	0	1	2	1	0	5	10	0	0
SELECTED MONTHLY OWNER COSTS									
SPECIFIED OWNER-OCCUPIED HOUSING UNITS	6,680	1,524	1,419	2,138	2,744	970	8,081	452	342
WITH A MORTGAGE	3,054	851	651	1,048	1,827	411	5,866	295	177
LESS THAN $100	0	0	0	0	0	0	25	6	12
$100 TO $149	60	0	0	13	29	0	54	16	0
$150 TO $199	36	25	18	30	38	47	127	6	32
$200 TO $249	115	62	25	133	215	95	204	50	48
$250 TO $299	374	122	98	181	373	64	659	44	8
$300 TO $349	583	184	134	219	309	86	1,108	88	28
$350 TO $399	491	121	148	207	457	26	1,120	25	23
$400 TO $449	520	110	129	81	229	35	900	22	15
$450 TO $499	257	62	44	95	93	0	754	18	0
$500 TO $599	381	92	33	74	69	12	582	12	0
$600 TO $749	193	56	22	10	15	14	243	8	11
$750 OR MORE	44	17	0	5	0	32	90	0	0
NOT MORTGAGED	3,626	673	768	1,090	917	559	2,215	157	165
LESS THAN $50	0	0	0	0	0	0	0	11	0
$50 TO $74	7	0	11	7	12	15	19	3	0
$75 TO $99	69	17	22	107	122	90	71	18	0
$100 TO $124	263	93	239	254	124	131	236	10	35
$125 TO $149	761	174	215	320	184	156	381	13	0
$150 TO $199	1,738	286	204	280	302	87	708	49	46
$200 TO $249	579	72	63	54	121	58	531	4	40
$250 OR MORE	209	31	14	68	52	22	269	49	44
GROSS RENT									
SPECIFIED RENTER-OCCUPIED HOUSING UNITS	9,312	3,786	8,262	21,145	13,757	25,191	25,186	6,979	7,805
LESS THAN $60	9	15	13	97	123	323	115	111	223
$60 TO $79	6	27	45	112	87	534	113	68	85
$80 TO $99	67	28	27	191	43	574	54	26	159
$100 TO $119	132	19	162	515	228	1,283	225	153	212
$120 TO $149	438	90	440	1,347	712	2,621	827	358	875
$150 TO $169	524	202	599	1,957	1,052	2,632	1,313	393	879
$170 TO $199	1,117	546	1,340	3,958	2,503	4,426	3,675	1,169	1,427
$200 TO $249	2,824	1,525	2,994	6,897	4,611	7,212	8,202	2,210	2,157
$250 TO $299	2,143	835	1,590	3,540	2,412	3,163	6,013	1,609	1,011
$300 TO $349	966	243	565	1,316	1,105	1,210	2,436	414	338
$350 TO $399	479	56	238	506	447	530	1,053	215	156
$400 TO $499	174	95	36	298	159	162	751	145	167
$500 OR MORE	41	14	7	46	52	95	162	32	28
NO CASH RENT	392	91	206	365	223	426	247	76	88
CONTRACT RENT									
SPECIFIED RENTER-OCCUPIED HOUSING UNITS	9,306	3,774	8,250	21,097	13,730	25,131	25,160	6,959	7,790
LESS THAN $50	33	11	48	180	147	576	175	112	198
$50 TO $99	357	123	503	1,338	648	4,183	322	242	524
$100 TO $119	400	179	539	1,462	823	3,453	562	279	633
$120 TO $139	506	273	815	2,394	1,475	4,526	1,320	736	1,221
$140 TO $149	200	153	371	1,220	905	1,773	948	476	702
$150 TO $159	588	324	775	2,262	1,740	2,874	1,864	846	1,095
$160 TO $169	513	254	588	1,930	1,463	1,683	2,276	686	768
$170 TO $199	1,915	920	1,952	4,619	3,658	2,958	7,097	2,066	1,550
$200 TO $249	2,735	1,127	1,888	3,830	2,129	1,999	7,581	1,216	834
$250 TO $299	1,230	266	445	1,105	451	436	2,275	204	138
$300 TO $399	438	49	114	319	60	111	405	36	30
$400 TO $499	8	3	5	43	2	27	25	3	2
$500 OR MORE	4	1	4	28	2	12	11	1	3
NO CASH RENT	379	91	203	367	227	520	299	56	92

TABLE III-8 FUELS AND FINANCIAL CHARACTERISTICS OF HOUSING UNITS,
BY COMMUNITY AREA: CITY OF CHICAGO, 1980

	28	29	30	31	32	33	34	35	36
OCCUPIED HOUSING UNITS	18,340	17,185	19,334	12,964	3,862	2,421	4,453	14,353	4,874
HOUSE HEATING FUEL									
UTILITY GAS	13,919	14,419	17,670	12,098	2,562	1,228	3,904	9,347	3,733
BOTTLED, TANK, OR LP GAS	497	652	145	93	33	38	42	188	107
ELECTRICITY	2,167	555	1,000	554	964	822	330	1,683	520
FUEL OIL, KEROSENE, ETC.	1,115	1,177	468	197	157	280	134	2,581	401
COAL OR COKE	204	222	35	5	33	23	0	148	27
WOOD	0	0	0	0	0	0	0	0	0
OTHER FUEL	402	122	0	0	113	30	15	347	81
NO FUEL USED	36	38	16	17	0	0	28	59	5
WATER HEATING FUEL									
UTILITY GAS	14,592	15,080	18,528	12,623	2,997	1,710	4,170	10,748	4,100
BOTTLED, TANK, OR LP GAS	898	1,102	455	161	9	68	125	294	187
ELECTRICITY	1,586	337	198	103	569	352	79	1,109	164
FUEL OIL, KEROSENE, ETC.	644	317	60	20	184	218	39	1,692	255
OTHER	483	281	40	11	95	57	21	483	146
NO FUEL USED	137	68	53	46	8	16	19	27	22
COOKING FUEL									
UTILITY GAS	15,368	16,355	18,745	12,719	2,005	2,307	4,145	12,952	4,599
BOTTLED, TANK, OR LP GAS	463	389	188	42	0	25	47	248	73
ELECTRICITY	2,200	323	386	184	1,593	51	244	847	119
OTHER	62	35	15	0	61	5	10	123	41
NO FUEL USED	247	83	0	19	203	33	7	183	42
SPECIFIED OWNER-OCCUPIED NON-CONDOMINIUM HOUSING UNITS	582	755	1,906	556	14	3	270	324	79
VALUE									
LESS THAN $10,000	52	46	44	57	0	0	7	20	9
$10,000 TO $14,999	69	86	141	77	0	1	20	31	10
$15,000 TO $19,999	64	116	267	105	1	0	15	46	7
$20,000 TO $24,999	78	124	350	117	0	0	21	62	10
$25,000 TO $29,999	48	114	279	77	0	0	22	16	2
$30,000 TO $34,999	28	100	283	49	0	1	24	21	17
$35,000 TO $39,999	16	47	215	30	0	0	15	7	9
$40,000 TO $49,999	26	68	223	24	0	0	51	19	6
$50,000 TO $79,999	105	49	93	19	0	0	50	39	6
$80,000 TO $99,999	41	2	7	0	10	1	24	23	0
$100,000 TO $149,000	41	2	2	1	3	0	18	37	2
$150,000 TO $199,999	3	1	0	0	0	0	3	3	1
$200,000 OR MORE	11	0	0	2	0	0	0	0	0
SELECTED MONTHLY OWNER COSTS									
SPECIFIED OWNER-OCCUPIED HOUSING UNITS	545	716	1,855	510	0	0	244	321	77
WITH A MORTGAGE	194	453	888	146	0	0	106	127	35
LESS THAN $100	0	14	0	8	0	0	0	0	0
$100 TO $149	6	15	40	14	0	0	0	19	0
$150 TO $199	0	7	32	28	0	0	6	0	0
$200 TO $249	0	100	116	25	0	0	13	0	0
$250 TO $299	17	108	165	15	0	0	0	0	12
$300 TO $349	19	92	143	8	0	0	9	0	0
$350 TO $399	23	62	162	8	0	0	13	21	0
$400 TO $449	0	22	113	18	0	0	7	12	0
$450 TO $499	9	27	50	4	0	0	25	6	0
$500 TO $599	25	6	45	13	0	0	33	50	23
$600 TO $749	79	0	16	5	0	0	0	16	0
$750 OR MORE	16	0	6	0	0	0	0	3	0
NOT MORTGAGED	351	263	967	364	0	0	138	194	42
LESS THAN $50	17	10	0	14	0	0	0	4	0
$50 TO $74	0	12	38	20	0	0	8	3	0
$75 TO $99	0	16	152	38	0	0	8	5	5
$100 TO $124	75	34	246	118	0	0	51	24	7
$125 TO $149	42	69	248	98	0	0	41	53	18
$150 TO $199	108	43	172	65	0	0	14	45	4
$200 TO $249	63	49	92	11	0	0	16	29	8
$250 OR MORE	46	30	19	0	0	0	8	31	0
GROSS RENT									
SPECIFIED RENTER-OCCUPIED HOUSING UNITS	15,908	13,480	12,171	9,716	2,234	2,407	3,409	13,549	4,616
LESS THAN $60	2,524	161	233	186	53	621	319	1,932	881
$60 TO $79	1,991	253	166	113	112	382	435	1,740	760
$80 TO $99	1,567	236	172	190	144	244	248	792	514
$100 TO $119	1,088	398	356	449	66	125	138	450	443
$120 TO $149	1,989	961	732	1,294	173	218	218	872	570
$150 TO $169	855	1,074	995	1,330	95	72	270	993	239
$170 TO $199	1,193	2,882	1,984	2,061	139	69	493	809	357
$200 TO $249	1,631	4,288	4,176	2,353	308	204	695	1,675	439
$250 TO $299	1,262	1,930	2,077	837	215	336	331	1,887	265
$300 TO $349	665	609	591	435	216	93	118	1,263	38
$350 TO $399	387	372	273	121	186	11	55	531	29
$400 TO $499	348	111	86	84	225	11	0	479	14
$500 OR MORE	116	6	10	15	236	0	0	64	0
NO CASH RENT	292	199	320	248	66	21	89	62	67
CONTRACT RENT									
SPECIFIED RENTER-OCCUPIED HOUSING UNITS	15,809	13,425	12,126	9,693	2,221	2,377	3,410	13,350	4,576
LESS THAN $50	2,210	349	411	349	55	499	392	1,074	976
$50 TO $99	5,132	1,085	1,263	1,913	353	862	956	3,633	1,735
$100 TO $119	1,330	1,104	1,102	1,534	56	98	335	501	279
$120 TO $139	1,954	1,817	1,966	2,082	62	117	447	728	363
$140 TO $149	571	1,112	1,095	723	65	63	153	470	158
$150 TO $159	694	1,859	1,917	1,074	24	31	283	453	188
$160 TO $169	442	1,501	1,240	543	48	31	125	418	111
$170 TO $199	775	2,822	1,707	675	132	96	323	691	280
$200 TO $249	957	1,273	873	440	291	186	199	2,149	338
$250 TO $299	670	248	174	75	254	342	85	1,395	97
$300 TO $399	675	78	44	29	462	36	10	1,422	21
$400 TO $499	144	11	13	3	147	0	1	270	2
$500 OR MORE	10	4	4	4	209	0	0	73	2
NO CASH RENT	245	162	317	249	63	16	101	73	26

TABLE III-8 FUELS AND FINANCIAL CHARACTERISTICS OF HOUSING UNITS,
BY COMMUNITY AREA: CITY OF CHICAGO, 1980

	37	38	39	40	41	42	43	44	45
OCCUPIED HOUSING UNITS	1,912	18,694	10,034	10,986	14,458	14,075	31,367	16,418	4,223
HOUSE HEATING FUEL									
UTILITY GAS	1,645	13,899	6,812	9,025	11,280	11,361	25,961	13,975	3,827
BOTTLED, TANK, OR LP GAS	17	538	202	242	202	444	947	413	60
ELECTRICITY	72	2,100	1,635	792	825	663	1,533	688	61
FUEL OIL, KEROSENE, ETC.	152	1,350	1,033	583	1,628	1,037	1,947	1,109	230
COAL OR COKE	17	210	202	126	251	252	461	117	25
WOOD	0	0	0	0	0	0	0	0	0
OTHER FUEL	9	560	120	212	272	293	491	109	20
NO FUEL USED	0	37	30	6	0	25	27	7	0
WATER HEATING FUEL									
UTILITY GAS	1,817	15,246	7,340	9,511	11,885	12,093	27,064	14,520	4,001
BOTTLED, TANK, OR LP GAS	41	716	239	413	246	703	1,280	521	122
ELECTRICITY	21	1,262	1,424	450	845	522	1,405	807	54
FUEL OIL, KEROSENE, ETC.	11	728	745	293	1,042	492	894	394	30
OTHER	22	630	270	274	324	252	659	156	16
NO FUEL USED	0	112	16	45	116	13	65	20	0
COOKING FUEL									
UTILITY GAS	1,846	17,213	6,927	10,390	12,294	13,115	27,377	14,248	3,783
BOTTLED, TANK, OR LP GAS	26	293	106	272	80	318	602	258	41
ELECTRICITY	26	841	2,942	180	1,795	446	3,236	1,870	385
OTHER	14	154	36	79	109	80	73	35	0
NO FUEL USED	0	193	23	65	180	116	79	7	14
SPECIFIED OWNER-OCCUPIED NON-CONDOMINIUM HOUSING UNITS	245	392	507	146	949	556	2,903	4,477	2,467
VALUE									
LESS THAN $10,000	16	30	7	13	0	21	12	30	8
$10,000 TO $14,999	23	50	15	19	6	43	35	46	29
$15,000 TO $19,999	36	65	33	31	6	92	168	228	114
$20,000 TO $24,999	50	76	16	27	8	93	327	378	273
$25,000 TO $29,999	35	38	19	10	11	88	352	505	326
$30,000 TO $34,999	18	32	29	12	11	66	310	562	286
$35,000 TO $39,999	20	22	19	9	13	40	283	577	293
$40,000 TO $49,999	21	30	28	17	50	65	481	980	519
$50,000 TO $79,999	25	38	68	7	195	43	644	1,048	588
$80,000 TO $99,999	0	1	41	1	194	2	132	79	22
$100,000 TO $149,000	0	6	101	0	273	1	118	31	6
$150,000 TO $199,999	0	1	60	0	113	0	34	8	1
$200,000 OR MORE	1	3	71	0	69	2	7	5	2
SELECTED MONTHLY OWNER COSTS									
SPECIFIED OWNER-OCCUPIED HOUSING UNITS	245	335	465	115	946	490	2,848	4,472	2,476
WITH A MORTGAGE	148	76	288	22	708	202	2,458	2,814	2,227
LESS THAN $100	0	0	8	0	0	0	9	14	17
$100 TO $149	0	0	0	0	10	0	15	56	21
$150 TO $199	6	28	2	4	9	9	26	131	20
$200 TO $249	24	5	0	0	12	39	101	151	133
$250 TO $299	37	10	19	4	40	25	289	522	484
$300 TO $349	18	5	16	0	100	30	427	638	557
$350 TO $399	48	7	17	10	76	70	439	517	395
$400 TO $449	11	21	30	0	77	0	334	357	272
$450 TO $499	0	0	14	0	63	7	234	187	139
$500 TO $599	4	0	58	4	92	14	353	146	131
$600 TO $749	0	0	28	0	106	8	134	74	41
$750 OR MORE	0	0	96	0	123	0	97	21	17
NOT MORTGAGED	97	259	177	93	238	288	390	1,658	249
LESS THAN $50	0	0	0	3	6	0	6	0	0
$50 TO $74	0	7	2	5	0	0	6	25	0
$75 TO $99	6	18	0	6	0	0	22	14	0
$100 TO $124	19	49	7	3	7	21	25	91	19
$125 TO $149	6	20	6	9	21	47	42	244	32
$150 TO $199	41	34	24	25	81	110	93	683	108
$200 TO $249	6	27	58	21	45	71	101	342	57
$250 OR MORE	19	104	80	21	78	39	95	259	33
GROSS RENT									
SPECIFIED RENTER-OCCUPIED HOUSING UNITS	1,348	17,324	7,737	10,319	10,751	12,070	25,278	9,897	1,142
LESS THAN $60	190	1,142	120	410	66	279	155	34	0
$60 TO $79	137	1,572	83	469	43	227	132	9	0
$80 TO $99	35	1,338	66	514	44	211	126	27	0
$100 TO $119	56	1,519	120	536	63	445	117	49	8
$120 TO $149	62	2,263	464	869	293	1,172	365	116	0
$150 TO $169	94	1,870	587	856	408	1,177	935	281	15
$170 TO $199	172	2,148	1,336	1,424	1,393	2,186	2,617	976	127
$200 TO $249	297	3,288	1,600	3,105	2,562	3,754	7,613	3,822	383
$250 TO $299	194	1,385	1,050	1,450	2,338	1,638	7,368	3,032	312
$300 TO $349	52	451	779	391	1,414	486	3,396	939	172
$350 TO $399	37	127	463	111	735	200	1,393	335	28
$400 TO $499	5	69	876	27	699	119	742	117	55
$500 OR MORE	0	12	123	0	554	46	145	60	17
NO CASH RENT	17	140	70	157	139	130	174	100	25
CONTRACT RENT									
SPECIFIED RENTER-OCCUPIED HOUSING UNITS	1,327	17,165	7,695	10,218	10,684	11,987	25,179	9,867	1,140
LESS THAN $50	214	2,010	93	659	58	264	227	28	2
$50 TO $99	300	3,260	208	1,189	133	698	287	72	2
$100 TO $119	151	1,588	200	581	78	602	233	102	16
$120 TO $139	181	1,862	520	823	312	1,013	449	213	37
$140 TO $149	66	857	287	386	103	697	403	175	24
$150 TO $159	122	1,352	476	675	276	1,053	823	429	48
$160 TO $169	71	1,182	531	830	294	1,091	1,164	469	66
$170 TO $199	120	2,543	1,419	2,358	1,695	3,158	4,790	2,267	260
$200 TO $249	60	1,825	1,163	2,117	2,697	2,416	9,170	4,274	444
$250 TO $299	17	454	925	417	2,228	616	5,008	1,418	169
$300 TO $399	4	103	1,132	81	1,674	243	2,160	313	44
$400 TO $499	0	6	564	6	465	27	306	13	4
$500 OR MORE	0	3	108	3	515	5	47	7	3
NO CASH RENT	21	120	69	93	156	104	112	87	21

TABLE III-8 FUELS AND FINANCIAL CHARACTERISTICS OF HOUSING UNITS, BY COMMUNITY AREA: CITY OF CHICAGO, 1980

	46	47	48	49	50	51	52	53	54
OCCUPIED HOUSING UNITS	14,471	1,039	6,194	18,113	3,367	5,627	7,458	11,745	3,395
HOUSE HEATING FUEL									
UTILITY GAS	12,850	977	5,521	16,361	2,992	5,032	6,911	10,703	2,709
BOTTLED, TANK, OR LP GAS	144	7	63	323	44	61	32	153	107
ELECTRICITY	516	30	137	413	108	55	113	423	309
FUEL OIL, KEROSENE, ETC.	812	14	460	955	217	429	397	443	120
COAL OR COKE	43	0	9	47	0	0	5	5	39
WOOD	4	0	0	0	6	0	0	0	0
OTHER FUEL	90	11	4	14	0	43	0	11	82
NO FUEL USED	12	0	0	0	0	7	0	7	29
WATER HEATING FUEL									
UTILITY GAS	13,357	997	5,923	16,620	3,091	5,356	7,215	10,971	2,910
BOTTLED, TANK, OR LP GAS	430	29	130	740	130	107	45	403	242
ELECTRICITY	292	5	94	481	90	72	155	320	103
FUEL OIL, KEROSENE, ETC.	211	0	27	164	14	63	32	40	24
OTHER	80	0	20	19	0	22	0	0	108
NO FUEL USED	101	8	0	89	42	7	11	11	8
COOKING FUEL									
UTILITY GAS	13,540	960	5,303	16,374	2,352	5,053	6,829	10,944	3,222
BOTTLED, TANK, OR LP GAS	189	16	61	197	29	7	29	87	92
ELECTRICITY	703	63	830	1,433	985	545	606	688	47
OTHER	6	0	0	21	5	0	0	16	18
NO FUEL USED	33	0	0	88	18	0	16	10	16
SPECIFIED OWNER-OCCUPIED NON-CONDOMINIUM HOUSING UNITS	3,205	520	3,938	9,203	1,476	3,221	4,046	6,802	471
VALUE									
LESS THAN $10,000	38	12	16	55	13	11	16	33	7
$10,000 TO $14,999	86	21	30	134	49	70	38	69	13
$15,000 TO $19,999	278	64	96	511	147	318	163	307	35
$20,000 TO $24,999	482	78	237	1,092	262	574	320	633	105
$25,000 TO $29,999	510	82	400	1,310	253	629	456	804	87
$30,000 TO $34,999	436	73	423	1,173	176	471	593	856	70
$35,000 TO $39,999	393	48	445	1,086	176	416	560	935	50
$40,000 TO $49,999	500	83	889	1,930	255	446	1,058	1,754	87
$50,000 TO $79,999	448	59	1,168	1,748	141	275	805	1,319	16
$80,000 TO $99,999	25	0	140	125	2	7	19	69	1
$100,000 TO $149,000	7	0	67	31	2	4	8	18	0
$150,000 TO $199,999	1	0	23	5	0	0	0	2	0
$200,000 OR MORE	1	0	4	3	0	0	0	3	0
SELECTED MONTHLY OWNER COSTS									
SPECIFIED OWNER-OCCUPIED HOUSING UNITS	3,149	520	3,938	9,204	1,480	3,230	4,050	6,809	453
WITH A MORTGAGE	2,421	418	3,543	7,617	1,186	2,560	1,873	6,189	400
LESS THAN $100	7	0	38	20	0	12	0	9	0
$100 TO $149	20	7	19	86	0	5	20	33	0
$150 TO $199	24	5	39	201	24	85	39	128	18
$200 TO $249	106	10	106	352	93	258	197	220	89
$250 TO $299	257	82	314	1,041	281	558	407	606	123
$300 TO $349	503	69	652	1,683	297	597	444	1,051	93
$350 TO $399	490	122	757	1,576	221	480	294	1,489	44
$400 TO $449	444	80	532	1,138	102	239	146	1,079	25
$450 TO $499	284	35	429	687	44	183	139	701	8
$500 TO $599	164	0	461	624	62	125	107	677	0
$600 TO $749	104	8	152	184	62	18	59	162	0
$750 OR MORE	18	0	44	25	0	0	21	34	0
NOT MORTGAGED	728	102	395	1,587	294	670	2,177	620	53
LESS THAN $50	5	0	0	0	0	0	0	0	0
$50 TO $74	8	2	9	7	79	18	21	18	0
$75 TO $99	54	3	17	75	43	20	107	37	0
$100 TO $124	158	44	49	229	49	117	334	65	12
$125 TO $149	157	16	100	243	55	108	589	154	6
$150 TO $199	196	27	134	641	49	253	864	160	31
$200 TO $249	96	10	60	256	6	114	212	91	0
$250 OR MORE	54	0	26	136	13	40	50	95	4
GROSS RENT									
SPECIFIED RENTER-OCCUPIED HOUSING UNITS	8,354	306	1,412	6,201	1,331	1,543	2,201	3,301	2,347
LESS THAN $60	194	0	12	27	0	168	7	7	344
$60 TO $79	196	0	0	10	12	9	9	12	412
$80 TO $99	166	0	0	40	25	49	23	15	351
$100 TO $119	291	6	0	153	21	35	62	43	144
$120 TO $149	558	0	14	209	96	163	202	131	224
$150 TO $169	670	10	28	292	72	92	177	209	65
$170 TO $199	1,290	25	135	725	142	152	429	264	105
$200 TO $249	2,330	103	373	1,924	369	234	597	809	330
$250 TO $299	1,481	87	410	1,358	344	161	389	595	212
$300 TO $349	612	23	213	685	120	124	106	626	106
$350 TO $399	216	20	96	380	59	22	47	229	12
$400 TO $499	67	8	80	240	44	121	42	275	20
$500 OR MORE	61	8	19	87	0	36	12	31	0
NO CASH RENT	222	16	42	71	27	49	106	55	22
CONTRACT RENT									
SPECIFIED RENTER-OCCUPIED HOUSING UNITS	8,311	309	1,422	6,193	1,329	1,564	2,199	3,272	2,344
LESS THAN $50	254	0	3	87	7	7	11	14	137
$50 TO $99	955	9	40	129	86	84	177	125	1,117
$100 TO $119	833	13	35	287	93	398	165	113	86
$120 TO $139	967	26	63	630	107	128	242	230	126
$140 TO $149	410	11	57	469	97	166	102	101	113
$150 TO $159	665	38	73	551	122	65	233	249	28
$160 TO $169	412	28	68	336	161	115	175	271	59
$170 TO $199	1,248	56	225	1,291	388	65	408	706	384
$200 TO $249	1,660	70	458	1,562	176	163	376	811	239
$250 TO $299	669	32	295	583	47	133	142	454	32
$300 TO $399	154	16	72	175	12	90	41	133	7
$400 TO $499	5	0	4	8	2	82	2	5	0
$500 OR MORE	1	0	0	2	0	18	1	2	0
NO CASH RENT	178	10	29	83	31	57	124	58	16

TABLE III-8 FUELS AND FINANCIAL CHARACTERISTICS OF HOUSING UNITS,
BY COMMUNITY AREA: CITY OF CHICAGO, 1980

	55	56	57	58	59	60	61	62	63
OCCUPIED HOUSING UNITS	4,127	12,611	3,710	12,193	4,867	11,336	17,010	4,863	9,303
HOUSE HEATING FUEL									
UTILITY GAS	3,208	11,850	3,459	11,537	4,493	10,820	15,669	4,487	8,796
BOTTLED, TANK, OR LP GAS	28	22	27	37	15	103	264	5	58
ELECTRICITY	329	328	102	245	120	216	467	219	137
FUEL OIL, KEROSENE, ETC.	545	411	112	362	225	163	510	134	285
COAL OR COKE	7	0	0	7	9	7	0	0	27
WOOD	0	0	0	0	5	0	0	0	0
OTHER FUEL	0	0	10	0	0	21	64	18	0
NO FUEL USED	10	0	0	5	0	6	36	0	0
WATER HEATING FUEL									
UTILITY GAS	3,312	12,244	3,486	11,894	4,726	11,068	15,902	4,675	9,018
BOTTLED, TANK, OR LP GAS	45	104	63	181	81	180	759	35	96
ELECTRICITY	744	239	123	99	38	79	176	153	119
FUEL OIL, KEROSENE, ETC.	11	24	32	14	22	9	53	0	49
OTHER	7	0	0	0	0	0	41	0	21
NO FUEL USED	8	0	6	5	0	0	79	0	0
COOKING FUEL									
UTILITY GAS	3,223	11,259	3,471	11,652	4,639	10,937	16,374	4,222	8,536
BOTTLED, TANK, OR LP GAS	424	21	17	70	19	25	182	23	23
ELECTRICITY	465	1,324	222	453	195	368	382	610	731
OTHER	5	0	0	0	14	0	33	8	13
NO FUEL USED	10	7	0	18	0	6	39	0	0
SPECIFIED OWNER-OCCUPIED NON-CONDOMINIUM HOUSING UNITS	2,135	9,122	1,575	2,228	1,111	1,776	2,436	3,205	3,878
VALUE									
LESS THAN $10,000	42	11	2	25	21	65	121	5	23
$10,000 TO $14,999	38	23	12	72	86	134	301	10	47
$15,000 TO $19,999	78	74	22	184	182	222	464	33	165
$20,000 TO $24,999	141	218	86	288	178	259	466	92	360
$25,000 TO $29,999	161	294	102	273	153	233	336	172	462
$30,000 TO $34,999	240	506	129	315	161	177	264	252	609
$35,000 TO $39,999	273	736	158	249	109	142	191	335	635
$40,000 TO $49,999	588	2,175	416	434	136	240	210	854	1,067
$50,000 TO $79,999	553	4,867	630	378	84	267	75	1,408	498
$80,000 TO $99,999	18	189	12	8	1	29	4	38	8
$100,000 TO $149,000	2	25	5	2	0	7	1	6	3
$150,000 TO $199,999	1	1	0	0	0	1	1	0	0
$200,000 OR MORE	0	3	1	0	0	0	2	0	1
SELECTED MONTHLY OWNER COSTS									
SPECIFIED OWNER-OCCUPIED HOUSING UNITS	2,136	9,127	1,575	2,213	1,083	1,757	2,413	3,204	3,880
WITH A MORTGAGE	1,223	4,459	554	1,129	491	741	1,317	1,141	1,729
LESS THAN $100	0	8	8	0	0	0	10	6	0
$100 TO $149	0	51	7	31	0	18	49	11	39
$150 TO $199	8	101	11	74	13	10	40	7	30
$200 TO $249	122	381	51	124	155	115	185	84	170
$250 TO $299	396	880	129	289	132	98	330	232	333
$300 TO $349	263	979	101	245	91	184	301	206	406
$350 TO $399	176	712	107	109	24	122	188	171	294
$400 TO $449	97	573	48	126	13	43	160	95	167
$450 TO $499	48	255	29	59	16	43	22	143	148
$500 TO $599	94	332	48	57	32	93	32	135	105
$600 TO $749	14	142	15	9	8	15	0	26	29
$750 OR MORE	5	45	0	6	7	0	0	25	8
NOT MORTGAGED	913	4,668	1,021	1,084	592	1,016	1,096	2,063	2,151
LESS THAN $50	0	0	0	4	0	19	12	0	0
$50 TO $74	15	18	0	6	20	34	21	8	18
$75 TO $99	125	90	19	129	117	196	134	55	115
$100 TO $124	141	254	134	265	158	255	256	204	431
$125 TO $149	163	1,049	242	250	131	193	267	490	617
$150 TO $199	355	2,498	461	325	125	179	282	993	767
$200 TO $249	93	620	160	67	41	133	99	270	134
$250 OR MORE	21	139	5	38	0	7	25	43	69
GROSS RENT									
SPECIFIED RENTER-OCCUPIED HOUSING UNITS	935	2,301	1,299	6,242	2,473	6,853	10,402	928	3,503
LESS THAN $60	0	12	0	4	9	11	17	0	0
$60 TO $79	8	18	0	57	17	103	80	15	14
$80 TO $99	45	74	18	80	91	175	194	0	27
$100 TO $119	30	86	5	212	117	202	438	0	68
$120 TO $149	87	162	29	577	276	870	1,003	35	206
$150 TO $169	70	62	111	623	235	825	1,019	47	234
$170 TO $199	195	206	150	1,062	343	1,260	1,937	82	630
$200 TO $249	245	491	324	1,903	786	1,918	2,936	196	1,107
$250 TO $299	76	343	350	974	377	751	1,519	236	735
$300 TO $349	44	353	171	274	86	317	612	147	157
$350 TO $399	43	172	50	75	38	83	154	51	114
$400 TO $499	5	132	20	65	7	48	116	52	58
$500 OR MORE	0	39	13	14	0	5	29	3	7
NO CASH RENT	87	151	58	322	91	285	348	64	146
CONTRACT RENT									
SPECIFIED RENTER-OCCUPIED HOUSING UNITS	928	2,299	1,299	6,226	2,481	6,853	10,397	938	3,499
LESS THAN $50	13	249	8	73	30	225	163	8	25
$50 TO $99	145	157	50	676	343	1,279	1,661	14	211
$100 TO $119	96	66	79	767	353	930	1,582	34	220
$120 TO $139	118	74	95	868	407	1,181	1,968	32	293
$140 TO $149	46	42	26	378	156	429	667	22	125
$150 TO $159	95	85	85	761	251	840	1,297	51	320
$160 TO $169	51	61	71	472	182	443	619	22	251
$170 TO $199	106	231	204	1,039	299	641	1,144	99	733
$200 TO $249	115	498	358	715	277	470	700	245	809
$250 TO $299	50	474	209	136	79	127	178	243	307
$300 TO $399	14	195	38	39	6	16	61	79	45
$400 TO $499	0	13	1	2	0	1	7	1	4
$500 OR MORE	0	0	1	1	0	3	7	0	1
NO CASH RENT	79	154	71	299	98	268	346	87	155

	64	65	66	67	68	69	70	71	72
OCCUPIED HOUSING UNITS	8,043	8,992	17,600	15,857	17,739	16,932	12,754	19,350	7,750
HOUSE HEATING FUEL									
UTILITY GAS	7,117	8,237	16,419	14,087	14,757	14,301	12,007	17,211	7,238
BOTTLED, TANK, OR LP GAS	22	38	136	354	442	383	46	332	21
ELECTRICITY	664	440	194	333	732	347	443	486	217
FUEL OIL, KEROSENE, ETC.	209	277	745	989	1,439	1,447	258	1,068	258
COAL OR COKE	0	0	58	23	152	131	0	117	10
WOOD	0	0	0	0	8	7	0	0	0
OTHER FUEL	31	0	48	65	186	304	0	88	6
NO FUEL USED	0	0	0	6	23	12	0	48	0
WATER HEATING FUEL									
UTILITY GAS	7,320	8,519	16,950	14,344	15,937	15,267	12,227	17,884	7,332
BOTTLED, TANK, OR LP GAS	50	109	177	889	859	586	86	566	64
ELECTRICITY	635	359	249	379	398	486	416	498	348
FUEL OIL, KEROSENE, ETC.	24	5	131	155	292	334	25	248	6
OTHER	6	0	85	78	192	241	0	120	0
NO FUEL USED	8	0	8	12	61	18	0	34	0
COOKING FUEL									
UTILITY GAS	6,973	7,743	16,289	15,093	16,865	15,985	10,793	18,093	5,506
BOTTLED, TANK, OR LP GAS	0	24	50	280	306	266	9	231	15
ELECTRICITY	1,045	1,225	1,216	463	433	580	1,952	998	2,229
OTHER	0	0	30	5	114	83	0	6	0
NO FUEL USED	25	0	15	16	21	18	0	22	0
SPECIFIED OWNER-OCCUPIED NON-CONDOMINIUM HOUSING UNITS	4,766	5,700	6,465	5,213	2,228	2,936	10,930	7,033	5,581
VALUE									
LESS THAN $10,000	3	4	18	81	85	25	3	24	5
$10,000 TO $14,999	10	14	40	213	170	90	6	60	11
$15,000 TO $19,999	41	54	163	697	404	267	47	285	24
$20,000 TO $24,999	117	148	523	1,099	481	475	119	555	94
$25,000 TO $29,999	164	245	701	964	360	516	272	794	178
$30,000 TO $34,999	303	378	937	666	264	399	557	933	285
$35,000 TO $39,999	382	514	997	543	163	353	783	1,015	295
$40,000 TO $49,999	995	1,472	1,869	652	184	467	2,847	1,899	916
$50,000 TO $79,999	2,692	2,804	1,174	287	107	316	5,917	1,404	2,788
$80,000 TO $99,999	53	49	32	6	8	24	330	49	627
$100,000 TO $149,000	6	15	11	2	0	3	46	13	307
$150,000 TO $199,999	0	3	0	1	1	1	1	0	42
$200,000 OR MORE	0	0	0	2	1	0	2	2	9
SELECTED MONTHLY OWNER COSTS									
SPECIFIED OWNER-OCCUPIED HOUSING UNITS	4,757	5,705	6,447	5,213	2,228	2,936	10,924	7,013	5,578
WITH A MORTGAGE	2,665	2,416	3,523	4,390	1,297	1,428	6,468	6,326	3,559
LESS THAN $100	0	0	6	15	25	0	0	13	0
$100 TO $149	7	12	26	52	34	37	34	35	0
$150 TO $199	88	32	48	104	52	71	99	96	19
$200 TO $249	219	140	235	285	169	79	487	223	55
$250 TO $299	574	437	655	711	247	274	1,322	870	342
$300 TO $349	513	494	825	977	303	280	1,265	1,438	451
$350 TO $399	427	408	647	871	241	255	1,036	1,257	602
$400 TO $449	335	359	453	698	120	237	822	974	597
$450 TO $499	220	193	338	285	30	90	527	665	381
$500 TO $599	208	254	225	280	72	82	597	575	629
$600 TO $749	68	87	57	83	0	16	227	166	332
$750 OR MORE	6	0	8	29	4	7	52	14	151
NOT MORTGAGED	2,092	3,289	2,924	823	931	1,508	4,456	687	2,019
LESS THAN $50	0	0	0	13	7	0	0	7	0
$50 TO $74	14	9	9	11	13	0	0	8	0
$75 TO $99	50	58	72	55	39	31	31	5	4
$100 TO $124	148	242	430	58	93	169	225	86	93
$125 TO $149	410	815	873	133	145	258	974	104	263
$150 TO $199	1,183	1,654	1,102	230	259	539	2,298	226	736
$200 TO $249	214	440	301	133	196	282	741	122	601
$250 OR MORE	73	71	137	190	179	229	187	129	322
GROSS RENT									
SPECIFIED RENTER-OCCUPIED HOUSING UNITS	2,411	1,863	8,066	7,569	12,462	11,310	1,092	9,320	1,495
LESS THAN $60	0	6	9	0	313	49	0	0	0
$60 TO $79	0	0	12	11	270	44	0	44	0
$80 TO $99	8	0	61	38	133	135	0	8	7
$100 TO $119	6	14	181	103	324	136	0	43	8
$120 TO $149	76	44	382	308	665	386	14	143	27
$150 TO $169	49	91	494	296	889	571	16	274	22
$170 TO $199	219	208	1,396	897	2,068	1,908	59	1,215	112
$200 TO $249	521	424	3,099	2,316	3,856	4,673	146	3,130	320
$250 TO $299	725	396	1,393	1,872	2,041	2,077	264	2,689	490
$300 TO $349	463	262	520	802	894	775	249	1,019	201
$350 TO $399	147	171	176	428	464	217	154	403	115
$400 TO $499	67	69	98	288	270	148	92	214	67
$500 OR MORE	25	35	29	131	90	33	0	77	51
NO CASH RENT	105	143	216	79	185	158	98	61	75
CONTRACT RENT									
SPECIFIED RENTER-OCCUPIED HOUSING UNITS	2,406	1,852	8,067	7,546	12,393	11,255	1,082	9,276	1,506
LESS THAN $50	6	8	8	12	402	53	0	19	2
$50 TO $99	44	45	192	165	748	255	5	52	14
$100 TO $119	59	68	289	325	774	416	14	131	7
$120 TO $139	68	90	390	640	1,384	603	23	275	22
$140 TO $149	38	49	227	365	760	444	5	233	11
$150 TO $159	78	122	530	895	1,371	961	32	502	37
$160 TO $169	62	65	483	725	1,295	925	17	605	41
$170 TO $199	231	228	2,279	2,145	3,049	3,543	76	2,573	116
$200 TO $249	807	499	2,508	1,642	1,984	3,074	238	3,369	508
$250 TO $299	717	334	772	436	368	759	356	1,229	451
$300 TO $399	188	177	155	89	89	85	211	194	185
$400 TO $499	9	22	9	6	7	4	5	7	29
$500 OR MORE	1	8	4	4	2	3	1	4	5
NO CASH RENT	98	137	221	97	160	130	99	83	78

TABLE III-8 FUELS AND FINANCIAL CHARACTERISTICS OF HOUSING UNITS,
BY COMMUNITY AREA: CITY OF CHICAGO, 1980

	73	74	75	76	77
OCCUPIED HOUSING UNITS	10,034	6,705	8,866	5,500	29,302
HOUSE HEATING FUEL					
UTILITY GAS	9,025	6,264	8,165	4,793	21,436
BOTTLED, TANK, OR LP GAS	119	28	42	59	431
ELECTRICITY	353	201	315	584	4,218
FUEL OIL, KEROSENE, ETC.	443	202	313	64	2,634
COAL OR COKE	42	10	7	0	278
WOOD	0	0	0	0	0
OTHER FUEL	45	0	24	0	291
NO FUEL USED	7	0	0	0	14
WATER HEATING FUEL					
UTILITY GAS	9,334	6,414	8,297	5,048	22,693
BOTTLED, TANK, OR LP GAS	253	61	150	90	564
ELECTRICITY	327	226	339	341	4,291
FUEL OIL, KEROSENE, ETC.	58	4	47	21	1,349
OTHER	51	0	28	0	369
NO FUEL USED	11	0	5	0	36
COOKING FUEL					
UTILITY GAS	9,118	5,561	7,487	5,166	20,045
BOTTLED, TANK, OR LP GAS	46	18	43	42	200
ELECTRICITY	870	1,126	1,336	292	8,909
OTHER	0	0	0	0	18
NO FUEL USED	0	0	0	0	130
SPECIFIED OWNER-OCCUPIED NON-CONDOMINIUM HOUSING UNITS	6,703	5,314	5,885	655	1,277
VALUE					
LESS THAN $10,000	28	4	34	0	1
$10,000 TO $14,999	42	16	45	0	5
$15,000 TO $19,999	203	47	134	0	13
$20,000 TO $24,999	487	164	311	0	22
$25,000 TO $29,999	652	251	391	1	33
$30,000 TO $34,999	800	327	462	1	46
$35,000 TO $39,999	957	480	616	2	74
$40,000 TO $49,999	1,907	1,422	1,384	11	181
$50,000 TO $79,999	1,553	2,503	2,248	142	713
$80,000 TO $99,999	58	86	193	166	132
$100,000 TO $149,000	11	10	50	301	47
$150,000 TO $199,999	0	0	13	27	7
$200,000 OR MORE	5	4	3	4	3
SELECTED MONTHLY OWNER COSTS					
SPECIFIED OWNER-OCCUPIED HOUSING UNITS	6,709	5,309	5,861	641	1,252
WITH A MORTGAGE	6,000	2,717	4,204	248	788
LESS THAN $100	13	0	18	0	0
$100 TO $149	51	17	42	0	0
$150 TO $199	151	99	103	6	14
$200 TO $249	293	198	201	0	42
$250 TO $299	879	476	525	16	49
$300 TO $349	1,495	644	787	15	146
$350 TO $399	1,378	507	833	25	152
$400 TO $449	705	272	599	29	103
$450 TO $499	395	234	403	24	62
$500 TO $599	489	157	421	56	118
$600 TO $749	105	88	207	48	75
$750 OR MORE	46	25	65	29	27
NOT MORTGAGED	709	2,592	1,657	393	464
LESS THAN $50	24	0	22	0	0
$50 TO $74	8	5	14	0	0
$75 TO $99	20	49	41	0	6
$100 TO $124	42	343	222	6	48
$125 TO $149	90	631	336	0	54
$150 TO $199	258	1,086	570	93	227
$200 TO $249	140	407	261	211	91
$250 OR MORE	127	71	191	83	38
GROSS RENT					
SPECIFIED RENTER-OCCUPIED HOUSING UNITS	2,278	992	2,157	3,669	21,712
LESS THAN $60	0	0	0	0	271
$60 TO $79	0	0	0	0	489
$80 TO $99	0	4	0	0	116
$100 TO $119	0	0	6	0	170
$120 TO $149	73	0	43	0	584
$150 TO $169	21	3	38	17	1,294
$170 TO $199	121	66	237	9	2,982
$200 TO $249	652	145	489	75	5,569
$250 TO $299	641	231	553	453	5,031
$300 TO $349	296	299	419	1,628	2,768
$350 TO $399	213	87	142	863	1,048
$400 TO $499	173	71	121	498	862
$500 OR MORE	56	8	39	113	335
NO CASH RENT	32	78	70	13	193
CONTRACT RENT					
SPECIFIED RENTER-OCCUPIED HOUSING UNITS	2,268	984	2,160	3,651	21,588
LESS THAN $50	4	2	5	2	271
$50 TO $99	12	15	69	3	587
$100 TO $119	20	12	80	1	207
$120 TO $139	89	5	113	6	477
$140 TO $149	63	9	48	4	383
$150 TO $159	82	38	149	5	816
$160 TO $169	99	27	113	2	1,128
$170 TO $199	459	87	320	12	3,696
$200 TO $249	916	120	506	124	6,141
$250 TO $299	374	338	350	757	4,174
$300 TO $399	111	243	306	2,260	2,551
$400 TO $499	5	11	13	371	594
$500 OR MORE	3	1	5	72	320
NO CASH RENT	31	76	83	32	243

432

Part IV
Summary Statistics, 1980 and 1970, Chicago Community Areas and Places of 10,000 or More Population

Table IV-1 Selected Census Statistics, 1980
Community Areas in Chicago and Places of 10,000 or More Population, 1980
In Chicago-Gary-Kenosha Ill.-Ind.-Wis. Standard Consolidated Statistical Area

	01 Rogers Park	02 West Ridge	03 Uptown	04 Lincoln Square	05 North Center	06 Lake View
1980 Population						
Total	55,525	61,129	64,414	43,954	35,161	97,519
Black	5,225	442	9,703	236	412	6,757
Spanish Origin	6,621	2,266	14,984	4,973	6,684	18,333
% Change 1970-1980						
Total Population	-8.7	-6.6	-13.9	-8.0	-10.8	-15.2
Black Population	585.7	385.7	218.7	314.0	194.3	657.5
% of Population, 1980						
Black	9.4	0.7	15.1	0.5	1.2	6.9
Spanish Origin	11.9	3.7	23.3	11.3	19.0	18.8
Under 18 Years Old	16.8	18.4	23.5	20.9	24.7	16.0
65 Years and Older	15.0	22.7	13.9	18.0	13.6	14.8
Persons 25 and Older						
Median Years School Completed	12.9	12.8	12.3	12.4	12.0	13.2
% with 4 or More Years College	30.7	24.6	19.2	16.4	10.9	33.1
% of All Workers in Manufacturing	18.8	18.9	25.3	26.3	30.8	18.6
% of All Workers in White Collar Occupations	66.6	71.6	52.0	55.5	48.8	69.8
% Riding to Work by Auto	42.7	67.4	45.8	56.6	56.7	39.7
% of Civilian Labor Force Unemployed	6.3	4.0	10.3	6.4	7.3	5.5
Families (1980)						
Total Number	11,288	17,150	12,515	11,038	9,070	19,698
Median Family Income	$18,784	$25,109	$14,455	$20,170	$19,361	$20,716
% Below Poverty	11.9	4.4	22.6	7.2	9.9	10.2
% with Income Greater than $29,999	22.3	37.3	14.7	23.4	20.8	30.0
% of Persons 5 & Older Living in Different House in 1975	66.4	45.4	66.8	50.3	45.3	61.2
% of Population Living in Group Quarters	5.1	1.9	6.5	1.8	0.2	1.0
Population Per Household	2.0	2.4	2.1	2.3	2.5	1.9
Housing Units, 1980						
Total Number	28,400	26,064	33,714	19,454	14,969	56,794
% in 1-Unit Structures	4.7	22.3	2.4	11.3	15.5	3.6
% Owner-Occupied	12.7	46.0	11.1	26.6	35.3	20.4
% Built in 1970 or Later	4.9	4.0	8.1	1.7	0.4	9.0
% Vacant	7.4	4.1	16.3	4.1	6.3	8.5
% with More than 1 Person per Room	6.3	2.3	12.2	4.7	4.4	4.5
Median Value, Owner Units (in 1-Unit Structures)	$66,100	$72,300	$61,400	$60,100	$42,900	$52,300
Median Contract Rent, Renter Uni	$235	$269	$196	$217	$183	$239
Median Number of Rooms	3.8	5.0	3.1	4.4	4.8	3.7

Table IV-1 Selected Census Statistics, 1980
Community Areas in Chicago and Places of 10,000 or More Population, 1980
In Chicago-Gary-Kenosha Ill.-Ind.-Wis. Standard Consolidated Statistical Area

	07 Lincoln Park	08 Near North Side	09 Edison Park	10 Norwood Park	11 Jefferson Park	12 Forest Glen
1980 Population						
Total	57,146	67,167	12,457	40,585	24,583	18,991
Black	4,909	22,000	0	7	5	11
Spanish Origin	5,991	1,944	120	390	395	295
% Change 1970-1980						
Total Population	-15.2	-4.4	-5.9	-3.0	-10.8	-7.5
Black Population	0.1	-15.6	-	600.0	150.0	175.0
% of Population, 1980						
Black	8.6	32.8	0.0	0.0	0.0	0.1
Spanish Origin	10.5	2.9	1.0	1.0	1.6	1.6
Under 18 Years Old	13.9	18.8	20.6	19.2	17.9	22.0
65 Years and Older	9.9	13.0	18.6	19.4	20.4	19.0
Persons 25 and Older						
Median Years School Completed	15.7	15.1	12.5	12.4	12.2	12.9
% with 4 or More Years College	48.6	44.6	13.2	12.1	10.1	25.9
% of All Workers in Manufacturing	15.4	11.5	24.0	24.6	28.7	20.3
% of All Workers in White Collar Occupations	78.5	80.4	61.8	56.9	58.3	68.9
% Riding to Work by Auto	41.3	24.9	73.1	73.0	67.6	73.5
% of Civilian Labor Force Unemployed	4.1	5.5	3.6	4.0	4.0	3.6
Families (1980)						
Total Number	10,285	12,426	3,505	11,601	7,078	5,526
Median Family Income	$24,509	$23,408	$27,325	$27,596	$25,083	$31,651
% Below Poverty	12.0	26.2	1.5	2.4	2.1	1.8
% with Income Greater than $29,999	41.2	44.6	43.7	42.2	34.9	54.2
% of Persons 5 & Older Living in Different House in 1975	63.1	55.4	29.0	28.2	31.0	25.9
% of Population Living in Group Quarters	3.4	5.0	0.0	1.1	0.0	0.0
Population Per Household	1.7	1.8	2.7	2.7	2.5	2.8
Housing Units, 1980						
Total Number	35,315	41,289	4,777	15,180	10,175	6,907
% in 1-Unit Structures	6.8	2.2	67.4	71.8	47.9	85.9
% Owner-Occupied	23.0	22.4	78.4	78.6	65.2	87.2
% Built in 1970 or Later	17.9	19.4	7.9	7.0	5.0	4.9
% Vacant	10.4	11.9	1.7	1.7	2.1	1.4
% with More than 1 Person per Room	2.9	4.9	1.9	1.8	1.9	1.5
Median Value, Owner Units (in 1-Unit Structures)	$123,700	$200,100	$72,500	$70,400	$64,800	$87,100
Median Contract Rent, Renter Uni	$269	$322	$275	$269	$233	$265
Median Number of Rooms	3.8	3.1	5.2	5.3	5.0	5.6

Table IV-1 Selected Census Statistics, 1980
Community Areas in Chicago and Places of 10,000 or More Population, 1980
In Chicago-Gary-Kenosha Ill.-Ind.-Wis. Standard Consolidated Statistical Area

	13 North Park	14 Albany Park	15 Portage Park	16 Irving Park	17 Dunning	18 Montclare
1980 Population						
Total	15,273	46,075	57,349	49,489	37,860	10,793
Black	143	279	51	63	183	0
Spanish Origin	846	9,074	1,486	4,267	613	179
% Change 1970-1980						
Total Population	-8.7	-2.2	-9.8	-9.9	-13.7	-7.6
Black Population	-66.9	830.0	142.9	133.3	-41.2	-100.0
% of Population, 1980						
Black	0.9	0.6	0.1	0.1	0.5	0.0
Spanish Origin	5.5	19.7	2.6	8.6	1.6	1.7
Under 18 Years Old	20.1	27.4	19.8	22.1	20.1	19.2
65 Years and Older	17.9	11.1	19.1	15.6	18.3	20.5
Persons 25 and Older						
Median Years School Completed	12.8	12.2	12.2	12.3	12.1	12.1
% with 4 or More Years College	27.9	14.4	9.0	12.4	6.7	6.2
% of All Workers in Manufacturing	19.1	32.7	29.5	30.2	30.3	30.0
% of All Workers in White Collar Occupations	68.1	49.9	54.7	54.3	50.9	49.9
% Riding to Work by Auto	62.1	61.1	66.4	62.3	74.8	70.8
% of Civilian Labor Force Unemployed	4.5	6.9	4.8	6.2	4.5	4.0
Families (1980)						
Total Number	3,953	11,555	15,756	12,739	10,745	3,013
Median Family Income	$25,975	$19,793	$23,402	$21,089	$24,446	$24,006
% Below Poverty	3.1	10.5	3.4	6.6	2.9	3.9
% with Income Greater than $29,999	39.3	23.8	30.0	24.8	34.8	31.1
% of Persons 5 & Older Living in Different House in 1975	49.1	59.6	36.9	43.5	29.1	33.1
% of Population Living in Group Quarters	7.6	0.8	0.6	1.0	1.3	1.1
Population Per Household	2.6	2.8	2.5	2.4	2.7	2.6
Housing Units, 1980						
Total Number	5,582	17,119	23,422	21,350	14,161	4,328
% in 1-Unit Structures	40.3	19.1	37.9	19.6	70.4	49.8
% Owner-Occupied	55.2	31.8	55.8	38.1	76.1	60.8
% Built in 1970 or Later	3.3	1.2	3.6	1.9	4.8	2.2
% Vacant	3.1	4.9	2.6	3.5	1.9	4.7
% with More than 1 Person per Room	2.2	9.0	2.0	2.9	2.3	2.8
Median Value, Owner Units (in 1-Unit Structures)	$75,000	$59,400	$61,100	$53,800	$63,500	$61,800
Median Contract Rent, Renter Uni	$253	$212	$216	$201	$240	$225
Median Number of Rooms	5.4	4.7	5.0	4.7	5.1	4.9

Table IV-1 Selected Census Statistics, 1980
Community Areas in Chicago and Places of 10,000 or More Population, 1980
In Chicago-Gary-Kenosha Ill.-Ind.-Wis. Standard Consolidated Statistical Area

	19 Belmont Cragin	20 Hermosa	21 Avondale	22 Logan Square	23 Humboldt Park	24 West Town
1980 Population						
Total	53,371	19,547	33,527	84,768	70,879	96,428
Black	43	74	60	2,236	25,215	8,671
Spanish Origin	3,072	6,101	6,863	43,829	28,872	54,693
% Change 1970-1980						
Total Population	-7.0	-1.5	-6.4	-4.3	-1.2	-22.7
Black Population	330.0	825.0	445.5	255.5	81.1	57.1
% of Population, 1980						
Black	0.1	0.4	0.2	2.6	35.6	9.0
Spanish Origin	5.8	31.2	20.5	51.7	40.7	56.7
Under 18 Years Old	20.1	27.0	23.4	31.6	38.5	34.7
65 Years and Older	18.8	12.9	13.6	9.4	6.5	8.6
Persons 25 and Older						
Median Years School Completed	11.9	11.4	11.6	10.5	10.3	9.2
% with 4 or More Years College	7.3	7.7	7.7	7.0	4.8	6.6
% of All Workers in Manufacturing	37.1	40.6	40.4	42.7	44.0	42.3
% of All Workers in White Collar Occupations	48.4	42.9	40.4	38.3	33.0	34.7
% Riding to Work by Auto	65.4	66.2	54.8	58.2	62.4	53.9
% of Civilian Labor Force Unemployed	6.0	7.8	8.3	9.4	12.9	10.9
Families (1980)						
Total Number	14,743	5,038	8,657	19,864	16,078	22,000
Median Family Income	$22,246	$19,118	$19,144	$16,224	$14,462	$12,974
% Below Poverty	4.0	10.0	8.7	18.7	25.9	27.2
% with Income Greater than $29,999	27.1	20.3	19.1	14.6	13.4	10.2
% of Persons 5 & Older Living in Different House in 1975	37.2	46.7	46.0	52.5	48.9	47.9
% of Population Living in Group Quarters	0.6	0.4	0.2	1.1	0.7	0.9
Population Per Household	2.5	2.8	2.5	2.8	3.3	3.0
Housing Units, 1980						
Total Number	22,183	7,372	13,986	32,514	23,746	36,790
% in 1-Unit Structures	34.7	25.2	13.5	9.9	16.4	5.3
% Owner-Occupied	53.0	44.3	35.4	25.6	32.1	18.7
% Built in 1970 or Later	1.6	1.2	0.4	1.3	1.6	2.5
% Vacant	5.0	4.3	5.5	9.3	9.9	12.7
% with More than 1 Person per Room	3.0	5.2	5.1	10.8	12.9	12.8
Median Value, Owner Units (in 1-Unit Structures)	$55,800	$43,000	$39,500	$30,500	$27,400	$23,500
Median Contract Rent, Renter Uni	$199	$187	$176	$168	$167	$138
Median Number of Rooms	4.9	5.0	4.6	4.7	5.0	4.6

Table IV-1 Selected Census Statistics, 1980
Community Areas in Chicago and Places of 10,000 or More Population, 1980
In Chicago-Gary-Kenosha Ill.-Ind.-Wis. Standard Consolidated Statistical Area

	25 Austin	26 West Garfield Park	27 East Garfield Park	28 Near West Side	29 North Lawndale	30 South Lawndale
1980 Population						
Total	138,026	33,865	31,580	57,305	61,534	75,204
Black	101,831	33,475	31,263	42,810	59,370	6,476
Spanish Origin	8,148	278	263	5,705	1,653	55,700
% Change 1970-1980						
Total Population	7.8	-30.1	-39.5	-27.2	-35.1	19.6
Black Population	144.9	-28.7	-38.9	-24.7	-35.0	0.4
% of Population, 1980						
Black	73.8	98.8	99.0	74.7	96.5	8.6
Spanish Origin	5.9	0.8	0.8	10.0	2.7	74.1
Under 18 Years Old	36.5	40.8	37.4	38.6	40.6	35.8
65 Years and Older	6.1	5.0	7.8	8.1	6.5	6.5
Persons 25 and Older						
Median Years School Completed	12.1	10.9	10.7	10.8	10.8	7.9
% with 4 or More Years College	6.4	1.9	2.5	12.9	3.0	2.8
% of All Workers in Manufacturing	33.2	34.3	26.1	23.7	31.9	52.7
% of All Workers in White Collar Occupations	43.1	34.9	37.5	46.9	37.8	25.7
% Riding to Work by Auto	64.2	60.2	51.6	41.2	58.0	64.4
% of Civilian Labor Force Unemployed	13.9	20.7	20.6	15.8	20.4	13.7
Families (1980)						
Total Number	31,819	7,088	6,674	11,581	13,463	15,339
Median Family Income	$16,566	$10,922	$9,682	$7,535	$9,902	$16,410
% Below Poverty	21.8	37.2	40.3	48.9	39.9	19.5
% with Income Greater than $29,999	18.9	10.8	7.9	8.2	8.3	14.0
% of Persons 5 & Older Living in Different House in 1975	45.1	40.7	37.8	40.3	34.1	53.6
% of Population Living in Group Quarters	1.0	1.3	0.3	3.3	1.0	6.3
Population Per Household	3.3	3.7	3.2	3.0	3.5	3.6
Housing Units, 1980						
Total Number	44,682	9,582	10,933	20,064	18,592	20,899
% in 1-Unit Structures	23.2	7.5	6.0	11.3	6.3	12.3
% Owner-Occupied	36.6	22.4	17.8	10.2	19.9	34.2
% Built in 1970 or Later	3.6	1.8	2.3	12.1	2.8	3.2
% Vacant	6.9	4.6	10.6	8.6	7.6	7.5
% with More than 1 Person per Room	11.4	16.4	14.7	18.0	16.8	24.7
Median Value, Owner Units (in 1-Unit Structures)	$41,600	$25,400	$22,800	$27,900	$25,200	$27,700
Median Contract Rent, Renter Uni	$191	$171	$155	$107	$156	$150
Median Number of Rooms	5.0	5.2	4.8	4.1	5.0	4.3

Table IV-1 Selected Census Statistics, 1980
Community Areas in Chicago and Places of 10,000 or More Population, 1980
In Chicago-Gary-Kenosha Ill.-Ind.-Wis. Standard Consolidated Statistical Area

	31 Lower West Side	32 Loop	33 Near South Side	34 Armour Square	35 Douglas	36 Oakland
1980 Population						
Total	44,951	6,462	7,243	12,475	35,700	16,748
Black	477	1,231	6,819	3,162	30,905	16,647
Spanish Origin	34,867	222	108	603	313	97
% Change 1970-1980						
Total Population	1.0	31.0	-17.4	-4.5	-13.5	-8.4
Black Population	-55.3	109.4	-9.0	-23.5	-26.1	-8.0
% of Population, 1980						
Black	1.1	19.0	94.1	25.3	86.6	99.4
Spanish Origin	77.6	3.4	1.5	4.8	0.9	0.6
Under 18 Years Old	36.1	3.8	41.7	26.1	30.7	47.7
65 Years and Older	7.0	21.3	9.4	14.8	11.9	6.3
Persons 25 and Older						
Median Years School Completed	7.9	12.7	11.7	10.6	12.4	11.1
% with 4 or More Years College	4.1	22.6	9.2	7.3	20.7	3.4
% of All Workers in Manufacturing	46.7	16.9	19.9	22.1	10.8	17.6
% of All Workers in White Collar Occupations	27.3	70.4	53.3	41.3	70.3	41.6
% Riding to Work by Auto	57.0	29.3	32.9	57.9	41.8	41.0
% of Civilian Labor Force Unemployed	16.2	7.0	20.3	7.7	11.3	29.5
Families (1980)						
Total Number	9,694	1,028	1,558	2,940	7,575	3,425
Median Family Income	$14,487	$26,790	$7,326	$15,211	$8,578	$5,555
% Below Poverty	23.5	4.7	42.7	23.4	42.6	60.9
% with Income Greater than $29,999	12.5	43.9	5.8	15.0	11.3	3.7
% of Persons 5 & Older Living in Different House in 1975	48.1	52.9	33.6	35.8	39.8	37.3
% of Population Living in Group Quarters	0.4	17.3	3.9	0.2	7.0	0.5
Population Per Household	3.5	1.4	2.9	2.8	2.3	3.4
Housing Units, 1980						
Total Number	14,673	4,182	2,487	4,679	15,168	5,209
% in 1-Unit Structures	7.0	6.1	0.0	12.7	4.4	8.6
% Owner-Occupied	22.0	38.9	0.5	20.3	4.7	3.9
% Built in 1970 or Later	3.4	33.5	14.9	12.8	8.8	19.6
% Vacant	11.6	7.7	2.7	4.8	5.4	6.4
% with More than 1 Person per Room	22.7	2.7	16.1	13.0	10.1	22.4
Median Value, Owner Units (in 1-Unit Structures)	$21,700	$92,000	$32,500	$42,200	$25,900	$30,400
Median Contract Rent, Renter Uni	$129	$249	$90	$118	$155	$87
Median Number of Rooms	4.3	2.9	3.8	4.3	3.6	4.1

Table IV-1 Selected Census Statistics, 1980
Community Areas in Chicago and Places of 10,000 or More Population, 1980
In Chicago-Gary-Kenosha Ill.-Ind.-Wis. Standard Consolidated Statistical Area

	37 Fuller Park	38 Grand Boulevard	39 Kenwood	40 Washington Park	41 Hyde Park	42 Woodlawn
1980 Population						
Total	5,832	53,741	21,974	31,935	31,198	36,323
Black	5,757	53,428	17,024	31,726	11,610	34,759
Spanish Origin	71	350	241	205	721	285
% Change 1970-1980						
Total Population	-20.9	-32.9	-18.3	-30.6	-7.0	-32.5
Black Population	-19.4	-32.9	-19.8	-30.5	11.3	-32.6
% of Population, 1980						
Black	98.7	99.4	77.5	99.3	37.2	95.7
Spanish Origin	1.2	0.7	1.1	0.6	2.3	0.8
Under 18 Years Old	33.2	36.9	23.6	36.7	15.8	29.6
65 Years and Older	16.9	13.7	13.3	12.0	10.3	14.4
Persons 25 and Older						
Median Years School Completed	10.2	10.5	12.9	11.0	16.1	11.8
% with 4 or More Years College	1.0	2.9	30.4	2.6	56.2	7.7
% of All Workers in Manufacturing	33.0	23.3	12.7	20.7	8.0	17.9
% of All Workers in White Collar Occupations	35.9	38.0	71.3	39.8	80.0	51.8
% Riding to Work by Auto	53.6	36.8	53.1	40.0	38.2	45.6
% of Civilian Labor Force Unemployed	22.2	24.2	10.0	21.0	5.5	19.3
Families (1980)						
Total Number	1,221	10,509	5,048	6,559	6,398	7,862
Median Family Income	$10,799	$6,945	$16,140	$8,158	$22,115	$10,546
% Below Poverty	34.5	51.4	20.2	43.2	9.1	32.3
% with Income Greater than $29,999	8.1	4.9	23.2	6.5	36.0	8.3
% of Persons 5 & Older Living in Different House in 1975	28.7	34.2	51.6	39.6	59.4	44.3
% of Population Living in Group Quarters	0.8	1.5	2.1	0.9	8.7	3.2
Population Per Household	3.0	2.8	2.1	2.9	2.0	2.5
Housing Units, 1980						
Total Number	2,023	20,852	11,256	12,085	15,493	15,747
% in 1-Unit Structures	22.1	3.9	6.2	3.1	7.9	5.2
% Owner-Occupied	27.6	6.3	20.1	5.2	23.8	12.6
% Built in 1970 or Later	19.3	7.4	16.1	4.1	3.4	5.9
% Vacant	5.5	10.3	10.9	9.1	6.7	10.6
% with More than 1 Person per Room	12.1	13.6	6.3	13.2	3.5	9.4
Median Value, Owner Units (in 1-Unit Structures)	$24,700	$23,400	$89,500	$21,900	$98,000	$26,600
Median Contract Rent, Renter Uni	$118	$138	$203	$169	$243	$175
Median Number of Rooms	4.9	4.3	3.6	4.4	3.7	4.2

436

	43 South Shore	44 Chatham	45 Avalon Park	46 South Chicago	47 Burnside	48 Calumet Heights
1980 Population						
Total	77,743	40,725	13,792	46,422	3,942	20,505
Black	73,929	40,113	13,258	22,186	3,491	17,795
Spanish Origin	917	271	109	18,229	100	1,481
% Change 1970-1980						
Total Population	-3.6	-13.9	-4.3	1.7	23.9	1.9
Black Population	32.8	-13.0	11.3	116.8	3736.3	96.9
% of Population, 1980						
Black	95.1	98.5	96.1	47.8	88.6	86.8
Spanish Origin	1.2	0.7	0.8	39.3	2.5	7.2
Under 18 Years Old	29.6	22.6	29.1	34.2	39.5	30.8
65 Years and Older	6.6	12.0	6.1	7.5	5.0	5.2
Persons 25 and Older						
Median Years School Completed	12.6	12.5	12.6	11.8	12.2	12.7
% with 4 or More Years College	15.0	12.7	16.5	8.1	6.9	18.0
% of All Workers in Manufacturing	16.6	18.4	19.1	34.8	33.1	21.1
% of All Workers in White Collar Occupations	59.0	56.2	59.0	43.5	41.3	61.4
% Riding to Work by Auto	56.7	58.7	66.6	61.3	61.2	72.8
% of Civilian Labor Force Unemployed	13.1	11.2	9.3	11.4	15.2	7.8
Families (1980)						
Total Number	18,659	10,880	3,424	10,850	866	5,284
Median Family Income	$15,969	$18,797	$24,209	$20,015	$20,625	$26,550
% Below Poverty	20.8	12.6	9.7	15.0	15.1	5.5
% with Income Greater than $29,999	19.1	23.4	37.5	22.9	19.0	40.9
% of Persons 5 & Older Living in Different House in 1975	48.3	32.8	23.5	36.2	48.1	22.0
% of Population Living in Group Quarters	0.4	0.1	0.2	0.3	0.3	0.2
Population Per Household	2.5	2.5	3.3	3.2	3.8	3.3
Housing Units, 1980						
Total Number	34,162	17,138	4,302	15,616	1,114	6,321
% in 1-Unit Structures	10.2	31.3	67.1	26.8	60.6	71.2
% Owner-Occupied	17.8	37.8	71.2	39.0	64.8	75.2
% Built in 1970 or Later	2.7	1.6	1.7	6.0	4.6	1.6
% Vacant	8.2	4.2	1.8	7.3	6.7	2.0
% with More than 1 Person per Room	6.7	4.4	5.4	12.0	13.5	6.1
Median Value, Owner Units (in 1-Unit Structures)	$39,400	$39,200	$38,400	$32,400	$30,200	$43,600
Median Contract Rent, Renter Uni	$223	$213	$212	$160	$183	$214
Median Number of Rooms	4.3	4.7	5.6	4.8	5.3	5.6

	49 Roseland	50 Pullman	51 South Deering	52 East Side	53 West Pullman	54 Riverdale
1980 Population						
Total	64,372	10,341	19,400	21,331	44,904	13,539
Black	62,749	7,896	10,631	25	40,701	13,089
Spanish Origin	550	642	4,763	2,678	2,309	176
% Change 1970-1980						
Total Population	3.0	-5.1	0.7	-13.5	11.4	-9.8
Black Population	82.1	50.6	246.6	8.7	510.2	-8.0
% of Population, 1980						
Black	97.5	76.4	54.8	0.1	90.6	96.7
Spanish Origin	0.9	6.2	24.6	12.6	5.1	1.3
Under 18 Years Old	34.1	32.4	34.5	24.2	40.6	49.0
65 Years and Older	6.4	8.2	6.3	13.3	3.5	2.7
Persons 25 and Older						
Median Years School Completed	12.4	12.4	12.2	11.9	12.3	12.1
% with 4 or More Years College	10.3	7.3	7.2	4.9	6.4	3.8
% of All Workers in Manufacturing	21.3	25.8	29.4	39.9	26.4	23.4
% of All Workers in White Collar Occupations	52.1	51.6	50.7	39.7	45.9	43.2
% Riding to Work by Auto	64.1	64.8	65.0	75.2	68.6	63.1
% of Civilian Labor Force Unemployed	13.6	12.9	12.7	7.3	13.5	25.3
Families (1980)						
Total Number	14,926	2,512	4,654	5,757	10,145	3,036
Median Family Income	$20,189	$21,388	$21,471	$24,582	$21,247	$9,434
% Below Poverty	15.2	13.4	11.5	5.1	13.5	44.8
% with Income Greater than $29,999	27.2	26.4	27.7	36.3	25.9	7.3
% of Persons 5 & Older Living in Different House in 1975	26.0	30.0	28.9	31.0	30.4	34.0
% of Population Living in Group Quarters	0.7	0.4	0.4	0.5	0.1	0.3
Population Per Household	3.5	3.1	3.4	2.8	3.8	4.0
Housing Units, 1980						
Total Number	18,771	3,525	5,804	7,754	12,281	3,505
% in 1-Unit Structures	64.8	69.4	72.3	59.4	66.8	57.4
% Owner-Occupied	62.2	53.5	68.4	67.6	68.4	16.5
% Built in 1970 or Later	2.9	0.8	2.8	3.6	4.3	5.8
% Vacant	3.5	4.5	3.0	3.8	4.4	3.1
% with More than 1 Person per Room	8.9	8.0	10.8	3.9	11.9	25.3
Median Value, Owner Units (in 1-Unit Structures)	$36,500	$30,400	$30,100	$38,800	$38,700	$29,300
Median Contract Rent, Renter Uni	$183	$169	$137	$166	$191	$96
Median Number of Rooms	5.5	5.0	5.2	5.2	5.4	4.6

Table IV-1 Selected Census Statistics, 1980
Community Areas in Chicago and Places of 10,000 or More Population, 1980
In Chicago-Gary-Kenosha Ill.-Ind.-Wis. Standard Consolidated Statistical Area

	55 Hegewisch	56 Garfield Ridge	57 Archer Heights	58 Brighton Park	59 McKinley Park	60 Bridgeport
1980 Population						
Total	11,572	37,935	9,708	30,770	13,248	30,923
Black	29	5,116	8	34	5	40
Spanish Origin	718	1,566	354	4,539	2,129	6,584
% Change 1970-1980						
Total Population	2.0	-11.8	-12.8	-13.6	-15.3	-12.1
Black Population	31.8	45.8	700.0	0.0	25.0	-11.1
% of Population, 1980						
Black	0.3	13.5	0.1	0.1	0.0	0.1
Spanish Origin	6.2	4.1	3.6	14.8	16.1	21.3
Under 18 Years Old	24.7	24.1	18.7	22.5	26.5	26.7
65 Years and Older	11.2	11.8	15.2	15.2	12.4	11.8
Persons 25 and Older						
Median Years School Completed	12.1	12.1	11.5	11.7	11.6	11.0
% with 4 or More Years College	2.7	5.4	6.0	5.7	4.6	4.9
% of All Workers in Manufacturing	34.9	31.3	34.8	31.3	25.8	25.8
% of All Workers in White Collar Occupations	43.6	49.9	46.6	45.2	51.0	47.3
% Riding to Work by Auto	75.4	70.3	63.8	61.2	58.9	56.8
% of Civilian Labor Force Unemployed	6.9	7.8	6.0	7.7	8.0	8.9
Families (1980)						
Total Number	3,167	10,516	2,761	8,184	3,461	7,788
Median Family Income	$25,681	$24,677	$23,230	$20,508	$19,989	$18,999
% Below Poverty	4.1	5.7	4.8	8.0	9.2	12.6
% with Income Greater than $29,999	35.4	34.8	32.0	23.8	23.0	20.5
% of Persons 5 & Older Living in Different House in 1975	23.4	22.5	26.9	37.3	34.4	36.8
% of Population Living in Group Quarters	0.0	0.1	0.1	0.5	0.1	0.2
Population Per Household	2.8	3.0	2.6	2.5	2.7	2.7
Housing Units, 1980						
Total Number	4,364	12,748	3,786	12,766	5,232	12,281
% in 1-Unit Structures	56.8	83.4	47.5	21.4	26.5	19.8
% Owner-Occupied	73.1	79.4	63.3	46.5	45.4	36.2
% Built in 1970 or Later	13.2	4.6	5.7	1.0	0.9	2.9
% Vacant	5.4	1.0	2.0	4.5	7.0	7.7
% with More than 1 Person per Room	4.8	6.6	4.0	4.9	5.0	6.3
Median Value, Owner Units (in 1-Unit Structures)	$41,600	$53,200	$46,600	$34,300	$27,900	$29,500
Median Contract Rent, Renter Uni	$151	$211	$199	$153	$144	$135
Median Number of Rooms	4.9	5.0	4.8	4.5	4.9	4.8

Table IV-1 Selected Census Statistics, 1980
Community Areas in Chicago and Places of 10,000 or More Population, 1980
In Chicago-Gary-Kenosha Ill.-Ind.-Wis. Standard Consolidated Statistical Area

	61 New City	62 West Elsdon	63 Gage Park	64 Clearing	65 West Lawn	66 Chicago Lawn
1980 Population						
Total	55,860	12,797	24,445	22,584	24,748	46,568
Black	12,239	7	163	5	52	4,782
Spanish Origin	19,945	297	2,701	916	599	4,940
% Change 1970-1980						
Total Population	-8.2	-9.0	-8.4	-9.3	-10.5	-3.9
Black Population	468.7	40.0	16200.0	400.0	420.0	47720.0
% of Population, 1980						
Black	21.9	0.1	0.7	0.0	0.2	10.3
Spanish Origin	35.7	2.3	11.0	4.1	2.4	10.6
Under 18 Years Old	36.0	18.4	22.8	23.8	21.1	25.3
65 Years and Older	7.5	18.0	17.9	10.4	16.4	17.7
Persons 25 and Older						
Median Years School Completed	9.9	12.1	12.0	12.2	12.2	12.2
% with 4 or More Years College	3.6	7.1	6.5	5.2	7.1	9.5
% of All Workers in Manufacturing	37.4	26.6	27.1	30.0	25.3	26.5
% of All Workers in White Collar Occupations	34.4	49.3	49.2	47.4	51.5	49.9
% Riding to Work by Auto	61.4	72.5	68.2	77.3	72.9	68.2
% of Civilian Labor Force Unemployed	12.4	5.1	7.8	6.3	5.4	6.8
Families (1980)						
Total Number	12,627	3,785	6,530	6,180	6,936	11,664
Median Family Income	$15,427	$23,560	$21,866	$25,176	$25,733	$21,058
% Below Poverty	21.9	3.7	5.1	4.4	2.7	7.8
% with Income Greater than $29,999	15.5	32.1	26.1	34.7	35.5	24.7
% of Persons 5 & Older Living in Different House in 1975	49.2	30.4	33.7	34.5	26.3	43.1
% of Population Living in Group Quarters	0.4	0.3	0.1	0.2	0.1	0.4
Population Per Household	3.3	2.6	2.6	2.8	2.7	2.6
Housing Units, 1980						
Total Number	18,603	4,910	9,603	8,297	9,152	18,164
% in 1-Unit Structures	18.1	72.2	46.7	63.0	69.2	40.8
% Owner-Occupied	35.2	79.7	60.3	67.8	77.9	52.2
% Built in 1970 or Later	3.4	7.9	1.1	10.9	4.3	1.1
% Vacant	8.6	1.0	3.1	3.1	1.7	3.1
% with More than 1 Person per Room	13.9	2.9	4.1	4.8	3.3	4.3
Median Value, Owner Units (in 1-Unit Structures)	$23,600	$48,200	$37,100	$54,100	$50,200	$39,300
Median Contract Rent, Renter Uni	$136	$229	$179	$235	$218	$194
Median Number of Rooms	4.6	4.9	4.9	4.9	5.0	5.0

	67 West Englewood	68 Englewood	69 Greater Grand Crossing	70 Ashburn	71 Auburn Gresham	72 Beverly
1980 Population						
Total	62,069	59,075	45,218	40,477	65,132	23,360
Black	60,882	58,395	44,660	1,084	64,093	3,178
Spanish Origin	686	497	266	905	463	308
% Change 1970-1980						
Total Population	0.3	-34.2	-16.9	-14.2	-5.4	-12.7
Black Population	103.5	-32.5	-16.3	115.5	35.5	10493.3
% of Population, 1980						
Black	98.1	98.8	98.8	2.7	98.4	13.6
Spanish Origin	1.1	0.8	0.6	2.2	0.7	1.3
Under 18 Years Old	40.8	37.3	26.6	24.6	33.2	28.7
65 Years and Older	4.1	8.6	14.3	11.9	5.1	15.4
Persons 25 and Older						
Median Years School Completed	11.8	11.2	12.1	12.4	12.3	13.7
% with 4 or More Years College	3.5	3.3	6.8	8.6	7.6	33.1
% of All Workers in Manufacturing	25.6	27.9	21.2	19.0	24.5	11.2
% of All Workers in White Collar Occupations	41.7	39.7	49.5	53.2	48.3	71.1
% Riding to Work by Auto	58.8	50.6	56.8	78.4	62.8	69.5
% of Civilian Labor Force Unemployed	20.6	18.2	14.2	5.2	13.2	4.1
Families (1980)						
Total Number	13,304	12,960	11,349	11,071	15,268	5,972
Median Family Income	$13,909	$10,597	$14,086	$27,291	$20,531	$29,756
% Below Poverty	29.4	35.8	22.4	2.4	13.3	2.7
% with Income Greater than $29,999	13.1	7.7	14.1	42.7	27.1	49.5
% of Persons 5 & Older Living in Different House in 1975	28.5	36.8	31.4	23.6	27.2	34.6
% of Population Living in Group Quarters	0.1	0.5	0.2	0.8	0.2	0.1
Population Per Household	3.9	3.3	2.7	3.1	3.4	3.0
Housing Units, 1980						
Total Number	16,980	19,301	17,671	12,875	20,122	7,885
% in 1-Unit Structures	41.3	17.7	22.6	90.8	40.6	79.1
% Owner-Occupied	48.3	27.1	31.4	90.6	49.7	79.1
% Built in 1970 or Later	3.2	4.5	2.6	3.1	2.0	0.5
% Vacant	6.6	8.1	4.2	0.9	3.8	1.7
% with More than 1 Person per Room	13.9	12.3	6.5	4.5	8.5	1.9
Median Value, Owner Units (in 1-Unit Structures)	$27,700	$24,700	$31,200	$54,200	$39,300	$60,600
Median Contract Rent, Renter Uni	$178	$165	$186	$261	$203	$246
Median Number of Rooms	5.4	5.0	4.8	5.3	5.3	5.6

Table IV-1 Selected Census Statistics, 1980
Community Areas in Chicago and Places of 10,000 or More Population, 1980
In Chicago-Gary-Kenosha Ill.-Ind.-Wis. Standard Consolidated Statistical Area

	73 Washington Heights	74 Mount Greenwood	75 Morgan Park	76 O'hare	77 Edgewater	Addison
1980 Population						
Total	36,453	20,084	29,315	11,068	58,561	29,759
Black	35,778	93	18,320	165	6,514	246
Spanish Origin	177	154	280	288	7,805	1,732
% Change 1970-1980						
Total Population	-0.2	-13.4	-5.5	74.5	-4.9	21.6
Black Population	31.0	322.7	23.8	1400.0	1646.4	846.2
% of Population, 1980						
Black	98.1	0.5	62.5	1.5	11.1	0.8
Spanish Origin	0.5	0.8	1.0	2.6	13.3	5.8
Under 18 Years Old	32.0	24.6	30.6	14.1	15.9	31.6
65 Years and Older	4.9	15.5	11.7	10.8	18.4	4.4
Persons 25 and Older						
Median Years School Completed	12.5	12.4	12.6	12.7	12.8	12.5
% with 4 or More Years College	10.8	10.6	16.4	18.4	25.9	12.6
% of All Workers in Manufacturing	23.1	13.8	16.1	19.7	18.9	35.0
% of All Workers in White Collar Occupations	52.0	52.0	59.5	64.1	64.9	52.6
% Riding to Work by Auto	68.3	76.6	71.1	81.5	45.1	91.2
% of Civilian Labor Force Unemployed	12.9	4.6	11.6	4.2	7.2	3.6
Families (1980)						
Total Number	8,503	5,345	7,038	2,920	12,524	7,701
Median Family Income	$23,422	$24,794	$23,735	$23,884	$19,860	$27,413
% Below Poverty	10.0	2.9	9.6	2.8	11.2	3.3
% with Income Greater than $29,999	33.7	34.8	34.1	33.5	28.1	42.1
% of Persons 5 & Older Living in Different House in 1975	20.8	25.2	25.8	61.0	60.1	49.3
% of Population Living in Group Quarters	0.4	1.7	1.1	0.0	3.6	0.1
Population Per Household	3.6	2.9	3.3	2.0	1.9	3.1
Housing Units, 1980						
Total Number	10,245	6,812	9,121	5,737	32,613	10,037
% in 1-Unit Structures	75.4	86.1	75.0	11.9	4.6	56.5
% Owner-Occupied	75.6	83.8	73.1	31.9	23.2	57.0
% Built in 1970 or Later	4.5	6.7	5.2	62.4	12.0	31.5
% Vacant	2.1	1.6	2.8	4.1	10.2	3.8
% with More than 1 Person per Room	8.8	4.8	6.4	1.7	5.9	4.6
Median Value, Owner Units (in 1-Unit Structures)	$41,000	$49,600	$46,900	$100,700	$61,100	$76,900
Median Contract Rent, Renter Uni	$216	$271	$214	$340	$225	$265
Median Number of Rooms	5.6	5.2	5.6	4.0	3.5	5.1

	Alsip	Arlington Heights	Aurora	Bartlett	Batavia	Bellwood
1980 Population						
Total	17,134	66,116	81,293	13,254	12,574	19,811
Black	101	288	8,459	130	584	6,956
Spanish Origin	441	1,149	14,482	346	397	1,105
% Change 1970-1980						
Total Population	47.6	1.6	9.3	278.6	38.8	-10.3
Black Population	359.1	966.7	73.8	261.1	31.2	4833.3
% of Population, 1980						
Black	0.6	0.4	10.4	1.0	4.6	35.1
Spanish Origin	2.6	1.7	17.8	2.6	3.2	5.6
Under 18 Years Old	30.1	29.2	32.0	35.2	30.3	29.8
65 Years and Older	6.6	7.7	9.9	3.7	11.1	8.6
Persons 25 and Older						
Median Years School Completed	12.5	13.8	12.4	12.9	12.8	12.4
% with 4 or More Years College	11.6	32.7	13.7	22.7	21.6	8.4
% of All Workers in Manufacturing	23.5	23.5	39.1	28.0	29.3	33.7
% of All Workers in White Collar Occupations	48.9	77.1	46.5	66.0	60.0	48.2
% Riding to Work by Auto	87.9	83.1	89.5	85.1	91.7	88.0
% of Civilian Labor Force Unemployed	5.4	2.9	6.8	4.0	5.5	5.9
Families (1980)						
Total Number	4,429	17,454	20,219	3,650	3,270	5,334
Median Family Income	$25,731	$33,323	$23,035	$28,360	$26,072	$24,959
% Below Poverty	4.0	1.9	6.6	2.0	2.4	3.8
% with Income Greater than $29,999	34.6	59.7	29.7	43.4	38.5	34.9
% of Persons 5 & Older Living in Different House in 1975	47.0	42.3	52.4	78.0	55.5	46.6
% of Population Living in Group Quarters	0.2	1.7	1.6	0.7	2.7	0.6
Population Per Household	2.8	2.9	2.9	3.1	2.8	3.0
Housing Units, 1980						
Total Number	6,269	23,194	29,406	4,640	4,573	6,609
% in 1-Unit Structures	51.0	68.7	62.3	75.5	68.8	73.5
% Owner-Occupied	54.8	71.1	58.3	79.8	63.1	76.8
% Built in 1970 or Later	38.3	25.1	18.6	78.9	35.0	2.1
% Vacant	3.7	4.4	5.9	9.1	4.2	2.2
% with More than 1 Person per Room	3.5	0.9	6.4	1.0	2.2	5.6
Median Value, Owner Units (in 1-Unit Structures)	$63,500	$93,400	$49,100	$76,100	$72,000	$58,000
Median Contract Rent, Renter Uni	$269	$333	$219	$320	$241	$245
Median Number of Rooms	4.8	5.6	5.2	5.6	5.6	5.1

Table IV-1 Selected Census Statistics, 1980
Community Areas in Chicago and Places of 10,000 or More Population, 1980
In Chicago-Gary-Kenosha Ill.-Ind.-Wis. Standard Consolidated Statistical Area

	Bensenville	Berwyn	Bloomingdale	Blue Island	Bolingbrook	Bridgeview
1980 Population						
Total	16,124	46,849	12,659	21,855	37,261	14,155
Black	44	13	213	1,077	2,539	44
Spanish Origin	1,353	1,128	267	3,469	1,689	488
% Change 1970-1980						
Total Population	24.5	-10.8	325.7	-3.4	387.0	13.0
Black Population	2100.0	62.5	508.6	32.6	253800.0	388.9
% of Population, 1980						
Black	0.3	0.0	1.7	4.9	6.8	0.3
Spanish Origin	8.4	2.4	2.1	15.9	4.5	3.4
Under 18 Years Old	25.6	18.5	33.8	25.0	40.3	29.0
65 Years and Older	8.9	22.3	5.8	14.0	1.7	10.1
Persons 25 and Older						
Median Years School Completed	12.5	12.2	12.9	12.3	12.9	12.2
% with 4 or More Years College	14.8	9.4	23.1	9.5	24.0	5.9
% of All Workers in Manufacturing	33.3	27.1	26.1	28.8	27.7	30.2
% of All Workers in White Collar Occupations	54.9	59.6	65.9	48.3	63.6	43.0
% Riding to Work by Auto	88.2	73.7	89.8	75.0	90.1	91.0
% of Civilian Labor Force Unemployed	4.2	5.3	4.4	7.3	4.4	8.5
Families (1980)						
Total Number	4,096	13,094	3,271	5,632	9,497	3,622
Median Family Income	$26,008	$23,178	$30,943	$20,772	$27,679	$24,764
% Below Poverty	3.1	4.0	2.8	7.3	2.8	3.2
% with Income Greater than $29,999	37.8	30.5	53.2	22.4	40.9	32.1
% of Persons 5 & Older Living in Different House in 1975	53.2	34.5	55.8	46.C	67.7	39.6
% of Population Living in Group Quarters	1.5	0.4	4.2	0.3	0.0	3.8
Population Per Household	2.7	2.4	3.0	2.6	3.4	2.9
Housing Units, 1980						
Total Number	6,236	20,464	4,333	8,855	11,773	4,747
% in 1-Unit Structures	51.7	46.3	71.4	41.9	79.9	58.3
% Owner-Occupied	52.4	58.0	76.3	47.0	77.2	73.9
% Built in 1970 or Later	36.8	2.3	81.3	8.5	80.9	31.4
% Vacant	6.1	3.1	8.2	3.9	6.8	1.9
% with More than 1 Person per Room	3.2	1.6	0.8	5.5	2.2	3.5
Median Value, Owner Units (in 1-Unit Structures)	$66,700	$58,500	$85,000	$42,000	$65,200	$60,800
Median Contract Rent, Renter Uni	$311	$213	$314	$208	$273	$251
Median Number of Rooms	4.8	5.0	5.6	4.7	5.6	4.9

	Brookfield	Buffalo Grove	Burbank	Calumet City	Carol Stream	Carpentersville
1980 Population						
Total	19,395	22,230	28,462	39,697	15,472	23,272
Black	11	142	5	2,360	618	224
Spanish Origin	351	345	887	1,521	618	2,141
% Change 1970-1980						
Total Population	-4.4	80.2	-4.8	19.9	248.9	-3.3
Black Population	83.3	4633.3	0.0	7051.5	1445.0	3100.0
% of Population, 1980						
Black	0.1	0.6	0.0	5.9	4.0	1.0
Spanish Origin	1.8	1.6	3.1	3.8	4.0	9.2
Under 18 Years Old	23.2	35.9	29.2	23.1	31.4	37.7
65 Years and Older	14.4	3.0	8.4	11.8	4.3	2.9
Persons 25 and Older						
Median Years School Completed	12.6	14.4	12.2	12.3	13.0	12.4
% with 4 or More Years College	15.2	37.5	5.0	9.4	24.0	7.5
% of All Workers in Manufacturing	27.3	23.1	28.4	32.1	28.3	41.4
% of All Workers in White Collar Occupations	63.0	76.7	46.2	50.5	63.7	42.2
% Riding to Work by Auto	80.2	90.4	89.2	87.0	88.7	92.8
% of Civilian Labor Force Unemployed	2.9	3.0	6.1	7.1	3.9	5.8
Families (1980)						
Total Number	5,574	5,870	7,446	10,985	4,124	5,952
Median Family Income	$25,679	$32,338	$26,367	$25,628	$23,892	$24,224
% Below Poverty	2.3	2.3	2.8	5.0	5.7	6.3
% with Income Greater than $29,999	34.4	57.5	37.3	36.8	28.6	28.4
% of Persons 5 & Older Living in Different House in 1975	32.6	60.5	31.2	40.7	81.8	48.4
% of Population Living in Group Quarters	0.4	0.0	1.1	0.0	0.0	0.0
Population Per Household	2.6	3.2	3.3	2.5	2.7	3.4
Housing Units, 1980						
Total Number	7,459	7,862	8,682	16,247	6,421	7,082
% in 1-Unit Structures	71.5	72.4	83.4	51.2	44.7	78.9
% Owner-Occupied	73.3	73.6	83.0	59.4	42.1	73.0
% Built in 1970 or Later	10.8	65.7	11.7	35.4	76.5	14.2
% Vacant	2.1	11.0	1.4	3.6	9.1	3.1
% with More than 1 Person per Room	1.8	1.2	4.8	2.8	2.1	6.0
Median Value, Owner Units (in 1-Unit Structures)	$63,000	$89,800	$59,100	$49,000	$75,200	$56,700
Median Contract Rent, Renter Uni	$262	$342	$262	$239	$278	$248
Median Number of Rooms	5.2	5.6	5.3	4.8	5.0	5.3

Table IV-1 Selected Census Statistics, 1980
Community Areas in Chicago and Places of 10,000 or More Population, 1980
In Chicago-Gary-Kenosha Ill.-Ind.-Wis. Standard Consolidated Statistical Area

	Chicago	Chicago Heights	Chicago Ridge	Cicero	Country Club Hills	Crestwood
1980 Population						
Total	3,005,072	37,026	13,473	61,232	14,676	10,852
Black	1,197,000	10,651	17	74	1,750	316
Spanish Origin	422,063	4,205	263	5,271	353	205
% Change 1970-1980						
Total Population	-10.8	-9.5	46.7	-8.7	112.1	88.1
Black Population	8.6	50.0	-	1380.0	19344.4	24.4
% of Population, 1980						
Black	39.8	28.8	0.1	0.1	11.9	2.9
Spanish Origin	14.0	11.4	2.0	8.6	2.4	1.9
Under 18 Years Old	28.4	32.3	27.6	23.3	37.6	28.5
65 Years and Older	11.4	9.6	8.1	15.9	3.0	9.1
Persons 25 and Older						
Median Years School Completed	12.2	12.3	12.4	11.9	12.8	12.5
% with 4 or More Years College	13.8	10.2	7.4	6.2	22.0	12.8
% of All Workers in Manufacturing	26.6	30.6	25.4	36.2	23.6	23.4
% of All Workers in White Collar Occupations	52.7	46.8	51.8	44.7	62.6	53.9
% Riding to Work by Auto	58.1	86.7	89.4	72.7	83.3	91.0
% of Civilian Labor Force Unemployed	9.8	8.9	6.7	6.4	4.3	6.6
Families (1980)						
Total Number	705,954	9,222	3,473	16,365	3,795	2,834
Median Family Income	$18,776	$21,206	$22,392	$20,804	$27,794	$24,604
% Below Poverty	16.8	12.9	5.5	6.8	2.5	3.8
% with Income Greater than $29,999	23.6	27.4	26.5	23.5	42.8	30.6
% of Persons 5 & Older Living in Different House in 1975	42.1	41.1	52.2	42.9	44.6	46.7
% of Population Living in Group Quarters	1.5	1.1	1.6	1.2	0.0	3.5
Population Per Household	2.7	3.1	2.7	2.5	3.5	2.8
Housing Units, 1980						
Total Number	1,173,758	12,728	5,183	25,861	4,357	3,972
% in 1-Unit Structures	24.6	58.0	34.3	31.5	91.3	49.8
% Owner-Occupied	36.3	57.9	45.3	47.3	89.9	65.3
% Built in 1970 or Later	5.9	13.1	49.0	2.7	63.7	58.6
% Vacant	6.8	5.9	4.1	6.4	3.5	4.4
% with More than 1 Person per Room	8.1	7.4	4.1	3.5	2.2	3.1
Median Value, Owner Units (in 1-Unit Structures)	$47,200	$45,800	$60,500	$50,800	$61,700	$60,900
Median Contract Rent, Renter Uni	$190	$186	$269	$186	$322	$275
Median Number of Rooms	4.6	5.2	4.4	4.7	5.6	4.9

	Crystal Lake	Darien	Deerfield	Des Plaines	Dolton	Downers Grove
1980 Population						
Total	18,590	14,536	17,430	53,568	24,766	42,572
Black	15	66	44	160	487	471
Spanish Origin	242	258	223	2,139	731	585
% Change 1970-1980						
Total Population	27.8	86.6	-7.7	-6.4	-4.5	30.0
Black Population	1400.0	-	69.2	240.4	1059.5	659.7
% of Population, 1980						
Black	0.1	0.5	0.3	0.3	2.0	1.1
Spanish Origin	1.3	1.8	1.3	4.0	3.0	1.4
Under 18 Years Old	32.7	32.5	32.8	25.5	26.4	27.5
65 Years and Older	8.3	5.3	5.7	10.5	9.9	9.4
Persons 25 and Older						
Median Years School Completed	13.0	12.9	16.1	12.6	12.5	13.5
% with 4 or More Years College	26.1	28.1	50.1	16.7	10.1	32.6
% of All Workers in Manufacturing	29.8	25.5	18.0	27.5	26.6	22.7
% of All Workers in White Collar Occupations	65.9	69.1	82.4	62.6	54.8	72.0
% Riding to Work by Auto	86.9	89.5	80.0	85.9	83.7	79.1
% of Civilian Labor Force Unemployed	3.8	3.1	2.3	3.4	4.9	3.3
Families (1980)						
Total Number	4,938	3,882	4,744	14,360	6,935	11,648
Median Family Income	$28,142	$33,428	$41,383	$28,807	$27,747	$31,478
% Below Poverty	3.8	1.8	1.4	2.1	2.3	1.9
% with Income Greater than $29,999	44.6	59.5	74.7	46.5	41.6	55.1
% of Persons 5 & Older Living in Different House in 1975	55.9	51.8	35.2	41.3	33.9	46.9
% of Population Living in Group Quarters	0.6	0.8	0.9	1.7	1.0	1.0
Population Per Household	3.0	3.2	3.2	2.8	3.0	2.8
Housing Units, 1980						
Total Number	6,540	4,800	5,489	19,281	8,473	15,865
% in 1-Unit Structures	73.4	71.5	91.6	71.2	81.1	69.9
% Owner-Occupied	69.7	79.3	87.4	75.0	83.0	74.4
% Built in 1970 or Later	34.8	56.1	13.3	14.2	21.0	33.3
% Vacant	5.3	6.8	2.4	2.6	2.2	3.7
% with More than 1 Person per Room	1.3	1.9	0.6	2.4	2.4	1.1
Median Value, Owner Units (in 1-Unit Structures)	$68,900	$90,800	$113,000	$73,800	$50,500	$79,300
Median Contract Rent, Renter Uni	$277	$328	$360	$285	$261	$283
Median Number of Rooms	5.6	5.6	5.6	5.6	5.4	5.6

Table IV-1 Selected Census Statistics, 1980
Community Areas in Chicago and Places of 10,000 or More Population, 1980
In Chicago-Gary-Kenosha Ill.-Ind.-Wis. Standard Consolidated Statistical Area

	Elgin	Elk Grove Village	Elmhurst	Elmwood Park	Evanston	Evergreen Park
1980 Population						
Total	63,798	28,907	44,276	24,016	73,706	22,260
Black	4,206	226	186	8	15,801	53
Spanish Origin	6,529	741	945	405	1,715	229
% Change 1970-1980						
Total Population	14.6	42.1	-4.6	-8.2	-8.0	-14.1
Black Population	57.5	737.0	9.4	60.0	23.0	960.0
% of Population, 1980						
Black	6.6	0.8	0.4	0.0	21.4	0.2
Spanish Origin	10.2	2.6	2.1	1.7	2.3	1.0
Under 18 Years Old	28.0	31.9	27.0	19.5	19.8	22.1
65 Years and Older	12.0	4.7	11.2	18.2	14.1	19.2
Persons 25 and Older						
Median Years School Completed	12.5	12.9	13.0	12.4	15.4	12.5
% with 4 or More Years College	16.2	22.6	28.3	11.5	46.2	15.1
% of All Workers in Manufacturing	31.4	28.9	22.3	24.3	14.0	20.9
% of All Workers in White Collar Occupations	53.3	68.4	68.6	59.3	77.7	63.2
% Riding to Work by Auto	88.6	92.4	83.9	79.5	55.2	80.3
% of Civilian Labor Force Unemployed	5.8	2.7	3.5	2.9	3.5	3.9
Families (1980)						
Total Number	16,476	7,525	12,006	6,664	16,198	6,066
Median Family Income	$23,193	$30,578	$30,407	$25,851	$28,264	$26,376
% Below Poverty	5.3	1.2	1.3	2.8	3.8	2.7
% with Income Greater than $29,999	29.6	52.3	51.4	39.4	46.1	40.9
% of Persons 5 & Older Living in Different House in 1975	53.5	50.1	37.5	34.3	55.0	25.1
% of Population Living in Group Quarters	2.8	0.4	1.9	0.9	11.1	2.4
Population Per Household	2.6	3.1	2.9	2.5	2.3	2.9
Housing Units, 1980						
Total Number	24,892	9,774	14,995	9,751	29,276	7,662
% in 1-Unit Structures	56.9	70.5	83.8	49.9	36.2	83.6
% Owner-Occupied	55.5	70.8	82.3	60.4	46.2	83.6
% Built in 1970 or Later	25.5	46.2	9.9	11.2	3.3	2.1
% Vacant	5.7	4.2	1.8	3.3	4.7	1.2
% with More than 1 Person per Room	4.2	1.7	1.7	2.0	2.2	2.7
Median Value, Owner Units (in 1-Unit Structures)	$62,200	$78,300	$74,200	$67,300	$88,600	$58,600
Median Contract Rent, Renter Uni	$229	$325	$288	$261	$312	$246
Median Number of Rooms	4.9	5.6	5.6	4.9	5.0	5.6

Table IV-1 Selected Census Statistics, 1980
Community Areas in Chicago and Places of 10,000 or More Population, 1980
In Chicago-Gary-Kenosha Ill.-Ind.-Wis. Standard Consolidated Statistical Area

	Forest Park	Franklin Park	Glendale Heights	Glen Ellyn	Glenview	Glenwood
1980 Population						
Total	15,177	17,507	23,163	23,649	32,060	10,538
Black	636	15	377	245	279	1,009
Spanish Origin	447	1,543	850	272	453	221
% Change 1970-1980						
Total Population	-1.9	-14.0	103.1	7.9	28.9	42.1
Black Population	12620.0	114.3	1008.8	218.2	1541.2	3154.8
% of Population, 1980						
Black	4.2	0.1	1.6	1.0	0.9	9.6
Spanish Origin	2.9	8.8	3.7	1.2	1.4	2.1
Under 18 Years Old	16.2	24.6	35.6	29.5	28.5	30.7
65 Years and Older	16.9	10.8	2.3	8.8	8.6	8.8
Persons 25 and Older						
Median Years School Completed	12.7	12.3	12.8	15.2	14.7	12.8
% with 4 or More Years College	24.7	6.7	22.7	43.7	39.7	19.9
% of All Workers in Manufacturing	19.7	39.8	30.6	20.1	21.4	23.9
% of All Workers in White Collar Occupations	68.8	48.4	57.6	78.0	79.8	64.9
% Riding to Work by Auto	67.6	86.6	91.6	76.4	82.3	84.9
% of Civilian Labor Force Unemployed	3.8	4.6	4.0	3.0	2.5	4.9
Families (1980)						
Total Number	3,706	4,817	5,838	6,400	8,879	2,833
Median Family Income	$23,040	$26,151	$27,496	$33,506	$36,344	$30,649
% Below Poverty	4.2	1.3	2.3	2.7	1.6	1.5
% with Income Greater than $29,999	24.8	38.5	41.4	59.7	62.9	52.4
% of Persons 5 & Older Living in Different House in 1975	55.2	28.5	65.5	44.7	38.7	42.2
% of Population Living in Group Quarters	2.1	0.0	0.0	0.0	1.3	2.1
Population Per Household	2.0	2.9	3.1	2.8	3.0	3.1
Housing Units, 1980						
Total Number	7,938	6,255	7,881	8,943	10,994	3,476
% in 1-Unit Structures	21.1	73.6	64.9	65.6	79.0	72.5
% Owner-Occupied	36.1	73.4	67.7	67.4	79.3	84.7
% Built in 1970 or Later	20.4	5.1	65.1	25.6	22.2	46.7
% Vacant	4.6	2.1	6.0	5.6	2.9	2.8
% with More than 1 Person per Room	2.3	5.4	2.8	1.0	0.8	1.2
Median Value, Owner Units (in 1-Unit Structures)	$52,100	$63,800	$68,100	$86,000	$111,900	$67,000
Median Contract Rent, Renter Uni	$246	$230	$276	$282	$322	$287
Median Number of Rooms	4.1	4.9	5.6	5.6	5.6	5.6

Table IV-1 Selected Census Statistics, 1980
Community Areas in Chicago and Places of 10,000 or More Population, 1980
In Chicago-Gary-Kenosha Ill.-Ind.-Wis. Standard Consolidated Statistical Area

	Hanover Park	Harvey	Hazel Crest	Hickory Hills	Highland Park	Hinsdale
1980 Population						
Total	28,850	35,810	13,973	13,778	30,611	16,726
Black	390	23,491	1,662	4	547	72
Spanish Origin	1,748	1,643	329	275	837	197
% Change 1970-1980						
Total Population	145.8	3.4	35.3	4.6	-5.1	5.1
Black Population	-	119.3	55300.0	100.0	-4.7	-7.7
% of Population, 1980						
Black	1.4	65.6	11.9	0.0	1.8	0.4
Spanish Origin	6.1	4.6	2.4	2.0	2.7	1.2
Under 18 Years Old	37.2	36.5	32.2	30.8	29.5	27.9
65 Years and Older	1.8	7.7	6.8	6.1	9.1	11.5
Persons 25 and Older						
Median Years School Completed	12.8	12.2	12.8	12.5	15.9	15.6
% with 4 or More Years College	18.6	5.4	23.0	12.3	49.4	46.7
% of All Workers in Manufacturing	33.2	30.4	23.1	23.5	14.0	18.2
% of All Workers in White Collar Occupations	59.3	40.1	63.5	54.9	81.2	78.1
% Riding to Work by Auto	88.6	83.2	80.9	93.2	74.8	72.0
% of Civilian Labor Force Unemployed	5.7	14.5	4.1	6.8	2.4	2.3
Families (1980)						
Total Number	7,505	8,434	3,715	3,590	8,568	4,636
Median Family Income	$27,036	$20,441	$28,057	$27,363	$42,903	$39,104
% Below Poverty	2.9	16.7	2.6	2.7	1.5	1.0
% with Income Greater than $29,999	38.1	23.9	44.6	40.4	69.5	68.8
% of Persons 5 & Older Living in Different House in 1975	62.3	40.7	51.1	37.7	36.9	41.4
% of Population Living in Group Quarters	0.0	1.7	1.4	0.6	1.0	2.2
Population Per Household	3.3	3.2	3.1	3.1	3.0	2.8
Housing Units, 1980						
Total Number	9,352	11,449	4,597	4,648	10,540	6,024
% in 1-Unit Structures	75.8	60.3	80.9	62.1	82.7	80.0
% Owner-Occupied	74.6	58.5	82.6	65.7	78.9	75.6
% Built in 1970 or Later	67.0	5.4	36.2	24.3	13.4	12.3
% Vacant	6.7	4.1	3.1	3.9	3.0	4.6
% with More than 1 Person per Room	3.3	10.8	2.6	1.9	1.2	1.1
Median Value, Owner Units (in 1-Unit Structures)	$67,000	$33,800	$56,000	$71,200	$124,800	$110,700
Median Contract Rent, Renter Uni	$276	$178	$284	$264	$286	$304
Median Number of Rooms	5.6	4.9	5.6	5.6	5.6	5.6

Table IV-1 Selected Census Statistics, 1980
Community Areas in Chicago and Places of 10,000 or More Population, 1980
In Chicago-Gary-Kenosha Ill.-Ind.-Wis. Standard Consolidated Statistical Area

	Hoffman Estates	Homewood	Joliet	Justice	La Grange	La Grange Park
1980 Population						
Total	37,272	19,724	77,956	10,552	15,445	13,359
Black	503	424	15,672	1,102	1,036	19
Spanish Origin	1,203	132	6,565	285	238	122
% Change 1970-1980						
Total Population	67.6	4.5	-1.1	11.4	-7.9	-13.6
Black Population	3492.9	3433.3	64.8	9918.2	144.3	375.0
% of Population, 1980						
Black	1.3	2.1	20.1	10.4	6.7	0.1
Spanish Origin	3.2	0.7	8.4	2.7	1.5	0.9
Under 18 Years Old	32.9	25.2	28.9	28.7	25.9	21.2
65 Years and Older	2.2	13.4	13.1	4.7	13.3	19.1
Persons 25 and Older						
Median Years School Completed	13.4	13.2	12.3	12.4	14.0	13.0
% with 4 or More Years College	29.4	30.9	12.8	8.6	34.9	27.3
% of All Workers in Manufacturing	25.9	18.8	28.1	32.1	21.5	27.9
% of All Workers in White Collar Occupations	69.0	74.6	48.7	42.1	73.6	72.8
% Riding to Work by Auto	91.7	76.7	91.8	92.2	72.0	78.1
% of Civilian Labor Force Unemployed	3.9	4.0	9.3	7.6	4.3	2.1
Families (1980)						
Total Number	9,601	5,619	19,022	2,840	4,185	3,825
Median Family Income	$29,865	$31,247	$22,694	$22,188	$31,915	$30,100
% Below Poverty	2.6	1.3	9.1	3.5	2.1	1.5
% with Income Greater than $29,999	49.5	53.8	30.7	23.4	55.8	50.4
% of Persons 5 & Older Living in Different House in 1975	60.5	39.6	47.3	68.3	42.1	34.1
% of Population Living in Group Quarters	0.5	1.1	4.8	0.5	1.8	2.9
Population Per Household	3.0	2.7	2.7	2.7	2.8	2.5
Housing Units, 1980						
Total Number	13,214	7,328	29,803	4,163	5,745	5,239
% in 1-Unit Structures	72.3	78.0	59.7	35.3	67.9	71.7
% Owner-Occupied	68.2	82.2	55.5	43.0	69.6	70.8
% Built in 1970 or Later	56.4	19.5	14.0	43.1	5.3	3.0
% Vacant	7.5	2.4	8.5	6.7	4.1	1.3
% with More than 1 Person per Room	1.5	0.7	4.8	3.1	1.0	1.0
Median Value, Owner Units (in 1-Unit Structures)	$76,900	$67,700	$45,700	$60,600	$84,800	$76,200
Median Contract Rent, Renter Uni	$324	$296	$184	$276	$273	$278
Median Number of Rooms	5.6	5.6	5.0	4.7	5.6	5.4

Table IV-1 Selected Census Statistics, 1980
Community Areas in Chicago and Places of 10,000 or More Population, 1980
In Chicago-Gary-Kenosha Ill.-Ind.-Wis. Standard Consolidated Statistical Area

	Lake Forest	Lansing	Libertyville	Lincolnwood	Lisle	Lombard
1980 Population						
Total	15,245	29,039	16,520	11,921	13,625	37,295
Black	218	321	28	12	402	220
Spanish Origin	166	598	327	254	192	575
% Change 1970-1980						
Total Population	-2.5	12.5	41.4	-7.8	155.7	9.6
Black Population	-35.9	2040.0	75.0	-65.7	3554.5	1471.4
% of Population, 1980						
Black	1.4	1.1	0.2	0.1	3.0	0.6
Spanish Origin	1.1	2.1	2.0	2.1	1.4	1.5
Under 18 Years Old	26.4	26.3	33.4	20.8	28.1	27.2
65 Years and Older	10.2	9.9	7.5	14.9	4.4	7.7
Persons 25 and Older						
Median Years School Completed	16.1	12.5	14.2	14.0	14.2	12.8
% with 4 or More Years College	51.8	12.7	37.6	35.4	35.8	23.8
% of All Workers in Manufacturing	17.3	27.9	27.5	14.8	23.6	21.1
% of All Workers in White Collar Occupations	82.3	54.9	73.7	82.6	68.7	67.8
% Riding to Work by Auto	68.1	90.9	87.1	83.7	78.4	85.5
% of Civilian Labor Force Unemployed	2.1	5.2	4.0	3.1	2.5	4.0
Families (1980)						
Total Number	3,870	8,136	4,289	3,661	3,440	9,933
Median Family Income	$52,691	$26,707	$34,953	$38,453	$30,141	$28,404
% Below Poverty	1.7	2.0	1.5	1.2	1.6	1.5
% with Income Greater than $29,999	76.7	40.4	64.9	67.3	50.4	45.2
% of Persons 5 & Older Living in Different House in 1975	41.8	32.6	56.7	29.3	75.3	43.0
% of Population Living in Group Quarters	7.5	0.2	0.8	0.0	1.3	0.6
Population Per Household	2.9	2.8	3.1	2.9	2.6	2.9
Housing Units, 1980						
Total Number	5,115	10,672	5,539	4,161	5,454	13,439
% in 1-Unit Structures	78.3	68.4	77.5	89.9	52.5	69.8
% Owner-Occupied	77.6	69.0	72.8	93.8	48.5	73.3
% Built in 1970 or Later	20.4	26.5	40.1	7.0	60.1	24.6
% Vacant	5.7	2.8	4.2	1.6	6.7	3.4
% with More than 1 Person per Room	0.5	1.9	0.9	0.8	1.6	1.5
Median Value, Owner Units (in 1-Unit Structures)	$180,900	$57,800	$104,500	$106,700	$88,600	$69,300
Median Contract Rent, Renter Uni	$321	$271	$282	$441	$312	$332
Median Number of Rooms	5.6	5.2	5.6	5.6	5.2	5.6

Table IV-1 Selected Census Statistics, 1980
Community Areas in Chicago and Places of 10,000 or More Population, 1980
In Chicago-Gary-Kenosha Ill.-Ind.-Wis. Standard Consolidated Statistical Area

	McHenry	Markham	Matteson	Maywood	Melrose Park	Midlothian
1980 Population						
Total	10,908	15,172	10,223	27,998	20,735	14,274
Black	5	10,592	1,266	21,015	46	25
Spanish Origin	80	217	333	1,893	3,060	321
% Change 1970-1980						
Total Population	61.1	-5.1	115.6	-3.5	-8.7	-1.0
Black Population	-	32.7	126500.0	69.3	-69.1	-86.6
% of Population, 1980						
Black	0.0	69.8	12.4	75.1	0.2	0.2
Spanish Origin	0.7	1.4	3.3	6.8	14.8	2.2
Under 18 Years Old	27.8	36.6	33.7	33.6	23.3	32.0
65 Years and Older	15.5	4.3	4.9	8.2	11.6	8.2
Persons 25 and Older						
Median Years School Completed	12.6	12.3	12.9	12.2	12.2	12.5
% with 4 or More Years College	15.0	5.6	19.6	8.2	8.6	9.2
% of All Workers in Manufacturing	26.6	24.8	21.1	31.8	34.3	23.3
% of All Workers in White Collar Occupations	56.4	41.1	67.0	46.9	49.0	51.8
% Riding to Work by Auto	90.0	85.6	80.5	86.4	87.4	82.8
% of Civilian Labor Force Unemployed	5.3	9.5	3.9	9.7	6.5	6.1
Families (1980)						
Total Number	3,029	3,571	2,745	6,435	5,611	3,703
Median Family Income	$23,814	$24,714	$29,168	$21,668	$22,503	$24,481
% Below Poverty	2.0	8.3	3.7	11.0	6.2	4.8
% with Income Greater than $29,999	28.1	32.9	46.4	29.0	28.8	30.9
% of Persons 5 & Older Living in Different House in 1975	53.3	25.2	61.0	36.0	42.3	34.8
% of Population Living in Group Quarters	1.7	0.0	0.7	1.3	0.2	0.8
Population Per Household	2.7	3.8	3.2	3.3	2.6	3.1
Housing Units, 1980						
Total Number	4,112	4,032	3,324	8,777	8,373	4,746
% in 1-Unit Structures	74.9	96.2	78.3	57.6	38.1	75.0
% Owner-Occupied	75.0	91.0	75.3	59.6	50.3	73.5
% Built in 1970 or Later	44.8	3.9	61.4	4.8	8.7	19.0
% Vacant	4.5	1.5	3.6	4.8	4.7	4.0
% with More than 1 Person per Room	1.5	10.6	2.0	8.7	5.1	4.2
Median Value, Owner Units (in 1-Unit Structures)	$63,700	$36,900	$67,200	$44,800	$66,000	$50,100
Median Contract Rent, Renter Uni	$260	$208	$282	$213	$215	$238
Median Number of Rooms	5.4	5.6	5.6	5.3	4.5	5.4

Table IV-1 Selected Census Statistics, 1980
Community Areas in Chicago and Places of 10,000 or More Population, 1980
In Chicago-Gary-Kenosha Ill.-Ind.-Wis. Standard Consolidated Statistical Area

	Morton Grove	Mount Prospect	Mundelein	Naperville	Niles	Norridge
1980 Population						
Total	23,747	52,634	17,053	42,330	30,363	16,483
Black	31	331	16	314	63	6
Spanish Origin	440	1,225	1,287	418	495	148
% Change 1970-1980						
Total Population	-9.9	50.4	5.7	51.6	-3.4	-3.7
Black Population	675.0	2264.3	14.3	630.2	250.0	-
% of Population, 1980						
Black	0.1	0.6	0.1	0.7	0.2	0.0
Spanish Origin	1.9	2.3	7.5	1.0	1.6	0.9
Under 18 Years Old	23.6	26.8	30.8	34.2	21.1	19.0
65 Years and Older	10.9	7.1	4.8	5.5	15.3	14.0
Persons 25 and Older						
Median Years School Completed	12.8	12.9	12.7	15.5	12.5	12.2
% with 4 or More Years College	22.0	24.3	20.1	46.4	15.1	7.4
% of All Workers in Manufacturing	25.9	27.1	30.0	23.1	28.6	31.2
% of All Workers in White Collar Occupations	71.3	68.5	58.2	79.4	62.9	54.2
% Riding to Work by Auto	85.3	86.3	90.3	79.1	85.3	83.8
% of Civilian Labor Force Unemployed	3.1	3.1	3.4	1.9	3.0	3.7
Families (1980)						
Total Number	6,793	14,103	4,414	10,998	8,097	4,547
Median Family Income	$31,898	$30,617	$27,394	$36,685	$28,447	$27,665
% Below Poverty	1.5	2.2	3.6	1.5	2.2	1.6
% with Income Greater than $29,999	55.9	51.9	43.1	69.2	45.9	43.4
% of Persons 5 & Older Living in Different House in 1975	28.3	44.4	50.0	61.8	34.5	25.5
% of Population Living in Group Quarters	1.1	0.0	1.3	2.0	5.9	2.5
Population Per Household	3.0	2.8	3.1	3.2	2.8	2.8
Housing Units, 1980						
Total Number	8,046	19,508	5,689	14,057	10,727	5,757
% in 1-Unit Structures	86.0	62.9	73.1	79.5	69.5	77.9
% Owner-Occupied	90.6	65.1	65.9	76.3	71.0	79.1
% Built in 1970 or Later	11.5	31.9	24.8	54.6	9.9	11.2
% Vacant	1.2	3.8	3.0	7.2	4.6	1.5
% with More than 1 Person per Room	1.9	1.5	3.4	0.6	1.8	2.7
Median Value, Owner Units (in 1-Unit Structures)	$84,900	$88,500	$67,400	$98,400	$79,700	$77,500
Median Contract Rent, Renter Uni	$246	$319	$291	$315	$282	$273
Median Number of Rooms	5.6	5.6	5.4	5.6	5.3	5.2

Table IV-1 Selected Census Statistics, 1980
Community Areas in Chicago and Places of 10,000 or More Population, 1980
In Chicago-Gary-Kenosha Ill.-Ind.-Wis. Standard Consolidated Statistical Area

	Northbrook	North Chicago	Northlake	Oak Forest	Oak Lawn	Oak Park
1980 Population						
Total	30,778	38,774	12,166	26,096	60,590	54,887
Black	73	10,495	21	522	38	5,929
Spanish Origin	533	1,963	1,013	443	753	1,364
% Change 1970-1980						
Total Population	21.1	-18.0	-14.3	35.4	0.5	-12.2
Black Population	87.2	33.9	250.0	-	533.3	4391.7
% of Population, 1980						
Black	0.2	27.1	0.2	2.0	0.1	10.8
Spanish Origin	1.7	5.1	8.3	1.7	1.2	2.5
Under 18 Years Old	30.7	24.6	25.8	33.4	25.1	24.4
65 Years and Older	7.9	4.0	11.0	6.9	14.4	14.1
Persons 25 and Older						
Median Years School Completed	15.4	12.5	12.2	12.6	12.5	14.5
% with 4 or More Years College	45.7	9.7	6.0	13.9	13.7	39.4
% of All Workers in Manufacturing	19.0	31.4	40.8	22.1	22.3	15.8
% of All Workers in White Collar Occupations	81.5	44.9	48.6	57.3	58.0	76.9
% Riding to Work by Auto	83.5	38.9	92.1	85.5	86.0	62.2
% of Civilian Labor Force Unemployed	2.4	5.3	6.6	4.7	5.9	4.4
Families (1980)						
Total Number	8,480	5,539	3,136	6,373	16,111	13,377
Median Family Income	$42,297	$16,850	$25,657	$28,027	$27,813	$27,413
% Below Poverty	1.5	7.5	2.5	2.2	2.6	2.8
% with Income Greater than $29,999	72.3	15.3	36.5	42.8	44.7	42.8
% of Persons 5 & Older Living in Different House in 1975	40.7	76.1	39.0	42.3	32.0	47.1
% of Population Living in Group Quarters	2.3	43.3	1.4	4.1	1.1	1.2
Population Per Household	3.1	3.1	2.8	3.2	2.9	2.4
Housing Units, 1980						
Total Number	9,930	7,462	4,545	8,036	21,189	23,438
% in 1-Unit Structures	87.8	39.6	63.4	72.4	66.9	41.6
% Owner-Occupied	88.1	37.1	67.3	76.0	76.5	48.3
% Built in 1970 or Later	33.8	23.4	10.0	34.9	23.8	4.6
% Vacant	3.8	6.2	7.0	4.1	2.2	4.0
% with More than 1 Person per Room	0.7	7.3	4.4	2.3	2.8	1.3
Median Value, Owner Units (in 1-Unit Structures)	$128,400	$45,200	$60,300	$65,600	$66,200	$68,000
Median Contract Rent, Renter Uni	$436	$219	$238	$270	$276	$258
Median Number of Rooms	5.6	4.9	5.1	5.6	5.4	5.1

Table IV-1 Selected Census Statistics, 1980
Community Areas in Chicago and Places of 10,000 or More Population, 1980
In Chicago-Gary-Kenosha Ill.-Ind.-Wis. Standard Consolidated Statistical Area

	Orland Park	Palatine	Palos Heights	Palos Hills	Park Forest	Park Ridge
1980 Population						
Total	23,045	32,166	11,096	16,654	26,222	38,704
Black	24	106	17	261	3,178	60
Spanish Origin	328	618	87	452	626	334
% Change 1970-1980						
Total Population	260.6	23.5	29.9	151.2	-14.4	-9.2
Black Population	2300.0	606.7	-34.6	26000.0	357.9	122.2
% of Population, 1980						
Black	0.1	0.3	0.2	1.6	12.1	0.2
Spanish Origin	1.4	1.9	0.8	2.7	2.4	0.9
Under 18 Years Old	33.8	30.6	28.4	28.8	31.4	24.7
65 Years and Older	4.9	6.5	8.3	6.9	5.8	13.4
Persons 25 and Older						
Median Years School Completed	12.7	13.7	12.9	12.6	13.4	13.3
% with 4 or More Years College	21.1	32.6	27.0	15.6	27.5	30.4
% of All Workers in Manufacturing	20.9	24.9	15.4	24.7	20.8	21.6
% of All Workers in White Collar Occupations	61.0	73.2	71.8	55.6	68.9	77.2
% Riding to Work by Auto	90.9	84.0	86.7	93.1	78.6	79.0
% of Civilian Labor Force Unemployed	4.9	3.8	3.5	4.5	5.0	2.7
Families (1980)						
Total Number	6,050	8,310	2,927	4,473	7,225	10,781
Median Family Income	$31,229	$33,443	$36,126	$28,939	$25,156	$34,131
% Below Poverty	2.7	1.6	2.3	2.1	3.4	1.3
% with Income Greater than $29,999	53.9	60.8	65.6	46.5	36.1	61.3
% of Persons 5 & Older Living in Different House in 1975	60.9	49.0	34.5	53.3	46.1	31.5
% of Population Living in Group Quarters	0.0	0.8	2.3	1.2	1.8	1.4
Population Per Household	3.3	3.0	3.3	2.9	2.9	2.9
Housing Units, 1980						
Total Number	7,571	11,091	3,328	5,848	9,247	13,535
% in 1-Unit Structures	69.0	69.1	86.3	56.8	81.0	80.1
% Owner-Occupied	72.0	71.3	93.7	68.5	61.5	84.2
% Built in 1970 or Later	74.1	36.2	34.9	64.8	6.7	7.6
% Vacant	8.0	4.2	2.6	4.1	2.8	1.9
% with More than 1 Person per Room	1.5	1.0	1.2	2.1	1.6	1.1
Median Value, Owner Units (in 1-Unit Structures)	$90,900	$88,900	$92,400	$82,800	$49,500	$92,900
Median Contract Rent, Renter Uni	$328	$327	$329	$284	$223	$298
Median Number of Rooms	5.6	5.6	5.6	5.4	5.6	5.6

Table IV-1 Selected Census Statistics, 1980
Community Areas in Chicago and Places of 10,000 or More Population, 1980
In Chicago-Gary-Kenosha Ill.-Ind.-Wis. Standard Consolidated Statistical Area

	Prospect Heights	Riverdale	River Forest	River Grove	Rolling Meadows	Romeoville
1980 Population						
Total	11,808	13,233	12,392	10,368	20,167	15,519
Black	218	36	106	1	249	244
Spanish Origin	630	321	188	202	1,303	1,401
% Change 1970-1980						
Total Population	-11.4	-16.3	-7.5	-9.6	5.2	22.4
Black Population	990.0	111.8	135.6	-66.7	982.6	8033.3
% of Population, 1980						
Black	1.8	0.3	0.9	0.0	1.2	1.6
Spanish Origin	5.3	2.4	1.5	1.9	6.5	9.0
Under 18 Years Old	24.5	21.2	23.9	19.9	28.0	39.1
65 Years and Older	4.5	18.6	15.9	15.7	4.8	1.7
Persons 25 and Older						
Median Years School Completed	12.9	12.4	15.4	12.3	12.7	12.3
% with 4 or More Years College	24.4	9.2	45.6	8.8	19.4	5.9
% of All Workers in Manufacturing	29.5	28.3	15.5	29.4	28.1	35.9
% of All Workers in White Collar Occupations	63.3	56.6	80.9	61.3	60.5	36.6
% Riding to Work by Auto	90.9	69.7	70.4	80.0	91.2	92.8
% of Civilian Labor Force Unemployed	3.8	5.8	2.3	4.6	2.9	8.4
Families (1980)						
Total Number	3,059	3,764	3,014	2,941	5,373	3,587
Median Family Income	$28,750	$24,047	$36,312	$23,278	$27,144	$25,453
% Below Poverty	3.1	3.1	2.4	3.1	1.7	3.5
% with Income Greater than $29,999	46.8	31.0	64.3	27.9	42.7	34.9
% of Persons 5 & Older Living in Different House in 1975	61.3	36.5	36.8	37.7	49.2	44.1
% of Population Living in Group Quarters	0.0	0.0	9.3	0.5	1.1	4.8
Population Per Household	2.5	2.4	2.8	2.4	2.9	3.8
Housing Units, 1980						
Total Number	5,148	5,671	4,162	4,414	7,667	3,921
% in 1-Unit Structures	42.8	59.5	64.5	46.6	58.2	99.3
% Owner-Occupied	47.7	58.8	76.3	54.6	60.0	92.8
% Built in 1970 or Later	42.4	2.9	6.0	14.3	31.7	27.5
% Vacant	9.1	1.1	2.7	3.6	9.9	2.1
% with More than 1 Person per Room	2.5	1.9	0.8	1.9	4.0	5.9
Median Value, Owner Units (in 1-Unit Structures)	$92,400	$41,600	$111,600	$64,000	$71,200	$46,700
Median Contract Rent, Renter Uni	$307	$239	$278	$268	$307	$340
Median Number of Rooms	4.7	4.8	5.6	4.4	5.1	5.6

Table IV-1 Selected Census Statistics, 1980
Community Areas in Chicago and Places of 10,000 or More Population, 1980
In Chicago-Gary-Kenosha Ill.-Ind.-Wis. Standard Consolidated Statistical Area

	Roselle	Round Lake Beach	St. Charles	Sauk Village	Schaumburg	Schiller Park
1980 Population						
Total	16,948	12,921	17,492	10,906	53,305	11,458
Black	141	28	78	154	645	72
Spanish Origin	312	985	474	830	986	751
% Change 1970-1980						
Total Population	173.0	126.0	35.1	45.8	184.6	-9.9
Black Population	-	1300.0	550.0	5033.3	3931.3	242.9
% of Population, 1980						
Black	0.8	0.2	0.4	1.4	1.2	0.6
Spanish Origin	1.8	7.6	2.7	7.6	1.8	6.6
Under 18 Years Old	30.0	40.4	30.2	41.5	31.2	25.8
65 Years and Older	4.7	4.6	8.8	1.9	4.7	5.6
Persons 25 and Older						
Median Years School Completed	13.1	12.3	12.9	12.3	13.0	12.3
% with 4 or More Years College	26.7	3.9	26.4	5.1	27.3	6.5
% of All Workers in Manufacturing	24.9	40.9	29.4	38.6	27.8	41.5
% of All Workers in White Collar Occupations	69.1	42.3	63.3	37.0	70.5	45.4
% Riding to Work by Auto	85.3	91.4	90.8	96.3	91.3	89.5
% of Civilian Labor Force Unemployed	3.1	8.3	4.8	8.9	3.3	4.7
Families (1980)						
Total Number	4,746	3,126	4,684	2,660	13,622	2,956
Median Family Income	$30,368	$23,849	$27,379	$25,046	$29,257	$25,457
% Below Poverty	4.5	4.3	2.0	4.8	1.9	5.0
% with Income Greater than $29,999	51.3	25.4	42.8	32.0	47.4	36.1
% of Persons 5 & Older Living in Different House in 1975	59.6	48.3	55.8	42.1	65.5	49.2
% of Population Living in Group Quarters	0.5	0.7	0.8	0.0	0.3	0.1
Population Per Household	2.9	3.6	2.8	3.8	2.7	2.7
Housing Units, 1980						
Total Number	6,049	3,738	6,451	2,997	20,929	4,507
% in 1-Unit Structures	82.9	93.3	69.5	88.7	56.0	45.5
% Owner-Occupied	78.9	84.1	64.2	84.3	60.9	47.6
% Built in 1970 or Later	67.5	53.8	38.0	44.1	76.2	14.0
% Vacant	4.2	3.4	4.4	5.0	6.9	5.8
% with More than 1 Person per Room	0.9	6.0	1.5	7.4	1.0	4.5
Median Value, Owner Units (in 1-Unit Structures)	$76,800	$49,300	$73,800	$44,100	$83,300	$66,800
Median Contract Rent, Renter Uni	$318	$246	$274	$298	$354	$262
Median Number of Rooms	5.6	5.6	5.6	5.5	5.4	4.5

Table IV-1 Selected Census Statistics, 1980
Community Areas in Chicago and Places of 10,000 or More Population, 1980
In Chicago-Gary-Kenosha Ill.-Ind.-Wis. Standard Consolidated Statistical Area

	Skokie	South Holland	Streamwood	Summit	Tinley Park	Villa Park
1980 Population						
Total	60,278	24,977	23,456	10,110	26,171	23,185
Black	613	120	172	1,637	463	102
Spanish Origin	1,612	395	1,213	2,022	405	456
% Change 1970-1980						
Total Population	-11.8	4.4	29.0	-12.6	108.2	-10.5
Black Population	472.9	900.0	5633.3	-26.2	75.4	537.5
% of Population, 1980						
Black	1.0	0.5	0.7	16.2	1.8	0.4
Spanish Origin	2.7	1.6	5.2	20.0	1.5	2.0
Under 18 Years Old	20.8	27.6	39.8	28.3	31.8	28.1
65 Years and Older	14.6	10.6	1.7	10.4	6.5	8.6
Persons 25 and Older						
Median Years School Completed	13.2	12.6	12.6	11.4	12.5	12.6
% with 4 or More Years College	28.6	16.3	12.8	6.0	12.7	17.5
% of All Workers in Manufacturing	20.1	23.5	29.6	42.4	22.8	26.0
% of All Workers in White Collar Occupations	79.0	59.6	55.0	39.1	55.8	59.8
% Riding to Work by Auto	80.4	85.4	92.6	80.4	84.5	86.0
% of Civilian Labor Force Unemployed	2.7	5.2	5.2	10.4	4.9	4.4
Families (1980)						
Total Number	18,043	6,841	5,922	2,551	6,664	6,265
Median Family Income	$30,858	$30,706	$26,947	$21,584	$26,901	$27,215
% Below Poverty	1.9	2.0	1.6	10.4	2.7	3.3
% with Income Greater than $29,999	52.3	52.3	36.5	27.3	39.5	41.8
% of Persons 5 & Older Living in Different House in 1975	36.0	29.0	49.6	38.5	50.0	34.8
% of Population Living in Group Quarters	1.0	2.5	0.1	0.0	4.1	0.0
Population Per Household	2.7	3.2	3.6	2.8	3.0	2.9
Housing Units, 1980						
Total Number	22,805	7,599	6,664	3,719	8,623	8,107
% in 1-Unit Structures	63.1	96.6	95.5	37.8	66.0	75.4
% Owner-Occupied	73.8	93.2	89.0	47.9	70.3	72.1
% Built in 1970 or Later	8.9	20.0	38.1	5.6	60.8	8.4
% Vacant	2.2	1.2	3.3	4.1	3.6	2.6
% with More than 1 Person per Room	1.4	1.7	3.4	10.0	1.7	2.6
Median Value, Owner Units (in 1-Unit Structures)	$84,400	$67,800	$65,000	$47,600	$65,300	$66,000
Median Contract Rent, Renter Uni	$311	$215	$351	$199	$273	$267
Median Number of Rooms	5.6	5.6	5.6	4.5	5.6	5.4

Table IV-1 Selected Census Statistics, 1980
Community Areas in Chicago and Places of 10,000 or More Population, 1980
In Chicago-Gary-Kenosha Ill.-Ind.-Wis. Standard Consolidated Statistical Area

	Waukegan	Westchester	West Chicago	Western Springs	Westmont	Wheaton
1980 Population						
Total	67,653	17,730	12,550	12,876	16,718	43,043
Black	12,484	14	202	19	293	1,068
Spanish Origin	9,253	182	2,094	115	328	615
% Change 1970-1980						
Total Population	3.9	-11.5	25.7	-1.2	89.3	38.2
Black Population	48.2	16.7	1583.3	90.0	4783.3	80.7
% of Population, 1980						
Black	18.5	0.1	1.6	0.1	1.8	2.5
Spanish Origin	13.7	1.0	16.7	0.9	2.0	1.4
Under 18 Years Old	29.1	20.2	31.3	28.3	22.7	27.1
65 Years and Older	9.9	15.3	8.3	11.1	9.9	7.9
Persons 25 and Older						
Median Years School Completed	12.4	12.6	12.5	15.4	12.8	14.7
% with 4 or More Years College	13.9	17.2	15.0	45.6	23.6	40.4
% of All Workers in Manufacturing	32.6	27.0	32.3	20.3	22.2	17.5
% of All Workers in White Collar Occupations	50.6	66.8	44.5	83.6	64.4	76.5
% Riding to Work by Auto	90.4	88.5	86.1	72.6	81.8	76.6
% of Civilian Labor Force Unemployed	7.9	2.6	6.8	2.2	3.5	3.2
Families (1980)						
Total Number	16,992	5,381	3,061	3,789	4,450	10,849
Median Family Income	$22,692	$30,391	$22,823	$36,210	$25,438	$31,185
% Below Poverty	7.2	1.4	3.7	0.9	3.1	1.9
% with Income Greater than $29,999	29.2	51.3	29.9	64.4	34.1	53.5
% of Persons 5 & Older Living in Different House in 1975	49.0	25.5	55.2	25.5	61.5	58.4
% of Population Living in Group Quarters	2.6	0.1	2.9	0.1	2.3	6.7
Population Per Household	2.7	2.9	3.0	3.0	2.4	2.8
Housing Units, 1980						
Total Number	25,671	6,230	4,362	4,338	7,101	15,232
% in 1-Unit Structures	52.2	91.3	58.6	95.2	43.5	69.7
% Owner-Occupied	51.7	91.2	54.0	93.3	45.4	68.2
% Built in 1970 or Later	16.0	5.3	31.8	5.7	54.0	42.9
% Vacant	6.0	1.0	6.0	1.3	5.6	5.6
% with More than 1 Person per Room	6.8	1.3	5.9	0.6	1.8	1.1
Median Value, Owner Units (in 1-Unit Structures)	$50,400	$71,500	$62,500	$97,300	$69,200	$81,100
Median Contract Rent, Renter Uni	$226	$331	$258	$349	$300	$292
Median Number of Rooms	4.7	5.6	5.1	5.6	4.8	5.6

	Wheeling	Wilmette	Winnetka	Wood Dale	Woodridge	Woodstock
1980 Population						
Total	23,266	28,229	12,772	11,251	22,322	11,725
Black	188	95	62	11	864	23
Spanish Origin	1,282	337	120	611	516	392
% Change 1970-1980						
Total Population	75.7	-12.2	-9.6	27.4	102.4	14.7
Black Population	2585.7	17.3	-47.0	-	2441.2	130.0
% of Population, 1980						
Black	0.8	0.3	0.5	0.1	3.9	0.2
Spanish Origin	5.5	1.2	0.9	5.4	2.3	3.3
Under 18 Years Old	25.8	27.4	30.9	29.1	32.3	26.9
65 Years and Older	5.1	12.7	11.6	7.3	2.0	13.4
Persons 25 and Older						
Median Years School Completed	12.9	16.1	16.1	12.5	13.9	12.5
% with 4 or More Years College	23.9	54.0	65.9	11.7	32.1	15.7
% of All Workers in Manufacturing	26.7	13.8	15.7	29.2	25.1	37.6
% of All Workers in White Collar Occupations	65.1	85.4	89.0	57.4	68.9	45.1
% Riding to Work by Auto	92.2	67.8	53.7	91.9	86.7	87.2
% of Civilian Labor Force Unemployed	3.7	2.6	2.3	4.8	4.8	5.8
Families (1980)						
Total Number	6,322	7,880	3,549	3,094	5,749	3,051
Median Family Income	$26,301	$41,304	$54,900	$29,113	$29,582	$22,671
% Below Poverty	2.3	2.0	1.3	3.5	2.8	4.1
% with Income Greater than $29,999	36.8	71.6	79.6	47.6	48.5	26.7
% of Persons 5 & Older Living in Different House in 1975	62.9	35.9	34.4	40.8	61.8	49.5
% of Population Living in Group Quarters	0.5	1.1	0.1	0.4	0.0	3.2
Population Per Household	2.6	2.9	3.0	3.1	2.9	2.6
Housing Units, 1980						
Total Number	9,617	9,982	4,383	3,737	8,527	4,610
% in 1-Unit Structures	47.6	82.8	85.5	77.1	53.7	61.3
% Owner-Occupied	60.9	83.1	81.4	83.1	56.7	55.2
% Built in 1970 or Later	59.6	5.3	6.1	30.0	62.0	22.8
% Vacant	6.0	2.6	2.8	2.2	8.3	4.1
% with More than 1 Person per Room	2.2	0.5	0.4	3.2	1.3	1.9
Median Value, Owner Units (in 1-Unit Structures)	$68,800	$121,800	$172,000	$75,800	$73,200	$61,000
Median Contract Rent, Renter Uni	$325	$374	$368	$255	$303	$216
Median Number of Rooms	5.0	5.6	5.6	5.6	5.4	5.1

	Worth	Zion	Crown Point, Ind.	East Chicago, Ind.	Gary, Ind.	Griffith, Ind.
1980 Population						
Total	11,592	17,861	16,455	39,786	151,953	17,026
Black	4	3,146	158	11,802	107,644	28
Spanish Origin	180	665	317	16,818	10,793	650
% Change 1970-1980						
Total Population	-3.4	3.4	50.5	-15.3	-13.4	-6.3
Black Population	300.0	34.2	71.7	-8.4	16.1	-65.0
% of Population, 1980						
Black	0.0	17.6	1.0	29.7	70.8	0.2
Spanish Origin	1.6	3.7	1.9	42.3	7.1	3.8
Under 18 Years Old	26.4	33.4	26.8	31.5	34.9	28.9
65 Years and Older	9.6	6.8	13.9	10.5	8.2	6.6
Persons 25 and Older						
Median Years School Completed	12.4	12.4	12.6	11.3	12.1	12.6
% with 4 or More Years College	7.8	11.9	15.7	5.5	7.6	13.9
% of All Workers in Manufacturing	23.1	34.0	23.8	51.0	42.9	37.1
% of All Workers in White Collar Occupations	49.0	45.5	52.5	32.0	36.4	50.7
% Riding to Work by Auto	87.8	93.8	93.9	82.9	88.9	94.4
% of Civilian Labor Force Unemployed	7.5	6.1	6.8	11.1	14.5	5.6
Families (1980)						
Total Number	3,088	4,647	4,211	9,650	37,178	4,600
Median Family Income	$24,918	$22,212	$27,365	$20,945	$19,477	$26,660
% Below Poverty	3.9	10.1	2.4	15.9	18.0	3.6
% with Income Greater than $29,999	33.8	25.6	42.8	25.8	23.7	39.7
% of Persons 5 & Older Living in Different House in 1975	36.1	54.2	47.3	36.0	38.0	42.9
% of Population Living in Group Quarters	0.0	1.6	7.1	0.7	0.5	0.0
Population Per Household	2.7	3.1	2.8	2.9	3.1	2.8
Housing Units, 1980						
Total Number	4,369	6,132	5,585	14,925	54,381	6,129
% in 1-Unit Structures	53.9	63.9	73.2	34.1	63.5	65.2
% Owner-Occupied	61.7	57.6	67.9	39.3	54.9	62.0
% Built in 1970 or Later	20.3	26.8	36.2	8.5	7.8	21.1
% Vacant	3.2	7.1	3.3	8.3	9.1	2.0
% with More than 1 Person per Room	2.4	5.6	1.8	9.3	8.7	2.2
Median Value, Owner Units (in 1-Unit Structures)	$61,500	$48,500	$59,200	$35,600	$25,200	$54,000
Median Contract Rent, Renter Uni	$253	$232	$256	$131	$142	$296
Median Number of Rooms	4.8	5.1	5.6	4.5	4.8	5.1

Table IV-1 Selected Census Statistics, 1980
Community Areas in Chicago and Places of 10,000 or More Population, 1980
In Chicago-Gary-Kenosha Ill.-Ind.-Wis. Standard Consolidated Statistical Area

	Hammond, Ind.	Highland, Ind.	Hobart, Ind.	Lake Station, Ind.	Merrillville, Ind.	Munster, Ind.
1980 Population						
Total	93,714	25,935	22,987	14,294	27,677	20,671
Black	5,995	29	43	3	36	23
Spanish Origin	7,777	652	759	1,476	1,343	431
% Change 1970-1980						
Total Population	-13.1	4.0	7.0	45.0	73.9	25.2
Black Population	28.2	1350.0	258.3	-94.4	1700.0	130.0
% of Population, 1980						
Black	6.4	0.1	0.2	0.0	0.1	0.1
Spanish Origin	8.3	2.5	3.3	10.3	4.9	2.1
Under 18 Years Old	28.3	29.7	29.3	32.8	28.4	28.6
65 Years and Older	10.7	6.8	9.3	7.3	9.4	10.0
Persons 25 and Older						
Median Years School Completed	12.2	12.6	12.4	12.0	12.5	12.9
% with 4 or More Years College	7.0	14.4	9.3	3.0	13.4	28.0
% of All Workers in Manufacturing	41.7	34.3	33.8	42.7	31.8	29.2
% of All Workers in White Collar Occupations	40.2	51.5	47.4	28.1	53.5	68.7
% Riding to Work by Auto	89.2	94.7	95.6	95.1	96.0	91.8
% of Civilian Labor Force Unemployed	8.8	4.5	7.8	10.7	5.9	3.8
Families (1980)						
Total Number	24,797	7,173	6,395	3,761	7,663	5,844
Median Family Income	$22,978	$29,039	$25,586	$22,049	$27,653	$33,259
% Below Poverty	6.9	2.3	3.5	8.3	2.5	2.5
% with Income Greater than $29,999	27.8	47.0	35.3	24.1	41.5	59.2
% of Persons 5 & Older Living in Different House in 1975	39.9	37.5	39.9	39.6	37.8	37.9
% of Population Living in Group Quarters	0.4	0.2	0.6	0.0	0.7	0.9
Population Per Household	2.7	3.0	2.9	3.1	3.0	3.0
Housing Units, 1980						
Total Number	36,075	8,637	8,154	4,749	9,282	6,883
% in 1-Unit Structures	63.7	82.0	80.8	87.6	80.5	86.1
% Owner-Occupied	61.7	79.3	76.9	77.8	78.8	86.4
% Built in 1970 or Later	5.9	22.2	22.3	11.6	29.9	34.4
% Vacant	5.0	1.4	2.9	3.8	1.6	1.8
% with More than 1 Person per Room	4.5	2.9	2.8	7.6	2.4	1.2
Median Value, Owner Units (in 1-Unit Structures)	$38,100	$58,500	$43,700	$29,700	$55,100	$74,300
Median Contract Rent, Renter Uni	$178	$259	$243	$188	$259	$286
Median Number of Rooms	4.9	5.3	5.2	4.9	5.6	5.6

Table IV-1 Selected Census Statistics, 1980
Community Areas in Chicago and Places of 10,000 or More Population, 1980
In Chicago-Gary-Kenosha Ill.-Ind.-Wis. Standard Consolidated Statistical Area

	Portage, Ind.	Schererville, Ind.	Valparaiso, Ind.	Kenosha, Wis.
1980 Population				
Total	27,409	13,209	22,247	77,685
Black	30	36	177	2,813
Spanish Origin	1,360	337	246	3,110
% Change 1970-1980				
Total Population	43.3	260.6	11.1	-1.4
Black Population	130.8	-	118.5	46.4
% of Population, 1980				
Black	0.1	0.3	0.8	3.6
Spanish Origin	5.0	2.6	1.1	4.0
Under 18 Years Old	32.7	29.6	23.1	28.4
65 Years and Older	5.4	4.2	10.1	11.6
Persons 25 and Older				
Median Years School Completed	12.4	12.7	12.8	12.3
% with 4 or More Years College	6.6	20.4	27.7	10.3
% of All Workers in Manufacturing	39.3	34.7	21.2	41.6
% of All Workers in White Collar Occupations	39.7	52.9	60.3	44.3
% Riding to Work by Auto	95.9	96.8	83.8	88.6
% of Civilian Labor Force Unemployed	8.9	5.1	4.5	7.6
Families (1980)				
Total Number	7,424	3,563	5,070	19,912
Median Family Income	$26,225	$27,568	$25,619	$22,313
% Below Poverty	4.6	2.9	3.2	6.4
% with Income Greater than $29,999	35.7	40.7	36.5	27.5
% of Persons 5 & Older Living in Different House in 1975	51.4	66.3	61.9	44.4
% of Population Living in Group Quarters	0.5	0.5	14.6	3.1
Population Per Household	3.0	2.8	2.5	2.7
Housing Units, 1980				
Total Number	9,591	5,058	7,848	29,384
% in 1-Unit Structures	67.3	52.2	63.4	61.2
% Owner-Occupied	72.2	51.9	55.7	61.8
% Built in 1970 or Later	46.8	73.0	27.0	18.1
% Vacant	4.6	6.0	4.6	4.8
% with More than 1 Person per Room	3.2	2.4	1.4	3.0
Median Value, Owner Units (in 1-Unit Structures)	$52,200	$73,400	$56,600	$45,700
Median Contract Rent, Renter Uni	$236	$280	$225	$188
Median Number of Rooms	5.1	5.0	5.2	4.9

	01 Rogers Park	02 West Ridge	03 Uptown	04 Lincoln Square	05 North Center	06 Lake View
1970 Population						
Total	60,787	65,432	74,838	47,751	39,410	114,943
Black	762	91	3,045	57	140	892
Spanish Language	2,802	1,129	9,955	1,995	2,127	15,504
% Change 1960-1970						
Total Population	6.9	2.4	23.7	-4.2	-10.2	-3.2
Black Population	1236.8	12.3	755.3	90.0	191.7	431.0
% of Population, 1970						
Black	1.3	0.1	4.1	0.1	0.4	0.8
Spanish Language	4.6	1.7	13.3	4.2	5.4	13.5
Under 18 Years Old	19.1	21.7	24.9	22.4	27.9	21.9
65 Years and Older	15.6	16.4	15.6	17.3	14.2	15.4
Persons 25 and Older						
Median Years School Completed	12.4	12.4	11.4	11.8	10.6	12.1
% with 4 or More Years College	18.4	14.6	11.3	8.7	4.1	15.4
% of All Workers in Manufacturing	20.6	18.5	31.8	27.4	37.5	26.9
% of All Workers in White Collar Occupations	40.6	48.6	27.8	29.0	19.8	35.2
% Riding to Work by Auto	44.9	63.3	44.4	51.1	53.0	42.5
% of Civilian Labor Force Unemployed	2.9	2.8	4.9	2.9	2.6	3.7
Families (1970)						
Total Number	15,614	19,792	16,807	13,397	10,822	27,492
Median Family Income	$11,306	$13,531	$8,524	$11,246	$10,600	$10,484
% Below Poverty	4.7	3.2	15.8	5.0	6.3	8.9
% with Income Greater than $14,999	27.8	41.4	18.1	27.6	20.6	26.6
% of Persons 5 & Older Living in Different House in 1965	65.2	46.4	70.8	46.6	42.2	59.6
% of Population Living in Group Quarters	3.4	1.6	3.8	1.3	0.4	1.1
Population Per Household	2.2	2.7	2.2	2.5	2.7	2.2
Housing Units, 1970						
Total Number	28,042	24,384	36,859	19,396	15,182	56,572
% in 1-Unit Structures	5.4	23.2	2.8	11.7	15.9	4.4
% Owner-Occupied	10.3	44.8	5.5	27.5	36.9	11.7
% Built in 1960 or Later	15.9	13.6	12.6	5.2	2.2	18.8
% Vacant	4.0	1.5	10.2	2.3	4.3	7.3
% with More than 1 Person per Room	3.7	1.7	10.7	4.0	4.8	5.3
Median Value, Owner Units (in 1-Unit Structures)	$24,500	$30,500	$21,900	$22,500	$17,400	$17,900
Median Contract Rent, Renter Uni	$132	$154	$111	$117	$93	$121
Median Number of Rooms	3.8	5.0	2.9	4.4	4.8	3.7

	07 Lincoln Park	08 Near North Side	09 Edison Park	10 Norwood Park	11 Jefferson Park	12 Forest Glen
1970 Population						
Total	67,416	70,269	13,241	41,827	27,553	20,531
Black	4,904	26,079	0	1	2	4
Spanish Language	9,880	2,227	38	281	115	82
% Change 1960-1970						
Total Population	-24.1	-6.9	5.4	2.1	0.2	54.5
Black Population	261.1	12.8	-	-91.7	-	-33.3
% of Population, 1970						
Black	7.3	37.1	0.0	0.0	0.0	0.0
Spanish Language	14.7	3.2	0.3	0.7	0.4	0.4
Under 18 Years Old	24.9	24.5	29.1	27.1	24.8	27.2
65 Years and Older	11.1	12.1	13.5	12.4	14.6	14.4
Persons 25 and Older						
Median Years School Completed	12.2	12.7	12.2	12.1	11.3	12.6
% with 4 or More Years College	21.8	27.9	8.8	7.3	5.8	20.8
% of All Workers in Manufacturing	27.5	18.4	30.7	34.7	36.1	27.1
% of All Workers in White Collar Occupations	39.8	49.3	31.7	27.4	24.8	46.2
% Riding to Work by Auto	39.9	24.6	67.2	67.5	63.2	71.7
% of Civilian Labor Force Unemployed	4.0	4.1	1.9	2.5	2.4	2.0
Families (1970)						
Total Number	14,291	12,591	3,630	11,631	8,002	5,925
Median Family Income	$9,652	$11,274	$13,536	$13,699	$12,353	$16,868
% Below Poverty	12.6	22.2	2.4	2.5	3.3	2.9
% with Income Greater than $14,999	24.0	39.4	38.3	40.8	31.3	57.0
% of Persons 5 & Older Living in Different House in 1965	59.0	59.9	27.8	27.8	31.4	31.8
% of Population Living in Group Quarters	2.9	4.8	0.2	0.8	0.2	0.1
Population Per Household	2.3	2.0	3.0	3.1	2.8	3.1
Housing Units, 1970						
Total Number	33,042	38,946	4,393	13,641	9,950	6,770
% in 1-Unit Structures	5.8	3.4	71.9	74.7	48.6	86.4
% Owner-Occupied	13.8	6.5	78.9	80.6	66.2	88.6
% Built in 1960 or Later	12.1	29.6	17.0	13.6	12.8	10.2
% Vacant	12.0	14.9	1.0	1.3	2.0	1.4
% with More than 1 Person per Room	7.0	9.0	4.1	4.6	3.7	2.2
Median Value, Owner Units (in 1-Unit Structures)	$19,500	$50,100	$29,500	$28,200	$25,200	$34,700
Median Contract Rent, Renter Uni	$111	$161	$157	$147	$128	$145
Median Number of Rooms	3.9	2.9	5.2	5.2	4.9	5.8

Table IV-2 Selected Census Statistics, 1970
Community Areas in Chicago and Places of 10,000 or More Population, 1970
In Chicago-Gary-Kenosha Ill.-Ind.-Wis. Standard Consolidated Statistical Area

	13 North Park	14 Albany Park	15 Portage Park	16 Irving Park	17 Dunning	18 Montclare
1970 Population						
Total	16,732	47,092	63,608	54,900	43,856	11,675
Black	432	30	21	27	311	1
Spanish Language	391	2,852	670	1,596	345	81
% Change 1960-1970						
Total Population	-6.3	-4.8	-3.5	-5.8	5.4	-1.1
Black Population	-16.4	57.9	23.5	35.0	15450.0	0.0
% of Population, 1970						
Black	2.6	0.1	0.0	0.0	0.7	0.0
Spanish Language	2.3	6.1	1.1	2.9	0.8	0.7
Under 18 Years Old	21.2	28.5	25.7	26.3	26.2	24.3
65 Years and Older	15.2	13.1	15.4	14.0	13.1	15.0
Persons 25 and Older						
Median Years School Completed	12.4	11.3	11.1	11.1	10.9	10.7
% with 4 or More Years College	16.0	6.4	4.8	4.9	4.2	3.6
% of All Workers in Manufacturing	20.0	32.1	34.7	35.5	35.8	36.8
% of All Workers in White Collar Occupations	47.0	23.2	24.0	21.8	24.8	21.2
% Riding to Work by Auto	60.8	55.6	61.5	56.2	66.3	62.4
% of Civilian Labor Force Unemployed	2.7	2.5	2.5	2.6	2.7	3.4
Families (1970)						
Total Number	4,502	12,885	17,945	15,114	12,059	3,343
Median Family Income	$13,695	$11,021	$11,916	$11,254	$12,129	$11,700
% Below Poverty	2.7	6.2	3.9	4.6	3.6	3.5
% with Income Greater than $14,999	43.8	23.7	29.1	24.5	30.8	28.3
% of Persons 5 & Older Living in Different House in 1965	42.7	49.9	36.2	45.3	34.5	37.1
% of Population Living in Group Quarters	10.4	0.6	0.5	0.8	3.8	1.4
Population Per Household	2.8	2.8	2.8	2.6	3.0	2.8
Housing Units, 1970						
Total Number	5,389	17,079	23,110	21,357	14,184	4,137
% in 1-Unit Structures	43.4	18.5	38.8	19.7	72.3	49.6
% Owner-Occupied	57.4	33.7	56.1	39.2	78.0	61.6
% Built in 1960 or Later	5.3	2.3	5.7	4.6	12.7	12.1
% Vacant	1.3	2.7	2.2	2.9	1.4	1.8
% with More than 1 Person per Room	1.6	5.5	3.9	3.8	4.8	4.4
Median Value, Owner Units (in 1-Unit Structures)	$31,000	$22,800	$23,600	$21,100	$25,300	$24,600
Median Contract Rent, Renter Uni	$137	$113	$116	$107	$131	$122
Median Number of Rooms	5.4	4.7	5.0	4.7	5.0	4.8

Table IV-2 Selected Census Statistics, 1970
Community Areas in Chicago and Places of 10,000 or More Population, 1970
In Chicago-Gary-Kenosha Ill.-Ind.-Wis. Standard Consolidated Statistical Area

	19 Belmont Cragin	20 Hermosa	21 Avondale	22 Logan Square	23 Humboldt Park	24 West Town
1970 Population						
Total	57,399	19,838	35,806	88,555	71,726	124,800
Black	10	8	11	629	13,924	5,518
Spanish Language	666	777	1,645	15,765	11,122	48,900
% Change 1960-1970						
Total Population	-5.7	-7.4	-9.9	-6.6	0.2	-10.6
Black Population	233.3	-	266.7	69.5	3176.2	133.2
% of Population, 1970						
Black	0.0	0.0	0.0	0.7	19.4	4.4
Spanish Language	1.2	3.9	4.6	17.8	15.5	39.2
Under 18 Years Old	24.0	27.5	27.0	31.7	35.9	36.7
65 Years and Older	14.8	13.6	12.9	10.4	8.7	7.9
Persons 25 and Older						
Median Years School Completed	10.3	10.5	10.0	9.8	9.2	8.6
% with 4 or More Years College	4.0	3.2	3.4	3.9	2.8	3.3
% of All Workers in Manufacturing	41.4	43.0	44.4	46.8	47.2	52.0
% of All Workers in White Collar Occupations	19.3	18.0	16.1	15.1	12.0	10.9
% Riding to Work by Auto	58.2	58.1	51.4	50.6	54.0	46.7
% of Civilian Labor Force Unemployed	3.0	3.2	3.3	4.9	4.8	6.0
Families (1970)						
Total Number	16,368	5,642	9,962	22,463	17,812	29,221
Median Family Income	$11,403	$10,799	$10,495	$9,915	$9,472	$8,021
% Below Poverty	4.7	4.8	6.4	10.0	13.0	19.4
% with Income Greater than $14,999	27.1	22.2	21.6	17.9	16.1	12.2
% of Persons 5 & Older Living in Different House in 1965	36.7	41.9	41.4	51.4	54.7	53.7
% of Population Living in Group Quarters	0.2	0.3	0.3	0.7	0.7	1.2
Population Per Household	2.8	2.8	2.7	2.9	3.2	3.1
Housing Units, 1970						
Total Number	21,185	7,275	13,751	32,301	23,323	43,188
% in 1-Unit Structures	35.3	23.5	12.2	9.8	14.5	6.2
% Owner-Occupied	55.4	44.8	36.6	28.0	35.5	21.4
% Built in 1960 or Later	5.3	1.8	1.3	0.8	2.3	3.3
% Vacant	2.1	2.6	4.6	5.5	5.7	9.2
% with More than 1 Person per Room	4.4	4.5	5.7	8.4	11.9	14.2
Median Value, Owner Units (in 1-Unit Structures)	$23,400	$20,600	$18,200	$15,300	$15,500	$12,500
Median Contract Rent, Renter Uni	$111	$102	$92	$91	$96	$72
Median Number of Rooms	4.8	4.9	4.6	4.6	4.9	4.4

Table IV-2 Selected Census Statistics, 1970
Community Areas in Chicago and Places of 10,000 or More Population, 1970
In Chicago-Gary-Kenosha Ill.-Ind.-Wis. Standard Consolidated Statistical Area

	25 Austin	26 West Garfield Park	27 East Garfield Park	28 Near West Side	29 North Lawndale	30 South Lawndale
1970 Population						
Total	127,981	48,464	52,185	78,703	94,772	62,895
Black	41,584	46,947	51,128	56,836	91,292	6,447
Spanish Language	4,577	344	534	6,989	1,501	20,044
% Change 1960-1970						
Total Population	2.3	6.3	-22.0	-37.8	-24.1	3.2
Black Population	134041.9	551.7	24.4	-16.6	-19.8	80.7
% of Population, 1970						
Black	32.5	96.9	98.0	72.2	96.3	10.3
Spanish Language	3.6	0.7	1.0	8.9	1.6	31.9
Under 18 Years Old	31.2	47.4	46.4	44.5	49.3	33.3
65 Years and Older	11.1	3.6	4.1	6.5	3.8	8.9
Persons 25 and Older						
Median Years School Completed	11.2	10.3	9.8	9.4	10.0	9.1
% with 4 or More Years College	6.0	1.3	1.2	4.5	1.8	2.9
% of All Workers in Manufacturing	35.0	40.6	36.3	31.0	37.4	50.2
% of All Workers in White Collar Occupations	19.7	8.8	8.3	16.2	9.4	12.1
% Riding to Work by Auto	55.1	54.7	46.7	37.9	49.1	54.3
% of Civilian Labor Force Unemployed	4.1	8.0	8.4	8.0	8.6	3.9
Families (1970)						
Total Number	32,936	10,371	10,921	15,433	19,899	14,816
Median Family Income	$10,631	$7,532	$6,357	$6,012	$6,972	$9,044
% Below Poverty	8.1	24.5	32.4	34.7	30.0	11.7
% with Income Greater than $14,999	23.8	9.9	7.8	7.1	10.5	15.8
% of Persons 5 & Older Living in Different House in 1965	57.1	52.2	50.9	44.1	44.4	50.5
% of Population Living in Group Quarters	0.6	1.2	0.9	6.1	1.2	5.6
Population Per Household	3.0	3.9	3.6	3.4	4.1	3.1
Housing Units, 1970						
Total Number	44,844	13,177	16,101	23,741	25,328	20,220
% in 1-Unit Structures	21.0	6.6	6.4	9.4	6.3	15.3
% Owner-Occupied	36.6	18.7	14.8	10.0	17.9	37.5
% Built in 1960 or Later	3.4	2.2	2.8	11.8	3.8	0.9
% Vacant	4.3	7.7	11.0	8.5	10.8	5.7
% with More than 1 Person per Room	8.2	22.0	22.4	22.8	27.1	14.0
Median Value, Owner Units (in 1-Unit Structures)	$20,900	$15,700	$13,500	$13,100	$15,500	$12,600
Median Contract Rent, Renter Uni	$116	$112	$103	$76	$105	$75
Median Number of Rooms	4.8	4.9	4.4	4.1	4.8	4.3

Table IV-2 Selected Census Statistics, 1970
Community Areas in Chicago and Places of 10,000 or More Population, 1970
In Chicago-Gary-Kenosha Ill.-Ind.-Wis. Standard Consolidated Statistical Area

	31 Lower West Side	32 Loop	33 Near South Side	34 Armour Square	35 Douglas	36 Oakland
1970 Population						
Total	44,498	4,933	8,767	13,058	41,276	18,291
Black	1,068	587	7,490	4,131	41,807	18,090
Spanish Language	24,463	83	131	796	588	125
% Change 1960-1970						
Total Population	-8.2	13.7	-15.3	-17.3	-21.1	-25.0
Black Population	101.5	30.7	-5.7	-16.7	-13.0	-24.5
% of Population, 1970						
Black	2.4	11.9	85.4	31.6	101.3	98.9
Spanish Language	55.0	1.7	1.5	6.1	1.4	0.7
Under 18 Years Old	38.6	2.6	41.5	35.5	39.5	52.2
65 Years and Older	6.8	19.1	11.0	12.1	7.7	6.6
Persons 25 and Older						
Median Years School Completed	8.5	12.5	10.0	8.9	11.4	9.6
% with 4 or More Years College	2.8	19.4	5.1	2.7	14.8	2.0
% of All Workers in Manufacturing	49.0	13.3	22.5	28.4	19.3	24.9
% of All Workers in White Collar Occupations	10.5	49.9	16.3	14.3	33.1	10.3
% Riding to Work by Auto	46.8	23.9	32.7	45.5	42.5	31.9
% of Civilian Labor Force Unemployed	6.1	5.3	7.0	4.9	5.4	13.4
Families (1970)						
Total Number	10,304	765	1,679	2,993	9,770	3,401
Median Family Income	$8,557	$20,929	$5,254	$7,835	$6,260	$4,879
% Below Poverty	15.5	5.0	37.2	19.3	30.2	44.4
% with Income Greater than $14,999	14.2	70.8	6.1	13.0	11.9	3.2
% of Persons 5 & Older Living in Different House in 1965	45.6	71.9	69.0	40.1	46.6	42.0
% of Population Living in Group Quarters	0.7	21.8	6.4	0.5	3.5	1.2
Population Per Household	3.4	1.3	2.8	3.2	2.9	3.6
Housing Units, 1970						
Total Number	14,557	3,083	3,240	4,270	17,010	5,686
% in 1-Unit Structures	9.2	1.1	2.1	12.2	5.8	8.2
% Owner-Occupied	25.9	0.0	0.5	19.5	4.3	5.0
% Built in 1960 or Later	0.9	52.0	39.3	13.2	19.8	28.9
% Vacant	10.1	6.0	9.8	5.2	5.4	11.7
% with More than 1 Person per Room	18.2	2.9	20.3	15.8	17.0	30.1
Median Value, Owner Units (in 1-Unit Structures)	$10,600	-	-	$15,500	$17,200	$15,200
Median Contract Rent, Renter Uni	$63	$173	$81	$69	$96	$81
Median Number of Rooms	4.4	1.7	3.4	4.4	3.7	3.7

Table IV-2 Selected Census Statistics, 1970
Community Areas in Chicago and Places of 10,000 or More Population, 1970
In Chicago-Gary-Kenosha Ill.-Ind.-Wis. Standard Consolidated Statistical Area

	37 Fuller Park	38 Grand Boulevard	39 Kenwood	40 Washington Park	41 Hyde Park	42 Woodlawn
1970 Population						
Total	7,372	80,150	26,908	46,024	33,559	53,814
Black	7,146	79,607	21,228	45,649	10,427	51,572
Spanish Language	58	451	275	197	882	755
% Change 1960-1970						
Total Population	-39.5	0.1	-35.2	5.3	-26.4	-33.8
Black Population	-38.9	0.1	-39.1	5.4	-39.2	-28.8
% of Population, 1970						
Black	96.9	99.3	78.9	99.2	31.1	95.8
Spanish Language	0.8	0.6	1.0	0.4	2.6	1.4
Under 18 Years Old	43.7	42.6	30.7	37.9	19.4	34.4
65 Years and Older	7.1	11.0	11.0	10.4	11.4	9.4
Persons 25 and Older						
Median Years School Completed	9.0	9.4	11.9	10.0	14.8	10.6
% with 4 or More Years College	2.1	1.7	14.9	1.7	43.9	4.6
% of All Workers in Manufacturing	29.6	26.7	19.8	30.9	10.8	28.6
% of All Workers in White Collar Occupations	10.3	9.7	30.9	8.6	56.1	12.8
% Riding to Work by Auto	46.8	34.8	48.7	38.7	43.2	39.6
% of Civilian Labor Force Unemployed	11.9	9.5	5.0	8.0	2.7	6.9
Families (1970)						
Total Number	1,566	15,551	6,471	9,926	7,917	14,087
Median Family Income	$6,492	$5,644	$8,053	$6,547	$11,244	$6,559
% Below Poverty	27.0	37.4	24.1	28.2	6.8	27.6
% with Income Greater than $14,999	8.6	5.6	20.1	8.3	32.9	7.6
% of Persons 5 & Older Living in Different House in 1965	44.2	41.2	50.9	43.5	65.6	57.0
% of Population Living in Group Quarters	1.0	1.6	2.7	1.3	7.2	2.4
Population Per Household	3.8	3.3	2.5	3.1	2.2	2.8
Housing Units, 1970						
Total Number	2,293	25,937	11,602	15,888	15,683	22,261
% in 1-Unit Structures	18.9	5.4	7.1	4.6	8.8	5.0
% Owner-Occupied	31.8	7.2	11.5	5.4	15.2	11.5
% Built in 1960 or Later	14.7	16.5	11.3	11.6	11.7	5.9
% Vacant	16.5	7.9	8.9	7.5	9.2	14.6
% with More than 1 Person per Room	21.1	21.6	13.4	17.4	4.5	13.3
Median Value, Owner Units (in 1-Unit Structures)	$12,400	$15,800	$34,400	$13,400	$39,800	$17,300
Median Contract Rent, Renter Uni	$88	$89	$112	$102	$134	$110
Median Number of Rooms	5.0	4.2	3.3	4.2	3.7	4.1

Table IV-2 Selected Census Statistics, 1970
Community Areas in Chicago and Places of 10,000 or More Population, 1970
In Chicago-Gary-Kenosha Ill.-Ind.-Wis. Standard Consolidated Statistical Area

	43 South Shore	44 Chatham	45 Avalon Park	46 South Chicago	47 Burnside	48 Calumet Heights
1970 Population						
Total	80,660	47,287	14,412	45,655	3,181	20,123
Black	55,649	46,128	11,912	10,233	91	9,038
Spanish Language	1,173	519	283	11,906	251	1,631
% Change 1960-1970						
Total Population	10.4	12.7	13.4	-8.5	-8.1	4.0
Black Population	692.9	72.4	198433.3	318.0	-	112875.0
% of Population, 1970						
Black	69.0	97.5	82.7	22.4	2.9	44.9
Spanish Language	1.5	1.1	2.0	26.1	7.9	8.1
Under 18 Years Old	25.8	28.0	36.2	32.9	29.5	33.0
65 Years and Older	11.5	7.2	6.6	9.5	12.2	6.6
Persons 25 and Older						
Median Years School Completed	12.3	12.2	12.4	10.3	9.4	12.3
% with 4 or More Years College	13.5	9.3	13.0	5.5	3.5	13.3
% of All Workers in Manufacturing	23.0	22.5	22.6	40.1	36.4	25.6
% of All Workers in White Collar Occupations	29.1	22.5	25.8	18.8	12.1	32.8
% Riding to Work by Auto	51.4	60.5	60.2	53.2	65.9	65.6
% of Civilian Labor Force Unemployed	4.2	3.5	4.0	4.2	2.7	2.8
Families (1970)						
Total Number	20,996	13,016	3,522	11,715	850	5,384
Median Family Income	$10,461	$10,772	$12,434	$9,970	$9,740	$13,319
% Below Poverty	7.8	7.7	5.1	9.7	6.1	3.8
% with Income Greater than $14,999	24.4	25.1	34.1	20.5	19.8	39.3
% of Persons 5 & Older Living in Different House in 1965	66.4	38.2	61.2	48.0	25.1	53.3
% of Population Living in Group Quarters	0.9	0.3	0.2	0.5	0.4	0.5
Population Per Household	2.5	2.9	3.5	3.1	3.1	3.3
Housing Units, 1970						
Total Number	33,368	16,912	4,206	15,756	1,036	6,108
% in 1-Unit Structures	11.8	31.7	70.9	26.4	60.8	72.1
% Owner-Occupied	17.7	40.1	71.8	40.8	64.0	77.6
% Built in 1960 or Later	10.8	13.4	7.8	4.3	6.3	14.7
% Vacant	3.7	2.9	2.0	6.4	1.8	2.0
% with More than 1 Person per Room	5.7	6.4	7.7	10.4	8.3	6.3
Median Value, Owner Units (in 1-Unit Structures)	$20,200	$21,300	$19,900	$18,400	$15,700	$22,700
Median Contract Rent, Renter Uni	$134	$133	$133	$86	$90	$125
Median Number of Rooms	4.1	4.7	5.5	4.7	4.9	5.4

454

Table IV-2 Selected Census Statistics, 1970
Community Areas in Chicago and Places of 10,000 or More Population, 1970
In Chicago-Gary-Kenosha Ill.-Ind.-Wis. Standard Consolidated Statistical Area

	49 Roseland	50 Pullman	51 South Deering	52 East Side	53 West Pullman	54 Riverdale
1970 Population						
Total	62,512	10,893	19,271	24,649	40,318	15,018
Black	34,454	5,244	3,067	23	6,670	14,232
Spanish Language	1,215	293	3,220	807	1,476	157
% Change 1960-1970						
Total Population	6.4	29.5	2.5	6.2	13.9	31.2
Black Population	159.9	-	2353.6	475.0	10658.1	38.1
% of Population, 1970						
Black	55.1	48.1	15.9	0.1	16.5	94.8
Spanish Language	1.9	2.7	16.7	3.3	3.7	1.0
Under 18 Years Old	34.1	34.1	36.9	31.5	34.3	56.0
65 Years and Older	10.3	8.0	7.1	9.3	9.0	2.6
Persons 25 and Older						
Median Years School Completed	12.0	11.6	11.6	10.8	11.5	10.7
% with 4 or More Years College	6.5	7.5	5.5	3.6	3.8	1.3
% of All Workers in Manufacturing	27.9	30.1	34.6	43.6	36.2	28.9
% of All Workers in White Collar Occupations	22.1	23.3	24.0	15.9	20.2	12.1
% Riding to Work by Auto	62.3	59.8	61.5	70.2	63.9	53.1
% of Civilian Labor Force Unemployed	4.0	4.0	3.3	2.8	3.2	12.1
Families (1970)						
Total Number	15,759	2,860	4,785	6,612	10,300	3,102
Median Family Income	$11,193	$10,549	$11,152	$11,509	$11,507	$6,273
% Below Poverty	5.7	6.0	5.4	4.4	5.6	37.8
% with Income Greater than $14,999	26.8	21.2	23.8	26.0	28.1	5.6
% of Persons 5 & Older Living in Different House in 1965	46.8	57.8	44.2	34.7	32.2	50.0
% of Population Living in Group Quarters	0.7	0.7	0.3	0.4	0.2	0.3
Population Per Household	3.3	3.1	3.5	3.2	3.3	4.4
Housing Units, 1970						
Total Number	19,533	3,683	5,699	7,945	12,507	3,470
% in 1-Unit Structures	60.5	66.1	73.0	54.8	63.0	64.4
% Owner-Occupied	64.0	65.6	71.5	70.2	70.7	27.3
% Built in 1960 or Later	9.1	24.6	10.6	14.7	17.8	33.1
% Vacant	2.9	4.2	2.6	2.4	2.5	2.7
% with More than 1 Person per Room	7.9	8.2	10.5	7.7	9.3	33.8
Median Value, Owner Units (in 1-Unit Structures)	$19,200	$17,200	$17,300	$17,800	$18,700	$17,600
Median Contract Rent, Renter Uni	$105	$83	$78	$87	$92	$85
Median Number of Rooms	5.3	4.8	5.1	5.0	5.1	4.5

Table IV-2 Selected Census Statistics, 1970
Community Areas in Chicago and Places of 10,000 or More Population, 1970
In Chicago-Gary-Kenosha Ill.-Ind.-Wis. Standard Consolidated Statistical Area

	55 Hegewisch	56 Garfield Ridge	57 Archer Heights	58 Brighton Park	59 McKinley Park	60 Bridgeport
1970 Population						
Total	11,346	42,998	11,134	35,618	15,632	35,167
Black	22	3,508	1	34	4	45
Spanish Language	392	971	178	2,329	970	4,418
% Change 1960-1970						
Total Population	27.0	6.3	5.2	-6.3	-7.5	-15.4
Black Population	-31.3	30.6	0.0	-5.6	-	-30.8
% of Population, 1970						
Black	0.2	8.2	0.0	0.1	0.0	0.1
Spanish Language	3.5	2.3	1.6	6.5	6.2	12.6
Under 18 Years Old	37.1	34.6	26.1	28.0	31.3	33.2
65 Years and Older	6.0	5.8	10.0	10.6	9.6	9.3
Persons 25 and Older						
Median Years School Completed	10.8	11.2	10.1	10.0	10.0	9.7
% with 4 or More Years College	2.8	3.1	4.6	2.9	2.7	2.7
% of All Workers in Manufacturing	43.6	37.3	38.7	37.6	31.2	33.3
% of All Workers in White Collar Occupations	17.2	17.0	17.4	14.3	14.6	13.9
% Riding to Work by Auto	64.0	66.3	59.0	55.9	53.0	49.7
% of Civilian Labor Force Unemployed	2.8	3.3	3.4	3.6	3.7	4.8
Families (1970)						
Total Number	2,915	11,122	3,034	9,529	4,041	8,955
Median Family Income	$11,433	$12,454	$12,129	$10,626	$10,662	$9,823
% Below Poverty	3.6	4.3	2.9	5.8	7.8	9.9
% with Income Greater than $14,999	22.2	31.9	28.8	21.1	22.1	18.0
% of Persons 5 & Older Living in Different House in 1965	27.6	26.3	31.8	35.4	34.3	37.7
% of Population Living in Group Quarters	0.2	0.1	0.2	0.9	0.7	0.3
Population Per Household	3.4	3.5	3.0	2.8	3.0	3.0
Housing Units, 1970						
Total Number	3,395	12,359	3,862	12,952	5,381	12,312
% in 1-Unit Structures	68.4	82.9	45.8	20.9	26.3	18.0
% Owner-Occupied	74.2	80.9	63.9	47.0	46.0	36.3
% Built in 1960 or Later	29.9	14.6	13.4	4.2	3.9	1.5
% Vacant	2.4	1.2	2.8	3.9	5.0	6.2
% with More than 1 Person per Room	9.8	12.2	7.4	7.6	8.5	9.6
Median Value, Owner Units (in 1-Unit Structures)	$19,100	$22,100	$21,000	$16,800	$13,200	$12,400
Median Contract Rent, Renter Uni	$79	$111	$103	$81	$75	$66
Median Number of Rooms	5.0	4.9	4.7	4.5	4.8	4.7

Table IV-2 Selected Census Statistics, 1970
Community Areas in Chicago and Places of 10,000 or More Population, 1970
In Chicago-Gary-Kenosha Ill.-Ind.-Wis. Standard Consolidated Statistical Area

	61 New City	62 West Elsdon	63 Gage Park	64 Clearing	65 West Lawn	66 Chicago Lawn
1970 Population						
Total	60,817	14,059	26,698	24,911	27,644	48,435
Black	2,152	5	1	1	10	10
Spanish Language	7,811	283	376	671	144	522
% Change 1960-1970						
Total Population	-9.8	-1.1	-5.5	32.5	2.7	-5.7
Black Population	1196.4	-	-50.0	-50.0	100.0	233.3
% of Population, 1970						
Black	3.5	0.0	0.0	0.0	0.0	0.0
Spanish Language	12.8	2.0	1.4	2.7	0.5	1.1
Under 18 Years Old	34.4	25.8	25.3	34.2	27.5	22.7
65 Years and Older	9.0	10.2	14.9	5.7	11.3	17.0
Persons 25 and Older						
Median Years School Completed	9.2	10.6	10.6	11.5	11.2	11.2
% with 4 or More Years College	1.6	3.4	3.9	2.7	4.9	6.4
% of All Workers in Manufacturing	35.9	37.2	32.7	39.0	34.0	30.3
% of All Workers in White Collar Occupations	12.6	19.6	19.6	18.3	22.3	23.5
% Riding to Work by Auto	55.4	67.9	59.8	69.3	66.2	58.4
% of Civilian Labor Force Unemployed	4.8	3.9	2.7	3.3	2.5	3.5
Families (1970)						
Total Number	14,915	4,033	7,439	6,448	5,021	13,696
Median Family Income	$9,808	$12,089	$11,479	$12,280	$12,467	$11,582
% Below Poverty	10.2	3.1	3.3	2.9	3.0	4.2
% with Income Greater than $14,999	16.1	31.8	28.1	29.8	32.0	29.2
% of Persons 5 & Older Living in Different House in 1965	41.4	26.6	35.0	34.9	31.5	34.7
% of Population Living in Group Quarters	0.8	0.4	0.3	0.3	1.3	0.4
Population Per Household	3.1	3.1	2.8	3.4	3.1	2.7
Housing Units, 1970						
Total Number	20,784	4,631	9,630	7,397	6,276	18,450
% in 1-Unit Structures	16.8	74.5	45.7	67.2	62.3	40.0
% Owner-Occupied	37.5	81.7	61.5	72.2	74.3	53.2
% Built in 1960 or Later	1.8	13.8	6.9	31.9	13.1	5.1
% Vacant	7.1	1.5	2.2	1.8	5.0	1.8
% with More than 1 Person per Room	11.4	6.8	5.7	10.7	7.0	4.1
Median Value, Owner Units (in 1-Unit Structures)	$12,700	$21,500	$18,400	$21,900	$21,100	$19,200
Median Contract Rent, Renter Uni	$69	$127	$104	$133	$126	$114
Median Number of Rooms	4.5	4.8	4.8	4.9	4.9	4.9

Table IV-2 Selected Census Statistics, 1970
Community Areas in Chicago and Places of 10,000 or More Population, 1970
In Chicago-Gary-Kenosha Ill.-Ind.-Wis. Standard Consolidated Statistical Area

	67 West Englewood	68 Englewood	69 Greater Grand Crossing	70 Ashburn	71 Auburn Gresham	72 Beverly
1970 Population						
Total	61,910	89,713	54,414	47,161	68,854	26,771
Black	29,917	86,503	53,374	503	47,312	30
Spanish Language	1,977	1,740	501	578	909	122
% Change 1960-1970						
Total Population	5.8	-8.1	-13.9	22.1	15.8	7.9
Black Population	337.3	28.7	-1.6	50200.0	51891.2	114.3
% of Population, 1970						
Black	48.3	96.4	98.1	1.1	68.7	0.1
Spanish Language	3.2	1.9	0.9	1.2	1.3	0.5
Under 18 Years Old	39.4	44.7	31.7	36.0	36.0	32.8
65 Years and Older	8.1	5.1	8.9	7.0	8.2	16.1
Persons 25 and Older						
Median Years School Completed	10.7	10.5	11.4	12.2	12.0	12.7
% with 4 or More Years College	2.9	2.0	5.1	6.7	5.6	23.6
% of All Workers in Manufacturing	30.7	32.5	25.8	24.7	27.3	14.8
% of All Workers in White Collar Occupations	14.5	10.9	15.2	27.7	17.8	53.5
% Riding to Work by Auto	56.4	50.0	54.4	73.4	60.4	66.5
% of Civilian Labor Force Unemployed	6.5	7.7	5.9	2.7	4.6	2.6
Families (1970)						
Total Number	14,474	19,348	13,863	11,665	16,806	6,649
Median Family Income	$9,654	$7,509	$8,667	$13,848	$10,860	$15,750
% Below Poverty	12.0	24.3	14.1	2.2	8.3	2.1
% with Income Greater than $14,999	15.9	11.1	16.5	41.8	24.6	52.4
% of Persons 5 & Older Living in Different House in 1965	48.8	50.8	36.8	28.3	57.7	36.0
% of Population Living in Group Quarters	0.4	0.9	0.5	0.2	0.4	0.3
Population Per Household	3.5	3.8	3.1	3.7	3.4	3.3
Housing Units, 1970						
Total Number	18,517	25,250	18,489	12,746	20,658	8,199
% in 1-Unit Structures	36.3	15.4	21.2	89.8	40.7	79.1
% Owner-Occupied	50.5	25.5	33.2	90.5	51.6	79.5
% Built in 1960 or Later	4.3	5.2	3.1	24.0	6.3	6.4
% Vacant	5.7	7.0	4.4	0.7	3.0	1.6
% with More than 1 Person per Room	13.6	20.6	9.6	11.0	10.1	4.9
Median Value, Owner Units (in 1-Unit Structures)	$14,900	$15,100	$17,900	$23,600	$18,900	$27,600
Median Contract Rent, Renter Uni	$103	$110	$121	$159	$128	$162
Median Number of Rooms	5.1	4.8	4.8	5.2	5.2	6.0

Table IV-2 Selected Census Statistics, 1970
Community Areas in Chicago and Places of 10,000 or More Population, 1970
In Chicago-Gary-Kenosha Ill.-Ind.-Wis. Standard Consolidated Statistical Area

	73 Washington Heights	74 Mount Greenwood	75 Morgan Park	76 O'hare	77 Edgewater	Addison
1970 Population						
Total	36,540	23,186	31,016	6,342	61,598	24,482
Black	27,307	22	14,799	11	373	26
Spanish Language	570	57	176	140	4,859	651
% Change 1960-1970						
Total Population	22.6	5.7	11.1	731.2	19.4	263.2
Black Population	635.8	450.0	51.1	-	767.4	2500.0
% of Population, 1970						
Black	74.7	0.1	47.7	0.2	0.6	0.1
Spanish Language	1.6	0.2	0.6	2.2	7.9	2.7
Under 18 Years Old	38.5	34.4	35.4	25.1	17.4	42.9
65 Years and Older	7.4	9.2	12.1	4.1	17.8	2.5
Persons 25 and Older						
Median Years School Completed	12.1	12.1	12.3	12.2	12.4	12.4
% with 4 or More Years College	8.2	7.2	11.9	11.3	16.7	9.0
% of All Workers in Manufacturing	25.2	21.0	21.6	32.2	23.0	35.2
% of All Workers in White Collar Occupations	23.1	27.1	30.4	59.5	40.4	34.0
% Riding to Work by Auto	65.4	67.9	64.8	86.6	43.5	88.5
% of Civilian Labor Force Unemployed	4.8	2.2	4.4	1.2	2.6	2.1
Families (1970)						
Total Number	8,620	5,803	7,468	1,971	15,222	6,084
Median Family Income	$12,086	$13,152	$12,620	$13,884	$11,844	$13,303
% Below Poverty	6.4	4.0	6.7	2.6	5.6	2.2
% with Income Greater than $14,999	30.8	36.8	36.5	40.8	32.0	34.7
% of Persons 5 & Older Living in Different House in 1965	56.9	27.8	43.5	68.0	61.8	56.7
% of Population Living in Group Quarters	0.6	2.2	1.4	0.3	3.1	0.3
Population Per Household	3.7	3.6	3.5	2.8	2.1	3.7
Housing Units, 1970						
Total Number	10,100	6,389	9,052	2,402	30,494	6,798
% in 1-Unit Structures	73.8	91.7	71.8	30.0	5.8	65.4
% Owner-Occupied	77.2	90.8	72.7	27.5	16.3	64.9
% Built in 1960 or Later	15.3	13.9	18.3	28.8	30.3	67.1
% Vacant	3.4	1.2	2.2	5.0	5.5	2.1
% with More than 1 Person per Room	11.3	11.7	9.6	4.3	4.5	8.4
Median Value, Owner Units (in 1-Unit Structures)	$20,200	$21,600	$22,500	$40,500	$21,600	$28,300
Median Contract Rent, Renter Uni	$137	$127	$125	$179	$135	$168
Median Number of Rooms	5.4	5.2	5.4	4.1	3.4	5.1

Table IV-2 Selected Census Statistics, 1970
Community Areas in Chicago and Places of 10,000 or More Population, 1970
In Chicago-Gary-Kenosha Ill.-Ind.-Wis. Standard Consolidated Statistical Area

	Alsip	Arlington Heights	Aurora	Bartlett	Batavia	Bellwood
1970 Population						
Total	11,608	65,058	74,389	3,501	9,060	22,096
Black	22	27	4,867	36	445	141
Spanish Language	128	617	5,412	23	215	530
% Change 1960-1970						
Total Population	207.9	133.4	16.8	127.3	20.9	6.6
Black Population	-29.0	575.0	118.5	38.5	81.6	14000.0
% of Population, 1970						
Black	0.2	0.0	6.5	1.0	4.9	0.6
Spanish Language	1.1	0.9	7.3	0.7	2.4	2.4
Under 18 Years Old	42.3	40.8	35.8	36.8	36.1	33.8
65 Years and Older	3.4	4.3	9.2	6.0	9.7	6.7
Persons 25 and Older						
Median Years School Completed	12.2	12.9	12.1	12.3	12.3	12.0
% with 4 or More Years College	5.1	28.0	9.4	11.3	9.1	4.9
% of All Workers in Manufacturing	28.5	27.2	43.3	26.5	40.5	38.8
% of All Workers in White Collar Occupations	24.9	55.7	27.3	32.3	26.6	25.4
% Riding to Work by Auto	89.9	78.3	84.6	82.4	85.6	78.8
% of Civilian Labor Force Unemployed	3.6	1.8	2.8	3.1	2.4	2.6
Families (1970)						
Total Number	2,731	15,673	18,638	910	2,316	5,992
Median Family Income	$12,687	$17,034	$11,274	$13,087	$11,808	$13,008
% Below Poverty	3.3	1.4	3.9	6.5	2.6	2.1
% with Income Greater than $14,999	30.8	59.0	24.7	38.8	25.2	34.3
% of Persons 5 & Older Living in Different House in 1965	55.0	60.5	46.7	62.0	42.0	35.7
% of Population Living in Group Quarters	0.4	0.6	1.9	2.9	0.4	0.1
Population Per Household	3.7	3.6	3.1	3.3	3.2	3.4
Housing Units, 1970						
Total Number	3,133	18,710	24,237	1,052	2,846	6,589
% in 1-Unit Structures	67.9	73.4	62.0	68.8	75.6	75.1
% Owner-Occupied	67.9	74.3	60.5	78.1	73.2	78.3
% Built in 1960 or Later	71.1	58.6	18.4	57.3	13.5	15.2
% Vacant	3.4	4.8	3.7	2.1	2.3	1.1
% with More than 1 Person per Room	11.6	3.2	8.0	4.7	6.8	8.5
Median Value, Owner Units (in 1-Unit Structures)	$22,500	$35,500	$18,800	$25,800	$20,300	$23,200
Median Contract Rent, Renter Uni	$172	$194	$121	$161	$116	$142
Median Number of Rooms	5.0	6.0	5.0	5.2	5.4	5.0

	Bensenville	Berwyn	Bloomingdale	Blue Island	Bolingbrook	Bridgeview
1970 Population						
Total	12,956	52,502	2,974	22,629	7,651	12,522
Black	2	8	35	812	1	9
Spanish Language	566	660	50	1,745	434	404
% Change 1960-1970						
Total Population	41.7	-3.2	135.7	15.3	-	70.7
Black Population	0.0	33.3	600.0	154.5	-	800.0
% of Population, 1970						
Black	0.0	0.0	1.2	3.6	0.0	0.1
Spanish Language	4.4	1.3	1.7	7.7	5.7	3.2
Under 18 Years Old	39.0	22.7	42.2	28.3	50.3	41.9
65 Years and Older	5.6	16.7	4.0	12.2	1.6	2.5
Persons 25 and Older						
Median Years School Completed	12.3	11.5	12.5	12.0	12.2	12.0
% with 4 or More Years College	8.9	5.9	12.7	7.1	4.2	2.7
% of All Workers in Manufacturing	37.1	35.7	37.1	27.5	40.6	38.1
% of All Workers in White Collar Occupations	27.6	26.9	30.1	26.1	23.0	19.5
% Riding to Work by Auto	85.2	68.7	87.8	69.2	92.6	91.7
% of Civilian Labor Force Unemployed	2.6	2.2	1.7	2.2	2.5	2.2
Families (1970)						
Total Number	3,257	15,141	680	6,347	1,598	3,121
Median Family Income	$13,374	$11,836	$13,422	$11,470	$12,070	$11,910
% Below Poverty	2.3	3.5	2.7	5.3	2.9	3.6
% with Income Greater than $14,999	37.4	29.7	35.1	26.6	21.2	22.7
% of Persons 5 & Older Living in Different House in 1965	42.7	33.0	57.7	47.0	44.9	43.7
% of Population Living in Group Quarters	1.0	0.5	6.0	1.0	0.1	1.0
Population Per Household	3.6	2.6	3.8	2.8	4.4	3.7
Housing Units, 1970						
Total Number	3,630	20,335	827	8,423	1,726	3,413
% in 1-Unit Structures	81.6	47.1	82.6	42.7	99.2	74.5
% Owner-Occupied	74.0	60.6	86.5	47.4	95.3	73.5
% Built in 1960 or Later	28.3	8.5	62.2	29.4	87.9	45.0
% Vacant	1.8	1.8	10.4	2.8	3.5	2.1
% with More than 1 Person per Room	9.1	2.8	6.6	5.8	6.7	11.3
Median Value, Owner Units (in 1-Unit Structures)	$24,300	$23,200	$31,600	$18,600	$21,300	$21,000
Median Contract Rent, Renter Uni	$151	$121	$162	$123	$145	$161
Median Number of Rooms	5.2	4.9	5.8	4.7	6.2	5.0

	Brookfield	Buffalo Grove	Burbank	Calumet City	Carol Stream	Carpenters-ville
1970 Population						
Total	20,284	12,333	29,900	33,107	4,434	24,059
Black	6	3	5	33	40	7
Spanish Language	293	129	597	447	148	979
% Change 1960-1970						
Total Population	-0.7	726.6	-	32.4	-	38.1
Black Population	50.0	-	-	43.5	-	600.0
% of Population, 1970						
Black	0.0	0.0	0.0	0.1	0.9	0.0
Spanish Language	1.4	1.0	2.0	1.4	3.3	4.1
Under 18 Years Old	29.9	48.9	42.1	34.6	46.1	47.8
65 Years and Older	10.3	1.3	3.7	6.4	1.5	2.2
Persons 25 and Older						
Median Years School Completed	12.2	12.9	11.8	12.1	12.8	12.1
% with 4 or More Years College	9.4	22.9	3.5	5.2	22.8	4.2
% of All Workers in Manufacturing	35.9	33.7	32.2	37.3	25.0	41.9
% of All Workers in White Collar Occupations	31.1	52.6	20.5	24.5	43.3	22.7
% Riding to Work by Auto	71.9	85.0	87.5	82.8	86.7	91.2
% of Civilian Labor Force Unemployed	2.1	1.8	2.9	2.9	0.9	2.4
Families (1970)						
Total Number	5,670	2,772	7,207	8,631	1,004	5,461
Median Family Income	$12,993	$14,833	$12,511	$11,823	$13,113	$12,491
% Below Poverty	3.1	1.8	3.2	3.4	1.4	4.3
% with Income Greater than $14,999	36.1	48.3	29.2	26.0	32.8	28.2
% of Persons 5 & Older Living in Different House in 1965	31.3	76.6	32.6	45.6	60.6	44.7
% of Population Living in Group Quarters	0.6	0.1	0.9	0.2	0.9	0.1
Population Per Household	3.1	4.2	3.9	3.1	3.8	4.2
Housing Units, 1970						
Total Number	6,686	3,092	7,671	10,862	1,390	5,904
% in 1-Unit Structures	77.4	97.8	88.5	60.5	61.0	87.0
% Owner-Occupied	80.2	96.0	87.2	64.6	64.6	82.8
% Built in 1960 or Later	10.0	89.4	36.8	34.1	83.1	34.8
% Vacant	2.1	8.6	1.0	3.3	15.8	2.2
% with More than 1 Person per Room	4.6	5.4	13.1	7.7	7.5	15.6
Median Value, Owner Units (in 1-Unit Structures)	$23,100	$34,000	$20,900	$19,300	$23,800	$19,000
Median Contract Rent, Renter Uni	$137	-	$151	$121	$190	$152
Median Number of Rooms	5.2	6.7	5.2	4.9	5.5	5.2

Table IV-2 Selected Census Statistics, 1970
Community Areas in Chicago and Places of 10,000 or More Population, 1970
In Chicago-Gary-Kenosha Ill.-Ind.-Wis. Standard Consolidated Statistical Area

	Chicago	Chicago Heights	Chicago Ridge	Cicero	Country Club Hills	Crestwood
1970 Population						
Total	3,369,357	40,900	9,187	67,058	6,920	5,770
Black	1,102,620	7,100	0	5	9	254
Spanish Language	247,343	2,884	144	890	153	116
% Change 1960-1970						
Total Population	-5.1	19.1	59.8	-3.0	102.3	375.7
Black Population	35.7	8.7	-	25.0	-	31.6
% of Population, 1970						
Black	32.7	17.4	0.0	0.0	0.1	4.4
Spanish Language	7.3	7.1	1.6	1.3	2.2	2.0
Under 18 Years Old	32.5	38.7	44.0	25.9	51.6	49.2
65 Years and Older	10.3	6.8	3.5	12.2	1.8	2.7
Persons 25 and Older						
Median Years School Completed	11.2	12.0	12.1	10.7	12.5	12.2
% with 4 or More Years Colleg	8.1	8.5	4.1	4.0	12.9	5.3
% of All Workers in Manufacturing	32.0	37.3	28.4	44.4	26.5	27.6
% of All Workers in White Collar Occupations	23.7	27.6	19.0	19.5	35.8	23.4
% Riding to Work by Auto	53.1	80.6	87.6	64.5	81.9	86.8
% of Civilian Labor Force Unemployed	4.4	3.9	4.0	2.8	3.0	3.5
Families (1970)						
Total Number	826,441	10,033	2,187	19,106	1,430	1,187
Median Family Income	$10,242	$11,153	$11,957	$11,265	$14,058	$11,750
% Below Poverty	12.2	8.4	6.4	4.2	1.5	5.3
% with Income Greater than $14,999	23.3	27.3	27.1	23.6	40.2	26.3
% of Persons 5 & Older Living in Different House in 1965	47.6	43.2	34.4	31.9	42.8	43.0
% of Population Living in Group Quarters	1.5	0.6	0.2	0.3	0.0	3.4
Population Per Household	2.9	3.4	3.8	2.7	4.6	4.2
Housing Units, 1970						
Total Number	1,208,327	12,339	2,450	25,388	1,628	1,309
% in 1-Unit Structures	23.7	57.1	72.9	32.7	99.6	93.9
% Owner-Occupied	34.8	60.2	78.2	50.9	95.5	90.3
% Built in 1960 or Later	10.6	21.7	40.5	9.4	55.3	60.2
% Vacant	5.8	3.9	2.3	2.9	7.9	2.2
% with More than 1 Person per Room	9.9	11.0	12.1	4.8	10.0	14.8
Median Value, Owner Units (in 1-Unit Structures)	$21,200	$21,000	$21,300	$21,000	$22,900	$21,400
Median Contract Rent, Renter Uni	$108	$94	$154	$107	$165	$113
Median Number of Rooms	4.6	5.1	5.1	4.7	6.4	5.4

Table IV-2 Selected Census Statistics, 1970
Community Areas in Chicago and Places of 10,000 or More Population, 1970
In Chicago-Gary-Kenosha Ill.-Ind.-Wis. Standard Consolidated Statistical Area

	Crystal Lake	Darien	Deerfield	Des Plaines	Dolton	Downers Grove
1970 Population						
Total	14,541	7,789	18,876	57,239	25,937	32,751
Black	1	0	26	47	42	62
Spanish Language	117	27	173	1,153	187	293
% Change 1960-1970						
Total Population	74.9	-	60.2	64.1	38.4	54.8
Black Population	-50.0	-	116.7	840.0	-	148.0
% of Population, 1970						
Black	0.0	0.0	0.1	0.1	0.2	0.2
Spanish Language	0.8	0.3	0.9	2.0	0.7	0.9
Under 18 Years Old	41.0	42.9	43.7	36.6	40.7	35.8
65 Years and Older	6.9	2.3	3.8	6.1	4.6	7.1
Persons 25 and Older						
Median Years School Completed	12.6	12.6	14.8	12.5	12.3	12.7
% with 4 or More Years College	17.8	18.2	41.2	12.7	7.4	23.4
% of All Workers in Manufacturing	32.5	35.5	25.3	31.4	31.0	27.2
% of All Workers in White Collar Occupations	44.9	43.8	66.5	36.8	32.1	49.5
% Riding to Work by Auto	80.8	85.4	78.3	83.2	78.4	76.6
% of Civilian Labor Force Unemployed	2.7	1.7	2.0	2.2	2.9	1.8
Families (1970)						
Total Number	3,584	2,095	4,671	14,804	6,507	8,826
Median Family Income	$13,734	$14,997	$20,050	$14,056	$13,282	$14,524
% Below Poverty	2.7	0.6	2.2	2.2	3.3	2.2
% with Income Greater than $14,999	41.6	50.0	69.6	42.8	35.9	46.9
% of Persons 5 & Older Living in Different House in 1965	57.5	69.2	51.2	43.0	39.4	54.8
% of Population Living in Group Quarters	0.3	0.0	0.0	0.6	0.2	0.3
Population Per Household	3.5	3.8	3.8	3.4	3.7	3.2
Housing Units, 1970						
Total Number	4,362	2,155	5,061	17,134	7,020	10,727
% in 1-Unit Structures	81.7	88.1	91.0	73.8	86.8	73.4
% Owner-Occupied	75.9	85.8	87.5	76.6	86.2	74.7
% Built in 1960 or Later	38.4	69.8	39.2	40.1	34.4	41.1
% Vacant	5.0	2.3	1.4	2.0	1.4	5.9
% with More than 1 Person per Room	4.6	4.7	2.3	5.1	9.6	4.0
Median Value, Owner Units (in 1-Unit Structures)	$26,200	$34,600	$42,000	$30,000	$21,700	$27,200
Median Contract Rent, Renter Uni	$140	$185	$190	$172	$151	$173
Median Number of Rooms	5.8	6.4	6.8	5.4	5.3	5.4

459

Table IV-2 Selected Census Statistics, 1970
Community Areas in Chicago and Places of 10,000 or More Population, 1970
In Chicago-Gary-Kenosha Ill.-Ind.-Wis. Standard Consolidated Statistical Area

	Elgin	Elk Grove Village	Elmhurst	Elmwood Park	Evanston	Evergreen Park
1970 Population						
Total	55,691	20,346	46,392	26,160	80,113	25,921
Black	2,671	27	170	5	12,849	5
Spanish Language	2,933	347	869	237	1,407	259
% Change 1960-1970						
Total Population	12.6	207.9	25.4	9.5	1.0	7.2
Black Population	67.5	-	844.4	-44.4	40.8	0.0
% of Population, 1970						
Black	4.8	0.1	0.4	0.0	16.0	0.0
Spanish Language	5.3	1.7	1.9	0.9	1.8	1.0
Under 18 Years Old	32.0	47.3	36.8	27.3	27.5	32.1
65 Years and Older	11.6	2.1	8.1	10.8	13.3	10.3
Persons 25 and Older						
Median Years School Completed	12.1	12.7	12.7	12.1	13.2	12.2
% with 4 or More Years College	9.7	18.2	21.3	7.9	33.7	9.7
% of All Workers in Manufacturing	31.8	33.5	27.4	32.8	15.8	21.7
% of All Workers in White Collar Occupations	30.2	43.9	46.3	33.2	49.9	35.5
% Riding to Work by Auto	84.0	89.0	78.1	74.6	56.7	76.3
% of Civilian Labor Force Unemployed	3.3	1.9	1.7	2.7	3.1	2.3
Families (1970)						
Total Number	13,848	5,724	12,904	7,524	19,905	7,170
Median Family Income	$11,555	$14,155	$14,955	$13,028	$13,932	$13,903
% Below Poverty	4.2	1.8	2.0	4.5	3.9	2.7
% with Income Greater than $14,999	27.3	42.9	49.7	37.8	44.4	42.8
% of Persons 5 & Older Living in Different House in 1965	50.0	58.8	39.1	39.0	50.8	29.7
% of Population Living in Group Quarters	7.3	0.1	1.7	0.0	8.0	2.2
Population Per Household	2.9	4.0	3.4	2.9	2.7	3.4
Housing Units, 1970						
Total Number	18,433	6,246	14,594	9,217	27,768	7,428
% in 1-Unit Structures	57.2	87.2	87.3	53.7	37.1	83.5
% Owner-Occupied	58.9	90.8	84.9	62.6	42.1	84.5
% Built in 1960 or Later	22.7	72.6	17.2	24.4	12.4	18.6
% Vacant	3.0	2.3	0.9	3.6	2.1	0.8
% with More than 1 Person per Room	5.6	5.6	4.9	4.2	3.4	7.2
Median Value, Owner Units (in 1-Unit Structures)	$20,700	$29,900	$28,600	$27,400	$33,700	$25,900
Median Contract Rent, Renter Uni	$124	$204	$153	$154	$165	$152
Median Number of Rooms	4.8	5.8	5.7	4.9	5.0	5.4

Table IV-2 Selected Census Statistics, 1970
Community Areas in Chicago and Places of 10,000 or More Population, 1970
In Chicago-Gary-Kenosha Ill.-Ind.-Wis. Standard Consolidated Statistical Area

	Forest Park	Franklin Park	Glendale Heights	Glen Ellyn	Glenview	Glenwood
1970 Population						
Total	15,472	20,348	11,406	21,909	24,880	7,416
Black	5	7	34	77	17	31
Spanish Language	249	408	336	226	346	44
% Change 1960-1970						
Total Population	-7.1	11.1	-	37.2	37.2	-
Black Population	-16.7	600.0	-	26.2	21.4	-
% of Population, 1970						
Black	0.0	0.0	0.3	0.4	0.1	0.4
Spanish Language	1.6	2.0	2.9	1.0	1.4	0.6
Under 18 Years Old	21.3	33.6	51.1	39.1	37.0	41.9
65 Years and Older	13.5	5.7	1.2	6.3	6.5	3.5
Persons 25 and Older						
Median Years School Completed	12.1	12.1	12.3	13.8	13.5	12.6
% with 4 or More Years College	10.2	5.0	6.9	34.8	32.8	14.8
% of All Workers in Manufacturing	28.3	41.3	40.6	24.0	25.3	29.1
% of All Workers in White Collar Occupations	31.8	21.4	29.4	60.4	59.1	44.4
% Riding to Work by Auto	64.0	79.6	87.2	72.7	77.6	81.8
% of Civilian Labor Force Unemployed	2.5	4.7	2.1	1.8	2.0	1.8
Families (1970)						
Total Number	4,297	5,343	2,479	5,524	6,453	1,742
Median Family Income	$11,941	$12,833	$12,927	$17,680	$19,137	$14,429
% Below Poverty	4.5	2.1	1.7	1.5	2.2	0.9
% with Income Greater than $14,999	28.9	33.8	30.8	61.5	64.4	45.7
% of Persons 5 & Older Living in Different House in 1965	50.5	32.2	63.2	50.4	43.7	69.2
% of Population Living in Group Quarters	1.8	0.2	0.1	0.3	0.9	2.9
Population Per Household	2.4	3.3	4.4	3.4	3.5	3.8
Housing Units, 1970						
Total Number	6,755	6,262	2,729	6,573	7,194	2,036
% in 1-Unit Structures	24.8	74.2	86.5	79.0	89.1	85.7
% Owner-Occupied	37.5	75.1	85.7	78.1	87.9	88.4
% Built in 1960 or Later	30.5	21.3	95.7	30.9	26.1	84.8
% Vacant	6.9	1.3	4.5	3.2	1.2	5.8
% with More than 1 Person per Room	3.2	8.2	12.0	3.7	2.5	5.3
Median Value, Owner Units (in 1-Unit Structures)	$20,300	$24,100	$23,900	$32,200	$41,900	$28,400
Median Contract Rent, Renter Uni	$139	$141	$189	$173	$213	$171
Median Number of Rooms	4.4	4.9	5.6	5.9	6.3	6.0

Table IV-2 Selected Census Statistics, 1970
Community Areas in Chicago and Places of 10,000 or More Population, 1970
In Chicago-Gary-Kenosha Ill.-Ind.-Wis. Standard Consolidated Statistical Area

	Hanover Park	Harvey	Hazel Crest	Hickory Hills	Highland Park	Hinsdale
1970 Population						
Total	11,735	34,636	10,329	13,176	32,263	15,918
Black	0	10,711	3	2	574	78
Spanish Language	578	457	59	196	522	292
% Change 1960-1970						
Total Population	-	19.1	66.5	386.7	26.4	23.8
Black Population	-	439.3	200.0	-	13.9	14.7
% of Population, 1970						
Black	0.0	30.9	0.0	0.0	1.8	0.5
Spanish Language	4.9	1.3	0.6	1.5	1.6	1.8
Under 18 Years Old	50.3	36.7	42.7	41.1	38.4	35.7
65 Years and Older	1.5	7.2	4.1	2.6	6.6	8.2
Persons 25 and Older						
Median Years School Completed	12.4	11.7	12.5	12.4	14.1	14.3
% with 4 or More Years College	7.7	5.1	16.2	11.1	37.0	37.1
% of All Workers in Manufacturing	38.7	35.5	29.5	31.2	17.3	22.3
% of All Workers in White Collar Occupations	31.2	19.7	42.8	33.0	61.6	60.5
% Riding to Work by Auto	87.3	76.7	77.3	90.8	68.6	64.6
% of Civilian Labor Force Unemployed	4.0	3.8	3.9	1.7	1.9	1.6
Families (1970)						
Total Number	2,694	8,821	2,524	3,417	7,973	4,136
Median Family Income	$12,902	$11,035	$14,101	$12,779	$20,749	$19,185
% Below Poverty	2.2	7.7	2.4	2.7	2.3	1.7
% with Income Greater than $14,999	28.2	23.5	43.9	33.5	67.3	63.9
% of Persons 5 & Older Living in Different House in 1965	62.7	47.1	47.6	59.0	42.1	46.0
% of Population Living in Group Quarters	0.0	0.7	0.1	0.7	0.9	0.9
Population Per Household	4.4	3.2	3.8	3.6	3.5	3.3
Housing Units, 1970						
Total Number	2,879	11,207	2,782	3,680	9,387	4,934
% in 1-Unit Structures	89.2	57.7	94.8	71.8	81.5	87.8
% Owner-Occupied	88.7	59.5	91.4	73.1	77.7	80.6
% Built in 1960 or Later	92.6	23.8	38.5	77.6	22.3	17.6
% Vacant	4.9	4.1	2.0	1.8	2.1	1.8
% with More than 1 Person per Room	7.7	10.7	6.9	5.8	2.5	2.6
Median Value, Owner Units (in 1-Unit Structures)	$28,200	$17,400	$23,000	$28,700	$46,100	$39,500
Median Contract Rent, Renter Uni	$176	$103	$124	$164	$161	$136
Median Number of Rooms	6.3	4.9	5.9	5.6	6.6	6.3

Table IV-2 Selected Census Statistics, 1970
Community Areas in Chicago and Places of 10,000 or More Population, 1970
In Chicago-Gary-Kenosha Ill.-Ind.-Wis. Standard Consolidated Statistical Area

	Hoffman Estates	Homewood	Joliet	Justice	La Grange	La Grange Park
1970 Population						
Total	22,238	18,871	78,827	9,473	16,773	15,459
Black	14	12	9,507	11	424	4
Spanish Language	561	113	3,195	197	122	80
% Change 1960-1970						
Total Population	168.1	41.1	18.0	238.0	9.7	12.1
Black Population	-	50.0	105.0	-	-60.9	100.0
% of Population, 1970						
Black	0.1	0.1	12.1	0.1	2.5	0.0
Spanish Language	2.5	0.6	4.1	2.1	0.7	0.5
Under 18 Years Old	48.3	35.5	34.4	35.6	35.4	30.3
65 Years and Older	1.5	9.2	10.1	3.0	8.5	10.1
Persons 25 and Older						
Median Years School Completed	12.7	12.8	12.0	12.2	12.9	12.8
% with 4 or More Years College	17.7	23.7	9.3	9.2	28.5	23.6
% of All Workers in Manufacturing	32.1	24.3	33.0	38.3	25.8	29.5
% of All Workers in White Collar Occupations	44.7	52.2	27.8	27.4	50.2	52.9
% Riding to Work by Auto	89.2	67.2	89.0	91.6	69.8	76.2
% of Civilian Labor Force Unemployed	2.2	2.2	3.7	2.0	1.5	1.4
Families (1970)						
Total Number	5,085	5,092	19,932	2,597	4,467	4,285
Median Family Income	$14,549	$15,758	$11,233	$11,745	$16,552	$15,237
% Below Poverty	1.7	2.5	6.1	3.1	3.0	0.9
% with Income Greater than $14,999	46.5	53.0	27.7	27.0	55.9	50.9
% of Persons 5 & Older Living in Different House in 1965	54.3	47.1	42.1	57.0	43.1	35.3
% of Population Living in Group Quarters	0.1	0.1	2.7	0.7	0.1	2.9
Population Per Household	4.2	3.3	3.1	3.1	3.3	3.0
Housing Units, 1970						
Total Number	5,808	5,843	26,514	3,173	5,194	5,056
% in 1-Unit Structures	82.1	86.2	62.0	36.7	76.0	73.2
% Owner-Occupied	82.3	86.7	62.1	56.5	76.0	74.1
% Built in 1960 or Later	70.2	35.7	17.0	63.2	17.0	18.3
% Vacant	8.1	1.6	4.4	5.8	1.8	0.9
% with More than 1 Person per Room	5.9	2.6	8.3	8.5	2.8	2.7
Median Value, Owner Units (in 1-Unit Structures)	$28,600	$27,800	$17,700	$18,400	$33,100	$31,800
Median Contract Rent, Renter Uni	$185	$161	$98	$175	$162	$174
Median Number of Rooms	6.3	5.8	4.9	4.4	6.1	5.3

Table IV-2 Selected Census Statistics, 1970
Community Areas in Chicago and Places of 10,000 or More Population, 1970
In Chicago-Gary-Kenosha Ill.-Ind.-Wis. Standard Consolidated Statistical Area

	Lake Forest	Lansing	Libertyville	Lincolnwood	Lisle	Lombard
1970 Population						
Total	15,642	25,805	11,684	12,929	5,329	34,043
Black	340	15	16	35	11	14
Spanish Language	193	263	208	78	34	448
% Change 1960-1970						
Total Population	46.4	42.6	36.5	10.1	26.3	50.9
Black Population	51.8	-	433.3	-20.5	1000.0	1300.0
% of Population, 1970						
Black	2.2	0.1	0.1	0.3	0.2	0.0
Spanish Language	1.2	1.0	1.8	0.6	0.6	1.3
Under 18 Years Old	35.7	36.8	39.5	30.1	40.7	40.2
65 Years and Older	9.3	5.7	6.8	8.4	3.8	5.1
Persons 25 and Older						
Median Years School Completed	14.5	12.3	12.7	12.9	12.5	12.6
% with 4 or More Years College	39.7	8.6	24.7	24.9	16.4	15.8
% of All Workers in Manufacturing	16.1	32.2	33.8	21.2	30.9	26.8
% of All Workers in White Collar Occupations	58.7	32.6	47.2	62.0	41.1	43.3
% Riding to Work by Auto	60.3	88.4	80.7	80.7	81.3	81.7
% of Civilian Labor Force Unemployed	2.8	2.1	2.3	2.1	1.5	2.3
Families (1970)						
Total Number	3,491	6,786	2,925	3,655	1,359	8,868
Median Family Income	$22,686	$13,069	$14,560	$21,365	$14,107	$14,087
% Below Poverty	2.0	3.2	3.1	3.1	4.2	1.9
% with Income Greater than $14,999	70.7	34.9	46.7	71.2	42.5	43.2
% of Persons 5 & Older Living in Different House in 1965	54.9	46.6	54.6	26.1	55.2	45.1
% of Population Living in Group Quarters	10.7	0.2	0.7	0.0	0.0	0.3
Population Per Household	3.3	3.4	3.4	3.4	3.6	3.6
Housing Units, 1970						
Total Number	4,402	7,685	3,512	3,814	1,612	10,500
% in 1-Unit Structures	84.0	78.9	74.4	93.8	81.5	81.2
% Owner-Occupied	77.7	78.2	70.6	94.8	81.0	83.0
% Built in 1960 or Later	31.4	38.3	31.3	19.9	40.7	38.6
% Vacant	4.2	1.5	4.0	0.6	8.8	6.2
% with More than 1 Person per Room	1.6	6.6	4.4	0.8	5.9	6.4
Median Value, Owner Units (in 1-Unit Structures)	$50,100	$21,100	$30,000	$45,300	$29,400	$26,200
Median Contract Rent, Renter Uni	$154	$149	$155	$264	$173	$172
Median Number of Rooms	7.1	5.2	5.8	6.6	5.9	5.5

Table IV-2 Selected Census Statistics, 1970
Community Areas in Chicago and Places of 10,000 or More Population, 1970
In Chicago-Gary-Kenosha Ill.-Ind.-Wis. Standard Consolidated Statistical Area

	McHenry	Markham	Matteson	Maywood	Melrose Park	Midlothian
1970 Population						
Total	6,772	15,987	4,741	29,019	22,716	14,422
Black	0	7,981	1	12,416	149	186
Spanish Language	13	519	68	1,083	1,186	297
% Change 1960-1970						
Total Population	103.0	36.6	47.0	6.2	1.9	118.3
Black Population	-	218.6	-	137.4	161.4	-
% of Population, 1970						
Black	0.0	49.9	0.0	42.8	0.7	1.3
Spanish Language	0.2	3.2	1.4	3.7	5.2	2.1
Under 18 Years Old	35.2	46.8	39.1	37.0	30.8	43.3
65 Years and Older	12.1	3.0	5.3	8.3	7.3	4.8
Persons 25 and Older						
Median Years School Completed	12.1	12.0	12.5	12.1	12.0	12.2
% with 4 or More Years College	9.6	5.4	13.4	10.0	6.4	5.7
% of All Workers in Manufacturing	24.2	32.5	27.0	35.8	36.7	29.6
% of All Workers in White Collar Occupations	33.3	20.5	42.4	22.7	24.8	24.4
% Riding to Work by Auto	80.1	86.4	72.7	78.8	84.3	78.0
% of Civilian Labor Force Unemployed	2.3	3.6	2.4	4.3	2.2	2.8
Families (1970)						
Total Number	1,769	3,404	1,169	7,318	6,225	3,697
Median Family Income	$11,912	$12,045	$14,045	$11,573	$12,121	$12,348
% Below Poverty	3.4	5.0	0.7	6.4	3.7	2.2
% with Income Greater than $14,999	25.9	28.8	42.5	27.3	30.7	27.0
% of Persons 5 & Older Living in Different House in 1965	49.2	40.1	45.9	43.6	42.0	42.8
% of Population Living in Group Quarters	0.3	0.6	0.9	0.9	0.3	1.1
Population Per Household	3.2	4.3	3.5	3.4	3.0	3.8
Housing Units, 1970						
Total Number	2,194	3,795	1,424	9,021	7,701	4,218
% in 1-Unit Structures	86.0	98.2	73.3	57.4	39.6	84.0
% Owner-Occupied	77.5	91.3	71.7	62.3	56.6	81.5
% Built in 1960 or Later	33.8	28.8	39.1	9.1	22.3	42.3
% Vacant	2.6	3.0	6.3	2.7	3.1	2.1
% with More than 1 Person per Room	6.0	17.4	6.6	9.8	6.9	11.2
Median Value, Owner Units (in 1-Unit Structures)	$21,100	$17,600	$21,500	$19,500	$24,700	$19,600
Median Contract Rent, Renter Uni	$121	$135	$159	$126	$129	$134
Median Number of Rooms	5.1	5.4	5.4	5.2	4.6	5.3

Table IV-2 Selected Census Statistics, 1970
Community Areas in Chicago and Places of 10,000 or More Population, 1970
In Chicago-Gary-Kenosha Ill.-Ind.-Wis. Standard Consolidated Statistical Area

	Morton Grove	Mount Prospect	Mundelein	Naperville	Niles	Norridge
1970 Population						
Total	26,369	34,995	16,128	27,924	31,432	17,113
Black	4	14	14	43	18	0
Spanish Language	325	370	387	152	479	153
% Change 1960-1970						
Total Population	28.4	85.1	53.2	115.9	54.1	21.5
Black Population	-81.8	366.7	1300.0	258.3	500.0	-100.0
% of Population, 1970						
Black	0.0	0.0	0.1	0.2	0.1	0.0
Spanish Language	1.2	1.1	2.4	0.5	1.5	0.9
Under 18 Years Old	39.0	40.6	44.6	41.7	35.7	34.2
65 Years and Older	5.1	4.5	3.3	5.3	5.8	5.9
Persons 25 and Older						
Median Years School Completed	12.5	12.7	12.4	13.1	12.3	12.0
% with 4 or More Years College	14.4	21.0	14.6	32.9	11.7	4.8
% of All Workers in Manufacturing	31.7	30.7	32.2	26.9	32.7	38.2
% of All Workers in White Collar Occupations	45.8	50.0	36.4	56.3	39.6	25.5
% Riding to Work by Auto	82.1	77.3	86.3	72.0	85.8	80.3
% of Civilian Labor Force Unemployed	2.0	2.3	3.2	1.9	1.8	1.6
Families (1970)						
Total Number	6,680	9,336	3,699	5,671	8,201	4,576
Median Family Income	$16,488	$16,503	$13,811	$16,818	$14,159	$13,996
% Below Poverty	2.3	1.8	3.3	2.9	1.4	2.7
% with Income Greater than $14,999	56.1	56.4	39.8	57.9	44.2	42.6
% of Persons 5 & Older Living in Different House in 1965	28.6	42.9	46.6	57.3	40.8	26.8
% of Population Living in Group Quarters	0.8	0.4	1.9	2.7	1.9	0.7
Population Per Household	3.7	3.7	3.9	3.6	3.4	3.5
Housing Units, 1970						
Total Number	7,114	9,699	4,247	6,602	9,064	4,912
% in 1-Unit Structures	95.1	84.5	81.9	79.9	76.7	82.2
% Owner-Occupied	93.4	83.2	75.7	77.7	77.5	85.4
% Built in 1960 or Later	26.2	41.7	34.5	46.2	40.8	35.2
% Vacant	0.6	2.9	5.0	3.3	1.1	2.5
% with More than 1 Person per Room	4.1	4.7	12.3	3.8	5.0	8.0
Median Value, Owner Units (in 1-Unit Structures)	$33,700	$32,900	$22,600	$35,700	$31,800	$31,100
Median Contract Rent, Renter Uni	$144	$182	$172	$157	$170	$171
Median Number of Rooms	5.9	5.9	5.2	6.4	5.4	5.2

Table IV-2 Selected Census Statistics, 1970
Community Areas in Chicago and Places of 10,000 or More Population, 1970
In Chicago-Gary-Kenosha Ill.-Ind.-Wis. Standard Consolidated Statistical Area

	Northbrook	North Chicago	Northlake	Oak Forest	Oak Lawn	Oak Park
1970 Population						
Total	25,422	47,275	14,191	19,271	60,305	62,511
Black	39	7,836	6	0	6	132
Spanish Language	304	1,124	440	335	640	1,190
% Change 1960-1970						
Total Population	118.5	106.1	15.2	417.5	119.5	2.3
Black Population	95.0	71.2	-	-	20.0	131.6
% of Population, 1970						
Black	0.2	16.6	0.0	0.0	0.0	0.2
Spanish Language	1.2	2.4	3.1	1.7	1.1	1.9
Under 18 Years Old	44.3	42.3	35.1	44.4	38.7	28.1
65 Years and Older	3.5	4.7	4.0	2.8	7.1	16.1
Persons 25 and Older						
Median Years School Completed	14.3	12.1	11.8	12.5	12.3	12.8
% with 4 or More Years College	37.3	7.9	5.0	10.3	9.6	24.6
% of All Workers in Manufacturing	26.5	35.7	42.1	27.0	25.3	19.9
% of All Workers in White Collar Occupations	62.5	19.2	20.0	34.9	35.7	49.4
% Riding to Work by Auto	78.9	33.0	87.4	81.1	82.3	57.4
% of Civilian Labor Force Unemployed	1.3	0.9	3.7	2.0	2.6	2.3
Families (1970)						
Total Number	6,529	5,385	3,545	4,359	14,864	16,129
Median Family Income	$19,994	$8,899	$12,561	$12,949	$13,824	$13,823
% Below Poverty	2.0	7.2	2.8	1.9	2.5	3.2
% with Income Greater than $14,999	69.5	15.2	34.1	33.4	41.5	43.0
% of Persons 5 & Older Living in Different House in 1965	65.4	81.1	35.3	67.2	43.0	45.6
% of Population Living in Group Quarters	1.7	53.2	1.3	0.1	0.8	1.2
Population Per Household	3.9	3.6	3.4	3.8	3.6	2.7
Housing Units, 1970						
Total Number	7,033	6,424	4,212	4,873	16,771	23,198
% in 1-Unit Structures	95.4	33.0	72.0	83.3	78.7	42.5
% Owner-Occupied	92.1	36.8	71.8	81.7	81.4	46.7
% Built in 1960 or Later	50.8	24.5	27.2	79.8	45.4	11.1
% Vacant	2.2	3.2	2.9	3.0	1.5	2.5
% with More than 1 Person per Room	2.5	13.1	7.5	7.0	8.5	3.0
Median Value, Owner Units (in 1-Unit Structures)	$48,500	$18,700	$21,200	$25,900	$26,500	$26,200
Median Contract Rent, Renter Uni	$212	$109	$160	$135	$171	$145
Median Number of Rooms	7.0	4.7	5.2	5.9	5.4	5.1

	Orland Park	Palatine	Palos Heights	Palos Hills	Park Forest	Park Ridge
1970 Population						
Total	6,391	26,050	8,544	6,629	30,638	42,614
Black	1	15	26	1	694	27
Spanish Language	75	246	48	345	478	431
% Change 1960-1970						
Total Population	146.6	126.4	126.3	76.0	2.2	30.5
Black Population	–	1400.0	–	–	8575.0	440.0
% of Population, 1970						
Black	0.0	0.1	0.3	0.0	2.3	0.1
Spanish Language	1.2	0.9	0.6	5.2	1.6	1.0
Under 18 Years Old	47.3	44.1	43.2	37.8	42.4	34.1
65 Years and Older	2.6	4.2	4.3	3.8	3.2	9.2
Persons 25 and Older						
Median Years School Completed	12.4	12.8	12.6	12.2	13.1	12.8
% with 4 or More Years College	12.3	25.2	16.9	10.5	30.2	23.6
% of All Workers in Manufacturing	25.7	30.9	22.2	35.7	24.9	26.4
% of All Workers in White Collar Occupations	32.9	50.5	49.6	30.3	59.4	54.1
% Riding to Work by Auto	90.8	78.0	86.1	92.7	69.5	76.1
% of Civilian Labor Force Unemployed	1.0	2.2	1.8	2.8	2.7	1.9
Families (1970)						
Total Number	1,469	6,206	2,333	1,646	7,886	11,036
Median Family Income	$13,741	$16,072	$17,082	$12,580	$13,951	$17,472
% Below Poverty	1.0	2.2	1.6	3.0	2.8	1.8
% with Income Greater than $14,999	38.5	54.6	57.7	32.5	43.3	59.7
% of Persons 5 & Older Living in Different House in 1965	53.0	55.3	44.3	53.4	56.6	37.6
% of Population Living in Group Quarters	0.0	0.3	0.1	2.2	0.0	1.0
Population Per Household	4.1	3.9	4.0	3.4	3.6	3.3
Housing Units, 1970						
Total Number	1,594	6,901	2,507	2,016	8,541	13,188
% in 1-Unit Structures	89.6	84.8	97.8	70.5	89.5	78.7
% Owner-Occupied	80.4	82.1	96.4	65.5	77.6	81.9
% Built in 1960 or Later	61.6	54.8	43.7	58.2	10.1	23.7
% Vacant	2.6	3.1	2.3	6.4	1.2	2.2
% with More than 1 Person per Room	10.2	3.8	4.0	8.0	4.2	2.9
Median Value, Owner Units (in 1-Unit Structures)	$23,700	$32,900	$33,900	$22,600	$21,100	$37,000
Median Contract Rent, Renter Uni	$166	$169	$151	$171	$143	$175
Median Number of Rooms	5.8	6.6	6.5	5.0	5.6	5.9

	Prospect Heights	Riverdale	River Forest	River Grove	Rolling Meadows	Romeoville
1970 Population						
Total	13,333	15,806	13,402	11,465	19,178	12,674
Black	20	17	45	3	23	3
Spanish Language	235	289	217	127	383	778
% Change 1960-1970						
Total Population	–	31.6	5.6	35.5	76.3	254.6
Black Population	–	466.7	28.6	0.0	–	–
% of Population, 1970						
Black	0.2	0.1	0.3	0.0	0.1	0.0
Spanish Language	1.8	1.8	1.6	1.1	2.0	6.1
Under 18 Years Old	41.9	27.8	31.0	28.1	41.7	51.7
65 Years and Older	3.5	11.1	14.3	7.5	2.2	0.9
Persons 25 and Older						
Median Years School Completed	12.7	12.3	14.0	12.1	12.6	12.0
% with 4 or More Years College	18.2	9.3	35.9	7.8	14.7	3.0
% of All Workers in Manufacturing	29.5	25.8	23.0	40.3	30.6	44.4
% of All Workers in White Collar Occupations	52.3	34.0	61.5	28.7	40.7	16.9
% Riding to Work by Auto	85.1	60.8	64.6	76.4	87.3	93.7
% of Civilian Labor Force Unemployed	2.1	1.4	2.1	2.8	1.7	2.6
Families (1970)						
Total Number	3,290	4,815	3,240	3,274	4,757	2,743
Median Family Income	$15,992	$12,520	$21,236	$12,480	$13,343	$12,565
% Below Poverty	3.1	3.4	2.4	1.9	2.3	2.7
% with Income Greater than $14,999	54.3	32.6	65.5	32.8	37.4	25.7
% of Persons 5 & Older Living in Different House in 1965	56.2	42.2	44.4	43.6	53.1	51.7
% of Population Living in Group Quarters	0.1	0.0	10.6	0.9	0.2	0.1
Population Per Household	3.8	2.8	3.1	2.9	3.6	4.5
Housing Units, 1970						
Total Number	4,038	5,660	3,921	3,991	5,763	2,833
% in 1-Unit Structures	81.0	58.9	69.0	49.3	62.9	99.6
% Owner-Occupied	86.6	59.3	72.7	56.5	63.8	94.5
% Built in 1960 or Later	62.8	39.1	9.0	42.9	55.1	70.6
% Vacant	12.6	1.8	1.9	2.4	7.7	1.7
% with More than 1 Person per Room	2.5	4.6	2.2	4.9	7.5	19.2
Median Value, Owner Units (in 1-Unit Structures)	$38,400	$19,500	$45,100	$23,800	$23,900	$18,900
Median Contract Rent, Renter Uni	$202	$152	$172	$159	$190	$146
Median Number of Rooms	6.6	4.7	6.4	4.5	5.0	5.2

Table IV-2 Selected Census Statistics, 1970
Community Areas in Chicago and Places of 10,000 or More Population, 1970
In Chicago-Gary-Kenosha Ill.-Ind.-Wis. Standard Consolidated Statistical Area

	Roselle	Round Lake Beach	St. Charles	Sauk Village	Schaumburg	Schiller Park
1970 Population						
Total	6,207	5,717	12,945	7,479	18,730	12,712
Black	0	2	12	3	16	21
Spanish Language	102	154	358	534	386	354
% Change 1960-1970						
Total Population	73.3	14.1	39.7	-	-	123.5
Black Population	-	100.0	-57.1	-	-	2000.0
% of Population, 1970						
Black	0.0	0.0	0.1	0.0	0.1	0.2
Spanish Language	1.6	2.7	2.8	7.1	2.1	2.8
Under 18 Years Old	45.5	41.4	36.1	53.4	45.4	30.9
65 Years and Older	3.8	6.8	8.3	1.1	1.7	3.3
Persons 25 and Older						
Median Years School Completed	12.4	10.5	12.4	11.7	12.6	12.2
% with 4 or More Years College	11.2	1.4	13.3	2.3	16.0	6.4
% of All Workers in Manufacturing	32.2	52.0	43.2	45.9	33.5	31.9
% of All Workers in White Collar Occupations	34.0	17.1	34.9	12.0	43.4	23.0
% Riding to Work by Auto	82.9	90.0	85.4	93.0	86.3	79.6
% of Civilian Labor Force Unemployed	2.2	3.7	2.0	2.0	1.4	1.3
Families (1970)						
Total Number	1,127	1,466	3,285	1,573	4,685	2,993
Median Family Income	$14,190	$10,723	$13,094	$12,245	$13,888	$12,695
% Below Poverty	2.4	4.3	1.0	3.2	3.1	4.2
% with Income Greater than $14,999	44.9	19.0	34.6	26.8	39.8	30.0
% of Persons 5 & Older Living in Different House in 1965	45.4	46.7	51.4	43.6	77.5	50.8
% of Population Living in Group Quarters	0.2	0.0	0.8	0.5	0.1	0.1
Population Per Household	4.0	3.6	3.2	4.7	3.9	3.0
Housing Units, 1970						
Total Number	1,173	1,751	4,116	1,613	5,013	4,287
% in 1-Unit Structures	91.9	97.6	70.7	99.2	91.5	45.6
% Owner-Occupied	89.7	86.5	66.9	94.5	90.3	49.5
% Built in 1960 or Later	44.7	16.9	30.9	42.6	92.2	60.8
% Vacant	1.9	10.2	2.2	2.7	4.2	2.6
% with More than 1 Person per Room	8.3	13.6	5.9	25.7	3.2	6.1
Median Value, Owner Units (in 1-Unit Structures)	$29,200	$14,200	$24,800	$17,000	$31,400	$26,700
Median Contract Rent, Renter Uni	$143	$112	$133	$151	$191	$170
Median Number of Rooms	5.8	5.1	5.2	5.1	6.5	4.4

Table IV-2 Selected Census Statistics, 1970
Community Areas in Chicago and Places of 10,000 or More Population, 1970
In Chicago-Gary-Kenosha Ill.-Ind.-Wis. Standard Consolidated Statistical Area

	Skokie	South Holland	Streamwood	Summit	Tinley Park	Villa Park
1970 Population						
Total	68,322	23,931	18,176	11,569	12,572	25,891
Black	107	12	3	2,219	264	16
Spanish Language	974	121	809	695	83	154
% Change 1960-1970						
Total Population	15.1	129.8	277.0	11.5	96.7	27.0
Black Population	-27.2	-	-	18.7	26300.0	-
% of Population, 1970						
Black	0.2	0.1	0.0	19.2	2.1	0.1
Spanish Language	1.4	0.5	4.5	6.0	0.7	0.6
Under 18 Years Old	32.2	41.9	51.0	34.9	42.6	38.9
65 Years and Older	7.3	4.6	1.2	6.6	4.4	5.9
Persons 25 and Older						
Median Years School Completed	12.8	12.4	12.3	10.3	12.3	12.4
% with 4 or More Years College	20.6	10.8	6.2	3.1	7.6	11.9
% of All Workers in Manufacturing	21.9	28.7	41.1	48.2	27.1	31.2
% of All Workers in White Collar Occupations	55.9	38.6	26.2	15.6	29.9	37.2
% Riding to Work by Auto	79.5	81.1	90.0	78.3	75.6	82.1
% of Civilian Labor Force Unemployed	2.3	1.3	2.9	4.3	1.4	2.7
Families (1970)						
Total Number	19,139	5,478	4,104	2,869	2,911	6,472
Median Family Income	$16,423	$14,495	$12,481	$10,281	$12,798	$13,616
% Below Poverty	2.3	1.7	2.2	7.3	3.5	3.4
% with Income Greater than $14,999	55.1	46.5	27.3	20.2	31.7	39.5
% of Persons 5 & Older Living in Different House in 1965	36.1	50.8	62.8	42.6	55.6	39.0
% of Population Living in Group Quarters	0.7	0.5	0.0	0.6	4.9	0.2
Population Per Household	3.3	3.9	4.3	3.1	3.8	3.6
Housing Units, 1970						
Total Number	21,153	6,169	4,272	3,952	3,265	7,354
% in 1-Unit Structures	67.9	96.3	97.9	30.9	86.0	80.7
% Owner-Occupied	75.4	93.7	96.0	42.6	83.2	79.2
% Built in 1960 or Later	23.6	54.1	76.1	20.5	47.7	23.3
% Vacant	1.1	1.2	2.0	7.1	4.6	1.6
% with More than 1 Person per Room	2.0	6.1	12.2	13.4	8.2	7.9
Median Value, Owner Units (in 1-Unit Structures)	$36,700	$29,500	$23,000	$19,300	$22,400	$24,100
Median Contract Rent, Renter Uni	$181	$104	$195	$117	$152	$160
Median Number of Rooms	5.7	6.0	5.5	4.3	5.6	5.3

	Waukegan	Westchester	West Chicago	Western Springs	Westmont	Wheaton
1970 Population						
Total	65,134	20,033	9,988	13,029	8,832	31,138
Black	8,421	12	12	10	6	591
Spanish Language	4,680	145	562	0	43	530
% Change 1960-1970						
Total Population	16.9	10.7	45.7	20.2	47.3	28.1
Black Population	87.8	300.0	-	66.7	-	70.3
% of Population, 1970						
Black	12.9	0.1	0.1	0.1	0.1	1.9
Spanish Language	7.2	0.7	5.6	0.0	0.5	1.7
Under 18 Years Old	35.2	32.2	40.1	36.0	30.1	38.5
65 Years and Older	7.6	7.4	6.2	8.0	8.1	6.6
Persons 25 and Older						
Median Years School Completed	12.2	12.4	12.2	14.0	12.2	13.1
% with 4 or More Years College	11.3	13.7	10.3	35.9	10.9	32.0
% of All Workers in Manufacturing	35.9	33.1	27.0	28.8	31.7	20.5
% of All Workers in White Collar Occupations	28.3	44.0	29.3	64.2	31.7	50.2
% Riding to Work by Auto	85.2	81.7	79.3	71.4	73.3	72.8
% of Civilian Labor Force Unemployed	3.2	1.7	3.0	1.3	2.3	1.6
Families (1970)						
Total Number	16,812	5,556	2,570	3,321	2,329	7,343
Median Family Income	$11,478	$15,812	$12,886	$19,502	$12,674	$15,055
% Below Poverty	6.4	1.3	1.8	0.8	2.4	3.5
% with Income Greater than $14,999	28.0	53.4	32.5	67.4	28.3	50.2
% of Persons 5 & Older Living in Different House in 1965	46.2	31.3	53.4	32.9	46.8	55.2
% of Population Living in Group Quarters	1.0	0.4	0.1	0.1	0.1	5.8
Population Per Household	3.1	3.4	3.5	3.4	2.9	3.4
Housing Units, 1970						
Total Number	21,784	5,890	2,963	3,577	3,098	8,754
% in 1-Unit Structures	55.8	92.4	76.0	95.9	61.7	80.4
% Owner-Occupied	57.9	93.2	69.1	94.3	60.6	76.1
% Built in 1960 or Later	23.0	17.9	31.9	18.7	41.3	28.9
% Vacant	3.8	0.7	3.0	0.8	6.2	2.3
% with More than 1 Person per Room	9.5	4.5	8.9	1.6	4.9	4.2
Median Value, Owner Units (in 1-Unit Structures)	$19,800	$31,300	$20,800	$38,100	$19,900	$29,000
Median Contract Rent, Renter Uni	$123	$215	$150	$184	$171	$155
Median Number of Rooms	4.7	5.4	5.2	6.4	4.7	5.8

	Wheeling	Wilmette	Winnetka	Wood Dale	Woodridge	Woodstock
1970 Population						
Total	13,243	32,134	14,131	8,831	11,028	10,226
Black	7	81	117	0	34	10
Spanish Language	497	486	132	332	361	160
% Change 1960-1970						
Total Population	84.7	13.7	5.7	187.6	-	14.9
Black Population	75.0	-48.1	-53.6	-	-	42.9
% of Population, 1970						
Black	0.1	0.3	0.8	0.0	0.3	0.1
Spanish Language	3.8	1.5	0.9	3.8	3.3	1.6
Under 18 Years Old	43.0	37.9	37.5	39.6	50.0	34.0
65 Years and Older	3.2	9.0	9.9	4.0	1.2	11.2
Persons 25 and Older						
Median Years School Completed	12.4	15.2	16.1	12.2	12.7	12.2
% with 4 or More Years College	11.7	44.2	53.9	6.6	19.9	10.6
% of All Workers in Manufacturing	32.3	17.9	16.9	38.8	30.1	38.2
% of All Workers in White Collar Occupations	36.6	68.2	73.7	27.8	50.3	27.8
% Riding to Work by Auto	87.5	69.4	53.8	87.4	83.3	83.5
% of Civilian Labor Force Unemployed	2.1	2.7	1.7	2.5	1.3	3.5
Families (1970)						
Total Number	3,581	8,060	3,476	2,198	2,559	2,648
Median Family Income	$13,398	$21,809	$28,782	$13,806	$13,870	$11,636
% Below Poverty	2.2	2.5	1.2	4.4	1.4	3.9
% with Income Greater than $14,999	38.0	71.8	79.3	40.5	37.2	23.3
% of Persons 5 & Older Living in Different House in 1965	50.3	37.6	42.7	59.3	70.6	46.3
% of Population Living in Group Quarters	0.8	1.4	0.2	0.9	0.1	2.3
Population Per Household	3.6	3.4	3.4	3.6	4.4	3.0
Housing Units, 1970						
Total Number	4,249	9,582	4,241	2,471	2,650	3,428
% in 1-Unit Structures	67.4	82.9	89.5	84.8	94.5	71.9
% Owner-Occupied	68.2	83.7	82.9	86.0	97.0	66.3
% Built in 1960 or Later	58.1	21.1	8.1	66.0	93.8	17.3
% Vacant	5.5	3.2	2.1	2.5	4.5	2.3
% with More than 1 Person per Room	8.1	1.5	0.8	6.4	6.5	4.5
Median Value, Owner Units (in 1-Unit Structures)	$24,900	$46,500	$50,100	$27,800	$29,200	$19,500
Median Contract Rent, Renter Uni	$185	$220	$171	$159	$191	$100
Median Number of Rooms	5.1	6.8	7.7	5.4	6.6	5.2

Table IV-2 Selected Census Statistics, 1970
Community Areas in Chicago and Places of 10,000 or More Population, 1970
In Chicago-Gary-Kenosha Ill.-Ind.-Wis. Standard Consolidated Statistical Area

	Worth	Zion	Crown Point, Ind.	East Chicago, Ind.	Gary, Ind.	Griffith, Ind.
1970 Population						
Total	11,999	17,268	10,931	46,982	175,415	18,168
Black	1	2,345	92	12,881	92,695	80
Spanish Language	151	447	121	12,582	14,241	268
% Change 1960-1970						
Total Population	46.4	44.6	29.5	-18.5	-1.6	91.6
Black Population	-	333.5	360.0	-6.4	34.1	515.4
% of Population, 1970						
Black	0.0	13.6	0.8	27.4	52.8	0.4
Spanish Language	1.3	2.6	1.1	26.8	8.1	1.5
Under 18 Years Old	39.0	41.3	37.5	35.7	38.8	40.6
65 Years and Older	4.8	5.1	8.9	8.8	7.6	3.5
Persons 25 and Older						
Median Years School Completed	12.1	11.8	12.4	9.8	11.1	12.4
% with 4 or More Years College	6.2	5.7	13.9	3.6	5.6	11.6
% of All Workers in Manufacturing	25.7	42.1	28.9	55.9	48.8	39.9
% of All Workers in White Collar Occupations	26.8	20.9	35.3	13.9	18.0	32.3
% Riding to Work by Auto	86.7	91.0	80.9	67.1	76.4	90.6
% of Civilian Labor Force Unemployed	2.9	4.0	4.1	4.2	5.5	2.7
Families (1970)						
Total Number	3,098	4,174	2,700	11,399	41,831	4,545
Median Family Income	$12,514	$10,302	$12,181	$9,208	$9,819	$12,308
% Below Poverty	2.5	6.7	3.2	11.5	13.5	1.9
% with Income Greater than $14,999	31.2	19.4	32.7	16.5	19.2	28.2
% of Persons 5 & Older Living in Different House in 1965	40.9	57.5	43.1	45.1	45.4	49.1
% of Population Living in Group Quarters	0.1	2.3	3.4	0.9	0.6	0.3
Population Per Household	3.4	3.5	3.3	3.2	3.4	3.5
Housing Units, 1970						
Total Number	3,583	5,123	3,234	15,659	54,244	5,170
% in 1-Unit Structures	63.1	55.9	83.9	31.7	59.2	75.1
% Owner-Occupied	66.1	55.0	76.3	40.3	58.6	71.5
% Built in 1960 or Later	44.7	36.2	24.9	7.9	10.6	48.5
% Vacant	2.6	4.8	2.5	6.5	4.9	1.1
% with More than 1 Person per Room	9.0	12.5	7.5	14.9	15.8	10.4
Median Value, Owner Units (in 1-Unit Structures)	$21,500	$18,200	$19,100	$16,700	$15,000	$19,900
Median Contract Rent, Renter Unit	$151	$125	$101	$72	$80	$153
Median Number of Rooms	4.9	4.7	5.3	4.4	4.6	5.0

Table IV-2 Selected Census Statistics, 1970
Community Areas in Chicago and Places of 10,000 or More Population, 1970
In Chicago-Gary-Kenosha Ill.-Ind.-Wis. Standard Consolidated Statistical Area

	Hammond, Ind.	Highland, Ind.	Hobart, Ind.	Lake Station, Ind.	Merrillville, Ind.	Munster, Ind.
1970 Population						
Total	107,790	24,947	21,485	9,858	15,918	16,514
Black	4,677	2	12	54	2	10
Spanish Language	3,316	527	280	299	573	196
% Change 1960-1970						
Total Population	-3.5	53.2	15.0	5.9	-	60.1
Black Population	92.2	-	71.4	2600.0	-	11.1
% of Population, 1970						
Black	4.3	0.0	0.1	0.5	0.0	0.1
Spanish Language	3.1	2.1	1.3	3.0	3.6	1.2
Under 18 Years Old	34.8	41.9	38.6	39.2	38.8	38.3
65 Years and Older	7.8	3.5	6.2	5.8	4.9	5.4
Persons 25 and Older						
Median Years School Completed	11.7	12.4	12.2	10.7	12.4	12.7
% with 4 or More Years College	5.1	9.9	7.5	1.3	10.4	20.6
% of All Workers in Manufacturing	45.7	41.6	39.8	53.6	38.3	31.6
% of All Workers in White Collar Occupations	20.9	29.8	24.3	12.0	29.1	47.7
% Riding to Work by Auto	82.7	90.8	90.3	91.2	89.9	89.6
% of Civilian Labor Force Unemployed	3.9	2.8	3.0	4.6	2.4	1.5
Families (1970)						
Total Number	27,793	6,168	5,492	2,469	4,023	4,343
Median Family Income	$10,899	$12,773	$12,052	$10,249	$13,965	$15,108
% Below Poverty	5.4	2.6	4.7	6.8	2.7	1.8
% with Income Greater than $14,999	22.4	32.8	29.4	17.1	42.5	50.4
% of Persons 5 & Older Living in Different House in 1965	38.8	35.0	34.8	41.8	33.6	46.3
% of Population Living in Group Quarters	0.3	0.1	0.0	0.0	0.2	0.5
Population Per Household	3.1	3.8	3.5	3.6	3.7	3.6
Housing Units, 1970						
Total Number	35,613	6,685	6,283	2,819	4,335	4,674
% in 1-Unit Structures	65.9	91.0	89.5	90.7	91.9	92.1
% Owner-Occupied	65.2	88.0	84.2	78.4	89.2	88.5
% Built in 1960 or Later	10.9	39.9	18.5	12.9	49.6	42.6
% Vacant	4.0	1.1	1.9	2.1	1.3	0.9
% with More than 1 Person per Room	9.9	11.6	9.4	14.6	7.5	4.8
Median Value, Owner Units (in 1-Unit Structures)	$16,400	$21,500	$16,400	$13,400	$24,300	$29,500
Median Contract Rent, Renter Unit	$97	$136	$101	$96	$144	$136
Median Number of Rooms	4.8	5.1	5.1	4.8	5.4	5.6

Table IV-2 Selected Census Statistics, 1970
Community Areas in Chicago and Places of 10,000 or More Population, 1970
In Chicago-Gary-Kenosha Ill.-Ind.-Wis. Standard Consolidated Statistical Area

	Portage, Ind.	Schererville, Ind.	Valparaiso, Ind.	Kenosha, Wis.
1970 Population				
Total	19,127	3,663	20,020	78,805
Black	13	0	81	1,923
Spanish Language	321	71	173	2,212
% Change 1960-1970				
Total Population	61.8	27.4	31.5	16.1
Black Population	0.0	-	710.0	103.9
% of Population, 1970				
Black	0.1	0.0	0.4	2.4
Spanish Language	1.7	1.9	0.9	2.8
Under 18 Years Old	43.2	41.8	29.0	40.4
65 Years and Older	3.0	4.3	7.9	10.0
Persons 25 and Older				
Median Years School Completed	12.1	12.2	12.5	11.9
% with 4 or More Years College	4.5	8.1	19.2	7.1
% of All Workers in Manufacturing	46.5	33.7	26.4	42.8
% of All Workers in White Collar Occupations	16.6	28.2	36.2	41.6
% Riding to Work by Auto	93.3	82.1	75.9	84.0
% of Civilian Labor Force Unemployed	3.8	2.3	3.1	4.3
Families (1970)				
Total Number	4,661	913	4,303	19,489
Median Family Income	$11,910	$12,388	$11,580	$10,191
% Below Poverty	3.5	5.5	3.6	6.1
% with Income Greater than $14,999	26.3	30.4	27.9	17.9
% of Persons 5 & Older Living in Different House in 1965	51.0	43.3	57.7	39.1
% of Population Living in Group Quarters	0.1	0.2	14.3	2.5
Population Per Household	3.8	3.8	2.9	3.2
Housing Units, 1970				
Total Number	5,181	998	6,038	24,848
% in 1-Unit Structures	82.7	85.8	70.5	63.2
% Owner-Occupied	84.5	83.0	64.6	64.7
% Built in 1960 or Later	51.6	31.2	25.9	17.6
% Vacant	2.1	2.7	2.7	3.8
% with More than 1 Person per Room	12.8	12.5	3.8	8.5
Median Value, Owner Units (in 1-Unit Structures)	$18,000	$21,300	$19,400	$16,400
Median Contract Rent, Renter Uni	$126	$113	$109	$91
Median Number of Rooms	5.1	5.2	5.1	4.9

DATE DUE

MAY 1 ~

JAN 0 2 2001

Demco, Inc. 38-293